Tourism
A Modern Synthesis

Tourism can be a challenging subject for students because it is both dynamic and susceptible to economic turbulence and shifts in trends. *Tourism: A Modern Synthesis* is an essential textbook for tourism students seeking a clear and comprehensive introduction to their studies that addresses these challenges. The authors apply a business approach to the subject, reflecting developments in the teaching and content of university courses, and the text covers both key principles and contemporary themes and issues at a global scale.

Among the new features and topics included in this fifth edition are:

- New and fully updated case studies to reflect current trends and emerging markets including Africa and Asia.
- Up-to-date content on disruptive technologies such as Airbnb, low-cost airlines, the e-travel revolution and future developments.
- Current debates in sustainable tourism including the anti-tourism movement, plastic use and the Sustainable Development Goals.
- New content on evolving topics such as future employment, human resource management in tourism and generational marketing.
- Fully updated statistics and data.
- A brand-new Companion Website including an instructor's manual, supplementary case studies, weblinks, multiple choice questions and PowerPoint slides.

This is the ideal guide to tourism for students across all levels, serving as a point of reference throughout a programme of study.

Stephen J. Page is Associate Dean (Research) and Professor of Business and Management, Hertfordshire Business School, University of Hertfordshire, UK.

Joanne Connell is Senior Lecturer in Tourism Management, University of Exeter Business School, Exeter, UK.

D1294612

Tourism
A Modern Synthesis

Fifth Edition

Stephen J. Page and Joanne Connell

Routledge
Taylor & Francis Group

LONDON AND NEW YORK

Fifth edition published 2020
by Routledge
2 Park Square, Milton Park, Abingdon, Oxon, OX14 4RN

and by Routledge
52 Vanderbilt Avenue, New York, NY 10017

Routledge is an imprint of the Taylor & Francis Group, an informa business

© 2020 Stephen J. Page and Joanne Connell

The right of Stephen J. Page and Joanne Connell to be identified as authors of this work has been asserted by them in accordance with sections 77 and 78 of the Copyright, Designs and Patents Act 1988.

All rights reserved. No part of this book may be reprinted or reproduced or utilised in any form or by any electronic, mechanical, or other means, now known or hereafter invented, including photocopying and recording, or in any information storage or retrieval system, without permission in writing from the publishers.

Trademark notice: Product or corporate names may be trademarks or registered trademarks, and are used only for identification and explanation without intent to infringe.

First edition published by Cengage Learning EMEA 2001
Fourth edition published by Cengage Learning EMEA 2014

British Library Cataloguing-in-Publication Data
A catalogue record for this book is available from the British Library

Library of Congress Cataloging-in-Publication Data
Names: Page, Stephen, 1963– author. | Connell, Joanne, author.
Title: Tourism : a modern synthesis / Stephen J. Page and Joanne Connell.
Description: Fifth Edition. | New York : Routledge, 2020. | "Fourth edition
    published by Cengage Learning EMEA 2014"—T.p. verso. | Includes
    bibliographical references and index.
Identifiers: LCCN 2019051589 (print) | LCCN 2019051590 (ebook)
Subjects: LCSH: Tourism.
Classification: LCC G155.A1 P25787 2020 (print) | LCC G155.A1
    (ebook) | DDC 910—dc23
LC record available at https://lccn.loc.gov/2019051589
LC ebook record available at https://lccn.loc.gov/2019051590

ISBN: 978-0-367-43737-4 (hbk)
ISBN: 978-0-367-43736-7 (pbk)
ISBN: 978-1-003-00552-0 (ebk)

Typeset in Sabon LT Std, Futura Std
by Apex CoVantage, LLC

Visit the Companion Website: www.routledge.com/cw/page

Brief contents

Contents

Part 1
Understanding tourism 1

Part 2
Understanding the tourism industry 93

Part 3
Managing tourist operations and communicating with the visitor 243

Part 4
The impact of tourism 353

Part 5
Trends and themes in the use of tourist resources 441

Part 6
Managing tourism activities 529

Preface

Welcome to the fifth edition of *Tourism: A Modern Synthesis*, which has been revised to meet the needs of the reader after extensive feedback from readers, adopters, students and reviewers. This new edition builds upon the embryonic book first published in 2001, and as tourism has continued to develop as a subject of study, the book has evolved to incorporate many of the new themes and debates which now impact upon the study of tourism.

The features of this book

The changes which have occurred in international and domestic tourism globally since the first edition in 2001 have been massive. Events such as 9/11, Ebola, terrorism, technological change and the global climate emergency to name but a few have led commentators to depict tourism as operating in turbulent times. But underpinning the current thinking associated with the highly volatile nature of tourism is over 50 years of academic endeavour in the study of tourism, which has built up a large collection of concepts, theoretical debates and industry examples. This new edition seeks to embody many new ways of thinking about the development, management and operation of tourism as a global activity, embracing many of the classic and popular concepts and approaches that have become firmly embedded in the subject. This is why it is called a *Modern Synthesis*. Unlike many journal articles you may now read, this book looks at the seminal studies which helped shape the subject under discussion, so it acts as a starting point and reference source. It then provides a road map of the subject and points to key studies to read to take the issues further. Above all the book sets out to link the conceptual issues with practical real-world examples in a cohesive and concise framework that is both logical, topical and interesting for the reader.

In this edition, a cohesive approach has been adopted to present a seamless transition through the book, with new material included to show how current thinking has moved on since the last edition. The book has been expanded and new material has been added in every chapter, particularly in the tourism industry section, as this has seen massive change, notably with the e-travel revolution, new methods of management and huge changes in the way tourism operates globally, as well as with new forms of supply such as low-cost airlines, and the impact of disruptive technologies such as Airbnb.

A new range of in-depth insights has also been incorporated throughout the book to illustrate particular themes and issues that will interest the book's global audience, while also updating many others. Above all, this is an up-to-date and comprehensive overview – a synthesis of all that is topical, important and relevant to the student and teacher of tourism, which is global in its focus.

This book is an invaluable global resource for any student or teacher of tourism, as a concise resource for classroom and independent study, especially given the additional features of the book, which make it highly desirable as a resource.

Chapter learning outcomes are used at the beginning of each chapter to focus the reader on the expected outcome they should derive after reading the chapter, which is helpful in identifying the key features a lecture or tutorial might seek to develop.

Discussion questions are included at the end of every chapter so that the reader can self-review the subject they have studied and see how the knowledge they have accessed on tourism can be applied to current themes in tourism.

Tourism insights have been introduced in this edition, as opposed to large unwieldy case studies. These are short in-depth discussions of a contemporary theme or issue in tourism. In some cases they focus on problems posed by tourism, in other cases they highlight good practice or current thinking on a theme.

Web-based case studies are also included on the Companion Website to provide more detailed analysis of key issues and to avoid diverting the reader's attention from the main flow of the book and important issues and concepts. They are a supplementary learning aid.

References are included at the end of each chapter. While the first edition minimized the number of references in each chapter, the second, third and fourth editions introduced many classic and contemporary studies appearing in the academic literature. As mentioned above, they act as a starting point for further research when writing essays, undertaking assignments or beginning extended projects and dissertations. The fifth edition continues with this tradition, so anyone can pick up a chapter and see how the subject has evolved in terms of academic thinking through time.

Further reading is identified at the end of every chapter to identify current thinking and literature which might help the reader to begin further research on the subject. As the tourism literature is growing at an exponential rate, this simple signpost to a key study is a starting point and a self-help feature.

Web-based sources are used throughout the text to highlight industry examples, good practice and additional sources of material to help with assignments and in-class discussion; since tourism is a commercial business subject, a blend of industry material was seen as essential.

Tables are used to provide illustrations of the current scale, impact and ways of summarizing key features of a tourism phenomenon. Current commercial data are also presented, together with snapshots of recent research studies on contemporary tourism themes.

Figures are used to explain key concepts, simplify complex issues and identify the context of tourism (i.e. locations, localities and places) as well as providing a road map of key issues for topics.

Images bring key elements of tourism to life, expanding upon specific themes discussed in the text.

A **Glossary of key terms** has been included to help guide the reader through the jargon, complex terminology and concepts introduced throughout the book.

The structure of the book

The principal feature of each chapter is that it is intended to cover the breadth and scope needed at an introductory level. It introduces basic principles and concepts which an introductory lecture on the topic might want to cover in an up-to-date and discursive way. The book is not a simple compendium of facts and figures. Instead, it is a balance of much-needed concepts associated with the analysis of tourism. Above all, the subtitle *Modern Synthesis* means exactly that: it introduces current thinking on many of the key themes in each chapter along with the essential concepts and issues in an unambiguous manner.

It is intended that this book will help students to have a thorough understanding of:

- the concepts and characteristics of tourism as an area of academic and applied study
- the structure of and interactions in the tourism industry
- the place of tourism in the communities and environments that it affects
- the nature and characteristics of tourists.

The book adopts a fairly straightforward approach to tourism. It has a series of integrated sections and chapters and their rationale is outlined next.

Part 1: Understanding tourism

Part 1 of the book provides the wide range of concepts and approaches developed over the last 50 years to understand the nature of tourism and characteristics of tourists. The underpinning concept of globalization is introduced as a theme running throughout the book, given the global nature of tourism. The volatility of tourism is outlined. This leads to a wide-ranging review of how to conceptualize and understand tourism as a fickle and volatile activity. The historical evolution of tourism demand, and its measurement and analysis, are also presented. The growing interest in tourists as consumers is also discussed, highlighting the growing recognition of tourism as a global consumer product, illustrated by the rise of medical tourism.

Part 2: Understanding the tourism industry

Part 2 of the book is essentially focused upon the concept of supply in tourism, and the tools which have evolved to analyze and manage it. The global expansion of new trends using technology, notably the e-travel revolution, is discussed, which provides a benchmark for further debate in subsequent chapters. This theme is apparent in the different components of supply (tourism intermediaries, transport, attractions and accommodation/hospitality services).

Part 3: Managing tourist operations and communicating with the visitor

Part 3 of the book builds upon Parts 1 and 2, identifying the tools, techniques and concepts associated with the management of supply and demand. As tourism is a people business, the first chapter discusses human resource issues, which is followed by the often neglected area of the role of entrepreneurship in creating innovation, which forces businesses to adapt, develop and accommodate change; this is presented along with examples of how entrepreneurs have established individual businesses. One consequence of change in tourism is the need for management of private-sector activity in tourism; this leads to an in-depth discussion of the public sector's role in tourism. This also provides a basis for the subsequent chapters on tourism marketing concepts, and how destinations are created and marketed by different agencies to explain how the tourism sector communicates with consumers.

Part 4: The impact of tourism

In Part 4, the natural outcome of tourism activity, resulting from supply and demand issues, is examined in terms of tourism impacts. The scope of economic, sociocultural and environmental impacts are presented, along with the tools used by researchers to understand and measure tourism impacts. This provides a background for the in-depth analysis of the concept of sustainability and its development as a tool for the planning and development of tourism, as well as a discussion of the current challenges to sustainable tourism such as global warming.

Part 5: Trends and themes in the use of tourist resources

In Part 5, the impact of tourism is examined in relation to the different resources and environments consumed by tourism. The examples of urban, rural, coastal and resort tourism and the less-developed world provide topical and insightful perspectives on different types of tourism destination.

Part 6: Managing tourism activities

In Part 6, the culmination of tourism in different environments raises the issue of how we need to plan and manage tourist activity. The role of tourism planning and its implementation is reviewed, and the current thinking on the concept of the tourist experience, the principles of service quality and how to enhance the visitor experience are discussed. The highly contentious and volatile nature of tourist health and safety, as impinging upon tourist decision-making and tourist development is outlined in detail, as a current theme affecting global tourism. This is followed by the example of events and festivals as activities to nurture and develop for tourism. The book then concludes with a series of debates associated with how to conceptualize, analyze and measure future change in tourism.

Companion Website material

 Visit the Companion Website at www.routledge.com/page for an extensive selection of teaching and learning materials accompanying *Tourism: A Modern Synthesis*.

Instructor resources:

- An instructor's manual
- PowerPoint slides

Student Resources:

- Multiple choice questions
- Additional case studies
- Links to useful websites and videos
- Glossary

Publisher acknowledgements

Thomas Cook for the excellent images and posters used throughout the book. Les Lumsdon, Eric Laws, Michael Hall, Mark Orams, Russell King, Airport Council International, ATAG, and ISEAS in Singapore.

Copyright material is duly acknowledged throughout the book and permission has been kindly granted by: Elsevier, Pearson Education, Routledge, and various other organizations. Every attempt has been made to contact owners of copyrighted material. If any unknowing use of copyrighted material has been made, please contact the authors via the publishers.

Stephen would like to thank Julie Franklin for her speedy and accurate translation of his scribbles to legible text, and both Joanne and Stephen would like to thank Rosie for her very adept editing of the chapters and Toby for his attention to detail in drawing some of the figures from statistical sources. Any omissions or errors are the authors', and if any inadvertent misuse of copyrighted material has occurred, please contact the authors via the publishers. Both Joanne and Stephen would also like to thank Emma Travis for her unstinting support for publishing the book, and Lydia Kessell for her ongoing input and advice during the development of the book and with image research, and Frances Tye for her excellent copyediting skills.

Guided tour

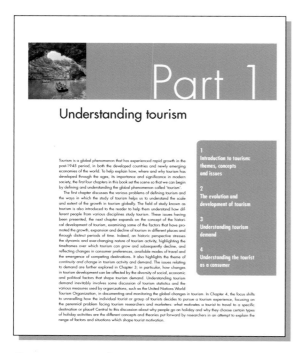

Chapter opener Bullet points at the start of each chapter highlight the concepts, each referenced in terms of expected learning outcomes.

Glossary terms Key terms are explained in more detail.

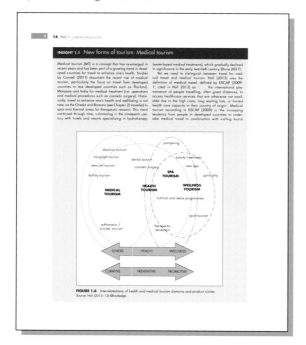

Insight box Insights provide more in-depth analysis of key and relevant themes discussed in each chapter.

Discussion questions Questions help reinforce and test your knowledge and understanding.

Case matrix

Insight = Mini case in the chapter

Insight no.	Insight Title	Country of Origin	Page number
1.1	New forms of tourism: Medical tourism	Thailand (and various)	14
2.1	The history of the Thomas Cook Company: Milestones in its development 1841–2019	UK/various	29
2.2	Holidays in inter-war Scandinavia	Scandinavia (various)	33
2.3	The Scandinavian tourism boom by air	Scandinavia (various)	36
3.1	BRIC countries: Emerging outbound markets	Various	47
3.2	Taxing the tourist: Air Passenger Duty in the UK	UK	49
3.3	Tourism demand and weather	General	56
4.1	Motivation to attend travel exhibitions	General	72
4.2	Conceptualizing household tourism demand	General	81
5.1	easyJet's growth as a tourist supply firm – a major success story of growth and competition	General	107
6.1	Marriott uses celebrities to promote renovations on Twitter	UK	121
7.1	Profile of the European tourist – implications for travel retailing	Europe	136
7.2	TUI AG – the world's largest integrated tour operator	General	141
7.3	Airline and tour-operator insolvency in the UK	UK/General	145
7.4	Travel agencies in Australia	Australia	155
8.1	Safety and security and cruise lines	General	173
9.1	Attraction of the coast: The role of coastal heritage as a tourist attraction	Global	192
10.1	The development of Surfers Paradise, Gold Coast Queensland, Australia	Australia	221
10.2	The evolution of the Chinese hotel industry since 1980	China	225
10.3	Rethinking tourism accommodation: The multi-ownership model	General	234
11.1	Human resource management and labour planning issues for the UK hospitality sector	UK	249
11.2	The future of work and implications for tourism employment and holidays	General	257
12.1	The role of Scottish Enterprise in driving innovation in tourism	Scotland	269
12.2	Social enterprises and tourism in sub-Saharan Africa	Africa	274
13.1	The role of local authorities in tourism in Scotland	Scotland	283
13.2	Destination management organizations (DMOs) and tourism	Global	292

Web case studies

Chapter	Case study title	Country of origin
1	An expanding niche market for youth travel: The student gap year and tourism	Global
1	Globalization and tourism: South Korean tourism activity in New Zealand	New Zealand
1	The impact of the London bombings on tourism	London
2	Thomas Cook 1919–1922: Battlefield tours and dark tourism	UK, France and Belgium
2	Literary tourism development – the Trossachs, Scotland: Evolution, continuity and change	Scotland
2	The evolution of tourism in Monaco as a high-class tourism destination	Monaco
3	The Chinese outbound boom	China
3	The United Kingdom's international passenger survey	UK
3	The United Kingdom Tourism Survey (UKTS)	UK
4	Motivations and activities of ecotourists at an ecolodge in Ecuador	Ecuador
4	Tourist motivation – adventure tourism as a global growth market	Global
5	Managing costs as a tool to stay competitive: The case of the airline sector	Global
6	The aims and objectives of DMOs and e-marketing and distribution	Global
6	Benefits of e-solutions for tourism value chains	Global
6	ICTs' impact on tourism organisations	Global
6	The impact of social media on the tourism sector	Global
6	The role and impact of the Internet on tourism distribution	Global
6	Tracking and monitoring Internet and social media use	Global
7	The Thomas Cook–MyTravel merger in 2007	Global
8	The evolution of cycle tourism in the USA	USA
9	Solar eclipses as a natural attraction	Global
10	J.D. Wetherspoon: The growth of a hospitality chain	UK
10	Second homes: Curse or blessing?	Global
10	The mega-resort hotel and Las Vegas	USA
11	Empowerment, HRM and the Southwest Airlines model	USA
11	The role of the World Travel and Tourism Council (WTTC): The Human Resources Taskforce and the future role of HRM	Global
12	Stelios Haji-Ioannou and the easyGroup	UK
13	The role of Scottish Enterprise in the development of tourism	Scotland
13	The Singapore Tourism Board's vision for tourism and Tourism 21	Singapore
14	fastjet – Launching Africa's first low-budget airline using digital marketing	Africa
15	The marketing and promotion of Berlin as a tourist destination	Germany
16	Gromit Unleashed: The economic impact of a film and TV tourism product	UK
17	The Arctic – sociocultural impacts of tourism in an emerging destination	Arctic
18	British Airways environmental report	UK
18	Whale and dolphin watching: A global growth sector	Global
19	Sardinia: Implementing approaches to sustainability at the destination level	Sardinia
20	Urban regeneration and tourism in the 'Big Apple': New York and the 2012 Olympic bid	USA
21	Rural tourism in Namibia	Africa
22	Margate: Cultural tourism and the British seaside towns	UK
23	Enclave tourism in Africa	Africa
24	Factors influencing the tourist experience at visitor attractions: Key studies and issues	Global
25	Accidents and injuries in adventure tourism	Scotland
26	Squamish and event development	Canada
27	Future changes in air travel: The role of technology – the A380	Global

Part 1

Understanding tourism

Tourism is a global phenomenon that has experienced rapid growth in the post-1945 period, in both the developed countries and newly emerging economies of the world. To help explain how, where and why tourism has developed through the ages, its importance and significance in modern society, the first four chapters in this book set the scene so that we can begin by defining and understanding the global phenomenon called 'tourism'.

The first chapter discusses the various problems of defining tourism and the ways in which the study of tourism helps us to understand the scale and extent of the growth in tourism globally. The field of study known as tourism is also introduced to the reader to help them understand how different people from various disciplines study tourism. These issues having been presented, the next chapter expands on the concept of the historical development of tourism, examining some of the factors that have promoted the growth, expansion and decline of tourism in different places and through distinct periods of time. Indeed, an historic perspective stresses the dynamic and ever-changing nature of tourism activity, highlighting the timeframes over which tourism can grow and subsequently decline, and reflecting changes in consumer preferences, available modes of travel and the emergence of competing destinations. It also highlights the theme of *continuity and change* in tourism activity and demand. The issues relating to demand are further explored in Chapter 3; in particular, how changes in tourism development can be affected by the diversity of social, economic and political factors that shape tourism demand. Understanding tourism demand inevitably involves some discussion of tourism statistics and the various measures used by organizations, such as the United Nations World Tourism Organization, in documenting and monitoring the global changes in tourism. In Chapter 4, the focus shifts to unravelling how the individual tourist or group of tourists decides to pursue a tourism experience, focusing on the perennial problem facing tourism researchers and marketers: what motivates a tourist to travel to a specific destination or place? Central to this discussion about why people go on holiday and why they choose certain types of holiday activities are the different concepts and theories put forward by researchers in an attempt to explain the range of factors and situations which shape tourist motivation.

1
Introduction to tourism: Themes, concepts and issues

2
The evolution and development of tourism

3
Understanding tourism demand

4
Understanding the tourist as a consumer

Introduction to tourism: Themes, concepts and issues

Learning outcomes

In this chapter, we explore the nature of tourism as a subject area and the problems of defining the terminology of tourism. After reading this chapter and answering the questions, you should be able to understand:

- why tourism is an important subject to study

- how different definitions of tourism have been developed, and the frameworks used to study tourism

- the different forms of tourism

- the difference between domestic and international tourism

- the changing nature of global tourism.

Overview

This chapter presents an introduction to the study of tourism and the concepts with which students need to be acquainted, including the meaning of 'tourism' and what is meant by the terms 'tourist', 'traveller', 'visitor' and 'excursionist'. Some of the leading studies in the growing field of tourism studies are reviewed in the chapter to provide an overview of the evolution of tourism as an area of study, and issues related to tourism development in the wider environment of global change are recognized.

Introduction

Tourism is not a new phenomenon: Smith (2004: 25) noted 'tourism and travel have been part of the human experience for millennia', describing tourism as a form of nomadism that characterizes *Homo sapiens*, and which is both normal and, under the right conditions, pleasurable. In the last 70 years, with the rise of the jet aircraft, tourism has grown in significance and emerged as a global phenomenon, affecting an increasing range of environments as opportunities for travel have widened. Although the latter part of this chapter will examine in detail what we mean by the terms 'tourism' and 'tourist', it is useful to outline a number of the essential ideas which are associated with tourism. In essence, tourism is associated with the following issues:

- travelling away from one's home for more than 24 hours
- using one's leisure time to travel and take holidays
- travelling for business.

While these three issues are a simplification of what is meant by 'tourism', this book aims to address many of the questions and themes that are important in developing an understanding of tourism, which is a convenient catch-all term often used without a clear understanding of its meaning, scope and extent. This book assumes no prior knowledge of the subject area, progressively developing the reader's understanding of the scope, complexity and range of issues that the tourism phenomenon poses for anyone who is serious about the study of the subject.

The late twentieth century and the new millennium have witnessed the sustained growth of the leisure society in which people place value on holidays, travel and the experience of visiting new places and societies. The growth of this consumer-focused society in the developed world since the 1950s, with its emphasis on discretionary spending on leisure activities, reflects greater disposable income and the increased availability of time to engage in leisure pursuits and holidays. Although this leisure society has its roots in the Western developed world, trends that emerged in the 1990s indicated an expansion in the global propensity to travel and engage in holidays. As a result of major economic, political, social and cultural changes, demand is escalating in countries formerly not engaged in international tourism activity such as post-Communist countries and in new world regions such as Asia, China, the Indian subcontinent and South America. At a global scale, international and domestic tourism have been transformed by changes to the economic climate which affect the propensity of people to travel for pleasure and business. Many Western countries are facing extended periods of slow economic growth and greater austerity amidst inflationary pressures from oil prices, making travel more expensive. In contrast, the fast-growing economies of Brazil, Russia, India and China (called the BRIC economies) have a rapidly expanding affluent middle class who are pursuing domestic and international travel in much greater volumes. There is also a growing interest in other countries that have been identified as emerging economies with major outbound travel potential via their emerging middle classes, such as Mexico, Indonesia, Nigeria and Turkey; these are known as the MINT economies.

This sharp contrast in the economic fortunes of countries explains why many governments have turned to the marketing and promotion of tourism to boost ailing economies, given the revenue generated by tourism as a consumer-led activity to improve their balance of payments from inbound tourists. Conversely, it also explains why the national tourism agency – VisitEngland – has promoted domestic tourism (people holidaying in their home country) using the staycation concept to try to retain holiday expenditure in the UK economy rather than such consumer spending being transferred overseas.

Tourism: A global activity

Tourism is part of a global process of change and development (known as globalization) which is no longer confined to the developed countries that traditionally provided the demand for world travel. In this respect, understanding the pace of change in tourism is more complex as the forces of change are diverse and not homogeneous. Increasingly, the development of tourism throughout the world is a function of complex factors that coalesce to generate dynamic processes that one must understand in a local context, while recognizing the national and international factors affecting change. Therefore, understanding how and why changes in tourism activity occur, what motivates people to travel and how their patterns of tourism affect tourism destinations and destination communities are pervasive challenges now facing tourism organizations, researchers and students. Increasingly, governments are recognizing the importance of tourism, in particular to national economies, but they are also recognizing the problems arising from tourism activity as a route to national economic development. As an example of a government boosting a tourism economy, in July 2004, the UK Culture Secretary launched the strategy *Tomorrow's Tourism Today* for England, with a vision of increasing the annual turnover of tourism from £76 billion in the UK in 2002 to £100 billion in 2010 (Department for Digital, Culture, Media & Sport (DCMS)). By 2017, the annual turnover from tourism reached £106 billion, supporting 2.6 million jobs.

It is easy to underestimate the global significance of tourism. However, as the following statistics suggest, tourism is one of the most important global industries. In 1991, the international tourism industry employed 112 million people worldwide and generated over US$2.5 trillion at 1989 prices. By 2006, the figure had reached 234.3 million people employed, and by 2012 this had grown to 260 million jobs and generated US$2 trillion for the global economy. By 2019, tourism was responsible for 1:10 jobs in the global economy and 1:5 of all newly created jobs as well as comprising 10.4 per cent of world GDP.

Therefore, it is not surprising that many analysts at the World Travel and Tourism Council (WTTC) argue that tourism is the world's largest industry. Seeking evidence to substantiate this claim was particularly difficult until an accounting process known as Tourism Satellite Accounts (TSAs) was developed to provide more reliable and comparable data generated by individual nations (see Chapter 16 on economic impacts), as it has been easy for governments to underestimate the real value tourism has in different countries. However, there is growing evidence that tourism is a volatile economic activity that can be subject to shock waves, such as the oil crisis in the 1970s, the Gulf War, the Asian economic crisis in 1997 and 1998, the effect of 9/11 and the impact of SARS, the double-dip recession in Europe (Bronner and de Hoog 2014) and terrorism. A useful illustration of the effect of one shock event was the impact of the Ebola epidemic on West Africa between 2014 and 2016. The effect on Sierra Leone's tourism sector was an immediate drop in international arrivals in May 2014 and a sustained drop to 50 per cent below pre-epidemic levels 2016–19. The WTTC estimated that the impact on Sierra Leone's tourism sector was a loss of US$67 million. Such crisis events rapidly change the economic fortunes of the tourism industry in specific countries and heighten public consciousness about global travel and the associated risks, particularly in the case of Ebola, in which tourists were advised not to travel to affected areas. This demonstrates that consumer confidence can be damaged by media reporting, resulting in changes in consumer behaviour, propensity to travel and choice of destinations.

This chapter now examines some of the key concepts that underpin the study of tourism, including:

- the scope of tourism as an area of study
- tourism as an integrated system
- definitions of tourism
- international and domestic tourism patterns
- tourism as a global activity and the implications of globalization.

In the process, several contemporary themes and issues that highlight the difficulties and nuances of both understanding and managing tourism as an activity are explored.

Tourism as an area of study

Tourism is now embraced as a subject for serious academic study, but it has not always been this way. Prior to the 1980s, the study of tourism as an intellectual pursuit was viewed by many academics and analysts as superficial and not really worthy of academic respect in the same way that established disciplines, such as history, economics and politics were, but with some notable exceptions (e.g. Hayner 1932; Crampon 1955 in the USA). Indeed, tourism was often perceived as a practitioner subject taught at craft level. This changed considerably in the 1990s. Yet tourism does have a much longer history of study, as Hall and Page (2014) chart, with reference to the work of geographers dating back to the 1920s. Today, many schools, colleges, polytechnics and universities around the world offer courses in tourism-related studies, with qualifications offered from certificate level through to PhD level (see Figure 1.1), and it is now maturing as a subject area in its own right (see Dredge, Airey and Gross 2014).

The majority of influential tourism textbooks which have popularized the study of tourism are a product of the 1980s and early 1990s, despite some notable exceptions in the 1970s (e.g. Burkart and Medlik 1974, 1975), and a rapid profusion of specialist texts emerged in the new millennium. The rapid expansion in the number of tourism textbooks and academic journal articles published in top journals such as *Annals of Tourism Research*, *Tourism Management* and the *Journal of Travel Research* are one indication of the emergence of the subject as a serious area of study at vocational, degree and postgraduate level throughout the world.

This literature base is supplemented by trade publications such as *Travel Trade Gazette* and electronic newswires such as TravelMole (http://www.travelmole.com), where research findings are also reported. However, textbooks

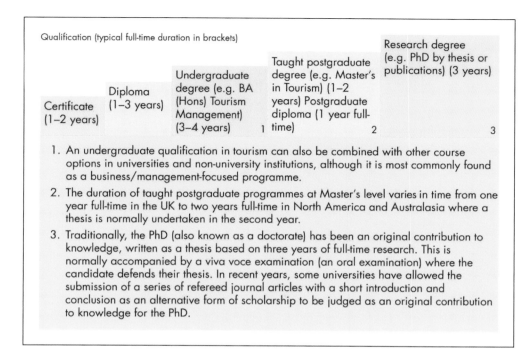

Qualification (typical full-time duration in brackets)

1. An undergraduate qualification in tourism can also be combined with other course options in universities and non-university institutions, although it is most commonly found as a business/management-focused programme.

2. The duration of taught postgraduate programmes at Master's level varies in time from one year full-time in the UK to two years full-time in North America and Australasia where a thesis is normally undertaken in the second year.

3. Traditionally, the PhD (also known as a doctorate) has been an original contribution to knowledge, written as a thesis based on three years of full-time research. This is normally accompanied by a viva voce examination (an oral examination) where the candidate defends their thesis. In recent years, some universities have allowed the submission of a series of refereed journal articles with a short introduction and conclusion as an alternative form of scholarship to be judged as an original contribution to knowledge for the PhD.

FIGURE 1.1 The staircase of tourism qualifications

are an important medium of communication, offering a synthesis of existing knowledge and opportunities to debate tourism, its concepts and development more fully than is possible in academic journals.

Difficulties in studying tourism

As a subject area, tourism is fraught by a number of problems which any student and researcher needs to be aware of. Some of the principal problems are:

1 *Recognition*: Tourism is not easily recognized as a subject because some analysts view it as an industry, while others view it as a subject or as a process. Consequently, there is no universal agreement on how to approach it.

2 *Conceptualization*: Academics argue that tourism is a subject that is conceptually weak, which means that there are no universally agreed sets of laws or principles that all researchers adopt as the starting point for the discussion of tourism. To add to the difficulties, tourism is a **multidisciplinary** subject (see Table 1.1) and different disciplines examine tourism from their own standpoints rather than from a universally agreed tourism perspective. In this respect, the different subject areas that inform tourism use concepts and modes of analysis that have been developed in their own disciplines. This means that, as a multidisciplinary subject area, tourism is not integrated between the different disciplines studying it and this severely limits the intellectual development of the area, as there is no cross-fertilization of ideas across disciplines.

3 *Terminology*: There is a wide range of jargon used (e.g. 'alternative', 'responsible' and 'sustainable' tourism) that refers to facets of the same issue (see Image 1.1), which is perplexing for students and researchers because of the semantic complexity and the lack of universally agreed definitions of phenomena being studied.

4 *Data sources*: The data sources available to tourism researchers are weak compared with those available for other subjects.

5 *Reductionism*: The different approaches used by researchers from different disciplines and industry backgrounds have led to what Cooper *et al.* (1998) call reductionism. This means that tourism is reduced to a series of activities or economic transactions and is not seen in terms of a wider series of concepts and overarching analytical frameworks that would help in the understanding and interpretation of tourism. One example is that sociologists often use the **postmodern** paradigm to explain tourist behaviour.

6 *Rigour*: In academic environments, there is still suspicion about the intellectual rigour with which tourism researchers approach their subject. This is made more difficult by the tendency for non-specialists to

TABLE 1.1 Disciplines contributing to the study of tourism

Discipline	Example of contribution to tourism studies
Geography	Spatial analysis of where tourism develops and why
Ecology	The impact of tourism on the natural environment
Agricultural studies	The significance of rural tourism to rural diversification
Parks and recreation	Recreation management techniques in natural areas such as national parks used by tourists
Urban and regional planning	The planning and development of tourism
Marketing	The marketing of tourism
Law	The legal framework and implications for tourists and tourism operators
Business and management science	The management of tourism organizations
Transport studies	The provision of tourist transport services
Hotel and restaurant administration	The provision of hospitality services and accommodation for tourists
Educational studies	Tourism curriculum design and development
Sociology	Sociological analyzes and frameworks to understand tourism as an element of people's leisure time
Economics	The economic impact of tourism
Psychology	Tourist motivation to explain why people travel
Anthropology	The host–guest relationship
Health sciences	The well-being of visitors and the positive and negative aspects of travel including elements of travel medicine
Safety management and ergonomics	The design and development of environments and activities which are safe for tourists

IMAGE 1.1 Researchers need to conduct surveys to understand which people are tourists, as a beach may be populated by tourists, residents and day trippers

dabble in this area of research, which is perceived by some as easy to understand and associated with 'fun' aspects, such as travel and leisure.

7 *Theory*: To date no theoretical constructs or theories which explain the development and internal dynamics of tourism as a process of global economic and social change have been developed. Most academics argue that a subject will not advance learning and understanding until theories are developed which can be tested, modified and rejected or redeveloped. Thus, tourism remains theoretically devoid as a subject area. In other words, much of the research in tourism has tended to be descriptive, lacking in contributions to the development of tourism knowledge and continuing to use established techniques and methodologies. Although there is evidence that this situation is changing slowly, the absence of theoretically derived research remains a major weakness for students and researchers. More insightful studies such as *The Tourist Gaze* (Urry and Larsen 2011), with its attendant postmodernist and sociological analysis of modern-day tourism, are the exception rather than the rule in tourism.

8 *Academic/practitioner divide*: There are inherent tensions in tourism research between the pursuit of knowledge by academics to advance their subject area and the practical and applied needs of the tourism industry and public-sector policymakers who wish to influence the research agenda by seeking usable results from academics.

As a consequence of these problems, one is forced to look around for a conceptual or organizing framework which helps the student of tourism to understand the holistic nature of tourism and how the main components of tourism can be integrated.

Tourism as part of a leisure spectrum

An initial important starting point for defining tourism is to consider how it relates to leisure and the time we have available to be travellers and tourists (see Page and Connell 2010 for more detail). Figure 1.2 shows that many researchers and organizations blur the distinction between leisure, recreation and tourism. Many traditional definitions viewed leisure as a non-commercialized pursuit in contrast to tourism, and the associated costs of travel and accommodation (excluding those who stay with friends and families). There was also a notable distinction between the commercialized tourism industry as predominantly a private sector and profit-oriented, and leisure activities, many of which did not generate the visitor spending of tourism. Many of these boundaries are increasingly blurring as leisure has become commercialized and involves travel (often by car). Consequently, leisure has no precise boundaries with tourism and recreation – they are interrelated and overlapping concepts. For this reason, our definitions suggest that:

- Leisure is viewed as the time, activities and experience derived, characterized by freedom to spend one's free time.
- Recreation is about the activities undertaken in one's leisure time leading to renewal.
- Tourism is travel to a destination (involving an overnight stay and at least 24 hours away from home) which incorporates leisure and recreation activities.

As Parker (1999: 21) notes:

It is through studying leisure as a whole that the most powerful explanations are developed. This is because society is not divided into sports players, television viewers, tourists and so on. It is the same people who do all these things.

This indicates the value of viewing tourism and recreation as part of a wider concept of a leisure continuum, as shown in Figure 1.2. The only major complexity here is that while work is differentiated from leisure, travel can

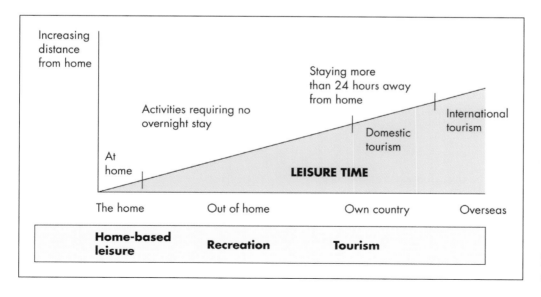

FIGURE 1.2 The leisure spectrum

occur in a work setting through business travel, which is seen as a work-oriented form of tourism in order to differentiate it from leisure-based travel; also, serious leisure, which refers to the breakdown between leisure and work pursuits and the development of leisure career paths with respect to their hobbies and interests (Stebbins 1979), has been discussed by Hall and Page (2006). However, the specific elements of tourism in the leisure spectrum also need an organizing framework in which tourism can be understood more fully as an activity.

One **methodology** used by researchers to understand the nature of tourism phenomena is a **systems** approach (Leiper 1990). The main purpose of such an approach is to rationalize and simplify the real-world complexity of tourism into a number of constructs and components that highlight the interrelated nature of tourism.

Tourism as an integrated system

Since tourism is a multidisciplinary area of study (Gilbert 1990), a systems approach can accommodate a variety of different perspectives because it does not assume a predetermined view of tourism. Instead, it enables one to understand the broader issues and factors which affect tourism, together with the interrelationships between different components in the system. According to Leiper (1990), a 'system' can be defined as a set of elements or parts that are connected to each other by at least one distinguishing principle. In this case, tourism is the distinguishing principle which connects the different components in the system around a common theme. Laws (1991: 7) developed this idea a stage further by providing a systems model of the tourism industry in which the key components were the inputs, outputs and external factors conditioning the system, for example the external business environment, consumer preferences, political factors and economic issues. As external factors are important influences upon tourism systems, the system can be termed 'open', which means that it is influenced by factors aside from the main inputs. The links within the system can be examined in terms of flows between components and these flows may highlight the existence of certain types of relationships between different components (see Figure 1.3). For example:

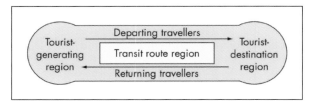

FIGURE 1.3 Leiper's tourism system

- What effect does an increase in the cost of travel have on the demand for travel?
- How does this have repercussions for other components in the system?
- Will it reduce the number of tourists travelling?

A systems approach has the advantage of allowing the researcher to consider the effect of such changes to the tourism system to assess the likely impact on other components. Leiper (1990) identified the following elements of a tourism system: a tourist; a traveller-generating region; tourism destination regions; transit routes for tourists travelling between the generating destination area and the destination region; and the travel and tourism industry (e.g. accommodation, transport, the firms and organizations supplying services and products to tourists). In this analysis, transport forms an integral part of the tourism system, connecting the tourist-generating and destination regions, represented in terms of the volume of travel. Thus, a tourism system is a framework which embodies the entire **tourist experience** of travelling. The analytical value of such an approach is that it enables one to understand the overall process of tourist travel from both the supplier's and the purchaser's (tourist's) perspectives (supply and demand) while identifying the organizations which influence and regulate tourism. This approach highlights the importance of:

- the tourist
- the integral relationships in the overall tourist experience
- the effect of transportation problems on travellers' perceptions
- the tourist's requirement for safe, reliable and efficient modes of transport and service provision
- the destination.

Defining tourism

As Williams and Shaw (1988: 2) observed, 'the definition of tourism is a particularly arid pursuit', but important if one is to understand the nature, scope, impact and magnitude of global tourism. The terms 'travel' and 'tourism' are often interchanged within the published literature on tourism, but they are normally meant to encompass the field of research on human and business activities associated with one or more aspects of the temporary movement of persons away from their immediate home communities and daily work environments for business, pleasure or personal reasons (Chadwick 1994: 65). These two terms tend to be used in differing contexts to mean similar things, although there is a tendency for analysts in the USA to continue to use the term 'travel' when in fact 'tourism' is meant. Despite this inherent problem that may be little more than an exercise in semantics (how to define things), it is widely acknowledged that the two terms are used in isolation or in unison to describe three concepts:

- the movement of people
- a sector of the economy or an associated set of industries
- a broad system of interacting relationships of people, their needs [*sic*] to travel outside their communities and services that attempt to respond to these needs by supplying products (after Chadwick 1994: 65).

From this initial starting point, one can begin to explore some of the complex issues in arriving at a working definition of the terms 'tourism' and 'tourist'. In a historical context, Burkart and Medlik (1981: 41) identify the development of the term 'tourism'. They also point to the problems of separating and differentiating between technical definitions of tourism by organizations and more abstract conceptualizations of the term 'tourism'.

The *concept* of tourism refers to the broad notional framework that identifies tourism's essential characteristics and distinguishes tourism from similar, often related but different phenomena. In contrast, *technical definitions* have evolved through time as researchers modify and develop appropriate measures for statistical, legislative and operational reasons; this implies that there may be various technical definitions to meet particular purposes. However, the concept of tourism and its identification for research purposes are important considerations in this instance for tourism statistics, so that users are familiar with the context of their derivation. While most tourism books, articles and monographs now assume either a standard definition or interpretation of the concept of tourism, which is usually influenced by a social science perspective (e.g. a geographical, economic, political or sociological approach), Burkart and Medlik's (1981) approach to the concept of tourism continues to offer a valid assessment of the situation, highlighting five main characteristics (see Table 1.2). Furthermore, Burkart and Medlik's (1981) conceptualization of tourism is invaluable because it rightly recognizes that much tourism is a leisure activity, which involves a discretionary use of time and money, and recreation is often the main purpose for participation in tourism. But this

TABLE 1.2 Conceptualizing tourism

- Tourism arises from the movement of people to, and their stay in, various destinations.
- There are two elements in all tourism: the journey to the destination and the stay, including activities, at the destination.
- The journey and the stay take place outside the normal place of residence and work, so that tourism gives rise to activities which are distinct from those of the resident and working populations of the places through which tourists travel and in which they stay.
- The movement to destinations is of a temporary, short-term character, with the intention to return home within a few days, weeks or months.
- Destinations are visited for purposes other than taking up permanent residence or employment remunerated from within the places visited (see Image 1.2).

Source: Adapted from Burkart and Medlik (1981: 42)

IMAGE 1.2 Theme parks, such as Disneyland, can create a large demand for visitors to a location, making it a destination in its own right

is no reason for restricting the concept of tourism, as new trends stretch the scope and extent of what we deem the term to mean. All tourism includes some travel but not all travel is tourism, while the temporary and short-term nature of most tourist trips distinguishes them from migration.

However, there is a growing body of knowledge in tourism which is beginning to look at the relationship between tourism and migration (Image 1.2). Migration patterns can influence the nature and scale of tourism patterns, especially where migration is related to ethnic populations who travel back to their family in their native country. Attention now turns to the technical definitions of tourism (also see Leiper 1990 for a further discussion).

Technical definitions of tourism

Technical definitions of tourism are commonly used by organizations seeking to define the population to be measured and there are three principal features which normally have to be defined, as Table 1.3 shows (see BarOn 1984 for a detailed discussion). As Smith (2004) discusses, attempts to define tourism are not new. The first attempt was by the Committee of Statistical Experts of the League of Nations in 1937, with other bodies progressing this work in the 1950s including the International Union of Official Travel Organizers (IUOTO), the United Nations (UN) and more recently the United Nations World Tourism Organization (hereafter WTO). Among the subsequent attempts to recommend appropriate definitions of tourism was the WTO International Conference of Travel and Tourism in Ottawa in 1991, which reviewed, expanded and developed technical definitions and stated that tourism comprises:

> *the activities of a person travelling outside his or her usual environment for less than a specified period of time and whose main purpose of travel is other than [the] exercise of an activity remunerated from the place visited. (WTO 1991)*

Here 'usual environment' is intended to exclude trips within the areas of usual residence, frequent and regular trips between the domicile and the workplace and other community trips of a routine character. 'Less than a specified period of time' is intended to exclude long-term migration, and 'exercise of an activity remunerated from the place visited' is intended to exclude migration for temporary work.

TABLE 1.3 Key technical issues in defining tourism

- Purpose of travel (e.g. the type of traveller, be he or she a business traveller, holidaymaker, someone visiting friends and relatives or someone visiting for other reasons).
- The time dimension involved in the tourism visit, which requires a minimum and a maximum period of time spent away from the home area and the time spent at the destination. In most cases, this would involve a minimum stay of more than 24 hours away from home and a maximum of less than a year.
- Those situations where tourists may or may not be included as tourists, such as cruise-ship passengers, those tourists in transit at a particular point of embarkation/departure and excursionists who stay less than 24 hours at a destination (e.g. the European duty-free cross-Channel day-trip market).

The definitions in Table 1.4 were developed by the WTO. Such definitions can best be thought of as how the majority of organizations define these terms, and Table 1.5, compiled by Lumsdon (1997), summarizes most of the key terms used to define tourism. There are, however, different interpretations in some countries where tourism statistics are gathered. Clearly, how the various terms are defined is crucial to the measurement of tourism demand (see Chapter 3). International comparisons on an equal basis can only be made if like for like is defined, collected and analyzed in a similar fashion. Goeldner *et al.* (2000: 17) note that the National Travel Survey conducted by the Travel Industry Association of America's US Travel Data Center reports on all trips, whatever the purpose, which are in excess of 100 miles and all trips involving an overnight stay, whatever the distance. In the UK, the United Kingdom Tourism Survey (UKTS) distinguishes between short holidays (one to three nights) and long holidays (more than four nights' duration). In order to improve statistical collection and improve understanding of tourism, the UN (WTO and UNSTAT 1994) and the WTO (1991) also recommended differentiating between visitors, tourists and excursionists.

From this classification of travellers, the distinction between international and domestic tourism needs to be made:

- 'Domestic tourism' usually refers to tourists travelling from their normal domicile to other areas within a country.

- In contrast, 'international tourism' normally involves a tourist leaving their country of origin to cross into another country, which involves documentation, administrative formalities and movement to a foreign environment.

TABLE 1.4 Definition of tourism developed by the WTO

International tourism:	Consists of inbound tourism, visits to a country by non-residents, and outbound tourism, residents of a country visiting another country.
Internal tourism:	Residents of a country visiting their own country.
Domestic tourism:	Internal tourism plus inbound tourism (the tourism market of accommodation facilities and attractions within a country).
National tourism:	Internal tourism plus outbound tourism (the resident tourism market for travel agents and airlines).

Source: WTO cited in Chadwick (1994: 66)

TABLE 1.5 Technical definitions: Tourism

Traveller, visitor or tourist	Terms used to describe a person travelling to and staying in a place away from their usual environment for more than one night but less than one year, for leisure, business and other purposes
International tourism	Travel between countries by various modes of travel for the purpose of tourism. This can be subdivided as follows:
Long haul	Travel which involves long distances (e.g. over 1000 miles) for example, between continents
Short haul	Travel between countries which involves shorter distances or travel time (e.g. 250–1000 miles)
Inbound	Visits to a country by non-residents (importation of overseas currency)
Outbound	Visits by residents of one country to another country (exporting currency to other countries)
Domestic tourism	Internal travel and inbound tourism in total
Excursionist or same-day	Visitors who begin and end their visit from the same base (home or holiday base) within the same 24-hour period

Source: Based on Lumsdon (1997: 6)

The WTO (1991) recommended that an international tourist be defined as:

a visitor who travels to a country other than that in which he/she has his/her usual residence for at least one night but not more than one year, and whose main purpose of visit is other than the exercise of an activity remunerated from within the country visited.

and that an international excursionist (e.g. a cruise-ship visitor), be defined as:

a visitor residing in a country who travels the same day to a country other than that in which he/she has his/her usual environment for less than 24 hours without spending the night in the country visited and whose main purpose of visit is other than the exercise of an activity remunerated from within the country visited.

Similar definitions were also developed for domestic tourists, with a domestic tourist's visit having a time limit of not more than six months (WTO 1991; WTO and UNSTAT 1994). The WTO (1983) suggested the following working definition of a domestic tourist:

any person, regardless of nationality, resident in a country and who travels to a place in the same country for not more than one year and whose main purpose of visit is other than following an occupation remunerated from within the place visited. Such a definition includes domestic tourists where an overnight stay is involved and domestic excursionists who visit an area for less than 24 hours and do not stay overnight.

Interestingly, the inclusion of a same-day travel, excursionist category in UN–WTO technical definitions of 'tourism', makes the division between 'recreation' and 'tourism' even more arbitrary and there is increasing international agreement that 'tourism' refers to all activities of visitors, including both overnight and same-day visitors (WTO and UNSTAT 1994: 5). Given improvements in transport technology, same-day travel is becoming increasingly important to some countries, with the UN (WTO and UNSTAT 1994: 9) observing, 'day visits are important to consumers and to many providers, especially tourist attractions, transport operators and caterers'. Chadwick (1994) moves the definition of tourists a stage further by offering a typology of travellers (tourists) which highlights the distinction between tourist (travellers) and non-travellers (non-tourists) and which is summarized in Figure 1.4. Figure 1.4 is distinctive because it highlights all sections of society which are involved in travel of some kind but also looks at the motivation to travel. One area which has expanded since Chadwick's development of Figure 1.4 is the growth in event tourism (see Chapter 26) as a reason to visit places to experience the planned events. Figure 1.4 is also useful because it illustrates where technical problems may occur in deciding which groups to include in tourism and those to exclude. As Figure 1.5 suggests, when operationalizing the typology of travellers, there are other key considerations: notably, the time spent as a tourist and travelling, evolving forms of tourism (e.g. **gap years**; **second home** ownership, which may also include **timeshare** ownership – see Image 1.3) and the geographical dimension (where, when and the form or forms of tourism engaged in), as travellers can engage in different forms of tourism. The concept of tourism is constantly evolving, pushing the boundaries of existing definitions and the scope of what has traditionally been categorized as tourism or leisure. As Figure 1.5 suggests, new forms of tourism are developing to add diversity and further scope for the development of opportunities for businesses and destinations. One example of this process of evolution is the rise of medical tourism (see Insight 1.1). One additional area of growth in tourism-related travel is the student gap year. Certain companies have developed this as a product, and different forms of travel and experiences can be developed with different rewards and risks for the participants. This concept has also begun to have some influence upon young professionals aged 25–40 who have careers but seek spiritual refreshment.

IMAGE 1.3 Timeshare properties, such as these in Malta, bring a diversity of visitors to stay at the property over a calendar year and may help with generating all-year round visitation

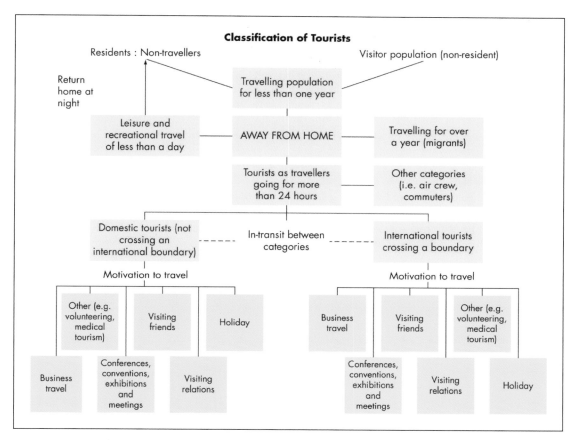

FIGURE 1.4 Chadwick's classification of travellers

Source: Adapted, expanded and simplified from *Travel, Tourism and Hospitality Research*, 2nd edition, Ritchie and Goeldner (1994)

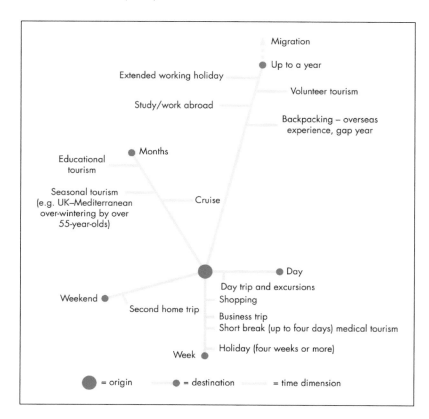

FIGURE 1.5 The temporary mobility in time and space nexus with typical profile of tourist activity

Source: Adapted from C.M. Hall (2005)

INSIGHT 1.1 New forms of tourism: Medical tourism

Medical tourism (MT) is a concept that has re-emerged in recent years and has been part of a growing trend in developed countries for travel to enhance one's health. Studies by Connell (2011) document the recent rise of medical tourism, particularly the focus on travel from developed countries to less developed countries such as Thailand, Malaysia and India for medical treatment (i.e. operations and medical procedures such as cosmetic surgery). Historically, travel to enhance one's health and well-being is not new, as the Greeks and Romans (see Chapter 2) travelled to spas and thermal areas for therapeutic reasons. This trend continued through time, culminating in the nineteenth century with hotels and resorts specializing in hydrotherapy

(water-based medical treatments), which gradually declined in significance in the early twentieth century (Durie 2017).

Yet we need to distinguish between travel for medical travel and medical tourism. Hall (2013) uses the definition of *medical travel*, defined by ESCAP (2009: 1, cited in Hall 2013) as '. . . the international phenomenon of people travelling, often great distances, to access health-care services that are otherwise not available due to the high costs, long waiting lists, or limited health-care capacity in their country of origin'. Medical tourism according to ESCAP (2009) is 'the increasing tendency from people in developed countries to undertake medical travel in combination with visiting tourist

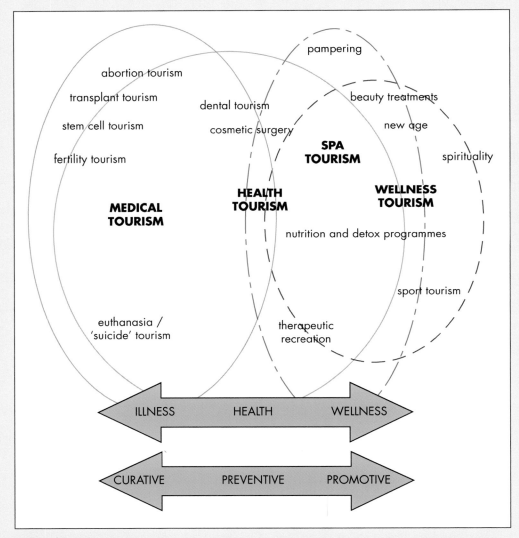

FIGURE 1.6 Interrelatedness of health and medical tourism domains and product niches
Source: Hall (2013: 12) ©Routledge

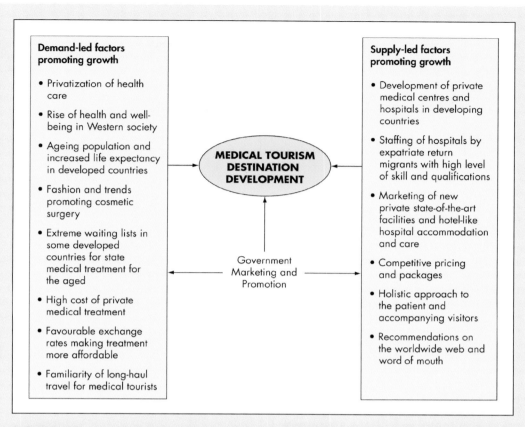

FIGURE 1.7 Key factors promoting the rise of medical tourism since the 1990s

attractions. Medical tourism is often seen as adding medical services to common tourism'. So in its simplest form this is tourist travel for medical treatment. Hall (2013) illustrates that medical tourism can be either international or domestic in scope, need not involve international travel and will involve some form of treatment. In the USA over 11 million people seek medical treatment overseas annually. This creates a demand for visitor services such as hotel accommodation, tours and trips, and a wider range of tourism and hospitality services. It is not surprising that some countries have seized upon the value of marketing and promotion of medical tourism, because it attracts relatively affluent visitors. Laesser (2011) suggests that this is the fastest growing area of tourist travel even though it remains a niche and highly specialized form of demand, and Hall (2013: 12) provides an excellent overview, as illustrated in Figure 1.6, in which the drivers of medical tourism are outlined across a spectrum ranging from traditional forms of spa tourism and the growing interest in wellness, to medical tourism to address illness. These are summarized in terms of supply and demand in Figure 1.7. With an ageing global population, the demand for medical tourism is likely to rise as people are living longer and likely to have more complex illnesses and conditions needing treatment that many state medical systems will not be able to easily cope with. As Connell and Page (2020: 81–85) argue, 'The UN has forecast the rise in the world's population over 60 from 500 million in 1990 to 3.2 billion by 2100 which indicates the long-term projections for a more ageing population structure globally that will create a wide range of societal challenges'. This will simultaneously also add an ageing dimension to future tourism demand, as we will discuss in later chapters. Consequently, medical tourism can be distinguished by a range of motives spanning curative domain for specific illnesses to wellness tourism and more preventative aspects of health. Among the leading medical tourism destinations globally are India, Malaysia, Brazil, Thailand, Turkey, Mexico, Costa Rica, Singapore, Taiwan and South Korea. Estimates of the scale of the global market and value of medical tourism have been put at USD 45.5–72 billion with 14 million travellers according to Global Health Care Resources (2017). Therefore opportunities for tourism and new forms of tourism can emerge from unlikely sources.

Further reading

Connell, J. (2011) *Medical Tourism*. Wallingford: CABI.

Connell, J. and Page, S.J. (2020) 'Tourism, ageing and the demographic timebomb – The implications of dementia for the visitor economy', *Tourism Review* 75 (1): 81–85.

Global Health Care Resources (2017) *2016–2017 Global Buyers Survey,* http://medicaltourismassociation.com/userfiles/files/GLOBAL_BUYERS_REPORT_BRIEF.pdf.

Hall, C.M. (2013) *Medical Tourism: The Ethics, Regulation and Marketing of Health Mobility.* Routledge: London.

Laesser, C. (2011) 'Health travel motivation and activities: Insights from a mature market – Switzerland', *Tourism Review* 66 (1/2): 68–82.

Questions

1 How would you set about defining medical tourism?
2 With reference to Figure 1.6, how do you think this continuum of provision will change in the future?
3 How will an ageing population change the demand for medical tourism in the future?
4 What factors might destinations consider when seeking a specialization in medical tourism?

Ritchie (1975, cited in Latham 1989: 55) argued that an important part of the maturing process for any science is the development or adaptation of consistent and well-tested measurement techniques and methodologies that are well suited to the types of problems encountered in practice. There is a need for a classification of tourism which can evolve and accommodate more complex forms of tourism, as Figures 1.4 and 1.5 demonstrated. A robust system is required to not only classify what we mean by 'tourism', 'tourist' and a 'trip', but how we measure these interactions between origin, destination and travel routes. In this context, the measurement of tourists, tourism activity and the effects on the economy and society in different environments is crucial to the development of tourism as an established area of study within the confines of social science and management disciplines. In relation to establishing demand, tourism statistics and the associated challenges and issues in measuring tourism are explored in Chapter 3. Yet one of the most enduring themes throughout this book, and one which affects all forms of tourism in the way they are produced and consumed by tourists in the twenty-first century, is the process of globalization.

Globalization and the production and consumption of tourism

This chapter has established that tourism is a global economic activity and as such is part of a much wider process of globalization. Meethan (2004) describes the growing importance of the term 'globalization' in everyday language, based upon the principles of a new economic order, with global markets, and which, as a process, shapes our purchases and preferences as consumers. While our daily lives are largely fixed to the localities we live, work and play in, globalization is an international process which transcends local and national boundaries, representing an international geographical entity which has eroded the autonomy of the nation state. The process of globalization has many facets, but its development since the 1980s has been aided by financial deregulation in many countries and the lifting of barriers to capital and private enterprise. An example of this in the tourism sector is the growth of multinational enterprises in tourism (e.g. transnational hotel chains with head offices outside the country/region of operation, to which profits are repatriated). The impact of information technology has also made the world a more interconnected place, compressing time and place and intensifying connections, with enterprises able to access and do business with global consumers via the Internet. However, globalization is much more than the internationalization of business.

To understand tourism and globalization in terms of the service sector, it is helpful to introduce two terms: production and consumption. In the global economy, tourism has increasingly become commodified (i.e. portrayed as a commodity to be traded, which as a service is consumed) so that consumers (the tourists) consume the destination as a product. This process requires a complex range of organizations involved in the supply of tourism to combine in order to 'produce' tourism experiences that the tourist consumes. For the tourist, globalization means that increasingly a global bundle of services and commodities are purchased. In this respect, 'globalization' is an umbrella term to describe a number of converging trends, particularly the ability of larger global companies to achieve economies of scale and to control the supply of products to consume. Researchers have also described circuits of production and consumption in tourism as a function of globalization in that these bundles of services and products are purchased and consumed across the world from the point of origin (e.g. purchase of travel) to the destination. Part of the globalization process is leading to global standards and expectations of standards. However, unlike global manufacturing and production, the production and consumption of tourism is not placeless, nor can it be located in the cheapest location, like call centres. Instead tourism is place-specific (i.e. the destination is the point of consumption) and production is fragmented across many sectors of the economy (e.g. accommodation, tour operators, transport, destinations).

Global **investment flows** are creating global forms of tourism production (i.e. hotel chains and integrated tourism companies) as tourism flows are now reaching all parts of the globe and intensifying activity at specific locations. As Ashworth and Page (2011) argue, this is manifest in the pivotal role of world tourism cities like London, Paris, New York and Rome, where global control of capital flows is often located. Similarly, at a regional level, tourism activity is intensifying in the three main regions that dominate global patterns: Europe, North America and East Asia-Pacific (Image 1.4). This globalization process, as they argue, is bringing cultures into contact with each other, highlighting inequities between the developed and the developing worlds. Underlying this culture contact is a growing dependency between those two worlds. Where global capital exploits tourism destinations, the local communities and resource base in order to profit from tourists, the inequalities are reinforced. As a result, Shaw and Williams (2004) point to globalization as part of a process of tightening interconnections which cut across national boundaries. Networks are based on the production–consumption exchange process in tourism manifest in terms of:

- economic interconnections – global flows of capital, activities of transnational companies such as multinational hotel corporations
- global consumerism
- global mobility of people for tourism or migration (after Shaw and Williams 2004: 42).

Some of the dimensions of globalization in tourism discussed by Shaw and Williams (2004) include:

- globalization of media images by satellite television and the Internet, which has assisted in the promotion of places to a global audience
- dynamic forms of place promotion by tourism agencies through advertising, especially via the Internet
- travel promotion by tour operators and transport
- the globalization of business
- the globalization of migration and the recognition of the linkage between homeland and the new area of settlement, generating a demand for travel to visit friends and relatives
- the 'McDonaldization' of tourism experiences – the standardization of the provision of hotel and restaurant experiences worldwide

IMAGE 1.4 World cities are a key resource for tourism in locations such as Shanghai

- investment flows from tourist-generating areas following the tourist to the destination area, such as the Japanese investment in Australia's Gold Coast since the 1980s and Korean investment in Rotorua, New Zealand's tour companies, retail shops and retail outlets. While globalization is a major process shaping international tourism, a number of other key issues which can be described as 'cross-cutting themes' will also shape the content of this book. For example, Figure 1.7, based on a study by UN–WTO (2011), depicts some of these themes that cut across a range of topics and subject areas. Two in particular, new *technology media* and *sustainability*, are embedded in each area of this book as well as having their own chapters, being interconnected with globalization. In the case of new technology, it has revolutionized every area of tourism activity, making information flows critical to the way tourism businesses operate and their relationship with consumers. In a similar vein, sustainability has emerged as a cornerstone of modern-day tourism, as a reaction to the excesses of mass tourism and the short-term exploitation of tourism-related resources. New sustainability-related agendas such as climate change and the depletion of natural resources have focused attention on the conspicuous consumption associated with tourism.

The sustainability debate has also seen growing concerns around the evolving concept of overtourism and the concerns within communities about the effects on daily life of too many visitors, reflected in the growing political movements and civil protest and unrest in some cities (e.g. Barcelona – see Chapter 20) that challenge economic growth,

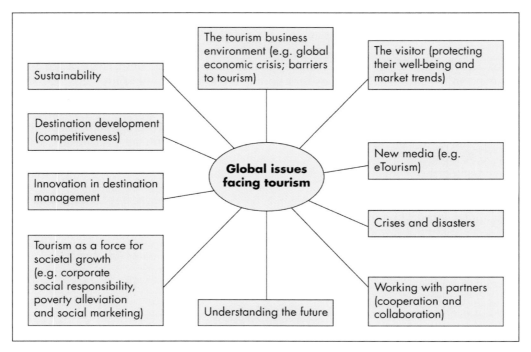

FIGURE 1.8 Key forces shaping global tourism.
Source: Developed from UN–WTO (2011)

which proponents of tourism point to as a benefit. We will pick up these themes later in the book, but they are new themes that are changing the nature of tourism as a phenomenon. Likewise, the growing impact of technology will be considered later in the book because it has made booking travel-related products easy and placed travel within the reach of a new generation of computer-literate consumers who are not necessarily going to a physically located travel agent to book the annual holiday. Technology now opens up the option of travel at the click of a computer mouse or mobile device. Technology is also changing the way travel experiences are promoted, created, consumed and instantaneously shared. More concerning for some sectors of the tourism industries are the effects of new technology on the way they do business and its impact on existing business models.

The harnessing of new technologies by some companies has been used to act as **disruptive innovations** (i.e. an idea or new service that disrupts existing provisions, such as Airbnb (Airbnb.com) – see Guttentag 2015) and disruptive technology (i.e. a new technology that displaces existing technology, such as mobile phones or apps that have enabled new businesses to be created, such as the taxi firm Uber (Uber.com)). By developing such innovations and technological changes, companies have created new concepts such as the **sharing economy** (see Cheng 2016), where existing organizational forms have been challenged by peer-to-peer transactions in which consumers may be both consumers and/or suppliers as opposed to organizations solely fulfilling the supply function. Airbnb epitomizes this trend in that it reduces the price of production, thereby undercutting other providers to create a new landscape of competition in a market, as the low-cost-airline phenomenon did in the 1980s and 1990s.

Conclusion

This chapter has introduced the conceptual issues associated with the study of tourism, highlighting the development of the subject area and some of the principal difficulties which students and researchers need to be aware of when attempting to define the subject. It has distinguished between the terms:

- a tourist
- domestic tourism
- international tourism

and acknowledged that tourism is a multidisciplinary subject rather than a discipline in its own right, because other subjects study and contribute to it. It has no core body of knowledge that is distinct, unique and not modified from other disciplines such as geography, marketing or economics, a feature debated by Hall *et al.* (2004). The lack of any theoretical core of knowledge has also impeded the intellectual development of tourism from making major leaps forward in understanding although, as Hall *et al.* (2004) acknowledge, the subject is in good health if a high level of research activity is a measure. But others still criticize tourism for being eclectic, disparate and under-theorized (e.g. Meethan 2001: 2). Intellectually, other disciplines have viewed tourism as a descriptive subject but the recent scale and significance of tourism as a global activity and process, with economic implications for governments, has elevated its acceptability as an academic area worthy of study. Crises such as 9/11 and Ebola have reinforced the public awareness of tourism as an academic subject, and as the volatile nature of an economic sector which many countries depend upon has reached centre stage. One of the most interesting changes in the status of tourism as a

subject area worthy of pursuit is the demand for students and skilled workers who have a grasp of the dynamic and ever-changing nature of tourism, and an ability to manage the detrimental impacts of tourism on the total population and natural environment.

Although this chapter has addressed a host of technical and semantic issues associated with the measurement and definition of tourists and tourism, which may appear dull and uninteresting, a fundamental understanding of these seemingly tedious issues is essential when wider issues of tourism impacts and effects are evaluated: without a baseline or an agreement on what one is observing or measuring, the results and recommendations will have little meaning – especially if the wrong assumptions or features are measured. One continued mistake which tourism researchers consistently make is that they fail to agree on clear parameters of what is being observed, measured and evaluated, and rarely refer to the technical issues necessary to precisely delimit what they are studying.

Discussion questions

1 What are the different subjects which contribute to the area known as tourism studies?
2 What are the main components of Leiper's tourism system?
3 What are the problems one may encounter in trying to calculate the number of tourists which arrive in a country in a given time period?
4 How will the process of globalization continue to affect tourism?

References

Ashworth, G. and Page, S.J. (2011) 'Urban tourism research: Recent progress and current paradoxes', *Tourism Management*, 32 (1): 1–15.

BarOn, R. (1984) 'Tourism terminology and standard definitions', *Tourist Review*, 39 (1): 2–4.

Bronner F. and de Hoog, R. (2014) 'Vacationers and the economic "double-dip" in Europe', *Tourism Management*, 40: 330–337.

Burkart, A. and Medlik, S. (1974) *Tourism, Past, Present and Future*. Oxford: Heinemann.

Burkart, A. and Medlik, R. (eds.) (1975) *The Management of Tourism*. Oxford: Heinemann.

Burkart, A. and Medlik, R. (1981) *Tourism, Past, Present and Future*, 2nd edition. London: Heinemann.

Chadwick, R. (1994) 'Concepts, definitions and measurement used in travel and tourism research', in J. R. Brent Ritchie and C. Goeldner (eds.) *Travel, Tourism and Hospitality Research:*

A Handbook for Managers and Researchers, 2nd edition. New York: Wiley.

Cheng, M. (2016) 'Sharing economy: A review and agenda for future research', *International Journal of Hospitality Management*, 57, 60–70.

Connell, J. (2011) *Medical Tourism*. Wallingford: CABI.

Connell, J. and Page, S.J. (2020) 'Tourism, ageing and the demographic timebomb – The implications of dementia for the visitor economy', *Tourism Review 75* (1): 81–85.

Cooper, C.P., Fletcher, J., Gilbert, D.G. and Wanhill, S. (1998) *Tourism: Principles and Practice*, 2nd edition. London: Pitman.

Crampon, J. (1955) 'Tourism research – a recent development at the University', *Journal of Marketing*, 20 (1): 28–35.

Dredge, D., Airey, D. and Gross, M. (eds.) (2014) *The Routledge Handbook of Tourism and Hospitality Education*. London: Routledge.

Durie, A. (2017) *Scotland and Tourism: The Long View, 1700–2015*. London: Routledge.

Economic and Social Survey of Asia Pacific (ESCAP) (2009). *Medical Travel in Asia and the Pacific. Challenges and Opportunities*. United Nations: New York.

Gilbert, D.C. (1990) 'Conceptual issues in the meaning of tourism', in C.P. Cooper (ed.) *Progress in Tourism, Recreation and Hospitality Management Volume 2*. London: Belhaven.

Global Health Care Resources (2017) *2016–2017 Global Buyers Survey*, http://medicaltourismassociation.com/userfiles/files/GLOBAL_BUYERS_REPORT_BRIEF.pdf.

Goeldner, C.R., Ritchie, J.R.B. and McIntosh, R.W. (2000) *Tourism: Principles, Practices and Philosophies*. New York: John Wiley and Sons.

Guttentag, D. (2015) 'Airbnb: Disruptive innovation and the rise of an informal tourism accommodation sector', *Current Issues in Tourism*, 18 (12): 1192–1217.

Hall, C.M. (2005) *Tourism: Rethinking the Social Science of Mobility*. Prentice Hall: Harlow.

Hall, C.M. (2013) *Medical Tourism: The Ethics, Regulation and Marketing of Health Mobility*. Routledge: London.

Hall, C.M. and Page, S.J. (2006) *Geography of Tourism*, 3rd edition. London: Routledge.

Hall, C.M. and Page, S.J. (2014) *The Geography of Tourism and Recreation*, 4th edition. London: Routledge.

Hall, C.M., Williams, A. and Lew, A. (2004) 'Tourism: Conceptualisations, institutions and issues', in A. Lew, C.M. Hall and A.M. Williams (eds.), *A Companion to Tourism*, 1st edition. Oxford: Blackwell.

Hayner, N. (1932) 'The tourist family', *Social Forces* 11 (1): 82–85.

Laesser, C. (2011) 'Health travel motivation and activities: Insights from a mature market – Switzerland', *Tourism Review* 66 (1/2): 68–82.

Latham, J. (1989) 'The statistical measurement of tourism', in C.P. Cooper (ed.) *Progress in Tourism, Recreation and Hospitality Management, Volume 1*. London: Belhaven.

Laws, E. (1991) *Tourism Marketing*. Cheltenham: Stanley Thornes.

Leiper, N. (1990) *Tourism Systems: An Interdisciplinary Perspective*, Palmerston North, New Zealand: Department of Management Systems, Occasional Paper 2, Massey University.

Lumsdon, L. (1997) *Tourism Marketing*. London: Thomson Learning.

Meethan, K. (2001) *Tourism in a Global Society*. London: Palgrave.

Meethan, K. (2004) 'Transnational corporations, globalisation and tourism', in A. Lew, C.M. Hall and A. Williams (eds.) *A Companion to Tourism*. Oxford: Blackwell.

Page, S.J. and Connell, J. (2010) *Leisure: An Introduction*. Harlow: Pearson.

Parker, S. (1999) *Leisure in Contemporary Society*. Wallingford: CABI.

Ritchie, J.R.B. and Goeldner, C. (eds.) (1994) *Travel, Tourism and Hospitality Research: A Handbook for Managers and Researchers*, 2nd edition. New York: Wiley.

Shaw, G. and Williams, A. (2004) *Tourism and Tourism Spaces*. London: Sage.

Smith, S.L.J. (2004) 'The measurement of global tourism: Old debates, new consensus and continuing challenges', in A. Lew, C.M. Hall and A. Williams (eds.) *A Companion to Tourism*. Oxford: Blackwell.

Stebbins, R. (1979) *Amateurs: On the Margin between Work and Leisure*. Beverly Hills, CA: Sage.

UN–WTO (2011) *Policy and Practice for Global Tourism*, Madrid: UN–WTO.

Urry, J. and Larsen, J. (2011) *The Tourist Gaze*, 3rd edition. London: Sage.

Williams, A. and Shaw, G. (1988) 'Tourism and economic development: introduction', in A. Williams and G. Shaw (eds.) *Tourism and Economic Development: Western European Experiences*. London: Belhaven Press.

WTO (World Tourism Organization) (1983) *Definitions Concerning Tourism Statistics*. Madrid: WTO.

WTO (World Tourism Organization) (1991) *Resolutions of International Conference on Travel and Tourism, Ottawa, Canada*. Madrid: World Tourism Organization.

WTO and UNSTAT (1994) *Recommendations on Tourism Statistics*. Madrid and New York: WTO and UN.

Further reading

Books

Colomb, C. and Novy, J. (2016) *Protest and Resistance in the Tourist City*. London: Routledge.

Gilbert, D.C. (1990) 'Conceptual issues in the meaning of tourism', in C.P. Cooper (ed.) *Progress in Tourism, Recreation and Hospitality Management Volume 2*. London: Belhaven.

Hall, C.M. and Page, S.J. (2014) *The Geography of Tourism and Recreation: Environment, Place and Space*, 4th edition. London: Routledge.

Lohmann, G. and Netto, A. (eds.) (2016) *Tourism Theory: Concepts, Models and Systems*. Wallingford: CABI.

Page, S.J. (2019) *Tourism Management*, 6th edition. London: Routledge.

Sigala, M., Christou, E. and Gretzel, U. (eds.) (2016) *Social Media in Travel, Tourism and Hospitality: Theory, Practice and Cases*. London: Routledge.

Smith, S. (2007) 'Duelling definitions: Challenges and implications of conflicting international concepts of tourism', in D. Airey and J. Tribe (eds.) *Developments in Tourism Research*. Oxford: Elsevier.

Journal articles

Dredge, D. and Gyimóthy, S. (2015) 'The collaborative economy and tourism: Critical perspectives, questionable claims and silenced voices', *Tourism Recreation Research*, 40 (3): 286–302.

Hughes, N. (2018) '"Tourists go home": Anti-tourism industry protest in Barcelona', *Social Movement Studies*, 17 (4): 471–477.

Hunt, J.D. and Layne, D. (1991) 'Evolution of travel and tourism terminology and definitions', *Journal of Travel Research*, 29 (4): 7–11.

Varma, A., Jukic, N., Pestek, A., Shultz, C.J. and Nestorov, S. (2016) 'Airbnb: Exciting innovation or passing fad?' *Tourism Management Perspectives*, 20: 228–237.

The evolution and development of tourism

Learning outcomes

After reading this chapter and answering the questions, you should be able to:

- understand the principal factors that have influenced the development of tourism through time and space

- recognize the theme of continuity and change as a central feature of tourism development

- understand that the development of tourism globally, in a given location or at a certain time, is explained by a combination of political, economic, social and technological influences.

Overview

Throughout history people have travelled for many different reasons and so tourism is as old as human activity, although its development from antiquity highlights its critical link – that one had to have the means by which to consume tourism. Travel for pleasure purposes is essentially a more recent phenomenon, which has grown rapidly in the last 200 years. From the end of the eighteenth century, when only the wealthy few could indulge in this activity, tourism has developed into something that many ordinary people now consider as a necessity.

Introduction

Tourism is by no means a new phenomenon, with its historical origins in the ancient cultures of the Greek and Roman social elite. While we may consider the seaside resort to be a feature of modern times, there were many seaside resorts in the Roman Empire where the upper classes and masses flocked each summer to get away from the overcrowded and unhealthy conditions in Rome. In the respect that these early 'tourists' pursued pleasure and relaxation in regions away from the main towns and cities, they epitomize modern-day tourism: the pursuit of pleasure in a location away from everyday life and the use of one's leisure time for non-work purposes. However, the root of modern-day tourism is to be found much later. As Inglis (2000: 1) observes, 'Vacation-taking and holiday-making turn up . . . at more or less the same moment as the consumer . . . from some time early in the second half of the eighteenth century when consumers begin to take holidays as a fashionable activity.' This trend-driven element of tourism is a considerable force in the pursuit of pleasure through history, as the status and recognition which are still afforded to travel experiences are considerable in Western society. However, as Table 2.1 shows, throughout history tourism has been dependent upon several factors which have facilitated its growth and development, particularly transport and access, along with the leisure time and means by which to afford to travel (in other words, disposable income and wealth). Turning to a different perspective on historical associations, the late twentieth century saw the rise of the heritage industry as a core interest within tourism, with a dramatic rise in, demand for and supply of heritage-based attractions. This meshing of tourism and history and the associated issues of interpretation, management and ownership provide some interesting debate in contemporary studies of tourism.

Tourism, history and the past: Its significance and analysis

How should we study a subject such as the historical development of tourism when it is as vast as human civilization itself? The historian has adopted different techniques towards the study of tourism in past times, notably those derived from the emergence of social history in the 1970s and 1980s, although many examples of the study of tourism can be dated to earlier periods, particularly the rise of seaside resorts in the 1930s. The historian's analysis of tourism is dominated by two complementary and yet divergent themes: the development of tourism and its *continuity* as a phenomenon through time; this often runs parallel to and sometimes in opposition with the process of *change*, where tourism is constantly evolving and changing often due to innovation in transport or products (Armstrong and Williams 2005). Perhaps one of the central features driving continuity and change in tourism was summed up by Löfgren (2002: 282).

> If today's tourists are no longer satisfied with sun and tour guides, history teaches us tourists never seem to be satisfied, whether in 1799 or 1999. Restlessness, frustration, and boredom are part of that great personal experience. A strange and often insatiable longing for transcendence gives tourism an element of secular religion, a quest for that fulfilment waiting out there somewhere – in the elsewherelands. As soon as our vacation is over we start to fantasise about the next one: the perfect holiday.

If this holds true through history, then the constant demands from tourists for places to visit and different experiences helps to keep the phenomenon of tourism growing. This is perhaps best illustrated by the example of Blackpool, one of Britain's most popular seaside resorts. Blackpool developed as a major day-excursion market, promoted by its main railway company, and as a working-class domestic tourism holiday resort in the Victorian period. The resort continued to grow through to the 1950s (despite the impact of the First and Second World Wars, in 1914–1918 and 1939–1945 respectively) and then started to decline in the 1970s, as overseas holidays became more fashionable. Despite attempts to attract conferences and conventions to Blackpool, the resort has changed and declined since its Victorian, Edwardian and Inter-war heyday.

Therefore, in any analysis of tourism the historical dimension has a great deal to offer the student of tourism. Yet as Durie (2003) notes, in spite of several good studies by historians (e.g. Walton 1983) and geographers (e.g. Towner 1996), the historical study of tourism remains a comparatively new field of study. However, since 2009 a new academic journal, the *Journal of Tourism History*, has expanded the knowledge base of the history of tourism. Any historical analysis of tourism will reveal a great deal of attention to empirical research (i.e. a concern for facts and figures) as well as interest in the factors promoting tourism development (e.g. transport) and the role of leading entrepreneurs as agents of change in developing non-tourism locations into tourism locations.

TABLE 2.1 Illustrations of the development of tourism: A range of historical forms of tourism and factors promoting their development

Era	Typical form of tourism	Facilitating factors	Main participants/tourists
Greeks Romans	Olympic Games Coliseums for events and leisure/tourism Business travel Seaside and inland spa tourism Urban and rural tourism	Leisure and sport ethic Expansion of the Roman Empire Construction of Roman roads Road/sea travel 200 holidays a year for leisured classes Business travel due to imperial expansion	Leisured classes staying in tented encampments Urban leisured elite construct second homes in rural locations away from main cities Imperial civil servants for business travel Middle classes – travel to seaside resorts and spas for health and spiritual reasons
Middle Ages	Festival and event tourism linked to religious events Jousting tournaments Pilgrimages Limited business travel	General population as day trippers in immediate locality related to holy days	Knights and landed classes Religious orders for pilgrimages and the nobility
Renaissance and Reformation	Continuity with fairs and events/festivals Second-home ownership	Holy days Dissolution of the monasteries and creation of landed estates with confiscated lands used to stimulate country-estate development and rural tourism Improved road access	Nobility
Sixteenth and seventeenth centuries	Continuity with festivals Grand Tour Spa tourism	Improved transportation – sea and rivers/land to allow touring and access to spas and inland resorts Rise of international travel New Protestant work ethic emerging to differentiate between classes and work/leisure	Nobility and pursuit of the Classical antiquities initially as part of an educational experience, followed by the pursuit of the picturesque
Eighteenth century	Continuity with previous forms of tourism (spas, Grand Tour and festivals) New forms of tourism – the rise of the seaside/coast	Royal patronage of bathing Improved road access by stagecoach to the coast Changing attitudes towards use of leisure time and willingness to explore the coast in Christian doctrines Fashion and taste promote the coast	Nobility
Nineteenth century	Spas Coastal tourism Urban tourism Rise of interest in wilderness areas Development of international business travel – imperial expansion in European countries Pleasure cruising	New technology, the steamship making urban areas and the coast more accessible to a mass market from the 1840s Reducing costs of travel Rise in holidays for industrial workforce	Growing social differentiation (upper, middle and working classes) with distinct forms of tourism and holidaytaking Tourism becoming a mass consumer product later in Victorian period
Twentieth century	All forms for Victorian period and expansion of sea travel	Reducing cost of sea and land-based travel, and greater prestige and status associated with foreign travel Rise of the car and charabanc in the 1930s making a wider range of areas accessible The rise of the aircraft and jet aeroplane post-1950	As for Victorian period but faster pace of diffusion of former upper/middle-class forms of tourism becoming more widely available to the population Innovations in the 1930s such as the holiday camp idea Emergence of mass tourism in the 1950s at the coast and then via package holidays

A more in-depth review of some of the ways historians analyze tourism reveals a wide range of themes which have begun to attract attention, including (but not exclusively) some of the following themes:

- The emergence of pleasure travel as a distinct activity (Walton 2009).
- The rise and continuing role of the seaside resort (e.g. Walton 1983, 2000).
- The cultural history of tourism and holiday-making (e.g. Löfgren 2002), particularly the role of the beach and coast and its use for tourism.
- The rise of tourism in specific countries (e.g. Durie 2003) and on entire continents (e.g. Towner 1996).
- The rise of the package holiday and mass tourism (Bray and Raitz 2001).
- The rise of commercialized leisure and tourism in the American city (Hannigan 1998) such as the development of Coney Island amusement parks as leisure attractions.
- The development of urban tourism locations, such as spas and resorts inland, and towns as service centres for visitors; this also provided development opportunities for individual entrepreneurs such as Billy Butlin in the 1930s in the UK.
- The emergence and role of heritage as part of the contemporary tourism product.
- The way in which the private and public sectors set about attracting and developing tourism in specific locations using public sector finance, such as rates.
- The role of private transport providers, such as railway companies, and the imagery and promotional material developed to promote the localities.
- The historian and techniques for analyzing tourism.

These themes also reveal two approaches used in historical research: the analysis of how changes have come about and their formative influences on the contemporary era, and the in-depth study of specific eras and phenomena in past times; this latter approach is described as taking a cross-section of a specific era. Some of the key questions which historians ask when examining the evolution and development of tourism include:

- When did the development process begin?
- How did the sequence of change induced by tourism development in the location, society, economy, built and natural environment and landscape occur?
- Why did development occur when and where it did?
- What were the formative influences on the development process (i.e. agents of change)?
- What was the scale of change induced by and contributed to by tourism?
- What role did the private and public sectors play in initiating, managing and promoting tourism development?

To address these questions, historical researchers focus on specific themes and issues dependent upon their interest or specialism (i.e. economic, social, cultural and political dimensions and the geographers' concern with place and localities in past times). This leads them to the all-important issue of how one reconstructs past experiences of tourism. Walton's (1983, 2000) seminal studies of the English seaside resort outlined a number of important source materials available to reconstruct the history of tourism, including:

- The census to illustrate the population composition, growth and impact of tourism on employment and the demand for migrant labour.
- Visitors' use of guide books in resorts and diaries of experiences of touring.
- Records of resort development by builders and entrepreneurs and the records of municipal corporations and their involvement in tourism.
- Records of tourist-related businesses (e.g. the Thomas Cook archive) where these records exist and are available for consultation (see Insight 2.1).

While this chapter cannot present a comprehensive review of tourism through history, nor the separate tourism histories of the world's regions, it is hoped that some of these principal features of the historical analysis of tourism will be portrayed. For example, historical analysis of tourism is used by the public sector through promoting oral history and perpetuating a living tradition. Public sector organizations have also used historical associations with literary figures to create and promote destinations. The use of oral history involves the recording of past histories, of how people remembered their experiences of tourism, to understand both the cultural meaning of tourism to people in past times and how the tourism system developed and functioned in the areas these people visited. As Barton's (2005) study depicts, using a range of different data sources, the working classes' experiences of tourism from the Victorian period onwards was one of *communal experiences*, using mass transport such as steamboats, trains and then charabancs (early coaches), and of staying in seaside boarding houses and then the holiday camps. In contrast, the history of middle-class tourism experiences was characterized by more individualistic pursuits and epitomized by tourists' purchasing of motor cars in the 1930s and the postwar period. Oral histories and diaries reported on in studies such as Kynaston (2008) depicted the crowds of train travellers who used this means of transport in the postwar period of austerity. Kynaston depicted the 1950s as a time in which holiday travel was juxtaposed with a daily life characterized by the rationing of food, queuing and shortages. Kynaston (2008) made extensive use of key studies such as the Mass Observation project. Mass Observation in the UK was conducted between 1937 and 1955 and has become a rich source of historical evidence on the holiday habits, activities and behaviour of the British population in the late 1930s (it was also used as methodology for monitoring British opinion and attitudes and morale during the Second World War) (http://www.massobs.org.uk/). The Mass Observation social research organization was set up in 1937 to collate an anthropology of the British population using a wide range of survey methods, including participant observation. Field researchers observed and recorded people's behaviour and activities, and their approach is outlined in Madge and Harrisson (1937). One interesting feature of this project was that it confirms what many historians suggest, that holidays were firmly embedded in working-class culture in the postwar years. For example, when a sample of the population was asked what they would economize on, holidays (irrespective of social class) were deemed to be important elements not to be sacrificed. Only limited evidence survives with which to reconstruct tourism prior to the eighteenth century (as we saw in Table 2.1). The period after 1700 is often acknowledged as the beginning of the rise of domestic travel (see Dove 2016); this evolved to become mass travel in the Victorian years in Europe, and digital archives on this offer many possible avenues for researchers (see http://www.masstourism.amdigital.co.uk/).

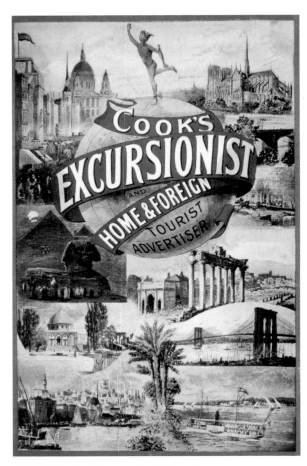

IMAGE 2.1 *Thomas Cook's* The Excursionist
Source: © Thomas Cook

The origins of modern tourism

It is impossible to pinpoint a precise point in time when tourism as we understand it today began. Rather, it evolved through time, building on the needs and desires of society and the opportunities that were presented. Pilgrimages in medieval Britain (brought to life for a modern audience by Chaucer's *Canterbury Tales*) show that both the supply and demand for what might be loosely termed 'tourism products and services' (such as accommodation and transport) were operating as far back as the fifteenth century. In the wider context, the sixteenth-century Elizabethan mansion became a social and cultural centre, and the early origins of the VFR (visiting friends and relatives) sector are easily identified in this period. From the seventeenth century, a form of tourism known as 'polite visiting' emerged: those in the upper classes travelled on circuits of the country or took day trips, visiting the country estates of associates or society figures to view the architecture, garden, parkland and works of arts. Such occupations are reflected in the literature of the time, perhaps the most well-known example being Jane Austen's *Pride and Prejudice* (1813), in which the protagonist's visit to Darcy's country estate is documented. Publications by respected writers stimulated travel to unknown and remote places from the late eighteenth century onwards. A good example is the Hebridean Islands off Scotland's west coast which, prior to the 1770s, were not visited for pleasure purposes. After the publication and success of Johnson's *A Journey to the Western Islands of Scotland* (1775) and Boswell's

Journal of a Tour to the Hebrides (1785), the islands became a magnet for travellers, most notably poets, artists and composers, who further popularized the region to others through their works. These early visits required special preparations, and a degree of discomfort in terms of accommodation, travel and food was to be expected. However, visits remained confined to a small number of academics and intellectuals until the introduction of regular steamship services from Glasgow around 1840.

A form of tourism based on social and cultural experiences and education for young aristocrats became particularly prominent during the eighteenth century; it was known as the Grand Tour. Historical evidence shows that several nationalities undertook Grand Tours, including the British, French, Germans and Russians, but most research on the subject concerns British outbound travellers. Towner (1985) suggests that the number of Britons undertaking Grand Tours per year was 15 000–20 000 at the peak in the mid-eighteenth century, from the landed and, as they grew in wealth, the middle classes. Towner (1996) presents a comprehensive review of the Grand Tour and notes some of the reasons for travel, which included a shift away from the increasingly unfashionable society and culture of Britain and the perception that travel would broaden the mind. Grand Tour itineraries were often influenced by travel literature. Tourists visited classical antiquities, principal works of art and architecture, picturesque landscapes, gardens and natural curiosities, as well as mixing with fashionable society on their travels. Similar to modern-day tourism, the Grand Tour was typified by distinct seasonal patterns of travel. As Towner (1996) notes, tourists wished to see particular places at particular times of the year: Venice was popular around May and June for the Ascension-tide, while Rome was favoured at Christmas, both for their renowned festivities. Other places were rarely visited when the climate was less hospitable: the heat of Rome and Naples in August, or the poor winter travel conditions in the Alps were usually avoided. The length of a Grand Tour varied from around three years in the seventeenth century to about six months or less in the nineteenth century. Stays of around three months were common in the cultural centres such as Paris and many of the Italian cities, while other locations were sometimes visited overnight or only for a short stay (Towner 1996).

The examples in this section have emphasized the importance of the 'continuity and change' theme within tourism. In terms of the influence of literature and culture on travel behaviour, historically this was significant, yet it is equally so in the twenty-first century, when media influences, such as travel writing, literature, film and television, play a crucial role in stimulating interest in visiting certain locations. Similarly, while the Grand Tour itself died out, the same patterns of travel are identifiable in contemporary forms of travel, such as the student gap year (see Chapter 1) or backpacking.

The rise of mass domestic tourism and the seaside resort

At the same time as the aristocracy and upper classes undertook their Grand Tours of Europe and beyond, within the UK and northern Europe those who could afford to visited seaside resorts and spa towns. Accordingly, domestic travel for pleasure purposes, akin to what we could recognize today, became popular in the eighteenth century.

The major form of tourism at this time might be more accurately described as health tourism, as the drinking of and bathing in mineral water and seawater was recommended by doctors, who believed it contained health-giving properties. Many inland spa resorts grew up in the eighteenth century across Europe, and this was later extended to resorts located at the seaside. In the UK, the first spa was in Scarborough (North Yorkshire), which developed very early, in the mid-seventeenth century, as a result of Dr Robert Wittie's treatise on the curative powers of the Scarborough seawater in 1667. Indeed, Scarborough was to become Britain's first seaside resort too, and was well established as a fashionable spa resort by the 1730s. By the end of the eighteenth century sea bathing had become popular among the upper classes. Visits to the seaside and 'taking the waters' were often stimulated by royal patronage, with George IV visiting places such as Brighton (where Dr Richard Russell had promoted the therapeutic qualities of the water in 1750) and Weymouth in the 1780s. The Royal Sea-Bathing Infirmary opened at Margate in 1796. According to Walton (1983: 216), referring to the writer William Hutton, who remarked in 1788 that 'wherever people in the high life take the lead, the next class eagerly follow', tourism began a process of democratization. This pattern, where either the elite or the adventurous first visit a destination or make an activity fashionable and are subsequently followed by others, is one that was to continue for the next 200 years, as we saw illustrated in Table 2.1. However, in the eighteenth century, it was only the money- and time-rich in society who possessed the resources required for travel outside their own immediate area. Another historical theme emerges here: as technological advances take place within a society, the impact on the economy

2

is such that a wider section of the society can take advantage of greater levels of disposable income and free time for leisure purposes. Certainly, the Industrial Revolution in northern Europe in the late eighteenth and nineteenth centuries saw the value of money increase, and the middle and upper classes found they could afford to travel to the coast.

The fact that some in society had the financial means to participate in leisure travel is only a partial explanation of the factors that initiated tourism. Time free from work or other responsibilities is also a key determinant. Working structures became more highly organized and rationalized in the later nineteenth century, and working hours were reduced (Urry 1990). In the UK, legislation to create public or bank holidays came in 1871 (establishing four days' holiday per year) and led to the emergence of the week's holiday. Walton (1983) states that longer, week-long breaks were pioneered in the north of England's textile regions, where total shutdown of factories would take place to enable workers to enjoy a holiday en masse as a community, giving all workers the same holiday entitlement. These 'Wakes weeks', as they were known, were favoured by employers in the hope that they would promote morale, and thereby efficiency and regular attendance at work. This mass exodus meant that many workers travelled at the same time to similar destinations. Cotton workers in Lancashire, with their relatively high incomes and stable employment, often saved for their holidays through 'going off clubs' for 51 weeks of the year. Holidays taken by the working class were common by the 1890s (Walton 2000). The more affluent classes took overseas trips, particularly to Europe, which grew in number from 418,003 in 1891 to 493,946 in 1895 and 669,292 in 1900.

As well as money and time, the supply of services such as accommodation in facilitating tourism is equally important in generating tourism demand. In the USA's Yellowstone **National Park**, demand for quality hotel accommodation outstripped supply in the late nineteenth century, and the park authority acknowledged the need for a new hotel to meet the needs of visitors. The Fountain Hotel, built in 1891, helped to popularize visits to the Park by offering luxury alongside easy access to wild land. As well as accommodation, the means of travel is a crucial factor in stimulating tourism. In the period from 1900, railways had a significant effect on leisure travel. It was the railway that brought an even bigger change in attitudes, for it changed the class structure of the English seaside holiday. Thomas Cook is widely credited with using railways for leisure travel in its guided tours from the early 1840s; these had expanded to European and Far East and Egypt tours by the 1860s (see Insight 2.1; Image 2.3). As an example of the level of leisure travel in the mid-Victorian period, there were some 5000 miles of railway in the UK by 1862, and Brighton received some 132 000 visitors by train in a single day in that year. The coming of the railway enabled people to travel further, faster and at a relatively affordable price. As Walton (1983: 218) observed:

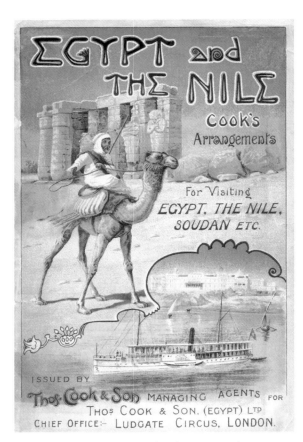

IMAGE 2.2 Thomas Cook advertisement for a tour of Egypt.
Source: © Thomas Cook

In the railway age . . . transport and distance from population centres came to have only secondary importance except on the remoter coastlines. The early arrival of a railway could give a resort a head start over actual and potential rivals . . . but communications arteries between population concentrations and coastlines tended to create wide areas of potential development . . . without determining the pace and character of that development in any particular place.

In line with growing affluence and free time and improved transport systems, seaside resorts developed quickly towards the end of the nineteenth century and firmly established themselves in the late Victorian years as sites of mass consumption. In England and Wales the number of rail travellers increased twenty-fold between 1840 and 1870 and the resorts accounted for their full share of this traffic (Walton 1983: 4). As more and more people were able to travel, a resort hierarchy developed where certain places (such as Southend) were seen as embodiments of mass tourism to be despised and ridiculed, while others were held in high esteem (such as Bournemouth). It is certainly the case that some places consolidated their position as premier seaside resorts (e.g. Brighton and Blackpool), while other locations were still at an earlier stage in their development. Walton (1983: 3) aptly summarizes:

The Victorian and Edwardian seaside resort was important not only as a repository for investment, consumer spending and social emulation, but also as a crucible of conflict between classes and lifestyles, as wealthy and status conscious visitors and residents competed with plebeian locals and roistering excursions for access to and enjoyment of amenities.

INSIGHT 2.1 The history of the Thomas Cook Company: Milestones in its development 1841–2019

1841 Thomas Cook organizes Leicester to Loughborough rail journey for 500 travellers

1845 Thomas Cook organizes tour to Liverpool with an extension to Caernarvon and Snowdon

1846 First tour of Scotland, 800 miles for a guinea, with 500 passengers. Sightseeing in Stirling, Ayrshire and on Loch Lomond
Initial bankruptcy but restarts business

1847 Two further trips to Scotland. Excursions to the Lake District, Fleetwood, Blackpool, Liverpool, Isle of Man and Belfast

1849 No excursions by rail; rail companies are trying to run their own and will not negotiate. Offers coach trips to areas of local interest

1851 First edition of *The Excursionist*
Great Exhibition hosted in London and Thomas Cook organizes tours from different parts of England (which arguably marks the first wide-ranging use of package trips involving accommodation, travel and excursions)

1855 First European tour

1862 Rail companies refuse to issue more tourist tickets to Scotland

1866 First North American tour

1869 First river cruise on the River Nile

1870 Opening of offices in four European cities

1872 Cairo office opened

1873 Thomas Cook publishes the first edition of their Compendium of Railway and Steamship timetables

1873 *Cook's Continental Timetable* issued

1874 Introduction of Thomas Cook Credit Note

1879 Publication of *The Excursionist* to promote travel products overseas (see Image 2.1)

1881 French edition of *The Excursionist* published; Eiffel Tower opened

1919 Sale of first airline ticket

1928 Company sold to Wagon-Lits, its main competitor

1939 Opened holiday camp at Prestatyn, North Wales on a 58-acre site, with holidays for £3/3/6d (£3.18) rising to £9 in 1965, with 900 chalets and capacity for 2,000 guests. This remained

the company's only foray into the holiday camp business

1948 State ownership of Thomas Cook as part of the British Transport Holding Company

1965 Profits exceed £1 million

1972 Sale to private-sector consortium of Midland Bank, Trust House Forté and the AA

1975 Prestatyn holiday camp sold to Pontins and then closed in 1985

1977 Midland Bank becomes sole owner

1990 Purchase of foreign-exchange company to become the largest foreign-exchange retailer

1992 Sold to LTU Group

1995 Company website launched and sale of products online

1999 John Mason Cook (JMC) brand launched
Pressaug AG buys the company

2001 C&N Touristic AG takes over the company and it is renamed Thomas Cook AG

2003 Thomas Cook Airlines launched

2007 Merger of Thomas Cook and MyTravel Group PLC to create Thomas Cook Group PLC

2010 Thomas Cook and Cooperative Travel merger

2011 30 per cent of Thomas Cook business is now online; £9.8 billion turnover with 236 million customers

2015 Company launches 'Customers at Our Heart' strategy to improve customer loyalty and to attract new customers (https://www.thomascookgroup.com/strategy)

2016 Thomas Cook celebrates its 175th anniversary

2018 The company has a fleet of 105 aircraft, 2,926 stores, 32,722 employees, and over 19.1 million annual customers and turnover of £9.5 billion.

2019 On 19 September the company entered administration and ceased trading after 178 years of successful operation. The various factors attributed to its collapse included the impact of the UK's withdrawal from Europe and the impact on consumer holiday booking behaviour; overheads from running high-street travel agents; and online competition undercutting its profitability. A total of 22 000 employees worldwide were affected by its closure, 9 000 based in the UK. The UK Civil Aviation Authority undertook the repatriation of 150 000 customers in the UK who were overseas on Thomas Cook holidays.

Cook is widely acknowledged for his early role in the marketing and promotion of domestic and international travel, initially printing handbills. In 1851 he published Cook's *Exhibition Herald and Excursion Advertiser*, which survived until 1939. This brochure promoted company products and services including excursions and special events, to encourage travel, and ran advertisements from hotels and transport companies. *The Excursionist* highlighted the power of advertising (see Image 2.1) to generate travel business, selling 100 000 copies a month in the 1880s in English and foreign editions. For example, in 1881 the company took 200 000 visitors to Paris to see the Eiffel Tower, making a record profit of £22 819. By 1891, the company was emerging as a truly global operation, with 84 offices, 85 agencies, and 2692 staff (of which almost 1000 were in Egypt, Image 2.2); it branched out into steamer tours to the West Indies in 1893 and conducted cycling tours of Europe in 1896. By 1899, the more adventurous tourists were travelling on the new Trans-Siberian Express; it was a record year in which 7 million travelling tickets were issued, double the company's volume of the previous decade.

Further reading

Barton, S. (2005). *Working-Class Organisations and Popular Tourism, 1840–1970*. Manchester: Manchester University Press.

Brendon, P. (1991) *Thomas Cook: 150 Years of Popular Tourism*. London: Secker and Warburg.

Smith, P. (ed.) (1998) *The History of Tourism: Thomas Cook and the Origins of Leisure Travel*. London: Routledge.

Withey, L. (1998) *Grand Tours and Cook's Tours: A History of Leisure Travel, 1750–1915*. London: Arun.

Questions

1 How did Thomas Cook innovate in the market for domestic travel in the mid-nineteenth century?

2 What strategy did Thomas Cook adopt towards marketing its products in the nineteenth century?

The seaside brought mutually incompatible modes of recreation and enjoyment into close proximity in ways that seldom happened inland (see also Chapter 22 and coastal tourism).

Understanding the development of resorts in time and space: The resort lifecycle model

Butler (1980) devised a model to show how tourism destinations develop over time (Figure 2.1). The model depicted resorts moving from the initial stage of being found (*exploration*), through the *involvement* and *development* stages to a *stagnation* stage. Beyond this a number of options are possible, from *decline* to *rejuvenation* (regeneration). The model in essence depicts the development process and if a geographical dimension is added, it is also possible to illustrate the pattern of development through time. In the case of British seaside resorts, the period 1750–1911 shows an initial growth of elite resorts focused on Kent and Sussex (and Weymouth); c. 1750 saw a wider spread around England and Wales (as well as in Scotland). During the nineteenth century many seaside resorts in the UK were in the involvement or development stages and were not to peak until well into the twentieth century, given an additional boost in the 1930s by the rise of holiday camps (discussed later). However, such growth was not uniform. Even locations in close proximity grew at different rates and excellent studies such as Walton (1983) outline these intricacies of different development trajectories for individual resorts.

Tourism in the twentieth century: c.1900–1939

The growing demand for leisure travel among the working population began as day trips, initially in the late eighteenth century and increasingly throughout the nineteenth century. It was this form of tourism that was to develop

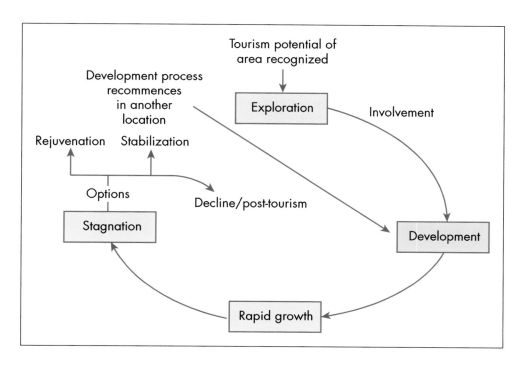

FIGURE 2.1 The resort lifecycle model
Source: Page (2019) developed and adapted from Butler (1980)

further in the twentieth century. The development of tourism in the early part of the twentieth century displays numerous themes and exogenous factors. Particularly important are the economic, social and political climates, as well as aspects discussed in the previous section such as affluence, holiday entitlement and technological advances.

In the early part of the twentieth century, travel was expanding due to growing affluence and continued improvements in transport systems, as depicted in the 1901 *Excursionist,* in which different destinations and modes of transport are highlighted. War, however, was to have a marked effect on many nations, and in many ways, in 1914 and again in 1939. Following the First World War (1914–1918) there was fluctuating prosperity, depression and recovery. Although there was a worldwide economic depression in the period between 1929 and 1931, such effects were not evenly distributed. The mass nature of the communal travel experiences was evident from the patronage of seaside holiday resorts in the 1930s, as Blackpool routinely received 7 million tourists and day visitors a year and Southend 5.5 million (Barton 2005).

As Table 2.2 shows, the 1920s and 1930s marked the embryonic stage of countries seeking to collect tourism statistics, albeit using different criteria. With the exception of inbound tourism to the UK, Norval's (1936) survey of statistics for selected countries (Table 2.2) illustrates the impact of the Wall Street crash and a slowdown in international tourism in selected countries during 1929–1934. This was particularly noticeable in the case of USA–Canadian cross-border automobile trips, which dropped almost 33 per cent in 1932–1933.

Immediately following the First World War, a global flu pandemic initially reduced the volume of international travel as well as domestic tourism. By 1919, after the pandemic had passed, most UK domestic resorts were 'bursting at the seams' as newspaper reports in Blackpool observed and the *Daily Telegraph* in the UK in 1919 reported on the pent-up demand for postwar travel which also saw Thomas Cook inaugurate sales of a new luxury travel product – a regular London-to-Paris air service. In 1919, Thomas Cook also began promoting motor coach tours throughout the UK, such as a 14-guinea tour to the West Country for one week. The company also began operating coach tours from provincial towns to destinations, following the postwar boom in demobbed troops purchasing surplus army vehicles and converting them into coaches and charabancs.

In terms of free time, there was a growing recognition of the value of a holiday. Whereas the UK's Bank Holidays Act of 1871 had ensured not only crowded trains, but crowded beaches, longer holidays were to become more typical. Similar experiences have also been recorded in the USA in the late nineteenth century, with Philadelphians crowding onto trains on Sunday mornings to visit Atlantic City and Cape May (Lenček and Bosker 1998). The similarities in European and North American experiences of coastal tourism led Lenček and Bosker (1998: 140) to argue that:

At the turn of the [nineteenth] century, seaside life at the [New] Jersey shore was a burlesque for the masses. Everyone was welcome, and the price of admission was the cost of a bathing suit – frequently, even that was not necessary. For Americans, as much as for Europeans, resort and public beach were very much about status, social climbing and health. And about vanity and fashion.

As they also noted, at the southern tip of New Jersey, Cape May (which was in the 1880s a hundred-mile stretch of coastline and 54 seaside cities) was a pioneer of American seaside resorts, with coastal towns receiving US$150 million in revenue and tourist spending each season. By 1900, Atlantic City had 400 hotels, some able to accommodate up to 1000 guests. Newport, Rhode Island also developed as the elite mecca of the American millionaire. Much of the development was based on second homes/villas, funded by industrial wealth, which led to a demand for summer houses after the 1860s to meet the needs of the rich on the north-east seaboard. In Australia, coastal resorts developed in the late nineteenth century in Queensland, South Australia and Victoria. However, here, as in New Zealand, daylight bathing was banned until the early years of the twentieth century. Hall (2003) noted that it was not until 1903 that it became legally permitted to swim at Sydney's Manly Beach and the emergence of the Australian beach culture was stimulated. In terms of the interior, Australia Railways made Australia's rural hinterland accessible to its metropolitan population, such as the Sydney–Blue Mountains railway after the 1850s which led to the development of inland tourist towns at locations such as Katoomba (Hall 2003).

Before the outbreak of the Second World War, the Amulree Report in the UK led to the Holidays with Pay Act 1938. Similar legislation was also enacted in Scandinavia and other countries (see Insight 2.2). While this only established voluntary agreements with employers, between 1931 and 1939 the number of workers entitled to paid holidays increased from 1.5 million to 11 million. This, coupled with a shorter working week (reduced from 54 hours in 1919 to 48 hours by 1939) and a doubling of average weekly wages over the same period, all contributed to the development of tourism, particularly in the form of the seaside holiday.

By the 1930s holidays had become an expected part of life for many in employment rather than a luxury preserved for the elite. Improvements elsewhere fuelled the demand for leisure travel. While the masses may have taken a short annual holiday by the sea, wealthier individuals took advantage of technological advances in transportation systems and took more exotic holidays by ocean liner, aeroplane or motor car (see Table 2.2). In 1931, 900 000 British tourists travelled to Europe. The freedom offered by the car was quickly recognized. In 1920 there were 200 000 cars on British roads, rising to 1 million by 1930 and 2 million by 1939. In addition to private cars, long-distance bus services in the form of charabancs began to challenge the railways for speed, comfort and convenience. For example, 37 million passengers were carried on long-distance services and tours in 1939. In continental Europe coach travel for holiday purposes was also widely used in France, Switzerland and Italy. The volume of passengers carried on the new Imperial Airways and British Empire routes rose from 11 000 in 1925 to 27 300 in 1928, dropping in 1929–1931 due to economic conditions, but increased to 48 000 in 1932 and exceeded 135 000 in 1934. These volumes doubled to 200 000 in 1935, peaking at 244 000 in 1937. In contrast, Pan Am developed routes from North to South America and KLM pioneered routes with its colonies in the Dutch East Indies (Indonesia). Imperial Airways routes connected London with its Empire in India, Africa and Australia. As Pirie (2009) shows, the tourism which resulted at refuelling

TABLE 2.2 International tourism – global estimates

	France	Canada (by automobile)	Canada (from overseas)	Australia	Austria	Germany	UK	Italy	Japan	New Zealand	USA
1913	300 000										
1925		7 748 613	15 766	23 236	1 204 196	465 550	365 568	1 340 000	23 839	12 118	
1926		6 615 637	11 722	24 795	1 253 165	491 429	366 224	1 150 000	24 706	13 442	2 054 731
1927		10 054 477	13 181	26 435	1 460 713	657 528	418 485	1 070 000	26 386	13 078	2 401 652
1928		12 206 014	13 132	26 721	1 849 463	758 503	441 243	1 093 000	37 707	13 642	2 660 742
1929	1 911 107	14 292 719	13 472	24 892	1 813 561	851 414	451 659	1 221 000	43 224	12 988	2 905 587
1930	1 668 831	18 592 691	12 578	22 186	1 808 868	969 574	444 479	1 290 000	33 572	11 203	2 405 918
1931	1 542 285	14 715 269	12 229	17 616	1 433 595		351 338	1 191 000	27 273	7 615	2 163 081
1932	944 353	13 243 198	10 755	19 031	1 326 983		318 720		20 960	7 283	1 502 108
1933	931 505	8 920 586	9 650	18 125	796 266		322 445		26 264		1 136 967
1934					602 573				35 196		

Source: Developed from A. Norval (1936) *The Tourist Industry: A National and International Survey.* Pitman: London

INSIGHT 2.2 Holidays in inter-war Scandinavia

In the study by Rowntree and Lavers (1951), *English Life and Labour: A Social Study*, evidence was collated on leisure-time pursuits in Scandinavia, observing the 1938 legislation enacted in Denmark, Norway, Sweden and Finland providing for paid holidays. In each country (excluding Finland), 12 days' paid holiday was provided for employees who typically worked 47-hour weeks, while in Finland three weeks' paid holiday was accrued by those who had been employed by a company for five years, two weeks after one year's service and one week after six months' service, plus one compulsory paid state public holiday and ten days' unpaid holiday which was available. In each country, holidays were promoted by workers' organizations set up by the trade unions similar to those in the Soviet Union, such as the Danske Folk-Ferier in Denmark, Norsk Folk Ferie in Norway and Reso in Sweden, all of which provided holiday camps and accommodation to promote domestic (and in some cases overseas) holidays. For example, in 1948, the Holiday Union in Finland had the capacity for 28 000 people a season in accommodation at camps (the population was 4.1 million); this capacity was complemented by some employers who provided holiday accommodation. This period also saw the continued growth of existing trends of mobility such as cycling, coastal holidays and the development of resort areas.

Further reading

Emanuel, M. (2017) 'Seeking adventure and authenticity: Swedish bicycle touring in Europe during the interwar period', *Journal of Tourism History*, 9 (1): 44–64.

Hundstad, D. (2011) 'A "Norwegian Riviera" in the making: The development of coastal tourism and recreation in southern Norway in the interwar period', *Journal of Tourism History*, 3 (2): 109–128.

Johnsen, B. (2013) 'Research on the history of Scandinavian summer and seaside tourism – transnational and transregional perspectives?' *Journal of Tourism History*, 5 (3): 246–264.

Kostiainen, A. (2007) 'A northern "Riviera": Tourism in Terijoki in the 1920s and 1930s', *Scandinavian Journal of Hospitality and Tourism*, 7 (4): 328–334.

and stopover locations was an 'incidental' form of tourism based on affluent leisure travellers as well as business travellers who could afford the cost of long-haul air travel.

In an international context, P&O steamer routes stimulated tourist travel from the UK and Europe to the Far East, especially the greater expansion of cruises after the opening of the Suez Canal in 1869. P&O's association with Thomas Cook and Sons, having rendered most of Europe safe for British travellers, undertook their first world tour in 1872–1873 (20 days at £1 a day), not surprisingly using P&O ships for the main sea travel. The Thomas Cook company ensured that greater numbers of visitors to India, Malaysia and often beyond were in the hands of British travel entrepreneurs. By 1886, Cook and P&O were organizing trips from Bombay to Jeddah for Muslim pilgrims, an activity for which the shipping company later built a special vessel, and the promotion of this form of travel is depicted in Images 2.3 and 2.4. In the case of the South Pacific, similar developments associated with cruising have also been documented by Douglas and Douglas (1996), who observed the impact of the Canadian Australian Royal Mail Steamship Line and the New Zealand Union Steamship Line in developing tourism in Fiji (with stopover traffic at Suva) after 1893. By 1930, monthly services provided by steamships had acted as a catalyst for international tourism and they formed the precursor of the modern-day luxury liners that called at South Pacific ports. Douglas and Douglas (1996) examined this process in other parts of the South Pacific including Melanesia and Hawaii as well as the emergence of the South Pacific as the playground of European and American tourists. There is also a degree of continuity in the decline and subsequent rebirth of the South Pacific as a cruise ship destination, with vessels calling at many of the ports which developed in the nineteenth century.

In terms of other forms of long-distance travel, transatlantic crossings between Europe and North America had been possible since 1838; the following year Samuel Cunard founded the Cunard Line after winning the

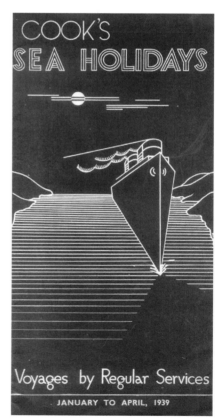

IMAGE 2.3 Thomas Cook sea-voyaging advertisement c.1939.
© Thomas Cook

IMAGE 2.4 Thomas Cook sea-voyaging advertisement, c.1949–50. ©Thomas Cook

lucrative North Atlantic mail contract. By the 1930s, however, sea travel had expanded considerably and cruising was a popular form of travel among those who could afford to travel this way. In the early twentieth century there were many economic and social changes, particularly during the Edwardian years (1901–1914) in the UK, Europe and North America. These changes impacted upon the recreation and leisure behaviour of the population, with some further expansion of tourism opportunities for the middle and working classes (Clarke and Critcher 1985). In fact, there is evidence of public sector involvement in promoting tourism at a local level (i.e. place-marketing by seaside resorts) (Ward 1998), and of some countries seizing the lead, e.g. New Zealand, which established the first national tourist board.

Increased leisure time, paid holidays and developments in transport inspired and enabled many to travel, expanding the geographical extent of domestic tourism in many countries, dependent upon the transport infrastructure available and its cost (see Durie 2017). At the same time, following the Edwardian period and aftermath of the First World War, a period of economic fragility ensued. The historical development of tourism was directly affected by economic austerity, unemployment and financial hardship followed which suppressed many of the initial opportunities made available in the Edwardian period. Alternative forms of tourist activity began to appeal to a larger number of participants, particularly those that could be enjoyed at relatively little cost in times of economic depression. In Britain, the inter-war period saw an enormous growth in the demand for outdoor recreation, such as rambling and cycling, and the accommodation favoured was either camping or the Youth Hostel. In England and Wales, the Youth Hostel Association had 300 establishments in the 1930s with a membership of 225 000 people walking or cycling. In Australia in the inter-war period, the growth of coastal resorts also gave way to the bush-walking movement. This led to the rise of the conservation movement (Hall 2003) and the formation in 1932 of the National Parks and Primitive Areas Council (NPPAC) in New South Wales.

Lower-cost forms of domestic tourism, particularly the rise of holiday homes on the fringe of urban areas such as London's green belt, provided a substitute for holidays in times of austerity. So too did working holidays among the working classes, whose families engaged in traditional activities such as hop-picking in Kent, living in often cramped conditions. What is apparent is that the development of mass tourism opportunities for the population in specific countries is very much a cyclical process linked to the economy and the availability of disposable income in households. When income is in short supply, cheaper alternatives are often selected.

The Second World War and tourism

According to many surveys of wartime, holidays were suspended: historians of UK conditions have pointed to the Railway Executive Committee slogan 'is your holiday really necessary?' (Sladen 2002), something which Page and Durie (2009) have questioned in relation to the First World War. Sladen (2002) shows that such advertising had only a minor impact on curbing travel behaviour, consistent with that observed during the First World War, when major fare rises were invoked to try to stifle demand. In the Second World War, Sladen (2002) shows that many railway companies ignored government instructions not to run extra trains at holiday times, and Lancashire Wakes week continued (the annual factory close-down period). As also occurred with newspaper advertising and articles in *The Times* newspaper 1914–1916, Sladen (2002) shows that domestic holidays were promoted in the Second World War, in spite of difficult travel conditions. Railway company statistics indicate that the volume of pleasure travel from

1939–1945 in the UK was broadly similar to pre-1939 levels, and in some years it may have exceeded the prewar levels. Even though the rationing of petrol was in force, this was not a major curb on demand as the number of cars registered at the end of the 1930s was less than 2 million for a 40-million population. Sladen (2005) shows that from 1943 to 1945, the volume of railway-passenger journeys increased from 1335 million to 1372 million, of which 28–30 per cent was excursion traffic, 17–20 per cent was accounted for by service personnel and 20–25 per cent by commuters. Therefore, while travel decreased in some classes of ticket, the shift to purchasing full-fare tickets instead of excursion tickets saw a growth after the initial outbreak of the war. The Great Western Railway serving western England saw the volume of excursion traffic drop from 44.7 million journeys in 1938 to 36.5 million in 1940 but it rose again to 54.4 million in 1943. Anecdotal evidence and oral history can expand upon the experiences of wartime travel, as many safe resorts which were not at risk of aerial bombardment, such as Blackpool, benefited from wartime, in spite of long queues for trains.

Tourism in the twentieth century: c.1945–1970

In most developed Western countries, there was rapid growth in tourism after the Second World War. In the case of Australia, Hall (2003: 52) confirmed that:

> The period after the Second World War witnessed an unparalleled development in leisure services for the Australian population. A new period of prosperity following the depression of the 1930s and the war years meant that people had greater disposable income and more leisure time in which to enjoy the prosperity, particularly as three weeks of annual holidays became standard. One of the greatest impacts was the growth in personal mobility through car ownership.

This was also mirrored in the USA on a much larger scale. One consequence in Australia and North America was the development of motels to meet the routeway demand for travellers. Many aspects, such as holiday entitlements and growing affluence, which affected growth in the previous period, continued in the period after 1945, illustrating the continuity as well as change in the way these processes and factors impact upon tourism behaviour. The immediate postwar period was one of continued and rapid growth and recognition of the tourism industry in the UK. For example, in 1946, 202 680 overseas tourists visited the UK, which rose to 504 360 in 1948 and exceeded 1 million by 1955. In many key tourist destinations, the hotel and catering sector employed between 8 and 20 per cent of the local working population in 1951. In terms of overseas visitors to the UK, in 1955 23 per cent of the visitors originated in the USA and 22 per cent from Britain's close links with the Commonwealth.

The 1950s and 1960s saw great changes in the nature of tourist travel with the introduction of package holidays by air using charter aircraft, and also in the development of home-centred forms of leisure (see Insight 2.3). Radio and television in the home challenged the cinema as a major form of leisure entertainment. Television advertising was gradually introduced by tour operators to promote domestic and overseas tourism. At the same time, growing affluence meant that overseas travel truly came within the grasp of the working classes, having previously been a luxury enjoyed by the upper and middle classes. In contrast to outbound and domestic tourism in the UK, and despite restrictions on overseas currency available for travel, visitors to the UK also became a valuable invisible export for the economy. One of the major features of tourism in Britain during the inter-war years and through to the 1950s and 1960s was the development of the holiday camp. Ward and Hardy (1986) provide a detailed history of the development of holiday camps in the UK, showing that they date back to 1897, with a camp for young men on the Isle of Man. The entrepreneur Billy Butlin is often credited with the concept and development of holiday camps after developing amusement parks in the UK over the period 1925–1937, and certainly Butlin's skill was important in the holiday camp's development in the UK. In 1936, the first Butlin's opened in Skegness with a capacity of 1000, followed in 1938 by Clacton, with a 2000 capacity. By 1948, it was estimated that 1 in 20 of all holidaymakers in the UK stayed at a Butlin's holiday camp each year (Ward and Hardy 1986: 75). However, from the 1960s the popularity of holiday camps diminished and many closures took place. The company then focused on three sites – Minehead, Skegness and Bognor Regis – in developing a new style of holiday resort (http://www.butlinsonline.co.uk). In 2001 it also entered the conference and event market to extend its markets. Holiday camps as a type of holiday are not restricted to the UK and, following the theme of continuity and change, have been refocused and reborn not just in the new Butlin's resorts but in the shape of ventures such as Center Parcs and the Disney theme parks.

INSIGHT 2.3 The Scandinavian tourism boom by air

According to Kaiserfeld (2010), in Scandinavia mass tourism expanded rapidly between the 1950s and 1960s, as package tours by coach were replaced by outbound air travel on charter aircraft. The result was that by 1965 Sweden had the greatest per capita consumption of package holidays in Europe. Given the population size of Sweden, this meant that package holidays were 2.5 times more common among the population than in the UK. A key driver of this growth in Sweden was the availability of paid holidays, where the minimum of two weeks' paid leave (see Insight 2.2) was increased to three weeks in 1951 (and five weeks in 1978). Growth was also fuelled by rising wage rates in the 1950s and 1960s, while the relative cost of travel fell, making travel cheaper. The result was a growth in charter traffic in Sweden from 75 000 outbound passengers in 1947, to 375 000 in 1950, to 1 104 000 in 1954. This began a cultural shift from domestic and international travel by coach and sightseeing/visiting cultural attractions, to hedonism focused on sun, sea and sand holidays and swimming in saltwater. Destinations which dominated were Majorca and the Canary Islands as well as destinations on the mainland. This was in spite of an almost 12-hour journey time from Scandinavia with numerous refuelling stops en route.

Further reading

Kaiserfeld, T. (2010) 'From sightseeing to sunbathing: Changing traditions in Swedish package tours; from edification by bus to relaxation by airplane in the 1950s and 1960s', *Journal of Tourism History* 2 (3): 149–163.

Tourism in the twentieth century: Post-1970

In the last 40 years, tourism activity has developed many of the features established in the earlier periods of the twentieth century, while new trends have altered the nature of demand and supply. The theme of continued expansion remains applicable into the new millennium. Some of the themes that are particularly significant in this period, many of which are interrelated, include:

- greater internationalization and globalization of tourism
- changes in technology
- the legislative environment
- increasing political recognition of tourism's economic impacts
- a rise in consumer spending
- emergence of new consumers
- changes in products
- development of marketing (Image 2.5), research and information.

The discussion of tourism history is somewhat Western-centric as, for many countries and areas, tourism development is a very recent phenomenon. Some of the most well-known and loved holiday destinations have only a recent history in terms of tourism. For example, tourism in the Maldives began in the early 1970s, with the arrival of the first tour group in 1972 and the first resort, Kurumba Village, completed in the same year. However, such destinations are still subject to the wider global changes: in many cases, they have evolved as tourism destinations as a direct result of these changes.

IMAGE 2.5 Innovative resorts such as Bournemouth, UK developed a conference/exhibition business to diversify their dependence upon domestic tourism

A greater internationalization and globalization of tourism

As Figure 2.2 shows, global tourism expanded significantly in the 1970s (excluding the effect of the oil crisis as shown in this trend line) and at a much faster rate after 1984, though the annual change in visitor arrivals worldwide has fluctuated since then between 1.5 per cent and 16 per cent depending on a wide range of factors. What is indisputable is the growing global reach of tourism, aided by declining relative costs of travel, increased consumerism in tourism and constant innovation in products and provision. The number of domestic trips (i.e. UK residents holidaying in the UK) has remained relatively constant, however.

Travellers are now becoming more adventurous, with long-haul travel to Australasia and Asia-Pacific growing, even though North America and Europe have remained the dominant destinations in terms of international arrivals. Accompanying this growth, an increasingly wide geographic range of destinations emerged in this period, not just in the more traditional holiday countries but including areas as diverse in product offering as Africa, East Asia-Pacific and Antarctica. There have also been significant increases in intra-regional travel, particularly in regions where tourism is a relatively new activity in which to engage. For example, tourism in East Asia-Pacific is dominated by demand generated from within the region.

A final area of change has been in the growth of the short-break market, initially within domestic markets but also increasingly in intra-regional and international destinations, which are competing for the short-break traveller. Cities such as New York, Paris and Brussels have traditionally been popular for Europeans taking a short break but an increasingly wide choice of further-flung destinations, such as New Orleans, Reykjavik, Prague and Las Vegas, have begun to compete in the marketplace. A number of factors have boosted the short-break market, including greater disposable income, political changes allowing travel into Eastern European countries and vast improvements in travel technology.

Changes in technology

Improvements in transport have been an enduring theme in the history of tourism, and are a major element which explain internationalization of tourism, especially the introduction of new technology, in the airline industry. The

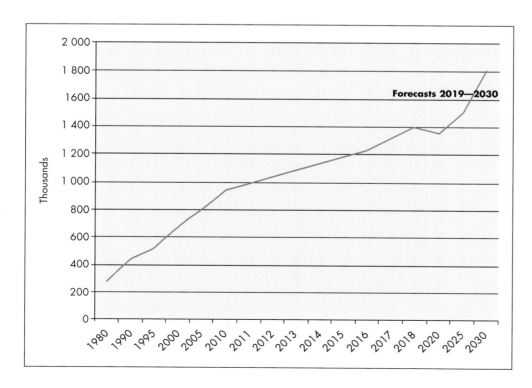

FIGURE 2.2 International arrivals 1980–2030

year 1970 brought a technological breakthrough in air transport, with the introduction of the DC-10, and the much bigger Boeing 747, on a global scale: the first wide-bodied jets. The earliest 747 (747–100), the first flight of which was a Pan Am service from New York to London, had a cruising speed of 600 mph, a range of 6000 miles and capacity for 370 passengers (later to increase). One of the implications of the new era aircraft were the economies of scale generated, meaning more people could travel more cheaply, more quickly and more easily, covering greater distances, than before. This has continued with the introduction of the Airbus A380. In addition to air travel, changing technology and developments leading to high-speed rail links and improvements in road travel have assisted land-based tourism in spite of concerns about climate change and sustainability.

The legislative environment

Since the late 1960s, a growing political recognition of tourism as a significant part of a nation's economy has developed in many countries or, in the case of countries where tourism activity has a longer tradition, has remained important as a strategic objective. In some countries, government policy was set out within a legislative structure during this period. For example, the 1969 Development of Tourism Act laid down a public sector structure in the UK, establishing a formal structure of tourist boards and financial mechanisms for stimulating tourism capital projects. Other legislation has also affected the private sector; for example, from 1970, tour operators were required to have an **Air Travel Organizer's Licence (ATOL)** (see Chapter 7 for a more detailed discussion).

Throughout Europe, legislation for tourism has been a feature of developments from the 1980s. State subsidies for tourism have been replaced with **EU**-funded regional incentives for development in areas of decline and high socio-economic deprivation, so that new employment opportunities can be created in peripheral regions. European legislation has also introduced measures to liberalize air and road transport, harmonize hotel classifications, relax frontier controls and has made efforts to balance VAT and duty-free regulations in a bid to ease the flow of tourism at a transnational level, so that barriers to tourism are removed, including the visa restrictions which control the flow of overseas visitors into many countries.

Political and economic events

The explanation of why certain events affect the tourism industry often lies within a combination of factors rather than a single influence. Political issues affecting the industry are difficult to explain without reference to economic factors. As tourism is demand-inelastic (see Chapter 16), variations in the economy have a direct impact on tourism demand (see Chapter 3). Particular factors that impact upon tourism demand include high unemployment, high interest rates and high levels of inflation. When such conditions prevail, tourism demand can be suppressed. Economic uncertainty due to high interest rates and fear of redundancy may cause many consumers to abandon plans for expensive overseas holidays.

Politics can influence the tourism industry in other ways too. Disputes can seriously impede travel, especially when conditions escalate. During the 1990s, ethnic conflict in the former **Yugoslavia** decimated the country's tourism industry. Statistics show that arrivals from the UK to Yugoslavia peaked at 656,000 in 1990, after which they fell to 22,000 by 1992. More recently, the 9/11 attacks and subsequent terrorist alerts have undoubtedly affected tourism demand on a global scale not seen since the oil crisis in the 1970s.

The rise of a consumer society

As Page (2019) argues, society has passed from the stage of industrialization to one now described as post-industrial, where new technologies and ways of communicating and working have evolved. Sociologists such as Baudrillard (1998) in *The Consumer Society: Myths and Structures* have argued that we have moved from a society dominated by work and production to one where leisure and tourism consumption now dominate. This has been reflected in social changes, such as the rise of new middle classes in many developed and developing countries, and these middle classes have a defining feature, which is the concern with leisure lifestyles and consumption. Since the 1970s there has been a general affluence for those in employment. For example, in the UK net wealth more than doubled in 1987–2000, and in 1990–2009, real household disposable income rose (ONS 2011). At the same time, the impact of the global financial crisis led to changes in the consumption habits of UK residents in terms of tourism. Between 2008 and 2009 overseas trips dropped by 15.1 per cent, the largest decline since 2000. Households took more UK domestic holidays, which rose from 75 million in 2008 to 84 million in 2009. Within these trends, the 45 to 54 age group took the most holidays, reflecting a greater disposable income. Disposable income is clearly an important determinant of short-term and much longer-term trends in holiday taking.

Changing products

Through time, destinations and their products which attract visitors are in a state of constant evolution akin to the resort lifecycle model we discussed earlier. The implications in terms of tourism history are that, through time, some destinations which evolved based on a mass tourism product have seen major changes in the demand and tastes of the visitor market. For example, in the UK many domestic resorts declined due to their lack of cost-competitiveness and lack of attraction compared to cheap overseas package holidays. The changes led to a legacy of landscape decline in the built environment of resorts, as examined in detail by Agarwal *et al.* (2019). However, tourism is not just concerned with seaside resorts. Increasingly in the last 35 years, niche products have emerged and developed, some of which have even become mainstream. Examples include ecotourism, film tourism, adventure tourism and heritage tourism, and many others which will be discussed in various parts of this book. Such product developments reflect the trend away from a product-led (**Fordist**) tourism industry to a more consumer-focused approach (**post-Fordist**), which is able to respond to, stimulate and predict consumer needs and wants. What is also important in this transition from what Poon (1993) describes as old to new tourism is an increasing demand for quality, service, flexibility and differentiation, very different from the standardized packages that dominated post-1945 tourism. The period from the 1970s saw the supply of and demand for tourism grow rapidly at an international level. This period also saw the development of powerful tour operators, segmentation of the tourist market and differentiation of tourism products, services and experiences, as new niches developed: for example, volunteer tourism as the new 'Grand Tour' (Wearing and McGehee 2013).

Linking history and tourism: The rise of heritage tourism

Tourism has a long and fascinating history, the surface of which has only been scratched briefly in this chapter. The link between tourism and history does not end there, however, as history itself is one of the essential components of the contemporary tourism industry. Throughout the world, the commercialization of history and culture as part of the process of developing tourism products is a recurrent theme. Indeed, historic buildings and places and those with cultural and religious significance, such as the Acropolis, the Pyramids, the Taj Mahal and the city of Nazareth, act as the focal point for many holiday excursions and a backdrop for many city breaks. In the UK, visits to National Trust historic house and garden properties continue to grow. Even recent history can quickly become integrated into tourism. For example, in South Africa the end of racial segregation has stimulated the growth of tourism attractions based on the apartheid theme and dark tourism. Indeed, since 1997 the Robben Island prison, where Nelson Mandela was in captivity, has been open to visitors as a museum and is deemed to be an example of **dark tourism** (Stone *et al.* 2018). Industrial heritage is often reflected in tourism products, particularly in the UK, where six such sites have attained World Heritage Site status. These include Ironbridge, New Lanark, Blaenavon, Saltaire, and Derwent Valley Mills and, in 2004, the maritime mercantile city of Liverpool, one of the world's major trading centres in the eighteenth and nineteenth centuries was added to the list (see whc.unesco.org for more information). Historic resources play an important role in tourism. However, the operation of historic and cultural sites for visitor use raises many competing and conflicting challenges for the planning and management of both tourism promotion and conservation of the historic environment. Such management-related issues will be discussed later in this book.

Conclusion

This chapter has shown that the development of tourism in the last 200 years has been inextricably linked to political, economic, social and technological influences. While the general theme has been one of growth, there are some exceptions and conditions. First, tourism is not and never has been a universal activity for all. Throughout history those without the financial means or time available have not been able to participate. While the proportion of those in this category has decreased, it has not been eliminated, and in recent years the proportion of those not taking a holiday has remained fairly constant.

As Crouch (1999) notes, even those in work are finding it increasingly difficult to take time from work, and holidays in the future may become more frequent, shorter, spread throughout the year and more intensive. This leads to a second conclusion, that of the development of the tourism product itself. This chapter has shown that destinations move through a cycle of development which lead to a stage of consolidation (at least) or decline (at worst), and where a catalyst for change can be mobilized, rejuvenation may occur to try to find a new economic rationale for such areas. Social changes in fashion and a theme of 'been there, done that' means that new types of holiday and activities are needed. A feature of the development of tourism in some locations is the obsolescence of the once popular accommodation stock, now being put to alternative uses or pulled down. A third feature of the development of tourism

that should be considered is the volatility of the market. Again, it is a combination of factors sometimes operating at a macro level that can have far-reaching effects on the industry. Aspects such as political and economic stability in the generating area and destination are crucial. At any time specific changes in tax policies, the value of currency and controls on tourist spending can affect the number of tourists travelling from a country. Similarly, price, competition and the quality or popularity of the product can influence the destination area. History has shown that such aspects can be susceptible to rapid change and greatly alter the tourism industry. When all of these are added to changing consumer tastes and fashion it can be seen why tourism may be volatile. Yet, as shown in Chapter 1, globalization and a greater competition for tourism mean places need to stay ahead of the game through reinvestment, to try to anticipate trends and to avoid areas losing their economic rationale once they lose popular appeal. Once tourism has become a mainstay of many communities, often over a long time frame, adaptation and change can be a difficult process. What a historical perspective shows is that adaptation, innovation (see Chapter 12) and understanding the tourist as a consumer are all critical to maintaining the tourism development process. For this reason, the next chapter focuses upon the tourist as a consumer to understand what motivates him or her to visit different places.

Discussion questions

1 Suggest how employment changes have affected tourism.

2 Suggest how economic changes have affected tourism in the last 100 years.

3 Show how changes in fashion have affected the popularity of selected destinations.

4 What different types of tourist go on holiday in the UK and why?

References

Agarwal, S., Jakes, S., Essex, S., Page, S.J. and Mowforth, M. (2019) 'Disadvantage in English seaside resorts: A typology of deprived neighbourhoods', *Tourism Management* 69: 440–459.

Armstrong, J. and Williams, D. (2005) 'The steamboat and popular tourism', *Journal of Transport History* 26 (1): 61–67.

Barton, S. (2005) *Working-Class Organisations and Popular Tourism, 1840–1970*. Manchester: Manchester University Press.

Baudrillard, J. (1998) *The Consumer Society: Myths and Structures*. London: Sage.

Bray, R. and Raitz, V. (2001) *Flight to the Sun: The Story of the Holiday Revolution*. London: Continuum.

Butler, R.W. (1980) 'The concept of the tourist area cycle of evolution: Implications for management of resources', *Canadian Geographer* 24 (1): 5–12.

Clarke, J. and Critcher, C. (1985). *The Devil Makes Work: Leisure in Capitalist Britain*. London: Macmillan.

Crouch, S. (1999) 'Relationship marketing', *Tourism – The Journal of the Tourism Society* 99: 13–15.

Douglas, N. and Douglas, N. (1996) 'Tourism in the Pacific: Historical factors', in C.M. Hall and S.J. Page (eds.) *Tourism in the Pacific: Issues and Cases*. London: Thomson Learning.

Dove, J. (2016) 'Geographical board game: Promoting tourism and travel in Georgian England and Wales', *Journal of Tourism History* 8 (1): 1–18.

Durie, A.J. (2003) *Scotland for the Holidays: A History of Tourism in Scotland 1780–1939*. East Linton: Tuckwell Press.

Durie, A.J. (2017) *Scotland and Tourism: The Long View, 1700–2015*. London: Routledge.

Hall, C.M. (2003) *Introduction to Tourism: Dimensions and Issues*. Frenchs Forest: Pearson Education Australia.

Hannigan, J. (1998). *Fantasy City*. London: Routledge.

Inglis, F. (2000) *The Delicious History of the Holiday*. London: Routledge.

Kaiserfeld, T. (2010) 'From sightseeing to sunbathing: Changing traditions in Swedish package tours; from edification by bus to relaxation by airplane in the 1950s and 1960s', *Journal of Tourism History*, 2 (3): 149–163.

Kynaston, D. (2008) *A World to Build*. London: Bloomsbury Publishing.

Lenček, L. and Bosker, G. (1998) *The Beach: The History of Paradise on Earth*. London: Pimlico.

Löfgren, O. (2002) *On Holiday: A History of Vacationing*. Berkeley and Los Angeles: California University Press.

Madge, C. and Harrisson, T. (1937) *Mass Observation*. London: Frederick Muller Limited.

Norval, A. (1936) *The Tourist Industry: A National and International Survey*. London: Pitman.

ONS (2011) *Social Trends* 41. London: Office for National Statistics.

Page, S.J. (2019) *Tourism Management*, 6th edition. London: Routledge.

Page, S.J. and Durie, A. (2009) 'Tourism in wartime Britain 1914–1918: A case study of adaptation and innovation by Thomas Cook & Sons', in J. Ateljevic and S.J. Page (eds.) *Tourism and Entrepreneurship*. Oxford: Elsevier.

Pirie, G. (2009) 'Incidental tourism: British Imperial air travel in 1930s', *Journal of Tourism History* 1 (1): 49–66.

Poon, A. (1993) *Tourism, Technology and Competitive Strategies*. Wallingford, Oxon: CABI.

Rowntree, S. and Lavers, G. (1951) *English Life and Leisure: A Social Study*. London: Longmans, Green & Co.

Sladen, C. (2002) 'Holidays at home in the Second World War', *Journal of Contemporary History* 37 (1): 67–89.

Sladen, C. (2005) 'Wartime holidays and the myth of the Blitz', *Cultural and Social History* 2 (2): 215–245.

Stone, P.R., Hartmann, R., Seaton, T., Sharpley, R., and White, L. (2018) *The Palgrave Handbook of Dark Tourism Studies*. London: Palgrave.

Towner, J. (1985) 'The Grand Tour: A key phase in the history of tourism', *Annals of Tourism Research* 15 (1): 47–62.

Towner, J. (1996) *An Historical Geography of Recreation and Tourism in the Western World, 1540–1940*. Chichester: Wiley.

Urry, J. (1990) *The Tourist Gaze*. London: Sage.

Walton, J.K. (1983) *The English Seaside Resort: A Social History, 1750–1914*. Leicester: Leicester University Press.

Walton, J.K. (2000) *The British Seaside: Holidays and Resorts in the Twentieth Century*. Manchester: Manchester University Press.

Walton, J.K. (2009) 'Prospects in tourism history: Evolution, state of play and future developments', *Tourism Management* 30 (5): 783–93.

Ward, C. and Hardy, D. (1986) *Goodnight Campers: History of the British Holiday Camp*. London: Mansell.

Ward, S.V. (1998) *Selling Places: The Marketing and Promotion of Towns and Cities 1850–2000*. London: E&FN Spon.

Wearing, S. and McGehee, N. (2013) 'Volunteer tourism: A review', *Tourism Management* 38: 120–130.

Further reading

Books

Cross, G. (1990) *Worktowners at Blackpool: Mass-Observation and Popular Leisure in the 1930s*. London: Routledge.

Cross, G. and Walton, J. (2005) *The Playful Crowd: Pleasure Places*. New York: Columbia University Press.

Journal articles

Salinas, E., Mundet, L. and Salinas, E. (2018) 'Historical evolution and spatial development of tourism in Cuba, 1919–2017: What is next?' *Tourism Planning and Development* 15 (3): 216–238.

Summerfield, P. (1985) 'Mass Observation: Social research or social movement?' *Journal of Contemporary History* 20 (3): 439–452.

Vallejo-Pousada, R., Vilar-Rodríguez, M. and Lindoso-Tato, E. (2018) 'The tourism economy in Spain, 1900–1939: New sources, new methodologies and new results', *Journal of Tourism History* 10 (2): 105–129.

Willcock, H.D. (1943) 'Mass Observation', *American Journal of Sociology* 48 (4): 445–456.

Understanding tourism demand

Learning outcomes

After reading this chapter and answering the questions, you should be able to:

- recognize the different forms of tourism demand

- understand the range of factors influencing tourism demand including particular factors at the destination and in generating areas

- be aware of those influences on tourism demand which the tourism industry can affect and those which are beyond its control

- recognize the procedures for measuring tourism demand

- understand the challenges and problems of collecting tourism statistics.

Overview

Demand is the basis upon which researchers conceptualize how visitors choose and pursue a range of opportunities in their leisure time. Thus, a consideration of demand in relation to tourism can assist in understanding **motivation**, needs and experiences, as well as being a useful indicator of changing trends. Hall and Page (2002: 60) state that 'an understanding of tourism demand is a starting point for the analysis of why tourism develops, who patronizes specific destinations and what appeals to the client market'. Quite simply, as Song and Witt (2000: 1) argue, 'tourism demand is the foundation on which all tourism-related business decisions ultimately rest'.

Introduction

Attempting to define 'demand' as a concept is a complex task and often depends on the disciplinary perspective adopted by the researcher. For example, the geographer is pre-eminently concerned with 'the total number of persons who travel, or wish to travel, to use tourist facilities and services at places away from their place of work or residence' (Mathieson and Wall 1982: 1). The geographer examines these issues in a spatial context to assess the impact on domestic and international tourism destinations. In contrast, the economist examines the tourist propensity to purchase tourism products or services at a specific price during a given period of time. Psychologists approach tourism demand with a particular focus on motivation and behaviour, while anthropologists and sociologists also focus on the impact of tourism on the societies hosting tourists and the social dimensions of the tourists visiting. An explanation of what demand means in simple terms is probably expressed most clearly by Pearce (1995) as the relationship between individuals' motivation to travel and their ability to do so. This means that a range of factors influence tourism demand in both the tourist-generating and destination areas. However, before examining the factors influencing demand, it is first necessary to consider more closely the different types of demand.

Based on Smith's (1995) observations, demand occurs at four different levels as shown in Figure 3.1, which builds upon other definitions such as that of Burkart and Medlik (1981), who divided the influences on the tourism market into two components:

- 'Determinants' refer to the exogenous or external factors that shape the general demand for tourism within society or a specific population. Such factors tend to be common to all world regions, although they are likely to show a different emphasis in every country (e.g. the economy in each country will have a greater or lesser effect on outbound tourism).

- 'Motivations' refer to the personal factors that directly affect the individual and are expressed as tourism desires and choices. Motivations can be influenced by internal (e.g. perceptions and personality) and external (e.g. culture, age and gender) aspects.

Essentially, leisure demand results from a variety of social, economic, demographic and psychological factors peculiar to the individual (Argyle 1996; Ryan 1997; Hall and Page 2002). Models of tourist motivation which explore the effect of these diverse influences are examined in the next chapter. However, extrinsic factors or determinants, such as government policy, media communications, marketing, societal norms and pressures, knowledge, information on and images of destinations, technological change and wider socio-economic determinants have an equally important role to play in shaping tourism destination demand (see Figure 3.2). These particular issues will form the focus of this chapter.

The term 'demand' is sometimes ambiguous in its use and meaning, often referring to different measures of tourism participation and behaviour. Subsequently, the study of tourism demand can be approached from differing perspectives. It is therefore important to understand the elements of tourism demand and how researchers and analysts use the terms which are shown in Figure 3.3.

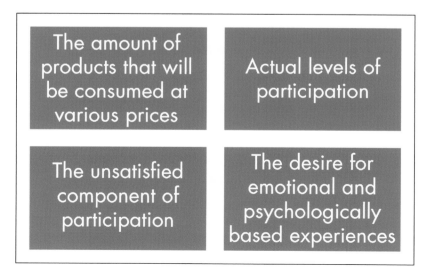

The amount of products that will be consumed at various prices

Actual levels of participation

The unsatisfied component of participation

The desire for emotional and psychologically based experiences

FIGURE 3.1 Approaches to tourism demand
Source: After Smith (1995)

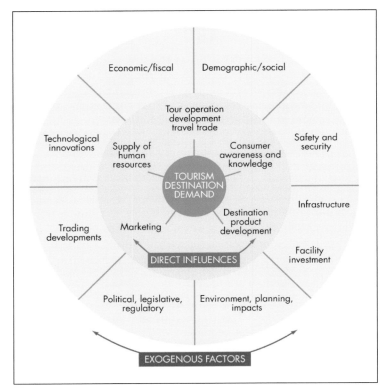

FIGURE 3.2 Factors shaping development of tourism destination demand.
Source: Adapted from WTO (1995)

- Aggregate/effective/actual demand
- Suppressed demand
- No demand
- Substitution of demand
- Displacement of demand

FIGURE 3.3 Elements of tourism demand

The elements of tourism demand

Aggregate/effective/actual demand

The term 'demand' is often used to specify actual or observed tourism participation and activity. This type of demand is known as 'effective' or 'actual' demand and refers to the aggregate number of tourists recorded in a given location or at a particular point in time. It is most easily visualized by reference to tourism statistical sources, where the total numbers of people are shown, travelling from one country to another or by purpose of visit. Clearly tourism suppliers require demand for their products, but too much effective demand poses the problem of exceeding the supply of products, such as overbooking of airline seats. Effective tourism demand within a population can be measured by means of gross **travel propensity**, which yields the total number of tourism trips as a percentage of the population.

Suppressed demand

It is often suggested that suppressed demand can be subdivided into 'potential' and 'deferred' demand (Cooper *et al.* 1998). Both refer to those who do not travel for some reason, the nature of that reason being the distinguishing factor. Those who might be classified as potential demand are more likely to become actual demand in the future when circumstances allow. It may well be additional income or holiday entitlement is needed for that suppressed, but potential, demand to become actual or effective. It can be seen that the reason behind potential demand relates more specifically to factors associated directly with the individual.

With deferred demand, the reasons for the 'suppression' are down to problems on the supply side, with perhaps accommodation shortages, transport difficulties or the weather preventing people from travelling to their chosen destination. Again, though, once such problems are overcome, those in this category move upwards and become effective or actual demand. For the tourism industry, ensuring that those classified within either of the suppressed demand categories turn into effective demand is crucial, as such individuals represent potential new customers.

No demand

Generally, there is a proportion of the population that does not participate in tourism. Reasons for this may be a lack of money (which may be resolved later in life), an unwillingness or inability to find the time necessary or a desire to enjoy holiday time at home rather than away from it. Whether the reasons are, through choice or otherwise, those in this category represent 'no demand'. Studies of poverty suggest that in low-income households, holidays are one luxury that families cannot afford. With holidays in developed countries now perceived as 'essential' elements of many people's lifestyles, the inability of poorer households to participate in holidays reinforces a sense of material deprivation and explains why 'no demand' exists in some households.

Other aspects of demand

There are other ways of viewing demand in addition to the three elements discussed above, which build on these basic concepts. Cooper *et al.* (1998) refer to 'substitution of demand' when demand for an activity is replaced by another form of activity, for example staying in a hotel rather than self-catering. In addition, redirection of demand occurs when the geographical holiday location is changed, perhaps as a result of overbooking in one destination. Demand may also be displaced where an absence of capacity (i.e. due to the hosting of an event such as the Olympics or other sporting event) means that people choose to visit an alternative destination.

Having established the parameters of tourism demand, it is now appropriate to conduct an analysis of the ways in which demand is influenced by exogenous factors. Such externally driven influences can be divided into two forms: those affecting demand in the tourist-generating region and those affecting demand in the tourist destination.

Factors influencing demand in the tourist-generating area

There are numerous factors influencing demand from the tourist-generating area, which in simple terms can be grouped as shown in Figure 3.4.

- economic determinants
- social determinants
- political determinants.

These determinants act as significant enabling or constraining variables on individuals within a tourist-generating region.

Economic determinants

Personal incomes The availability of the necessary finance is perhaps the most obvious variable influencing tourism demand. Incomes and tourism expenditure are closely linked, and it is possible to examine this relationship through observing statistics on economic trends and tourism activity in any country. An interesting example is Brazil, where the emerging middle class is made up of over 113 million people, who are among the top spenders in the USA according to the Brazilian Central Bank. As a product, tourism has traditionally been considered as 'demand-elastic' (see Chapter 16), which means that consumers tend to be sensitive to a price rise. Put simply, as prices rise, demand reduces; similarly, if incomes

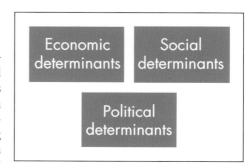

FIGURE 3.4 The determinants of tourism demand

rise and prices remain the same, then demand increases. In 2012 President Obama announced changes to visa restrictions to enable the Global Entry Program to expand the volume of visitors from the expanding economies of Brazil and China. This involved raising the capacity of visa processing at US embassies in each country as well as conducting background checks to reduce delays in customs on arrival in the USA. This was in response to the relatively poor performance of international tourist arrivals since the 9/11 terrorist attack in 2001 and the imposition of greater security restrictions.

Distribution of incomes Within a tourist-generating nation, income distribution is likely to affect tourism demand. A skewed income distribution, for example, where there are relatively few wealthy and many poor households, is likely to limit the proportion of people who can afford to travel internationally. In wealthier developed countries, a more equal income distribution may result in a high overall level of tourism demand. Clearly there must also be a willingness to spend on tourism products. According to the Office for National Statistics (ONS 1999), in 1995 4:10 households in the UK felt that they could not afford a week's holiday, compared to 6:10 in Portugal and 1:10 in Germany. This is a point often overlooked by tourism researchers who naturally assume that such barriers do not exist when looking at the tourism-generating propensity of the population in individual countries. The Family Holiday Association in the UK reaffirmed in 2006 that the continued poverty among families in the UK meant that 1:3 families cannot afford a one-week holiday and 1:5 cannot afford a day trip. This was amplified in one-parent families, where 57 per cent were unable to afford a holiday and 40 per cent unable to afford a day trip. The UK Department of Work and Pensions and the government's Social Exclusion Unit regard the lack of a one-week break as a measure of poverty. Martins *et al.* (2017) also examined the impact of world GDP and currency changes, which have boosted world tourism growth. However, as these statistics suggest, this growth in tourism was socially and economically divisive. In France 30 per cent of the population did not take holidays for financial reasons in 2004, around 47 per cent of the Latin American population did not take a holiday in 2006, and in the USA around 35 million people live in poverty. There are also trends in some countries where employees do not take their full holiday entitlement, as reported in 2018 (McCulloch 2018); in this study, 40 per cent of employees took only half of their leave entitlement; a further 23 per cent regularly checked emails while on holiday and 15 per cent continued working while on holiday for fear of getting behind. The propensity not to take a holiday was greatest among those in the 18–24 age group. Only half of employees stated they could relax and not be contactable on holiday. This is somewhat at odds with other sample surveys, which report high rates of holiday-taking among the people surveyed. What is apparent is that the propensity for holiday-making, especially multiple trips to different destinations, is greater among higher occupational and income groups, a feature observed by the Civil Aviation Authority (2006) study of low-cost airlines, which found that higher social groups were the main beneficiaries of the growth in travel by air.

Those not taking a holiday are more numerous among the lower income groups, for whom paid holidays are a much less common occurrence in the USA. Added to this are differences in the patterns of domestic and outbound demand within countries. As with other aspects in society (e.g. unemployment), tourism activity is not evenly distributed across all social groups or geographically within countries. In the UK for example, higher income and socio-economic groups are over-represented as are those living in the more prosperous areas of the south-east, and these groups show a higher propensity towards taking holidays. Conversely, while some sections of society enjoy holidays during school vacations, some families face the daily struggle of food poverty and insecurity – the daily struggle of how to feed their families. A holiday to these groups is a pure luxury. In 2017 alone, in the months of July and August 2017, the Trussell Trust (a UK food charity – www.trusselltrust.org/) provided 204 525 three-day emergency-supply food packages in the summer vacation period. Some 74 011 of these went to feed children, from the total of around 1.6 million food parcels it provided annually. In China a higher propensity for travel exists in the major urban centres on the southern coastal seaboard, with its expanding middle-class population seeking overseas travel experiences.

Value of currency/exchange rates A destination's exchange rate has a far-reaching influence on tourism demand from a generating area, and international tourism is highly susceptible to exchange-rate fluctuations that can alter the cost of a holiday considerably. The potential consequences of changes in exchange rates are immediately acted upon by the tourism industry and travellers alike. Crouch (1994) identified the impact of an unfavourable exchange rate to include less travel abroad, a reduction in expenditure of length of stay, changes in the method or length of travel time and a reduction in spending by business travellers. A movement in exchange rates of at least 10 per cent is necessary before a consequential correlation in visitor movement can be traced, according to some studies, and for some destinations (with high international appeal or very strong economies) movements of 20 per cent have been necessary to seriously change tourism demand. Research in 2010 by Tourism Australia found that such bilateral currency fluctuations influenced the decision to visit in the source area and that this was cyclical and related to periodic changes in economic performance.

Social determinants

Demographic variables Although Chapter 4 examines the demographic variables in more detail in terms of tourist motivation to travel, it is evident that a range of demographic variables affects demand. For example, the stage in the lifecycle of a family or an individual in that family (see Figure 3.5) will often exert an influence on the type of travel product and destination they choose.

Figure 3.5 combines some of the thinking on the family lifecycle stages people are often classified into. These stages will be a key determinant of the type of travel they consume (which we will return to in Chapter 4). For example, research on youth tourism and the backpacker market indicates how influential age is on the

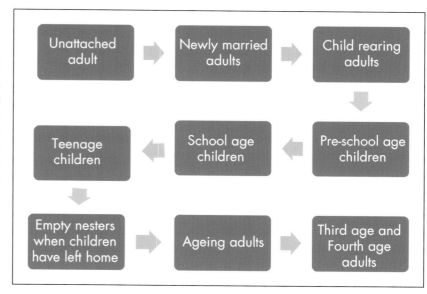

FIGURE 3.5 Stages in the family lifecycle

selection of this type of experience as the numbers of such tourists in their late teenage years and early 20s demonstrate. In contrast, other studies of ageing have distinguished between groups of people living longer and made a distinction between third-age and fourth-age travellers. Laslett (1989) described the third age as an era of personal achievement and fulfilment in later life. In contrast, Laslett described the fourth age as one of growing dependence, leading to death. This approach to ageing adopted a focus on the functional attributes of individuals so as to determine a person's position in the cycle of ageing (see Connell and Page 2020). The impact of education can also be a major determinant of both employment type and income-earning potential, and therefore of the type of tourism experience one seeks. Similarly, the availability of time and disposable income for tourism (see Insight 3.1) can influence holiday-taking propensity. Other factors such as home ownership, occupation, gender and ethnic group are increasingly being recognized as major determinants of tourism demand.

INSIGHT 3.1 BRIC countries: Emerging outbound markets

At a global scale, many of the mature tourism markets in North America and Europe have seen relatively slow growth in international arrivals, with niche markets offering much of the expansion (e.g. the youth travel market and backpacking and the low-cost market). In contrast, the booming BRIC economies (Brazil, Russia, India and China) have seen major growth among their rapidly expanding middle classes. The caveat here is that the economic crisis in Brazil saw the market for outbound travel slump in 2015–2016 as residents took shorter international trips and replaced outbound trips by air with car-based domestic travel. The UN–WTO and the European Tourism Commission examined the characteristics of the growing markets of Russia, China and India, identifying their potential as major drivers of future international tourism growth. For example, only around 15 per cent of the 140 million-strong Russian population have travelled overseas. The majority of trips outbound from Russia are

predominantly for business purposes, highlighting the potential for growth in holiday trips overseas. Existing studies (i.e. UN–WTO 2011) suggest that previous rates of growth in outbound travel from the BRIC countries have been extremely buoyant with rates of around 10 per cent growth per annum, compared to average global rates of outbound growth of between 2 and 4 per cent. The rising middle classes and extreme rich (i.e. billionaires) make this a major growth market for Europe given the existing provision of air routes. The influence of the BRIC market has also spread widely as a recent study of tourism in South Africa found BRIC arrivals accounted for less than 3 per cent of international visitors but spent three times the amount of those from other countries. The majority of the BRIC visitors to South Africa are on business trips, supporting up to 26 000 tourism jobs. In 2017, the outbound spending of BRIC countries among the top 25 outbound spending markets internationally was as follows: Brazil was placed 16th; Russia was in 8th place; India was 17th; and China was first, with an outbound expenditure of US$ 258 billion).

In the case of India outbound growth has risen in excess of 16 per cent per annum since 2004. Data from the UN–WTO (2011) shows that expenditure by outbound Indian tourists rose from US$1.3 billion in 1997 to almost eight times that amount in 2007, and then to US$8.2 billion and US$ 18 billion by 2017. The existing patterns of travel are dominated by middle-class, well-educated travellers who are predominantly male or travelling as couples/in groups. Key UN–WTO research suggests the ease of gaining a visa, together with other variables such as safety and security, combine with the image of the destination, quality of visitor facilities, variety of activities and attractions and level of infrastructure to shape this outbound market. The UN–WTO research also identifies other key determinants of outbound travel (i.e. availability of vegetarian food, cultural affinity, priced packages and a welcoming environment).

Much of the growth in both Russia and India is driven by available disposable income resulting from the fast growth of these economies alongside the trend of associating outbound travel with prestige and status. Similar patterns of development in other BRIC countries (i.e. China and Brazil) exist as these countries contain half of the world's population.

Further reading

UN–WTO (2011) *Policy and Practice for Global Tourism*. Madrid: UN–WTO.

UN–WTO and European Tourism Commission (2009) *The Russian Outbound Travel Market with Special Insight into the Image of Europe as a Destination*. Madrid: UN–WTO.

UN–WTO and European Travel Commission (2009) *The Indian Outbound Travel Market with Special Insight into the Image of Europe as a Destination*. Madrid: UN–WTO.

Questions

1 Will the BRIC countries follow a similar route to outbound travel as other Western countries did in the 1980s and 1990s?

2 How does poverty and inequality in BRIC countries impact the future prospects of growth in the BRIC markets?

3 Are BRIC countries going to see their domestic tourism industry develop to absorb other forms of tourism demand not met by outbound travel?

4 Search for other growing outbound markets with similar characteristics to BRIC countries (e.g. the MINT economies – Malaysia, Indonesia, Nigeria and Turkey).

Holiday entitlements The growth of leisure time over the last two centuries has greatly increased the amount of time available for tourism, especially in the developed world, but since the 1980s there has been some reversal. In Germany and Italy typical holiday entitlement amounts to 28 days, in addition to 12 or 14 public holidays, whereas 10 days is normal in Japan. Increases in holiday entitlement are likely to result in increases in tourism demand, as the extra time may allow trips to more distant destinations or longer stays. The patterns of public- and school-holiday periods give rise to seasonal patterns of tourism demand in developed countries. One result of this is the growth of supplementary, shorter holidays in addition to the main holiday, often referred to as 'short breaks'. Low levels of holiday entitlements do act as a real obstacle upon the opportunities for recreational travel, while a high level of entitlement encourages such travel.

Political determinants

Government tax policies and controls on tourist spending Approaches taken by governments can greatly influence tourism demand. Examples include exchange control, currency export prohibition, taxation of tourists and residents and visa regulations. Visitors also respond to political events, such as the Arab Spring in the Middle East, with Spain reporting growth as visitors replaced North African visits with those to Spain in 2011. Bull (1995) shows that government fiscal and control policies can change tourist flows and specific destinations can gain or lose potential profitability. For example, exchange-rate fluctuations in Europe can make the UK dearer or cheaper for those using the euro. In March 2008, the euro was 18 per cent dearer than in the preceding year, pushing up the price of UK-to-Europe travel and vice versa. VisitBritain has shown that, in the case of US non-business visitors to the UK, when sterling is expensive in relation to the US dollar, the volume of travel drops and vice versa. This assumes a greater significance as hotel accommodation in London may be up to 40 per cent more expensive than other UK cities, making price an important determinant.

Many governments have used tourism as a source of tax revenue, and Bull (1995) notes three specific types:

- taxes on commercial tourism products
- taxes imposed on consumers in the act of being tourists
- user-pays charges.

Some countries also impose exit or travel taxes on their residents who wish to travel overseas. A study in 2006 for Edinburgh Tourism Action Group (ETAG) reviewed the issue of taxing visitors and the notion of Transient Visitor Taxes (TVTs) (those levied and paid by tourists and transient visitors, and non-specific taxes paid by visitors and residents alike). In their survey of cities around the world, they found that most cities with tourist-specific taxes used hotel or accommodation bed levies. Some cities used airport departure taxes. If a TVT was introduced, based on a bed levy in Edinburgh, it was estimated that it would generate £1.1–£4.9 million in revenues in 2006. However, ETAG identified a risk to tourism demand associated with this strategy. Interestingly, in 2005 both Rotterdam and Amersfoort in the Netherlands abolished bed-levy charges to make the destinations more competitive. In contrast, Vancouver, Canada has a 2 per cent bed levy which has been used to help fund Tourism Vancouver, an approach also adopted in many US states (see also Chapter 15). In 2019, Edinburgh City Council revisited the tourist tax. and the City Council approved plans to introduce a tax (subject to approval by the Scottish Parliament) of £2 a night per room which it estimated would generate £11–14 million a year in revenue, following the trend set by Paris and Barcelona, which had both introduced such a tax.

INSIGHT 3.2 Taxing the tourist: Air Passenger Duty in the UK

There have been comparatively few studies of tourist taxation by researchers, the most notable being Mak's (2006) review. One such method of taxing tourists is Air Passenger Duty. As Song *et al.* (2012) show, this is a regressive tax that is proportionally more costly for lower-priced tickets. This has led to a decline in outbound travel from the UK for certain categories of travel and destinations. The arguments for taxing air travel by the UK government were premised on reducing environmental pollution, as

according to the . . . White Paper 'The Future of Transport' carbon emissions from [the] aviation sector are expected to amount to be 18 million tons by 2030 and domestic flights will be responsible for only 3 percent of this, illustrating the relative importance of outbound trips by air and their contribution to environmental pollution. The total emissions from air travel could represent almost 25 per cent of UK's contribution to global warming by 2030 (Seetaram et al. 2014: 477).

The UK government chose, in 1993, to develop an Air Passenger Duty Tax (APD) which it introduced in 1994. According to Seetaram *et al.* (2018: 86), in its current form the scheme comprises

two bands of APD. Band A covers destinations zero to 2000 miles from London with a sliding scale of duty according to the class being travelled in. Band B is for

travel to destinations over 2000 miles from London. There are three categories of APD for each band, depending on the class of travel. The top rate of APD is for smaller aircraft, typically personal jets of 20 tonnes or more that are equipped to carry fewer than 18 passengers.

This tax has been heavily criticized by the tourism industry in the UK (e.g. see the Travel Association in its A Fair Tax on Flying (AFTOF) campaign, http://www.afairtaxonflying.org/), which focuses on arguments about its limiting effects on tourist travel. The taxation is estimated to raise £3.4 billion for the UK Treasury annually and is absorbed into general revenue as a taxation with no tagging to sustainability activity. Seetaram *et al.* (2014) noted the negative effects on some overseas destinations and travellers have been prepared to pay more to travel. For this reason, Seetaram *et al.* (2018) undertook a study to assess how much travellers would be willing to pay before such costs impacted their travel behaviour. This study used the economic valuation method known as Willingness to Pay, and again the results showed that, for holidays, people were prepared to pay more to travel. Seetaram *et al.* (2018: 94) found that:

- The MWTP (mean or average Willingness to Pay) for short-haul trips is £16.543 in economy class and £24.116 in business class. In comparison, the current APD rate (enforced from 1 April 2017 to 1 April 2018) is £13 for economy class and £26 for business class

(HM Revenue & Customs 2017). It is evident that the 'average tourist' is prepared to accept the current APD rate for short-haul trips.

- For medium- and long-haul trips, the MWTP ranges from £22.88 to £36.79. In contrast, the current APD rates are £75 for economy class and £150 for business class (HM Revenue and Customs 2017), which are far beyond what the average tourist is willing to accept. Therefore, the current rate for medium- and long-haul trips may largely decrease outbound travel demand, confirming the validity of many of the concerns raised by trade lobby groups about the perceived effects of APD on air travel.

What these findings demonstrate is that APD has a limited effect on short-haul travel but for longer-haul travel, pricing can be used to limit travel.

Further reading

Choi, A. and Ritchie, B. W. (2014) 'Willingness to pay for flying carbon neutral in Australia: An exploratory study of offsetter profiles', *Journal of Sustainable Tourism* 22 (8): 1236–1256.

HM Revenue and Customs (2017) *Excise Notice 550: Air Passenger Duty*. https://www.gov.uk/government/publications/excise-notice-550-air-passenger-duty.

Jou, R. and Chen, T. (2015) 'Willingness to pay of air passengers for carbon-offset', *Sustainability* 7(3): 3071–3085.

Mak, J. (1988) 'Taxing hotel room rentals in the U.S.', *Journal of Travel Research* 26 (1): 10–15.

Seeley, A. (2014). *Air passenger duty: Recent debates and reform*. House of Commons Briefing Paper, http://www.sasig.org.uk/wp-content/uploads/2014/05/2014.05.16_HoC_StandardNote_APD.pdf.

Seetaram, N., Song, H. and Page, S.J. (2014) 'Air passenger duty and outbound tourism demand from the United Kingdom', *Journal of Travel Research* 53 (4): 476–487.

Seetaram, N., Song, H., Ye, S. and Page, S.J. (2018) 'Estimating Willingness to pay air passenger duty', *Annals of Tourism Research* 72: 85–97.

Questions

1 How much extra would you be prepared to pay to fly short-haul and long-haul?

2 How should government taxation levied on APD be used?

3 What alternative measures to achieve environmental goals or raise money might there be, instead of levying APD?

4 What are the costs and benefits of using APD as a tax on tourism?

Factors influencing demand in the tourist destination area

In a similar vein, the level of demand at a tourist destination is influenced by economic and political factors, but tourism products and services also have a role to play here. Dominant among these are the price of the tourism products, the supply of tourism products and services and their overall quality. Moreover, the government of the destination area can affect the trading operations of suppliers or the way tourists purchase goods and services, and thereby influence demand.

Economic

Price Tourism suppliers, such as in the accommodation and transport sectors, may well price their goods or services independently, but a close watch on the behaviour of their competitors is clearly necessary (Burkart and Medlik 1981). With the growth of online platforms to sell capacity, businesses can match prices more closely to demand as well as monitor competitor's prices. The relationship between price and demand is an inverse one. Higher prices result in lower demand and vice versa. Low prices in Spain and the Balearic Islands caused huge demand from UK tourists in the 1960s, 1970s and 1980s. However, in a volatile market, fashion and environmental damage have combined to cause a downturn in the region's popularity. In addition to the price of what might be thought of as the central part of the tourist product (accommodation and transport), the demand for tourism is also influenced by other forms of expenditure associated with the holiday. In this respect, the influence of price is not straightforward. While tourists are sensitive to the cost of a holiday and changes in the price, a reduction in cost may result in the perception of a lower-quality product.

Supply-related

Competition If the number of suppliers providing goods and services in the destination increases with demand, the level of competition among suppliers also increases, as will be discussed in Chapter 5. As Dogru *et al.* (2019: 27) argue 'In a competitive market, an increase in supply while keeping demand relatively constant would decrease prices and revenues'. The extent of this form of supply competition will relate to both the number and size of the suppliers involved. This has been seen in the case of Airbnb as a disruptive form of technology that has disproportionately affected that part of the accommodation sector which is at the lower end of the quality spectrum (Dogru *et al.* 2019). In contrast, in Norway, Airbnb has been reported as being beneficial in stimulating demand for tourism in some areas (see Strømmen-Bakhtiar and Vinogradov 2019). Price competitiveness between countries is also an issue (see Chapter 16) and Han *et al.* (2006) identified that the US outbound market to mainland Europe showed a propensity to substitute one country for another depending on price. The analysis of global tourism competitiveness for 136 countries can be seen in the World Economic Forum *Travel and Tourism Competitiveness* report (World Economic Forum 2017).

Political

Government controls at the destination Just as governments in the generating area can influence demand, so can those at destinations. Regulation can directly limit the number of tourists, through visa restrictions, and a case in point is those in force in Bhutan. Other countries restrict the number of charter flights that can enter, again influencing demand, but possibly more as an attempt to promote the national airline. It is possible for countries to control the amount of tourist expenditure (e.g. Egypt) or restrict the amount of currency that can be exchanged. Moreover, governments at tourist destinations can manage capacity through planning regulations and thereby restrict competition.

Other factors influencing tourism demand

While there are some factors which mainly influence tourism demand at the destination or from the generating area, there are others which fall between these categories, but are nevertheless important determinants. Among these are the promotional efforts of the destination and the time/cost of travel.

Promotional efforts of the destination

While it could be argued that the promotional efforts of a destination are largely due to the destination itself, aspects of imagery and how such efforts are received make this influence distinctive. As a product, tourism is intangible, which means that it is impossible for the consumer to 'test' the product before purchase (see Chapter 14). As such, tourism promotion is different from promotion in other industries. When contemplating a visit to a new destination, the consumer must use various means to secure information that will enable them to make a decision. Brochures once dominated the range of promotional tools, but the Internet has quickly proved to be one of the most valuable marketing tools for tourism suppliers, with customers able to check availability and book online without the need for a third party. The success of promotional efforts can influence tourism demand; however, such efforts are beyond the control of some suppliers at a destination, especially when media images of negative issues (see Chapter 25) portray the destination in poor light (see Pike 2008). This is also now more immediate, due to the impact of social media and instant messaging and communication tools like Twitter and Facebook, which have a global reach.

3

Health, safety and security issues

Reductions in demand at both regional and international levels have been a marked pattern in tourism activity in the new millennium, as the 2001 9/11 attacks on the USA affected tourism demand dramatically (also see Chapter 25) and political, war-related and terrorist activity have long featured as a constraint on the freedom of tourism travel. Corbet *et al.* (2019) examined the effect of such attacks and found that due to the duty of care among European employers, business travel using flights slowed down after terrorist attacks. Other events, such as SARS and the outbreak of foot-and-mouth disease in the UK in 2001, had short-term effects on tourism demand in these regions, as noted in Chapter 1. These issues and their implications are of great contemporary significance for national tourism industries, and this is now being recognized by politicians, decision makers and the tourism industry in terms of destination development and tourists' willingness, when a crisis occurs, to change travel plans or to seek places 'off the beaten track' (see Images 3.1. & 3.2). This type of demand substitution, or the displacement

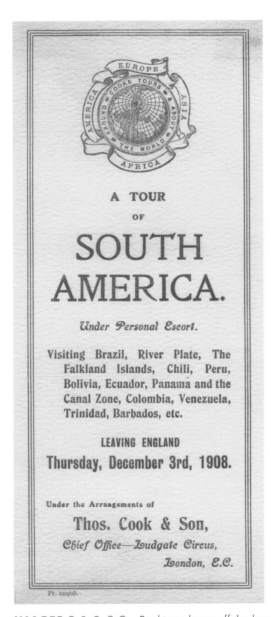

IMAGES 3.1 & 3.2 Seeking places off the beaten track is not a new trend within tourism, as these posters promoting travel to South America in 1908 and 1928 by Thomas Cook illustrate that exploration of new places is a well-established theme in tourism ©Thomas Cook

of one form of demand from an affected destination to a non-affected destination, adds an additional competitive pressure for the tourism industries.

Time and cost considerations

The cost and time involved in the travel component itself is important. While some distance is needed, the time and cost of travel over very long distances may be prohibitive and influence demand. As such, it is likely that the faster people can travel to destinations, the more popular the tourism product will be. This has been most noticeable in the expansion of Eastern European tourism destinations, as low-cost airlines have made it easier to access these areas. Time and cost considerations also have a significant role in countries with large land borders, such as in the EU and along the USA–Canada border, which amount to some of the largest tourist flows at a global scale, due to convenience and opportunities for ease of travel. The USA–Mexico border has 48 crossings and around 350 million crossings a year, a significant proportion of which will be for tourism. The USA–Canada border is the largest border in the world, at 5525 miles long with 119 crossings, 13 ferry crossings and 39 railway crossings (of which only two carry international passengers). Research on cross-border tourism has generated considerable interest in terms of the impact on areas within the border zone (see Gao *et al*. 2019 for the example of the China–Myanmar border).

Seasonal variations

Seasonality is a well-documented aspect of tourism demand, and an important determining factor in relation to providing the motivation for tourists to escape to warmer climes or experience different climatic regions: Antarctica, for example. A long tradition of seasonality research exists in tourism, as shown in Table 3.1, and Butler and Mao (1997) identified three types of seasonality in destinations:

- *one-peak seasonality*, with a distinct summer season
- *two-peak seasonality*, with a summer and winter season
- *non-peak seasonality*, mainly occurring in urban areas where the urban centre has all-year-round use, but seasonal demand from different domestic and international visitors.

Among the factors influencing seasonality of different markets are the interaction of temperature, rainfall (see Image 3.3) and daylight in the origin and destination areas (see Insight 3.2), pricing policies of tourist operators (see Image 3.4), airlines, the different holiday habits of travellers, and the importance of fashion, tastes and

IMAGE 3.3 Rainfall can be a major deterrent to outdoor activities even in the peak visitor seasons, as illustrated by these visitors seeking indoor activities to avoid the rain at a major attraction

IMAGE 3.4 Pricing can be a major element impacting upon visitor behaviour and to attract group visits, family tickets are often advertised, as illustrated here, to offer greater value for money

IMAGE 3.5 Events are often used to attract visitors in the low season, as illustrated at this attraction, with its provision of a Halloween theme, encouraging children to dress up and join in games, such as guessing the weight of the pumpkin, as well as a Halloween tour

provision of events and attractions at the destination (Image 3.5). An inclement climate, such as the winter in Canada, may lead to the development of indoor facilities, like West Edmonton Mall, to create a demand for leisure shopping. Ferrante *et al.* (2018) observed that the most seasonal regions for tourism in Europe were the colder regions where the season for visiting was shorter. Yet they also observed that retired and more aged travellers were less affected by school holidays.

Seasonally distorted patterns of holiday-taking occur as a result of institutionally driven holiday periods, such as school holidays and calendar-related events like Thanksgiving and Christmas. In the Balearic Islands, more than 80 per cent of arrivals fall in the May–September period, and this is typical of many holiday resorts. Many destinations seek to reduce patterns of seasonality that show marked peaks by creating interest and promoting off-peak short breaks, sometimes based around event strategies, as observed by Connell *et al.* (2015). Connell *et al.* (2015) examined Scottish visitor attractions and how they used events to address seasonality, particularly the very concentrated patterns of tourism visitation in Scotland. As Figure 3.6 shows, the analysis of seasonality and tourism has to span various disciplines (i.e. geography, economics, politics, and policy analysis and management) to understand the various attributes of seasonality. Managers then have to make decisions on the type of strategy they may wish to embrace to address seasonality, as illustrated by Figure 3.7. From a tourism-demand perspective, this highlights how the substitution of demand from tourism markets can be adapted to include residents and the school markets in terms of building the business opportunities through off-peak events in visitor attractions. This also demonstrates the broader links between tourism, leisure and events, which were introduced in Chapter 1 as visitor attractions do not just rely on tourists as their market, a theme we will return to in Chapters 9 and 26. A key element of seasonality is the link with weather as the patterns of weather change with the seasons, in countries that have distinct seasons.

TABLE 3.1 Perspectives on tourism and seasonality that inform events research
<ul><li>Hartmann (1986) argued that the complexity of seasonality is created by the interplay of factors in both origin and destination areas, where flows of tourism are conditioned by a wide range of social and cultural factors (e.g. imagery), economic (e.g. price) and physical factors (e.g. the availability of skiing in winter periods).</li><li>Seasonality has both a distinct time-based element and a more neglected spatial component. Hartmann (1986: 12) defined tourism seasonality as 'temporal variance in the phenomenon of tourism activities', and acknowledged the existence of a spatial element.</li><li>Butler (2001: 5) argued that 'little research has addressed the problem of whether seasonality varies in nature and intensity on a spatial basis either within or between destination areas'. The point is further reaffirmed by Baum and Lundtorp (2001), who argue that there is no concept or theory of tourism seasonality.</li><li>Butler and Mao (1997) recognize that urban tourism is often the least seasonally affected form of tourism; seasonal spatial patterns within destinations are not readily charted and understood.</li><li>Seasonal variations in destination characteristics can act as a magnet for visitors seeking ephemeral experiences linked with climate or nature, such as the fall market (Spencer and Holecek 2007), as well as economic-driven destination experiences such as Christmas markets (see Haid 2006).</li></ul>

Source: © Elsevier, reproduced from Connell, J., Page, S.J. and Meyer, D. (2015) 'Visitor attractions and events: Responding to seasonality', *Tourism Management* 46: 285.

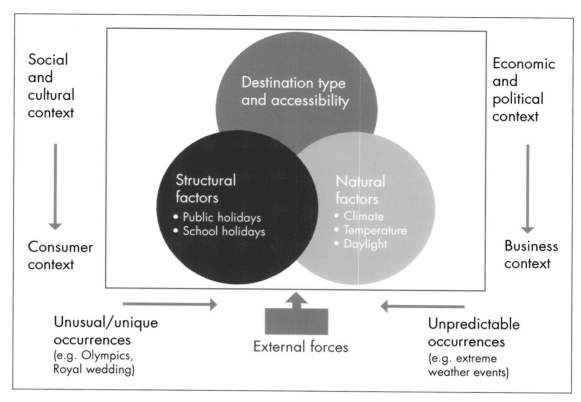

FIGURE 3.6   Seasonal influences on tourism demand

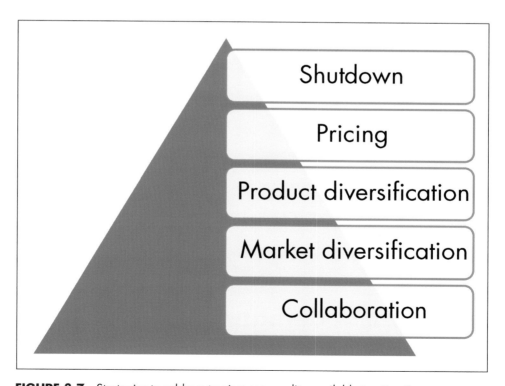

FIGURE 3.7   Strategies to address tourism seasonality available to attraction managers

INSIGHT 3.3 Tourism demand and weather

The demand for tourism may also be affected by environmental factors such as the climate and weather, which do help to shape seasonal patterns of visitation. Climate may also be a key determinant of tourist activities (e.g. hours of sunshine, temperature, snow, wind and precipitation). At the same time, climate is a highly variable parameter, subject not only to annual or seasonal, but also daily variations (i.e. the diurnal range from the highest to lowest temperature). The inability to 'guarantee' good weather from one day to the next (Martín 2005) means that the daily demand for tourist activities can be expanded during good weather, and during inclement conditions, it can lead to a switching from outdoor to indoor activities. This means that to accommodate demand and unpredictable weather, destinations need to ensure that a wide range of visitor attractions (see Chapter 9) are available, including indoor venues. In extreme weather events (e.g. cyclones, heavy or torrential rain, heavy snowfall, floods, heat waves and avalanches), the demand for tourism will be suspended due to the climatic constraints on tourism, when public warnings are issued.

Climate is also a clear attraction or the main appeal of a destination or product selection, and remains a key element in the advertising of resorts and countries to influence tourist decision-making (see Chapter 4). Indeed, Besancenot (1991: 208) claims that 'the iconographic analysis of tourist brochures and careful reading of the accompanying text only confirm the obsessive presence of references, direct or indirect, to the climate'. Tables of data on air temperature, sun hours and rainfall are used to extol the virtues of a destination's climate by tour operators. Favourable representations are frequently used to create longer tourist seasons, thereby promoting a less seasonal industry. However, climate does shape the 'what' and 'when' of tourist activities, and with concerns over the impact of global warming on freak weather events (see Chapter 27), these concerns are only likely to be exacerbated. Climate will certainly influence tourist enjoyment and psychological reactions to a destination, particularly satisfaction.

Research in Michigan, USA found that a 1-degree increase in a day's high temperature led to a 1 per cent increase in traffic on state roads and vice versa. In the summer of 2007, a particularly wet season caused by an Atlantic jet stream over England led to 180 per cent average rainfall in May, 241 per cent in June and 219 per cent in July. The impact on domestic tourism was a switching from outdoor and beach locations to other pursuits (i.e. demand displacement) as visitors amended or adapted their planned activity to suit the weather.

Further reading

Becken, S. and Wilson, J. (2013) 'The impacts of weather on tourist travel', *Tourism Geographies* 15 (4), 620–639.

Day, J., Chin, N., Sydnor, S. and Cherkauer, K. (2013) 'Weather, climate, and tourism performance: A quantitative analysis', *Tourism Management Perspectives* 5: 51–56.

Jeuring, J. (2017) 'Weather perceptions, holiday satisfaction and perceived attractiveness of domestic vacationing in The Netherlands', *Tourism Management* 61, 70–81.

Martín, M. (2005) 'Weather, climate and tourism', *Annals of Tourism Research* 32 (3): 571–591.

Questions

1 How does climate impact tourist's perceptions of where to go on holiday?

2 Can you construct a table of different climate types and how the markets for their products vary by season?

3 Using examples, identify the effect of extreme climate events on tourism destinations.

4 How do tourism destinations address the effects of seasonality on the demand for tourism?

So far, this chapter has identified the main determinants of tourism demand. However, an essential aspect of understanding demand for tourism is an appreciation of how tourism activity is measured, evaluated and reported; these are central to the appropriate planning and management of tourism activity in destinations.

Measuring tourism demand: Tourism statistics

Smith (2004: 29) recognizes that 'the fundamental concept in measuring tourism is, of course, tourism':

Tourism is the set of activities engaged in by persons temporarily away from their usual environment, for a period of not more than one year, and for a broad range of leisure, business, religious, health and personal reasons, excluding the pursuit of remuneration from within the place visited or long-term change of residence[.]

which highlights the scope of what we might measure – the scale of tourism as an economic activity, the reasons for becoming a tourist, where one goes on holiday, through to an endless range of possible issues. Accordingly, measurement of such a diverse activity poses many methodological problems. Such issues will be explored later, but first, why is it important to measure tourism activity?

What do tourism statistics measure and how are they used?

Burkart and Medlik (1981) provide a useful insight into the development of measurements of tourism phenomena by governments during the 1960s and their subsequent development through to the late 1970s. While it is readily acknowledged by most tourism researchers that statistics are a necessary feature to establish effective demand for tourism, Burkart and Medlik (1981: 74) identify the principal reasons for statistical measurement in tourism:

- to evaluate the magnitude and significance of tourism to a destination area or region
- to quantify the contribution of tourism to the economy or society, especially the effect on the balance of payments
- to assist in the planning and development of tourism infrastructure and the effect of different volumes of tourists with specific needs to assist in the evaluation and implementation of marketing and promotion activities where the tourism marketer requires information on the actual and potential markets and their characteristics.

Consequently, tourism statistics are essential to the measurement of demand in terms of the volume, scale, impact and value of tourism at different geographical scales from the global to the country level down to the individual destination. In order to assist in activities such as the planning and development of tourism and in impact assessments and to inform promotional campaigns and market research, tourism statistics crucially provide data on several issues:

- volume of tourism
- value of tourism.

These are typically measured by:

- frontier arrivals
- accommodation arrivals
- nights spent
- tourist receipts.

We will now examine the organizations that measure tourism activity and methodologies used, with some discussion of the inherent problems in data collection. In addition, insights on international and domestic tourism activity are now presented.

International and domestic tourism: Statistics and insights

The two principal organizations that collate data on international tourism are the United Nations World Tourism Organization (UN–WTO) and the Organization for Economic Cooperation and Development (OECD). The UN–WTO provides the main source of data, collated from a survey of major government agencies responsible for data collection and the trend in international arrivals since 1950. As shown in Chapter 2, there has been an almost constant growth in tourism arrivals since the 1970s despite temporary setbacks in the growth due to crises (e.g. the oil crisis in the 1970s, Gulf War in the 1980s and SARS). While most international tourists are expressed as frontier arrivals (i.e. arrivals determined by means of a frontier check), the use of arrival/departure cards (where used) provides additional detail to the profile of international tourists, and where they are not used, periodic tourism surveys often are. UN–WTO statistics are mainly confined to all categories of travellers and in some cases geographical disaggregation of the data may be limited by the collecting agencies, and the use of descriptions and categories for aid of simplicity (e.g. rest of the world) rather than listing all categories of arrivals.

The major publications of the UN–WTO and OECD in relation to international tourism are:

- the WTO's *Yearbook of Tourism Statistics*, which contains a summary of the most salient tourism statistics for almost 150 countries and territories
- the OECD's *Tourism Policy and International Tourism*, referred to as the Blue Book; this is less comprehensive, covering only 25 countries, but it does contain most of the main generating and receiving areas. While the main thrust of the publication is government policy and the obstacles to international tourism, it does expand on certain areas not covered in the WTO publication.

In addition, international regional tourism organizations such as the Pacific Asia Travel Association, the ASEAN Tourism Working Group, APEC and the EU (Europa) also collect international tourism statistics. National Tourism Organizations (NTOs) also collect data on international arrivals and many of their websites contain tables of statistical data.

Domestic tourism statistics

Data on domestic tourism volume, expenditure and patterns are normally coordinated by NTOs, often with the assistance of regional tourism bodies. Tourism data are also collected by commercial organizations and those requiring the results can subscribe to or purchase reports from a range of bodies, such as the European Union's statistical agency – Eurostat (https://ec.europa.eu/eurostat). Moreover, consultants can be commissioned to specifically collect the data required. However, in both cases the expense is such that most turn to national government organizations for tourism data.

According to the UN–WTO, domestic tourism is estimated to be up to *ten times greater* in volume than international tourism, and yet comparatively little research has been undertaken on this neglected area of tourism activity. Pearce (1995: 67) argues that this may be attributed to the less visible nature of much domestic tourism, which is often more informal and less structured than international tourism, and a subsequent tendency by many government agencies, researchers and others to regard it as insignificant. Where government agencies and other public sector organizations undertake data collection on domestic tourism, the results are not often directly comparable, limiting the identification of general patterns and trends (Pearce 1995: 67) although the study by Singh (2009) examines the situation in Asia. Yet one of the enduring problems in tourism research is that organizations that collect data are often beset with methodological difficulties, which must be clearly identified and understood when interpreting statistics. These, and associated problems, will now be explored.

Measuring demand: Problems and challenges

Despite the clear need for statistical input, an information gap exists between the types of statistics provided by organizations and the needs of users. The compilation of tourism statistics provided by organizations associated with the measurement of tourism have established methods and processes to collect, collate and analyze tourism statistics, yet these have only been understood by a small number of researchers and practitioners. A commonly misunderstood feature which is associated with tourism statistics is the assumption that they are a complete and authoritative source of information (i.e. they answer all the questions posed by the researcher and are completely reliable). Other associated problems are that tourism data are subject to considerable time lag in their generation, analysis, presentation and dissemination to interested parties. Accordingly, available statistics are not always recent and may not relate to the previous year or season.

In fact, most tourism statistics are typically measurements of arrivals, trips, tourist nights and tourist expenditure, and these often appear in total or split into categories such as business or leisure travel (Latham and Edwards 2003) (see http://www.unwto.org, and consult the webpage which provides up-to-date lists of arrivals and visitor expenditure along with the World's Top Tourism Destinations). Furthermore, the majority of published tourism statistics are derived from sample surveys, with the results being weighted or statistically manipulated to derive a measure which is supposedly representative of the real-world situation. In reality, this often means that tourism statistics are subject to significant errors depending on the size of the sample, so may not effectively represent actual demand.

Latham and Edwards (2003) identify a number of distinctive and peculiar problems associated with the tourist population, as Table 3.2 shows. Even where sampling and survey-related problems can be minimized, one has to treat tourism statistics with a degree of caution because of additional methodological issues that can affect results. For example, Table 3.3 shows that tourism research typically comprises a range of approaches towards tourist populations which can be grouped into four categories.

In an ideal world, where resource constraints are not a limiting factor on the generation of statistics, each of the aforementioned approaches should be used to provide a broad spectrum of research information on tourism. In reality, organizations and government agencies select a form of research that meets their own particular needs. In practice, most tourism statistics are generated with practical uses in mind and they can usually, though not exclusively, be categorized as shown in Table 3.4. The tourism industry requires reliable statistical data to inform decision-making in public- and private-sector organizations alike. Many countries attach a high priority to the collection and analysis of tourism data. Despite this, national and international tourism data sources are often criticized for lacking consistency and coherence.

The effectiveness of the national organizations as providers of related tourism data depends on a variety of factors. These include the scope and frequency of the data collection as well as the methods used in the data collection and analysis. Here, aspects such as sampling techniques and sample size will greatly influence data reliability. Even

---

TABLE 3.2 Problems associated with the statistical measurement of tourist populations

- Tourists are a transient and highly mobile population, making statistical sampling procedures difficult when trying to ensure statistical accuracy and rigour in methodological terms.
- Stopping and sampling respondents often has practical problems, due to accompanying passengers and the time required.
- Some people avoid interviewers and interviews.
- The environment in which interviews are often conducted (i.e. airports, seaports and points of entry and departure) are problematic, with the many distractions associated with the presence of large numbers of people sometimes leading respondents to curtail long interviews.
  Other variables, such as the weather, may affect the responses.

Source: Adapted from Latham and Edwards (2003: 56) with authors' additions

---

TABLE 3.3 The scope of research on tourist populations

- Pre-travel studies of tourists' intended travel habits and likely choice of destination (intentional studies).
- Studies of tourists in transit to provide information on their actual behaviour and plans for the remainder of their holiday or journey (actual and intended studies).
- Studies of tourists at the destination or at specific tourist attractions and sites, to provide information on their actual behaviour, levels of satisfaction, impacts and future intentions (actual and intended studies).
- Post-travel studies of tourists on their return journey from their destination or on-site experience or once they have returned to their place of residence (post-travel measures).

Source: Adapted from Latham (1989)

TABLE 3.4 Categorizing tourism statistics

- Measurement of tourist volume, enumerating arrivals, departures and the number of visits and stays.
- Expenditure-based surveys which quantify the value of tourist spending at the destination and during the journey.
- The characteristics and features of tourists are used to construct a profile of the different markets and segments visiting a destination.
- Tourism Satellite Accounts.

3

in large-scale surveys, such as the UK's International Passenger Survey, sampling errors for particular countries vary. Countries with low visitation rates from and to the UK have high sampling errors, whereas popular generating and destination nations have low sampling errors in the survey. Both the World Travel and Tourism Council (WTTC) and the International Monetary Fund (IMF) have recommended that governments effectively collect and analyze tourism data and represent them in the country's national accounts, and there is evidence that these recommendations are being adopted.

Establishing international tourism demand

In contrast to domestic tourism, statistics on international tourism are normally collected to assess the impact of tourism on a country's balance of payments. However, as Withyman (1985: 69) argued:

> *Outward visitors seem to attract less attention from the pollsters and the enumerators. Of course, one country's outward visitor is another country's (perhaps several countries') inward visitor, and a much more welcome sort of visitor, too, being both a source of revenue and an emblem of the destination country's appeal in the international market. This has meant that governments have tended to be generally more keen to measure inward than outward tourism, or at any rate, having done so, to publish the results.*

This statement indicates that governments are most concerned with the direct effect of tourism on their balance of payments. Indeed, outbound travel can assume a greater significance for the receiving countries. However, it is the inbound, or 'arrivals', which are statistics of significance for marketing arms of NTOs to base their decisions on in terms of who to target in international campaigns. The wider tourism industry also makes use of such data as part of its strategic planning and for more immediate purposes where niche markets exist. However, it is increasingly the case that only when the economic benefits of data collection can be justified will national governments continue to compile tourism statistics. Where resource constraints exist, the collection and compilation of tourism statistics may be impeded. This also raises important methodological issues related to what exactly is being measured. As Withyman (1985: 61) argued:

> *In the jungle of international travel and tourism statistics, it behoves the explorer to step warily; on all sides there is luxuriant growth. Not all data sources are what they appear to be; after close scrutiny they show themselves to be inconsistent and often unsuitable for the industry researcher and planner.*

The key point Withyman recognizes is the lack of comparability in tourism data in relation to what is measured (i.e. is it visitor days or visitor nights?) and the procedures and methodology used to measure international tourism (Table 3.5). Yet the principal difficulty which confronts tourism researchers is whether business travel should continue to be considered as a discrete part of tourism. Chadwick (1994: 75) notes that the consensus of North American opinion seems to be that, despite certain arguments to the contrary, business travel should be considered part of travel and tourism. Latham (1989: 59) suggests that the main types of international tourism statistics collated relate to:

- volume of tourists
- expenditure by tourists
- the profile of the tourist and their trip characteristics.

As is true of domestic tourism, estimates form the basis for most statistics on international tourism, since the method of data collection does not generate exact data. For example, volume statistics are often generated from counts of tourists at entry/exit points (i.e. gateways such as airports and ports) or at accommodation. But such data relates to numbers of trips rather than individual tourists, since one tourist may make more than one trip a year and each trip is counted separately. In the case of expenditure statistics, 'tourist expenditure' normally refers to tourist spending within a country and excludes payments to tourist transport operators. Yet the derivation of such statistics is often an indirect measure based on foreign currency estimates derived from bank records, from data provided by tourism service providers or, more commonly, from social surveys undertaken directly with tourists. Tourist statistics are usually collected in one of five ways (see Table 3.3) and a range of such statistics can easily be viewed in the Organisation for Economic Cooperation database (see https://stats.oecd.org/) by searching under Industry and Services and then by selecting Tourism. The OECD data is very accessible and contains the material as shown in Figure 3.8.

TABLE 3.5 How international tourism statistics are collected

- Counts of all individuals entering or leaving the country at all recognized frontier crossings are made, often using arrival/departure cards where high volume arrivals/departures are the norm. Where particularly large volumes of tourist traffic exist, a 10 per cent sampling framework is normally used (i.e. every tenth arrival/departure card). Countries such as New Zealand actually match the arrival/departure cards, or a sample, to examine the length of stay.
- Interviews are carried out at frontiers with a sample of arriving and/or departing passengers to obtain a more detailed profile of visitors and their activities within the country. This will often require a careful sample design to gain a sufficiently large sample, with details required from visitors on a wide range of tourism data including places visited, expenditure, accommodation usage and related items.
- A sample of arrivals is selected, and they are provided with a self-completion questionnaire to be handed in or posted. This method is used in Canada but it fails to incorporate those visitors travelling by road via the USA.
- Sample surveys are carried out of the entire population of a country, including travellers and non-travellers, though the cost of obtaining a representative sample is often prohibitive.
- Accommodation arrivals and nights spent are recorded by hoteliers and owners of the accommodation types covered. The difficulty with this type of data collection is that accommodation owners have no incentive to record accurate details, particularly where the tax regime is based on the turnover of bed nights.

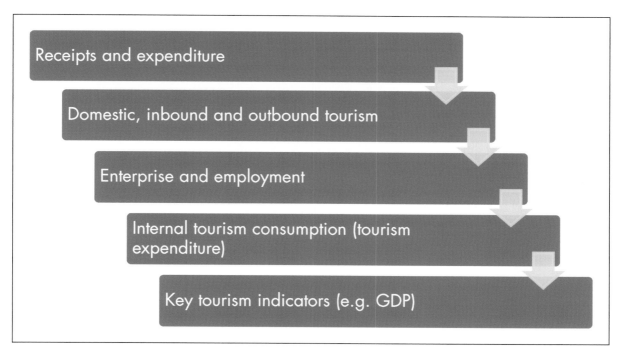

FIGURE 3.8 The OECD Tourism online database: Categories of data
Source: Listing developed and adapted from OECD.org

The last area of data collection is that of profile statistics, which examine the characteristics and travel habits of visitors. For example, the UK's International Passenger Survey (IPS) is one survey that incorporates volume, expenditure and profile data on international tourism. For example, in 2009 the IPS employed a multi-stage random sample of over 311 000 people (representing about 0.2 per cent of all travellers to and from the UK), who were interviewed at all the major airports, sea routes, Eurostar terminals and on Eurotunnel trains (see Coshall *et al.* 2015 for further detail).

3

Establishing demand for domestic tourism

Pearce (1995) acknowledges that the scale and volume of domestic tourism worldwide exceeds that of international tourism, although it is often viewed as the poorer partner in the compilation of statistics. For example, in 1996 domestic tourism in China generated 639 million trips, but by 2017 this had risen to 1.4 billion trips, while international arrivals grew from 51.1 million in 1996 to 139 million in 2017, illustrating the greater volume of domestic tourism. So it is difficult to understand demand in a domestic context, because most domestic tourism statistics tend to underestimate the scale and volume of flows, and some aspects of domestic tourist movements are sometimes ignored in official sources (Table 3.6). For the most part, visits to friends and relatives, the use of forms of accommodation other than hotels (for example, second homes, camp sites and caravan sites) and travel by large segments of a population from towns to the countryside are not included (Latham 1989: 65).

Moreover, some countries rely exclusively on the traditional hotel sector, thereby leaving out of the account the many travellers staying in supplementary accommodation establishments or with friends and relatives. Therefore, the collection of domestic tourism statistics requires the use of different data sources aside from the more traditional sources such as hotel records, which identify the origin and duration of a visitor's stay. UN–WTO (1981) identified four uses of domestic tourism statistics, as Table 3.4 shows. Many countries also collate supplementary information beyond the minimum standards identified by UN–WTO, whereby the socio-economic characteristics of tourists are identified, together with their use of tourist transport and purpose of visit, although the cost of such data collection does mean that the statistical basis of domestic tourism in many less developed countries remains poor. The methods used to generate domestic tourism statistics are normally based on the estimates of volume, value and scale derived from sample surveys due to the cost of undertaking large-scale surveys of tourist activities. The immediate problem facing the user of such material relates to the type of errors and degree of accuracy which can be attached to such data.

TABLE 3.6 Uses of domestic tourism statistics

- To calculate the contribution of tourism to the country's economy, whereby estimates of tourism's value to the gross domestic product are made due to the complexity of identifying the scope of tourism's contribution
- To assist in the marketing and promotion of tourism, where government-sponsored tourism organizations seek to encourage its population to take domestic holidays rather than to travel
- To aid with the regional development policies of governments which harness tourism as a tool for area development, whereby domestic tourists in congested environments are encouraged to travel to less developed areas and to improve the quality of tourism in different environments
- To achieve social objectives, as in when socially oriented tourism policies may be developed for the underprivileged; this requires a detailed understanding of the holiday-taking habits of a country's nationals[.]

Source: WTO (1981)

Future demand for tourism

One way in which the tourism sector seeks to identify how demand will change in the future is to try to understand how the different components of tourism demand may change and be affected by specific factors affecting change, known as drivers. These drivers for one destination (Scotland) include:

- *Economic drivers* – including the overall performance of the economy, levels of unemployment, economic development of developing nations, structure of the workplace, enterprise in Scotland, income and wealth structure and Scottish oil.
- *Social and cultural drivers* – including the impact of increasing affluence, individualization, new trends in luxury, youth markets, hedonism, subcultures, healthy hedonism, obesity, liberalism, tolerance, demography, migration, family relationships, anxiety, society, home ownership, second homes, sophisticated consumers, gender roles, time pressures, networked society.

- *Political drivers* – including devolution, identity politics and confidence, regional renaissance, Scottish iconography and pilgrimage, transport.
- *Technology drivers* – including information and communications technology, digital divide, aviation technology, energy.
- *Environmental drivers* – including sustainability, climate change, change in land use, rural tourism and environmental impact of rural tourism.
- *Leisure and tourism trends* – including hobbies, extreme sports, the new tourism model, short breaks, business travel, authenticity, new experiences and cultural capital.

These drivers are often analyzed using a variety of tools and techniques to depict future scenarios of change in tourism; this may involve different specialist skills such as forecasting as well as scenario planning, which seeks to consider how uncertain futures may evolve in relation to tourism. Scenario planning embraces a wide variety of techniques to help create choices based on looking at alternative possibilities framed around three key questions: *what may happen* (possible futures), *what is the most likely to happen* (probable futures) and *what we would prefer to happen* (preferable futures). In each case, the tourism sector is trying to understand how tourism demand will change in the future. For example, Figure 3.9 illustrates a key determinant of future demand – the growth in the world's population and how the proportion of over-60-year-olds will expand as a proportion of the total.

The implications for tourism demand are that the tourism sector will need to be more attuned to the needs of this growing market (i.e. it will need to become more *age-friendly*), as many of these people in the over-60 age group will have experiences of overseas travel and a travel history (i.e. the stock of experiences accumulated through their lifetime of travel). This will make them a discerning and lucrative market, in spite of changes to pension provision and expected changes in welfare provision. As the Barclays (2015) report *An Ageing Population – The Untapped Potential for Hospitality and Leisure Business* found: 20 per cent of the hospitality businesses derived their turnover from the over-65s, but only 5 per cent of businesses saw this as an important market, illustrating the types of changes which the tourism sector will need to make towards becoming more age-friendly.

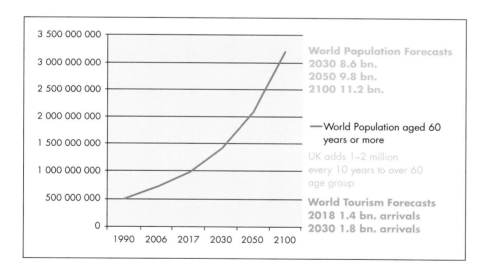

FIGURE 3.9 World population aged 60 years or more

Conclusion

The demand for tourism products is clearly crucial to the survival of the tourism industry. Recognition of the barriers to demand is, in part, particularly important for marketers in terms of pricing products and promotional efforts to attract people. In some countries, there are growing moves by employers to recognize that holidays are essential to the health and well-being of the workforce, as well-being is becoming a major concept for businesses to understand

3

in terms of extolling the virtues of how tourism can enhance one's quality of life (see Uysal *et al.* 2016; Hartwell *et al.* 2018; de Bloom *et al.* 2017). Some other studies (e.g. Kroesen and Handy 2014) have also pointed to how holiday-taking can positively enhance one's happiness, reinforcing the arguments around tourism as a positive enhancer of well-being. Indeed, a study of the link between paid holiday time and depression found that increasing the number of paid days' holiday leave by 10 days for workers could eliminate 568 442 cases of depression in women in the USA annually, with a cost saving of US$2.94 billion each year (see Kim 2019). We will pick up these arguments again in the next chapter in relation to the benefits of tourism for consumers, but there is evidence emerging to demonstrate the relationship between holidays and work (see Chen 2018), and the impact of not being able to get away from work and its influence, due to the role and use of smartphones (see Wang *et al.* 2016; Voase 2018). For people to enjoy these potential positive benefits, they must have the available leisure time (for workers this means leave entitlement), despite the growing precariousness of some workers in society associated with the **gig economy** (a term used to describe short-term or temporary work contracts) which has also been associated with a growth of companies outsourcing jobs so the staff are effectively self-employed without any of the benefits of being employed (e.g. pension and holiday rights and regular work, see Taylor 2016). In other cases, there are growing concerns in Europe that hours of work are increasing overall in countries like the UK, while in other countries they are declining, providing more leisure time. Whatever the situation, this chapter has shown that a complex array of factors affects the demand for tourism.

There are numerous dynamics that influence demand and which are beyond the control of those within the tourism industry. While exogenous factors such as terrorist acts or economic stability are obvious examples of how tourism demand can be suppressed, attitudes of governments in the generating or destination areas have also been shown to be influential.

The chapter also recognized that tourism is measured and evaluated by governments and agencies in different and sometimes conflicting ways, often making data sources little more than an indication of the order of magnitude of tourism rather than a precise delineation of its scale and volume. Official statistics and data sources have to be treated with caution, as tourism statisticians observe, since problems of accuracy, methodology and consistency confront researchers and students. Much of the research which the private sector commissions to examine tourism-related problems is kept confidential even though it sometimes uncritically uses public data sources, supplemented with face-to-face interviews with decision makers, where tourism structure plans are being developed for governments. This type of unpublished material in reports is sometimes described as grey *literature*; although the reliability of its contents and findings may be perceived to be less reliable than peer-reviewed scientific research, it still has an important role to play. Classifying and enumerating tourists remains a complex problem, not least because the population is highly mobile and tourists consume an experience rather than a tangible product. As a result, any analysis of tourism is highly dependent upon the tools and methods of analysis one employs.

Discussion questions

1 How are the different types of tourism demand defined?
2 What are the main economic-related determinants influencing tourism demand?
3 To what extent is price important in influencing tourism demand?
4 What are the main factors influencing demand at the tourist destination area?

References

Argyle, M. (1996) *The Social Psychology of Leisure.* Harmondsworth: Penguin.

Barclays (2015) *An Ageing Population – The Untapped Potential for Hospitality and Leisure Business.* London: Barclays.

Baum, T. and Lundtorp, S. (eds.) (2001) *Seasonality in Tourism.* Oxford: Pergamon.

Bloom, J. de, Nawijn, J., Geurts, S., Kinnunen, U. and Korpela, K. (2017) 'Holiday travel, staycations, and subjective well-being', *Journal of Sustainable Tourism,* 25 (4): 573–588.

Bull, A. (1995) *The Economics of Travel and Tourism,* 2nd edition. Melbourne: Pitman.

Burkart, A. and Medlik, S. (1981) *Tourism: Past, Present and Future,* 2nd edition. London: Heinemann.

Butler, R. (1994) 'Seasonality in tourism: Issues and implications', in A.V. Seaton (ed.) *Tourism: The State of the Art* (pp. 332–339). Chichester: Wiley.

Butler, R. (2001) 'Seasonality in tourism: Issues and implications', in T. Baum and S. Lundtorp (eds.) *Seasonality in Tourism* (pp. 5–21). Oxford: Elsevier.

Butler, R. and Mao, B. (1997) 'Seasonality in tourism: Problems and measurement', in P. Murphy (ed.) *Quality Management in Urban Tourism* (pp. 9–23). Chichester: Wiley.

Chadwick, R. (1994) 'Concepts, definitions and measures used in travel and tourism research', in J.R. Brent Ritchie and C. Goeldner (eds.) *Travel, Tourism and Hospitality Research: A Handbook for Managers and Researchers,* 2nd edition. New York: Wiley.

Chen, C. (2018) 'Examining stress relief benefits of tourism experiences: A study of American workers', *Tourism Analysis,* 23 (3): 421–426.

Civil Aviation Authority (2006) *No Frills Carriers: Revolution or Evolution?* London: Civil Aviation Authority.

Connell, J. and Page, S.J. (2020) 'Tourism, ageing and the demographic timebomb: The implications of dementia for the visitor economy', *Tourism Review* 75 (1): 81–85.

Cooper, C.P., Fletcher, J., Gilbert, D., Wanhill, S. and Shepherd, R. (1998) *Tourism Principles and Practice,* 2nd edition. London: Longman.

Corbet, S., O'Connell, J., Efthymiou, M., Guiomard, C. and Lucey, B. (2019) 'The impact of terrorism on European tourism', *Annals of Tourism Research* 75: 1–17.

Coshall, J., Charlesworth, R. and Page, S.J. (2015) 'Seasonality of overseas tourism demand in Scotland: A regional analysis', *Regional Studies,* 49 (10): 1603–1620.

Crouch, G. (1994) 'The study of tourism demand: A review of findings', *Journal of Travel Research* 33 (1): 2–21.

Dogru, T., Mody, M. and Suess, C. (2019) 'Adding evidence to the debate: Quantifying Airbnb's disruptive impact on ten key hotel markets', *Tourism Management* 72: 27–38.

Ferrante, M., Lo Magno, G. and De Cantis, S. (2018) 'Measuring tourism seasonality across European countries', *Tourism Management,* 68: 220–235.

Gao, J., Ryan, C., Cave, J. and Zhang, C. (2019) 'Tourism border-making: A political economy of China's border tourism', *Annals of Tourism Research,* 76: 1–13.

Haid, O. (2006) 'Christmas markets in the Tyrolean Alps: Representing regional traditions in a newly created world of Christmas', in D. Picard and M. Robinson (eds.) *Festival Tourism and Social Change – Remaking Worlds* (pp. 209–221). Clevedon: Channel View.

Hall, C.M. and Page, S.J. (2002) *The Geography of Tourism and Recreation: Environment, Place and Space,* 2nd edition. London: Routledge.

Han, Z., Durbarry, R. and Sinclair, M.T. (2006) 'Modelling US tourism demand for European tourism destinations', *Tourism Management* 27(1): 1–10.

Hartmann, R. (1986) 'Tourism, seasonality and social change', *Leisure Studies* 5 (1): 25–33.

Hartwell, H., Fyall, A., Willis, C., Page, S.J., Ladkin, A. and Hemingway, A. (2018) 'Progress in tourism and destination well-being research', *Current Issues in Tourism,* 21 (16): 1830–1892.

Kim, D. (2019) 'Does paid vacation leave protect against depression among working Americans? A national longitudinal fixed effects analysis', *Scandinavian Journal of Work, Environment and Health* 45 (1): 22–32.

Kroesen, M. and Handy, S. (2014) 'The influence of holiday-taking on affect and contentment', *Annals of Tourism Research* 45: 89–101.

Laslett, P. (1989) *A Fresh Map of Life: The Emergence of the Third Age.* London: Weidenfeld and Nicolson.

Latham, J. (1989) 'The statistical measurement of tourism', in C.P. Cooper (ed.) *Progress in Tourism, Recreation and Hospitality Management Volume 1.* London: Belhaven.

Latham, J. and Edwards, C. (2003) 'The statistical measurement of tourism', in C. Cooper (ed.) *Classic Reviews in Tourism.* Clevedon: Channel View Publications.

McCulloch, A. (2018) 'UK employees fail to use holiday entitlement', *Personnel Today,* 25 May 2018. https://www.personneltoday. com/hr/uk-employees-fail-to-use-holiday-entitlement.

Mak, J. (2006) 'Taxation of travel and tourism', in Larry Dwyer and Peter Forsyth (eds.), *International Handbook on the Economics of Tourism* (pp. 251–265). Cheltenham: Edward Elgar.

Martins, L.F., Gan, Y., and Ferreira-Lopes, A. (2017) 'An empirical analysis of the influence of macroeconomic determinants on World tourism demand', *Tourism Management,* 61: 248–260.

Mathieson, A. and Wall, G. (1982) *Tourism: Economic, Physical and Social Impacts.* Harlow: Longman.

ONS (Office for National Statistics) (1999) *Social Trends 29.* London: ONS.

Pearce, D.G. (1995) *Tourism Today: A Geographical Analysis,* 2nd edition. Harlow: Longman.

Pike, S. (2008) *Destination Marketing.* Oxford: Elsevier.

Ryan, C. (ed.) (1997) *The Tourist Experience.* London: Cassell.

Singh, S. (2009) (ed.) *Domestic Tourism in Asia.* London: Earthscan.

Smith, S.L. (1995) *Tourism Analysis: A Handbook,* 2nd edition. Harlow: Longman.

Smith, S.L. (2004) 'The measurement of global tourism: Old debates, new consensus and continuing challenges', in A. Lew, C.M. Hall and A. Williams (eds.) *A Companion to Tourism.* Oxford: Blackwell.

Song, H., Page, S.J. and Seetaram, N. (2012) 'The long-term effects of APD on outbound tourism from the UK', *BESTEN Think Tank XXI,* Provence, France, 24–27 June 2012.

Song, H. and Witt, S. (2000) *Tourism Demand Modelling and Forecasting: Modern Econometric Approaches.* Oxford: Pergamon.

Spencer, D. and Holecek, D. (2007) 'Basic characteristics of the fall tourism market', *Tourism Management,* 28 (2): 491–504.

Strømmen-Bakhtiar, A. and Vinogradov, E. (2019) 'The effects of airbnb on hotels in Norway', *Society and Economy* 41 (1): 87–105.

Taylor, M. (2016) *Good Work: The Taylor Review of Modern Working Practices.* Department for Business,

Energy and Industrial Strategy: London. https://www.gov.uk/government/publications/good-work-the-taylor-review-of-modern-working-practices.

Uysal, M., Sirgy, M.J., Woo, E. and Kim, H. (2016) 'Quality of life (QOL) and well-being research in tourism', *Tourism Management*, 53: 244–261.

Voase, R. (2018) 'Holidays under the hegemony of hyper-connectivity: Getting away, but unable to escape?' *Leisure Studies*, 37 (4): 384–395.

Wang, X., Li, X., Zhen, F. and Zhang, J. (2016) 'How smart is your tourist attraction? Measuring tourist preferences of smart tourism attractions via a FCEM-AHP and IPA approach', *Tourism Management*, 54: 309–320.

Withyman, W. (1985) 'The ins and outs of international travel and tourism data', *International Tourism Quarterly*, Special Report No. 55.

World Economic Forum (2017) *World Travel and Tourism Competitiveness Report 2017*. Geneva: WEF. https://www.weforum.org/reports/the-travel-tourism-competitiveness-report-2017.

WTO (World Tourism Organization) (1981) *Guidelines for the Collection and Presentation of Domestic and International Tourism Statistics*. Madrid: World Tourism Organization.

WTO (World Trade Organization) (1995) *Global Tourist Forecasts to the Year 2000 and Beyond*. Madrid: WTO.

Further reading

Books

Baggio, R. (2019) 'Measuring tourism: Methods, indicators, and needs', in E. Fayos-Solà and C. Cooper (eds.) *The Future of Tourism*. Cham, Switzerland: Springer.

Department for Business, Energy and Industrial Strategy (2018) *Good Work: The Taylor Review of Modern Working Practices*. https://www.gov.uk/government/publications/good-work-the-taylor-review-of-modern-working-practices.

Journal articles

Duro, J. and Turrión-Prats, J. (2019) 'Tourism seasonality worldwide', *Tourism Management Perspectives* 31: 38–53.

Pratt, S. and Tolkach, D. (2018) 'The politics of tourism statistics', *International Journal of Tourism Research* 20 (3): 299–307.

On tourism statistics associated with measuring tourism demand, see:

Dupeyras, A. and MacCallum, N. (2013) *Indicators for Measuring Competitiveness in Tourism: A Guidance Document*. OECD Tourism Papers, No. 2013/02. Paris: OECD Publishing. DOI: https://doi.org/10.1787/5k47t9q2t923-en.

OECD (2016) *An OECD Review of Statistical Initiatives Measuring Tourism at Subnational Level*. OECD Tourism Papers, 2016/01. Paris: OECD Publishing. DOI: http://dx.doi.org/10.1787/5jln3b32hq7h-en.

Understanding the tourist as a consumer

Learning outcomes

After reading this chapter and answering the questions, you should be able to:

- recognize the role of consumption in tourism
- understand theories and models relevant to the explanation of tourist motivation
- recognize the importance of those factors that influence motivation
- identify the factors that affect the tourism decision-making process in selecting tourism products.

Overview

The question of why people go on holiday is fundamental to the study of tourism. What motivates people to participate in different forms of behaviour concerned researchers and academics long before it was applied to the field of tourism. This chapter sets out to explain contemporary patterns of tourism activity as they relate to the individual. It contends that tourism activity is not merely an outcome of people's freedom to choose where they go on holiday; there are many factors at work which initiate the desire to travel and then influence the ultimate selection of destination.

Introduction

According to Hall and Page (2002: 60), one of the fundamental questions tourism researchers consistently seek to answer is: *why do tourists travel?* And this seemingly simple proposition remains one of the principal challenges facing tourism research. This area of tourism research is more firmly bedded in social psychology. At one level people may choose where they wish to travel to, so the patterns of tourism activity could be explained in terms of individual choice. Consider Table 4.1 which outlines how holiday-taking behaviour in the UK has changed in a decade: There are a wide range of factors which explain these trends and they reflect the importance of what we discussed in Chapter 2 (*continuity* and *change*). Table 4.1 also illustrates what we will seek to explain in this chapter – that as individuals, we do not have limitless choice and our actions are inevitably influenced by a combination of opportunities and constraints. These may include available finance and time (which can be affected by price), trends in travel, the effect of new technology (e.g. social media and the Internet) and personal preferences that are affected by a wide range of factors such as perceptions of risk. As we highlighted in Chapter 1, new trends in tourism consumption have also arisen that have impacted consumers, including the sharing economy. As Cheng (2016) noted, the sharing economy has changed the nature of consumption as consumers may be both consumers and/or suppliers as opposed to the traditional model of organizations fulfilling the supply function. This is illustrated by the example of Airbnb that we will return to in the accommodation chapter. Other key influences associated with technology are associated with the rise of the smartphone as we indicated in Chapter 3. For example, the UK's Office for National Statistics noted in 2017 how influential these devices were in relation to leisure time: young people spent a third of their leisure time on devices such as mobile phones, tablets and other portable technology making us connected virtually. This has challenged the existing notion of escapism and relaxation when on holiday as key motives for tourism. It is commonplace, as Chapter 3 highlighted, to see people on holiday sitting with their mobile phones checking work emails and messages as part of the addiction to the dopamine that is released every time we check a text or email. When we check the messages, dopamine that is released transmits messages to our brain that make us feel good and experience a sense of enjoyment. Conversely, there is also an ethos of staying connected which has developed with the evolution of smartphones, 'and sharing travel photographs with others [which] is an important way of processing, remembering and prolonging these experiences' (Gretzel 2017: 115). These photographs are used to construct personal narratives of one's holidays that are now shared in real time rather than back at home with friends and relatives. Many of these photos are now 'selfies', defined by Lyu (2016: 85) as 'a photograph that one has taken of oneself, typically with a smartphone or webcam'. The selfie has evolved as a 'a ritualistic and routinized practice among tourists' (also see Lo and McKercher 2015) and as Chapter 20 will show, this has had serious environmental and cultural impacts on destinations from tourists who have no cultural awareness of the impact of their selfie-seeking behaviour. The selfies are typically shared on social media sites such as Instagram instantly, as Lo *et al.* (2011: 725) found: '89 per cent of pleasure travelers take photographs and . . . 41 per cent of them posted their photographs online. Social network sites (SNSs), instant messaging, online photo albums and personal blogs were the most popular media used', while common places photos were posted included: Flickr, Picasa, Digital Darkroom; using SNSs (i.e. Facebook, MySpace, Twitter); travel-themed sites (i.e. Travel Blog, Lonely Planet, Mook); online forums and instant messaging as well as personal blogs. There is an evolving debate over how social media affects what holiday-makers do, experience and choose to share through family, groups and the wider domain of the Internet. The *digitally enabled tourist* (see Chapter 6 for more discussion) is a key change as Wu and Pearce (2014: 263) observed:

> Tourism, a special component of our social life, has been strongly influenced by information and communication technologies and a new digital tourist era can be identified . . . Travel- and tourism-related topics are frequently discussed in online communities . . . Further, travel blogging and other styles of communication online have become part of the tourist experience. These online tourist activities provide an opportunity to investigate several components of tourist behaviour, especially at the post-consumption stage.

This generates additional data and forms of information to help us understand tourists' choices about holidays and their satisfaction with them in ways that were not possible 20 years ago. But we should not overlook the fact that a number of social divisions may also circumscribe choice in tourism. Just as there are inequalities in many countries in terms of education, employment, housing and income, so there are inequalities in tourism. Argyle (1996) acknowledges the significance of gender, age, social class, retirement, unemployment, social relationships, personality and socialization in affecting leisure behaviour, which is a determinant of tourism. So, while choice is an important factor in tourism decision-making, individuals are rarely 'free' to make those choices, being constrained (see Lai *et al.* 2013) and influenced by personal and situational circumstances. While there is no universally accepted theory of tourist motivation, several researchers have developed frameworks to use in the

TABLE 4.1 Changing trends in UK outbound holidays

According to the ONS (2017) study *Holidays in the 1990s and Now*, UK holiday-taking demand has changed, which has impacted upon the popularity of destinations and the way people travel. Among some of the most marked changes are:

- A shift from traditional long holidays of over 7 days to short breaks (3–5 days in duration) and week-long trips.
- The rise of the Internet in terms of the way holidays are booked and how the smartphone has made destination-related activity more accessible.
- The residents of the UK are going on holiday more: In 1996, 27 million overseas holidays were taken; in 2016 this had risen by 68 per cent to 45 million holidays. In contrast, the UK population rose by 12 per cent in 1996–2016.
- The top destinations visited have changed. The top destination remained Spain, seeing an 87 per cent growth to almost 12 million a year in 2016. Trips to France, the second-most-visited destination dropped below 6 million a year, with car-based travel supplanted by low-cost airline travel. Trips to Italy, Portugal, USA, Greece, the Netherlands and Germany, and cruises all saw increases.
- Destinations which saw drops due to the impact of terrorist attacks were: Turkey, Egypt, Kenya and Tunisia.
- Countries that have grown in popularity between 1996–2016 are: United Arab Emirates, Poland, Croatia, Iceland and Romania. The popularity of Dubai and development of tourist infrastructure have contributed to the rise of travel to the Middle East. Eastern European travel reflects the flows of migrants to the UK since 2004 and visits to see family and friends. In the case of Iceland, the devaluation of the Icelandic krona after 2008 stimulated travel from the UK, as it became a more affordable destination.

Source: ONS (2017) *Holidays in the 1990s and Now*, http://www.ons.gov.uk/peoplepopulationandcommunity/leisureandtourism/articles

understanding of why people go on holiday (e.g. Pearce 2005). This chapter identifies and explains some of the critical arguments in understanding the less than straightforward questions of why people go on holiday and what influences certain holiday choices.

Motivation and decision-making in tourism

Moutinho (1987: 16) argued that motivation is 'a state of need, a condition that exerts a push on the individual towards certain types of action that are seen as likely to bring satisfaction'. Essentially, in relation to tourism, motivation is a part of the consumption process and is stimulated by a complex mixture of economic, social, psychological, cultural, political, industry-related and wider environmental influences. Motivation as a subject is an integral part of the study of consumer behaviour in tourism. Motivation acts as a trigger which stimulates the chain of events in the tourism process.

Understanding tourist motivation and decision-making is important for two main reasons:

- *Planning considerations*: All destinations require some form of planning and management, and control of negative impacts, where it may be appropriate to divert tourists or particular activities away from vulnerable areas.
- *Economic considerations*: Growth and development of the tourism industry in a region or corporate growth are dependent on understanding consumer behaviour, particularly through market segmentation strategies.

The term 'motivation' is open to interpretation and is often used to merely describe the purpose of a holiday, such as visiting friends and relatives (which is really a motive rather than a motivation). However, the study of motivation is really concerned with more deeply rooted psychological needs and desires. Accordingly, it is a very complex area of research. Researchers are charged not just with explaining behaviour but with understanding it too.

Hall and Page (2002: 61) note that 'the factors which shape the tourist decision-making process to select and participate in specific forms of tourism is [*sic*] largely within the field of consumer behaviour and motivation'. As Mill and Morrison (1992: 17) argued, 'the key to understanding tourist motivation is to see vacation travel as a satisfier of needs and wants . . . it is the difference between those travel agents who see themselves as sellers of airline seats and those who view themselves as dealers in dreams', and a useful starting point for understanding motivation is to study the decision-making process in tourism that affects what products a tourist purchases (a theme also discussed in Chapters 14 and 15).

The decision-making process in tourism is viewed in two ways by researchers. First, it may be likened to the basic decision-making process aligned with all product purchasers, where the consumer identifies a need, looks for information on the product, its cost and where it might be purchased, weighs up the alternative products and suppliers, makes a choice, consumes and finally makes a judgement on the experience of that product which may then influence future purchasing decisions. Most models of consumer behaviour reflect this basic outline, although many other factors influence this process, some of which the consumer is barely conscious of. Imagery, advertising, word-of-mouth recommendation and peer pressure are just a few examples of the more obvious influences, but other more intrinsic factors should not be underestimated. The tourism decision-making process is affected by personal, behavioural and destination-specific qualities, as well as the exogenous factors influencing demand illustrated in the last chapter. Based on Ryan (1997), these include:

- social and personal interactions, such as the needs of others with whom the individual is travelling, whether there are children in the group, likely contact with service staff and host community
- travel experience, expectation of delays, comfort and ease of travel to destination
- destination-specific factors, such as the quality of the accommodation and facilities, and historical or other interests, which may act as a particular draw for tourists
- personal factors, such as self-confidence, personality, experience, lifestyle and life stage
- behaviour patterns, which may dictate an individual's propensity to experience new places and activities, or to search for holiday information pre-booking
- responsive mechanisms, desire for authentic experiences, social skills and feeling at ease in a strange environment.

Post-holiday, all of these aspects will combine to influence future holiday choices. But not all tourism consumers are intricate planners who will compare brochures, online information, destinations, packages and prices. Some make impulse purchases, many attracted by imminent departures at discounted cost. The Internet has made such purchases even easier to obtain from the comfort of home. Despite this, the consumer will still be motivated but will demonstrate a more minimal decision-making process. The theme of constraints and opportunities, then, is one that dominates this area of tourism. As Patmore (1975: 7) remarked, 'there are three broad constraints, including *desire*, *ability* and *mobility* . . . desire has first to be aroused; the wish to participate – so often an imitative wish, the desire to imitate something at least of the lifestyle of those ranked higher'. These issues will form an important focus later in the chapter, but prior to a more detailed exploration of the concepts of tourism motivation, it is first important to establish what is meant by the term 'consumer', why it is important to understand tourism behaviour and how the consumer has changed in contemporary times.

The tourist as a consumer

A consumer is an individual who, through a process of decision-making, obtains goods and services for personal consumption. In basic terms, such a process involves a 'purchase', but in tourism the importance of *experiencing* a destination environment must also be recognized where the tourist becomes a consumer of place or culture, as well as a purchaser of tourism products. Howie (2003) suggested that the changes that have occurred in tourism activity since 1945 have meant that tourism has evolved into a more sophisticated model than its previous status as a product-led industry dominated by standardized and limited holiday choices, in which consumers were inexperienced as purchasers of the new tourism packages. Through the latter part of the twentieth century and into the new millennium, as part of the growth of consumer culture, tourists have become more experienced, aware, discerning and demanding in relation to holiday experiences. No longer are the basic sun, sand and sea ('3S') holidays sufficient to meet the demands of the modern tourist, but a more individualized quality product, that the tourist is more ready to put together without the assistance of a travel agent, is emerging. The contemporary tourism and leisure industries have had little choice but to become more consumer-oriented in order to meet, and where possible exceed, the increasingly sophisticated needs of the market.

Hogg (2003) outlines the various changes that have occurred and paved the way for the new consumer in the twenty-first century, and states that consumers have become more knowledgeable, demanding and thinking. Middleton and Clarke (2001) argued that the rise of a more demanding tourism consumer has occurred globally due to a number of factors, some of which include:

- increased affluence
- better education
- more experience of travel, including international travel

- a more culturally diverse travelling population
- greater exposure to the media and other forms of information (which now includes the Internet and digital age).

There is also a growing debate (Kozak and Kozak 2018) that marketing theory has become far more important in this context, as tourists are seeking experiences which motivate them to be tourists, notably with the development of the experience economy.

The experience economy and tourism

The evolution on thinking on the experience economy has meant that in the evaluation of tourists' motivation, a fundamental shift has occurred: tourists have become more involved in co-creating the experiences they consume. The influential study that stimulated thinking in this area is Pine and Gilmore's (1999) *The Experience Economy*, which suggested that this was the next stage in the evolution of a society from a service economy. Pine and Gilmore argued businesses need to create experiences that are memorable, given the increased levels of education of many consumers and their pursuit of value-added elements within the experience they purchase. The central feature of Pine and Gilmore (1999) is the production of experiences (also see Sundbo and Sorensen 2016 and Smit and Melissen 2018 for subsequent assessments of the key thinking behind the experience economy). For tourism organizations it means that they will need to focus on:

- the need to create a sensation
- the need to personalize the experience; to develop trust and a bond with the consumer which has been embodied in the use of brands.

Other studies, such as Bentley (1924) noted that 'experience is complex. It is complex in both its temporal course and in its momentary phases' (Bentley 1924: 50). Bentley (1924) outlined the constituent of experience around the concept of stimuli (i.e. things that stimulate the experience) and receptors (i.e. our senses that receive and help formulate our experience). Bentley (1924) pointed to the sensational elements of the human experience that are grouped around:

- Visual qualities of what we see, that are affected by colour and light
- Auditory (i.e. hearing) elements that are affected by the concept of tones
- Taste and smell
- Touch

and the body's ability to receive messages about each of these elements, as shown in Figure 4.1.

A study by Toraldo (2013) highlighted the paucity of research on sensory issues, particularly the impact on experience and hedonism. Toraldo (2013) suggested many sensory differences exist between humans who are socially and culturally conditioned. Therefore, to understand these sensory issues, we need to focus on one concept – *anticipation*. The experience is dependent upon the expectation and anticipation of the experience and whether or not it is met. The experience economy concept suggests that we need to focus on four areas of experience in tourism as shown in Figure 4.2. Even so, as we highlighted at the beginning of this chapter, this has to be counterbalanced with the effects of the digital age for tourists as consumers, in also affecting the anticipation process.

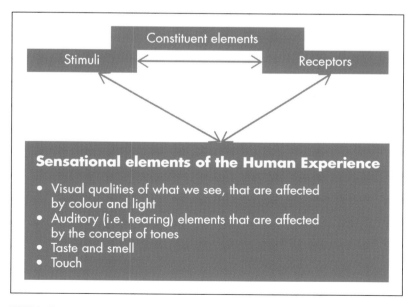

FIGURE 4.1   Interactions in the constituent and sensational elements of the human experience

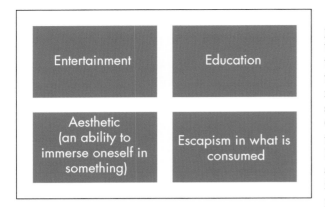

FIGURE 4.2 Implications of the experience economy for tourism

Consequently, tourism needs experiences designed to allow participants to engage in discrete ways ranging from absorption through to immersion. Any tourism experience will need to be able to accommodate different modes of participation, from passive through to very active forms of involvement. They also need to engage all of our senses (i.e. hearing, sight, touch, smell and taste) and permit co-creation to occur. Co-creation means that a business (organization) and customer (or potential audience) share in the creation of value by allowing customers to shape experiences to suit their needs and desires. This is in stark contrast to the idea of consuming a single product, with experiences shaped entirely by the producers. It recognizes that personal experiences are at the heart of the tourism experience and able to meet the motives of tourists. Attention now turns to tourist motives.

Tourist motives

Demand for tourism is highly segmented and is distinguished through a number of different markets. For example, day visitors, while not strictly tourists, are a major component of the market for many destinations, motivated by the access to the area and availability of activities to undertake (e.g. shopping) within the confines of one day. Conversely, other forms of travel due to business may have a different set of motivating factors according to the purpose of the business trip (i.e. to attend a meeting or conference at home or overseas; to attend a training course; to attend an exhibition or trade show where the audience is informed about a new product or service; as 'incentive travel', a reward for employees for good performance). Each of these forms of tourist travel has different motives. Motives for travel are not the same as motivations, as we have already pointed out, but are useful categorizations of tourists whose main reason for travel is to participate in a particular niche interest.

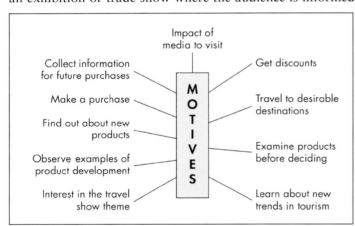

FIGURE 4.3 Reasons for attending exhibitions

Some of the major motives for travel include a desire to participate in one or more of a number of activities while on holiday. Such motives may be given by tourists in visitor surveys when asked 'for what reason did you visit here today?', which to some extent is useful, but the deeper motivation is often veiled, as shown in Insight 4.1, in terms of motivation to attend travel exhibitions. That is why an understanding of needs, desires and personal goals in a tourism context is necessary.

INSIGHT 4.1 Motivation to attend travel exhibitions

A study by Rittichainuwat and Mair (2012) that examined the motivation of visitors to attend travel fairs identified multiple motivations: to acquire information about purchasing; an attraction to the theme of the travel show; the impact of media coverage in promoting a visit. This suggests that trade shows and exhibitions in tourism have considerable potential to reach a wide range of public audiences who may be attracted by a diversity of motives. In the study by Rittichainuwat and Mair (2012), five domestic travel shows in Thailand were surveyed and Figure 4.3 illustrates the reasons given by visitors for attending the exhibitions.

Further reading

Getz, D. and Page, S.J. (2019) *Event Studies*, 4th edition. London: Routledge.

Theoretical and conceptual approaches to tourist motivation

Much of the literature on tourist motivation emerges from a social psychological perspective, and many of the studies are based on models, which seek to simplify the complexity we see in the real world to a more abstract and series of concepts – hence the term conceptual model. Where these conceptual models are developed in more depth and linked to prevailing arguments in social psychology and other disciplines, these are often rooted in theories of human behaviour. We will now explore some of these models. However, it is worth bearing in mind the recent assessment of tourist motivation research by Albayrak and Caber (2018: 169) that 'no single model can explain tourist's destination selection process' (also see Yoo *et al.* 2018).

Maslow's hierarchy of needs

Maslow (1943) is acknowledged as the best-known work on motivation. Although originally related to the field of clinical psychology, his work has been more widely applied and often cited in tourism studies. Maslow argued that our individual needs fall into five broad categories, as shown in Table 4.2. Maslow suggested that these five categories formed a hierarchy, beginning with lower-order physiological needs moving through to higher-order self-actualization needs. This is based on the premise that each of the needs expressed in a category should be satisfied before the individual seeks motivation from the next category of need. It can be seen that once the basic human requirements of thirst and hunger have been met, the need for these to motivate the behaviour and actions of an individual may no longer apply. At this point the individual may be motivated by higher-order classification rising to self-actualization. Several tourism researchers have applied Maslow's model in the context of tourism motivation (for example, Pearce and Caltabianco 1983). For example, tourists visiting friends and relatives may show needs for belonging and love, while those choosing a holiday out of a need to keep up with their friends and neighbours demonstrate esteem needs. The framework is easy to apply, although tourists are often motivated by more than one factor, which limits the application of the theory.

Push and pull factors

Maslow's hierarchy of needs can be useful in demonstrating the source of our initial needs and wants, where the satisfaction of these needs may ultimately lead to the purchase of a holiday. Another way of considering this process is, as Dann (1977) described, **push factors** and **pull factors**. Push factors are those that propel a desire to travel; pull factors are those that influence which destination is selected, given the initial push, and arise from a desire to travel. As Sharpley (1994: 99) states 'the motivation to satisfy needs, combined with personal preferences, pushes the tourist into considering alternative products; the final choice depends on the pull of alternative holidays or destinations'. The themes of push and pull, or escaping and seeking, were commonly applied in early classic tourism motivation studies (see Crompton 1979; Krippendorf 1987; Mannell and Iso-Ahola 1987). A study by Caber and Albayrak (2016) adopted the push/pull dichotomy in an analysis of rock-climbing tourists and the satisfaction derived was based on their experience level. Murdy *et al.* (2018) examined ancestral tourist visits, which is travel to

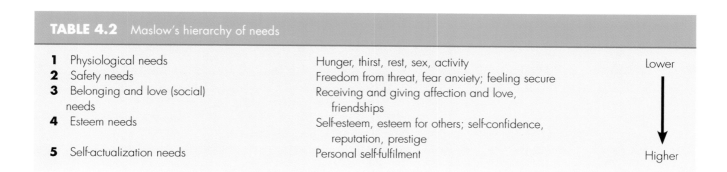

TABLE 4.2 Maslow's hierarchy of needs

1	Physiological needs	Hunger, thirst, rest, sex, activity	Lower
2	Safety needs	Freedom from threat, fear anxiety; feeling secure	
3	Belonging and love (social) needs	Receiving and giving affection and love, friendships	
4	Esteem needs	Self-esteem, esteem for others; self-confidence, reputation, prestige	
5	Self-actualization needs	Personal self-fulfilment	Higher

trace ancestral roots. Murdy *et al.* (2018) found four groups of pull motives associated with the desire to trace one's roots that allows tourists to be grouped into: full heritage immersion; the ancestral enthusiast; general interest; and heritage-focused tourists.

Gilbert (1991) acknowledges the push and pull factors influencing the tourism consumer-decision process, and suggests that the process has four distinct stages:

1 *Energizers of demand*: These are the various forces, including motivation, which initiate the decision to visit an attraction or go on holiday at the outset.

2 *Effectors of demand*: Information about a destination will have been received by various means (brochures and media). The consumer will have developed their own ideas and perceptions about the destination and this perception may enhance or reduce the likelihood of a visit.

3 *Roles and decision-making*: The role of the tourist as a consumer will influence the final choice of holiday. For example, different members of a family will have a varying impact on where and when the family will take the holiday and what they will do there.

4 *Filterers of demand*: The decision to travel is heavily influenced by a series of demographic and socio-economic constraints and opportunities. While there may be a strong 'push', demand is filtered through such constraining factors.

Dann's perspectives on tourism motivation

To this point, our investigation of tourist motivation could, perhaps, be most easily related to what might be termed a 'leisure' holiday (with the exception of the study of ancestral tourism by Murdy *et al.* 2018). However, tourism takes many forms, and visiting friends and relatives or business travel may result from different motives or even be more related to the actual purpose of the visit (for example a family reunion) than the needs and wants of the tourist. Dann (1981), in a study of tourist motivation, identified seven perspectives (Table 4.3), which provide a more in-depth

TABLE 4.3 *Seven perspectives on tourist motivation based on Dann (1981)*

Travel as a response to what is lacking yet desired	Tourist motivation may result from a desire for something new or different that cannot be provided in the individual's home environment
Destination pull in response to motivational push	The distinction between the needs, wants and desires (push factors) of the individual and how these are shaped by perceptions of the destination (pull factors)
Motivation as fantasy	Tourists may be motivated to travel to engage in forms of behaviour or activities that are not culturally acceptable in their home environment. One context of this is travel to enable deviant behaviour such as gambling, drugs or prostitution where, because such activities may be illegal in the home country but not in others, this creates the desire to travel
Motivation as classified purpose	Some are motivated to travel or 'caused' to travel by the nature or purpose of the trip. Visiting friends and relatives is one example, the opportunity to undertake specific leisure activities another
Motivational typologies	Different types of tourists may influence the motivation to travel
Motivation and tourist experiences	Tourism often involves travel to places not visited previously. As such, some are motivated to travel by what they expect to experience in contrast to their home area and other holiday experiences
Motivation as auto-definition and meaning	The ways in which tourists define their situations and respond to them may provide a better understanding of tourist motivation. Such an approach is seen in contrast to simply observing behaviour as a means to explain tourist motivation

TABLE 4.4	Forms of the tourist gaze
Romantic	Object of vision or awe consumed in solitude, involving a prolonged immersion, e.g. the early tourists to the Trossachs or the Lake District, whose gaze resulted in works of art and literature
Collective	Social activity involving a series of shared encounters based around familiar objects, e.g. a domestic coach tour
Spectatorial	Again, a social activity based on a series of brief encounters, which encompass collecting symbols of the visit, e.g. sightseeing tour with much photography and souvenir purchase
Environmental	Collective organization of a sustained and multifaceted nature, involving study and inspection of the environment, e.g. rainforest conservation holiday
Anthropological	A solitary pursuit, involving a prolonged contact with the object of the gaze and involving study and interpretation, e.g. backpacker trip where tourist lives as a local resident

Source: Adapted from Urry (1995: 191)

attempt to identify the principal elements of tourist motivation. In terms of Dann's sixth point, tourism experiences, or rather the anticipation and expectations of a holiday, can act as strong motivators in relation to push factors. A useful way of thinking about this is what the sociologist Urry (1990) terms the **tourist gaze** (also see the latest edition – Urry and Larsen 2011).

The tourist gaze

Tourism demand as a form of consumption has emerged as a theme in the literature on the sociology and geography of tourism. Most notably, the work of Urry (1990) on the notion of the tourist gaze has gained wide recognition. Developing Foucault's (1976) idea of the medical gaze and MacCannell's (1976) earlier work on sightseeing as consumption, Urry (1990: 1) suggests that tourists observe the environment with 'interest and curiosity . . . in other words, we gaze at what we encounter'. So, the gaze is one way of understanding the experiential elements of tourism motivation as it relates to expectation. Viewed as 'visual consumption of the environment', five forms of the tourist gaze are outlined by Urry (1995: 191) (see Table 4.4). While the idea of the tourist gaze is not concerned solely with motivation, it is valuable to the process of understanding why people visit certain environments and assists in attaching meanings to tourist settings. Thus, the tourist gaze provides an interesting introduction to the consumer of tourism.

A range of factors are involved in producing the tourist gaze, but the main premise rests on the identification of differences from everyday/ordinary experiences. According to Urry (1990), objects suitable for the tourist gaze include a unique object, a particular sign, an unfamiliar aspect of what was previously considered ordinary, an ordinary aspect of life undertaken by people in unusual contexts, a sign which indicates that a certain object is extraordinary, and familiar tasks being carried out in unusual environments. The gaze concept, like most attempts to conceptualize the more nebulous aspects of tourism motivation and the tourism experience, has gained some criticism. For example, Meethan (2001: 83) argues that the notion of the gaze is problematic and that it 'cannot adequately account for multiple, different, conflicting – interpretations . . .'. While the gaze notion may not be universally accepted, the concept does give a functional framework for appreciating the way in which demand is constructed. It is their visual distinctiveness which sets many destinations apart and which is instrumental in attracting visitors. Accordingly, the consumption idea is a central tenet.

Tourist roles

One of Dann's perspectives (motivational typologies) (see Table 4.3) suggests that tourist types, the personality traits of tourists that enable us to classify them, could provide an explanation for why some travel to certain destinations.

In the 1970s, several studies attempted to classify tourists according to observable behaviour. One of the first researchers to do this was Cohen (1972), who established four categories of tourist:

1 *The organized mass tourist* takes a highly organized package holiday and has minimal contact with the host community, holidaying within an 'environmental bubble'.

2 *The independent mass tourist* uses similar facilities to the organized mass tourist but also wants to break away from the norm and to visit other sights not covered on organized tours in the destination.

3 *The explorer* arranges their travel independently and wishes to experience the social and cultural lifestyle of the destination.

4 *The drifter* does not seek any contact with other tourists or the organized tourism industry, preferring to live with the host community.

This type of classification is problematic, since it does not take into account the increasing diversity of holidays undertaken and the different locations chosen. Along these lines, one of the best-known theories was developed by Plog (1974), and was based on the US population. Plog identified two opposite types of tourist each at the end of a continuum (Table 4.5). Allocentrics are tourists who seek adventure on their holidays and are prepared to take risks. As such, they prefer holidays in more exotic locations and prefer to travel independently. At the other extreme are psychocentrics. These tourists look rather inwardly and concentrate their thoughts on the small problems in life. On holiday they are not adventurous, but prefer locations that are similar to their home environment. Such tourists may repeatedly return to the same destination where they have experienced a satisfying experience, safe in the knowledge of the familiar. In between these two extremes other categories exist such as near-allocentric, mid-centric and near-psychocentric.

While Plog's typology provides a simple model that can explain, to some extent, aspects of tourist motivation, there are some difficulties in its application. One aspect, for example is that both tourists and destinations change over time. A young adult may well be allocentric at certain stages in their lifecycle and more mid-centric at other stages: when children are present, for example.

Tourism researchers have developed other systems for defining tourists, but much of this early work was based on non-empirical research and it was not until the 1980s that researchers began to undertake quantitative studies of tourist motivation. Pearce (1982) developed 15 **tourist roles** (tourist, traveller, holiday-maker, jet-setter, businessman, migrant, conservationist, explorer, missionary, overseas student, anthropologist, hippie, international athlete, overseas journalist and religious pilgrim) and by using statistical techniques, identified five major tourist types:

- environmental
- high contact
- spiritual
- pleasure first
- exploitative travel

but this classification did not distinguish solely leisure-based roles. Table 4.6 draws together many of the arguments and summarizes many of the points discussed to date on tourist motivation.

TABLE 4.5 Plog's tourist types

Type	Characteristics
Allocentric	Enjoy travelling independently, cultural exploration, often in above-average income groups, seek adventurous experiences on holiday.
Mid-centric	The majority of the population go to known destinations, but do not go for exploration and adventure. May travel to destinations previously 'found' and made popular by allocentrics.
Psychocentric	Tend to be rather unsure and insecure about travel. Go to places similar to their home environment.

TABLE 4.6 Travel motivation – Key points

- People in the larger, more established source markets are increasingly seeing themselves as 'travellers', rather than 'tourists'. They are looking for immersion in a culture, an understanding of the destination's human and physical environment, and personal fulfilment from their holiday experience.
- Tourism is experiential: The total experience of the holiday has become larger than the sum of its individual parts and travellers are looking for new sensations and unique experiences, even at established traditional destinations.
- Tourism is experimental: Holiday-makers seek out adventure and 'freedom from the limits imposed by things familiar and owned'.
- Tourism is existential: Travellers are striving for purpose and self-realization, whether indulging in sporting challenges, learning a new skill, participating in an exciting new activity, or just searching for personal space in natural surroundings and an emotional reconnection with their own soul or with their partner.
- People are increasingly focusing on the personally regenerating, fulfilling power of a holiday, and on the opportunity to reconnect with a partner and sometimes with the family.
- People are increasingly seeking escape, authenticity, emotional recharge and exploration, rather than passive sightseeing or just relaxing on a beach.

Source: UN–WTO (2009: 2) © UN–WTO

The travel career ladder

Researchers recognize that tourist motivation changes over time and tourists may have several 'motives' to travel. Pearce (1993) suggested that individuals exhibit a 'career' in terms of tourism behaviour. Individuals thus start out at different levels and are likely to change levels as they progress through the various lifecycle stages and can be constrained from progressing by money, health and other people. The model also recognizes that tourists can 'retire from their travel career, or by not taking holidays at all they are not a part of the system' (Pearce 1993: 125). Pearce's model builds on the pyramidal system conceptualized by Maslow, with five motivational levels, and suggests that tourist motivation is an ever-changing process and individuals move up the 'ladder', now modified to Travel Career Patterns (Pearce 2005). Pearce (2005) explained the Travel Career Pattern concept as three layers of travel motivation:

- The core motives, which are the most important ones, such as the pursuit of novelty, escape, relaxation and the desire to enhance relationships.
- A layer surrounding the core, where moderately important travel motives exist such as self-actualization, which change from inner-focused to externally oriented motives.
- An outer layer comprising the most commonly cited and less stable motives which are of less importance. For example, nostalgia and the pursuit of isolation fall into this category.

Pearce (2005) suggests that as the travel career level develops, and tourists become more experienced, their moderately important motives will shift from inner- to outer-focused needs such as experiencing nature and involvement with hosts. In terms of emotional elements in tourism, Hosany and Gilbert (2010) noted that the three most common emotions expressed by tourists as part of hedonistic behaviour were joy, love and positive surprise, further expanding our understanding of the outcome of tourist motivation in tourist behaviour as these emotions were linked to satisfaction and affected future behavioural intentions as tourists.

Current thinking on tourist roles

Building on Pearce's (1982) work, Yiannakis and Gibson (1992) derived a comprehensive classification of leisure tourists, and more recent work has added two more roles to this original typology (Foo *et al.* 2004) (Figure 4.4). Yiannakis and Gibson (1992: 287) suggested that individuals 'enact preferred tourist roles in destinations which provide an optimal balance of familiarity–strangeness, stimulation–tranquility, and structure–independence'.

In other words, some types of tourists on holiday seek unusual environments where others seek familiar ones, some want peace and quiet where others want activity, and some require an organized holiday or itinerary and others do not. Each tourist role seeks something different. Yiannakis and Gibson (1992) found that, in terms of strangeness–familiarity, the archaeologist and the seeker prefer strange environments, while the sport tourist prefers a familiar environment. The organized mass tourist prefers a tranquil environment, and those seeking a high degree of structure include the jet-setter, drifter and action seeker, while the sun lover and escapist prefer low-structured environments. In more recent research, Gibson and Yiannakis (2002) investigated the relationship between tourist role preferences according to gender and adult life-course and psychological needs. This research showed that there are three trends in tourist role preferences over the course of adult life. These are:

- Roles where preferences mostly *decrease* through life-course, which include certain roles that people are less likely to assume as they grow older. Such roles are the action seeker, the active sport tourist, the thrill seeker, the explorer, the drifter and the sun lover. Needs driving these roles vary but, to take the example of the active sport tourist, for males the push to participate includes a combination of unsatisfied and satisfied needs: unsatisfied needs for play, sexual needs, the home and family, and satisfied needs for setting goals and control over their life.

- Roles where preferences mostly *increase* through life-course, which include roles that people are more likely to adopt as they grow older. These include the anthropologist, the high-class tourist, the educational tourist and the organized mass tourist.

- Roles where preferences *vary* through life-course include the seeker, the jet-setter, the independent mass tourist and the escapist.

The findings of this research indicate that tourist roles serve as a medium for tourists to satisfy their needs and wants at various stages of the life-course. As Lepp and Gibson (2008) suggest, individuals are different in terms of the level of stimulation required in their leisure behaviour, which shows stability through time. This has led to research on sensation seeking (SS) by Zuckerman (1979: 10) that defined SS as a 'trait defined by the need for varied, novel and complex sensations and experiences and the willingness to take physical and social risks for the sake of such experience'. As a result, research suggests those with higher levels of SS may have a higher propensity for more high-risk forms of tourism activity.

Sun lover: Interested in relaxing and sunbathing in warm places with lots of sun, sand and ocean

Action seeker: Mostly interested in partying, going to night clubs and meeting the opposite sex for uncomplicated romantic experiences

Anthropologist: Mostly interested in meeting local people, trying the food and speaking the language

Archaeologist: Mostly interested in archaeological sites and ruins; enjoys studying history of ancient civilizations

Organized mass tourist: Mostly interested in organized vacations, package tours, taking pictures and buying lots of souvenirs

Thrill seeker: Interested in risky, exhilarating activities which provide emotional highs, such as sky diving

Explorer: Prefers adventure travel, exploring out-of-the way places and enjoys challenges involved in getting there

Jetsetter: Vacations in elite world-class resorts, goes to exclusive night clubs and socializes with celebrities

Seeker: Seeker of spiritual and/or personal knowledge to better understand self and meaning of life

Independent mass tourist: Visits regular tourist attractions but makes own travel arrangements and often 'plays it by ear'

High-class tourist: Travels first class, stays in the best hotels, goes to shows and dines at the best restaurants

Drifter: Drifts from place to place living a hippie-style existence

Escapist: Enjoys taking it easy and getting away from it all in quiet and peaceful places

Sport tourist: Primary emphasis while on vacation is to remain active, engaging in favourite sports

Educational tourist: Participates in planned study programmes or education-oriented vacations, primarily for study and/or acquiring new skills and knowledge

---

FIGURE 4.4 A typology of 15 leisure-based tourist roles.

Source: Reprinted from *Annals of Tourism Research*, vol. 31: Foo, McGuiggan and Yiannakis, 'Roles tourist play', 408–427: copyright (2004), with permission from Elsevier

So, it can be seen that there are several ways in which we can explain the push factors in tourism motivation. Once the motivation to embark on a holiday has been determined, numerous pull factors effectively influence our choice of destination. Within this, aspects such as the purpose of the holiday and tourist typologies may well be particularly influential. However, the circumstances that affect us as individuals, both personal and wider external influences, greatly affect the nature of the holiday and the final selection of a particular destination. These influences on tourist motivation will now be investigated.

Factors influencing tourist motivation

While we have seen that the decision to go on holiday is an outcome of personal motivation, the selection of a destination/type of holiday is set against a series of constraints of which individuals are aware. The choice of the final holiday is limited because some holidays are too expensive, are not suited to the time we have available, are too far away, or may even involve activities that are beyond our capabilities. There are numerous ways that such constraints could be organized, but the ensuing discussion will focus on two broad categories:

- *personal and family influences*, including age, stage in the family lifecycle and gender issues
- *social and situational influences*, including the tourism and work relationship, social class and income issues.

Age

Variations in tourism participation are strongly related to age, and this is evident in the style in which many tour operators segment their holiday products by age such as Club 18–30 and Saga (for the over-'50s) in the UK. There are many inequalities in terms of age and tourism. In the UK, statistics indicate that those aged 16–24 and over 65 are more likely to not have a holiday than other age groups, and one of the main constraints for both groups is limited income. Overseas holidays are more likely to be taken by those aged 35–54, while the retired population generates the largest proportion of domestic holidays.

Typically, young adults are shown in advertising as backpackers, or else attracted to fun-seeker package holidays aimed specifically at the age group in destinations such as Ibiza. To some extent, tourism participation could be seen as a wage-earning symbol of adulthood for young people. Young adulthood is a time to experiment, to develop confidence in one's own identity, to establish independence, to broaden horizons and to experience sexuality and relationships, and tourism can provide a useful outlet for such needs. By the time of old age there is an inevitable reduction in an individual's physical and mental facilities and as such a reduction in the more active holiday pursuits. Disincentives for travel include falling ill, availability of medical services, personal security, safety and hygiene, whereas motivations include health and well-being, socializing, companionship and opportunity to participate in activities. However, it is clearly incorrect to equate retirement with old age. In the Western world, there is an ageing population which includes the 'baby boomer' generation, who contrary to traditional analyzes, have both the time and the budget for travel. People for whom retirement has come in their 50s represent an attractive 'target' for tourism operators. Often the over-50s are free from family commitments but may still have limited free time and an attractive pension. Thus, such individuals may approach early retirement as a welcome gift. Opportunities may well expand as the individual enters retirement, and only retract when the individual becomes elderly. Some tourism markets benefit substantially from the more mature population, such as the coach travel market (see Chapter 8). For some, retirement stimulates a move to a favoured holiday destination and the holiday experience is therefore recreated on a permanent basis, linking tourism and migration within a domestic and sometimes overseas context.

Family lifecycle

As we introduced briefly in Chapter 3, the lifecycle concept helps us to understand variables such as age in a more dynamic context where other variables interact to shape the propensity to take certain types of holiday (e.g. age, the family lifecycle groups people are located within, and their marital status and whether they have children). Numerous classifications have been developed over the years, including the generic one we introduced in Chapter 3, that reflect the societal structure and dynamic of the time in which they were developed. To give an example, the framework set out by Rapoport and Rapoport in 1975 defined four stages:

1 Adolescence (15–19 years old).
2 Young adult (to late 20s).
3 Family establishment (25–55).
4 Later years (55+).

A European/North American model outlining eight stages has superseded the earlier basic formats of lifecycles (Table 4.7). Such classifications, while useful, need constant updating. Looking at the two examples it can be seen that little account is made in either of single-parent families, gay people and extended families. Such models imply the stages to be the 'norm' and pay little attention to those choosing not to have children or cultural differences in families by ethnic class. Despite these concerns, it is fair to say that different stages in a lifecycle are characterized by different interests, activities and opinions. These translate to different holiday requirements at each stage, and some companies can effectively 'capture' loyalty at an early stage and maintain this throughout the lifecycle, the Disney Corporation for example.

Since the 1950s, it has been considered that women made holiday decisions. However, more recent research has indicated that the holiday choice of a heterosexual couple is made jointly, particularly in the case of high-income households. Women tend to dominate the information-search stage. It is in reality very difficult to judge how decisions are made as tourism decisions often involve a string of choices, including travel, time, accommodation, activities, destination and duration.

TABLE 4.7 The family lifecycle (European/North American model)

Stage	Characteristics	Tourism behaviour
1. Early childhood	Entirely dependent on parent or guardian. Classic sea and sand holidays	Seeking seaside or inland resorts with entertainment facilities for children
2. Early teenager	More influence on decision-making process but still dependent on parent	Resort-based holidays with nightlife. Also youth hostels and semi-independent activity holidays. Group-based holidays
3. Young person	Young, single, not living at home	Holiday-taking dependent on time and resources, therefore wide-ranging – 'sun-lust' to activities. High on adventure, backpacking and experiences
4. Partnership stage	Couples living together with busier lifestyles. Time is a major barrier to travel	Wide-ranging, more short breaks to fit in with dual careers
5. Family stage – early	Includes single parent or separated partners. Financial and school constraints are key factors. Seeking family-centred holidays	Key interest in main holidays, or VFR at other times
6. Family stage – late	Still major constraints regarding education. Holiday-taking patterns breaking up	Mix of holidays and children seeking semi-independence
7. Empty nest	Children leave home and parent or parents have increased freedom and spending power	Wide-ranging but higher prosperity to take more expensive explorer holidays and second breaks
8. Retired	One person or partners retired; income fixed but time available	Continued search for quality. As age increases seeking more passive holidays. Old age no longer a barrier to travel

Note: This generalized model does not include the increasing number of people who remain single or do not have a family. It does, however, recognize different family structures, particularly single-parent families.
Source: Lumsdon (1997: 44)

The presence of children in a household has a significant influence on tourism participation and patterns, and can often create a substantive diversion from the type of pre-family holidays taken by a couple. Households with children tend to have a more limited choice in terms of travel date and duration, dominated by school holidays. People with very young children are constrained by the abilities and tolerances of their children, in terms of travel time and accommodation flexibility. Couples without children tend to take more short breaks throughout the year and some very long trips (more than two weeks). Children are an important determining factor of parental holiday satisfaction and can often play a role in the decision-making process, in terms of identifying a holiday desire and negotiating activities. Carr (2011) observed that children certainly have an effect on tourism behaviour, and Connell and Meyer (2009) highlights the emergence of toddler tourism, where young children's pester power has played an important role in choice of destination: as is the case of the film location of the children's TV programme *Balamory*. It has also been shown that grandparents play a role in taking younger children on trips, particularly day trips and short breaks, as well as within the visiting friends and relatives (VFR) sector.

Gender

Gender as an influence in tourism decision-making is not widely researched or discussed. Much gender-related tourism research concentrates on employment patterns and sex tourism, focusing on women as producers rather than consumers (Pritchard 2004). Yet one of the primary relations between individuals in any society is based on gender. Clarke and Critcher (1985) argue, in the context of leisure participation, that women have less leisure time than men, undertake fewer leisure activities and spend a higher proportion of their time in and around the home and family. If this is accepted, then there are also clear implications for gender to be an issue in tourism participation and motivation. One illustration may well be that for those women who have primary responsibility for household organization and childcare, a self-catering holiday may not fully provide a means of escape from the home environment when this is an important motivator. However, if tourism is part of a family ritual, then all members participate. So, it is not necessarily participation in tourism that is an issue for women with primary care roles, but the type and quality of that participation. Women's caring roles do not just relate to children, since around 70–80 per cent of those caring for an elderly or infirm relative or partner are women, so a holiday may be a rest from caring or caring in a different location (Gladwell and Bedini 2004).

Contemporary tourism, reflecting wider societal changes, has witnessed the empowerment of women and the rise of the lone female traveller. As Kinnaird and Hall (1994) argued, women's travel is often associated with spiritual destinations (e.g. Tibet, Bhutan) or voluntary environmental work, with tracing routes (such as backpacker routes) or just getting away from being a carer (e.g. going to a spa or on a pampering short break). In addition, female group travel is much in evidence in the European youth market. The industry tends to negate the lone traveller, male or female, and tourism tends to be promoted as a couple or family pursuit. Packages are sold on a double-occupancy basis, and single-room supplements can be exorbitant.

INSIGHT 4.2 Conceptualizing household tourism demand

Much of the existing research on tourism demand examines how households respond to different constraints, which has been extensively examined in leisure research where three interconnected themes are examined: personal factors (e.g. fear and anxiety of travel), interpersonal factors (e.g. opportunities to travel with friends/family members) and structural constraints (e.g. available time, money and availability of transport). This area of research offers interesting insights if it is integrated with other concepts from social science such as the family lifecycle, to reveal household demand in time and space, albeit with a focus on poverty and income.

The concept of the family lifecycle can be traced to the seminal work of Rowntree (1901) examining household poverty. The concept of the family lifecycle describes how families pass through distinct stages that place pressure on household finances. In addition, the concept helps us to understand life in a holistic manner, while also recognizing that life events (e.g. getting married, having children and getting old) will impact upon a household budget and ability to engage in tourism. Other unpredictable events, such as unemployment and illness, will provide random impacts on household budgets. Therefore by fusing Rowntree's concept with the notion of household demand, we see that a series of lifecycle factors will mediate the ability to engage in tourism, particularly when associated leisure constraints are also superimposed. While some social psychologists

4

INSIGHT 4.2 continued

have developed the notion of individual's travel careers through time, we can see that there are difficulties in predicting demand when it is such an individual process. Nevertheless, the combination of the family lifecycle and leisure constraints helps us to understand that visitors will have very specific needs as consumers at different stages of the lifecycle, ranging from family-friendly resources and infrastructure to those which an increasingly ageing Westernized population requires. What is also significant is that since Rowntree's original family lifecycle concept, life expectancy has risen significantly in many developed countries, with some studies now predicting that for the current generation

born after 2000, a proportion of these people will reach 100 years of age, stretching and adding new age-related circumstances for households. With ageing a key issue in the demographic structure of most developed countries, it poses new challenges for tourism demand in later life, associated with a growth forecast in the number of people who will develop dementia-related conditions that will affect how the tourism sector has to adjust to these new challenges.

Reference

Rowntree, S. (1901) *Poverty: A Study of Town Life*. London: Macmillan.

Men and women tend to be viewed differently by society in terms of being travellers. For example, men who travel alone might be considered as seeking adventurous activity, expedition or sex tourism. Women may be thought of as brave, vulnerable or even abnormal (Kinnaird and Hall 1994). Some women decide not to travel independently or to avoid certain countries for safety reasons (see Seow and Brown 2018). Many women recognize increased vulnerability in an unfamiliar destination but will take calculated risks; however personality as well as gender affects perception of risk (Yang *et al.* 2018). Kinnaird and Hall (1994) noted that the differing socialization process in leisure experience seems to affect tourism behaviour, but as Foo *et al.* (2004) illustrates motivation is a function of the role of the tourist (e.g. sun lover, jet-setter). Foo *et al.* (2004) found that women are more likely to take a passive role in strange environments than men and that men pursue a wider range of leisure opportunities in unfamiliar environments.

Disability

Some of the barriers to tourism participation faced by the less able are outlined in Table 4.8. Murray and Sproats (1990) identified financial constraints as a major issue for disabled tourists, and it is true that some disabled persons live on modest incomes if they are reliant on state benefits. However, as a group of travellers, this is a large and growing sector, often with more money to spend than most would acknowledge (Ray and Ryder 2003). Mobility-challenged consumers tend to form the focus of much of the development work in the tourism sector, although they form only about 5 per cent of the total disabled population. In tourism, there is little research on visual, hearing, learning difficulties and mental impairments including dementia. The scope of the tourism accessibility debate is outlined in Figure 4.5. A range of studies that are emerging around accessible tourism include:

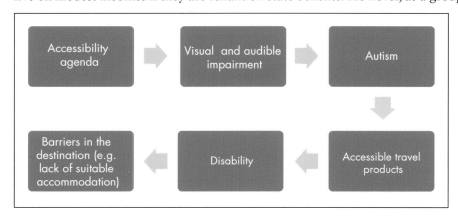

FIGURE 4.5 The scope of the tourism accessibility debate

- *General studies*: Altinay *et al.* (2016); Darcy and Dickson (2009); Israeli (2002).
- *Autism*: Dattolo and Luccio (2016); Hamed (2013).
- *Visual and audible impairments*: Hersh (2016); Kong and Loi (2017); Mesquita and Carneiro (2016); Tutuncu and Lieberman (2016).
- *Disability*: McKercher and Darcy (2018).

Specific conditions such as dementia have also attracted research interest as the studies by Innes *et al.* (2016), Page *et al.* (2015), Connell *et al.* (2017) and Connell and Page (2019) indicate.

Increasingly, the tourism industry is able to offer improved products and services to the disabled market as a consumer market (Shi, Cole and Chancellor 2012). Airlines are particularly good at accommodating wheelchair users; they provide allocated seats and special narrow wheelchairs that can be used to move along aisles, although other forms of transport are often more problematic. Tourism operators often do not know what sort of modifications are required to meet the needs of a range of disabled people, and often do not achieve the right standards. However, this is changing. In many countries, there are strict legal requirements placed on businesses to provide accessibility and the tourism industry is not exempt. In the UK, VisitBritain operates the National Accessible Scheme, which assists accommodation operators in making their products more accessible by providing standards for visual and physical impairments and downloadable guides on visitors with autism and hearing difficulties. Other guides such as Klug *et al.* (2017)

have extensively reviewed how to make visitor sites more dementia-friendly, with industry examples of best practice and guidance on how to address the issue. The Disability Discrimination Act (1992) in Australia and (1995) in the UK places a responsibility on all public and private organizations to make services fully accessible to disabled persons; this was updated in 2010 in the UK in the Equality Act that legally protects people in the workplace and society from discrimination based on the nine protected characteristics listed in Figure 4.6. This more holistic approach to equality is now evident in many countries in order to seek to create a socially inclusive society where people are not excluded from activities.

A growing number of specialist organizations and tour operators now offer both domestic and overseas tourism experiences for those with special needs. One good example

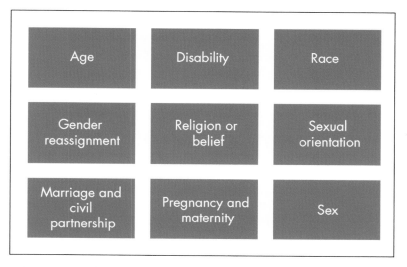

FIGURE 4.6 The 2010 Equality Act – Nine protected characteristics

is Access Africa, which has established wheelchair-accessible lodge accommodation in South Africa, with adapted safari vehicles and personal carers available in a tailor-made itinerary. In the UK, Dementia Adventures provide holidays for people with dementia. Gladwell and Bedini (2004) state that the Internet is a favoured mechanism for planning holidays for disabled people. Websites such as disabilityworld.com assist the disabled tourist to find

TABLE 4.8 Barriers to tourism participation faced by persons with a disability

Internal intrinsic barriers	Economic barriers	Exogenous environmental barriers	Interactive barriers
Lack of knowledge	Affordability	Architectural/accessibility of accommodation etc.	Skills challenges and incongruities
Ineffective social skills	Income disparities	Ecological, paths, trails, hills, etc.	Communication challenges
Health-related barriers	Need for travel companions/special facilities	Transport	Lack of encouragement to participate
Physical or psychologically related barriers		Rules and regulations	Attitudes of travel and hospitality industry workers
Is travel seen as a right?		Safety	Availability and accuracy of information

Source: Reprinted from *Tourism Management*, vol. 24, McKercher, Packer, Yau and Lam, 'Travel agents as facilitators or inhibitors of travel: Perceptions of people with disabilities', 465–474, copyright (2003), with permission from Elsevier

IMAGE 4.1 Beach wheelchairs provide much easier access to beaches than conventional wheelchairs

accessible attractions and accommodation and allow informed choices to be made for planning day trips and holidays. The disabled tourist is often quite a loyal one to destinations that are sensitive to needs. A further issue relates to carers. Gladwell and Bedini's (2004) research identified that those able-bodied individuals who act as full-time carers to a disabled, infirm or elderly relative or partner suffer from 'leisure loss', in that carers have less time and energy to devote to leisure and tourism and may be more prone to illnesses themselves. Some tour operators take such issues into consideration, offering a personal assistant while on holiday to relieve the carer. Other carers take holidays alone while the patient takes respite care. Some beaches have also sought to be more accessible by providing beach wheelchairs, as illustrated in Image 4.1.

Nationality and national identity

Leisure participation rates vary with ethnicity and nationality. However, these patterns are complicated by socio-economic and lifecycle influences. Early work on tourism patterns and race was conducted in North America, and this shows evidence of differences between non-white and white Americans, although there were many variations and no real conclusive findings (Shaw and Williams 1994). In general, there is a lack of research evidence as to whether tourism motives and destination choices vary between nationalities, although several recent studies indicate that differences exist. For example, Foo *et al.* (2004) identified some differences in motivation between American and Australian tourists, Kozak (2002) found differences between English and German tourists to Majorca and Turkey, and some of this research suggests that different nationalities perceive destinations slightly differently. Tourists from cultures that are viewed as extrovert are more likely to adopt adventurous forms of tourist behaviour, and tourists who are culturally dissimilar to the destination are less likely to visit lots of attractions and different areas within the destination.

Pizam and Sussman (1995) examined the behaviour of Japanese, American, French and Italian tourists, and identified differences in five behavioural characteristics, including:

- social interaction (e.g. Japanese tend to stay within their own group)
- commercial transaction (e.g. Americans buy the most)
- preference for activities (e.g. Italians and French are the most adventurous)
- bargaining and trip planning (e.g. Japanese plan the most, Italians the least)
- knowledge of destination (e.g. French, Italians and Americans are interested in authentic experiences).

For overseas travel, language barriers may act as a disincentive to travel, although in many cases legal requirements for visas prove to be most problematic. In recent times, certain nationalities have been deterred from visiting certain countries due to the threat of terrorism and other safety concerns. Accordingly, there is a need for tourism marketers to understand each nationality and develop strategies appropriate to the needs and aspirations of each of the major markets for a country. The role of nationality and cultural characteristics is fully recognized by NTOs charged with marketing to overseas tourists. They prepare market reports on the key overseas segments according to market research, profiling each nationality, and examining their needs and expectations. Such work assists individual operators to cater for each nationality that they are likely to encounter, as well as in the wider marketing effort alongside issues of national identity (Frew and White 2011).

Tourism and work

Work provides a means for tourism and, often, escaping from work provides the motivation for tourism. Whatever the balance, leisure, tourism and work are inseparable. However, leisure and work both compete for an individual's time. If one increases then the other decreases. The nature of work, however, is an important influence on tourism not just in terms of competition for time. Where an individual's work is boring, arduous or monotonous, tourism may well represent an escape. Opposing this, some are fortunate enough to find their work exciting, enjoyable and possibly difficult to disassociate from their leisure. Here a holiday may be seen as a means to extend one's work interests. Zuzanek and Mannell (1983) identified four hypotheses in terms of a work/leisure relationship:

1 *The Trade-off Hypothesis*: Work and leisure are competitors for time and an individual chooses between them.

2 *The Compensation Hypothesis*: Leisure and holidays compensate for the boredom and troubles associated with work and everyday life.

3 *The Spin-off Hypothesis*: The nature of an individual's work produces a similar pattern of leisure activities.

4 *The Neutralist Hypothesis*: There is no discernible relationship between leisure and work.

What can be seen here is that in the vast majority of cases different types of work produce different levels of satisfaction, which in turn influence individual needs and wants and hence leisure and tourism motivations.

Social class and income

Lumsdon (1997: 42) suggests that social class be 'considered to be one of the most important external factors, assessed primarily by occupation and level of income'. However, social class is an awkward concept in that there are numerous dimensions associated with power, money, prestige, culture and background. Nevertheless, social class is used throughout social research and as a means of segmenting the population (along with gender and age) for the purposes of surveys and opinion polls, although class is now more commonly established by occupational grading schemes.

So what is social class and how might it be an influence in terms of tourism motivation? Social class was defined for the UK population census in 1911, to facilitate the analysis by arranging the large number of occupational groups. This initial system took no account of differences between individuals in the same occupation groups (e.g. in terms of remuneration) and over the years other systems have been introduced. For example, in 1951 (amended 1961) the seven social class groups were replaced by 17 socio-economic classes for the UK census. Here the aim was to bring together people with jobs of similar social and economic status. In common use is a system devised by the Market Research Society:

Class

A   *Professional/senior managerial*

B   *Middle managers/executives*

C1 *Junior managers/non-manual*

C2 *Skilled manual*

D   *Semi-skilled/unskilled*

E   *Unemployed/state-dependents*

The implications for leisure and tourism participation are that, moving from the professional occupational grouping to the unskilled, there is an increase in television viewing, a decline in library membership and book reading, and a decline in holiday-making, sports participation and countryside recreation. The statistical data suggest that professional occupations enjoy a more active and varied range of leisure activities. As tourism is price elastic (i.e. small price increases may result in many people seeking cheaper alternatives) and as incomes are generally synonymous with occupational groups, these classifications have an influence on the tourism patterns.

While it is fair to accept that aspects of occupational grouping do influence tourism, such assumptions should be approached with caution. The categories do not relate to lifecycle, hence a young professional worker with four children may have less disposable income than a working couple in the skilled manual class who have no dependents.

It is also pertinent to note that there are other more subjective dimensions of social class, more associated with class imagery. An individual's accent, style of speech, residence, social network, job, educational background, dress, car, income, race, family background and leisure activities may be more influential than their occupation.

The subjective judgements associated with the upper, middle or working classes may also affect the nature and type of holiday as well as other aspects of life. Tourism destinations have traditionally been associated with certain social groupings, and marketers are often charged with repositioning a destination as part of a wider tourism strategy.

Inequalities in tourism among occupational groups are more evident in the type of holiday taken than the participation rates. The AB groups are more likely to take overseas holidays than the DE groups, despite the existence of cheap package deals which have 'democratized' foreign travel (Shaw and Williams 1994: 49). Higher-status consumers tend to travel independently more often and the short-break market is dominated by the AB groups. Attempts to make tourism and leisure more socially inclusive abound, most notably in the social tourism movements of northern Europe (see the example of the North Yorkshire Moors Bus, http://www.northyorkmoors-npa.gov.uk).

Tourist motivation and segmentation

So far this chapter has shown that people are motivated to travel for a variety of reasons. However, understanding the tourist and their motivations is far from easy. For instance Laws (1991) argued that however convenient it is to categorize travellers, not all individuals fall neatly into behavioural models or typological classifications. Moreover, it is not realistic to assume that the accurate descriptions of tourists through their reasons for travel that were gained at the time of purchase will remain constant throughout the travel experience. Despite such concerns, by identifying types of customers and classifying them into groups or market segments, a process called segmentation, tourism suppliers may be able to deliver their products more effectively. Through segmentation, marketers can establish common reasons behind the purchase of tourism products within a market segment. For example, the importance of children is one market segment which some holiday companies have seen as a key component of the family holiday market and worthy of investment; thus they target markets with family-friendly products. Through an understanding of this common purchasing behaviour by market segment, it becomes possible to target market segments with particular products. Clearly, different groups of tourists will make varying economic contributions as a result of their activities. Wealthier tourists may be more valuable to destinations than other tourist types (see Image 4.2), thus efforts may be specifically made to target such groups and, to do this, marketers use segmentation techniques ranging from the simple to the more complex, as we shall now examine.

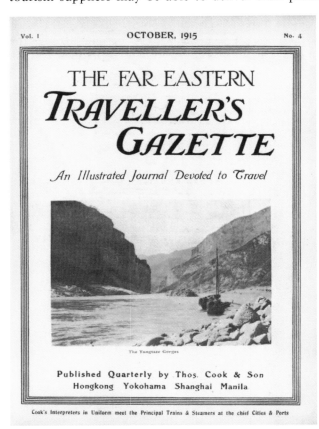

Vol. 1   OCTOBER, 1915   No. 4

THE FAR EASTERN TRAVELLER'S GAZETTE

An Illustrated Journal Devoted to Travel

The Yangtze Gorges

Published Quarterly by Thos. Cook & Son
Hongkong Yokohama Shanghai Manila

Cook's Interpreters in Uniform meet the Principal Trains & Steamers at the chief Cities & Ports

IMAGE 4.2 Affluent travellers, such as the colonial administrators who were based in the Far East during the early twentieth century, were targeted for both the business and leisure travel they undertook when located on assignment overseas, as illustrated in Thomas Cook's 1915 Far Eastern Travellers Gazette. ©Thomas Cook

Segmentation by purpose of travel

The purpose of a trip is used to divide groups of tourists. Commonly, business travellers are separated from those on a leisure holiday, with those visiting friends and relatives making a third group. Occasionally, the leisure holiday might be further subdivided into groups reflecting sun, sea and sand or sun-lust holidays from a sightseeing or wanderlust tour (Images 4.3 and 4.4). Travel for health and for sport may be additional subdivisions, both of which are growth areas internationally. Yet one of the most neglected areas of study is VFR, and as Backer (2007) has shown, it is also widely misunderstood and its volume and scale is often underestimated in destinations.

IMAGE 4.3 Authentic visitor attractions, such as this traditional Fijian village, form part of many sightseeing tours

IMAGE 4.4 Many tour operators provide regimented tours of the key sites of a region or country deemed 'must-see' attractions, such as this geyser and thermal park in Rotorua, North Island, New Zealand

Psychographic segmentation

Segmentation based on lifestyle factors or activities, interests, attitudes and opinions is known as 'psychographic segmentation'. Such behavioural characteristics can help to build a picture of common purchasing behaviour. This enables tourism suppliers to target certain types of individuals with their products in the knowledge that such groups may be more receptive than the population at large. One example is the adventure tourism market, where operators aim to target thrill-seekers and adventurous people.

Behaviourist segmentation

This form of segmentation is multifaceted and aims to group consumers according to their relationship with a product. Aspects that marketers consider include the benefits sought by the consumer (e.g. value for money with no frills on budget airlines), loyalty (e.g. frequent flyers schemes), purchase regularity, attitude to product and awareness of product. In addition to these, there are a number of other techniques, such as geographic segmentation and socio-economic segmentation, which rely on the delineation of occupational grouping and purchasing power. An example is the allocation of categories to residential areas where certain groups of people reside. The **ACORN** system is one of these classifications, and marketers have used it to target promotions to groupings of households that are likely to display certain socio-economic or sociocultural characteristics using census data at a neighbourhood level. A more recent development of the behaviourist approach is the focus on tourists and the notion of travel for lifestyle reasons. Prentice (2004) attributes this approach to a growing recognition that travel is multi-motivational in nature, as tourists undertake 'journeys as experiences'. These experiences are part of the individual's pursuit of specific lifestyle attributes linked to the concept of cultural capital, where the experiences are accumulated to develop a repertoire of attributes associated with visiting or undertaking specific activities. Yet, as Prentice (2004) suggests, these lifestyles no longer allow the division of tourists into neat social groups, such as mass tourist or ecotourist. Instead, a more 'pick and mix' approach exists, where the pursuit of cultural capital and meaning from tourism experiences will see tourists mixing the consumption of high forms of culture (e.g. the arts and opera) alongside travelling on a low-cost airline. Consequently, tourism is no longer an exceptional item in the lives of many people in developed countries but part of their lifestyles, where travel to both familiar and unknown places to enrich their lives is a complex multi-motivational process. Much of the emphasis from the tourism industry is on how it can appeal to these 'lifestyle' motivators to enrich the tourists' journey, from booking through to consuming the products in the destination. In the case of Destination Iceland, its focus is on visitor segmentation into what they describe as Affluent Adventurers, Older Relaxers, Emerging Market Explorers, City Breakers and those travelling for business meetings and conferences and events (known as MICE). In the case of Mexico, the Mexico Tourism Board had been planning to move away from mass advertising and mass appeal towards digitally targeting visitors through its new digital ecosystem approach, and to personalize content, moving away from sun and sand to also include heritage, culture, culinary and nature-based tourism in its key international markets. However, in early 2019 the government dissolved the organization, pushing the onus onto the tourism sector to market itself. In contrast, New York City identified two key market segments driving visitation to the city (Family Markets, who comprised 13 million visitors a year) and the Luxury Market. In the case of Dubai, its Tourism 2020 strategy identified a number of key market segments it wanted to attract to develop festivals and events (including MICE events) and Dubai as a cruise destination, including a focus on attracting ageing visitors. The development of tourist shopping, theme parks and other infrastructure has allowed the country to target specific visitor segments associated with its airline – Emirates.

Conclusion

As Hogg (2003) argues, consumption now dominates our lives and not only does it mark social differences, but it has also come to represent how people relate to one another. No longer is a holiday just viewed as an opportunity to have a break away from everyday life; the tourist as consumer now demands to know 'what's in it for me?' In other words, a complex array of benefits and experiences combine to form the individual's motivation for tourism within the context of the experience economy and the growing significance of digital technology. While the literature on tourism motivation is still evolving, the problems of determining tourist motivation may be summarized in Figure 4.7.

As UN–WTO (2009: 3) argues:

Travel motivation is increasingly characterized by a search for leisure, emotional recharge, authenticity, fulfilling experience, outdoor activities/adventure, and a general desire to participate and explore, rather than merely relax. In particular, there is a need to 'get away from it all', and to use travel and holidays as discovery of place, culture and of self.

This chapter set out with the question of 'why do people go on holiday?' akin to the question posed by Dann (2018). At the outset it has been shown that a variety of push factors may motivate the desire to travel. Such factors may result from the particular relationship an individual has with their work or home environment. Alternatively, the motivation to travel may be driven by other forces as in the case of needing to visit relatives or go on a business trip. Other types of tourist may be motivated by higher-order psychological needs, such as for self-esteem. While people are instrumental in their motivation, once a decision to travel has been made, a variety of pull factors influence that decision. While in theory we may be free to choose our tourism activities, our choice is inevitably limited by an awareness of constraints which influence and circumscribe the range of

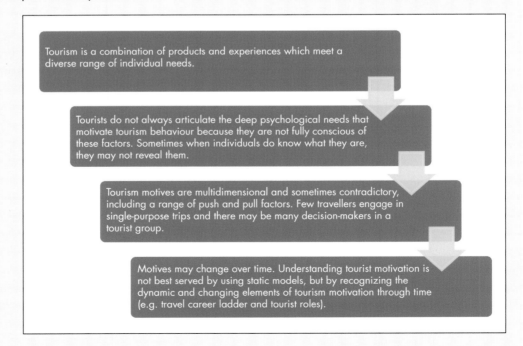

FIGURE 4.7 The problems of determining tourist motivation

opportunities. As Murdy *et al.* (2018: 13) argue, 'Push factors have been identified to consist of psychological forces, for example, desire for escape, adventure, self-exploration, or social interaction . . . Contrastingly, pull factors consist of features of a destination that attract visitors, for example, nature, and sports facilities'. As Wong *et al.* (2018)

demonstrate, people's motivations for tourist travel change through time and expanding our understanding of what affects visitors' emotions to in turn affect their destination experience is becoming better understood, especially associated with the emotions of anticipation and trust as tourists (Rahmani *et al.* 2019).

Discussion questions

1 What models aid our understanding of tourist motivation?

2 Discuss the extent to which people are free to choose where they go on holiday.

3 How important is social class in understanding tourist motivation?

4 What are the main uses of tourist segmentation?

References

Albayrak, T. and Caber, M. (2018) 'Examining the relationship between tourist motivation and satisfaction by two competing methods', *Tourism Management* 69, 201–213.

Altinay, Z., Saner, T., Bahçelerli, N. and Altinay, F. (2016) 'The role of social media tools: Accessible tourism for disabled citizens', *Educational Technology and Society* 19 (1): 89–99.

Argyle, M. (1996) *The Social Psychology of Leisure*. London: Penguin.

Backer, E. (2007) 'VFR travel: An examination of the expenditure of VFR travellers and their hosts', *Current Issues in Tourism* 10 (4): 366–377.

Bentley, M. (1924). *The Field of Psychology*. London: D. Appleton and Company.

Caber, M. and Albayrak, T. (2016) 'Push or pull? Identifying rock climbing tourists' motivations', *Tourism Management* 55: 74–84.

Carr, N. (2011) *Children's and Families Holiday Experiences*. London: Routledge.

Cheng, M. (2016) 'Sharing economy: A review and agenda for future research', *International Journal of Hospitality Management* 57: 60–70.

Clarke, J. and Critcher, C. (1985) *The Devil Makes Work*. Basingstoke: Macmillan.

Cohen, E. (1972) 'Towards a sociology of international tourism', *Social Research* 39 (1): 64–82.

Connell, J. and Meyer, D. (2009) 'Balamory revisited: An evaluation of the screen tourism destination-tourist nexus', *Tourism Management* 30 (2): 194–207.

Connell, J. and Page, S.J. (2019) 'Destination readiness for dementia-friendly visitor experiences: A scoping study', *Tourism Management* 70: 29–41.

Connell, J., Page, S.J., Sherriff, I. and Hibbert, J. (2017) 'Business engagement in a civil society: Transitioning towards a dementia-friendly visitor economy', *Tourism Management* 61: 110–128.

Crompton, J. (1979) 'Motivations for pleasure vacation', *Annals of Tourism Research* 6 (4): 550–568.

Dann, G. (1977) 'Anomie to ego-enhancement and tourism', *Annals of Tourism Research* 4 (4): 184–194.

Dann, G. (1981) 'Tourist motivation: An appraisal', *Annals of Tourism Research* 8 (2): 187–219.

Dann, G. (2018) 'Why, oh why, do people travel abroad?' in N. Prebensen, J, Chen and M. Uysal (eds.) *Creating Experience Value in Tourism*, 2nd edition (pp. 44–57). Wallingford: CABI.

Darcy, S. and Dickson, T. (2009) 'A whole-of-life approach to tourism: The case for accessible tourism experiences', *Journal of Hospitality and Tourism Management* 16 (1): 32–44.

Dattolo, A. and Luccio, F. (2016) 'A review of websites and mobile applications for people with autism spectrum disorders: Towards shared guidelines', in *International Conference on Smart Objects and Technologies for Social Good* (pp. 264–273). Cham: Springer.

Foo, J., McGuiggan, R. and Yiannakis, A. (2004) 'Roles tourists play: An Australian perspective', *Annals of Tourism Research*, 31 (2): 408–427.

Foucault, M. (1976) *The Birth of the Clinic*. London: Tavistock.

Frew, E. and White, L. (eds.) (2011) *Tourism and National Identity*. London: Routledge.

Gibson, H. and Yiannakis, A. (2002) 'Tourist roles: Needs and the lifecourse', *Annals of Tourism Research* 29 (2): 358–383.

Gilbert, D.C. (1991) 'An examination of the consumer decision process related to tourism', in C.P. Cooper (ed.) *Progress in Tourism, Recreation and Hospitality Management, Vol. III*. London: Belhaven.

Gladwell, N. and Bedini, L. (2004) 'In search of lost leisure: the impact of caregiving on leisure travel', *Tourism Management* 25 (6): 685–694.

Gretzel, U. (2017) '#travelselfie: A netnographic study of travel identity communicated via Instagram', in S. Carson and M. Pennings (eds.) *Performing Cultural Tourism: Communities,*

4

Tourists and Creative Practices (pp. 115–127). London, Routledge.

Hall, C.M. and Page, S.J. (2002) *The Geography of Tourism and Recreation: Environment, Place and Space,* 2nd edition. London: Routledge.

Hamed, H. (2013) 'Tourism and autism: An initiative study for how travel companies can plan tourism trips for autistic people', *American Journal of Tourism Management* 2 (1): 1–14.

Hersh, M. (2016) 'Improving deafblind travelers' experiences: an international survey', *Journal of Travel Research* 55 (3): 380–394.

Hogg, G. (2003) 'Consumer changes', in S. Hart (ed.) *Marketing Changes*. London: Thomson.

Hosany, S. and Gilbert, D. (2010) 'Measuring tourists' emotional experiences toward hedonic holiday destinations', *Journal of Travel Research* 49 (4): 513–526.

Howie, F. (2003) *Managing the Tourist Destination*. London: Continuum.

Innes, A., Page, S.J. and Cutler. C. (2016) 'Barriers to leisure participation for people with dementia and their carers: An exploratory analysis of carer and people with dementia's experiences', *Dementia* 15 (6): 1643–1665.

Israeli, A. (2002) 'A preliminary investigation of the importance of site accessibility factors for disabled tourists', *Journal of Travel Research* 41 (1): 101–104.

Kinnaird, V. and Hall, D. (eds.) (1994) *Tourism: A Gender Analysis*. Chichester: Wiley.

Klug, K., Page, S.J., Connell, J., Robson, D. and Bould, E. (2017) *Rethinking Heritage: A Guide to Help Make Your Site More Dementia-Friendly*. London: Historic Royal Palaces.

Kong, W. and Loi, K. (2017) 'The barriers to holiday-taking for visually impaired tourists and their families', *Journal of Hospitality and Tourism Management* 32, 99–107.

Kozak, M. (2002) 'Comparative analysis of tourist motivations by nationality and destinations', *Tourism Management* 2 (3): 221–232.

Kozak, M. and Kozak, N. (eds.) (2018) *Tourist Behaviour: An Experiential Perspective*. New York: Springer International Publishing.

Krippendorf, J. (1987) *The Holidaymakers*. Oxford: Butterworth-Heinemann.

Lai, C., Li, X. and Harrill, R. (2013) 'Chinese outbound tourists' perceived constraints to visiting the United States', *Tourism Management* 37 (1): 136–146.

Laws, E. (1991) *Tourism Marketing, Services and Quality Management Perspectives*. Cheltenham: Stanley Thornes.

Lepp, A. and Gibson, H. (2008) 'Sensation seeking and tourism: Tourist role, perception of risk and destination choice', *Tourism Management,* 29 (4): 740–750.

Lo, I. and McKercher, B. (2015) 'Ideal image in process: Online tourist photography and impression management', *Annals of Tourism Research* 52: 104–116.

Lo, I.S., McKercher, B., Lo, A., Cheung, C. and Law, R. (2011) 'Tourism and online photography', *Tourism Management* 32(4): 725–731.

Lumsdon, L. (1997) *Tourism Marketing*. London: Thomson International Business Press.

Lyu, S.O. (2016) 'Travel selfies on social media as objectified self-presentation', *Tourism Management* 54: 185–195.

MacCannell, D. (1976) *The Tourist: A New Theory of the Leisure Class*. London: Macmillan.

Mannell, R. and Iso-Ahola, S. (1987) 'Psychological nature of leisure and tourism experience', *Annals of Tourism Research* 14 (3): 314–341.

Maslow, A.H. (1943) 'A theory of human motivation', *Psychological Review* 50: 370–396.

McKercher, B., Packer, T., Yau, M.K. and Lam, P. (2003) 'Travel agents as facilitators or inhibitors of travel: Perceptions of people with disabilities', *Tourism Management,* 24 (4): 465–474.

McKercher, B. and Darcy, S. (2018) 'Re-conceptualizing barriers to travel by people with disabilities', *Tourism Management Perspectives* 26: 59–66.

Meethan, K. (2001) *Tourism in Global Society: Place, Culture, Consumption*. Basingstoke: Palgrave.

Mesquita, S. and Carneiro, M. (2016) 'Accessibility of European museums to visitors with visual impairments', *Disability and Society* 31 (3), 373–388.

Middleton, V.T.C. and Clarke, J. (2001) *Marketing in Travel and Tourism,* 3rd edition. Oxford: Butterworth-Heinemann.

Mill, R. and Morrison, A. (1992) *The Tourism System: An Introductory Text*. Harlow: Prentice Hall.

Moutinho, L. (1987) 'Consumer behaviour in tourism', *European Journal of Marketing,* 21 (10): 3–44.

Murdy, S., Alexander, M. and Bryce, D. (2018) 'What pulls ancestral tourists "home"? An analysis of ancestral tourist motivations', *Tourism Management* 64: 13–19.

Murray, M. and Sproats, J. (1990) 'The disabled traveller: Tourism and disability in Australia', *Journal of Tourism Studies* 1 (1): 9–14.

Page, S.J., Innes, A. and Cutler, C. (2015) 'Developing dementia-friendly tourism destinations: An exploratory analysis', *Journal of Travel Research* 54 (4), 467–481.

Patmore, J.A. (1975) 'People, Place and Pleasure', inaugural lecture, University of Hull, UK, 30 April.

Pearce, P. (1982) *The Social Psychology of Tourist Behaviour*. Oxford: Pergamon.

Pearce, P. (1993) 'Fundamentals of tourist motivation', in D.G. Pearce and R.W. Butler (eds.) *Tourism Research: Critiques and Challenges*. London: Routledge.

Pearce, P. (2005) *Tourist Behaviour: Themes and Conceptual Schemes*. Clevedon: Channel View.

Pearce, P. and Caltabianco, M. (1983) 'Inferring travel motivation from travellers' experiences', *Journal of Travel Research* 22 (2): 16–20.

Pine, B. and Gilmore, J. (1999) *The Experience Economy: Work Is Theatre and Every Business a Stage*. Boston, MA: Harvard Business School Press.

Pizam, A. and Sussman, S. (1995) 'Does nationality affect tourism behavior?' *Annals of Tourism Research,* 22 (4): 901–917.

Plog, S. (1974) 'Why destination areas rise and fall in popularity', *Cornell Hotel and Restaurant Administration Quarterly* (February): 55–58.

Prentice, R. (2004) 'Tourism motivations and typologies', in A. Lew, C.M. Hall and A. Williams (eds.) *A Companion to Tourism*. Oxford: Blackwell.

Pritchard, A. (2004) 'Gender and sexuality in tourism research', in A. Lew, C.M. Hall and A. Williams (eds.), *A Companion to Tourism*. Oxford: Blackwell.

Rahmani, K., Gnoth, J. and Mather, D. (2019) 'A psycholinguistic view of tourists' emotional experiences', *Journal of Travel Research* 58 (2): 192–206.

Rapoport, R., Rapoport, R. N. and Strelitz, Z. (1975) *Leisure and the Family Life Cycle*. London: Routledge & Kegan Paul.

Ray, N. and Ryder, M. (2003) '"E-bilities" tourism: An exploratory discussion of the travel needs and motivations of the mobility-disabled', *Tourism Management* 24 (1): 57–72.

Rittichainuwat, B. and Mair, J. (2012) 'Visitor attendance motivations at consumer travel exhibitions', *Tourism Management* 33 (5): 1236–1244.

Ryan, C. (ed.) (1997) *The Tourist Experience. A New Introduction*. London: Cassell.

Seow, D. and Brown, L. (2018) 'The solo female Asian tourist', *Current Issues in Tourism* 21 (10): 1187–1206.

Sharpley, R. (1994) *Tourism, Tourists and Society*. Huntingdon: Elm.

Shaw, G. and Williams, A. (1994) *Critical Issues in Tourism*. Oxford: Blackwell.

Shi, L., Cole, S. and Chancellor, C. (2012) 'Understanding leisure travel motivations of travelers with acquired mobility impairments', *Tourism Management* 33: 228–231.

Smit, B. and Melissen, F. (2018) *Sustainable Customer Experience Design: Co-creating Experiences in Events, Tourism and Hospitality*. London: Routledge.

Sundbo, J. and Sorensen, F. (eds.) (2016) *The Experience Economy*. Cheltenham: Edward Elgar.

Toraldo, M. (2013) 'Mobilising the cultural consumer through the senses: Festivals as sensory experiences', *International Journal of Work Organisation and Emotion*, 5 (4), 384–400.

Tutuncu, O. and Lieberman, L. (2016) 'Accessibility of hotels for people with visual impairments: From research to practice', *Journal of Visual Impairment and Blindness*, 110 (3): 163–175.

UN–WTO (2009) *Handbook of Destination Branding*. Madrid: UN–WTO.

Urry, J. (1990) *The Tourist Gaze: Leisure and Travel in Contemporary Societies*. London: Sage.

Urry, J. (1995) *Consuming Places*. London: Routledge.

Urry, J. and Larsen, J. (2011) *The Tourist Gaze 3.0*. Sage: London.

Wong, I. A., Law, R. and Zhao, X. (2018) 'Time-variant pleasure travel motivations and behaviors', *Journal of Travel Research* 57 (4): 437–452.

Wu, M. and Pearce, P. L. (2014) 'Appraising netnography: Towards insights about new markets in the digital tourist era', *Current Issues in Tourism*, 17 (5): 463–474.

Yang, E.C.L., Khoo-Lattimore, C. and Arcodia, C. (2018) 'Power and empowerment: How Asian solo female travellers perceive and negotiate risks', *Tourism Management* 68: 32–45.

Yiannakis, A. and Gibson, H. (1992) 'Roles tourists play', *Annals of Tourism Research* 19 (2): 287–303.

Yoo, C.-K., Yoon, D. and Park, E. (2018) 'Tourist motivation: An integral approach to destination choices', *Tourism Review* 73 (2): 169–185.

Zuckerman, M. (1979) *Sensation Seeking: Beyond the Optimal Level of Arousal*. Hillsdale, NJ: Lawrence Erlbaum Associates.

Zuzanek, J. and Mannell, R. (1983) 'Work leisure relationships from a sociological and social psychographical perspective', *Leisure Studies* 2 (3): 327–344.

Further reading

Books

Kozak, M. and Kozak, N. (eds.) (2016) *Tourist Behaviour: An International Perspective*. Wallingford: CABI.

Prebensen, N., Chen, J. and Uysal, M. (eds.) (2018) *Creating Experience Value in Tourism*, 2nd edition. Wallingford: CABI.

Robinson, M. and Picard, D. (eds.) (2018) *Emotion in Motion: Tourism, Affect and Transformation*. London: Routledge.

Journal articles

Cohen, S. and Cohen, E. (2019) 'New directions in the sociology of tourism', *Current Issues in Tourism* 22 (2): 153–172.

Dickson, T., Misener, L. and Darcy, S. (2017) 'Enhancing destination competitiveness through disability sport event legacies: Developing an interdisciplinary typology', *International Journal of Contemporary Hospitality Management* 29 (3), 924–946.

Guttentag, D. (2016) 'Why tourists choose Airbnb: A motivation-based segmentation study underpinned by innovation

concepts', *UWSpace*, https://uwspace.uwaterloo.ca/handle/10012/10684.

Knobloch, U., Robertson, K. and Aitken, R. (2017) 'Experience, emotion, and eudaimonia: A consideration of tourist experiences and well-being', *Journal of Travel Research* 56 (5): 651–662.

Leong, A., Yeh, S., Hsiao, Y. and Huan, T (2015) 'Nostalgia as travel motivation and its impact on tourists' loyalty', *Journal of Business Research* 68 (1): 81–86.

Otoo, F. and Kim, S. (2018, in press) 'Analysis of studies on the travel motivations of senior tourists from 1980 to 2017: Progress and future directions', *Current Issues in Tourism*.

Sie, L., Patterson, I. and Pegg, S. (2016) 'Towards an understanding of older adult educational tourism through the development of a three-phase integrated framework', *Current Issues in Tourism* 19 (2): 100–136.

Weiler, B., Torland, M., Moyle, B. and Hadinejad, A. (2018) 'Psychology-informed doctoral research in tourism', *Tourism Recreation Research* 43 (3): 277–288.

Part 2

Understanding the tourism industry

This section addresses the way in which the demand for tourism is managed by 'suppliers' by commencing with a review in Chapter 5 of the term 'tourism supply' and what the scope and nature of the tourism sector is. This should not be seen in isolation from tourism demand, but, for the ease of explanation, the supply issues are explained separately. In the discussion of supply, the challenge of managing a tourism enterprise is highlighted along with some of the prevailing issues for tourism operators such as competition and the need to make cost savings to remain competitive. Having provided a broad overview of what exactly constitutes tourism supply, attention shifts to one of the most dramatic changes which has revolutionized the landscape of tourism supply – the introduction of new technology. The impact of this on the tourism sector, for both supply and demand, has been tremendous, with new forms of travel distribution emerging – e-tourism. Chapters 5 and 6 should not be seen in isolation from the chapters that follow them, where we examine the processes of globalization and the impact of technology that are simultaneously occurring in time and space to create a truly globalized tourism industry, returning to one of the all-embracing themes of the book developed in Chapter 1.

More detailed analysis of each sector of the travel and tourism market is presented in each of the subsequent chapters so that the reader can appreciate the wide range of suppliers and sectors which exist and interact to produce the tourism experience. Chapter 7 reviews the nature of travel and tourism intermediaries, which assemble and distribute tourism products to the consumer through various distribution channels. The transportation sector is discussed in Chapter 8 and the wide range of modes of transport which the tourist utilizes as well as the significance of transport as an integral part of the tourism experience are examined. This is followed by a discussion of the scope and nature of visitor attractions (Chapter 9) as a vital part of the visitor's experience at a destination. Lastly, the hospitality sector is introduced in Chapter 10.

5

Understanding and managing tourism supply: An introductory framework

Learning outcomes

After reading this chapter and answering the questions, you should:

- be familiar with the concept of tourism supply

- understand how different sectors are involved in tourism supply

- be aware of issues relating to supply and the interconnections which exist in the tourism supply chain

- understand the significance of management as a tool to guide the development of supply in tourism enterprises.

Overview

The purpose of this chapter is to provide the reader with an appreciation of the many types of tourism supplier, providing key examples of organizations involved and the scale of operations together with some of the issues facing them, notably the management of tourism and strategy issues. The significance of the travel distribution sector, transport, visitor attractions, accommodation and hospitality sector as components of supply are introduced, together with the challenges involved in ensuring the supply is able to meet demand.

Introduction

The study of tourism supply is often seen as an abstract economic concept and difficult to visualize and, for that reason, this chapter presents an introductory framework which introduces supply and different approaches used to explain its significance. This chapter provides an overview of the various approaches and concepts related to tourism supply, which are subsequently developed in the ensuing chapters on supply issues (Chapters 6–10). The analysis of the tourism sector by economists has traditionally distinguished between the demand for goods and services and the ways in which the demand is satisfied, and how this affects the *consumption* of tourism goods and services. Economists also examine how the supply of tourist services is produced (i.e. the *production* side). In the real world, the tourism industry consider supply in terms of three basic questions: 'what to produce?', 'how to produce it?' and 'when, where and how to produce it?' according to Bull (1991). Some analysts, however, argue that the tourism industry only really grapples fully with supply issues in conditions of oversupply, which may occur in times of economic downturn when demand drops and surplus capacity ensues. Yet it is also argued that many examples of mismanaging tourism supply exists in the competitive environment. For example, the oversupply which exists on transport corridors such as the English Channel crossing by air, rail and sea has led to overprovision and deep discounting, which has undermined the profitability of supply.

March and Wilkinson (2009: 455) summarize the importance of looking at supply issues, as:

People, organisations and firms depend on other people, organisations and firms in important ways in carrying out their tasks and achieving their goals. They rely on key inputs from others in the form of various products and services, including material goods, personal and professional services, information and funds; they depend on others to use, transfer, transform and combine their outputs into meaningful goods and services for others; they depend on regulators, communities and industry bodies to protect and sustain them and their workers; they depend on competitors to challenge and inform them about new possibilities and threats.

Few studies provide a conceptual framework to incorporate this wide range of issues in which supply issues can be examined, although geographical studies of tourism (e.g. Shaw and Williams 1994; Hall and Page 2002) have argued that the production of tourism services and experiences offer new directions for research, alongside Song (2012). March and Wilkinson (2009) provide an illustration of the scope of tourism businesses involved in the supply of products and experiences in the Hunter Valley in Australia, where thicker lines in the connections between businesses indicate stronger relations and interactions.

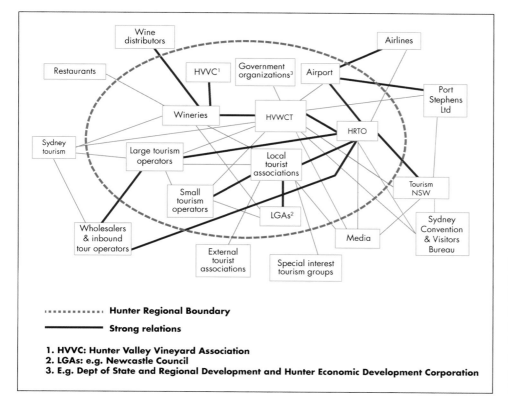

FIGURE 5.1 Overview of the Hunter Valley tourist region business network
Source: Reproduced with permission from Elsevier from March, R. and Wilkinson, I. (2009) 'Conceptual tools for evaluating tourism partnerships', *Tourism Management* 30 (3): 458.

.... **Hunter Regional Boundary**

———— **Strong relations**

1. HVVC: Hunter Valley Vineyard Association
2. LGAs: e.g. Newcastle Council
3. E.g. Dept of State and Regional Development and Hunter Economic Development Corporation

With the rise of the experience economy discussed in Chapter 4, this also raises different issues about the type of experiences that tourism suppliers will create and the opportunities they offer for co-creation. In the case of Hunter Valley in Figure 5.1, March and Wilkinson (2009) outline the type of relationships that exist where there are:

- *Competitors* whose outputs reduce the value of the focal actor's output (other tourism actors, intra and interregional competitors, indirect competitors);
- *Complementors* who enhance the value of the focal actor's outputs (other tourism actors, support services, government organizations, trade and industry organisations);
- *Suppliers* (of staff, provisions, materials, technology, finance, services and other component inputs); and
- *Customers* (tourists, and channel intermediaries linking a tourist operator with actual and potential tourists).

(March and Wilkinson 2008: 458)

These relationships are demonstrated in more detail in Figure 5.2, which illustrates that the scope and nature of tourism supply issues is vast. This is because of the scope of those businesses which are directly or indirectly involved in tourism production, which extends beyond what we might immediately see as tourism. For this reason, it is important to understand many of the conceptual issues on supply that arise in this chapter, illustrated by the example of the Hunter Valley. This is followed by more in-depth studies in subsequent chapters. One difficulty is that the tourism industry remains sceptical of academic researchers and their ability to understand complex business issues, which they do not face in centres of learning. This is compounded by a gap between the research needs of industry, the sensitive nature of much of their commercial data and the perspectives of academic researchers, who are often inexperienced in the business and managerial aspects of tourism (unless they have worked in the industry). Despite this, the more able academic researchers who have industry experience and skills which industry seeks do work as consultants to industry to try to address specific business problems.

What is supply?

Sessa (1983: 59) considers 'tourism supply is the result of those productive activities that involve the provision of goods and services required to meet tourism demand and which are expressed in tourism consumption'. Sinclair and Stabler (1992: 2) indicate that supply issues can be classified and divided into three main categories:

1 Descriptions of the industry and its operation, management and marketing.
2 The spatial development [the geographical development] and interactions which characterize the industry on a local, national and international scale.
3 The effects which result from the development of the industry.

Although the tourist is a mobile consumer at different geographical scales, much of what can be deemed tourism supply is geographically fixed at specific places. Yet there are also trends, which are examined in other chapters (e.g. Chapter 10 on accommodation and hospitality services), that show that transnational corporations are relocating capital and finance to a wider range of international locations to fulfil the demand for tourism services. As Meethan (2004) indicates, the development of production and consumption chains means that bundles of services can be purchased and consumed, highlighting the globalized nature of tourism activity. As part of this, both transport and information technology (IT) are key elements in forming inter-sector linkages and this is discussed in the case of easyJet, as well as in Chapters 6 and 8.

Tourism supply issues are critical in the analysis of tourism because they help to understand how the tourism industry is both organized and distributed geographically, particularly if one adopts a holistic perspective using the tourism system and the supply aspects as critical inputs to the system. Tourism supply issues also exist in an environment in which policy, planning, development issues and political factors impinge upon the regulatory framework and influence the extent to which the tourism industry operates in a regulated through to deregulated environment.

The determinants of tourism supply

According to Sinclair and Stabler (1997: 58):

Tourism supply is a complex phenomenon because of both the nature of the product and the process of delivery. Principally, it cannot be stored (i.e. it is a perishable product), it is intangible in that it cannot be examined prior to purchase, it is necessary to travel to consume it, heavy reliance is placed on both natural and human-made resources and a number of components are required, which may be separately or jointly purchased and which are consumed in sequence.

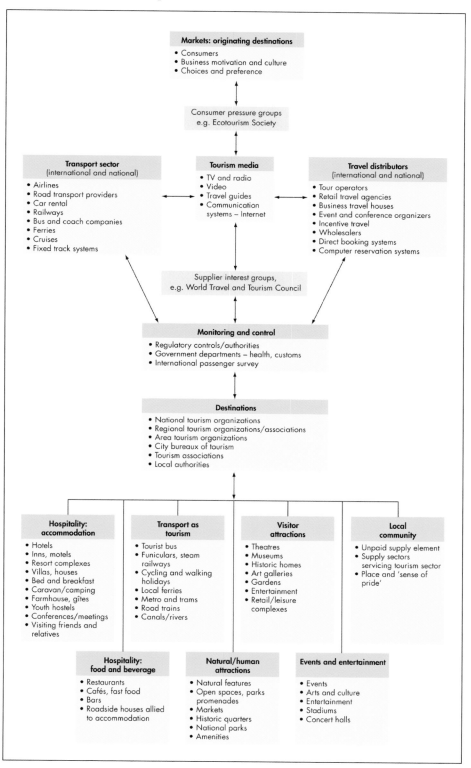

FIGURE 5.2 The scope and nature of tourism supply
Source: Lumsdon (1997: 13)

It is a composite product involving transport, accommodation, catering, natural resources [see Image 5.1], *entertainment, and other facilities and services, such as shops and banks, travel agents and tour operators.*

What this quotation illustrates is that the scope of tourism supply issues is extremely broad and wide-ranging and comprises many disparate suppliers providing a combination of tangible and intangible products. For the purposes of this chapter (to be discussed in more detail in other chapters), the key aspects of tourism supply are:

- tour operators and intermediaries (e.g. travel agents or service providers like Internet travel agencies such as Expedia)
- attractions (Images 5.1 A & B) and activities
- accommodation
- transportation
- other tourist facilities and services (e.g. hospitality, catering and entertainment).

It is also apparent that the precise form of supply in different tourism origin and destination areas is conditioned by the actors involved in tourism supply, in other words the nature of provision. It needs to be emphasized that three types of business forms exist in supply terms:

- *The public sector*, with its provision of services and facilities, and infrastructure from taxes and the public purse to facilitate and manage tourism activity (see Chapter 13 for more detail). One interesting example here which is often misunderstood and underemphasized is the local authority working at the local level in tourism provision, managing and coordinating services which meet the needs of tourists and residents alike. The scale of provision in Scotland was identified by the COSLA report (2002, annex 1) *Review of the Area Tourist Boards*:

  Local authorities are an essential contributor to the Scottish tourism product, through their responsibilities for economic and social development, licensing, planning, trading standards, roads and transport, environmental health, support for events and the operation of facilities such as museums, galleries, country parks and entertainment venues. This role is vital in ensuring that visitors have a satisfying and rewarding experience once they are in the area. This involves ensuring, among many other things, that:

  - necessary infrastructure to support the tourism product is in place at the local level
  - visitor attractions are easily accessible, well signposted and well cared for
  - there is adequate, quality information available on local attractions and events that will enhance the visitor's experience
  - high standards of environmental care are maintained
  - there is particular attention to security and safety, for example through lighting, policing and inspection of premises
  - new and enhanced tourism products are developed and supported.

- *The private sector*, which dominates provision and is driven by profit motives in most cases (although lifestyle businesses which seek to maintain marginal profitability to meet family and social motives also exist). At a global scale, small businesses dominate the tourism sector, although much of the power and control of the tourism sector is a function of the growing role of transnational and global companies which control different aspects of supply.

- *The voluntary and not-for-profit sector*, which has more aesthetic and esoteric reasons for being involved in tourism, such as volunteering to help heritage bodies to maintain national historic assets. Some business interests in this sector receive public sector grants to act as custodians of state resources (e.g. the National Trust). This sector provides a counterbalance to organizations with profit-driven motives that may not necessarily have the long-term protection of natural and built assets as their main objective, especially if it affects profits and shareholder interests.

Collectively, these actors vary in their significance in different tourism supply situations but they do condition the mix of supply available to the tourism sector, with state regulation and private-sector profitability often in a state of tension in many countries. There are also globalization processes at work which will impact upon tourism supply and that transcend individual countries.

The influence of global transnational companies

Research by Hall and Page (1996) in the South Pacific highlighted the interrelationships which exist between tourism and international business. For example, the way in which tourism is organized constitutes a form of international business, especially the way it is managed by global transnational companies (TNCs) where its organizational behaviour, methods of financing and approach to marketing and promotion comprise global activities in their own right. However, in tourism studies the link between these activities and international business remains weakly articulated as Hall and Page (1996) identified. Studies in economic geography have broached this subject, but many of these issues are subsumed in more simplistic notions of the supply of tourism. Yet what remains clear is that tourism is inherently a form of international business which manifests itself in:

- tourists and host cultures interacting with each other
- the movement of capital and labour to facilitate international business, especially the international investment in the tourist infrastructure
- the formation of supply chains which are organized internationally as the key function of TNCs, or where TNCs organize these elements of tourism to package and supply tourism.

What is interesting from a tourism perspective is the power and control which these key businesses now wield over the global supply, particularly in Europe with the rise of large TNCs such as TUI and Thomas Cook in Europe, discussed in Chapter 7. While many national and international bodies, especially competition commissions, seek to control the power of TNCs because they attempt to merge and create large entities, the involvement of airlines in strategic alliances helps to overcome competition issues (see later in the chapter). Yet there are also larger entities that have developed, such as the integrated tourism companies like TUI (see Chapter 7) which operate globally and have a strong strategic vision of the market conditions they operate in and the way they need to respond to develop their products. For example, in 2005 Thomson, which is part of the TUI group, began developing low-cost products and destinations such as Egypt to combat the low-cost airline phenomenon, which was impacting upon its traditional holiday business and leading to flight-only travel. It also introduced other measures to allow holidaymakers to compile their own packages from a portfolio of products to respond to the growth of online booking, and launched a low-cost airline. A competitive response by the low-cost airline industry saw easyJet launch easyJet Holidays in 2007 (see Image 5.2),

IMAGE 5.1 A & B Attractions are subject to extremes in visitor demand, as these two contrasting queues in July and October show. Approaches to addressing seasonality include pricing strategies and scheduling events to manage demand

linking its daily flights and 900 departures with 10 000 hotels across Europe serving 75 destinations. This provides a flexible, customizable product for the consumer with a choice of departure times. Compulsory periods required to stay at the destination (typically seven days) do not exist on easyJet Holidays.

It is also important to recognize that the tourism industry and individual firms are directly influenced by the market conditions, which will vary according to demand and supply, and which affect the economic/business environment in which tourism and other economic activities operate. Although there is not space within this chapter to examine these issues in detail (see Sinclair and Stabler 1997 for more depth), four market situations normally prevail in the tourism sector.

Perfect competition

Within economic models of perfect competition, economists make a number of assumptions related to tourism issues. These are that there is a large number of consumers and firms that exist so that neither can affect the price of the undifferentiated product; and that there is free entry to and exit from the market with no barriers to the market. However, in the real world few conditions exist where perfect competition can prevail.

Contestable markets

Contestable markets exist where there are 'insignificant entry and exit costs, so that there are negligible entry and exit barriers. Sunk costs [known more commonly as capital], which a firm incurs in order to produce and which would not be recoupable if the firm left the industry, are not significant' (Sinclair and Stabler 1997: 61). What this means is that producers cannot react immediately, despite the onset of information technology and greater market intelligence, whereas consumers can react immediately. In other words, businesses compete with each other for the consumer by adopting different pricing strategies so that market segmentation can occur and operators can contest the price. Yet firms in contestable markets charge similar prices because it is frequently a mass market and little product differentiation may exist. In economic terms, this means that existing operators cannot charge more than the average cost because more competitors would enter the market to compete. This is due to the low sunk costs and low entry/exit barriers which rivals would have.

Oligopoly

Oligopoly exists where there is a limited number of suppliers who dominate the tourism sector. This is particularly the case where 'tourism has a dualistic industrial structure which is polarized between large numbers of small firms (typically in retailing, accommodation services) and a small number of large companies (for example in air transport)' (Williams 1995: 163). What this means is that in an oligopoly, a firm can control its price and output levels because there are entry and exit barriers. Many of the supply conditions are ultimately dependent upon the suppliers who determine the output and pricing level. Although, in an ideal world, oligopolies set prices where profits are maximized and may even collude to establish a monopoly and increase profit levels, in the real world producers may alter prices and output without reference to competitors to gain market advantage. Sinclair and Stabler (1997: 81) argue in the case of the air transport market that:

> Although a domestic monopoly or oligopoly structure has been common, with a single state supported airline or a small number of competing airlines, deregulation has made some markets competitive in the short run. In the international market some routes are competitive, being served by many carriers. Most of the others are served by at least two carriers, indicating an oligopolist market, although a few routes are served by a single carrier which may be tempted to exercise monopoly powers.

Thus, where a large number of small firms operate in the tourism industry, a competitive market exists. However, where a limited number of operators or tourism businesses exist, an oligopolistic situation may also verge on the conditions akin to monopoly if the competition is limited.

Monopoly

This is probably easily described as the opposite of perfect competition, since it is where a company or firm can exercise a high degree of control over a product or level of output. This means that businesses can charge a price which is above the average cost of production, indicating that consumers pay a higher price than would be the case in a more competitive market situation. Quite often monopoly situations exist which are detrimental to the interests of consumers, but in the transport sector monopolies may exist where the state is the main provider of a service due to the lack of a viable service from the private sector. Even where governments have privatized monopolies on tourism provision (e.g. with air travel), the enterprises can react in a way where the free market leads to oligopolistic or monopolistic behaviour prevailing in specific areas, which has been the case in the airline industry in the USA.

Therefore, in any analysis of tourism supply issues and market conditions, Sinclair and Stabler (1997: 83) argue that a number of factors need to be considered in evaluating tourism, which include:

- the number and size of firms
- entry and exit barriers to specific tourism businesses
- the extent to which market concentration exists in a specific tourism sector (i.e. where a small number of large operators control the majority of the market, such as the UK tour operator sector, which has a small number of large integrated operators controlling the business)
- economies and diseconomies of scale
- the costs of capital and operation
- the extent to which price discrimination exists and products are differentiated
- pricing policies.

Yet these factors do not occur in isolation, and in many cases they can be understood in a more dynamic context by looking at the tourism supply chain to show how the businesses working in tourism fit together, and what types of relationships exist between them.

The tourism supply chain

Tapper and Font (2004: 1), in their *Tourism Supply Chains* study, described this concept as:

> *all the goods and services that go into the delivery of tourism products to consumers. It includes all suppliers of goods and services whether or not they are directly contracted by tour operators or by their agents . . . or suppliers (including accommodation providers): Tourism supply chains involve many components . . . bars and restaurants, handicrafts, food production, waste disposal, and the infrastructure that supports tourism in the destination.*

Many of these supply chains are managed by business-to-business relationships, using what is known as supply chain management to improve the performance and output in the chain. A typical tourism supply chain will have four components: a tourism supplier, a tour operator, a travel agent and the customer, linked together in a chain. What Figure 5.3 shows is that these chains, which can often encompass a wide range of tourism and non-tourism sectors, can determine the visitor's overall experience of the destination, in relation to those elements of the supply chain they interact with. The supply chain may also help operators to understand where efficiency gains, cost savings and investment may be needed to add value to the customer's experience of tourism, including the use of measures to improve sustainable business performance (Schwartz *et al.* 2008).

The emergence of the concept of Tourism Supply Chain Management (TSCM) has created a focus within the study of tourism supply issues centred on understanding how to organize and optimize the efficient delivery of tourism services and experiences. Song (2012) argued that we need to recognize a number of underlying characteristics of tourism as a business that make supply chain management essential to the efficiency and profitability of tourism enterprises, as shown in Figure 5.4.

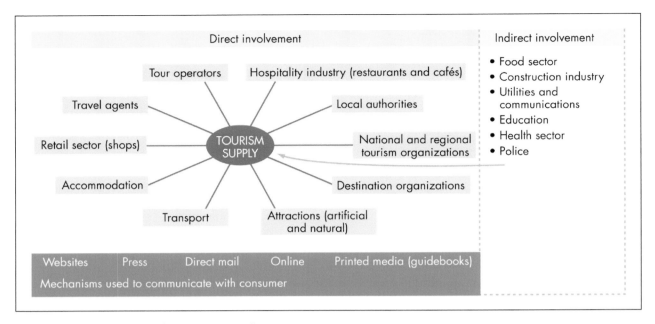

FIGURE 5.3 The supply of tourism – a production system

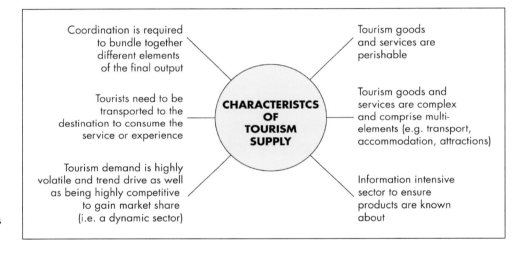

FIGURE 5.4 Characteristics of tourism supply

As a result of these characteristics, Zhang *et al.* (2009) identified a range of TSCM-related issues, as shown in Figure 5.5, which tourism managers need to be cognizant of. What Figure 5.5 shows is that for destinations to have sufficient capacity to accommodate seasonal increases in a visitor population, forecasting is crucial to the assessment of the management of demand. In terms of TSCM, Song (2012) argued that any supply chain will be characterized by relationships between suppliers and between suppliers and consumers, termed two-party relationships. These relationships may be created by a legally binding agreement and so relationship management is a key element of TSCM to ensure the relationships thrive, prosper and perform their intended outcome (i.e. through performance management examining financial, operational and overall performance). This is essentially supply management which can create collaboration and cooperation between supply chain partners to control inventory (i.e. hotel rooms and airline seats) to ensure the sale of available inventory. Likewise, this may also involve provision of additional inventory when demand peaks, to maximize profitable operations. As Vanhove (2011) argues, this requires supply chain partners to have a sound grasp of the lifecycle of a product, from its evolution and development, to growth and maturity. This indicates that as a dynamic changing sector, the life of a particular product or service needs to be understood along with the role of innovation and new product development. For supply chain partners to do this, and to understand the needs of customers, coordination of partners is crucial so that organizations work towards agreed goals and objectives. Information flow from customers to supply-chain businesses and between businesses (Business to Business, B2B) is vital to the coordination and product development. Therefore, as Figure 5.5 shows, tourism supply chains are complex, with fundamental linkages and relationships between the characteristics of tourism and TSCM. Against this background, it is pertinent to focus on the role of management and to demonstrate why it is crucial to the supply of tourism. In any assessment of the supply of tourism, there are a wide range of factors that can affect the operation notwithstanding the wider market conditions, and the supply chain is a critical element in the management and development of the tourism sector. In other words, the products and services that tourism businesses provide are a function of changing market conditions, and businesses need constantly to consider the market and adapt their business strategies to remain competitive. An interesting illustration of this is Figure 5.6, which shows the corporate strategy of a major low-cost airline in Europe (easyJet) which we will return to later in the chapter. For this reason, it is useful to examine the relationship between management, tourism supply issues and the way businesses adapt through their use of management strategies to achieve a competitive position in the marketplace.

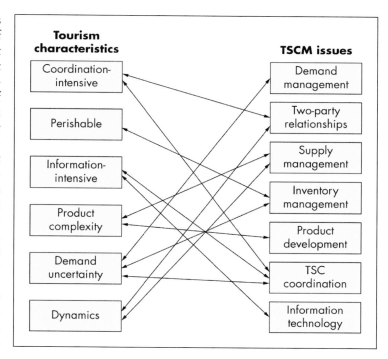

FIGURE 5.5 Tourism characteristics and TSCM issues

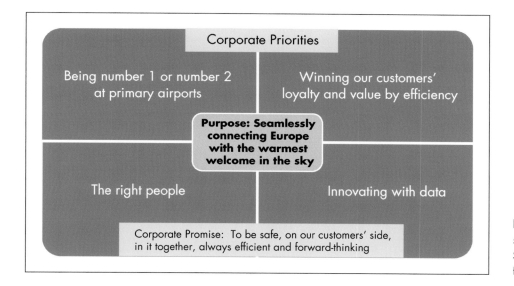

FIGURE 5.6 easyJet company strategy.
Source: Developed and adapted from easyjet.com

The management of tourism supply

Management normally occurs in the context of a formal environment – the organization. Within **organizations** (small businesses through to multinational enterprises), people are among the elements which are managed. As a result, Inkson and Kolb (1995: 6) define management as 'getting things done in organizations through other people'. In a business context, organizations exist as a complex interaction of people, goals and money to create and distribute the goods and services which people and other businesses consume or require.

Organizations in tourism are characterized by their ability to work towards a set of common objectives (e.g. the sale of holidays to tourists for a profit). To achieve their objectives, organizations are often organized into specialized groupings or departments to achieve particular functions (e.g. sales, human resources management, accounts and finance). In addition, a hierarchy usually exists where the organization is horizontally divided into different levels of authority and status, and a manager often occupies a position in a particular department or division at a specific point in the hierarchy. Within organizations, managers are grouped by level:

- *Chief executive officer* (CEO) or *general manager* at the top, who exercises responsibility over the entire organization and is accountable to a board of directors or other representatives for the ultimate performance of the organization.
- *Top managers* are one level down from the CEO and their role is usually confined to a specific function, such as marketing or sales. They may act as part of an executive team that works with other top managers and the CEO to provide advice on the relationship between different parts of the organization and contribute to corporate goals.
- *Middle managers* fill a niche in the middle of the hierarchy, with a more specialized role than the top managers. Typically they may head sections or divisions and be responsible for performance in their area. In recent years, corporate restructuring has removed a large number of middle managers to cut costs and placed more responsibility on top managers or the level below – first-line managers.
- *First-line managers* are the lowest level of manager in an organization, but arguably perform one of the most critical roles – the supervision of other staff who have non-managerial roles and who affect the day-to-day running of the organization (after Page 2005).

Yet the existence of different theories of management means that organizations may choose different structures to manage their businesses, as epitomized by the less hierarchical and team-based approach at Southwest Airlines, which is discussed further in Chapter 11 along with the concept of empowerment and new styles of management in the digital age.

Managers can also be classified according to the function they perform (i.e. the activity for which they are responsible). As a result, three types can be discerned:

- *Functional managers* manage specialized functions such as accounting, research, sales and personnel. These functions may also be split up even further where the organization is large and there is scope for greater specialization.
- *Business unit, divisional or area managers* exercise management responsibilities at a general level lower down in an organization. Their responsibilities may cover a group of products or diverse geographical areas and combine a range of management tasks, requiring the coordination of various functions.
- *Project managers* manage specific projects which are typically short-term undertakings, and may require a team of staff to complete them. This requires the coordination of a range of different functions within a set time frame (after Page 2005).

The goals of managers within organizations are usually seen as profit-driven, but as the following list suggests, they are more diverse and encompass:

- *Profitability*, which can be achieved through higher output, better service, attracting new customers and by cost minimization.
- In the public sector, other goals (e.g. *coordination, liaison, raising public awareness and undertaking activities for the wider public good*) dominate the agenda in organizations. Yet in many government departments in developed countries, private sector, profit-driven motives and greater accountability for the spending of public funds now feature high on the agenda and this has led to many public-sector tourism organizations, like national tourism organizations (NTOs), being restructured.
- *Efficiency*, to reduce expenditure and inputs to a minimum to achieve more cost-effective outputs.
- *Effectiveness*, achieving the desired outcome; this is not necessarily a profit-driven motive.

Managers are therefore necessary to implement the management process and there are four commonly agreed sets of tasks. McLennan *et al.* (1987) describe these as:

- *Planning*, so that goals are set out and the means of achieving the goals are recognized.
- *Organizing*, whereby the work functions are broken down into a series of tasks and linked to some form of structure. These tasks then have to be assigned to individuals.

- *Leading*, which is the method of motivating and influencing staff so that they perform their tasks effectively. This is essential if organizational goals are to be achieved. Leadership is a critical role in the success of any enterprise, but has been attributed to the success of key low-cost airlines such as Southwest Airlines, Ryanair and Air Asia.
- *Controlling*, which is the method by which information is gathered about what has to be done.

Managing requires one to gather and analyze information on the stated organizational goals and, if necessary, take action to correct any deviations from those overall goals.

Above all the management process is associated with the need for managers to make decisions, which is an ongoing process. In terms of the levels of management, CEOs make major decisions which can affect everyone in the organization, whereas junior managers often have to make many routine and mundane decisions on a daily basis but may be interacting directly with tourists. In each case, decisions made have consequences for the organization. To make decisions, managers often have to balance the ability to use technical skills within their own particular area with the need to relate to people and to use 'human skills' to interact and manage people within the organization and clients, suppliers and other people external to the organization. Managers need these skills to communicate effectively to motivate and lead others. They also need cognitive and conceptual skills. Cognitive skills are those which enable managers to formulate solutions to problems. In contrast, conceptual skills are those which allow them to take a broader view, often characterized as 'being able to see the wood for the trees': the manager can understand the organization's activities, the interrelationships and goals and can develop an appropriate strategic response (Inkson and Kolb 1995).

In recent years, there has been a growing recognition that to perform a managerial task successfully, a range of competencies are needed. A 'competency', according to Inkson and Kolb (1995: 32) is 'an underlying trait of an individual – for example a motive pattern, a skill, a characteristic behaviour, a value, or a set of knowledge – which enables that person to perform successfully in his or her job'. The main motivation for organizational interest in competency is the desire to improve management through education and training. Competencies can be divided into three groups (Page *et al.* 1994: 25) with some of the required competencies (in brackets):

- understanding what needs to be done (i.e. critical reasoning, strategic vision and business know-how)
- getting the job done (i.e. confidence, being proactive, control, flexibility, effectiveness)
- taking people with you (i.e. motivation, interpersonal skills, persuasion and influence).

One of the key skills here is the strategic ability of a tourism business to compete in the marketplace, and its ability to change to new conditions and the business strategies it adopts.

Tourism business strategies and supply issues

According to Evans *et al.* (2003: 9), strategy is one of the most important factors which determines the success or failure of tourism businesses in both the public and private sectors. They point to the use of the term 'strategy' by management theorists such as Mintzberg (1988), who identified that it may constitute:

- a pattern of behaviour
- a position in relation to someone else or a perspective
- a plan
- a ploy.

This involves a range of strategic elements including identifying long-term objectives. In particular, this requires different courses of action – strategic alternatives to be recognized and planned for at different levels within the organization, from the strategic level of the CEO or board through to the tactical level of middle managers or at the operational level of customer delivery. This very hierarchical approach does not, however, account for the success of strategic approaches by airlines such as Southwest, where the policy of empowering staff to work as teams and to work towards set corporate objectives around the company vision of the CEO has raised questions about many of the established approaches to managing organizations (see Chapter 11 for more detail).

Shaw and Williams (2004) discuss the strategic reactions of tourism companies to competition in the marketplace. Intermodal competition, for example, is a key element of transport (except in cases of monopoly provision, or where there is one mode of transport such as a ferry to cross between two islands and no air access). Chamberlin (1933) observed that where different companies provide similar products, consumers will prefer one supplier to another, indicating the importance of differentiation between suppliers. Shaw and Williams (2004) show that where contestable markets exist, as in the airline sector in the USA, different strategies may result. Evans *et al.* (2003) point to the influential work of the strategic management theorist Porter (1980, 1985) (see also Chapter 14) in setting out the strategic reactions in maintaining a competitive advantage, which could involve:

- differentiation (i.e. making your product look different and more attractive to the competitor)
- cost leadership
- the use of either approach to set out a narrow focus on the market such as one segment.

Mintzberg (1988) suggested that companies may adopt different approaches to product and service differentiation based upon issues such as quality, design, support, image and price. Shaw and Williams (2004) indicate that the most common response to competition is cost competition (i.e. reducing the price), which will require reducing the cost of production, typically labour inputs, although other options exist such as developing strategic alliances or takeovers. For example, Claver-Cortés *et al.* (2007) show how entire destinations can adopt new development strategies to address competition and declining market share. This may involve reorganizing the type of product offered by making service quality improvements, repositioning (i.e. rethinking the image of the destination) to shift from low-spending tourists to appealing to higher-spending special interest-tourists. Other measures which can be used include collaboration and adapting to the needs of visitors. Benidorm in Spain has repositioned its market position towards higher-spending visitors and diversified its product base, exploiting local assets to develop business tourism, conference tourism and domestic short breaks. This was in response to a stagnation in the volume of visitors at around 10.5 million a year. Knowles *et al.* (2004) highlight the various growth strategies and competitive models that tourism organizations use to gain competitive advantage, as shown in Table 5.1. These strategies are often combined in the most successful companies through innovation to maintain a competitive edge, as Insight 5.1 on easyJet shows.

Given the nature of competition in the tourism sector, especially in the transport sector, one response among some airlines has been the development of strategic alliances. Evans (2001) highlights a range of motives, objectives and different outcomes. Evans summarized the strategic process by which airlines entered into collaborative arrangements in terms of:

- *internal drivers* (i.e. risk sharing, economies of scope and scale, accessing assets such as limited slots at airports and shaping the competition), and
- *external drivers* (i.e. the changes induced by information technology and turbulent economic climates, rapid product and market changes as well as global competition).

Although some alliances and **collaborations** are successful, they can be very unstable and subject to what is called 'churn' (i.e. partners enter and leave as business needs and objectives change). This highlights what Evans *et al.*

TABLE 5.1 Growth strategies and competitive methods

Growth strategies	Competitive methods
Joint ventures	Technology-based systems
Franchising	Brand development
Strategic alliances	Product quality
Management contracts	Sophisticated pricing
Conversions	Global marketing and advertising
Sale and leaseback	
Acquisition of small firms	

Source: Knowles *et al.* (2004: 162)

(2003) point to as 'strategic fit', the need for partnerships to be workable as well as able to offer compatibility, commitment and a sense of partnership.

In the airline sector, research has distinguished between the following:

- *Tactical partnerships*, comprising a loose form of collaboration designed to derive marketing benefits, characterized by code sharing among cooperating partners. This is reflected in the smaller feeder and regional airlines being aligned with key hub-based carriers.

- *Strategic partnerships*, where an investment or pooling of resources by partners aims to achieve a range of common objectives focused on the partners' strategic ambitions.

INSIGHT 5.1 easyJet's growth as a tourist supply firm – a major success story of growth and competition

easyJet is one of the great success stories of tourism in the late 1990s and new millennium, from its humble origins in 1995 to its dominance of the low-cost market in Europe, where it is one of Europe's largest online retailers. Its massive growth is shown in Figure 5.7, which is based on passengers carried, and its success is not dissimilar to that of other low-cost rivals such as Ryanair. For example, Ryanair summarized a typical day in the company's airline operations as including:

- 1.5 million visits to its website (Ryanair.com, accessed September 2019)
- 382 605 km flown by its fleet
- Over 400 Boeing 737s in flight, travelling to 200 destinations, serving 215 airports.

Yet, as the marketplace shows, numerous low-cost rivals in the USA and Europe failed due to a lack of good management skills, strategic vision and a rigid concern for costs and consumer service. A number of notable failures exist among large carriers who responded to competition on full-service routes by developing low-cost offshoots (e.g. British Airways' Go and United Airlines' Shuttle). Many of the principles of success in the case of easyJet can be attributed to its visionary founder – Stelios Haji-Ioannou, whose family provided much of the start-up capital.

easyJet attributes its success to using the Internet to reduce distribution costs, maximizing the use of its assets to reduce the unit cost of travel, ticketless travel, eliminating free catering on-board and the efficient use of airports as well as embracing the paperless office concept. Figure 5.8 illustrates how it explains its operational advantages. In the low-cost airline business, success really hinges upon cost control of operations, as shown in Table 5.2, which illustrates its appeal to consumers. One of easyJet's real selling points for consumers is the low cost. Profit margins on operations are slim, with the 2011 financial results showing that it achieved profitable operations with an 87.3 per cent load

factor generating £55.27 for each seat sold against costs of £51.30 per seat. By 2018 the position had improved to a load factor of 92.2 per cent for its operations at 156 airports in 33 countries and 979 routes. Its overall profit per seat in 2018 was £6.07, and the company had revenue per seat of £61.94 and a total of £5898 million in revenue. It also acquired one of its competitors – Air Berlin in 2018 from Tegel at a cost of €40 million, and in 2019 the company was expected to spend £1 billion on capital expenditure. One of its principal competitive advantages, following the global trend towards low-cost airline operations based on the model of the highly successful US airline Southwest, is the way in which it has harnessed the use of technology.

As Page (2019) shows, the main advantages which easyJet along with other low-cost airlines have derived relate to the development of much simpler products that consumers can understand and purchase without lots of caveats and restrictions. There is a one-class service and simple pricing of each flight segment. In supply terms, the creation of a simple mechanism by which to distribute the

IMAGE 5.2 easyJet continues to add new destinations every year and is a market leader

INSIGHT 5.1 continued

product has led to the establishment of both call centres and incentivized Internet sales, with a discount over and above the call centre price. easyJet now receives over 93 per cent of its bookings from the Internet. It has also made extensive use of incentivized newspaper promotions along with very aggressive media campaigns. This has led to a strong brand proposition, where the company's orange livery is also very prominent on the Internet even with partnered products.

Behind the scenes, the basic principles of financial success with its passenger profitability relate to the use of yield management systems where seats are priced at different rates according to popularity of departure times and cost.

In some cases, new routes are given an impetus by very low prices to establish a market demand in situations where this may not have existed before, since some relatively unknown secondary airports may be used, with low landing and service costs. In 2010, the company also introduced flexible fares aimed at business travellers to further refine its market position.

In information technology terms, easyJet has also created what are termed **complementary services**, by offering additional services on their websites using independent suppliers and adding value to the purchasing experience, in many cases replacing the role of the travel agent. This is known in the trade as dynamic packaging,

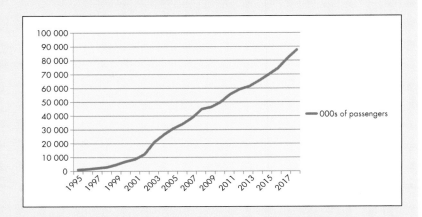

FIGURE 5.7 Growth in easyJet passenger numbers 1995–2018 (including Tegel operations from September 2018)
Source: easyJet (http://www.easyjet.com)

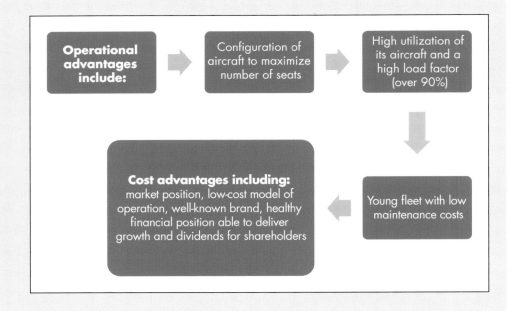

FIGURE 5.8 Summary of easyJet's operational advantages
Source: Developed from easyjet.com

so that consumers can buy the total travel experience online rather than having to search various sources for products.

Further reading

Cattaneo, M., Malighetti, P., Redondi, R. and Salanti, A. (2018) 'Changes in frequencies and price variations on point-to-point routes: The case of easyJet', *Transportation Research Part A: Policy and Practice* 112: 60–70.

Dobruszkes, F. and Wang, J. (2019) 'Developing a low-cost airline in a semi-protected regime: Comparing China to Europe and the US', *Journal of Transport Geography* 77: 48–58.

easyJet PLC (2019) '2019 full year results', *easyJet PLC* website. http://corporate.easyjet.com/investors/results-centre.

Morlotti, C., Cattaneo, M., Malighetti, P. and Redondi, R. (2017) 'Multi-dimensional price elasticity for leisure and business destinations in the low-cost air transport market: Evidence from easyJet', *Tourism Management* 61: 23–34.

Questions

1 How would you explain the popularity of low-cost airlines like easyJet?
2 How has easyJet diversified its business offer to broaden its consumer base?
3 What are the key characteristics of flying with a low-cost airline like easyJet?
4 What is the long-term future for low-cost air travel?

French (1997) by contrast, outlined the principal features which may be included in strategic alliances developed by airlines, including equity stakes, code sharing, joint services, block-seat booking or joint booking arrangements, joint marketing, joint fares, franchise agreements, wet-leasing (where one airline company hires the aircraft and crew

---

TABLE 5.2 Key characteristics of low-cost carriers which make them more competitive than other carriers

- Single/one-way fares replacing former advanced purchase (APEX) prices
- No complimentary in-flight service (no frills) to reduce operating costs 6–7 per cent
- One-class cabins (in most cases)
- No pre-assigned seating (in most cases)
- Ticketless travel
- High-frequency routes to compete with other airlines to popular destinations
- Short turnarounds, often in less than half an hour
- Higher aircraft rotations (i.e. the level of utilization is higher than other airlines)
- Less time charged on the airport apron and runway
- The use of secondary airports
- Point-to-point flights
- Lower staffing costs (i.e. fewer cabin crew)
- Flexibility in staff rostering, a lack of overnight stays for staff at non-base location
- Streamlined operations (e.g. on some airlines, toilets on domestic flights are only emptied at cabin crew request, to reduce costs)
- Many of the aircraft are leased, reducing the level of depreciation and standardizing costs
- Many airline functions are outsourced, such as ground staff and check-in, minimizing overheads and reducing overhead costs by 11–15 per cent
- Standardized aircraft types are used to reduce maintenance costs
- Limited office space at the airports
- Heavy emphasis on advertising, especially billboards, to offset the declining use of travel agents
- Heavy dependence upon the Internet and telephone for bookings
- Small administrative staff, with many sales-related staff on commission to improve performance

Source: Adapted from Page (2011)

to another company) and frequent-flyer programmes. In studies of strategic alliances, it is apparent that some of the competitive reasons for adopting this business strategy include:

- gaining economies of scale to improve profitability and to gain from economies of scope (i.e. one purchasing cost for the alliance members)
- accessing other airlines' assets
- reducing risk by sharing it, given the highly volatile nature of the tourism business environment
- helping share the market, which may help reduce incapacity in mature markets and could reduce competition
- achieving a high degree of adaptability to the industry (e.g. deregulation and privatization), to stay ahead of the competition.

One other strategy actively pursued by most global and, to a lesser degree, small- and medium-scale enterprises is to control costs.

Cost control has become a key priority for many tourism organizations following the credit crunch in late 2008 and the associated concerns over recession in the global economy. One immediate response among many transport companies, especially airlines, has been to reduce capacity in response to a drop in demand. For example, charter airlines, low-cost carriers and scheduled airlines have cut back their winter timetables and grounded aircraft to cut costs as opposed to flying aircraft partially full and incurring large operating losses on every flight. In the USA, this has been accompanied by difficult trading conditions: the industry announced the first year of profitability in 2007 after consecutive years of losses since the 9/11 attacks in 2001. In the case of JetBlue in the USA, after a year of losses in 2005, it pursued a cost-saving strategy to reduce losses and bring it back into profitability. This involved wide-ranging cost savings including removing seats from its Airbus A320 fleet so that it carried fewer passengers, under the threshold necessary to have three cabin crew. This resulted in reduced fuel costs, despite lost revenue from fewer seats, which was more than compensated for by reduced staff costs. What this strategy demonstrates is a good understanding of the factors outlined in Figure 5.9 in a study by Seristö and Vepsäläinen (1997). Their study also developed a more complex model (Figure 5.10) to show how costs for airlines were dominated by the composition of a fleet, personnel issues, its route network and the composition of traffic, route structure and staff remuneration. As a result, the study highlighted areas for cost savings which many airlines now regularly review to improve profitability.

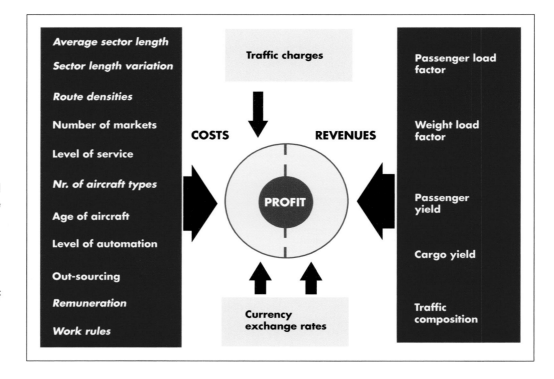

FIGURE 5.9 Cost and revenue factors in airline operations
Source: Reproduced with permission from Elsevier in Seristö, H. and Vepsäläinen, A.P.J. (1997) 'Airline cost drivers: Cost implications of fleet, routes, and personnel policies', *Journal of Air Transport Management* 3 (1): 12.

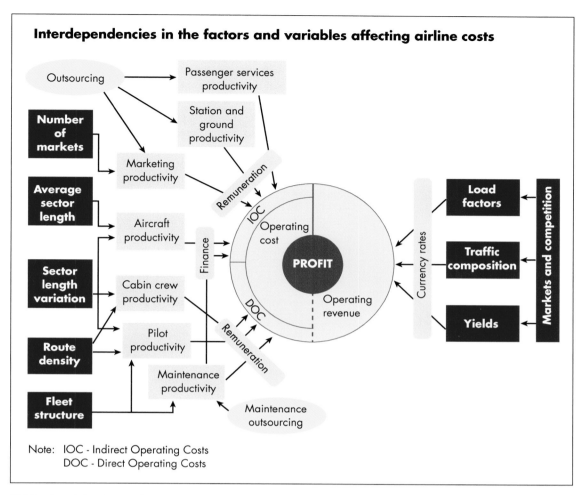

FIGURE 5.10 Comprehensive interdependence model

Source: Reproduced with permission from Elsevier in Seristö, H. and Vepsäläinen, A.P.J. (1997) 'Airline cost drivers: Cost implications of fleet, routes, and personnel policies', *Journal of Air Transport Management*, 3 (1): 19.

Conclusion

Tourism supply issues illustrate that the tourism sector operates in a dynamic business environment which is subject to constant change in both the tastes and trends which tourists pursue (i.e. consumption) and the regulatory environment in which tourism operates. The business environment is always in a state of constant flux, and effective, responsive and strategic management is vital for both the private and public sector if tourism is to remain competitive and consumer-focused in the global marketplace. The management strategy must combine ways of reducing costs with pursuing growth strategies. One also has to have a clear understanding of what the competition is doing.

It is evident that attempts to conceptualize and develop frameworks and models of tourism supply have been limited within tourism studies, and largely descriptive

sector-by-sector studies have prevailed. But the concepts of TNCs and TSCM help to overcome these weaknesses. As a result, the consumption of tourism services and goods are often emphasized by researchers to the neglect of the production of tourism goods and the complexity involved in decisions made by businesses in this context. What one often overlooks is that although tourism is a dynamic business activity based upon discretionary spending, especially within specific tourism businesses, it is the constraints upon production which inhibit a situation of perfect competition. The retailing of tourism goods and services is highly competitive in most countries where the formulation of tourism products based upon different elements (e.g. accommodation, transport and attractions) is increasingly subject to a greater degree of control by regulatory bodies. The increased

5

competition is also manifest in the pressure which multinationals and large national corporations are placing on the existing suppliers of tourism services due to the financial leverage and control which they exert through increased concentration of their activities, particularly through integration in the tourism sector. At the same time, tourism businesses are being forced to re-examine their traditional methods of production because of reduced profit margins and competition from new entrants using technology such as the Internet. Although the tourism sector has a chequered history of adopting technology successfully to improve business processes, the Internet is helping businesses to communicate with customers and to perform business processes more efficiently, as well as to communicate directly with new growth sectors such as the over-50 age group (the 'silver surfers'). For this reason, the next chapter examines the role of technology and the e-tourism revolution and the impact on tourism supply for consumer choice and competition.

Discussion questions

1 Why is an understanding of tourism supply fundamental to the analysis of how the tourism sector is organized and operates?

2 How do transnational tourism companies impact upon the organization and management of tourism?

3 What are the principal features of management relevant to the supply of tourism?

4 What types of business strategy have airlines pursued to address competition?

References

Bull, A. (1991) *The Economics of Travel and Tourism*. Melbourne: Pitman.

Chamberlin, E. (1933) *The Theory of Monopolistic Competition*. Cambridge, MA: Harvard University Press.

Claver-Cortez, E., Molina-Azorín, J. and Pereira-Moliner, J. (2007) 'Competitiveness in mass tourism', *Annals of Tourism Research*, 34 (3): 727–745.

COSLA (2002) *Review of the Area Tourist Boards*. Edinburgh: COSLA.

Evans, N. (2001) 'Collaborative strategy: An analysis of the changing world of international airline alliances', *Tourism Management* 22: 229–243.

Evans, N., Campbell, D. and Stonehouse, G. (2003) *Strategic Management for Travel and Tourism*. Oxford: Butterworth-Heinemann.

French, T. (1997) 'Global trends in airline alliances', *Travel and Tourism Analyst* 4: 81–101.

Hall, C.M. and Page, S.J. (1996) 'Australia and New Zealand's role in Pacific tourism: Aid, trade and travel', in C.M. Hall and S.J. Page (eds.) *Tourism in the Pacific: Issues and Cases*. London: International Thomson Business Press.

Hall, C.M. and Page, S.J. (2002) *The Geography of Tourism and Recreation: Environment, Place and Space*, 2nd edition. London: Routledge.

Inkson, K. and Kolb, D. (1995) *Management: A New Zealand Perspective*. Auckland: Longman Paul.

Knowles, T., Diamantis, D. and El-Mourhabi, J. (2004) *The Globalisation of Tourism and Hospitality: A Strategic Perspective*. London: Thomson.

Lumsdon, L. (1997) *Tourism Marketing*. London: Thomson.

March, R. and Wilkinson, I. (2009) 'Conceptual tools for evaluating tourism partnerships', *Tourism Management*, 30 (3): 455–462.

McClennan, R., Inkson, K., Dakin, S., Dewe, P. and Elkin, G. (1987) *People and Enterprises: Human Behaviour in New Zealand Organisations*. Auckland: Rinehart and Winston.

Meethan, K. (2004) 'Transnational corporations, globalisation and tourism', in A. Lew, C.M. Hall and A. Williams (eds.) *A Companion of Tourism*. Oxford: Blackwell.

Mintzberg, H. (1988) 'Generic strategies: Towards a comprehensive framework', *Advances in Strategic Management* 5: 1–67.

Page, S.J. (2003) *Tourism Management: Managing for Change*. Oxford: Butterworth.

Page, S.J. (2005) *Transport and Tourism*, 2nd edition. Harlow: Pearson.

Page, S.J. (2011) *Tourism Management: An Introduction*, 4th edition. Oxford: Elsevier.

Page, S.J. (2019) *Tourism Management*, 6th edition. London: Routledge.

Page, C., Wilson, M. and Kolb, D. (1994) *On the Inside Looking In: Management Competencies in New Zealand*. Wellington: Ministry of Commerce.

Porter, M. (1980) *Competitive Strategy: Techniques for Analysing Industries and Competitors*. New York: The Free Press.

Porter, M. (1985) *Competitive Advantage: Creating and Sustaining Superior Performance*. New York: The Free Press.

Schwartz, K., Tapper, R. and Font, X. (2008) 'A sustainable supply chain management framework for tour operators', *Journal of Sustainable Tourism* 16 (3): 298–314.

Seristö, H. and Vepsäläinen, A. (1997) 'Airline cost drivers: Cost implications of fleet, routes, and personnel policies', *Journal of Air Transport Management* 3 (1): 11–22.

Sessa, A. (1983) *Elements of Tourism*. Rome: Cantal.

Shaw, G. and Williams, A. (1994) *Critical Issues in Tourism: A Geographical Perspective*, 1st edition. Oxford: Blackwell.

Shaw, G. and Williams, A. (2004) *Tourism and Tourism Spaces*. London: Sage.

Sinclair, M.T. and Stabler, M. (eds.) (1992) *The Tourism Industry: An International Analysis*. Wallingford, Oxon: CAB International.

Sinclair, M.T. and Stabler, M. (1997) *Economics of Tourism*. London: Routledge.

Song, H. (2012) *Tourism Supply Chain Management*. London: Routledge.

Tapper, R. and Font, X. (2004) *Tourism Supply Chains, Report of a Desk Research Project for the Travel Foundation*. Leeds: Leeds Metropolitan University.

Vanhove, N. (2011) *The Economics of Tourism*. Oxford: Elsevier.

Williams, A. (1995) 'Capital and the transnationalism of tourism', in A. Montanari and A. Williams (eds.) *European Tourism: Regions, Spaces and Restructuring*. Chichester: Wiley.

Zhang, X., Song, H. and Huang, G. (2009) 'Tourism supply chain management: A new research agenda', *Tourism Management* 30 (3): 354–358.

Further reading

Books

Song, H. (2012) *Tourism Supply Chain Management*. London: Routledge.

Stabler, M., Papatheodorou, A. and Sinclair, M.T. (2009) *The Economics of Tourism*. London: Routledge.

Journal articles

Huang, Y., Song, H., Huang, G.Q. and Lou, J. (2012) 'A comparative study of tourism supply chains with quantity competition', *Journal of Travel Research* 51 (6): 717–729.

Richards, P. and Font, X. (2019) 'Sustainability in the tour operator–ground agent supply chain', *Journal of Sustainable Tourism* 27 (3): 277–291.

Schwartz, K.C., Tapper, R. and Font, X. (2008) 'A sustainable supply chain management framework for tour operators', *Journal of Sustainable Tourism* 16 (3): 298–314.

Sigala, M. (2008) 'A supply chain management approach for investigating the role of tour operators on sustainable tourism: The case of TUI', *Journal of Cleaner Production* 16 (15): 1589–1599.

Smith, S.L.J. and Xiao, H. (2008) 'Culinary tourism supply chains: A preliminary examination', *Journal of Travel Research* 46 (3): 289–299.

Véronneau, S. and Roy, J. (2009) 'Global service supply chains: An empirical study of current practices and challenges of a cruise line corporation', *Tourism Management* 30 (1): 128–139.

Technology and tourism:
Themes, concepts and issues

Marianna Sigala, University of South Australia

Learning outcomes

After reading this chapter and answering the questions, you should be able to:

- understand the scope of information technology and its impact on the tourism sector
- distinguish between a computer reservation system and a global distribution system
- understand the scope of the Internet, the e-travel revolution and the role of travel services now provided online
- identify the changes which technology are bringing to the future of tourism industry and services.

Overview

This chapter examines the interface between tourism and information technology. It introduces the concept of information technology, one of the major drivers of change within the tourism sector, and describes its impact on the industry. Technology has revolutionized the pace, scale and nature of business processes in the tourism industry, changing the parameters and scale of business operation as well as the structure of the industry. It is now possible for small businesses to operate globally through the use of technology (e.g. website, email and Web-based booking). Technology has also transformed the nature of tourism supply, questioning the role of intermediaries (see Chapter 7) and allowing the consumer greater autonomy, choice and empowerment in deciding what tourism products to purchase, consume, promote and/or co-produce.

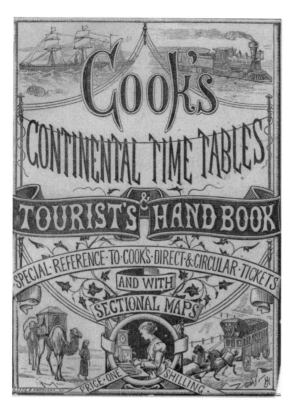

IMAGE 6.1 This image of the first *Thomas Cook Compendium of Railway and Steamship Timetables* in 1873 illustrates the importance of information for tourists in planning their travel. Despite the advances in technology making information more accessible on mobile devices, this guide was still being produced in a hard copy over 140 years after its first publication, albeit by a different company since 2014. Up until 1963, its main competitor was the Bradshaw railway guide, popularized in television series like *Great Railway Journeys*.
Source: ©Thomas Cook

Introduction

IT is defined by Poon (1993) as 'the collective term given to the most recent developments in the mode (electronic) and the mechanisms (computers and communications technologies) used for the acquisition, processing, analysis, storage, retrieval, dissemination and application of information'. It is a subject embedded throughout the book as technology has changed many aspects of the way tourism operates as a business, and the way in which the demand for tourism experiences has created a need to disseminate multimedia information from tourism suppliers to potential visitors (Image 6.1).

IT aids the identification, selection, booking and payment as well as the after-sale evaluation of tourism goods. IT also empowers tourists to become co-designers, co-marketers and / or even co-producers of their tourism experiences (e.g. tourists sharing their travel experiences and reviews online, tourists exchanging and buying tourism services on peer-to-peer platforms). As information is the lifeblood of tourism, Information and Communication Technologies (ICTs) are the backbone of the tourism industry. Tourists need to use ICT to support their trip planning processes, for example for searching and booking tourism services, receiving and paying for travel, and sharing tourism experiences and reviews. Currently the number of tourists who design and buy personalized packages online (known as dynamic packaging) exceeds the number who buy static premade packages developed by tour operators. In addition, annual accommodation bookings on Airbnb have surpassed the number of bookings made by the largest hotel chain (Cheng and Edwards 2019). This means that tourism operators have had to redefine their business models and mode of operation to exploit the business opportunities as well as the threats resulting from ICTs, as emphasized in Chapter 1 in relation to disruptive technologies. This chapter examines the major applications and impacts of ICTs, especially the impact of the Internet on tourism demand and supply, focusing on the use of ICTs at both a micro- and macro-level by illustrating their impact on tourism suppliers and Destination Management Organizations (DMOs) (see Chapters 14 and 15 for more detail on DMOs). Factors influencing the adoption and use of ICTs are considered in this chapter in order to distinguish ways of enhancing ICT exploitation by the tourism industry. As Sigala (2018: 151) suggests, 'technologies are also a transformational driver of the industry structure and operations as well as the role and functions of its stakeholders'. Technological advances are causing fundamental disruptions in tourism by empowering (traditional but also new) tourism actors to form new markets, offerings, management practices and competitive strategies. These new technologies are democratizing the management of the relationships between suppliers and consumers. In the early stages of the introduction of tourism technologies, their use was relatively static and utilitarian (where managers and tourists used technologies as tools for specific functions such as booking or to capture information), later moving to a transformative role where tourism markets and actors (tourism providers, stakeholders, intermediaries and tourists) both shape and are shaped by technology. In other words, the relationships are interactive and interconnected as well as mutually dependent. Sigala (2018: 151) indicates that this has meant that the new technologies have evolved to:

- simultaneously disrupt and transform tourism actors (i.e. businesses and consumers)
- affect the way these actors interact to (co-)create and (co-)destruct tourism value
- transform the context in which tourism actors traditionally interacted from a tourism 'industry' and linear supply and distribution chain approach to a complex socio-technical smart tourism ecosystem perspective (see Figure 6.1 and Table 6.1).

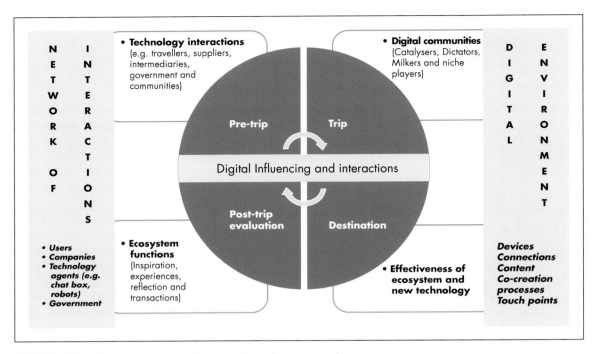

FIGURE 6.1 Digital ecosystem characteristics, functions and actors

TABLE 6.1 Smart tourism and big data

- Smart tourism is 'an ability to exploit operational, near-real-time real-world data, integrate and share data, and use complex analytics, modelling, optimisation and visualisation to make better decisions' (Benckendorff et al. 2019: 294). Smart tourism is being fuelled by smart devices and technologies connecting tourism actors and enabling them to exchange resources as well as by big data representing the 'oil' of the new digital economy (Sigala et al. 2019a). Big data is also seen as a key output from these various digital interactions in the ecosystem, which creates 'huge datasets that an organisation can mine for information' (Benckendorf et al. 2019: 15), related to the digital interactions, transactions and activities that occur in the ecosystem.

- Smart tourism comprises three areas of activity:

  - *Smart experiences*, e.g. how technology is used to: enhance the tourist experience such as personalization and real-time information (e.g. the exact time a bus will arrive at a specific stop, where the bus has a tracking device, typically a Global Positioning System (GPS) that has a sensor for identifying and tracking the bus location in real time); and to support tourists to manage their whole tourism journey (before, during and after the trip) in a seamless way (e.g. identify tourism experiences to consume, book, pay and reflect-share on tourism experiences)

  - *Smart destinations* where the ICT infrastructure is harnessed to manage tourism-carrying capacity and resources in an optimal and sustainable way that enhances the tourists but also the residents' satisfaction and well-being

  - *Smart business ecosystems* where the range of businesses involved in the ecosystem deliver and exchange the digital resources to enable the tourist to consume and co-create or co-destruct their tourism experience.

- Technology advances (sensors, social media, Web-based tools) generate data in high volumes (large-scale data), at high velocity (high-speed real-time data), in wide variety (data variability in the form of e.g. soft and hard data, text-based data and numerical data), and with a high level of veracity (multiple interpretations and a lot of 'noise', e.g. big-data quality and reliability). To that end, big data is traditionally described in terms of Vs: volume, variety, velocity, validity, veracity, value, visibility, visualization, and virility in spreading (Sigala et al. 2019b).

- Big data enable new business models (i.e. Uber becoming a supplier of critical data about people's mobility patterns to urban developers) and foster innovation (e.g. what products people prefer) as well as empowering real-time decision-making and performance improvement (e.g. location of rented cycles and the need to inform the logistics team to relocate the cycles to where the demand exists).

TABLE 6.1 continued

- Big data as a concept has meant that the marketing and strategic planning for meeting consumer needs can now be undertaken with a large pool of data collected from devices and digital channels from the personal activities of individuals. While this area of research has proved very controversial due to the privacy of personal information and the growing digital footprint of tourists as travellers, it has generated a new research agenda around big data (Sigala *et al.* 2019a).
- According to Li *et al.* (2018), big data has arisen from three sources: users (e.g. user-generated content such as online reviews), devices (i.e. GPS data) and operations (e.g. transaction data from online books and Web views). This has been stimulated by the use of the Internet, devices and social media and the growing importance of the Internet of Things (which is the use of the Internet to connect with everyday things we use such as televisions) alongside the growth in sensor-based data associated with the tracking of tourists' movements and activities using Bluetooth, GPS data and mobile roaming data.
- As Sigala (2018: 152) concludes, 'connected smart actors create and operate within a smart socio-technical tourism ecosystem whereby they interact and exchange resources (e.g. information, computing power, skills, know how, software, cloud-based services) with the aim to achieve three major goals: [to] *optimise use of resources* (e.g. space, energy, carrying capacity); *enhance and enrich tourists' experiences and residents' quality of life*; and *empower tourism suppliers to take smart data-driven decisions'*.

Figure 6.1 shows that, as Benckendorff *et al.* (2019) argue, a digital ecosystem is a living entity with a range of components and features; these include its network of interactions made up of its users, companies and governments, all of whom shape the technology interactions in parallel with the digital environment. A range of ecosystem functions, technology interactions and networks/subnetworks of online communities shape the ecosystem. These include a range of digital communities, for example *catalysers* (i.e. DMOs), who seek to shape their interests, such as the destination and visitor experience delivered by various stakeholders. Another group, the *dictators*, seeks to control one element such as the Destination Management System; *milkers* seek to utilize the supply elements such as online travel agents, while other niche groups like Airbnb see opportunities for disruptive activities to create their own niche (Benckendorff *et al.* 2019).

What this means is that 'complex tourism ecosystems that enable and support various forms of interactions and collaborations among a variety of actors are now possible using ICTs (e.g. firm-to-firm, known as business-to-business;

TABLE 6.2 The functions of technology in tourism

Technology as a:

- **means of 'individual' expression** (e.g. tourism brands communicating and forming their image, tourists sharing experiences and information to self-construct their social image and identity)
- **decision-support tool for firms** (e.g. logistics and pricing tool) **and tourists** (price-comparison tools, meta-search engines, recommender systems)
- **market intelligence source**: for collecting, storing, analyzing, sharing, visualizing and interpreting big data (characterized by volume, variety, velocity, veracity and value)
- **e-learning tool**: transforming education and knowledge management from an instruction-led and self-service-paced learning mode to collaborative, constructivism, dialectic and open connectivism learning models (e.g. MOOCs which are modes of study offered over the Internet for free)
- **automation tool, substituting labour and 'predictable' programmable tasks** (e.g. self-driven cars): augmenting labour by creating information to optimize decision-making processes and outputs
- **game changer**: enabling new business models (e.g. cyber-intermediaries, multi-sided markets, sharing economy) and new management practices (open innovation, crowdsourcing, crowdfunding, gamification)
- **a transformer of tourism experiences** (e.g. virtual tours, technology-mediated or -augmented tourism experiences)
- **co-creation platform** (e.g. review websites, wiki-based tourism guides, peer-to-peer marketplaces): empowering and providing the space, functionality and connectivity to all tourism actors to actively engage and participate in value co-creation

Source: Based on Sigala (2018: 152)

customer-to-firm; machine-to-customer; or machine-to-machine interactions). The most notable disruptive influence of these new technologies, as highlighted in Chapter 1, has been the peer-to-peer market that is at the heart of the sharing economy, disrupting all traditional tourism sectors (e.g. accommodation, transportation, social dining, guiding and tour operations and travel intermediaries) (Sigala 2018). The most notable transformation is the rise of an asset-light/zero-fixed-costs economy, epitomized by Airbnb, which is arguably the largest global hotel chain that owns none of its rooms. Similarly, Uber is the world's largest taxi company that owns none of its own vehicles. In other words, technology has expanded the range and scope of the functions now possible in the tourism supply chain and beyond, as shown in Table 6.2, providing niches for new forms of economic activity such as the sharing economy.

Consequently, technology is creating advances and tools that are driving tourism change including: machine learning, artificial intelligence, an industrial web, big data, the Internet of Things, smart devices, robots, drones, sensors, beacons, virtual and augmented reality, near-field communications, ubiquitous computing and many other examples as new technology evolves, which we will examine later in the chapter. However, the chapter starts by identifying the capabilities of ICTs and the way in which they are transforming business practices and strategies.

ICT capabilities and their role in tourism organizations

ICTs include a continuously increasing number of tools enabling the capture, processing, storage, dissemination and use of information, such as computers, tablets, the Internet, smartphones, management information systems (MIS), Radio Frequency Identification (RFID), Bluetooth and wireless networks. ICTs have expanded our ability to manipulate data by enabling the simultaneous analysis of a huge amount of data to produce structured information and visual tools so that we can use the information to extract knowledge and take decisions. ICTs also enable the storing of an unlimited amount of information which can be accessed, searched, and retrieved or updated quickly and easily. Therefore, information in electronic databases is available for automating business operations. Communication links and networks offer the third most significant contribution of ICT. This new, combined functionality is characterized by the speed of distribution of networked databases that enhances the capabilities for networking, cooperation and coordination within, but also beyond, the organizational and functional borders, as well as geographical limits of individual organizations. This communication functionality of ICTs has facilitated a great number of changes including the centralization of activities and the increase in both the quality and range of knowledge held by staff who have become flexible and multi-skilled, which has redefined organizations and their business models (Buhalis and Law 2008).

The capabilities of ICTs can be grouped into a 4 C's model of ICT functionality: *cost, control, coordination*, and *communication*. ICT can reduce costs by automating and increasing the accuracy of repetitive tasks such as payments, accounting and payroll functions. ICTs also enable firms to increase their control over operations, whole processes and employees, as outlined in Chapter 11 on human resource management. The automatic capture of data and their quick analysis offer managers real-time information about all departments and tasks. ICTs foster and nurture communications and share data at all levels (e.g. across departments, among staff and with business partners). Information flows within and across firms enable more intra-firm and inter-firm coordination and the synchronization of supply chains at lower costs and in real time. As a result, organizational structures are flattening (i.e. levels of organizational hierarchies are reduced as ICT replaces human coordination previously provided by middle managers) and a broadening out of these structures to incorporate various business partners (i.e. creation of business webs, clusters and highly networked, decentralized organizations). Yet as technology moves forward rapidly in the field of ICTs, new developments such as Web 2.0 have induced substantial changes to the way tourism operates.

Current technological advances such as machine learning, human language processing, image recognition and artificial intelligence also mean that the new technological applications in tourism afford intelligences that can replace almost all types of human jobs and tasks in tourism operations (Ivanov *et al.* 2019). Specifically, modern technology applications like robots (see Figure 6.2) and chatbots afford:

- Mechanical intelligence that can automate and replace human tasks related to standardized repeated operations (i.e. check-in processes, payments).
- Analytical intelligence that can enrich, augment but also replace human decision-making processes by processing a greater volume and type of multimedia data in a faster and more accurate way and with higher

prediction accuracy. For example, a robot can now take revenue management decisions by considering real-time data about capacity, availability, prices and availability of competitors, customer's profile data and preferences.

- Intuitive intelligence that can replace human wisdom in taking decisions by understanding and reacting to human behaviour and patterns. For example, a robot taking an order from a guest at a restaurant that understands and processes information about the guest's eating patterns, the weather conditions and the meal occasion.

- Empathetic intelligence, (i.e. an ability to recognize and understand people's emotions, respond appropriately emotionally), and the ability to influence others' emotions, such as a chatbot managing a customer making an online complaint by understanding and reacting to his voice tone, face reactions and words used, in order to describe the complaint and reaction to the complaint management process.

In the very near future technological advances will be able to fully substitute all human intelligence. Staff in tourism and hospitality will need to redefine their roles and tasks in order not to be substituted by technology but instead to be enhanced and augmented by technology and to focus on excelling in tasks that only human beings are able to do (e.g. take decisions and responsibility for actions based on ethical criteria and trade-offs, apply emotional labour with a human meaning and purpose and not with an automated/mechanical identification of and response to human emotions). Technology and human cooperation might show the emergence of a workforce whose intelligences and capabilities are augmented with technology.

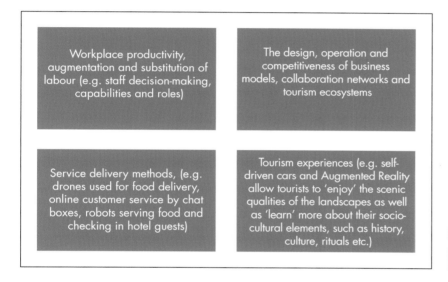

FIGURE 6.2 How technology agents are providing 'near-human' experiences and how they transform and disrupt tourism

Internet advances: Social media, its functionality and impact on tourism

Since the early 1990s, the Internet has revolutionized tourism, providing low-cost efficient and effective Web tools to any size of tourism organization to globally promote and sell its services. During the last decade, Web 2.0 has developed as a platform for information sharing, inter-operability, user-centred design and collaboration. While the original focus of the Web was on information publication and dissemination to the users (consumers), in Web 2.0 the users are no longer passive receivers and viewers of information created for them. Instead, a Web 2.0 site allows users to interact and collaborate in a social media dialogue as (co-)creators (prosumers) of user-generated content (UGC) in a virtual community or social network (see Stepchenkova and Zhan 2013 on destination photography).

An important part of Web 2.0 is the social web, which consists of a number of online tools and platforms social media where people can create, share and comment on content (be it textual, aural or visual). Social media is a group of online media which share the following characteristics: *participation, openness, conversation, community* and *connectedness*. Examples of social media include blogs, social networks, wikis, mashups, video-sharing websites and folksonomies. Recently, many social media tools have been enriched with web-mapping applications (e.g. GeoBlog,

TABLE 6.3 The social media landscape	
Types of social media	*Major examples*
Social news sites	Digg, reddit, Twitter, Slashdot
Social bookmarking sites	Delicious, StumbleUpon
Social networking	Facebook, MySpace, Eventful, Orkut, XING, LinkedIn, Plaxo
Social media sharing	YouTube, Flickr, SlideShare, Picasa, Vimeo, Last.fm
Social knowledge	Wikipedia, Yahoo! Answers
Social gaming	Second Life, Zynga, (FarmVille, ChefVille and other games on Facebook)

wikimapping and geoRSS) which enable users to store, search, visualize and share multimedia content on top of a map. Social web-mapping gives rise to what is called the geospatial web, which has many new applications and implications in the tourism industry, as more than 80 per cent of travel content is geographically defined (Sigala and Marinidis 2012b). Social media has changed the way people search for, find, read, gather, share, develop and consume information, and the way people communicate with each other and collaboratively create new knowledge (Sigala 2011). Thus, social media are considered to be 'tools of mass collaboration' that in turn enable the creation and exploitation of the 'social intelligence' through the online collection, analysis, sharing, discussion and visualization of UGC (Sigala 2012). Table 6.3 categorizes the social media tools based on the type of social intelligence activity that they support.

To summarize, social media enable the following mass-scale and interactive functionalities in tourism (termed the 4 C's):

- *communication:* multimedia-enabled conversations in various formats and timing (e.g. many-to-many, one-to-many, simultaneously or asynchronous)
- *cooperation:* sharing of content in a structured (e.g. by using tags) or unstructured way
- *collaboration:* collaboration of individuals to solve a specific problem
- *connection:* making connections with and between both content and other people.

Social media is fundamentally changing the way travellers search, find, read and trust, as well as produce information about tourism suppliers, destinations and experiences (Sigala *et al.* 2012). By browsing UGC and social media, travellers are becoming co-marketers, co-designers, co-producers and co-consumers of tourism and hospitality products and services. They gain inspiration for travel destinations to select and become motivated to design their personalized travel itineraries and share these itineraries with their social networks and then comment on them via e-word-of-mouth (e-WOM) with real-time commentary on their real-life experiences (Sigala 2012a). In other words, social media has an *AISDAS* effect on consumer behaviour: at first, it will attract the traveller's **A**ttention; the traveller then develops an **I**nterest in the service: they then **S**earch online for information, which in turn creates a **D**esire to consume the service; they then need an **A**ction to purchase the service, which the traveller experiences and **S**hares; and then feeds back with others after the consumption and evaluation of the service. Social media can also facilitate and support several grass-roots (social) actions for anyone, irrespective of their location and time zone. Examples of such actions can be related to community-based destination governance practices (Sigala and Marinidis 2012a) or crisis and environmental management in destinations (Sigala 2012c). For instance, http://crisiscommons.org is a social media platform which provides wikis, Twitter feeds, social networks and blogs to facilitate the coordination and mobilization of various stakeholders (e.g. citizens, policymakers, activists' groups, rescue teams, police forces and companies) to assist in crisis management. Examples of the application of this platform for crisis management include the management of the earthquake in Haiti and the riots in London. Thus, the new generation of travellers are the *C travellers*, characterized by social cultures and values related to *c*onversation, *c*ommunication, *c*onnectedness, *c*ollaboration, *c*ooperation, *c*o-creation and *c*ommunity responsibility. One way that the tourism sector has responded to such changes, as Insight 6.1 shows, is through harnessing new technology such as Twitter.

INSIGHT 6.1 Marriott uses celebrities to promote renovations on Twitter

- The UK division of Marriott International is promoting the completion of a £120 million refurbishment project across 41 UK hotels with an innovative review campaign via Twitter.

- Marriott has invited several well-known Twitter users, including celebrities and journalists, to communicate their experiences at selected properties to followers live on the micro-blogging site. 'We wanted to communicate this news in an original and forward-thinking way that would resonate well with our guests', said Osama Hirzalla, Marriott's vice president of brand marketing and e-commerce for Europe. Because of social media's immediacy and presumed authenticity, Marriott hopes the strategy will convey a message of confidence in its product.

- Participants are personally invited by Marriott to review a refurbished hotel of their choice. Beyond that, however, they will experience the property in the same way any guest would, Hirzalla states. 'All we ask in return for their stay is that they tweet regularly about their experiences at the hotel, providing a good overview of the refurbished property and its services. It's just like any other review, really, only communicated instantly via Twitter to their followers'.

- The campaign is believed to be the first organized Twitter promotion of its kind in the hotel industry. 'By using Twitter effectively and by leveraging Facebook, in addition to our more traditional communication channels, we have been able to reach many more thousands of members of the general public with news about our refurbished hotels', Hirzalla claimed.

- UK celebrities who have participated so far include TV presenter Gail Porter, actor Noel Clarke, actress Kaya Scodelario and E! Entertainment network personality Sam Mann. Among the hotels reviewed to date are London Marriott Grosvenor Square Hotel; Forest of Arden, a Marriott Hotel and Country Club in Maidstone, Kent; London Marriott County Hall Hotel; and Liverpool Marriott Hotel City Centre.

- The campaign launched in January 2012, with initial plans to roll out over the course of three months. 'We have received a lot of interest from both celebrities and journalists active on Twitter wanting to review a refurbished Marriott hotel, so it is definitely something we would consider extending and developing into an ongoing campaign in the UK', Hirzalla reported.

The use of ICT in the management of tourism suppliers

ICT supporting the value chain of tourism firms

ICTs provide tourism firms with the capability to digitize the operation of their **value chain** (Figure 6.3) in order to increase their performance by automating, increasing information flows by migrating value chain operations to Internet platforms by adopting e-business applications (the prefix *e* can be assigned to this operation, e.g. e-commerce, e-marketing, e-procurement, e-learning, e-recruiting). An e-operation provides firms with the additional benefits of Internet technologies such as the use of inter-operable technology standards which enable the firm to easily integrate this e-operation with other business partners' applications to form inter-organizational networks and develop collaborative practices to gain performance benefits of a virtual firm. It can also enable global sourcing and partnering to increase cost-efficiency, and the adoption of effective business applications offered by the Internet. The Internet also allows customization and personalization of services, real-time management, operational and strategic flexibility, and the ability to respond quickly to the market and competitive trends. The wide diffusion of the Internet in tourism firms' value chain has led to the emergence to what is usually called e-tourism.

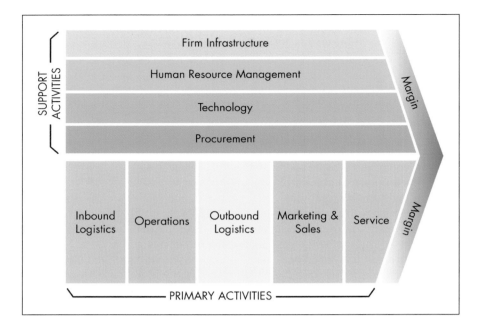

FIGURE 6.3 The value chain

ICT, supply chains and their impact on tourism firms

In recent years, the most decisive impact of ICT and specifically of interactive Internet capabilities is related to technology functionality which allows firms to actively involve customers in all their business processes from service design to service production and service marketing (see Figure 6.4). Consequently, travellers become the co-designers, co-producers and co-marketers of their tourism experiences (also see Chapter 14 on tourism marketing). By getting involved in the service value chain, travellers are usually more satisfied, as they take control of the service process and its timing and customize services to personal needs, potentially becoming more emotionally attached and loyal to the firm (Sigala 2009a). On the other hand, by exploiting travellers as partial employees, tourism firms enjoy benefits such as: lower operational costs and higher productivity; interactive customer touch points from which they can gather and exploit good-quality customer intelligence; lower market research expenses; and increased opportunities to up-sell and cross-sell to loyal customers.

As Chapter 5 argues, information is the glue connecting all stakeholders involved in a value and supply chain. Hence, ICT and Internet applications that enable the real-time exchange and share of information within and beyond the firm's borders are crucial for integrating processes and fostering collaborative practices that increase business performance.

Overall, ICTs enable tourism firms to enhance their business performance and competitiveness by achieving:

- *Cost leadership*, by reducing administration and labour costs in the coordination of business processes in value and supply chains.
- *Product differentiation*, where ICTs are used to add value to services and/or to differentiate a product from the competition, e.g. through customization.
- *Improved customer focus*, with ICTs helping to establish more targeted and detailed micro- or niche markets through better use of market intelligence and market research (Image 6.2).
- *Market leadership*, where ICTs help to set the market conditions and enhance the ability to innovate, because they can be used to communicate more quickly with consumers.
- *Quality leadership*, defined by the provision of personalized services meeting the needs of customers on a one-to-one basis (i.e. mass customization strategies). ICT also help to monitor quality and respond to customer complaints in real time, while UGC is a valuable source of information for continuous quality improvement.
- *Re-engineering of business processes*, to create synchronized and customer-focused operations as well as to integrate and actively engage customers in business operations as partial employees.
- *Improved integration of the supply chain*, as ICTs foster process re-engineering and can result in enhanced business networking and inter-firm collaborative practices that improve the performance of tourism business clusters (see Chapter 7 and the role of integrated tour operators such as TUI and their supply chain).

- *Improved communication with consumers and customer communities*, with one-to-one marketing, one-to-many and many-to-many communication through social media, email and other technology applications (e.g. mobile phone email alerts).
- *Better response to competition*, by using ICT as a barrier to entry and conducting continuous environmental scanning, improving supplier–supplier and consumer–supplier relationships.
- *Continuous innovation*, by adopting open innovation, co-creation and crowdsourcing practices (see Chapter 12).

IMAGE 6.2 Online airport check-in is one example of ICT improving the flexibility of travel options using new technology such as the smartphone

Many of the above-mentioned ICT business benefits are soft and qualitative in nature, meaning that they can be very difficult to measure and to link to profit and loss. Many benefits only materialize in the longer term, while all of them are dependent on many other factors such as the change of organizational structures and management cultures, business process re-engineering practices, and the absorptive capacity of the firm (that is the ability of the firm to recognize, assimilate and use new knowledge for productive purposes) and its staff's capacity to exploit ICT. In other words, ICTs do not create business value in a 'plug-and-play' form. In addition, business performance is vulnerable to many internal and external factors (such as mismanagement, economic crises and new competition). These are some of the major reasons why many researchers and professionals cannot capture, measure or demonstrate the performance impact of ICT. This has resulted in many studies talking about the ICT *productivity paradox* (i.e. that ICT investments do not lead to related performance improvements). Due to the ICT

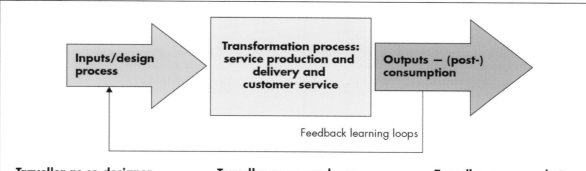

FIGURE 6.4 Customer engagement in the e-value chain of tourism firms
Source: Sigala (2006)

productivity paradox, many tourism firms are cautious about investment in ICT, as funds invested in ICT may not bring quick or significant return on investment compared to funds invested on other projects. Direct benefits for businesses are in the application of ICTs to the distribution chain.

Internet and tourism distribution chains: e-channels and intermediaries

A channel of distribution is a set of interdependent companies or individuals (including customers, suppliers and intermediaries) who participate in the flow of goods, services, information and finance from the producer to the customer in order to make a product available for use or consumption. To make a product available for sale, a distribution channel should perform various functions, usually referred to as *marketing flows* in order to emphasize that these functions flow through the channel at different points in time and through different channel members (intermediaries, suppliers or customers). Flows may move forward through the channel (e.g. promotion), move up the channel from customers to suppliers (e.g. cancellation of flights), move in either direction (e.g. product and customer information) or may be engaged in by pairs of channel members (e.g. negotiation). There are nine marketing flows going through distribution channels (Table 6.4).

Every flow contributes to the production of valued services to suppliers and/or customers, but it also carries an associated cost for implementing them. By helping suppliers to perform the marketing flows, intermediaries provide the following product, possession, place, credibility and time utilities:

- *product utility*: intermediaries enable customers to find, buy and combine a large variety of goods in one place by buying in bulk and performing sorting and allocation functions
- *possession utility*: intermediaries facilitate tasks (e.g. exchange of documents, transactions) that enable the exchange of possession of a product from the supplier to the customer/purchaser
- *place utilities*: intermediaries operate (e-)retail outlets located in more convenient and easily accessible places for potential customers
- *credibility utilities*: customers cannot know and evaluate all potential suppliers and their offers; intermediaries possess specialized knowledge and brand credibility to recommend appropriate suppliers and goods according to customers' needs and can enforce the quality and reputation of suppliers and offers
- *time utilities*: intermediaries provide potential customers time convenience in relation to the purchase and/or change of an order.

A new generation of tourism intermediaries has risen for supporting Internet distribution, which are usually referred to as cyber-intermediaries. Hence, although it may seem that Internet distribution is cheap and goes directly to the customers, tourism firms wishing to distribute their services through the Internet may have to pay for numerous technology-based distribution services and involve various cyber-intermediaries in their Internet distribution chain, which increases the costs, the complexity and the management sophistication of that chain. The multiplication of the number and types of cyber-intermediaries and e-channels has also created another operational challenge for tourism firms. Although tourism suppliers can gain online visibility by distributing their goods through numerous websites/ cyber-intermediaries, in doing so they also face the risk of losing control of their online inventory and prices. For example, when cyber-intermediaries purchase tourism services and become the owners of this inventory (e.g. tour operators), then they also have the ability to determine the price and the website at which this inventory will be sold. Provided that many cyber-intermediaries also conduct forward distribution (i.e. distributing and sharing their databases to many other websites), one can easily understand a major reason why tourism suppliers may lose control of their inventory and prices. In addition, many tourism suppliers also fail to synchronize, monitor or update inventory and prices across channels due to a lack of time or technology support or poor management practices. Loss of inventory and price control has serious impacts on both tourism firms and travellers. Firms failing to implement a sophisticated strategy across distribution channels to optimize yield performance, risk overbooking and/or under-booking and cannibalization of price optimization, and this may lead to online price wars and the provision of heavy discounts to attract travellers. Travellers also become confused and dissatisfied by being offered different availabilities and prices for the same product on different websites, which in turns ruins the brand image and reputation of the supplier. It may also lead travellers to become more price-sensitive. To effectively manage prices and inventory online, tourism firms can use channel management systems which provide sophisticated functionality such as:

TABLE 6.4 Value creation and costs of marketing flows in distribution channels

Marketing flow	Value-added services	Cost represented
Information flow: involves two directions – from the supplier to the consumer and from the consumer to the supplier.	Multimedia presentation of goods, live cameras online for product provision, virtual environments and product simulations. Collection, analysis and dissemination of customer data and feedback as well as of market and competitive intelligence.	Costs for presenting the product; costs for allowing customers to try a product prior to purchase. Costs related to information collection, analysis and distribution related to: consumer behaviour and goods' evaluation; competition; market trends, etc.
Physical/product flow possession: the actual physical movement of the product from the supplier through all of the parties to the consumer.	Logistics and transportation services. Services for digitizing a service and delivering it through the Internet.	Storage and delivery/logistics costs. Service digitization costs.
Ownership flow: the movement of the title of the product from one stage in the process to another.	Buying goods in bulk, assorting and combining them to be sold as a package.	Costs of buying and maintaining inventory of products and services (high costs due to service perishability). Costs of overbookings and under-bookings.
Promotion flow: refers to the flow of persuasive communication for supporting the marketing of the product/supplier.	Provision of various forms of marketing communication such as personal selling, advertising, sales promotion, publicity and public relations.	Personal selling, advertising, sales promotion, publicity, public relations costs.
Negotiation flow: the interplay of the buying and selling functions associated with the transfer of title or rights of ownership.	Provision and support of auction services (e.g. traditional, reversed auctions). Supporting two-way processes involving mutual exchange between buyer and seller.	Time and legal costs.
Financing flows: backward and forward funds transfers among distribution members.	Services supporting the (real-world or electronic) transfer of funds between customers and suppliers, payment of goods, compensations, cancellation returns and between channel members for performing marketing flows (e.g. logistics, promotion).	Credit terms, terms and conditions of sale.
Risking flows: provision of price and quality guarantees of products to buyers. Guaranteeing to suppliers the materialization of an order or the sale of a (perishable) product (reducing the risk of lost sales for suppliers).	Provision of best price and (service) quality guarantees. Developing and maintaining a system evaluating quality and/or sustainability practices of suppliers and goods.	Costs related to: price guarantees, warranties, insurance, repair and after-sales service. Risks of overbookings and under-bookings.
Ordering flows: processes facilitating the taking, monitoring and management of an order.	Operating ordering systems such as booking systems, call centres, mobile booking services.	Order-processing costs.
Payment flows: determination of what is paid for the product and how, e.g. processes related to the collection and handling of funds.	Provision of multiple payment methods (e.g. credit cards, online payments, bank transfers). Dynamic pricing methods changing prices online in real time based on demand and supply (availability) levels.	Collection faults, bad debt costs.

Source: Author; multiple sources

having one platform for allocating and managing inventory and prices across many websites (i.e. one manual entry in one screen/interface or one system integration between the company CRS with the channel management system, with automatic onward promotion of the information to many websites); integration of the channel management platform with yield management systems to optimize capacity and price allocation across channels; integration of reputation management through social media with yield and channel management systems, so customer feedback can be considered when deciding prices and offers; and the provision of market intelligence, such as competitors' information about numbers of online bookings and level of prices at various channels, and statistical data about online demand evolution and trends. The increasing need to use a channel management system has also led to the establishment of new types of intermediaries in the tourism distribution chain that can offer such services (e.g. http://www.travelclick.com/), while it has also forced existing players (e.g. Global Distribution Services [GDS], which followed on from the CRS developed by the major airlines) to integrate and offer channel management functionality in their distribution services.

However, the Internet has not only influenced costs, distribution services and the structure of the electronic tourism distribution chain, it has also distorted power relations, dynamics and the ways of achieving competitive advantage in distributing goods and services. Three major concepts reflect the Internet's impact on tourism distribution dynamics:

- *disintermediation:* bypassing of a tourism intermediary, when the tourism supplier goes directly to the source of demand
- *re-intermediation:* the redefinition of the strategy and distribution services/functions of an existing tourism intermediary in order to survive and compete in the tourism distribution chain
- *cyber-intermediation:* the new types of tourism e-intermediaries that have evolved either because of Internet functionalities and/or the new distribution needs that the Internet has created.

Competition is an interesting challenge, as researchers observe that while it may be possible to eradicate intermediaries (or even substitute them) in a tourism distribution channel, this in itself will not remove the need for these flows. So another supplier will normally develop the skills to fill the void. Thus, when using the Internet to bypass an intermediary, the distribution flows once performed by this intermediary are either automated and substituted by ICT applications and/or they are performed by other player(s) (e.g. suppliers and customers). Internet distribution has created the need for new distribution services (e.g. online authentication of users and e-payments), which have also given rise to new types of intermediaries. Irrespective of how these new or technology-automated distribution flows and services occur, or who uses them, their cost has to be borne by someone: Internet distribution is not cheap and definitely not free. Green and Lomanno (2012) suggest online commissions represent between 15 and 20 per cent of a hotel's room revenue, while this percentage is expected to increase to 30 per cent. Thus e-distribution expenses represent a substantial part of the suppliers' revenue. In summary, the Internet has not only created disrupting change in e-tourism distribution by challenging the survival of intermediaries and traditional players, but has also provided tools to existing tourism firms to redefine their strategy to compete within the new virtual space. It is not the Internet per se that creates the change, but rather the way in which the Internet is exploited by the firms in integrating it into their distribution chain and creating innovative new distribution services. To explore this theme further, the Web materials will help you understand re-intermediation, disintermediation and cyber-intermediation.

A typology of new tourism cyber-intermediaries

As new cyber-intermediaries develop in the tourism distribution chain, it has becomes more difficult for tourism firms to identify and select which cyber-intermediaries to use in order to optimize distribution and yield management performance by selling different amounts of inventory, at different prices, to different market segments, across different e-channels and at different times. There are many different approaches to categorizing cyber-intermediaries. An e-business model determines what is being sold online, the members of the distribution chain and their roles/functions, the direction and process of marketing flows among the members of the distribution chains, and the pricing model used (e.g. auction, standard prices, commissions for referrals, online sales/bookings or promotion/advertising services). The most useful type of categorization uses e-business models of cyber-intermediaries, mainly based on the pricing mechanism used to gain access to tourism products and information and then to sell/price the products and information online to achieve the profit margin. The pricing mechanism is a critical issue, as it significantly influences the appeal of the e-business model to suppliers and travellers (and the market adoption of the cyber-intermediary model), because it determines the profit margin that intermediaries can achieve and thus the profitability and sustainability of their business. According to this criterion, cyber-intermediaries can follow one or more of the following e-business models:

Merchant model

Examples of the merchant model include: hotels.com, travelocity.com, orbitz.com, where the cyber-intermediary buys a certain amount of inventory from tourism suppliers (e.g. hotels, cruise operators and airlines). In this model inventory ownership and the risk of selling it moves from the suppliers to the cyber-intermediary, who can determine when, on which website and at what price to sell the inventory individually and/or as part of a package. Tourism suppliers usually sell at a lower price than the rack rate but they have a secure payment. The 'merchant model' also means that the supplier provides a third-party vendor with a net rate that is often 17–35 per cent below retail levels. The merchant model website (an online wholesale travel agency) then decides what rate to post on its site to sell to the consumer. Some suppliers are able to negotiate limits on markup for different rooms at different times, but this is not always possible. The consumer pre-pays for the product and the online vendor pays the supplier later at the agreed net rate. These agencies seek year-round partnerships to ensure they have inventory 'on their shelves' at all times and that the consumer views them as a reliable storefront to deliver fresh and desirable products.

Commissionable or retail model

Examples of the commissionable or retail model include: expedia.com, booking.com (see Image 6.3); where the cyber-intermediary provides information about inventory levels and prices from the suppliers, makes the products available for sale online and then receives a commission on sales/bookings. In this way, suppliers can retain control over their inventory and prices, but they have to pay commission costs and assume the risk of not selling the inventory online.

Opaque model

Examples of the opaque model include: priceline.com, hotwire.com, lastminute.com, where the cyber-intermediary provides a platform whereby the customers can determine the type of tourism services required and the range of prices they are willing to pay (e.g. one room for one night in Paris, at a price between €60 and €80, at a three-star hotel property, 2 km away from the Eiffel Tower). The cyber-intermediary communicates the travellers' requests to tourism suppliers with whom they cooperate, suppliers bid for the offer, the consumers are presented with the suppliers' offer but with hidden information about the suppliers' identity. The suppliers' identity is disclosed to the traveller only when they select and pay for a specific offer. By using this cyber-intermediary, the tourism suppliers can get rid of 'distressed' unsold inventory at the last minute without associating their brand name with low prices. Cyber-intermediaries receive commission from the suppliers for the online bookings achieved. Instead of commission, some cyber-intermediaries keep the difference between what the buyer pays and the pre-negotiated product rate. Typically, the percentage of the room rate kept by the cyber-intermediaries is in the range of 35 to 50 per cent.

Auction model

An example of the auction model is ebay.com: the cyber-intermediary provides platforms enabling suppliers to meet buyers and conduct various types of auctions using a traditional model (i.e. suppliers presenting their product and buyers giving their bids; the buyer giving the highest price gets the product) or reversed auctions (e.g. conference organizers advertising their meeting space and food and beverage needs online, suppliers provide their offers for this specification and the buyer-conference organizers select the best offer for their needs). Auctions are used by tourism suppliers for several reasons including: creating online buzz and promotion of a new service (e.g. a new flight) as

IMAGE 6.3 Booking.com uses the commissionable model as a cyber-intermediary

auctions tend to create a lot of e-WOM; disposing of distressed inventory; optimizing prices for a product of low capacity levels (e.g. tickets to special events); and identifying and targeting new market segments.

Coupons

Examples of the coupon model are: groupon.com, feecation.com, www.touristorama.com/deals. Companies wishing to promote their services through these websites create and sell online coupons at a major markdown (e.g. up to 90 per cent off a usual price), while they also have to pay a substantial amount of the coupon face value (sometimes up to 50 per cent) to the coupon-distributing website. Group-buying websites introduce new coupon deals every day and they keep their customers updated through automated emails to customers' databases, RSS and other social media tools. However, coupons do not actually become available as soon as they are advertised. Instead, online coupons are valid and can be used by customers only when a minimum number of people (set by the retailers) have committed to buy them. If the minimum number of coupons is not sold, the credit card of the customer is not charged and the coupon is cancelled. The online coupons represent a very effective and measurable form of advertising and customer acquisition method, because: firms get exposure even if the online coupon does not materialize (i.e. the minimum number of coupons is not sold); there are no up-front and 'wasted' advertising costs, as the firms are not charged any marketing fee before reaching the deal and customers are brought to them (i.e. firms pay commissions only for the sold coupons); the promotion achieved through online coupons is more effective, as the firm is exposed and becomes known to market segments that are likely to be interested in its goods; the online coupons generate (e-)WOM that enhances the reach and the effectiveness of the advertising message; the online coupons assist in collecting valuable customer details and marketing intelligence to improve marketing practices; and the online coupons help to drive revenues, as they drive customers to the company, and they may be motivated to spend beyond the coupon face value (Dev *et al.* 2011).

Referral service model or meta-search engines

Examples of the referral service model or meta-search engines are: kayak.com, mobissimo.com, travelaxe.com, travelfusion.com, hotelfinder.com, roomkey.com, fly.com, where these cyber-intermediaries do not get access to and/or ownership of inventory, but their software is allowed access to the tourism supplier's website, so it can trawl it and provide customers with consolidated results about the suppliers' products and prices on one screen and one search at the cyber-intermediary website. These intermediaries are popular with travellers as they save them a lot of time and online comparison, while suppliers have to pay them a commission/referral fee when travellers select and click their offer in order to be diverted to the supplier's website and complete the purchase. Suppliers may agree to allow access to their websites to meta-search engines and allow the price comparison and perhaps price wars, because customers use them heavily and will do the online price comparisons anyway (either manually or through other meta-search engines).

Peer-to-peer platforms/marketplaces

Examples of the Peer-to-peer platforms/marketplaces are: Uber, Airbnb, toursbylocals.com, rvshare.com, www.eatwith.com. Peer-to-peer marketplaces are platforms enabling anyone to become a micro-entrepreneur (e.g. micro-hotelier, micro-taxi driver, micro-restaurateur). Peer-to-peer platforms are marketplaces enabling demand and supply stakeholders to find and establish trust and exchanges among each other; i.e. micro-entrepreneurs promoting and providing their own 'idle' resources, or tourists searching, evaluating and booking a shared tourism service. Platforms enable exchanges between the two parties in various ways (e.g. exchange, barter, gifting, renting, sales), while they mainly use a two-sided reputation and review system for establishing trust between the two parties (e.g. guests evaluating hosts and hosts evaluating guests in Airbnb; guests and hosts obtaining badges, awards and ranking that contribute to their online reputation and trust). Peer-to-peer platforms are two-sided markets that can make money by charging both sides for the services that they provide to them.

ICT, Internet and social media adoption

Travellers differ not only in the way in which they use technologies, but also in their abilities and motivations for doing so (Sigala *et al.* 2012). Indeed, numerous studies confirm that travellers use technologies because they seek both functional (e.g. saving time, place convenience, supporting decision-making) and hedonistic benefits (e.g. fun, entertainment, helping others online, self-expression and self-presentation, creating their own profile and identity). Numerous factors affect travellers' adoption and uses of technologies (Table 6.5). Based on travellers' use and adoption of the Internet, firms have traditionally divided travellers into *lookers* and *bookers* for numerous purposes, such as identifying and addressing problems related to Internet adoption and website design features (e.g. increased security assurances for online bookings), and better customer targeting of online campaigns, but Web 2.0 has changed that situation. Travellers have become partial employees by (collaboratively) designing, distributing and promoting tourism services online. As travellers use the Internet not only for looking, but also for booking services, their technology usage profile expands from lookers to bookers to travellers using the Internet for one or more of the following tasks: searching and reading UGC and travel information (Image 6.4); sharing and distributing travel content with social networks; critiquing and discussing travel content online; evaluating travel content and content writers (e.g. like buttons on Facebook); and writing and creating travel content.

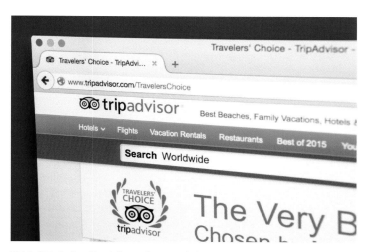

IMAGE 6.4 TripAdvisor hosts UGC

TABLE 6.5	Examples of factors affecting technology adoption and use	
Type of factor	*Travellers, adoption and use of technology*	*Firms' adoption and use of technology*
Factors related to the stakeholder	User personality, attitude to technology, abilities/ skills to use technology, type of benefits sought from technology use, user demographics (e.g. gender, age, education level), user lifestyle, user perception of the ease of use of technology, user perception of the technology benefits, perceived risks of using technology	Firms' characteristics such as size, management and ownership style, management support and commitment, availability of funds to invest in technology, firm's attitudes towards technology innovation and use, firms' and staff's skills and abilities to exploit ICT
Factors related to the technology	The benefits and functionality of the technology, ease of use, technology interface, security and privacy issues, assurances afforded by the technology, the innovativeness of technology and the compatibility of the technology with the users' profile and working patterns	Technology functionality, technology integration with existing information systems and application, security issues of technology, cost of technology, technology's return on investment, technology's alignment with the firm's strategy
Factors related to the environment	Peer pressure, technology use at work	Competitors' use of technology, suppliers' push for using technology, partners' push for using technology, use technology for increasing the professionalism and image of the firm to that of a high-tech firm

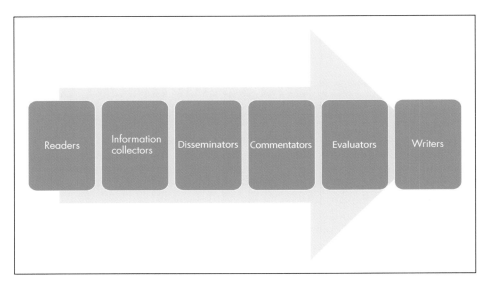

FIGURE 6.5 A technographic profile

The travellers add value to the firm's value and distribution chain by engaging in a variety of uses of the Internet, from the very basic to the more Web 2.0-enhanced. Thus, to better exploit travellers' use of technology and their active involvement in the firm's value chain, tourism firms need to understand the technographic profile of travellers and the factors influencing it. For example, what are the demographic characteristics of travellers with different technographic profiles (e.g. readers, commentators, critics, writers and distributors of information, as shown in Figure 6.5, see old fig 6.3) and what are the factors (e.g. personality) that influence the travellers to adopt a different technographic profile? Answers to such questions can help firms to improve the design and functionality of their technology applications, to target technology applications to a better profile of customers that are more likely to use them, and increase the level of the travellers' participation in the value chain (and thus the business benefits provided by travellers) by elevating their technographic profile from that of simple readers to writers of UGC.

Destination Management and Marketing Systems (DMSs)

The totality of the ICTs developed by a DMO for marketing their destinations represents the Destination Management and Marketing System (DMS) of the destination. In general, DMSs are regarded as inter-organizational ICTs aiming to link the geographically separated tourism supply with the tourism demand. A comprehensive DMS definition was recently developed by Frew and Horan (2007: 63):

> . . . DMSs are systems that consolidate and distribute a comprehensive range of tourism products through a variety of channels and platforms, generally catering for a specific region, and supporting the activities of a DMO within that region. DMSs attempt to utilize a customer-centric approach to managing and marketing the destination as a holistic entity, typically providing strong destination related information, real-time reservations, destination management tools and paying particular attention to supporting small and independent tourism suppliers.

It becomes clear from the above definition that the major role of a DMS is to act as an electronic intermediary providing functionalities related to e-distribution, e-marketing and e-sales for the entire destination and its tourism suppliers. Indeed, the impact and the necessity of a DMS for the survival and the competitiveness of small and medium tourism and hospitality enterprises is considered indispensable, as such enterprises represent the majority of firms at many destinations, but they lack the technological, managerial and financial resources to exploit ICTs for e-commerce and e-marketing. Therefore, these enterprises depend heavily on a DMS for having an e-presence and an alternative e-distribution channel to reduce their dependency on intermediaries.

The role of DMSs has evolved and expanded to provide several other online services and functionalities that allow DMOs to achieve their major roles in destinations (i.e. destination developer, manager and collaboration leader).

Such DMS roles and services may include inter-firm collaboration and networking; destination knowledge management through supporting knowledge exchanges among firms; the operation of a tourism observatory collecting and disseminating tourism intelligence to tourism stakeholders; the support of e-procurement and other collaborative practices among tourism firms; e-learning opportunities for tourism stakeholders (e.g. for accommodation providers or tourism intermediaries for B2B destination marketing and complementing travel trade familiarization trips to destinations); destination customer relationship programmes aimed at increasing travellers' loyalty and visitation to the destination as well as the diffusion of travellers' spending to many tourism firms and destination locations, e.g. destination cards and loyalty programmes (Sigala 2012d).

DMSs represent a technology platform (a mixture of software and hardware) comprising three basic elements that are closely interrelated and interdependent:

- content (creation, aggregation and distribution–promotion): destination content and UGC
- processes (transactions, CRM, customer service, dynamic packaging): internal DMO processes such as provision of tourist information as well as inter-firm processes such as collaborative destination decision-making and management, dynamic packaging and destination loyalty cards
- community (users, stakeholders and their interrelationships): Web 2.0 tools have enabled the active involvement and engagement of tourists and local communities in DMOs' traditionally 'internal' processes such as marketing, new product development, decision-making and policy development. Tourists become co-marketers and co-developers of travel experiences, while stakeholders can propose and monitor the implementation of destination tourism policies.

However, despite the increasing importance of DMSs in supporting and fostering sustainable destination management, their adoption has been slow and low because of several factors (Sigala 2009b): *inter-organizational factors* (e.g. lack of trust among partners, unwillingness to share firm data of prices and availability with others, low collaboration culture); *intra-organizational factors* (e.g. firms' limited knowledge and understanding of DMS benefits; lack of internal information support systems); *technological factors* (e.g. difficulty in maintaining and using DMS functionality; cost for promoting a firm through the DMS); and *environmental/competitive factors* (e.g. lack of DMO support, commitment, peer pressure). Destinations wishing to enhance the role of a DMS in their destination management and marketing would need to identify and address all these factors (Hays *et al.* 2012).

Future technology developments

ICT tools and capabilities continuously advance, enriching and disrupting the way firms and sectors operate and compete. As Sigala (2018: 152) argues in relation to the future of tourism ICTs, there are three words characterizing the features of emerging and future technologies: *connectivity, data* and *smartness*. Smartness is an emerging area which depends on smart connectivity, the smart data components as well as the smartness of technology agents such as chatbots and robots. Currently, technological agents are capable of recognizing, identifying, replicating and reacting to human emotions, but they are not able yet to understand what the human emotion is (i.e. how it feels to be annoyed, unhappy or in pain). Technological advances are currently automating, and augmenting as well as enriching human labour and tasks, but until technological advances can fully understand and replicate human intelligence, humans will still be required to provide the human touch of a tourism service. Future scenarios might also see the creation of workers whose human intelligence is complemented and works collaboratively with technological intelligence (which we could call super-humans). Such developments do not only affect the type and the efficiency/effectiveness of tourism services to be provided, but they also redefine and transform concepts such as: how the service quality of a technology supported and augmented tourism service will be evaluated; how tourists interact, perceive and work with technology agents; how tourism staff will work and collaborate with technology agents; what will be the ethos and values as well as the legal responsibilities of technological agents; what the future of tourism workers and professions will be; what legislation would need to be changed, updated and created to take into account human–computer labour relations and/or customer–staff–technology relations, privacy, safety and security issues. Smart tourism scenarios are revolutionizing the tourism industry by bringing in changes, but we do not know what these changes will be, or even their implications and the side-effects of these implications in other spheres of human activity and behaviour.

ICTs advances also further revolutionize the role of travellers in the tourism value and distribution chain. Travellers have become the co-creators, co-designers, co-producers of their own experiences. Peer-to-peer marketplaces enable anyone to become a tourism supplier and disrupt tourist supply chains. Traditionally, companies aimed to 'own' the customer by collecting, analyzing and using customer data to build customer relations and loyalty. Technological advances such as Blockchain enable customers themselves to 'own' their personal profiles and transaction data and trade them to companies that wish to use them to personalize their offerings and who aim to build a relationship with them. Thus, the tourism companies would need to change their management mindset and paradigm from trying to 'own' and 'control' customer relationships to trying to 'earn' and 'get' the customer relationships. ICTs evolve and change at a rapid pace, and as a result, the tourism industry and all its constituent elements are also undergoing constant, fast and dynamic change if not a total transformation. Coping with change by being able to react to changes and also able to create them has always been the critical success factor of any tourism actor, namely tourism operators, destinations, workers and researchers, but also tourists.

Conclusion

ICTs have profoundly changed the way tourism has operated over the last 20 years, particularly with the onset of the Web and Web 2.0. While technology was very much a stand-alone issue 20 years ago, now it is central to everything related to tourism. Technology has changed the relationship between demand and supply, the management of tourism, and the creation of tourism services and experiences and added a greater degree of complexity for those who seek to understand the relationships that now exist within the tourism system. Above all, technology has enabled supply and demand to be connected in a far more sophisticated manner, where the old models of transaction-based relationships between buyer and seller have been replaced by much deeper relationships through technology. Tourism experiences are now consumed and communicated in real time by social-media-savvy travellers, as part of their repertoire of cultural capital that is shared among their community of friends, family and contacts. Technology has also changed the business landscape as the relationship between consumer and retailer has changed, with trust and branding becoming a key element in the online booking process. While this chapter has examined discrete themes and trends that are affecting the tourism sector and consumers, technology is a common theme running through every chapter of the book that now connects together all relationships in the tourism system in some way directly or indirectly. This means that technology is one of the most pervasive influences upon global tourism, alongside the other big issues of the day such as climate change; although it is far less media-worthy and sits in the background, transforming the way tourism operates, is managed and is delivered to consumers. The digital age is a remarkable new era for tourism, connecting, facilitating and enabling it to be a more global process, since technology transcends borders in most cases (except for countries where the state regulates and controls access to technology in a globalized world), and continues to stimulate innovations that keep changing the way tourism is produced and consumed.

Discussion questions

1 What are the major ICT capabilities affecting the tourism industry?
2 Analyze and discuss how ICT enables tourism firms to increase their operational efficiency and effectiveness.
3 Debate how ICT can empower tourism firms to transform their business model and adopt competitive and sustainable strategies.
4 Discuss how Internet tools enable tourism intermediaries to develop a competitive strategy, giving examples.
5 Critically evaluate the impact of ICTs' advances on tourist workers and tourists.

References

Benckendorff, P.J., Xiang, Z. and Sheldon, P.J. (2019) *Tourism Information Technology*. Wallingford, Oxon: CABI.

Buhalis, D. and Law, R. (2008) 'Progress in tourism management: Twenty years on and 10 years after the Internet: The state of e-tourism research', *Tourism Management* 29 (4): 609–623.

Cheng, M. and Edwards, D. (2019) 'A comparative automated content analysis approach on the review of the sharing economy discourse in tourism and hospitality', *Current Issues in Tourism*, 22 (1): 35–49.

Dev, C.D., Falk, L.W. and Stroock, L.M. (2011) 'To Groupon or not to Groupon: A tour operator's dilemma', *Cornell Hospitality Report* 11 (19): 4–18.

Frew, A.J. and Horan, P. (2007) *Destination Website Effectiveness: A Delphi Study-based eMetric Approach*. HITA Conference, Orlando, FL: 49–80.

Green, C.E. and Lomanno, M.V. (2012) *Distribution Channel Analysis: A Guide for Hotels*. USA: HSMAI Foundation Publications. https://pdfs.semanticscholar.org/ab72/40f8da5f503a05a90ff8e8d198a9b358b263.pdf.

Hays, S., Page, S.J. and Buhalis, D. (2012) 'Social media as a destination marketing tool: Its use by national tourism organizations', *Current Issues in Tourism*, 16 (3): 211–39.

Ivanov, S., Gretzel, U., Berezina, K., Sigala, M., and Webster, C. (2019) 'Progress on robotics in hospitality and tourism: a review of the literature', *Journal of Hospitality and Tourism Technology*, 10 (4): 489–521.

Li, J., Xu, L., Tang, L., Wang, S. and Li, L. (2018) 'Big data in tourism research: A literature review', *Tourism Management*, 68: 301–323.

Poon, A. (1993) *Tourism, Technology and Competitive Strategies*. Wallingford: CAB International.

Sigala, M. (2006) 'e-Procurement diffusion in the supply chain of foodservice operators: An exploratory study in Greece', *Information Technology and Tourism*, 8 (2): 79–90.

Sigala, M. (2009a) 'E-service quality and Web 2.0: Expanding quality models to include customer participation and inter-customer support', *The Service Industries Journal*, 29 (10): 1341–1358.

Sigala, M. (2009b) 'Destination management systems: A reality check in the Greek tourism industry'. 16th International Conference on Information Technology and Travel and Tourism, ENTER 2009 'eTourism: Dynamic Challenges for Travel and Tourism' organized by the International Federation of IT, Tourism and Travel (IFITT), 28–30 January 2009, Amsterdam.

Sigala, M. (2011) 'eCRM 2.0 applications and trends: The use and perceptions of Greek tourism firms of social networks and intelligence', *Computers in Human Behaviour*, 27 (2): 655–61.

Sigala, M. (2012a) 'The impact of geocollaborative portals on group decision making for trip planning', *European Journal of Information Systems*, 21 (4): 404–26.

Sigala, M. (2012b) 'Social networks and customer involvement in New Service Development (NSD): The case of www.mystarbucksidea.com', *International Journal of Contemporary Hospitality Management*, 24 (7): 966–90.

Sigala, M. (2012c) 'Social media and crisis management in tourism: Applications and implications for research', *Information Technology and Tourism*, 13 (4): 269–84.

Sigala, M. (2012d) 'Developing destination management systems (DMS): Roles, functionality and future trends', in G.P. Fernandes, A. Oliveira da Naia Sardo and A. da Silva Melo (eds.) *Innovation in Tourism and Hospitality* (with proceedings of the international symposium on innovation in tourism and hospitality – ISITH). Seia, Portugal: Instituto Politecnico da Guarda.

Sigala, M. (2018) 'New technologies in tourism: From multi-disciplinary to anti-disciplinary advances and trajectories', *Tourism Management Perspectives*, 21: 151–155.

Sigala, M., Christou, E. and Gretzel, U. (2012) *Web 2.0 in Travel, Tourism and Hospitality: Theory, Practice and Cases*. Aldershot: Ashgate.

Sigala, M. and Marinidis, D. (2012a) 'e-Democracy and Web 2.0: A framework enabling DMOs to engage stakeholders in collaborative destination management', *Tourism Analysis*, 17 (2): 105–120.

Sigala, M. and Marinidis, D. (2012b) 'Web map services in tourism: A framework exploring the organisational transformations and implications on business operations and models', *International Journal of Business Information Systems*, 9 (4): 415–434.

Sigala, M., Rahimi, R. and Thelwall, M. (2019a) *Big Data and Innovation in Tourism, Travel, and Hospitality: Managerial Approaches, Technologies and Applications*. Cham: Springer.

Sigala, M., Beer, A., Hodgson, L. and O'Connor, A. (2019b) 'Big data for measuring the impact of tourism economic development programmes: A process and quality criteria framework for using big data', in M. Sigala, R. Rahimi and M. Thelwall (eds.) *Big Data and Innovation in Tourism, Travel, and Hospitality: Managerial Approaches, Technologies and Applications*. Cham, IL: Springer.

Stepchenkova, S. and Zhan, F. (2013) 'Visual destination images of Peru: Comparative content analysis of DMO and user-generated photography', *Tourism Management*, 36: 590–601.

Further Reading

Books

Sigala, M., Christou, E. and Gretzel, U. (2012) *Web 2.0 in Travel, Tourism and Hospitality: Theory, Practice and Cases*. Aldershot: Ashgate.

Journal Articles

Jovicic, D. (2019) 'From the traditional understanding of tourism destinations to the smart tourism destinations', *Current Issues in Tourism*, 22 (3): 276–282.

Li, Y., Hu, C., Huang, C. and Duan, L. (2017) 'The concept of smart tourism in the context of tourism information services', *Tourism Management*, 58: 293–300.

Travel intermediaries: Tour operators and agents

Learning outcomes

After reading this chapter and answering the questions, you should be able to:

- understand the functions of travel and tourism intermediaries

- be able to identify the characteristics of integrated tourism companies

- have an awareness of the significance of travel distribution channels in tourism

- outline some of the challenges facing the travel agency sector in travel retailing.

Overview

The travel product, be it a flight or hotel room, differs from manufactured goods in that it must be sold or lost; it cannot be stocked indefinitely. This feature has led to the creation of thousands of intermediaries around the world packaging two or more complementary travel elements. This chapter considers the diverse range of intermediaries in the travel and tourism industry and the challenge of technology for the travel agency sector. The issues associated with regulating the tour-operator sector are discussed together with the impact of large integrated operators and the effects of consolidation and concentration in the tourism sector.

Introduction

Retailing tourism products to consumers is a key element in the production, selling and distribution of tourism services, where different organizations link the supply to the source of demand. To connect supply and demand, the tourism industry has to communicate, trade and interact with the tourist, and it does this through the distribution channel (i.e. how it is sold to the consumer) using intermediaries, who are agents who sell products for the industry. A distribution channel is a combination of intermediaries who seek to cooperate to sell a product, while a product may be sold through a variety of distribution channels, each of which may have different distribution channels (Figure 7.1). What the intermediaries do is transform the goods available by bundling together the raw components into a product that can be both purchased and consumed (Figure 7.2), and the pace of change in this sector can be observed by consulting industry news sites such as http://www.travelmole.com and http://www.ttgmedia.com.

Historically, tourism products were retailed through travel agents (intermediaries) who offered products from tour operators (who are known as principals), but, as Chapter 6 has shown, the e-tourism revolution and impact of the digital consumer has dramatically changed that mode of distribution. In Europe, Eurostat estimated that the tour operator and travel agency sector has 109 000 businesses involved in these activities (classified as *Travel Agency, Tour Operator and other Reservation Systems enterprises*) within the 28 countries of the EU, where over 190 million package holidays are sold. The largest concentration of activity exists in the four main countries of: Germany, with 12 339 businesses; Italy, with 16 800 businesses; France, with 8929 businesses and the UK with 8134 businesses (see Fuentes 2011 on the growth of travel agents in Spain). The use of different distribution forms of travel products traditionally varied across the EU before the onset of online booking. Belgian, Danish, German, Greek and Austrian tourists had preferred to book direct with operators, whereas in other countries travel agents were a preferred form of booking, usually for package holidays. The exception was Spain, where travel agents were and are still used to book

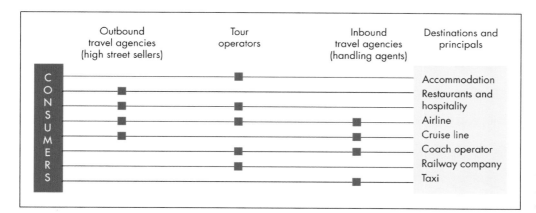

FIGURE 7.1 Tourism distribution mechanisms
Source: Modified from Buhalis and Laws (2001: 11)

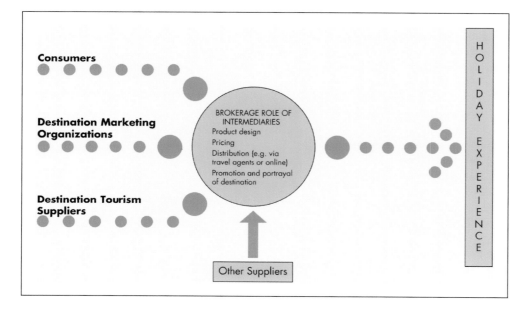

FIGURE 7.2 The role of intermediaries in travel retailing

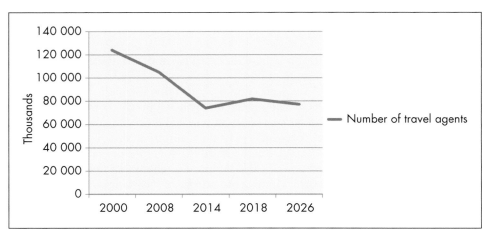

FIGURE 7.3 Changing numbers of travel agents in the USA 2000–2026
Source: Data from United States Bureau of Labor

domestic travel, especially for late booking in Spain and Italy. Yet as Quintana *et al.* (2016: 98) observed in the case of Spain, 'the traditional travel agency in particular, is currently going through a quite complex, dynamic and uncertain operating environment. This is due to factors such as technological innovations, increasingly demanding consumers, fierce competition, and changes in the tourism distribution system, with lower commissions being paid to agencies'. One consequence was that online agencies replaced the traditional agent, with 5000 closing in 2008–2012 alone. The growth in online sales rose by 18 per cent in 2014–2015, with the shift to online retailing (Quintana *et al.* 2016). Similar patterns have also been discerned in the USA since 2000, as shown in Figure 7.3.

More recent trends, such as direct selling, have changed the relationship between the tourism sector and the public and cut out the travel agent. In recent years this relationship has changed again with the impact of information communication technologies (ICTs) such as the World Wide Web and ease of communication by email, to create a new form of distribution – a virtual distribution channel. It is estimated that there are over 5 billion mobile phone users globally, which illustrates the scale of the digital revolution for tourism suppliers, as a self-service trend towards booking has developed facilitated initially by the iPhone and Android phone apps and then via tablets, with their greater visualization capacity compared to a phone screen. The diversity of markets such as the EU (see Insight 7.1) has meant that different countries and types of traveller have different needs which the digital distribution channels have effectively targeted. Therefore, tour operators and travel agents need to be aware of the patterns of demand they are dealing with, as demonstrated in Insight 7.1.

INSIGHT 7.1 Profile of the European tourist – implications for travel retailing

The European statistics agency Eurostat produces a report – *Tourism Trips of Europeans* (2018) in which it outlines the travel behaviour of over 500 million Europeans and which illustrates the scale and volume as well as activities they undertake. The main findings have to be viewed against other statistics that suggest around 1:3 Europeans cannot afford to take a holiday each year, particularly those with children, illustrating the social disparities in some of the 28 countries that currently form the European Union, as highlighted in Chapter 4. The lowest rates of exclusion were in Sweden where less than 10 per cent fell into this category. In stark contrast, at the other end of the spectrum, those countries with over 50 per cent of their population unable to afford a week's holiday included Hungary, Cyprus, Greece, Bulgaria, and Croatia; and Romania with the highest at 66 per cent. In contrast, over 85 per cent of the population in Europe has a mobile phone with 80 per cent of users surfing the Internet on mobile devices such as mobile phones and tablets. These statistics demonstrate the digital footprint that consumers of tourism services now have and the profile of the European traveller includes the following key characteristics:

- EU residents made 1207 million tourism trips in 2017
- They spent an average of 5.1 overnight stays per trip
- Some 58 per cent of these trips were short trips of one to three nights
- The remaining 42 per cent were trips of four nights or more
- Europeans spent 85 per cent of their holidays in the country they lived in (i.e. as domestic tourists)
- Some 75 per cent of all trips they took were domestic destinations and they spent an average of 3.9 nights away from home
- For international trips, which were 35 per cent of the total number of trips taken, the length of stay was around 8.4 nights

- Where business trips were taken, these tended to be 1:9 of all trips
- Air travel was used in 54 per cent of all trips
- The proportion of people participating in holidays ranged from almost 90 per cent of the population of Finland to much lower proportions in many of the new accession countries in Eastern Europe
- The main destinations selected by the European tourist are shown in Figure 7.2, where Spain dominates, with over 20 per cent of the market share
- Some 1:4 holidays are taken in the months of July and August, which tend to be the longer holidays, followed

by the Christmas holidays, highlighting the highly seasonal nature of European holiday-taking

- An average of €355 was spent per trip equating to a €428 198 million expenditure on tourism trips for all Europeans.

Source: Eurostat (2018)

Further reading

Eurostat (2018) *Tourism Trips of Europeans*. Brussels: Eurostat, https://ec.europa.eu/eurostat/statistics-explained/index. php?title=Tourism_trips_of_Europeans.

Ferrante, M., Lo Magno, G.L., and De Cantis, S. (2018) 'Measuring tourism seasonality across European countries', *Tourism Management*, 68: 220–235.

Medeiros, E. (2019) 'Cross-border transport and cross-border mobility in EU border regions', *Case Studies on Transport Policy*, 7(1): 1–12.

Questions

1 How will these patterns of holiday-taking change in the next five years?

2 Why are there such disparities in holiday-taking propensity within the 28 countries of the European Union?

3 What opportunities and problems will the profile of the European tourist pose for the travel and tourism industry in the next five years?

4 What can Destination Management Organizations do to promote greater cross-border tourism?

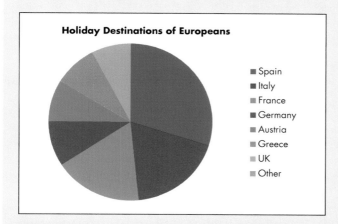

FIGURE 7.4 The top destinations chosen by Europeans when taking holidays
Source: Eurostat (2018)

As we discussed in Chapter 6, tourism has undergone profound changes in recent years via the use of ICTs but also due to industry changes. These changes to the distribution channels have not removed the need for intermediaries, as they still exist. Instead the e-tourism revolution has expanded the range and scope of these for consumers and for businesses seeking to sell their products. Nevertheless, as Cooper *et al.* (2005: 422–423) reiterate, travel intermediaries, in spite of changes in ICTs, still bestow a range of advantages for:

- *producers*, in terms of bulk selling, thereby transferring risk to the tour operator and reducing promotion costs
- *consumers*, via reducing time and costs of searching for products by purchasing an inclusive tour product and by gaining the specialist knowledge and advice of the tour operator. The bulk purchasing power of tour operators may reduce consumer prices by up to 60 per cent of the price a consumer would have to pay for a non-packaged product
- destinations, by bringing volume business. But critics point to the growing marketing control and influence which tour operators exert, as this chapter will show in terms of concentration and consolidation.

The tour operator

Defining 'the tour operator' is a far from easy process because its role, activities and form have changed dramatically from the early days, when Thomas Cook first organized a package trip by rail in the 1840s (see Chapter 2).

IMAGE 7.1 1968 brochure for Thomas Cook holidays to Spain and Portugal
© Thomas Cook

HOLIDAYS BY RAIL AND AIR 1969

Spain & Portugal

COOKS

SEE SEPARATE PROGRAMME FOR COOKS SILVER WING HOLIDAYS AT REDUCED PRICES ON FIXED DEPARTURE DATES

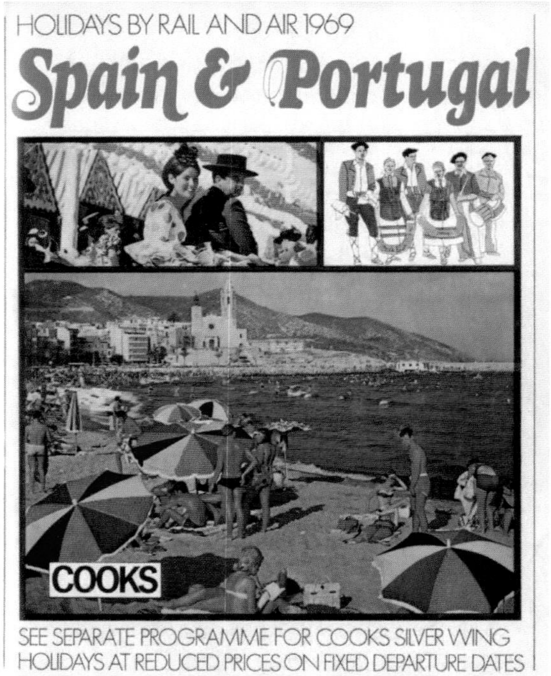

IMAGE 7.2 1969 brochure for Thomas Cook holidays to Spain and Portugal, © Thomas Cook abroad © Thomas Cook

One useful approach is to identify what a tour operator does, as a means of establishing its characteristics and form. In simple terms, a tour operator will organize, package together (i.e. assemble) different elements of the tourism experience and offer them for sale to the public either through the medium of a brochure, leaflet or advertisement (see Images 7.1 and 7.2), or using ICT to display its offering. For a tour operator to offer a package, also known as an 'inclusive tour', this will normally have to have at least two elements which are offered for sale at the inclusive sale price and will involve a stay of more than 24 hours in overnight accommodation. These elements would normally include transport (aircraft seat), accommodation at a destination, return transfer from airport to accommodation, services of a tour representative, insurance and other tourist services such as car hire and excursions. The position of 'packages' in the UK tourism industry was reviewed in 2008 (BERR 2008) to clarify their position in terms of the growth of self-packaged holidays purchased online and the implications for regulation, which is discussed in more detail later.

The nature of those packages sold by the tourism industry can normally be divided into two types: those using the traditional charter flight and those which use scheduled flights, where it is uneconomic for the tour operator to purchase charter flights. Other types of package may also exist, including multi-destination types that visit more than one country/destination, and linear tours or itineraries provided by coach holidays.

The types of packages are often segmented according to:

- those focused on a mode of travel, such as ferry or coach holidays, typified in the UK by Shearings. The package may also be based on twin-transport packages such as fly–drive, which are very popular with inbound tourists in the USA
- mode of accommodation, where hotel chains become tour operators by packaging their surplus capacity to offer weekend or short breaks in business-oriented hotels, selling rail or air transport and visits to attractions as an all-inclusive package for holidaymakers
- whether they are international or domestic packages
- length of holiday: short breaks (i.e. less than four nights away) or long holidays (of more than four nights)
- distance, where the market is divided into short-haul and long-haul: over 90 per cent of UK outbound packages are short-haul
- destination type (e.g. city breaks, beach holidays, adventure holidays).

Source: Page 2003

These tours may be organized by small independent tour operators, who specialize in certain segments, or larger operators such as TUI AG, which has global operations. In addition, there are over 300 inbound tour operators who organize the itineraries, activities and logistics of inbound visitors to countries. The British inbound tour operators are represented by their trade organization – the British Incoming Tour Operators Association (BITOA). But why do tour operators exist and why do people use them? The answer is reflected in the way they operate and the economic benefits they provide to the customer.

The business of tour operation

Tour operators have the ability to purchase services and elements of the tourism experience from other principals or suppliers at significant discounts by buying in bulk. They fulfil a major role in the tourism sector as they allow the different tourism sectors to sell their capacity in advance – often a long time in advance, as contracts are drawn up a year prior to tourists using accommodation or services. This obviates the need for smaller, specialized businesses to market and distribute their product with a wide range of potential retailers, hoping that customers will choose their product or service over and above others. The bulk purchase agreements in large resort areas mean that, in the summer season, the complete capacity of hotels, self-catering and other forms of accommodation may be block-booked leaving the firm free to develop its own expertise in running or managing its business. Similarly, the tour operator connects together with all the ancillary services to negotiate contracts and deals which will allow a holiday to be sold and be delivered on the ground.

In operational terms, the tour operator will bulk purchase airline seats, airport transfer services from coach operators and taxis in the destination area and a whole host of local entertainment and visitor attraction opportunities to sell them to clients at the booking stage or in the destination. Tour operators have traditionally provided a guaranteed level of sales which allowed principals to fix their costs in advance and allowed the operators to achieve economies of scale by giving them heavily discounted rates on their purchase. This is a business opportunity for the tourism sector, with the tour operator creating a package, product or experience by assembling the elements, and advertising and selling them using the third-party agents to deliver each element on the ground. It is obvious that tourist dissatisfaction is possible under this system: service interruptions or breakdowns can occur in the delivery since so many interconnected elements are involved. For example, TUI AG, which is Europe's largest integrated tourism company, has a network of incoming agencies to manage around 20 million inbound visitors a year, and provide a friendly welcome, a smooth transfer from the airport to booked hotel, the services of a company representative, the provision of sightseeing and excursions in the destination and other services such as booking car rental. Therefore, for tour operators, managing the tourist experience to ensure the holiday experience is an enjoyable and rewarding one is a key element of customer care, to which we will return later. The tour operator will often add a mark-up on the product they are selling by calculating all the input costs, their overheads, profit margin and then producing a price.

Among the risks the tour operator takes in planning a holiday are:

- estimating the likely market
- competing with long-established tour operators in a destination who have a recognizable brand
- putting major investment in human resources and infrastructure to set up a destination.

Source: Page 2003

The business performance of tour operators is determined by the company's ability to buy its product components (i.e. aircraft seats, accommodation and transfers) at a competitive price, and resell at a price lower than a consumer could find when assembling the same product. One consequence is that tour operators standardize packages which differ little between destinations, to keep prices low. Technology (e.g. the Internet) is a challenge to this process as it may help the consumer to try to beat such prices, but tour operators have managed to remain competitive in their pricing and buying strategies (Romero and Tejada 2012).

Tour operators may keep their prices low by:

- negotiating low prices from the supplier
- reducing profit margins
- cutting their cost structures.

Source: Page 2003

Where tour operators have become integrated tourism companies and operate their own aircraft, prices for air travel can be reduced by heavy usage of an aircraft (i.e. the number of flights it can make each day).

To achieve cost savings, charter flights need high load factors to break even, typically 80–90 per cent, compared to 50–70 per cent for scheduled flights (depending on the cost base of the carrier). This means that any unsold seats may be unloaded on to the market at cost or less to fill the aircraft, either as seat-only sales/cheap holidays or for purchase through consolidators (air brokers). Consolidators purchase surplus capacity and have the responsibility for marketing and selling such seats. For the airline/tour operator, additional passengers may yield extra revenue from onboard duty-free sales or through purchasing the company's holiday package even if a loss is made on the flight.

With charter operators, costing their price is a complex process, as 'dead legs' at the beginning and end of a season have to be incorporated. At the beginning of a season, an aircraft will fly out with tourists but return empty, and vice versa at the end of the season. To extend the season, operators may provide inducements such as low-cost accommodation to attract low-season business to fill capacity. One such example is the winter flows of elderly people from Northern Europe wintering in the Mediterranean. Hotels discount their rates, hoping guests will spend money in their premises and thus compensate for discounts given at a quiet time of year.

7 Regulating tour operating

Since the 1960s, the UK has seen a number of massive tour-operator collapses (including XL in 2008 – see Parton and Ryley 2012), which led ABTA, the Association of British Travel Agents (renamed the Travel Association in 2007), to set up its bonding scheme in the 1970s. In 1975, the government introduced a compulsory contribution of 2 per cent of operator turnover by tour operators to ABTA's bonding scheme. This is to safeguard tourists from company insolvencies and being stranded overseas, as happened in the 1990s with the collapse of the International Leisure Group, which severely depleted the fund. From April 2008 the levy on turnover was replaced by a £1 levy on each package holiday sold. For tour operators wishing to operate specific programmes, a licensing scheme which the Civil Aviation Authority (CAA) operates in the UK requires them to obtain an Air Travel Organizer's Licence (ATOL) with a £2.50 levy on each passenger booked, although this is currently under review.

Trends in the European holiday market: Integration, consolidation and concentration

The European market is one of the most highly developed and complex areas of activity in the development of tour operators globally. It has seen a great deal of activity, particularly in investment, acquisitions and mergers. For example, in February 2005, the UK leading coach operators Shearings and Wallace Arnold merged, to create a combined passenger base of 1 million and 3400 employees; the venture capitalist 3i owned 67 per cent of the shares. This reflects issues of strategy and scale in seeking to reduce competition and develop a pan-European business. As Insight 7.2 suggests, there is a much stronger propensity for people from the more affluent Western European regions to travel than those from other EU regions.

The markets that dominate outbound travel are Germany, the UK and Scandinavia. A significant proportion of the holiday traffic is on inclusive tours to the main destinations of Spain, France and Germany, with Asia Pacific the fastest-growing area of activity.

In Europe, large integrated tour operators dominate channels via integration:

- *vertically*, via the value chain, to include transport, business travel, tour operating and travel retailing
- *horizontally*, by amalgamations, takeovers and mergers of competing companies in the same business (e.g. TUI AG's purchase of Thomson Holidays)
- *in destination areas*, by acquiring, developing or buying equity stakes in accommodation as well as incoming tour and locally based coach operators.

Much of the growth in the European tour-operator market has exhibited this pattern of concentration into fewer large integrated operators with aggressive commercial strategies of high-volume sales, purchasing or providing capacity at low cost with a resulting low profit margin. The commercial strategy seeks to grow the control of the tourism sector, with profitability based on cost control, the use of ICTs and profit based on high-volume turnover, with low profit margins per unit sold. As Huang *et al.* (2010) suggest, two distinct competition strategies used for package holidays are those based on quantity competition (volume) and price competition in the supply chain. Alegre *et al.* (2012) adopt a more historical analysis in the analysis of package holiday prices in the Balearic Islands, where price competition exists. Yet as the discussion of ATOL data later in the chapter will show, the competition posed by low-cost carriers (including the airlines like Monarch who adopted a low-cost model – see Insight 7.3 later), profit margins have caused significant problems for the sale of holidays alongside the online competition. In the UK, the pressures posed by uncertainty around the effect of Brexit in 2019 also suppressed demand, leading major tourism companies like TUI and Thomas Cook to report poorer than expected financial, with Thomas Cook going into receivership in September 2019.

However, at the individual country level, the real significance of tour operators such as TUI is evident in their overall control of the package holidaymaker in terms of volume and extent (see Insight 7.2). For this reason, attention now turns to the UK.

The UK outbound package tour market

In the UK, licensing of tour operations by the CAA via ATOL provides a good insight into how far the main concerns of consumer groups and government regulatory bodies are warranted regarding the control which integrated groups have over the market. Critics have pointed to the potentially anticompetitive practices of large groups in forcing smaller operators out of the market to gain market share and control, as many Monopoly and Mergers Committee reports on the tour-operator market indicated. Up to 2007, four main groups emerge in terms of passengers carried, dominated by TUI UK Ltd, Thomas Cook Group, First Choice and MyTravel. However, the rapid expansion of the e-tourism market, represented by the Expedia Group, marks a major shift in tour operating.

INSIGHT 7.2 TUI AG – the world's largest integrated tour operator

The company evolved from the German company Preussag AG in the 1990s, when it chose to focus on services, having been an industrial conglomerate. Its entry into tourism is a significant example of corporate restructuring and repositioning to enter a growth sector – tourism. This involved divestment of former assets and investment in others, including the acquisition in 1997 of Hapag-Lloyd AG, which had a global logistics, airline and travel agency chain. This was closely followed by the acquisition of TUI Deutschland, which was a brand leader for quality package holidays. The company invested in other tourism assets in tourism distribution (vertical and horizontal integration), to develop an integrated value chain. That means that, by owning companies performing key functions throughout the tourism distribution chain, it can create synergies, enter into international partnerships, form strategic alliances (see Chapter 5 for more detail) and establish quality levels across all elements of the tourism product (i.e. purchasing, transport, incoming tour handling, accommodation and ground transport). The complete integration of the product through the distribution also allows the company to provide a seamless tourism experience (Image 7.3).

In 2000, the company continued its rapid growth in developing tourism operations, purchasing the Thomson travel group in the UK, which had a prominent brand and market position with a quality association. Further acquisitions followed in other European countries, including Eastern Europe. By 2003, 65 per cent of the Preussag AG group turnover was from tourism and in 2006 this rose to 70 per cent, with shipping accounting for 30 per cent.

In terms of the company image, it was rebranded in 2004 to TUI AG under the aegis of the World of TUI, and Figure 7.5 summarizes the company's corporate profile in tourism. It is clearly the most integrated tourism operator in Europe and has developed a strong market presence in most European countries' outbound markets (and China). This distribution of tour operators within the TUI AG group highlights the key outbound markets of the UK, Germany, France and Scandinavia, as well as the Netherlands, with affluent consumers taking overseas holidays. The company's consolidation of the tour-operator market is also illustrated by its investment in airlines-to-service packages and

IMAGE 7.3 TUI has a range of products for different markets, such as cruises for couples
© TUI

7

the growing low-cost market. In 2005 it launched its low-cost airline, Thomsonfly, which served 20 UK airports and 85 destinations until it merged with Thomson Airways in 2008. The company integrated operations in tourism cover retailing (travel agents, Internet and other ICTs), tour operation, transportation, accommodation, business travel, incoming tourism and cruising, to provide control over the distribution channels in the destination.

The company is both visionary and strategic in its development of new markets and products, including its understanding of the fundamental changes in consumer behaviour towards the modular consumer who needs to be accommodated by innovative approaches rather than a complete, 'take it or leave it' package. For example, TUI offers seat-only sales in the UK and Belgium. The move into China with the TUI China joint venture has tapped the growing inbound, outbound and domestic Chinese tourism market. The company has also developed a joint venture in Russia (TUI Mostravel) with the expansion of outbound travel among Russians to conventional Eastern European areas and new travel to the Mediterranean. Above all, innovation remains a hallmark of TUI AG, as epitomized by its establishment of a travel agency of the future in a Berlin shopping mall. This uses virtual reality to allow the consumer to view the product as a sensory experience.

In September 2007, TUI AG merged with First Choice and sought to improve profitability with cost savings from the merger of £150 million. This involved the closure of 100 of its 1100 travel agencies, and it envisaged a growth in long-haul travel as new long-range aircraft were introduced to its European fleet. By 2011, TUI had 200 brands in 180 countries, serving 30 million customers, employing 53,000 staff in the 31 countries which it viewed as its main source markets. The company had grown its turnover from £13,514 million in 2010 to £14,687 million in 2011, with profits of £471 million in 2011. This rose to over €19.7 billion in 2018. In terms of turnover, the three largest markets are Germany, France and the UK. As Figure 7.5 shows, the company has reoriented itself to four key areas of operation, with around a third of the European tour-operator market. Among the hallmarks of TUI's success are a strategic focus on selling leading brands, offering mainstream package holidays and diversifying into new markets and products while driving sales by online tools. For example, in 2011 the company sold 30 per cent of its holidays online. The scale of operation has enabled TUI to offer competitive prices by achieving economies of scale (i.e. the company sold 150 million room nights), while entering new markets (e.g. Brazil and India). As the company's Annual Report outlined in 2011, TUI sought to innovate, building profitable supplier relationships, controlling costs, utilizing yield management and selling high volumes while being customer-oriented. By catering for established mainstream and emerging markets, TUI is constantly evolving and is seen as a market leader. The company's 2018 Annual Report observed that it had grown turnover.

Owing to the strategic transformation from a traditional tour operator and trader to a developer, investor and operator of hotel and cruise companies initiated in 2014, TUI's business delivers considerably higher margins and is less seasonal, reducing its dependence on the summer months . . . and [thanks to our] use of state-of-the-art IT and intelligent customer systems, we have considerable potential for new business, turnover and earnings. We will continue our successful transformation: The next step will transform TUI into a digital and platform organisation.

(TUI Annual Report 2018)

More in-depth analysis from ATOL examines the recent trends in the price of ATOL holidays but this does not cover the rapid development of flight-only purchases from low-cost airlines which is dealt with elsewhere (CAA 2006). If we compare Figures 7.6 and 7.7 it is clear that in a 17-year period, a significant change has occurred in tour operating in the UK in relation to how holidays are sold.

Figure 7.6 shows that in 2002, the large tourism companies like MyTravel, TUI, First Choice and Thomas Cook Group dominated the market and volume of sales with 53 per cent of the total number of ATOL passengers licensed with a total of over 17 million passengers. By 2019, this had dropped to 13.6 million passengers for the Top 4 companies with Jet2holidays reaching the second position in 2019. Jet2holidays is part of the Dart Group which owns the airline Jet2.com (the fifth largest airline operator in the UK operating 100 aircraft in the peak season) serving destinations in the Mediterranean, the Canary Islands and European cities. The company saw an 18 per cent growth in revenue in 2018 on a turnover of £2.3 billion in the Dart Group reflecting its rising position in UK package holiday sales offering holiday flights from £49. In 2018 it sold 5.3 million flight only seats reflecting the shift

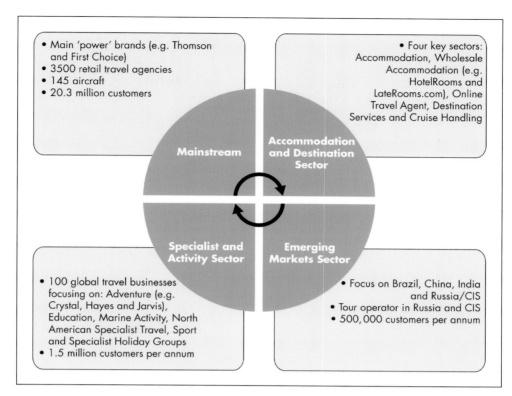

FIGURE 7.5 TUI business sectors

from packages to self-packaging in contrast to the 2.5 million package holidays it sold. The company carried over 10 million passengers in 2018 and in the peak operating season it provides 312 weekly flights.

The scale of growth in the online travel companies and control which the large integrated tourism companies have on the holiday market is reflected in Figure 7.7 over the last decade in particular. Figure 7.7 shows that not only have online retailers emerged to challenge the large tourism companies like TUI, but low-cost airlines like easyJet have also diversified their portfolio of businesses to become more than low-cost airlines by offering holidays. The UK government concerns for competition in this area of holiday purchasing led to a Department of Trade and Industry Foreign Package Holiday Order which stated that travel agents owned by a tour operator controlling

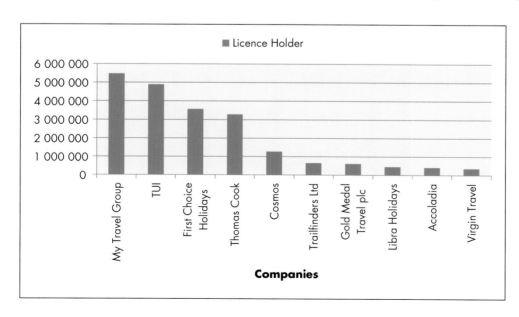

FIGURE 7.6 Top 10 ATOL Licence Holders, 2002
Source: Compiled from ATOL CAA (2002), *ATOL Business*, Issue 20

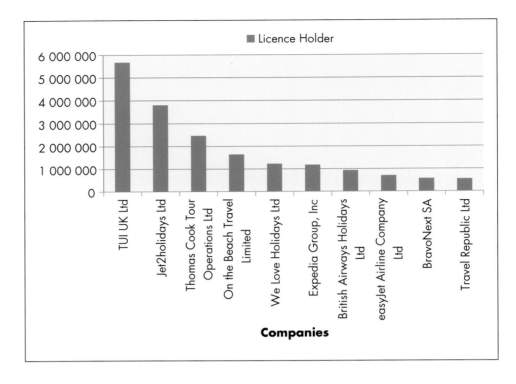

FIGURE 7.7 Top 10 ATOL Licence Holders, 2019
Source: Compiled from ATOL database

more than 5 per cent of the package market should identify their links with suppliers in brochures and shop interiors. Above all, the volatile nature of the package holiday market has seen the integrated companies pursue different market strategies as they:

- seek to expand market share, market dominance and position in consumers' minds
- seek to convert domestic holiday-taking to outbound travel by conveying images of low-cost holidays
- drive down the cost from suppliers and from repackaging the product, so that no-frills packages (i.e. no airport transfers, no holiday representative or in-flight meals) are provided in the market, appealing to the lower end of the consumer spectrum
- drive out the smaller operators in the long term, to further consolidate market dominance.

(Page 2003)

Other strategies have been to develop new markets such as long-haul markets which now exceed 20 per cent of outbound UK business. Seat-only sales on charter flights have also seen some operators expand their business, as illustrated by TUI AG. More common strategies are to seek new, cheaper destinations as over 50 per cent of UK holidaymakers are choosing packages when travelling overseas abroad at some time. One consequence has been product diversification to grow the range of possible holiday options including:

- city breaks and additional short breaks as secondary airports open up new potential destinations such as Iceland Air's service to Reykjavik
- long-haul and adventure travel such as ecotourism and nature holidays
- greater flexibility and tailoring of the packages to the client needs

(Page 2003)

Clearly competition will result in further consolidation among tour operators as the e-tourism revolution continues. One consequence is that, in 2001, 23 ATOL-licensed companies went bankrupt and £3 million in compensation was awarded to travellers. This led Barclays Bank to launch a new bonding scheme for small operators with less than 800 passengers a year to help address the issue of insolvency. In the period 1985–2001, £159 million was paid to 190 000 people for 300 ATOL operators failing, which was paid from the ATOL bond it retains from tour operators. The CAA pays the shortfalls in compensation from the bond from its Air Travel Trust Fund, which in 2002 was, reportedly, £8 million in debt, highlighting the need for a re-evaluation of the role of bonds and tour operators' solvency. In 2011–2012 the ATOL Air Travel Trust Fund paid repatriation costs of tourists stranded overseas and reimbursed the costs of those who had booked, and the company was in a £42.2 million deficit. The scale of the deficit was caused by 29 ATOL licence holders failing in 2011, with 47 000 passengers repatriated and 145 000 people receiving refunds. In the period May 2011–May 2012 a total of 21 failures occurred, also reflected in the 40 company failures reported by ABTA, where £542,000 was paid out to clients from its funds. Clearly 2010–2012 also proved to be turbulent times for the tour-operator sector, with the Thomas Cook Group also receiving refinancing loans. Numbers of passengers paying the Air Passenger Contribution of £2.50 per head rose from 17 to 19 million between 2012 and 2013 and ATOL's income rose from £42 million to £48 million. The year 2012–2013 saw only 11 businesses fail, resulting in £813,000 in claims against the Air Transportation Fund (also see Insight 7.3). By 2018, the Fund was sufficiently robust to accommodate the challenges it faced in 2017 as discussed in Insight 7.3, when the largest airline collapse in UK history occurred with the demise of Monarch Airlines.

INSIGHT 7.3 Airline and tour-operator insolvency in the UK

In 2017, the largest airline failure which ATOL had to contend with was the collapse of Monarch Airlines with its fleet of 36 aircraft when 110 000 people were repatriated in a two-week operation. At the time it was the fifth largest airline in the UK, having operated for 50 years. This was the largest single repatriation of people in the UK since the Second World War and involved 60 aircraft from 24 airlines. The explanations for the collapse are attributed to several factors:

- The impact of terrorism in the Middle East targeting tourists in its core markets of the Mediterranean and North Africa

- The devaluation of the UK currency, the pound sterling, after the announcement of Brexit that impacted the exchange rate and made UK overseas holidays more expensive

- Falling revenue and rising costs, such as the price of aviation fuel

- The failure to compete using a low-cost airline business model (e.g. in 2016 it made a loss of £291 million, by carrying 14 per cent more passengers but receiving £100 million less in revenue due to cost-cutting by competitors

- It switched from long-haul flights after 2014 when it was rescued by Greybull Capital, a private investment company

- The uncertainty posed by Brexit for consumers taking overseas holidays

- Competition from other companies.

The scale of the repatriation cost the UK government £60 million for uninsured passengers and ATOL £21 million from 32 000 claims. In total a further 600 000 passengers had their travel arrangements cancelled and the government announced a review of airline insolvency (Department for Transport 2018) that reported in 2018. The report assessed airline insolvency risk, concluding that there was a 25 per cent risk of an airline failing in the next 15 years, which would impact 0.5 per cent of holiday travellers up to 2033, reflecting the competitive environment for operations. In fact the International Air Transport Association (IATA) argued in its 2018 Annual Report that the average profit per airline passenger was US$9.7 on a US$38 billion profit for the entire aviation sector. It is not surprising that such low profit margins require expert management to ensure ongoing profitability in a sector where crisis events (e.g. terrorism) can remove the market for a product (as discussed in earlier chapters). The report also highlighted other schemes such as Denmark's levy on all outbound passengers. The ATOL scheme was under scrutiny due to the ability to manage future collapses given the cost to the UK government of the Monarch collapse. As part of the review, the report also outlined the protection landscape for consumers where two distinct areas existed:

- **Statutory Protection**
  - The 1992 Package Holiday Directive and subsequent amendments
  - The ATOL scheme
  - The UK Consumer Credit Act 1975 which provides cover for consumers on purchases for the sale and supply of goods and in this case travel services

- **Non-Statutory Protection**
  - The IATA's billing and settlement arrangements for travel agents may allow them to make refunds to the agents and to offer 'rescue fares' when an insolvency occurs to help repatriate passengers cheaply (although the 2018 report notes the lack of capacity in the European airline market in the peak season to accommodate large insolvencies)

INSIGHT 7.3 continued

- o Insurance where consumers may gain cover for airline insolvency
- o In the UK, the Credit Card Act allows consumers to ask for a credit card company to reverse a disputed purchase where insolvency occurs, called a charge-back.

The collapse of several larger airlines and the inquiry into insolvency in the UK airline market demonstrates the various options of protecting the outbound package holiday consumer. Given the scale and volume of holiday-taking in the UK and Europe, it reinforces the need for mechanisms able to facilitate the effective operation of airline operations. It also illustrates the risk and challenges posed by high levels of competition which were discussed in Chapter 5, which in extreme cases can cause business insolvency, where profit margins are extremely low and so dependent upon volume sales.

Further reading

Department for Transport (2018) *Airline Insolvency Review: Interim Report*. London: Department for Transport.

di Giulio, M. (2018) 'Alitalia, or the inability to align regulation with industrial policies', *Contemporary Italian Politics*, 10(4): 377–392.

Hoggan, K. (2017) 'Monarch: Four reasons behind its failure', *BBC News* 2 October 2017, https://www.bbc.co.uk/news/business-41466722.

Parton, J. and Ryley, T. (2012) 'A business analysis of XL airways: What lessons can be learned from the failure?' *Journal of Air Transport Management*, 19 (1): 42–48.

Questions

1 Why are airlines ending up insolvent?
2 How does insolvency affect consumer confidence in tourism products and services?
3 If you were advising the government on what action to take to restore consumer confidence, what measures might you consider introducing?

TABLE 7.1 Changes in travel retailing

Period	Trading environment	Type of travel retailing
1950s	Limited demand for holidays or other travel. Reconstruction of war-damaged city centres	Full-service travel specialists located in major urban and business centres. Limited competition
1960s	Gradual increase in city centre travel retailers with the development of demand for leisure travel	Coach and other domestic holidays sold by small coach companies and through newsagents
1970s	Rapid expansion in demand for holidays	Successful retailers expand the number of outlets – proliferation of high-street retailers
1980s	Development of out-of-town shopping malls and large-scale town centres. Many high streets suffer from shop closures and temporary tenants	First computerized reservations system for inclusive holidays. Larger travel agency chains grow by acquiring smaller 'miniples', consolidating ownership and putting pressure on independents. Development of specialized holiday shops, and decline of full-service travel agencies
1990s	Increasing financial pressure on travel retailers, increasing rate of acquisition and mergers	Increasingly selective racking policies. Technological developments enable customers to create their own holiday packages by booking direct from home

Source: © Eric Laws (1997: 122), reproduced with permission from the author

---

To summarize, the outcome of changes in the European tour-operator market is likely to be further integration and consolidation with:

- expansion via acquisitions, especially as some of the large tourism concerns have
- integration of air and hotel businesses

- further widening of distribution channels, especially with the digital revolution and enhancements with new technologies such as artificial intelligence
- widening geographical coverage of markets and tour operators merging/entering into strategic alliances
- the impact of the euro, which may allow operators to buy capacity cheaper from weaker currencies, providing lower-priced holidays
- a gradual levelling of package holiday prices across the EU
- greater cost controls
- new business strategies towards products (i.e. focus on core business versus diversification)
- a greater alignment of business towards changing consumer behaviour.

(developed from Page 2019; other sources)

One consequence of these changes, as the examples have shown, is the growing internationalization of the tour operator. Many become TNCs (see Chapter 5) and seek further economies of scale, a wider market spread internationally and the use of multiple distribution strategies, advertising and ICTs using yield management systems (see Chapter 8 for more detail of yield management). The result in highly developed outbound markets such as the UK and Germany is that a small number of large companies now control the supply to consumers. Two casualties were MyTravel and First Choice, which sought to grow and consolidate their market positions but were taken over in 2007. Above all, it is important for tour operators to be cognizant of market trends, changes to consumer behaviour and the effect on their business as well as the profitability of their business operations, which partly explains the major takeovers in 2007.

The role of the 'new' consumer and future trends in tour operating

A very influential study by Poon (1993) identified the changing nature of tourists as consumers, which had implications for tourism purchasing habits. In particular Poon identified a shift from the old tourists, the less experienced travellers who purchased a homogeneous, mass-produced product that was supply-driven (Chapter 4). Much of the consumption was mass resort, 'sun, sea and sand'-oriented for consumers to escape the routines of daily life. In contrast, 'new' tourism is characterized by more experienced travellers who have a growing environmental concern

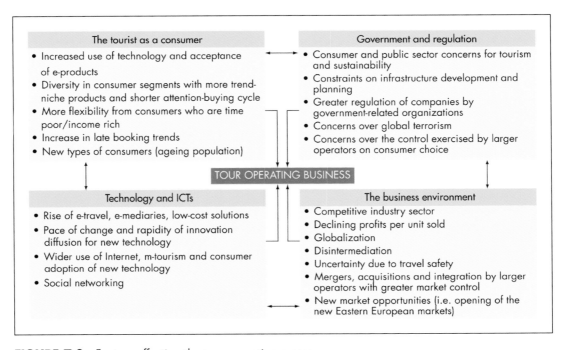

FIGURE 7.8 Factors affecting the tour operating sector

about the impact of their holidays on the places they visit and require more individualized products rather than the mass products, that are less predictable, and products that are full of surprise, discovery and memorable experiences rather than simply a repetition of last year's beach holiday (Page 2003). Although 'old' and 'new' tourism coexist, 'new' tourism offers the tourism industry many growth opportunities given that tourism businesses can react to the demand for increased flexibility through greater use of ICTs. The types of factors operators need to consider are highlighted in Figure 7.8, which reveals the increasingly complex business environment which the tour-operator sector now faces globally. As Insight 7.1 shows, integrated companies such as TUI are pursuing a dual strategy towards the holiday market: nurturing the existing 'old' or what they term 'the mainstream' package holiday market, and the more flexible and more customized products. Perhaps one of the most dominant issues to arise, however, is the growth of consumer rights, consumer action and a more discerning approach to purchasing. Yet one anomaly here is that despite consumer interest in the environment, the numbers of tourists travelling is increasing – ultimately placing more pressure on the environment.

Tour operating and consumerism

One consequence of 'new' tourism and more experienced travellers is the rise of a more demanding consumer combined with a demand for higher quality at lower cost. According to ABTA, 90 per cent of UK package holidays are ABTA-bonded and in 2000 almost 5 per cent of the UK's 20 million package-holiday-takers were fairly or very dissatisfied with their holidays. In 2003, ABTA received 17,000 complaints and all but 1200 were resolved quickly, with the remainder going to arbitration. By 2011 this had dropped to 12,566 complaints with only 151 going to arbitration. However, this does not include those tourists who directly litigated via the small claims court or by other means. Complaints concerned the quality of accommodation, perceived safety standards of overseas chartered aircraft, surcharges, and failure to provide what was advertised. For example, £2.5 million in compensation was agreed in an out-of-court settlement for 790 holidaymakers who caught the norovirus stomach bug, salmonella and campylobacter while staying at a hotel in Spain between 2000 and 2003. The case reflects the likely cost of such failures in maintaining adequate standards of hygiene and cleanliness in a hotel when it impacts upon tourist health and well-being. The most common complaints are shown in Figure 7.9.

These issues remain problematic due to the gap between the consumers' perception of what they are purchasing and the reality of consumption. In the EU, the 1993 EC Directive on Package Travel required greater precision from the tour operator. As the DTI response to the directive, the following measures were implemented so that:

- all tours were licensed
- there was a greater degree of honesty in holiday brochure description
- an obligation was placed on travel agents to take responsibility for the information contained in brochures they stocked and for ensuring adequate advice to clients on:
  - health
  - passport and visa requirements
  - insurance needs

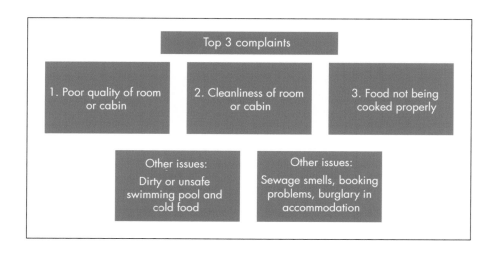

FIGURE 7.9 Common issues which tourists complain about from their holiday experience
Source: Holiday Travel Watch survey data, 2016

and makes the tour operator liable for losses resulting from misleading information or where suppliers do not provide the services paid for and contracted(Page 2003).

For the tour operator, the DTI response highlights the need for support staff in the destination, namely the holiday representative ('the Rep'), so they can act as trouble-shooters to remedy problems or complaints *in situ*. The Rep's job is very demanding as they are the public relations agent of the company, often on call 24 hours a day, 7 days a week in the peak season. They typically combine a number of roles including:

- meeting and greeting incoming and departing passengers at the airport to ensure airport transfers drop the right passengers at the correct accommodation
- handling a wide range of destination-specific inquiries, requests and provision of social events
- giving publicity to tours and services endorsed by the company for which a commission is paid to the company by the suppliers
- dealing with special requests (i.e. arrangements for disabled guests) and acting as a go-between for the tourist and hotel, local police, medical services and other agencies when required

(Page 2003)

However, there are also moves among some tour operators to remove the Rep, given that they may not add value for experienced travellers. They are replacing the Reps with 24-hour contact with the company head office and quality information.

The business of tour operating: Developing the holiday brochure

The holiday brochure remains the most powerful marketing tool in reaching the consumer increasingly via online tools, since the intangible nature of tourism makes it imperative that the potential customer can read about what they may want to purchase (although much of this is also available electronically). To develop a brochure, a tour operator will need to plan, organize and implement a tour programme as part of its marketing and advertising process (see Chapters 14 and 15). The tour operator has to undertake a series of stages of work including:

- research and planning
- negotiation with suppliers
- administration
- marketing

all of which are now highly dependent upon the use of ICTs. It can take up to 18 months from identifying a resort and product to brochure production.

The holiday brochure has evolved from its modern-day predecessor which was introduced in 1953 by Thomas Cook (Laws 1997) (see Images 7.4 and 7.5 for an example), although the company also produced much simpler brochures during the 1920s and 1930s. The changes from the 1960s can be seen by comparing Images 7. 1 and 7.2 with subsequent changes in the 1970s in brochure design. During the 1970s, brochure design assumed a greater sophistication (Images 7.6 and 7.7) to nurture a generation of travellers who had already experienced overseas travel in the late 1960s with the more sophisticated brochure imagery of the 1970s. This used a similar format to that of women's magazines, reflecting the important role of women as holiday decision-makers. The 1960s saw holiday brochures become glossier and packed with information and their role change to that of a modern-day holiday catalogue. One possible format is shown in Figure 7.10.

Holiday brochures and the electronic equivalents allow travel agents and e-mediaries:

- to obtain sales
- to provide information to assist purchasers' decision-making in relation to the destination, product offerings, timing (summer/winter), price, ancillary services
- to afford cost-effective distribution for the tour operator, with an attractive cover, being prominently racked in travel agents and able to generate business among agents

- to provide an effective tool to allow agents to sell holidays with detailed products/booking codes
- to allow a contract to be agreed between the tour operator and customer, providing information on procedures for changing the booking, complaints, refunds, the details of the product purchased, the client details and insurance premium paid.

(Page 2003)

As Laws (1997) describes, a brochure will go through a design process to:

- identify the market audience and product
- utilize an appropriate company brand
- produce a mock-up, using a computer with illustrations and professional photographs of the hotel, destination, product offerings and services
- use a desktop publishing system which will help with brochure layout and design
- produce a proof, which is checked, and inaccuracies identified prior to printing.

Accuracy and a need to be honest and truthful in holiday brochures are now enshrined in consumer legislation in many countries. Operator groups such as ABTA with its *Code of Conduct for Tour Operators* indicate that the brochure is a legal document to which complaints may refer in future claims for compensation.

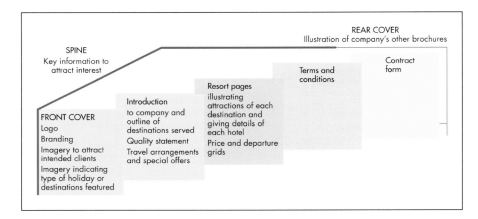

FIGURE 7.10 Structure of inclusive holiday brochures.
Source: © Eric Laws (1997), reproduced with the author's permission

IMAGE 7.4 Thomas Cook brochure for holidays to Italy, 1958. © Thomas Cook

Holloway (2001) identifies the following information, which must be provided in a holiday brochure for the tour operator to obtain a licence:

- the name of the firm responsible for the IT
- the means of transport used, including, in the case of air transport, the name of the carrier(s), type and class of aircraft used and whether scheduled or charter aircraft are operated
- full details of destinations, itinerary and times of travel
- the duration of each tour (number of days'/nights' stay)
- full description of the location and type of accommodation provided, including any meals
- whether services of a representative are available abroad
- a clear indication of the price for each tour, including any taxes
- exact details of special arrangements, (e.g. if there is a games room in the hotel, whether this is available at all times and whether any charges are made for the use of this equipment)
- full conditions of booking, including details of cancellation conditions
- details of any insurance coverage (clients should have the right to choose their own insurance, providing this offers equivalent coverage)

- details of documentation required for travel to the destinations featured, and any health hazards or inoculations recommended.

Source: Holloway: 2001: 253–254

Once a booking needs to be made, the tour operators will distribute the product via a wide range of channels including agents and CRSs, the Internet, direct by phone and the different mechanisms discussed earlier in Figure 7.1.

Prior to the digital age, the continued consolidation meant that 80 per cent of inclusive tours were sold through 20 per cent of agents, with commissions paid to agents, plus an override (1–5 per cent) in addition to the basic 10 per cent for high performance. This has changed with disintermediation.

Travel agents and retailing

Travel agents perform a role in the tourism distribution system, and in the UK they accounted for the dominant element of sales of package holidays in the late 1990s, though online retailing by tour operators and e-mediaries (see Chapter 6) has begun to challenge the travel agent's role. Yet if the consumer requires information, then the travel agent's role in tourism is to recognize and highlight that tourism is:

- *intangible*, meaning tourism is a speculative investment and an expensive purchase where the product is conveyed to the customer usually in a brochure
- *perishable*, and so can only be sold for the period it is available (it cannot be stored). This highlights the importance of last-minute bookings to sell surplus capacity
- *dynamic*, meaning that it is forever in a state of flux, especially as a product where prices can rise and fall
- *heterogeneous*, meaning it is not a standardized product which is produced and delivered in a homogeneous manner. It varies, and interactions can enhance or adversely affect it since it is dependent upon people and many unknown factors
- *inseparable*, meaning that in the consumer's mind it is purchased and consumed as an overall experience; so communicating what is being offered, its value and scope is important. Since the consumer is transported to the product, it is an unusual form of distribution, where there is a need for timely information on all of the elements as outlined in the brochure (Page 2003), where the imagery seeks to create an impression of fun for young people (see Images 7.5–Image 7.7).

However, the rise of a new trend, disintermediation, has also impacted upon the traditional role of the travel agent. Disintermediation has been brought about by the rise of e-tailing and e-mediaries, which have removed the dominance of the traditional high-street travel agent, as discussed previously in Chapter 6. Combined with changes brought about by ICTs, a number of processes in the tourism business environment are impacting upon travel agents to increase the effect of disintermediation, as Figure 7.11 shows. This is reinforced by Figure 7.8, which outlines changes to the environment of tour operating which are also relevant to travel agencies. Disintermediation

IMAGE 7.5 1955 holiday brochure for Prestatyn Holiday Camp owned and operated by Thomas Cook, © Thomas Cook

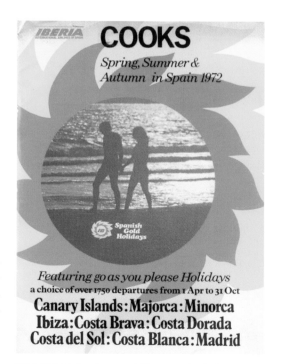

IMAGE 7.6 A typical Thomas Cook Spain brochure, *c.*1972
© Thomas Cook

IMAGE 7.7 Thomas Cook Summer Sunshine brochure, 1978
© Thomas Cook

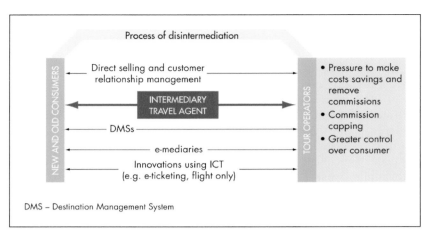

FIGURE 7.11 Disintermediation in the distribution chain

effectively unlocks the broker role that the tour operator and travel agent have traditionally provided by allowing consumers alternatives and the information from the Internet to book holidays and travel. Despite disintermediation, travel agents remain a key intermediary in the distribution chain, and are characterized by many features although the impact of decommissioning trends by low-cost airlines who do not pay a travel agent's commission has been a major threat to their commission-based model (Benckendorff *et al.* 2019).

The evolution of travel agents

Travel agents in their most commercial form can be traced back to Thomas Cook, and most then were independent agents, with the exception of Thomas Cook. They largely performed an agent's role in selling travel tickets for rail-, sea- and land-based services as well as accommodation. This was largely a brokerage role, receiving a commission on each sale. In the 1930s, air-based travel emerged (Image 7.8) but agents had not reached a mass market. It was in the 1960s that the greatest changes in travel agencies occurred, with commissions, licensing and greater airline–agency relations, particularly in the sale of group travel (Laws 1997). By developing increased levels of information, service and specialized products, agents began to become more involved in the tour operation side of travel, organizing tours and selling cruises from block allocations. During the 1970s, these changes saw many travel agents expand with the growth of package travel, basing their business on volume sales. Further market change occurred in the 1980s as agencies entered into tour operating, while mergers, acquisitions and consolidation occurred. Grouping into formal alliances or consortia enabled agencies to seek greater commissions, using increased levels of technology to assist in distribution, while the high street has seen large chains emerge. In the 1980s and 1990s, travel agents bore the brunt of tour-operator practices of fuel and currency surcharges which significantly impacted upon the image of the tourism sector. Similarly, in the 1990s, major challenges have included the loss of commission from airline ticket sales and other cuts in earning potential. One response for some agencies is to now charge a consultancy fee in lieu of agency fees, since commissions are the lifeblood of their revenue. One consequence is the diversification into other products such as travel insurance, where the commission may counterbalance cuts in other areas of their work. Yet the Internet is also allowing the cost-conscious traveller to compare insurance costs now, making this revenue more contested. Laws (1997) examined many of these changes, as shown in Table 7.1, looking at the entire postwar period and the style of travel retailing which evolved to characterize each era.

Travel agents: Roles and activities

Globally it is estimated that there are about 400 000 travel agents using Global Distribution Systems like Amadeus which has an around 40 per cent share in the global market for travel bookings. In the UK, there are almost 5000 travel agency branches affiliated to ABTA via its 1200 members; many of these are retail multiples (i.e. chains also owned by tour operators). Like tour operating, the structure of travel agents has changed in recent years as consolidation led to greater pressure on independent agents and less choice for the consumer, as multiples dominate the retailing of products. Interestingly, travel agents have no stock, acting on behalf of the tour operators, and so they have little financial risk and do not purchase products themselves. They receive a commission for each sale and, as agents, do not become part of the contract of sale, which is between the tour operator and the customer. Some agencies specialize, such as in airline tickets; others may aim at the larger mass-package market. Agents use the GDS (introduced in Chapter 6) and the scale of travel bookings is reflected in the following summary statistics from Amadeus, who use a transaction business model for selling travel products and services from suppliers, with their inventory in 2019 comprising:

- 440 airlines
- 2 million hotel and shopping options
- 90 railway companies
- 40 car rental companies
- 30 insurance providers
- 50 cruise ship companies
- airport transfer companies and local tour companies.

Source: Amadeus (2019) Global Report 2018, Amadeus.com

Such GDSs are used by a range of travel agent types, including travel management companies selling corporate travel, online travel agencies, high-street and physically located agencies as well as tour operators.

High-street agents do not specialize in business and corporate travel, although the market for specialist agents is worth over £10.5 billion a year in the UK. One very controversial area of debate in travel agents' behaviour is the process of racking, where the agents emphasize/display certain businesses' products (perhaps their own company's in the case of integrated businesses) to favour them as they promise higher commissions. This has concerned government bodies like the MMC, who call this directional selling (where an agent tries to sell a product from a vertically integrated tour operator). This complex process is then developed by the travel agent through a purchase process, where matching client needs with product offerings has a key role to play. As Figure 7.12 shows, the travel agent has to establish a rapport with clients, then understand their needs, while keeping them interested

IMAGE 7.8 Leaflet advertising charter trips to attend the Grand Prix horse race Feb. 1933 or ski races at a cost of £22 and £44, respectively, on a 'Heracles' airliner
© Thomas Cook

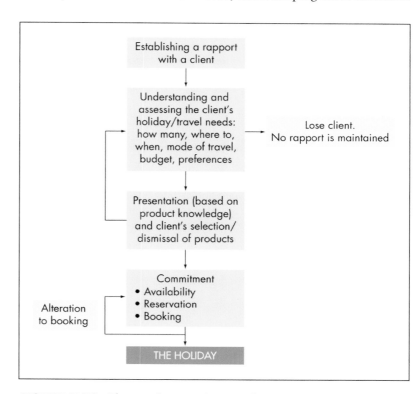

FIGURE 7.12 The travel agent–client purchase process

7

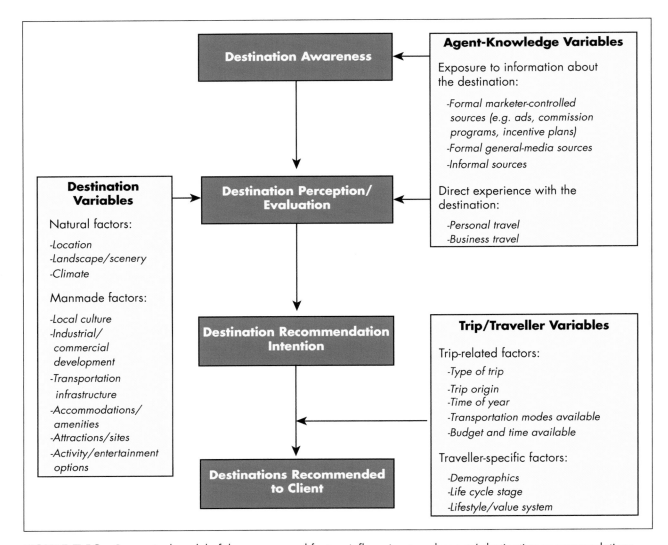

FIGURE 7.13 Conceptual model of the process and factors influencing travel agents' destination recommendations. Source: Reproduced with permission from Elsevier from Klenosky, D. B. and Gitelson, R. E. (1998), 'Travel agents' destination recommendations', *Annals of Tourism Research*, 25 (3): 664.

and presenting various options based on product and destination knowledge. This also highlights the critical role which agency recommendation may play in shaping consumer choice of destination. Klenosky and Gitelson (1998) have produced a conceptual model to explain this which is outlined in Figure 7.13, highlighting the key role of agent knowledge in matching customer and trip variables to destination variables.

However, at a more practical level, travel agents typically deal with a diverse range of tasks including:

- making reservations
- planning itineraries (including complex around-the-world travel)
- calculating fares and charges
- producing tickets
- advising clients on destinations, resorts, airline companies and a wide range of travel products
- communicating with clients verbally and in writing
- maintaining accurate records on reservations

- ensuring racks are stocked well or supplies are kept in-house
- acting as intermediaries where customer complaints occur

(Page 2003)

and an illustration of their scale, significance and organization in Australia can be found in Insight 7.4, which examines travel retailing.

INSIGHT 7.4 Travel agencies in Australia

The Australian tourism sector has experienced considerable growth in recent years, with the sector employing almost 500 000 people. As in Europe, the Australian tourism industry has seen a contraction in the number of travel agencies, with the number of businesses dropping from 3174 in 2000–2001 to 2968 in 2005. The sector has a high staff-agency ratio with around 23 000 employees, who account for around 75 per cent of travel agency overheads. As in Europe, the market has seen considerable consolidation with the top four retailers controlling 40 per cent of revenue, which equates to around AU$2338 million for the entire sector. The top four retailers are:

- Flight Centre
- Jetset Travel World
- Harvey World Travel
- Travelscene.

Flight Centre dominate with a 34 per cent market share.

The three markets which the Australian travel agency sector serves are: Australians travelling overseas (65 per cent), Australians travelling domestically (15 per cent) and international visitors to Australia (20 per cent). The Internet has had a major impact on the travel agency sector, supplanting it in 2005 as the most popular booking method.

Among the principal challenges facing Australian travel agents is the way they respond to the decline in commissions from airlines and online competition. Some opportunities exist in non-price-based elements, such as the ease of access they provide to their corporate clients and the role of word-of-mouth recommendation. Opportunities also exist in terms of charging for professional services they offer and in developing new niches such as group travel.

The challenges of a rapidly changing market are exemplified in the case of Flight Centre, originally established in 1981, which expanded from 200 outlets to 1181 in 2005, to 1500 in 2007 in 30 countries employing over 5800 staff, which rose to 13 000 globally in 2011. By 2018 it was operating its Corporate Travel Management business in 90 countries and had 19 000 staff across 2800 businesses. The company located its outlets initially in central city areas and popular shopping malls. It moved into Internet ticket sales in 2000 and in Australia built alliances with airlines such as Qantas and Virgin Blue to sell airline seats, and as airline seat commissions dropped, it began selling land-based transport and cruises. The company had a turnover measured on the value of sales of AU$7.8 billion in 2007, 12.2 billion in 2011 and 21.8 billion in 2018, of which 7.7 billion was from corporate travel. In 2018 it received over 50 per cent of its turnover from its Australian activities followed by 14.6 per cent from the USA, 10 per cent from the UK, 7 per cent from Canada and 6 per cent from New Zealand, with operations in South Africa, Europe, the United Arab Emirates, South East Asia, China, India and Latin America. Its retail leisure brands include: Flight Centre Limited, Travel Managers, Student Universe, Round the World Experts, Aunt Betty, Top Deck, Back Roads Touring, Travel Associates (selling luxury travel), GapYear.com, Liberty Travel and BYO jet. It also has brands in the corporate travel market as well as in student travel (e.g. Campus Travel): Executive Travel, FCM Travel Solutions, Corporate Traveller, Cievents, Stage and Screen, Travel Club Getaways and 4th Dimension. The major investment of AU$10 million in ICTs in 2004 to improve online bookings led the company to also purchase travelthere.com in 2005, and by 2006 it was cited as the top Australian travel agency website (flightcentre.com.au). This investment in digital technology saw further developments in 2018 in GDS technology. The company also announced its expansion of homeworking travel agents in the USA via Liberty Travel to expand its number of homeworking agents in North America to 500.

Figure 7.14 portrays the combination of positive strengths which have helped create the success of Flight Centre globally, while counterbalancing that with the risks and issues it highlighted in its 2011 Annual Report, which continue as the company seeks sustainable growth year on year. As Figure 7.14 shows, Flight Centre's global operations are trading in profit, and it is a forward-looking company which is innovative and entrepreneurial. Much of the company's success may be attributed to the way in which it tries to stay ahead of its competitors, such as through global expansion and use of ICTs.

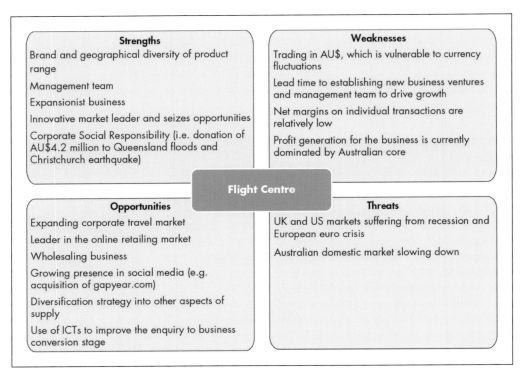

FIGURE 7.14 Generalized Strengths, Weaknesses, Opportunities and Threats (SWOT) analysis of Flight Centre

Business travel agents

Some travel agents also specialize in business travel. According to Davidson (2001) business travel comprises:

- individual business travel (corporate travel), involving business trips related to employer needs
- occasional work activities – such as conferences, conventions, events and incentive programmes.

Figure 7.15 highlights the nature of each category of business travel, the key purchases, the range of intermediaries and who may supply the product.

Globally, Amadeus suggest the market for corporate travel is worth €1.3 billion and is set to grow at 7 per cent per annum between 2018 and 2022, with its GDS's used by 16,000 corporations globally in travel organizing. What is evident from Figure 7.15 is that both private-sector businesses and public-sector employees (i.e. local, regional and national government bodies and charitable bodies) also engage in business travel. Not surprisingly, travel agencies specialize in this market due to the high value of much business travel, which is often sudden, unplanned and may involve premium-priced travel (i.e. business-class travel). In addition, travel management is increasingly questioning the necessity of face-to-face meetings and the importance of 'virtual meetings' in the electronic age, especially with organizations seeking to reduce their carbon footprint (and costs). Business travel costs are substantial for many organizations and so the services of a travel manager may be a mechanism to manage demand and reduce costs. In fact travel management has a long history in the corporate world according to Gustafson (2012), dating to the 1940s in the USA, with professional travel managers emerging in the 1960s as a common element in large organizations. A more common arrangement is for a business travel agency to be engaged in smaller organizations to manage all the clients' travel arrangements. Where a travel manager is employed in an organization, they will work with a travel agency, and the wider range of activities will be ensuring the agency conforms to the company's travel policy (i.e. ensuring certain grades of staff are entitled to travel economy or business class).

The real dilemma for many business travel agencies is that in using e-ticketing, especially for air travel, they may see disintermediation occur where direct purchasing and e-ticketing replace some of their organizing function. The largest business travel agencies in Europe have traditionally been American Express, BTI Hogg Robinson and

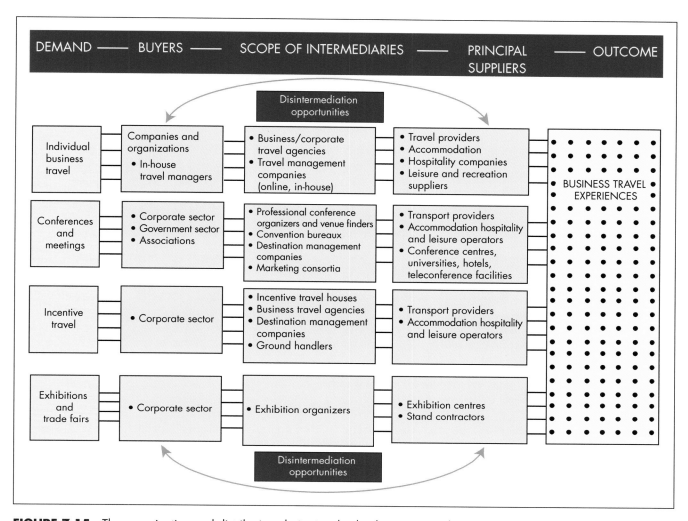

FIGURE 7.15 The organization and distribution chains involved in business travel

Carlson Wagonlit, as consolidation has occurred through mergers and takeovers. However, as the inroads are made by online providers such as Expedia's Egencia, no areas are free of significant digital competition. Where companies use these agencies, contracts can be constructed in a number of ways, but above all this seems to provide companies with greater cost controls on corporate travel and reduces costs. Increasingly the range of activities has expanded, including obtaining visas and passports, ensuring that employers meet their duty of care for employees travelling with a tracking service for overseas travel, and repatriation processes and a helpline if things go wrong. The corporate solution also offers procurement departments of organizations a single point of contact for the implementation of corporate travel policies (e.g. ensuring all staff fly economy class, for example). It also offers monthly management information reporting, removing the need for internal organizational staff to oversee travel.

The online travel revolution and the future of travel agents

The e-tourism revolution identified in Chapter 6 highlights a major problem for the travel agency sector in its current shape and form. E-mediaries, such as Microsoft's Expedia in the USA, which rose from a newcomer to one of the top US travel agencies in four years (Buhalis 2003), have grown phenomenally due to the impact of ICTs and new forms of intermediary and distribution electronically on the conventional high-street travel agent. Expedia purchased US business travel management firm Metropolitan Travel as it also moved into business travel. Figure 7.16 summarizes some of the principal challenges that the sector is facing (see Quintana *et al.* 2016).

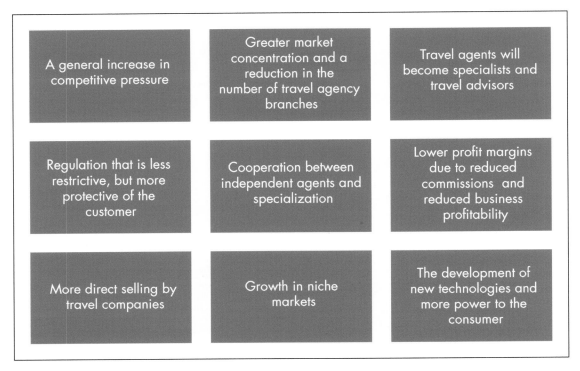

FIGURE 7.16 Trends affecting the travel agent sector
Source: Developed from Quintana *et al.* (2016)

In fact Xiang *et al.* (2015: 244) argue that further trends within digital purchasing are occurring that also impact upon the travel booking process, as:

while traditional means of Internet use for travel planning appears to be widespread across all customer segments, higher-order Internet uses (i.e., social media) are now prevalent among some segments, particularly among travelers of Generation Y. Also, there seems to be an important bifurcation in the traveler population in that the traditional online consumers remain unchanged with their pattern of use of online tools while sizable groups are adopting emergent information sources and transaction channels.

In other words, specific digitally savvy market segments like Generation Y (born in the 1980s and 1990s) and millennials (born after 2000) are providing the division of the online population into two groups, described as bifurcation, as new transaction channels become available through new technology such as apps. For example, Amadeus observed in 2019 that its app CheckMyTrip is used by 2 million people. This means that travel agents with an online presence need to understand these new trends and how consumer preferences are changing as technology evolves. In fact Buhalis (2003) has gone as far as to suggest that the successful future travel agency will take less of a booking-office role and more of a travel management and advisor role, while adding value not accessible from online booking. In the USA, this saw the rebranding of the American Society of Travel Agents to the American Society of Travel Advisors (ASTA.org, originally founded in 1931 as the American Steamship and Tourist Agents' Association). This has also led to an expansion of homeworking in the UK and USA, so agents can be available when clients want to speak to them.

In view of the success of online travel and characterization of travel agencies as struggling to compete, there is adequate evidence of travel agents embracing new technology when its proprietary products are at a price that makes their acquisition cost-effective. The notion of travel agents as technophobic is a poor representation: they have embraced technology since its inception. The main lag has been in their response to the speed of change with the Internet. In fact some GDSs such as Sabre have even added European low-cost airlines to their booking systems. They have also responded to the evolution of dynamic packaging technology. In 2004, Sabre launched a MySabre Internet-based agency tool to combine its product range within one site for travel agents. Deregulation of the European GDS market for travel agents in 2005 has provided agents with access to different systems and will most likely see use of this combined with more Internet-based travel solutions. Agents able to combine face-to-face and online options are likely to retain their business, though e-ticketing is now commonplace. It would seem that partnering with the low-cost airlines in providing tailored travel solutions, and moving away from the rapid growth in low-cost seat-only sales, may help agents to add value in the travel purchase process. Disintermediation will not disappear from the travel agency sector, but the introduction of dynamic packaging into this sector has allowed them to compete with the online e-tourism boom. A number of studies have examined the future outlook for travel agents (e.g. Assaf *et al.* 2011) and the strategic importance of online travel agencies (e.g. Chiou 2011) and the efficiency of travel agency operations (e.g. Fuentes 2011) although this is such a fast-changing area of activity that continued analysis of industry press such as *Travel Weekly* and *Travel Trade Gazette* track the innovations in such areas.

Conclusion

In summary, it is clear that technology has had a phenomenal impact on the distribution of travel products, illustrated by the comparison of Figures 7.6 and 7.7 in relation to the ATOL data. This is not confined to the UK but a process occurring globally, particularly in terms of the way in which each intermediary accesses the consumer. Technology has also made packaging products more flexible for those businesses investing in ICTs. Yet the business environment for travel distribution is changing rapidly and the consolidation of both tour operators and travel agent networks into global operations now raises issues of competition, discussed in Chapter 5. Some critics point to the impact of the multiples and global players on small businesses (SMEs) (Buhalis and Laws 2001), especially the power these yield in contract negotiation, particularly in destination areas. In some smaller, more marginal tourist destinations dependent upon a number of key tour operators for their tourism market, they can have an undesirable control and power over how the country's tourism industry develops.

At a global scale, many of the trends identified in this chapter highlight the variability in the adoption of new technology and the effect it has had to date on travel distribution. No two countries have had similar experiences. Likewise, the importance of different stakeholders in the integrated tourism distribution chain has been highlighted as one area which the larger companies can nurture and use to add value

to customers through improved quality and greater consistency using ICTs. Companies such as TUI AG demonstrate this trend by using technology to manage supplier quality, although collaboration rather than more competitive models of doing business may make these relationships more productive where non-integrated companies provide products for tourists. Above all, supply-chain issues in tourism are highly complex and less predictable, and the outcomes in terms of consumer expectations do not necessarily follow predefined outcomes. Consumers are very heterogeneous and the growing diversity of needs as tourists highlights the importance of the use of ICTs in distribution and also the role of personal involvement and contact with people. Intermediaries should always remember they are dealing with people who are the customer in the service delivery process associated with distributing tourism products. Tour operators and travel agencies are operationally driven, dealing with customers, and as distribution channels they are there first and foremost to provide information for tourists to purchase products and to enable suppliers to deliver these products effectively. Therefore ICTs in the intermediaries sector need to be harnessed to bring together buyers and sellers and create a market for a product and service as well as to help the market to function more smoothly or to expand. One element of the travel product which is integral to travel is transport, and this is the focus of the next chapter.

Discussion questions

1 What is a tourism distribution channel?

2 Why is the European tour-operator sector becoming controlled by integrated tourism companies? How is this impacting upon other operators and consumers? How has the digital revolution affected these tourism companies?

3 How will travel agents evolve to compete with disintermediation?

4 How important is the e-revolution to consumer purchasing of travel products?

References

Alegre, J., Cladera, M. and Sard, M. (2012) 'The evolution of British package holiday prices in the Balearic Islands, 2000–2008', *Tourism Economics*, 18 (1): 59–75.

Assaf, G., Barros, C.P. and Machado, L. (2011) 'The future outlook for Portuguese travel agents', *Tourism Economics*, 17 (2): 405–423.

ATOL CAA (2002) *ATOL Business Issue 20.* London: Civil Aviation Authority.

Benckendorff, P., Xiang, Z. and Sheldon, P. (2019) *Tourism Information Technology*, 3rd edition. Wallingford: CABI.

BERR (Department for Business Enterprise and Regulatory Reform) (2008) *What Is a Package? A Guidance Note for Travel Organisers.* London: BERR.

Buhalis, D. (2003) *eTourism: Information Technology for Strategic Tourism Management.* Harlow: Pearson Education.

Buhalis, D. and Laws, E. (eds.) (2001) *Tourism Distribution Channels: Practices, Issues and Transformation.* London: Continuum.

CAA (Civil Aviation Authority) (2006) *No Frills Airlines: Evolution or Revolution?* London: Civil Aviation Authority.

CAA (Civil Aviation Authority) (2007) *Business Issue 29.* London: Civil Aviation Authority.

Chiou, W., Lin, C. and Perng, C. (2011) 'A strategic website evaluation of online travel agencies', *Tourism Management,* 32 (6): 1463–1473.

Cooper, C., Fletcher, J., Fyall, A., Wanhill, S. and Gilbert, D. (2005) *Tourism: Principles and Practice,* 3rd edition. Harlow: Pearson Education.

Davidson, R. (2001) 'Distribution channel analysis for business travel', in D. Buhalis and E. Laws (eds.) *Tourism Distribution Channels: Practices, Issues and Transformations.* London: Continuum.

Department for Transport (2019) *Airline Insolvency Review: Interim Report.* London: Department for Transport. www.gov.uk/dft.

Fuentes, R. (2011) 'Efficiency of travel agencies: A case study of Alicante, Spain', *Tourism Management,* 32 (1): 75–87.

Gustafson, P. (2012) 'Managing business travel: Developments and dilemmas in corporate travel management', *Tourism Management,* 33 (2): 276–284.

Holloway, J.C. (2001) *The Business of Tourism,* 6th edition. London: Pearson Education.

Huang, G., Song, H. and Zhang, X. (2010) 'A comparative analysis of quantity and price competitions in tourism supply chain networks for package holidays', *Service Industries Journal,* 30 (9/10): 1593–1606.

Klenosky, D. and Gitelson, R. (1998) 'Travel agents' destination recommendations', *Annals of Tourism Research,* 25 (3): 661–674.

Laws, E. (1997) *Managing Packaged Tourism.* London: Thomson Learning.

Page, S.J. (2003) *Tourism Management: Managing for Change.* Oxford: Butterworth-Heinemann.

Page, S.J. (2019) *Tourism Management,* 6th edition. London: Routledge.

Parton, J. and Ryley, T. (2012) 'A business analysis of XL airways: What lessons can be learned from the failure?' *Journal of Air Transport Management,* 19 (1): 42–48.

Poon, A. (1993) *Tourism, Technology and Competitive Strategies.* Wallingford, Oxon: CABI.

Quintana, T.A., Gil, S.M., and Peral, P.P. (2016) 'How could traditional travel agencies improve their competitiveness and survive? A qualitative study in Spain', *Tourism Management Perspectives,* 20, 98–108.

Romero, I. and Tejada, P. (2011) 'A multi-level approach to the study of production chains in the tourism sector', *Tourism Management,* 32 (2): 297–306.

Xiang, Z., Magnini, V.P., and Fesenmaier, D.R. (2015) 'Information technology and consumer behavior in travel and tourism: Insights from travel planning using the internet', *Journal of Retailing and Consumer Services,* 22: 244–249.

Further reading

Books

Benckendorff, P., Xiang, Z. and Sheldon, P. (2019) *Tourism Information Technology*, 3rd edition. Wallingford: CABI.

Department of Transport (2019) *Airline Insolvency Review: Final Report.* London: Department for Transport. www.gov.uk/dft.

Journals and articles

Quintana, T.A., Gil, S.M. and Peral, P.P. (2016) 'How could traditional travel agencies improve their competitiveness and survive? A qualitative study in Spain', *Tourism Management Perspectives,* 20: 98–108.

Tom Dieck, M.C., Fountoulaki, P. and Jung, T.H. (2018) 'Tourism distribution channels in European island destinations', *International Journal of Contemporary Hospitality Management,* 30 (1): 326–342.

Wall-Reinius, S., Ioannides, D. and Zampoukos, K. (2019) 'Does geography matter in all-inclusive resort tourism? Marketing approaches of Scandinavian tour operators', *Tourism Geographies,* 21 (5): 766–784.

Wu, Y., Lee, H. and Liao, P. (2018) 'What do customers expect of travel agent–customer interactions? Measuring and improving customer experience in interactions with travel agents', *Journal of Travel and Tourism Marketing,* 35 (8): 1000–1012.

8

Transporting the tourist

Learning outcomes

After reading this chapter and answering the questions, you should:

- be able to recognize the principal forms of tourist transport and their characteristics
- be familiar with the development of tourist transport and how it facilitates tourism development
- understand how important the experience of transport is to the mobility of tourists.

Overview

The purpose of this chapter is to introduce the concepts used to understand the relationship between transport and tourism and the characteristics of different forms of tourist transport. Transport remains the dynamic element facilitating tourist travel and it provides the opportunity for holiday-making to occur. The scope of the transport sector is explored, focusing on the different travel modes used by tourists (e.g. land, air and sea-based modes).

Introduction

Transport is a fundamental component of the tourism industry. Transport is a precondition for travel: it facilitates mobility and the movement of tourists from their place of origin (i.e. their home area) to their destination and back, thereby forming the bridge to the barrier of distance. As McKercher (2018: 905) argues. 'Distance has a profound, though often unappreciated impact on all aspects of tourism, extending well beyond the volume of tourist movements. It also reflects changes in the type of tourists who are most likely to visit a destination and their subsequent behaviour'. McKercher (2018) identified the impact of distance and how the effect of distance decays the nearer the demand is to the supply in tourism. For example, 'land neighbours account for 57 per cent of all [tourist] arrivals, while, collectively, destinations within 1000 km of a source market's border attracted 80 per cent of all arrivals' (McKercher 2018: 905). Therefore, overcoming distance as a barrier remains a key element in the movement of tourists from their origin to destination along with other non-transport barriers (see McKercher and Darcy 2018). Transport is frequently neglected in the analysis of tourism, often being relegated to a passive element of the tourist experience. Yet transport remains an essential service element of tourism, and in some cases it can form the focus of the tourism experience *per se* (e.g. cruising, scenic and heritage train journeys – also see Chapter 9) (Page and Connell 2014). Various forms of transport have been associated with the development of tourism, and technological developments in transport combined with the rise in personal disposable incomes have led to the expansion of both domestic and international tourism facilitated by those transport innovations.

Conceptualizing transport and tourism

Despite the overriding significance of transport as a mode of transit, from origin to destination, there have been few attempts to conceptualize this vital function in the tourism system. In essence there are three distinct methods of human transport: *self-propelled modes* (e.g. walking); *augmented modes* (using technology or tools to amplify our bodily effort such as skiing) and *fuelled modes* (especially motorized transport) (Stradling and Anable 2008). 'What these three modes of transport suggest are that without the infrastructure and the mode of transport, then tourism could not possibly occur. Tourism has become one of the most visible signs of human movement at a global level, benefitting from increased prosperity, a desire to travel and the benefits which new transport technology has brought to aid increased accessibility of destinations to tourists and other travellers' (Page 2009: 3). Two basic approaches have dominated the analysis of transport and tourism:

1 *Transport for tourism:* this is transport as a utilitarian or functional act which involves a mode or modes of travel in moving from origin to destination and for travel in the destination. At a global scale, Lumsdon and Page (2004: 5) point to the importance of this approach in international travel where the balance of different modes of transport remain fairly constant as:

    o international air travel accounts for 43 per cent of international tourist trips

    o road transport accounts for 42 per cent of trips

    o rail travel comprises 8 per cent of trips

    o sea transport accounts for 7 per cent (based on UN-World Tourism Organization).

    Yet the relative importance of these different forms of transport varies by region of the world. For example, air travel is more important for international tourist travel in Latin America and car travel is more important in Finland. In contrast, the existence of a well-developed alternative transport infrastructure in Europe means that air travel's importance is counterbalanced by the importance of road travel and other options such as sea travel and other land-based transport modes such as rail and metro/trams.

2 *Transport as tourism:* the mode of transport is integral to the overall experience of tourism such as cruising or taking a scenic railway journey. Some of the most luxurious tourist products available, such as the Orient Express and exclusive cruises, utilize the elegance, opulence and quality service attributes of the mode of travel. In other cases, historic modes of transport such as trams or heritage trains may be given a new lease of life by tourist demand. A good example of this is the use of the *cyclo*, a three wheeled variant of the rickshaw in Vietnam, introduced in the 1930s by the French colonial rulers. It has survived, despite the huge impact of motorized transport such as the car and motorbike, and 300 survive in Ho Chi Minh City, patronized by tourists.

What Lumsdon and Page (2004) identify is a tourist transport continuum in which transport for tourism offers a low intrinsic value in relation to the overall tourist experience (i.e. typified by using a mode of transport to simply get from origin a to destination b) through to the position where transport is developed, designed and harnessed as the containing context and the central element – as tourism (see Figure 8.1). A more in-depth study of tourism and transport linkages by Moscardo and Pearce (2004) helps to refine this continuum a stage further since it explores the tourists' motivations and interface with transport, concluding that there is a clear distinction between:

- a core motivational element related to whether people choose to travel on a particular mode of transport for tourism purposes
- a series of additional motivational elements.

This classification highlights the multiple role of transport in tourism, the influence of consumer choice and the motivating factors which contribute to the overall travel experience in terms of the continuum discussed by Lumsdon and Page (2004). This is depicted in Figure 8.2, and what the conceptual map helps us to understand is how the transport sector can create transport as a tourism product by emphasizing core and additional motivating

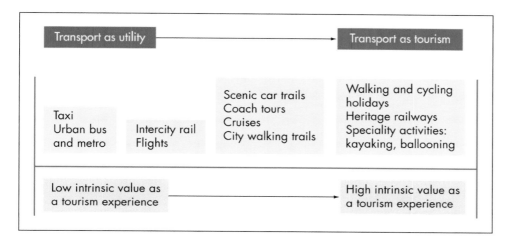

FIGURE 8.1 The tourism transport continuum
Source: Reprinted from *Tourism and Transport: Issues and Agenda for the New Millennium*, Lumsdon and Page, p. 7, copyright (2004), with permission from Routledge

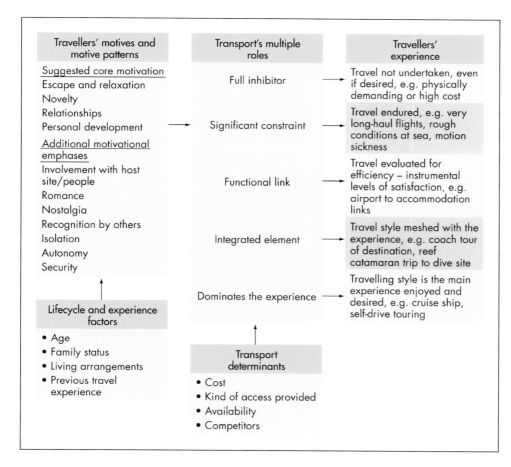

FIGURE 8.2 A conceptual map of the links between motivation, lifecycle, transport roles and the traveller's experience
Source: Reprinted from *Tourism and Transport: Issues and Agenda for the New Millennium*, Lumsdon and Page, p. 32, copyright (2004), with permission from Routledge

factors to aim at different markets. Figure 8.2 also helps to understand how to unlock latent demand (i.e. people wanting to travel if the price/service is right), as many low-cost airlines have done (i.e. via cost) or by adding improvements in the tourism value chain by raising satisfaction levels in the transport for tourism element. Above all, Moscardo and Pearce (2004) concur with the view that transport can perform multiple roles in tourism and show how successful transport operators have combined a core motivation (e.g. novelty) with an additional motivation (e.g. romance or nostalgia) to create world-class products such as the Orient Express rail journeys (http://orientexpress. co.uk). With these different modes of transport in mind, attention now turns to an overview of tourist travel modes.

Tourist travel modes: A global overview

At an international scale, few studies exist to document tourists' use of different modes of transport. Even where data exist, they are specific to a certain form of transport such as air travel. At an EU level, it is possible to gauge the importance of different modes of transport for non-tourist/tourist use. Figure 8.3 illustrates the trends in the use of various modes of transport 1970–2015, which indicates the dominance of two key modes: the car and air travel, as well as the growth attributed to the expansion of the EU to 28 member states. In the case of the car, widening access has made it a dominant mode of travel for leisure and recreation trips, and increasingly for tourist trips in the EU. One interesting example is the July/August annual holiday in Paris, France, and the massive temporary migration by car to the south of France and other destinations for holidays. This causes massive congestion, with the peak Saturday departure called Black Saturday (*samedi noir*), and travellers are advised to avoid using the motorway network that day. This example highlights the problems of managing car-based tourism, with reports of over 700 km of accumulated traffic jams on Black Saturday. The rise of air travel globally as a mode of transport for short- and long-haul travel is reflected in Figure 8.3 in the context of Europe; this was fuelled initially by package holidays and more recently by the revolution in low-cost air travel, a phenomenon affecting many countries after being pioneered in the USA and diffused to Europe, Asia and Australasia as shown in Figure 8.4.

In contrast, the trends in rail and bus/coach travel in Europe also mirror many international trends in tourist use of these travel modes, which have recorded relative declines or modest increases in their use. These modes of transport do not perform the same function in moving high volumes of mass tourists that they did historically in the nineteenth and up to the mid-twentieth century. They may best be described as complementary modes of transport compared to the tourist preference for car and air-based travel. This reflects a shift from tourist use of transport in the public domain unless it is faster, more accessible and time-efficient. Exceptions do exist such as the use of the TGV and high-speed rail services, which are time-competitive with air and road transport. The relative importance of different modes of transport used to visit a destination will vary depending on the attributes and accessibility of the place. For example, UK tourist travel to Scotland is dominated by land-based travel, using the car.

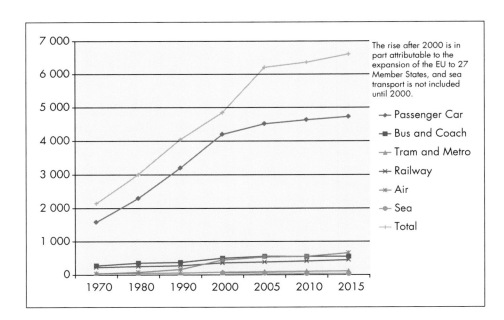

FIGURE 8.3 Performance of
EU passenger transport modes
1970–2015 (billion passenger km)

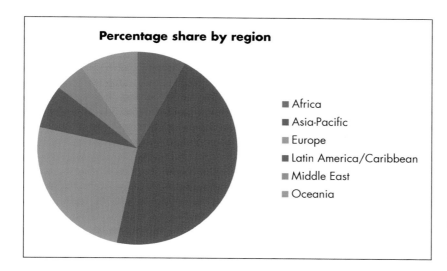

Percentage share by region

- Africa
- Asia-Pacific
- Europe
- Latin America/Caribbean
- Middle East
- Oceania

FIGURE 8.4 Distribution of low-cost airlines by continent
Source: ICAO data; Wikipedia; other sources

Land-based transport

The car

The car is still widely neglected in tourism studies because it is now such an accepted part of everyday life that its impact and use in tourism is taken for granted and overlooked. In Europe, the car comprises 83 per cent of all journeys by land. Both the early study by Wall (1971) and Patmore (1983) identify the fundamental changes in mobility in the postwar period in Western industrialized society and the rise in car ownership. One of the principal changes to take place in the postwar period in both outdoor recreation and domestic tourism is the major effect of the car on patterns of travel: it has made travel more convenient and less dependent upon public transport. The car offers considerable flexibility in the way people can travel and access tourism resources and sites outside urban areas (Prideaux and Carsen 2011). What the car has done is transform tourists' ability to organize and develop their own itineraries and activity patterns, so that they are no longer dependent upon existing transport provision. For the resource managers of sites such as National Parks, one outcome has been the need to manage the impact of the car on key sites (e.g. 'honeypots', which are high-use sites) and popular locations which tourists visit. In some cases, in key tourism and recreational sites where overuse is a potential threat to the local resource base (e.g. the Goyt Valley in the Peak District National Park), the use of cars has been managed through the provision of alternative forms of transport.

Dickinson *et al.* (2004) pointed to the problems which the car posed to sustainable tourism as shown in Figure 8.5, problems also examined by Martín-Cejas and Sánchez (2010). Despite these problems, there remains an insatiable demand from car users in many of these environments, where mobility forms a central component of the holiday experience or an element of a tour. Despite the importance of car-based travel, McKercher and Lew (2004: 36) argue that 'little empirical or conceptual work has been conducted examining and modelling tourism itineraries, in spite of the long understood need to study this phenomenon', identifying four specific itinerary types:

- Single destination movement with or without side trips
- Transit leg and circular tour at the destination
- Circular tour
- Hub and spoke system of movement from home or destination area

Further research by McKercher *et al.* (2008) identified the complexity of tourist movement styles in an urban destination, as demonstrated in Figure 8.6. What Figure 8.6 demonstrates is that tourists tend to structure their trips according to the resources available (e.g. attractions – see Chapter 9), activities (e.g. shopping) and established forms of infrastructure and different modal forms of transport to facilitate the movement, typically involving walking at some point. The different movement styles could be classified into 11 specific types. The study also questions the repetitive nature of tourist itineraries, since the most common type of movement style was a 'direct trip to and from a distant place, with an intermediate stop, combined with local exploration'.

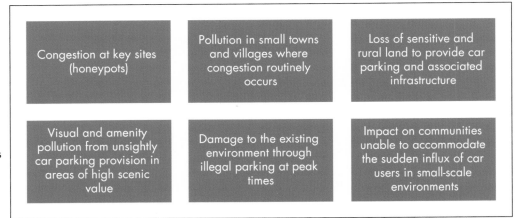

FIGURE 8.5 The problems which tourist use of the car poses for destinations
Source: Developed from Dickinson *et al.* (2004)

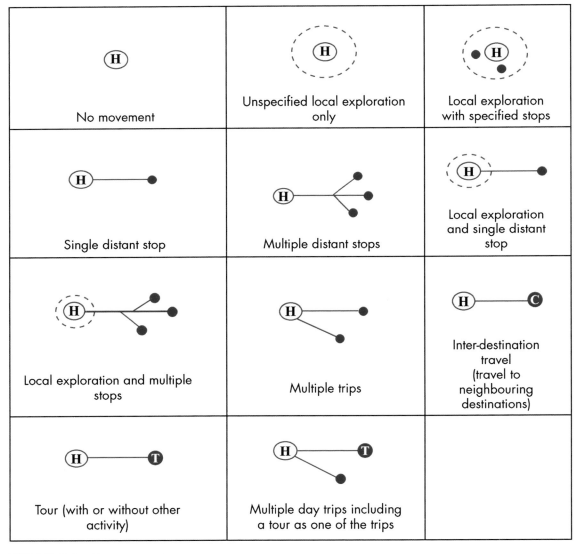

FIGURE 8.6 Movement styles
Source: Reproduced from McKercher *et al.* (2008: 366) with permission from Routledge

Where research has been undertaken with a policy focus (e.g. Connell and Page 2008) it illustrates that tourist itineraries are critical to understanding the dynamic ever-changing nature of tourist travel behaviour to understand the impact on transport and tourism of infrastructure provision. As Connell and Page (2008) illustrated, studying tourist movement to and within a destination, such as a National Park, helps identify the services required based on the timing of tourist visits in terms of seasonality and peak use. In the case of the Loch Lomond and Trossachs National Park, this meant the need to prepare appropriate planning measures to manage/control/restrict car use within sustainable tourism strategies to balance the use of the resource base with the objectives of National Park plans.

Yet as Page (2005) shows, many National Parks in the UK are concerned about their ability to accommodate the forecast growth in car use to these sites of 267 per cent between 1992 and 2025. The essential problem posed by the car is that its use is subject to the whim of the individual and its users cannot be controlled. In urban areas, the car is also a major problem for small historic cities such as Canterbury, York, Chester and Cambridge which have provided out-of-town car parking to address the environmental impact of congestion on the town centre environment which is used by tourists.

Dickinson *et al.* (2004: 105) highlight the range of initiatives developed to try to manage the tourist's use of the car, given that in Western developed countries such as the UK, 30–40 per cent of mileage travelled is for leisure use. Dickinson *et al.* (2004) point to leisure travel initiatives which have sought to:

- encourage closer travel to home
- develop containment/restriction strategies such as encouraging visitors to park their cars at a gateway location in a National Park (Beunen *et al.* 2008)
- generate tourist traffic to support uneconomic public transport, such as the seasonal use of rail routes to peripheral areas
- make improvements to cycling and walking opportunities such as those introduced by **SUSTRANS** in the UK.

But barriers to the adoption of these solutions to managing tourist demand relate to inadequate expenditure on promoting and raising awareness of alternatives to the car, failing to make access to alternatives easier, and a lack of supply-led solutions such as expanding parking provision.

In historic cities, Orbasli and Shaw (2004) identified the need to reconfigure the road network to reroute tourist cars away from city centres to catchment areas with **park-and-ride** schemes. Such a scheme also requires the separation of the car from tourists on foot by provision of pedestrian-only and cycle tracks to reduce pollution, noise and conflicts. For many government agencies, the car poses a fundamental contradiction: it brings the volume of visitors many towns and cities local economies depend upon, and measures to limit or deter its use, or make city-centre access inconvenient (i.e. by pricing mechanisms) or promote park-and-ride schemes are opposed by business groups. Consequently environmental concerns related to congestion remain dominant arguments for implementing such measures, but concerns over the possible loss of business leave many local authorities in a quandary – whatever solution they adopt, opponents will be vociferous.

Coach and bus transport

In the road-based transport sector (excluding the car) a number of different forms of passenger transport serve the needs of tourists (Figure 8.7). What is interesting in coach travel is that its decline in the evolution of domestic holiday-making in the postwar period has now been reversed as investment in high-quality services and coach travel's redevelopment as a budget-priced option for tourist travel in the 1990s have led to a resurgence of interest. In the EU, the bus/coach mode of travel for tourism and leisure purposes is used by around 9.3 per cent of the population, and the countries with the greatest use were Greece, Denmark, Germany and Spain. The lowest levels of use – under 5 per cent – were in the UK, Ireland, Italy and France. At a European level, over 10 million people are employed in the bus/coach sector, which is much higher than the air transport sector with almost 4 million employees and railway sector with almost 9 million employees. Policy changes in the EU as expressed in the White Paper *European Transport Policy for 2010* (European Union 2002) outlined the potential of this sector to substitute road-based car travel for bus/coach travel. However, critics of reducing car-based travel such as Stopher (2004) indicate the practical and logistical issues of seeking to promote modal switching from car to alternative modes, in the absence of government policy shifts, and considering the central role of the car in the mobility of modern-day society. Furthermore, the potential of the bus can only be realized, as it has been in London, when a radical measure like the

Express scheduled coach services (domestic and international services)	Private hire services for group travel	Packaged tours on coaches
Urban and rural bus services to tourist locations	Airport taxi and shuttle services	Excursions, day trip, sightseeing tours in urban and rural areas

FIGURE 8.7 The structure of bus and coach provision for tourists
Source: Developed from ECMT (1999)

IMAGE 8.1 The iconic London Routemaster was withdrawn from service in December 2005: a heritage service remains on one route in Central London and it was closely associated with London as a unique experience for visitors

congestion charge is accompanied by massive investment in buses on the road networks. This saw bus patronage rise 13 per cent 1986–2000 and a further 8 per cent in 2001–2002, although introducing one-person-operated vehicles, thereby replacing icons of London such as the 1950s Routemaster (Image 8.1), may impact upon tourist use of such services. To attempt to rekindle the iconic Routemaster, Transport for London introduced 1000 new Routemaster buses as hybrid diesel/electric-powered vehicles at a cost of £355K each, although critics have pointed to the vehicles bringing about a less significant reduction in emissions than was promised. This was to address the polluting effects of transport, which contributes 20 per cent of London's CO_2 emissions. The EU has shown that more controlled competition in bus and coach transport, as has been used in London, has been more beneficial so that the model of uncontrolled competition in the UK following the 1980 and 1985 Transport Acts is not repeated. In 2015, France deregulated aspects of its coach services, with Isilines. In many mainland European countries, state monopolies still exist, although Scandinavia's limited competition model and its use in France have helped these countries to use public subsidies more effectively. The extent of public subsidies for bus travel range from 29 per cent of costs in Scotland, to 32 per cent in the UK, to 60–70 per cent in Austria, Belgium, Italy and the Netherlands. These subsidies are dependent upon government transport policy.

These different policy approaches have led to different market structures for the management of bus and coach travel, from a public-ownership model to market-led approaches and major competition. One outcome in the UK is the development of large integrated bus-coach-rail operators such as Arriva, First Group, Stagecoach and National Express. Some of these operators have European and global operations. In February 2008, First Group in the UK acquired Laidlaw International Inc. in the USA which operates the famous North American long-distance coach services – Greyhound. The company serves 3800 destinations in the USA and Canada and carries around 20 million passengers a year using 2100 vehicles and generated £634 million for First in 2011. In May 2019, FirstGroup put Greyhound up for sale after shareholder pressure. National Express as a company carries 1 billion passengers a year.

The more notable and leisure-focused services are in the express coach market. The ECMT (1999) *Regular Inter-urban Coach Services in Europe* report documented the growth of motorway inter-urban express services. These are epitomized in the UK by National Express. Since the ECMT (1999) report, the market has seen significant changes with the introduction of new products such as the Megabus brand in recent years in the UK and more recently in the USA (having sold its European operations to the German company Flix). Megabus is a low-cost inter-urban coach operator that has established a low-cost product and online booking and is owned by Stagecoach. The company launched a series of long-distance routes in the UK and then in the USA with its striking brand and has become a major success in the scheduled coach market. The initial success of Megabus has seen the company further invest in new vehicles to offer comfortable, low-cost travel, which it demonstrated as being less environmentally damaging than low-cost air travel. In the competitive market for low-cost travel, Stagecoach's success reflects a degree of change in the consumer preferences for this option, particularly for leisure travel. The expansion into the USA and Canada also reflects a market opportunity to compete with long-distance intercity transport modes such as Greyhound and low-cost air travel. In contrast, the coach holiday market has seen significant change in the UK in recent years with the merger of the two market leaders – Wallace Arnold and Shearings – now under the Shearings brand. The new combined company has invested in new Grand Tourer coaches costing £10 million for 45 luxury vehicles. The company has also continued its popular independent holidays programme with self-drive car holidays since it owns 50 hotels in the UK, as part of its diversified holiday business under the Bays and Coast and Country brands. In Scotland, smaller examples of this diversified model of coach holiday operation have been highly successful, using a personalized approach to clients, high quality coaches and staff to deliver high levels of occupancy in the coach hotels and repeat business.

In the EU, the express Eurolines business established in 1985 comprises 32 independent coach companies under the National Express subsidiary serving 300 cities and 500 destinations with 29 companies remaining in the consortium. The profile of its passengers shows that they are largely aged 16–30 years of age, most of them use the Internet and over half travel alone, of whom over 55 per cent are female and 37 per cent are students. Quality enhancement to the operators' vehicles mean that the services are competitive in price with rail and air and offer an assured standard of service. The company's quality policy identifies five areas which determine the travellers' impression and satisfaction level (Figure 8.8) with communication being the most important characteristic. In contrast, the UK-based National Express coach network carries around 19 million passengers a year serving 800 destinations.

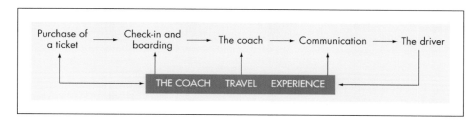

FIGURE 8.8 Model of Eurolines' quality policy

Cycling

The cycle is arguably the most sustainable form of tourist transport one can use because, being non-motorized, it does not require fuel and does not always have a major impact on the built and physical environment (the exception being mountain biking where it constitutes a recreational activity). As Lumsdon and Tolley (2004) argue, after walking, cycling is the most important form of transport globally, given its significance for leisure use in developing countries such as China where it comprises 65 per cent of all trips made. In a European context, cycling is a popular form of transport in Denmark, Germany and the Netherlands, even though motorized transport has dominated transport policy in the inter-war and postwar period in most Westernized countries. Cycling also symbolizes many of the key principles of sustainable tourism: it has minimal environmental impact and limited infrastructure requirements, and it is part of a wider renaissance of interest in walking and cycling in North America, Australasia and Eastern Europe, where quality of life is moving higher up the political agenda (Lumsdon and Tolley 2004: 147). This is in contrast to developing countries seeking to emulate symbols of modernization and affluence such as car ownership.

'Cycle tourism', according to SUSTRANS (Sustainable Transport), is recreational visits, either overnight or visits away from home, which involve leisure cycling as a fundamental and significant part of the visit (cited in Lumsdon and Tolley 2004: 149) including:

- the recreational cyclist (e.g. the day excursionist)
- the cycle tourist (e.g. on holiday)

and may exemplify tourism as transport.

Infrastructure needs and patterns of cycle tourism Tourist cycling is now a well-established form of tourism in many countries, particularly where provision has been made through the development of cycle routeways (Bíl, Bílová and Kubeček 2012). In the case of New Zealand, distinct patterns of cycle tourism exist (e.g. see Ritchie 1998). In the UK, developments in recreational and tourist cycling, often using redundant railway lines, are exemplified by the work of SUSTRANS, the civil engineering charity formed in 1979, which is coordinating the National Cycle Network in Britain. This covers around 17 000 miles of cycle route 4000 miles of which passes through dedicated pathways, green spaces and woodlands. It reflects the importance of cycle routeways in the destination, which may include a network of links and loops, using a long-distance linear route or circuit trip from origin back to the origin. The national network in the UK has been planned with the intention of linking visitor attractions, and the National Trust and SUSTRANS have worked on a number of joint initiatives which make journeys for cyclists more enjoyable and are largely traffic-free. During 2006, over 338 million trips were made on the Sustrans network which had risen to 420 million in 2010 and 786 million by 2019, 75 per cent for non-commuting purposes, and Belgium has also promoted cycle tourism (Cox 2012).

Cycling is also a popular pastime for domestic tourists, and increasingly many cities are now making provisions for cycle paths within the built environment which visitors can enjoy through hiring cycles. This is even evident in locations such as the Norfolk Broads in the UK where cycle routeways have been developed and managed to encourage low-impact tourism on a fragile environment. This follows good practice which is epitomized by the tourism and recreational activities that are planned and managed in the Netherlands. Here, cycling is a pastime and a sustainable form of day-to-day transport. The nature and profile of cycle users for tourism purposes is now becoming well documented as reflected in the work of Lumsdon (1997). SUSTRANS observed that cycle tourism generated £2.5 billion for the UK visitor economy. As Lumsdon (1997: 115) suggests, the growing importance of cycle tourism means that the market is growing and definite segments exist, including:

- *half-day/day excursionists*: occasional users who are home based and touring, typically aged 24–41 years of age and cycling 10–20 miles
- *half-day and day casual mountain bikers*: based at home and occasional users, aged 24–45 years and cycling 10–20 miles; they transport their bikes by car
- *half-day and day cycle hirers*: infrequent riders aged 18–55 years of age with a strong family element
- *the holiday tourists*: organize day rides or may be cycle tourists; they are in the upper socioeconomic groups, often transporting bikes by car
- *the holiday do-it-yourself mountain bikers*: like the previous group, but seeking harder routes
- *organized, independent self-guided cycling tourists*: organize holidays and travel as a pair or group
- *organized group cyclists*: like the previous group but take guided routes
- *groups on holiday*: the cycle element is part of a multi-activity or cycle holiday
- *club riders*: self-arranged, long-distance riders
- *sports competitors*: undertake cycling as a sport
- *event riders*: undertake charity rides as part of a leisure experience (developed from Lumsdon 1997).

Clearly, in some contexts, cycling as an element of transport in a package or as a reason for tourism is seeing a resurgence, but one of the principal challenges for tourism planners and local authorities in destination areas is its integration into other forms of transport provision. The evidence in Loch Lomond and Trossachs National Park currently is that cycle tourists have to enter and access cycle routes by car. This is negating the principles of sustainable tourism as it adds to road-based congestion and access points by cycle are needed prior to tourists entering the park boundary. Cycle tourism provision can create a vital attraction for many destinations, but strategic planning in integrating its role and use is essential for success. There is also a wider role for cycling as discussed earlier in the case of the *cyclo* in Vietnam, as the rickshaw and its motorized and non-motorized variants perform an important mobility role in tourism. For example, they are commonplace in Madagascar, Macau, India and Bangladesh. In Bangladesh there are around 750,000 vehicles employing 1 million people with the motorized version known as *tuk tuks* in Thailand.

Rail travel

Train transport for tourism takes two forms: combined leisure and business, which is scheduled, and predominantly leisure-based services, 'where train travel becomes the focus of the tourist experience' (Prideaux 1999: 73). Rail transport was one of the prime movers of the leisure revolution in Victorian and Edwardian times, linked with the rise of seaside resorts since it offered an efficient mode of moving volumes of urban passengers from a city to a coastal destination. Yet, for rail transport to operate effectively, a vastly expensive **capital investment** in built infrastructure is needed. Many current-day rail networks were funded by private investment in Victorian times, and have been added to and further developed by the state. Tourist use of these networks for leisure purposes has been classified by Page (2009) thus:

- the use of dedicated rail corridors which connect major gateways (airports and ports) of a country to the final destination, or as a mode of transit to the tourist accommodation in the nearby city
- the use of rapid transit systems and metros to travel within urban areas
- the use of high-speed and non-high-speed intercity rail corridors to facilitate movement as part of an itinerary or city-to-city journey, typically for business and leisure travel. These journeys may cross country borders in the EU and form part of a pan-European network
- the use of local rail services outside urban areas, often used in peak hours by commuters to journey to/from mainline/intercity rail terminals en route to other destinations
- the use of peripheral rail services which serve remote communities in the tourist season for scenic sightseeing and special interest travel (based on ECMT 1992).

In the case of tourist journeys by rail, the market for rail holidays has seen competition emerge with low-cost airlines although leisure day trips remain a key element of rail travel and, as discussed earlier, its use in Europe for leisure and business use on high-speed routes has seen significant growth. In Europe, rail has been subject to deregulation and it remains an expensive sector with ongoing investment requirements. Rail travel is portrayed as a more sustainable mode of travel than the car and its safety record is impressive in most countries where the infrastructure is well maintained. However investment needs to occur on a rolling basis to ensure it is designed for modern-day tourist needs (i.e. time savings and convenience), examples of this being France's TGV network and dedicated city-to-airport rail routes like the British Airport Authority-funded Heathrow Express. In the years leading up to privatization, the market for leisure rail travel declined in the period 1990–1995. Since privatization in 1994 (and excluding the impact of several rail crashes and the impact of foot and mouth), rail volumes have grown. In Europe, around 441 billion passenger km are travelled annually on the national rail networks, 54 per cent of the volume resulting from rail travel in France, Germany and the UK. In contrast, international rail travel in Europe is around 20 billion passenger km annually, dominated by France with almost 30 per cent of trips and France and Germany jointly accounting for 54.5 per cent of trips. In fact, France, Germany, Italy, the UK, the Netherlands, Austria and Belgium are responsible for 82 per cent of international passenger trips. In contrast, rail travel in some countries (e.g. the USA) is perceived as a poorer alternative to flying but in the UK a renaissance has occurred. Investment in terminal facilities, state-of-the-art new trains or high quality refurbishments of rolling stock have all created a new ambience for rail travel in the UK so the tourist or leisure traveller feels relaxed, refreshed and comfortable, and able to access the central areas of cities with ease compared to flying or via car use. Yet some of the most profound changes in rail travel have occurred with the 'transport and tourism' luxury market such as the Orient Express and variants of this with sleeper train services across the world are shown in Table 8.1 which are popular with tourists (Image 8.2). Similar examples have been developed in many countries, an example being Queensland Rail which has packaged scenery and sightseeing as key elements, as discussed by Prideaux (1999). In addition, rail infrastructure can perform a major role in improving the accessibility of destinations within a country and the connectivity between destinations through a well-integrated public transport network.

IMAGE 8.2 Sleeper services promote an experience of travel that is relaxed and nostalgic, reflecting an age of rail travel in a bygone era devoid of crowds and congestion

Water-based transport

Water-borne transport is frequently overlooked in many studies of tourism since air travel dominates the world patterns of travel. It is certainly the case that the need to cross bodies of water, particularly where tourists

TABLE 8.1 Countries with sleeper trains and examples of routes

Australia (Sydney–Melbourne–Brisbane; Brisbane – Cairns; Adelaide–Perth)

Canada (Toronto – Vancouver; Windsor – Quebec)

China (e.g. Beijing – Lhasa)

Europe

- Extensive Deutsche Bahn (DB) network in Europe largely withdrawn in 2017
- Australian Railways Nightjet brand has taken over many German routes from DB
- UK (London-Penzance; London – Edinburgh/Glasgow and Inverness; Fort William and Aberdeen)
- Spain Tenhotel Service (Madrid – Lisbon)
- Poland (Wroclaw – Budapest, Gdansk – Bielsko-Biala; Budapest – Warsaw; Gdynia – Przemyśl; Gdynia – Zakopane)
- France (Paris, Cannes, Antibes, Toulouse, Perpignan, La Tour de Carol, Rodez, Briancon)
- Italy (Milan – Paris/Venice – Paris)
- Finland (Helsinki – Moscow)
- Sweden (Gothenburg/Stockholm to Lulea/Narvik)

Russia (Trans-Siberian Express)

- Kiev – Warsaw, Moscow – Nice; Moscow – Prague

United States – On long-distance Amtrak services

India – Extensive network

Argentina (Buenos Aires – Tucuman; Cordoba)

Vietnam (Hanoi – Ho Chi Minh City)

Thailand (Bangkok – Chiang Mai and Pedang Besar and Kuala Lumpur)

Egypt (Alexandria – Cairo – Luxor – Aswan)

Namibia (Desert Express Windhoek return tour)

South Africa (Cape Town – Johannesburg, Durban, Port Elizabeth and East London)

Iran (Tehran – Shiraz)

Malaysia (Kuala Lumpur – Singapore)

Myanmar (Rangoon – Mandalay, Thazi)

Tanzania (Dares Salaam – Kapir Mposhi in Zambia)

Zimbabwe (Victoria Falls to Hwange National Park is being introduced)

use recreational vehicles (e.g. motor homes) or cars and who then pursue land-based touring, means that crossing bodies of water presents transport operators with seasonal markets that can help offset the costs of all-year-round operation. Within the water-based transport sector, three main forms of transport can be identified: cruising, ferries and pleasure craft.

Cruising

According to Papathanassis (2012: 1148), 'The cruise sector has been experiencing exponential growth . . . From an estimated 17.5 million passengers in 2009, approximately 60 per cent originated [in] the US and Canada and 27 per cent from Europe.' By 2018 this volume of passengers had grown to 26 million generating around US$45 billion a year (cruisemarketwatch.com). The cruise product can take many forms; small-scale, specialist ships exist to take niche market clients to Antarctica and the Galapagos Islands, and, at the other end of the spectrum, there are gigantic mass-entertainment ships which are themselves the destination. As tour operators have expanded the market for these products to a mass market (e.g. Thomson Holidays), a budget product has emerged, whereas new luxury ships such as the Eagle Class have a higher capacity ratio. The product, obviously, comprises both transport and accommodation – and a number of cruises out of Asia go 'nowhere' since

they are provided for the gambling market. As an activity, cruising has been growing at a dramatic rate and large cruising companies dominate the market (e.g. Carnival Cruises, http://www.carnival.com). An associated trend is the growing size of cruise ships with the major operators now ordering 100,000-ton-plus ships which bring significant economies of scale. Peisley (2006) indicated that the Caribbean was the dominant destination. For example, the Bahamas receives around 2 million cruise passengers each year. The market for cruises is dominated by three global players: Carnival Corporation (incorporating P&O Cruises, Cunard, Holland America Line, Seabourne, AIDA and Costa cruise brands with 104 ships); Royal Caribbean (with 25 ships) and the Star Cruises Group (with 5 ships) which generate over US$22 billion a year in revenue (Peisley 2006) from 12 million passengers a year. These forms of luxury travel have led to a revival of cruise tourism at a global scale after the decline of the cruise liner in the postwar period when aircraft offered much lower costs of transatlantic and world travel and the luxury element lost favour. This is another example of how changes in tastes can shift demand to alternative forms of transport. In the case of cruising, its development on the late Victorian period was a supply-led innovation by shipping companies to fill their available capacity by developing a new product. Recently, cruising has been relaunched as a luxury activity which is now more accessible to greater numbers of people, but a much wider range of people from different age groups (including families) now choose this as a holiday option. In addition, the growth in new larger ships is leading cruise operators to discount their prices to fill capacity, with the new innovation of the easyCruise, another product to enter a crowded market. Cruise lines have diversified their product offerings as they have evolved from 'line voyages' in the 1960s between two locations to include more complex itineraries visiting multiple ports, to fly-cruises, cruise and stay destination cruises, around the world cruises, river cruises and the special interest cruises. This remains a very major growth sector for the tour operator sector such as TUI that reported strong growth in 2019 amid flat performance in other areas of holiday-taking activity, reflected in the fact that Carnival had grown their berth capacity from 212 000 in 2014 to 237 000 in 2018 and had a further 21 new ships on order for delivery by 2025. There has also been a growing interest in safety and security issues in cruising (see Insight 8.1).

INSIGHT 8.1 Safety and security and cruise lines

Clare Bowen, Paul R. Fidgeon, Stephen J. Page

The cruise industry has experienced continued growth in the 1990s and new millennium, largely as the sector has nurtured new markets and reinvented itself. This has combined with a need to fill capacity on expanding vessel size (i.e. many 'third generation' vessels now accommodate over 2000 passengers and 5000 crew). As Mancini (2011) argues, only 20 per cent of cruise passengers are over 60 years of age as the 25–40-year age group has embraced cruising as a new leisure activity. In addition, cruise lines have diversified their routes and ports of call from the predominant Caribbean and Mediterranean focus to include a diverse range of regions (e.g. the African and Atlantic Islands, the Far East, South Pacific, the Baltic, Antarctic, Middle East and Australasia). However, accompanying this diversification strategy has been an increased risk of terrorist attack on cruise ships as they operate in more volatile political regions and become targets for global terrorism in all areas of operation.

Henderson (2007: 68) defines terrorism as 'the use of terror and violence by individuals or groups outside legitimate structures and processes to achieve desired ends which are political in nature'. While a great deal of research attention to tourism has been focused on the terrorist impact on destinations (e.g. 9/11 and the USA; 7/7 and the UK), there is a growing recognition that many cruise ships are 'floating destinations' in their own right. To date, terrorist and piracy incidents have been comparatively rare in the context of cruising, although the 2012 accident associated with the cruise ship *Costa Concordia* off the coast of Italy illustrated the potential effects of a crisis-related event for a large-scale cruise liner. There has been a rise in piracy events in recent years off the Malacca Straits, Suez Canal, Indonesia and East Africa, the cruise liner *Seabourn Spirit* being attacked by pirates in 2005.

As a consequence of these increased security concerns for cruise liners, researchers and analysts have examined the measures which the international aviation sector adopted post-9/11 as examples of best practice to assess the application of such measures for the maritime sector including:

- installation of explosive detection equipment at airports
- use of air marshals in the USA
- introduction, albeit controversially, of full body scanners
- baggage checks for explosives
- manual searching of passengers
- reinforced cockpit doors
- enhanced training of airport staff
- greater airport perimeter security
- use of sniffer dogs
- passenger profiling systems and checks prior to departure.

To strengthen security measures for cruise liners, the International Maritime Organization reviewed existing measures, introducing a new Ship and Port Security Code in 2004. This has been adopted by 108 countries to increase levels of security for cruise ship operations so that all ships and ports are expected to provide:

- company/port security officers to assess both the threat and vulnerability of ships and ports
- company and port-based security plans
- annually updated audits of ship and port-based security measures
- three-monthly ship and port drills to prepare for crisis events
- a continuous record of ship operations and movements
- security alert systems on-board ships designed to inform land-based authorities of potential security events such as hijacking, terrorist attack or acts of piracy.

INSIGHT 8.1 continued

What this demonstrates is that, even though cruising is deemed to be a safe mode of tourism compared to other forms of travel, the impact of global terrorism has meant even this sector has had to adopt greater security measures to protect passenger safety.

Further reading

Bowen, C., Fidgeon, P. and Page, S.J. (2014) 'Maritime tourism and terrorism: Customer perceptions of the potential terrorist threat to cruise shipping', *Current Issues in Tourism*, 17 (7): 610–639.

Praduroux, S. (2015) 'Italy', in K. Roach (ed.) *Comparative Counter-Terrorism Law* (pp. 269–296). Cambridge: Cambridge University Press.

Questions

1 Why are cruise ships an important terrorist target?
2 What measures can cruise ships take to safeguard their visitors?
3 How have previous terrorist attacks affected the cruise market?
4 How vulnerable are tourists when the cruise docks at a port and when they take local tours?

TABLE 8.2 Selected river cruise routes in Europe

Some rivers cross several European borders, so the main concentration of cruise activity comprises:

- The Danube, Germany
- The Rhine, Germany and Holland
- The Rhone, France
- The Douro, Portugal and Spain
- The Seine, France
- The Elbe, Germany
- The Po and Venice Lagoon, Italy
- The Oder, Germany
- The Volga, the Svir, the Dnieper, Russia and Ukraine

One further area of significant growth in cruise-related activity has been the rapid development of inland river cruises, especially in Europe. The capacity in Europe has doubled 2004–2018 with 348 vessels operating with over 50 000 berths (inland-navigation-market.org) and over 1.4 million passengers a year attracting North American, German and UK/Eire visitors in the main as the principal source markets. The range of routes which the river cruises operate on are shown in Table 8.2.

Ferries

Ferries are used to cross water where it constitutes a barrier to travel. One of the busiest waterways in the world is the English Channel and a ferry service has been recorded in history between Dover and Calais since Roman times. Evidence in medieval records also confirms the vital strategic and trade route which existed between these two ports. It remained the main crossing point between the UK and mainland Europe for many years. However, it is only since the end of the Second World War that a truly comprehensive 'product' has become available, with the size of ships increasing in order to provide more of an 'experience' for travellers and a major business activity on board the vessels for the ferry operators. The opening of one of the largest-ever European tourist transport infrastructure projects, in the form of the Channel Tunnel, altered services on this route by the end of the 1990s and provided a new form of competition with the sea-based services which were subsequently rationalized, reorganized and repositioned to compete with the new operator.

However, in some peripheral locations which have a highly seasonal tourist market, such as the Highlands and Islands of Scotland, the ferry services not only operate under a **public service grant** to subsidize the operation, but are a vital lifeline to a scattered series of communities. The volume of traffic on these Scottish services is around 6 million passenger journeys a year including nearly 2 million car crossings. The tourist market remains a key element of their business, supporting the highly seasonal tourism trade on remote and dispersed islands. In the UK, competition between the ferry operators on the North Sea and other crossings has led to their promotion of the 'cruising' qualities of sea travel to highlight the tranquillity and relaxation compared to the low-cost airline alternative, with some operators using catamaran services to offer a high-speed alternative to ferries. The UK has a particularly dense network of ferry services which are used by domestic and international tourists (as well as cross-Channel day trippers) as shown in Figure 8.9. Innovation in transport technology and solutions to address problems of road-based congestion have seen the potential of river crossings and water-borne transport investigated by various companies, partly where the linear nature of the waterway links to key destinations. In London, for example, the river bus concept has been developed alongside river tours.

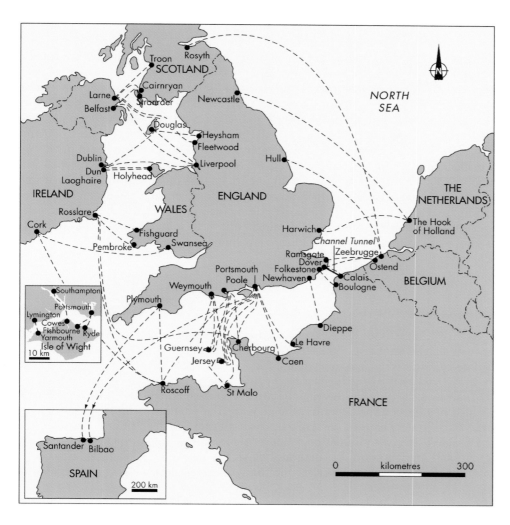

FIGURE 8.9 Ferry routes map

Pleasure craft on inland waterways

Jennings (2007) pointed to around 20 million private pleasure craft globally, with over 12 million in the USA although only a proportion of these are used on inland waterways. Within countries which have an industrial heritage based on canals and inland waterways (e.g. northern European countries, the UK and Eire) a significant vacation market has developed based on pleasure boats designed to use the former canal and waterways that were previously developed to serve the transport needs of a former era. For example, in Ireland, the Lower Shannon navigation which extends from Meelick to Limerick has 5729 registered vessels and 10 per cent are available for hire. The area has developed a tourism industry to serve this market with accommodation, attractions and cafés to meet boat users' needs. In cities

IMAGE 8.3 Since the 1990s, river tourism has become a fast-growing market in many European countries, as the appeal of cruises and trips on waterways has enjoyed a renaissance, including canal boats

such as Birmingham and Gloucester in the UK, the network of canals is so extensive that it has become the focus of urban regeneration projects. Tourist use of pleasure craft is an integral part of the strategy by the British Waterways Board to relaunch the area's appeal to the tourist seeking a heritage product (Image 8.3). The extent of the canal network in the UK still offers considerable potential for expansion as a tourism and leisure resource using the historic canal boats, converted for holidays as companies such as Hoseasons have promoted.

To illustrate the scale and significance of this growing market for pleasure craft as part of a holiday experience, the example of the Norfolk Broads in the UK suggests that even seemingly sustainable modes of tourist transport, such as the canal or pleasure boat, are not without environmental impacts. The Norfolk Broads is a wetland region in East Anglia created through the flooding of peat diggings in the medieval period. The region comprises a number of rivers and their tributaries which offer opportunities for recreational and tourism-related boating activities. The hire-boat industry was pioneered by John Loyne in the 1880s and popularized in 1908 by H. Blake and Company, which set up purpose-built vessels for hire aimed at the rail-based visitors. In 1995, the boat companies in the region owned 1481 motor cruises and launches hired to approximately 200 000 visitors a year but there are over 13 000 licensed boats using the Broads each year. The single most important environmental impact of the hire boat and recreation and boat industry has been the damage to the river banks caused by the wash from vessels together with a number of other impacts induced by the visitors' effect on wildlife and the potential conflict with other activities such as angling. Yet the economic impact of boating in the region is estimated to contribute £25 million to the local economy and supports over 1600 jobs, while indirect tourist spending contributes to over 5000 jobs.

Air transport

Apart from so-called 'air taxis', all civil aviation falls into one of two categories: scheduled and charter traffic. Scheduled airlines are those which operate to a clearly defined, published timetable, irrespective of whether a flight is full or not. Until the 1980s, many scheduled airlines were state-owned and run for reasons of national prestige; a classic example of privatization occurred in 1987 when the British government sold British Airways. In contrast, chartered aircraft, by definition, are chartered out to a third party; this may be a seat-broker who will sell smaller blocks of seats to small tour operators or it may be a large tour operator who requires the whole aircraft for a summer or winter season's flying. In reality, the large tour operators possess their own airlines. The evolution of air travel is a complex area which is historically determined by international bodies such as the International Civil Aviation Organization (ICAO) and the International Air Transport Association (IATA). The regulations they established have, combined with bilateral agreements, established the framework for international air travel up until the deregulation era in the late 1970s.

One of the most complex areas is the political regulation of air travel, which dates to the 1930s and includes the 1944 Chicago Convention. Current-day aviation is regulated by international aviation law and this provides the context in which national and global carriers operate. At the national level, different countries have varying approaches to aviation competition and regulation. In the USA, anti-trust laws exist to encourage competition and reduce price fixing. This was extended under the 1978 Airline Deregulation Act. In Europe, similar legislation exists with anti-competition law in existence. In the USA, deregulation has seen the patterns of larger carriers take over many of the smaller operators and develop a hub and spoke operation. Here, the hub is a centralized point of operation where local flights feed passengers to the hub, to avoid operating large aircraft on local, uneconomic routes (Figure 8.10). One of the exceptions to this rule is the growth of low-cost carriers, like Southwest Airlines in the USA, which use smaller secondary airports and offer point-to-point services, rather than a national and international network.

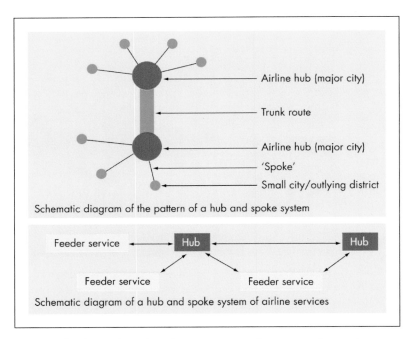

Airline hub (major city)

Trunk route

Airline hub (major city)

'Spoke'

Small city/outlying district

Schematic diagram of the pattern of a hub and spoke system

Feeder service — Hub ↔ Hub

Feeder service   Feeder service

Schematic diagram of a hub and spoke system of airline services

FIGURE 8.10 Hub and spoke operation and point-to-point services
Source: Page (1994)

At an international scale, the right of airlines to fly is governed by the five freedoms of the air, outlined in Figure 8.11. Airlines can gain technical and traffic rights to operate between countries, based on the 1944 Chicago Convention. The rights have also been developed in subsequent years with sixth and seventh freedoms being added.

A key feature of international civil aviation in the last 20 years has been 'deregulation'. This started in the USA in 1978, when the federal government relaxed its control over route allocation and pricing leading, inevitably, to the establishment of numerous small airlines, many of which no longer exist; although it pre-dates 1978, Southwest Airlines benefited from the ability to fly on any route and has pursued a policy of issuing boarding cards instead of tickets, serving no meals and operating as many flights a day as possible (see Page 2009 for a detailed analysis of air travel in a climate of deregulation). Southwest remains one of the USA's most successful airlines. One consequence of excessive competition in the airline sector was evident after 9/11 when many US airlines were already burdened with debt and only six weeks away from collapse, even though they provide the vital link for domestic and international tourism.

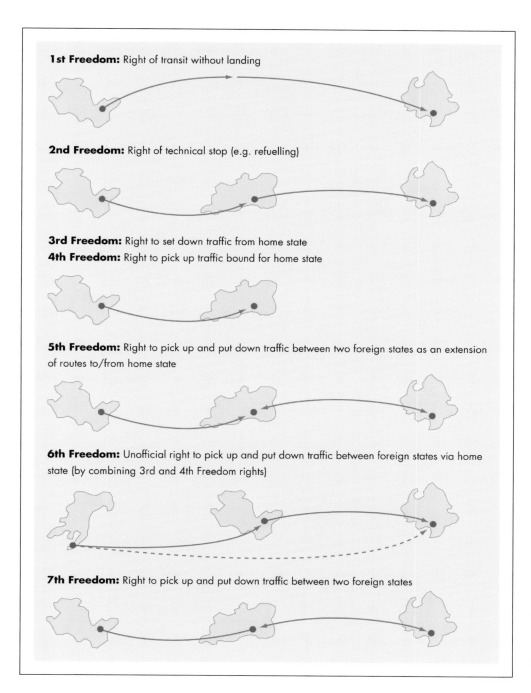

1st Freedom: Right of transit without landing

2nd Freedom: Right of technical stop (e.g. refuelling)

3rd Freedom: Right to set down traffic from home state
4th Freedom: Right to pick up traffic bound for home state

5th Freedom: Right to pick up and put down traffic between two foreign states as an extension of routes to/from home state

6th Freedom: Unofficial right to pick up and put down traffic between foreign states via home state (by combining 3rd and 4th Freedom rights)

7th Freedom: Right to pick up and put down traffic between two foreign states

FIGURE 8.11 Freedoms of the air
Source: Redrawn from 'Figure G. 1: Air transport freedom rights' which first appeared in *Asia Pacific Air Transport. Challenges and Policy Reforms*, edited by Christopher Findlay, Chia Lin Sien and Karmjit Singh, p. 193 with the kind permission of the publisher, Institute of Southeast Asian Studies, Singapore http://bookshop.iseas.edu.sg

Airline deregulation: Globalization and alliances

Aviation has not been immune from deregulation, as many governments have sought to reduce investment requirements by privatizing the state airline, which has provided some airlines with opportunities to become global businesses. In Asia and South America, however, many airlines are still state-owned and enjoy a degree of protectionism. The protectionism means that many of the state-owned airlines are less competitive, leading to high fares for Asian travellers (Findlay *et al.* 1997) (except where they operate low staffing cost structures), and are not operating at their optimum performance. Figure 8.12, based on Evans's (2001) conceptualization of

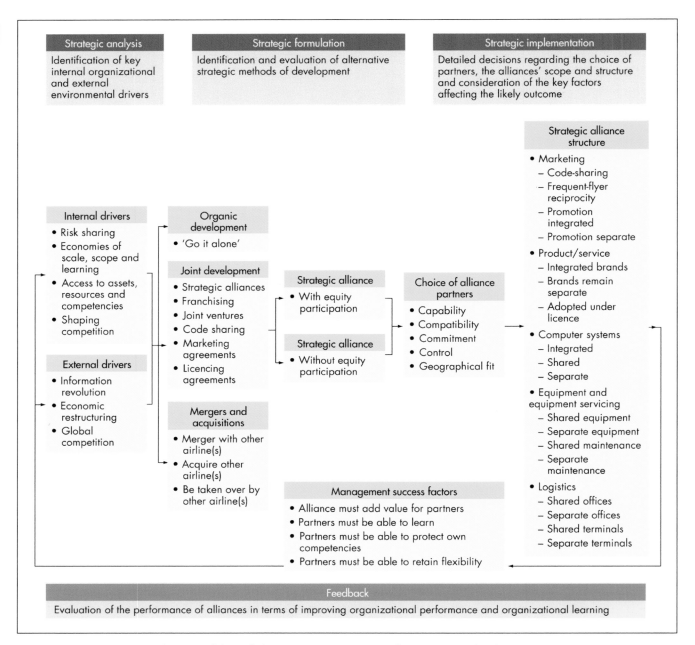

FIGURE 8.12 Conceptualization of the collaborative strategy process for international airlines

Source: Reprinted from *Tourism Management*, vol. 22, Evans, 'Collaborative strategy: An analysis of the changing world of international airline alliances', 229–243 © 2001 with permission from Elsevier

the alliance and collaboration process for international airlines, highlights the range of motives associated with entering into such arrangements, especially the potential for airlines to cooperate; for example, an alliance may offer passengers a global network without one airline having to provide all the services. This has assisted many of the larger airlines to establish a global presence through the three existing large airline alliances – Oneworld, Star Alliance and Sky Team.

The structure of the air transport sector

The complexity of the aviation sector is shown in Figure 8.13 which highlights the wide range of stakeholders involved in the aviation industry, and their significance to the wider tourism economy. For example, aviation transports over 4 billion passengers a year, 40 per cent of whom are international tourists, which supports over

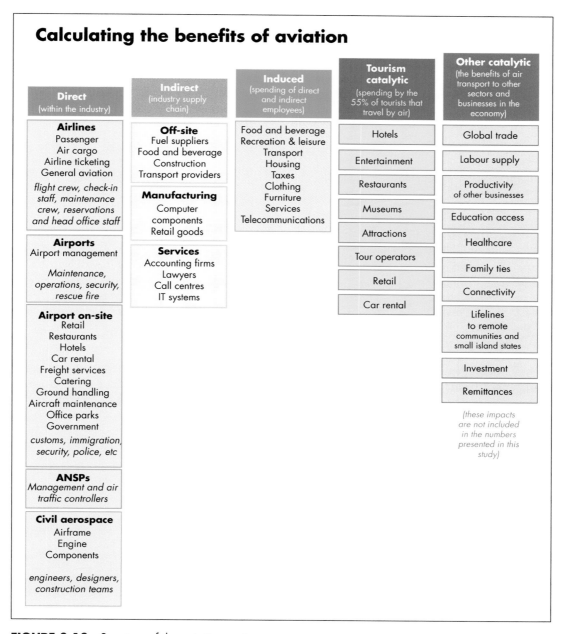

FIGURE 8.13 Structure of the aviation sector
Source: ATAG, reproduced with permission

65 million jobs and generates an estimated US$2.7 trillion in economic activity comprising (reflecting the categories in Figure 8.13 from ATAG):

- US$704.4 billion from aviation directly
- US$637.6 billion from direct indirect spending
- US$454 billion induced from direct and indirect spending
- US$896.6 from tourism based on the 57 per cent of tourist who travel by air according to ATAG (2018).

This activity is generated by 1303 airlines with around 34 000 aircraft serving 3759 airports and 45 000 routes and 41 million scheduled flights a year generating 7.75 trillion passenger km a year globally (ATAG 2018). For a vibrant airline sector to function, collaboration and a strong industry body is needed.

What the airline alliance literature shows is that a number of airline alliances have grown from 'inter-line' agreements into substantial, coordinated reservation and marketing agreements for groups of airlines. Bennett (1997) identified two forms of alliance: *tactical* (informal) and *strategic* (informal). The tactical partnership provides marketing advantages at low risk to the parties; 'code-sharing' allows one airline to market flights from regional airports to an international one (a so-called 'hub') for onward connection to intercontinental destinations. Bennett (1997: 214) considers strategic partnerships are where longer-term commitment results in 'shared airport facilities (check-ins, lounges), improved connections (synchronized schedules), reciprocity on frequent flyer programmes . . . and marketing agreements'. Ongoing consolidation in the airline industry has led to changes in alliance membership within a short space of time but one way airlines have addressed costs is through yield management.

Yield management and airlines

According to Kimes (2000: 3):

'yield management originated with the deregulation of the US airline industry' as the People's Express low-priced, no frills airline model of operation saw full-service operators such as American Airlines and United compete by offering a small number of similar seats on each departure. This created a diversity of passenger types and the yield (or revenue) management, a method for managing capacity profitability, has since gained widespread acceptance in the airline and hotel industries. The term 'yield' originated in the airline industry and refers to yield (or revenue) per available seat mile . . . Yield management is a method which can help a firm to sell the right inventory unit to the right customers, at the right time and for the right price . . . to maximize profit and revenue.

The concept of yield management has come to have equal validity for the hotel and cruising businesses since any capacity not sold cannot be held onto; for example, an unsold bed-night cannot be retained – it is lost revenue and better to achieve some price than none at all. Kimes (2000) identified a number of conditions that are essential for yield management to work:

- fixed capacity
- high fixed costs
- low variable costs
- time-varied demand
- similarity of inventory units.

Added to these conditions, there are a number of required features of the business, namely:

- market segmentation capability
- historical demand and booking pattern data
- knowledge of competitor pricing
- development of an over-booking policy
- links to the corporate management information system.

Importantly, airline yield management systems enable some seats to be retained for those premium fare passengers who always book late. Page (2009) refers to research which shows 2–5 per cent revenue gains resulting from implementation of such a system.

Such systems have been successfully used by the rapidly expanding low-cost airlines in the 1990s. For example, the growth of Southwest Airlines in the USA in the 1970s has been replicated by Ryanair and easyJet in the UK. This model of operation using yield management has also filtered through to Australia with Virgin Blue, Air Asia in Malaysia and many other competing operators in Asia such as Sky Asia and Tiger Airways (the latter two airlines developed from larger flag carriers – Thai International Airlines and Singapore Airlines) to generate new markets without diluting the full-cost and high-quality service brand of the parent company. These airlines use yield management successfully to maximize revenue and passenger loadings, with low operational costs and using a distinctive business model similar to that of the highly successful Southwest Airlines (Gittell 2003).

Low-cost airline growth: Expanding capacity versus profitability

Competition in this market, as discussed in Chapter 7, has led tourism growth and development (Akguc *et al.* 2018), being supply-led through the provision of seat capacity in many EU countries, to stimulate new demand. Akguc *et al.* (2018) outline the patterns of concentration in the low-cost airline market in Europe with the major low-cost carriers being: Ryanair (120 million passengers a year), easyJet (80 million passengers a year) and Wizz (28.3 million passengers a year). The other large player they did not have data for was Vuelling, who carried 29.5 million passengers a year. By 2017, low-cost carriers offering international flights ranged from 12 per cent market share in Finland to 52 per cent in Ireland, 55 per cent in Italy, 56 per cent in Spain, 57 per cent in the UK and 50 per cent in Poland. In the domestic markets, the low-cost carriers dominated the UK (66 per cent share) with just under half the market share in Italy with a 47 per cent share and Spain with a 48 per cent share. But as Budd *et al.* (2014) found, the low-cost airline market is a very fluid one (observed in Chapter 7 in relation to insolvency and risk) as between 1992 and 2012, of 43 low-cost airlines which began operation in Europe, only 10 remained operational. The failure rate of 77 per cent can be attributed to a wide range of factors including start-up date, the nature and size of the airline's operation (including route selection) and the size and composition of its aircraft fleet. Despite this, constant innovation characterizes the sector. For example, the IAG Group launched a new low-cost international carrier – LEVEL (operated by Iberia) in 2017 and in 2018 were operating flights from Barcelona to Los Angeles, Guadeloupe, Buenos Aires, Boston, Montreal and San Francisco using two A330–200 aircraft, with an aim to grow the company to 15 aircraft. One-way flights from Barcelona to Boston started at US$149 and San Francisco for US$160 and Montreal for US$239 in 2018 (see www.flylevel.com).

Terminal facilities and tourist travel

One of the most neglected and poorly understood areas of tourist travel is the role and significance of terminal facilities (Page 2005). These provide a wide range of functions from simple interchanges in the public transport setting (e.g. a coach terminal such as London's Victoria Coach Station) to the more advanced integrated transport interchanges such as Singapore Changi Airport where air, rail, coach, taxi and car modes are fully integrated. In the airline industry, terminals have traditionally been viewed as transfer points from air to other modes or air-to-air transfers. But the 1970s and 1980s have seen a revolution in airport terminal design since they offer a wide range of retailing opportunities for passengers to make the waiting and journey more pleasurable. This has also led to a growth in non-aviation revenue for airports (Graham 2013) for highly successful global airline companies such as British Airports Authority (http://www.baa.co.uk). Airlines have developed specialist facilities in these terminals for high-yield passengers such as first-class travellers, namely first-class lounges or VIP lounges which cater for the needs of these groups (e.g. a place to relax, work or to hold meetings) (see Halpern and Graham 2013).

These facilities have to be integrated with a wide range of other functions at airports including (estimates of employment globally based on ATAG 2018):

- Airlines (472 000 jobs, 28 per cent of total employment)
- Ground handling, which involves managing the aircraft on the ground (241 000, 14 per cent of total employment)

- Food and beverage (130 000 jobs, 8 per cent of employment)
- Retail and in-terminal jobs (including check-in and baggage handling, 107 000 jobs, 6 per cent of total employment)
- Airport security and passenger screening (106 000 jobs, 6 per cent of total employment)
- Airport ground transport (79 000 jobs, 5 per cent of employment)
- Customs, immigration and government jobs (90 000 jobs, 5 per cent of employment)
- Airport and air traffic control (238 000, 14 per cent of jobs)
- Mechanical and repairs services/engineering (102 400 jobs, 6 per cent of employment)
- Other (127 000 jobs, 7 per cent of employment).

The scale and significance of such terminals in terms of the volume of traffic they handle is recorded by the global organization, the Airport Council International (ACI). Table 8.3 provides more detailed insight for 2018. The situation has changed significantly in the last five years as the traditional dominance of the USA and Europe has been complemented by the growth of Asian airports, especially Chinese airports. As Table 8.3 shows, Hong Kong, Tokyo and Beijing have prominent positions in the Top 19 rankings, challenging the traditional dominance of North American and European airports with Asian airports now almost rivalling the North American and European dominance. A further notable feature is how Dubai has developed a Middle East hub for two purposes: to generate inbound visitors to visit the region, especially Dubai; and as a hub for cross-world travel from Europe to Asia and other key trunk routes, rivalling Kuala Lumpur, Bangkok, Singapore Changi airport and Los Angeles. It is also clear in the case of China it is replicating the position in the USA with its highly developed domestic and long-haul airline market as volumes of travel build to a point that the key airports have international significance. What ACI statistics also demonstrate is the dominance of airports in accommodating tourist travel and the need for long-term development strategies (Graham 2013), since building a new terminal can take over a decade from inception, including the planning, development and opening phases. Airport privatization, like airline privatization, has occurred at a global scale due to the high investment costs to governments of building new airport capacity.

TABLE 8.3 Top 19 airports by passenger numbers for 2018

Rank	Region	Country	City	Airport Name	IATA Code
1	North America	United States	Atlanta, GA	Hartsfield-Jackson Atlanta International Airport	ATL
2	Asia-Pacific	China	Beijing	Beijing Capital International Airport	PEK
3	Middle East	United Arab Emirates	Dubai	Dubai International Airport	DXB
4	North America	United States	Los Angeles, CA	Los Angeles International Airport	LAX
5	Asia-Pacific	Japan	Tokyo	Tokyo International (Haneda) Airport	HND
6	North America	United States	Chicago, IL	O'Hare International Airport	ORD
7	Europe	United Kingdom	London	Heathrow Airport	LHR
8	Asia-Pacific	Hong Kong	Hong Kong	Hong Kong International Airport	HKG
9	Asia-Pacific	China	Shanghai	Pudong International Airport	PVG
10	Europe	France	Paris	Aéroport de Paris-Charles de Gaulle	CDG
11	Europe	Netherlands	Amsterdam	Amsterdam Airport Schiphol	AMS
12	Asia-Pacific	India	New Delhi	Indira Gandhi International Airport	DEL
13	Asia-Pacific	China	Guangzhou	Guangzhou Bai Yun International Airport	CAN
14	Europe	Germany	Frankfurt	Flughafen Frankfurt/Main	FRA
15	North America	United States	Dallas/Fort Worth, TX	Dallas/Ft Worth International Airport	DFW
16	Asia-Pacific	Korea, Republic Of	Incheon	Incheon International Airport	ICN
17	Europe	Turkey	Istanbul	Atatürk International Airport	IST
18	Asia-Pacific	Indonesia	Jakarta	Soekarno-Hatta International Airport	CGK
19	Asia-Pacific	Singapore	Singapore	Singapore Changi Airport	SIN

Source: © Airports Council International (ACI) World 2018 Annual World Airport Traffic Dataset, reproduced with kind permission

For example, China invested US\$17.4 billion up to 2010 to cope with the growth in demand to 100 million arrivals by 2020. To cater for this demand, China built a further 92 airports between 2008 and 2020.

Future issues for tourist transport: Will it continue to be used as a tool to expand tourism?

The continued growth in the tourist demand for travel has seen a largely upward trend in the expansion of car use for domestic travel and air for domestic and international travel. However, there is a growing recognition that nothing in the future is certain or predictable with regard to transport and tourism, given the current concerns over global issues such as climate change, oil as a future fuel and more variable elements such as safety and security concerns emanating from terrorism and personal security. Airline pollution, according to ATAG (2018), accounts for 2 per cent of global CO_2 emissions, but 80 per cent of these emissions arise from flights of over 1500 km, and the sector has spent \$1 trillion on new aircraft since 2009 to reduce emissions and fuel consumption. But one has to question the need for so much air travel in an age where technology can be a good substitute for business travel, and awareness of climate change issues has clearly not led to a drop in long-haul flying despite measures such as air passenger duty. While ATAG (2018: 7) argues that 'aviation is indispensable for tourism', one can see a position where extreme measures to limit human mobility and CO_2 emissions could lead to the imposition of individual carbon budgets. These could transform international air travel into a more user-pays activity, especially if aviation fuel is taxed in line with other fuels such as diesel and petrol. The subsidy that aviation enjoys through aviation fuel gives it a competitive advantage. Even so, ATAG (2018: 16) points to the dependency of developing nations on air-facilitated tourist travel as

> for developing countries in particular, air links provide a vital economic lifeline to communities. In Africa . . . an estimated 4.9 million people are employed in areas supported by a steady influx of overseas visitors, most of whom arrive in the region by air. In addition, these arrivals by air supported an estimated \$35.9 billion contribution to GDP in African economies in 2016 . . . For small island states, the economic input provided by international tourists is invaluable. These countries, many of which are in remote parts of the world enjoy tourism-induced economic boosts which would not be available without air links.

This quotation illustrates the dependent relationship which air transport has with tourism, and its relationship at a national and local level. But this current thinking on transport-led tourism growth as knowing no limits is likely to change in the next 15 to 20 years, if not sooner (see Chapter 19). Tourism will also be affected by changes in transport technology (i.e. the use of greener fuels and cleaner aircraft engines) although whether these will compensate for the growth in volume of tourist travel or mitigate the environmental costs and impacts is debatable. Most important of all will be the way governments and people think about transport for tourism as unconstrained and available to those who can pay for it. For example, tourism will be affected by a range of new challenges and different potential scenarios such as the future role of transport and CO_2 emissions by 2030 in the UK (see Hickman and Bannister 2007) and elsewhere. Future policy measures will shape this debate and become critical as a way of guiding the actions of governments.

A critical debate is already occurring among different political groups related to the role of air travel and the necessity of expanding it to promote further transport-led tourism growth. For example, in the UK the Environment Change Institute (ECI) (2006) questioned many of the Department for Transport's assumptions (2003) in *The Future for Air Transport* over the need for new airport projects. It questioned the argument that growth in air travel is *inevitable* since it is the consequence of growth in GDP, as the expansion of air travel has tended to follow the growth in GDP. Yet the report argues that while income and GDP growth affect the demand for air travel, it does not mean aviation is a key driver of GDP. There is a broad relationship apparent that as GDP growth increases the number of passengers travelling by air increases, but the relationship is *not* direct, and can be altered by policy intervention. The ECI report also questioned the potential impact if air fares rose to reduce overseas travel for UK residents and the consequences of additional spending on UK domestic tourism and the net effect in regenerating many destinations through new investment. It showed that for every £1 spent by overseas visitors, UK residents spend £2.32 abroad. Consequently the ECI report criticizes the aviation industry for having a negative effect on UK tourism, running contrary to popular opinion. Such debates at a policy level are beginning to question the environmental basis of continued growth in transport to promote tourism growth. Yet this has not stopped subsequent governments approving further airport capacity to remain economically competitive with other countries. To a large degree this makes the sustainability policies in place redundant when there is no fundamental change to the societal ideologies on economic growth. We would do well to reconsider many of the 1960s and 1970s classic studies on limiting economic growth, which we will revisit in Chapter 19 on sustainability. Therefore debates on the future role of transport in tourism development continue but it is only changes brought about by environmental legislation and concerns (see Chapters 18 and 19) which are likely to see a significant shift in the unrestricted use of transport to promote tourism development. In this respect, the sustainable development agenda we will discuss in Chapter 19 remains outside of the influence of mainstream politics associated with transport and tourism despite the mounting evidence on the impact on global climate (Dubois *et al.* 2011) and the prevailing climate emergency we will examine in Chapter 19.

Conclusion

The tourist's use of transport begins when the tourist leaves their home and boards a form of transport. Without the transport mode, access to tourism would be very limited and restricted. It is really the postwar period that has seen the greatest revolution in transportation, making tourist destinations more accessible to a much greater population as living standards and income have increased per capita, making travel relatively cheap and freely available. Expanding car ownership has also made accommodating the car a major problem for destinations (Image 8.4).

IMAGE 8.4 Accommodating the car can be detrimental to destinations in the peak season when sensitive areas are used as car parks to address congestion

What is also clear from this chapter is the pace of change and development in the transport sector, particularly in air travel, which provides new opportunities for tourist travel, realizing latent demand (i.e. facilitating travel where demand may not have existed because of the prohibitively high cost of travel for low-income groups). The introduction of budget travel, especially the low-cost carriers, remains a major driver of tourist development that has expanded the range of destinations for the budget-conscious traveller. This

also leads to change in the marketplace and fierce competition between carriers to gain market share.

Among some of the current trends that are also likely to affect tourist travel in different transport modes over the next decade are:

- *Air travellers' price sensitivity has increased*, as low-cost travel has challenged models of provision which have dominated many carriers, especially in markets that have only limited elements of internationalization.
- *Collaboration among transport providers*, especially airlines, has enabled greater cost-competitiveness and an interconnected transport system at a global level and these will continue to grow in significance.
- *Quality service remains a constant pressure upon the suppliers of transport services*, especially as travellers seek more for less in terms of price. However, quality hallmarks and customer service still distinguish many well-established and successful companies that offer premium services, and there is no shortage of demand in key markets for premium services. The success of the Orient Express is a case in point.

Among key management considerations to meet increasing customer expectations in transport provisions are:

- *efficient cost controls*, as discussed in Chapter 5, continued savings in operational budgets and a greater use of technology to achieve these goals
- *a clear understanding of strategic issues*, especially the implications of transport policy changes such as the greater liberalization of air travel and process of globalization and privatization
- *a need for effective and influential leadership skills* to ensure operators stay ahead of the competition
- *managing yields* so that existing capacity and infrastructure can be used more efficiently and profitably.

A thorough understanding of the relationship between transport and tourism is a major prerequisite for any analysis of the factors which facilitate and constrain the development of tourism and any discussion of its role cannot ignore the importance of governments in shaping policy and infrastructure development to encourage inbound and outbound tourism.

Discussion questions

1 Why is transport important to the study of tourism?

2 Has the development of cruising in the new millennium become a new product based on the concept of luxury and leisure experiences?

3 Identify the impact of low-cost airline carriers on the European airline market.

4 The interaction between transport and tourism is poorly understood. Why is this the case?

References

Akguc, M., Beblavy, M. and Simonelli, F. (2018) *Low Cost Airlines: Bringing the EU Closer Together.* Brussels: Centre for European Policy Studies. www.ceps.eu.

ATAG (2018) *Aviation Benefits without Borders.* Geneva: ATAG. www.atag.org.

Bennett, M. (1997) 'Strategic alliances in the world airline industry', *Progress in Tourism and Hospitality Research,* 3: 213–23.

Beunen, R., Regrierns, H. and Jaarsma, C. (2008) 'Gateways as a means of visitor management in National Parks and protected areas', *Tourism Management,* 29 (2): 138–145.

Bíl, M., Bílová, M. and Kubeček, J. (2012) 'Unified GIS database on cycle tourism infrastructure', *Tourism Management,* 33: 1554–1561.

Budd, L., Francis, G., Humphreys, I. and Ison, S. (2014) 'Grounded: Characterising the market exit of European low cost airlines,' *Journal of Air Transport Management,* 34: 78–85.

Connell, J. and Page, S.J. (2008) 'Exploring the spatial patterns of car-based tourist travel in Loch Lomond and Trossachs National Park, Scotland', *Tourism Management,* 29 (3): 561–80.

Cox, P. (2012) 'Strategies promoting cycle tourism in Belgium: Practices and implication', *Tourism Planning and Development,* 9: 25–39.

Department for Transport (2003) *The Future for Air Travel.* HMSO: London.

Dickinson, J., Calver, S., Watters, K. and Wilks, K. (2004) 'Journeys to heritage attractions in the UK: A case study of National Trust visitors in the South West', *Journal of Transport Geography,* 12 (1): 103–113.

Dubois, G., Peeters, P., Ceron, J. and Gössling, S. (2011) 'The future tourism mobility of the world's population: Emission growth versus climate policy', *Transportation Research Part A: Policy and Practice,* 45: 103–143.

ECI (Environmental Change Institute) (2006) *Predict and Decide: Aviation, Climate Change and UK Policy.* ECI: Oxford.

European Union (2002) *European Transport Policy for 2010.* Brussels: EU.

Evans, N. (2001) 'Collaborative strategy: An analysis of the changing world for international airlines', *Tourism Management,* 2 (2): 229–43.

Findlay, C., Sieh, L. and Singh, K. (eds.) (1997) *Asia Pacific Air Transport: Challenges and Policy Reforms.* Singapore: Institute of South East Asian Studies.

Gittell, J. (2003) *The Southwest Airlines Way.* New York: McGraw-Hill.

Graham, A. (2013) *Managing Airports,* 4th edition. London: Routledge.

Halpern, N. and Graham, A. (2013) *Airport Marketing.* London: Routledge.

Henderson, J. (2007) *Tourism Crises: Causes, Consequences and Management.* Oxford: Butterworth Heinemann.

Hickman, R. and Bannister, D. (2007) 'Looking over the horizon: Transport and reduced CO_2 emissions in the UK by 2030', *Transport Policy,* 14 (5): 377–387.

Jennings, G. (ed.) (2007) *Water-based Tourism, Sport, Leisure and Recreation Experiences.* Oxford: Butterworth-Heinemann.

Kimes, S. (2000) 'Yield management: An overview', in U. McMahon-Beattie, I.I. Yeoman and A. Ingold (eds.) *Yield Management – Strategies for the Service Industries,* 2nd edition. London: Continuum.

Lumsdon, L. (1997) 'Recreational cycling: Is this the way to stimulate interest in everyday urban cycling?', in R. Tolley (ed.) *The Greening of Urban Transport Planning for Walking and Cycling in Western Cities,* 2nd edition. Chichester: Wiley.

Lumsdon, L. and Page, S.J. (eds.) (2004) *Tourism and Transport: Issues and Agenda for the New Millennium.* Oxford: Elsevier.

Lumsdon, L. and Tolley, R. (2004) 'Non-motorised transport: A case study of cycling', in L. Lumsdon and S.J. Page (eds.)

Tourism and Transport: Issues and Agenda for the New Millennium. Oxford: Elsevier.

Mancini, M. (2011) *The CLIA Guide to the Cruise Industry*. Clifton Park, NY: DELMAR, CENGAGE Learning.

Martín-C. and Sánchez, P. (2010) 'Ecological footprint analysis of road transport related to tourism activity: The case for Lanzarote Island', *Tourism Management*, 31 (1): 98–103.

McKercher, B. (2018) 'The impact of distance on tourism: A tourism geography law', *Tourism Geographies*, 20 (5): 905–909.

McKercher, B., Chan, A. and Lau, C. (2008) 'The impact of distance on international tourist movements', *Journal of Travel Research*, 47 (2), 208–224.

McKercher, B. and Darcy, S. (2018) 'Re-conceptualizing barriers to travel by people with disabilities', *Tourism Management Perspectives*, 26, 59–66.

McKercher, B. and Lew, A. (2004) 'Tourist flows and the spatial distribution of tourists', in A. Lew, C.M. Hall and A. Williams (eds.) *A Companion of Tourism*. Oxford: Blackwell.

Moscardo, G. and Pearce, P. (2004) 'Life cycle, tourist motivation and transport: Some consequences for the tourist experience', in L. Lumsdon and S.J. Page (eds.) *Tourism and Transport: Issues and Agenda for the New Millennium*. Oxford: Elsevier.

Orbasli, A. and Shaw, S. (2004) 'Transport and visitors in historic cities', in L. Lumsdon and S.J. Page (eds.) *Tourism and Transport Issues and Agenda for the New Millennium*. Oxford: Elsevier.

Page, S.J. (1994) *Transport for Tourism*. London: Routledge.

Page, S.J. (2009) *Transport and Tourism*, 3rd edition. Harlow: Prentice Hall.

Page, S.J. and Connell, J. (2014) 'Transport and tourism', in A. Lew, C.M. Hall and A. Williams (eds.) *A Companion to Tourism*. Oxford: Blackwell.

Papathanassis, A. (2012) 'Guest to guest interaction on board cruise ships: Exploring social dynamics and the role of situational factors', *Tourism Management*, 33 (5): 1148–1153.

Patmore, J.A. (1983) *Recreation and Resources*. Oxford: Blackwell.

Peisley, T. (2006) *The Future of Cruising – Boom or Bust? A Worldwide Analysis to 2015*. Colchester: Seatrade Communications.

Prideaux, B. (1999) 'Tracks to tourism: Queensland Rail joins the tourist industry', *International Journal of Tourism Research*, 1 (2): 73–86.

Prideaux, B. and Carson, D. (2010) *Drive Tourism: Trends and Emerging Markets*. London: Routledge.

Ritchie, B.W. (1998) 'Bicycle tourism in the South West of New Zealand: Planning and management issues', *Tourism Management*, 19 (6): 567–582.

Stopher, P. (2004) 'Reducing road congestion', *Transport Policy*, 11: 117–31.

Stradling, S. and Anable, J. (2008) 'Individual transport patterns', in R. Knowles, J. Shaw and I. Docherty (eds.) *Transport Geographies: Mobilities, Flows and Spaces*. Oxford: Blackwell.

Wall, G. (1971) 'Car owners and holiday activities', in P. Lavery (ed.) *Recreational Geography*. Newton Abbot: David and Charles.

Further reading

Books

Arup (2017) Future of Air Travel. London: Arup. https://www.arup.com/en/perspectives/publications/Research/Section/Future-of-Air-Travel.

ATAG (Air Transport Action Group) (2007) *The Economic Benefits of Air Transport*. Brussels: ATAG.

Graham, A. (2013) *Managing Airports*, 4th edition. London: Routledge.

Hall, C.M., Ram, Y. and Shoval, N. (2017) *The Routledge International Handbook of Walking*. London: Routledge.

Journal articles

Albalate, D. and Fageda, X. (2016) 'High speed rail and tourism: Empirical evidence from Spain', *Transportation Research Part A: Policy and Practice*, 85: 174–185.

Budd, L., Francis, G., Humphreys, I. and Ison, S. (2014) 'Grounded: Characterising the market exit of European low cost airlines', *Journal of Air Transport Management*, 34: 78–85.

McKercher, B. and Darcy, S. (2018) 'Re-conceptualizing barriers to travel by people with disabilities', *Tourism Management Perspectives*, 26, 59–66.

Rico, A., Martínez-Blanco, J., Montlleó, M., Rodríguez, G., Tavares, N., Arias, A. and Oliver-Solà, J. (2019) 'Carbon footprint of tourism in Barcelona', *Tourism Management*, 70, 491–504.

Wang, K., Zhang, A. and Zhang, Y. (2018) 'Key determinants of airline pricing and air travel demand in China and India: Policy, ownership, and LCC competition', *Transport Policy*, 63: 80–89.

Visitor attractions

Learning outcomes

After reading this chapter and answering the questions, you should be able to:

- understand the scope and importance of visitor attractions
- identify and discuss the main issues influencing the development and management of attractions
- outline future issues and themes affecting the attractions sector.

Overview

Visitor attractions are one of the key components of the tourism industry, adding to the appeal of destinations through natural and built features, as well as the hosting of special events. This chapter reviews the nature and scope of visitor attractions and explores a number of issues associated with their development, operation and management.

Introduction

Visitor attractions form one of the basic components of the tourism industry, along with transport and accommodation, and play a crucial role in the appeal of destinations. For many tourists, the attractions on offer at a destination form the major reason for visiting. Indeed, attractions are frequently used as the basis for destination marketing campaigns (see Chapter 15). Attractions are a central component of leisure day visits as well as tourism trips, serving the resident community as well as those on holiday away from home. The attractions sector comprises a wide range of built environment and natural environments, as well as cultural resources, products, festivals and events, which are developed and managed to provide interesting and enjoyable experiences to the visitor (also see Chapter 26 on event tourism).

As well as providing appeal in a destination, attractions act as a focal point for visitor activity and spending, which is particularly important where tourism forms part of a wider development or area rejuvenation strategy. Therefore, a thriving attraction industry is part of an area's basic tourism infrastructure, providing opportunities for the local community, businesses and the local economy as well as visitor enjoyment. The management of attractions, however, is highly complex and beset with difficulties. Throughout this chapter, a key theme is the development, operation and management of visitor attractions as part of a prosperous tourism economy. Where examples of failed attractions are apparent, then the basic infrastructure of the tourism sector is diminished, and throughout the chapter it is apparent that those attractions that do not embrace the positive features of attraction development will either face financial problems or, more likely, fail.

The evolution of visitor attractions

While visitor attractions might be considered as a modern creation, the evolution of tourism was dependent on the existence and development of attractions. Even as far back as Roman times, travellers went to look at the Pyramids and, much later, the Grand Tour circuits were based around the major cultural attractions of Europe (see Chapter 2). As Table 9.1 indicates, some of today's major attractions existed in an embryonic form in the late nineteenth century (e.g. Blackpool Pleasure Beach, UK) and early twentieth century (e.g. De Efteling, Netherlands). However, it was not really until the post-war period that visitor attractions really developed into a form that we recognize in contemporary tourism, including theme parks where the experience is highly sophisticated, using marketing and technology. A study by Hansen (2018) examined visits to 40 museums in 1864–2015 and found a relationship between average earnings and visitation, indicating that such visits were dependent upon disposable income.

The USA is considered to be the pioneer in the development of theme parks, the first of which was Disneyland created by Walt Disney in California in 1955. The Disney vision to create a magical place which children and parents could enjoy attracted nearly 4 million visitors in its first year of opening and set the standard for the future development of the newly emerging attractions sector. Disney's second, larger resort, Walt Disney World in Florida, is now the world's most visited holiday destination. In a more global context, attractions became more prolific in number in the 1980s, with demand stimulated by tourism growth. The global distribution of major brands then became a key feature (see Table 9.1), emphasizing the central theme of globalization of tourism.

Since 1955, the initial investment of US$17 million in Disneyland and 3.8 million visitors in its first year of opening accelerated the trend towards theme park visitation in the USA. By 1975, the top 30 theme parks attracted 65 million visitors rising to 95 million in 1985, 160 million in 1995 and over 200 million today. Almost half of the visitors now visit Walt Disney attractions (see Theme Park Tourist 2016). The development of the attraction sector is not simply concerned

TABLE 9.1 Selection of the world's most popular theme parks		
Year opened		*Country*
1896	Blackpool Pleasure Beach	UK
1923	Tivoli Gardens, Copenhagen	Denmark
1951	De Efteling	Netherlands
1955	Disneyland, Anaheim	USA
1964	Universal Studios, Hollywood	USA
1971	Magic Kingdom, Orlando	USA
1971	Sea World, Gold Coast	Australia
1977	Ocean Park	Hong Kong
1982	EPCOT, Orlando	USA
1983	Tokyo Disneyland	Japan
1989	Lotte World, Seoul	South Korea
1990	Universal Studios, Orlando	USA
1992	Disneyland Paris	France
2001	Universal Studios, Japan	Japan
2001	Disney Californian Adventures	USA

with the major global theme parks. Since the 1980s, there has been a rapid growth in all types of attractions, from **country houses** to industry-related visitor centres. Thus let us turn first to the definition of the term 'visitor attraction'.

Defining attractions

As Richards (2002) argues, the study of tourism attractions is not as advanced as some other areas of tourism, and defining the scope of attractions can be problematic. With regard to basic terminology, it should be noted that visitor attractions are also known as 'tourist attractions', but because the client base of many attractions includes local residents, day visitors and tourists, the term 'visitor attraction' is a more appropriate one to use for this chapter.

The definition of attractions adopted by the NTOs in the UK states that an attraction is:

where the main purpose is sightseeing. The attraction must be a permanent established excursion destination, a primary purpose of which is to allow access for entertainment, interest or education; rather than being primarily a retail outlet or a venue for sporting, theatrical or film performances. It must be open to the public, without prior booking, for published periods each year, and should be capable of attracting day visitors or tourists as well as local residents. In addition, the attraction must be a single business, under a single management, so that it is capable of answering the economic questions on revenue, employment . . . (VisitScotland 2004: 8)

While this definition is helpful in harmonizing the collection of statistics that ascertain the volume and value of the attractions sector, it is very specific and deliberately narrow in perspective. Importantly, it excludes:

- The growing significance of shopping as a destination attraction. City centre retailing experiences increasingly form a significant draw for tourists, as well as shopping malls, clusters of specialist shops, street markets and farmers' markets. Individual shops often form an attraction in their own right, including landmark stores like Harrods through to small ventures like the House at Pooh Corner, England. Retail outlets that combine visitor services and retailing are increasingly common in tourist areas, such as the Gretna Gateway Outlet Village on the main route between Scotland and England, which attracts over 1 million visitors per year.

- Unique, periodic or non-permanent events and festivals (sporting, cultural and natural), which although they may be one-off or infrequent, still have the capacity to create demand and associated management issues. Such events include major international events such as the Olympic Games through to the viewing of natural phenomena such as the Northern Lights.

- Images and locations viewed in films and television programmes stimulate tourist interest in destinations and have created a niche form of attraction, seen globally.

- A destination's natural, social, architectural (Image 9.1) and cultural resources act as an attraction too (Image 9.2), including important facets of a region such as food, wine, crafts, **vernacular buildings** and indigenous people. Importantly, while such features and activities may not be deemed as part of an attractions *sector*, they are nonetheless significant in defining the *attractions* of a destination.

IMAGE 9.1 Historic attractions such as Bath's Roman Baths are a key drawcard for a destination

IMAGE 9.2 As this tomato-throwing event in Spain indicates, large numbers of people and crowds require management

Therefore, a broader definition allows a wider range of attractions to be recognized. Pearce (1991: 46) presented an operational definition of a tourist attraction, which encompasses a broad spectrum of locations:

A tourist attraction is a named site with a specific human or natural feature which is the focus of visitor and management attention.

As Swarbrooke (2002: 9) emphasizes, attractions must be differentiated from destinations since:

attractions are generally single units, individual sites or very small, easily delimited geographical areas based on a single key feature. Destinations are larger areas that include a number of individual attractions together with the support services required by tourists.

Despite this, some attractions, such as Walt Disney World, Orlando, are of such a scale, providing substantial serviced accommodation, that they can be classed as a destination according to this definition. In terms of statistics on the visitor attraction sector internationally, there is a lack of comparable data to allow comparisons between countries. This is complicated by the different ways in which countries collect data and classify attractions.

With this debate in mind, it is clear that the scope of visitor attractions is large, and therefore it is useful to consider ways in which attractions can be categorized.

Classifications of attractions

One of the challenges for seeking to bring some order and logic to the scale and scope of visitor attractions is to find a framework that assists in the categorization process. Figure 9.1 provides one such overview. What Figure 9.1 highlights is the main attractor of visits – the core product, and structured around that are different factors and perspectives that assist in any attempt to categorize attractions (e.g. the nature of the environment it is located in, the charge to enter, structure of ownership, nature of the markets it attracts from residents through to international visitors as well as the different consumer groups within these visitor markets that typify attractions). We now look at some of these characteristics in more detail.

Type

The core product offered by an attraction is one method of classification, which is commonly used by NTOs. For example, attractions can be grouped as:

- historic houses
- museums and galleries
- wildlife attractions
- castles
- gardens

- steam railways
- visitor centres
- country parks
- leisure parks.

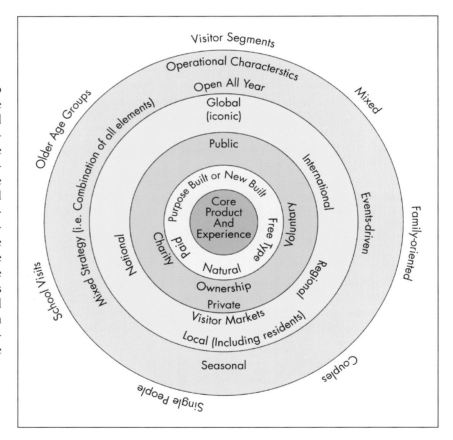

FIGURE 9.1 Categorization framework for visitor attractions
Source: Adapted and developed from Fyall *et al.* (2008)

Physical environment

Attractions can be located in the:

- natural environment, such as forests, mountains, National Parks. A further distinction can be made according to whether the natural environment is managed for visitors or left to nature
- built environment and adapted, but not originally designed for, visitor purposes, such as historic houses, workplaces, steam railways and castles
- built environment and designed for visitor purposes, such as visitor centres and leisure parks.

In addition, attractions may be located in the outdoor or indoor environment.

Ownership

Attractions are owned and managed by a range of organizations, trusts and individuals, working in the public, private and not-for-profit sectors. The shape of the attractions sector is by no means dominated by large commercial ventures. A high level of state involvement in attraction funding is evident across Europe and in other parts of the world like Canada and Singapore. In Singapore, many of the attractions are owned by the public sector (see also Chapter 13, which examines the role of the public sector as an attraction operator in Scotland). Conversely, there is little public sector intervention in attractions in the USA, although many are subsidized by charitable donations and the voluntary sector. The voluntary sector includes organizations that own and manage attractions on a not-for-profit basis, and has a particularly important role in the heritage sector.

Perception

Some visitors may perceive an attraction as an attraction but others may not. For example, sites associated with disaster and death have become tourism attractions, known as 'dark tourism' (Light 2017). While this area of research and visitation expanded in the 1990s, it is not new, as Thomas Cook tours of the First World War battlefields of France and Belgium indicated, and a focus on death has been described as thanatourism. This distinguishes it from the broader notion of dark tourism, which Light (2017: 276) described thus: 'Dark tourism is a way of conceptualising visits to places associated with death, disaster and human suffering'. Light further refines the definition to distinguish between dark tourism and thanatourism, describing the former 'as an umbrella term for any form of tourism that is somehow related to death, suffering, atrocity, tragedy or crime. As originally formulated, it is a phenomenon rooted in the circumstances of the late twentieth century. Thanatourism is a more specific concept and is about long-standing practices of travel motivated by a specific desire for an encounter with death'. Whether a location such as the former Second World War concentration camp at Auschwitz should be viewed as a visitor attraction poses an ethical and philosophical dilemma, one which is likely to be perceived differently by different groups of people.

Events such as memorial day commemorations, while not visitor attractions as such, still require a great deal of preparation by tourism organizations to cope with the participant demand for accommodation and other services. What undeniably 'turns a tract of land, monument, park, historic house or coastline into a heritage attraction is often the attitude of the public' (Millar 1999: 6). Allied to this aspect is the fact that public motivation to visit a site varies over time. Uzzell (1989: 14) refers to the war generation visiting battlefield sites after 1945, but as those individuals cease 'to be with us, [there is] . . . less to do with remembrance and more to do with a day-trip excursion, less of a memorial and

IMAGE 9.3 Historic infrastructure, such as San Francisco's cable car, can be an attraction in its own right where television and film exposure creates a 'must see and must do' experience

more of a tourist attraction'. There has recently been a resurgence in interest in this area, with the commemoration of the centenary of the end of the First World War in 2018, and the 75th anniversary of the 1944 D-Day landings to liberate Europe, both occurring in 2018.

Similar interest exists where a long-term association with television and film promotes visits to an area and its iconic elements, such as San Francisco and its unique cable car (Image 9.3).

Admission policy

Some attractions charge admission fees, while others are open freely to the public. Attractions operated by membership subscription organizations allow members in for no charge, an example being the National Trust for England and Wales (Calver and Page 2013). Other attractions operate friends' schemes, which allow subscribers free entry. Voluntary donations are requested in other attractions, such as cathedrals and churches, although some of these attractions also charge as a means to offset long-term maintenance costs.

Appeal

The market appeal of attractions can be viewed at a geographic level, where attractions might appeal: just to a local market, regionally, nationally or internationally. While the market for visitor attractions tends to be dominated by the domestic, there are strong variations according to attraction type. In Scotland, the largest proportion of visits to distilleries and castles was made by overseas tourists, whereas more domestic visitors were recorded at steam railways and country parks. The strong appeal of attractions to the domestic market was examined by Molinillo and Japtura (2017) noting that cultural attractions, especially festivals and events were major drawcards (also see Chapter 26). Additionally, certain attractions may only appeal to niche markets, or particular market segments. Some attractions, like farm parks, are clearly aimed at a family market, while others, like historic houses and gardens, tend to attract larger volumes of mature visitors. Events of national significance, particularly where a range of events are held within the event itself (such as the Queen's Diamond Jubilee Celebrations in London, 2012), are more likely to attract a diverse demographic and socio-economic profile. A major growth area in recent years has been the expansion of escape rooms as visitor attractions, where the visitors are given a time limit and challenge to follow clues to escape from a series of locked rooms. These attractions, which have developed globally, with around 4000 businesses operating 8000 escape room sites, have been examined by Kolan (2017) and Dilek and Dilek (2018). Kolan (2017) depicts the niche appeal of the attraction as novelty comprising an emotional learning experience, requiring practical problem-solving skills and potentially a transformational experience for individuals. The notion of escapism has been described by Dilek and Dilek (2018) as a form of game that can be themed around stories that are based on drama, mystery, crime, horror, science fiction, espionage or war. Certain types of attractions also have an iconic appeal worldwide, as the example of coastal heritage resources in Insight 9.1 shows.

INSIGHT 9.1 Attraction of the coast: The role of coastal heritage as a tourist attraction

With the historical development of coastal areas for tourism (also see Chapter 2 and 22), a wide range of built facilities and attractions have been developed to cater for tourist needs, such as promenades and piers (see http://www.piers.co.uk), with Southport in Lancashire developing the first iron pier in the UK in 1861. The same resort also opened its Bathing Rooms in 1871 and the Winter Gardens and Concert Pavilion in 1874, during its Victorian heyday. Many of these features have become icons of the coastal tourism product, and as a result have been saved from dereliction, destruction and redundancy, since they often have high maintenance costs. This highlights the need for ongoing investment in coastal tourism attractions in order for them to stay competitive and to attract visitors. For example, Hastings in the UK has undergone a £6 million regeneration funded by the public sector. Yet the built environment that predates mass tourism development also has a major role to play as an attraction for coastal tourism. For example, the following historic castles in prominent and commanding positions on the UK coastline are an integral part of the tourism attraction system: Bamburgh Castle, Northumberland; Conwy Castle, Wales; Lindisfarne Castle, Northumberland; Tintagel Castle, Cornwall; Dover Castle, Kent; St Michael's Mount, Cornwall. A further element of the built landscape that predates mass coastal tourism around the world and that is proving to be a popular attraction is the lighthouse.

Lighthouses have a long history in coastal locations to protect shipping from dangerous physical features, but their current form as permanent structures with a distinctive architectural style date to the eighteenth and nineteenth centuries, with the influential work of Trinity House. Studies such as Azevedo (2018) highlight the meanings, symbolism and emotion associated with lighthouse visiting and the dark aspects of history such as shipwrecking, death, danger and risk. Added to these features are the architectural history and landscape appreciation of these iconic features within coastal settings.

At a global scale, there are still over 8300 lighthouses worldwide in coastal locations, despite the newer global satellite technology that has reduced their critical role in ship navigation. As Williams (2004) observes, their conservation and conversion to tourism-related uses (e.g. heritage centres; visitor centres, such as Hook in Ireland; novel accommodation units in Norway, for example; and as working museums) has led them to become a popular coastal attraction worldwide. In the USA around 40 per cent are open to the public. Cape Otway in Victoria, Australia, overlooking the Bass Straits, receives over 70 000 visitors a year. In fact lighthouse visiting has a long history, dating back to the Victorian period when Trinity House issued guidelines to lighthouse keepers on this function. In the UK, some 12 of the 72 remaining lighthouses are open to the public, and steps to retain them as part of our coastal heritage are reflected in the work of bodies such as the World Lighthouse Society, National Trust and Trinity House. In New South Wales, Australia, lighthouses are used as a key promotional tool in attracting visitors to coastal locations: (www.lighthouses.net. au) which is also the case in Maine, USA, and Brittany, France. In Finland and Estonia a Lighthouse Tourism Development Plan has been developed. For example, in Finland Bengtskär opened in 1995 and received 1000 visitors, which was expected to grow to 20 000 in 2016. The opening for visitors of seven lighthouses in Estonia, and 12 in Finland, was planned for the period 2008–2013, with around 12 in Estonia and 20 in Finland on tourist routes to create iconic visitor destinations. The Lighthouse Tourism Development Plan aims to grow visitor numbers to around 60 000 for Estonia and Finland combined. In Scotland, 2012 marked the bicentenary of the Bell Rock Lighthouse in Arbroath, and it was the focus of the Year of Light programme of events in 2015. Lighthouses are also being used to create unique tourist coastal routes such as Nova Scotia's Lighthouse Route to visit the South Shore and the renowned Peggy's Cove Light. India is also developing this theme, with the Ministry of Shipping and Directorate General of Lighthouses and Lightships (DGLL) identifying 78 lighthouses that could be incorporated into major tourism development projects following the example of other countries such as Croatia, where they have been used as sites to stay in or as planned focal points for coastal tourism development.

Further reading

Azevedo, A. (2018) 'Lighthouse tourism: Is there a "dark" side?' *International Journal of Tourism Cities*, 4 (1): 54–67.

Lawrence, M. (2002) 'One hundred years of light: A cause for a community celebration', *Journal of Sport and Tourism*, 7 (3): 39–40.

Stanivuk, T., Juričević, I. and Žanić Mikuličić, J. (2018) 'Maritime lighthouses in the Republic of Croatia – Safety of navigation and/or tourist attraction', *Transactions on Maritime Science*, 7 (1): 33–40.

Williams, P. (2004) *Beacon on the Rock: The Dramatic History of Lighthouses from Ancient Greece to Present Day*. Edinburgh: Birlinn.

Websites

Lighthouse Tourism Development Plan for Finland and Estonia 2008–2013: http://www.lighthousetourism.net/Development_plan_english.pdf

Indian lighthouse tourism: http://www.dgll.nic.in/content/320_0_TOURISMATLIGHTHOUSES.aspx

The UK's 10 lighthouse visitor centres can be accessed at: https://www.trinityhouse.co.uk/lighthouse-visitor-centres

Norway and lighthouses as accommodation options: https://www.visitnorway.com/hotels-more/lighthouses/

The Brittany lighthouse route: https://www.brittanytourism.com/matching-what-i-want/ideas/on-the-lighthouse-route/

Lighthouse visiting in Maine: https://visitmaine.com/things-to-do/lighthouses-sightseeing/lighthouses

The Irish tourism initiative to boost tourism linked to lighthouses: https://www.greatlighthouses.com/

Lighthouses to stay in in Scotland: https://www.visitscotland.com/blog/attractions/lighthouses-to-visit-and-stay-in/

Questions

1 What is the appeal of coastal heritage, such as lighthouses to tourism?

2 How have lighthouses been used to revitalize visitation to coastal areas?

3 What are the aspects of 'dark tourism' associated with lighthouses?

4 How would you set about harnessing the promotional role of lighthouses in marketing an area for tourism?

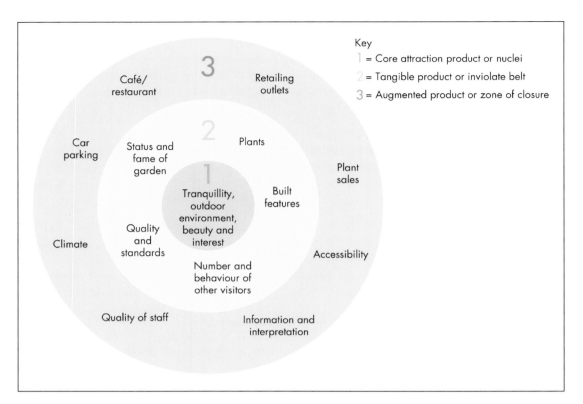

FIGURE 9.2 Spatial arrangement of a garden visitor attraction. Adapted from Gunn (1972), Kotler (1994) and Swarbrooke (2002)

Size and capacity

Attractions vary in land coverage, with some housed in tiny buildings and others covering several hectares. Some are designed for a mass audience and are able to absorb large numbers of visitors compared with others. Such attractions form destinations in their own right, and may incorporate a range of resort services and facilities that enable visitors to prolong their stay, overnight or even longer. Understanding the capacity of sites is important in terms of management and marketing, as well as protection of the resource base, which may be damaged as a result of poor visitor management, as examined in Northern Norway by Jensen *et al.* (2017).

Composition

While many attractions are nodal in character, i.e. they are located at or around a specific point or feature such as a capital city, some are linear in that they follow a line or route. Good examples of linear attractions are Blackpool's Golden Mile, UK, and the Great Ocean Road, Australia, which follows Victoria's coast for over 400 km. Events may also be nodal, i.e. fixed in one venue, or may occur at a variety of locations as part of a festival: the Edinburgh Festival which, across the city, attracts 2.6 million, equivalent to the attendance at the 2002 FIFA World Cup in South Korea, is an example. In the case of nodal attractions, they may also help to create an iconic element for the destination, such as a large tower. For example, the Eiffel Tower in Paris is a major landmark and icon which visitors associate with Paris, while also a major visitor attraction. The tower opened initially in 1889 for the World Trade Fair, receiving 1.9 million visitors in that year. By the 1920s, it was receiving 400 000–500 000 visitors a year, which dropped in the 1930s and it ceased operation during the Second World War (1939–1945). By 1949, it was receiving 1 million visitors a year, which grew to over 2 million by the late 1960s, almost 3.5 million by the mid-1970s and over 5 million in the 1980s and has remained around 6 million a year most recently. The tower is one of 27 visitor attraction towers globally which belong to the World Federation of Great Towers that receive over 27 million visitors a year, of which the tallest tower is the CN Tower in Canada.

Degree of permanence

Built visitor attractions are designed with a degree of permanence. In the case of events and festivals, a short duration is expected and temporary sites, buildings or a mobile infrastructure are often used. Such events may also take part within established attractions, forming an effective method of reaching new audiences or developing an existing audience's appreciation of a site: for example, a weekend festival at a historic house. Sporadic non-permanent natural events, which are neither designed nor staged for visitors, can also attract substantial visitor interest.

Visitor numbers

Like size and capacity, visitor attractions may also be differentiated according to the volume of visitors received over a given period of time. Some attractions regularly record visitor figures of over 500 000, while others may attract more modest numbers. As a general guide, many analysts classify visitor attractions by visitor numbers using a breakdown of 'small' attraction (up to 50 000 visits a year), 'medium' attraction (51 000–300 000) and 'large' attraction (of over 300 000). Yet these visitor numbers may rise substantially when the notion of an 'event' is included under the heading of a visitor attraction, such as Scotland's Hogmanay Celebrations, held on New Year's Eve each year and attracting large crowds as well as global media coverage. While events may form an important element of the visitor attraction sector, a more detailed account of their role as a contemporary issue in tourism development is provided in Chapter 26.

Organizational complexity and risk

Extending the debate, Shone and Parry (2004: 7) suggest that a typology relating to the degree of organizational complexity and risk offers another perspective, with reference to events as a form of attraction. The complexity of the 'attraction' relates to the degree of organization needed to coordinate the specific event, which increases with the scale and nature of the visitor market it targets. The level of risk also poses an added layer of complexity due to the unpredictable nature of visitor markets and individuals sought for each event. The level of uncertainty is not just associated with individual events, a feature which highlights the risks associated with staging events to promote a destination as an attraction at different geographical scales. Therefore, while events can become a key attraction for destinations, this has an element of commercial risk which has to be managed.

Understanding the concept of visitor attractions

Several seminal studies were published from the 1970s enabling the development of understanding of visitor attractions. At an applied level, Gunn (1972) identified three zones in relation to the spatial or physical layout of an attraction, as illustrated in Figure 9.2:

1 The central nucleus contains the core attraction.
2 The zone of closure that surrounds the nucleus contains the ancillary services associated with the attraction, such as shops, car park and tea room.
3 The inviolate belt is an area which protects the core product from the commercialized areas of the zone of closure.

At a more conceptual level, and drawing on a more cognitive approach to understanding visitor attractions, MacCannell (1976) identified three elements that comprise a tourism attraction:

- a tourist – a consumer with certain needs, searching for an experience
- a sight – the visitor attraction
- a marker – form of information about the attraction that stimulates decision-making and motivation to visit.

This analysis is interesting, as the focus of attention may be regarded as falling simply on the 'sight', 'site' or 'nucleus'. Instead, the attraction system integrates the visitor and information about the attraction. Leiper's (1990) study of attractions developed the notion that attractions form part of a system, and expressed the idea in a model (Figure 9.3). Leiper suggests that tourists are not simply pulled or attracted, but *motivated* by the opportunity to experience the core product and its markers. Accordingly, when the visitor, the nucleus and the marker are linked together, the attraction system develops. If we think about attractions as a system, it becomes more apparent how a destination 'attracts' visitors, and knowing this can assist in the development of policy and strategy (Leiper 1990). A further refinement to Leiper's (1990) model was proposed by Kang *et al.* (2018) in their analysis of an attraction system in South Korea. Their study argued that in any region, a series of multiple anchor points existed, and that hierarchies of attractions existed even with the major drawcards or primary attractions. What Kang *et al.* (2018) proposed was based on the anchor-point theory developed in behavioural geography by Golledge (1978), where primary or major attractions function as landmarks, nodes or places that are easily recognized by visitors as part of their spatial cognition of the built environment (which is discussed in detail in Chapter 20 on urban tourism). What this study also links to is the discussion of tourists' mobility in the built environment and visits to attractions, as introduced in Chapter 8.

Visits to attractions comprise a strong element of consumption (of which experience is a key element – see Pine and Gilmore 1999), characteristic of the shift to a post-modern society in industrialized countries. As Page and Connell (2010) suggested, Pine and Gilmore's (1999) *The Experience Economy* argues that the experience economy is the next stage in the evolution of society from a service economy, as introduced in Chapter 4. The essence of Pine and Gilmore's arguments are that businesses, like visitor attractions, need to create experiences that are memorable, given the increased levels of education of many consumers and their pursuit of value-added elements within the experience

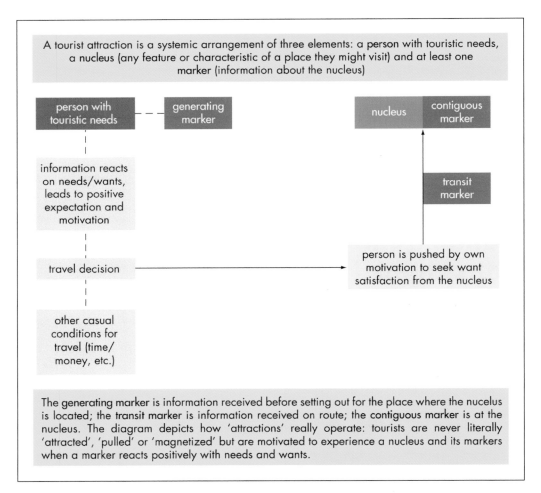

FIGURE 9.3 Leiper's model of an attraction system

Source: Reprinted from *Annals of Tourism Research*, Vol. 17, Leiper, 'Tourist attraction systems', 367–384 © (1990), with permission from Elsevier

they purchase. The essence of the Pine and Gilmore (1999) study was that the production of experiences (as were introduced in Chapter 4) will need to focus on a number of aspects of consumption, including:

- the need to create a sensation
- the need to personalize the experience; to develop trust and a bond with the consumer which has been embodied in the use of brands.

The experience economy concept suggests that we need to focus on four areas of experience in visitor attractions:

- entertainment
- education
- aesthetic (i.e. an ability to immerse oneself in something)
- escapism in what is consumed.

Consequently, attractions need to be developed in such a way as to allow participants and audiences to engage in discrete ways ranging from absorption through to immersion. Such experiences need to be able to accommodate different modes of participation, from passive through to very active forms of involvement. An attraction also needs to engage all of our senses (i.e. hearing, sight, touch, smell and taste) as 'companies stage an experience whenever they engage customers, connecting with them in a personal, memorable way' (Pine and Gilmore 1999: 3).

In essence, the themes adopted by many attractions as their core product enable the visitor to experience a particular subject, issue or location, which has been commoditized and packaged for easy viewing or consumption and that will appeal to visitors, with a sense of surprise and immersion. Good examples include heritage interpretation centres and workplace attractions, which tell a story based on real events made palatable (but perhaps less authentic) for the pleasure-seeking visitor. Lew (1987) recognized that a cognitive perspective, which places an emphasis on understanding visitor perceptions and experiences of an attraction, is crucial for those concerned with gaining an appreciation of what motivates a visit to an attraction and identifying the most enjoyable facets of a site. It is important for managers of attractions to recognize visitor experiences if they wish to capture repeat visits and stimulate recommendations, as well as provide a good core product. One key element in improving the visitor experience and satisfaction with attractions relates to the types of interpretation provided. Interpretation may be used to help create the visitor experience as well as enrich it, adding value to how the visit is perceived. Many of the services and activities provided at attractions are forms of interpretation (e.g. signage, guided tours, display boards, exhibits and audiovisual displays) used to communicate ideas and to help people understand what they are viewing or experiencing. As a communication process, interpretation helps to create the visit as a memorable event in the mind of the visitor, ideally seeking to stimulate a positive emotional or affective response among the audience (Pine and Gilmore 1999) to increase the positive receptiveness to the experience. Among key factors in promoting this receptiveness are: good levels of orientation for the visitor; attention to visitor comfort; relevance of the experience to the individual; variety and diversity in the experience; a degree of personal control and choice in the interpretation; an ability to interact with objects and people at the attraction (and event); and a growing recognition of the importance of technology in helping to create multisensory experiences (i.e. those appealing to our sight, taste, smell and hearing).

Understanding visitor motivations is vital in terms of marketing, product development and management of the site or event. While it might be argued that the main motivator for visiting attractions is enjoyment, specific motivators tend to vary according to attraction type and between individuals. Such an analysis is quite complex because what one individual might define as enjoyment, another might not, and individuals exhibit quite varying needs at different times.

What needs to be addressed next are the factors that contribute to the success or otherwise of visitor attractions.

Influences determining the success of visitor attractions

Factors that contribute to the success of a tourist attraction comprise those associated with the operator or organization in charge of the attraction, the visitor and the managed features of the attraction (Table 9.2). Accordingly,

TABLE 9.2 Factors influencing the success of tourist attractions

The organization and its resources	Experience of developing and managing attractions	Financial resources	Marketing – see 'the management of the attraction'				
The product	Novel approach or new idea	Location	On-site attraction	High-quality environment	Good customer service	Visitor facilities	Value for money
The market	Growth markets – targeting markets which are likely to expand						
The management of the attraction	Experienced professional managers	Adequate attention to market research	Realizing that marketing is not just about brochures and adverts	Long-term strategic view	Accepting importance of word of mouth	Planned marketing strategy with proper financing	Staff training

Source: Adapted from Swarbrooke (2002)

the range of elements that constitutes a visitor attraction stretch far beyond the core focus of the attraction. In many cases, a successful attraction is one that captures the right market in the right location at the right time at the right price.

These factors include:

- professional management skills and the operator's available resources
- the type of attraction or 'product offering'
- market demand for the product
- ease of access from major routes and centres of tourist and resident populations
- appropriate hours of opening
- provision and quality of on-site amenities, such as parking, visitor centre, signs and labels, shops, guides, refreshments, toilets, litter bins, seating and disabled provision
- proximity to and quality of near-site amenities, such as signposting, local accommodation, local services and other attractions
- quality of service, including staff appearance, attitude, behaviour and competence
- the mood, expectation, behaviour and attitude of visitors
- value for money.

The attractions market is very competitive and those developing and managing attractions increasingly understand the need to base them on innovative concepts which create a sensational experience or, as it is often termed, a 'wow' factor for the visitor. Understanding the visitor experience is a key concept for contemporary visitor attraction management, and is explored further in Chapter 24. Creating the right appeal and ambience in a fiercely uncompromising sector is crucial for visitor attractions. Neglect of an element of a visitor attraction, whether it is poor toilet cleaning or an unjustifiably high entry charge, has the potential to harm the overall experience, affecting both return visits and recommendations.

Research undertaken in Hong Kong by McKercher, Ho and du Cros (2004) revealed the aspects which influence the popularity of a cultural tourism attraction. Table 9.3 indicates that product development, visitor experience and marketing are more important in determining popularity than the historic significance of an attraction, or its meaning to local people and intrinsic worth. This research suggests that the marketing and management of an attraction are crucial and that the core product attributes alone are insufficient in determining appeal and success. Such findings only emphasize the importance of understanding the visitor experience. Visitor experiences are likely to be affected by numerous factors, some of which are inevitably not linked with the destination per se, but which hinge on the mood and personal circumstance of the visitor. Figure 9.4 illustrates the range of factors that affect the visitor's experience of an attraction.

TABLE 9.3 Attributes of popular cultural tourism attractions

Category	Attribute
Product	Site
	Setting
	Scale
	Access
	Purpose-built or extant facility
	Complementary adaptive reuse
Experiential	Uniqueness
	Relevance to tourist
	Ease of consumption
	Focus on 'edutainment'
Marketing	Position
	Does the asset have tourism potential?
	Identification of viable market segments
	Place in attraction's hierarchy
	Product lifecycle stage and ability to rejuvenate product lifecycle
Cultural Leadership	Local vs. international social values
	Attitude to tourism
	Vision
	Ability to assess tourism potential realistically
	Ability to adopt a marketing management philosophy to the management of the asset

Source: Reprinted from *Annals of Tourism Research*, vol. 31, McKercher, Ho and du Cros, 'Attributes of popular cultural attractions in Hong Kong', 393–407 © (2004), with permission from Elsevier

Understanding the visitor experience is a basic facet of visitor attraction management. However, attractions are subject to a number of issues, threats and opportunities which impact on effective management. Kempiak *et al.* (2017) observed the key elements that emerged in the visitor experience at heritage attractions were: the audiovisual communication, the atmospherics (linking to Pine and Gilmore's elements), the on-site engagement and information on issues like heritage preservation. What this also highlights is the significance of engagement of visitors, described by Loureiro and Ferreira (2018) as the means by which one can initiate social interaction with the visitor. One technique advocated by Swacha and Itterman (2017) is **gamification**, a term that describes the use of games outside of the area of games to engage people in specific activities, which in this instance is designed to increase visitors' motivation to visit an attraction to make the engagement more interesting. Xu *et al.* (2017) suggest that gamification has its roots in marketing and can aid brand awareness, enhancing visitor experiences so they are encouraged to explore the site as in the example of the REXexplorer app at the Regensburg UNESCO World Heritage Site in Germany, which engages visitors in active learning. Xu *et al.* (2017: 249) also point to 'Sighter . . . [a] location based game developed by Waterways Ireland. Players select a site, find it and snap a photo of it to win points'. This type of activity is called geocaching and uses

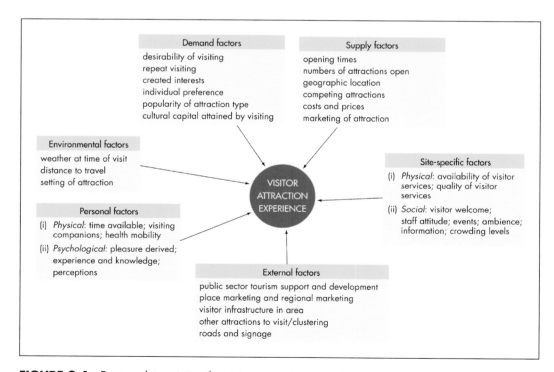

FIGURE 9.4 Factors determining the visitor attraction experience

GPS-enabled devices like smartphones and IPads to engage in an activity similar to the concept of a treasure hunt. This brings more fun and entertainment to the visitor experience through collaboration, sharing and working with clear goals during the visit. Swacha and Itterman (2017) point to the potential for visitor attractions to engage visitors through gamification before the visit, during the visit (e.g. a reward or discount obtained by travelling by public transport or by visiting at a less busy time, and puzzles for children to solve during the visit) and after the visit by encouraging visits to other attractions the operators might own. Yet as Hall and Ram (2019) show, walking to attractions in urban areas where the attractions are accessible on foot is also a major challenge in cities like London, and attempts to promote this form of active transport requires major incentives. The chapter now moves on to consider a range of themes and issues involved in managing visitor attractions.

Themes and issues in the management of visitor attractions

Attractions face a number of threats from the external and internal environment that pose risks to both product quality, operational viability and the visitor experience. Large operators such as Merlin with over 67 million visits to its attraction portfolio exemplify the scope and scale of the management issues attraction businesses face. Merlin was established in 1999 and operates in 25 countries, 70 per cent of its profits arise from outside of the UK (www.merlinentertainments.biz) and it has three specific revenue streams, as shown in Figure 9.5. As observed in Merlin's 2018 Annual Report, the competition it faces is limited in the markets it operates within. This is due to high entry barriers (i.e. large capital investment is required to operate in this sector), and the fact that it is working within a highly fragmented market, which gives it opportunities for acquisitions and partnerships. Its application of digital technology is focused on enhancing the 'guest experience' and its overall strategy is 'To create a high growth, high return, family entertainment company based on strong brands and a global portfolio that is naturally balanced against the impact of external factors' (www.merlinentertainments.biz). The company also has a strategic focus on developing its attractions, as shown in Figure 9.6 which is divided into existing development of the attraction estate and new business opportunities.

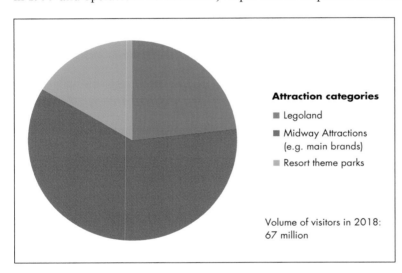

FIGURE 9.5 The structure of Merlin Entertainments' visitation by attraction type

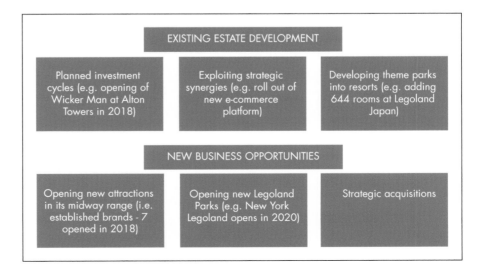

FIGURE 9.6 Merlin Entertainment's strategic focus on attraction development

It is essential for attraction managers to derive a strategy that recognizes threats and opportunities and focuses on managing potential impacts in an attempt to strive for long-term viability. To do this, Merlin maintains a focus on costs and productivity, as shown in its stated objective of strict financial discipline and its investment criteria. It also invests in markets with strong growth potential (e.g. China) and attractive markets that will deliver this growth, as well as having a diversified portfolio so it can ride out short-term fluctuations in demand, such as the dip in London that occurred following the 2017 terrorist attacks, and other factors that can impact demand, such as poor weather. However, in 2019, Merlin was taken over by a consortium comprising the Lego family and the Canadian private equity firm Blackstone in a £5.9 billion purchase, making it one of the largest global operators. This example also illustrates the volatility in demand and how market forces may affect supply.

Management planning

Benckendorff and Pearce (2003) found in a study of Australian tourist attractions that attractions with the highest level of management planning tend to perform the best, be more profitable and have a sounder basis for the future. Accordingly, the larger the attraction, the more likely its management will engage in planning. Higher levels of planning in attractions are associated with:

- higher visitor numbers
- larger asset value
- higher admission prices
- better growth

- more gross revenue
- greater total profit
- longer length of stay
- greater confidence.

Like those in any business, the managers of an attraction must plan ahead by deciding what actions will be necessary, identifying objectives, time scales, funding and implementation of projects. Planning underpins the dynamic nature of the visitor attraction sector and is essential for the attraction's long-term survival based on renewal and innovation, which are discussed later in the chapter. One of the key challenges for visitor attraction managers is to ensure the continued viability of an attraction, since the sector is littered with examples of business failure that can be attributed to poor financial management, a lack of understanding of the markets (including over-optimistic forecasts of visitor use and spending) that would be interested in the attraction, and an inability to move with the times. For the attraction manager the range of issues they will often have to grapple with is varied and diverse, ranging from simple issues such as customer dissatisfaction or a complaint through to more protracted strategic and planning problems such as accommodating the car as a form of transport that connects the visitor with the attraction site. The management issues associated with the impact of visitors require a multitalented team of staff able to grapple with these challenges, including the day-to-day operational issues associated with human resources and finance and general management. For example, common issues reported in studies of attractions include: overcrowding, wear and tear (especially at natural and historic sites), vandalism, traffic-related problems - often associated with the car – and accommodating peak numbers at popular times. In addition, the location of the attraction may indirectly lead to community impacts that occur between visitors and local residents, who may feel 'under siege' at peak times. Other impacts which may arise for the attraction which can compromise the authenticity of the product and its portrayal to visitors is the need to alter or adapt the structure of the site or venue to accommodate the flow of visitors, make provision for disabled visitors, and legal requirements such as complying with health and safety legislation that can affect the experience, as illustrated in Figure 9.7 in the case of visitors with dementia.

Attraction managers have an arsenal of methods to manage the impacts, including supply-led measures:

- *Queue management.* For example, large 3D screens adjacent to queuing areas to keep visitors entertained.
- *Making the capacity at the attraction more flexible* (extending the opening hours and providing additional staff at locations to cope with additional demand).
- *Increasing the capacity by hardening the site,* such as the Tower of London's Jewel House, which has a travelator that is switched on during busy periods to limit the amount of time visitors can dwell at the point of interest.

and demand-led measures including:

- Price incentives to encourage visitation, as many visitors to attractions are price-sensitive.
- Marketing to encourage off-peak use.

- Education and interpretation to promote responsible behaviour and the provision of alternative routes to reduce pressure on sensitive sites.

Source: Fyall *et al.* (2008)

However, many of these measures can culminate in a range of environmental impacts.

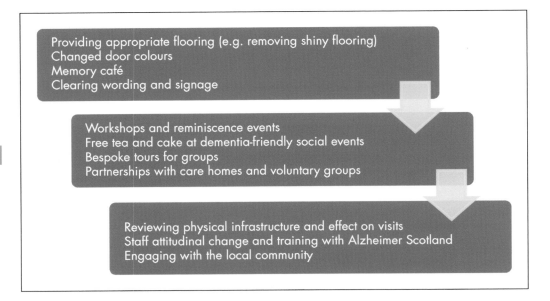

FIGURE 9.7 Selected practical steps taken by visitor attractions to become more accessible to people with dementia Source: Reproduced with permission from Elsevier in Connell, J., Page, S.J., Sheriff, I., and Hibbert, J. (2017) 'Business engagement in a civil society: Transitioning towards a dementia-friendly visitor economy', *Tourism Management*, 61:120.

Environmental impacts

The environmental impacts caused by visitors raise a number of issues for managers of natural, built and event attractions. For example, the heritage site Hadrian's Wall, in the vicinity of the English–Scottish border,

TABLE 9.4	Environmental impacts relating to attractions
Overcrowding	Overcrowding of parts of a site is generally considered to be more significant than overcrowding of the site as a whole in attractions which were not designed to accommodate visitor flow (e.g. castles).
Wear and tear	Actions causing wear and tear are often unintentional. Erosion of footpaths, graffiti covering artefacts, control of humidity and temperature, dirty hands on glass cabinets, walls and windows, carpet wear, are examples.
Litter, vandalism and stealing	Usually intentional actions. Connell (2004) found that acts of theft in garden attractions ranged from digging up plants to more professionally organized robbery of valuable statues.
Transport-related	Many visitors arrive by car or coach and there is a need to accommodate vehicles on-site by building and maintaining car parks. Road access can be a major issue. Where on-site parking is limited, vehicles may spill over into residential areas. Vehicular traffic also causes pollution, noise and visual impacts.
Behaviour	The local community and visitor interface can often be problematic as visitors may be perceived in positive or negative ways. If an attraction encourages visitors to explore the local area in a sensitive way and spend money in local businesses, the overall effect might be positive. Where visitors simply go to the attraction and have little benefit on the local area, a more antagonistic attitude is likely to develop. Where the actions of visitors frustrate locals, visitor management intervention is required to alleviate practical problems.
Effects of visitor management on authenticity	Visitor management techniques are vital for protecting the resource or providing information but may be intrusive on the visitor's enjoyment. Such tools include interpretation panels, rope cordons and covers on furniture. To comply with legislation on accessibility, attractions have to provide means by which less able visitors can enjoy the resource, including lifts, rails and ramps; however, these may detract from heritage architecture.

receives 400 000 walking visitors following a trail alongside the wall, which is a unique and fragile attraction now under threat from tourism. The construction of visitor attractions alone inevitably causes environmental impact, although some attractions positively aim to assist environmental conservation, like the Scottish Seabird Centre in North Berwick, UK. Natural attractions and built attractions are prone to visitor impacts, and religious or sacred sites are vulnerable too. A range of such attraction impacts, as shown in Table 9.4, and additional problems such as waste generation can be added to this.

Seasonality

In many parts of the world, seasonality is a significant issue affecting demand for tourism (see Chapter 3), and the attractions sector is particularly susceptible. In Scotland, the majority of visits to attractions are made between April and September. Some types of attractions show a greater susceptibility to seasonality. Historic properties and monuments, steam railways, industrial/craft attractions and those that charge for admission show the highest seasonal peaks and troughs in visitor numbers. Places of worship and country parks tend to suffer the least from seasonal visits, as each exhibit strong local appeal. Attractions in cities suffer less from seasonality than those located in peripheral areas. For example, in Scotland, visitor numbers to attractions in the cities of Glasgow and Edinburgh show little variation through the year, compared with the Highlands and the Western Isles, areas which are subject to much stronger patterns of seasonal visiting (also see Chapter 3 and Tables 3.1 and 3.2).

According to Goulding (2008), the main operational effects of seasonality for visitor attractions include:

- staffing issues
- recruitment costs and difficulties
- cost of training and development
- commitment of seasonal staff
- loss of trained staff at the end of the season
- capacity utilization
- peak season over-utilization and the consequent impacts
- opportunity costs of under-utilization
- peaks and troughs in cash flow and revenue generation, and potential to deter capital investment due to risks of long-term payback.

Several management responses to seasonality are widely applied in visitor attractions. These include:

- accepting peak season highs by deploying more resources to generate maximum potential revenues and using the low season to develop the business or undertake maintenance and refurbishment obligations
- extending the season through product development and extension, including events and community festivals, corporate events, hiring out of the attraction and promotion of the attraction to local residents and educational groups. Initiatives to extend the season are most often effective when a number of attraction and visitor-related services collaborate in the promotion of out-of-season leisure opportunities. Such promotions allow potential visitors to become aware of activities and places to eat and stay at times of the year when they might not consider there to be any offerings for visitors. And as discussed earlier, innovations such as gamification can be added to this list.

Visitor numbers

Factors positively affecting visitor numbers at attractions are diverse, but the main determinants appear to be promotions and holding events, and in negative terms, global issues affecting the supply of visitors and disruptions caused by refurbishment. The most significant factor that affects visitor numbers both positively and negatively is one that attraction operators have little control over – the weather (see Chapter 3 for a fuller discussion). The issue of visitor demand for an attraction is relevant in management terms, depending on whether an attraction aims:

- to increase visitor numbers
- to decrease visitor numbers

• to maintain current levels of visitors
• to change the composition of an existing visitor profile

which is underpinned by an understanding of current visitor numbers. Mechanisms for recording visitor numbers include admission tickets, car parking receipts, and manual or mechanical counts. Recording visitor numbers at some sites is problematic, of course, where entry is free, where the site has multiple entry points and where the installation of mechanical counting devices (such as magic eye counters) is uneconomic. One example of a country that collects visitor data across the visitor attraction sector is England, with the annual Visitor Attraction Monitor. Figures 9.8 and 9.9 depict the recent Top 20 Visitor Attractions for paid and free entry to a range of attractions. As attractions can opt out of this survey, it means that this data is not necessarily comparable with previous years where leading attractions are no longer comparable as a time series. However, what Figures 9.8 and 9.9 show is that among the Top 20 attractions, free attractions have approximately twice the volume of visits than the equivalent ranked paid entry attractions.

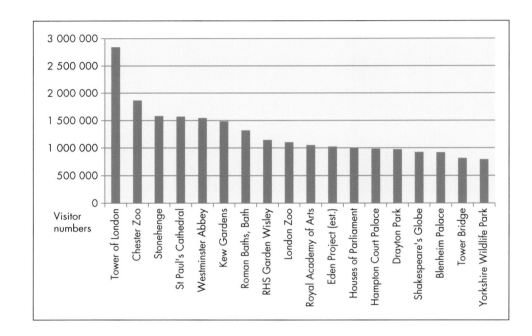

FIGURE 9.8 Top 20 most visited paid admission attractions in England
Source: Data from VisitEngland (2017) Annual Survey of Visits to Visitor Attractions

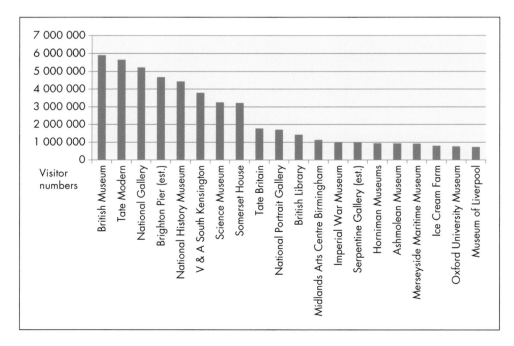

FIGURE 9.9 Top 20 most visited free admission attractions in England.
Source: Data from VisitEngland (2017) Annual Survey of Visits to Visitor Attractions

Where there is significant visitor activity, some attractions have developed strategies to manage numbers through estimating a site's carrying capacity, i.e. deciding how much use can be accommodated at a given site. In reality, each attraction has a range of capacities depending on the type of visitor experience intended and the extent of resource protection required, which must be balanced against accessibility and revenue considerations. As a result, the application of carrying capacity models is a controversial issue. While physical carrying capacity is easy to determine through car park size, numbers allowed on theme park rides or number of seats in a café, more personal experiences of overcrowding, known as 'perceptual carrying capacity', are difficult to define and evaluate. One method for achieving this objective is to identify primary indicators of the quality of the visitor experience, and to identify where the number of visitors at any one time exceeds both preferred and acceptable limits, and where subsequent management intervention is necessary. On Alcatraz Island (within the Golden Gate National Recreation Area, San Francisco), which receives several hundred thousand visitors a year, the primary indicator was determined to be the number of other people in the prison cellhouse (the core or 'icon' attraction of Alcatraz Island) (Manning *et al.* 2002), reflecting the interest in dark tourism. Other indicators of quality in attractions might include the amount of time required to queue for a theme park ride, to use a toilet facility or to wait for a table in a café.

Attractions and destination planning

Gunn (1988) states that attractions function most effectively when they are clustered together. Many areas have adopted a strategy of clustering attractions and events, to provide a critical mass of activity with appeal to visitor markets. The rationale for clustering has become clear with regard to greater tourist mobility, competition between tourist areas, stronger marketing mechanisms and higher investment in development. These principles are embodied in theme park development where the attractions are all clustered and concentrated in one accessible area although this can give rise to issues with tracking patterns of mobility (see Solmaz *et al.* 2015) to understand how to overcome perennial issues of queuing and crowding in time and space. As we will demonstrate later in the chapter, technology does offer some solutions to these issues. Managers of attractions need to be able to work in collaboration with one another to attract visitors to an area rather than to a single attraction, with encouragement to visit all attractions, often through discount schemes and visitor passes such as in London and Stockholm and initiatives in US cities such as City Pass and Go Cards.

The development of industry coordination mechanisms is a useful tool in boosting the profile of attractions as a key segment of the tourism product offering within a geographic area. Some of the advantages of collaboration include: collective branding and theming of the visitor attraction product; economies of scale from pooling resources; scope to reduce risk and uncertainty by sharing market intelligence; joint marketing and promotion at reduced cost. Yet as Fyall (2008) demonstrates, such collaboration among visitor attraction operators can also lead to: unhealthy competition between large attractions and smaller ones; mutual distrust where the outcome of collaboration produces uneven results; and conflict among attraction operators who have different objectives for collaboration. Yet there are many successful examples where collaboration has led to the creation of high-quality groupings of attractions, such as New Zealand's Leading Attractions and the Cornwall Association of Tourist Attractions, formed in the 1970s with a membership of 40, with a desire to improve the visitor experience across the south-west region of England. Collaboration allows attractions to become more receptive to changes in the marketplace and assists in the formation of strong regional identities through destination marketing, rather than marketing that concentrates on specific attractions (Fyall *et al.* 2001). Investment in flagship attractions can act as a tool for regeneration, as seen in the example of the Guggenheim Museum, Bilbao.

Diversification: The case of industry-based tourism

Many attractions have developed from an existing business, like farm attractions, where visitor incomes act as an essential component of a diversified agricultural business. Industry or workplace attractions have also developed through a similar process (e.g. the Legoland theme park in Billund, Denmark, opened in 1968), where a company identifies an opportunity to promote its products and engender brand awareness through the visitor market. While visits to such attractions tend to be considered a phenomenon of modern tourism, Donnachie (2004) identified that tourists visited workplaces and factories as early as the eighteenth century in Britain and in 1962, in Milwaukee there were 35 factory tours advertised. Industry-based attractions fall into two categories:

1 Those where visitors can watch the production process.

2 Those where the emphasis is on the product plus other facets, such as amusements or retailing (e.g. a visitor center selling souvenirs), the product not necessarily being produced on-site.

Internationally, there are many examples of companies that operate visitor centres or visitor experiences that are linked to a production process or product offering, as diverse as nuclear energy production and chocolate (Table 9.5). The World of Coca-Cola is one of the world's top industry-based experiences, with over 11 million visitors recorded in the 15 years following its opening in 1990. Australia offers a multitude of food and drink experiences, from its renowned range of wineries and vineyards, to a lobster factory and a ginger processing plant. In the USA, there are over 1500 brewery tours on offer. In many of the coffee- and tea-producing countries of the world, such as Costa Rica, tourists can visit working plantations. In Alaska, even oil installations are considered tourist attractions. According to the Scottish Whisky Association, in 2011 there were 1.2 million visits to 42 distilleries in Scotland, which provides an indication of the impact of one specific industrial tourism sector in one country and in Ireland, Guinness received 18 million visits 2000–2018.

Renewal and innovation

As Chapter 12 explains, innovation is a key concept in all tourism businesses. However, innovation is particularly important in the attractions industry and initiatives to extend the attraction **product lifecycle** must be built in to long-term planning, as illustrated above with the case of Merlin Entertainment. With the significant increase in competition for visitor expenditure since the 1990s across the leisure and tourism sector, a distinct visitor attraction lifecycle may be observed. Lennon (2001) argues that paid and free attractions with over 10 000 visitors a year in Scotland tend to show the following pattern after opening:

- growth in years 1–2
- a decline in visitation in year 3
- there is a greater stability in visitor numbers to paid attractions, up to year 4
- non-paid admission attractions, on the other hand, experience a decline in years 3 and 4, then stabilization in numbers.

TABLE 9.5 Examples of industry-based attractions

Company	Product	Location	Approximate annual visitor numbers
Tillamook	Cheese	Oregon, USA	1 000 000
Volkswagen Autostadt	Cars	Wolfsburg, Germany	2 200 000
Guinness Storehouse	Stout	Dublin, Ireland	1 700 000
Cadbury World	Chocolate	Birmingham, UK	648 000
Cheddar Gorge Cheese Company	Cheese	Cheddar, UK	300 000
Ben & Jerry's Visitor Centre	Ice cream	Vermont, USA	300 000
Carlsberg	Lager	Copenhagen, Denmark	170 000
The Famous Grouse Experience	Whisky	Crieff, Scotland	120 000
Cadbury World	Chocolate	Dunedin, New Zealand	180 000
Newbridge Silverware	Silver making	Ireland	350 000
Crayola Experience	Crayon making	Orlando, USA	300 000
Zotter Schokoladenmanufaktur	Chocolate making	Bergl, Austria	260 000
Zotter Schokoladenmanufaktur		Styria, Czech Republic	200 000

Source: Company Websites

A decline in visitor numbers is often a reflection of a failure to innovate, refresh or expand the components of the attraction. Many attraction operators find that it is necessary to invest in major refurbishment to nurture existing customers and reinvigorate visitor interest, often using new forms of interpretation or technology. For example, a **virtual reality** trip through New York, called New York Skyride, has been developed at the Empire State Building (see http://www.skyride.com/index2.cfm). Further, some attraction managers constantly introduce innovations, where diversification of the product offering and upgrading of facilities bucks the trend of the attraction lifecycle model through intervention and ongoing re-investment. It is common to see promotional literature for attractions that boast 'New for 2020 . . .', in an attempt to retain loyal or repeat visitors and to stimulate new visitor interest. Such strategies are commonly adopted, a good example being Cedar Point, the second-oldest theme park in the world, located in Ohio, USA. Since 1989, nine record-breaking rides have been introduced at Cedar Point, breaking the 200- and 300-foot-high barriers. Cedar Point also boasted the world's tallest and fastest ride by 2003, 420 feet high and involving a speed of 120 miles per hour, with a capacity for 1500 passengers and covering eight acres of land. In Germany, the Science Center in Heilbron has pioneered experiences such as what it is like to be in the eye of a storm and what it looks like for a body to be turned into ice, bringing science and entertainment together as edutainment. In the case of the Carnival cruise ship *Mardi Gras*, a 220 m roller coaster is being installed, with passengers able to control the speed the roller coaster proceeds at.

Harnessing economic impacts

Attractions, and in particular events, often stimulate huge economic benefits for the areas in which they are located, and it is important for tourism organizations to gauge economic impacts in order to justify spending and publicize the effects to the local community. Local tourism economies can benefit from hosting *peripatetic* events, i.e. those that are held in different locations each year, or *rolling* events, which run on an annual basis in the same location. A good example of a rolling event is New Orleans' annual Mardi Gras, 'the greatest free show on earth', which attracts large numbers of visitors, both staying visitors and day trippers, generating significant expenditure in the city. The range of festivals throughout the year in New Orleans creates a substantial income. This impact is estimated to be approximately US$145 million in direct income with around US$332 million for the wider New Orleans economy in indirect spending across the economy. While the Mardi Gras is an independent event that is not coordinated by a particular organization, it is much more common for tourism and economic development organizations to collaborate in order to attract peripatetic events and/or to provide pump-priming funds. In the case of New Orleans, the attraction of its international and domestic event programme has been instrumental in rebuilding the tourism economy post-Hurricane Katrina. Economic impacts from events are variable and often imply an opportunity cost, where public sector investment might be more effectively spent on other developments that benefit local communities. In the case of New Orleans, the economic contribution of tourism events and attractions to the local economy makes a net contribution, reducing residents' taxes and supporting local services. While the examples above show very positive outcomes, some events run at a loss. Therefore, running special events, and creating new visitor attractions in general, is best viewed as one option for stimulating or regenerating a local economy rather than a panacea, such as the example of the Titanic visitor attraction in Belfast that received 760 000 visits in 2017 (Paraskevaidis and Weidenfeld 2019), second to the largest attraction in Northern Ireland with 1 million visits a year (the Giant's Causeway). However, to put this in perspective attractions such as Times Square and Central Park in New York receive over 40 million visits a year, and the Great Wall of China receives 10 million visitors over its 13 000-mile length, with 30 million visits a year to Niagara Falls on the USA/Canada border. Therefore, ensuring attractions are able to accommodate the volumes of visitors where they are iconic is a key management challenge, alongside developing new ones.

The future of visitor attractions

Pearce *et al.* (2000) identify four areas of potential influence that will affect the future shape and success of tourist attractions. These are:

- management
- marketing
- product development
- interpretation and communication.

New approaches to the management and training of staff (Watson and McCracken 2008), marketing and information provision focusing on the quality and experience of the core product are a necessary part of attraction management in the twenty-first century.

Improving performance in the management of tourism has led businesses to examine the experiences of successful and innovative organizations in and outside of the tourism sector to understand their business practices. This has been termed 'best practice' and a Best Practice Forum exists across the leisure, hospitality and tourism sector in the UK comprising industry membership from professional bodies such as the Association of Leading Visitor Attractions. The value of best practice to improving business performance in tourism has often been based on examining case studies of successful tourism businesses to understand their business processes, corporate culture and the application of management concepts in practice including:

- Leadership – does the organization have a visionary leader with a clear strategy?
- Customer focus – does the organization build their business around the needs of the customer as well as listen to, and exceed their expectations?
- Value-adding processes – does the organization set out to find ways to add value to the experiences received by visitors?
- Process-led – does the business measure its internal processes and performance, through systematic measures to manage financial and operational practices?
- People-oriented – does the business value its employees and manage business relationships with suppliers effectively?
- Continuous learning and innovation – does the organization seek to find new ways of doing things to constantly improve existing products and seek to develop new products?

These elements of the management process have been widely recognized as helping to build successful tourism and service-led organizations where best practice studies have been undertaken, and these experiences are often built into new projects.

Management: Revenue generation

Globally, attractions face many difficulties in the new millennium. Big-name attractions such as Disney have witnessed a slump in visitor numbers and some, like Universal Studios Japan and Disneyland Paris, have experienced severe financial pressures. In the UK, several of the major attractions funded by the National Lottery have gone out of business or have failed to be as successful as predicted. Many were high-risk projects with unrealistic business plans, such as the Millennium Dome, the Earth Centre and the National Centre for Pop Music in the UK, which opened in an era of fierce competition for visitor spend. For many attractions, creating diverse income streams is a prerequisite for achieving financial viability and success. Apart from ticket sales, attractions can generate revenue through a number of means, as shown in Table 9.6. The success of such ventures is highly dependent on marketing, as well as efficient management.

Marketing

Recent slumps in visitor numbers to some attractions indicate a need for attraction operators to engage in the marketing process. Marketing is central to the success of attractions. As Chapter 14 explains, marketing is not simply concerned with promotion and advertising, both of which are important to visitor attractions, but also with pricing, products and distribution channels. Most attractions produce a promotional leaflet (either as a single attraction or as a collective of attractions in a region), which can be displayed in tourist information centres or in leaflet racks maintained by distribution companies in key visitor locations. Most have websites, displaying essential information for visitors. Other means of promotion include advertising in tourist brochures, magazines, newspapers and on television, although few visitor attractions have the necessary funds for advertising. Luckily, word-of-mouth (WOM) recommendations remain the most powerful promotional tool for many attractions, which underlines the need for a good product that visitors will tell their friends and relations about. The most successful attractions in the world have produced professional media kits for use in public relations work, which include photographs, a brochure, maps, posters and information for different markets.

TABLE 9.6 Alternative mechanisms for revenue generation in attractions

- Encouraging educational visits
- Providing a venue for corporate hospitality, meetings and product launches
- Hosting weddings and birthday parties
- Generating rental income from alternative usage of infrastructure, such as retail outlets, clubs and offices, which utilize redundant buildings or space on-site
- Introducing car parking charges or leasing of the car park to a management company
- Improving retail and catering initiatives that reflect the ethos of the attraction
- Attracting more visitors and more frequent repeat visits
- Increasing length of stay by offering more activities
- Extending opening hours such as night-time visiting
- Introducing members or friends schemes, giving privileges and discounts
- Hosting high-profile events
- Attracting corporate sponsorship

Where new attractions open and they engage in 'awareness-raising' campaigns to promote their existence and the visitor experience, an integrated communications programme comprising printed billboard advertisements and radio coverage may help to develop the visitor market. A marketing campaign can prove to be a costly activity, with a three-week poster at a major railway station costing around £10 000–15 000 plus the cost of producing the advertisement. Television advertising will be considerably more expensive, typically upwards of £50 000 for a short information advertisement at non-peak time on a regional television channel in the UK.

In relation to pricing, operators of attractions must be cognizant of market conditions. The market for tourism and visitor attractions is demand-elastic (see Chapter 3), so the degree of disposable income available affects an individual's propensity to visit an attraction. Many built attractions can be relatively expensive to visit, compared with the price of a holiday. If, during a family holiday, there are sufficient funds to visit only one major attraction, then individual attractions must prepare effective marketing strategies to appeal to that consumer, while offering the right product to the right person at the right time in the right place.

Braun and Soskin (2003) note that during periods of growing or high attendance to theme parks, as in the 1980s, entry prices tend to increase, sometimes faster than inflation. Conversely, when attendance falls, increases in price may slow or prices may even decrease. Prices charged by market leaders and premium attractions, like Walt Disney World, usually act as a guide for other attractions, but such premium products often attempt to retain customer interest through heavy investment and multi-day discounting, which acts to limit the residual market available to competitors. Some attractions can exist in compatibility where they appeal to a different demographic, i.e. Disneyland and Universal Studios tend to charge similar entry prices, but Disney appeals more to younger families and older people, while Universal holds greater attraction for teenagers and 'twenty-somethings'. Central to this debate is the issue of product development.

Product development: Creating world-class destinations

In the dynamic attraction sector, product development is a crucial aspect of economic sustainability, and is a process in which managers of attractions must constantly engage. Innovations tend to be based on the development of a new concept, new technology, such as virtual reality, or animation or enlivening the product offering through tours, re-enactments and personal forms of interpretation. Following the lead set by Disney, attractions are increasingly developing into visitor destinations in their own right, with a capacity to attract international and domestic staying visitors on-site as also illustrated by Merlin Entertainment. A new era of all-inclusive, multidimensional attractions that operate all year round and offer something for everyone are developing across the world, particularly in newly emerging economies in South America, South East Asia and Eastern Europe, as well as in existing markets. Such attractions have the potential to assist in urban regeneration schemes and to put less well-known places on the tourist map. Such attractions offer retail, relaxation, entertainment and catering facilities, some with accommodation on-site as well. A key feature of new developments is striking architecture that creates a 'wow' factor for visitors on arrival and becomes part of the experience.

Other product developments result from a requirement to maintain or improve standards, especially in the case of making attractions accessible and appealing to all customers. Adjustments to the layout and design of an attraction may be required to allow for easy access by wheelchair users, or adaptations to labels and announcements for those with hearing or visual impairments. Attractions that have appeal to young families must be prepared to adapt products to suit their needs: basics include a nappy-changing toilet, a child-friendly restaurant and interests for all age groups. The key feature in creating a world-class destination is creating a product that is equal or superior to any similar product internationally, firmly centred around a clear understanding of the visitor experience, the principles of human resource management and a commitment to product development. Inherent in this process for operators is understanding and anticipating consumer needs and expectations, understanding the wider market and the supply of competing products, and being able to innovate. In terms of theme parks as visitor attractions, recent thinking in social science has examined the effect of these new cultural forms of visitor entertainment. Globally, commercial data do exist for the themed attractions and are collated by the Themed Entertainment Association which provides up-to-date statistics on theme park attendance and global trends. There have been a range of ways of thinking about such attractions as *themed spaces* (Shaw and Williams 2004), which can be classified into three distinct areas: tourism and leisure spaces that could include heritage theme parks and literary landscapes; new retail and leisure spaces that can be used to create new visitor locations from a blank canvas, such as the Eden Project in Cornwall, UK; and those locations with global iconic status for their theme parks, such as Disney World in Florida and Universal Studios in Los Angeles. Researchers have also focused on the significance of such landscapes based on the underlying notion of a visitor attraction to create a wider destination appeal in a commercialized and controlled environment that is man-made, emphasizes fun and has an underlying artificiality that is carefully scripted and managed around the need to provide pleasure and stimulation, as discussed by Bigne *et al.* (2005). Ultimately these highly commercialized and themed spaces are designed to be memorable and exhilarating as well as capable of filling a day or multiple-day visits that meet a wide range of motivations for visitation.

Interpretation and communication

In relation to interpretation and communication, two broad themes are of significance:

- the role of technology (known as 'high tech')
- the role of personal interactions (known as 'high touch') (see Image 9.4).

The high-tech aspects have led to two distinct areas of activity in relation to the attractions:

1 Industry use of social media and other tools to build visitor loyalty and to enhance the visitor experience, as illustrated earlier in the chapter. One of the principal areas of building greater visitor engagement is via the use of Twitter (Light and Cerrone 2018; Padilla *et al.* 2018). As Light and Cerrone (2018) show, this can help keep visitors up to date with the attraction in a concise manner, and Padilla *et al.* (2018) examined the Twitter content to show where visitors got the most enjoyment, through a focus on tourist emotions.

2 The application of technology in situ to enhance the visitor experience and to drive audience growth (Chiwara and Chipangura 2018), as summarized in Figure 9.10. What Figure 9.10 shows is the scope of new technologies, and Oh and Ma (2018) illustrate how animation and narration can enhance the visitor experience.

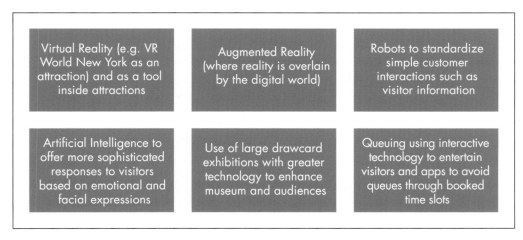

FIGURE 9.10 The future use of technology to enhance the visitor experience at attractions

One of the greatest continuing developments for many attractions is the use of interactive technology to appeal to all audiences. There are several reasons why operators of attractions invest and develop technology-based elements, including:

- *Creating a unique product*, such as the example of Newseum, the world's only interactive museum of news and journalism in Arlington, Virginia, USA. Newseum offers a highly interactive product, including a newsroom and a broadcast room, where visitors find out what it is like to investigate a story and produce news programmes. It cost $50 million to develop, and 2.25 million visitors were recorded between 1997 and 2002. The creation of a tropical rainforest-themed visitor attraction announced in South Wales in 2008, costing £45 million on a 9290 m² site, with visitors exploring the Indonesian Malay rainforest canopy via a series of elevated walkways and a visitor centre, will focus on climate change, conservation and sustainable technology.

IMAGE 9.4 High-touch exhibits, which allow children to interact with exhibitions and learn about the attraction, prove popular with families

- *Enhancing the visitor experience* through interpretation based on entertainment and education, where visitors are exposed to the core element of the visitor attraction product and provided with information in a fun or interactive style, different to the traditional guide book or audiovisual. Sights, sounds and smells can be replicated, a story woven into a series of exhibits and the visitor transported into a simulated environment, in which absorption of key messages may be more effective or where the thrill factor can be maximized. As an example of the last point, at the 'Borg Invasion' 3D Star Trek Experience, Las Vegas Hilton, visitors embarked on a tour of a simulated research station, then to be subjected to an alien assault accompanied with physical and visual effects. The 'transporter', or theatre, had 3D main and ceiling screens, with powerful lighting and sound systems to create a formidable effect.

- *Competition*, where an attraction can boast of a unique or unusual experience, outstripping that offered by competitors. Some attractions, while not necessarily unique in nature, can create a niche through offering a particular experience that cannot be found elsewhere. Many museums have adopted technological approaches to boosting interest in their collections and artefacts. The Museum of World Religions opened in 2001 in Taipei, Taiwan. It incorporates a range of technologies including an acoustically active elevator to the main entrance, plasma screens, interactive displays, video theatres and video walls, creating a unique interplay of spirituality, religion and technology. One aim is to inspire young people to visit the museum, which has been designed with the idea that education and pleasure are compatible (see https://www.mwr.org.tw/mwr_en).

- *Managing visitors*, where larger numbers of visitors can be formally moved through a site and its experiences by means of a technology-driven transport system, such as that found in the Yorvik Museum, York, and the New Millennium Experience at New Lanark in the UK.

- *Systems management*, where the functional activities of attraction management can be looked after by technology (Image 9.5), including computerized ticketing, online booking, customer feedback and client databases, as highlighted by Merlin with its investment in an e-commerce platform. There is also potential in the introduction of 5G to capture a greater variety of visitor data and begin to use AI to help make recommendations in real-time to the future visitor and begin to use smart technology to make the time use at attractions far more efficient.

IMAGE 9.5 Visitor attractions have harnessed technology to help reduce queues by pre-booking

Technological approaches in visitor attraction development are important, but so too are the personal interaction and services elements. In this respect, small and less well-resourced attractions have potential to compete with larger organizations by providing a specialized, differentiated product with an emphasis on personal service. In some attractions, a high degree of interpretation based on technology may not be required by the visitor (see Image 9.6), such as with heritage railways or in the case of gardens, where visitors may be more content to wander freely and ask a question or two of the garden staff. More generally, helpful and friendly staff remain a crucial element in any visitor

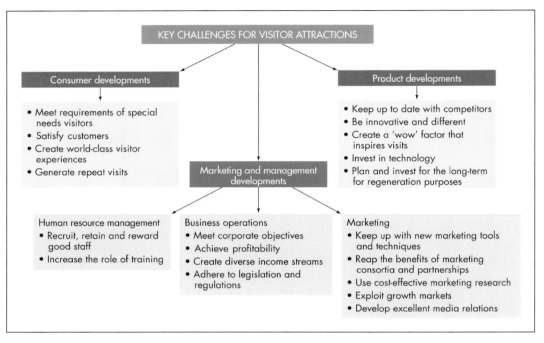

FIGURE 9.11 Key challenges for visitor attraction management
Source: Adapted and expanded from Swarbrooke (2001)

IMAGE 9.6 Former transport infrastructure can become the focal point for a tourist attraction, such as this Darjeeling tea train from India built in 1889 now used as a tourist train

IMAGE 9.7 Timed ticketing for site tours is a useful tool to manage demand

attraction, even where technology plays a big role in the attraction experience, and provision of a welcoming and interesting café or restaurant may also provide an important revenue stream for attractions. Such revenue streams have become critical to the financial viability of many attractions, and cafés can help to extend the dwell time. This may give visitors the opportunity to reflect on the memorable and most enjoyable aspects of the visit, while offering them time to relax and enjoy the surroundings including guided tours (Image 9.7). Therefore the ambience and setting of the café or restaurant is a key element of the experience.

Conclusion

Attractions increased in volume and diversity through the twentieth century and continue to develop in an increasingly global marketplace, as well as for local audiences, in the new millennium. Success in attraction management is never guaranteed, even with the major global brands, and the future for attractions is likely to show a mix of winners and losers. Swarbrooke (2001) presents several key challenges that face managers of visitor attractions, which have been extended to incorporate more recent developments and are summarized in Figure 9.11. Most successful attractions seize new and interesting ways of stimulating visitor interest, provide multiple activities and experiences and generate multiple streams of revenue to attain financial viability.

A key tool in the future development and renewal of attractions is the augmentation of the distinctiveness of an attraction to form a 'wow' factor, or sensational experience.

Such developments must be based on innovation, a commitment to investment and re-investment, and a clear recognition of market trends and visitor needs. In this respect, visitor attractions must not simply meet expectations but exceed them. In a competitive market, contemporary attraction development centres on constant innovation and development, creating must-see places that visitors will want to return to again. Simultaneously, attractions must be developed and managed sensitively, to sustain, reflect and care for environmental, cultural and community interests. Attractions form just one part of the tourism and leisure industry, but display many of the key themes and issues central to other sectors. The next chapter continues the theme of supply and explores the role of accommodation and hospitality as a key part of tourism infrastructure.

Discussion questions

1 Why is the term 'visitor attraction' more appropriate to use than 'tourist attraction'?

2 Explain the approaches used to classify visitor attractions.

3 How important is the role of technology in visitor attractions?

4 What issues are likely to affect the future development of visitor attractions?

References

Benckendorff, P. and Pearce, P. (2003) 'Australian tourist attractions: The links between organizational characteristics and planning', *Journal of Travel Research*, 42 (1): 24–35.

Bigne, J.E., Andreu, L. and Gnoth, J. (2005) 'The theme park experience: An analysis of pleasure, arousal and satisfaction', *Tourism Management*, 26 (6): 833–844.

Braun, B. and Soskin, M. (2003) 'Competitive theme park strategies: Lessons from central Florida', in A. Fyall, B. Garrod and A. Leask (eds.) *Managing Visitor Attractions: New Directions*. Oxford: Butterworth-Heinemann.

Calver, S. and Page, S.J. (2013) 'The value of service to the hedonic aims of visitors to heritage attractions: A structural model to measure the influence on visit behaviour', *Tourism Management*, 39: 23–36.

Chiwara, D. and Chipangura, N. (2018) 'Digital technology: The panacea to improve visitor experience and audience growth?' *Museum International*, 70(1–2): 114–123.

Connell, J. (2004) '"The purest of human pleasures": The characteristics and motivations of garden visitors in Great Britain', *Tourism Management*, 25 (2): 229–247.

Connell, J., Page, S.J., Sheriff, I. and Hibbert, J. (2017) 'Business engagement in a civil society: Transitioning towards a dementia-friendly visitor economy', *Tourism Management*, 61: 110–128.

Dilek, S. and Dilek, N. (2018) 'Real-life escape rooms as a new recreational attraction: The case of Turkey', *Anatolia*, 29(4), 495–506.

Donnachie, I. (2004) 'Historic tourism to New Lanark and the Falls of Clyde 1795–1830. The evidence of contemporary

9

visiting books and related sources', *Journal of Tourism and Cultural Change*, 2 (3): 145–162.

Fyall, A. (2008) 'Marketing visitor attractions: A collaborative approach', in A. Fyall, B. Garrod, A. Leask and S. Wanhill (eds.) *Managing Visitor Attractions: New Directions*, 2nd edition. Oxford: Butterworth-Heinemann.

Fyall, A., Garrod, B., Leask, A. and Wanhill, S. (eds.) (2008) *Managing Visitor Attractions: New Directions*, 2nd edition. Oxford: Elsevier.

Fyall, A., Leask, A. and Garrod, B. (2001) 'Scottish visitor attractions: A collaborative future?', *International Journal of Tourism Research*, 3 (3): 211–228.

Golledge, R. (1978) 'Representing, interpreting, and using cognized environments', *Papers of the Regional Science Association*, 41: 169–204.

Goulding, P. (2008) 'Managing temporal variation in visitor attractions', in A. Fyall, B. Garrod, A. Leask and S. Wanhill (eds.) *Managing Visitor Attractions: New Directions*, 2nd edition. Oxford: Butterworth-Heinemann.

Gunn, C.A. (1972) *Vacationscape: Designing Tourist Regions*. Austin, TX: University of Texas.

Gunn, C.A. (1988) *Tourism Planning*, 2nd edition. New York: Taylor and Francis.

Hall, C.M. and Ram, Y. (2019) 'Measuring the relationship between tourism and walkability? Walk Score and English tourist attractions', *Journal of Sustainable Tourism*, 27(2): 223–240.

Hansen, M. (2018) 'Analysing visits to English museums 1850–2015: A research note', *Cultural Trends*, 27(4), 296–305.

Jensen, Ø., Li, Y. and Uysal, M. (2017) 'Visitors' satisfaction at managed tourist attractions in Northern Norway: Do on-site factors matter?' *Tourism Management*, 63, 277–286.

Kang, S., Lee, G., Kim, J. and Park, D. (2018) 'Identifying the spatial structure of the tourist attraction system in South Korea using GIS and network analysis: An application of anchor-point theory', *Journal of Destination Marketing and Management*, 9: 358–370.

Kempiak, J., Hollywood, L., Bolan, P. and McMahon-Beattie, U. (2017) 'The heritage tourist: An understanding of the visitor experience at heritage attractions', *International Journal of Heritage Studies*, 23(4): 375–392.

Kolar, T. (2017) 'Conceptualising tourist experiences with new attractions: The case of escape rooms', *International Journal of Contemporary Hospitality Management*, 29(5): 1322–1339.

Kotler, P. (1994) *Marketing Management: Analysis, Planning, Implementation and Control*, 8th edition. Hemel Hempstead: Prentice Hall.

Leiper, N. (1990) 'Tourist attraction systems', *Annals of Tourism Research*, 17 (3): 367–384.

Lennon, J. (ed.) (2001) *Tourism Statistics*. London: Continuum.

Lew, A. (1987) 'A framework of tourist attraction research', *Annals of Tourism Research*, 14: 533–575.

Light, D. (2017) 'Progress in dark tourism and thanatourism research: An uneasy relationship with heritage tourism', *Tourism Management*, 61: 275–301.

Light, D. and Cerrone, M. (2018) 'Science engagement via Twitter: Examining the educational outreach of museums, zoos, aquariums and other science organizations', *Visitor Studies*, 21 (2): 175–188.

Loureiro, S. and Ferreira, E. (2018) 'Engaging visitors in cultural and recreational experience at museums', *Anatolia*, 29 (4): 581–592.

MacCannell, D. (1976) *The Tourist: A New Theory of the Leisure Class*. London: Macmillan.

Manning, R., Wang, B., Valliere, W., Lawson, S. and Newman, P. (2002) 'Research to estimate and manage carrying capacity of a tourist attraction: A study of Alcatraz Island', *Journal of Sustainable Tourism*, 10 (5): 388–404.

McKercher, B., Ho, P. and du Cros, H. (2004) 'Attributes of popular cultural attractions in Hong Kong', *Annals of Tourism Research*, 31 (2): 393–407.

Millar, S. (1999) 'An overview of the sector', in A. Leask and I. Yeoman (eds.) *Heritage Visitor Attractions: An Operations Management Perspective*. London: Cassell.

Molinillo, S. and Japutra, A. (2017) 'Factors influencing domestic tourist attendance at cultural attractions in Andalusia, Spain', *Journal of Destination Marketing and Management*, 6 (4): 456–464.

Oh, J. and Ma, H. (2018) 'Enhancing visitor experience of theme park attractions: Focusing on animation and narrative', *Journal of Advanced Research in Dynamical and Control Systems*, 10 (4 Special Issue): 178–185.

Padilla, J., Kavak, Lynch, C., Gore, R. and Diallo, S. (2018) 'Temporal and spatiotemporal investigation of tourist attraction visit sentiment on Twitter', *PLoS ONE*, 13 (6): e0198857.

Page, S.J. and Connell, J. (2010) *Leisure: An Introduction*. Harlow: Pearson.

Paraskevaidis, P. and Weidenfeld, A. (2019) 'Sign consumption and sign promotion in visitor attractions: A netnography of the visitor experience in Titanic Belfast', *International Journal of Contemporary Hospitality Management*, 31 (4): 1937–1955.

Pearce, P. (1991) 'Analysing tourist attractions', *Journal of Tourism Studies*, 2 (1): 46–55.

Pearce, P., Benckendorff, P. and Johnstone, S. (2000) 'Tourist attractions: Evolution, analysis and prospects', in B. Faulkner, G. Moscardo and E. Laws (eds.) *Tourism in the Twenty-First Century*. London: Continuum.

Pine, I.B. and Gilmore, J. (1999) *The Experience Economy*. Boston, MA: Harvard Business School Press.

Richards, G. (2002) 'Tourism attraction systems: Exploring cultural behaviour', *Annals of Tourism Research*, 29 (4): 1048–1064.

Shaw, G. and Williams, A. (2004) *Tourism and Tourism Spaces*. London: Sage.

Shone, A. and Parry, B. (2004) *Successful Event Management: A Practical Handbook*, 2nd edition. London: Thomson.

Solmaz, G., Akbaş, M. and Turgut, D. (2015) 'A mobility model of theme park visitors', *IEEE Transactions on Mobile Computing*, 14 (12): 2406–2418.

Swacha, J. and Ittermann, R. (2017) 'Enhancing the tourist attraction visiting process with gamification: Key concepts', *Engineering Management in Production and Services*, 9(4): 59–66.

Swarbrooke, J. (2001) 'Visitor attraction management in a competitive market', *Insights,* A41–A52. London: English Tourism Council.

Swarbrooke, J. (2002) *The Development and Management of Visitor Attractions*, 2nd edition. Oxford: Butterworth-Heinemann.

Theme Park Tourist (2016) 'The top 50 theme parks in the world', *Theme Park Tourist.* https://www.themeparktourist.com/features/20140228/16441/top-50-theme-parks-world.

Uzzell, D.L. (1989) 'The hot interpretation of war and conflict', in D.L. Uzzell (ed.) *Heritage Interpretation: Volume 1 The Natural and Built Environment.* London: Belhaven.

Watson, S. and McCracken, M. (2008) 'Managing human resources in visitor attractions', in A. Fyall, B. Garrod, A. Leask and S. Wanhill (eds.) *Managing Visitor Attractions: New Directions*, 2nd edition. Oxford: Butterworth-Heinemann.

Williams, P. (2004) *Beacon on the Rock: The Dramatic History of Lighthouses from Ancient Greece to Present Day.* Edinburgh: Birlinn.

Xu, F., Buhalis, D. and Weber, J. (2017) 'Serious games and the gamification of tourism', *Tourism Management*, 60: 244–256.

Further Reading

Books

Benckendorff, P., Xiang, Z. and Sheldon, P. (2019) *Tourism Information Technology*, 3rd edition. Wallingford: CABI: Chapter 10.

Weidenfeld, A., Butler, R. and Williams, A. (2016) *Visitor Attractions and Events.* London: Routledge.

Journal articles

Beck, J., Rainoldi, M. and Egger, R. (2019) 'Virtual reality in tourism: A state-of-the-art review', *Tourism Review*, 74 (3): 586–612.

Blumenthal, V. and Jensen, Ø. (2019) 'Consumer immersion in the experiencescape of managed visitor attractions: The nature of the immersion process and the role of involvement', *Tourism Management Perspectives*, 30: 159–170.

Isaac, R.K., Nawijn, J., van Liempt, A. and Gridnevskiy, K. (2019) 'Understanding Dutch visitors' motivations to concentration camp memorials', *Current Issues in Tourism*, 22 (7): 747–762.

Kolar, T. (2017) 'Conceptualising tourist experiences with new attractions: The case of escape rooms', *International Journal of Contemporary Hospitality Management*, 29 (5): 1322–1339.

Leask, A. (2016) 'Visitor attraction management: A critical review of research 2009–2014', *Tourism Management*, 57: 334–361.

Light, D. (2017) 'Progress in dark tourism and thanatourism research: An uneasy relationship with heritage tourism', *Tourism Management*, 61: 275–301.

Tourism accommodation and hospitality services

Learning outcomes

After reading this chapter and answering the questions, you should:

- understand the scope and nature of the hospitality industry

- be aware of the diverse range of accommodation for tourism

- be familiar with the operational issues affecting the accommodation sector

- be able to identify the different types of accommodation and hospitality services used by tourists.

Overview

The purpose of this chapter is to provide the reader with an appreciation of the various types of accommodation and hospitality services and some of the issues which impact upon the sector. The growing diversity of the accommodation sector mirrors trends in the wider tourism sector, as it focuses on attracting customers and profitability as well as quality issues. The sector is often a trendsetter and innovator in its pursuit of ways to stay ahead of the competition as well as its anticipation of changing tourist behaviour and the pursuit of niche products.

Introduction

The concept of **hospitality** underpins much of what the tourist experiences as a traveller, namely the consumption of food, drink and accommodation away from the home environment. As Lashley (2000) observed, it is this context where such activities create a range of relationships, some of which occur in commercial, social and private settings. As Lashley (2000) explains, hospitality may occur in three domains:

- *The private domain* – guests experience the provision of food, drink and accommodation in domestic settings. This involves hosting and hospitality by the **host**. This personal relationship sometimes has a reciprocal nature (i.e. if you host a friend there is often an expectation that they will host you at some point in the future), where the **guest** may be the host on a future occasion (i.e. involving family and friends) and may also characterize some of the relationships experienced by guests in bed-and-breakfast establishments.
- *The social domain* – historically many societies valued the social setting in which hospitality occurs, particularly the trait to act with generosity as a host to visitors. This traditionally involved being charitable to strangers, especially travellers in pre-industrial societies, and bestowed status on the host.
- *The commercial domain* – now characterizes many industrial societies where the experience of hospitality is a purely commercial relationship and not based on charitableness or social reciprocity in the main. A commoditized relationship now exists where the guest pays the host for the services/products consumed via a bill. However, being treated as a valued customer does not infer that a business is offering personal hospitality. Indeed, the cost controls used by large hospitality businesses in terms of portion control, well-defined limits to the scope and extent of the hospitality experience to be delivered, are certainly very distant from the notions of hospitality in the private domain. Nevertheless, hospitality is a relationship between host and guest, and the different contexts in which tourists consume such hospitality is the focus of this chapter.

10

The hospitality industry

Historical studies of the hospitality sector indicate that 'commercial hospitality has its roots in supplying to travellers through the market, the basic human needs of food, drink, shelter and rest' (Walton 2000: 57). From the early ale houses of medieval times, to inns and the emerging public houses, such establishments met travellers' needs. Yet it was the Victorian era that saw the rise of the hotel, restaurant and large-scale caterer in the form of public dining rooms in London from the 1820s, and Mac Con Iomaire (2013) examines the phenomenon in Dublin between 1700 and 1900. As Littlejohn (2003) indicated, the concept of a hotel developed in mid-seventeenth-century Paris. In 1780 it crossed to London with the founding of Nero's Hotel, aimed at an affluent clientele. In the mid-Victorian period, the provision of railway hotels catering for middle-class travellers created a major development boost to the urban expansion of hotels. Littlejohn (2003) argued that a hotel is a culturally bound phenomenon, given that cultural rules and customs affect hospitality provision and certain behaviour and social codes prevail (i.e. certain codes of conduct are encouraged/discouraged). National codes of regulation also affect hospitality establishments, impacting upon what they provide and the roles they fulfil in tourism. This can complicate attempts to define the scope and nature of hospitality services in tourism.

Defining the scope of the hospitality industry

According to Jones (2002), various criteria and measures have been used to define the scope of the hospitality sector. He points to the use of the UK's Standard Industrial Classification (SIC) developed initially in 1948 to statistically track the development of industry. Revised in 1968 and 1980, the SIC divides hospitality into its constituent parts of establishments providing meals and light refreshments, drink and accommodation. Much of the hospitality industry is classified under the Division 6, services, Class 66 – hotels and catering, which is then subdivided into six groups. An indication of the scale of the hospitality sector is demonstrated by the following statistics: in Europe, HOTREC (the umbrella Association of Hotels, Restaurants, Bars and Cafes in Europe: see https://www.hotrec.eu/about-us/mission-vision/) and similar establishments in Europe estimated that the sector employed 9.5 million people in 1.7 million hospitality enterprises (equivalent to 4.4 per cent of total European employment and 8 per cent of businesses). It is a fast-growing sector that has seen employment rise from 7.4 million employees in 2003 to 9.3 million in 2008 and 9.5 million in 2010, despite the conditions of slow growth in recent years. In the UK, the British

10

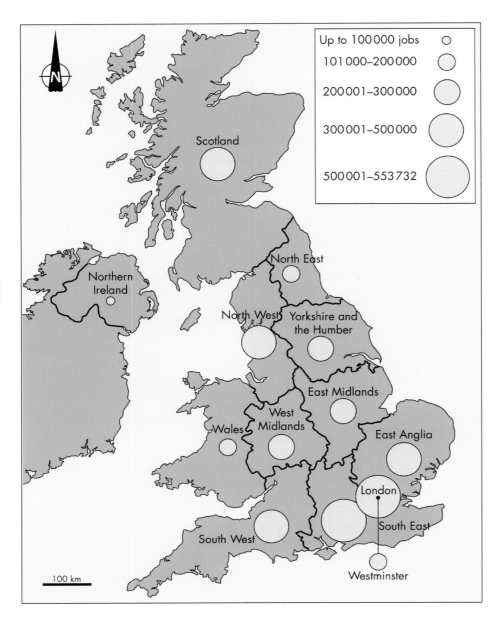

FIGURE 10.1 The geographical distribution of hospitality employment in the UK
Source: Data from BHA (2011)

Hospitality Association (BHA) (2011) found that hospitality employed 2.4 million people in 206 000 businesses and over the period since 2001, 1 000 new hotels had been constructed. The BHA report also observed the regional impact of the industry, where the economic impact of the sector is broken down by region of the UK. The salient features of Figure 10.1 are the geographical concentration in central London (i.e. Westminster, with 860 00 hospitality jobs in the borough representing 16 per cent of all employment) which was the largest concentration in the UK. Alongside London in the top ten locations were Birmingham, Glasgow, Edinburgh, Manchester, Leeds, Cornwall, Camden in London, Liverpool, and Kensington and Chelsea in London, and tourist resort regions (e.g. Cornwall), and the major cities demonstrate a growing dependence upon the hospitality sector as driver of their local economies. The BHA report also indicated the significance of this sector of the service economy, with an annual turnover of £90 billion. Page (2019) provides an indication of the scale of the hospitality sector, as follows:

- The sector employs 3 million people, predominantly in catering and restaurants with smaller numbers in hotels and accommodation
- It is the fourth largest economic sector in the UK, employing 9 per cent of the workforce and the third largest private sector employer
- It generates an estimated £130 billion a year

- It is one of the fastest growing sectors, experiencing a 17 per cent growth in employment 2010–2014, although one needs to look at the nature of these jobs and their status (i.e. part-time and hourly-paid employees)
- It has a high reliance upon migrant labour, estimated at up to 30 per cent of all employees in London, to maintain its churn and growth patterns. The British Hospitality Association estimated that it required 60 000 EU migrant workers every year to maintain its employment needs
- Around 97 per cent of hospitality businesses are small- to medium-sized ventures with less than 50 employees and wages comprise around 35 per cent of costs.

In contrast, Table 10.1 illustrates the scale of the sector in Australia, where it equally has a large contribution to make to the economy, but highlights that the key feature of small businesses are dominant but larger players produce the greater economic benefits.

There are also alternative ways of defining hospitality as Page (2019) suggests, namely the visitor economy. Connell *et al.* (2017: 111) described it thus:

> *It embraces the hospitality and tourism sector (food and drink provision via cafes, restaurants and accommodation), travel agencies, transport providers, cultural activities like galleries, events and retailing. There is often a blurring of the terms visitor economy, tourism and leisure as residents may also use the facilities and services in their leisure time. The term broadly refers to the supporting infrastructure that caters for the needs of visitors and residents especially in their leisure time and so is very wide ranging in what is included in such a categorisation.*

TABLE 10.1 Characteristics of the Australian tourism and hospitality sector

- According to Tourism Research Australia (2015) the sector comprises 267 000 businesses comprising 13 per cent of the total 2.1 million businesses in Australia in 2013
- 80 per cent of the total sector-related businesses are in New South Wales, Victoria and Queensland, reflecting the concentration of the sector within these regional economies
- 95 per cent of the businesses are micro/small businesses, accounting for 32 per cent of turnover
- 5 per cent of businesses contribute 68 per cent of turnover

For the purposes of the survey, the employment structure of the sector comprises:

114 812 businesses (43 per cent) do not employee any staff or are self-employed
86 146 businesses (32 per cent) employ 1–4 employees
51 640 businesses (14 per cent) employ 5–19 employees
13 376 businesses (5 per cent) employ 20–199 employees
675 businesses (0.3 per cent) employee 200 or more employees

- Tourism spending in Australia in tourism businesses is worth AU$110 billion (2013)

Source: Tourism Research Australia (2015), reproduced from Page *et al.* (2018)

Accommodation

According to Medlik and Ingram (2000: 4):

> *hotels play an important role in most countries in providing facilities for the transaction of business, for meetings and conferences, for recreation and entertainment . . . In many areas hotels are important attractions for visitors who bring to them spending power and who tend to spend at a higher rate than when they are at home.*

What Medlik and Ingram's key study of the hotel sector shows is that for many forms of tourism (excluding visiting friends or visiting relatives), the tourist requires some form of accommodation for an overnight stay or longer. And part of that accommodation consumption often involves discretionary spending which is at a higher rate than their normal leisure spending or household expenditure. Accommodation provides the base from which tourists can engage in the process of staying at a destination, and a number of studies of the sector are identified in Table 10.2.

TABLE 10.2 Selected books on accommodation and hospitality
Brotherton, B. (ed.) (2003) *International Hospitality Industry: Structure, Characteristics and Issues*. Oxford: Elsevier.
Clark, A. and Chun, W. (2015) *International Hospitality Management*. London: Routledge.
Davis, B., Lockwood, A., Pantelidis, I. and Alcott, P. (2008) *Food and Beverage Management*. Oxford: Elsevier.
Ivanova, M., Ivanov, S. and Magnini, V. (eds.) (2016) *The Routledge Handbook of Hotel Chain Management*. London: Routledge.
Kaufman, T., Lashley, C. and Schreier, L. (2009) *Timeshare Management*. Oxford: Elsevier.
Lashley, C. (ed.) (2016) *The Routledge Handbook of Hospitality Studies*. London: Routledge.
Pantelidis, I. (ed.) (2014) *The Routledge Handbook of Hospitality Management*. London: Routledge.
Rutherford, D. and O'Fallon, H. (2010) *Hotel Management and Operations*. Oxford: Elsevier.
Timothy, D. and Teye, V. (2009) *Tourism and the Lodging Sector*. Oxford: Elsevier.
Wood, R. (2015) *Hospitality Management*. London: Sage.
Wood, R. (2018) *Hotel Accommodation Management*. London: Routledge.

The accommodation sector is among the capital-intensive infrastructure which tourists utilize and is very labour-intensive in servicing visitors' needs. But it has the advantage in that by hosting guests it also has the potential to generate additional revenue from **food and beverage** services. In that sense accommodation in the tourism and wider hospitality sector has the potential to realize spending from visitors at different rates, particularly as the diversification of the accommodation sector into a wide variety of niche markets and products based on price has offered a new range of opportunities for the tourist in recent years (e.g. the growth of budget accommodation). The accommodation sector is one of the most visible and tangible elements in the tourist's trip and experience, since the premises host the visit. Therefore, the underlying premise in accommodation provision, aside from operating profitably, should be to provide a conducive environment where the visitor feels comfortable and welcomed (Image 10.1). This involves considerable investment in the accommodation infrastructure. The accommodation sector is perhaps one of the most capital-intensive areas of the tourism industry given the real-estate value of accommodation venues.

The accommodation product, according to Medlik and Ingram (2000), comprises:

- the *location* of the establishment (i.e. where it is based in terms of a city or rural area and its relative accessibility to tourists and customers)
- its *facilities* (i.e. its bedrooms, bars, restaurants, meeting rooms and sports and recreation facilities) (see Image 10.1)
- its *service* (i.e. what level of service the provider offers will depend upon its grading and facilities and market niche)
- its *image* (i.e. how it is portrayed to customers and the way it is marketed)
- its *price*, which is a function of the location, facilities, service and image (Image 10.2).

IMAGE 10.1 Resort hotels, such as this one in Fiji, epitomize the concept of the perfect getaway to a tropical island

IMAGE 10.2 Hotel room. The way the room is designed, furnished and its ambience are important elements in the image a hotel seeks to portray

In addition, the price will also depend upon the customers being sought, since accommodation units appeal to a range of users. Tourist accommodation has been developed, over time, to a position where virtually all tastes are catered for: from holiday villages and resort hotels that encourage guests to spend their time on-site, to basic bunkhouse barns that cater for a single-night stay at very low cost. Another variation is the concept of timeshare, which provides an investment for one or two weeks per year in a property with the option of exchanging weeks for locations elsewhere.

Forms of accommodation have been developed to meet the purposes of individual and group travellers. En route accommodation has evolved with changes in modes of transport such that the railway terminus hotel of the nineteenth and twentieth centuries is today represented by the airport hotel where accommodation at major gateways now comprises a significant sector of the accommodation stock in many countries. Motels represent the logical extension of the coaching inn, although some companies have restored these older properties to high-standard contemporary business use, and in the USA and Australasia they represent a major sector of accommodation supply. An illustration of the growth of accommodation in one location – the Gold Coast – is shown in Insight 10.1.

INSIGHT 10.1 The development of Surfers Paradise, Gold Coast Queensland, Australia

10

In Australia, the Gold Coast is the country's main tourist destination (after Sydney). Located in the south-east corner of Queensland, the region is 70 km south of the state capital, Brisbane. Tourism accommodation has developed since the early 1900s (Warnken *et al.* 2003) when the region first became known as a recreational destination, and when the accommodation consisted of tents, boarding houses and small hotels in Coolangatta. As Table 10.3 shows, five phases can be discerned in the growth of accommodation, as the initial development at Coolangatta reached its peak along the coastal strip along Surfers Paradise, Broadbeach, Barleigh and Carrumbin. The growth of tourism accommodation along the Gold Coast was promoted by the extension of rail services from Brisbane and the entrepreneurial activities of early guest houses and accommodation.

Warnken *et al.* (2003) observed that in the 1950s and 1960s demand for more sophisticated leisure and entertainment options saw Coolangatta decline and Surfers Paradise grow. This was at a time when all the coastal plots had been divided into 500–900 m² sections and developed into holiday homes. High-rise development did not occur until the 1960s, although three-storey hotels emerged. The infilling of land for tourism use and upgrading of Coolangatta airport in the 1960s widened access to the region from domestic and overseas markets, although the area still only had a population of 38 000. The growth of high-rise buildings in the 1960s and 1970s was followed by the area's further development as a tourism node. This was followed by a growing intensity of accommodation development to serve tourists, and new infrastructure provision. In the 1980s and 1990s, high-rise accommodation resulted, with some low-value, low-density residential properties being redeveloped to create the tourist destination – the Gold Coast, focused on Surfers Paradise.

As Warnken *et al.* (2003) show, condominium development (self-catering apartments and properties) and different development booms created a distinctive accommodation landscape, and southern Surfers Paradise enjoyed a massive building boom in the early 1980s. These condominiums can operate with much lower overheads than hotels, especially in the number of employees needed to service them. Yet as such properties may be driven by property development opposed to tourism demand, occupancy levels rarely exceed 70 per cent. Where such infrastructures age and deteriorate and do not have ongoing reinvestment (in contrast to luxury hotels), the only option may be lower prices. A downward spiral of decay may begin as the properties do not get maintained as profits drop. On the Gold Coast, Warnken *et al.* (2003) point to the threat that condominium development may pose to the long-term sustainability of tourism, if investors in such developments leave when financial returns are no longer attractive, further intensifying the spiral of decline. In the Surfers Paradise case, the clustering of buildings of a similar age has the potential for long-term environmental deterioration and a negative aesthetic impact when they age, so that an entire district will have a visual and image problem 20–25 years after development. This highlights the wider importance of individual accommodation providers to the image of a destination and the consequences of market forces, oversupply and the link between a condominium's visual attractiveness and ongoing demand for its use.

Further reading

Warnken, J. and Guilding, C. (2009) 'Multi-ownership of tourism accommodation complexes: A critique of types, relative merits, and challenges arising', *Tourism Management*, 30 (5): 704–714.

10

INSIGHT 10.1 continued

Warnken, J. and Guilding, C. (2014) 'Quo Vadis Gold Coast? A case study investigation of Strata Titled tourism accommodation densification and issues arising', *Journal of Travel Research*, 53 (2): 167–182.

Warnken, J., Russell, R. and Faulkner, B. (2003) 'Condominium developments in maturing destinations: Potentials and problems of long-term sustainability', *Tourism Management*, 24 (2): 155–168.

Questions

1 What is a condominium?
2 What impact has condominium development had on the urban landscape of the Gold Coast?
3 How has the landscape of hotel and condominium development evolved on the Gold Coast? How does it fit with other resort development time horizons such as Spain?
4 What are the future debates that will emerge around this style of accommodation development in relation to sustainability?

TABLE 10.3 Succession of accommodation facilities on the Gold Coast

Stage	Type of tourist accommodation	Location, distribution
One (pre-WWII)	Early days: tents, boarding houses and small hotels	Mostly around headlands, along protected beaches
Two (post-WWII)	Low-key development: summer holiday houses, small motels (one storey), two- or three-storey hotels	Development spreading north from headlands
Three (1950s–1960s)	Intermediate phase: multi-storey holiday apartment complexes, two-storey motels, multi-storey hotels	Development filling in area between headlands and main coastal road running parallel to the beaches
Four (1960s–1970s)	First high-rise buildings: 6–10-storey brick and concrete condominium complexes, 10–20-storey hotels	Establishment of major tourism node: Surfers Paradise
Five (1980s–1990s)	Built-up: >20-storey high-rise condominium resorts, >20-storey hotels	Consolidation of destination's tourist centre, Surfers Paradise

Source: Reprinted from Warnken *et al.* 2003 © 2003, with permission from Elsevier

In some countries, the state is or has been directly involved in the operation of accommodation. The former Eastern European countries are an example. Here, the state identified the supply in relation to the demand, although state involvement has been waning globally due to costs of operation and high capital requirements for upgrading schemes and an absence of management skills. As state involvement has waned, private sector involvement, especially through global interests, has grown and this is reflected in the trends in many countries. Page (2019) outlined the global impact of trends in the accommodation sector, as the case of the UK shows.

Global trends in the accommodation sector

Major trends affecting the accommodation sector globally include:

- internationalization of many hotel and accommodation chains (e.g. represented in the three- to five-star category)
- disruptive innovations such as Airbnb
- greater product differentiation and the use of brands by larger operators (and multiple brands by some hotel companies)
- the growth of the non-serviced sector internationally, with serviced apartments and self-catering providing greater flexibility and individuality for tourists

- new ownership models (e.g. franchising and management contracting, joint ventures) as well as the rise of investment portfolios in the self-catering market as it has grown in popularity

- the growing importance of second homes in domestic and international settings as greater affluence has created new opportunities for developers and investors

- increasing use of technology, such as the World Wide Web for marketing and purchasing by consumers, which has reduced the time horizon for booking. It has also created new tools for the discerning consumer to track the rating of accommodation by consumers

- the creation of new forms of demand (e.g. the growth of short breaks induced by the introduction of low-cost airlines serving a wider range of destinations)

- the expansion of niche and novelty forms of accommodation

- increased competition between accommodation providers in different destinations and within destinations as epitomized by the shifting trend towards self-catering in some locations, such as the Lake District National Park in the UK, where it has begun to outperform serviced accommodation

- a perception that some sectors of the market for accommodation are being displaced (e.g. bed and breakfasts) by budget brands and changes in hostel accommodation

- a more discerning consumer, seeking more for less from accommodation products in the low to mid range

- growth in social-media-informed consumers, who increasingly review brands, products and services using social media following the expansion in consumer access to Web 2.0 technology, as discussed in Chapter 6 (see Figure 10.2). These consumers review products, services and experiences post-purchase, a phenomenon which is described as e-word of mouth or eWoM. eWoM increasingly reviews service experiences such as

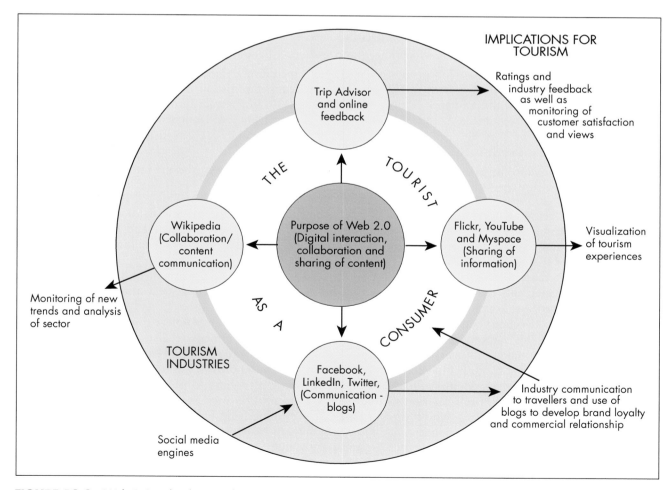

FIGURE 10.2 Web 2.0 technology and tourism
Source: Page (2019)

service failures (e.g. this may be presented to a service provider as a complaint) via online travel communities (i.e. TripAdvisor). Research on eWoM, reviewing the responses and approaches adopted by companies to eWOM, especially in the hospitality sector, illustrates its value as a means of engaging with consumers. This type of engagement can be viewed as a tool to aid in service recovery (i.e. putting things right after a poor experience or at least apologizing for that experience). Such approaches are increasingly being used as part of a corporate marketing strategy to help develop greater consumer loyalty through the increasing use of social media to target communities of consumers. A useful review of this expanding area of research within tourism and marketing can be found in Nieto *et al.* (2014)

- a demand for luxury in accommodation experiences by some consumers, for which they will pay a premium (e.g. being pampered with chocolate, flowers and champagne in a top-of-the-range hotel suite)
- a greater use of yield management among hotels to increase profitability
- mixed development where a hotel project incorporates an office or residential development as well as further splitting of the brand and property – a bricks and brains split which will lead to divestment in the hotel sector.

Source: Page (2019)

Within the UK, this has manifested itself as a key driver of tourism in most destinations. As Page (2019) observed, in the UK, budget hotels form a fast-growing sub-sector, and key trends affecting the market include:

- an increase in amenities and costs at properties, termed *amenities creep*
- a drop in the number of business travellers using budget hotels
- the necessity of attracting more leisure business
- a growing average size of budget properties
- greater pressure on room rates, due to more flexibility in pricing policies by operators such as Travelodge
- improvements in full-service hotels which have put pressure on budget hotels to cut prices
- the market leader, Premier Inn (785 properties in locations including Ireland, the UAE and Germany), was closely followed by Travelodge, with 560 properties (after acquiring Mitchell and Butler Innkeepers) in the UK, Ireland and Spain, and a further 20 properties opening in 2018. Premier Inn plans to grow its room capacity from 72 000 rooms in 2018 to 85 000 by 2020. Premier Inn also launched its streamlined budget brand – the Hub – in 2014 and aims to have 3500 rooms operational by 2020 by using digital technology to reduce running costs such as check-in
- 'breakfast included in the price' is the single greatest attractor in guest stays (despite the market leaders not offering this), with Express by Holiday Inn providing free breakfast.

The market for budget hotel development in the UK has become fiercely contested, with major expansion in budget property development in non-central city locations on cheaper land. In the UK, Premier Inn and Travelodge are seeking to also be the number one provider of budget accommodation in London, with Premier Inn having launched a new low-cost brand in major cities.

Internationally, capacity growth has been directly affected by high fixed investment costs in the sector and new modes of management (e.g. Holiday Inn moving from a hotel owner/operator to a management company) as well as the competition in many locations between tourism and offices for land. Equally, small and marginal hotel properties have also been converted to accommodation and residential uses where the return on investment from a booming housing market has offered short-term gains. Second homes are also growing alongside the self-catering sector, particularly in overseas locations (e.g. Cape Verde off the Senegal Coast and Eastern Europe). However, the UK Survey of English Housing found that 582 000 households in 2006/2007 had a second home. In addition, UK domestic demand for holidays has been declining in volume since 2002 from 42.2 million to 41 million in 2006, while in the self-catering sector, there is a demand for increased quality in terms of standard of property and facilities required – with a greater emphasis on home from home, with some residential homes now having a wider range of luxury fittings and features than many holidays properties would traditionally have had. Self-catering appeals to a wider range of customers with high disposable income, but the market is highly seasonal due to the focus on domestic holidays. However, self-catering accounts for around 60 per cent of UK overseas holidays.

INSIGHT 10.2 The evolution of the Chinese hotel industry since 1980

Since economic reform was introduced in China in 1978, China's hotel properties have grown at around 20 per cent per annum according to Gu *et al.* (2012), with the greatest increases occurring in 1991 (36.34 per cent), 1994 (31.2 per cent) and 2000 (59.7 per cent). As Table 10.4 shows, the number of hotels has risen from 853 in 1991 to 13 991 in 2010. The greatest increase has occurred in the proportion of four- and five-star hotels, as the sector has progressively increased provision in the higher quality properties. As Gu *et al.* (2012) argue, the initial phase of growth in China's hotel sector after 1978 was focused on attracting international visitors, although between 1978 and 1988 international-standard hotels were in short supply. To put this in perspective, international tourism demand in China has been remarkable in its growth from 716 000 overseas arrivals in 1978 to 55.7 million in 2010. However, the

first decade of growth in demand provided the country with experience of dealing with visitors and their expectations, and highlighted the need to develop a service culture. Such growth was also assisted by inward investment from overseas as well as importing skilled hotel managers. However, domestic tourism demand has also expanded from 1994, when the demand was 524 million, to 2100 million in 2010 as a result of an increase in holiday entitlement and disposable income and a rise in affluence as the national economy boomed, as shown in Figure 10.3. This has created an additional source of demand for accommodation. Travel agents in China are increasingly promoting international travel alongside domestic travel.

As the hotel sector has grown, the nature of financing hotel investment and development of hotel projects has shifted from the model of joint ventures funded by

10

TABLE 10.4 Number of hotels in China by star classification

Year	Hotels	Hotels according to star rating				
		5 star	4 star	3 star	2 star	1 star
1991	853	21	21	235	393	156
1992	1028	24	24	280	470	187
1993	1186	32	32	337	541	198
1994	1556	35	35	452	737	236
1995	1913	38	38	591	930	248
1996	2349	46	46	743	1148	284
1997	2724	57	57	895	1339	276
1998	3248	64	64	1085	1610	313
1999	3856	77	77	1292	1898	385
2000	6029	117	352	1899	3061	600
2001	7358	129	441	2287	3748	753
2002	8880		635	2846	4414	810
2003	9751	198	727	3166	4864	796
2004	10 888	242	971	3914	5096	665
2005	11 828	281	1146	4291	5497	613
2006	12 751	302	1369	4779	5698	603
2007	13 583	369	1595	5307	5718	594
2008	14 099	432	1821	5712	5616	518
2009	14 639	462	1968	6436	6705	676
2010	13 991	595	2219	6268	4612	297

Source: Annual Tourism Statistics of China National Tourism Administration (1992–2010), Beijing, China Travel & Tourism Press, 2011: Gu *et al.* (2012) © Elsevier

INSIGHT 10.2 continued

TABLE 10.5 Major hotel groups operating in China in 2010

Rank	Hotel name	Hotels (worldwide)	Rooms (worldwide)	Hotels (China)	Rooms (China)
1	IHG (InterContinental Hotels Group)	4432	643 787	227	50 440
2	Wyndham Hotel Group	7112	597 674	326	48 821
3	Hilton Hotel Corp	3526	587 813	24	8695
4	Marriott International	3329	580 876	58	21 970
5	Accor	4111	492 675	107	28 002
6	Choice Hotels	6021	487 410	3	455
7	Best Western International	4048	308 477	34	6396
8	Starwood Hotels and Resorts Worldwide	979	291 638	72	26704
9	Carlson Hotels Worldwide/Rezidor	1059	159 756	9	3817
10	Global Hyatt Group	399	120 031	17	NA
11	Shangri-La	72	30 000	36	NA
12	Banyan Tree	30	NA	5	502
13	Ascott	NA	NA	40	7000

Sources: Data gathered from company websites, accessed on 10 December 2011.
H. Gu, C. Ryan and L. Yu (2012) 'The changing structure of the Chinese hotel industry: 1980–2012', *Tourism Management Perspectives*, 2 (1): © Elsevier. NA = Not Available.

government agencies and Chinese overseas investors. This was supplemented by international hotel corporations entering China's emergent tourism sector in the 1980s. As Gu *et al.* (2012) show, the main mode of entry into the Chinese hotel market was through management contracts and joint ventures. For example, by 1991, 202 hotels were classified as joint ventures and 215 hotels were managed by international hotel companies. Initially, the high-quality international hotel brands entered the main cities of Shanghai, Guangzhou and Beijing. This was followed by brands moving into secondary cities and major tourist destinations. Through time, international management expertise has passed into domestic hotel companies and the international hotel companies have established a major presence throughout China's major cities (Table 10.5).

Unlike the international hotel chains, domestic hotel brands have also moved into the budget hotel market, though such operations have proved challenging to manage in terms of the revenue generated per room compared to the more lucrative luxury brands. Such challenges have led some domestic hotel brands in the budget market to seek capital from overseas to fund expansion in China and in other countries, sometimes through mergers and acquisitions. After such a rapid pattern of growth, some areas of China have seen the growth in hotel supply matched by demand from a growing economy, although since 2008 a global financial recession has led to a drop in export-led economic growth and pressures on domestic demand. Some regions of China, according to Gu *et al.* (2012) will see supply exceeding demand, impacting upon prices and profitability. Increased competition from new hotel capacity is a new theme in China's hotel performance alongside a growing demand from mass tourists for select budget hotels (Ren *et al.* 2018) with a focus on the aesthetics, staff, location and sensory elements of the hotel visit being important in the selection of budget hotels (Ren *et al.* 2016). Other

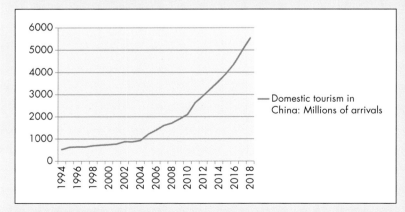

FIGURE 10.3 Domestic tourism in China

trends emerging as a challenge to the hotel sector include the rise of Airbnb (Bie *et al.* 2018), with many positive reviews of this sector, although the issue of trust still remained a key issue for consumers when selecting Airbnb.

Further reading

Andreu, R., Claver, E. and Quer, D. (2017) 'Firm-specific factors and entry mode choice: An analysis of Chinese hotel chains', *Tourism Economics*, 23 (4): 756–767.

Bie, Y., Wang, J. and Wang, J. (2018) 'Airbnb in China: The impact of sharing economy on Chinese tourism', *Advances in Intelligent Systems and Computing*, 594: 11–19.

Gross, M.J., Huang, S. and Ding, Y. (2017) 'Chinese hotel firm internationalisation: Jin Jiang's joint venture acquisition', *International Journal of Contemporary Hospitality Management*, 29 (11): 2730–2750.

Gu, H., Ryan, C. and Yu, L. (2012) 'The changing structure of the Chinese hotel industry: 1980–2012', *Tourism Management Perspectives*, 4 (1): 56–63.

Ren, L., Qiu, H., Ma, C. and Lin, P. (2018) 'Investigating accommodation experience in budget hotels', *International Journal of Contemporary Hospitality Management*, 30 (7): 2662–2667.

Ren, L., Qiu, H., Wang, P. and Lin, P. (2016) 'Exploring customer experience with budget hotels: Dimensionality and satisfaction', *International Journal of Hospitality Management*, 52: 13–23.

Questions

1 Over what time frame has hotel development experienced a major growth in China?
2 What is the difference between the effect of domestic and overseas tourism brands on market development?
3 What has been the effect of budget hotel development in China?
4 How have mergers and acquisitions affected the Chinese hotel market?

Globalization and the accommodation sector

As we discussed in Chapter 1, the term 'globalization' refers to the process of internationalization which is now associated with a growing worldwide trend towards products and tastes among consumers that are now being recognized and fulfilled by international companies (see Insight 10.2). Some critics of globalization in the accommodation sector argue that this is leading to the McDonaldization of the tourism product line, where the experience of a hotel stay in one country is identical to that in another country. In other words, the experience of products and services is becoming homogenized by the global operators, especially in the accommodation sector, where the consumer can be assured of a standard level of service and provision regardless of the country they visit. Yet this standardization may in fact be running contrary to the wider changes in consumer tastes for different experiences but still with a guaranteed quality threshold. Within the accommodation sector, any company pursuing a global strategy can operate in countries where their head office is not located, through a number of strategies:

- franchising its operation to other businesses in other countries (see Altinay *et al.* 2013 on franchising)
- licensing other companies or premises to operate using its brand, logo or trademark
- making non-investment management agreements
- acquiring overseas properties and interests
- engaging in mergers to horizontally integrate business interests to operate in a number of countries.

In the field of international business, these approaches are called 'market entry choices': a company decides to enter a foreign market and chooses the best mode of entry into that market; other approaches may involve forming strategic alliances, as discussed in Chapters 5 and 8, and joining consortia which can support those companies that choose franchising options. In some cases, companies will choose to become sole owners of a hotel but, whatever entry mode is chosen, strategic planning will be important to set out the business case and logic for a particular entry mode.

Hotel chains

As Page (2019) observed, almost 30 per cent of all of the world's accommodation stock is chain controlled (chains in this case are international businesses operating globally) while the International Hotel Corporation stated in Page (2019) that it controlled around 9 per cent of branded rooms globally. Chain hotels often expropriate profits back to the country in which the hotel chain is based. The importance of the USA in the evolution of hotel chains can be dated

IMAGE 10.3 Two important global brands for the hotel sector are the Holiday Inn and InterContinental logos

to the period after 1952, when Kemmons Wilson established Holiday Inn to produce a standardized product across a chain of properties (Image 10.3). This standardization created a focus on a guarantee of quality but also enabled operators to set and control prices and operational costs. Over 50 years after this evolution of the chain concept, 67 per cent of US accommodation is branded (see Chapter 15 for more discussion of branding), most of which is franchised, compared to just over 25 per cent in Europe. In addition, many of the chains have highly developed distribution channels, being affiliated to major global distribution systems that distribute the product electronically to travel agents. The Horwarth and Horwarth Worldwide Hotel Industry report predicted that by 2050 up to 60 per cent of hotels will be affiliated to global chains, continuing the consolidation trend.

According to the World Tourism Organization (UNWTO), global hotel rooms have increased in number from 14 million in 1997 to around 17 million in 2008 and other studies currently estimate the 21 million, a figure which is a broad estimate of the scale of rooms. The bulk of investment has arisen from private sector finance, although some governments provide incentives to hotel developers (e.g. tax breaks and tax holidays) to encourage investment in this sector. With hotel room construction costs now in excess of £3250 per m² for a five-star hotel in the UK, and higher outlays in London, one can see the enormous capital costs of development.

There are important global differences between the more historic and ageing stock in Europe and the relatively new properties in the USA and Asia. The impact of chain development in Europe varies by country, with the greatest activity in France, the UK and the Netherlands, Germany and Spain. In some countries, such as France, the chains have focused on the lower-grade properties (up to two-star) for chain development. In the UK the major growth in chain ownership has been in the establishment of budget brands. For example, budget capacity in the UK has expanded sharply in recent years and the major players in the UK are:

- Travel Inn, Travelodge, Premier Inn, Express by Holiday Inn; many of these are controlled by diversified pub and restaurant groups (e.g. Whitbread) highlighting the wider importance of integration in the tourism and hospitality sector
- new entrants, including the Cendant Corporation with its Days Inn brand.

TABLE 10.6 Top 30 Chinese hotel brands (2011)

Rank	Group Name	Rooms	Hotels
1	Jinjiang Hotels International	105 149	703
2	New Century Hotels & Resorts	24 610	83
3	CTS HK Metro Park Hotels	23 964	74
4	Jinling Hotels & Resorts	23 057	92
5	BTG-Jianguo Hotels & Resorts	20 283	67
6	Blue Horizon Hotels Group	16 239	51
7	Biguiyuan Phoenix	15 707	50
8	Guangzhou Lignan International	14 511	55
9	Ladison	13 782	70
10	Hunan Huatian Hotel Group	13 266	63
11	SGF International Hotels	12 346	37
12	Zhejiang Narada Hospitality Services	12 032	42
13	Guangdong (International) Hotels	12 024	41
14	Plains Hotel, Henan	11 998	62
15	Minshan Hotel	10 132	69
16	Soluxe Hotel Group	9698	53
17	Nanyuan Hotel Group	9566	69
18	Shandong Silver	8585	66
19	Shaanxi Provincial Tourism	7810	46
20	Centuries	7400	16
21	Tianlun Hotels International	7105	28
22	Gloria Plaza	6754	27
23	Shanghai Hengshan	6504	26
24	Oriental Jasper Hotels	5606	18
25	CTS Fujian	5580	29
26	Hangzhou Tourism	5121	31
27	Shenzhen Airlines Hotel	4983	24
28	Fuzhou Westlake	4496	24
29	Sichuan Jinjiang	4298	15
30	Zhejiang Tourism	4041	18
	Total	426 647	2049

Source: Gu *et al.* (2012). © Elsevier

In a European context, the most important chains are Accor, Intercontinental, Best Western and Hilton International, and as Table 10.5 shows, there has also been a considerable growth in the concept of chain hotels within China (also see Insight 10.2 for more detail earlier in the chapter). Table 10.5 shows that the rate of international expansion has internationalized China's hotel industry, creating competition and a strong presence among the major hotel brands. Aside from the internationally recognized brands evident in Table 10.5, specific brands have also been developed for the Chinese market (e.g. Accor's Pullman brand) as the local market has gradually accepted Chinese brands. As a result, Chinese hotel groups have developed, as Table 10.6 shows, with Jin Jiang Hotels now considered to be the thirteenth largest hotel company globally (Gu *et al.* 2012). Yet the expansion of development of hotels as part of a corporate strategy also depends upon the professional and high-quality management of individual properties and, for this reason, attention now focuses on hotel management.

Hotel management

According to Jones and Lockwood (2002: 1) a hotel 'is an operation that provides accommodation and ancillary services to people away from home', and the elements of what a hotel provides can be classified into 'tangible components', such as rooms, and more 'intangible' elements, such as room ambience, which are assessed by visitors as part of their experience of staying at a property. This molecular model of hotel management highlights the central element for hotel management – the human element (i.e. the staff) and the way they interact with guests to create a favourable impression where the intangible and tangible elements come together. However, at a more generic level, hotel management needs to ensure that each accommodation unit can function profitably. It also needs to ensure high levels of customer satisfaction and a quality experience by generating income and profit from customer demand while managing the supply elements (i.e. asset protection and development, employees, service standards and quality and productivity levels). The assets include the buildings, rooms and infrastructure which the customer experiences, and the scope of the areas to manage are shown in Figure 10.4. This illustrates the wide range of skills which a hotel manager must possess in seeking to integrate all elements of the hotel to ensure they run smoothly and work towards a common set of goals. As demand and supply for hotels varies, hotels will also need to utilize technology to manage different situations which may arise, including where supply exceeds demand or where demand exceeds supply, so as to maximize the business and revenue opportunities.

Yet these operational issues also have to be balanced against developments in the area of distribution channels (i.e. e-solutions such as last-minute.com to sell surplus capacity), and in making pricing decisions and capacity decisions on how much to sell and at what price to generate sales and profit. For example, in 2004, the world's largest hotel company, Marriott International, Inc., agreed to sell rooms in over 2000 of its worldwide stock of hotels via Expedia.com and Hotels.com as one additional distribution channel for its products. One part of this strategy is to attempt to improve room occupancy and sales, and to this end such companies employ sophisticated yield management systems, as discussed in Chapter 8.

Different studies on the performance of the worldwide hotel industry exist, mainly undertaken by large global consulting firms with the resources to track and monitor it. One of the most detailed is Deloitte's *HotelBenchmark Survey* (www.hotelbenchmark.com) which surveys 6000 hotels worldwide (excluding the USA). The study has many key features, but for the purpose of analyzing hotel performance, three useful indicators are:

FIGURE 10.4 Functional areas for hotel management

- *occupancy rates* (i.e. how many people stayed in the hotel as a percentage of the number of available rooms, where complete occupancy would be 100 per cent)
- *average room rate (ARR)*, which is the average price charged for a room, taking into account the highest and lowest rates which are then averaged
- *revenue per available room* (Rev Par), being the amount of revenue from each guest which is received after costs of supplying the room have been deducted, as a form of profit.

Deloitte's survey examines the operational performance of hotels in the main capital cities around the world, and highlights:

- the relatively high occupancy rates in Asia Pacific and Europe
- high room rates in Europe, particularly in Paris, London and Madrid, which are rivalled in Asia by Tokyo
- the high Rev Par rates for Tokyo, Amsterdam, London, Madrid, Paris and Rome.

Characteristics of the accommodation sector

All types of accommodation are confronted with some common characteristics – for example *seasonality*, which affects those properties where one market, such as 'summer sun', dominates. In these situations, marketing efforts attempt to fill rooms at off-peak times through short breaks or other incentives (see Chapter 20 for more discussion of seasonality and urban tourism). Many accommodation providers work with their regional tourist board to develop local products such as festivals in the spring and autumn to spread the demand across seasons which may be quieter. Related to seasonality is the issue of *occupancy level*, as discussed above. For large hotels occupancy levels have been assisted with the development of yield management systems which seek to achieve a better fit with the market so that occupancy is spread across the week, month and year to avoid too many peaks and troughs in their business. Location can be of paramount importance in the siting of accommodation units. Ashworth (1989) proposed a model of urban hotel location based on one simple principle: distance decay – the prestigious properties are those located in the central locations with the greatest accessibility to the market and adjacent to convention centres and other large venues. There is a tendency for hotels to locate in urban areas and to seek out the most accessible locations, as railway hotels did in the nineteenth century, next to the source of demand. In some situations, conversion of former office blocks and redundant warehouses (the Palace Hotel in Manchester is located in a listed insurance building) are used as prestigious locations for upmarket hotels. At the same time, gateways such as airports remain high-value locations. Intersections on major routeways (e.g. motorways) are also assuming a significant role for mid-range hotels in the absence of available in-town sites. In rural environments, location is often related to the scenic and aesthetic qualities of the landscape so that visitors can enjoy the rustic image and landscape attraction and, in coastal locations, sea views assume a premium price in the location of accommodation (Alegre *et al.* 2013).

Grading systems, according to Cooper (2005), incorporate classifications and grading of accommodation, and the former relates to the assignment of hotels to a category in relation to its facilities and services. In contrast, grading emphasizes the internal quality elements of the property. The result is that classification and grading schemes are used to establish a standardized approach to service and product range and to communicate with consumers on what is provided at each property. They also enable accommodation providers to market, segment and compete on the basis of their property's distinctive features while setting minimum standards for consumers. In 1999, the UK finally harmonized the tourist board 'crown' scheme with the 'stars' awarded by the two motoring organizations, the RAC and the AA. The result: stars for hotels and diamonds for other serviced accommodation. England does not operate a statutory registration scheme for tourist accommodation; at a major conference organized by the English Tourism Council (now subsumed into VisitBritain) in 1999, some of the arguments given for the introduction of one were: 'the unacceptable level of customer dissatisfaction . . . no formal channel for complaints . . . no mechanism for taking action against persistent offenders . . . [the] enforcement of fire regulations, building controls, environmental health is poorly resourced' and a similar debate has been ongoing in other countries over compulsory registration. Opponents of statutory grading schemes argue that further regulations stifle enterprise and that there is no firm evidence that in countries where they have been implemented standards have been raised. Furthermore, the tourist experience includes visits to theatres, restaurants and shops but these are not subject to grading; despite the latter point, there is little doubt that, for many tourists, their accommodation acts as a 'base' while on holiday and although they may tolerate low standards in some shops the same cannot be applied to where they sleep.

Classifying the accommodation sector

The accommodation sector is a diverse and complex phenomenon which is in a state of constant change and evolution. As a result, it is impossible to come up with a definitive classification that will embrace all forms of accommodation at any one point in time because of the pace of change in this sector, although Figure 10.5 attempts to develop a typology based on the form of journey/visit being undertaken and the purpose of the trip, which highlights

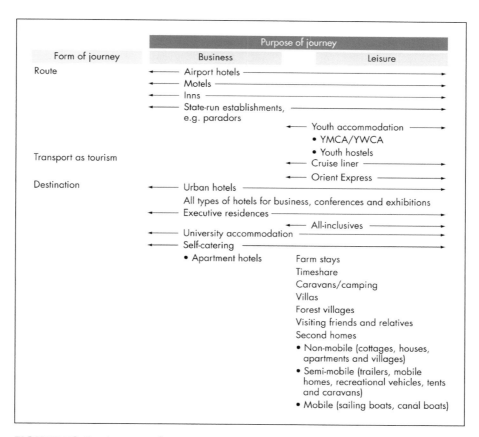

FIGURE 10.5 Accommodation types

Source: Adapted from Hall and Page (1999); Hall and Müller (2004)

the complexity of classifying the sector. However, for the purpose of simplifying the nature of the accommodation sector, the first major distinction one can make is between the serviced and non-serviced sectors. The serviced sector is accommodation with services and facilities provided, which can be included in the charge for the product. In the non-serviced sector, the product is accommodation only.

Serviced accommodation

Hotels

As mentioned already, the hotel is among the most visible and easily identifiable subsectors within the accommodation business (and is referred to as the 'lodging sector' in the USA), employing large numbers of staff. While globally the sector is dominated by small family-owned businesses, the competition with chains and reinvestment costs have forced many out of this sector. Many of the surviving hotels in the small family sector have identified distinct niches although small hotels of less than 50 rooms are considerably more at risk of insolvency. Alongside this operators need to ensure they plan to regularly refurbish properties to remain competitive and to attract consumers with the right facilities, room design and services. The ownership of hotels is a complex area, typically grouped under three forms (based on the discussion earlier of entry mode):

- those hotels owned and operated by hotel companies under their own name
- those which are franchised, which may use a brand (in the USA the Hospitality Franchise Systems company operates many franchises on behalf of brands but owns few properties; it is reputed to be the largest global hotel company, although it does not have an identifiable physical presence)
- management of the hotel on behalf of an owner – such as Hilton and Marriott.

What has characterized hotels in the last 20 years is the low rates of return on investment, with many city centre hotels purchased more for their long-term asset value than for profitability, as occupancy levels have posed problems in achieving profit thresholds. However, the last decade has seen a greater pressure on hotel chains to meet profit thresholds given their investors' demands for greater returns.

Recent developments in the hotel sector include the growth of health resorts (which is one of the fastest-growing sectors of the business in Europe, particularly the luxury end of the market with tariffs of £1000 a night) and the introduction of long-stay five-star hotels such as Marriott Executive Residences, including their recently opened property in Budapest, and TownePlace Suites which has properties in different American states.

According to Jones (2002), the different sources of demand for accommodation include:

- government officials
- business travellers
- leisure travellers
- tour groups
- conference participants
- other users

from both domestic and international markets. Some hotels specialize in certain markets, such as city centre business and conference hotels with premium prices which use weekend capacity for short-break leisure travellers at significant reductions on mid-week rates. Similarly, airport hotels are a growth market in many countries, with the rise in air travel, and the market for accommodating flight crews and transiting passengers as well as inbound and outbound travellers. Periods which sometimes prove problematic for airport hotels are weekends and holiday periods such as Easter and Christmas, and some have diversified by catering for weddings.

The rise of the hotel chains, the development of newer, more innovative forms of hotel accommodation and the decline of the traditional seaside resorts in many western European locations have seen a shift towards urban and rural properties and a focus on areas of potential and growth at a global scale that are apparent; in some cases, niche and novelty forms of accommodation are a means to create new market opportunities, as Figure 10.6 shows. In many respects, the small family-owned hotel is in decline and is being superseded by the globalization of the high-yield locations in cities and resorts. The small family-run sector is left with the less profitable and lifestyle properties with much smaller profit margins. One notable exception is the growth of smaller prestigious boutique hotels. This is evident in the evolution of new luxury health resorts and hotels, which are moving the hotel sector into new market segments.

Traditional family-run businesses relying upon domestic tourists are facing increased competition in many countries from the larger hotels and the appeal of cheap package holidays and new products (e.g. cruises and motoring holidays).

One example of a response to the development of chain hotels has been the formation of independent groupings, and a number of consortia have developed in recent decades in order to compete with the power of the hotel chains; independent hotels group together to obtain the benefits of national and international marketing and bulk-purchasing discounts. A range of other developments, including the rise of the resort offering a more diverse range of accommodation and services such as the mega

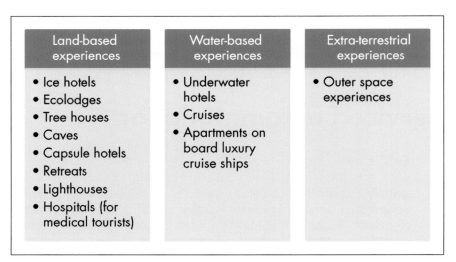

FIGURE 10.6 Niche and novelty forms of tourist accommodation
Source: developed from Timothy and Teye (2009)

resort hotel in Las Vegas. These resorts indicate that the accommodation sector cannot easily be separated from the tourism sector since it is a key element of the tourism economy and is linked to the image and concept of the destination, although in some cases it can create an enclave where the tourist stays within the resort and has little interaction with the area they are staying in.

The resort and accommodation

The term 'resort' is here taken to mean the provision of accommodation and substantial other services at one location. Poon (1998: 62) defines all-inclusive resorts as those 'which include virtually everything in the prepaid price – from airport transfers, baggage handling, government taxes, rooms, all meals, snacks, drinks and cigarettes to the use of all facilities, equipment and certified instructors . . . the result is that the use of cash is eliminated'. The all-inclusive concept originates from holiday camps and villages such as Butlin's in Britain and the French-based Club Méditerranée (Club Med). Club Med, which developed in the 1950s, now dominates the league table of all-inclusive chains, and is the market leader in France for French holidays, with 25 000 rooms and 2 million customers in 2004. Its global operations cover France, Mediterranean Europe, Asia, the Caribbean, Africa, the South Pacific and the USA.

Budget accommodation

At the low-cost end of the serviced market are forms of budget accommodation, as discussed earlier. Some forms have developed as a result of transport improvements and the innovation by entrepreneurs and these include motels, budget hotels (e.g. the easy.com brand) and some guest houses. Branding assists the process of marketing as it informs the customer that a Travelodge at one end of the country is likely to offer the same facilities 300 miles away; there are over 190 of these lodges in the UK, all offering en-suite rooms with satellite television and easy check-in/out. What is apparent in the budget hotel sector is its rapid response to consumer demand since the 1980s, as the demand for low-cost accommodation shifted from bed and breakfasts and small family-owned hotels to new low-cost, high-quality room-only priced units. This has also meant greater competition at the one- or two-star accommodation level and a rise in business travel, which can account for up to 50 per cent of budget hotel business in the UK. This has been because budget hotels offer many of the facilities of higher-grade hotels (en-suite facilities, direct dial telephones, televisions) and are often on sites easily accessed by car. In 2013, Whitbread announced a new budget 'Hub' brand, with prices 25 per cent cheaper at the 40 city-centre properties it planned to develop by 2018 to run in parallel with the Premier Inn brand in the UK.

The Days Inn concept of 'budget-luxury' is another example of market segmentation. As a result of travelling in New England, Cecil B. Day, the founder of Days Inns, realized that there was a gap in accommodation for the typical American family travelling on a limited budget. Day opened his first motel, which combined budget and luxury features, in Tybee Island, Georgia, in April 1970 on the premise of providing quality lodging at a fair and reasonable price. Since then, Days Inn has grown into one of the largest franchised lodging systems in the world, opening its 1900th hotel in November 1999. There are now Days Inns in Canada, China, Colombia, the Czech Republic, Hungary, India, Mexico, Philippines, South Africa, the UK and Uruguay in addition to the USA, and the chain is now owned by Cendant Corporation. At a lower cost, the Youth Men's Christian Association (YMCA), Youth Women's Christian Association (YWCA) and Youth Hostels Association (YHA) (http://www.yha.org.uk) are notable. The market has also grown as entrepreneurs have set up backpackers' establishments to cater for the global growth in dormitory-style accommodation for backpackers in youth and mature markets. The rise of more luxurious backpacker establishments akin to budget hotels also highlights one of the trends in this growing market. Yet one of the most established forms of budget accommodation is the YHA.

The non-serviced accommodation sector

In contrast to the serviced sector the growth of self-catering accommodation has been a major change for the postwar accommodation industry in many countries and much of this growth has been at the expense of the traditional guest house and small family-run hotel sector. Some self-catering complexes have provided recreational and entertainment facilities such as Center Parcs (http://www.centerparcs.co.uk), a company that has sites in Germany, Belgium, France and the Netherlands, from where it first developed. When it took over the Oasis holiday village, it acquired 750 villas at the Penrith location on the edge of the English Lake District. The all-inclusive nature of this complex means that there is no reason to leave the site (the Oasis Penrith location covers 400 acres) and, given that the villas are let on a self-catering basis, the clientele are encouraged to buy from the on-site supermarket if they do not patronize the restaurants. What is notable about Center Parcs is that occupancy rates are around 90 per cent and repeat visits are running at 60 per cent, which is a significant achievement for this innovative form of accommodation. In the early years of operation, the Rural Development Commission in the UK concluded that Center Parcs Sherwood Forest and Elveden Forest villages had an economic impact of £4 million on the local economy, with visitors also spending £2 million locally. Through the multiplier effect (see Chapter 16 for an explanation of how this works) Center Parcs' impact on the local area of each village is £14 million based on initial estimates. This highlights the impact which the accommodation sector can have on the local economy.

Apartments form a central component of the accommodation provided in self-catering units, and in the Mediterranean, the USA and Australasia this market has been a popular addition to both coastal and urban locations. This sector also includes developments such as gîtes (French holiday cottages) and second homes. In some cases self-catering accommodation is also being packaged in the mass markets by specialist operators, while new innovations (e.g. house swaps) have also added additional capacity for holiday accommodation to compete with the serviced sector following the 1980s boom in global timeshare.

Timeshare and holiday rental intermediaries

Holiday rental intermediaries link owners and clients of holiday properties together, and are part of the global growth in the market for a new type of non-serviced accommodation. The consumer purchases a week, or more, on a lease from a property developer who provides the maintenance and management contract for the holiday product. These are called condominiums and timeshares. These companies are beginning to compete with hotels, as condominiums and timeshares continue to become more fashionable, especially for families with young children. The rise of the low-cost airlines has made this accommodation-only option more accessible to holidaymakers. The market is experiencing growth as niche operators enter, such as Internet-based companies (e.g. Vacation Rentals by Owner and hotelrentals.com) (Insight 10.3). Further forms of accommodation which are notable are university campus accommodation (see Connell 2000), camping and caravan sites, while specialist operators such as Eurocamp have developed sited tents and caravans for the budget-conscious family and small groups of travellers.

INSIGHT 10.3 Rethinking tourism accommodation: The multi-ownership model

Warnken and Guilding (2009) reviewed the development of multi-ownership forms of tourism accommodation (MOTA) where ownership is divided into smaller ownership units. It is somewhat different to the traditional model of tourism accommodation funding by private-sector investors through models such as joint-stock companies (i.e. ownership by shares), where the investment motive may also be combined with the owner's desire to also spend their leisure time in such an acquisition. The early forms of second-home ownership characterized the desire to own a residence away from the normal home environment, which can be dated back to the most affluent in history seeking non-urban locations in which to spend their leisure time. What Warnken and Guilding (2009) show is that three types of MOTA can be discerned:

- *Contractual Timeshare*, including traditional and new timeshare models in Europe and the North American model of one- to two-week ownership. Other developments such as vacation and destination clubs have entered this market (i.e. typically for a set period of time, a week a year for up to 50 years).

- *Deeded Title Timeshare*, which overlaps with some forms of North American timeshare where access has expanded from two weeks up to several months. Other models of deeded timeshare include private residency clubs and fractional timeshare of 3 to 14 weeks.

- *Undivided Title Interests*, which are not able to provide uninterrupted periods of accommodation usage by unit owners. In this category are holiday and second-home apartments, serviced apartments, aparthotels and condotels.

As Warnken and Guilding (2009) show, this can pose serious problems for destinations, particularly in terms of planning, as MOTA development can rapidly increase the rate of urbanization in the absence of planning restrictions. It can also lead to a shifting of hotel capacity to new uses, reducing the availability of serviced accommodation. This not only shows how the usage of such MOTA capacity may change the visitor profile but also challenges our conventional categorization and classification of tourism accommodation from the tourists' perspective, in that MOTA stock is potentially used as residential living units by retirees. This may also lead to inflated land prices which can then lead to prospective hotel developers having to compete for land at higher prices, impacting upon the profitability of the operation or reducing the prospective return on investment. As Warnken and Guilding (2009) observe, this may also change the destination landscape as developers lobby planners to relax urban density and height restrictions on MOTA developments.

Further reading

Warnken, J and Guilding, C (2009) 'Multi-ownership of tourism accommodation complexes: A critique of types, relative merits and challenges arising', *Tourism Management* 30 (4): 704–714.

Caravanning and camping

In Europe one of the leading caravanning organizations, the Caravan Club, points to 315 000 touring caravans in use. The volume of members has seen a growth from 50 000 in 1966 to 100 000 in 1972 with the greatest rise occurring 1972–1990, when membership exceeded 250 000. The organization offers over 5 million pitch nights each year on 200 sites and via a further 2700 certified sites in private ownership on farms and rural sites. It accounts for 17 per cent of UK holiday spending and is worth £2 billion a year in the UK, employing 90 000 people as a result of the UK's 18 million bed nights spent in caravans. The average caravanner spend is relatively low in the UK at £25 a night, but this generates £210 million for the local economies in which caravans are pitched. However, there is an ongoing debate on the aesthetic impact of mobile and static caravans on the rural and coastal environment, given that many campsites were constructed prior to planning legislation becoming formalized in many countries, and remains a contentious issue in many national parks, where they are often viewed as a blight on the landscape. In Europe, the European Camping Federation assessed the impact of caravanning as €14.4 billion, based on 400 million overnight stays by tourist campers. Tourist travel by touring caravan is dominated by French, German, Dutch and UK tourists while motor home use is greatest among French, German and Italian tourists.

One of the least-known and understood sectors, which is not strictly non-serviced, is the visiting relatives (VFR) category. In some cities, such as Auckland in New Zealand, up to 50 per cent of the inbound UK visiting relatives market stay in the home of a relative or acquaintance. While this makes a major contribution to the local tourism economy, it is poorly understood in relation to domestic tourism. Similarly, the growth of global family networks in an age of increasing travel among certain ethnic groups such as the Chinese may also create a market for visiting relatives who do not use serviced accommodation or non-serviced accommodation, but stay with a network of family and friends in different countries. Yet, at some point during a visit, tourists will make use of non-accommodation hospitality services.

Non-accommodation hospitality services

The hospitality services which are often associated with the accommodation sector are not always provided by this sector. In many locations, these services are also provided outside accommodation establishments and comprise restaurants, fast-food outlets, cafeterias and public houses, bars, clubs and canteens. This sector has undergone massive change in the UK, reflected in employment change in hotel and catering. One of the greatest changes has occurred in the fast-food sector, which has grown nationally in the UK, while other sectors have expanded through the use of part-time employment. The dominance of transnational corporations such as McDonald's, KFC and Burger King have resulted in the market being dominated by a limited number of brands. For the tourist, this has meant that the fast-food sector has competed directly with other forms of food retailing in city and small-town locations and is a good illustration of the theme of globalization.

'Restaurant' is a wide-ranging term used to incorporate establishments serving food, from full-service gastronomy through to fast-food establishments. Shifting lifestyle trends affecting the way people eat in their leisure time have impacted upon the sector. In the UK, eating out may be related to greater disposable income, following trends in North America. The boom in fast-food consumption, however, has been challenged by concerns over healthy eating, leading many fast-food chains to launch healthy options, most notably McDonald's with its deli range, and a greater tailoring to consumers' needs. However, this eating-out trend saw major contraction of consumer spending during the credit crunch.

The restaurant sector is a highly volatile sector as it relies on a mix of tourism and leisure trade, with high rates of business failure and ownership change. Among key drivers of change in this sector of leisure consumption are service, quality and branding. In the coffee consumption expansion in many cities across the world, chains such as Starbucks and Costa have increased competition, and coffee as a takeaway and casual drink has become a key consumption experience for visitors and non-visitors alike, leading to comments that we now live in a cappuccino society where the café is a central element of socializing and enjoying hospitality. While the eating-out expansion in many countries has seen massive growth, in part fuelled by tourism and leisure spending, the competition and involvement of chains have also impacted upon this sector. Competition remains intense as the restaurant sector takes a major part of the tourist spend. One measure of the importance of the dynamic nature of this sector is the growth of one chain in the UK: J.D. Wetherspoons.

In certain destinations, for example the tourist-historic city, those establishments offering food and possibly other entertainment tend to cluster. This causes major difficulties with quantifying the impact of both the accommodation and more complex and diverse hospitality sectors in terms of the users. This is demonstrated most clearly in many Dutch cities where entertainment facilities (e.g. sex shops and brothels) are located in a distinct area, with other food and hospitality services developing nearby given the nature of the attraction and visitor appeal of these icons of the built environment. Yet hospitality and the consumption of food and drink may also have wider uses in tourism, since regional specialization (e.g. the use of local seafood) (Images 10.4 and 10.5), marketing and promotion may lead to themed forms of tourism based on these experiences, which can be integrated with local accommodation providers to develop new forms of tourism.

IMAGE 10.4 Advertising local produce to create unique meal experiences linked to a destination's image of seafood is a powerful tool for hospitality businesses

IMAGE 10.5 The local food produce advertised also has to be delivered and presented in such a way as to ensure the visitor experience is as expected

Contemporary issues in hospitality management

Managing accommodation and hospitality premises poses many complex issues for those in a managerial role. In Western Europe, the impact of government and transnational bodies like the EU has generated a wide range of legislation with which managers need to be conversant. As Table 10.7 illustrates, in the accommodation sector the legislation covers a wide range of concerns, many of which are related to providing a safe experience and environment for guests and employees. However, for many smaller businesses this has led to criticisms of unnecessary red tape which increases compliance costs; an example of such a piece of legislation is the 2002 Disability Act in the UK, enacted to make public places such as hotels accessible to the less able (now superseded by the 2010 Equality Act, which brought together discrimination and disability legislation in a much more holistic manner, as discussed in Chapter 4). In extreme cases, some businesses cease operating when compliance costs cannot be financed or will push the business into a loss, although it does offer new opportunities to reach new markets (see Ozturk 2008).

TABLE 10.7 Principal legislation issues for accommodation providers

- Planning permission and building regulations
- Fire safety (including fire certificates)
- Signage
- Business rates for the premises
- Utility supplies (water, gas and electricity)
- Health and safety
  - for guests, the public and employees
  - insurance cover
  - workplace-based safety
  - food safety (hygiene, handling and labelling)
  - liquor licensing

- The business of tourists/visitors as consumers
  - pricing and charging
  - accepting guests (i.e. disabled access)
  - cancellations
  - recording guests
- Other areas of regulation as an employer
  - national minimum wage
  - paternity and maternity leave
  - employee rights
  - taxation

Source: Adapted from VisitBritain (2004)

Attracting and retaining staff also remains a problem area for the hospitality sector, as Chapter 11 will show later. Rates of high staff turnover in many European countries have led some hotel managers to recruit economic migrants from the former Eastern Europe to fill gaps in the hospitality workforce. To address these labour shortages in recruiting skilled workers, resulting from poor wage rates compared to other industries, employers have de-skilled some vital areas of hospitality work. A response to this is the use of contract caterers (Haywood and Wilson 2003), who provide systems solutions with prepacked chilled prepared food which does not need skilled food preparation. Among the successful companies operating in this sector are The Compass Group plc, now one of the world's largest food service companies, with revenue in excess of £10 billion; the group also owns brands such as Burger King and many catering franchises, employing 360 000 people in 64 countries. Many hotels now rely upon just-in-time delivery from contract caterers, such as Brake Brothers in the UK. Globally, this market is estimated to be worth in excess of US$290 billion.

Management skills have also assumed a growing importance now larger hotel chains seek increased profits for shareholders. As Riley (2003) observes, in the hotel sector, two sources of uncertainty characterize hospitality: demand and the consumer's subjective evaluation of products and services. The increasing role of technology has meant that hospitality managers are needing to use e-solutions for securing customers, in-house management (especially yield management) and procuring supplies via supply chains to achieve economies of scale.

Mergers and acquisitions and corporate strategy in hospitality and changing operational conditions have led many international firms to choose a strategy of either concentration or of obtaining scale economies by offering a uniform product with preferred management approaches including strategic alliances, franchising, management contracts, joint ventures and acquisitions, as discussed in Chapter 5. This has meant change is the only constant in the sector. The need also to understand the lifecycle of a product, the effect of competitors, and technology has become critical for managers. Innovative marketing by new entrants may remove the existing competitive advantage of a product, particularly where consumer sales and promotion expenditure are targeted at encouraging brand switching. Operating in a global marketplace, expanded by the impact of technology and the bypassing of existing intermediaries, has seen e-mediaries and dedicated accommodation sites gain ground. As a result, accommodation businesses will need to harness new marketing techniques such as relationship marketing (see Chapter 14) and to embrace new approaches such as one-to-one marketing, using information and communication technologies (ICTs) to individualize the interaction (i.e. via email). They will also need to make a greater effort to retain customers, since it is cheaper to retain an existing customer than to recruit a new one. Hotels in particular are facing a growing pressure to deliver customer value, to meet expectations and to have quality as an all-embracing feature throughout all levels of their organization. The challenge for the hotel sector of online hotel review sites such as TripAdvisor (see Chapter 6) led HOTREC to argue that the sector needs to embrace these new ways of interacting with consumers, but with clear guidelines in place to protect the sector from manipulation and unfair evaluations. There is also growing research (e.g. Heide *et al.* 2007) which suggests that the design and management of aesthetic features in hotels and their ambience can have a definite impact upon consumer satisfaction. Yet there is a recognition among researchers that agreeing to a method of assessing quality and the effectiveness of rating systems, such as Scotland's Quality Assurance scheme (Briggs *et al.* 2007) which focuses on tangible aspects, often neglects the more intangible aspects rated by consumers such as ambience.

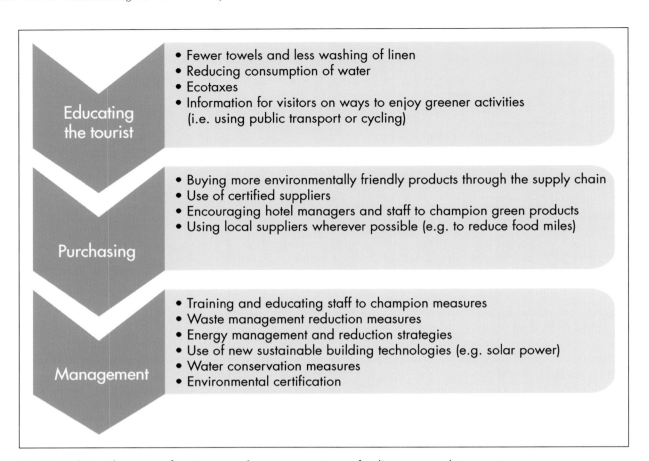

FIGURE 10.7 The scope of environmental management issues for the accommodation sector

A particularly important and emerging area for the hospitality sector, especially hotels, is environmental management, which is the way in which organizations deal with their impact and effect on the environment as a business (including meeting the needs of their visitors). This has been a significant area of interest for the hospitality sector because around 21 per cent of all CO_2 emissions in tourism are from the accommodation sector. To address the effects of such emissions, environmental research on hotels has shown that there are three main areas where the organization may help to address their footprint on the environment (Figure 10.7): in terms of *educating visitors* to reduce their consumption of resources such as water, directly, and indirectly through changing their linen and towels less frequently); in *purchasing*; and through a *commitment by management* to drive forward these agendas. To help with such agendas, various green quality assurance schemes such as the Green Tourism Business Scheme in the UK have voluntary accreditation to help drive up the quality of commitment of businesses to such environmental management, which often needs a stimulus in the form of showing businesses how much they can save financially by adopting more green measures. As Spenceley (2019) found in Africa, only a very small proportion of hotels have engaged in such schemes. Research on one of the most contentious issues for hotels in locations with highly seasonal tourist visitation (e.g. the Balearic Islands) where rainfall and water availability is in short supply in the summer, highlights the problems facing hoteliers. Many tourists consume far more water daily than local people, where luxury hotels may use 500 to 800 litres a day and tourists may consume a year's water supply in one month in extreme cases where there are finite sources of water. This is against average tourist consumption of water of 440 litres a day, which may be double the use by local people. Understanding how to manage and control such excessive water use is crucial as it may have even more disastrous effects for countries in the developing world, where water used for tourism may be at the expense of local people or agriculture. This raises major problems in the area known as water equity (see tourismconcern.org.uk). Areas where hotels need to focus their efforts are around the key consumptive drivers of water use by tourists at resorts and hotels as shown in Figure 10.8. Above all, as studies such as Gössling *et al.* (2012) show, tackling water usage requires a concerted public sector strategy as well as action by individual hotels

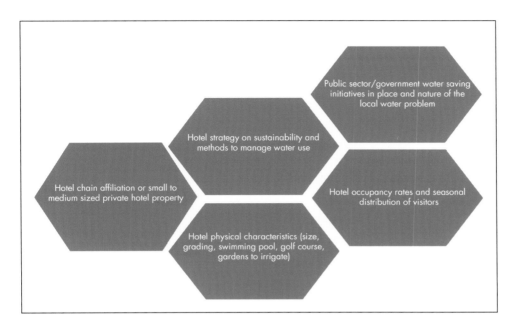

Public sector/government water saving initiatives in place and nature of the local water problem

Hotel strategy on sustainability and methods to manage water use

Hotel chain affiliation or small to medium sized private hotel property

Hotel occupancy rates and seasonal distribution of visitors

Hotel physical characteristics (size, grading, swimming pool, golf course, gardens to irrigate)

FIGURE 10.8 Variables affecting the management of water consumption at hotels

10

and also educating tourists. The case for engaging in sustainability schemes, as Kularatne *et al.* (2019) demonstrated in Sri Lanka, was that it enhanced hotel efficiency and performance, especially in water use and waste management. But to engage more businesses in such behaviours, Martinez-Martinez *et al.* (2019: 381) argue, businesses need 'knowledge agents [who] are those individuals who can provide information and knowledge that enables the firm to deal with environmental issues effectively' within their organizations to champion the idea.

Conclusion

Within the accommodation and hospitality services sector, the global brand has emerged as one of the most significant developments and is an ongoing trend alongside the rapid growth of social media and online hotel booking, especially with the rise of mobile technology like smartphones (Tao *et al.* 2018; Wu *et al.* 2018). The process of globalization and the increasing domination of brands is evident from the hotel sector to restaurants and even cafés, where it serves as a reassurance of quality. The consequence for the built environment and the tourist experience, as critics would argue, is the growing McDonaldization of the accommodation and hospitality services sector where the same style of experience is available globally to a set standard. Yet one trend running contrary to this is the development in local and regional cuisine and hospitality as reflected in wine and food festivals and the theming of tourism products to emphasize local and regional distinctiveness.

The market for accommodation is very diverse with the product and price range being developed for an increasingly sophisticated tourist market. This is evident in the rise of the Internet as a search tool for consumers to identify a wider range of products to consider in booking accommodation and travel services. Added to this is the rise of the environmental lobby, reflected in consumer demands for a greater attention to environmental sensitivity. Hotels are now achieving cost savings as a result, by seizing on the environmental advantages of less laundering, savings in water consumption and reduction in the use of consumables. Thus, the accommodation sector cannot be separated from trends in the wider tourism sector and in some cases this sector is leading the way forward in environmental management, where such initiatives are developed and implemented. The accommodation sector is also a key element of the tourist's experience of a destination and is often sold as part of a product; therefore quality standards and tourists' satisfaction levels with their holiday experiences are intrinsically linked to the accommodation sector. The consumer is consuming an experience where tourism, hospitality and accommodation are integrated. Yet the constant theme in this sector is the quality of the staff who interface with visitors, and for this reason the next chapter examines human resource issues in tourism.

Discussion questions

1 What image does the hotel sector have within the tourism and hospitality industries?

2 Discuss the problem of staff turnover in the hospitality industry.

3 How has the development of self-catering accommodation villages such as Center Parcs impacted upon the serviced sector in European coastal resorts?

4 The rise of budget accommodation in the serviced sector is now driven by the demand for quality at a lower cost. How far does this result from wider developments in the tourism industry?

References

Alegre, J. Cladera, M. and Sard, M. (2013) 'Tourist areas: Examining the effects of location attributes on tour operator package prices', *Tourism Management*, 38: 131–141.

Altinay, L., Brookes, M. and Aktas, G. (2013) 'Selecting franchise partners: Tourism franchise approaches, processes and criteria', *Tourism Management*, 37: 175–185.

Ashworth, G.J. (1989) 'Urban tourism: An imbalance in attention', in C.P. Cooper (ed.) *Progress in Tourism, Recreation and Hospitality Management Volume 1*. London: Belhaven.

Bie, Y., Wang, J. and Wang, J. (2018) 'Airbnb in China: The impact of sharing economy on Chinese tourism', *C3 - Advances in Intelligent Systems and Computing*, 594: 11–19.

Briggs, S., Sutherland, J. and Drummond, S. (2007) 'Are hotels serving quality? An exploratory study of service quality in the Scottish hotel sector', *Tourism Management*, 28 (4): 1006–1019.

BHA (British Hospitality Association) (2011) *Hospitality Driving Local Economies*. London: BHA.

Connell, J. (2000) 'The role of tourism in the socially responsible university', *Current Issues in Tourism*, 3 (1): 1–19.

Connell, J., Page, S.J., Sheriff, I. and Hibbert, J. (2017) 'Business engagement in a civil society: Transitioning towards a dementia-friendly visitor economy', *Tourism Management*, 61: 110–128.

Cooper, C., Fletcher, J., Fyall, A., Gilbert, D. and Wanhill, S. (2005) *Tourism: Principles and Practice*, 3rd edition. Harlow: Pearson Education.

Gössling, S., Peeters, P., Hall, C.M., Ceron, J., Dubois, G., Lehmann, L. and Scott, D. (2012) 'Tourism and water use: Supply, demand and security: An international review', *Tourism Management*, 33 (1): 1–15.

Gu, H., Ryan, C. and Yu, L. (2012) 'The changing structure of the Chinese hotel industry: 1980–2012', *Tourism Management Perspectives*, 2 (1).

Hall, C.M. and Müller, D. (2004) 'Introduction: Second homes, curse or blessing? Revisited', in C.M. Hall and D. Müller (eds.) *Tourism, Mobility and Second Homes*. Clevedon: Channel View.

Hall, C.M. and Page, S.J. (1999) *The Geography of Tourism and Recreation: Environment, Place and Space*, 2nd edition. London: Routledge.

Haywood, K. and Wilson, G. (2003) 'Contract food service', in B. Brotherton (ed.) *The International Hospitality Industry: Structure, Characteristics and Issues*. Oxford: Butterworth-Heinemann.

Heide, M., Laerdal, K. and Grønhang, K. (2007) 'The design and management of ambience – implications for hotel architecture and service', *Tourism Management*, 28 (5): 1315–1325.

Jones, P. (ed.) (2002) *Introduction to Hospitality Operations: An Indispensable Guide to the Industry*, 2nd edition. London: Continuum.

Jones, P. and Lockwood, A. (eds.) (2002) *The Management of Hotel Operations: An Innovative Approach to the Study of Hotel Management*. London: Continuum.

Kularatne, T., Wilson, C., Månsson, J., Hoang, V. and Lee, B. (2019) 'Do environmentally sustainable practices make hotels more efficient? A study of major hotels in Sri Lanka', *Tourism Management*, 71, 213–225.

Lashley, C. (2000) 'Towards a theoretical understanding', in C. Lashley and A. Morrison (eds.) *In Search of Hospitality: Theoretical Perspectives and Debates*. Oxford: Butterworth-Heinemann.

Littlejohn, D. (2003) 'Hotels', in B. Brotherton (ed.) *The International Hospitality Industry: Structure, Characteristics and Issues*. Oxford: Butterworth-Heinemann.

Mac Con Iomaire, M. (2013) 'Public dining in Dublin: The history and evaluation of gastronomy and commercial dining 1700–1900', *International Journal of Contemporary Hospitality Management*, 25 (2): 227–246.

Martinez-Martinez, A., Cegarra-Navarro, J., Garcia-Perez, A. and Wensley, A. (2019) 'Knowledge agents as drivers of environmental sustainability and business performance in the hospitality sector', *Tourism Management*, 70: 381–389.

Medlik, R. and Ingram, S. (2000) *The Business of Hotels*, 4th edition. Oxford: Butterworth-Heinemann.

Nieto, J., Hernández-Maestro, R.M. and Muñoz-Gallego, P.A. (2014) 'Marketing decisions, customer reviews, and business performance: The use of the Toprural website by Spanish rural lodging establishments', *Tourism Management*, 45: 115–123.

Ozturk, Y., Yayli, A. and Yesiltas, M. (2008) 'Is the Turkish tourism industry ready for a disabled customer's market?' *Tourism Management*, 29 (2): 382–389.

Page, S.J. (2003) *Tourism Management: Managing for Change.* Oxford: Butterworth-Heinemann.

Page, S.J. (2019) *Tourism Management*, 6th edition. Abingdon: Taylor and Francis.

Page, S.J., Bentley, T., Teo, S. and Ladkin, A. (2018) 'The dark side of high performance human resource practices in the visitor economy', *International Journal of Hospitality Management*, 74: 122–129.

Poon, A. (1998) 'All-inclusive resorts', *Travel and Tourism Analyst*, 6: 62–77.

Ren, L., Qiu, H., Ma, C. and Lin, P. (2018) 'Investigating accommodation experience in budget hotels', *International Journal of Contemporary Hospitality Management*, 30(7): 2662–2667.

Ren, L., Qiu, H., Wang, P. and Lin, P. (2016) 'Exploring customer experience with budget hotels: Dimensionality and satisfaction', *International Journal of Hospitality Management*, 52: 13–23.

Riley, M. (2003) 'Operational dilemmas', in B. Brotherton (ed.) *The International Hospitality Industry: Structure, Characteristics and Issues.* Oxford: Butterworth-Heinemann.

Spenceley, A. (2019) 'Sustainable tourism certification in the African hotel sector', *Tourism Review*, 74 (2): 186–200.

Tao, M., Nawaz, M. Nawaz, S., Butt, A. and Ahmad, H. (2018) 'Users' acceptance of innovative mobile hotel booking trends: UK vs. PRC', *Information Technology and Tourism*, 20 (1–4): 9–36.

Timothy, D. and Teye, V. (2009) *Tourism and the Lodging Sector.* Oxford: Elsevier.

Tourism Research Australia (2015) 'Home'. Tourism Research Australia (website). www.tra.gov.au.

VisitBritain (2004) *The Pink Booklet: A Practical Guide to Legislation for Accommodation Providers.* London: VisitBritain.

Walton, J. (2000) 'The hospitality trades: A social history', in C. Lashley and A. Morrison (eds.) *In Search of Hospitality: Theoretical Perspectives and Debates.* Oxford: Butterworth-Heinemann.

Warnken, J., Russell, R. and Faulkner, B. (2003) 'Condominium developments in maturing destinations: Potentials and problems of long-term sustainability', *Tourism Management*, 24 (2): 155–168.

Warnken, J. and Guilding, C. (2009) 'Multi-ownership of tourism accommodation complexes: A critique of types, relative merits, and challenges arising', *Tourism Management*, 30 (5): 704–714.

Wu, J., Law, R. and Liu, J. (2018) 'Co-creating value with customers: A study of mobile hotel bookings in China', *International Journal of Contemporary Hospitality Management*, 30 (4): 2056–2074.

Further reading

Books

KPMG (2004) *Global Hotel Distribution Survey.* London: KPMG.

Wood, R. (2015) *Hospitality Management.* London: Sage.

Wood, R. (ed.) (2017) *Hotel Accommodation Management.* London: Routledge.

Journal articles

Bevan, M. and Rhodes, D. (2005) *The Impact of Second and Holiday Homes in Rural Scotland.* Edinburgh: Communities Scotland.

Grimmer, L., Vorobjovas-Pinta, O. and Massey, M. (2019) 'Regulating, then deregulating Airbnb: The unique case of Tasmania (Australia)', *Annals of Tourism Research*, 75: 304–307.

Hajibaba, H., Boztuğ, Y. and Dolnicar, S. (2016) 'Preventing tourists from canceling in times of crises', *Annals of Tourism Research*, 60: 48–62.

Randle, M. and Dolnicar, S. (2019) 'Enabling people with impairments to use Airbnb', *Annals of Tourism Research*, 76: 278–289.

10

Part 3

Managing tourist operations and communicating with the visitor

The major challenge for the tourism sector is the maximization of demand to meet its supply. This management challenge is one which concerns tourism managers globally and dominates both strategic long-term goals and day-to-day tourism operations where the tourism sector seeks to fill demand and meet the customer's needs through a range of mechanisms.

Tourism is a people business and so having the right kinds of people doing the right kinds of jobs to delight the tourist must be central to the management of successful tourism enterprises. This is discussed in Chapter 11 in relation to the global issues of human resource management which affect the tourism industry. Surprisingly, finance is largely neglected in many studies of tourism despite its key role in understanding how businesses operate and the financial management required for them to remain profitable and able to develop. Therefore, the finance chapter on the Companion Website introduces some of the broad concepts and principles which tourism managers need to understand; while Chapter 12 examines the vital area of tourism and entrepreneurship and the characteristics and activities of key individuals who have had a major impact on a specific sector of the tourism industry. The chapter highlights the influence of key individuals who are responsible, along with companies they own and operate, for the provision of tourism services and experiences.

In Chapter 13 the emphasis is on the role which the public sector plays at all geographical scales, from the international level right down to the role of the local authority, in helping to manage tourism as well as promoting, facilitating and pump-priming tourism in some cases. Chapter 14 introduces many of the key marketing concepts used by businesses to develop a customer-focused organization, through a marketing orientation. One context in which this occurs in a highly visible manner is the destination. Therefore, Chapter 15 discusses the concept of destination marketing and its role in promoting places for tourism. Critical issues and concepts such as the marketing mix, communicating with the tourist and the role of advertising in tourism are discussed.

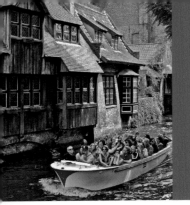

Human resource management in tourism

Learning outcomes

After reading this chapter and answering the questions, you should be able to:

- understand the people dimension in tourism as a fundamental element in the success of tourism enterprises

- assess the scope of the human resource manager's job in tourism

- consider how agencies are involved in human resource management issues in tourism

- examine how future changes in work patterns will affect human resource issues in tourism

- assess the role of human resource issues in small tourism businesses

- understand how empowerment impacts upon the success of human resource issues in tourism organizations.

Overview

Human resource management issues are vital in the successful operation, development and long-term sustainability of tourism organizations. These issues are global in nature, although they may also have local ramifications, but the indisputable feature of tourism is its reliance on people as the vital ingredient in making an experience a success or failure. Even where experiences may be affected by negative events, empowered staff with initiative and a grasp of how to make a difference can often rescue a negative tourism experience. At the same time, many countries are reporting problems in recruiting and retaining staff, and many new initiatives and developments are occurring globally to try to address some of these issues.

Introduction

Tourism is a people industry: tourists are people, customers and clients, and their activities are subject to the normal vagaries of human behaviour (i.e. decision-making about what to buy and consume) which are both predictable and unpredictable depending on the situation and context. As Fáilte Ireland (2005: 8) suggests:

The story of successful tourism enterprises is one that is largely about people – how they are recruited, how they are managed, how they are trained and educated, how they are valued and rewarded, and how they are supported through a process of continuous learning and career development.

The tourism experience or product is entirely dependent upon people for its delivery – or, more simply put, it is dependent upon the human factor in a service sector such as tourism, which is characterized by high levels of human involvement in the development and delivery of services or vacation experiences. Watson, D'Annunzio-Green and Maxwell (2004: 1) acknowledge that delivering hospitality and tourism products and services across international frontiers to discerning customers in highly competitive and dynamic market conditions presents a range of organizational challenges. **Human resource management (HRM)** presents a valuable tool for meeting many of these challenges and adding value in organizations and it frequently involves contact with people from different backgrounds, locations and cultures. Therefore, tourism can be conceptualized as a client purchasing 'the skills, service and commitment of a range of human contributors to the experience that they are about to embark upon' (Baum 1993: 4) and, as Baum and Kokkranikel (2005: 86) argue, 'The human resource dimension is one of the most important elements of any industry sector, none more so than for the tourism experience to be successful; managers within the tourism industry need to ensure that the tourism product or experience is "mediated" to the customer' which by its very nature means a wide range of human resource issues emerge.

As Baum and Kokkranikel (2005) indicate, the distinctive features of tourism as a human contact industry, based on service delivery, means that a number of issues impact upon HRM in tourism settings. Figure 11.1 summarizes some of these issues, which highlight the perishability of tourism products and services (i.e. they cannot be stored), their intangibility and the critical importance of employees in making the visitor's experience memorable and enjoyable. Figure 11.1 highlights that, as a service delivered in specific places (i.e. destinations or in settings like a restaurant), tourism has a people-intensive nature. As a result, human resource managers need to be aware, at the very least, of a number of key issues as shown in Table 11.1. Yet Baum and Kokkranikel (2005) argue that HRM in tourism is characterized by 'adhocism', since managers and industry leaders have often had ambivalent attitudes to investing in the human capital (i.e. the people) who are the lifeblood of the tourism sector. One consequence of the long history of underinvestment in the human capital in the tourism sector is the development of global concern over how future labour requirements will be met if the growth of the sector is to be maintained. Labour shortages will constrain the growth ambitions of many governments that see tourism growth as one way of expanding and

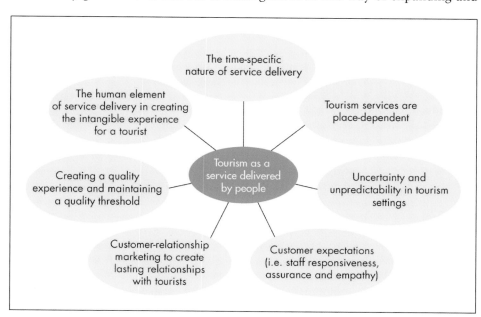

FIGURE 11.1 The nature of tourism as a service and the human resource component
Source: Adapted from Baum (1993)

TABLE 11.1 The scope of human resource management issues for a tourism industry manager

1 A critical awareness of the scope and nature of the labour market
2 The design of jobs
3 Recruitment, selection, appointment and retention of staff
4 Induction, equal opportunities, training and development
5 Evaluation of staff performance
6 Salaries and incentives
7 Employment termination, grievance and dispute procedures
8 Industrial relations and employment law
9 Motivation of staff

Source: Adapted from Baum (2006)

diversifying their economies: this hinges upon recruiting and training the right staff for the jobs available. This poses many challenges for individual businesses at the destination level and globally, where transnational operators concerned with their growth strategies will require labour to meet expansion plans. For the individual firm, these issues can be best summarized in Table 11.1 which outlines the scope of the activities a manager might have to consider.

Since tourism is a global business, with many enterprises operating transnationally or as multinational enterprises across several continents, certain sectors of the industry (e.g. the hotel sector) also have to adopt an international or global approach to HRM. Within the published studies of HRM in tourism, there is a common range of themes that consistently emerge which help to identify a number of elements that need to be considered when attempting to define the nature and scope of HRM in tourism. Baum (1993: 9–10) cites the following 'universal themes' (summarized in Figure 11.2) which consistently feature in the analysis of HRM in tourism and these remain in force more than a decade later:

- demographic issues related to the shrinking pool of potential employees and labour shortages, which surface when the economy is performing well and other career options offer higher rates of pay
- the tourism industry's image as an employer: it is seen as a low payer, providing routine and mundane work roles
- cultural and traditional perceptions of the tourism industry
- rewards and compensation for working in the sector
- education and training and the need to constantly upgrade skills in a growing technical age
- skill shortages at the senior and technical levels, especially in developed countries
- linking human resource concerns with service and product quality
- poor manpower planning, especially a lack of

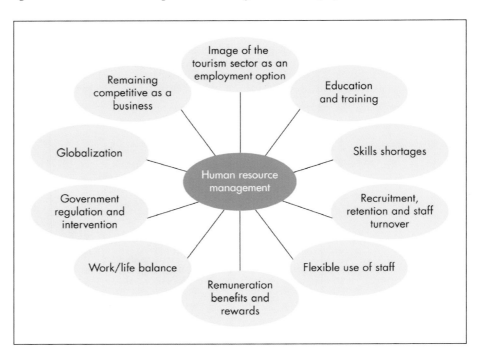

FIGURE 11.2 Contemporary themes in human resource management in tourism
Source: Adapted from Baum (1993)

innovation and empowerment of staff and the reluctance to introduce boundary-spanning roles for staff, breaking down traditional functional job roles to meet customer needs
- a remedial rather than a proactive approach to human resource issues.

Aside from the scope of HRM issues identified in Table 11.1, it is evident that the tourism sector also has a number of unique problems which need to be considered when attempting to define the scope of HRM in tourism.

So what do we mean by the term 'human resource management'?

In simple terms, HRM can be termed as a form of employment management which is focused on the managerial need for human resources to be provided and deployed. In line with the functions of management, the concern within HRM is the planning, monitoring and control of the human resource as a management activity. More complex analyzes of HRM identify the need for the individual human resource system within any organization to realize the strategic objectives of the organization (i.e. the delivery of excellent customer service to tourism consumers). One can also distinguish between 'hard' and 'soft' HRM approaches. 'Hard' approaches are essentially financially driven and concerned with controlling the salary cost; they are extremely directive and this type of approach is therefore described as utilitarian and managerialist. In contrast, 'soft' approaches to HRM are centred on the principle of the development of the employees and are much more humanist, with employees as assets rather than liabilities. In practice most organizations adopt a pragmatic approach to HRM depending on a wide range of factors including the economic and operating environment, the size of the organization, the extent to which the labour market is supplied with adequate staff and the corporate culture. What should be evident from this brief discussion of HRM is that it is far more than simple personnel management and in its most highly effective state it should adopt a holistic approach to employment management. In a 'people' business such as tourism, this approach assumes a significant role because of the need to derive quality from the employees and their interaction and exchanges with customers so that it becomes critical that the people with the right skills are in the right jobs. Since tourism is a global business which operates at a wide range of scales, this chapter will examine HRM issues in tourism at the international and the individual levels of tourism enterprise to illustrate the issues which students need to be aware of when examining the tourism sector. (For a more specific discussion of the detailed nature of HRM functions, readers are directed to Baum 2007 and Nickson 2007.) To analyze the issues around workforce development research, Baum *et al.* (2016) outlined three distinct domains which are interconnected in analyzing human resource management issues in tourism where there are:

1 **Macro issues** that are associated with the role of tourism work in society and examine broad demand and supply issues at different geographical scales from the global to local level. These issues include labour mobility, state regulation of employment and state policies towards the tourism workforce such as legislation around trade unionism.

2 **Meso issues** that are predominantly associated with organizational systems and the traditional notion of HRM such as the nature of roles, the workplace and managerial practices within the organization.

3 **Micro issues** that focus on the individual worker(s) and their attitudes and behaviours along with issues such as stress and working conditions and mode of working such as working in teams (after Baum *et al.* 2016).

IMAGE 11.1 Human resource issues and training are vital in face-to-face encounters such as check-in at airports where tourists rate the efficiency and friendliness of the encounter

Agencies and HRM issues in tourism: International perspectives

Among the existing studies of HRM in tourism, there is a reasonably consistent view on the human problems which face the tourism industry, and at the international scale there is a wide range of approaches and responses to the problems (Baum 2006; Ladkin 2011). They assume a key role for governments in countries seeking to expand their tourism economy. For example, in Croatia international tourism generated a ratio of 1:13.3 jobs that equates to around 300 000 jobs in total. One important scheme which has helped Croatia to capitalize upon its HR potential is the EU's *Travel and Tourism Capital Investment Programme* which aims to help provide a trained and responsive workforce, given Croatia's growing high dependence upon this growth sector compared to some of its neighbours (e.g. the Czech Republic has 12.4 per cent of employment based on tourism, Bulgaria 12.1 per cent, Hungary 10.3 per cent and Romania 5 per cent). With tourism employment set to grow 3.8 per cent per annum, training and HRM will prove to be key issues. Not surprisingly, in many of the tourism master plans developed for countries, human resource issues assume a significant position. There is also a range of bodies which have an active involvement in HRM issues in tourism such as the World Travel and Tourism Council (WTTC).

In some countries, the public sector is actively involved in the provision of organizations and assistance for the tourism sector to assist in human resource development, through policies, planning and the implementation of initiatives. A good example of this is the establishment of CERT (the state training agency responsible for providing a trained workforce for the hotel, catering and tourism industry) in Ireland over 40 years ago as a national initiative funded by the state government. However, where the state is involved, it may often be the case that a range of bodies have overlapping responsibilities. The organizations which are typically involved are state education provision, private training and educational providers, national employment or manpower agencies, and associated bodies such as trade unions and the national, regional and local tourism agencies. Coordinating and liaising with such a host of bodies can be complex and time-consuming. Furthermore, changes in political philosophy, such as in the UK after 1979, have seen state assistance progressively cut back and the emphasis being placed on the private sector. Where national tourism organizations (NTOs) are involved in training, their function can range from direct control of the training system at one extreme through to a limited policy role.

The World Tourism Organization (WTO) collates information from time to time and publishes it in reports, but even those data are partial. More progressive countries such as Singapore, with its Singapore 21 Strategy, have a key concern for human resource issues in tourism and this reflects the vast investment and significance of tourism to their national economies. At a pan-European level, the EU (2001) report *Working Together for the Future of European Tourism* identified a number of priorities for concerted EU action in the field of tourism including:

- the need to upgrade skills in the tourism workforce, which is characterized by low skill levels, with potential barriers to improvement being high levels of staff turnover

- the need for holistic solutions to training, including creating partnerships between training institutes, the tourism sector and other stakeholders through the concept of learning areas. The report advocated the use of structural funds to support innovative solutions

- the need to monitor the tourism labour environment better, with a focus on the staff in this sector

- the development of a handbook for learning areas in tourism to turn learning to innovation

- an improvement in the quality of tourism products in the EU, which will require a better trained and skilled workforce.

IMAGE 11.2 Airline service. Emirates has developed a high-quality brand based on the service its staff provides on board its flights

In the UK, the Department of Culture, Media and Sport's (2004) *Tomorrow's Tourism Today* identified the importance of skills and education to provide a workforce to deliver a quality product. It also indicated the need for high-quality training strategies from hands-on skills to management to improve the workforce. It cited the launch in 2004 of yet another agency with an input to HR issues in tourism, the sector Skills Council on Hospitality, Leisure, Travel and Tourism – People First, which needed to engage with other stakeholders to develop a cooperative approach to:

- identify skills shortages affecting the industry and regional variations
- develop proposals building on best practice to improve training, recruitment and skills
- ensure government initiatives in skills and training are available to the tourism industry.

To implement *Tomorrow's Tourism*, public sector agency support from regional development agencies, the Local Government Association and the business group, the Tourism Alliance were all actively involved. Yet not all state agencies adopt a singularly supportive view of tourism development based on investing in this sector. However, political changes such as the expansion of the EU in 2004 to include a further ten countries has been widely welcomed by Western Europe's hotel sector. This has provided opportunities for east to west urban migration to fill employment vacancies, given the wage rate differential between Eastern and Western Europe. Many hotel chains in the UK quickly responded to this political change by recruiting Eastern European chefs and staff, although other hotels pursue a 'grow your own' policy via investing in the training and retention of their staff, as other companies also do (Image 11.2). Janta *et al.* (2011) examined Polish migrant workers in the UK hospitality sector and found their motivation for seeking such employment opportunities was self-development to improve their long-term career prospects. A considerable body of research has emerged which explores the issues associated with migrant workers (Joppe 2012) to address labour shortages, and in some countries, such as the UK, they now comprise a significant element of the hospitality and tourism sector (also see Insight 11.1). It is also the case that hotels have used social media to assist with recruitment to reach a wider audience as outlined by Gibbs *et al.* (2015).

11

INSIGHT 11.1 Human resource management and labour planning issues for the UK hospitality sector

The scope and nature of the HR issues facing the wider hospitality sector, of which tourism services are a component, were the focus of a People 1st (2011) *State of the Nation* report which was a wide-ranging review of five key themes (economic performance, workforce size and characteristics, recruitment and retention, employee engagement, workforce skills and development). As People 1st (2011: 4) argue, 'whilst the sector has generally fared well [in the midst of a recession], high labour turnover, over-reliance on transient workers, and stubbornly high skills gaps continue to hamper businesses'. The significance of the hospitality sector is demonstrated by the size of the UK workforce, comprising 2.1 million workers (equivalent to 7.2 per cent of the working population) and represents 1 in 14 jobs in the UK. In terms of economic output, tourism comprises travel services (18 per cent). 'Tourist services' is only 2 per cent of the total while self-catering accommodation is a further 2 per cent. Output is dominated by restaurants (18 per cent), pubs/bars/nightclubs (18 per cent) and gambling (15 per cent). Therefore, the hospitality sector is a dominant element with its high staff: visitor ratios.

The sector is dominated by small and medium-sized enterprises, with half of all businesses employing less than five people, and 24 per cent are sole traders. However, almost half of the workforce is employed by large employers with over 100 employees. The sector is dependent upon part-time employees as almost half of the workforce fall into this category (compared to 28 per cent for the national economy, which is also on the increase). Many of these workers are aged under 30 and almost two-thirds are female, although they are under-represented in senior management posts. In terms of the structure of the workforce, 21 per cent of employees are not UK nationals (i.e. they were born overseas), two-thirds of whom are from outside the European Economic Area. These are often migrant workers who assist in filling the lower-skilled roles, since at any time 17 per cent of employers have vacancies. The most difficult posts to recruit are chef and managerial roles. This is compounded by high levels (23 per cent) of staff turnover which has dropped slightly due to recessionary effects on the labour market. Such levels of turnover are a huge cost for employers.

People 1st (2011) estimate that this costs businesses in the sector £33 million a year in terms of recruitment and training. This is why it is economically important for employers to build good working relationships with staff; this is

INSIGHT 11.1 continued

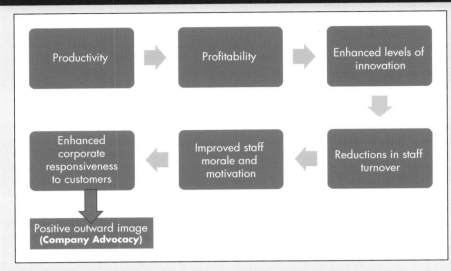

FIGURE 11.3 Reasons to foster good employer–employee relationships

described as employer–employee engagement because it will improve the performance of the business, as shown in Figure 11.3.

To enhance employee engagement, People 1st (2011) found that more employee-focused work practices were important to employee engagement, as Figure 11.3 shows.

With a reliance upon female workers, Figure 11.4 illustrates how important flexibility is among employers to attract workers and retain them. Improving the productivity of employees to enhance their effectiveness can be achieved by investment in ongoing training, and the sector spends around £4.2 million on training annually, with around two-thirds spent on customer service training.

Although the data are now somewhat old, they do illustrate the challenges of operating in the small business sector.

In terms of the characteristics of the sector, almost 185 000 businesses opened in 2010, encouraged by low entry barriers. While the rate of new business start-ups was higher than the national average, at 12 per cent per annum (equivalent to 21 580 businesses), the sector also had a high exit rate. The failure rates for businesses were high, with 25 510 closing in contrast to the 21 580 start-ups. The food and service management category has the highest rate of closure (17.6 per cent), while the self-catering/holiday parks/hostel category had the lowest failure rate (9.4 per cent). This is often because, as People 1st (2011) found, few businesses sought or obtained business advice before setting up a new venture. This may be a function of the owner of a new venture not perceiving any need for assistance, or because this level of advice was not available.

The People 1st (2011) study found that businesses adapted to the effects of economic slowdowns in terms of:

- putting staff on shorter working time
- asking staff to work longer hours
- reducing expenditure on recruitment

which is compounded by the effects of seasonality on workforce needs, which often leads to a use of part-time seasonal workers (especially transient workers).

People 1st (2011) also outlined long-term workforce projections for the sector, which accounted for 'replacement demand' (i.e. those needed to replace those who have left their jobs). Figure 11.5 shows that at least an extra 1 million staff will be needed by 2022 and these estimates have grown further with the effect of Brexit on migrant labour.

The implications are that recruitment and retention will be major concerns for the sector, with retention a much bigger problem given the estimates of staff turnover of 30 per cent. This combines with major skill shortages facing the sector, where around 10 per cent of employees are not completely proficient in their job, particularly in customer-handling skills in a sector that is based on customer interaction. This is compounded by employee shortages and

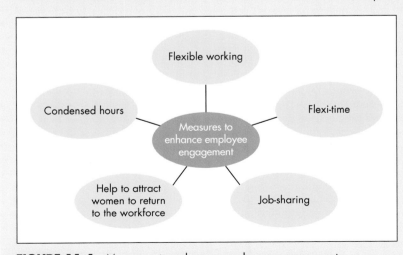

FIGURE 11.4 Measures to enhance employee engagement

recruiting staff that do not have all the skills required. The most obvious problem is where customer service skills are lacking in a people-centred, experience-focused sector: it limits the business's ability to build an immediate and long-term relationship with the customer. What this overview of the UK hospitality sector shows is that the demand for skilled labour will become more acute by 2022. That, combined with an ageing worker profile, poses profound challenges for the long-term labour market.

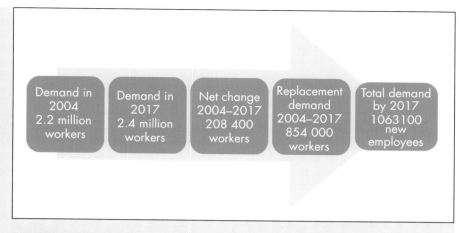

FIGURE 11.5 Employment demand projections for the UK hospitality and tourism sectors to 2017

Further reading

People 1st (2011) *State of the Nation Report 2011: An Analysis of Labour Market Trends, Skills, Education and Training within the UK Hospitality, Leisure, Travel and Tourism Industries*. London: People 1st.

Questions

1 Why are employment forecasts for labour force planning important?

2 What is the effect of an ageing population on recruitment in tourism and hospitality?

3 Why is a high rate of staff turnover a problem for the sector? What might the sector do to address these issues?

4 To what extent will technology be a solution for replacing human–customer interactions? How might this affect the customer experience?

TABLE 11.2 Human resource management problems in the Latin American tourism industry

1 A lack of effective managerial training
2 Educational institutions have inappropriate provision for the needs of the tourism industry
3 Lack of coordination between the educational sector and the tourism industry
4 Limited number of tourism instructors
5 Inadequate investment in training by the private sector
6 Insufficient and inadequately designed in-house training programmes
7 Limited exposure to foreign language training
8 A lack of travel agency training programmes
9 Service delivery and customer relations given inadequate attention together with inadequate levels of education among employees
10 Too few internship opportunities for tourism students
11 Poor regulation of training institutions
12 Inadequate government fiscal incentives to facilitate industry training
13 Limited public sector support for tourism
14 Low wages and salary levels for employees in the tourism industry
15 Negative attitudes towards service occupations

Source: Adapted from Pizam (1999)

As Insight 11.1 shows, the scope and extent of many HR issues in countries seeking to develop their tourism industry are evident in Table 11.2, where the range of problems which the state and private sector need to address through a more coordinated approach to HRM in tourism is apparent. However, focusing on the role of the state and public sector as the agents responsible for HRM issues overlooks the fact that individual businesses need to take an active role and for that reason the discussion now turns to this issue.

Tourism and HRM issues: The response and role of the individual business

For the individual business, there is a need to recognize the macroeconomic processes which are at work within the business environment. For example, one of the greatest challenges for the future development of tourism employment is the change to the nature of work. For medium-sized and large tourism enterprises, HR issues and the factors affecting their performance are usually linked to the staff and workforce, and therefore recognizing the role of recruitment and ongoing development of the staff resource to achieve strategic goals becomes essential. A reinvestment in the human resource, through ongoing training and development of the employees' skills and abilities to create and add value to the organization, is an inherent quality which successful tourism enterprises are recognized for throughout the world. The scale of the HR function will often reflect the size of the organization and the specific functions (e.g. training and development) that may be allocated to specific individuals, whereas, in smaller organizations, a commitment to core functions (recruitment and retention) may be all that is possible due to work pressures and constraints on staff time. However, one also has to recognize that in some countries, the larger tourism organizations (e.g. airlines and hotel chains) may be major employers, but the backbone of the tourism industry is the small business sector with its own range of issues.

11 HRM issues in small tourism businesses

According to Morrison (1996: 400):

> *a small tourism business is financed by one individual or small group and is directly managed by its owner(s), in a personalized manner and not through the medium of a formalized management structure . . . it is perceived as small, in terms of physical facilities, production/service capacity, market share and the number of employees.*

The definition of a small tourism business according to employee size varies with each research study. For example, Thomas *et al.*'s (2011) study acknowledged that in the EU a small business could range up to 50 employees, with micro enterprises employing fewer than ten employees. Morrison (1996: 401) has argued that 'traditionally the tourism industry has been dominated by the small business and this still remains true in the 1990s. Currently in Ireland . . . firms with less than 15 employees account for around 79 per cent of all Irish tourism businesses.' In New Zealand, it is nearer to 90 per cent. In this sector of the tourism industry, the literature on small businesses indicates that four types of firm can be discerned which has a bearing on HRM. Table 11.3 highlights the typology (which we will return to in more detail in Chapter 12). This is also reflected in the different management differences between small and large firms as highlighted in Table 11.4. The short-term time horizon of small businesses and owner-managed structure relies more on personal skills, especially leadership qualities and experience (Thomas *et al.* 2011). The implications for HRM in small tourism firms are as follows:

- small businesses normally have constraints on their resource base and therefore are unable to fund developments in HRM to the same degree as large firms
- HRM is widely acknowledged as a major component in small businesses becoming more competitive and productive as well as in organizational success
- HRM is often of marginal interest for family-owners where a family business exists
- the most important area for small businesses to improve their performance is in the recruitment and selection of personnel
- small firms tend to use marginally qualified staff in the tourism sector, especially in the rural environment
- management training is normally limited among owner-managers, with time constraints and a perception of no need for training limiting the development of HR processes
- many managers in small businesses do not apply strict principles of HRM, being unable to delegate, and fail to define lines of authority and responsibility for employees.

TABLE 11.3 Organizational structures and entrepreneurial characteristics

Category	Entrepreneurial characteristics
Self-employed	Use of family labour, little market stability, low levels of capital investment, tendency towards weakly developed management skills
Small employer	Use of family and non-family labour; less economically marginalized but shares other characteristics of self-employed group
Owner-controllers	Use of non-family labour, higher levels of capital investment, often formal system of management control but no separation of ownership and control
Owner-directors	Separation of ownership and management functions, highest levels of capital investment

Source: Adapted from Goffee and Scase (1983)

TABLE 11.4 Management differences between small and large firms

Small firms	Large firms
Short-term planning horizon	Long-term planning horizon
Reacts to the environment	Develops environmental strategy
Limited knowledge of the environment	Environment assessment
Personalized company objectives	Corporate strategy
Communication informal	Formal and structured communication
Informal communication systems	Formalized control systems
Loose and informal task structure	Job descriptions
Wide range of management skills	Highly specialist/technical skills demanded
Income directly at risk in decision-making	Income derived from a wider performance base
Personal motivations directly affect performance	Broader-based company performance

Source: Adapted from Carter (1996)

As Morrison and Teixeira (2004: 245) argue, 'human resource management appears consistently as an aspect that significantly challenges small firms'. In some cases, some SMEs opt for an approach to management where family members report fewer HRM problems than paid employees (Morrison and Teixeira 2004). Habberson and Williams (1999) report this as:

● creating a more unique, family-oriented workplace with more customer care
● having more flexible work practices
● experiencing family members as more productive than non-family employees
● communicating effectively through a common family language
● unusual motivation, improved trust and improved loyalties generated by family relationships
● low transaction costs
● informal and efficient decision-making (cited in Morrison and Teixeira 2004: 25).

Managing HRM issues in the tourism sector in the new millennium

The major challenges for the tourism industry in the new millennium are associated with developing a high-quality staff who do really make a difference in what is undoubtedly a people business. Yet within many of the international research studies of HRM in tourism, there are concerns that there is and will continue to be a severe shortage of trained and able staff. One of the greatest challenges which faces any employee in the tourism sector is the ability to respond and adapt to change, especially at a managerial level. In a high-technology sector where knowledge and managerial skills are vital, managing staff and the recruitment and retention of high-calibre staff are also vital. The 1980s and early 1990s can best be described as years of unsophisticated and reactive HR policies in the tourism sector, and in the new millennium a new economic climate in which tourism operates combined with the growth of the knowledge economy means that change and competition will continue to intensify. Those businesses which are not adopting progressive HR policies in line with other sectors of the service sector will be left behind and will find it difficult to compete when much of the work is people and skills based. More sophisticated HR policies need to be developed and implemented in the following areas for the tourism sector to be responsive to add value to its staff and change the sector's image as an employer:

- induction of staff
- appraisal and staff performance evaluation
- effective staff communication
- reward of initiative and excellence
- empowerment of staff
- industry–education collaboration.

One of the real solutions in the hotel sector in accommodating staff and demand, is the introduction of flexible working as illustrated in Insight 11.1. This may help with:

- workforce development
- improving employee job satisfaction, particularly work–life balance
- attracting and retaining staff
- reducing risks in some areas, especially the problem of stress for those staff working in face-to-face delivery of services and those involved in long hours of work.

But these issues are part of the growing recognition in some tourism and hospitality organizations of the need for greater flexibility in the way staff are able to perform their tasks. One strand of that change in thinking is the rise of empowerment. Empowerment of staff is a growing area of interest in building workforce engagement so that they are given more authority, autonomy and flexibility to perform their roles and adapt to situations as they arise. This is vital in service encounters that are very fluid and ever changing. To achieve greater levels of empowerment, it is important to see how this needs to be part of the corporate culture where a series of questions and steps needs to be followed (Figure 11.6) that can be analyzed in a very rational manner. Implementing these principles of

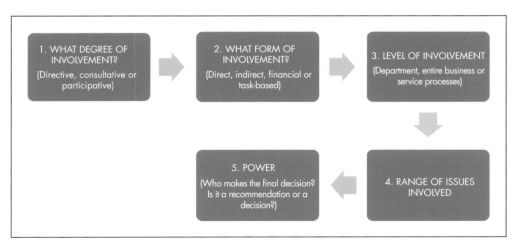

FIGURE 11.6 Rational components of empowerment
Source: Developed from Lashley (2004)

empowerment at an individual staff/team member level means that competence and skills need to be developed to accommodate this style of leadership in an organization (Figure 11.7).

One other area of activity among tourism businesses has been the investment in service quality training for employees to deliver high-quality tourism experiences in the service encounter between tourist and staff. Baum and Kokkranikel (2005)

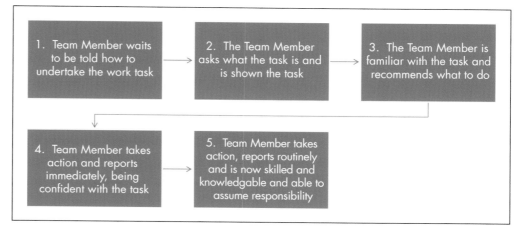

FIGURE 11.7 Five stages of individual empowerment
Source: Developed from Lashley (2004)

summarize the importance of this and the criteria used by Grönroos (1988) which hinge upon the staff–customer interaction around a number of the customer's perceived tangible and intangible elements of the service encounter, including:

- professionalism and skill in the service encounter
- staff attitudes and behaviour
- customers being able to access staff and feeling they are flexible and able to respond to their needs
- reliability and trustworthiness of staff
- recovery of a situation when things go wrong
- ensuring the brand image of a product has a reputation and credibility.

Since quality is seen as critical to being competitive in tourism, and most of the tangible and intangible criteria of perceived good service are largely HR-related, this illustrates the critical nature of employing staff with the skills or ability to be trained to add value to these service encounters.

For employers, legislative changes have also placed many additional functions and procedures upon HR managers. For example, a growing legislative requirement in many countries to monitor issues of gender, age, social inclusion and employee well-being means that employers have additional legal commitments as well as employment costs. In some developing countries, the human capital and potential of the tourism sector is attracting growing interest (Liu and Wall 2005). There is also a considerable interest in best practice and excellence in the HR area for tourism based on eight recurring themes: flexibility; participation in decision-making by staff; performance management; recognition; reward; communication and dialogue with staff; learning and development; and empowerment (Baum 2007) which emerge in Insight 11.1 and the work of People 1st.

Future issues in HRM and tourism

With tourism being a 'people' industry (Baum *et al.* 2016), there are growing concerns about issues associated with the impact of service delivery, particularly emotional labour. In broad terms, emotional labour is where employees need to use their feelings and emotions in productive interactions with customers and other staff. In a people-facing, experiential sector like tourism, much of the service experience is made or broken by the staff–customer interactions. The area of emotional labour was popularized by Hochschild (1983) who defined the term simply as displaying certain emotions to meet the job requirements that are particularly important in worker–customer interactions that:

- Involve face to face (or phone interactions such as call centre staff).
- Necessitate an employee producing a desired emotional state in another person(s), typically evaluated through customers' satisfaction scores.
- Commodify the employers' goals and outcomes into a standardized service delivery process to seek maximum customer satisfaction.

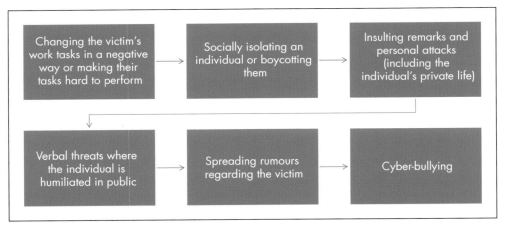

FIGURE 11.8 The scope of bullying in the workplace

Source: Based on Ram (2018)

This often means in service interactions a mantra of the 'customer' (or tourist) is always right. Combine these emotional requirements with the growing concerns about low pay, zero hours contracts and instability in tourism employment, there are numerous calls to improve working conditions for tourism employees, who are often from younger age groups (under 30 years of age). There are also growing concerns in relation to emotional labour demands in tourism that are combined with significant problems associated with bullying and harassment in tourism employment, as shown in Figure 11.8. As this figure shows, the scope of bullying and harassment includes many undesirable issues that can affect tourism employees due to the high-pressure-people contact that is associated with work roles. As Ram (2018) and Page *et al.* (2018) argue, these issues have a significant effect on the three areas of tourism employment: the firm, the perception of the tourism and hospitality sector as an employer and the individual, as illustrated in Figure 11.9. This has led some countries, such as Australia, to develop a code of practice in 2015 for employers and employees to address systemic problems related to bullying and harassment. In extreme cases, it can lead to employees taking legal action where legislative frameworks permit this to be deemed an employment issue under equality legislation.

Tourism is also a fast-moving area of activity and Baum (2015) has outlined some of the changes affecting the tourism workplace (Table 11.5). Some of the principal changes are affecting the type of skills employees need (especially with the rise of the digital consumer), the impact of new work processes, employment practices and the effect on work–life balance. It is no surprise that HR organizations like People 1st report turnover rates of 31 per cent in the sector which cost £414 million a year in recruitment issues. It is not surprising that businesses also use social media to recruit staff (Gibbs *et al.* 2015).

In the larger companies, to utilize technology more effectively, businesses have embraced E-hrm. E-hrm is the devolution of different HR functions to management and employees. The use of technology has focused on three distinct areas of E-hrm:

- Operational issues, such as payroll and other back-office functions such as managing personal data (which has to meet strict guidelines in Europe since the 2018 General Data Protection Regulation was introduced).

- Relationship issues, such as external and internal recruitment and performance management.

- Transformational issues, such as knowledge management, training and development courses using pre-purchased modules on health and safety at work and appraisals.

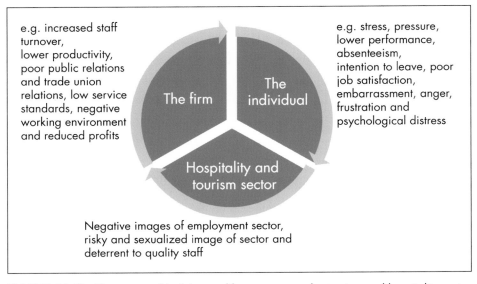

FIGURE 11.9 The impact of bullying and harassment on the tourism and hospitality sector

Source: Developed from Ram (2018)

TABLE 11.5 Impact of tourism change on work and the workplace

Influencers/drivers of change in tourism	Implications for work
The nature of the tourism industry itself, with changing patterns of travel with respect to both originating and destination markets	New skills and service demands – for example social media-based marketing and the need for a wider portfolio of language and cultural skills
The growing maturity of tourists as independent travellers, with less dependence on pre-packaged programmes and tours (Babu 2014)	More bespoke/individualized service delivery
Fluctuating economic conditions resulting in efforts to drive down costs from key sectors in tourism, notably air transport (CAPA 2013), the emergence of retrenchment strategies such as the 'staycation', a clear luxury–budget polarization and an increasing focus on dynamic packaging	Elimination of key work areas, especially in tourism intermediaries such as travel agents
The impact of social media on customers and their decision-making (Xiang et al. 2015)	Pressure on workforce to adopt new communications strategies
Changing tourism distribution systems, primarily through evolving technologies (Mistilis et al. 2014)	Altering or eliminating existing skills, creating new skills and new jobs
Growing awareness of environmental concerns within tourism	Emergence of a demand for new range of 'green' skills from those working in the sector

Source: Baum, T. (2015) Human resources in tourism: Still waiting for change? – A 2015 reprise. *Tourism Management*, 50: 206.

The objective of E-hrm is to shift a great deal of rudimentary record keeping and data management onto employees to make them become employee-managed, freeing up resources for HR departments to work more closely with managers and individuals on strategic issues. In this sense it represents a shift from operational to strategic priorities.

A further trend emanating from HR practices is the rise of green HRM. This is the engagement with the sustainability debates so that human resource departments roll out and embed the policies and procedures on sustainability in the workplace. These policies often seek to achieve greater eco-efficiencies and to reduce human impacts on the environment. For example, the promotion of paper reduction measures such as electronic filing, car-sharing, the promotion of public transport to travel to work and greater use of technology to reduce the organizations' carbon footprint by using technology rather than travelling. It also encompasses energy-efficiency measures in offices and buildings as well as recycling and waste reduction measures. Other transport-related measures might include encouraging car-sharing, cycling to work and subsidizing public transport. By gathering and monitoring HR data on these measures, employers can reduce their expenditure on some areas of work and enhance their green credentials. Green issues are an important facet of consumers' attitudes to tourism companies when making judgements about the environmental stewardship of the businesses they purchase from and work for. Mishra (2017) provides an example of India and the growing interest in green HRM and Renwick et al. (2016) provide a review of this emerging field of HR practice. As Insight 11.2 shows, there are also more sweeping changes expected in the area of tourism employment with the greater use of technology and automation.

INSIGHT 11.2 The future of work and implications for tourism employment and holidays

Lund et al. (2019) take a futurist look at the future of work in the USA and it has implications for other developed countries and their tourism and hospitality sectors. The Lund et al. (2018) study *The Future of Work in America* suggests that by the mid-2020s intelligent machines will be commonplace in the workplace, a feature introduced in Chapter 6.

This will mark a new wave of automation in the workplace, but the geographical impact of these changes will be focused on high-growth centres of innovation adopters like fast-growing cities while rural areas will be low-growth areas. The implications for tourism employment are that these forms of automation may enhance the key challenge that many governments raise about the tourism and hospitality sector – productivity. By replacing menial and routine tasks, automation may enhance the productivity of companies. For employees, this will mean that there will be a greater demand for workers with higher levels of education as well as altering day-to-day employment. Automation will redefine the way in which people employed are deployed in organizations, and Lund *et al.* (2019) suggest that the most affected sectors related to tourism will be the food service sector, office support functions, customer service roles and the transportation sector. One consequence will be the creation of new career pathways while displacing large numbers of workers. In the USA the Lund *et al.* (2019) study forecast that 11.5 million workers over the age of 50 could be displaced by automation, as companies seek to innovate and enhance productivity levels. For the worker of tomorrow this will mean that they will need to engage with lifelong learning and constant retraining to stay ahead of the impact of technological trends. In the USA, Lund *et al.* (2019) suggest that these changes in employment may create a surplus of workers and depress wage rates while reducing the purchasing power of certain groups of workers. Such reduced earnings will filter through to diminished capacity for tourism spending.

Automation will mean the greater use of robots using artificial intelligence (AI) and could replace 1 million jobs in the USA. For example, a greater use of self-service screens could be used in food service outlets. This reflects the role of technology as a disrupter but we also have to recognize that technology could also create new job types we cannot even envisage currently. Lund *et al.* (2019) suggest that these new jobs could add a further 8–9 per cent of jobs to the economy while the transport sector's future adoption of semi-autonomous and automated technology (e.g. self-driving vehicles) could remove a range of job types. For employees in the tourism and hospitality sector, the key to

career progression and development will be a range of key skills that Lund *et al.* (2019) identify:

- Adaptability
- Initiative
- Critical thinking
- Creativity and innovation

and specific skill sets to develop in managerial roles associated with socio-emotive skills (e.g. leadership and management of people such as conflict resolution). Current developments in robot technology are likely to see a much greater use in the tourism and hospitality sectors given their ability to provide accurate information although the acceptance of this technology by tourists still has a long way to go as studies by Travelzoo have shown.

Further reading

Lund, S., Manyika, J., Segel, L., Dua, A., Hancock, S., Rutherford, S. and Maron, B. (2019) *The Future of Work in America: People and Places, Today and Tomorrow*. New York: McKinsey and Company. https://www. mckinsey.com/featured-insights/future-of-work/the-future-of-work-in-america-people-and-places-today-and-tomorrow.

See the following reports based on the TravelZoo study:

https://press.travelzoo.com/robophiles--robophobes--britons-divided-over-use-of-robots-in-travel/

https://www.businesstraveller.com/news/2016/03/09/robots-working-in-travel-industry-would-improve-service/

Questions

1 Can you think of examples of key functions that companies perform with humans that may be automated in the next five years?

2 How do you think tourists will accept robots in five years' time?

3 What are the likely problems of using robots in the tourism sector?

4 What will the typical holiday experience be like in 2025 if predictions for robot use gather momentum?

Conclusion

Tourism education and training globally need to take stock of what HR requirements are needed in each area: a theme highlighted by WTTC and other governmental bodies as seeking to understand the productivity and wastage rates (i.e. staff leaving the industry). Looking at the Australian tourism sector, Hall (2003) outlined its productivity rates and its relatively low outputs compared to some other sectors of the economy, as well as its lower operating profit margins of 15.2 per cent compared to 22 for other industries. This has also arisen in studies of other countries. Herein lies the problem for the sector: it needs to improve labour productivity so it can raise profit margins and thereby invest further in human capital. Of course tourism is not alone in having low profit levels, since this characterizes many areas of service provision. Adding value to the tourism experience is one obvious way of being able to levy higher profits. Understanding these concepts is critical to education and training as well as investing in lifelong learning and upskilling. What is interesting is the continued existence of ongoing problems in HRM and tourism, which have altered little in the last decade. If anything, changes in the demand for tourism labour have intensified the pressure on employers. As the WTTC Task Force report observed, the demand for workers will continue to increase. At the same time, an ageing population in developed countries will reduce the pool of employees and while technology may offer some options, face-to-face interactions will also remain that require staffing. The telling recommendation of the Task Force is that companies must place learning and education for their workforce centre-stage in their business strategy. This is because, increasingly, the performance of a business in tourism will be based on the quality of its human talent. At the front line of delivery, quality of service will continue to be a surrogate of corporate performance, especially given the need to impress first-time visitors and also to nurture repeat customers. The importance of word-of-mouth recommendation to build a loyal customer base will grow in significance, and delivering consistent quality will be a challenge. New ways of working within organizations will need to be found to address the high turnover of first-time employees who leave disenchanted with an industry, associated with glamour in some sectors, but also involving long hours of work and poor training opportunities. There are many examples of good practice now being developed across the tourism and hospitality industries to overcome these negative images, by developing career paths for employees so that tourism careers rather than jobs become the norm. Only by raising global awareness of tourism's critical role in the economy, and through more innovative and attractive labour market policies, will tourism address future HRM issues.

Discussion questions

1 What is the purpose of HRM?
2 What problems do tourism businesses face in relation to HR issues?
3 How do the HR problems facing small and large tourism businesses differ?
4 What types of role does an HR manager play in a large tourism organization?

References

Babu, S. (2014) 'Mass customerisation: Next generation mass customisation for tourism', *International Journal of Social Science and Management*, 1 (1): 115–119.

Baum, T. (1993) *Human Resource Issues in International Tourism.* Oxford: Butterworth-Heinemann.

Baum, T. (2006) *Human Resource Management for Tourism, Hospitality and Leisure.* London: Thomson Learning.

Baum, T. (2007) 'Human resources in tourism: Still waiting for change', *Tourism Management*, 28 (6): 1383–1399.

Baum, T. (2015) 'Human resources in tourism: Still waiting for change? – a 2015 reprise', *Tourism Management*, 50: 204–212.

Baum, T. and Kokkranikel, J. (2005) 'Human resource management in tourism', in L. Pender and R. Sharpley (eds.) *The Management of Tourism.* London: Sage.

Baum, T., Kralj, A., Robinson, R.N.S., and Solnet, D.J. (2016) 'Tourism workforce research: A review, taxonomy and agenda', *Annals of Tourism Research*, 60: 1–22.

CAPA (2013) 'European airlines' labour productivity. Oxymoron for some, Vueling and Ryanair excel on costs', accessed at http://centreforaviation.com/analysis/european-airlines-labour-productivity-oxymoron-for-some-vueling-and-ryanair-excel-on-costs-97635, 15 February 2013.

Carter, S. (1996) 'Small business marketing', in M. Warner (ed.) *International Encyclopedia of Business and Management.* London: International Thomson Business Publishing.

Department of Culture, Media and Sport (2004) *Tomorrow's Tourism Today.* London: DCMS.

Eichaikul, R. and Baum, T. (1998) 'The case for government involvement in human resource development: A study of the Thai hotel industry', *Tourism Management*, 19 (4): 359–370.

EU (2001) *Working Together for the Future European Tourism.* Brussels: EU.

Fáilte Ireland (2005) *A Human Resource Development Strategy for Irish Tourism: Competing through People 2005–2012.* Dublin: Fáilte Ireland.

Gibbs, C. MacDonald, F. and MacKay, K. (2015) 'Social media usage in hotel human resources: Recruitment, hiring and communication', *International Journal of Contemporary Hospitality Management* 27 (2): 170–184.

Gittell, J. (2003) *The Southwest Airlines Way.* New York: McGraw-Hill.

Goffee, R. and Scase, R. (1983) 'Class, entrepreneurship and the service sector: Towards a conceptual clarification', *Service Industries Journal*, 3: 146–160.

Grönroos, C. (1988) 'Service quality: The six criteria of good perceived service quality', *Review of Business*, 9 (3): 10–13.

Habberson, T. and Williams, M. (1999) 'A resource based framework for assessing the strategic advantage of family firms'. Working Paper Series, No. 101. The Wharton School, University of Pennsylvania.

Hall, C.M. (2003) *Introduction to Tourism in Australia: Dimensions and Issues*, 4th edition. Frenchs Forest, NSW: Hospitality Press.

Hochschild, A. (1983) *The Managed Heart: Commercialisation of Human Feeling.* Berkeley: University of California Press.

Janta, H., Ladkin, A., Brown, L. and Lugosi, P. (2011) 'Employment experiences of Polish migrant workers in the UK hospitality sector', *Tourism Management*, 32 (3): 1006–1019.

Jappe, M. (2012) 'Migrant workers: Challenges and opportunities in addressing labour shortages', *Tourism Management*, 33 (3): 662–671.

Ladkin, A. (2011) 'Exploring tourism labour', *Annals of Tourism Research*, 38 (3): 1135–1158.

Lashley, C. (2004) 'A feeling for empowerment?', in N. D'Annunzio-Green, G. Maxwell and S. Watson (eds.) *Human Resource Management: International Perspectives in Hospitality and Tourism.* London: Thomson.

Liu, A. and Wall, G. (2005) 'Human resources development in China', *Annals of Tourism Research*, 32 (3): 689–710.

Mishra, P. (2017) 'Green human resource management: A framework for sustainable organizational development in an emerging economy', *International Journal of Organizational Analysis*, 25 (5): 762–788.

Mistilis, N., Buhalis, D. and Gretzel, U. (2014) 'Future eDestination marketing: perspective of an Australian tourism stakeholder network', *Journal of Travel Research*, 53 (6): 778–790.

Morrison, A. (1996) 'Marketing the small tourism business', in A. Seaton and M. Bennett (eds.) *Marketing Tourism Products: Concepts, Issues and Cases.* London: International Thomson Business Publishing.

Morrison, A. and Teixeira, R. (2004) 'Small firm performance in the context of agent and structure: A cross cultural comparison in the tourist accommodation sector', in R. Thomas (ed.) *Small Firms in Tourism: International Perspectives.* Oxford: Elsevier.

Nickson, D. (2007) *Human Resource Management for the Hospitality and Tourism Industries.* Oxford: Elsevier.

Page, S.J., Bentley, T., Teo, S. and Ladkin, A. (2018) 'The dark side of high performance human resource practices in the visitor economy', *International Journal of Hospitality Management*, 74: 122–129.

Pizam, A. (1999) 'The state of travel and tourism human resources in Latin America', *Tourism Management*, 20 (5): 575–86.

Ram, Y. (2018) 'Hostility or hospitality? A review on violence, bullying and sexual harassment in the tourism and hospitality industry', *Current Issues in Tourism*, 21 (7): 760–774.

Renwick, D., Jabbour, C., Muller-Camen, M., Redman, T. and Wilkinson, A. (2016) 'Contemporary developments in green (environmental) HRM scholarship', *International Journal of Human Resource Management*, 27 (1–2): 114–128.

Thomas, R., Shaw, G. and Page, S.J. (2011) 'Understanding small firms in tourism: A perspective on research trends and challenges', *Tourism Management*, 32 (5): 963–976.

Watson, S., D'Annunzio-Green, N. and Maxwell, G. (2004) 'Human resource management issues in international hospitality and tourism: Identifying the priorities', in N. D'Annunzio-Green, G. Maxwell and S. Watson (eds.) *Human Resource Management: International Perspectives in Hospitality and Tourism.* London: Thomson.

Xiang, Z., Magnini, V. and Fesenmaier, D. (2015) 'Information technology and consumer behavior in travel and tourism: Insights from travel planning using the internet', *Journal of Retailing and Consumer Services*, 22 (1): 244–249.

Further reading

Books

Brela, M. (2017) *Human Resource Management in the Hotel and Catering Industry.* London: Routledge.

Hochschild, A. (1983) *The Managed Heart: Commercialisation of Human Feeling.* Berkeley: University of California Press.

Journal articles

Baum, T. (2015) 'Human resources in tourism: Still waiting for change – a 2015 reprise', *Tourism Management*, 50: 204–212.

Baum, T., Kraij, A., Robinson, R. and Solnet, D. (2016) 'Tourism Workforce research: A review, taxonomy and agenda', *Annals of Tourism Research*, 60 (1): 1–22.

Madera, J., Dawson, M. and Guchail, P. (2017) 'Strategic human resource management in hospitality and tourism: A review of the current literature', *International Journal of Contemporary Hospitality Management*, 29 (1): 48–67.

11

Tourism and entrepreneurship

Learning outcomes

After reading this chapter and answering the questions you should be able to:

- understand the range of characteristics common to entrepreneurs
- outline how entrepreneurship is linked to tourism
- analyze the factors affecting entrepreneurs
- identify the features of innovation and its significance to tourism
- comprehend the wide variety of successful tourism entrepreneurs.

Overview

Tourism throughout history has been dependent upon entrepreneurs identifying business opportunities and turning their ideas into businesses. This process has largely driven new firm development in tourism, and governments support this type of activity on the premise that these types of ventures create wealth and employment, while the small firm of today may be the large company of tomorrow if it succeeds. Much of the success in the business field is dependent upon individual entrepreneurs and their vision, business acumen and ability to see opportunities.

Introduction

Entrepreneurship is a major force in economic development, since it is responsible for generating growth and acts as a vehicle for innovation and change in the economy. Tourism is one of the sectors of the service economy that is in a constant state of change and flux, and innovation and change are vital if businesses are to grow and provide the diversity of products to accommodate changing patterns of tourism consumption. Our knowledge and understanding of entrepreneurship in tourism have progressed substantially since the comments of Shaw and Williams (1990: 67) that there is 'relatively little appreciation of the specific operating characteristics of tourism firms, and especially of tourism entrepreneurship'. Indeed as Shaw (2004: 122) notes, 'during the last 20 years there has been a growing recognition of the importance of entrepreneurship within the tourism industry', especially as small tourism businesses become more fully understood alongside the large research literature on tourism as an element of international business (Thomas *et al*. 2011). There are many important examples within the history of tourism, such as Thomas Cook, Richard Branson and V. Raitz, Michael O'Leary and Ryanair, and Tony Fernandez and Air Asia, in innovating to generate significant tourism businesses and many of their successes have evolved into global brands and products we are all familiar with (i.e. Thomas Cook, Virgin and package holidays and low-cost air travel with Air Asia, Ryanair and easyJet). There have also been subsequent examples with the growth in disruptive technologies such as Uber, Airbnb and other businesses that have harnessed the power of Web 2.0 to change the distribution of the existing supply and demand relationships. Such success can be found in many countries and underpins the economic vitality of the tourism sector. Many studies of tourism and entrepreneurship show that the private sector is a fundamental element driving the growth of business activity, as Stokes (2012) illustrated in relation to events and business tourism and competitiveness in destinations (Kompulla 2014).

This chapter examines the nature of tourism entrepreneurship, especially the importance of innovation and small business development. This is assuming a growing international significance, as Chapter 5 explained, with changes in the nature of how businesses are organized in an increasingly globalized world. To keep ahead of the competition, innovation and change are vital and, while many tourism enterprises are small-scale in nature, there has been a significant paradigm shift in how firms are organized. Globalization is now making business networks increasingly important, with opportunities emerging for small firms able to use new technology to develop into flexible entities. This is creating a need for flexible working to accommodate change and innovation in the digital age. For entrepreneurs and innovators within organizations, an ability to harness technology to nurture business-to-business (B2B) relationships in the tourism supply chain and business-to-consumer (B2C) relationships in terms of demand will lead to a redefining of how organizations interact with each other, with customers and how they are operated as organizations. We should also not forget the discussion of C2C (consumer-to-consumer relationships) that have evolved through disruptive technologies with Airbnb. As a result, the need for 'enterprise' and 'enterprising people' has never been greater in tourism as the digital era and networked society offer many opportunities that can be exploited by entrepreneurs.

Understanding the nature of entrepreneurship

According to Drucker (1985: 12) there is no explanation 'as to why entrepreneurship emerged as it did in the late nineteenth century and as it seems to be doing again today . . . The changes are likely to lie in changes in values, perception, and attitude, changes in demographics, in institutions . . . perhaps changes in education as well.' Besides the lack of explanation for entrepreneurship, there is little in the way of economic theory for the entrepreneur. Casson (1982: 9) considers that the subject has become the domain of 'sociologists, psychologists and political scientists'; in his view, this is because of the assumption that we all have 'free access' to the information needed for decision-making which, therefore, becomes 'the mechanical application of mathematical rules for optimization . . . trivializes decision-making, and makes it impossible to analyze the role of entrepreneurs in taking decisions of a particular kind', implying that it is a complex area to understand. Medlik (1996: 94) argues that an entrepreneur is 'a person who undertakes an enterprise, makes decisions on and controls its conduct, and bears the risk'. Youell (1996: 79), similarly, emphasizes that it is 'an individual who is prepared to take a risk and accept a challenge or undertake a venture that has no guarantee of success'. The challenge and risk elements are evident when many tourism businesses are reviewed. Significantly, the process of entrepreneurship is 'more holistic and dynamic' (Morrison 1998: 1) than any one perspective can explain: nonetheless, the focal point is the individual. More recent research in management science has identified the need to understand the individual characteristics and the stories of individual entrepreneurs so as to appreciate the diversity of experiences and successes.

Shaw (2004) points to the fact that entrepreneurs have traditionally been perceived as innovators contributing to economic development by Schumpeter (1934). This perspective highlights the entrepreneur as a business pioneer driven by profit motives. But as we will show later in the chapter, this strand of thinking has also evolved into a much broader concept of entrepreneurship that also includes social entrepreneurship. This draws upon research on social innovation (e.g. see van der Have and Rubalcaba 2016) and this has a major bearing on addressing societal issues as we will explore later. An important building block in understanding how entrepreneurship can be applied for other motives beyond profit in a capitalist society is developed in Porter and Kramer's (2011) notion of creating shared value. Porter and Kramer argue that by bringing business and society together to create economic value can also create value for society. Porter and Kramer (2011: 4) argue that 'businesses acting as businesses, not as charitable donors, are powerful for addressing pressing issues we face'. The practical application of shared value as Porter and Kramer (2011: 5) argue can be achieved in three areas of business activity 'by reconceiving products and markets; by redefining productivity in the value chain; by enabling local cluster developments'.

Shaw (2004) is critical of established notions of entrepreneurship, arguing that few small-scale entrepreneurs actually pioneer: they tend to be 'reproducers', taking ideas from elsewhere and making them work in their context. This has led Shaw (2004) to identify different entrepreneurial types in tourism, such as classical entrepreneurs interested in being their own independent boss, managerial types and the artisan entrepreneur. There is a tendency to classify small-scale tourism entrepreneurs into:

IMAGE 12.1 Ryanair founder Michael O'Leary is now a well-known entrepreneurial figure in the tourism and leisure sector with the increasing visibility of low-cost brands such as Ryanair

- *lifestyle entrepreneurs*, who often have low managerial skills and expertise and focus on niche products with limited capital which Morrison *et al.* (1999) observed as comprising the majority of small businesses in the UK where non-economic motives are important in tourism entrepreneurship
- *business-oriented entrepreneurs*, who are motivated by profit.

Whatever categorization one adopts (and many exist in the research on this theme), what is clear is that the entry into entrepreneurship is in itself a life-changing experience for most people and is often related to a desire to exercise some control over their working lives as well as to seek to seize the economic potential of perceived opportunities. Not surprisingly, the majority of studies of tourism entrepreneurship have been focused on small businesses, although examples of individual successes in the low-cost airline market exist in relation to popular biographies of influential entrepreneurs and the companies they have set up (Image 12.1). Yet what are some of the reasons for people seeking to become tourism entrepreneurs?

Characteristics of entrepreneurs

A common belief is that entrepreneurs are born rather than made and, indeed, some personalities appear to have an innate ability: Casson (1982: 6) argued that 'many of the qualities with which the heroic stereotype is imbued are simply a reflection of contemporary cultural attitudes . . . the stereotype is useful as an articulation of the view that there is a correlation between various personal characteristics and entrepreneurial activity'. There can be no doubt that entrepreneurship comprises a number of elements. McMullan and Long (1990) consider these to be a combination of creativity and/or innovation, uncertainty and/or risk taking, and managerial and/or business capabilities. Shaw and Williams (1994: 133) recognize that entrepreneurs at the owner-manager level may well have '*non-economic motives* for entering the business'. In Getz and Petersen's (2005) study of profit-oriented entrepreneurship among family business-owners in tourism and hospitality, lifestyle and autonomy were key attributes. Interestingly, they found that owners of restaurants and forms of accommodation are more motivated by profit and growth than owners of arts and crafts and bed and breakfasts (B & Bs), who are more motivated by lifestyle and autonomy. Lifestyle motives comprise a need for independence, the need to achieve, job satisfaction – or self-actualization – and 'environmental factors'.

TABLE 12.1	Organizational structures and entrepreneurial characteristics
Category	Entrepreneurial characteristics
Self-employed	Use of family labour, little market stability, low levels of capital investment, tendency towards weakly developed management skills
Small employer	Use of family and non-family labour; less economically marginalized but shares other characteristics of self-employed group
Owner-controllers	Use of non-family labour, higher levels of capital investment, often formal system of management control but no separation of ownership and control
Owner-directors	Separation of ownership and management functions, highest levels of capital investment

Source: Adapted from Goffee and Scase (1985); Shaw and Williams (1994)

Not surprisingly perhaps, there are also differences in motivation between males and females, as discussed in Fielden and Davidson (2005). The 'overwhelming majority' of women in Goffee and Scase's (1985: 62) survey who had started their own businesses were 'university graduates who had been employed in a variety of middle-management positions . . . [whose] career prospects were limited because of the existence of various gender-related prejudices'. Of particular interest is the observation that many of these female entrepreneurs 'organize their businesses on the basis of trust . . . employees are committed to the employer's goals' and will accept lower wages because of greater individual autonomy and job satisfaction; the 'pay-off' for the entrepreneur is that a 'high trust organizational culture, then, has important economic advantages' (Goffee and Scase 1985: 68). One of the most widely cited classifications of entrepreneurs remains Goffee and Scase (1985), as shown in Table 12.1. This outlines their model of organizational structures and entrepreneurial characteristics, where the self-employed and small firms tend to dominate the accommodation sector. This raises the issue of what constitutes a small firm. Definitions vary, as discussed by Page *et al.* (1999), where up to 70 exist, a feature reiterated by Thomas (2004). The term 'small or medium enterprise' (SME) tends to complicate things, since the EU definition of 'medium enterprise' is of 100–499 employees while 'small' is 10–99 employees. The only agreement is on the micro-enterprise, employing fewer than ten people with the majority located in this category in the tourism and hospitality sector in many countries, a theme explored by Wanhill (2000). Drucker (1985) considers that longer years in education played a part in the emergence of the entrepreneurial economy in the UK. Ultimately, 'personal qualities which are rewarded through entrepreneurship are imagination and foresight, and skill in organizing and delegating work' (Casson 1982: 347). In seeking to understand what shapes the process of becoming and/or being an entrepreneur, a range of issues exist which can be broadly classified as the political/economic environment, the social/cultural environment, and innovation and creativity.

The political/economic environment

Not surprisingly, larger tourism economies 'have a wider range of entrepreneurial opportunities' (Shaw and Williams 1994: 121) and political changes such as deregulation and privatization which have provided opportunities in the tourism sector for entrepreneurs to succeed. The advent of the 1979 Conservative government in Britain led to sweeping changes to many national policies: 'rolling back the frontiers of the state' created opportunities for both established and budding entrepreneurs. In the USA the deregulation of civil aviation in 1978 immediately spawned a range of low-cost carriers; the deregulation of the coach transport business came in 1982 and led to the creation of many small-scale businesses with only Greyhound surviving out of the two large operators. Greek-born entrepreneur Stelios Haji-Ioannou developed the direct-sell, low-cost carrier easyJet which was discussed in Chapter 5. Again this reinforces the importance of opportunities in the wider context of why entrepreneurs set up new ventures. Research on the concept of **effectuation**, which argues that the future is unpredictable but can be controlled, has been cited as one factor associated with such activity (Sarasvathy 2005). Effectuation research also argues that rather than simply focusing on the traits of entrepreneurs, one should also look more closely at their expertise as a key element in setting up new ventures and success, as explored by Eyana *et al.* (2018) in the case of Ethiopian entrepreneurs.

British deregulation of the passenger coach business, created by the 1980 Transport Act, allowed brother and sister Brian Souter and Ann Gloag, with their company Stagecoach, to develop national bus routes (http://www.stagecoach.co.uk). They also bid for railway interests with the privatization of British Rail and the acquisition of various interests in rail franchises and a recent success is the megabus.com brand for low-cost coach travel (see Page 2019 for an in-depth case study of Megabus, its innovative practices and global expansion into a major transport brand). Music and aviation entrepreneur Richard Branson expanded his travel interests by acquiring the West Coast Inter-City franchises, thereby creating Virgin Rail – having already benefited from the 'liberalization' of flights within the European Union and Virgin Blue in Australia (Branson 1998).

The sociocultural environment

Drucker (1985: 1) observed in the USA, 'a profound shift from a "managerial" to an "entrepreneurial" economy'. This has been further enhanced by social innovation, just as the commercial bank and civil service resulted from the Industrial Revolution: 'the present age of entrepreneurship will be [as] important for its social innovations – and especially for innovations in politics, government, education and economics – as for any new technology or material product' (Drucker 1989: 247). Entrepreneurship is an integral part of North American culture and is, indeed, 'taught in school from kindergarten through to the twelfth grade, it has been integrated into college and university curricula, and is . . . promoted through . . . government Small Business Development Centers in every state' (Welsch 1998: 59). Entrepreneurs on that continent have the status of 'modern hero'.

However, in societies which show a marked respect for 'seniority' and authority, the environment is unlikely to be conducive to the creation of large numbers of entrepreneurs. Dondo and Ngumo (1998: 18) consider the education, especially in primary schools, received by Kenyans is not only very conformist but that 'natural curiosity is suppressed'. When this factor is coupled with respect for 'rank', they believe the cultural environment is a poor base for entrepreneurship. Shaw (2004) also noted the cultural brokerage role tourism entrepreneurs play within host communities, acting as a bridge between the world of the tourist and the local community, which is most vivid in developing countries. Getz and Carlsen (2000) found in Australian family-run businesses that social motives were very dominant, particularly in their prioritization of family life as opposed to business. Here the household has a major role to play in production. In Ghana, Gartner (2004) observed the importance of extended family being employed in these settings. Yet for businesses to remain viable, the process of innovation is crucial to success as Alsos *et al.* (2014) demonstrate.

Innovation, tourism and creativity

According to Hjalager (2002: 465), 'innovation' has been used to describe the behaviour of tourism enterprises, destinations and the tourism sector and can occur in a variety of contexts. 'Innovation' is a comparatively recent term to be examined in entrepreneurship (Schumpeter 1952), and Ateljevic and Page (2009) and Hall and Williams (2008) provide an excellent overview of contributions to this area. Hirsrich and Peters (1992: 8) observe that innovation 'is one of the most difficult tasks for the entrepreneur. It takes not only the ability to create and conceptualize but also the ability to understand all the forces at work in the environment' and yet it is now one of the most all-embracing terms used in the tourism sector.

Tourism and innovation: The conceptual basis

There is a growing recognition by transnational agencies such as the OECD (2006) that tourism is a highly fragmented industry sector, often reliant upon SMEs, with a high labour intensity (i.e. a high ratio of staff to clients). It is also characterized by low levels of productivity. For example, Blake *et al.* (2006) observed that productivity levels in the hotel and restaurant sector were 49 per cent of the UK average. These low levels of productivity also translate into low levels of competitiveness, compounded by poor awareness of, and involvement in, the process of innovation, especially in the SME sector, which is well documented in academic studies. Interestingly, the OECD (2006) argues that innovation should now be a matter of routine for many businesses, and can be incorporated into normal business practices as a series of incremental steps. When a failure to innovate across the tourism sector occurs at a destination level, there is a high likelihood that a loss of destination comprehensiveness could lead to a downward spiral of decline in the destination lifecycle. This would then require, as is the case in many former UK seaside resorts, a massive capital reinvestment programme to reposition and regenerate the resort to stimulate further development of the lifecycle stage from decline and decay to growth. Therefore, pursuing a strategy based on innovation in a destination while it is still developing to avoid stagnation is a more cost-effective intervention and business-led rather than needing to regenerate an entire destination.

What is innovation?

Innovation is a process whereby change can occur in the way businesses and organizations perform their activities and functions in more efficient, profitable and meaningful ways to remain competitive. The term originates from the Latin *innovatio* which means 'to create something new' (Peters and Pikkemaat 2005), which embodies the essence of tourism as a service sector to remain competitive as well as ensuring continuous improvement to the visitor experience. Within tourism, Sundbo *et al.* (2007) observed that innovation normally occurred at the level of the firm, at the level of a network and at a systems level (i.e. within government, institutions and organizations which influence the management and operation of tourism). Hjalager (2002) expands upon the typical areas of innovation, basing her observations on the initial work of Schumpeter which outlined the main areas for industrial innovation: they include product innovations, process innovations (e.g. new ways of delivering services), market innovations (i.e. new ways of communicating with the customer such as the Internet) and logistical innovations (i.e. innovations in supply chain delivery of services such as vertical integration to deliver a seamless tourism experience).

Hjalager (2002) has reviewed many of the academic studies of tourism and innovation, highlighting that it is not an insurmountable problem to repair the limited levels of innovative behaviour which characterize the tourism industry, a feature also observed by Hall and Williams (2008). Indeed, Sundbo *et al.* (2007) suggest that most innovation which occurs in tourism is not technological; it comprises a change in behaviour by businesses – a culture shift. One of the principal factors which affects the culture of innovation in a country is the attitude, support structures and approach of the state. International research suggests that fostering innovation to promote competitiveness and improved business performance requires leadership to champion the notion and to create a focal point to increase adaptation and implementation of innovation-fostering initiatives.

Schumpeter's seminal work in this area identified five types of innovation:

- introduction of a new product – or an improvement in the quality of an existing product
- introduction of a new method of production
- opening of a new market
- conquest of a new source of supply of raw materials or half-manufactured product
- creation of a new type of industrial organization.

Some of these types can be observed by reviewing Branson's Virgin Atlantic airline: quality has been raised across the board through competition, true sleeper-beds have been introduced, new markets were opened to Tokyo (1991), Hong Kong (1994), Washington, DC and Johannesburg (1996) and St Lucia (1999). This was made possible by the introduction of the Airbus A340–300 with its configurations and greater operational economies available for medium- to long-haul operations.

Hjalager (2002) outlined five types of innovation:

- *product innovations for new services* (e.g. airline loyalty programmes)
- *process innovations* to improve the performance of operations, such as information communication technologies (ICTs)
- *management innovations* (e.g. staff empowerment, as discussed in Chapter 11)
- *logistics innovations*, such as vertical links between restaurants and food producers
- *institutional innovations*, where new regulations such as government legislation provide new opportunities such as the deregulation of the aviation sector

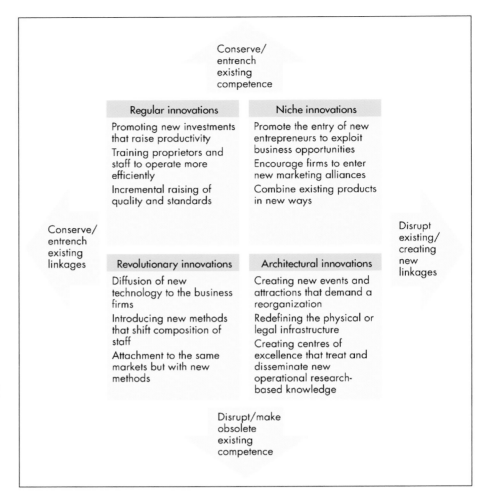

FIGURE 12.1 The Abernathy and Clarke model

Source: Reprinted from *Tourism Management*, vol. 5, Hjalager, 'Repairing innovation defectiveness in tourism', 464–474, © 2002, with permission from Elsevier

while Wan *et al.* (2005) simplify this typology into:

- technical/administrative innovation (e.g. booking via the Internet)
- product and process innovation
- radical and incremental innovation.

Hjalager (2002) points to the Abernathy and Clark model (Figure 12.1) which explains whether innovation makes business linkages redundant (the horizontal axis) or leads to retrenchment. The vertical axis points to the knowledge and competencies used to produce things, leading to four types of innovation:

- *regular innovation*, such as ongoing investment in upgrading a hotel
- *niche innovations*, where new suppliers may enter the tourism supply chain or the creation of a marketing alliance
- *architectural innovations*, creating new infrastructure or capacity to develop a new product such as an event-led destination, remodelling the concept of tourism in that locality
- *revolutionary innovations*, such as the use of e-services to reach customers.

For innovation to occur, the innovator has to acquire the knowledge and then be able to use it. As Chapter 11 argued, the EU (2001) saw that obstacles to innovation diffusion might be removed by better dissemination of existing knowledge by a guidebook. This is why Scottish Enterprise (see Franchetti and Page 2009) has pursued a wide range of strategies to encourage innovation as shown in Insight 12.1, including knowledge exchange via cases of best practice. The major problem facing the tourism sector is its dominance by small firms, especially the micro-enterprise (Wanhill 2000). This was one reason for the EU's financial support for the industry to help facilitate entrepreneurial activity and job creation. Not surprisingly, many of the cases of best practice in innovation tend to be large enterprises, such as the Disney Corporation discussed by Page (2011). It is widely emulated and studied in the tourism sector for its customer care programme, attention to detail, high level of repeat business (50–70 per cent) and desire to exceed customer expectations based on three propositions:

- *a quality staff experience*, since each individual staff member impacts on the customer experience
- *a quality customer experience*, based on being customer-driven and seeking to exceed customers' needs and expectations rather than simply meeting them
- *a quality set of business practices*, where knowledge, marketing, innovation and other elements are blended to ensure commercial success.

Disney empowers its staff to put things right when they go wrong, with its 'How can I help?' philosophy and focus on what it describes as service debugging. It is also widely admired for its innovation in being able to manage massive numbers of visitors in its theme parks with visitor management tools such as an Early Bird Programme, Fast Passes and Tip Boards to advise on waiting times. Loeffler and Church (2015) explored what made the Disney model unique and its focus on creating an exceptional experience, as shown in Figure 12.2. They point to the five principles that create the 'Exceptional Experience'. What this demonstrates is a more responsible method of

12

INSIGHT 12.1 The role of Scottish Enterprise in driving innovation in tourism

In 2001, a Tourism Innovation Group was formed by the tourism industry to promote such processes to make Scottish tourism more competitive. One intended outcome of their actions and why they are engaged in such a process as a result of intervention by Scottish Enterprise, is to promote greater levels of innovation. Much of their work in this area is world leading, since few other public sector agencies have pursued and championed such an ambitious innovation programme. Scottish Enterprise, which covers 93 per cent of the Scottish population through its regional offices, has a fourfold approach to involvement in tourism to promote a competitive edge and improvement to the visitor experience. The areas are:

- business leadership
- destination development
- product development
- innovation.

It embraces:

- *the Tourism Innovation Group*, with its resulting Pride and Passion programme for encouraging new ideas, with passionate people able to promote it
- *Learning Journeys* to destinations deemed to be innovative and able to provide learning experiences for participants, generating ideas to introduce into their businesses

- *a Tourism Innovation Day*, where members of the tourism industry can gather to hear about and share new ideas and best practice in innovation
- *a Tourism Innovation Toolkit* and training programme to facilitate in-company innovation and training
- *an annual Innovation Development Award* to help fund promising new ideas by financially assisting the development of a feasibility study to implement the idea
- *a Destination Development programme* to help focus resources geographically into leading destinations to foster excellence in key areas
- *an Ambassadors Scheme* aimed at encouraging enhanced product development.

Each initiative is driven by a desire to see innovative businesses fostered to cater for tomorrow's tourists and their changing needs, while also acting as a high-profile model for other businesses to learn from. To drive forward innovation based on sound business intelligence, the organization has fostered the establishment of Tourism Intelligence Scotland (tourism-intelligence.co.uk) with industry-focused reports and information with over 5000 businesses making use of the resource.

Source: Page (2011: 262)

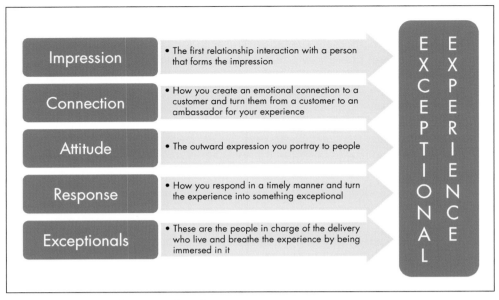

FIGURE 12.2 The five principles of Disney service

Source: Developed from Loeffler and Church (2015)

managing the organization where the traditional hierarchical model of management is inverted. The focus of the organization is in the customer contact zone, the interface between staff and guests/visitors, and everything in the organization is focused on that relationship. This was depicted by Carlzon (1987: 4) as 'if you're not serving the guest, your job is to serve those who are', a principle inherent in the Disney model. In this inverted model of management where front-line staff are the service deliverers, management is less about control and more about facilitating the work of front-line staff. However, competition and the global diffusion of innovations mean that a market leader will be quickly replicated, unless the product is patented and licensed. Yet even when an innovative idea has been created, it needs to be developed and commercialized in the tourism sector if it is to be marketed and this faces many obstacles. To exploit the idea, one of the most significant obstacles is funding it, and, where a business is set up to progress the concept, it may go through a series of growth stages which will have many barriers and constraints. One way to understand these is to look at how small firms grow; thus one will understand better what problems entrepreneurs and innovators face and therefore how to develop the business idea, concept or innovation.

How do small tourism firms grow?

Much of what we understand about tourism firms is based on large enterprises but, as many researchers acknowledge, the growth of small firms today in a number of cases may create the large company of tomorrow. This explains why governments support this activity. The role of economic geography (e.g. Hjalager 1999) and small firm researchers (e.g. Thomas 2004) have traditionally examined the dynamics of small firm growth in terms of:

- births (creation of new enterprises)
- deaths (business failures, where firms enter into receivership, go bankrupt or cease operation for personal reasons).

Morrison *et al.* (1999) interestingly observed the following stages of growth which small firms pass through after establishment (failure typically occurs in the first couple of years of operation), as shown in Figure 12.3. The experiences of the business in each stage will be dependent upon

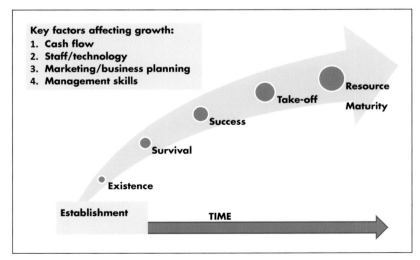

FIGURE 12.3 How small firms grow in their early years

Source: Developed from Morrison et al. (2009)

the management style and skills, style of organization and problems faced by the company. Finance and working capital are key problems in the set-up and existence stages and it is here that the management skills and abilities of the entrepreneur are crucial. Even in the survival stage, Shaw (2004) pointed to the weakness of formal management systems and the result is that many tourism lifestyle businesses remain in the survival stage, staving off failure. Where businesses enter the success stage, they may opt for a steady-state, stable option to meet lifestyle choices, or go for growth. Yet the main constraint to growth which many studies identify (e.g. Page *et al.* 1999), is a lack of finance. Other key features which will impact upon the business in the growth stage as shown in Figure 12.3 are cash flow, staff and technology, marketing and business planning and management skills (i.e. personal skills and qualities and formal management skills). These all affect the performance of small tourism ventures, and have also been observed among the critical factors for businesses. Yet entrepreneurship does not just exist in the private sector, as the case of intrapreneurship will show.

Public sector entrepreneurship: Intrapreneurship in tourism

As Morrison *et al.* (1999) discuss, in existing private and public sector organizations, the process of intrapreneurship may occur. This is when an individual or group of people may envision something and make it happen. These types of entrepreneur are often branded as 'product' or 'business' champions, epitomized by First Scotrail's rail franchise in Scotland (http://www.firstscotrail.com) and its customer service 'champion' to bring continuous improvements. Such a change master requires important personal qualities to overcome those resistant to innovation and change – the 'laggards'. As Neessen *et al.* (2019: 545) found, 'innovativeness, proactiveness, risk-taking, opportunity recognition /exploitation and internal /external networking are important behavioral dimensions of intrapreneurship. A certain skillset, a perception of their own capabilities, personal knowledge, past experience, the relation with the organization, motivation, satisfaction and intention are the determinants of intrapreneurial behavior' based on the findings of their study. Intrapreneurs therefore have a wide skill set to help overcome organizational barriers to innovation (e.g. being risk-averse); innovators will need to progress the following strategies to win over staff, highlighting the benefits to employees and the importance of change as shown in Figure 12.4, where many of the stages may be occurring simultaneously where multiple actors are progressing the intrapreneurial actions. For example, Maria Glot, Eddie Fenn and Ian Page performed this role at Bradford City Council in the early 1980s by putting an industrial city on the tourist map in what was described as a difficult area (Buckley and Witt 1985). What is interesting in this case is the role which the public sector and key drivers of change (the intrapreneurs) did in the 1980s. Davidson and Maitland (1997: 177) note that in the public sector, in Britain, there was 'an element of hegemonic change . . . in the face of evidence that the Thatcher values of enterprise and initiative were actually taken up by local government staff. In many cases, there was a change in attitude from regulation to entrepreneurship' making it possible to use tourism as a process for urban regeneration, with the public sector taking a lead role (see Chapter 13 for more detail on the public sector) (see Image 12.2 A & B).

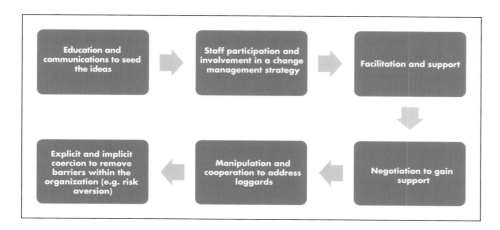

FIGURE 12.4 Strategies to overcome resistance to innovation in public sector organizations used by intrapreneurs

IMAGES 12.2 A & B Creating an innovative experience to encourage visitors to travel around a destination through promoting 'must do' activities and trail, such as locating uniquely painted otters at participating businesses in Dartmoor National Park, Devon, UK

The demise of traditional manufacturing in the early 1980s prompted Bradford City Council to set aside funds for the development of tourism in the area; textiles and engineering had dominated up until the 1970s but, by the 1980s, the city's image was one of bleak de-industrialization. Themed packages, such as 'The Flavours of Asia' and ones based on the Brontë Sisters, were developed: 2000 were sold in 1981/82 rising to 25 000 over the following two years (also see Hope and Klemm 2001). This confirms that there can be entrepreneurship in a public service institution although it is likely to be 'far more difficult to innovate than even the most bureaucratic company' (Drucker 1985: 163). Davidson and Maitland (1997: 176) argue that 'a new approach to planning is emerging which seeks to combine private-sector requirements with a greater sense of public purpose: entrepreneurial planning' although the research by Hope and Klemm (2001) also pointed to changes in public sector involvement and emphasis in the 1990s. One of the key features of developing a destination such as Bradford is the role which innovation played across the entire city and the need for collaboration and joint working so that organizations could realize the wider tourism objectives for the city. For this reason, it is useful to examine the strategies which SMEs can develop in relation to innovation in tourism.

Strategies for SME innovation in tourism: Collaboration

In the pursuit of innovation, many SMEs are widely acknowledged to be at a disadvantage compared to large businesses due to their isolation, lack of resources and inadequate networking. Here one of the most powerful tools which has been recognized is the process of collaboration. As tourism is a fragmented and diverse industry, with many linkages across sectors, joining up some of these links may prove beneficial to SMEs. The formation of partnerships to develop collaborations can have win–win outcomes for SMEs and destinations and these have been widely encouraged by public sector agencies in the creation of business networks. The culture of business-to-business networks and public–private partnerships can help with information sharing and in influencing policymaking to lobby agencies for support; they are also well known in sustainable tourism projects for bringing stakeholders together. This may help with developing new products where inter-organizational collaboration may lead to a supply chain being formed. The application of the idea in rural tourism is also well developed.

Hallenga-Brink and Brezet (2005) identified potential innovation strategies which might result in microtourism enterprises where a brainstorming method is used (i.e. getting the stakeholders together at a meeting to explore the range of potential innovations perceived by business owners). Possible innovations include:

- *at the company level*, introducing a level of socially responsible entrepreneurship by an ecovolunteer programme and business collaboration to create new products such as a laundry service for hotels
- *for local infrastructure development*, clustering tourist activity to reduce seasonal pressure
- *at the product level*, developing quiet beaches where low-impact activities could be developed
- *aimed at the guest*, green marketing on menus.

What collaboration may also achieve is a greater competitive advantage, by allowing SMEs to concentrate on their core competencies, pooling their resources, creating economies of scale, reducing costs and creating a model which competitors cannot easily imitate. As a result, to foster innovation, collaboration may be horizontal, cooperating with similar businesses undertaking similar activities, as well as vertical, with businesses undertaking different activities. With the use of ICTs, some of these organizations may be virtual.

Collaboration is preferable to competition in the SME sector which, in its most highly developed form, can lead to value chains, creating interdependencies which provide the competitive advantage. Much of the thinking in this area results from the influential work of Michael Porter (1985) on how to gain competitive advantage. Some of the forms which these collaborations may take include, as Shaw and Williams (2004a) show:

- informal inter-firm relationships
- supply strategies, such as those used by tour operators
- long-term strategic alliances
- mergers and acquisitions.

although the latter two categories are much more common in larger tourism firms. For example, 'micro-clusters' of small firms in a defined geographical area may be useful for collaborating businesses to identify a niche product as a network of interested businesses. In New Zealand, this approach was actively pursued by the New Zealand Trade and Enterprise organization to facilitate the development of wine tourism clusters, where a range of formal and informal linkages and relationships develop to add value to the product for tourists. The OECD (2008) emphasized the importance of such networks for SMEs and tourism development. However, much of the success of entrepreneurship is dependent upon the individual entrepreneur. While tourism remains characterized by relatively easy access in forming a business, personal traits still play a powerful role and the following section examines the characteristics of some influential entrepreneurs in the tourism sector.

Travel and tourism entrepreneurs

Brian Souter and Ann Gloag, representing rail and coach operation, and Richard Branson, with airline and rail businesses, have already been mentioned. When it comes to tour operating, there are few barriers to entry into the business: the single greatest in Britain is probably the Civil Aviation Authority's ATOL (Air Travel Organizer's Licence) financial requirement. This is one reason why tourism is so attractive to entrepreneurs: thus, in the SME sector, entry barriers and capital needs may be low (unless a major technological investment is envisaged – see Image 12.3).

IMAGE 12.3 Innovative technologies introduced in the late 1960s such as the Hovercraft revolutionized cross-Channel sea travel, competing with the ferry companies. They were replaced by more fuel-efficient technology such as the catamaran in 2000

In the USA, Sheldon (1995: 405) cites the growth from 588 tour operating firms in 1978 to 1001 by 1985, although only 34 per cent of those operating in 1978 were still in business seven years later; she notes that 'the situation is similar in European countries and seems to be characteristic of the industry'. Instability is largely a result of the easy entry and exit from this sector of tourism. When reviewing tour operations, Yale's (1995: 24) comments are particularly apposite: 'starting a new tour operating company can be seen as a creative business requiring imagination and strong nerves, so it has tended to attract entrepreneurial characters with strong personalities, most of them men'. The British tour operating industry is strewn with well-known names and their former brands: Harry Goodman and Intasun, Freddy Laker – whose Skytrain Holidays evolved out of the airline – and Vic Fatah, founder of SunMed and managing director of Inspirations, to name but three. However, a large number of contemporary entrepreneurs are simply emulating names from the past such as Vladimir Raitz who, many would argue, first established the mass market for package holidays by air charter in 1950. (See Bray and Raitz 2001 for a detailed analysis of Raitz's entrepreneurial activities.)

Shifting the focus of entrepreneurship: Social entrepreneurship and tourism

While entrepreneurship is fundamental to the development of businesses in the tourism domain, with an explicit focus on profit within a capitalist system, a new paradigm has developed over the last 30 years – social entrepreneurship (SE). It has a deeper set of ambitions associated with the underlying goal of finding solutions to major societal issues, as well as cultural and environmental problems. There are many reasons behind the growth in SE as shown in Figure 12.5.

In short, the aim of SE is to make a sustained contribution to the social good as well as creating a profit through its business activities to reinvest in its business mission. Social entrepreneurship is not a new concept, since the work of Robert Owen (1771–1858) who founded the modern day co-operative movement is often credited with popularizing this way of conducting business (Bornstein 2004). A wide range of types of SE exist, many with a community development focus, and their key success factors are usually characterized by a charismatic leader, with a single focus on the issue they wish to address. Other characteristics of social enterprises are illustrated in Table 12.2.

There are many examples of successful implementation of SE in tourism (see Sheldon and Roberto 2017) where individual success stories are typically represented as case studies, as exemplified by Kimbu and Ngoasong (2016). The growing significance of SE in tourism has also been viewed as a relatively new research direction, related to debates on sustainability to address issues around spreading the benefits of tourism to broader groups of people beyond the existing supply chain of tourism distribution. These points are evident in the review by Rey-Martí *et al.* (2016) and the potential for implementation of the idea in sub-Saharan Africa as illustrated in Insight 12.2.

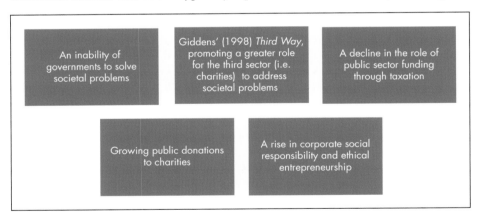

FIGURE 12.5 Factors promoting the growth of social entrepreneurship in society

12

INSIGHT 12.2 Social enterprises and tourism in sub-Saharan Africa

Rivera-Santos *et al.* (2015) highlighted the comparative neglect of sub-Saharan Africa even within research studies of Africa. The region comprises 50 countries with a range of common development issues, with district historical differences related to their diverse colonial histories and national politics. One common theme has been political conflict and severe socio-economic inequalities and continuous governmental failure to address protracted social and economic problems around development. Various United Nations Development Programme (UNDP) indices place countries in the region among the lowest ranked on education, life expectancy and health care. The region also faces many barriers to establishing new businesses with a very large informal economy (see Chapter 23) with large numbers employed in these sectors. This combines with low levels of income and high levels of poverty. Conversely, Rivera-Santos *et al.* (2015) point to data that sub-Saharan countries are experiencing high rates of GDP growth which are above world average rates of growth. The consequence is that the region offers many opportunities and challenges for SE, especially poverty alleviation. This combines with the growth in tourism in the region observed by Adu-Ampong and Kimbu (2019). In fact Kimbu *et al.* (2019) point to how women's tourism entrepreneurship can by harnessed by developing better collaborative networks. Kimbu and Ngoasong (2016) discussed women as 'vectors of social entrepreneurship' in tourism as owner-managers of socially focused small tourism firms. To support such SE ambitions, Ngoasong and Kimbu (2016) highlight the vital support role of informal microfinance (which are institutions providing credit, support and outreach to facilitate entrepreneurship). Littlewood and Holt (2018) also highlighted the importance of resilience for these types of business venture in the region to survive many challenges in running such enterprises. This draws upon the notion of resilience from Linnenlueke (2017) who defined business resilience in several ways: '(a) resilience as an organizational response to external threats; (b) resilience as organisational reliability; (c) resilience through employee strengths;

(d) resilience and business model adaptability; and (e) resilience through design principles that reduce supply chain vulnerabilities and disruptions' (Littlewood and Holt 2018: 55), all of which illustrate the scope of challenges which were illustrated in Figure 12.3 in terms of SME survival, particularly with some such enterprises operating in the informal economy. As von der Weppen and Cochrane (2012: 509) concluded, the key success factors in social enterprises operation in tourism in Africa were '. . . awareness of market conditions, including the need for a good product (and, by extension, the need to match product to market), and for strong leadership to shape a coherent organizational culture that provides the context for different stages of enterprise growth, and to create a balance between financial and social/environmental aims . . . Ultimately, the success of any social enterprise relies on maintaining a balance between mission and profit.' They also indicated that 'the entrepreneurs . . . had all started their venture based on belief in the power of commerce to effect change and after identifying a gap in the market, rather than doing so after reading a manual'. They represent the "transformational leaders"' which is a key element of the social enterprise paradigm.

Questions

1 Why has the social entrepreneurship idea become a key area of development in tourism?
2 What are the key principles of social entrepreneurship?
3 What are the range of business opportunities which social entrepreneurship offers in sub-Saharan Africa?
4 As a government charged with growing SMEs in an African country, how would you go about stimulating social entrepreneurship in tourism?

12

TABLE 12.2 Characteristics of social entrepreneurship and social enterprises

- a focus on innovation and change
- meeting and discovering unmet needs
- a non-profit focus (with profit reinvested back in the business rather than being disseminated to shareholders)
- a desire to initiate and make social changes
- the use of social media to canvass support for the cause being promoted
- the creation of employment for vulnerable and poorer people in society
- long-term planning horizon to meet a global or local societal need
- a social mission
- key organizations such as trusts and charities willing to provide practical and financial support to support new ventures
- the generation of profits to reinvest to address the problem the business is focused on
- a reciprocal relationship between innovation and change to create social wealth and value
- a transformative business agenda that harnesses opportunities that may be associated with technology, products, services or new processes
- compassion and commitment to relieving others' suffering
- varied types of enterprise which may have an economic, social, political or human focus.

Source: Developed from Perrini (2006); Rivera-Santos *et al.* (2015); other sources

INSIGHT 12.2 continued

Further reading

Black, R. and Cobbinah, P. (2017) 'On the rim of inspiration: Performance of AWF tourism enterprises in Botswana and Rwanda', *Journal of Sustainable Tourism*, 25 (11): 1600–1616.

Chell, E. (2007) 'Social enterprise and entrepreneurship: Towards a convergent theory of the entrepreneurial process', *International Small Business Journal*, 25: 5–26.

Manyara, G. and Jones, E. (2007) 'Community-based tourism enterprises development in Kenya: An exploration of their potential as avenues of poverty reduction', *Journal of Sustainable Tourism*, 15 (6): 628–644.

von der Weppen, J. and Cochrane, J. (2012) 'Social enterprises in tourism: An exploratory study of operational models and success factors', *Journal of Sustainable Tourism*, 20 (3): 497–511.

Conclusion

What emerges from the discussion of entrepreneurs and entrepreneurship is an understanding that successful entrepreneurs are likely to possess a number of personal characteristics although no two will be alike: one individual may exhibit a high degree of innovation but wish to limit the amount of risk exposure, while another will perceive the 'self-actualization' process as more important. A good track record in a previous business is undoubtedly of great help and provides a network of contacts to draw upon. These skills are vital in the early stage of business formation to survive and then to make informed decisions on how to grow the business. As SMEs dominate the tourism sector worldwide, the issues they face in the twenty-first century in the foundation by entrepreneurs is a valuable area of study, and researchers have begun to try to recognize what characteristics contribute to success. An example is the BBC series *The Apprentice* (Sugar 2005) which tested many of the characteristics needed to be successful in business. Besides these individual features, the wider economic and political environment is extremely important; in a highly regulated environment, there is little incentive for personal enterprise. What is widely acknowledged is that certain sectors such as the restaurant and catering sector have high failure rates, while other SMEs in tourism may hover around financial viability due to lifestyle reasons and cost subsidization from the use of family labour. Yet identifying the scale and extent of business failure in the tourism sector is notoriously difficult due to the sector's wide-ranging nature and data limitations in many countries. Even so, business failure does not deter serial entrepreneurs, especially as the experience of the dot-com boom illustrates: many of those who failed started up again later. While crises like foot and mouth and 9/11 tipped many small businesses into liquidation, other companies got stronger by weathering such events. In developing countries, Gartner (2004) for example, notes the links between entrepreneurs and working in the informal economy where regulations or a lack of capital prohibit a formal business structure. Finally, the sociocultural environment must be considered to have a major effect. Media portrayal of entrepreneurs in the USA frequently show success as something to be admired whereas respect tends to be more grudging in Western Europe.

Understanding entrepreneurship in tourism, particularly the process of innovation, is critical to fostering a competitive tourism sector. As agencies such as Scottish Enterprise show (http://www.scottish-enterprise.com), fostering innovation via its Tourism Innovation Development Awards, supporting an online innovation exchange and providing online case studies of successful innovation are all part of the wider support structure entrepreneurs and businesses require if they are to aim to do things better. Tourism innovation will continue to be one of the key buzzwords which remains associated with supporting entrepreneurial and intrapreneurial activity to raise the standards, invest in new products and to drive tourism forward in all areas of the industry.

Discussion questions

1 Why is the study of entrepreneurship important in tourism?

2 What makes a successful tourism entrepreneur?

3 Identify the preconditions in the wider economy conducive to tourism entrepreneurship.

4 Why does the tourism sector have low entry barriers to starting a new business, and is this detrimental to the long-term viability of the sector?

References

Adu-Ampong and Kimbu, A. (2019) 'The past, present and future of sustainability in tourism policy and planning in sub-Saharan Africa', *Tourism Planning and Development*, 16 (2): 119–123.

Alsos, G., Eide, D. and Lie, E. (eds.) (2014) *Handbook of Research on Innovation in Tourism Industries*. Cheltenham: Edward Elgar.

Ateljevic, J. and Page, S.J. (eds.) (2009) *Tourism and Entrepreneurship*. Oxford: Elsevier.

Blake, A., Sinclair, M. and Soria, J. (2006) 'Tourism productivity: Evidence from the UK', *Annals of Tourism Research*, 33 (4): 1099–1120.

Bornstein, D. (2004) *How to Change the World: Social Entrepreneurship and the Power of New Ideas*. Oxford: Oxford University Press.

Branson, R. (1998) *Losing my Virginity – the Autobiography*. London: Virgin Publishing.

Bray, R. and Raitz, V. (2001) *Flight to the Sun: The Story of the Holiday Revolution*. London: Continuum.

Buckley, P. and Witt, S. (1985) 'Tourism in difficult areas: Case studies of Bradford, Bristol, Glasgow and Hamm', *Tourism Management*, 6 (3): 205–213.

Carlzon, J. (1987) *Moments of Truth*. Cambridge, MA: Ballinger.

Casson, M.C. (1982) *The Entrepreneur: An Economic Theory*. Oxford: Martin Robertson.

Davidson, R. and Maitland, R. (1997) *Tourism Destinations*. London: Hodder and Stoughton.

Dondo, A. and Ngumo, M. (1998) 'Africa: Kenya', in A. Morrison, M. Rimmington and C. Williams (eds.) *Entrepreneurship in the Hospitality Tourism and Leisure Industries*. Oxford: Butterworth-Heinemann.

Drucker, P.F. (1985) *Innovation and Entrepreneurship*. London: Heinemann.

Drucker, P.F. (1989) *The New Realities*. London: Heinemann.

EU (2001) *Working Together for the Future of European Tourism*. Brussels: EU.

Eyana, S., Masurel, E. and Paas, L. (2018) Causation and effectuation behaviour of Ethiopian entrepreneurs: Implications on performance of small tourism firms', *Journal of Small Business and Enterprise Development*, 25 (5): 791–817.

Fielden, L. and Davidson, M. (eds.) (2005) *International Handbook of Women and Small Business Entrepreneurship*. Cheltenham: Edward Elgar.

Franchetti, J. and Page, S.J. (2009) 'Innovation in tourism: The public sector response in Scotland', in J. Ateljevic and S.J. Page (eds.) *Tourism and Entrepreneurship*. Oxford: Elsevier.

Gartner, W. (2004) 'Factors affecting small firms in tourism: A Ghanaian perspective', in R. Thomas (ed.) *Small Firms in Tourism International Perspectives*. Oxford: Elsevier.

Getz, D. and Carlsen, J. (2000) 'Characteristics and goals of family and owner-operated businesses in rural tourism and hospitality sectors', *Tourism Management*, 21 (6): 547–560.

Getz, D. and Petersen, T. (2005) 'Growth and profit oriented entrepreneurship among family business owners in the tourism and hospitality industry', *Hospitality Management*, 24 (2): 219–242.

Giddens, A. (1998) *The Third Way: The Renewal of Social Democracy*. Cambridge: Polity.

Goffee, R. and Scase, R. (1985) *Women in Charge: The Experiences of Female Entrepreneurs*. London: Allen and Unwin.

Hall, C.M. and Williams, A. (2008) *Innovation in Tourism*. London: Routledge.

Hallenga-Brink, S. and Brezet, J. (2005) 'The sustainable innovation design diamond for micro-sized enterprises in tourism', *Journal of Cleaner Production*, 13: 141–149.

Have, van der, R. and Rubalcaba, L. (2016) 'Social innovation research: An emerging area of innovation studies', *Research Policy*, 45 (9): 1923–1935.

Hirsrich, R.D. and Peters, M.P. (1992) *Entrepreneurship – Starting, Developing and Managing a New Enterprise*, 2nd edition. Irwin, IL: Homewood.

Hjalager, A. (1999) 'The ecology of organizations in Danish tourism: A regional labour perspective', *Tourism Geographies*, 1 (2): 164–182.

Hjalager, A. (2002) 'Repairing innovation defectiveness in tourism', *Tourism Management*, 23 (4): 464–474.

Hope, C. and Klemm, M. (2001) 'Tourism in difficult areas revisited: The case of Bradford', *Tourism Management*, 22 (6): 629–635.

Kimbu, A. and Ngoasong, M. (2016) 'Women as vectors of social entrepreneurship', *Annals of Tourism Research*, 60: 63–79.

Kimbu, A., Ngoasong, M., Adeloa, O. and Afenyo-Agbe, E. (2019) 'Collaborative networks for sustainable human capital entrepreneurship: The role of tourism policy', *Tourism Planning and Development*, 16 (2): 161–176.

Kompulla, R. (2014) 'The role of individual entrepreneurs in the development of competitiveness for a rural destination', *Tourism Management*, 40: 361–371.

Linnenlueke, M. (2017) 'Resilience in business and management research: A review of influential publications and a research agenda', *International Journal of Management Reviews*, 19 (1): 4–30.

Littlewood, D. and Holt, D. (2018) 'Social enterprise resilience in sub-Saharan Africa', *Business Strategy and Development*, 1 (1): 53–63.

Loeffler, B. and Church, B. (2015) *The Experience: The 5 Principles of Disney Service and Relationship Excellence*. New York: Wiley.

McMullan, W. and Long, W. (1990) *Developing New Ventures: The Entrepreneurial Option*. London: Harcourt Brace Jovanovitch.

Medlik, S. (1996) *Dictionary of Travel, Tourism and Hospitality*, 2nd edition. Oxford: Butterworth-Heinemann.

Morrison, A. (ed.) (1998) *Entrepreneurship – An International Perspective*. Oxford: Butterworth-Heinemann.

Morrison, A., Rimmington, M. and Williams, C. (1999) *Entrepreneurship in the Hospitality Tourism and Leisure Industries*. Oxford: Elsevier.

Morrison, A., Rimmington, M. and Williams, C. (2009) *Entrepreneurship in the Hospitality Tourism and Leisure Industries*. London: Routledge.

12

Morrison, A., Rimmington, M. and Williams, C. (2011) *Entrepreneurship in the Hospitality Tourism and Leisure Industries*. London: Routledge.

Neessen, P., Caniëls, M., Vos, B. and de Jong, J. (2019) 'The intrapreneurial employee: Toward an integrated model of intrapreneurship and research agenda', *International Entrepreneurship and Management Journal*, 15 (2): 545–571.

Ngoasong, M. and Kimbu, A. (2016) 'Informal microfinance institutions and development-led tourism entrepreneurship', *Tourism Management*, 52: 430–439.

OECD (2006) *Innovation and Growth in Tourism*. Paris: OECD.

OECD (2008) *Tourism in OECD Countries, 2008: Trends and Policies*. Paris: OECD.

Page, S.J. (2011) *Tourism Management: Managing for Change*, 3rd edition. Oxford: Elsevier.

Page, S.J. (2019) *Tourism Management*, 6th edition. London: Routledge.

Page, S.J., Forer, P. and Lawton, G.R. (1999) 'Small business development and tourism: *Terra incognita*?', *Tourism Management*, 20: 435–459.

Perrini, F. (ed.) (2006) *The New Social Entrepreneurship: What Awaits Social Entrepreneurial Ventures*. Cheltenham: Edward Elgar.

Peters, M. and Pikkmaat, B. (2005) 'Innovation in tourism', in M. Peters and B. Pikkmaat (eds.) *Innovation in Hospitality and Tourism*. Binghampton, NJ: The Haworth Hospitality Press.

Porter, M. (1985) *Competitive Advantage: Creating and Sustaining Superior Performance*. New York: The Free Press.

Porter, M. and Kramer, M. (2011) 'Creating shared value', *Harvard Business Review*, Jan.-Feb.: 1–17.

Rey-Martí, A., Ribeiro-Soriano, D. and Palacios-Marqués, D. (2016) 'A bibliometric analysis of social entrepreneurship', *Journal of Business Research*, 69 (5): 1651–1655.

Rivera-Santos, M., Holt, D., Littlewood, D. and Kolk, A. (2015) 'Social entrepreneurship in sub-Saharan Africa', *Academy of Management Perspectives*, 29 (1): 72–91. https://doi.org/10.5465/amp.2013.0128

Sarasvathy, S. (2005) *Effectuation: Elements of Entrepreneurial. Expertise*. Cheltenham: Edward Elgar.

Schumpeter, J. (1934) *The Theory of Economic Development*. Cambridge, Mass.: Harvard University Press.

Schumpeter, J. (1952) *Can Capitalism Survive?* New York: Harper & Row.

Shaw, G. (2004) 'Entrepreneurial cultures and small business enterprises in tourism', in A. Lew, C.M. Hall and A. Williams (eds.) *A Companion of Tourism*. Oxford: Blackwell.

Shaw, G. and Williams, A. (1994) *Critical Issues in Tourism: Geographical Perspective*. Oxford: Blackwell.

Shaw, G. and Williams, A. (2004a) 'From lifestyle consumption to lifestyle production: Changing patterns of tourism consumption', R. Thomas (ed.) *Small Firms in Tourism: International Perspectives*. Oxford: Elsevier.

Shaw, G. and Williams, A. (2004b) *Tourism and Tourism Spaces*. London: Sage.

Shaw, G. and Williams, A.M. (1990) 'Tourism, economic development and the role of entrepreneurial activity', in C. Cooper (ed.) *Progress in Tourism, Recreation and Hospitality Management*, Volume 2. London: Belhaven.

Sheldon, P. and Roberto, D. (eds.) (2017) *Social Entrepreneurship and Tourism: Philosophy and Practice*. New York: Springer.

Sheldon, P.J. (1995) 'Tour operators', in S.F. Witt and L. Moutinho (eds.) *Tourism Marketing and Management Handbook*. Hemel Hempstead: Prentice Hall.

Stokes, R. (2012) 'The private sector and events', in S.J. Page and J. Connell (eds.) *The Routledge Handbook of Events*. London: Routledge.

Sugar, A. (2005) *The Apprentice*. London: BBC Books.

Sundbo, J., Orfilas-Sintes, F. and Sørensen, F. (2007) 'The innovative behaviour of tourism firms – comparative studies of Denmark and Spain', *Research Policy*, 36 (1): 88–106.

Thomas, R. (ed.) (2004) *Small Firms in Tourism: International Perspectives*. Oxford: Elsevier.

Thomas, R., Shaw, G. and Page, S.J. (2011) 'Progress in tourism management: Understanding small firms in tourism: A perspective on research trends and challenges', *Tourism Management*, 32 (5): 963–976.

Wan, D., Ong, C. and Lee, F. (2005) 'Determinants of firm innovation in Singapore', *Technovation*, 25 (3): 261–268.

Wanhill, S. (2000) 'Small and medium tourism enterprises', *Annals of Tourism Research*, 27 (1): 132–147.

Welsch, H. (1998) 'America: North', in A. Morrison (ed.) *Entrepreneurship – An International Perspective*. Oxford: Butterworth-Heinemann.

WTTC (2001) *HR Opportunities and Challenges, a Report by the WTTC Human Resources Task Force*. London: WTTC.

Yale, P. (1995) *The Business of Tour Operations*. Harlow: Longman.

Youell, R. (1996) *The Complete A–Z Leisure, Travel and Tourism Handbook*. London: Hodder and Stoughton.

Further reading

Books

Ateljevic, J. and Page, S.J. (eds.) (2009) *Tourism and Entrepreneurship*. Oxford: Elsevier.

McKercher, B. (1998) *The Business of Nature Tourism*. Melbourne: Hospitality Press.

Sheldon, P. and Roberto, D. (eds.) (2017) *Social Entrepreneurship and Tourism: Philosophy and Practice*. New York: Springer.

Sotiriadis, M. (ed.) (2018) *The Emerald Handbook of Entrepreneurship in Tourism, Travel and Hospitality*. Bradford: Emerald Publishing.

Journal articles

Connell, J. and Page, S.J. (2019) 'An exploratory study of creating dementia-friendly businesses in the visitor economy: Evidence from the UK', *Helyion 5*, eO1471: 1–30.

Dionisio, M. (2019) 'The evolution of social entrepreneurship research: A bibliometric analysis', *Social Enterprise Journal*, 15 (1): 22–45.

Getz, D. and Carlsen, J. (2005) 'Family business in tourism: State of the art', *Annals of Tourism Research*, 32 (1): 237–258.

Tapscott, D. and Caston, A. (1993) *Paradigm Shift: The New Promise of Information Technology*. New York: McGraw-Hill.

Morley, A. and Peattie, K. (2008) 'Eight paradoxes of the social enterprise research agenda', *Social Enterprise Journal*, 4 (2): 91–107.

Peters, M. and Kallmuenzer, A. (2018) 'Entrepreneurial orientation in family firms: The case of the hospitality industry', *Current Issues in Tourism*, 21 (1): 21–40.

12

The role of the public sector in tourism

Learning outcomes

After reading this chapter and answering the questions, you should be able to understand:

- the rationale for public sector intervention in tourism
- the function and role of the public sector in tourism activity
- the development and implementation of tourism policies in the public domain
- the role and responsibilities of national tourism organizations and other public sector agencies in the tourism sector.

Overview

This chapter discusses the role of the government and other agencies in the facilitation and development of tourism. The structure and activities of national tourism organizations and their regional partners are explored along with their coordination and liaison roles. The main focus of the chapter is on the reasons for public sector involvement in tourism, the activities of the sector and the mechanisms through which public sector objectives in tourism are achieved. International examples of public sector involvement and intervention in tourism are also discussed to highlight the impact and effect of policies and interventions on the tourism sector.

Introduction

The private sector, largely typified by profit-driven motives and entrepreneurial activity operating in a free market economy, forms a significant driver in tourism. However, as Pearce (1989) states:

> *Provision of services and facilities characteristically involves a wide range of agents of development. Some of these will be involved indirectly and primarily with meeting the needs of tourists, a role that has fallen predominantly to the private sector in most countries. Other agents will facilitate, control or limit development . . . through the provision of basic infrastructure, planning or regulation. Such activities have commonly been the responsibility of the public sector with the government at various levels being charged with looking after the public's interest and providing goods and services whose cost cannot be attributed directly to groups or individuals.* (Pearce 1989: 32)

This quotation from Pearce summarizes the basic issues that this chapter will examine:

- Why is the public sector involved in tourism?
- How do different organizations in the public sector manage tourism?

The development of tourism in specific countries is a function of the individual government's predisposition towards this type of economic activity. In the case of outbound tourism, governments may curb the desire for mobility and travel by limiting the opportunities for travel through currency restrictions, as South Korea did in the 1980s, while still encouraging inbound travel. Similarly, in the USSR, under the former Communist rule, the opportunities for domestic tourism were controlled by a limited supply of holiday infrastructure. However, such examples are not usual because most governments seek to maximize the domestic population's opportunities for mobility and travel by the provision of various modes of transport to facilitate the efficient movement of goods and people at a national level. To achieve the objective of encouraging tourism, policies must be formulated to guide the organization, management and development of tourism, which is where the public sector has an important role to play. The government is a major influence in society and in tourism, and Elliot (1997) argues that the success of entrepreneurs like Thomas Cook would not have been possible without a stable and supportive government. The public sector plays a very significant role in facilitating, controlling and/or providing the context for tourism development. As Joppe (2018: 201) explains:

> *The public sector – composed of elected and appointed officials as well as bureaucrats – plays a key role in both fostering and controlling the movement of tourists, as well as the activities of the businesses and organizations that provide the goods and services they need to complete their trip. The objectives pursued are to maximize particularly the economic benefits of this highly fragmented and dynamic activity, while minimizing potential problems for society, the environment, consumers, and businesses. Every aspect of its intervention (or non-intervention) is the result of policy decisions, most of which are made in branches of government or departments not directly concerned with tourism.*

Defining the public sector

The public sector is a somewhat nebulous grouping of organizations which comprises a range of government and government-based organizations. Their unifying focus is to deliver government policy and they have power to make decisions on aspects of strategic importance. Public sector bodies with an interest in tourism are linked together in a complex set of working relationships, designed to achieve objectives for wider good. To do this, the public sector uses taxation revenue to develop and implement policies and initiatives that benefit the community that it serves. Organizations that comprise the public sector are not commercially oriented institutions, although increasingly they operate with commercially driven objectives to ensure internal and external efficiency in utilizing limited resources.

The public sector operates at a number of different geographic levels in tourism, including:

- *Supra-national organizations*, working in the international or regional arena and involving a number of countries working in cooperation, the organization having greater power than individual countries on issues that transcend national interests. These organizations are likely to influence tourism planning and policy (e.g. United Nations, EU, ASEAN, APEC).

- *International organizations*, working on particular issues on an international policy area, often in an advisory capacity (e.g. UN–WTO, UNESCO).
- *National governments*, working at the level of the state or country and often operated by a democratically elected group that represent the wider populace, supported by an employed civil service. However, other styles of governance include dictatorships and non-democratic systems. National governments usually oversee tourism development through a ministry which may have tourism among a portfolio of other interests or which may be specifically focused on tourism. The level of national government involvement in tourism differs significantly between countries.
- *Government-funded agencies*, often working within a particular policy or geographic area. These bodies are charged with implementing national or local government policy but with the freedom to manage their own affairs. They are termed quangos (quasi-autonomous non-governmental organizations) in the UK, and in many Western countries there has been a proliferation of such organizations since the 1980s (van Thiel 2004). Many NTOs fall into this category.
- *Local authorities*, working at the local level of a county or administrative area, and, in a democratic system, elected by the local community and supported by an employed staff. Local councils often play an important part in tourism development and promotion at the local level, as Insight 13.1 shows (see Image 13.1).

A further dimension that complements the work of the public sector is the third sector or charitable sector. It has a major role to play as a voluntary body and while there is not a great deal of research in this field, Hunter-Jones and Thornton (2012) point to the three specific types of charitable organizations that co-exist with the tourism sector: those that work outside of the sector but use it as a basis for fundraising; those working within it, such as the National Trust, which rely upon it for donations and visitors to continue their charitable work; and those which exist above the tourism sector, which challenge current norms and thinking in relation to how the tourism sector operates. A good example of this is the long-established lobbying body Tourism Concern (http://www.tourismconcern.org), which relies upon donations and strategic partnerships with organizations to support its work on tourism.

IMAGE 13.1 Local and regional governments provide visitor information services for tourists, as this large centre on the waterfront in Auckland, New Zealand shows

Public sector interest in tourism stretches across all of these organizational and geographic dimensions. However, tourism development usually requires support and guidance from national government through policy. As Gunn and Var (2002: 114) state, governments 'have the choice of doing nothing or doing something constructive about public tourism policy'. In many countries the state's role in tourism is not new, as Chapter 2 illustrated. For example, as shown in Table 13.1, Almeida Garcia (2014) demonstrated the background of the government's role in tourism in Portugal and Spain:

In Portugal, the efforts of the Sociedade de Propaganda de Portugal (Propaganda Society of Portugal), a private institution founded in 1906 to encourage foreign tourism in Estoril and Lisbon and on the island of Madeira . . . [and in] . . . Spain [led to the creation of] its own Comisión Nacional para Fomentar las Excursiones Turísticas (National Commission for the Promotion of Tourist Excursions) in 1905. As the Spanish government's initial response to the demands of the business community, this focused on both generating revenue and raising the country's profile in the rest of Europe. The Commission was conceived primarily as a publicity tool, with the improvement of tourist facilities a secondary issue.

What Almeida Garcia (2014) also reinforces is that changes in policy and government direction meant that the state had a significant role in shaping tourism development in Spain and Portugal, which went through three stages, as shown in Figure 13.1.

While policy issues will be explored later in the chapter, this example of Portugal and Spain illustrates how important the state was in promoting tourism, but now the discussion moves on to consider why public sector interest in tourism exists.

TABLE 13.1 The beginnings of tourism in Spain and Portugal in the early twentieth century

Spain	Key factors	Portugal
Society Propaganda Climate of Malaga (1898) Tourist initiative associations	The first private initiatives	Society Propaganda of Portugal (1905) Tourist initiative associations
National Commission for the Promotion of Tourist Excursions (1905)	The first government initiatives	National Propaganda and Tourism Department (1911)
Royal Commission for Tourism and Artist Culture (1911)	1911	IV International Congress of Tourism in Lisbon
1st tourist museums 1st *Parador* (State hotel chain) Gredos mountains (1928)	Improved hotel accommodation	1st Pousada (State hotel chain) Elvas (1942)
National Tourism Board (1928)	Other government agencies	Portuguese Commission for the Promotion of Tourism (1930)

Source: Reproduced with permission from Elsevier from Almeida Garcia, F. (2014). A comparative study of the evolution of tourism policy in Spain and Portugal. *Tourism Management Perspectives*, 11, p. 44.

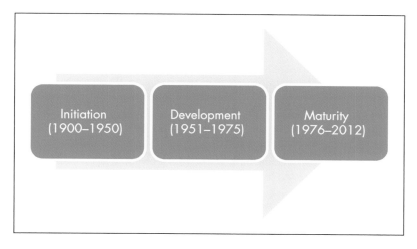

FIGURE 13.1 The trajectory of tourism growth and development in Portugal and Spain
Source: Developed from Almeida Garcia (2014)

INSIGHT 13.1 The role of local authorities in tourism in Scotland

There are 32 local authorities (known also as councils) across Scotland, and the role that they play in tourism is of crucial importance to ensuring that visitors have a satisfying and rewarding experience in the area. The main areas of involvement for local authorities include:

- providing and maintaining infrastructure to support tourism
- ensuring that attractions are accessible
- providing useful information on local attractions and events
- achieving a high standard in the maintenance of the physical environment

- paying attention to safety, for example through street lighting, policing and inspection of premises
- assisting in the development of new and enhanced tourism products.

From this, it is clear that Scottish local authorities play a multifarious role in tourism facilitation and development. However, they also function as a major stakeholder in tourism, providing direct and proactive contribution to the tourism product, as well as performing a support role. Tourism functions of local authorities are now explored below under two main headings.

INSIGHT 13.1 continued

Tourism support role

Within their area of jurisdiction, local authorities:

- are responsible for roads, planning, signposting, environmental health, public safety, licensing, trading standards and public transport coordination, all of which have a role to play in the potential success of an area's tourism product

- own, fund and manage public amenities, including museums and galleries, country parks, leisure facilities and public parks to serve the local community, but which facilities are also attractive to visitors

- employ a tourism officer or person whose portfolio includes tourism development

- provide information about their area and operate a website.

Such functions are fairly typical among local authorities on an international level. However, where Scotland differs from many regions is in the more direct role that the local authority plays in tourism, as illustrated below.

Tourism operations role

Funding

Scottish local authorities fund tourism through various means, for example:

1 They supply the main source of funding for the area-based tourism organizations, providing one-third of revenue income overall. For some areas, local authority funding is as high as 60 per cent of revenue.

2 Local authorities are a major promoter of tourism-related initiatives that are eligible for EU funding (dependent upon the outcome of **Brexit**), and, during the period 1994–1999, expenditure by Scottish councils on tourism-related projects funded by EU schemes was estimated at £71.8 million, mainly focused on the range, quality and marketing of the tourism product. Such a level of funding reflects the importance of tourism as part of a holistic approach to improving social and economic development.

Visitor attraction ownership

Contrary to the ethos that many governments have adopted with regard to tourism operations, in Scotland many local authorities own visitor attractions, and thus directly interact with and profit from visitors. Local authorities own

47 per cent of the 1999 attractions not charging an admission fee, and 6 per cent of all 318 paid attractions. Of these attractions, local authorities are charged with running 21.5 per cent of the total. Another particularly important feature of the tourism asset in Scotland is the provision of genealogical services for those seeking their ancestral roots, a service provided by the local authority library services.

In addition, the range of assets owned by local authorities which tourists use is diverse, from harbours and fisheries to arts venues, car parks, golf courses and even a racecourse, as well as the more traditional conference centres, parks and sporting facilities. Local authorities also fund and coordinate festivals and events, such as the Highland Games and Hogmanay celebrations.

Tourism development and marketing

Local authorities are also major funders of direct services and partnership arrangements to support tourism development and marketing. Examples include:

- design and implementation of promotional campaigns
- film location support
- coordination, promotion and sponsorship of events
- town twinning
- interpretation of sites, such as town trails and country park guided walks
- tourism brochures and 'what's on' guides for the local area
- town centre management and enhancement schemes
- advice and support to tourism businesses through Small Business Gateway and Scottish Enterprise.

Local authorities are charged with applying commercial values in the operation and delivery of services, and adhere to a strict policy of 'best value'. This means that much of the work of Scottish local authorities in tourism is achieved through collaborative working with other public sector organizations and, where appropriate, the private sector, to achieve maximum efficiency.

Yet this Insight also raises the issues of governance of tourism which have emerged and how these different organizations are integrated to achieve their goals. Hall (2011) pointed to four types of governance that affect tourism:

1 Hierarchies (state governance)
2 Markets (private economic actors and their associations)
3 Networks (dominated by various forms of public–private partnerships and associations)

4 Communities (governance at the local level by local authorities with direct public involvement)

Source: Joppe (2017); Hall (2011)

As Dredge and Jamal (2015: 285) suggest, 'tourism planning and policy is, arguably, one of the most significant influences on how tourism develops, who wins and loses, and how benefits and impacts of tourism are distributed' within the system of governance outlined by Hall (2011), in which local government is just one layer of a complex multilayered decision-making.

Source: Adapted from SLAED (2002); COSLA (2002); Economic Development and Planning Executive Group and VisitScotland (2004)

Further reading

Edgell, D. and Swanson, J. (2018) *Tourism Policy and Planning: Yesterday, Today and Tomorrow.* London: Routledge.

Questions

1 Why should local authorities be involved in tourism?
2 What is the scope of local authority involvement in tourism?
3 How would you justify local authority funding to residents and taxpayers?
4 Is the local authority the right type of organization to be involved in tourism provision and management?

The rationale for public sector involvement in tourism

Lickorish and Jenkins (1997) argued that tourism is too important for governments to leave to market forces alone due to the array of positive and negative impacts that tourism can create (see Chapters 16–19 for further discussion of impacts) that require some form of intervention. Such mitigating activity transcends the scope of the private sector.

The scope and extent of national government involvement in tourism varies between countries and regions, depending on political ideology (i.e. a system of belief about an issue that structures our thoughts), level of national economic development and the importance of the industry. Ooi (2002) compared the different approaches taken by the governments of Singapore and Denmark, as shown in Table 13.2, where Singapore retained strong state control in promoting a profit-driven culture, while in Denmark the state maintained a clear separation between private and public sectors and only offered the infrastructure necessary to stimulate business. Often, there is a direct and positive relationship between the importance of the industry and the amount of government involvement, so where tourism is a very significant part of a country's economy, or where tourism impacts are prominent, it is likely that government involvement will be high (Kerr 2003) (see Image 13.2). For example, tourism has grown rapidly since the late 1980s in Ireland as a result of the govern-

IMAGE 13.2 Stimulating local supply chains by organizing farmers' markets is a key activity for the public sector in attracting and engaging visitors

ment's policy of developing and maintaining the growth and success of the sector within the nation's economy (Deegan and Dineen 1997), and government involvement remains strong. However, the tourism boom of the 1990s has been replaced by a relative decline in recent years, with the exception of continued growth in tourism to Dublin. As a result, the public sector is actively examining ways to revitalize tourism to encourage new growth. In Paris, on the other hand, tourism was never highlighted as a key policy area but subsumed in a wider urban strategy. Since the 1990s, tourism

TABLE 13.2 Different approaches of the Danish and Singaporean tourism authorities

	Copenhagen: Wonderful Copenhagen (WoCo) and Danish Tourist Board (DTB)	Singapore: Singapore Tourist Board (STB)
Cooperation with industry	Build cooperation with other business agencies WoCo coordinates five tourism-related business networks	Cooperates with other state agencies in their social engineering programmes Cooperates with and offers policy support and financial resources to tourism businesses, such as retailers, attraction operators and travel agencies
	DTB licenses tourist information centres around Denmark	Licenses attraction operators, travel agencies and guides in Singapore
Role of tourism authorities	Provide infrastructure for tourism businesses	Provides infrastructure for tourism businesses Initiates, manages and provides financial and institutional support for tourism activities. Engages in state social engineering programmes
Public–private separation	Maintains separation between public and private sectors	Merges private sector interest with public social interests
Business and culture relations	Advocates that business influences on culture should be balanced by letting these two spheres of activities decide for themselves	Advocates that business and culture complement each other

Source: Reprinted from Ooi (2002): 689–706, © reprinted with permission from Elsevier

13

in the city has been addressed more directly by the public sector due to the negative impacts of traffic congestion and parking, rather than a direct approach to develop tourism (Pearce 1998).

Normally, the public sector does not have an involvement in tourism to directly profit from interaction with tourists, although conversely, in some regions, the public sector is a major stakeholder in tourism. Indeed, the work of the public sector in fulfilling its primary responsibility to its taxpaying citizens creates spin-offs from which tourists benefit, such as providing and maintaining infrastructure. The public sector also subsidizes and manages facilities and services for local people, from museums to swimming pools, and official events to national attractions, such as New Year celebrations, which are equally attractive to visitors and assist in developing tourism products and economic benefits for local communities.

In England, a report by the Local Government Association (2008), expanded this remit for tourism to include 'the cultural industries' (i.e. industries based on creativity such as music, the performing arts, literature, art and film) since these have helped create a cultural economy, a major element of many local tourism industries. The Local Government Association identified their role in terms of using cultural facilities to lead regeneration and growth (via their planning role); capital investment in new facilities; providing leadership such as in setting up the Liverpool Culture Company to develop the programme of works for Liverpool as European Capital of Culture 2008; assisting with innovation via strategic alliances with education and training providers. This not only helps to create unique competitive advantages for destinations in growing their cultural appeal to visitors, but also expands the scope and range of tourism-related employment opportunities associated with the cultural industries.

The traditional rationale for public sector activity in tourism is to generate economic benefits, although in the new millennium a much wider rationale exists. The dominant policy of economic growth through tourism has been superseded in many destinations around the world by a broader base of objectives, including:

- community welfare
- visitor satisfaction
- environmental and cultural protection
- economic benefits.

Finding the balance to make these often conflicting goals work is fraught with difficulties, as Chapter 19 on sustainable tourism will further explore. Accordingly, government involvement in tourism crosses the spectrum of economic, environmental, social and political interests. The factors outlined in Table 13.3 characterize public sector interest in tourism. Underpinning that interest in intervention are a number of important theoretical perspectives which illustrate how the process of public sector policy occurs. Dredge and Jenkins argue that:

> *tourism planning and policy is a result of thoughts, ideas, actions, collusions and collaborations of diverse actors, agencies and institutions . . . the social and relational characteristics of government, business and community have a powerful influence on tourism planning and policy development. Put simply, issues are identified, information is collected and exchanged, alternatives are discussed and even discarded and actions are taken.* (Dredge and Jenkins 2011: 2)

What is important is how the political process occurs in formal and informal settings so decisions are influenced and taken. Hall and Wilson (2011) point to the rise in neoliberalism in the public sector as a change to the relationship between the state and the private sector (i.e. the market) where the notion of public good is changing. In other words, the changing relationship between the state and corporate interests under neoliberalist approaches mean that what constitutes the public good changes, whereby public sector funding is used to benefit private sector interests with an expectation this will have public benefits (e.g. in the subsidization or support for major infrastructure projects such as stadia development). Under neoliberalist policies, the role of the state in tourism (and leisure) has been redefined (see Page and Connell 2010 for more detail) along with the notion of how we define the public good. As a result the politics of tourism policy formulation and implementation have changed in line with these new political realities. Indeed, Dredge and Jenkins (2011) point to the blurring of the boundary between the public sector and corporate interests under neoliberalism that has led to the favouring of corporate interests over those of the community and common pool (i.e. the wider public resources we all depend upon such as water, air and land). What this shows is that tourism policy-making is a highly politicized and fluid process with multiple layers of influencing and interests

13

TABLE 13.3 Public sector interest in tourism: Influential factors

Economic factors	Social and cultural factors
• To improve the balance of payments in a country by generating hard currency through tourism • To aid regional or local economic development and economic restructuring • To help diversify the economy and encourage commercial developments • To increase income levels in a country, region or specific locality • To increase state revenues from taxation of tourism activity • To generate new employment opportunities	• To ensure the well-being of the individual, by legislating for paid holiday time and supporting 'social tourism', exemplified by the Soviet Union's network of holiday centres for workers • To act as a catalyst of social change, for example facilitating closer interaction between host cultures and those from other countries • To promote cultural awareness, appreciation and development through tourism

Political factors	Environmental factors
• To achieve political goals in relation to promoting a country's political acceptability as a place to visit, for example in Spain in the 1960s, the government promoted tourism to stimulate political acceptance of the Franco regime as well as foreign exchange • To promote the development process through tourism, especially in less developed countries • To ensure that development is consistent with political ideology, e.g. in Cuba, where there was an embargo on American visitors	• To address market failure, where unrestricted operation of the private sector results in, for example, degradation of the environment, exploitation of labour or erosion of culture • To coordinate and undertake environmental enhancement works and visitor management schemes to manage the effects of tourism, as well as improving areas to attract visitors • To raise awareness and support for environmental initiatives and regeneration schemes, such as visitor payback schemes

each seeking to get their viewpoint adopted. So, having established the basic reasons as to why the public sector has an interest in tourism activity, the mechanisms through which involvement becomes manifest and the multiple roles that the sector plays are now explored.

The role of the public sector in tourism

A number of public sector tourism roles can be identified, which will vary in importance according to place. Drawing from the work of the International Union of Official Travel Organisations (IUOTO) in identifying the role of the state, Hall (2007) argues that the government now plays eight roles in tourism, as follows.

Coordination

Duplication of resources between government-based tourism bodies and private bodies can be better avoided through greater coordination and information sharing, based on a common strategy which is founded on cooperation between agencies. However, as van Westering and Niel (2003) highlight, public sector organizations at different levels sometimes experience difficulties in working together towards collective goals, and communications may be impaired due to differing political loyalties.

Planning

13

The wide remit of planning including the application and enforcement of development control strategies and tourism development strategies, as well as tourism development strategies allow the state to identify the wide remit of planning, which includes the application and enforcement of development control strategies as well as tourism development strategies (Chapter 24 provides a more detailed discussion on tourism planning processes). More recent functions which the public sector has assumed in view of the increasingly volatile nature of international tourism is the preparation of crisis management plans in anticipation of impending events, including scenario planning exercises associated with global issues such as the potential flu pandemic.

IMAGE 13.3 Enforcing local regulations, such as dog-free beaches, is a key responsibility for local authorities to safeguard hard-won environmental awards and to attract visitors

Legislation and regulation

Legislation and regulation not directly aimed at the tourism sector impinges upon its growth and development: examples range from immigration and visa regulations to employment policy. These and other statutory responsibilities are not an active form of intervention in tourism in most cases, but form the regulatory framework to which tourism activity must adhere. In some instances, regulations for tourism businesses have been proven to be unnecessarily bureaucratic, as the UK government recognized in the 'Tomorrow's Tourism' policy (Department of Culture, Media and Sport 2004). Conversely, in other parts of the world, increased regulation of tourism has been argued for with respect to environmental (see Image 13.3) and human rights issues.

Entrepreneurship

Governments and public sector bodies often own and operate tourism ventures or may own or manage land resources. This type of entrepreneurial activity appears to be declining particularly in countries where less public sector intervention is sought, where there is an increase in public–private partnerships (see Chapter 12); in the latter case a direct financial return is sought by the public sector rather than development being undertaken for the public good. It is exemplified in urban and rural as well as seaside regeneration schemes where the lifecycle model has reached stagnation.

Stimulation

Mill and Morrison (1985) argue that stimulation may occur in three ways:

1 The public sector stimulates tourism supply through financial incentives such as providing tax relief to overseas investors in tourist developments to encourage foreign investment and generate employment. This may be necessary in destinations where there is insufficient experience or capital to finance tourism projects.

2 Sponsoring research to assist the development of the sector through knowledge and understanding of markets and product innovation. A good example of this is provided by the partnership work of VisitScotland, Scottish Enterprise and Tourism Intelligence Scotland, where dissemination of research is facilitated through a website to industry (see http://www.tourism-intelligence.co.uk). This initiative was based on similar knowledge-transfer activities undertaken in other countries.

3 Stimulation of demand through marketing and promotion, which is a significant area of work for the public sector (see below) and is explored more fully in Chapter 15 on destination marketing.

Marketing and promotion

One of the primary roles of the public sector in tourism is marketing and promotion aimed at increasing consumer interest in a destination (see Chapters 14 and 15). Such activity is undertaken at different geographic levels but is normally coordinated through an NTO, which reflects national tourism policies. The curiosity in this is that the public sector promotion rarely has much control over the products that are being marketed, which are largely owned, managed and operated within the private sector. But NTOs have embraced the concept of destination branding globally, as well as unique selling propositions (USPs), as discussed earlier in relation to the cultural economy (Local Government Association 2008): these are the unique features of a locality and area which gives it a distinct competitive advantage, which are explored further in Chapter 15. Such marketing activities are outside the scope of the private sector alone, although the private sector is an integral part of the marketing process.

Providing social tourism

Historically, many governments actively participated in or issued policy statements on social tourism: providing holiday opportunities to marginalized groups such as those on low incomes, or for the general population within a state-supported framework, as seen in the former USSR. There has been a substantial decline in social tourism in recent years, reflecting a reduced governmental intervention. The focus has been on the individual as a consumer as opposed to the public interest reflected in social tourism objectives. An exception is Kyrgyzstan, which is actively developing mechanisms for social tourism. Social tourism activity now occurs more in the not-for-profit sector (e.g. the Family Holidays Association in the UK) and is more common in Scandinavia and Europe. Examples can be found on the International Bureau of Social Tourism website (https://www.linkedin.com/company/international-social-tourism-organisation-isto-) (also see Minnaert *et al.* 2012) and in Spain (Cisneros-Martinez *et al.* 2018).

Protector of the public interest

The government's role is to serve as an intermediary between competing interests and act as a balance between those seeking short-term gain and those with long-term interests. The public sector's responsibility is to act in the collective interest to prevent abuses and resolve conflict (Jeffries 2001). This is not the case in non-democratic countries with a centralized approach to development, in instances where the democratic process is brought into question or simply when dubious decisions are made within democratic processes. Indeed, governments can sometimes act against community interests in the cause of generating economic benefits from tourism, as in the case of the build-up to Visit Myanmar Year in 2000, where the military government of Myanmar forced communities to move in order to build new tourist accommodation (see Chapter 23). Pearce (1989) contests that the public sector does not have clearly defined responsibilities in relation to tourism and because there are often a large number of different bodies with a tourism interest, a resultant lack of coordination, duplication of effort or in some cases, neglect occurs. Such a diverse set of functions and roles normally require a *policy* to guide public sector activity (Edgell and Swanson 2013). Although by no means a panacea, a defined policy and integrated system for implementation can help to achieve strategic objectives more effectively.

Tourism policy

The term 'policy' is frequently used to denote the direction and objectives an organization wishes to pursue over a set period of time. Policy tends to focus at the macro level, while planning (see Chapter 24) normally focuses more at the micro level and implementation of policy (Hall 2007). According to Turner (1997), the policy process is a function of three interrelated issues:

- the intentions of political and other key actors
- the way in which decisions and non-decisions are made
- the implications of these decisions.

The policy-making process is a continuous process, and Figure 13.2 outlines a simplified model of that process which is applicable to the way tourism issues are considered by government bodies. Hall and Jenkins (1995) argue that state policy is a consequence of the political environment, values and ideologies, the distribution of power, institutional frameworks and the decision-making process within a country. Tourism policy reflects the strategic direction that a government deems appropriate to follow, although, in a democratic context, the process of policy formulation is also open to industry stakeholders, communities, development agencies and those with an interest in tourism development. Hall (2007) argues that it is more effective for countries to follow a tourism policy than a wider economic development strategy that incorporates tourism (Edgell *et al.* 2008).

Some countries have followed tourism policies for many years, while others have more recently developed a framework for tourism as they have emerged as international players, e.g. the Baltic States. In the case of India, which issued its first tourism policy in 1982, the key elements of the redesigned 2002 National Tourism Policy aim to position tourism as a major engine of economic growth and to harness the potential of India as a destination. The policy acknowledges the critical role of government acting as a proactive facilitator and catalyst, working in partnership with other bodies. In the UK, national government

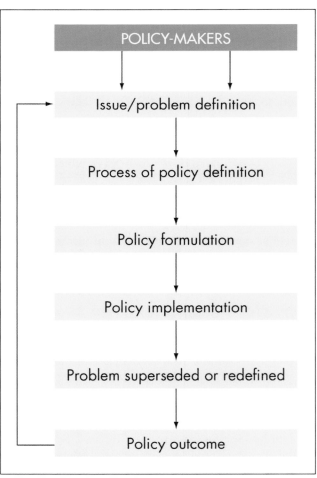

FIGURE 13.2 The policy-making process

policy focuses on promoting a favourable economic climate for enterprise and investment and therefore assisting the industry to develop. Part of this strategy, for example, focuses on reducing or simplifying burdensome regulations for businesses. However, the national approach also acknowledges a need for integrated or 'joined-up' thinking in tourism as an industry that is impacted on by a number of government areas, such as transport, planning, operational regulations and licensing, employment regulations and strategic funding.

While there are certainly some generic features of tourism policy, particularly in terms of economic impacts, some governments are particularly focused on other aspects of development and the role that tourism can play in fostering growth in specific parts of the economy. One example is Nigeria, where the main thrust of the government policy on tourism introduced in 1990, aside from the more universal objectives of generating foreign exchange and employment, is to encourage rural development by promoting tourism-based rural enterprises and accelerating rural–urban integration and exchange. It is pertinent to now focus on the public policy framework in which tourism is developed and managed.

The public policy framework for tourism

At a global scale, there are a number of agencies who have an influential impact upon tourism (Kennell and Chaperon 2013). The most significant of these is the United Nations World Tourism Organization (UN–WTO), a specialist agency of the United Nations Development Programme established to maximize the benefits of tourism while minimizing the negative impacts. The WTO was originally set up as the International Congress of Official Tourist Traffic Associations in 1925, becoming the WTO in 1975. The WTO encourages government involvement in tourism in partnership with other stakeholders, including the private sector, local authorities and non-government organizations (NGOs). It promotes international cooperation, serves as a forum for tourism issues globally and provides more practical assistance for its members, such as tourism planning, market intelligence, statistical information (as outlined in Chapter 3), education and training. The WTO also plays an advisory role in relation to, for example, technological development in tourism, harmonization of policies and practices in terms of trade, quality and safety, achieving sustainable development through tourism and funding sources. The WTO is based in Madrid and has a very useful website (https://www.unwto.org) which provides regular newsletters and press releases as well as a statistics database (for subscribers) and a list of the reports it produces. At an international level, a number of associated organizations also undertake activities which impact upon tourism, including transport industry bodies such as the International Air Transport Association (IATA), the International Civil Aviation Organization (ICAO) and interest groups such as the Air Transport Action Group (ATAG). The Organization for Economic Cooperation and Development (OECD) also has an involvement in tourism, producing publications for its member countries. These bodies have a coordinating and influencing role in terms of governments and, at a regional level, bodies such as the Pacific Asia Tourism Association (PATA) exercise considerable influence over tourism organization and policy. The European Union (EU) is a good example of a transnational body which provides a policy framework for tourism and this seeks to coordinate and liaise with the diverse stakeholders' interest groups and organizations that need to be taken into consideration.

According to Cooper *et al.* (2005), the EU's role in tourism is one of simplifying, harmonizing and reducing restrictions on trade, which in this case is travel. The main thrust of the EU's tourism activities is directed towards improving the quality of tourism services, encouraging the development of inbound tourism from outside the EU as well as improving the business environment for tourism enterprises and ensuring a sustainable environment for tourism. Given the diversity of tourism products and experiences within member states, the EU effectively leaves tourism policy to those states. However, the EU's main action occurs in relation to the gathering of tourism statistics, improvements to transport infrastructure that impacts upon tourism and the easing of frontier formalities and image promotion with the European Travel Commission (a non-profit-making body with 21 member countries). Beyond the standard arguments for unification, the reasons for the EU's intervention in tourism, as Hall (2007) and Cooper *et al.* (2005) argue, can be summarized as follows:

- the transnational character and operation of some tourism business calls for a European-wide policy framework
- there are concerns about environmental, social and cultural dimensions of tourism development, necessitating the drive towards safeguarding natural and cultural resources and sustainable and balanced tourism growth
- supporting the development of regional policy, particularly in disadvantaged areas, where public sector financial support is required to kick-start and sustain businesses as well as providing or improving essential infrastructure

- improving the quality and competitiveness of the tourism product, through funding programmes, dissemination of best practice, market information and training
- retaining cultural identity and the promotion of the concept of 'Europe'.

Information on EU tourism activity can be found on the website europa.eu and is discussed by Estol and Font (2016). While organizations working in the international arena play an important role in tourism, it is national governments and agencies that exercise the greatest level of influence over tourism activities within a country.

National tourism organizations

There are wide variations in the administrative frameworks developed within countries to manage and promote tourism. The NTO is usually a state-funded or hybrid organization which is state/private-sector funded and often located within a ministry of tourism. The NTO may be inside or outside the ministry of tourism, depending on whether the state wants a government or semi-government agency to direct tourism. It normally has a board of directors, a constitution enacted by law and a degree of independence from the political system. The funding of the NTO is usually agreed by the ministry by a purchasing or direct funding agreement, typically annually. In some countries, the NTO is termed a 'convention and visitor bureau', where revenue is raised from a range of sources (such as the private sector and sometimes through tourist taxes). Many NTOs operate overseas offices from where overseas marketing can be more effectively organized, and work with the local media and travel trade to stimulate interest in visiting their particular country.

Not all nations have government-funded NTOs. Despite being one of the country's largest industries, the United States Congress voted to suspend funding of its tourism office (US Travel and Tourism Administration) in 1996. Without a nationally funded and coordinated tourism marketing agency, the Travel Industry Association of America (TIA), a non-profit industry association, stepped in. The TIA created the universal brand for the US tourism product 'See America' (see Chapter 15), in partnership with more than 2000 leading travel industry organizations, to promote the USA as the world's premier tourism destination. However, while there is no federal body in charge of tourism in the USA, there are a large number of state tourism offices and a small number of regional organizations consisting of states, such as Discover New England. In addition, there are many destination management organizations that work on a much smaller scale such as counties, resorts and towns (see Insight 13.2). Government funding is made available to support tourism development objectives, for example the US$10 million approved by Congress in November 2004 to build on efforts to promote the USA as an international travel destination, after a dramatic decline post-9/11, following the terrorist attacks on the USA that were watched all around the globe (also see Chapter 25).

INSIGHT 13.2 Destination management organizations (DMOs) and tourism

The term DMO is a highly contested one within the tourism literature, and our understanding of these dynamic organizations has not kept pace with the profound changes affecting their rationale and role, as many have come under intense scrutiny as publicly funded organizations responsible for tourism at a subnational level. The key change that has affected these bodies is the shift away from public sector funding (except for the USA where public funding has been a small component) to other forms of support (see Paddison and Walmesley 2018 for a more theoretical discussion on new public management). In Scandinavia, Jørgensen (2017) identified the challenges facing DMOs as ranging from survival to development, from whether to focus on market experiences or to focus on communication and

on internal versus external governance. Other studies have identified the importance of value creation in DMO survival, a theme we explore in Chapter 14 around value creation in the marketing process (see Serra *et al.* 2017; Reinhold *et al.* 2018).

Dredge (2016) argues that the DMO's role is to stimulate growth, create value and support network development among stakeholders through a combination of market-enhancing, product-enhancing policies with those designed to address market failures. The underlying experience of many DMOs is a greater requirement to generate income to fund their activities by engaging with stakeholders in collaboratively funded projects, as the state exits from many areas of tourism activity. While many national DMOs retain their funding, a considerable shift in emphasis has occurred in the last two decades to such an extent that DMOs are now little more than marketing organizations (see Pike and Page 2014 for a discussion of this). This is because much of the expenditure by DMOs is directed towards marketing activities in different areas. The consequence is a growing debate on the terminology 'management organization', given the reduced funding and these organizations' weakened role in terms of being able to 'manage' as opposed to 'influence, guide and advocate'. The consequence, as Paddison and Walmesley (2018) demonstrate, is that by adopting new public sector management approaches, a decline in local accountability has occurred as a result of outsourcing the function to a private sector organization. One of the most salient studies that advances thinking around DMOs is Pearce (2015). Pearce provides an excellent overview of the nature of DMOs in one country, producing a wide-ranging typology (e.g. city/district-council focused, regional tourism organizations, economic development agencies and macro regional marketing alliances), to which the national DMO can be added with its strategic countrywide overview. Pearce (2015) draws upon the organizational behaviour literature to depict the types of DMO based on organizational competencies such as those that are operational, marketing and inter-functional (e.g. quality control) and general competencies such as coordination. While the organizational structures adopted by DMOs vary from a formal and tightly structured form to a more loosely and informally organized one, the underlying rationale is to perform an enabling role as well as enforcement of regulatory issues.

Yet Pearce's (2015) model does not fit well with the growing recognition of the role disruptive technologies perform in business (e.g. the impact of the peer-to-peer sector such as the example of Airbnb, the role of social media, the role of online travel agencies in removing DMO traditional booking functions) and how the state may contribute to that disruptive process when they remove existing funding regimes and introduce a new model based on political ideology. This was the case in England, where a very structured model of provision was removed in 2010 and a new framework introduced which allowed DMOs to emerge and form around new principles. In the UK, funding dropped dramatically in the second decade of the twenty-first century, and is now estimated at £70 million including business support services by local government bodies (Department for Communities and Local Government Statistics 2016). The new structure that evolved in England was initially focused around the closure of former Regional Development Agencies as economic-development-focused bodies that funded many DMOs and the transition to Local Enterprise Partnerships (LEPs) (Ward 2019). Since 2010, 41 LEPs have been formed, funded by two government departments. However,

the LEPs are not the sole conduit for development in the new landscape of funding for DMOs because in the intervening years a variety of organizations have evolved that are not driven by government policy, but rather by commercial reality and local action. Indeed, there are now different forms of DMO of all shapes and sizes, from those with a wide remit from management to those with a much more limited role in marketing and promotional roles only. There are also spatially or resource-focused DMOs that are state entities (e.g. a National Park), while London has a specific body reflecting its world city status (London and Partners). The underlying rationale of these new DMOs is to coordinate stakeholders, fulfilling the higher-level competency identified by Pearce (2015), with a much stronger focus on tourism businesses, the community and other associated interests (e.g. transport operators). In management terms, VisitEngland is the lead organization within the new DMO landscape, which includes public sector bodies located and funded by the Local Authority, organizations focused on defined boundaries, private companies, Community Interest Companies, public/private-sector partnerships through to pan-geographical bodies. The situation is complex and multilayered, reflecting local politics, power relationships and local needs. Beritelli and Laesser's (2011) examination of power dimensions illustrated that DMOs must navigate significant power relationships in the horizontal associations they develop with stakeholders, especially businesses. LEPs also have to align their activities to the national government's Industrial Strategy (Department for Business, Energy and Industrial Strategy 2017) and its ambitions to address national priorities, especially productivity. While Ward (2019) reviews the reviews of LEPs from different agencies and bodies, the mixed results in their progress and ability to leverage funding is reflected in the range of experiences and types of DMOS established around tourism.

Further reading

Pearce, D. (2015) 'Destination management in New Zealand: Structures and functions', *Journal of Destination Marketing and Management*, 4 (1): 1–12.

Ward, M. (2019) *Local Economic Partnerships*. House of Commons Briefing Paper No. 5651, 28 March 2019, House of Commons Library, https://researchbriefings.parliament.uk/ResearchBriefing/Summary/SN05651#fullreport

Questions

1 What different types of DMO can you identify?
2 What different models of funding DMOs exist?
3 Why are DMOs important for the tourism sector?
4 How would you design a DMO for your country? And what would be its marketing focus?

Recent years have seen many changes to NTOs, particularly to their funding, as states have sought to encourage the private sector to contribute more to the running of NTOs (as discussed in Insight 13.2 with reference to DMOs) with some countries using tourist taxes as a means of funding the NTO. The structure of the Singapore Tourism Board (STB), which can be consulted at https://www.stb.gov.sg/content/stb/en.html, shows that the STB is one of the larger NTOs in an international context. It is funded by the state and was established in 1964 to promote Singapore as a tourist destination. In 1996, the STB launched its 'Tourism 21: Vision of a Tourism Capital' which was a public–private sector initiative for developing tourism in Singapore in the new millennium so Singapore would become a regional tourism capital in South East Asia.

Clearly, the NTO performs a wide range of roles but its main functions can largely be categorized into:

- development (including research and tourism plans)
- information provision
- pricing
- controlling access to key tourist sites
- marketing.

It is the latter function – marketing – to which attention now turns.

Marketing tourism and the NTO

Marketing is usually the primary function of an NTO. Oppermann and Chon (1997) highlight a key factor associated with the growth of tourism in less developed countries (LDCs), which is the aggressive marketing by NTOs. However, NTO finances are quite variable and the budgets of some of the US state travel offices exceed that of some countries' national tourism budgets. Pike (2008) identified the budgets of NTOs, and globally, most countries have some form of NTO or equivalent DMO. In some cases the DMO is part of the country's National Tourism Administration (NTA) but in many cases it is a separate organization. Recent years have seen NTO budgets cut back, which has impacted upon the range and scope of activities they typically under-take, as shown in Figure 13.3. However, as research by the UN–WTO (2010) demonstrated, in spite of these challenging times for NTOs, with public sector budget cuts due to austerity measures, the spending by NTOs is predominantly around marketing (especially advertising and increasingly through the use of social media – see Chapter 6). As UN–WTO (2010) indicated, the average spend per international arrival for the 62 NTOs it surveyed was US$4.6 per arrival, although this ranged from US$0.16 per arrival in China and $1.32 in the UK to $9.6 in Australia and $40 in the Bahamas. When one compares the proportion of the budget which NTOs spend on international marketing (based on 2009 figures), this varied from 63.9 per cent in Australia to 86.8 per cent in Malaysia, 93.9 per cent in Denmark and 100 per cent in Brazil. The range of expenditure per country also varies significantly, with larger destinations spending considerably more, such as France, which spent US$113 million on the NTO and $100 million on promotion in South Africa. This compares to the declining spend on overseas marketing in the UK in the run-up to the Olympic Games from £35.5 million in 2004/05 to £24.6 million in 2014. Yet as Pike (2008) rightly argues, the sums being spent on marketing and advertising tourism by NTOs are relatively small compared to the budgets of other global

FIGURE 13.3 Typical activities undertaken by national tourism organizations

Source: Developed from UN–WTO (2010) and other sources

brands and fast-moving consumer goods (FMCG) corporations. For example, New York state spends around US$50 million in its city marketing office, of which US$42 million is spent on advertising and promotion.

The marketing activity of an NTO includes a number of tasks, from preparing a marketing plan and subsequent advertising campaigns to organizing familiarization tours for the press or travel industry, creating newsletters and attending trade and consumer exhibitions (also see Pike and Page 2014). The NTO is increasingly charged with creating a brand image of a destination, which is discussed in Chapter 15. The process of identifying a destination's key tourism resources is a key component of marketing planning, as discussed in the next chapter, which shows that tourism assets can be a competitive advantage. For example, the Canadian Tourism Commission created a vision and a mission statement for tourism using an audit process. This illustrates the initial assessment of Canada's market position and natural tourism assets. From this, a vision and mission was developed, and the mission was:

> Canada's tourism industry will deliver world-class cultural and leisure experiences year round, while preserving and sharing Canada's clean, safe, natural environments. The industry will be guided by the values of respect, integrity and empathy. (Smith 2003: 130)

In terms of developing this mission, Smith identified a number of challenges: 'For example, while the vision was seen as laudable for the nation as a whole, not every business or destination has a realistic opportunity to develop into a world-class, four-season operation' (Smith 2003: 130).

Other agencies involved in tourism in the public sector

Below the NTO in most countries there is often a complex web of organizations which complement the work of the NTO at the regional and local level. While their activities are often a scaled-down version of the NTO's work at a regional level, they often implement national policy and pursue integrated activities with the NTO providing guidance in a top-down approach. Pearce (1992) examines the activities of the regional tourism organizations (RTOs) in different countries and discusses their varied roles. Other organizations also exist with a wide remit for enhancing economic development in a locality, such as Enterprise Companies, which often have a tourism interest in this respect, with an agenda to boost or diversify the economy. In addition, public sector bodies also encompass agencies like National Park Authorities, which have a substantial interest in tourism planning and visitor management at park level.

One of the growing areas of activity in the 1980s and 1990s in the public sector was an increase in interest and response at the local level, often at the city or area level, where tourism has become a major issue to manage. Page and Thorn (1997, 2002) examine the situation in New Zealand where the Resource Management Act and its principles of sustainable planning combined with a market-led approach to tourism policy and planning placed the emphasis on the public sector in the regions and localities to plan and manage tourism growth, which was followed by the creation of a National Tourism Strategy. Page and Thorn (1997, 2002) illustrate that the role of local and regional councils in New Zealand highlighted that many localities were unprepared for the impact of tourism. As a consequence, there is a greater role for the public sector, as Dredge and Moore (1992: 20) mooted, where

> increased tourism growth will result in greater challenges for the integration of tourism and town planning. These challenges will be brought about by the need for the development of attractions, transport, support services and infrastructure to cater for increased visitor numbers, and the implications this will have for land use planning . . . Planners have a responsibility to meet challenges offered by the growth in tourism and to understand how their activities affect tourism.

The outcome of this statement is reflected in many destinations around the world, where local government becomes responsible for implementing visitor management measures to manage tourism more effectively. For example, some 600 coaches (often old, noisy and polluting) used to visit Salzburg per day in the 1990s, and passengers often spent less than two hours in the city. The city council prohibited coaches from entering the centre unless passengers were staying overnight. However, businesses complained of a decline in patronage as a result of fewer coach visitors (Orbasli and Shaw 2004).

Local authorities play an important role in shaping the role and impact of tourism in local areas, often in tandem with other public and private sector organizations. Local authorities in the UK have also seen a new expansion, since 2003, in their role in managing the impact of the Licensing Act (2003) which extended opening hours of many entertainment establishments, creating an expanded 'late night economy'. Among the issues which this has raised in many UK cities is an inadequate provision of night-time transport, increased costs of litter collection, street cleaning costs (due to increased fouling/urination in streets), a rise in perceptions of city centres as 'unsafe areas', increased public rowdiness, vandalism and crime, as well as overcrowding in public spaces (Civic Trust 2007). This has also increased the costs of policing as well as increasing pressure for leisure and tourist use of urban environments. This illustrates how a change in legislation can lead to a growth in leisure use of the urban environment and in the hidden role of local authorities who have to manage, fund and plan for such impacts. Studies in other countries have also pointed to the concerns over expanding this night-time economy (see Pinke-Sziva *et al.* 2019 for the example of Budapest).

However, Hope and Klemm (2001) argue that support for tourism from local government cannot be relied on for two reasons. First, local authorities do not have a statutory responsibility to promote tourism and, second, it is difficult to obtain data that prove that tourism contributes to the local economy. In addition, as Ashworth and Tunbridge (2000: 66) argue, tourism can sometimes be viewed 'as a problem to be contained, not an opportunity to be welcomed' in cities such as Venice (see Chapter 20).

Public sector intervention in tourism

While some governments view the market economy as an adequate arena for tourism to operate within, others actively pursue interventionist policies to produce desired outcomes. Governments that are more likely to use interventionist policies are those whose countries are dependent on tourism as an economic agent or where tourism is creating significant problems. Two examples of intervention are discussed below.

1 Incentives to developers

The government has the capacity to alter regulations in order to provide an appealing climate for developers, particularly foreign investors able to bring in capital to start projects and developments that will bring economic benefits to a country or region in the longer term (see Dela Santa 2018 on the case of the Philippines, and Puciato and Dziedzic 2017 on the case of Poland). The Indian government views tourism as a major growth area and generator of economic benefits and the new tourism policy aims to assist the development of physical infrastructure. Incentives to developers that have been approved there include:

- concession rates on customs duty of 25 per cent for goods that are required for the initial setting up or substantial expansion of hotels
- 50 per cent of profits derived by hotels, travel agents and tour operators in foreign exchange are exempt from income tax. The remaining profits are also exempt if reinvested in a tourism-related project
- approved hotels are entitled to import essential goods relating to the hotel and tourism industry up to the value of 25 per cent of the foreign exchange earned by them in the preceding licensing year. This limit for approved travel agents/tour operators is 10 per cent
- hotels in locations other than the four major metro cities (Mumbai, Delhi, Calcutta and Madras) are entitled to a 30 per cent deduction from profit, for a ten-year period, as are hotels in designated tourist areas or heritage areas (adapted from http://www.tourismofindia.com).

2 Tourist taxes

Governments often levy taxes on the tourism sector, most commonly in the form of taxes on airport departure (see Seetaram *et al.* 2014 for a review of these taxes) and hotel occupancy, for the sole purpose of raising revenue. More recently, taxes have been levied on tourists for environmental reasons. Byron Bay in Australia, which receives in excess of 1.7 million tourists per year, is a town that has witnessed huge tourism growth. As a result of an influx of tourists and second-home owners, the local authority has a funding crisis, and is unable, for instance, to place adequate resources into improving sewerage capacities, which places pressure on other services, such as hospitals and public transport. One of the main reasons why this situation has arisen is that the revenue gained from the small permanent population through rates is insufficient to cover the costs associated with the tourist population. Suggestions to improve the flow of funding have included imposing a fee on day visitors and tourists by designating Byron Bay as a National Park. Recommendations being considered more widely in Australia include imposing a surcharge on airline tickets, provision of a fee from state government to the local authority based on numbers of tourists, placing a 50 per cent surcharge on the rates payable on second-home owners and charging a toll on certain highways. In Brisbane, a local government consortium suggested placing a levy of $200 on international tourists to cover tourism infrastructure costs. Such measures represent mechanisms by which local authorities can shift the burden of expenditure from their own budgets (and local residents) to visitors, but are often contentious, as many believe that increases in holiday costs may motivate tourists to find alternative destinations. In the USA, lodging taxes of between 11 and 15 per cent are levied at a state level and a proportion of these find their way back to the state DMO.

Conclusion

This chapter has examined the role of the public sector in the management and organization of tourism, emphasizing the role of different agencies and bodies in this process. The formulation and implementation of tourism policies is not a static unchanging process. Tourism is highly politicized as, in practice, tourism policies are often vehicles of national political ambitions by countries seeking to harness the economic and political benefits of a buoyant tourism industry. One of the key objectives of the NTO is to assist in the development of supply and promote the growth and management of demand to meet supply. Through the policy dimension, the NTO and government departments may use a range of instruments and other government measures such as land-use planning and control measures, building regulations and measures to regulate and direct the market as well as investment incentives. The state can also play a major role in non-tourism areas such as the provision of transport infrastructure, and this area is not always planned with tourism interests in mind, although in countries with an increasingly private-sector-demand-driven focus, the needs of the tourism sector are more carefully programmed into new developments such as airports and new infrastructure projects. There is also growing evidence of the NTOs seeking private sector finance through partnerships with industry to develop areas of their work for the tourism industry. Without a strong public sector role in tourism, the wider public good of the tourism sector and society is not easily reconciled with the needs of the private sector for profit and development. There is growing concern across NTOs and RTOs that state funding for tourism is increasingly being targeted towards marketing-led activities, given the strong business lobby which is associated with tourism in many countries. For example, in 2008, the Hong Kong Tourist Board received an additional HK$30 million to promote the convention and exhibition business, aimed at promotion overseas. This illustrates the performance focus on much of the public sector investment in tourism, which is marketing- and target-focused. The public sector acts as an anchor and counterbalance to the private sector, although it needs to work in harmony with the private sector rather than in opposition to it for a viable and successful industry. One area of cooperation is marketing, as Chapter 14 will now examine.

Discussion questions

1 What is the significance of declining government funding for the tourism sector, and should the private sector play a greater role in funding this activity?

2 Do governments need tourism ministers? If so, why and what functions should they undertake?

3 Review the roles which national, regional and local tourism organizations might play in tourism. Do they have overlapping roles, and if so, how would you address this problem?

4 What are tourist taxes? What role can they play in funding the tourism sector?

References

Almeida Garcia, F. (2014) 'A comparative study of the evolution of tourism policy in Spain and Portugal', *Tourism Management Perspectives*, 11: 34–50.

Ashworth, G. and Tunbridge, J. (2000) *The Tourist-Historic City. Retrospect and Prospect of Managing the Historic City*. Oxford: Elsevier.

Beritelli, P. and Laesser, C. (2011) 'Power dimensions and influence reputation in tourist destinations: Empirical evidence from a network of actors and stakeholders', *Tourism Management*, 32 (6): 1299–1309.

Cisneros-Martinez, McCabe, S. and Fernandez-Morales, A. (2018) 'The contribution of social tourism to sustainable tourism: A case study of seasonally adjusted programmes in Spain', *Journal of Sustainable Tourism*, 25 (1): 85–107.

Civic Trust (2007) *First National Survey: Evening and Night-Time Activities in England*, London: Civic Trust. http://www.civictrust.org.uk.

Cooper, C., Fletcher, J., Fyall, A., Gilbert, D. and Wanhill, S. (2005) *Tourism: Principles and Practices*, 3rd edition. Harlow: Prentice Hall.

COSLA (2002) *Review of the Area Tourist Boards*. Edinburgh: COSLA.

Deegan, J. and Dineen, D.A. (1997) *Tourism Policy and Performance – the Irish Experience*. London: International Thomson Business Press.

Dela Santa, E. (2018) 'Fiscal incentives for tourism development in the Philippines: A case study from policy networks and advocacy coalition framework', *Tourism Planning and Development*, 15 (6): 615–632.

Department for Business, Energy and Industrial Strategy (2017) *National Industrial Strategy*. London: Department for Business, Energy and Industrial Strategy.

Department for Communities and Local Government Statistics (2016) 'Local authority revenue expenditure and financing', Gov.uk (website) https://www.gov.uk/government/collections/local-authority-revenue-expenditure-and-financing.

Department of Culture, Media and Sport (2004) *Tomorrow's Tourism Today*. London: DCMS.

Dredge, D. (2016) 'Are DMOs on a path to redundancy?' *Tourism Recreation Research*, 41 (3): 348–353.

Dredge, D. and Jamal, T. (2015) 'Progress in tourism planning and policy: A post-structural perspective on knowledge production', *Tourism Management*, 51: 285–297.

Dredge, D. and Jenkins, J. (2011) 'New spaces of tourism planning and policy', in D. Dredge and J. Jenkins (eds.) *Stories of Practice: Tourism Policy and Planning*. Aldershot: Ashgate.

Dredge, D. and Moore, S. (1992) 'A methodology for the integration of tourism in town planning', *Journal of Tourism Studies*, 3 (1): 8–21.

Economic Development and Planning Executive Group and VisitScotland (2004) *FAQs on the Tourism Review*. VisitScotland.com

Edgell, D., Del Mastro Allen, M., Smith, G. and Swanson, J. (2008) *Tourism Policy and Planning*. Oxford: Butterworth-Heinemann.

Edgell, D. and Swanson, J. (2013) *Tourism Policy and Planning: Yesterday, Today and Tomorrow*. London: Routledge.

Elliot, J. (1997) *Tourism: Politics and Public Sector Management*. London: Routledge.

Estol, J. and Font, X. (2016) 'European tourism policy: Its evolution and structure', *Tourism Management*, 52: 230–241

Gunn, C. and Var, T. (2002) *Tourism Planning: Basics, Concepts, Cases*. London: Routledge.

Hall, C. and Wilson, S. (2011) 'Neoliberal urban entrepreneurial agendas. Dunedin Stadium and the Rugby World Cup: Or "If you don't have a stadium, you don't have a future"', in D. Dredge and J. Jenkins (eds.) *Stories of Practice: Tourism Policy and Planning*. Aldershot: Ashgate.

Hall, C.M. (2007) *Tourism Planning: Policies, Processes and Relationships*, 2nd edition. Harlow: Prentice Hall.

Hall, C. M. (2011) 'A typology of governance and its implications for tourism policy analysis', *Journal of Sustainable Tourism*, 19 (4–5): 437–457.

Hall, C.M. and Jenkins, J. (1995) *Tourism and Public Policy*, 4th edition. London: Routledge.

Hope, C. and Klemm, M. (2001) 'Tourism in difficult areas revisited: The case of Bradford', *Tourism Management*, 22 (6): 629–635.

Hunter-Jones, P. and Thornton, A. (2012) 'The Third Sector responses to accessible/disability tourism', in D. Buhalis, S. Darcy and I. Ambrose (eds.) *Best Practice in Accessible Tourism*. Bristol: Channel View.

Jeffries, D. (2001) *Governments and Tourism*. Oxford: Butterworth-Heinemann.

Joppe, M. (2018) 'Tourism policy and governance: Quo vadis?' *Tourism Management Perspectives*, 25: 201–204.

Jørgensen, M. (2017) 'Developing a holistic framework for analysis of destination management and/or marketing organizations: Six Danish destinations', *Journal of Travel and Tourism Marketing*, 34 (5): 624–635.

Kennell, J. and Chaperon, S. (2013) *Tourism and Public Policy*. London: Routledge.

Kerr, W. (2003) *Tourism Public Policy, and the Strategic Management of Failure*. Oxford: Elsevier.

Lickorish, L.J. and Jenkins, C.L. (1997) *An Introduction to Tourism*. Oxford: Butterworth-Heinemann.

Local Government Association (2008) *Local USP-Boosting the Creative Economy*. London: Local Government Association.

Mill, R.C. and Morrison, A.M. (1985) *The Tourism System: An Introductory Text*. Englewood Cliffs, NJ: Prentice Hall International.

Minnaert, L., Maitland, R. and Miller, G. (eds.) (2012) *Social Tourism: Perspectives and Potential*. London: Routledge.

Ooi, C. (2002) 'Contrasting strategies: Tourism in Denmark and Singapore', *Annals of Tourism Research*, 29 (3): 689–706.

Oppermann, M. and Chon, K. (1997) *Tourism in Developing Countries*. London: International Thomson Business Press.

Orbasli, A. and Shaw, S. (2004) 'Transport and visitors in historic cities', in L. Lumsdon and S.J. Page (eds.) *Tourism and Transport: Issues and Agendas for the New Millennium*. Oxford: Elsevier.

13

Paddison, B. and Walmesley, A. (2018) 'New Public Management in tourism: A case study of York', *Journal of Sustainable Tourism*, 26 (6): 910–926.

Page, S.J. and Connell, J. (2010) *Leisure: An Introduction*. Harlow: Pearson.

Page, S.J. and Thorn, K. (1997) 'Towards sustainable tourism planning in New Zealand: Public sector planning responses', *Journal of Sustainable Tourism*, 5 (1): 59–77.

Page, S.J. and Thorn, K. (2002) 'Towards sustainable tourism development and planning in New Zealand: The public sector response revisited', *Journal of Sustainable Tourism*, 10 (3): 222–38.

Pearce, D. (2015) 'Destination management in New Zealand: Structures and functions', *Journal of Destination Marketing and Management*, 4 (1): 1–12

Pearce, D.G. (1989) *Tourist Development*. London: Harlow.

Pearce, D.G. (1992) *Tourist Organizations*. Longman: Harlow.

Pearce, D.G. (1998) 'Tourism development in Paris: Public intervention', *Annals of Tourism Research*, 25 (2): 457–476.

Pike, S. (2008) *Destination Marketing Organizations*. Oxford: Butterworth-Heinemann.

Pike, S. and Page, S.J. (2014) 'The Destination Marketing Organization and destination marketing: A narrative analysis of the first 40 years of literature', *Tourism Management*, 41: 202–227.

Pinke-Sziva, I., Smith, M., Olt, G. and Berezvai, Z. (2019) 'Overtourism and the night-time economy: A case study of Budapest', *International Journal of Tourism Cities*, 5 (1): 1–16.

Puciato, D. and Dziedzic, E. (2017) 'Attractiveness of South-West Poland municipalities for independent hotel investors', *Tourism Economics*, 23 (3): 702–711.

Reinhold, S., Beritelli, P. and Grünig, R. (2018) 'A business model typology for destination management organizations', *Tourism Review*, 74 (6): 1135–1152.

Seetaram, N., Song, H. and Page, S.J. (2014) 'Air passengers and outbound tourism from the United Kingdom', *Journal of Travel Research*, 53 (4): 476–487.

Serra, J., Font, X. and Ivanova, M. (2017) 'Creating shared value in destination management organisations: the case of Turisme de Barcelona', *Journal of Destination Marketing & Management*, 6 (4): 385–395.

SLAED (Scottish Local Authority Economic Development Group) (2002) *The Role of Scottish Councils in Tourism*. Edinburgh: SLAED.

Smith, S.L.J. (2003) 'A vision for the Canadian tourism industry', *Tourism Management*, 24 (1): 123–133.

Turner, J. (1997) 'The policy process', in B. Axford, G. Browning, R. Huggins, B. Rosamond and J. Turner (eds.) *Politics: An Introduction*. London: Routledge.

UN-WTO (2010) *Budgets of NTOs 2008–2009*. Madrid: UN-WTO.

van Thiel, S. (2004) 'Trends in the public sector: Why governments prefer quasi-autonomous organisations', *Journal of Theoretical Politics*, 16 (2): 175–201.

van Westering, J. and Niel, E. (2003) 'The organization of wine tourism in France: The involvement of the French public sector', *Journal of Travel and Tourism Marketing*, 14 (3/4): 35–47.

VisitScotland (2001) *Visitor Attraction Monitor*. Edinburgh: VisitScotland.

Ward, M. (2019) *Local Economic Partnerships*. House of Commons Briefing Paper No. 5651, 28 March 2019, House of Commons Library, https://researchbriefings.parliament.uk/ResearchBriefing/Summary/SN05651#fullreport

13

Further reading

Books

Andriotis, K., Stylidis, D. and Weidenfeld, A. (eds.) (2019) *Tourism Policy and Planning Implementation: Issues and Challenges*. London: Routledge.

Dredge, D. and Jenkins, J. (2007) *Tourism Planning and Policy*. Milton, Qld: John Wiley and Sons Australia Ltd.

Dredge, D. and Jenkins, D. (eds.) (2011) *Stories of Practice: Tourism Policy and Planning*. Aldershot: Ashgate.

Journal articles

Dredge, D. (2016) 'Are DMOs on a path to redundancy?' *Tourism Recreation Research*, 41 (3): 348–353.

Dredge, D. and Jamal, T. (2015) 'Progress in tourism planning and policy: A post-structural perspective on knowledge production', *Tourism Management*, 51: 285–297.

Tang, X. (2017) 'The historical evolution of China's tourism development policies (1949–2013) – A quantitative research approach', *Tourism Management*, 58: 259–269.

14

Marketing tourism

Learning outcomes

After reading this chapter and answering the questions, you should be able to:

- understand some of the main terms associated with marketing and the concept of value and the challenge of marketing tourism in the digital era

- recognize the consequences of marketing in the tourism industry, and be aware of its distinguishing features as a service activity

- realize the importance of understanding the customers' needs, the marketing mix and market segmentation

- explain the role and nature of marketing plans, describing some of the main analytical techniques used.

Overview

Marketing is central to tourism to enable organizations to create value through their transactions with consumers. Core marketing concepts and issues are fairly universal but far from constant, with the impact of digital technology and Web 2.0 that has created a new landscape for tourism marketing, reflecting some of the special characteristics of tourism as an experience business. This chapter introduces a range of concepts and issues related to tourism marketing, emphasizing the role of value in the marketing process, the importance of understanding the marketing mix, understanding customers' needs, and the role of marketing planning and various techniques used to analyze the marketing environment.

Introduction

In the evolution of tourism, the practice of marketing has a long tradition, evident from the early work of Thomas Cook in using promotional material for tourism (see Chapters 2 and 7). Yet the formal identification of the concept of marketing emerged in the 1950s, and reviews of the evolution of marketing in tourism highlight a number of different stages including:

- *a production era*, based on the notion that if products were priced cheaply, they would sell regardless of consumer preferences. This was deemed an inward, product-oriented focus with little concern for consumers
- *a sales era*, when selling was the prime focus regardless of the market's willingness to accept the product
- *a marketing era*, replacing the preceding approaches: businesses now produced products they could sell which were tailored to consumer needs to satisfy the purchaser, effectively making the organization more outward looking
- an additional era has also emerged through the development of Web 2.0, which may be characterized as *the digital era of marketing*.

As Gretzel and Yoo (2014: 491) explain:

> *Web 2.0 refers to the technological base including programming languages and protocols that support the participatory nature of the Web . . . [and] . . . social media represent the platforms and channels through which content is created and shared. Thus, social media are Web-based applications built on the philosophical and technical foundations of the Web 2.0 that make it possible to create and easily transmit content. . . . The text, pictures, videos, audio files . . . created and shared through social media are called user-generated content (UGC) . . . or consumer-generated media (CGM).*

This shows that marketing has become more sophisticated as a process than in previous eras when printed and visual methods of reaching consumers (e.g. television and bill boards) were dominant. The digital age and Web 2.0 offers a growing range of tools for businesses to nurture customers and to add value to their experience of tourism, as well as opportunities to develop customer loyalty. Consumers now also exist as virtual communities and marketing has also become more immediate and interactive with the rise of digital platforms focused around notions of engagement, trust and creating lasting relationships with people to build consumer loyalty. Yet marketing is not a substitute for good business performance and vice versa. The cost of marketing (especially advertising) had made marketing an expensive activity for many SMEs, but the digital age has reduced these costs considerably. The low-cost airline sector and accommodation sector exemplify the role of marketing-oriented tourism organizations with their effective use of technology, as Chapters 5, 6 and 8 have shown.

14

The concept of marketing

As approaches to marketing have evolved, the consumer has also evolved in sophistication. The tourism sector has responded to meet their needs, as markets and sub-markets have developed, reflected in the use of segmentation techniques. A number of useful texts exist on tourism marketing (e.g. Kotler *et al.* 2017) and there is a general acceptance of the definition provided by the UK Chartered Institute of Marketing that marketing is 'the management process responsible for identifying, anticipating and satisfying customer requirements profitably'. This definition can be expanded to incorporate the growing sophistication of the consumer and the need to deliver value. As Kotler *et al.* (2004: 6) argue, marketing is:

> *A social and managerial process by which individuals and groups obtain what they need and want through creating and exchanging products and value with others.*

This definition has been revised more recently to recognize the impact of technology and a growing sophistication and breadth of marketing, especially the focus on relationship building in the digital age to connect with consumers:

> *Marketing is 'the process by which companies create value for customers and build strong customer relationships in order to capture value from customers in return'* (Armstrong *et al.* 2019: 11).

While Chapters 3 and 4 have highlighted the importance of human needs, wants and demand, the key feature here to stress is how marketing is based on a *value* proposition, which are the benefits which organizations put forward to satisfy consumers' needs (see Insight 14.1) as the *marketing offer* (i.e. the combination of products, services, experiences) to satisfy needs and wants. Consumers make decisions based on the perceived value of an overall product's capacity to satisfy their needs/wants and the marketing process is based on the concept of an *exchange* occurring between an organization and consumer (often a commercial transaction but not in every case). For this exchange to take place, two parties or more need to agree on the basis for the exchange, which will usually be a transaction, where these parties trade value, usually in response to some marketing offer made by the organization (see Kotler *et al.* 2004 for more detail). In tourism, the adding of value to the transaction has become a core concept in marketing, especially in the development of *relationship marketing* to build long-term relationships between customers and suppliers, with consistent quality and value-laden transactions that are mutually beneficial. The tangible outcome of value in tourism is often framed in terms of perceived notions of product and service quality, which we will return to in Chapter 24 on the tourist experience. For the tourism company, this means that they need to develop both marketing know-how and expertise to understand how to interpret customer needs. This may involve the training of staff to add value or, in extreme cases, re-engineering an organization to be more customer-focused, as British Airways did in the 1980s. Thus, marketing in tourism needs to be a philosophy adopted towards one's business operations that transcends simple notions of selling to the consumer: all the core elements of marketing (i.e. research, product, value creation, promotion and sales) should be integrated around a core focus on the consumer.

Therefore, to summarize, there are five core customer and marketplace concepts which are the foundations of the marketing process:

1   needs, wants and demands
2   market offerings (products, services and experiences)
3   value and satisfaction
4   exchanges and relationships, and
5   markets

Source: Armstrong *et al.* (2019: 11).

Some of these key concepts are outlined in Table 14.1.

Therefore, tourism marketing requires organizations to understand both the short-term needs to recruit customers and long-term goals to retain and nurture them, in a cost-effective and efficient manner.

TABLE 14.1   Key concepts in marketing

- **Wants** – the nature of human needs ranging from basic needs (i.e. for shelter, food, water, income and the resources to live to more consumer-oriented needs like taking holidays and purchasing branded products)
- **Demands** – how needs are turned into consumer items to be purchased
- **Market offering** – how businesses create services, experiences and products to meet a need or want, characterized by their construction of a consumer proposition or market offer with a value to be derived by a consumer from its purchase and consumption
- **Exchange** – the process by which a market offer is provided and a response occurs, typically as a purchase of the offer and its consumption
- **Market** – this comprises the range of possible buyers of a product, service or experience

---

Tourism marketing

In most organizations, marketing is a key component where consumer products are sold, and Lumsdon (1997: 27) outlined some of the characteristics which marketing orientated tourism businesses might exhibit (Table 14.2).

This orientation may be informed by one or more of the different philosophies that have developed in marketing, as shown in more detail in Table 14.3. In practice, different organizations define and apply their marketing activities in a way that is most relevant to their product or service. As we see shortly, new opportunities have also arisen with the digital age. Organizations, having examined their own marketing needs, should also:

- *develop a marketing information system* to undertake market research on customers, competitors and internal effectiveness to operate in particular markets
- *develop* marketing planning, to analyze the marketing environment and strategy to operate in certain markets and segments
- *plan tactical campaigns*
- *develop marketing operations*, including coordinating the internal marketing functions and communications internally and externally (i.e. public relations functions) as well as a monitoring and control function to manage the marketing function (after Lumsdon 1997).

TABLE 14.2   Marketing orientation

An organization would exhibit some or all of the following characteristics:

- A clearly defined approach to existing, potential and long-term markets.
- Policies and actions which reflect concern for consumer wants in relation to societal and environmental requirements.
- Implementation which involves internal marketing (own staff), consumer orientation and consideration of stakeholders including host communities.
- Market environmental scanning which includes short- and long-term scenarios.
- Marketing planning process which is part of the culture of the organization and includes genuine reappraisal of internal resources.
- A structure and culture which leads to long-term vision.

Source: Lumsdon (1997: 27)

TABLE 14.3   The marketing concept: Different approaches

The product concept An approach that assumes that customers are mainly interested in the quality, performance or features of the product. Thus marketing activities focus on product development and improvement.

The production concept An approach which believes that customers are generally price-sensitive. Here the aim will be to make products efficiently and distribute them widely enough to raise volume and drive down costs.

The selling concept Assumes that customers need to be persuaded to buy enough of the firm's products. Here a greater emphasis will be placed on advertising and promotion.

The marketing concept Has, as its basis, the importance of understanding customer needs and the aim to fulfil them more effectively than the competition.

The societal concept Here a concern for society is expressed, rather than simply satisfying customers and generating profits. Marketing approaches aim to encompass the interests of society as well as the customers concerned. More recently this has been termed social marketing.

Source: Adapted from Peattie (1992)

INSIGHT 14.1 The concept of perceived value in tourism marketing

There is a growing interest among marketers in the concept of value for tourists, given its potential to provide businesses with a competitive advantage if it is understood and built into the marketing offer. Sánchez *et al.* (2006) recognized

INSIGHT 14.1 continued

the dynamic nature of this seemingly subjective concept which is perceived by tourists in several ways:

- before a purchase
- at the moment of purchase
- at the point of use
- post-use.

Different elements of what tourists value may receive attention or focus at the various stages of purchase or use. For example, price may be a dominant issue at the point of purchase, whereas at the point of consumption other elements may be more significant than price.

Perceived value is a key element in the concept of relationship marketing and the nurturing of consumers. Perceived value is a complex concept which may best be understood as a multifaceted phenomenon based upon elements such as:

- notions of quality
- emotional responses
- monetary price
- behavioural price
- reputation.

Tourism experiences based on the notion of fun, pleasure and emotional responses are assuming a growing importance in seeking to understand tourist behaviour. One of the underpinning methods of explaining perceived value in consumer behaviour is the Cognition–Affect–Behaviour approach (Chapter 15), which argues that:

- *cognition* is associated with how consumers process information in consumption experiences, and how they develop meanings and beliefs about what they buy
- *affect* is associated with emotional elements (e.g. anxiety, hate and pleasure) which help to understand the types of feelings consumers develop
- *behaviour* relates to the purchasing and consumption element, where the enjoyment of a purchase or experience manifests itself.

This approach to consumer behaviour is a more complex one than more simplistic notions that all human behaviour in a consumption context is rational, which certainly would not help in studying hedonistic activities like tourism. To try to measure perceived value in tourism,

different dimensions have been examined: *perceived quality* through social value, *emotional elements* (perceived quality of the product) and the *functional value* (price and value for money). Sánchez *et al.* (2006) noted that in the case of a tourism package, the consumer has a holistic notion of its perceived value which is more complex than simplistic notions of quality and price, since affective elements have a key role to play. This is reflected in the social value attached to tourism purchases. For example, a family may place a great deal of value on being able to spend their leisure time together, and so a family tourism product will need to emphasize some of the affective elements that can be perceived as adding value to the marketing offer (see Chapter 15 on affective elements). As a result, the marketing implications of perceived value in tourism are clear. Tourism businesses need to focus on the intangible elements of tourism products, communicating these to consumers.

Further reading

Fang, B., Ye, Q., Kucukusta, D. and Law, R. (2016) 'Analysis of the perceived value of online tourism reviews: Influence of readability and reviewer characteristics', *Tourism Management*, 52: 498–506.

Sánchez, J., Callarisa, L., Rodriguez, M. and Moliner, A. (2006) 'Perceived value of the purchase of a tourism product', *Tourism Management*, 27 (3): 394–409.

Schoeman, K., Van Der Merwe, P. and Slabbert, E. (2016) 'The perceived value of a scuba diving experience', *Journal of Coastal Research*, 32(5): 1071–1080.

Williams, J., Ashill, N. and Thirkell, P. (2016) 'How is value perceived by children?' *Journal of Business Research*, 69 (12): 5875–5885.

Questions

1 How can value be examined in the purchasing stage through which people consider and purchase tourism products and experiences?
2 What are the elements of perceived value?
3 How do we explain perceived value?
4 How might we set about measuring perceived value?

This will also require an organization to be able to understand the external marketing environment (Table 14.4) at both the firm level and macro level, to understand how tourism operates and how different factors may affect its business. As the tourism industry is regarded as a 'service' industry, there are several attributes that distinguish the marketing needs of tourism from those of marketing a specific product. These characteristics are reflected in Table 14.5 and include intangibility, perishability, heterogeneity and inseparability. These can be expanded to also include a number of other considerations as shown in Table 14.6. As Tables 14.5 and 14.6 suggest, the tourism product

TABLE 14.4 The external marketing environment

Factor	Examples
1 Political environment	• Environmental awareness and legislation. • Growth of interest (lobbying on behalf of commercial sectors) and pressure group influence.
2 Economic environment	• Growth in economies, such as Asia. • Differential rates of personal discretionary income available for tourist expenditure.
3 Social/cultural environment	• Changing patterns of cultural values. • Fragmentation of societies into subcultural groupings.
4 Technological environment	• Accelerating pace of technological change. • Accessibility and rapid diffusion of technology in Western countries.
5 Ecological environment	• Increasing consumer and governmental awareness of ecological issues especially pollution and depletion of resources. • Continued questioning of short-termism by increasingly articulate groups.
6 Demographics	• Population growth in developing countries. • Ageism in Western economies.

Source: Lumsdon (1997: 15)

TABLE 14.5 The underlying principles of services marketing

Principle	Explanation	Implications
Intangibility	Unlike products, services are mainly intangible by nature. It is impossible for the consumer to touch, smell, feel or hear the service offering in the same way as they can test a product.	Tourism marketers tend to 'tangibilize' the tourism offering in brochures and videos – visual displays of the real thing.
Perishability	It is not possible to store services. An unoccupied seat on a train or bed in a guest house is lost forever, unlike a product which can be stockpiled until demand rises once more.	The management task emphasizes managing demand and capacity to a degree of fine tuning. For example, airlines offer standby fares to those willing to fill unexpected empty seats at short notice.
Heterogeneity	It is difficult for service marketers to standardize service provision given the close contact between staff and consumers. Performance varies regardless of processes designed to minimize this factor.	Tourism marketers design processes to minimize differences in service encounters and provision between different outlets or between different shifts at a hotel, for example. Provision of uniforms and of similar physical surroundings illustrates evidence of standardization.
Inseparability	The service provision and consumption occur at the same time and both provider and consumer interact in the process of delivery. This obviously is why standardization of service is so difficult as consumer involvement is high.	Marketers attempt to devise systems which ease interaction, and invest in campaigns to educate staff and consumers as to how to get the best from the interaction. Training in hotels emphasizes how staff can manage the interaction.
Lack of ownership	The consumer does not take title of goods as in product marketing. They bring back memories and feelings from a holiday.	The marketer emphasizes pictorial reference and souvenirs to reinforce image of holiday experience.

Source: Lumsdon (1997: 29)

14

can be more accurately thought of as a combination of several different services. While some of the basic principles of marketing apply to all products, there are clearly some special considerations to take into account in investigating the tourism industry. Lumsdon (1997) has shown that there is a conceptual continuum between goods and services where either tangible or intangible elements are dominant, and Figure 14.1 shows that, in most cases, tourism is an intangible offering. Therefore, in a business context, organizations providing tourism service need to have:

- a customer orientation
- a focus on the firm's external environment
- accurate marketing research information, particularly in relation to customers and competitors
- products that meet tourists' needs
- a strategy of differentiation, i.e. that the tourism firm's products are different in some way from the competition
- the ability to manipulate various marketing opportunities in such a way to create customer satisfaction.

TABLE 14.6 Additional features of tourism that highlight the need for service marketing

Inelasticity of supply Tourism products are inelastic in that often they cannot be easily adapted. If demand suddenly falls, this is unlikely to have a significant effect on the price. Tourism products are dependent on existing structures (hotels, transport and facilities) at destinations.

Elasticity of demand While it is more difficult to quickly adapt tourism products, demand is very elastic. Sudden events, such as fuel price rises, terrorist acts and exchange rate changes can quickly influence demand. Moreover, certain destinations can quickly become less fashionable.

Complementarity When a holiday is purchased, often it is not just a single service, but several sub-products that complement each other. Failure in one of these areas (e.g. airport delays) can seriously affect the overall experience.

High fixed costs The cost of developing tourism products, such as a holiday, involves high fixed costs (hotels, aircraft and trains). Such investment is not a guarantee of future profits.

Labour intensity Tourism is a labour intensive industry and the tourist's experience is greatly influenced by the skill of the staff they come into contact with.

Source: Adapted from Baker (1993); Cannon (1992); Vellas and Becherel (1999)

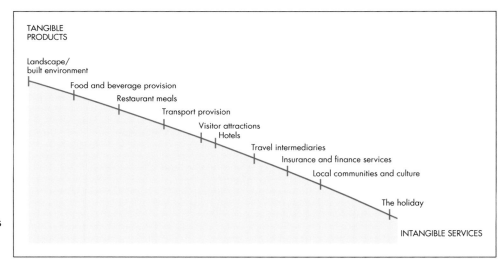

FIGURE 14.1 Good–services continuum in tourism
Source: Lumsdon (1977: 27)

It is against this background that marketing managers in tourism need to operate, since the marketing function is at the heart of an organization's strategy. Here, the most crucial question the marketing manager must ask is: 'Why should my customers buy my products, rather than those of my competitors?' (Holloway and Robinson 1995: 23). The remainder of this chapter will introduce some of the relevant concepts and issues associated with addressing this question. However prior to examining this proposition, we need to understand that marketing does not occur in a vacuum and the digital age has radically transformed these traditional approaches to marketing both as a process of deriving value and in how it has meant companies have had to embrace new ways of engaging with consumers. This is shown in Table 14.7 in relation to

TABLE 14.7 Marketing paradigm shift

Classic marketing	21st-century marketing	Social media marketing
Product	Experience	Relationship
Price	Exchange	Return on engagement
Place	Everyplace	Reach based on relevance
Promotion	Evangelism	Reputation

Source: Adapted from Birch (2011) in Gretzel, U. and Yoo, K.H. (2014) 'Premises and promises of social media marketing in tourism', in S. McCabe (ed.), *The Routledge Handbook of Tourism Marketing*, pp. 491–504. London: Routledge.

TABLE 14.8 Social media marketing functions (adapted from Gretzel and Yoo 2014)

Traditional marketing	Marketing functions	Social media marketing
- One-way communication		- Interaction
- Offline customer service centre		- Online customer service
- Limited customer data		- Customer identification with data mining
- B2C communication	Customer relations	- Virtual customer communities
- Prescribed solutions; scripted responses		- Crowd sourcing
- Delayed response		- Real-time communication
- One-off interaction		- Relationship
- Limited product information		- Value-added info on products: Pictures, video, catalogue, consumer reviews, etc.
- Mass products for mainstream markets		
- Company-created products	Product	- Product customization
		- Co-creation with consumers
		- Digital/virtual product
- One-price pricing		- Flexible pricing (Price transparency)
- Limited payment options	Price	- Online payment
		- Social buying
- Offline promotions		- Online promotions- Customized promotion messages
- One promotion message		
- Partnerships with traditional partners	Promotion	- Non-traditional partnerships
- Targeting customers		- Customer participation
- Mediated through mass media		- Viral spread facilitated by Web 2.0 tools
- Intermediaries		- Dis-/ Re-intermediation
- Required time to process order/booking	Place	- Real-time ordering and processing
- Offline distribution of products		- Online distribution of products
- Delayed results		- Real-time info through RSS or email alerts
- Push		- Pull
- Encouraged through incentives		- Based on altruistic motivations
- No follow-up		- Immediate reaction
- Mediated	Research	- Unmediated
- Sporadic		- Continuous
- Costly		- Free data
- Response limited to numbers and text		- Multiple formats
- Leads		- Conversations
- Discrete times	Performance measurement	- Continuous
- Hard sales/visitor numbers		- Consumer sentiment

Source: Gretzel, U. and Yoo, K.H. (2014) 'Premises and promises of social media marketing in tourism', in S. McCabe (ed.), *The Routledge Handbook of Tourism Marketing*, pp. 491–504. London: Routledge.

14

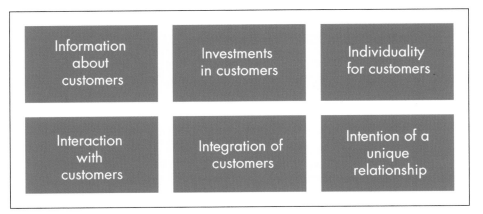

FIGURE 14.2 The 6Is of relationship marketing
Source: Developed from Diller, H. (2000) 'Customer loyalty: Fata Morgana or realistic goal?' in Hennig-Thurau, T. and Hansen, U. (eds.), *Relationship Marketing: Gaining Competitive Advantage through Customer Satisfaction and Customer Retention* (pp. 29–48). Berlin: Springer.

how Web 2.0 and the development of social media marketing have created a paradigm shift. In an age of social media, traditional marketing concepts have changed to adopt a very different approach to customer engagement. Birch (2011) has suggested that this marks a shift to the 4 R's rather than the traditional 4 P's as shown in Table 14.7. Here the focus is on how interactions with potential and actual customers occur and create a different set of principles in marketing associated with social media that are explored in more detail in Table 14.8. Table 14.8 illustrates the transformation of different marketing functions when using social media as a platform for connecting with consumers and how this is very different to more traditional approaches to marketing that characterized marketing in the pre-social-media era.

Both Table 14.7 and 14.8 illustrate the focus on customer relationships which are summarized in Figure 14.2 based on Diller's (2000) notion of the building blocks of relationship marketing that underpin social media marketing.

The marketing planning process and the marketing mix

Within the services marketing literature, there is a considerable debate over the precise nature of tourism as a consumer activity and its marketing needs. At a generic level, there is a debate over the nature of tourism consumption compared to the conventional consumption of goods through the pre-consumption (Stage 1), consumption (Stage 2) and post-consumption stages (Stage 3). As Jones and Lockwood (2002) point out, in the marketing process within tourism and hospitality firms, the marketing planning process usually occurs in Stage 1, but has a lesser role in services marketing as much of the 'production' or 'delivery' occurs in Stage 2, which is contact- or people-dependent. They also point to the element of remixing which often occurs in services in Stage 2, meaning the readjustment of pricing levels by monitoring consumer activity, typically through ICTs. Thus, Stage 2 is critical in tourism marketing and this highlights the importance of different marketing tactics and strategies which focus on the marketing mix.

The marketing mix

Marketers need to have a thorough understanding of the tourism products they offer, and long-term success requires an understanding of how potential tourists respond to a number of variables when deciding whether to respond to the marketing offer and purchase a product or service. It is the mix of these variables that will help to determine the extent to which an organization satisfies the needs of the market. These variables are referred to as the 'marketing mix' and are outlined in the Booms and Bitner

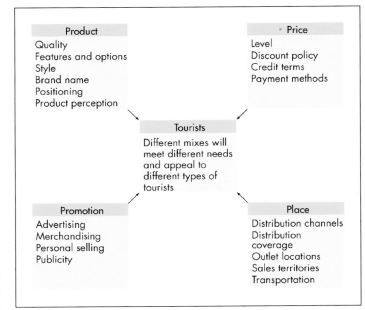

FIGURE 14.3 The marketing mix
Source: Developed from Cannon (1992); Holloway and Robinson (1995)

INSIGHT 14.2 The role of price in international tourism marketing in Africa

Oyewale (2004) examined the price competitiveness of African tourism destinations using a Tourism Price Competitiveness Index. This examined prices of tourism goods and services (i.e. food, beverages, tobacco, purchased transport, equipment and services for recreational hotel costs). In terms of the top five rankings, the most competitive were:

- Ethiopia
- Senegal
- Zimbabwe
- Mauritius
- Malawi

while the least competitive were:

- Congo
- Tanzania
- Botswana
- Côte d'Ivoire.
- Egypt

Oyewale (2004) explained that the price competitiveness of a country's international tourism product is a function of the export-nature of tourism resulting from:

- the exchange rate (external cost of money), and
- the inflation rate (internal cost of goods and services in a country).

The price competitiveness of a country's tourism product is not static, since it varies through time. For countries with a low price competitiveness, government policies directed at the tourism sector may help reduce this problem, such as reducing tax on hotel rooms and sales tax on goods.

Therefore, for countries promoting international tourism, the least price competitive may need to concentrate on market niches and particular segments which are less concerned with price (e.g. safari tourism in Botswana, as discussed in Chapter 23) as well as joint marketing campaigns focused on regional tourism to combine a price-competitive and less-price-competitive destination. Above all, the issue of price when combined with issues of product and destination marketing illustrates the need for marketers to have a sound understanding of the external environment and the changing position of one's competitors. Since Oyewale's (2004) study, the World Economic Forum's *Travel & Tourism Competitiveness Report* (2017) compared the price competitiveness of individual countries. It listed the five most price-competitive countries in Africa (Egypt, Algeria, Tunisia, Botswana and Gabon) as well as the five least price competitive (e.g. Sierra Leone, Ivory Coast, Ghana, Democratic Republic of Congo and Senegal). What is interesting is that the top 5 most price competitive also featured in the top 25 most price-competitive destinations to visit globally.

Further reading

Oyewale, P. (2004) 'International tourism in Africa: An assessment of price competitiveness using the purchasing power parities of the ICP', *Journal of Travel and Tourism Marketing*, 16 (1): 1–15.

World Economic Forum (2017) *The Travel & Tourism Competitiveness Report 2017*. https://www.weforum.org/reports/the-travel-tourism-competitiveness-report-2017.

model shown in Figure 14.3. These are often simplified to the 4 P's of product, price, place and promotion, as discussed in Insight 14.2 and in Table 14.7. It is the contribution of these variables which constitutes the total product and provides the basic opportunity for satisfying customer needs.

The interaction of factors shaping the marketing mix is illustrated in Figure 14.3, and different types of marketing decisions/marketing mixes will need to be made for different types of tourists since 'different markets require different marketing mixes at different times in their life cycle' (Vellas and Becherel 1999: 98). But there is some debate as to whether the four Ps are comprehensive enough to reflect the nature of marketing decisions in the tourism industry, with Vellas and Becherel (1999) referring to an additional three P's being necessary in the case of service providers. These are:

People In the tourism industry, people (i.e. staff) are important particularly in terms of their skills of customer care, how friendly they are and their appearance.

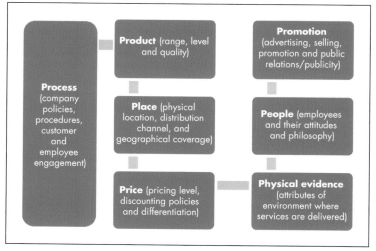

FIGURE 14.4 Boom's and Bitner's 7 P's marketing mix for services marketing, revised and adapted

Physical evidence Within accommodation, for example considerations of the furnishings, decor, environment, ambience, layout, cleanliness and noise level are all important.

Process Here aspects such as how efficiently procedures work, for example service time, waiting time, customer forms and documents all need to be evaluated, as illustrated in Figure 14.4, which is derived from Booms and Bitner (1981). However, marketing-mix decisions need to aim at the right target market and be consistent with the marketing concept of the particular tourism organization. Insight 14.3 reveals how the marketing mix needs to understand cultural issues in a growing market, Chinese outbound tourism.

Evolutions in marketing thinking on the 4 P's and shift to the 4 C's and rise of generational marketing

Traditionally the marketing mix has been focused on the 4 P's (or 7 P's, if one adopts the services marketing paradigm) but Armstrong *et al.* (2019: 58) argue that the 4 C's is a more balanced approach. The 4 C's is an approach that aims to include more than the seller's perspective of the market, and consists of:

- *The consumer solution* as the replacement for product, since the product is the marketing solution to a want/need.
- *Customer cost* as a replacement for price, since it includes both the purchase price but also the cost of production by the seller.
- *Convenience* as the replacement for place, since the digital age has meant that place is not necessarily fixed in time and space. The place can also be a virtual place or retailer, meaning that technology has adapted the conventional nature of place as a physical place where the marketing process occurs. As the Internet has made accessing and selling to consumers a more convenient means of accessing products and services, convenience is a better description of place.
- *Communication* is the replacement for the term promotion, as consumers now use a wide range of information services beyond physical print and advertising in the digital age. Therefore, for the marketing process to occur, sellers and buyers need to communicate with each other and in more diverse ways with the rise of the digital age, especially given the impact of social media. This makes the forming of relationships between businesses and consumers more important. Where businesses sell products, services and experiences through intermediaries (i.e. resellers and agents), communication with the seller and buyer involves more complex communication channels.

Traditional methods of marketing according to segments such as age, gender and socio-economic group have seen new methods of marketing emerge. These have been termed *Generational Marketing*, where the beliefs, values and behaviours of consumers can be aligned in a more complex manner with age and socio-economic variables. As Chaney *et al.* (2017: 180) argue, this represents a shift from an age-focused approach to marketing:

brand and product managers often consider age as a way to segment the market – often along with other demographic factors such as gender, marital status, occupation, and household size. This perspective is both obvious and inescapable. It is obvious because human morphology, tastes, attitudes, perceptions, and lifestyles change significantly over a lifetime, leading to substantial changes in buying behaviors. Marketing specialists may then note that specific behaviors match specific age groups, and use this match for segmentation, targeting, and positioning.

As Chaney *et al.* (2017: 180) go on to explain,

One way of going beyond age-based segmentation, which is often criticized as one-dimensional, is to place it in a broader theoretical field: Generational Cohort Theory. Anchored in sociology, this theory considers that individuals who experience the same historical, social, cultural, political, and economic events during their coming-of-age years – more specifically between 17 and 23 – share common core values and behaviors over the course of their lives.

What this approach does is shift the focus from individuals to groups, focusing on their consumption power and experiences that shape their behaviour. Some of the principles of generational marketing include associating a group of consumers by their birth years as groups and then identifying broad behavioural characteristics associated with their lifestyles, values, preferences and generational attributes. These are then targeted through marketing communications to appeal to them through more individualized messages. The common classifications of generations used include:

- *The GI Generation* – The name refers to the American servicemen associated with this generation who served in the Second World War.

- *The Silent Generation* – who were born between 1927 and 1945 experienced the Second World War and/ or its aftermath and may have been shaped by the austerity of wartime and post-war reconstruction; this group benefited from the growth in full employment, rising incomes, home and car ownership and pensions, making them affluent consumers in later life with a strong work ethic. This group would have been the first to experience mass tourism through overseas package holidays in the 1960s and 1970s.

- *Baby Boomers* – those groups born between 1946 and 1964 after the Second World War, and with a similar work ethic to the *Silent Generation*, who are respectful of authority and now nearing retirement. They benefited from the tail end of full employment, pensions and rising incomes, being able to spend money on travel with a widening range of tourism options in the late 1960s onwards.

- *Generation X* – people located in this group were born between 1965 and 1980 and are now in the family lifecycle stage with children. They possess technological skills and are often characterized as being independent, resourceful, and self-sufficient. They value freedom and responsibility in the workplace and are less respectful of authority than previous generations.

- *Generation Y (or the Millennials)* – these people were born between 1981 and 2000 and are characterized as being family-oriented, seeking work/life balance. Like Generation X, they are willing to challenge people in authority, and seek meaningful work experiences.

- *Generation Z (or the IGeneration or Centennials)* – people in this group were born after 2001and are characterized as very independent, with some of the features of Generation Y, but they are far less reliant on their parents compared to previous generations. Criticisms of this generation include their short attention spans, and immersion in technology (including social media), making them the most tech-savvy generation (for more detail on generation marketing and the groups – see Chaney *et al.* 2017).

According to Armstrong *et al.* (2019), a number of key considerations in generational marketing are:

- *The changing family*, with declining numbers per household in many developed countries. In Europe, the traditional nuclear family household of two adults and two children has declined as single-parent households have increased. This reflects wider societal trends of marital changes and second marriages, as well as more people living alone, including young financially independent women pursuing careers.

- *Geographical changes to population distribution*, as migration (especially labour migration) modifies the composition of countries' populations. In Europe, the mass migration of ethnic groups from Eastern Europe to Western Europe to work, and from South to North America, have added more diversity and complexity to consumer segments. One of the major developments in the greater diversity of consumer markets is the identification of religious groups and the need to appeal to multiracial groups. This also extends to sexual orientation (e.g. gay, lesbian and transgendered groups) and those with a disability.

- *Growing trends in consumer concerns for environmental issues*, reflected in concerns over ethical consumption.

- *A rise in direct marketing*, where businesses connect directly with their consumers to generate an immediate response and long-term customer relationships, often to nurture repeat business.

- *The growth of the digital age* and the ability to capture consumer data, often described as e-marketing, as the process of a company communicating with its customers digitally to nurture e-commerce to facilitate the exchange process to sell to consumers. The Internet age has changed the nature of purchasing, making

14

it private and more impersonal and removing sales people from the process, where the consumer can access more information on products and experiences. The Internet has made purchasing *immediate* and *interactive*, thereby making the consumer more knowledgeable. For business, the Internet age has created opportunities for greater relationship management, to nurture customer's wants and needs and to more accurately segment and segment them with tailored experiences.

● The Internet has led to a *reduction in production costs* (i.e. removing printed brochure costs for tour operators) and the cost of communications has reduced compared to mail and telephone. For businesses selling tourism products it also allows more flexibility in adjusting price in relation to their supply of products to avoid unsold capacity.

Various models for Web-based marketing have also emerged including:

● *Click-only versus click-and-mortar e-markets*. The early stages of the Internet spawned an entire generation of dot-com businesses which were click-only businesses with no physical premises or presence (brick-and-mortar presence), which led traditional non-digital business with a physical presence to add e-marketing operations.

● *Click-only* companies include e-tasters (e.g. dot-coms) such as Expedia. Other businesses in this category are Internet service providers and portals such as Yahoo and Google. A further group is price-comparison sites.

Knowing the customer and meeting their expectations is the only way to succeed, as the next section emphasizes.

14

INSIGHT 14.3 The marketing implications of Chinese cultural values

Mok and DeFranco (1999) note that China has one-fifth of the world's population and the greatest number of potential customers in any country of the world and the Chinese tourism industry is growing significantly now that travel restrictions have been relaxed and disposable income levels of a growing middle class are increasing. Mok and DeFranco (1999) outlined a series of Chinese cultural values which need to be considered in designing the marketing offer and in the marketing mix:

● Chinese tourists are more likely to engage in shopping activities during their trips.

● Chinese consumers are more likely to be influenced by opinion leaders than are Westerners.

● Chinese consumers are more responsive to relationship marketing techniques.

● Chinese consumers are more likely to be brand conscious than Westerners.

● Tourism services consumption decisions for individuals in China are likely to be the result of group decisions.

● Chinese consumers are less responsive to advertising which is openly critical of competitors.

● Chinese consumers are more sensitive to products or services which concern numbers, e.g. certain numbers (8)

are associated with luck or getting rich, while other numbers (4) have negative associations.

As China's economy grows, the demand for consumer products and services has grown. However, if tourism businesses wish to enter this market, understanding Chinese cultural values and how the Chinese shape their preferences and expectations is a first step in deciding on the type of marketing mix to develop. In addition, Zhu (2013) argued that there were specific issues to address when marketing to Chinese consumers, including: Chinese consumers are price-sensitive, but brand conscious; a lack of trust exists within China; children are a central part of the family and society due to the one-child policy; the Chinese consumer is becoming more informed and sophisticated in their use of social media and their activities.

Further reading

Kemp, S. (2015) 'Marketing in China: A five-step guide', *The Guardian*, 6 October, https://www. theguardian.com/media-network/2015/oct/06/marketing-china-social-media-consumers.

Sethi, A. (2019) *Chinese Consumers: Exploring the World's Largest Demographic*. London: Palgrave Macmillan.

Zhu, R. (2013) 'Understanding Chinese consumers', *Harvard Business Review*, 14 November, https://hbr.org/2013/11/understanding-chinese-consumers.

Knowing the customer

Marketers in the tourism industry need to understand the buying behaviour of the customers within their target markets. Some of the questions tourism marketers need to answer in respect of tourist buying behaviour include:

- Who are the customers/tourists?
- What types of tourism products do they buy?
- With whom do they travel (alone, couple, family)?
- Which suppliers do they use?
- What are the needs they aim to satisfy?
- Where/how do they buy their tourism products?
- When do they buy them (last minute, in advance)?

- How long do they go on holiday for?
- How often do they travel?
- How much are they prepared to pay?
- How do they decide which tourism products to buy?
- What influences their travel decisions?
- How do previous holidays affect future plans?

The answers to these questions will clearly help the marketer to decide how best to market their products, as well as any natural advantages of their location (Image 14.1). For most tourism businesses it is unlikely that their range of products will appeal equally to all types of potential tourists. Rather, the products are aimed primarily at particular types of tourists (e.g. young adults who are singles, travelling with friends, without children). Within the context of China. Bao *et al.* (2019) point to the three stages of outbound tourism growth which reflects the different market segments, comprising:

- The *first wave* of unsophisticated and package tourists of an older age profile
- A *second wave* of younger tourists born in the 1980s and 1990s, typically childless or with young children, and who are more sophisticated and independent. This group has been particularly prominent since 2005. These consumers tend to have experience of overseas education; they are English-speaking, self-organizing and seek a diverse range of experiences
- An emergent *third wave* of older, middle-class affluent outbound travellers.

Such groups represent the 'target market' for marketing, and Vellas and Becherel (1999: 59) refer to three options for targeting such markets:

Undifferentiated marketing

This is where a tourism business tries to sell as much as possible and their products have the broadest appeal. This would be a characteristic of mass-market tour operators, although, as Chapter 7 illustrated, even integrated operators such as TUI differentiate in mass markets.

Differentiated marketing

Here the company aims at particular target markets, and designs separate products and marketing programmes for each market. The costs to the firm of this are larger, but total sales may be greater if they can nurture new markets and their interest.

Concentrated marketing

In this approach the business concentrates on a specific target market. Rather than aim at all tourists, it chooses a specific market and aims to capture a large share of this particular market. Dacko (2004) examined

IMAGE 14.1 Iceland – Northern Lights, a significant natural attraction which can be used to market the destination

the price-sensitive online last-minute market including the three largest providers (Travelocity.com, Expedia.com and Orbitz.com) and the strategies used to target this type of consumer. These forms of purchasing reflect the global growth of Internet use. Tourism organizations may choose different virtual marketing solutions in seeking to target the online consumer, including the following:

- *a virtual face*, to achieve a low-cost approach to market products and services via the Web
- *a co-alliance* (a shared partnership), joining part of a consortium with a more sophisticated website
- *a star alliance*, comprising a number of core companies surrounded by others who draw on the expertise of the core
- *a value alliance*, based on a supply-chain model, using ICTs not previously available and facilitating the packaging of services and products in one place and able to respond quickly to the market
- *a market alliance*, with non-competing products and as a portal for the group
- *a virtual broker*, where third-party suppliers provide a virtual structure for different services
- *a virtual space*, which is entirely based on virtual contact with the customer, with an online marketing channel for distribution (Source: Burn and Barnett 1999; Lee *et al.* 2004).

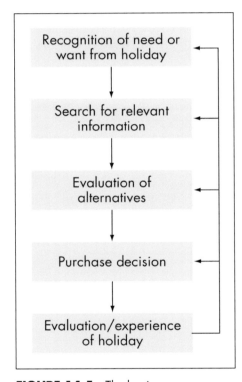

FIGURE 14.5 The buying process

This highlights that a strategy is necessary for approaching a target market, but tourists buy their holidays in different ways. Some people buy a holiday after careful study of travel brochures and guides and online press reviews, and after discussions with their friends and colleagues and a careful comparison of competing products. Others, who purchase the same holiday, may do so on impulse, after happening to see it advertised. For the purchase of most products, there is a buying process, as discussed in Chapter 4. The holiday-purchasing process is shown in a simplified form in Figure 14.5; this topic will be returned to in Chapter 15 in relation to the impact of advertising on this process.

At each stage in the buying process there are implications for the tourism marketer. Of particular importance is how potential tourists search for relevant information on which to base their decisions. This is of special relevance in the tourism industry, where attracting new visitors to a destination or new customers to a tourism service is always necessary. Here, marketers need to communicate their products to new customers, but to do this they need to know where the potential customer searches for that information and, as Chapter 6 highlighted, the Internet is increasingly being used to fulfil this role as 'lookers' search the millions of sites available. This has meant many tourism organizations have to have a Web presence in order to be more outwardly facing in this new environment for marketing products and services. Increasingly, organizations in the tourism sector are having to be more cognizant of the wider external environment discussed earlier as well as the diverse range of information sources now influencing tourist holiday-buying behaviour, as shown in Table 14.9.

The buying behaviour for a holiday is a complex process, and marketing communications have to be targeted at specific markets and types of consumers, as Chapter 15 will show. One technique developed and widely used in marketing, as discussed in Chapter 4, is market segmentation to identify target markets. For example, the National Tourism Organization of Argentina has previously segmented the inbound market into specific target markets comprising:

- active tourism (i.e. adventure activities)
- world heritage (i.e. it has nine UNESCO World Heritage sites)
- ecotourism

- thermal tourism
- rural tourism
- youth tourism.

The National Tourism Organisation, or Ministerio de Turismo (www.turismo.gob.ar) recorded 5.7 million international arrivals in 2019 but has plans to grow this number to 12.4 million by 2027 focusing on this product portfolio, supplemented by its diverse gastronomy and wines and the appeal of a wide range of landscapes ranging from deserts to glaciers. As Vellas and Becherel (1999: 60) state, market segmentation can improve the 'competitive position and better serve the needs of customers'. Achieving advantage over the competition introduces a new dimension in marketing, which is discussed next.

Competition

Identifying a market and presenting a distinctive service to a market segment are only the first stages of effectively developing a market. Having developed the tourism product, the business must hold onto it. As Chapter 5 discussed, competition for markets and consumers is intense in tourism and this illustrates the need for a well-developed strategy towards marketing and the marketplace. One of the most widely cited studies of the degree of competitive intensity a company will face is Porter's (1980) research into competitive strategy. Porter pointed to five key forces (degree of rivalry, new entrants, buyers, suppliers, substitutes) which impact upon a tourism setting and Lumsdon (1997) discusses this in the context of visitor attractions. This illustrates the importance of marketers undertaking competitor analysis using the tools and techniques which are discussed later in this chapter (e.g. SWOT analysis) and the need for ongoing monitoring of the marketplace. This helps to explain why market intelligence reports from organizations can command premium prices as they track the market and identify trends, future scenarios and the level of competition in the marketplace. Such research is critical for organizations who wish to develop or retain competitive advantages, seeking to cement the three-way relationship between the company, its products and consumers. Kotler (1988) argues that businesses need to know the following about their competitors:

- who are they
- what are their strategies
- what are their objectives
- what are their strengths and weaknesses
- how do they react.

14

TABLE 14.9 Sources of information used by tourists to decide on travel

The following sources of information for travel decision-making are commonly used:

- experience of previous visit
- friends and family
- travel guide books
- newspaper advertisements
- newspaper articles
- the Internet and social networking sites (e.g. YouTube, Instagram and Facebook)

- destination websites
- television advertising
- travel programmes on television
- magazine advertising
- travel fairs
- radio

Planning for the future: Marketing planning and analysis

Most commercial organizations in the tourism industry aim to survive, make a profit and, in many cases, grow. To do this requires that the firm have a strategic marketing plan in place which is flexible and a regular feature of managerial activity. According to Lumsdon (1997: 79), 'Marketing planning is the process by which an organization attempts to analyze its existing resources and marketing environment in order to predict the direction it should take in the future.' This is a necessary long-term strategy. One needs to be forward-thinking and innovative while thinking about the markets one serves/will serve, thereby ensuring that the organization is outward-facing. While different researchers adopt various approaches to outline the nature of the marketing planning process, it is likely to have many of the features outlined in Figure 14.6. Planning like this will apply to larger tourism organizations; Chapter 12 has already highlighted the lack of planning by many tourism SMEs. Yet marketing planning may be one of many planning processes for tourism organizations (e.g. financial planning, HRM (human resource management) planning and other lower-profile activities such as environmental planning to reduce waste).

As part of the marketing planning process, a number of questions to consider are:

- What is the core business and what are the firm's overall objectives?
- What is the current position in the marketplace?
- What are the firm's marketing objectives?
- What is the nature of the environment in which the firm operates and how will this change in the future?
- What strategies are there to achieve marketing objectives?
- What tactics are there to achieve the strategies (see Image 14.2)?
- Is there a sufficient budget for this activity?

IMAGE 14.2 Attractions are an important element in marketing an area and in providing family-friendly activities

As Figure 14.6 illustrates, these questions will be dealt with in a systematic manner to address wider management concerns over corporate strategy and the type of tourism business the organization in question aspires to be. One of the first steps in the marketing planning process is the marketing audit, to identify the company's strengths, weaknesses and ability to react to opportunities and threats. This wider analysis of the marketing environment may involve a **PEST** or **SWOT** analysis (see definitions in the next subsection), since to overlook these issues may mean that competition or events erode a company's competitive advantage.

PEST analysis

PEST analysis is an acronym for 'political, economic, sociocultural and technological', and refers to the external environment within which the firm operates. To inform future plans, this method provides a framework to help investigate the various factors that will affect the firm. While some of these are beyond the control of the individual business, an awareness of them is important.

- *Political*: What is the political environment of the destination area? Are there visa restrictions? Is there political stability or government elections? What is the government's attitude to tourism?
- *Economic*: What are the economic positions of both generating and destination areas? What effect will exchange rates, inflation, credit charges and labour costs have on the business?
- *Sociocultural*: What are the attitudes of the host community to tourism? What are the attitudes of tourists in the target market? What effect will new fashions and preferences have? What is the role of the family?
- *Technological*: What effects will new electronic forms of promotion, distribution and ticketing have?

PEST analysis is particularly important in the tourism industry due to the rapidity of change, and this highlights the importance of the marketing planning process. While PEST provides an awareness of the external environment, SWOT analysis is one of the main tools in developing business strategies.

SWOT analysis

SWOT is an acronym for 'strengths, weaknesses, opportunities and threats'. This technique provides a framework that enables an organization to assess their position within a market in relation to the competition. Information

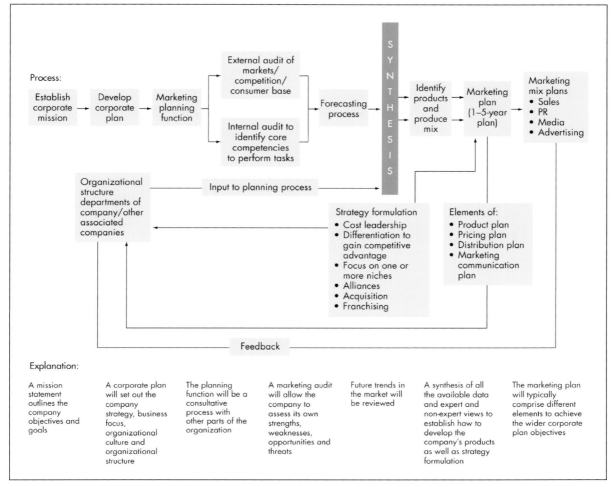

FIGURE 14.6 The marketing planning process in tourism
Source: Adapted from Atkinson and Wilson (1996); Lumsdon (1997)

TABLE 14.10 SWOT analysis of Iceland

STRENGTHS	WEAKNESSES
• Unique geological features and environment (e.g. geysers, lava deserts, glaciers). • Cultural heritage (i.e. Viking past). • International air access (Keflavik Airport). • International air access (international airlines serving Iceland including the flag carrier Icelandair, Air Canada, Norwegian, British Airways, Lufthansa and a number of low-cost carriers like JetBlue and easyJet).	• Damage to brand image by Iceland banking crisis. • Perceived remoteness. • Expensive destination to visit. • Highly seasonal visitor market and relatively recent tourism expansion emerging from a comparatively small international market (i.e. 540 000 international visitors in 2011 to 2.1 million in 2017) which has seen rapid growth. • Lack of a family-friendly image. • Infrastructure to access the interior is limited.

OPPORTUNITIES	THREATS
• Major growth potential for emerging high yield markets such as sustainable tourism, adventure tourism and wildlife tours. • Stopover opportunities for long-haul flights to the USA via Iceland.	• Numerous competing destinations in Scandinavia with similar products. • Low brand awareness. • Cost-competitiveness of destination and high cost of living relative to Europe, including import tariffs and Value Added Tax at 24 per cent that affect price-sensitive travellers.

Source: Various sources; compiled by authors

gathered in a marketing audit can assess the company's internal strengths and weaknesses and the external opportunities and threats that it faces. SWOT analysis is not limited to marketing; it can be applied to the whole company, to destinations or tourism products. Some of the common factors that could be considered are:

- *Strengths and weaknesses – internal*: Products, people, the organization, financial position.
- *Opportunities and threats – external*: Competition, nature of the market, new technology, economic position, legal framework, political situation.

These are illustrated by the SWOT analysis for Iceland (Table 14.10), which should also take into account the context of tourism that is examined in Frenţ (2018) and Gil-Alana and Huijbens (2018).

Approaches to marketing planning

Marketing plans are central to company strategy and, in tourism, short-term activities such as festivals or events may equally need professional marketing to make them a success and to attract the target market. An event, like any other tourism product or service, will seek to target potential visitors (i.e. buyers) as well as sponsors, and the budget available to implement the marketing plan will often reflect the scale and significance of the event. Edgell *et al.* (1999) suggest a six-stage framework to help marketers analyze the marketplace and develop a strategic marketing plan. While such plans will obviously differ, in accordance with the particular tourism product, these stages represent a useful structure, based on Edgell *et al.* (1999).

Needs analysis

Here the first step is to articulate the general objectives of the organization. This might include increasing the number of customers, the services they purchase and their repeat customers.

Research and analysis

Detailed analysis in all respects is an important second stage. Such methods may include SWOT and other types of examination of the marketing function within the organization. Externally, PEST analysis is useful, as are other forms of competitor analysis. Customer research is also important, to include market segmentation and target market identification.

Creative infusion

Edgell *et al.* (1999) suggest that after reviewing the results of the research, a stage of creativity, of finding ideas to distinguish the organization's marketing plan from its competitors, should be undertaken. Creativity is widely being recognized as an important driver in developing marketing and tourism products, as discussed by Richards (2011).

Strategic positioning

This will involve reviewing the organization's position in terms of its current and future customer needs, competitive advantage and competitor's position, together with a creative component that has helped to shape the strategic position.

Marketing plan development

Each market segment should have a separate marketing plan to capture new and repeat customers. Such plans have SMART goals ('specific, measurable, achievable, relevant and time-bound'). The accomplishment of goals is achieved through an identification of critical success factors (tasks that are vital to overall success). A definition of the marketing mix is also important, and should include aspects of pricing and promotion strategies.

Training, implementation, evaluation and adjustment

Training all who might be involved with the tourism product or service (including other organizations) is essential to remain competitive, aware of consumer needs and maintain a viable business. Following this, once implemented, continual evaluation and adjustment of plans are needed so that particular marketing campaigns can be examined in terms of their success. Recent developments in marketing practice are also outlined in Insights 14.5 and 14.6.

INSIGHT 14.4 Innovations in marketing theory and implications for tourism practice

As we discussed at the outset in the chapter, marketing as a subject has passed through a series of stages of development which culminated in the 1990s with a predominant focus on issues of service quality (SERVQUAL), which we will return to later in the book. While SERVQUAL has been a long-serving concept associated with the quality of service delivery in service businesses such as tourism, a new way of thinking (a paradigm) has evolved in recent years to challenge this approach. Whereas SERVQUAL has focused on services and their output (i.e. service quality), new thinking from mainstream marketing has refocused attention to services as a process. This has been described as service-dominant logic, and the new way of thinking has been described by Vargo and Lusch (2008: 258) as comprising a change, as embodied in Figure 14.7. This approach to service delivery and the focus on value creation reflects a step change in thinking which fits with the theoretical research on the experience economy, where consumers are looking for value in the experiences they engage in. This type of thinking emanates from the changing sophistication of tourists as consumers, especially the middle classes with their pursuit of authentic and unique experiences. This is part of what Pine and Gilmore

(1999) identified as the *experience economy*, which is the next stage in the evolution of society from a service economy. They argue that businesses need to create experiences which create a sensation and that can be personalized in order to build a relationship with the consumer, and they suggest four areas of experience that we need to focus on:

- entertainment
- education
- aesthetic (i.e. an ability to immerse oneself in something), and
- escapism in what is consumed.

This has major implications for the types of tourism we are developing now and will develop in the future, and for how tourism is marketed and promoted, with the growth of the Internet that now allows consumers to seek out these experiences globally. In particular, as Chapter 6 has shown, this has implications for National Tourism Organizations (NTOs) in terms of developing strategies to develop an ongoing and electronic relationship with potential visitors through the use of social media, as demonstrated in Insight 14.6.

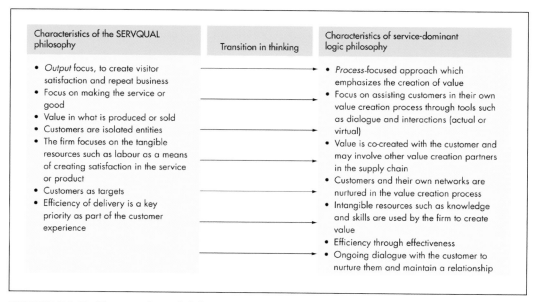

FIGURE 14.7 The paradigm shift from SERVQUAL to service-dominant logic
Source: Based on Vargo and Lusch (2008)

INSIGHT 14.5 The use of social media by destination marketing organizations

Stephanie Hays and Stephen J. Page

Social media are gaining prominence as an element of destination marketing organizations' (DMOs') marketing strategy at a time when public sector cuts in their funding are requiring them to seek greater value in the way marketing budgets are spent. Social media offers DMOs a tool to reach a global audience with limited resources. Social media is a constantly evolving phenomenon involving consumer-generated content (CGC) shared online. Brake and Safko (2009: 6) define it as:

> . . . activities, practices, and behaviours among communities of people who gather online to share information, knowledge, and opinions using conversational media. Conversational media are web-based applications that make it possible to create and easily transmit content in the form of words, pictures, videos and audios.

Social media refers to 'participatory', 'conversational' and 'fluid' online communities focused on user-generated content. Current marketing campaigns and initiatives suggest that a limited number of tourism organizations are beginning to study social media and develop strategies to use it to their advantage. Two areas where a great deal of activity has occurred in recent years are the use of Twitter and Facebook, because they have millions of users, strong participation from companies and organizations, and differ widely in services, reach and usage. This Insight represents the first research undertaken on Twitter and Facebook use in its early use in tourism and so provides an important benchmark of how its use has evolved.

Facebook, launched on 4 February 2004, has over 2 billion active users, 50 per cent of whom log on to the website daily. Businesses and organizations create and maintain an official presence on Facebook to engage with consumers. Twitter is a micro-blogging website that was launched on 13 July 2006 and users can send 140-character messages, called 'tweets', that answer the question 'What's happening?' Twitter is primarily about now, as it is excellent for current events and crisis communications. According to statistics, in July 2011 Twitter had 175 million users, a figure which had grown to over 300 million by 2019, making it by far the most popular micro-blogging website. Whereas most 'friends' on Facebook have met offline, it is common for users of Twitter to 'follow' accounts of those they have not met in real life, such as celebrities, bloggers, new organizations, comedians or other personal users with whom they share similar interests. Organizations see Twitter as a new, ground-breaking way of reaching out to, interacting with and understanding the consumer behaviour of millions around the world. Research by Hays *et al.* (2013) evaluated the use of these social media platforms by NTOs based in London to assess the activities

IMAGE 14.3 Icons, such as Westminster Abbey, are core elements used to market world cities like London

TABLE 14.11 Average number of daily posts and total number of posts in June 2011

Country	Average no. of daily Facebook posts, June 2011	Total no. of Facebook posts, June 2011	Average no. of daily tweet(s), June 2011	Total no. of tweet(s), June 2011
Mexico	0.33	10	0.8	24
Malaysia	1.53	46	2.33	70
Germany	0.57	17	1.1	33
UK	0.73	22	11.63	349
Turkey	n/a	n/a	0.37	11
France	0.5	15	0.67	20
Spain	0.7	21	0.77	23
Combined	0.73	131	2.52	530

by the top 10 international destinations in using this technology to interact with potential visitors.

Three main themes emerged in the use of social media by NTOs: *post frequency*, *interaction*, and *content*. Twitter is centred on micro-blogging – short (mostly) textual content. Facebook, on the other hand, is much more multifaceted: users can upload pictures and videos to photo albums, communicate privately with other friends, and post information for their entire network to see. Both sites are pull-based, as users choose a network of users from whom they wish to receive updates and can block other users or feeds any time. Table 14.11 shows that the average number of daily posts by DMOs on Facebook is 0.73 compared to 2.52 Twitter posts a day. This aligns with the general public's use of the two platforms: 12 per cent of Facebook users update their status each day, whereas 52 per cent of users on Twitter post daily. Status updates are more integral to the purpose of Twitter, for businesses and individuals alike. While Twitter is driven by and excels at providing timely updates, Facebook is a good platform to increase consumer loyalty. VisitBritain accounts for 66 per cent of the total monthly tweets of the combined DMOs, clearly skewing the total number of tweets for all DMOs. Furthermore, VisitBritain's Facebook page received 53 million views in 2010 compared with 18 million on VisitBritain's website, which is a measure of the changing significance of electronic communication (Image 14.3).

It is apparent that some DMOs are using social media as they would any other marketing tool, neglecting the full potential of its ability to engage and invoke informal conversation. However, it is different from traditional marketing strategies since it is far more fluid and interactive and requires different skills. Thus, accepting social media as a beneficial tool that is part of an integrated marketing strategy while still understanding its uniqueness as a medium is something that DMOs struggle with; this reflects what social media researchers acknowledge as a series of crucial steps for social media marketing: attract the users initially and then engage end-users' interest and participation; retain their loyalty and then learn about their preferences so as to provide customized and relevant information that they will find interesting so as to keep them engaged.

Further reading

Hays, S., Page, S.J. and Buhalis, D. (2013) 'Social media as a destination marketing tool: Its use by Destination Marketing Organizations', *Current Issues in Tourism*, 16 (3): 211–39.

Mariani, M.M., Mura, M. and Di Felice, M. (2018) 'The determinants of Facebook social engagement for national tourism organizations' Facebook pages: A quantitative approach', *Journal of Destination Marketing and Management*, 8: 312–325.

Oliveira, A. and Huertas-Roig, A. (2019) 'How do destinations use Twitter to recover their images after a terrorist attack?' *Journal of Destination Marketing and Management*, 12: 46–54.

Önder, I., Gunter, U. and Gindl, S. (2019) 'Utilizing Facebook statistics in tourism demand modeling and destination marketing', *Journal of Travel Research*. In press; https://doi.org/10.1177/0047287519835969

Vyas, C. (2019) Evaluating state tourism websites using Search Engine Optimization tools. *Tourism Management*, 73: 64–70.

Questions

1 Why have social media tools like Facebook and Twitter become important in tourism marketing?
2 How can NTOs use Facebook and Twitter to enhance their destination marketing?
3 What other social media tools might NTOS use to connect with potential visitors?
4 How would you go about measuring the impact and effect of Facebook and Twitter on your marketing activity if you were working in an NTO?

14

Introduction

Destinations are often seen by the tourist as the outwardly facing element of a tourism service or product, being a place where their consumption occurs. Morrison (2019: 4) defines a destination as a 'geographic area that attracts visitors', which we will explore in more detail in this chapter. At a global scale, the growth of international and domestic tourism has seen the exponential expansion of places seeking to develop their tourism potential. Even very unlikely and unattractive places have developed a tourism economy, based on the principles of creating a destination and a demand for the products and services they offer. This chapter examines the concept of a destination and how it has been used in a marketing context, and it develops many of the ideas covered in Chapter 14 on the role of the public sector, as well as the marketing and advertising concepts covered in Chapter 13. In this respect, it provides a synthesis of how destinations harness marketing principles and implement them. One of the central themes of this chapter is also to show how tourists perceive destinations, and how they develop destination images. In a strategic management context, this chapter also highlights the role played by marketing and management in terms of seeking to ensure the long-term sustainability and prosperity of destinations, the need to delight the visitor and engender notions of satisfaction from their experiences (often appealing to visitors' emotions to delight and excite the visitor – see Chapter 4) and to ensure that the area does not decline. One of the very early tourism marketing texts by Wahab *et al.* (1976: 24) outlined the scope of tourism destination marketing as:

> *The management process through which the National Tourist Organizations and/or tourist enterprises identify their selected tourist, actual and potential, communicate with them to ascertain and influence their wishes, needs, motivations, likes and dislikes, on local, regional, national and international levels and to formulate and adapt their tourist products accordingly in view of achieving optimal tourist satisfaction thereby fulfilling their objectives.*

Within the fields of tourism studies and marketing, destination marketing has emerged in recent years as a popular area of study and research, illustrated by the growth in key texts on the field, a selection of which are shown in Table 15.1 (see Pike and Page 2014 for a detailed review). In operational terms, destination marketing has a crucial role in ensuring that the destination lifecycle does not enter into a stage of saturation or decline, by communicating

15

TABLE 15.1 Key texts on destination marketing

Avraham, E. and Ketter, E. (2007) *Media Strategies for Marketing Places in Crisis: Improving the Image of Cities, Countries and Tourist Destinations.* Oxford: Butterworth-Heinemann.

Avraham, E. and Ketter, E. (2016) *Tourism Marketing for Developing Countries.* London: Palgrave Macmillan.

Baker, B. (2012) *Destination Branding for Small Cities: The Essentials for Successful Place Branding,* 2nd edition. Portland: Creative Leap Books.

Gursoy, D. and Chi, C. (eds.) (2018) *The Routledge Handbook of Destination Marketing.* London: Routledge.

Hallet, R. and Kaplan-Weinger, J. (2010) *Official Tourism Websites: A Discourse Analysis Perspective.* Bristol: Channel View Publications.

Kolb, B. (2006) *Tourism Marketing for Cities and Towns: Using Branding and Events to Attract Tourists.* Oxford: Butterworth-Heinemann.

Lewis-Cameron, A. and Roberts, S. (eds.) (2010) *Marketing Island Destinations: Concepts and Cases.* Oxford: Elsevier.

Morgan, N., Pritchard, A. and Pride, R. (eds.) (2011) *Destination Brands: Managing Place Reputation,* 3rd edition. Oxford: Butterworth-Heinemann.

Morrison, A. (2019) *Marketing and Managing Tourism Destinations,* 2nd edition. London: Routledge.

Pike, S. (2008) *Destination Marketing: An Integrated Marketing Communication Approach.* Oxford: Butterworth-Heinemann.

Richards, G. and Duif, L. (2019) *Small Cities with Big Dreams.* London: Routledge.

Sigala, M., Christou, E. and Gretzel, U. (2012) *Social Media in Travel, Tourism and Hospitality.* Aldershot: Ashgate.

Wang, Y. and Pizam, A. (eds.) (2011) *Destination Marketing and Management: Theories and Applications.* Wallingford: CABI.

Woodside, A.G. (2010) *Tourism Marketing Performance Metrics and Usefulness Auditing of Destination Websites.* Bradford: Emerald Publishing.

with the target markets at each stage of development (i.e. to raise visitors' awareness at the initial stage of development, to inform in the growth stage, to persuade visitors to come in a mature and saturation stage, and to retain visitors and introduce new markets in the declining stages). As Chapter 14's explanation of the resort lifecycle suggests, marketing is also vital since other destinations develop in competition, thus destinations have to formulate strategies to differentiate themselves. As Porter's model in Chapter 14 shows, destinations need to compete but are held back by one critical constraint, the resource base and its sustainability, since once the resource base is destroyed it cannot be replaced. Nevertheless, those working in destination marketing have to make critical decisions on strategic issues related to product, promotion, price and distribution strategies for tourism, since the resort lifecycle means that the destination is constantly evolving and changing, making strategic marketing a necessity. In extreme cases, destinations overrun by visitors may also have to use marketing to de-market their locality through dissuading visitors from coming at peak times in conjunction with visitor management tools.

One interesting attempt to set the destination in a competitive framework was made by Gilbert (1990), who argued that destinations could be classified along a continuum. At the initial stages of development, a destination achieves a status at which its unique attributes are not substitutable, so consumer loyalty and willingness to pay to visit are high. Through time, as the destination develops and competing destinations come on stream, decisions to visit it are based more on price-competitiveness, and high-spending visitors are not attracted. In some cases, destinations have sought to develop niche markets as a process of continuous innovation, in order to diversify their market base and remain competitive, retaining their unique appeal. However, in locations that have followed cost-leadership strategies, mass tourism has caused irrevocable damage to the resource base, often causing what has been dubbed overtourism, which we will address in Chapter 19 on sustainability and in Chapter 20 on urban tourism. Whatever approach to destination marketing an area develops, the starting point must be a fundamental understanding of the elements, which coalesce to form the destination (Brey *et al.* 2007).

The destination concept

Tourist destinations are a mix of tourism products, experiences and other intangible items promoted to consumers. This is not a new concept, since resorts and many areas which developed large tourism industries in the eighteenth and nineteenth centuries used guide books, posters and brochures to promote travel to their area. At a general level, this concept of a destination can be developed to represent geographically defined entities such as groups of countries, countries, regions in a country (i.e. the Rockies in North America), a city (e.g. London), a rural area (e.g. the Swan Valley, a wine tourism region in Western Australia), a resort or a wide range of experiences created by tourism marketers. Increasingly, the notion of a destination is something perceived by consumers, although most conventional definitions emphasize the geographical element of a specific place. From a tourist's perspective, a destination may usually be classified into one of the following: conventional resorts; environmental destinations; business tourism centres; places where one stops en route to another place; a short-break destination and day-trip destinations. In essence, destinations are places which tourists visit and stay at. Whatever way one approaches the concept of a destination (i.e. from an industry-supply perspective or from the consumer's viewpoint), there are a range of six components which comprise a destination, as Figure 15.1 shows.

The destination is often referred to as an amalgam of the six A's:

- available packages
- accessibility
- attractions
- amenities
- activities
- ancillary services,

and in the most developed destinations, a public/public–private or private sector organization may be responsible for the coordination, planning and promotion of the destination. This is expanded upon in Figure 15.2,

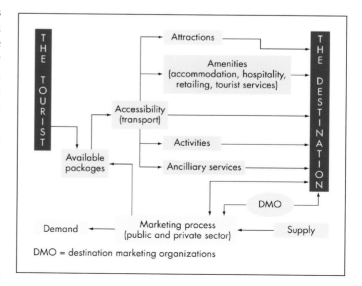

FIGURE 15.1 The elements of a tourist destination

which shows Morrison's (2019) development of the scope and extent of the characteristics of a tourist destination. When one then considers these characteristics and asks the key question – *What makes a destination successful?*, then one needs to refer back to Figures 15.1 and 15.2 again, and also begin to reflect on the content of the different chapters in the book we have covered to date. At this point, one should consider what the rest of this chapter will examine in terms of how to understand the tourism destination and what we need to do to create a successful place visitors want to visit, as outlined in Figure 15.3. Morrison (2019) argues that there are various ways to gauge success as a destination attribute, from simple measures such as the number of visitors

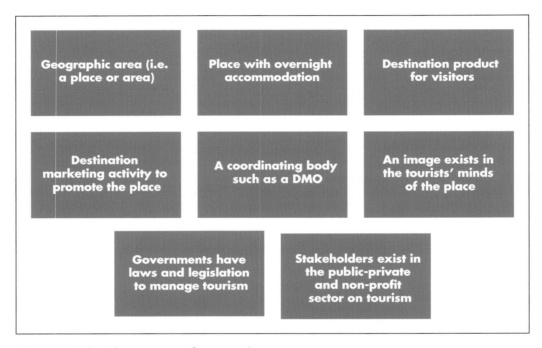

FIGURE 15.2 Characteristics of a tourist destination.
Source: Developed from Morrison (2019: 4)

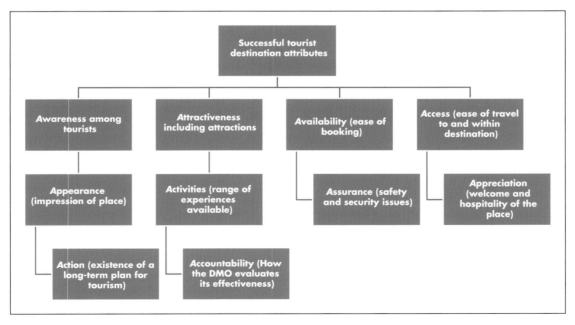

FIGURE 15.3 The 10 A's that contribute towards a successful tourist destination.
Source: After Morrison (2019: 21)

annually through to more qualitative measures assessments. These assessments may range from recommendations in guidebooks, such as Lonely Planet, and positive social media coverage, through to more objective measures such as compliance with best practice guides, such as the Global Sustainable Tourism Council Best Practice Criteria for Destinations, as summarized in Table 15.2. This table illustrates the scope and breadth of issues that a location would need to consider in seeking to meet the criteria to be deemed a sustainable destination, which is a theme we will return to in more detail in Chapter 19, which focuses on sustainability. What is clear from Table 15.2 is that management of the destination requires a lead body like a DMO and champions within the destination to achieve the sustainable criteria.

TABLE 15.2 Global Sustainable Tourism Council Criteria for Destinations with headline criteria and implications for destination management and compliance

Criterion: Demonstrate effective sustainable management

The destination needs:

- a multi-year tourism strategy
- a destination marketing organization (DMO) to coordinate the approach with stakeholders
- a system to monitor and report progress with sustainability
- to find ways of mitigating the effects of seasonality to identify all-year opportunities
- a system to identify and take mitigation and adaptation measures on climate change
- to have an up-to-date inventory of tourism assets and attractions
- to have planning regulations that integrate sustainability into its policies on tourism and activities allied to tourism
- to be accessible to all
- to have policies on property acquisitions to ensure indigenous rights
- to have measures in place to monitor visitor satisfaction and enhance it where necessary
- to have in place a system to promote the GSTC criteria on sustainability and publicly communicate it
- to have a system to record, report and monitor safety and security-related issues such as crime, including a crisis management plan for emergency situations (e.g. a natural hazard or terrorism).

Criterion: Maximize economic benefits to the host community and minimize negative impacts

The destination needs:

- a system to capture and record economic data on tourism at least annually
- to promote local career opportunities and fair wages for all
- to have a system that promotes public participation in planning that affects tourism
- to have a mechanism to capture local community opinion and the means to report it
- to assure local people have access to the natural and cultural sites and the resources to protect these resources
- to promote education and awareness of sustainability and tourism
- to have policies to prevent the exploitation of people by the tourism sector, including sexual exploitation and harassment
- to support local enterprises and community ventures, especially those that support sustainability
- to support the principles of fair trade and local entrepreneurs.

Criterion: Maximize benefits to communities, visitors, and culture; minimize negative impacts

The destination needs:

- to identify environmental risks and have measures in place to address these
- to have measures in place for wildlife protection
- to measure, monitor, minimize, publicly report, and mitigate greenhouse gas emissions from businesses including their use of energy and water
- to ensure a supply of safe drinking water and the treatment of waste water and solid waste (i.e. sewage)
- to have a system in place to minimize light and noise pollution
- to have a system in place to increase the use of low-impact transportation including the promotion of active transportation (e.g. walking and cycling).

Source: Developed from the Global Sustainable Tourism Council Criteria for Destinations (2013) (https://www.gstcouncil.org/gstc-criteria/gstc-destination-criteria/)

15

Early forms of destination marketing

The history of such organizations can be traced to the nineteenth century in the USA, where much of the focus was on attracting meetings and conventions, which is one facet of the events industry (Ford and Peeper 2007). In the USA, the formation of the Detroit Convention and Businessmen's League in 1896 is seen as the formal beginning of the US destination promotion industry, the management of which was handled by the League's Convention and Visitor Bureau organizations. While much of these organizations' initial interest was focused on domestic tourism, New Zealand was the first country to begin overseas promotion, as shown in Insight 15.1. Other countries, like Portugal and Spain (see Chapter 13), also made significant progress towards destination marketing in the Edwardian period (1901–1914). In the UK, many individual resorts began to advertise in parallel with developments in North America and mainland Europe. For example, in 1879 Blackpool Town Council levied a local tax on the rates in order to undertake advertising at railway stations, attractions and amusements via its Advertising Committee, initially using leaflets and after 1881, with posters. As attractions were added to the town's tourism infrastructure (e.g. Blackpool Tower in 1894 and the Illuminations in 1912) these featured in posters. Such advertising, sometimes produced in conjunction with railway companies, was aimed at the domestic tourism and day-trip market. Despite attempts by central government in the UK to limit municipal spending on promoting tourism, this became a highly competitive activity prior to 1914. Yet even during the First World War, with government restrictions imposed on domestic travel and tourism, destinations were still promoted by some of the most influential place-promoters of the time – the private railway companies. The most prominent advertiser was the Great Western Railway Company (GWR), with its literary and visual representations drawing upon the concept of departure and the aesthetic appeal of the coast. In some GWR posters, travel embodied a sense of adventure, or might involve a glamorous event as well as the pleasure of the journey itself. In the UK in 1921 the Health Resorts and Watering Places Act formally approved municipalities' expenditure of a one-penny rate to undertake certain forms of destination advertising to attract existing rail-borne travel and the potential of car and charabanc (early coaches) trips to the coast. This development of formally funded place-marketing in the 1920s, typically through guidebooks, posters and newspaper advertising, helped to provide the modern-day foundations of the destination marketing organization.

One of the principal tasks of destination management organizations (DMOs) is to increase visitation levels in a marketing context, as Chapter 13 illustrated in Insight 13.2.

However, DMOs also have a management function which consists of the coordination of planning, economic development, and of the role of stakeholders, who include the host community, private sector tourism interests, the

15

INSIGHT 15.1 The establishment of the first National Tourism Organization, the New Zealand Tourist and Health Resorts (THR) in 1901

In 2001, the New Zealand Tourism Board celebrated 100 years of public service to tourists, emphasizing its long history and associations with tourism and indigenous people, and its country's status as the first in the world to market and promote itself formally overseas. New Zealand was receiving international visitors after the establishment of the country in the 1840s, with domestic tourists travelling north of Auckland to Wairewa to the hot springs and making visits to the thermal resort area of Rotorua in the central North Island to see one of the wonders of the world – the Pink Terraces (destroyed by an earthquake in 1886). Much of the hospitality and tour guiding was provided by the local Maori iwi (tribe) – the Te Arawa.

In 1901, the New Zealand government established the New Zealand Tourist and Health Resorts (THR), the forerunner of the New Zealand Tourism Board, to encourage and develop tourism, particularly the facilities, marketing and publicity necessary to attract overseas visitors. Its success can be gauged in the development of international arrivals, as shown in Figure 15.4, which depicts the rapid expansion in the early 1990s: by 2019, international tourism represented a NZ$20 billion industry (also see Chapter 16 on New Zealand's Tourism Satellite Account). This is a major achievement for a country so distant from many of the world's major tourism-generating regions and whose primary means of transport prior to mass jet travel was by sea. In 1902 the THR also established a network of tourist information centres to advise and help tourists in Auckland, Rotorua, Wellington, Christchurch, Invercargill and Dunedin. In 1903, revenue from international tourism had reached £5490, and by 1913 this had grown to £28 000. In 1927, the THR also established a network of overseas offices to promote the country in the UK, USA, South Africa and Australia, which were key source markets, and offered links for visiting friends and family and for business travel.

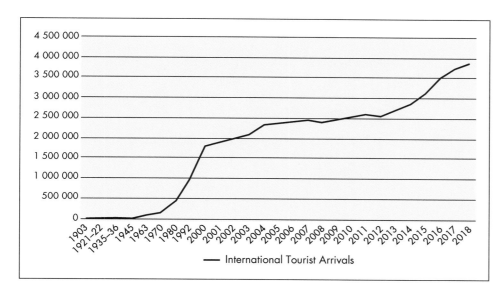

FIGURE 15.4 International tourist arrivals in New Zealand 1903–2018

public sector (including local and national government), tourists and other bodies such as pressure groups, as discussed in Chapter 13. These different stakeholders are an important focus for planning, since they may have diverging political agendas which makes seeking to derive a consensus about destination marketing a complex task and illustrates the importance of collaboration.

Formulating the destination marketing mix: The role of the DMO

A central feature of any destination marketing strategy will be the formulation of a destination product. In some cases, a destination may find that competitive forces have caused it to begin to decline. This may be due to a wide range of reasons such as lacklustre performance or complacency by the DMO or NTO or both, since NTOs will market countries as destinations, while DMOs will develop their own distinctive approach at the local destination level to develop a unique selling point and highlight key factors to appeal to visitors. For example, Sharpley and Pearce (2007) examine the tourism marketing undertaken by English National Parks and their ability to champion sustainable tourism as the principal challenge of balancing visitor needs and the environment. As Middleton *et al.* (2009) suggest, most DMOs do not have the ability to control tourist travel to destinations: they can only influence it because, as Chapters 3 and 4 have shown, a wide range of factors impact upon demand. DMOs are only part of the total marketing spend for a destination, since the private sector also uses brochures, websites and other campaigns to promote the products available for sale in the destination, as Figure 15.1 shows. In the best-case scenario, only a small proportion of these suppliers will have formal links with an NTO or DMO, although experiments in online DMOs such as VisitScotland.com have started to change this situation.

One starting point for DMOs is the marketing strategy, which will identify the marketing mix needed to promote the area after a marketing plan has been created. At a generic level, destination marketers need to constantly evaluate the strategic fit of the destination product with changing consumer tastes. This emphasizes the need for a DMO to provide leadership and a focus for industry coordination and planning of marketing efforts to gain synergies, consistent marketing messages to consumers and partnerships to facilitate joint marketing campaigns.

In formulating the destination product, the DMO will always have an intentional focus, meaning that it will be directly seeking to influence visitors to come in the short term as well as aiming to raise general awareness for future visits. One of the core functions of any DMO in communicating to stakeholders its direction and focus will be its strategy document. Middleton *et al.* (2009) point to the wider role which NTOs can play in support of DMOs:

- providing market intelligence and research data
- running web-based advertising (and social media activity)
- organizing trade shows
- hosting familiarization trips for foreign travel agents, travel writers and tour operators

15

- providing online travel trade manuals as reference guides
- participating in joint marketing
- running a Destination Management and Marketing System, or DMS (see Chapter 6) to provide direct access to consumers and bookings
- running destination quality schemes to raise standards and engender a wider concern for tourist well-being (see Chapter 25 for more detail).

What these potential roles and support functions of the DMO highlight is the need to undertake the following generic tasks in a marketing (and destination management) context:

- understanding consumer markets
- ensuring accessibility to the market
- understanding and communicating the core offering
- recognizing, analyzing and addressing the competitive forces affecting the destination
- identifying the tourism development needs of the destination to nurture visitors and to improve their experiences, as Insight 15.1 illustrates
- coordinating and leading destination marketing activities
- reformulating the marketing mix
- monitoring sustainability to ensure that activities do not destroy the long-term marketability and resource base in the destination, as illustrated by Table 15.2 (also see Chapter 19)
- identifying new ideas, trends and how to be an outwardly facing organization able to understand the global marketplace and adopt a creative approach to destination marketing.

DMOs also have a key role in understanding the pricing of the destination product, even though this is largely in the control of the private sector businesses. In the case of the large European tour operators who have been accused of driving down the prices paid to local operators, their size and power illustrates that small local businesses must address reduced profit margins by new strategies (i.e. overpricing local services and products). DMOs have a central role to play in working with intermediaries (including e-mediaries) such as those involved in staging meetings, incentives, conferences and exhibitions (MICE) who may bring lucrative business travellers. As Chapter 14 has shown, DMOs may have a communication role in promoting the destination by organizing a coordinated campaign. This may include *above-the-line promotional activity*, such as advertising, to develop the destination brand; this is discussed later. *Below-the-line promotion*, such as attending trade fairs and distributing brochures while meeting with intermediaries, is also undertaken. Avraham and Ketter (2016) outlined the particular challenges of attracting visitors to developing countries which are often beset with crises and have insufficient resources to manage the situation. Tourists' negative perceptions of a destination arise as a result of images in the media portraying it as unsafe to visit and emphasizing its undeveloped nature. This is an obstacle to marketing, especially given the associations with terrorist attacks in some locations, and other problems they may face, like natural disasters and long-standing issues such as crime, poverty and political instability. As Perles-Ribes *et al.* (2018) found in the case of the Arab uprisings in Tunisia and Egypt, crises displace visitors, and so this led to visitor growth in Morocco and Turkey during the Arab Spring movement. But how do tourists select a destination to visit, given the highly competitive marketing which many places are now undertaking?

Selecting a tourist destination

According to Seddighi and Theocharous (2002), understanding how tourists select the destinations they visit is central to destination marketers so they can decide upon which marketing strategies to use to influence consumer behaviour. At a simplistic level, any traveller is faced with a range of motives. In the case of business travel, this is often not a choice-related form of travel and is dictated by employment needs, although conference and incentive travel may be influenced by choice. It is the leisure holiday which has attracted the greatest amount of research, where the initial choice of destination facing the tourist is either a domestic or overseas destination(s), the decision being partly based upon the purchasing power of the consumer. The attitudes and perception of the prospective tourist towards alternative destinations leads to different preferences, as a multi-stage process. As Chapter 4 discussed, a wide range of demographic, gender, income and level of education impact upon holiday-taking. Seddighi and Theocharous (2002) also develop the importance of destination-specific factors including:

- whether the visitor has been to the destination before
- the cost of living at the destination
- the price of the tourist package
- facilities at the destination
- the cost of transportation and time taken in travelling
- the quality of the promotion and advertising
- the quality of services
- any political instability at the destination.

This highlights the importance of destination marketing, as Buckley and Papadopolous (1986: 86) argued, where

Greater attention must be paid to the characteristics of visitors when trying to develop a marketing strategy . . . a clear market segment must be identified and an investigation made of the buying decision factors, which predominate in that segment . . . It is, however, important to recognise that the tourist product is a composite product and that there is more than one type of client.

This also indicates the importance of buyer behaviour as a key element in destination choice. As Middleton *et al.* (2009) indicate, models of consumer behaviour have traditionally emphasized price as the key determinant of a purchase. But growing consumer sophistication has seen branding and other non-rational considerations and attitudes influence buyer behaviour. In a simplified form, this process can be summarized as follows:

- destinations promote competitive products to consumers direct, and via the travel trade/intermediaries
- advertising, promotion and the interplay of personal recommendation, family, friends, consumer trends, taste and the Internet combine to shape buyer characteristics
- these buyer characteristics are filtered by the learning behaviour of consumers, which has been influenced by marketing/recommendation. For example, Ashworth and Goodall (1988) observed that if a tourist is dissatisfied, they will not recommend the destination to others; a reminder of the importance of visitor satisfaction and word of mouth. It is also shaped by the perceptions of consumers of brands and images of the destination, and their experience of travel (i.e. prior travel to destinations)
- these characteristics combine in the buyer decision-making process where learning, perceptions and experience lead to the motivation to buy
- at the motivation stage, the characteristics of the consumer (i.e. demographic, economic and social profile) combine with their psychographic characteristics as well as their attitudes, to create: needs, wants and goals. In tourism purchases, the family often acts as a single decision-making unit and Zalaton (1998) noted male–female differences in purchases
- the consumer then chooses between different goods or services to purchase a product or brand to fulfil their motivation.

Within buyer behaviour research, which derives from the sub-area of marketing called 'consumer behaviour', the DMO may apply marketing segmentation techniques as described in Chapter 4. Yet one of the most influential factors in the consumer's choice of destination is the destination image, which is not necessarily grounded in experience or facts but is a key motivator in travel and tourism. Images and the expectations of travel experiences are closely linked in prospective customers' minds and the ultimate objective of destination marketing is to: find ways in which the potential visitor can be influenced through the image they have or which is created about the destination through various marketing activity such as advertising and the use of branding, which we will return to later in the chapter. Again, this reiterates the importance of marketing research in seeking to understand the intrinsic attractiveness of a destination's image to a visitor, as well as how the perceived image can be used to position the destination to derive a competitive advantage.

15

The tourist destination image

Within the literature on tourism marketing, the study of destination imagery is one of the major areas of academic endeavour and a selection of recent studies are shown in Table 15.3. For this reason, this section will examine the factors which impact upon destination image including how to approach the study of image formation. According to Gallarza *et al.* (2002: 58), the initial development of destination image research can be dated to Hunt (1975), as highlighted by Pike and Page (2014). Most academic studies have focused on:

- the conceptualization and dimensions of the tourism destination image (TDI)
- the destination image formation process
- the assessment and measurement of destination image
- the influence of distance on destination image
- destination image change over time
- the active and passive role of residents in the image of destinations
- destination image management (i.e. positioning and promotion).

This proliferation of studies has made the definition of TDI a complex task, with no consensus of the term and its scope, although it is broadly concerned with the way individuals and groups develop mental constructions about destinations, focusing on different attributes which are shaped by their beliefs, values, ideas, perceptions and impressions. As Beerli and Martin (2004b) suggest, the image of the destination might be classified into nine items as shown in Table 15.5:

- natural resources (e.g. weather and beaches)
- general infrastructure (e.g. roads and airports)
- tourist infrastructure (e.g. accommodation and restaurants)
- tourist leisure and recreation (e.g. theme parks and trekking)
- culture, history and art (e.g. museums and festivals)

15

Table 15.3	Illustrations of recent studies of tourism destination image

Chaulagain, S., Wiitala, J. and Fu, X. (2019) 'The impact of country image and destination image on US tourists' travel intention', *Journal of Destination Marketing and Management*, 12: 1–11.

Han, H., Al-Ansi, A., Olya, H. and Kim, W. (2019) 'Exploring halal-friendly destination attributes in South Korea: Perceptions and behaviors of Muslim travelers toward a non-Muslim destination', *Tourism Management*, 71: 151–164.

Iordanova, E. and Stainton, H. (2019) 'Cognition, emotion and trust: A comparative analysis of Cambodia's perceived and projected online image', *Tourist Studies*, 19 (4): 496–519.

Iordanova, E. and Stylidis, D. (2019) 'International and domestic tourists' "a priori" and "in situ" image differences and the impact of direct destination experience on destination image: The case of Linz, Austria', *Current Issues in Tourism*, 22(8): 982–1005.

Isaac, R. and Eid, T. (2019) 'Tourists' destination image: An exploratory study of alternative tourism in Palestine', *Current Issues in Tourism*, 22 (12): 1499–1522.

Jacobsen, J., Iversen, N. and Hem, L. (2019) 'Hotspot crowding and over-tourism: Antecedents of destination attractiveness', *Annals of Tourism Research*, 76: 53–66.

Oliveira, A. and Huertas-Roig, A. (2019) 'How do destinations use Twitter to recover their images after a terrorist attack?' *Journal of Destination Marketing and Management*, 12: 46–54.

Su, M., Wall, G. and Ma, Z. (2019) 'A multi-stakeholder examination of destination image: Nanluoguxiang heritage street, Beijing, China', *Tourism Geographies*, 21 (1): 2–23.

Tasci, A., Khalilzadeh, J. and Uysal, M. (2019) 'Network analysis of the Caucasus' image', *Current Issues in Tourism*, 22 (7): 827–852.

Vinyals-Mirabent, S. (2019) 'European urban destinations' attractors at the frontier between competitiveness and a unique destination image: A benchmark study of communication practices', *Journal of Destination Marketing and Management*, 12: 37–45.

TABLE 15.4 Dimensions and attributes determining the perceived tourist destination image		
Natural resources	**General infrastructure**	**Tourist infrastructure**
Weather 　Temperature 　Rainfall 　Humidity 　Hours of sunshine Beaches 　Quality of seawater 　Sandy or rocky beaches 　Length of beaches 　Overcrowding of beaches Richness of the scenery 　Protected nature reserves 　Lakes, mountains, deserts, etc. Variety and uniqueness of flora and fauna	Development and quality of roads, 　airports and ports Private and public transport facilities Development of health services Development of commercial 　infrastructures Extent of building development	Hotel and self-catering accommodation 　Number of beds 　Categories 　Quality Restaurants 　Number 　Categories Bars, discotheques and clubs. Ease of 　access to destination. Excursions at 　the destination Tourist centres Network of tourist information
Tourist leisure and recreation	**Culture, history and art**	**Political and economic factors**
Theme parks Entertainment and sports activities Golf, fishing, hunting, skiing, scuba, etc. 　Water parks 　Zoos 　Trekking 　Adventure activities 　Casinos 　Nightlife 　Shopping	Museums, historical buildings, 　monuments, etc. Festival, concerts, etc. Handicraft Gastronomy Folklore Religion Customs and ways of life	Political stability Political tendencies Economic development Safety 　Crime rate 　Terrorist attacks Prices
Natural environment	**Social environment**	**Atmosphere of the place**
Beauty of the scenery Beauty of the cities and towns Cleanliness Overcrowding Air and noise pollution Traffic congestion	Hospitality and friendliness of the 　local residents Underprivileged and poverty Quality of life Language barriers	Luxurious place Fashionable place Place with fame and reputation Place oriented towards families Exotic place Mystic place Relaxing place Stressful place Happy, enjoyable place Pleasant place Boring place Attractive or interesting place

Source: Reprinted from Beerli and Martin (2004b) © with permission from Elsevier

- political and economic factors (e.g. political stability)
- natural environment (e.g. the cleanliness and appeal of the environment)
- social environment (e.g. the hospitality and friendliness of the place)
- atmosphere of the place (e.g. ambience and appeal to visitor emotions),

based on the attributes of the destination, which are vast and very difficult to reduce to a series of simple constructs (you may wish to go back and compare these with Figures 15.1 and 15.2 and see the degree of similarity in these attributes). A study by Echtner and Ritchie (1991) has added some clarity to the wide range of definitions which exist by pointing to the existence of three axes that support the image of a destination:

- a psychological/functional dimension
- the common/unique dimension
- holistic/attribute axes.

As Beerli and Martin (2004a) suggest, a number of attributes have been studied in TDI studies which can be classified according to the functional–psychological axis. These studies can help in understanding what Gunn (1988) described as the personal factors affecting the tourist formation of a destination image:

- accumulating of images of the destination
- modifying the initial image after gathering more information, creating an induced image
- deciding to visit the destination
- visiting the destination
- sharing the destination
- returning home
- modifying the image based on experience to create an organic and induced image. This organic image, based upon non-commercial sources of data, is influenced by the media and friends. In contrast, the induced image is the result of commercial data and information such as destination or industry advertising.

One consequence of these studies of TDI is that whatever measures are developed to understand imagery, one needs a framework within which to understand image formation.

A model of destination image formulation

Baloglu and McCleary (1999) provided a framework to analyze TDI, which is conditioned by two key elements:

- stimulus factors (external stimuli, physical objects, personal experience)
- personal factors (social and psychological characteristics of the consumer).

As a result, three determinants of TDI were identified by Baloglu and McCleary (1999):

- tourism motivations
- sociodemographic factors
- information sources.

These determinants help shape the TDI as an attitudinal construct that comprises a consumer's mental understanding of knowledge, feelings and global impression of a destination. As we discussed in Chapter 14, the image has a perceptual/cognitive as well as an affective element, which generates responses to create an overall image of the destination, as shown in Figure 15.5. The construction of images of a destination is clearly an area which can be studied using quantitative research methods to measure the elements of a TDI and the visitors'

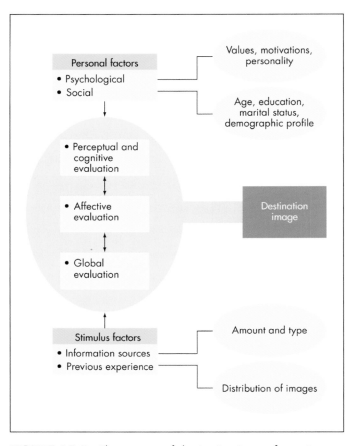

FIGURE 15.5 The process of destination image formation
Source: Adapted from Baloglu and McCleary (1999)

preferences. Yet there is also a growing interest in more qualitative studies which seek to examine the images portrayed in brochures by marketers to promote destinations.

Connell (2012) points to a similar effect that may be generated by motion pictures on destination images. Such images enter the domain of popular culture and the impact on place images can be very influential. In fact Gartner (1993) highlighted the interrelationship of cognitive and affective elements of destination images which have a strong impact on the decision to visit. One example of this effect occurred in Scotland following the launch of a children's programme, *Balamory*, set on a fictitious island of the same name, which was, in real life, the Isle of Mull, in the town of Tobermory (see Figure 15.6), with its painted houses. This led to a tourism boom, following the rise of toddler tourism (Connell 2005). The local area tourist board, AILLST, promoted the area using Tobermory on the front cover of their 2004 holiday brochure, adding to the tourist boom. As Connell (2005) has shown, such place imagery can have

IMAGE 15.1 *Works of fiction, such as Daphne du Maurier's* Jamaica Inn, *form a central focus for destination marketing based on literature and film interests*

an immediate impact on a destination, particularly when the images generated by popular culture (e.g. the BBC) are not matched in reality, and small-scale destinations find themselves besieged in the peak tourist season (see Insight 15.2). The stimulus may come from a wide range of media-generated sources including film (Image 15.1), televised dramas, televised light entertainment and the staging of events such as the Olympic Games, as well as more subliminal sources of advertising that use locations as backdrops.

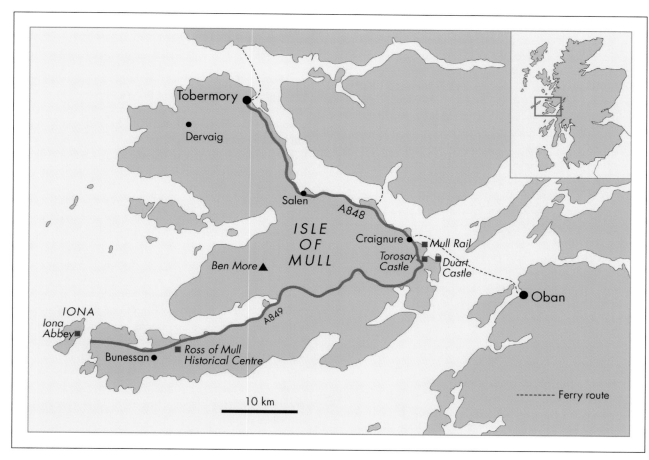

FIGURE 15.6 Location of *Balamory*
Source: Copyright J. Connell (2005)

INSIGHT 15.2 The impact of film and screen tourism as a form of destination promotion

There is a growing recognition of the importance of global forms of media in promoting visitation to places depicted in television programmes and films, known collectively as screen tourism (Olsberg/SPI 2007). For example, in 2019 the filming of the television series associated with the Chernobyl nuclear reactor in Russia that exploded in 1986 has seen a sharp increase to visitors to the area, which may reflect a form of dark tourism (see Chapter 9 for a discussion of dark tourism) given the large number of people estimated to have died from the accident. Wen *et al.* (2018) demonstrated that in China, film tourism was an important motivator of destination choice due to the filming activity in South Korea, Thailand and the USA. This is reinforced by the impact of the world's largest film industry – India with its 'Bollywood' movies, which attracts visitors to its locations – while holidaymakers also make decisions to visit particular locations in Europe to see where popular movies were filmed. Similarly other television series such as *Game of Thrones* have had significant impacts, as have films, some of which have proved controversial. For example, the two films about life in slums (e.g. *Slumdog Millionaire*, released in 2008 and based on the Dhavari neighbourhood of Mumbai and *City of God*, released in 2003 based on the favelas in Rio de Janeiro) have generated significant visitation. In Mumbai the development of 'slumdog tours' has generated around 20 000 visits a year and similar tours and publicity in Rio have helped bring in around 40 000 visitors to the favelas annually. Slum tourism, which originally developed in Victorian London with visits to the East End to observe the extreme poverty and deprivation there (visits which also stimulated charitable interventions), has also proved very controversial because of the issues it raises: it has been interpreted by some as patronizing and exploitative. Yet potentially it also offers opportunities for social entrepreneurship (see Chapter 12) to help local people through tourism (see Tourism Concern's blog on this issue at https://www.tourismconcern.org.uk/slum-tourism/, which summarizes many of these arguments).

The deliberate and indirect impact of film and screen tourism can help in creating a destination image for a wide market which has resulted in tourism organizations beginning to understand that screen tourism can boost the popularity of a destination in the following ways:

- The increase of visitation to location(s) that characters visit in a storyline or programme.
- In the case of literature-oriented films, tourists visit the locations used, and wider screen tourism impacts occur where the filming features historic/religious buildings, stately homes and rural village landscapes. This may have long-term effects, as shown in Table 15.5, as well as the more short-term effects related to trends in television and film, as shown in some of the examples in Table 15.7.
- The programmes and films also help to provide a brand for a destination, such as Tourism New Zealand's use of the filming of the *Lord of the Rings* trilogy. The benefit here is in sustaining visitor awareness and visitation beyond the immediate screening. In other words, the brand helps the destination to become more enduring even if peak visitation tails off.
- Where the storyline of the production has an emotional connection with the audience, the impact in promoting visitation can be long-lived: the BBC television programme *All Creatures Great and Small* generated long-term visitation to Thirsk in Yorkshire and the creation of a visitor attraction based on the writer James Herriot and his books.
- Where the programme or film becomes a 'cult' classic, such as the film *Trainspotting*, unusual and almost bizarre visitor activity can occur which seeks to replicate scenes in the film. For example, pilgrimages to Corrour Station in the Scottish Highlands, which features in the *Trainspotting* film, have meant that even long after the film's initial release, the location remains an enduring theme to visit.

For destination marketers, collaboration with film-makers and appropriate marketing to ensure destinations can cater sustainably for visitors, may help to create new locations for tourism. In the case of Northern Ireland, the £13.2 million subsidy provided to attract the filming of the *Game of Thrones* series yielded a significant payback from the effect of this injection of filming expenditure on the locality from the studios. It also created visits to the region and other impacts, as shown in Table 15.5. Other locations featured in films, such as St Abbs in Scotland, which was featured in the Marvel film *Endgame*, will also most certainly continue to generate visits.

Visit Britain's Movie Map of the UK is seen as a cost-effective method of building on the popularity of film tourism, creating regional tourism activity. For example, visitors were encouraged to 'See Britain through Paddington's eyes' and to take *selfies*. The campaign was launched in tandem with the release of a film about Paddington Bear (Image 15.2) as part of Visit Britain's 'Britain is Great' campaign in 2014, with the strapline 'Paddington is GREAT Britain', and the creation of a Paddington trail in London, with 50 individually designed bear statues. Over 70 000 people visited the trail website hosted by VisitLondon.com. When *Paddington 2* was launched in 2017 the film portrayed many iconic locations in London, promoting the city's global identity. Locations

IMAGE 15.2 The two motion picture films about Paddington Bear provided VisitBritain with an opportunity to use the interest generated by the films to develop a Paddington tour, and a brass statue of the fictional bear was installed at London's Paddington Station

featured in the film include Tower Bridge, St Paul's Cathedral, and London Paddington Station.

The effect of film tourism on shaping visits in the UK has been estimated at £2 billion. More organized packaging by destinations to create film tours, akin to the concept behind the Universal Studios film-set tour in Hollywood, can provide an additional method of tourism marketing. Stirling in Scotland demonstrated an early example of an initiative in this area as a Local Authority and Tourist Board by bringing the premiere of *Braveheart* to Stirling University, with press coverage and associated promotion that is widely acknowledged for creating the 'Braveheart effect' there in the late 1990s. Tourism in the city was boosted, and visits to the Wallace Monument increased from 40 000 in 1995 to 200 000 in 1996. To develop these film tourism locality effects, some countries positively nurture film-making to portray the country globally. Locations providing incentives for film-makers, such as tax incentives, include France, Hungary, the Czech Republic, Georgia, Serbia and New York. What many film-makers look for is a simplified one-stop shop for gaining licences and approvals within the country to reduce delays in filming. Some locations have film offices to attract filming and expedite such licences. There is also a growing interest in the long-term associations of screen tourism and destinations, as illustrated in Table 15.5, which looks at the ability to sustain visitors.

TABLE 15.5 Long-term screen associations and visitor activity

Location	Title	Type	Year of first release	Current activities
Doune Castle, Central Scotland	*Monty Python and the Holy Grail*	Film (but associated with comedy TV series *Monty Python's Flying Circus*)	1975	Film fans from all over the world contribute about one-third of visitors to Doune Castle every year (2006 visitor numbers: 35 401). An annual themed event is held every September for film fans (since 2004). The growth in visitor numbers to Doune Castle 2005–2006 was 29.2 per cent, compared with 2.1 per cent growth in visits to all castles in Scotland
Portmeirion, North Wales	*The Prisoner*	Cult TV series, 17 episodes	1967	About 10 per cent of annual visitor numbers (250 000) are film fans. Shop in village sells *Prisoner*-themed gifts. Annual convention held since 1978 for members of the Prisoner Appreciation Society (1000 members globally)

15

INSIGHT 15.2 continued

Table 15.5 continued

Location	Title	Type	Year of first release	Current activities
Thirsk, North Yorkshire	*All Creatures Great and Small*	Two feature films based on the James Herriot novels	1974–1975	Thirsk is home to *The World of James Herriot*, a visitor attraction based at the home of the infamous real-life vet, attracting about 45 000 visitors per year. The centre also features sets from the TV filming
		Prime-time Sunday night TV series	1978–1990	
		Remake of the *All Creatures Great and Small* series by UK's Channel 5 in 2019 for screening in early 2020	2020–	
Kircudbright, South West Scotland	*The Wicker Man*	Film (cult horror/thriller)	1972	Between 2002 and 2015, an annual weekend festival based loosely on the film was held in July. 'The Wickerman Festival' offered cult music, dance and art. In 2006, 16 000 attendees were recorded, from a baseline of 5000 in 2002
Holmfirth, West Yorkshire	*Last of the Summer Wine*	TV comedy – longest running in the world	1973–2010	Industry built on strength of the programme. Exhibition, gift shop, Wrinkled Stocking Team Room, Sid's Café, merchandise, location tour, 10-mile vintage bus tour, online promotions
Jersey	*Bergerac*	TV crime detective series	1981–1991	Remains one of the most important factors influencing a visit to Jersey, particularly for first-time visitors. More important than a range of traditional advertising forms
Goathland, North Yorkshire	*Heartbeat*	TV police drama series	1991–2010	Visitor numbers grew from about 200 000 per year prior to *Heartbeat* to nearly 1.5 m in 1995, stabilizing at about 1.2 m. Economic effect estimated at over £9 m per year at height of popularity
Thetford, Norfolk	*Dad's Army*	TV comedy (and some radio episodes)	1968–1977	Vintage bus tours, gifts, website *Dad's Army* experience, walking tour, museum, stage shows, statue of Captain Mainwaring (2010)
		Film	1971	

Source: Adapted and extended from Connell and Meyer (2009)

TABLE 15.6 Selected film tourism impacts in the UK (visitor numbers)

Film/television programme	Years involved and impacts
Balamory	In 2003, the children's television programme generated an extra 160 000 visits.
Da Vinci Code	Visitor numbers to Roslyn Chapel rose from 38 000 in 2003 to 68 000 in 2004, and from 120 000 in 2005 and 175 000 in 2006. By 2017 this had risen to almost 182 000.
Game of Thrones	In 2018 this was responsible for a boost to Northern Ireland's tourism industry of 350 000 visits a year and €58 million.
	In Dubrovnik, a UNESCO World Heritage Site, the association with the TV series has seen a 12 per cent annual growth in visitors rising to around 75 000 per annum, many arriving by cruise ship. The fact that 500 cruise ships now dock in a town with 43 000 residents is a serious concern for local authorities.
	Iceland has also reported a positive boost to visitor numbers as a result of being featured in the series.
Gosford Park	Visitor numbers at Beningbrough Hall rose from 10 218 to 94 032 in one year after the film was released and 131 000 in 2015.
Harry Potter	North Yorkshire Moors railway visits rose from 245 000 in 2001 to 297 000 in 2002 and 303 000 in 2004: 15 per cent of visits were due to the Harry Potter film and 38 per cent due to *Heartbeat*. The visitor numbers have now stabilized at around 300 000.
	The Glenfinnan monument, adjacent to the iconic Glenfinnan Viaduct, shown in scenes in the films featuring the Hogwarts Express, now receives 400 000 visits a year.
	Alnwick Castle saw a 120 per cent increase due to its use as Hogwarts. Alnwick Garden's visitor numbers rose from 13 627 in 2001 to 515 813 in 2003, a proportion of which can be attributed to the Harry Potter association. By 2017, visitor numbers had stabilized at 347 000.
	Lacock Abbey saw visitor numbers rise from 55 000 in 2000 to 93 000 in 2003 then fall to 88 000 in 2004, after it was featured as a location in *Harry Potter and the Half-Blood Prince* in 2001.
The Lords of the Rings Trilogy and The Hobbit	*Fellowship of the Ring* (2001), *The Two Towers* (2002) and *The Return of the King* (2003) films generated US$771 million for the New Zealand economy. In 2012, Tourism New Zealand indicated 47 000 international visitors had visited a *Lord of the Rings* film location in New Zealand
	Various surveys have suggested between 6 and 8% of international visitors gave the Lord of the Rings Trilogy as a reason for visiting New Zealand.
Zindagi Na Milegi	This Bollywood film with filming undertaken in Spain was the highest grossing Indian film of 2011. In 2012, over 60 000 Indians sought visas to visit Spain, a doubling of the normal volume of visitors. By 2015, this had risen to 85 000.

Source: Adapted from Olsberg/SPI (2007) *Stately Attraction: How Film and Television Programmes Promote Tourism in the UK*. London: UK Film Council, Scottish Screen, EU Media, East Midlands Tourism, Screen East, South West Screen, Film London and VisitLondon; EY and PHD Chamber of Commerce and Industry (2019) *Building Brand India through Film Tourism*. https://www.ey.com/Publication/vwLUAssets/ey-building-brand-india-through-film-tourism/%24File/ey-building-brand-india-through-film-tourism.pdf; J. Connell (2014) *The Impact of Broadchurch on Tourism Business in 2013*. Exeter: Exeter University Business School.

15

Further reading

Connell, J.J. (2012) 'Film tourism — evolution, progress and prospects', *Tourism Management,* 33 (5): 1007–1029.

Connell, J.J. and Meyer, D. (2009) 'Balamory revisited: An evaluation of screen destination-tourist nexus', *Tourism Management*, 30 (2): 194–207.

Li, S., Li, H., Song, H., Lundberg, C. and Shen, S. (2017) 'The economic impact of on-screen tourism: The case of The Lord of the Rings and the Hobbit', *Tourism Management*, 60: 177–187.

Questions

1 In what ways can destinations harness the power of film and screen tourism to their benefit?

2 What are the advantages and disadvantages to developing film and screen-based tourism as an element of a destination image?

3 How would you go about assessing the success or failure of a film tourism strategy for a destination?

4 How can businesses benefit from film tourism?

Using destination imagery to gain competitive advantage

With growing global competition for tourists, destination marketers are constantly seeking new ways to overcome the problem of destination substitutability. The global expansion of destination advertising is highly competitive as the use of print media and the World Wide Web along with the travel sections of European Sunday newspapers show. Competitiveness is a byword for destinations in the twenty-first century. One method developed is destination positioning (DP). As Pike and Ryan (2004) observe, DP is based on three propositions:

- in modern society, people are bombarded with information on a daily basis
- the mind has developed a defence mechanism against this process of information overload
- the only way to reach the consumer is through simplified and focused messages.

The core element of DP is image, that is the simplified messages and information associated with destination marketing (see Image 15.3). These messages try to influence buyer behaviour, given the intangible nature of tourism and its experiences. DP requires a DMO to create a lasting favourable image or perception among prospective consumers. In technical terms, the destination marketer will need to understand the cognitive, affective and choice element in the decision or intent to visit a destination (the 'conative image'). To operationalize this, marketers will need to identify the important attributes which visitors perceive in the destination, and its attractiveness to the target market. This needs to be understood in relation to how the competition performs. Through complex statistical analysis (e.g. factor analysis and importance–performance analysis), it is possible to group destinations in a matrix. This allows marketers to identify one or two key features to differentiate the destination image from that of the competition, while providing a mechanism to communicate that image to consumers. A typical affective response matrix for competing destinations in the adventure tourism destination market is shown in Figure 15.7. For example, Destination 1 is perceived as a relatively low-risk but challenging place to undertake adventure tourism whereas Destination 3 is perceived as a relatively passive and boring location and should reconsider the suitability of its image for the market it is trying to attract. Figure 15.7 shows that this type of competitor analysis is helpful in that each destination can see how suited it is to specific promotional messages which are aligned to consumer perception.

IMAGE 15.3 The restoration of Henry VIII's flagship the Mary Rose has helped to position Portsmouth, UK, as a naval heritage destination

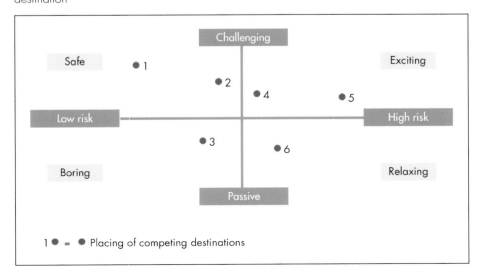

FIGURE 15.7 Affective response matrix for competing adventure tourism destinations

Communicating the destination image: The role of advertising

Marketing concepts in tourism allow us to understand some of the tools and techniques used to communicate with consumers, yet to the consumer these may seem abstract and very distant from the real world. This is because the tourist only sees the outwardly facing elements of marketing by businesses and destinations, and the most visible element of this is advertising. According to Middleton and Clarke (2001: 237), advertising and public relations

are primary means of manipulating demand and influencing buyer behaviour. Simply stated, they enable businesses to reach people in their homes or other places away from the places of production and delivery, and to communicate to them messages intended to influence their purchasing behaviour.

This suggests that buyer behaviour is a very complex process. Advertising is one of the most widely used marketing communication tool in tourism, mainly because the product or service is intangible. It is often based on real or perceived images of tourism and destination. What is notable in tourism is the massive scale of advertising spend. According to Middleton and Clarke (2001), advertising spend on display advertising for tourism in the UK in the late 1990s was £425 million. The tourism sector is a high spender on tourism advertising to get its messages across as any review of post-Christmas television advertising by European tour operators will show. This is designed to influence consumers in the traditional December–January period when they are looking to book summer holidays.

Destination marketing is most established in the USA with its model of Convention and Visitor Bureaus (CVBs), with their funding from a mix of state tourism budgets (set annually) and bed or tourism taxes, initially introduced in New York in 1946 with a 5 per cent levy on rooms, followed by Las Vegas in 1955. The critical point, as Ford and Peeper (2007) demonstrate, is the shift from residents funding all promotion to businesses and visitors paying for promotional activity. Their budgets, prior to the current economic downturn, have historically been significant topped by Hawaii with an annual budget of US$69 million. The justification for investment in promotion was to increase visitor trips and spending to create employment and tax revenues, since tourism supports 15.7 million jobs in the USA based on tourism spending of US$76 billion. The US Travel Association (USTA) provided a convincing argument of tourism as a fast-growing sector capable of generating new employment as a major contributor to new employment growth. In 2019, the USTA found that one-third of people re-entering the workforce found jobs in this sector. In fact, the tax revenue is some US states is sufficient to pay for basic services and so maintaining its vitality via marketing and promotion is essential. However, some states have been forced to make major cuts in promotional budgets, including Washington which closed its tourism office in 2011, passing some of its functions to the travel industry. The USTA pointed to a cut in Wisconsin's budget; this led to a decline in visitors, reflecting the highly competitive business of attracting visitors, especially the wider MICE market. For example, while Washington cut its tourism budget, the adjacent Canadian province of British Columbia was spending US$50 million on tourism promotion. The underlying problem is that when state legislations are forced to make cuts in public expenditure, tourism is a soft target. This is despite the prevailing evidence from the USTA on the return on investment by US states from tourism promotion, where every dollar invested in promotion generated the following sums of additional spending: California (US$20), Missouri (US$2.54), Nevada (US$31) and Indiana (US$16). More specifically, the USTA pointed to the success of Philadelphia's 'With Love' campaign which cost US$4.3 million and resulted in:

- an additional 3.7 million trips
- a growth of US$432 million
- an additional US$11 for each US$1 of state revenue spent on 'With Love'
- the creation of 7000 new jobs.

But it is expensive to undertake advertising and hard to assess its impact in any definitive way without expensive tracking and conversion studies. In 2019, Brand USA (the country's DMO), which is focused on growing international visitors, was attributed with generating 6.6 million additional visitors to the USA over a six-year period which generated US$22 billion and a combined economic impact of $47.7 billion. Brand USA, established in 2011, is

the nation's first public-private partnership to spearhead a globally coordinated marketing effort to promote the United States as a premier travel destination and to communicate U.S. visa and entry policies . . . [and is funded] . . . by a combination of non-federal contributions from destinations, travel brands, and private-sector organizations plus matching funds collected by the U.S. government from international visitors who visit the United States under the Visa Waiver Program (see https://www.thebrandusa.com/about/whoweare).

Yet for the highly developed and competitive tourism marketplace, social media is not the only tool used to inform, persuade and attempt to induce consumer activity in the fast-moving consumer goods sector, where products such as holidays have a limited shelf life. Brand USA's market intelligence noted the differences in the use of social media among different markets, in that 'Emerging markets rely on social media usage more than developed markets when it comes to destination selection. In India, over half of respondents turn to social media for help with their planning. In contrast, France has the lowest usage, with eight percent of respondents using social media'. Brand USA noted the influence of bloggers on shaping opinion for people seeking to visit the USA, now replacing the former travel guide writers as opinion leaders. Advertising in a marketing context is part of the promotional mix identified in marketing plans and strategies, but it has to be viewed as part of a more integrated communication strategy enabling businesses and NTOs to speak with one voice to their existing or potential customers.

Advertising and tourism: An integral relationship?

The consumer buying process in tourism often involves the consumer seeing imagery of places, products and services, rather than being able to physically experience them before buying. Consequently, advertising is important in developing the buyer attitudes, behaviour and the perceived image of a prospective purchase. Advertising is designed to move the consumer from an awareness of a product to a situation where it can be comprehended in relation to its features and benefits. The consumer then has to accept that the product meets their needs, which is where the advertising process is crucial. Here, providing a compelling reason for the consumer to prefer the product, ideally as a unique offering means that advertising exists to help create a purchase. Advertising not only helps to aid purchase but reinforces the importance of the purchaser in meeting their satisfaction. By understanding the process by which advertising will influence consumers, the advertiser may look at the wide range of tools they have at their disposal to use advertising to communicate with their target group. For example, destination advertising may use media such as television, press and billboards as well as the Internet and trade publications. They may also use public relations to provide media exposure as unpaid advertising. Major exhibitions such as the World Travel Market and ITB in Berlin will provide exposure to consumers, wholesalers and retailers who may wish to visit the destination. Other tools, such as direct mail or email, may help build up an advertising relationship with key groups along with sponsorship. For example, in 2008 VisitScotland promoted its 'white' winter campaign by sponsorship of small advertisements on milk cartons to target domestic tourists. However, destinations may employ a wide range of promotional tools to create an attractive destination proposition.

The holiday brochure, combined with powerful television images, is a major mechanism used by tour operators to seek to influence consumers that they will derive personal value and benefits from their holiday product. At the same time, such intentional advertising is often supported by destination marketing in terms of posters, billboards, brochures and media advertising to reinforce and encourage an interest in a certain destination. In the case of website advertising, Brand USA (2014) noted that a set process could be followed in web advertising including:

setting a primary objective (e.g., increase brand awareness, drive content engagement . . .); defining a call to action (what exactly do you want the consumer to do?); measuring results; and optimizing buys toward the best performing creative/media.

In terms of measuring web advertising effectiveness, Brand USA examines four issues:

1 cost per impression (CPM)
2 cost per on-ad engagement (CPE)
3 cost per click-through (CPC)
4 cost per net visit (CPNV)

including those visitors who 'bounce' (i.e. people who leave the website without engaging with the content or other pages).

The process of communicating the destination image

In its simplest form, advertising in tourism is a process and much of the discussion which follows is as relevant to destination marketing as it is for tourism businesses. In an operational context Middleton and Clarke (2001: 241) point to the six stages of advertising:

- advertising objectives (i.e. what is one seeking to achieve?)
- target audience identification
- creative planning (the pictures, images and symbols to use to convey the advertising message)
- media planning (i.e. what forms of advertising to use)
- media costs
- measuring the results and effectiveness of advertising; this typically falls into response measurement (i.e. in relation to a brochure request advertisement) and more in-depth market research studies of the communication effect. This will often be a costly market research exercise to test measures of awareness, interest, attitudes and recall of advertising.

The outcome of the advertising, as a communication process for destinations (and individual businesses), is shown in Figure 15.8. This combines much of the conventional research from consumer behaviour, which suggests that advertising will be targeted at consumers, but only around 12 per cent of the target is reached, since messages are filtered out by the consumer subconsciously. Once the message reaches the final proportion of consumers, a variety of different models of consumer behaviour suggest that potential visitors go through a series of steps before deciding to visit a destination. One model, shown in Figure 15.8, is the AIDA (attention–interest–desire–action) approach which dates to Strong (1925). Alternative models include the Awareness to Reinforcement Process as described by Morgan and Pritchard (2000) as well as that discussed by McWilliams and Crompton (1997).

To convert consumers to buyers, advertisers need to be aware of the following issues:

- *advertising objectives*: the identification of what a DMO or business wishes to achieve in its target markets, namely awareness, interest and activity resulting in a visit or purchase
- *target audience identification*, by examining their media habits
  - *creative planning*, where pictures, symbols and words are used to convey the message simply, as discussed under DP above. An example is British Airways and the World's Favourite Airline image. The tourism sector, like many other industries, uses the creative talents of private sector advertising agencies to develop a

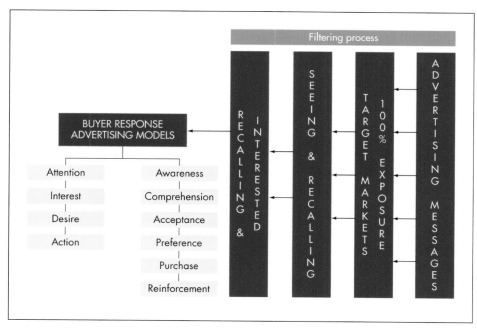

FIGURE 15.8 The advertising communication process in destination marketing
Source: Developed from Middleton and Clarke (2001); Morgan and Pritchard (2000); McWilliams and Crompton (1997)

creative set of concepts, which are tested on consumers using focus groups before launching the campaign. One strategy adopted by Brand USA in 2019 was its Brand USA's United Stories (a storytelling campaign) to capture local and authentic travel experiences to communicate globally. For example, a campaign run in South Dakota saw '1.7 million engagements (comments, likes and shares) on Facebook and Instagram': this campaign was focused on a traditional American road trip using a VW camper van and vintage Chevrolet. The six influencers on the South Dakota trip had 7 million followers and reached 75 million people, illustrating the advertising power of social media compared to traditional advertising media.

- *media planning*, identifying and programming which advertisements will be shown. This involves identifying which audiences to target, the cost of reaching them (as discussed above in terms of web advertising), the scope for creative activity depending on the media used, the space sought and receptiveness of the audience
- *media costs*, where advertising costs are identified as cost per thousand reached.

To reach the target market, various rules of advertising have been developed since the 1950s which include:

- have a unique selling proposition (USP)
- a memorable slogan is needed
- a logo is needed in any advertisement
- humour is not necessary
- the product needs to be visible in the advertisement (adapted from Morgan and Pritchard 2000).

However as Morgan and Pritchard (2000) demonstrate, these rules have been developed during the last decade to reflect the importance of creativity in gaining consumer attention through the use of social media. Conventional thinking on advertising suggests that advertising which is bright and irrelevant will grab consumer attention rather than more staid advertising that is relevant but dull. The key is in grabbing consumer attention and — in the case of a destination – standing out from the crowd, although the rise of social media has changed these ideas, as Chapter 14 highlighted. Thus, the USP may be replaced with emotional selling propositions and irrational appeals, while humour is valid, as are slogans and logos. The shift in marketing as a process as discussed in Chapter 14 also illustrates the changing landscape for advertising destinations. As Santos (2004) found in the case of Portugal, the opinions of travel writers can also be extremely influential in the promotion and advertising of tourism products and destinations. In some cases, this can also lead to misrepresentations of destinations. Historically, such writers have been important opinion leaders and influencers of tourist visitation, creating images that have even been incorporated into the advertising of destinations. These intangible elements of a destination image have led many DMOs to use more sophisticated tools to develop this emotional link between the consumer and the destination, through branding.

Destination branding

Branding is about helping destinations to harness their USP to promote their attractive features (e.g. history, culture, landscape, the people and destination attributes) by building a brand. Branding is designed, as Morgan and Pritchard (2002: 216) argue, to connect the consumer with the destination in the present or future. 'Modern branding is not just about developing appealing communication strategies, it is also about defining and delivering leading edge product or service quality to match or exceed customer expectations.' It requires a vision for the brand to be established so that consumers will buy into it; this can be expressed as the brand's core values. These values should be credible, plausible, drivable and deliverable. These values are consistently reinforced through the product, the service and in all marketing communications in all media to maintain a brand presence. In the case of destination branding, it is the image of the place held in the tourist's memory which needs to be developed in a positive way through the brand development process. As Qu *et al.* (2011) argue, destination branding is one way of differentiating a destination's identity and characteristics from those of competitors. The resulting brand should have a special meaning and attachment to the place, and so its identity should create positive associations with the destination, including feelings that give a compelling reason to visit. Modern-day brands have an emotional appeal, evoking trust, quality and reliability. Building a brand is a long process, but destination advertising is crucial where a brand has been developed to position the destination firmly in the target markets. Among the benefits of branding are:

- it allows consumers to identify with the product or place. These are constantly evolving propositions: New York's Convention Bureau and Visitors' Bureau coined the 'Big Apple' in the 1970s, and the State of New

York also developed the 'I Love New York' slogan at the same time. In 2005, the city of New York filed an application to trademark a new slogan – 'The World's Second Home'

- it helps to create an image of the product or service and raises visibility. In a more sophisticated use of branding, it may help a destination to target different markets, where multiple brands are developed. For example, in 2006, the resort company Sandals used branding to differentiate its resorts into Signature and Classic brands according to service levels. The Signature brand became the elite product with five-star restaurants and butler service

- it helps to reinforce imagery among customers and intermediaries selling tourism experiences and may add prestige to the destination

- a corporate logo, symbol or trademark may help to distinguish the destination from competitors.

Even so, there is also a growing interest in subsuming destination marketing within new ways of thinking about destinations, namely the role of place-making. For this reason, Insight 15.3 examines the ways in which small towns and cities may have bold ambitions to put themselves on the global map through a programme of events (a theme we will return to in Chapter 26). Therefore, Insight 15.3 reviews the experience of one successful small city and what the success factors were in creating a new image and sense of place.

INSIGHT 15.3 How small towns and cities can use an events programme to change their image: Place-making in action

A great deal of research has examined how destination marketing has focused on place-marketing to enhance the image and position of major cities as destinations. This Insight focuses on the experiences of small towns and cities and how they have also embraced these principles to create a successful approach to destination development using place-making.

Richards and Duif (2019) examined how one small Dutch city, s'-Hertogenbosch, created itself as a destination through a programme of cultural events. As a small city of 150 000 people, it used the 500th anniversary of the death of the painter Hieronymus Bosch to host a year of events with a global appeal. The city attracted 422 000 visitors. This follows on from other examples of art-led tourism events hosted by small towns such as Dubuque, Iowa, USA, which attracts 1.5 million visitors a year. Another example is Hobart, Australia, where an events and festival programme and the MONA museum have contributed to attracting 1.4 million visitors a year to the city. These types of small cities have been described by Landry (2013) as *cities of ambition*, achieving destination development beyond people's expectations.

Richards and Duif (2019) distinguish between the process of place-marketing, with a focus on selling the city to visitors and place-making. **Place-making** as a process is much deeper and seeks to generate improvements to the recognition of the place for visitors, residents and potential residents as a place to live. In place-making, creating a positive place image is a by-product rather than the sole focus. Richards and Duif (2019) identify three elements to place-making which small towns and cities have successfully embraced:

- The resources of the place (tangible and intangible)
- Engaging with stakeholders on the meanings and emotions linked to the place and changes needed to improve the place image

- Capturing and harnessing local creativity and innovation to improve the qualities of the place.

To enact successful place-making, a programme of action is required to build an ambitious plan (i.e. the dream) to enact change structured around:

- Attracting attention for the city through a well-designed programme of actions (e.g. a series of events hosted in the city).
- Building confidence to achieve the programme of actions.
- Developing the locality's attractiveness for residents, visitors and businesses to encourage investment in the city.
- Generating catalytic effects to quickly enhance the city's potential.

Many small towns and cities have wide-ranging advantages including higher quality of life than larger cities and higher levels of resident happiness and are based on a human scale. Successful small town and city place-making will need to overcome a range of inherent weaknesses such as a lack of distinctiveness, an absence of strategic planning, lack of vision and ambition. One of the key elements around place-making is branding and Kavaratzis and Ashworth (2005) pointed to three principal strategies used in cities:

- Personality branding
- Flagship construction (i.e. building a large attraction like the MONA in Hobart)
- Events branding, where the place is associated with events, such as Wellington in New Zealand or Edinburgh in Scotland.

15

INSIGHT 15.3 continued

Richards and Duif (2019) point out that a brand has to have meaning and this will need a story or narrative to describe the uniqueness of the place and its offering. In the case of s'-Hertogenbosch, it told the story of the place's most famous resident and his legacy, despite a lack of any of the artist's paintings in the city. By launching the Bosch 500 programme, the city attracted 1.4 million people in 2016 based on a limited number of elements to its successful narrative: it appealed to nostalgia, via the return of the paintings to the city for the exhibition; and it linked the event to contemporary culture, and made wide-ranging use of social media and television to raise interest. S'-Hertogenbosch's small-city success story was attributed to the following factors:

- Vision, with a clear focus on culture as a means to put the location on the map for visitors and residents alike.
- Ambition to realize the vision.
- Consistency and continuity in the leadership of the developments and implementation of the programme of place-making activity and flexibility to accommodate changes.
- Building relationships and collaborations across the city.
- Creating a story for the small city communicated by means of a wide range of strategies to stimulate audiences with engaging content, provoking emotions and attracting an international audience.
- Risk-taking, using research to scope out the risks and to understand how other locations have successfully implemented similar programmes.
- Knowing what to measure and how to measure it to quantify progress and success.
- Embedding the programme in the local community to gain support.

- Ensuring there is a legacy which may be tangible and intangible.
- Using a place-making approach to create real change to improve the quality of life for everyone who engages with the place (i.e. the stakeholders).
- Using a programme of events and projects as part of the place-making process.

References

Kavaratzis, M. and Ashworth, G. (2005) 'City branding: An effective assertion of identity or a transitory marketing trick?' *Tijdschrift voor economische en sociale geografie* 96 (5): 506–14.

Landry, C. (2013) 'Cities of ambition', *Charles Landry* (blog). http://charleslandry.com/blog/cities-of-ambition.

Further reading

Richards, G. (2017) 'From place branding to placemaking: The role of events', *International Journal of Event and Festival Management* 8 (1): 9–23.

Richards, G. and Duif, L. (2019) *Small Cities with Big Dreams: Creative Placemaking and Branding Strategies*. London: Routledge.

Richards, G. and Palmer, B. (2010) *Eventful Cities: Cultural Management and Urban Regeneration*. London: Routledge.

Questions

1 What are the opportunities for small cities in seeking to build a new external image?
2 What are the differences between place-marketing and place-making?
3 How does a programme of events enhance the image of a place?
4 Based on the experience of s'-Hertogenbosch, what are the success factors in creating a visitor destination?

But how can destinations evaluate the efficiency of their marketing efforts? One approach now being considered is destination benchmarking.

Destination benchmarking

Benchmarking is a technique which has gained increased popularity in the tourism industry since the 1990s. It looks at the performance of similar businesses or sectors to gauge how one is performing relative to competitors (Kozak 2003; Zins 2014). It has seen applications in measuring destination competitiveness, particularly in relation to productivity and the effectiveness of advertising and marketing in relation to measurable outcomes (e.g. visitor arrivals, bed nights and receipts) as well as for more subjective measures (Lennon *et al.* 2006). Wöber and Fesenmaier (2004) used Data Envelopment Analysis (DEA) to assess the efficiency of destination marketing in the USA. By examining the 48 state tourism offices (excluding Alaska and Hawaii), they identified three advertising elements:

- total state tourism office domestic advertising budgets
- total state tourism office international advertising budgets
- other budget services.

This highlighted that 15 states were extremely efficient while 33 faced challenges in justifying the advertising budgets given the visitor expenditure and employment generated. This highlights the value of DEA in benchmarking performance based on observed operations. It may also be useful when reviewing promotional campaigns, advertising and the long-term value of branding. In the case of branding, benchmarking may help to point to the brand lifecycle to see if it is achieving the desired effects. As Morgan and Pritchard (2002) argue, brands (like the destination lifecycle) pass through stages of growth when the brand is fashionable through to being famous, then familiar and then fatigued, at which point they need to be refreshed, relaunched or redeveloped. The key point here is that a destination's brand values will need to be reviewed, and benchmarking may be a technique to evaluate performance in a competitive context. In 2008, the World Economic Forum (WEF) produced a Travel and Tourism Competitiveness Index, with 14 'pillars' that accommodate variables which enable the index to be compiled (updated in subsequent years). These 'pillars' are outlined in Figure 15.9.

In 2017, Spain was the top-ranked destination in terms of competitiveness, followed by France, Germany, Japan and the UK. Of the 136 destinations ranked in the index, the bottom 11 were African countries, which scored poorly on critical factors. The area south of the Sahara received only 29 million visitors annually, which is low compared to the scale of the region but indicative of the constraints upon tourism highlighted in Chapter 12. The WEF explained Spain's top-ranked position in terms of:

> Its unique offer of both cultural (2nd) and natural (9th) resources, combined with sound tourism service infrastructure (2nd), air transport connectivity (9th) and strong policy support (5th). Spain's T&T [travel and tourism] sector has not only benefited from the recent ease of its fiscal policy, but also from diverted tourism from security troubled Middle East. (World Economic Forum 2017: 10)

While such benchmarking exercises are not without their critics, they do provide a framework in which elements of destination competitiveness may be examined using quantitative and qualitative measures which vary each time they are undertaken, reflecting the fluidity with which tourism changes and destination fortunes change at a country level.

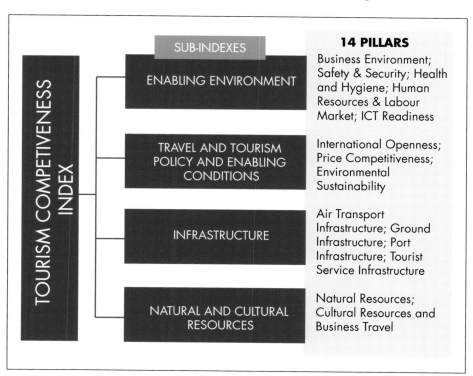

FIGURE 15.9 The structure of the World Economic Forum Travel and Tourism Competitiveness report for countries as destinations

Source: Developed from World Economic Forum

Conclusion

With the rapid changes in consumer behaviour brought about by technology and changing tastes and trends, destination marketing will need to harness market research to understand how such changes impact upon a destination. DMOs have many challenges to face and innovation will be a critical component, when harnessed with creative solutions to attract the future visitor. Among the critical issues facing DMOs in the immediate future include:

- understanding the potential of social media and information communication technologies (ICTs) to communicate and build long-term relationships with visitors
- realizing the potential of branding and its role in enhancing the unique attributes of the destination
- building flexible relationships with the changing public sector climate and fiscal restraints, to pool resources to market destinations to remain competitive
- responding tactically and strategically to new developments in tourism markets and understanding the changing needs of visitors, such as the ageing nature of many Western nations' visitor profiles.

Understanding how tourists select a destination is clearly important, as are the more specific aspects of destination image, promotion and segmentation within the marketing planning process as discussed in Chapter 14. There is a constant process of change in tourism destinations as they pass through various stages of the destination lifecycle and, within any region or country, destinations will be at various stages of development. Destinations compete with each other for both domestic and international visitors to ensure their viability, and the growth of greater cooperative marketing efforts among destinations adjacent to each other can assist in a wider regional marketing of regions with a cluster of destinations and attractions. These types of collaborative efforts are beginning to affect the way destinations within defined regions see the benefits of collaboration rather than wasteful competitive marketing. Destination marketing in the future will be increasingly dependent upon achieving a competitive advantage, and this will be done through more sophisticated research, creative marketing and the use of ICTs. The global marketplace is now a reality for many destinations, but more responsible, sustainable and product-driven marketing will be the key to successful destination development. In the case of Australia, the effect of bushfires in 2019 and 2020 led Tourism Australia to 'pause' its Matesong multi-million dollar advertising campaign in the UK featuring Kylie Minogue. The campaign featured bush locations, wildlife and blue skies, all of which were affected by the bushfires. This is in spite of this being the largest UK investment in destination marketing by the Australian DMO in a decade in the UK market. What this illustrates is the volatility of tourism as an activity and the impact of external factors which can have major repercussions for planned marketing activity that is often months in the planning stage. Yet one of the ongoing issues for all destinations will be the stage of development they have reached in the destination lifecycle, and the impacts which tourism development generates. This will be the focus of Part 4 of the book, which aims to understand the effects of tourist demand, the supply by the industry and effect upon localities and destinations.

The destination policy formulation process needs to consider the various stakeholders and external influences that will impinge upon future marketing strategies. Given the wide variety of people involved, disagreements are inevitable. Laws (1995: 39) notes that parties can be 'poles apart', with some arguing for 'further development, others opposing it, perhaps even arguing for a reduction of current levels of tourism activity'.

Discussion questions

1 Identify and describe the main components of a selected destination.
2 What activities do DMOs undertake in order to market a destination?
3 How do tourists choose which destination to visit?
4 How significant is the advertising process to destinations? What types of advertising can you identify for a destination you are familiar with?

References

Ashworth, G. and Goodall, B. (eds.) (1988) *Marketing in the Tourism Industry: The Promotion of Destination Regions.* Beckenham: Croom Helm.

Avraham, E. and Ketter, E. (2007) *Media Strategies for Marketing Places in Crisis: Improving the Image of Cities, Countries and Tourist Destinations.* Oxford: Butterworth-Heinemann.

Baloglu, S. and McCleary, K. (1999) 'A model of destination image formation', *Annals of Tourism Research,* 26 (4): 868–897.

Beerli, A. and Martin, J. (2004a) 'Factors influencing destination image', *Annals of Tourism Research,* 31 (3): 657–681.

Beerli, A. and Martin, J. (2004b) 'Tourists' characteristics and the perceived image of tourist destinations: A quantitative analysis – a case study of Lanzarote, Spain', *Tourism Management,* 25 (5): 623–636.

Brand USA (2014) 'Defining digital advertising success', Brand USA (website). https://www.thebrandusa.com/research-analytics/insights/defining-digital-advertising-success.

Brey, E., Morrison, A. and Mills, J. (2007) 'An examination of destination resort research', *Current Issues in Tourism,* 10 (5): 415–442.

Buckley, P. and Papadopolous, S. (1986) 'Marketing Greek tourism – the planning process', *Tourism Management,* 7 (2): 82–100.

Connell, J. (2005) 'Toddlers, tourism and Tobermory: Destination marketing issues and television-induced tourism', *Tourism Management,* 26 (5): 763–776.

Connell, J. (2012) 'Film tourism — evolution, progress and prospects', *Tourism Management,* 33 (5): 1007–1029.

Connell, J. (2014) *The Impact of Broadchurch on Tourism Business in 2013.* Exeter: Exeter University Business School.

Echtner, C. and Ritchie, J.B. (1991) 'The meaning and measurement of destination image', *Journal of Tourism Studies,* 2 (2): 2–12.

EY and PHD Chamber of Commerce and Industry (2019) *Building Brand India through Film Tourism.* https://www.ey.com/Publication/vwLUAssets/ey-building-brand-india-through-film-tourism/%24File/ey-building-brand-india-through-film-tourism.pdf.

Ford, R. and Peeper, W. (2007) 'The past as prologue: Predicting the future of the convention and visitor bureau industry on the basis of its history', *Tourism Management,* 28 (6): 1104–1114.

Gallarza, M., Saura, I. and Garciá, H. (2002) 'Destination image: Towards a conceptual framework', *Annals of Tourism Research,* 29 (1): 56–78.

Gartner, W. (1993) 'Image formation process', in M. Uysal and D. Fesenmaier (eds.) *Communication and Channel Systems in Tourism Marketing.* New York: Haworth Press.

Gilbert, D. (1990) 'Strategic marketing planning for national tourism', *The Tourist Review,* 1 (1): 18–27.

Global Sustainable Tourism Council (2013) 'Criteria for destinations'. https://www.gstcouncil.org/gstc-criteria/gstc-destination-criteria/.

Gunn, C. (1988) *Vacationscape: Designing Tourist Regions,* 2nd edition. New York: Van Nostrand Reinhold.

Hunt, J. (1975) 'Image as a factor in tourism development', *Journal of Travel Research,* 13 (3): 1–17.

Kavaratzis, M. and Ashworth, G. (2005) 'City branding: An effective assertion of identity or a transitory marketing trick?' *Tijdschrift voor economische en sociale geografie* 96 (5): 506–14

Kozak, M. (2003) *Destination Benchmarking.* Wallingford: CABI.

Landry, C. (2013) 'Cities of ambition', *Charles Landry* (blog). http://charleslandry.com/blog/cities-of-ambition.

Laws, E. (1995) *Tourist Destination Management.* London: Routledge.

Lennon, J., Cockerell, N. and Trew, J. (2006) *Benchmarking National Tourism Organizations and Agencies: Understanding Best Practice.* Oxford: Elsevier.

McWilliams, E.G. and Crompton, J. (1997) 'An expanded framework for measuring the effectiveness of destination advertising', *Tourism Management,* 18 (3): 127–137.

Middleton, V. and Clarke, J. (2001) *Marketing in Travel and Tourism,* 3rd edition. Oxford: Butterworth-Heinemann.

Middleton, V.T.C., Fyall, A., Morgan, M. and Ranchhod, A. (2009) *Marketing in Travel and Tourism.* Oxford: Butterworth-Heinemann.

Morgan, N. and Pritchard, A. (2000) *Advertising in Tourism and Leisure.* Oxford: Butterworth-Heinemann.

Morgan, N. and Pritchard, A. (eds.) (2002) *Destination Branding: Creating the Unique Destination Proposition.* Oxford: Butterworth-Heinemann.

Morrison, A. (2019) *Marketing and Managing Tourism Destinations,* 2nd edition. London: Routledge.

Olsberg/SPI (2007) *Stately Attraction: How Film and Television Programmes Promote Tourism in the UK.* London: UK Film Council, Scottish Screen, EU Media, East Midlands Tourism, Screen East, South West Screen, Film London and VisitLondon.

Perles-Ribes, J., Ramón-Rodríguez, A., Moreno-Izquierdo, L. and Torregrosa Martí, M. (2018) 'Winners and losers in the Arab uprisings: A Mediterranean tourism perspective', *Current Issues in Tourism,* 21 (16): 1810–1829.

Pike, S. and Page, S.J. (2014) 'The Destination Marketing Organization and destination marketing: A narrative analysis of the first 40 years of literature', *Tourism Management,* 41: 202–227.

Pike, S. and Ryan, C. (2004) 'Destination positioning analysis through a comparison of cognitive, affective and conative perceptions', *Journal of Travel Research,* 42 (May): 333–342.

15

Qu, H., Kim, L. and Im, H. (2011) 'A model of destination branding: Integrating the concepts of the branding and destination image', *Tourism Management*, 32 (3): 465–476.

Richards, G. and Duif, L. (2019) *Small Cities with Big Dreams*. London: Routledge.

Santos, C. (2004) 'Framing Portugal: Representational dynamics', *Annals of Tourism Research*, 31 (1): 122–138.

Seddighi, H. and Theocharous, A. (2002) 'A model of tourism destination choice: A theoretical and empirical analysis', *Tourism Management*, 23 (4): 475–487.

Sharpley, R. and Pearce, T. (2007) 'Tourism, marketing and sustainable development in the English National Parks: The role of National Park Authorities', *Journal of Sustainable Tourism*, 15 (5): 557–573.

Strong, E. (1925) 'Theories of selling', *The Journal of Applied Psychology*, 9: 75–86.

Wahab, S., Crampon, L. and Rothfield, L. (1976) *Tourism Marketing*. London: Tourism International Press.

Wen, H., Josiam, B., Spears, D. and Yang, Y. (2018) 'Influence of movies and television on Chinese tourists' perception toward international tourism destinations', *Tourism Management Perspectives*, 28: 211–219.

Wöber, K. and Fesenmaier, D. (2014) 'A multi-criteria approach to destination benchmarking: A case study of state tourism advertising programs in the United States', *Journal of Travel and Tourism Marketing*, 16: 1–18.

World Economic Forum (2017) *The Travel & Tourism Competitiveness Report 2017*. Geneva: World Economic Forum.

Zalaton, A. (1998) 'Wives' involvement in the tourism decision process', *Annals of Tourism Research*, 25 (4): 890–903.

Zins, A. H. (2014) 'Internal benchmarking for Regional Tourism Organizations: A case example', *Tourism Analysis*, 19 (4): 413–424.

Further Reading

Books

Gursoy, D. and Chi, C. (eds) (2018) *The Routledge Handbook of Destination Marketing*. London: Routledge.

Heeley, J. (2015) *Urban Destination Marketing in Contemporary Europe*. Bristol: Channel View.

Kolb, B. (2017) *Tourism Marketing for Cities and Tourism*. London: Routledge

Pike, S. (2016) *Destination Marketing Essentials*. New York: Routledge.

Journal Articles

Choe, Y., Stienmetz, J. and Fesenmaier, D. (2017) 'Measuring destination marketing: Comparing four models of advertising conversion', *Journal of Travel Research*, 56 (2): 143–157.

Galvez–Rodriguez, M., Alonso–Cafiadas, J., Haro-de-Rosario, A. and Caba–Perez, C. (2020) 'Exploring best practices for online engagement via Facebook with local destination management organisations (DMOs) in Europe: A longitudinal analysis', *Tourism Management*, 34: 100636.

Ma, W., Schraven, D., de Bruijne, M. de Jong, M and Lu, H (2019) 'Tracing the origins of place branding research: A bibliometric study of concepts in use (1980–2018)', *Sustainability*, (11): 2999.

Oliveira, A. and Huertas, A. (2019) 'How do destinations use twitter to recover their images after a terrorist attack', *Journal of Destination Marketing and Management*, 12: 46–54.

Scott, N., Green, C. and Fairley, S. (2016) 'Investigation of the use of eyetracking to examine tourism advertising effectiveness', *Current Issues in Tourism*, 19 (7): 634–642.

Tussyadiah, I. and Sigala, M. (2018) 'Shareable tourism: Tourism marketing in the sharing economy', *Journal of Travel and Tourism Marketing*, 35 (1): 1–4.

15

Part 4

The impact of tourism

In this section of the book, the impacts associated with tourist activities and effects are considered as a way of understanding some of the costs and benefits of tourism. Impacts are a major element of tourist activity and their scope, effect and duration on the host society are complex. They vary in terms of their intensity and effect according to the specific location and nature of the impacts. In Chapter 16, the most frequently cited impact used by governments and private sector enterprises to justify tourism activity – economic impacts – are reviewed. The chapter critically examines both the costs and benefits of tourism as an activity that can generate employment and foreign currency while contributing to the balance of payments at a national level. This is followed by Chapter 17, which discusses some of the social and cultural impacts that are inevitably associated with tourism development. The chapter evaluates the problems of gauging the extent to which tourism-induced changes to societies and their cultural values are a direct result of tourist activity. The chapter considers many of the concepts and frameworks developed by anthropologists and sociologists to evaluate the effect of tourism on host societies. Chapter 18 focuses on tourism's impact on the built and natural environment. The environment is viewed as a finite resource which is also directly affected by tourism development, and examples of impacts and measures to ameliorate these impacts are discussed. The tourism impacts associated with the environment have also generated a wide range of opinions and views on how to accommodate both tourism and the environment, given their symbiotic relationship. Therefore, Chapter 19 considers the challenge of sustainability, and reviews the evolution of the debate on the extent to which tourism can be a sustainable development option along with the wide range of issues associated with sustainability, including the climate emergency. However, before developing our understanding of the specific types of impacts arising from tourism, it is useful to outline a number of general principles applicable to all impacts.

A wide range of issues arise in relation to the impact of tourism, which include positive headline benefits in the economic and sociocultural/environmental domain, as illustrated in Figure 1. Conversely, there are rarely benefits without some form of impact, as the growth of tourism raises key issues including:

- What are the environmental impacts? (see Figure 2)
- Who benefits from tourism, when and where?
- Does tourism generate social problems when strategies for development claim it will solve underlying societal problems (e.g. poverty alleviation)?

FIGURE 1 Headline benefits of tourism for destinations

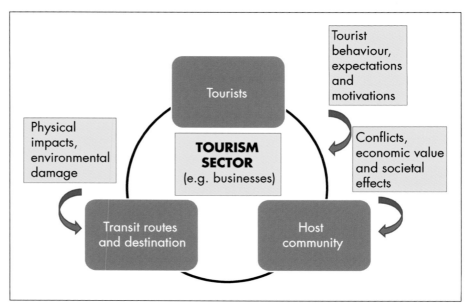

FIGURE 2 Concerns about the tourism–environment relationship

- Does tourism lead to a rejuvenation of local and indigenous culture?
- Does investment in tourism by the public sector come at a cost to other areas of society?
- Does tourism lead to resource destruction?

Yet seeking to understand how tourism generates impacts is far from straightforward, as Wall and Mathieson (2006) and Hall and Lew (2009) suggest. Among the problems are:

- A frequent lack of baseline data upon which to measure or gauge change induced by tourism.
- An inconsistent use of research methods and lack of compatibility between studies.
- A lack of understanding about the capacity of different environments to deal with and absorb change.
- A difficulty in establishing cause and effect around what change is due to the impact of tourism and what is due to non-tourism effects (i.e. disentangling the effects of tourism from other activities).
- The understanding of scale and the geographical focus of impacts (i.e. do they occur at a national, regional or local level of analysis).
- The difficulty of attributing the diverse range of impacts from tourism, as shown in Figure 3, which may be dispersed geographically while others occur at specific geographical locations. Consequently, in assessing any measure of impact, a combination of dispersed and concentrated impacts need to be incorporated.

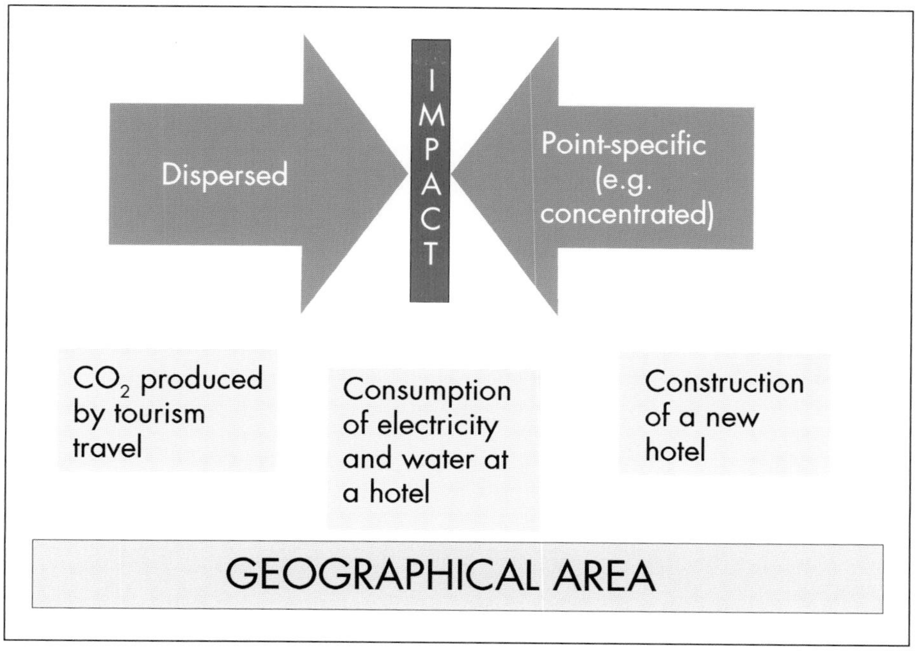

FIGURE 3   Understanding the impact of tourism: Concentrated versus dispersed impacts

References

Hall, C. M. and Lew, A. A. (2009) *Understanding and Managing Tourism Impacts: An Integrated Approach.* Abingdon: Routledge.
Wall, G. and Mathieson, A. (2006) *Tourism: Change, Impacts, and Opportunities.* Harlow: Pearson.

16

Economic impacts

Learning outcomes

After reading this chapter and answering the questions, you should be able to:

- explain what is meant by the terms 'economics', 'supply' and 'demand'
- define the positive and negative economic impacts of tourism
- outline methods for measuring tourism's economic impacts.

Overview

Among the most significant reasons used by government and private sector tourism businesses for developing tourism is the associated economic gain. Tourism can assist in generating foreign exchange, and improve the economy and employment prospects of countries, regions and cities. While the economic advantages of tourism are certainly clear, many negative aspects are apparent. To understand the nature of the economic impacts of tourism, it is important to have an understanding of economic concepts and how they relate to tourism. In addition, the tools used to measure the impact of tourism are introduced as an insight into the ways economists have developed new approaches to depicting how tourism interacts with the national economy.

Introduction

The economic aspects of tourism have been widely studied and extensively published in academic journals such as *Tourism Management* and *Tourism Economics*. Much of the early research on tourism impacts tended to be rather uncritical, and focused on the positive economic gains rather than any negative aspects relating to the environment and society. The justification for tourism development generally focuses on the potential for positive economic impacts and tourism has flourished across the world because of its perceived benefit: it is heralded as the world's largest industry. The global economic importance of tourism is illustrated by the World Travel and Tourism Council (WTTC 2019). Globally, tourism generates:

- 10.4 per cent of gross domestic product (GDP) (which has grown from 9.1 per cent in 2012)
- 319 million jobs (i.e. 1 in 10 of all jobs globally)
- 10 per cent of total employment, a growth of 2 per cent since 2012
- In the period 2013–2018, tourism was responsible for creating 20 per cent of all new jobs globally.

Although there are concerns about the validity of such measures, due to the problems of validating such estimates of global tourism activity, they are widely cited. As a result, several authors argue that the potential economic benefits of tourism are exaggerated for political reasons, particularly in the case of hosting events (see Chapter 26) where the tourism impacts are much smaller than predicted (Dwyer and Jago 2020). Even so, the WTTC data do indicate the broad dimensions of tourism, where 78.5 per cent of spending arises from tourism for leisure purposes (e.g. to take a holiday), with 21.5 per cent due to business-related travel. In 2018, the WTTC found that 71.2 per cent of all tourist spending arose from domestic tourism, with growth rates the strongest in developing countries (see Chapter 23). The main driver of global tourism growth was attributed, by the WTTC, to growth in the number of middle-class households, with the greatest growth in Asia and North Africa.

As the WTTC (2019) report notes, the regional economic significance of tourism growth means that for 2018 the value and growth rates in tourism were:

- North America: US$1.9 trillion contribution to GDP; tourism comprises 8.2 per cent of GDP
- The Caribbean: US$62 billion contribution to GDP; tourism comprises 15.5 per cent of GDP
- Europe: US$2.2 trillion contribution to GDP; tourism comprises 9.7 per cent of GDP
- Latin America: US$336 billion contribution to GDP; tourism comprises 8.7 per cent of GDP
- Africa: US$194 billion contribution to GDP; tourism comprises 8.5 per cent of GDP
- Middle East: US$278 billion contribution to GDP; tourism comprises 8.7 per cent of GDP
- North East Asia: US$2.1 trillion contribution to GDP; tourism comprises 9.6 per cent of GDP
- South Asia: US$296 billion contribution to GDP; tourism comprises 8.8 per cent of GDP
- South East Asia: US$373 billion contribution to GDP; tourism comprises 12.6 per cent of GDP
- Oceania: (Australia, New Zealand and the Pacific Islands) US$206 billion contribution to GDP; tourism comprises 12.2 per cent of GDP

Source: WTTC (2019)

According to Mathieson and Wall (1982), the magnitude of the economic impacts of tourism is influenced by five factors:

- the type of tourism facility and attraction for tourists
- the volume and level of tourist spending
- the level of economic development in the region
- the extent to which tourist spending is maintained and recirculated in the region
- the extent of seasonality in the region.

These factors determine whether economic impacts are positive or negative.

Tourism gives rise to different benefits and costs, and the nature and scope of economic impacts tend to depend on geography and socio-economic structures. There are distinctions between developed and less developed countries and core and peripheral areas within a country. For this reason, establishing the economic impact of tourism for specific countries is a difficult exercise. To derive a greater understanding of tourism and the economic impacts it generates, attention now turns to the nature of economics to explain the concepts which are used to study the economic effects of tourism.

What is economics?

Like many social science subjects, there is little agreement on how to define the area of study that is economics. However, according to Craven (1990: 3) 'economics is concerned with the economy or economic system . . . [and] . . . the problem of allocating resources is a central theme of economics, because most resources are scarce'. Therefore Craven (1990: 4) argues that economics is the study of methods of allocating scarce resources and distributing the product of those resources, and the study of the consequences of these methods of allocation and distribution.

What is meant by scarcity and resources? The term 'scarcity' is used to illustrate the fact that most resources in society are finite and decisions have to be made on the best way to use and sustain these resources. Economists define resources in terms of:

- natural resources (e.g. the land)
- labour (e.g. human resources and entrepreneurship)
- capital (e.g. artificial aids to assist in producing goods).

Collectively these resources constitute the factors of production which are used to produce commodities. These commodities can be divided into:

- goods (e.g. tangible products, such as an aircraft or a hotel room)
- services (e.g. intangible items, such as services of a tour guide).

The total output of all commodities in a country over a period of time, normally a year, is known as the *national product*. The creation of products and services is termed *production* and the use of these goods and services is called *consumption*. Since, in any society, the production of goods and services can only satisfy a small fraction of consumers' needs, choices have to be made on the allocation of resources to determine which goods and services to produce (Lipsey 1989). The way in which goods and services are divided among people has been examined by economists in terms of the distribution of income and the degree of equality and efficiency in their distribution. Many of these issues are dealt with under the heading of *microeconomics*, which Craven defines as:

> the study of individual decisions and the interactions of these decisions . . . [including] . . . consumers' decisions on what to buy, firms' decisions on what to produce and the interactions of these decisions, which determine whether people can buy what they would like, whether firms can sell all that they produce and the profits firms make by providing and selling. (Craven 1990: 4)

Therefore, microeconomics is concerned with certain issues, namely:

- the firm
- the consumer
- production and selling
- the demand for goods
- the supply of goods.

Economists also examine a broader range of economic issues in terms of *macroeconomics* which is concerned with:

> the entire economy and interactions within it, including the population, income, total unemployment, the average rate of price increases (the inflation rate), the extent of companies' capacities to produce goods and the total amount of money in use in the country. (Craven 1990: 5)

Therefore, macroeconomics is mainly concerned with:

- how the national economy operates

- employment and unemployment
- inflation
- national production and consumption
- the money supply in a country.

Within micro- and macroeconomics, tourism economists examine different aspects of the tourism system, based on the analysis of the concepts of demand and supply.

Demand

Within economics, the concern with the allocation of resources to satisfy individuals' desire to travel means that transport economists examine the demand for different modes of travel and the competition between such modes in relation to price, speed, convenience and reliability. Economists attempt to understand what affects people's tourism behaviour and the significance of tourism in a destination. Tourism economists have examined the demand for travel and tourist products, recognizing the significance of demand as a driving force in the economy. This stimulates entrepreneurial activity to produce the goods and services to satisfy the demand (Bull 1995). More specifically, tourism economists examine the effective demand for goods or services: the aggregate or overall demand over a period of time. Since income has an important effect on tourism demand, economists measure the impact using a term known as the elasticity of demand.

As Bull (1995) has shown, it is measured using a ratio calculated thus:

$$\text{Elasticity of demand} = \frac{\text{percentage change in tourism demand}}{\text{percentage change in disposable income}}$$

in relation to two equal time periods. The significance of this concept is that the demand for goods to fulfil basic needs (e.g. food, water and shelter) is relatively unchanging or *inelastic* while the demand for luxury items, such as holiday and pleasure travel, is variable or *elastic*, being subject to fluctuations in demand due to factors such as income or price. Thus, 'elasticity' is used to express the extent to which tourists are sensitive to changes in price and service. For example, primary demand is usually more elastic than derived demand. The different elements which comprise the tourism product (e.g. transport, accommodation and attractions) are complementary and it is difficult to separate out one individual item as exerting a dominant effect on price since each is interrelated in terms of what is purchased and consumed.

To assess the impact of price on the demand for tourism, economists examine the price elasticity of demand, where an inverse relationship exists between demand and price (Bull 1995). For example, it is generally accepted that the greater the price, the less demand there will be for a tourism product due to the limited amount of the population's disposable income which is available to purchase the product.

It is calculated thus:

$$\text{Price elasticity} = \frac{\text{Percentage change in quantity of tourism product demanded}}{\text{percentage change in tourism product price}}$$

The concept of cross-elasticity needs to be considered as destinations tend to be considered substitutes when they are in a similar area or offer a similar product. For example, Vu and Turner (2011) used an economic research technique called shift-share analysis to assess whether the growth of tourism in one country impacts on other neighbouring countries. The study focused on Vietnam examined how its growth affected or was affected by nearby Thailand and China. Their research concluded that Vietnam had a cost advantage over Thailand and attracted more long-haul visitors from the Americas, Europe and Australasia. Yet Vietnam had lost ground to attracting tourists from Asian markets.

Other contributory factors which influence the demand for tourism include the impact of tourist taxation and the amount of holiday entitlement available to potential tourists, as well as the effects of weather, climate and cultural preferences for holidaymaking which are expressed in terms of seasonality. These factors also need to be viewed in the context of the economics of each specific part of the tourism product, and the aggregate impact upon tourism demand leads economists to look ahead and forecast the likely growth which will occur in the future (i.e. tourism forecasting, see Chapter 27).

Supply

Economists are also interested in the *supply* of a commodity (e.g. hotel rooms) which is often seen as a function of its price and the price of alternative goods. Price is often influenced by the cost of the factors of production. Bull (1995) suggests that the principal questions in which economists are interested from the supply side are:

- what to produce
- how to produce it
- when and where to produce it.

Supply may be viewed from two perspectives. First, increasing demand requires an increase in facilities and infrastructure to cope with added pressure – this centres on the concept of extending capacity. Second, tourism may be stimulated by the provision of more facilities – this is creation and/or anticipation of demand. Borooah (1999) suggests that, for hotels, it is those who are already constrained by capacity who are responsible for most room increases. For commercial operators, the main objective in supply terms is to maximize profitability from the available capacity, as discussed in Chapter 10.

The economic characteristics of the tourism sector

There are numerous debates within the tourism literature on the extent to which tourism is a business, an industry, a service or just a phenomenon (see Leiper 2008). The WTTC outlines the extent to which the terms of tourism industry and tourism economy can be defined, where the 'travel and tourism industry' describes the direct effect of travel demand and relates to services such as accommodation, catering, entertainment, transport and attractions. The WTTC portrays this as the tip of the iceberg. In contrast, the 'travel and tourism economy' refers to the wider effects of flow-through of travel demand across the economy. This includes the 'travel and tourism industry' but also those businesses which support it, such as printers, publishers, wholesalers, utilities, administration, computing and security. The WTTC argues that to appreciate the total contribution of tourism to an economy, we need to incorporate the indirect effects that include:

- the amount of investment spending on travel and tourism
- government spending across all areas of tourism-related activity
- purchases of goods and services by the sectors which deal with tourists

to help identify the 'induced' contribution of tourism including those directly and indirectly employed in tourism.

One of the main justifications for tourism development is the potential for economic benefits. Tourism is often encouraged to draw in much-needed foreign exchange, generate employment and improve economic and social prospects in a destination area. There are a number of characteristics of tourism which distinguish it from other industries, goods and services. These are as follows:

- *Tourism is an invisible export industry* – there is no tangible product and consumers tend to make a purchase without seeing the product first-hand.
- *Tourists require supporting goods and services* – the expansion of existing infrastructure and services may be required or new ones created.
- *Tourism is a fragmented product* – it consists of a number of elements, such as transport and accommodation as well as landscape and cultural resources.
- *Tourism is a highly price- and income-elastic product.*
- *Tourism is a perishable product* – if a hotel room is not booked one night, then that income is lost.
- *Tourism is subject to unpredictable external influences*, such as currency, politics, tourist motivation and taste, and these features are discussed in more detail in Chapter 27.

Murphy (1985) states that the only constant in tourism is *change*. It is an industry dependent on a complexity of external factors (see Dwyer and Forsyth 2006). At a general level, the demand for tourism is governed by three economic cycles, which impact upon tourism, and consequently, tourism cycles may also emerge that shape tourism demand. As Guizzardi and Mazzocchi (2010) found, business cycles have a delayed effect on tourism cycles, since international tourism is more income-elastic than domestic tourism. The three economic cycles are as follows.

Short-term economic cycles

This type of economic cycle defines periods of dramatic change. Short-term cycles tend to be highly visible and predictable. Good examples of these manifest themselves as tourism cycles and include seasonality, such as summer peaks and winter troughs and the period in-between, and shoulder seasons. The problems with short-term cycles such as seasonality are pressure on the resource (congestion, overcrowding, staff stress) and issues of economic efficiency (too much summer trade, insufficient off-peak trade). For some tourism services, it might be necessary to maximize revenue during the summer season to ensure all-year-round survival (Murphy 1985). A commitment to a quality industry, including maintaining acceptable staff levels year-round, and a thriving industry is a challenge, requiring knowledge of the market and the tools which may assist in reducing fluctuating demand. In some instances, reduced demand out of season is desirable for environmental reasons or as part of a business strategy.

Medium-term economic cycles

Medium-term cycles relate to changes over a period of several years. These changes tend to reflect consumer attitudes and the demand for specific tourism products. Consumer preferences tend to be fickle. Natural events, such as floods, hurricanes and earthquakes, can also affect tourism in the medium term. Research by Coshall (2005) points to the role of intervention analysis and economic modelling to understand the impact of events such as disasters and terrorism in economic cycles. Coshall concluded that tourist spending was to return to normal in the 1980s but less so in the period 1990–2010 in the case of UK inbound and outbound travel. Yet there are no set rules on the recovery of tourist destinations after unpredictable events. Other economic aspects, such as currency devaluation and the strength of currencies, have significant effects on tourist numbers. For example, Alegre *et al.* (2012) examined the evolution of package holiday prices for British tourists visiting the Balearic Islands 2000–2008. They found that the actual price of holidays had dropped for British consumers but the market was not sufficiently sensitive to fuel a boom in demand.

Long-term economic cycles

Much of the work by economists seeking to model such cycles is derived from the ideas of Kondratiev, based in turn on the economic ideas of Schumpter in 1939, where four phases in long economic cycles could be discerned: boom, recession, depression, recovery. In the Kondratiev model, these waves last around 40–50 years (Berry *et al.* 1993) but they are becoming much shorter in the global economy. Much of the focus in tourism research has been on the implications of long-term economic cycles on the evolution, development and effect on destinations, utilizing the work of Butler (1980) on the tourism area lifecycle. However, there is also evidence that current ideas on long-term economic cycles as shaping the destination lifecycle may need a greater economic theorization around the notion of globalization, global capital flows, the positions of economic development and localities and how tourism fits into these new agendas, as examined in the chapter on urban tourism.

Economic benefits

The balance of payments

The balance of payments account for a country is a record of transactions during a period of time between residents of that country and the rest of the world. This includes all imports and exports. Improving the balance of payments is probably the most significant justification used by governments to promote tourism. The contribution of tourism to the overall balance of payments of a nation is calculated by working out the difference between the amount spent by overseas visitors in that country and the amount spent overseas by residents of the country. This figure will either be a net surplus or deficit on the tourism account of a national economy. Tourists are viewed as 'invisible exports' which have an impact on national economies. Some of the highest negative travel accounts in the world are displayed by Germany and Japan as residents spend more on tourism trips than incoming visitors do. The USA had the most positive account. For example, in response to a parliamentary question in the UK Parliament, it was disclosed that the UK had a deficit of £20 billion on its tourism accounts due to more tourist spending occurring overseas than the UK generated from inbound and domestic tourism. In contrast, Spain had a £24 billion surplus, France an £8.6 billion surplus and the USA a £17.9 billion surplus on its tourism account. In the case of France, this may be attributed to around 60 per cent of French summer holidays being taken within France (i.e. as domestic tourism). These amounts will vary annually, depending upon the effect of various factors like the state of the economy, exchange rates, economic and political stability and trends in inbound, outbound and domestic tourism.

The industrial structure of developing countries is often highly problematic in terms of tourism development, with the national economy comparatively weakly developed, with less scope for exporting manufactured goods. Reliance is on low-cost primary products and imported high-cost products; particularly in the case of luxury hotel developments, this means that the products used are imported. Tourism development can improve the balance of payments by bringing in foreign spending to the local economy (see Insight 16.1 on tourism in Cuba). But in the case of developing countries, this has to be balanced against imported goods.

INSIGHT 16.1 Economic aspects of tourism in Cuba

According to Jayawardena (2003), tourism developed in Cuba through three phases: the pre-revolution era (1945–1958), the post-revolution era (1959–1988) and the tourism revolution era (1989–2002), with a free tourism market emerging after 1989. In 1959, the Cuban revolution led by Fidel Castro (who subsequently ruled Cuba from 1959 to 2008), established a communist regime which ousted the Cuban dictator Batista. Castro's government introduced progressive social reforms to provide citizens with access to basic human needs, nationalizing key sectors of the economy and introducing land reforms, premised on reducing inequality and poverty. The country also pursued an interventionist foreign policy supporting conflicts and rebels in Angola and Nicaragua, being at odds with the USA.

Tourism in Cuba suffered greatly as a result of the revolution in 1959, with numbers dropping from 350 000 in 1958 to a negligible number in 1962. Following political changes and the collapse of the Soviet Union as a source of foreign aid, tourism expansion was identified as a mechanism for economic development. Tourism has been presented as the most successful sector of the Cuban economy and has been depicted as a 'model industry' because of its ability to generate foreign currency and investment. Government objectives for tourism in the tourism revolution era were to:

1 Increase tourism revenue and profitability.
2 Increase tourist arrivals year on year.

The strategy taken by the government is that of 'price leadership'– low price, low cost, high volume. For this to work effectively, costs must be lower than the price charged. However, there are problems in trying to increase tourist numbers.

- *The problems of inelastic demand.* There is a high substitution elasticity, which means that aggressive marketing by one Caribbean country will affect the tourist volume to another. A price war could cripple the tourism industry in Cuba.

- *A limitation in infrastructure constrains tourism growth.* An increase in visitors will require improvements in the supply of tourism facilities. The government cannot afford to undertake this work.

- *A high level of external competition from other Caribbean countries.* Low brand loyalty and increasing standards of quality mean that the tourism industry has to continually improve if tourist volumes are to be retained. There is a low level of internal competition as government policy has stifled privatization.

- *Cuba is unable to tap into the American market* like other Caribbean countries because there is an embargo in place which prevents American citizens visiting the country.

- *There is high leakage* so economic benefits are not fully appreciated and it is impossible to be a true low-cost producer. Repatriation of profits takes place due to a large number of international hotels and managers.

16

- *A lack of management skill* exists in Cuba, limited by the communist style of production. Management has to be sourced from overseas. Cubans will gain the necessary skills in time, the gap in the meantime will increase the costs of tourism to the country.

Recent tourism growth amid political change

Despite the constraints on tourism development, Cuban inbound tourism has grown from 1.17 million in 1997 to 1.6 million in 1999 and reached 2.6 million in 2012 and 4.7 million arrivals in 2017. Tourism is around 11.4 per cent of GDP and employs 126 000 jobs directly and 519 000 in total. The visitors are largely from Canada, who spend around nine nights there, followed by Italy, the UK, Spain, Germany and France. Cuba now features as one of the top Caribbean destinations, after Mexico and Jamaica. However, in July 2004 travel restriction were imposed by the USA so Cuban-Americans can only travel back once every three years compared to the once a year prior to 2004, which has been licensed only to visit close relatives. Ironically, this resulted after positive moves by Cuba to attract those visiting friends and relatives (VFR) and former migrants to visit, as 1.3 million people of Cuban origin live in the USA. US government restrictions have also made official US visits to Cuba more difficult. An investment programme in the island's 41 000 bed spaces, which have virtually doubled since 1995, meant the Cuban government encouraged foreign investment, especially joint ventures.

Continued sanctions by the USA have led to reprisals by Cuba, which added a 10 per cent levy on payment of goods and services in US$, and US visitors do visit, albeit via an indirect route through Mexico or the Bahamas. In addition, following financial concerns at the state-run Cubanacan (hotel, restaurant and travel agency business), direct control of the travel group has been assumed by the Ministry of Tourism, after a period of decentralization in tourism administration. Many of the government-appointed executives from the tourism revolution era have been removed, as central control of the tourism economy is strengthened. In June 2019, President Trump announced new restrictions, closing the 'People to People' visitor category as a result of Cuba's support for the socialist-led Venezuelan government. A range of approved categories of travel for US citizens wishing to visit Cuba, includes:

- Family visits
- Those on official US government business
- Journalist travel
- Professional research and meetings
- Educational travel by schools, colleges and universities
- Religious activities
- Support for the Cuban people
- Humanitarian projects.

Despite this, a ban on cruise ships visiting Cuba has meant cancelling 800 000 advance bookings in 2019. The extent to which these restrictions will impact on visitation is unclear, with 639 000 US citizens having visited Cuba in 2018. The debate among analysts is whether Cuba will reassert its formal dominance as the top Caribbean destination, a position it enjoyed prior to 1959, and the implications of centrally planned development. According to the WTTC (2018), the number of international visitors to Cuba is forecast to rise from almost 5 million in 2018 to 6.8 million by 2028.

Further reading

Babb, F. (2010) 'Che, Chevys, and Hemingway's daiquiris: Cuban tourism in an age of globalization', *Bulletin of Latin American Research*, 20 (1): 50–63.

Padilla, A. and McElroy, J. (2007) 'Cuba and Caribbean tourism after Castro', *Annals of Tourism Research*, 34 (5): 649–672.

Taylor, H. and McGlynn, L. (2009) 'International tourism in Cuba: Can capitalism be used to save socialism?', *Futures*, 41 (6): 405–413.

Wilkinson, S. (2008) 'Cuba's tourism book: A curse or blessing?', *Third World Quarterly*, 29 (5): 979–993.

Questions

1 What is unique about the Cuban model of tourism?
2 How has a new political regime affected tourism since 1959?
3 What has been the impact of state ownership of tourism in Cuba?
4 How will Cuba continue to develop its tourism industries in the post-Castro era and what political relationships will the state need to develop with inbound tour operators?

Income

As tourism stimulates economic activity in a destination, it assists in improving the overall economic status of a country. The measurement of economic production and nation wealth is **gross domestic product (GDP)** as outlined earlier with the WTTC data. Tourism can lead to increases in GDP, and other measures such as the gross value added (GVA) by tourism are widely used by economic development agencies to assess the effects. For example, in the Caribbean and Pacific Islands, over 40 per cent of GDP for many small islands is derived from tourism, which rises to 88 per cent in the case of the Maldives. At the microlevel, this can also mean such islands need to be aware of the value of tourism. Orams (1999) examined the economic value of whale watching to the economy of the South Pacific island of Vava'u in Tonga and highlights the significance of one major tourist activity for the local economy (see Table 16.1). From this, Orams notes that whales are worth about $750 000 in revenue to the community of Vava'u each year.

Employment

There are three types of employment which may be generated by tourism:

- **direct employment** – jobs created as a result of visitor expenditure and directly supporting tourism activity, e.g. hotels
- **indirect employment** – jobs created within the tourism supply sector but not as a direct result of tourism activity
- **induced employment** – jobs created as a result of tourism expenditure as local residents spend money earned from tourism.

Several factors influence tourism-related employment patterns. The type of tourist activity has an effect on employment as some forms of tourism are more labour intensive than others. Farm tourism, particularly farm accommodation, does not necessarily create new employment, whereas resort development will create a variety of new jobs. Employment opportunities for host communities may also be questioned as the benefits of tourism employment may not always be widely felt by local people. Employment of local people will be based on the local skill base. In most cases, there will be few managerial posts in local tourism development but many jobs requiring minimal skill – with low pay and little reward. Managerial-grade jobs may be advertised across a wide geographic area to attract well-qualified and experienced candidates and, in less developed countries and small island states, expatriate workers are often imported on higher salaries. Employment benefits may often be disguised as tourism jobs to attract people from other sectors or people not normally part of the economic workforce. This includes those who take second jobs, holiday work or those who generate extra revenue from an existing business (such as farm tourism).

Economic benefits to the tourism environment may be directly induced from tourism spending. While it is accepted that spending to a greater or lesser extent assists in local economic development, more refined ways of ensuring a flow of money to specific development projects requires a more innovative approach. One of the ways this is currently being evaluated is the **visitor payback** concept – visitor payback schemes.

TABLE 16.1 The economic value of whale watching in Vava'u, the kingdom of Tonga

	Direct expenditure of visitors on whale watching[1]	Other expenditure of whale tourists[2]	Whale watch operators' expenditure in Vava'u[3]	Whale watch business employees' expenditure in Vava'u[4]	TOTAL
Estimated totals for all permitted whale watch operators	$78 000– $116 000	$570 000	$47 000	$44 000	$739 000– $777 000

Source: © Mark Orams (1999) reproduced with permission

1 Direct expenditure includes items such as boat fares, food, camera film and souvenirs. Given as a range.
2 Other expenditure includes accommodation, transport, other food and souvenirs, other attractions.
3 Whale watch operators' expenditure includes wages, fuel, boat maintenance, supplies and administrative costs.
4 Estimate of the proportion of wage bill spent in the local community.

As tourism continues to grow, many destinations do not have budgets and resources to cope with environmental damage and the costs associated with tourist development. In many places, there are no entrance fees and public sector finance is often unable to meet the demands for conservation and restoration work, particularly in game reserves and national parks in Africa. Tourist taxes on businesses often do not directly benefit those managing tourism. Bearing this in mind, visitor payback schemes (see the Tourism Company 1998) give an opportunity of generating revenue which can be used to fund projects in the local area in a targeted way.

Economic costs

Inflation

Tourism development often creates inflationary effects on local economies, relating to land, property and goods. Inflation is typically measured through official government instruments such as the Consumer Price Index that tracks the changing price of a bundle of goods/services often on a monthly basis. The increased demand for land increases the price. While this is beneficial to those selling land, there is a negative side effect on the local population, particularly those who are not involved in tourism. Local people are then forced into competition for land and housing with tourism development interests. The consequences for local residents in places such as Polperro in Cornwall is social exclusion from their own community, even though they provide local labour. Inflation also increases the cost of tourism prices for specific destinations/countries, making them less competitive with those they compete with.

Opportunity costs

Opportunity costs relate to the time, effort and money spent in developing tourism at the expense of other activities or areas of investment. If a government invests in tourism, then the money spent is unavailable for other uses. This may be detrimental to the well-being of local communities or other sectors of the economy requiring investment. Tourism investment can, of course, benefit local people through improved infrastructure, services and employment potential. This necessitates a cost–benefit approach to the analysis of tourism impacts, which is often expressed in terms of the leverage of additional investment or tourist spending, where a public sector investment occurs. The WTTC tracks the amount of investment globally and by specific destinations in the travel and tourism sector.

Dependency

Heavy reliance on a single industry in any region or country is a risky strategy in the long term. Economic dependency on tourism is a much criticized policy, particularly for less developed countries and peripheral regions in the developed world. Some less developed countries rely on tourists from a small number of generating countries, which is the case for many small islands. For example, in Scotland tourism is the fourth largest sector of the economy and a major employer, but in the Highlands of Scotland it is a much larger contributor to more fragile and peripheral locations. The dependency is increased by the highly seasonal nature of visitors from central Scotland and fewer employment opportunities in remote rural and island communities. Changes in their markets are not controllable and decreases in demand for tourism will have huge effects on the receiving country. The Concentration Index is used to identify the level of dependency on one or more generating countries and is calculated as follows:

$$\frac{\textit{Tourist arrivals from primary markets}}{\textit{All tourist arrivals}} \times 100$$

It is more favourable for a destination to attract a broad base of tourists so that if there is a downturn in one particular market then the consequences are not so damaging.

Seasonality

Seasonality is one of the major disadvantages in tourism and can cause negative economic effects on a destination. Although the high season may bring the opportunity to generate significant revenue from tourism, the economic gain must be sufficient to allow an income which will support individuals and the economy throughout the year. A high incidence of seasonality generally means that employees have jobs for only part of the year. It also means that the investment made in the tourism business is idle for part of the year. So, profits that have to be made in a shorter time period than in most industries and spread across the year may not seem as lucrative as imagined. Some hotels, attractions and other tourism-related enterprises close down entirely in the off-peak season. Others, depending on location and climate, attempt market diversification, promotion and incentives to retain a more even spread of business or may stage events such as farmers' markets. Seasonality remains a major limitation for private sector investment in tourism capital where it has a limited peaked usage, particularly in peripheral locations. Consequently, attracting investment to all-year-round destinations with good accessibility and infrastructure such as capital cities or major urban centres is less problematic than for more remote rural areas with climatic constraints, as will be shown in Chapter 26 and Insight 26.2 on using events in the winter season.

Leakage

In many cases, foreign exchange generated by tourism activity may not benefit the economy of the destination. Foreign investors in the shape of multinational corporations (MNCs) which control accommodation, travel and tour organizations receive substantial proportions of tourist spending. **Leakage** may occur through:

- repatriation of profits generated from foreign capital investment
- vertical integration
- not sourcing services and goods locally
- payment for holidays made in the generating country
- ownership of transport (e.g. the national airline).

Bull (1995) notes that large, well-developed destinations demonstrate the lowest leakage rates, as they contain supply industries which can compete with foreign imports and therefore retain more money within the local or regional economy. In less developed countries, there is a higher propensity to import due to a lack of supporting industries (see Chapter 23). In this case, the **tourism multiplier** effect cannot develop to its full potential as most of the tourist revenue filters out of the destination. In the coastal area in Belize, for example, around 90 per cent of tourist development is in foreign hands.

Oppermann and Chon (1997) found leakage rates of 27–38 per cent in Singapore and Fletcher and Snee (1989) found 53 cents of every dollar leaked out of the Pacific island of Palau. Figure 16.1 shows this process of leakage, which can occur at each stage of tourist spending; it also shows how the infusion of spending into the local community is passed on, via tourist employees, to the community or destination. Yet Mitchell and Ashley (2010) are highly critical of the concept of leakage, particularly in terms of the tourism and poverty literature (as discussed in Chapter 24). They point to the lack of data to make robust claims rather than citing data which is out of date, implying that 'it is another example of how loose and conflicting terms lead to claims that are not useful for policy but instead obfuscate important development choices' (Mitchell and Ashley 2010: 81). Instead, they advise that by analyzing the linkages in the tourism economy to boost tourist discretionary spending in the destination and stimulating linkages in other parts of the economy, we can reduce leakage. In the case of developing countries, this may include enhancing linkages that involve local people and boost small enterprises.

Income and employment

While promoters of tourism promise jobs and improved income to host communities, in many cases there is a negative aspect to this. Better paid, managerial posts may not be available to local people. The income generated by tourism activity may not benefit the poorest in a society. First, it may leak out of the destination to a foreign investor and, second, it may only filter to those who have direct interest in a tourism business or those who exist within a certain type of economy. Oppermann and Chon (1997) question whether tourism is a useful tool in

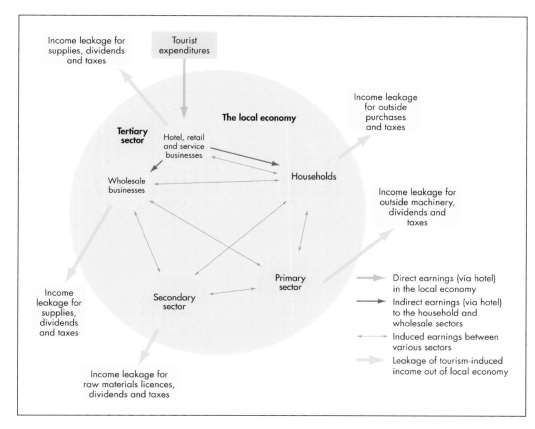

FIGURE 16.1 The economic impact of tourism in a locality and leakage effect
Source: Adapted from Kreutzwiser (1973), Murphy (1985) and Page (1995)

securing regional economic development in developing countries. For example, in the case of the Kruger National Park in South Africa, Saayman and Saayman (2006) found that, while it made a small overall impact on some districts, it was important in employment generation. In Hong Kong, the retail sector has a high dependency upon tourists, where sales to tourists represent 2 per cent of GDP (Wong and Law 2003). In Sydney, tourist shopping and expenditure on retailing generates US$1.1 billion a year just from domestic visitors, which led the tourism agency, Tourism New South Wales, to produce a 92-page *Sydney Shopping – The Official Guide* featuring 350 retail outlets. This illustrates how tourist spending may be used to support ancillary sectors of the economy and employment in retailing via tourist shopping. A study of the regeneration of Bilbao, Spain, by the construction of the Guggenheim Museum by Plaza *et al.* (2011) questioned the supposed creation of 4000 jobs by the project. The study found that only 1000–1200 jobs are supported by tourism, equivalent to 1.25 jobs for every 1000 visitors.

Measuring the economic impacts of tourism

There has been considerable debate over methodological problems in the economic analysis of tourism. These debates focus on three areas:

- economic multipliers and cost–benefit analyzes
- evaluation of opportunity costs
- the role of tourism in economic development.

There are significant problems in trying to obtain accurate measures of the economic impacts of tourism but several measures can be used to give an overview of the effect of tourism. Multipliers are used extensively to examine the effect of revenue generation from tourism.

The tourism multiplier

A multiplier is a statistical expression of how much income or employment (depending on whether one is referring to income or employment multipliers) is generated by a certain amount of tourist spending. The multiplier concept is based on the premise that tourist expenditure will inject additional cash flow into the regional economy and increase regional income. The size of the multiplier is based on the proportion of additional income spent within the region. The income is received by other businesses who also spend within the region and so on. The income multiplier is the ratio of income to the tourist spending that generated it. There are three types of spending:

- *direct spending* – this is the money spent by tourists on the services they need on holiday, such as accommodation, food, shops, attractions
- *indirect or generated spending* – this represents the expenditure of tourism businesses on goods and services
- *induced or additional spending* – this is expenditure by the resident community of income earned directly or indirectly from direct spending (tourist expenditure).

The multiplier does not show how income generation through tourism affects each sector of the local economy. To do this, another method is utilized called the input–output model (IO). This shows the flow of current transactions through a given economy for a given time period. Various types of businesses are grouped together into industrial sectors and arranged in a matrix. The total value of all sales made by each sector is calculated. This is a slightly more satisfactory method. Studies that demonstrate the IO model in operation include Leones *et al.*'s (1998) study of ecotourists in Arizona, and La Lopa *et al.*'s (1998) use of multiplier and IO methods to assess the economic impact of the 1996 Oldsmobile Classic (golfing tournament) on the Greater Lansing area of Michigan, USA. The total spending by those who attended the event was $1 811 055. The IO analysis showed a 76 per cent capture rate ('capture rate' indicates the amount of spending retained in the local economy), giving a total of $1 376 401.46. The multiplier generated a figure of 2.39, indicating a significant economic effect. This means that for every $1 spent by a visitor to the tournament, the total economic impact was $2.39, which illustrates the significance of event-led strategies to promote tourism, particularly where annual events are staged such as Edinburgh's New Year Hogmanay celebrations and Festival. To minimize the amount of leakage from tourism spending, Telfer and Wall (2000) illustrated that strategies to reduce import leakage resulting from imported food and drink and export leakage through salaries and profits that go elsewhere are rare. Telfer and Wall (2000) highlighted that by strengthening backward linkages in supply chains (e.g. with food producers) and forward linkages (e.g. with tour guides), leakage may be reduced.

Alternative measures

Despite the development of different techniques to examine the economic aspects of tourism, Dwyer *et al.* (2004: 307) argue that 'the fundamental problem with Input-Output analysis is that it is incomplete: it ignores key aspects of the economy'. This fails to adequately model the economy and 'in nearly all cases, the changes in economic activity which they come up with, whether relating to output, income or value added, are much greater than the net increase in activity in the economy overall . . . The old models give results which are hazardous to use for policy purposes' (Dwyer *et al.* 2004: 308). One of the newer techniques used to rectify these imperfections in estimating the economic impact of tourism, is the computable general equilibrium model (CGE). While the CGE model incorporates an IO framework, it also models a wider range of elements, ranging from basic to more complex forms, and may be static (i.e. for one point in time) or dynamic (see Dwyer *et al.* 2010 for more detail). But CGE models are often expensive to undertake, despite the availability of computer models (see Insight 16.2).

One of the most widely adapted elements of CGE models is their development of static snapshots in the form of *tourism satellite accounts* (TSAs) (WTO 1999). TSAs set out to measure the economic contribution of tourism in a fairly descriptive, yet detailed manner. The example of New Zealand illustrates how a TSA has been developed and the impacts it has on the national economy. The TSA for New Zealand has been produced since 1999 by Statistics New Zealand and it uses a range of commonly agreed measures by UN-WTO and OECD to measure:

- the direct tourism value added and its contribution to GDP
- the amount of tourist expenditure by tourist types and how this expenditure contributes to total tourist expenditure
- the amount of tourism-related employment that arises from direct and indirect employment
- the amount of tax generated from the New Zealand goods and services tax (GST) via tourist spending and the following is a summary for the TSA in 2018:

   o Total tourism expenditure was $39.1 billion, an increase of 7.7 per cent ($2.8 billion) from the previous year o International tourism expenditure increased 9.6 per cent ($1.4 billion) to $16.2 billion, and contributed 20.6 per cent to New Zealand's total exports of goods and services

o Domestic tourism expenditure increased 6.5 per cent ($1.4 billion) to $23.0 billion

o Tourism generated a direct contribution to GDP of $15.9 billion, or 6.1 per cent of GDP

o The indirect value added of industries supporting tourism generated an additional $11.1 billion, or 4.3 per cent of GDP

o 216 012 people were directly employed in tourism (8.0 per cent of the total number of people employed in New Zealand), an increase of 2.6 per cent from the previous year

o Tourists generated $3.7 billion in GST revenue, with $1.7 billion coming from international tourists

o Overseas visitor arrivals to New Zealand increased 7.8 per cent.

Source: Stats New Zealand (2018: 7)

TABLE 16.2 Tourism expenditure by component[1]: Year ended March 1999–2018

Year ended March	Direct tourism value added	Indirect tourism value added [2]	Imports sold to tourists [3]	GST paid on purchases by tourists	Total tourism expenditure	Value added as a percentage of total industry contribution to GDP		
						Direct tourism value added	Indirect tourism value added	Total tourism value added
	$(million)						Per cent	
1999	5197	4277	4846	1173	15 494	5.2	4.3	9.5
2000	5755	4713	5782	1293	17 542	5.5	4.5	9.9
2001	6013	5454	5932	1437	18 836	5.4	4.9	10.3
2002	6562	5670	6411	1549	20 192	5.5	4.7	10.2
2003	7548	5699	6782	1667	21 696	6.0	4.5	10.5
2004	8059	5747	6480	1719	22 006	6.0	4.3	10.3
2005	8558	5907	6422	1825	22 710	6.0	4.1	10.1
2006	8929	6166	6427	1920	23 442	5.9	4.1	10.0
2007	9288	6556	6913	2013	24 769	5.8	4.1	10.0
2008	9936	7035	6880	2071	25 992	5.8	4.1	9.8
2009	9279	6528	8561	2120	26 488	5.3	3.7	9.0
2010	9582	6769	7191	2071	25 613	5.3	3.8	9.1
2011	9756	6833	7310	2248	26 147	5.2	3.6	8.9
2012	10 085	7063	7165	2456	26 768	5.2	3.6	8.8
2013	10 329	7234	7197	2483	27 242	5.2	3.6	8.8
2014	10 953	7687	7347	2617	28 605	5.1	3.6	8.7
2015	12 664	8828	7527	2921	31 940	5.7	4.0	9.7
2016	14 443	10 078	7615	3315	35 451	6.2	4.3	10.5
2017	14 698	10 300	7924	3409	36 331	6.0	4.2	10.1
2018P	15 852	11 109	8500	3684	39 145	6.1	4.3	10.4

1. Individual figures may not sum to stated totals due to rounding.

2. Results from IO tables for 2013 have been used in the calculation of indirect tourism value added.

3. Imports used in production of goods and services sold to tourists; imports sold directly to tourists by retailers.

Note: Figures for all years prior to 2018 have been revised.

P means provisional.

Source: Stats New Zealand (2018) Tourism Satellite Account: 2018. Retrieved from www.stats.govt.nz.

Reproduced under the Creative Commons Attribution 4.0 International Licence.

IMAGE 16.1 Economic modelling, such as New Zealand's TSA, helps to understand the impact for remoter rural areas, such as Mount Cook National Park

(Source: Getty Images)

Figure 16.2 illustrates the expenditure for the year ending March 2018 and shows that tourism contributes 6.1 per cent to GDP (which has increased from 3.8 per cent to GDP in 2011). It shows that tourism generates NZ$39.1 billion for the national economy, employs 216 000 people and represents 8 per cent of the population. Table 16.2 outlines the historical changes in tourism expenditure measured by the TSA in New Zealand since 1999, which illustrates the trends in direct tourism value added, indirect tourism value added, imports sold to tourists, tax paid on purchases (i.e. GST, a goods service tax) and the contribution of these variables to the tourism sector's contribution to GDP (see Image 16.1).

Other techniques used to evaluate economic values include 'contingent valuation' (Lindberg and Johnson 1997) and the use of a 'social accounting matrix' (SAM). A useful study by Akkemik (2012) which used a SAM approach to quantify the impact of tourism on GDP and employment in Turkey found that international tourism had only a modest impact on employment generation. In particular, Akkemik (2012) highlighted the structural problem of large multinational and overseas tour operators controlling the demand effects. This suggests the importance of developing domestic tourism as a counterweight to potential shock effects that may occur in international arrivals. Walpole and Goodwin (2000) provide an alternative method of researching the economic impact of tourism, stating that macroeconomic techniques (such as IO analysis) are inappropriate for use at local levels due to lack of existing data. Walpole and Goodwin's study of the effects of ecotourism in the Komodo National Park of Indonesia set out to examine employment, distribution effects and tourism-induced change rather than regional economic impact. Techniques used included estimations from survey-based data and use of secondary data sources, referred to as 'local economic inquiry' (Walpole and Goodwin 2000: 565). This may be the only feasible approach to assessment if there is a lack of data for the area.

Tourism and economic development

The economic effects of tourism do not occur in isolation from the area and regions in which tourism develops. In destination areas and different regions of countries where tourism has been developed, the effect of tourism translates into economic development. That development occurs in time and space and follows distinct economic cycles; it may need public sector intervention to pump-prime it, via incentives such as tax benefits. Within the field of economics, there is an ongoing debate related to how tourism affects a national economy and whether the decision to develop this form of economic activity leads to a growth in GDP. For example, Figini and Vici (2010) argue that the evidence on whether tourism contributes to economic growth and thereby development in countries specializing versus those not specializing in tourism is inconclusive. In contrast, Fayissa *et al.* (2011) examined the contribution of tourism to economic growth in Latin American countries and saw a short-run growth in GDP, arguing that this was an important sector to strengthen to promote development. Yet as the discussion above by Akkemik (2012) cautions, there may be caveats to this.

Since tourism is a powerful tool in stimulating economic development, it has been widely used by governments to diversify a country's economic base, to stimulate a new economic sector and/or as part of the regeneration of urban, rural and coastal areas (Image 16.1), to underpin property redevelopment and to create new attractions and activities for tourists. In some cases, governments have developed purpose-built tourist resorts, such as Languedoc-Roussillon in southern France, to achieve regional economic development benefits via tourism. This highlights the significance of tourism and economic policies, with long-term growth in this productive activity. More commonplace is the intervention at the local level by the public sector as part of an urban regeneration scheme (see Chapter 20) to assist in the redevelopment of an urban environment. This intervention is often justified, as Chapter 13 has shown, to break the cycle of decline or to rectify a failure in the local economy. Through such an intervention, public investment is often seen as a positive step to stimulate and leverage additional public

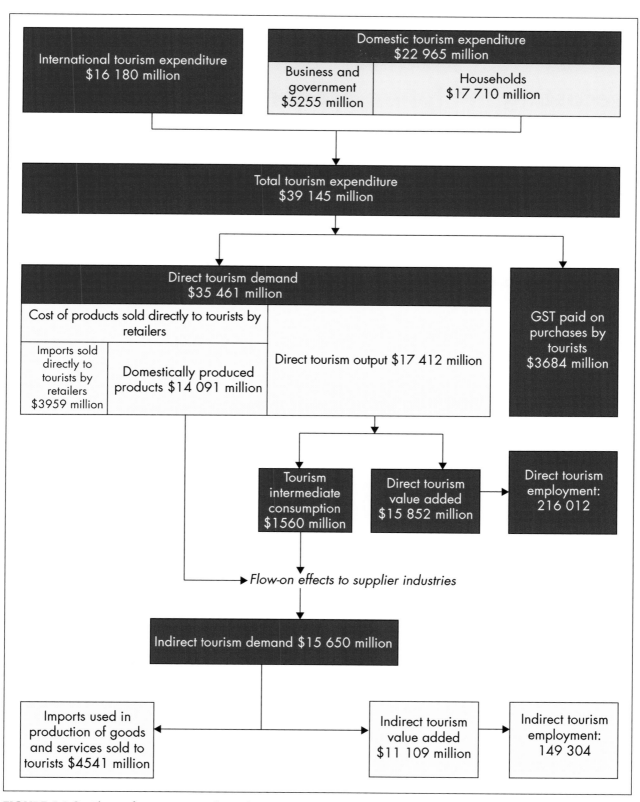

FIGURE 16.2 Flows of tourism expenditure through the New Zealand economy, year ended March 2018[1,2]

Source: Stats New Zealand (2018) Tourism Satellite Account: 2018. Retrieved from www.stats.govt.nz. Reproduced under the Creative Commons Attribution 4.0 International Licence.

1. Totals may not add to the stated totals, due to rounding.

2. Tourism expenditure is measured in purchaser prices. Other monetary aggregates are measured in producer prices.

and private sector investment focused around a dedicated tourism project or mixed tourism and other uses development. In theory, this is supposed to kick-start economic development, as exemplified by the spectacular redevelopment of Cardiff's waterfront and Tiger Bay area.

Forecasting the future economic value of tourism to 2022

Research by the WTTC regularly monitors and evaluates the economic contribution of tourism at a global and regional scale (e.g. for Africa, Europe and other regions), as well as for individual countries and groups of countries with growth characteristics (e.g. the BRIC countries of Brazil, the Russian Federation, India and China, APEC countries, OECD countries and the G20 nations). To try to understand how the economic significance of tourism as both a global and regional activity will change through time, the WTTC employ Oxford Economic Forecasting to assess the likely changes which will occur in the future (i.e. by 2022). Between 2012 and 2022, the WTTC argues that travel and tourism's direct contribution to GDP is likely to grow by 7.2 per cent per annum for South Asia, 6.4 per cent in North East Asia and 5.8 per cent in South East Asia. In contrast, lower growth rates will occur in the Caribbean (3.1 per cent) and Oceania (3 per cent), which includes Australia, New Zealand and the South Pacific region.

Conclusion

Tourism is a major global industry that provides huge opportunity for economic growth, foreign exchange earnings, employment and income generation. It has been seen that tourism results in a range of economic impacts, both positive and negative, depending on the location and socio-economic foundation of a destination. Future challenges for the industry include:

- reducing leakage of tourism revenue from the destination economy
- ensuring wider and more equal distribution of economic benefits
- developing strategies to ensure appropriate return on investment (ROI)
- balancing the needs of commercial operators with socio-economic stability in destination areas.

For any government seeking to develop tourism, greater attention to these aspects will assist the tourism industry in striving towards a more sustainable future. All too often, a critical awareness of the true economic costs of tourism to host communities and regions is obscured or glossed over in attempts to develop employment in declining regions or cities as well as in the less developed world. Yet, for tourism to reach its full potential, developing a tourism product and visitor industry based on the ability of the local economy and environment to support tourism-related growth needs careful planning and management. The economic aspects of tourism cannot be seen in isolation from the wider economic growth and development of countries, regions and places since they need to be carefully integrated into the existing social and cultural structures. In this respect, development planning in less developed countries needs to adopt a broader evaluation of tourism so that the expected benefits are balanced with the costs and impacts to the area being developed. In developed countries, the challenge for the tourism economy is in beginning to understand how it operates at a local level, its relationship to the national and regional economy and how to enhance the value chain for local economies.

Discussion questions

1 Explain the effect of leakage on a tourism destination.
2 What is the tourism multiplier and how does it work?
3 Discuss the positive and negative economic impacts of tourism.
4 Explain the meanings of 'macroeconomics' and 'microeconomics'. Discuss how these concepts relate to the tourism industry.

References

Akkemik, K. (2012) 'Assessing the importance of international tourism for the Turkish economy: A social accounting matrix', *Tourism Management*, 33 (4): 790–801.

Alegre, J., Magdalena, C. and Sard, M. (2012) 'The evolution of British package holiday prices in the Balearic Islands 2000–08', *Tourism Economics*, 18 (1): 59–79.

Berry, B., Kim, H. and Kim, H. (1993) 'Are long waves driven by techno-economic transformations? Evidence for the US and the UK', *Technological Forecasting and Social Change*, 44: 111–135.

Blake, A., Eugenio-Martin, J., Gooroochurn, N., Hay, B., Lennon, J. Sugiyarta, G., Sinclair, M.T. and Yeoman, I. (2004) *Tourism in Scotland: The Moffat Model for Tourism Forecasting and Policy in Complex Situations*, Tourism: State of the Art Conference, Strathclyde University, Glasgow, June.

Borooah, V.K. (1999) 'The supply of hotel rooms in Queensland, Australia', *Annals of Tourism Research*, 26 (4): 985–1003.

Bull, A. (1995) *The Economics of Travel and Tourism*, 2nd edition. Melbourne: Longman.

Butler, R. (1980) 'The concept of the tourist area life cycle of evolution: Implications for management of resources', *Canadian Geographer*, 14 (5): 5–12.

Coshall, J. (2005) 'Interventions on UK earnings and expenditure overseas', *Annals of Tourism Research*, 32 (3): 592–609.

Craven, J. (1990) *Introduction to Economics*, 2nd edition. Oxford: Blackwell.

Dwyer, L. and Forsyth, P. (eds.) (2006) *International Handbook on the Economics of Tourism*. Cheltenham: Edward Elgar.

Dwyer, L., Forsyth, P. and Dwyer, W. (2010) *Tourism Economics and Policy*. Clevedon: Channel View.

Dwyer, L., Forsyth, P. and Spurr, R. (2004) 'Evaluating tourism's economic effects: New and old approaches', *Tourism Management*, 25 (3): 307–317.

Dwyer, L. and Jago, L. (2020) 'The economic contribution of special events', in S.J. Page and J. Connell (eds.) *The Routledge Handbook of Events*, 2nd edition. Abingdon: Taylor and Francis.

Fayissa, B., Nsiah, C. and Tadesse, B. (2011) 'Tourism and economic growth in Latin American countries', *Tourism Economics*, 17 (6): 1365–1373.

Figini, P. and Vici, L. (2010) 'Tourism and growth in a cross section of countries', *Tourism Economics*, 16 (4): 789–805.

Fletcher, J. and Snee, H. (1989) 'Tourism in the South Pacific Islands', in C. Cooper (ed.) *Progress in Tourism, Recreation and Hospitality Management, Volume 1*. London: Belhaven.

Guizzardi, A. and Mazzocchi, M. (2010) 'Tourism demand for Italy and the business cycle', *Tourism Management*, 31 (3): 367–377.

Jayawardena, C. (2003) 'Revolution to revolution: Why is tourism booming in Cuba?', *International Journal of Hospitality Management*, 15 (1): 52–58.

Kreutzwiser, R. (1973) 'A methodology for estimating tourist spending in Ontario counties', unpublished MA thesis, University of Waterloo, Ontario.

Leiper, N. (2008) 'Why "the tourism industry" is misleading as a generic expression: The case for plural variation, "tourism industries"', *Tourism Management*, 29 (2): 237–251.

Leones, J., Colby, B. and Crandall, K. (1998) 'Tracking expenditures of the elusive nature tourists of Southeastern Arizona', *Journal of Travel Research*, 36: 56–64.

Lindberg, K. and Johnson, R.L. (1997) 'The economic values of tourism's social impacts', *Annals of Tourism Research*, 24 (1): 90–116.

Lipsey, R.G. (1989) *An Introduction to Positive Economics*, 7th edition. London: Weidenfeld & Nicolson.

Mathieson, A. and Wall, G. (1982) *Tourism: Economic, Social and Physical Impacts*. Harlow: Longman.

Mitchell, J. and Ashley, C. (2010) *Tourism and Poverty Reduction*. London: Earthscan.

Murphy, P. (1985) *Tourism. A Community Approach*. London: Routledge.

Oppermann, M. and Chon, K. (1997) *Tourism in Developing Countries*. London: International Thomson Business Press.

Orams, M. (1999) *The Economic Benefits of Whale Watching in Vava'u, the Kingdom of Tonga*. Auckland, New Zealand: Centre for Tourism Research, Massey University at Albany.

Page, S.J. (1995) *Urban Tourism*. London: Routledge.

Plaza, B., Galvez-Galvez, C. and Gonzalez-Flores, A. (2011) 'Testing the employment impact of the Guggenheim Museum, Bilbao via TSA', *Tourism Economics*, 17 (1): 223–229.

Saayman, M. and Saayman, A. (2006) 'Estimating the economic contribution of visitor spending in the Kruger National Park to the regional economy', *Journal of Sustainable Tourism*, 14 (1): 67–81.

Telfer, D. and Wall, G. (2000) 'Strengthening backward economic linkages: Local food purchasing by three Indonesian hotels', *Tourism Geographies*, 2 (4): 421–447.

The Tourism Company (1998) *Visitor Payback: Encouraging Tourists to Give Money Voluntarily to Conserve the Places They Visit*. Ledbury: The Tourism Company.

Vu, J. and Turner, L. (2011) 'Shift-share analysis to measure arrivals' competitiveness: The case of Vietnam, 1995–2007', *Tourism Economics*, 17 (4): 803–812.

Walpole, M.J. and Goodwin, H.J. (2000) 'Local economic impacts of dragon tourism in Indonesia', *Annals of Tourism Research*, 27 (3): 559–576.

Wong, J. and Law, R. (2003) 'Difference in shopping satisfaction levels: A study of tourists in Hong Kong', *Tourism Management*, 24 (3): 401–410.

WTO (World Tourism Organization) (1999) *Tourism Satellite Account: The Conceptual Framework*. Madrid: World Tourism Organization.

WTTC (2018) *Travel and Tourism Economic Impact 2018 Cuba*. London: WTTC. https://www.wttc.org/economic-impact/country-analysis/country-reports/.

WTTC (2019) *The Economic Impact of Global Travel and Tourism: World*. London: WTTC.

16

Further reading

Books

Dwyer, L., Forsyth, P. and Dwyer, W. (2020) *Tourism Economics and Policy*, 2nd edition. Bristol: Channel View.

Hall, C.M. and Lew, A. (2009) *Understanding and Managing Tourism Impacts: An Integrated Approach*. London: Routledge.

Wall, G. and Mathieson, G. (2006) *Tourism: Change, Impacts and Opportunities*. Harlow: Pearson.

Journal articles

Blake, A. and Sinclair, M.T. (2003) 'Tourism crisis management: US responses to September 11', *Annals of Tourism Research*, 30 (4): 813–832.

Li, S., Pratt, S. and Song, H. (2016) 'Developments in the field of tourism economics', *Tourism Economics*, 6 (1): 1171–1173.

Sainaghi, R. (2012) 'Tourist expenditures: The state of the art', *Anatolia*, 23 (2): 217–233.

Song, H., Dwyer, L., Li, G. and Can, Z. (2012) 'Tourism economics research: A review and assessment', *Annals of Tourism Research*, 39 (3): 1653–1682.

Song, H. and Li, G. (2008) 'Tourism demand modelling and forecasting – a review of recent research', *Tourism Management*, 29 (2): 203–220.

16

Social and cultural impacts

Learning outcomes

After reading this chapter and answering the questions, you should be able to:

- define the social and cultural impacts of tourism
- explain the factors which affect the extent of social and cultural impacts
- understand a range of current issues illustrating social and cultural impacts.

Overview

For many nations, tourism is seen as an easy way of generating income, particularly foreign exchange (see Chapter 16). In some cases, little capital expenditure is required by the host society as external investment is available. The economic spin-offs are viewed as the most important aspect of tourism development. As the economic impacts of tourism are more readily measurable, other types of impact tend to remain more hidden, in particular, the social and cultural effects. However, insidious social and cultural change may incur more significant costs than economic benefits in the long term. This chapter explores the nature of the impacts of tourism from this perspective.

IMAGE 17.1 The cultural dimension in tourism has seen many indigenous people, such as the Maori in New Zealand, provide interpretation of their rich cultural past, as embodied here in visits to Maori community meeting houses (Marae)

Introduction

The history of tourism indicates that tourism is a social event (Forster 1964). Resort development and sightseeing came about partly through fashions and social responses to the natural and built environments. Tourism is a global phenomenon which is essentially taste driven, with regions coming in and out of fashion and often the topic of social conversation and which is captured in social media, particularly through photographic images of tourism taken by tourists shared on platforms like Instagram. This is often embodied in the concept of which places are 'in vogue' and 'must see' destinations. In this respect, tourism is about people and how people as tourists interact with other locations and peoples (Image 17.1), engaging in experiences that may influence their own or the host community attitudes, expectations, opinions and lifestyles.

For example, Zaidan *et al.*'s (2016) study of the United Arab Emirates highlighted the scope of such concerns from local communities that revolved around religion, culture and ethnicity and the challenge to the authenticity of residents' local culture. This domain of study within tourism studies is normally identified with anthropology (Nash 2005) and, to a lesser degree, sociology (Cohen 2004). This interest is reflected in a number of seminal studies in tourism and its social and cultural impact embodied in MacCannell's (1976) *The Tourist*, Smith's (1977) *Hosts and Guests* and De Kadt's (1979) *Tourism: Passport to Development*. Each of these studies confirms what Murphy (1985: 117) argued, that tourism is a 'sociocultural event for the traveller and the host' (it is sometimes difficult to separate social and cultural elements and so the term 'sociocultural' tends to be used frequently in tourism literature).

The nature of sociocultural impacts

17

Sociocultural impacts relate to changes in societal value systems, individual behaviour, social relationships, lifestyles, modes of expression and community structures. The focus of sociocultural impacts tends to be the host community

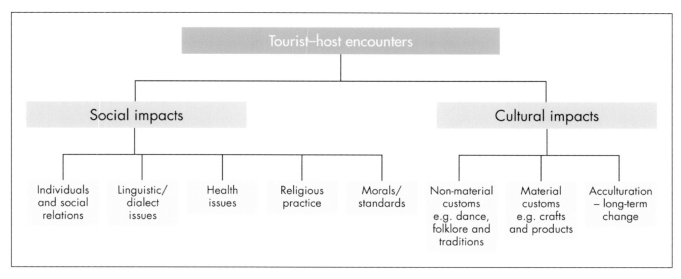

FIGURE 17.1 The dimensions of tourist–host encounters
Source: Modified from Shaw and Williams (1994: 87)

(i.e. the people who reside in tourist destinations), rather than the tourist-generating region. Mathieson and Wall (1982) state that sociocultural impacts are 'about the effects on the people of host communities, of their direct and indirect associations with tourists'. Lea (1988) outlines the dimensions of tourist–host encounters and provides a useful starting point from which to define social and cultural aspects. This is illustrated in Figure 17.1.

Elements of culture

According to Mathieson and Wall (1982: 158), culture is the 'conditioning elements of behaviour and the products of that behaviour', consisting of 12 elements:

- handicrafts
- language
- traditions
- gastronomy
- art and music
- history
- local work
- architecture
- religion
- educational system
- dress
- leisure activities.

Sharpley (1994) states that from a social and cultural perspective, the rapid expansion of tourism is important in two respects:

1 The development of tourism as a vehicle for economic modernization and diversification almost invariably leads to changes and developments in the structure of society. These may be positive and negative. In the positive sense, there may be society-wide improvements in income, employment opportunities, education, local infrastructure and services. On the negative side, there may be a threat posed to traditional social values, the creation of factions of society who may take advantage of others and adaptation or weakening of cultural values.

2 All tourists, to a lesser or greater extent, inevitably take on holiday their own beliefs, values and behavioural modes: what may be termed cultural baggage. Cohen (1972) states that people tend to travel in an environmental bubble (see Murphy 1985: 6). Therefore, the scope for mixing of cultures is great.

This gives rise to two ideas about the sociocultural effect of tourism. First, that the interaction between host and guest could dilute or destroy traditional cultures. This reflects the literature that considers tourism primarily as a threat to culture and peoples (Smith 2009). Second, that the interaction between host and guest could create new opportunities for peace and greater understanding and heritage preservation in the developing world (Timothy and Nyanpane 2009), as well as becoming a tool for enhancing destination attractiveness (OECD 2009). This alternative perspective acknowledges the benefits that tourism can have in allowing exchange of cultures in promoting greater awareness on both sides (see Image 17.1). There is evidence to prove both of these aspects exist and a consensus is by no means easy to generate.

There is, conversely, growing evidence of the negative social impact of tourism in some developing countries where tourist harassment, such as persistent badgering of tourists by local vendors and hawkers, has become a significant problem. Kozak (2007) also examined this issue in Turkey, noting the cultural differences among shopkeepers inviting tourists to visit their establishment and tourists who interpreted this as harassment. These cultural misunderstandings illustrate the social and cultural polarity between hosts and guests. While it is possible to generalize about sociocultural impacts, it is more problematic to define the extent to which they have occurred. The study of impacts on society and culture is complicated by the nature of more general social and cultural change. The forces of change are many and varied, tourism being just one factor. Other aspects which must be acknowledged include the role of advertising and media, the effect of multinational corporations, the aspirations of government, education and immigrants. Given the complexity of influencing factors, it is hard to extrapolate tourism as a single example of potential sociocultural impact. It might be argued that if cultures are continually changing, what is wrong with change as a result of tourism? Leaving this debate to one side, the main assumption about sociocultural impacts is that if the tourist-generating country has a 'stronger' economy and culture than the receiving country, then the sociocultural impact is likely to be higher than if the other way around. The greater the difference, the greater the impact. Thus, for example, the sociocultural effect of British holidaymakers to France is less than it would be on an undeveloped region such as Tibet.

Factors influencing sociocultural impacts

Having explored the general context, it is now apposite to consider the range of factors which influence the nature and extent of sociocultural impacts. Sharpley (1994) outlines four factors which shape the effects:

- *Types and numbers of tourists*: The traditional view is that low numbers of tourists, particularly independent travellers, result in a low impact, therefore a high tourist volume results in a high impact. In other words, those who integrate with local services and people have less impact than those who rely on externally provided mass tourism facilities. MacNeill and Wozniak (2018) examined the development of an additional cruise port terminal at Trugillo, Honduras, and the impact on the local community of large volumes of visitors disembarking and visiting the area. To develop the site, land was usurped (i.e. taken illegally) from the indigenous people to permit development, causing animosity and protest. The study illustrated that the economic benefits were limited as tourists had already visited and purchased goods at another Honduran port. However, a rise in visitation was associated with an increase in policing to assure tourist safety and a rise in sewage and rubbish dumping for the local community. A minimal benefit from economic development arose, much of which was related to new jobs in the informal tourism economy of this developing country. Cruise ship tourists arriving en masse are also viewed as a problem of overtourism, when residents are outnumbered by visitors, a feature we will return to in Chapters 20 and 23. Yet the independent traveller may have more effect on an isolated community that has not been exposed to outside influence than on a large, established resort. Therefore, it might be argued that mass tourism in self-contained resorts e.g. **Club Méditerranée** may have less impact. This is a much debated point.

- *Importance of the tourism industry*: The primary purpose of tourism as an industry is economic growth and/or diversification of the local economy. The impacts of tourism are likely to be less in a mixed economy than on an economy reliant on tourism.

- *Size and development of the tourism industry*: A large number of tourists in a small community will tend to have a large impact. Larger communities may remain less affected. In relation to the tourism lifecycle model (see Figure 2.1), there are more likely to be impacts in the developmental stage as facilities grow and changes take place. Many countries and destinations now want smaller numbers of higher-spending tourists to visit and some countries are following this particular mode of development (e.g. the Seychelles). Established resorts are likely to experience less change than newly emerging destinations.

- *Pace of tourism development*: Some destinations have witnessed rapid growth which has been relatively uncontrolled. Social impacts are likely to be higher in these areas. Local communities need to adapt gradually to the needs and benefits of change and tourists.

17

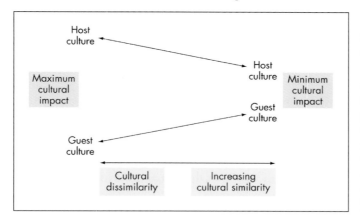

FIGURE 17.2 Host and guest relationship
Source: Modified from Williams (1998)

Other related aspects which need to be considered include the nature of the host–guest encounter, the nature of the destination and cultural similarities. Williams (1998) comments that cultural similarity or dissimilarity is one of the major factors in shaping sociocultural impacts. Impacts tend to be greater where the host and guest relationship is both culturally and geographically distant. This is represented in Figure 17.2, and Tourism Concern (www.tourismconcern.org.uk) point to the way in which cultural dances and artefacts are just commodities for tourists. They also point to destinations where cultural conflicts occur (e.g. Argentina, Australia, Bali, Brazil, Cambodia, China, Egypt, Ethiopia, Honduras, India, Jordan, Kenya, Namibia, Peru, Senegal, South Africa, Tanzania, Thailand, Tibet and Zanzibar). Thus, where the tourist and the host are culturally similar, then the sociocultural impacts will be limited.

The nature of the **host–guest relationship** and community attitudes to tourism generally depends on:

- type of contact between host and guest
- importance of the tourism industry to the community
- community tolerance threshold (De Kadt 1979).

Contact between host and guest may arise in three scenarios:

- tourist purchase of goods and services from local people (shops, hotels)
- tourist and local resident use of same facilities (beaches, shops, bars)
- purposeful meeting to exchange ideas and information.

The demonstration effect

De Kadt (1979) defines the demonstration effect as 'changes in attitudes, values or behaviour which can result from merely observing tourists'. This may be advantageous or disadvantageous to the host community. It is said that observing other peoples may encourage hosts, particularly in developing countries, to adapt or work for things they lack; in other words, it may assist development. More commonly it is detrimental, causing discontent and resentment because the degree of wealth and freedom of behaviour displayed by the tourist imposes an impossible goal. Local people may turn to illegal means to obtain the level of wealth they desire, thus crime rates may increase as a result of tourism in a destination. The demonstration effect has the greatest influence on young people and may create generation gaps and class differences between those who desire change and those who wish to retain traditional ways of life. The young and especially the educated tend to migrate. Norberg-Hodge (1992: 98) observes the effect of a sudden influx of Western tourists in Ladakh, Nepal, on young men and states that feelings of inferiority have resulted. 'They rush after the symbols of modernity: sunglasses, Walkmans, and blue jeans several sizes too small – not because they find those jeans more attractive or comfortable, but because they are symbols of modern life.' An increase in aggression was also noted. The young people want the material side of modern life but cannot see so readily the negative aspects of it – such as stress, unemployment, environmental degradation, disenfranchisement. This type of change may be a disruptive force to traditional kinship over time.

Acculturation

Many impacts of tourism appear relatively quickly while others tend to manifest themselves more gradually. Cultural change falls into this last category and, over time, more long-term cultural change may result from tourism. External influences and the evolution of society result in change, regardless of the existence of tourism. Enhanced networks of communication, technology and the emergence of the global market are all part of this process. However, the role of tourism needs to be understood to ensure that culture is not unnecessarily damaged. The infiltration of Western culture into less developed countries is viewed as problematic, as different views, attitudes, behaviour patterns, aspirations and expenditure patterns may not be easily adapted from one culture to another. In addition, unique and interesting ways of life may be pushed aside for Western ideals which are not necessarily appropriate for the future of global society. Sharpley (1994) notes the example of tourism in Nepal, now becoming a mainstream tourist destination where a visible Westernization of Kathmandu is occurring as a result of tourism. This type of change is sometimes referred to as coca-colonization. Ritzer (1996) has considered this in terms of the effects of globalization in the fast-food industry as 'McDonaldization' – the wider implications of this are worthy of consideration as this relates to acculturation through tourism.

International tourism is thought to influence sociocultural change through the process of acculturation. The theory of acculturation rests on the notion that contact between cultures results in sharing and adoption of one another's values and attitudes. A major concern is that when a culturally weak society comes into contact with a culturally strong one, the process will be more one way; that is, the values and attitudes of the strong nation are transferred to the weak one. Thus, acculturation is more pronounced in less developed countries, particularly those which have had less contact with Western society in the past. Tourism-induced acculturation may be difficult to disentangle from wider cultural change.

Two arguments dominate the literature on the cultural impacts of tourism:

1 Tourism results in the transformation of cultural events into commercialized products or spectacles which are devoid of all meaning. Culture may be trivialized by tourism in an attempt to make it a product for tourists to consume. The process of cultural commodification is much criticized by authors such as Urry (1990).

2 Tourism results in the preservation and revitalization of traditional cultural practices by providing financial support and engendering community pride. This is seen as positively contributing to the goals of sustainable tourism.

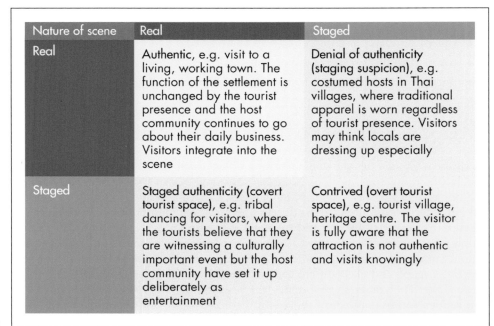

FIGURE 17.3 Tourist perception of a scene
Source: Adapted from Cohen (1972)

Furze *et al.* (1996) state that the development of consciousness assists in defending indigenous societies against the might of multinational companies, developers and governments and cite the example of Australian Aboriginal communities. Pedregal (cited in Bossevain 1996) talks about the idea of self-consciousness in the south Spanish coastal community of Zahara de los Atunes in response to tourist arrivals. The summer season is said to drive the locals crazy and they feel hostile towards the presence of tourists or 'others'. The end result is that local people close themselves off from tourists and continue their own cultural pastimes but away from the eyes of tourists. Host communities may be subject to what is termed 'zooification' if tourists are curious about local people and their way of life. This refers to tribal people being turned into sights to be viewed by the tourist. This is particularly marked for tribal people. Tribal people may put on special events for visitors such as demonstrations of dancing or traditional customs. The danger is that these events may lose their cultural significance if performed at inappropriate times or for inappropriate reasons. The Padaung women of Thailand have become victims of this.

From the tourist perspective this raises questions of authenticity and for the host, objectification of culture. Mathieson and Wall (1982) outline the developed world's interest in the material culture of Aboriginals. The ancient sand paintings of desert tribes have been adapted to the use of acrylics and canvas for the export market. This cheapens and degrades the traditional artwork because the aesthetic qualities are deemed to be more important than true meanings and function. Cohen (1972) constructed a framework to illustrate tourist settings in relation to authenticity (see Figure 17.3).

The sociocultural effects of tourism

Language

As a social vehicle of communication, language is a key indicator of acculturation. Tourism can lead to language change in three ways:

- economic changes through the hiring of immigrant or expatriate labour. Seasonal workers and second-home owners may exacerbate this. In some areas, there may be a diminishing trend of local dialects due to migration patterns (e.g. on the Isle of Skye, Scotland)
- demonstration effect, where the local community aspires to achieving the status of the visitor
- direct social contact and the need to converse to make commercial transactions. Sometimes, the host is obliged to learn the main incoming tourist language in order to deal with their requirements and to ease the transition to a foreign destination.

Religion

In some tourist regions, religion has become a commodity. Religious buildings and events are spectacles to view. Many religious sites attract large numbers of visitors, who may or may not possess the beliefs of that particular religion. Some of the most well-visited sites have religious connections, such as cathedrals, abbeys and spiritual centres, such as Mecca, Bethlehem and Lourdes. Increasing conflict exists between local worshippers, devout visitors and sightseers. Traditional ceremonies, rites and practices are not always recognized by the tourist, who may view such events in a frivolous and disrespectful way. It has been known for tourists to be spectators at burials and weddings. In Bhutan, tourists are not permitted to visit certain monasteries in a bid to prevent tourism from disrupting religious life. In many countries, particularly Islamic ones, tourist clothing can cause offence. For example, in the Gambia, with its predominantly Muslim population, female tourists who wear tight clothes, shorts or a short skirt and men wearing short-sleeved shirts are viewed as indecent. In the Maldives, where the population is Islamic, no topless bathing is allowed. In Zanzibar, Islamic beliefs are offended by improper tourist clothing and behaviour. In Japan some religious sites have been closed to foreign tourists due to poor visitor behaviour, among visitors from other Asian countries. For example, taking selfies and not respecting the temple code of conduct has meant that the Nanzoin Temple banned visitors, particularly because of being deluged by cruise ship visitors. These are just a few examples.

Host perceptions of impacts

There is substantial literature on the host perception of tourism impacts (e.g. Deery *et al.* 2012). Variables which contribute to host perception of tourism can be categorized as:

- extrinsic
- intrinsic.

Extrinsic factors are those factors that affect the community at a broader level, such as the pace of tourism development, type of tourism, cultural differences between host and guest and the tourist–host ratio. *Intrinsic factors* relate more specifically to the people, such as their demographic structure, employment in the tourism industry and proximity of residence to tourism areas. In fact many studies of the social impacts of tourism have been undertaken in less developed countries. While this research is important, there must be caution in applying research findings from one culture to another. Page and Lawton (1996) found that in the case of a host community in Devonport, Auckland, New Zealand, residents would be prepared to accept a growth in tourist numbers if the growth was appropriately managed, despite initial concerns by local politicians that tourism growth should be halted. This illustrates the importance of developing locally based research to understand these highly contentious issues and the influence of politics on tourism development.

17

INSIGHT 17.1 New theoretical approaches to tourist–host encounters

Within the rich history of research on the sociocultural impact of tourism, there has been a growing disenchantment with the failure to address deep-seated issues. As Deery *et al.* (2012: 65) argue, 'Research into the social impacts of tourism appears to be in a state of arrested development . . . while there is a reasonable agreement as to the nature of the impacts (e.g. overcrowding, disruptive tourist behaviour, high employment dependence on tourism for income), recent quantitative research in this area has analyzed specific impacts or used particular methods without providing in-depth insights into the reasons for residents' perceptions

and the subsequent consequences of such perceptions'. In fact, Ward and Berno (2011) point to the absence of theoretical frameworks to help predict and explain the way hosts interact with tourists. While there is adequate empirical evidence of the nature of sociocultural impacts as the following factors outlined by Deery *et al.* (2012) (e.g. economic benefits, opportunity costs, disruption, delinquent behaviour, environment effects, inflationary impacts, changes to the character of the locality) suggest, more theoretical frameworks are needed to investigate the exchanges which occur between tourists and hosts. These theoretical frameworks are

INSIGHT 17.1 continued

what help a subject area to progress our understanding of the phenomena we are studying.

Ward and Berno (2011) argue that social exchange theory is the exception to this, as it provides a framework, originally developed to examine the social psychology of groups. Ward and Berno (2011: 1557) explain that it focuses on 'the perceptions of the relative costs and benefits of relationships and their implications for relationship satisfaction'. The theoretical proposition which such an approach will help develop in relation to tourism, is that individuals' attitudes towards tourism will be evaluated by:

a Their level of support for development arising from tourism.

b How the resulting outcomes for a community/group are judged.

As Ward and Berno (2011) demonstrate, this theoretical model has been the basis for research that has looked at the way costs and benefits of tourism are judged in relation to support for development. In other words, those who are the beneficiaries of tourism development are more likely to adopt more positive attitudes to tourism. Ward and Berno (2011) have also proposed other frameworks derived from social psychology which may advance an understanding of

tourist–host relationships. They introduce new concepts such as integrated threat theory to examine how tourism threatens and competes in inter-group attitudes. What is clear is that the research on tourist–host encounters is still developing, as new frameworks and concepts in social science are introduced to expand our understanding of the field.

Further reading

Deery, M., Jago, L. and Fredline, L. (2012) 'Rethinking social impacts of tourism research: A new research agenda', *Tourism Management*, 33 (1): 64–73.

Ishii, K. (2012) 'The impact of ethnic tourism on hill tribes in Thailand', *Annals of Tourism Research*, 39 (1): 290–310.

Ward, C. and Berno, T. (2011) 'Beyond social exchange theory: Attitudes towards tourists', *Annals of Tourism Research*, 38 (4): 1556–1569.

Questions

1 What is a tourist–host encounter?

2 What are the nature and extent of tourist–host impacts?

3 How would you set about testing the notion of social exchange theory in tourist–host encounters? What types of research approach might be suitable?

4 How do visitors perceive their impact upon destinations?

Frameworks for measuring sociocultural impacts

Ways of assessing the extent of social impacts have emerged over the last 30 years in an attempt to provide some evidence of the effects of tourism on host communities. Doxey's Irridex (irritation index) (Figure 17.4) was developed following research in Barbados, the West Indies and Ontario in 1975 and remains one of the most widely cited frameworks for thinking about host responses to tourism. The model supposes that impacts of tourism on the host community may be translated to degrees of resident irritation. It is based on four stages of response which increase through time in sequence as the destination lifecycle unfolds and resident attitudes change. The initial stage – euphoria – arises at the outset of tourism and describes the scenario where a small number of travellers arrive in a location. There is little tourist infrastructure so visitors use local accommodation and services. Hence, there is a high degree of informal contact between host and guest and high economic benefits as local people benefit directly from tourism activity. Tourists are welcomed and the host population feels euphoric. As time progresses and tourism development begins, the host population may start to take tourism for granted (apathy). This may reflect an increasingly formal type of contact between host and guest as more services are developed, foreign investors begin to take control of the industry and local people begin to get used to servile roles. The annoyance stage generally reflects the stage when a destination reaches the saturation point, where tourism has become a dominant force in the environment and adaptations are necessary to cope with the numbers of tourists. The final stage of the Irridex – antagonism – is an extreme point where the host population blames tourism for all the negative aspects of life in the area. This antagonism may also lead to community pressure within destinations to seek to restrict and control tourist behaviour, as illustrated in Image 17.2 where UK coastal resorts have created alcohol-free zones and introduced antisocial behaviour orders.

Teo's study of the sociocultural impacts in Singapore (1994) illustrates the negative effects of lack of contact between the host and guest. The average length of stay, three days, implies minimal contact and no opportunity to

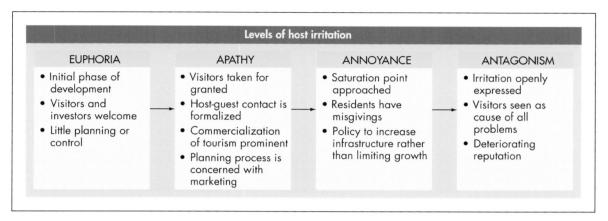

FIGURE 17.4 Doxey's Irridex
Source: Modified from Doxey (1975)

engage. Tourists tend to remain in enclaves or 'ghettoes'. Teo's attempt to measure the host response to tourism using Doxey's *Irridex* showed that:

- 75 per cent welcomed tourists for economic purposes
- 75 per cent thought that locals received poorer levels of service than tourists
- 99 per cent thought that tourists were overcharged
- 78 per cent rarely communicated with tourists – if they did, it was to give directions.

The results of a survey of residents indicated that the appropriate measure using the Irridex was apathy. Ap and Crompton (1998) have developed a tourism impact scale which has yielded valid and reliable data on resident perceptions of impacts and is more reliable than the widely cited study by Doxey and other research which has imitated the same conceptual framework. This is

IMAGE 17.2 To reduce conflict with local residents, some councils have imposed no-drinking areas in resorts to reduce the noise and nuisance experienced by residents

because Ap and Crompton (1993) recognize that host communities are not homogeneous. Many published studies still using unidirectional and redundant models such as Doxey have still not grasped the major progress made in the analysis of social and cultural impacts in tourism research. Krippendorf (1987) defined four categories of local person: those who are in continuous and direct contact with tourists; those who own tourism businesses but have little contact with tourists; those who are in direct and frequent contact with tourists but only gain part of their income from tourism; and those who have little or no contact with tourists. People in each category are likely to have a different view of tourism and its impacts. There is also a growing interest in how communities learn to adapt to tourists (Tucker 2003) and the cultural implications.

There is concern about how tourism relationships between developed and developing countries may represent a form of postcolonialism, a feature discussed in Chapter 23. These relationships may highlight how the culture of the host society in the developing country is commercialized through niche products such as cultural tourism which then brings the host into greater contact with visitors, thereby accelerating the impact on host populations.

Wider issues relating to social and cultural impacts of tourism

It is also important to recognize some of the wider ramifications of tourism development where economic objectives have been placed before community concerns. One of the most significant debates over recent years has centred on the displacement of local communities to make way for tourism such as with the Olympic Games. Tourism has also caused governments to act in ways which contravene the rights of local people and socially excluded them. This has been a primary issue for indigenous peoples as they enter into tourism as both spectacles and managers. Berno (1999) suggests that where the expectations of tourists and residents are similar, tourism can be a beneficial exchange process, but where the two do not meet, local culture can be compromised and indigenous people may find tourism contributes to low self-esteem and is exploitative.

Displacement

Various instances of local people being moved away from their place of residence to make way for tourism development have been recorded. This is termed 'spatial displacement'. In the case of spatial displacement, land is taken for various reasons, such as the construction of hotels, tourist infrastructure, golf courses and reserves. Tourism Concern (http://www.tourismconcern.org), the non-governmental organization that works to protect communities affected by tourism, has run many successful campaigns on these issues which can be seen on their website. Displacement illustrates the nature of the power relation between the forces of tourism development, government and local communities. It is usually the local people who lose out. For example, Bloch (2016) examined the UNESCO site of Hampi in India, a Hindu medieval site, from an anthropological perspective. Bloch documented how local farmers, who had also become petty entrepreneurs to develop tourism income, were evicted from their homes. The residents were relocated to a new site. The bazaar which was the location of local businesses was demolished and the UNESCO site put under the ownership of the Archaeological Survey of India. This was reinforced in the local masterplan for the area, effectively creating an outdoor living museum (Bloch 2017). Bloch (2016) described this process as *spatial cleansing*.

Tourism and local communities: Planning and management issues

Much work has been undertaken to identify ways in which the impact of tourism on local communities might be lessened. In conjunction with this, attempts to involve the local community in the tourism development and management process should be noted.

17

TABLE 17.1 Contravention of human rights associated with tourism development

- The right to freedom of movement including access to beaches.
- The right to health and well-being including not being subjected to pollution from tourism.
- The right of the child to protection so that children are not employed as cheap labour or as prostitutes.
- Right to work in appropriate conditions of employment and not one based on exploitation.
- The right to land, water and natural access resources.
- The right to respect and dignity so that local cultures are not treated as 'zoos for tourists'.
- Right to compensation for land confiscated by developers and government agencies for tourist development.

Source: Various; Tourism Concern (2009) Putting Rights to Tourism: A Challenge to Human Rights abuses in the tourism industry (http://www.tourismconcern.org.uk); also see the Roundtable Human Rights in Tourism website (www.humanrights-in-tourism.net) for examples of best practice and industry debates on these issues and its report Human Rights in Tourism: An Implementation Guideline for Tour Operators; Baumgartner and Beyer (ND).

Theme/control	Low degree of control	High degree of control
Indigenous theme present	Culture dispossessed, e.g. Padaung women, Burma	Culture controlled, e.g. Masai, Kenya and Tanzania
Indigenous theme absent	Non-indigenous tourism, e.g. all-inclusive resort	Diversified indigenous, e.g. Quichua Indians, Ecuador

FIGURE 17.5 Indigenous culture, control and tourism

Source: Adapted from Butler and Hinch (1996)

If one of the objectives of tourism development is to benefit the host population, some consideration must be given to the host perspective on impacts and local community carrying capacity values (see Chapter 18) should be part of tourism planning. This is important in all host communities but is a more sensitive issue in relation to tourism which affects tribal and indigenous peoples.

Indigenous tourism

According to Butler and Hinch (2007), indigenous tourism relates to a form of tourism that is directed by indigenous peoples or where indigenous culture is the tourist attraction. Figure 17.5 illustrates the theoretical nature of tourism as it relates to indigenous culture. The value of indigenous culture in allowing tourism destinations to promote the distinctive cultural features, may contribute to a cultural revival if the local culture is managed appropriately. Yet where it does not occur in a sensitive manner, it may illustrate the link between the notions of culture and control (see Carson and Pennings 2017). Altman and Finlayson (1993) outline some of the previous research on Aboriginal tourism which has tended to find that Aboriginal people are reluctant to participate directly in tourism activity because they feel that involvement with non-Aborigines is intrusive and negative (see Insight 17.2). Sociocultural considerations are put before economic ones as Aborigines do not feel it important to participate in the formal labour market. Aboriginal people tend to be directly involved in the manufacture and sale of artefacts and so are based in the cultural tourism sphere. However, there are many examples of successful ventures where there is a high degree of Aboriginal control, appropriate scale of enterprise, accommodation of social and cultural factors and an element of consumer and industry education.

INSIGHT 17.2 **The impact of tourism on ethnic women in North Vietnam**

Bott (2018) examined the role of tourism in marginalizing ethnic women in Sapa, North Vietnam, within an area of 6000 residents. Using an anthropological approach, Bott (2018) initially examined how women were portrayed in promotional materials such as web-advertised tours and other sources. As Table 17.2 shows, the representations of ethnic women suggest they were increasingly being commodified, compounded by the expansion of tourism from around 18 000 visits to the area in 2000, predominantly backpackers, to 125 000 tourists by 2012. The emergence of larger-scale tourism in the region, promoting visits to experience ethnic and tribal life, were described by Bott (2018) as 'orientalist' representations that depicted ethnic women as 'innocent, picturesque, colourful, simplistic and traditional' (Bott 2018: 1305), as reflected in Table 17.2.

TABLE 17.2 Frequency and type of descriptors of indigenous people in sample of literature promoting ethnic tours in Sapa

Photographic Depiction	Frequency (out of total of 24 sources)	Written Description	Frequency (out of total of 24 sources)
Tribal Dress	24	Unique	18
Woman/Women	22	Authentic	18
Field Labour	20	Tribal	14
Handicrafts	20	Traditional	13
Smiling Faces	18	Simple	12
Children	15	Colourful	12
Elderly (woman)	12	Friendly	11
Musical Instruments	7	Untouched	8

Source: Bott (2018: 1296) based on data from 14 tour operators/travel agencies, 4 newspaper/magazine travel articles and 6 travel blogs

INSIGHT 17.2 continued

Assessing the impact of the expanding scale of tourism on Sapa ethnic women, Bott (2018: 1305) concluded that tourism had led to a

loss of 'authentic lifestyles' and behaviour of indigenous women who were not faithfully replicating their portrayals in advertisements, guidebooks, as passive objects. Entrepreneurialism and hustling represent a loss of authenticity to tourists who are purposefully travelling to 'exotic' and under-developed parts of the world for distinctive, rarefied, pre-capitalist experiences and encounters (Bott 2018: 1305).

This quotation encapsulates many of the complex arguments which this chapter has put forward on the sociocultural impact of tourism, particularly on fragile cultures that are unprotected from the exploitative nature of tourism. Some of these issues will be returned to in Chapter 21.

Bott's (2018) study illustrates the inherent inequality and power relations between visitor and host community where a commercialized product is sold to tourists:

'Tourists expect to gaze upon, and be at liberty to photograph, the working bodies of Others' (Bott 2018: 1305) irrespective of the norms, behaviour or cultural wishes of the host community.

Further reading

Bott, E. (2018) 'Among the piranhas: The troubling lifespan of ethnic tropes in "tribal" tourism to Vietnam', *Journal of Sustainable Tourism*, 26 (8): 1291–1307.

Questions

1 What is the appeal and attractions to tourists of visiting ethnic groups?
2 What codes of behaviour should visitors be expected to confirm to when visiting ethnic groups?
3 What scale of visitation is appropriate to develop in promoting ethnic groups?
4 What are the long-term consequences for the Sapa women of a continued growth in the scale and intensity of tourist visits? How might you manage this situation to moderate the impacts?

Involving the community in tourism planning

Involving local communities in managing tourism is one of the precepts of sustainable tourism development and, as Ap and Crompton (1998: 120) state, 'for tourism to thrive in an area it needs support from the area's residents'. The rationale for involving the host community in tourism decision-making includes allowing those who will be involved with or affected by tourism to have their say in how it should be developed. Another reason is that local people often have knowledge of their home environment which can assist in planning tourism development. The overall aim of community involvement is to reduce the conflict between tourism and the host community. Methods of community involvement are varied but may include consultation with the host community about tourism plans and proposals or allowing some input to policies. Yet as Teye *et al.* (2002) found in a review of projects funded by aid donors in Ghana, local people were effectively excluded from involvement which failed to meet their expectations and created resentment among those working in the tourism sector. The host community with the assistance of a supporting organization may promote codes of conduct for incoming tourists as Tourism Concern do on their website. In some instances, local people have been the progenitors of tourism projects. The Quicha Indians in Ecuador are a good example. While some social and cultural change is inevitable, it seems more appropriate for local communities to control the rate of change through tourism. The fast pace of change in North Sulawesi has meant that it has been difficult for the host community to contribute and adapt to the development of tourism. Tour operators have taken control of the industry and policies have not been imposed to ensure appropriate forms of development which benefit local people.

A crucial component of the community-based tourism concept is empowerment of local people in the development process (Sofield 2003), a precursor in encouraging participation. Central to this process is ensuring that access to information is sufficient and that systems of governance actively promote meaningful interaction between the public sector, developers and local people, resulting in a collaborative approach to decision-making. Techniques used by the public sector that seek to advocate community approaches to tourism development often extend beyond consultation. Common tools include establishing marketing partnerships with groups of tourism providers, facilitating links between stakeholders and assisting with skills development through training. Examples of community-controlled projects, where a group of residents take charge of developing, promoting and operating a particular tourism product that produces economic and social benefits for that community, are increasingly common in both developed and less developed countries. However, the outcome and effectiveness of community approaches show substantive variation, according to cultural and business environments, strength and direction of governance, levels of existing tourism infrastructure development and degree of community interest.

Community-based tourism

More recent debates on community-based tourism have evolved since Murphy's (1985) initial study and these are reviewed in Simpson (2008), who presents the case for examining the concept of community benefit tourism initiatives (CBTIs) based on the transfer of benefits to a community in a responsible and sustainable manner. Among the benefits of CBTIs are:

- economic benefits (creating local direct and indirect employment opportunities and local economic development as well as providing opportunities for entrepreneurs)
- environmental benefits (improved understanding of natural resources as community assets and their stewardship)
- sociocultural benefits (improved social infrastructure for residents, workforce development, benefits for all community stakeholders, better cultural understanding).

This approach to tourism may also help in building the capacity of a community as illustrated in Chapter 12 in relation to social entrepreneurship, empowering it to engage in tourism as a viable economic activity. Community participation in the CTBI was seen as important to deliver the maximum benefits. In addition, government involvement at a local level can be crucial in terms of providing a supportive policy framework, funding and destination management strategies. Non-governmental organizations (NGOs) may also play a positive role in CBTIs as a key stakeholder to help build the local tourism potential of the community through collaboration with the community. There is also private sector interest in including community development in a more responsible approach to tourism in terms of the tour operators now promoting such objectives, as Chapter 19 shows. In many cases, Simpson (2008) found CBTIs to be based on an SME which face many of the perennial problems and barriers, including access to funding combined with community-related problems (e.g. disparate opinions within the stakeholder groups), a silent majority within the community, a lack of understanding over community needs and criticism that there is a lack of understanding over the market for the product or service being proposed. However, Simpson (2008) did point to a number of key success factors in CBTIs which, based on best practice, should be established on some of the following principles:

- interaction (with open communication, engagement and consultation with all community stakeholders)
- transparency (in terms of ownership structure, areas of responsibility and liaison officers who coordinate the stakeholder groups)
- analysis and evaluation (using best practice from either CBTIs, monitoring procedures and performance)
- practical issues/skills (including training and capacity building, financial skills, funding to pump-prime the project as well as marketing and operational skills).

CBTIs continue to represent an area in tourism whereby communities can develop tourism opportunities under their own direction, pace and scale in a manner which fits with the local culture, needs of the society and environmental resource base. Much of the interest in this area has also been subsumed in the tourism and entrepreneurship literature within social entrepreneurship which runs alongside social CBTIs, and readers should also consult Chapter 12.

Conclusion

Tourism results in a range of social and cultural impacts of varying magnitude. Several factors influence the extent of social and cultural impacts. It must be acknowledged that while tourism may have economic benefits which are generally easy to assess, it is likely that there will be some impact on the host community in both the short and long term. Discussion of social and cultural impacts often emphasizes the negative aspects but it must be remembered that there are positive angles too. It is difficult to make accurate assessments of the extent to which tourism causes social and cultural change because it is just one force of change which operates. This type of change is not really tangible and occurs gradually. Despite this, it is certainly clear that those who control tourism activity must take some responsibility for the cost to host communities. It is also apparent that in some cases tourism has been developed at the expense of the host community, where economic gain has been placed as a higher priority than the well-being and integrity of the local people. There are signs that more innovative ways of managing host–guest conflict are emerging but there is still a great deal of concern about the long-term implications of an ever-growing global tourism industry.

Discussion questions

1 Discuss whether tourism results in communication or corruption of culture.

2 Explain why local community involvement in tourism development and management can reduce sociocultural impacts.

3 Discuss the factors which seem to influence the extent of sociocultural impacts in relation to tourism.

4 Why do the sociocultural impacts of tourism appear to be more pronounced in developing countries?

References

Altman, J. and Finlayson, J. (1993) 'Aborigines, tourism and sustainable development', *Journal of Tourism Studies*, 4 (1): 38–50.

Ap, J. and Crompton, J.L. (1993) 'Residents' strategies for responding to tourism impacts', *Journal of Travel Research*, 22 (1): 47–49.

Ap, J. and Crompton, J.L. (1998) 'Developing and testing a tourism impact scale', *Journal of Travel Research*, 37: 120–130.

Baumgartner, C. and Beyer, M. (ND) Human Rights in Tourism: Findings and Results. Federal Ministry for Economic Cooperation and Development, Bonn. www.responseandability.com.

Berno, T. (1999) 'When a guest is a guest: Cook Islanders view tourism', *Annals of Tourism Research*, 26 (3): 656–675.

Bloch, N. (2016) 'Evicting heritage: Spatial cleansing and cultural legacy at the Hampi UNESCO site in India', *Critical Asian Studies*, 48 (4): 556–578.

Bloch, N. (2017) 'Barbarians in India: Tourism as moral contamination', *Annals of Tourism Research*, 62: 64–77.

Bossevain, J. (ed.) (1996) *Coping with Tourists. European Reactions to Mass Tourism*. Oxford: Berghahn.

Bott, E. (2018) 'Among the piranhas: The troubling lifespan of ethnic tropes in "tribal" tourism to Vietnam', *Journal of Sustainable Tourism*, 26 (8): 1291–1307.

Butler, R. and Hinch, T. (eds.) (1996) *Tourism and Indigenous People*. London: Routledge.

Butler, R. and Hinch, T. (eds.) (2007) *Tourism and Indigenous People: Issues and Implications*. Oxford: Butterworth-Heinemann.

Carson, S. and Pennings, M. (eds.) (2017) *Performing Cultural Tourism: Community, Tourists and Creative Practices*. London: Routledge.

Cohen, E. (1972) 'Rethinking the sociology of tourism', *Annals of Tourism Research*, 6 (1): 18–35.

Cohen, E. (2004) *Contemporary Tourism*. Oxford: Elsevier.

Deery, M., Jago, L. and Fredline, L. (2012) 'Rethinking social impacts of tourism research: A new research agenda', *Tourism Management*, 33 (1): 64–73.

De Kadt, E. (1979) *Tourism – Passport to Development*. New York: Oxford University Press.

Doxey, G.V. (1975) 'A causation theory of visitor–resident irritants, methodology and research inferences', *Conference Proceedings: Sixth Annual Conference of Travel Research Association*, San Diego, 195–198.

Forster, J. (1964) 'The sociological consequences of tourism', *International Journal of Comparative Sociology*, 5: 217–227.

Furze, B., De Lacy, T. and Birckhead, J. (1996) *Culture, Conservation, and Biodiversity: The Social Dimension of Linking Local Level Development and Conservation through Protected Areas*. Chichester: John Wiley.

Kozak, M. (2007) 'Tourist harassment: A marketing perspective', *Annals of Tourism Research*, 34 (2): 384–399.

Krippendorf, J. (1987) *The Holidaymakers*. Oxford: Butterworth-Heinemann.

Lea, J. (1988) *Tourism and Development in the Third World*. London: Routledge.

MacCannell, D. (1976) *The Tourist: A New Theory of Leisure Class*. London: Macmillan.

MacNeill, T. and Wozniak, D. (2018) 'The economic, social, and environmental impacts of cruise tourism', *Tourism Management*, 66: 387–404.

Mathieson, G. and Wall, A. (1982) *Tourism: Economic, Social and Environmental Impacts*. Harlow: Longman.

Murphy, P. (1985) *Tourism: A Community Approach*. London: Routledge.

17

Nash, D. (2005) *Beginnings of an Anthropology of Tourism.* Oxford: Elsevier.

Norberg-Hodge, H. (1992) *Ancient Futures. Learning from Ladakh.* London: Rider.

Organization for Economic Cooperation and Development (OECD) (2009) *The Impact of Culture on Tourism.* Paris: OECD.

Page, S.J. and Lawton, G. (1996) 'The impact of urban tourism on destination communities: Implications for community-based tourism in Auckland', in J. Jenkins, G. Kearsley and C.M. Hall (eds.) *Tourism Planning and Policy in Australia and New Zealand.* Melbourne: Irwin.

Ritzer, G. (1996) *The McDonaldization of Society.* Thousand Oaks, CA: Pine Forge Press.

Sharpley, R. (1994) *Tourists, Tourism and Society.* Huntingdon: Elm.

Shaw, G. and Williams, A. (1994) *Critical Issues in Tourism.* Blackwell: Oxford.

Simpson, M. (2008) 'Community-benefit tourism initiatives – a conceptual oxymoron?', *Tourism Management*, 29 (1): 1–18.

Smith, M. (2009) *Issues in Cultural Tourism.* London: Routledge.

Smith, V. (ed.) (1977) *Hosts and Guests: An Anthropology of Tourism.* Philadelphia, PA: University of Pennsylvania Press.

Sofield, T. (2003) *Empowerment for Sustainable Tourism Development.* Oxford: Elsevier.

Teo, P. (1994) 'Assessing sociocultural impacts: The case of Singapore', *Tourism Management*, 15 (2): 126–136.

Teye, V., Sönmez, S. and Sirakaya, E. (2002) 'Resident attitudes towards tourism development', *Annals of Tourism Research*, 29 (3): 666–686.

Timothy, D. and Nyanpane, G. (eds.) (2009) *Cultural Heritage and Tourism in the Developing World.* London: Routledge.

Tucker, H. (2003) *Living with Tourism.* London: Routledge.

Urry, J. (1990) *The Tourist Gaze.* London: Sage.

Ward, C. and Berno, T. (2011) 'Beyond social exchange theory: Attitudes towards tourists', *Annals of Tourism Research*, 38 (4): 1556–1569.

Williams, S. (1998) *Tourism Geographies.* London: Routledge.

Zaidan, E., Taillon, J. and Lee, S. (2016) 'Societal implications of UAE tourism development', *Anatolia*, 27 (4): 543–545.

Further reading

Books

Gursoy, D. and Nunkoo, R. (eds.) (2019) *The Routledge Handbook of Tourism Impacts.* London: Routledge.

Sharpley, R. (2018) *Tourism, Tourists and Society.* London: Routledge.

Journal articles

Bott, E. (2018) 'Among the piranhas: The troubling lifespan of ethnic tropes in "tribal" tourism to Vietnam', *Journal of Sustainable Tourism*, 26 (8): 1291–1307.

Helgadottiv, G., Einarsdottir, A., Burns, G., Gunnardottier, G. and Maria, J. (2019) `Social sustainability of tourism in Iceland: A qualitative inquiry', *Scandinavian Journal of Hospitality and Tourism*, 19 (4–5): 404–421.

Hughes, H. and Allen, D. (2005) 'Cultural tourism in Eastern Europe: The views of induced image formation agents', *Tourism Management*, 26 (2): 173–184.

Olsen, K, Avildgaard, M., Brattland, C. and Muller, D. (2019) *Looking at Arctic Tourism through the lens of Cultural Sensitivity: ARCTISEN – a Transnational Baseline Report*, diva – portal.org.

Richards, G. (2018) 'Cultural tourism: A review of recent research and trends', *Journal of Hospitality and Tourism Management*, 36: 12–21.

Santana-Talavera, A. (2017) 'Julio Aramberri: A sociological review of tourism studies', *Anatolia*, 28 (1): 122–128.

17

Environmental impacts

Learning outcomes

After reading this chapter and answering the questions, you should be able to:

- understand the importance of the environment as a tourism resource
- recognize the positive and negative impacts of tourism on the natural environment
- identify a range of examples of environmental impacts.

Overview

One of the phrases most frequently used by tour operators and tourism marketers to describe a destination is 'unspoilt'. For many tourists, the desire to escape to a seemingly untouched environment is strong, and tourism generally takes place in the world's most attractive environments. Since the onset of mass travel, concern has developed about the desirability of tourism. In many locations, tourism development has taken place with little regard for the natural environment. While it is recognized that tourism is an important contributor to the economy, there is a growing body of knowledge that recognizes the importance of managing and protecting the environment. This chapter outlines the major environmental impacts of tourism and future challenges for tourism such as climate change.

Introduction

Tourism development in many places has led to a deterioration in environmental quality and numerous studies have highlighted the growing scale of the problem (Gössling and Hall 2006). The growth of tourism has prompted debate about environmental consequences and the desirability of further development (Holden and Fennell 2012) including debates associated with over tourism and mass tourism. Some studies have called for a radical rethink about the rationale for tourism. For example, Higgins-Desbiolles *et al.* (2019) have pointed to the inequality tourism causes where communities and their resources are impacted by business interests that utilize the natural resource base for short-term profit. One consequence is the call for 'degrowth' in tourism, redefining the rights of local communities and areas to challenge destructive growth agendas. In the 1960s, the effects of mass tourism and increasing awareness of the human impact on the environment led to a general realization that nature is not an inexhaustible resource, and this was embodied in the seminal study by Young (1973), *Tourism: Blessing or Blight*? This was a notable turning point in the analysis of tourism's impact on the natural and built environment, questioning the validity of uncontrolled growth. Yet these lessons have not been heeded in the pursuit of growth in visitor numbers as countries and destinations have embarked on a race to join the global expansion of tourism (a theme we will return to in Chapter 27). Studies in the 1980s and 1990s such as Krippendorf's (1987) *The Holidaymakers* and Wood and House's (1991) *The Good Tourist* continued to highlight the finite nature of the environmental resources upon which tourism depends. These studies are symptomatic of the fact that not only have total international tourist numbers risen rapidly at a global scale but also the regional distribution has shifted away from a European focus to a more widespread pattern, covering less developed countries and new, exotic and extreme locations. Tourism is now a global phenomenon impacting every country in the world: nowhere is safe from the effects of tourism, a theme which explorers seek to capture in popular television series to demonstrate there are still very inaccessible locations (i.e. untouched areas) which intrepid tourists as *explorers* might want to seek out. There has also been a switch to more environmentally sensitive forms of tourism such as ecotourism and wildlife-based tourism, which still bring with them major environmental concerns. For some destinations, the environmental effects of tourism have led to direct threats to the industry, as the success in attracting tourists leads to negative impacts on the attractiveness of the environment.

Attributing environmental damage to tourism is difficult for a number of reasons, as outlined by Mathieson and Wall (1982) and Wall and Mathieson (2006) as we discussed in the preface to this section of the book. To recap, the main problem is that of disentangling the effects of tourism from the effects of human existence. Coupled with the complex and fragmented nature of tourism provision, the problem is further compounded. Nevertheless, Edington and Edington (1986: 2) point out that 'a proper understanding of biological, or more specifically, ecological factors can significantly reduce the scale of environmental damage associated with recreational and tourist development'.

As Gössling (2002: 284) observed, globally tourism contributes to:

- changes in land use, as tourism is a major consumer of land (e.g. airport development)
- energy use, as tourism may be a major consumer of fossil fuels
- extinction of wild species
- changes to the perception of the environment, which becomes a resource to be consumed, as part of an experience affecting human–environment relations, which is summarized in Figure 18.1. As Gössling (2002) noted, in the case of the Seychelles, a study by the World Wildlife Fund for Nature found that 97 per cent of the energy footprint from tourists was due to air travel. In fact, Gössling and Hall (2006) argued that despite a growing concern with environmental impacts in the 1980s, these problems have got worse. Gössling (2002) accepts that while travel may foster environmental knowledge, this does not necessarily lead to positive changes in environmental behaviour, a point reaffirmed by Page *et al.* (2014).

The relationship between tourism and the environment is complex but may be viewed from three perspectives. This demonstrates the holistic approach to the term 'environment', which includes the natural and sociocultural interface. The three perspectives are:

- tourist–environment interactions
- tourist–host interactions
- host–environment interactions.

When these relationships break down, problems inevitably ensue. While the term 'environment' may be used to denote an all-encompassing view of both the natural and social worlds, for the purposes of this chapter, attention is

18

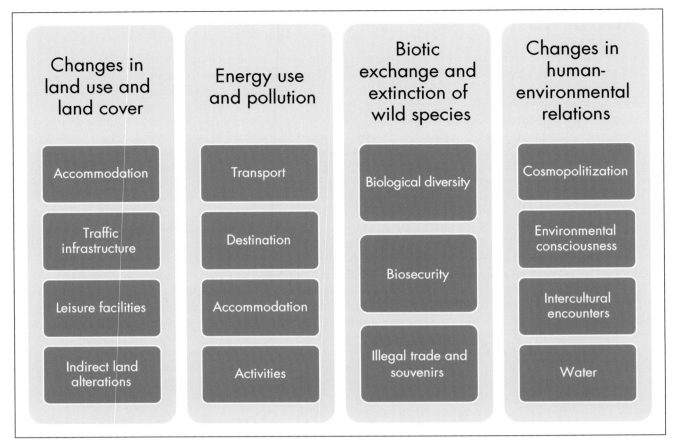

FIGURE 18.1 The global environmental consequences of tourism
Source: Adapted from Gössling (2002)

focused on the natural or physical environment, defined by Mieczkowski (1995: 8) as the 'combination of non-living, i.e. abiotic, physical components, with biological resources, or the biosphere, including flora and fauna'. Tourism and the environment are closely linked – without an attractive environment, tourism cannot succeed and, in some cases, without tourism, environmental conservation is at risk. In other words, a symbiotic relationship exists between tourism and the environment: each is dependent upon the other for maintaining a balance, so that if the environment deteriorates it will directly impact upon tourism. Mathieson and Wall (1982: 97) argue that 'In the absence of an attractive environment, there would be little tourism. Ranging from the basic attractions of sun, sea and sand to the undoubted appeal of historic sites and structures, the environment is the foundation of the tourist industry.' Farrell and Runyan (1991: 26) also suggest that 'natural resources, the ecosystem, regional ecology . . . contribute to all tourist locations', emphasizing the need to recognize environmental impacts.

The nature and scope of the environmental impacts of tourism

To facilitate the study of environmental impacts of tourism, it is advisable to break 'tourism' into its component parts. While there is some overlap between these categories, this provides a satisfactory basis for analysis. Broadly, tourism comprises:

1 travel
2 tourism destination development
3 tourism associated activities.

Travel

Much concern has been expressed about increasing levels of transport on roads and in the air in industrialized nations, and the consequent wider effects on the environment and human health. Awareness of pollution emanating from various transport modes as well as direct effects on landscape and amenity values have escalated as transport infrastructure is further developed. The study of transport is one aspect of tourism which highlights the conflict between the environment and the industry. On the one hand, enabling travel is an essential criterion for tourism: roads, cars, aircraft and airports are all needed to permit the easy passage of tourists from home to destination and back again. Conversely, the negative effects are the pollution of the natural environment and damage to the quality of landscapes. Balance is required between these two aspects, but this is not readily achievable. Gössling *et al.* (2005) examined the eco-efficiency of tourism by examining its energy efficiency in relation to economic performance. Tourist travel is responsible for around 50 per cent of all global travel and is a major consumer of fossil fuel. In locations such as the Seychelles, tourism was seven times less eco-efficient than tourism in France, which consumed only 10 per cent of the global average for tourism. Gössling *et al.* concluded that at current estimates tourism is not sustainable as an economic activity. This is compounded when one considers the following figures for air travel in the UK:

- during 1970–2002, passengers travelling by air travel rose from 32 million per annum to 189 million passengers per annum, a five-fold increase
- by 2017, there were 284 million passengers, and this could grow to 435 million by 2050. (Department for Transport, 2018)

This is a useful insight into why air travel is such a contentious issue, not least because of its environmental impacts and the increasing demand including the land take required to expand airports to accommodate such growth. For example, Beijing's second international airport will have seven runways and capacity to handle 72 million passengers a year. The International Air Transport Association data outlined in Chapter 8 illustrates that by 2037, the global demand for air travel will almost double from 4.2 billion passengers a year in 2017 to 8.2 billion in 2037, with Asia-Pacific key source markets.

Air travel

Worldwide, over 1 billion people (one-fifth of the world's population) now travel by air. The damage caused to the environment starts before the aircraft even takes off. Airports require substantial tracts of land in order to operate safely and efficiently. The scale of destruction linked with building an airport is significant – for example, Frankfurt's third runway resulted in the felling of half a million trees. Aircraft account for 13 per cent of total transport fuel consumption. Jet kerosene is currently the only significant fuel used, and the aviation sector does not pay the full economic cost of fuel, since it is exempt from taxation compared to other fuel sources. Like all fuels, on combustion kerosene produces:

- carbon dioxide (CO_2)
- water (H_2O)
- carbon monoxide (CO)
- hydrocarbons (HCs)
- nitrogen oxide (No_x)
- sulphur dioxide (SO_2).

Emission standards for unburned hydrocarbons, CO_2 and No_x are laid down for new aircraft by the International Civil Aviation Organization, but these only apply to take-off and landing. The key factor in the environmental effect of air travel is altitude. Although aircraft are responsible for only a small amount of hazardous pollutants, emissions have a greater impact because of the highly sensitive regions where they are emitted – particularly in the upper atmosphere. Nitrogen oxides (1–1.5 million tonnes per year) in the lower atmosphere (35 000–39 000 feet) lead to ozone formation at ground level and urban smog, and contribute to global warming, which is discussed later. As the Royal Commission on Environmental Pollution (2002) noted, these concerns are related to:

- climate change, including greenhouse gases
- the reduction of ozone in the stratosphere, contributing to increased surface ultraviolet (UV) radiation
- regional pollution downwind from airports and local pollution in terms of noise, decreased air quality and additional ground transportation pollution from airport expansion.

18

As Gössling and Peeters (2007) argue, there is a psychology of denial among many in the aviation sector who point to future energy-efficient technology to reduce emissions in spite of the year-on-year growth in air travel. For example, in the Department for Transport (2018) consultation on air transport to 2050, the argument used to justify meeting further demand for air travel (aside from economic competitiveness) was reduced environmental impacts. The study suggests future technology such as electric batteries to be developed for hybrid aircraft will help decarbonize aviation (we will return to decarbonization later and in Chapter 27). In other words, the logic of the Department for Transport argument is that we should grow now and hope that technology will catch up and provide the solution by 2035 with future development of hybrid aircraft. One response from the aviation sector has been the introduction of voluntary carbon offsetting schemes as a method of compensating for the production of greenhouse gases by air travel (Gössling *et al.* 2007), given the obligations on governments to reduce these emissions under the Kyoto Protocol (see Chapter 19). British Airways was the first airline to introduce a voluntary carbon offset scheme for passengers to offset the effects of their journey by donating money to help fund renewable energies. The airline has also joined a carbon trading scheme. Carbon trading is based upon the principle of establishing an upper limit for carbon emissions for an entire economy. Companies receive a carbon allowance and if they exceed that allowance, they have three options: cut their emissions through the use of new technology; purchase carbon allowances from other companies; or a combination of purchasing allowances and investing in new technology. For example, some airlines are experimenting with the use of biofuels, made from coconut and babassu oil. Long term, scientists are also experimenting with solar energy to power an aircraft to reduce emissions.

Tourism destination development

Tourism destinations comprise a wide diversity of environments, from purpose-built resorts to remote natural areas. In general it is possible to identify broad categories of impact that may affect all destinations to a greater or lesser extent: inappropriate development, loss of habitat, extinction of species, pollution, and loss of spirit. According to the European Environment Agency (1998), tourism creates significant contributions to the following environmental problems:

- waste
- reducing levels of biodiversity
- pollution of inland waters
- pollution of marine and coastal zones.

Lake environments – known as lacustrine systems – illustrate many of the impacts which visitors may pose to natural resources including damage to fauna, algal growth, discharge of sewage, bank erosion, trampling on lakeshores, increased turbidity due to water-skiing and jet-skiing and the impact on water birds due to noise pollution and disturbance. These tourism-generated impacts may combine with wider environmental problems not specifically attributed to tourism. In arid areas, excessive tourism impacts can also lead to desertification since these are fragile natural environments.

In a European context, the environments which tend to be most directly affected by tourism are coastal and alpine areas. (Table 18.1) illustrates a range of environmental impacts in relation to specific habitats. A habitat is defined as 'the place in which a species of animal or plant lives, providing a particular set of environmental conditions' (Cordrey n.d.).

There are two types of environmental impacts which occur in destination development:

- those affecting the integrity and composition of the natural environment
- those affecting the tourist experience of the environment.

In essence, these two categories overlap but need to be viewed from different perspectives. For example, the effects of trampling on vegetation induce direct environmental change, whereas overcrowding affects tourist enjoyment but has a different overall impact on the natural environment (Image 18.1). It is also interesting to consider the question of responsibility for tourism impacts. Kavallinis and Pizam (1994) found in a study of the perception of tourism impacts on the Greek island of Mykonos that tourists were more critical of impacts than the host community. Tourists considered residents and entrepreneurs to have greater responsibility than them for producing negative environmental impacts. Residents believed that tourists were to blame for much of the environmental impact. WWF

TABLE 18.1 Summary of environmental impacts in specific habitats

Habitats influenced	Effect of tourism development	Habitats influenced	Effect of tourism development
Marine waters	Pollution from sewage outfall Dumping of waste in the sea Oil pollution from tourist boats Litter and threat to marine creatures	Upland heaths, mires and tundra Agricultural land	Erosion Habitat loss and fragmentation Disturbance to nesting birds Loss of area for production Conflict between adjacent agricultural uses and tourism
Coastal habitats	Habitat loss and fragmentation Deterioration in ecological diversity Destabilization of sand dunes Erosion of coastal landscape	Semi-natural grasslands	Loss of open landscape Habitat loss
Inland waters	Sewage pollution Eutrophication Oil pollution from boats and barges Disturbance of bird communities by watercraft	Heathlands, scrub, rocky area Forests	Habitat loss and fragmentation Habitat loss and fragmentation Disturbance from recreational activities

Source: Adapted from European Environment Agency (1998)

(2002) developed an **ecological footprint** to help tourists to understand how different types of holidays affect the environment in terms of the consumption of resources and impacts.

The following sections outline the major environmental impacts of tourism in destinations.

1 Inappropriate development

Tourism development, whether it takes place on the micro or macro scale, may be classed as inappropriate where it fails to be sensitive to the natural environment. Large tracts of the Mediterranean coastal strip are now covered by urban sprawl to cater for the mass tourism market. Theroux (1996: 35) describes the Spanish coast as 'utterly blighted' and continues 'I felt intensely that the Spanish coast, especially here on the Costa del Sol, had undergone a powerful colonization, of a modern kind . . . It had robbed the shore of its natural features, displaced headlands and gullies and harbours with futile badly-made structures.' This type of development occurs as a result of short-term planning in environmental terms. Resort developments, while contained on specific sites, are normally built on green-field sites in undeveloped areas, often with no planning control. A chain reaction of tourism-related development often follows. The Waikiki area of Honolulu has also been subject to high-density tourism development with skyscraper hotels obscuring views of the coast. Newly developing resorts in less developed countries also display signs of unplanned development, such as Pattaya, in Thailand, which is considered to be overdeveloped. In a few cases, inappropriate development has been removed: the poorly built hotels of Calvià, Majorca (Mallorca), were demolished in the late 1990s to make way for environmental enhancements (see Chapter 22). In England, the National Trust has been active in turning the tide of inappropriate developments. At Kynance Cove, Cornwall, the Trust demolished unsightly cafés and shop buildings, which had contributed to site erosion as visitors would follow a particular route past them. The Trust rerouted the paths, restoring the damaged ground surface and controlling the movement of visitors to reduce the physical impact of visitors to the site. However, this has been seen to cause conflict with the local community in some cases, for some local businesses are dependent on visitors who stay on such sites.

2 Loss of natural habitat and effects on wildlife

Development of facilities and subsequent tourist use may result in rapid or more gradual effects on habitats. In Nepal, deforestation resulting in the felling of thousands of trees for building tourist lodges and provision of hot water, heating and cooking fuelwood has resulted in a dramatic depletion of the country's forest cover: one trekker consumes

IMAGE 18.1 Trampling and foot-damage has led to the hardening of this part of the Dorset Coast path

five to ten times more wood than a Nepali in a day and a single lodge may consume one hectare of virgin forest per year for running facilities (see Insight 18.1 later). Trampling, for example, through walking or horse riding, causes disturbance to vegetation and soil. Reduced ground vegetation cover or loss of tree seedlings through trampling causes soil to become exposed and therefore vulnerable to both erosion and compaction. Trail widening and muddiness may result.

There is much research on the effects of tourism on wildlife and nature conservation. As a result of habitat effects and as a direct result of tourism activity, wildlife can be disturbed. There is a debate about whether tourism and nature conservation can coexist in mutual benefit and it is possible to identify a number of examples of instances where tourism has incurred both costs and benefits. One example is the golden toad, only known to have existed in the Monteverde Cloud Rain Forest in Costa Rica, which is now extinct. This orange-coloured toad, depicted on postcards and on entrance signs to one of the most popular lodges in the area, declined in numbers at the same time as ecotourism evolved in the area. It is possible that an alien organism brought in by ecotourists may have caused a plague. Two contrasting examples illustrate the dichotomy between studies which demonstrate tourism is beneficial for wildlife and those which adopt the opposite view. Schuhmann *et al.*'s (2019) study of Barbados found that visitors were willing to pay between USD$36 and USD$52 per visit to Barbados to support wildlife conservation. In contrast, D'Cruze *et al.* (2018) examined wildlife tourism interaction experiences in Latin America using TripAdvisor. They found 249 wildlife attraction webpages in 21 countries involving 73 species, 19 of which are considered to be threatened by the International Union for the Conservation of Nature, offering direct contact with animals. D'Cruze *et al.* (2018) concluded that despite the economic benefits which ecotourism generate, these experiences have adverse effects on wildlife conservation and animal welfare.

Another species more directly affected by tourism activity is the loggerhead turtle. Prunier *et al.* (1993) provide evidence for this, having studied the turtles on the Greek island of Zakynthos, one of the most important nesting areas in the Mediterranean. Nesting takes place in the peak tourist season between June and August and, of the hatchlings, only one or two in every thousand will reach adulthood. Concern was expressed in 1979 about this 'endangered species'. The development of tourism threatens the turtle in six ways:

1 *Loss of beach nesting areas* – developers and tourists encroach on the habitat, and tree planting to provide shade for tourists may cause a barrier to successful nesting.

2 *Nesting females and young turtles disoriented by artificial illumination* – the turtle is phototactic and moves towards a light source. The usual movement is towards the reflection of the sun on the sea but lights from beachfront developments attract the turtles inland, where they dehydrate or become road casualties.

3 *Noise* – turtles are confused by loud noises.

4 *Traffic* – on the beach, traffic causes sand compaction, creates an imbalance of gases absorbed by the eggs and may activate hatchlings at the wrong time.

5 *Pollution* – litter and boat oil may be consumed and cause choking and death.

6 *Activities in water* – turtles become entangled in fishing lines, drown in nets and are injured in collision with watercraft.

The Galapagos Islands, 600 miles off the coast of Ecuador, are considered to be one of the foremost locations for wildlife tourism. Organized ecotourism started in the late 1960s with visitor numbers of about 6000 per year. In 1996, these visitor numbers were up to 40 000 and now exceed 225 000 (plus 132 000 land-based visitors) and generate between US$250 and US$350 million from international tourism. Each international visitor pays a US$100 entry fee for adults and US$50 for children. The environment of the Galapagos is the main attraction – sea lions, marine iguanas, giant tortoises, penguins and an array of unusual reptiles, birds, plants, insects and fish. Strict rules on tourist activity apply. Visitors must follow guides, stay on paths, not take food, not drop litter and wash off before going to another island. Despite this, red- and blue-footed boobies have been observed to change their nesting locations and display behaviour in relation to tourist use of trails. Iguanas wait for tourists to feed them bananas. Even so, in 2007 the World Conservation Union and Unesco added the location to a list of World Heritage Sites in danger, largely due to tourism, in-migration of population to benefit from the tourism boom, and overfishing. For example, the islands had a population of 3500 in the 1970s and it is now 18 000. In 2018, 35 tour operators on the Galapagos Islands wrote to the Ecuadorian Minister of Tourism to complain about the unregulated nature of land-based tourism in Galapagos. The crux of the argument was that this was contributing to invasive non-native species being introduced that affect the islands biodiversity.

Wildlife viewing is increasing in popularity and forms one of the major activities associated with ecotourism (Image 18.2). The impacts of this are trampling of vegetation by foot and vehicular traffic and disruption of wildlife behaviour. In the Amboseli National Park, Kenya, cheetahs have learned to avoid tourists and delay their activities according to tourist presence. Feeding and harassment of wildlife causes unnatural behaviour changes which may result in spatial and temporal displacement leading to lower-quality food sources, inferior cover and increased competition. Longer-term changes may lead to the alteration of the structure and size of the population and local extinction. Whale watching has become one of the boom sectors in ecotourism, but even this has impacts on wildlife.

IMAGE 18.2 Ecotourism trips, Galapagos Islands. What impact does this tourist behaviour have on the giant tortoises?

3 Pollution

Water quality and sewage treatment are often neglected following tourism development, sometimes due to lack of planning controls, sometimes due to lack of finance to back schemes. In the Mediterranean, horror stories of raw sewage being pumped straight out to sea have been prolific. This results in a number of different impacts. Increased nutrients in the water robs the water of oxygen causing eutrophication in lakes and subsequent death to aquatic life. Plagues of jellyfish feed on the increased nutrients and float ashore, causing problems for sea-bathing tourists. Water-borne diseases such as diarrhoea and typhoid can also occur, reflected in many European beaches seeking to acquire annual awards to reassure visitors of their cleanliness and safety. There has been a move towards limitation of problems, and preventative measures have been installed in many locations. Tighter regulations, new technology, improved waste-water management systems and innovations such as ultraviolet treatment systems are important environmental measures for resorts (we will return to pollution and the issues surrounding plastic and pollution in Chapter 19). One of the most controversial examples is the impact of adventure tourism on Mount Everest (Insight 18.1).

18

INSIGHT 18.1 Pollution and adventure tourism on Mount Everest

The remote mountain communities in the Nepalese Himalayas, located between China and India, have seen over 30 years of tourism linked to adventure travel and mountaineering. Nepal has eight of ten of the world's highest mountain peaks. The first American and European tourists did not enter the area until the 1950s, and until 1964 only mountaineering expeditions were permitted to visit there. By 1971 around 1000 visitors a year entered the area, but by 1981 it had risen to over 5000 visitors a year, and by the late 1980s it was around 8000 visitors a year, rising to 300 000 in the 1990s. It is now around 500 000, with government plans to attract 1 million visitors a year. Most visitors are attracted to trekking, generating over US$60 million a year in income. However, as Nepal (2005) has shown, this has had a pronounced effect on the local rural population and settlements, as less than 10 per cent of visitor spending filters down to those communities. The environmental consequences of tourist trekking have led to the growing environmental pollution of the Everest area.

There have been numerous studies of the impacts of trekking, with the visible overcrowding on trails causing erosion as well as overcrowding at 'teahouses', the Nepalese Sherpa homes for overnight guests. There are also major concerns over the massive deforestation of the Himalayas, with the trekker-generated demands for firewood and wood for construction material. For example, wood is needed to heat water for cooking and bathing, and it has been estimated that one trekker consumes five times more wood a day than a Sherpa family. Rubbish is also a problem for the Everest region; estimates suggest over 18 tons of rubbish have been dumped at Everest, which could cost over half a million dollars to clean up. The National Park in which Everest is located, Sagarmatha, has seen extensive changes to the landscape as a result of trekking and rubbish dumping in forest areas as deforestation has made the Nepalese government insist on the use of kerosene fuel for cooking during trekking expeditions.

Some media reports have described Everest as the 'highest junkyard' in the world, entirely the result of adventure tourism, largely from wealthy visitors from Europe and North America and other developed countries. This is the environmental cost of tourism where limited controls are placed upon the behaviour of high-value tourism. Environmental groups have described this as an impending ecological disaster, as pressure groups try to lobby the government to temporarily close the mountain to let it recover. The tens of thousands of feet which impact upon the fragile ecosystem have been compounded by pollution induced by tourism, as restaurants and Internet cafés have also moved into the area. While climate change is impacting upon the mountain ecosystem and water supplies, there is evidence that glaciers are receding due to global warming. The Khumbu region and the city of Kathmandu, which is the capital of Nepal, can accommodate around 40 000 visitors a year, and in the peak season visitor numbers can rise to 700 000. Of these 700 000, around 20 000–40 000 will ascend the Himalayas and many thousands will trek to the base of Everest. As the Nepalese government receives £50 000 in royalties for a team of seven climbers who ascend Everest, the pressure to close the mountain is problematic due to the foreign revenue it generates. With so many climbers discarding climbing equipment, food, plastics, tin cans, glass, clothes, tents and larger items, the mountain embodies all of the environmental problems of uncontrolled tourism. Although many researchers criticize the impact of mass tourism on destinations, Everest is an example of a destination where its carrying capacity and poor environmental standards by trekkers and mountaineers have polluted a unique and pristine resource.

There is little doubt in the mind of any environmentalist that Everest should be closed to visitors, but the consequences will be profound to the Sherpas and businesses now dependent upon this form of tourism. Similarly, the government has generated a major form of tourist taxation from climbing Everest, but the long-term environmental cost may be such that no royalty or climbing fee will be sufficient to repair a unique environmental resource that has exceeded its carrying capacity.

Further reading

Nepal, S. (2005) 'Tourism and remote mountain settlements: Spatial and temporal development of tourist infrastructure in the Mount Everest region, Nepal', *Tourism Geographies*, 7 (2): 205–227.

Questions

1 Why are mountains sensitive areas that are largely incompatible with intensive tourist use?
2 How has mountain tourism impacted the Nepalese population around Mount Everest?
3 What environmental impacts arise from tourism in the vicinity of Mount Everest?
4 What action should be taken to manage tourism around Mount Everest?

4 Loss of spirit

Much less of a tangible effect but still crucial is the impact of tourism on the ambience of a location. A loss of atmosphere might be individually perceived but it may also have wider implications for tourism. The spirit of a place might be the main attraction and once that spirit is diminished, then tourists may no longer desire to visit. That is over and beyond the ramifications for the integrity of the environment and the host community. Changes in character may be incremental, so the loss of spirit may occur gradually or may take place more rapidly, as in the instance of resort development or through too many tourists at visitor attractions like the Taj Mahal.

5 Overcrowding and traffic congestion

When the volume of tourists exceeds the capacity of an environment, then overcrowding occurs. Geographical and temporal considerations are required when assessing overcrowding because in general it affects certain parts of a site and/or certain times of the day or year. Overcrowding is a problem for two reasons:

- it poses an increased risk of environmental damage through erosion
- it restricts visitor appreciation of the destination.

Traffic, particularly the private car, attracts much attention as an area of research. In the UK, concern is directed at both rural and urban tourism. While tourist traffic is not generally the major cause of congestion, at certain times of the year and in particular regions and destinations, it adds significantly to the pressures of general road use. A large proportion of rural tourists visit the countryside by car and the biggest increase in car use is predicted for rural areas. For towns and cities, growing congestion from commuter and tourist traffic is leading to restrictions being imposed on use of roads at certain times. Road traffic can damage the built environment through pollution and vibration as well as negatively affecting tranquillity and atmosphere. Car parks are required to contain traffic volume at destinations, but in some locations inappropriate parking causes damage to verges and vegetation, for example off-road parking on moorlands. The increasing popularity of off-road driving damages vegetation, causes erosion and adds to localized pollution. At the extreme end of the spectrum, in some of the National Parks of the UK and the USA, road closures have been necessary to stem the untenable flow of traffic, and air quality problems have been perceived to be a significant effect of tourism – mainly from exhaust fumes from tourist vehicles in these environments. Koenen *et al.* (1995) calculated that about 19 per cent of carbon monoxide air pollution in Las Vegas is caused by tourism. Congestion often results in new journey patterns where people travel to different places to avoid queues and/or where they know they are able to park. This spreads the problem to a wider area.

6 Wear and tear

Physical damage to the environment is often more marked in the countryside but is also an issue for urban areas. Sensitive locations, such as peat moorlands and sand dunes, are prone to serious damage by a range of users, such as horse riders, mountain bikers, walkers and off-road vehicles.

Riverbanks are subject to the wash from pleasure boats, a problem suffered in the Norfolk Broads, UK, where the problem is exacerbated by the weakening of reeds by fertilizer run-off. Other problems of wear and tear include litter. On Dartmoor, UK, up to 250 trailer loads of litter are collected every year from one small area. Antarctica has seen visitor numbers rise from 6000 in the 1990s to over 28 000 in the new millennium and rubbish and waste from cruise ships have generated a problem for one of the world's most pristine environments. In Rome, coins thrown by tourists into the Trevi Fountain are chipping the marble. The English Tourist Board and Employment Department Group (1991) reported that Westminster Abbey's 3 million annual visitors were causing damage to the physical fabric of the interior (see Image 14.3). The thirteenth-century Cosmati pavement in front of the high altar is literally being worn away. Pieces of statuary are stolen and the increased exposure to humidity, light and dust from the volume of visitors is a threat to artwork, materials and ornamentation. The famous caves at Lascaux in the Dordogne, southern France, containing 17 000-year-old Quaternary cave paintings, illustrate a case where action was needed to eliminate the effect of tourism on the integrity of the resource base. Perspiration and breath from the large numbers of tourists to the caves altered the microclimate, leading to an increase in carbon dioxide, temperature and humidity. In addition, artificial lights used to illuminate the interior gave favourable conditions for the growth of mosses, algae and bacteria. This began to have a damaging effect on the quality of the paintings. The caves were closed to visitors in 1963 and are now only open to scholars by arrangement. They must go through a disinfectant chamber before entry, must not speak once inside and are allowed a maximum of 20 minutes in the caves. A replica, named 'Lascaux Two' was constructed in 1983 to enable 2000 tourists per day to experience something of the paintings.

7 Activities

In relation to the impact of tourism activities, it is worth drawing out examples to indicate to what extent popular holiday activities can affect the natural environment.

Skiing/alpine tourism Mountain ecosystems are generally quite fragile but many are prone to intensive use, through skiing, trekking and other mountain/snow sports. Skiing is seen by many as a damaging activity because it requires associated developments, such as lodges, resorts, roads and ski slopes and causes severe erosion and deforestation. A great deal of damage is caused in the initial construction and development stages. In some resorts, lack of snowfall and tourist demand for the snow experience means that snow cannons have been employed. These require large amounts of water to produce sufficient snow to form a satisfactory slope for skiing and lead to a shorter growing season, reduced river currents affecting fish populations and destruction of forest cover causing soil erosion.

Ecotourism While the premise of ecotourism is to assist in conservation and the well-being of local communities, it is often the case that ecotourism-based activities lead to deterioration in environmental quality. The problem is that what is ecotourism today may be a mass product next year. Early ecotourism destinations such as Kenya, the Galapagos Islands and Thailand have already suffered extensive negative impacts as a result of increased numbers of ecotourists. Cater (1993) cites the example of Belize, where development has involved the clearance of mangrove swampland, drainage and infilling using topsoil literally shaved off the wetland savannah a few miles inland. Thus, two distinctive ecosystems have been destroyed. Well-documented cases of lack of planning, improper management and negative impacts indicate that a desire for short-term benefits has in some cases resulted in inappropriate forms of development as well as the wider distribution of tourism across the globe to sensitive environments like Antarctica. Despite researchers claiming that tourism and wildlife are compatible in these environments, it is clear that if a catastrophic human-related event destroyed a single breeding ground, with a high proportion of a single species, the consequences would be severe. In the Antarctic, despite controls on ship size, around 30 ships operate there each year. The MS *Explorer* hit ice in Antarctica with 154 passengers and sunk in 2007. While all passengers were safely rescued, the incident highlighted how a cruise ship accident such as a major loss of fuel oil could impact on a breeding ground, as previous oil slicks from oil tankers have done in other parts of the ocean (albeit at a much greater scale). The issue is – *whose responsibility would an environmental clean-up be given the multinational treaty signed in 1959 by 12 nations?*

Positive environmental impacts of tourism

The damaging aspects of tourism are significant and receive deserved attention. However, it is essential to recognize that positive impacts may be gained from tourism activity. Doswell (1997) notes that tourism can focus attention on significant environmental issues and stimulate initiatives to conserve and enhance the environment. The main areas to examine are three-fold.

Conservation of redundant and/or historic buildings for alternative uses

Tourism can provide the impetus for converting disused buildings into foci for tourism activity, often in the guise of regeneration schemes. Many buildings retain their character yet can be carefully modernized to form new visitor attractions. Examples are old woollen mills and industrial premises, which may be given an alternative role through tourism use. Tourism may provide the financial means to restore and/or maintain historic buildings in an appropriate way. This may also provide the basis for future development in tourism, with planning approvals likely to be more easily obtained for building conversion or brownfield sites rather than new, greenfield locations. If existing buildings can be used in creative yet sensitive ways, tourism can prove to be a beneficial force of redevelopment. Use of derelict land for development of urban parks or country parks is widespread in industrialized nations. Despoiled land, such as the old open-cast coal mines of Northumberland, have been restored to both agricultural land and recreational areas and polluted brownfield sites in cities have been redeveloped for tourism uses, as the Millennium Dome project showcased. This is a vital part of all Olympic City bids (see Chapter 26), to leave an environmental legacy.

Enhancement of local environments

If tourism is viewed as an important source of income (Image 18.3), it is likely that local government will seek to retain and increase visitor numbers by improving the general amenity value of the local environment. This is relevant to a range of environments, including rural, coastal and urban areas. For many historic cities, improvements may consist of landscaping which reflects the heritage character of the townscape and simultaneously assists the visitor experience. However, it might be said that such enhancements detract from the original form. The Center Parcs development in Sherwood Forest, UK, resulted in the planting of 500 000 trees, the seeding of native grasses and wild flower species, heathland recreation and management and an overall increase in ecological diversity. While developments of this type tend to be criticized for their scale and siting in natural areas, in most cases, the environmental management which accompanies development improves the environment, which might have been subject to previous intensive use, such as forestry plantation. Heathland fauna, such as the nightjar and grass wave moth, are reappearing. Creation of waterways has attracted 12 species of dragonfly and damselfly (sufficient number to meet Natural England's criteria for selection as a Site of Special Scientific Interest). The first recorded sighting in Nottinghamshire of an emperor dragonfly has been recorded at Sherwood Forest.

IMAGE 18.3 Elephants in African national parks are a means of generating revenue for conservation

Protection of wildlife

It has been seen in various locations worldwide that tourism discourages poaching because it places economic value on wildlife and protection of natural resources. In many less developed countries, tourism acts as a force of conservation as it offers an alternative economic use. National parks, such as Amoseli in Kenya and Etosha in Namibia, are viewed as tools of conservation and economic development. Tourist spending generates local employment, demand for local goods and crafts and helps to justify protection of natural resources. Doswell (1997) comments that tourism draws attention to issues relating to biodiversity, endangered species and the human impact on the environment. However, Sindiga and Kanuhah (1999) state that in some of the Kenyan National Parks tourist-carrying capacities have been exceeded and animals are harassed by tourist vehicles, which disrupt their usual habits and behaviour. Appropriate environmental policy and management is required to ensure protection of the environment and a satisfactory visitor experience. But one of the main environmental problems affecting tourism as a global issue is global warming and climate change.

Tourism, global warming and climate change

One of the most serious global environmental issues facing the tourism industry is the issue of climate change (Hall and Higham 2005; Patterson *et al.* 2006) (see Image 18.4). According to the current forecasts for tourism activity, by 2050 tourism is expected to see its contribution to greenhouse gas emissions rise from its current 3 per cent to 7 per cent. One consequence of global warming is the negative effects it may have on tourism and the environments it occurs in. The first international tourism and climate change conference hosted by the World Tourism Organization

(WTO) in 2003 in Djerba (WTO 2003) endorsed the need for action to reduce tourism's global impacts by endorsing the Kyoto Protocol on reducing emissions (the Djerba Declaration), which highlights the expected impacts of climate change on different environments, a theme we will examine in more detail in Chapter 19. One of the most widely discussed issues is that of rising sea levels and the effect on small islands, combined with extreme climatic events such as a decrease in rainfall in some areas and increases elsewhere. These are significant, since climate and temperature are important determinants of destination selection. These will thus lead to a greater analysis of tourism comfort indices (i.e. mean temperature, maximum temperature, humidity, precipitation, sunshine hours and wind) in choosing destinations. Some of the expected effects may be as follows:

- a decline in European sun, sea and sand holidays in the Mediterranean due to the increased temperatures (Amelung and Viner 2006) in a region which receives over 100 million tourist trips each year
- rising temperatures in central European culture cities in peak season will lead to a decline in visitors
- specific ecosystems such as coral reefs will be affected as they have shown great sensitivity to minor changes in temperature; an increase of 1–2°C causes coral bleaching
- rising temperatures on the USA seaboards will trigger a move inland for holidays in the peak season, leading to people taking coastal holidays in the spring and autumn as Florida and California lose their popularity
- in the Caribbean, erosion may make their products less attractive
- in Alpine areas, shorter skiing seasons may arise
- in France, temperatures may rise by 2°C by 2050, with 15 per cent less rainfall in summer and 20 per cent more in winter. There may be a drop in winter snow for ski fields while in coastal areas, erosion and rising sea levels will impact upon the environment
- water shortages in the tourism sector may be exacerbated, as Kent *et al.* (2002) discuss in the case of Majorca, and as explored in Insight 22.1.

IMAGE 18.4 Coral reefs on the Great Barrier Reef are under significant threat from climate change

A number of global organizations are currently working in the field of global warming as experts begin to understand how climate change may lead to reverses in the shape of seasonality, with a growing demand for coolness in summer, leading to increased energy consumption for air conditioning, along with a greater number of extreme weather events which could disrupt tourism, such as flooding, sandstorms, droughts and summer fires. These challenges are nowhere more serious than for many Small Island Developing States (SIDS) (see Chapter 24). As UN–WTO (2012) demonstrate, many such SIDS in the Caribbean, the Pacific Ocean and Indian Ocean are among the most vulnerable environments to climate change. As many have a high dependence upon tourism issues such as the availability of fresh water, threats to food production and their fragile ecosystems mean they are extremely vulnerable to the consequences of climate change (i.e. changes in temperature of between 1.4 and 3.7°C, long dry seasons punctuated by heavy rain episodes and extreme weather events) which will disrupt the tourism economy. Above all this highlights the need for stakeholders (e.g. governments, the tourism sector, tourists and other bodies as well as scientists) to develop solutions to this global problem. However, one of the biggest stumbling blocks remains the reliance upon fossil fuel, and the rapid industrialization of developing countries such as China which poses major problems for progress towards reducing energy consumption, as China is expanding its demand for fuel and energy at an exponential rate. As recent studies show (e.g. Scott *et al.* 2007), climate change is among one of the most complex environmental issues to address, and the role of *mitigation* (i.e. reducing impacts) and *adaptation* (i.e. adapting how tourism operates) are important: measures to take including carbon management as a form of mitigation (Gössling 2010), a theme we will revisit in the next chapter.

Conclusion

Many environmental impacts resulting from tourism have been acknowledged. In some cases, programmes of work have been established to reduce these effects and a pledge towards developing more responsible forms of tourism has been made. In other instances, effects are less well known and/or accepted by those who seek to gain maximum economic benefits, regardless of the environmental costs. It is likely that the future will involve closer examination of environmental impacts, as the case of climate change has shown – the environmental impacts of tourism have come centre stage. Research is at a relatively early stage of development and there is still much work to be undertaken to establish clear knowledge of cause, effect, systems and interactions, but tourism's polluting role and massive fossil fuel consumption is now being recognized through techniques such as eco-efficiency and ecological footprinting, both of which we will examine in the next chapter. Wider uptake of auditing procedures and improvements in corporate environmental management through legislation and consumer demand will invoke a higher degree of environmental consciousness in tourism-based enterprises. These aspects are more fully discussed in Chapter 20.

Discussion questions

1 Why might it be argued that the ultimate success of tourism relies on an understanding of the environmental impacts?

2 Argue the case that tourism and the environment are mutually beneficial.

3 Which impacts are more serious – those which directly affect the physical environment or those which directly affect tourist enjoyment?

4 To what extent is the tourist responsible for environmental impacts of tourism?

References

Amelung, B. and Viner, D. (2006) 'Mediterranean tourism: Exploring the future with the Tourism Climatic Index', *Journal of Sustainable Tourism*, 14 (4): 349–366.

Cater, E. (1993) 'Ecotourism in the Third World: Problems for sustainable tourism development', *Tourism Management*, 14 (2): 85–90.

Cordrey, L. (ed.) (n.d.) *The Biodiversity of the South West. An Audit of the South West Biological Resource.* RSPB and County Wildlife Trusts and South West Regional Planning Conference.

D'Cruze, N., Niehaus, C., Balaskas, M., Vieto, R., Carder, G., Richardson, V. A., Moorhouse, T., Harrington, L. and Macdonald, D. W. (2018) 'Wildlife tourism in Latin America: Taxonomy and conservation status', *Journal of Sustainable Tourism*, 26 (9): 1562–1576.

Department for Transport (2018) *Aviation 2050: The Future of UK Aviation: A Consultation.* London: HMSO.

Doswell, R. (1997) Tourism: *How Effective Management Makes a Difference.* Oxford: Butterworth-Heinemann.

Edington, J.M. and Edington, M.A. (1986) *Ecology, Recreation and Tourism.* Cambridge: Cambridge University Press.

English Tourist Board and Employment Department Group (1991) *Tourism and the Environment: Maintaining the Balance.* London: English Tourist Board and Employment Department Group.

European Environment Agency (1998) *Europe's Environment: The Second Assessment.* Luxembourg: OOPEC.

Farrell, B.H. and Runyan, D. (1991) 'Ecology and tourism', *Annals of Tourism Research,* 18 (1): 26–40.

Gössling, S. (2002) 'Global environmental consequences of tourism', *Global Environmental Change*, 12 (4): 283–302.

Gössling, S. (2010) *Carbon Management in Tourism: Mitigating the Impacts on Climate Change.* London: Routledge.

Gössling, S., Broderick, J., Upham, P., Ceron, J.P., Dubois, G., Peeters, P. and Strasdas, W. (2007) 'Voluntary carbon offsetting schemes for aviation: Efficiency, credibility, and sustainable tourism', *Journal of Sustainable Tourism*, 15 (3): 223–248.

Gössling, S. and Hall, C.M. (2006) *Global Environmental Problems. Tourism?* London: Routledge.

Gössling, S. and Peeters, P. (2007) 'It does not harm the environment! An analysis of industry discourses on tourism, air travel and the environment', *Journal of Sustainable Tourism*, 15 (4): 402–417.

Gössling, S., Peeters, P., Ceron, J., Dubois, Patterson, T. and Richardson, R. (2005) 'The eco-efficiency of tourism', *Ecological Economics*, 54 (4): 417–434.

18

Hall, C.M. and Higham, J. (eds.) (2005) Tourism, Recreation and Climate Change. Clevedon: Channel View.

Higgins-Desbiolles, F., Carnicelli, S., Krolikowski, C., Wijesinghe, G. and Boluk, K. (2019) 'Degrowing tourism: Rethinking tourism', *Journal of Sustainable Tourism,* 27 (12): 1926–1944.

Holden, A. and Fennell, D. (eds.) (2012) *The Routledge Handbook of Tourism and the Environment.* London: Routledge

Kavallinis, I. and Pizam, A. (1994) 'The environmental impacts of tourism – whose responsibility is it anyway? The case study of Mykonos', *Journal of Travel Research,* 23 (2): 26–32.

Kent, M., Newnham, R. and Essex, S. (2002) 'Tourism and sustainable water supply in Mallorca: A geographical analysis', *Applied Geography,* 22 (4): 351–374.

Koenen, J.P., Chon, K.S. and Christianson, D.J. (1995) 'Effects of tourism growth on air quality: The case of Las Vegas', *Journal of Sustainable Tourism,* 3 (3): 135–142.

Krippendorf., J. (1987) *The Holidaymakers.* Oxford: Butterworth-Heinemann.

Mathieson, A. and Wall, G. (1982) *Tourism. Economic, Physical and Social Impacts.* Harlow: Longman.

Mieczkowski, Z. (1995) *Environmental Issues of Tourism and Recreation.* Lanham, MY: University Press of America.

Nepal, S. (2005) 'Tourism and remote mountain settlements: Spatial and temporal development of tourist infrastructure in the Mount Everest region, Nepal', *Tourism Geographies,* 7 (2): 205–227.

Page, S.J., Essex, S. and Causevic, S. (2014) 'Tourist attitudes towards water use in the developing world: A comparative analysis', *Tourism Management Perspectives,* 10: 57–67.

Patterson, T., Bastianoni, S. and Simpson, M. (2006) 'Tourism and climate change: Two-way street, or vicious/virtuous circle', *Journal of Sustainable Tourism,* 14 (4): 339–348.

Prunier, E., Sweeney, A. and Geen, A. (1993) 'Tourism and the environment: The case of Zakynthos', *Tourism Management,* 14 (2): 137–141.

Royal Commission on Environmental Pollution (2002) *The Environmental Effects of Civil Aircraft in Flight.* London: HMSO.

Schuhmann, P.W., Skeete, R., Waite, R., Lorde, T., Bangwayo-Skeete, P., Oxenford, H., Gill, D., Moore, W. and Spencer, F. (2019) 'Visitors' willingness to pay marine conservation fees in Barbados', *Tourism Management,* 71: 315–326.

Scott, D., Amelung, B., Bechen, S., Ceron, J., Dubois, G., Gössling, Peters, P. and Simpson, M. (2007) *Climate Change and Tourism: Responding to Global Challenges.* Madrid: UN–World Tourism Organization.

Sindiga, I. and Kanuhah, M. (1999) 'Unplanned tourism development in sub-Saharan Africa with special reference to Kenya', *Journal of Tourism Studies,* 10 (1): 25–39.

Theroux, P. (1996) *The Pillars of Hercules.* London: Penguin.

UN–WTO (2012) *Climate Change and Tourism – Responding to Global Challenges.* Madrid: UN–WTO.

Wall, G. and Mathieson, A. (2006) *Tourism: Change, Impacts, and Opportunities.* Harlow: Pearson.

Wood, S. and House, K. (1991) *The Good Tourist.* London: Mandarin.

WTO (2003) *The Djerba Declaration on Tourism and Climate Change.* Madrid: World Tourism Organization.

WWF (2002) 'Ecological footprint'. WWF (website). https://footprint.wwf.org.uk.

Young, G. (1973) *Tourism: Blessing or Blight?* Harmondsworth: Penguin.

Further reading

Books

Chen, J. and Prebensen, N. (eds.) (2017) *Nature Tourism.* London: Routledge.

Epler-Wood, M. (2017) *Sustainable Tourism on a Finite Planet.* London: Earthscan.

Holden, A. and Fennell, D. (eds.) (2013) *The Routledge Handbook of Tourism and the Environment.* London: Routledge.

Sharpley, R. (2009) *Tourism Development and the Environment.* London: Routledge.

Journal articles

Buckley, R. (2011) 'Tourism and environment', *Annual Review of Environment and Resources,* 36: 397–416.

Marsiglio, S. (2015) 'On the carrying capacity and the optimal number of visitors in tourism destinations', *Tourism Economics* 23 (3): 632–646.

The challenge of sustainability

Learning outcomes

After reading this chapter and answering the questions, you should be able to:

- understand the principles of sustainable development
- outline the approaches used to define the term sustainable tourism
- identify forms of sustainable practice in managing tourism development and activity
- evaluate the challenges in achieving sustainable tourism.

Overview

One of the most important aspects of tourism in the twenty-first century is reducing the negative impacts of tourist-related development and activity, while improving environmental performance within tourism operations and maximizing benefits for local communities. This aspect of tourism management is known as 'sustainable tourism', an idea that has become a central facet of tourism policy in both developed- and developing-world contexts. The premise of sustainable tourism is to protect the resources on which tourism relies, although it is a complex concept and its implementation is challenging. This chapter explores the principles of sustainable development, the implications for tourism and the evolution and progress in developing practices that address social and environmental agendas in local and global contexts.

Introduction

In the early years of mass tourism development, there was little recognition of tourism as an activity that could destroy natural environments, and negative effects were considered less important than the potentially powerful economic and developmental benefits. However, as outlined in Chapters 16 to 18, significant concerns about environmental and sociocultural impacts of tourism have prompted questions about the planning and management of tourism development and activity. As Chapter 18 illustrates, concern has been expressed in relation to global issues such as climate change and the measures that can be taken to adapt to, or mitigate, its impact (see Becken 2013). These ideas have great salience for this chapter in terms of the need to shift tourism behaviour, development, planning, policy and management towards more sustainable resource use.

The study of the relationship between tourism and environmental impacts highlights two issues:

1 *A conceptual issue*: The natural environment is exploited for commercial purposes in pursuit of human progress, and its intrinsic value and importance are little considered. Tourism in this sense is grouped with other economic activities that impact the natural environment and its resources, the implications of which are not fully understood;

2 *A business issue*: Most forms of tourism depend on the quality of the destination environment to attract tourists, so not managing the environment can lead to degradation of the resource and a decline in destination appeal and profitability.

These two issues have stimulated interest in forms of tourism practice that recognize alternative economic, environmental and social agendas since the 1970s. Underpinning this shifting interest is the principle known as sustainable development, which has become a central aspect of policies affecting a wide range of human actions in a global context. In tourism, sustainable development principles are translated into a field of interest known as sustainable tourism, which focuses on minimizing negative impacts while maximizing the more positive aspects of tourism activity that can help to sustain human and natural resources over the longer term (Image 19.1). Some studies have gone as far as to argue that sustainable tourism is the most researched area of tourism with over 5000 articles produced up to 2012 and one that has continued to expand in scale and breadth (see Ruhanen *et al.* 2015). The consequence is that the field of study has become difficult to navigate and controversially raises the question of whether such a large output has generated research with real impact on global policy or practice. Compare this to the huge impact of one schoolgirl, Greta Thunberg, who in August 2018 protested about climate change outside the Swedish Parliament (see Thunberg 2019). In March 2019, her campaigning went global and was taken up by approximately 1.4 million students in 112 countries with a series of strikes and protests. These protests gave voice to young people concerned about their future and helped to get governments to recognize the climate emergency posed by climate change. Gaining the world's attention and vocalizing how thinking and behaviour around climate change must change has become a hot issue. Beyond the academic world, leadership in sustainable tourism-related activity has been boosted by visionary leaders that understand the power of the green lobby and the need to adapt mainstream business practices towards future-proofed propositions as consumer trends change. Two examples illustrate this:

1 Plastic pollution has become a widely acknowledged problem (see also Chapter 22 on coastal pollution and plastics), and public horror at the infiltration of plastic in the environment has started to shift thinking and practice. This is often attributed to the impact of David Attenborough's BBC TV programme *Blue Planet 2*, which graphically highlighted the massive global scourge of plastic and micro-plastics in our oceans and the impact on marine creatures and habitats: a wake-up call to a non-expert audience. Wider actions relating to plastic waste are outlined in Insight 19.1.

2 The Governor of the Bank of England in July 2019 (Busby 2019) pointed to the mounting costs of economic dependence upon fossil fuels and/or activity that is vulnerable to climate change. Global capital and finance will judge where green investment needs to supplant higher-risk economic activity. This idea supports an earlier report by UN–WTO and UNEP (2012) that suggests that investment in green alternatives could stimulate the value of tourism beyond a 'business-as-usual' scenario, as well as reducing resource consumption and negative impacts.

These two examples illustrate more than ever before that climate change and environmental impacts are associated with unsustainable living and highly consumptive lifestyles that cannot be sustained (such as taking multiple holidays every year). The climate emergency is now seen as directly impacting tourism (see Table 19.1).

INSIGHT 19.1   Using nudge behaviour to address environmental problems – plastic use

An important concept is the notion of nudge behaviour to make us change our habits. As UNEP (2017: n.p.) argued, 'Nudges can take many forms, but describe policy design choices or actions that apply insights from behavioural science to improve consumers' existing choices', to make them more environmentally friendly. One good example is the move away from single-use plastics such as non-biodegradable plastic bags, bottled water, coffee cups, straws and polystyrene food containers, which have become socially unacceptable in a very rapid time period.

An EU ban on single-use plastic items such as straws, stirrers and cutlery comes into force in 2021. Environmental pioneers have raised popular awareness through the media, most notably Ellen MacArthur and Hugh Fearnley-Whittingstall, by challenging companies to rethink their reliance on plastic.

But how is the global tourism industry tackling the plastic problem?

- A growing number of music festivals are working towards plastic-free status by, for example, banning single-use plastics, swapping to bio-glitter and asking attendees to take home and reuse tents (see Association of Independent Festivals for more information; https://www.ukfestivalguides.com/aif/). Innovative enterprises have seized opportunities to collect discarded tents and other materials to send to aid organizations or repurpose into new products.

- Tour operators, hotels and airlines are starting to respond to the plastic crisis (see UNEP 2019). Most commonly, major hotel groups have removed plastic straws and stirrers (see e.g. Four Seasons Hotels), while some plan to be fully single-use-plastic-free within a short period (see e.g. Akayrn Hotel Group in South-East Asia). Thomas Cook's #noplaceforplastic campaign launched in 2018 included a scheme in Rhodes to collect discarded plastics left by holidaymakers, like pool inflatables that could be repurposed into new products, such as bags. Airlines such as Etihad and Alaska Airlines are striving to eliminate plastic use, while in the budget market Ryanair have set out a five-year plan to become plastic free by 2023 and are introducing wooden cutlery and other initiatives.

- Whole cities and tourist destinations have banned single-use plastics – examples include Seattle, Bali and

Capri. This approach may be far more effective than relying on individual behaviour alone, as UNEP (2017: n.p.) argued that a chasm exists between our good environmental intentions and actual actions – an intention–action gap. This explains why our pro-environmental attitudes may not necessarily be followed through with action. The problem is compounded in tourism, where pro-environmental behaviours at home are not replicated on holiday.

Further reading

Heidbreder, L.M., Bablok, I., Drews, S. and Menzel, C. (2019) 'Tackling the plastic problem: A review on perceptions, behaviors, and interventions', *Science of the Total Environment*, 668: 1077–1093.

Lehner, M., Mont, O. and Heiskanen, E. (2016) 'Nudging – A promising tool for sustainable consumption behaviour?' *Journal of Cleaner Production*, 134 (A): 166–177.

UNEP (2017) 'Nudge to action: Behavioural science for sustainability', *UN Environment Programme* (website). https://www.unenvironment.org/news-and-stories/story/nudge-action-behavioural-science-sustainability.

UNEP (2019) 'Paradise lost? Travel and tourism industry takes aim at plastic pollution but more action needed', *UN Environment Programme* (website). http://web.unep.org/environmentassembly/paradise-lost-travel-and-tourism-industry-takes-aim-plastic-pollution-more-action-needed.

World Economic Forum, Ellen MacArthur Foundation and McKinsey & Company (2016) *The New Plastics Economy - Rethinking the Future of Plastics*. http://www.ellenmacarthurfoundation.org/publications.

Questions

1 Why is nudging needed with respect to environmental issues?

2 How might nudging be used with reference to reducing holiday consumerism? What resistance might there be to this?

3 Why is a destination approach to environmental issues important?

4 Are there methods you can think of that might bridge the intention–action gap in relation to tourism?

Interest and activity in sustainable tourism is increasingly widespread across the public sector and in the tourism sector, while consumer-related research suggests a growing awareness of sustainability issues among tourists. The scale of the climate emergency declared in 2019, initially by the UK government and then by other countries, has brought sustainability-related issues into everyone's consciousness through the global media. In many ways this has

TABLE 19.1	Dimensions of the climate crisis in 2019 and the effect on tourism

Climate change crisis issue	Impact on tourism
Melting glaciers in the Arctic region, and Iceland launching a memorial in August 2019 to the loss of the first of 400 glaciers (Glacier Okjokull)	Loss of a major element of the county's visitor economy
Wildfires in Alaska and Russia in the summer of 2019 attributed to a dryer and hotter summer season, emitting more CO_2 emissions than Sweden in a given year	Loss of ecological diversity and landscapes of pristine wilderness for tourism
Warming of the UK average temperature by 0.9°C between 2003 and 2019 compared to average temperatures 1961–1990	Greater dependence upon fossil fuels to cool tourist environments like hotels with air conditioning to address the tourist comfort index
Reliance upon non-sustainable resources for everyday consumption (e.g. the World Wide Fund for Nature (see Alessi and Di Carlo 2018) estimates 7 million coffee cups are thrown away every day in the UK; 1 in 2 marine turtles have plastic in their stomachs; climate change is impacting upon the habitats of many endangered species)	Increased pressure to see disappearing species and places through 'last-chance tourism' and unsustainable tourist behaviours of detriment to pristine tourism environments through plastic pollution and species loss
The UK Committee on Climate Change indicated 1.5 billion trees need to be planted to reach the net zero emissions target the government set for 2050. This requires 30 000 hectares to be planted every year compared to the current 13 400 hectares	Landscape change and new environments for tourism activities and different visual characteristics in tourist preferences for places to visit
Increase in extreme weather events (e.g. cyclone in Mozambique and Tanzania – Cyclone Kenneth killing 1000 and displacing 3 million people and a drought in South Africa 2018–2019 in the Western Cape)	Disruption to the tourism sector due to a cyclone disaster and loss of tourism opportunities; in Western Cape, water restrictions on water consumption for tourists who are normally far more consumptive than local residents and selected businesses which had water contingency plans in place
Heatwave in Europe in July 2019	Trains were placed on slow running and were subject to running restrictions due to points failures and signal issues disrupting tourist travel; cracks in roads and road surfaces limiting travel; sinking water levels in the River Danube making it barely navigable while cruises depend on the flow of this river; if temperatures rise above 47°C there are potential risks to aircraft being grounded, as has happened previously in Arizona, due to safety issues
Australian bushfires in 2019/2020	A dry spring, drought conditions, hot temperatures and a build-up of combustible material in the bush areas contributed to conditions for the country's worst recorded bushfires. Estimates of the economic impact on the fires are placed at more than $AU 4.4 billion, after 8.9 million hectares of the country were affected by the fires, exceeding the 400 000 hectares affected in 2009 fires. Smoke and haze leading to poor air quality from the fires reduced visitation in the peak season for tourism. Visitor evacuations from sites such as Kangaroo Island and other destinations impacted visitor confidence. Tourism Australia also paused its advertising campaign in the UK (see Chapter 16). This will have caused major reputational damage to the tourism image of the country

19

rekindled the environmental protest movement of the late 1960s and early 1970s with sustainable resource use at its heart. However, evidence has shown that the application of sustainable principles in tourism is beset with challenges, especially with the year-on-year global growth in tourism demand and supply.

As previously mentioned, since the 1990s sustainable tourism has been one of the most prevalent areas of academic tourism research, a feature reflected in the comprehensive review by Page and Connell (2008), and there is even a journal dedicated to the topic (the *Journal of Sustainable Tourism*). In parallel, government and non-governmental organizations have been active in developing strategies to engage with sustainable tourism ideas. Thus, this is a very active area of interest for academic study and practitioners. Prior to exploring the concept and practice of sustainable tourism, this chapter turns to the context of sustainability and the evolution of environmental perspectives to help position contemporary practice and ways of thinking, to illustrate the principles, ideas and origin of this mode of thinking.

The rise of environmental concern

Our understanding of sustainability in the twenty-first century has a long and fascinating developmental history (see Pepper 1996 for a detailed exploration of the evolution of environmentalism). It is often believed that sustainability is a recent invention but the roots of concern about the human impact on the environment can be traced back to ancient civilizations (Hardy *et al.* 2002). Ancient Greek literature reveals a philosophy of the Earth as a living goddess (Gaia), while written evidence exists of land degradation and soil erosion in Roman times. In sixteenth- and seventeenth-century Europe, the dominant view of the environment emerged based on the idea of mastery over nature, conquering the natural environment and using its resources for human progress. This view is known as the imperial or **anthropocentric** perspective on the environment and it has dominated human thinking to the present day. Conversely, the scientific study of nature from around the late 1700s promoted an understanding of the interrelationships of the natural world and a valuing of flora and fauna, a perspective known as the Arcadian, or **ecocentric perspective**, as illustrated in Figure 19.1. The anthropocentric view still remains dominant, with supporters of continued growth in GDP and economic activity arguing that future technological solutions will solve environmental problems, not least climate change, by reducing CO_2 emissions. This perspective is readily illustrated in the arguments for expanding aviation and airport capacity globally.

In the early period of industrialization in the Western world, critics began to question the implications of industrial and population growth and to challenge the dominant world view of uncontrolled economic growth without respect to environmental capacity. This has shaped thinking on how environmental issues have contributed to building the concept of sustainability, which can be represented as a series of waves. Figure 19.2 depicts the upward trajectory of environmentalism, with indicative examples of how specific tipping points (i.e. the point at which a series of small changes or specific incidents contribute to a much more profound change) were reached through key events that accelerated the growth in environmental awareness and actions.

The academic discipline **ecology** became recognized from the 1850s, particularly following the publication of Darwin's *On the Origin of Species* in 1859, which emphasized the complex interrelations in the natural world, and gave rise to a new era in environmental thinking. While the early science of global warming emerged in the nineteenth century, this burgeoning awareness did little to change the course and impact of

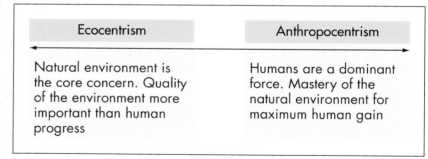

FIGURE 19.1 A simplified illustration of environmental thinking

industrialization. As Figure 19.2 suggests, the rapid social, environmental and economic changes of the nineteenth century stimulated resource management and preservation, best exemplified by the emergence of wilderness preservation societies and early proponents of the National Parks movement in North America (e.g. John Muir) who were concerned about the infiltration of exploitative industries in natural areas. Yellowstone was the first National Park (1872) (see also Chapter 2), followed by the Royal National Park in Australia (1879), Banff National Park in Canada (1885) and in New Zealand, Tongariro National Park (1887). There are now over 4000 National Parks globally,

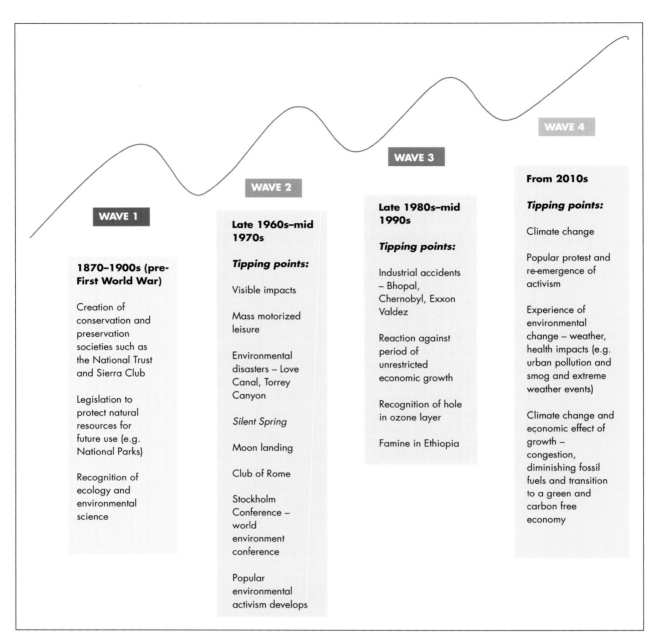

FIGURE 19.2 Waves of popular environmental interest

and a much larger number of protected areas, for example 3000 such areas in Africa alone. These are often highly valued tourism and recreational environments, but significant management and investments are required to conserve resources and deal with visitor impacts.

In the early twentieth century, groups dedicated to preserving and conserving habitats, species, built heritage and access to open areas were formed (e.g. the National Trust of England and Wales in 1895). Like National Parks, many of these protected sites are now key resources for tourism and recreation. Conservation issues, as Figure 19.2 shows, arose in the 1930s in many countries, not least Australia, where the culling of 4.1 million koalas from 1915 to 1927 saw the species become extinct in South Australia. Similar concerns were also raised about mammal conservation, with the hunting of the thylacine (also referred to as the Tasmanian tiger or wolf) to extinction by 1930.

It was not until the 1960s that environmental change became high profile in a social and political sense. Policies for economic growth post-1945 worked on the premise of 'maximum utility': the more goods the industrial system produced, the more satisfied consumers would be. While the age of consumerism and industrial production did little to recognize environmental responsibility, the conventions of economic growth began to be particularly questioned following several high-profile environmental catastrophes (such as the *Torrey Canyon* oil disaster in 1967). The contemporary environmental movement was born at this time and many global environmental pressure groups, including Friends of the Earth and Greenpeace, originate from this period. For example, in Australia, the damming projects in the 1970s (e.g. Lake Pedder and Franklin dam) inspired the world's first political party to focus on green issues, while the Keep Australia Beautiful (n.d.) movement was established to respond to the growing waste problems linked to consumer goods. Political leaders had little choice but to acknowledge that complex and significant problems had developed and solutions must be debated. Eventually, these discussions developed into the concept of 'sustainable development'.

The emergence of sustainability as a concept

Advocates of a new approach to the economy and the environment included a range of renowned academics, from economists (e.g. J.K. Galbraith) to biologists (see particularly Rachel Carson's book *Silent Spring* (1962), which became a bestseller) and ecologists (e.g. Garrett Hardin's (1968) application of the tragedy of the commons), as well as pressure groups working at global and local levels. By this point, the interconnections between environmental and societal issues were acknowledged politically, and increasingly appeared on the agendas of government and intergovernmental agencies, most notably in these major milestones that bring us up to the present day:

- 1972: representatives from the governments and non-governmental organizations of 119 countries met to consider environmental problems at the United Nations (UN) Conference on the Human Environment in Stockholm. The outcome was agreement that development and the environment could exist together in mutual benefit but not how this might be achieved.

- 1980: the International Union for the Conservation of Nature and Natural Resources (IUCN) published the World Conservation Strategy, which promoted sustainable development principles.

- 1984: the UN General Assembly appointed the World Commission on Environment and Development – headed by the Norwegian Prime Minister Gro Harlem Brundtland – to explore environmental and development philosophies and put forward proposals for change and action. The resulting publication *Our Common Future* (1987) set out critical objectives for the future of economic growth and the environment, stating that governments would have to make some painful decisions. One of the significant outcomes of this report was that it popularized the term 'sustainable development', a concept which has come to underpin social and environmental policy and practice ever since.

- 1988: Intergovernmental Panel on Climate Change (IPCC) established to assess climate change and its implications, and set out recommendations for action.

- 1992: UN Conference on Environment and Development, Rio de Janeiro (known as the Earth Summit), the first major global conference designed to co-ordinate global activities and encourage collaboration between countries and organizations. This created Agenda 21, an action plan for sustainable development, subsumed by the more recent Sustainable Development Goals (2015); and the UN Framework Convention on Climate Change (UNFCCC) – the signatories to which continue to meet at Conferences of the Parties (COP) events.

- 1997: the Kyoto Protocol (UNFCCC) established binding obligations on signatory countries to reduce greenhouse gases.

- 2000: Millennium Summit, New York: set out the Millennium Development Goals (MDGs) to reduce poverty, hunger and disease, with targets to reach by 2015.

- 2002: UN World Summit on Sustainable Development, Johannesburg (known as Rio + 10) focusing on sustainable production and consumption. Tourism mentioned explicitly in Chapter 43 of the *Implementation of the Johannesburg Summit Plan* as a means to benefit host communities while protecting cultural, natural and heritage resources. Sustainable tourism development and capacity-building to strengthen rural communities, particularly those in the developing world as well as countries with economies in transition, was recognized.

- 2012: UN Conference on Sustainable Development, Rio de Janeiro (known as Rio + 20) was the biggest ever UN conference. The major document produced, entitled *The Future We Want*, recognized significant failings in the policies developed at Rio in 1992 and that global problems had become more acute. One of the main strategies identified was the green economy concept (see Jiang *et al.* 2013), focusing on ways of mainstreaming sustainable development, harnessing green innovations and contributing to social and

19

environmental enrichment. Tourism was highlighted as a cross-sector theme that had further potential to contribute to sustainable development.

- 2011: Durban Conference and Climate Change Summit (COP17) to discuss the end of the Kyoto Protocol in 2012. The Momentum for Change initiative was launched to identify transformative carbon reducing schemes across the world.
- 2012: Doha conference, Qatar (COP18), with a commitment to uphold the Kyoto Protocol principles to 2020.
- 2014: IPCC launches 5th Assessment of Climate Change Report; UN celebrates 20 years of the Framework Convention on Climate Change to make climate change a global issue of consideration.
- 2015: UN Sustainable Development Conference, New York, 'Transforming Our World: The 2030 Agenda for Sustainable Development' created 17 goals known as the Sustainable Development Goals, with 169 targets, adopted by all UN member states (see Hall 2019 for a critique).
- 2016: COP21 Paris Agreement achieved agreement to target climate warming to well below 2°C above pre-industrial levels and to pursue efforts to limit the temperature increase even further to 1.5°C.
- 2017: COP22 in Marrakesh where nations pledged to move the COP21 agreement forward, while at the Bonn meeting (COP23) the USA announced its decision to leave the Paris Agreement.
- 2019: IPCC launches its 1.5°C goal to reduce climate warming (see IPCC 2018).
- 2019: UK Parliament first in the world to declare a climate emergency.
- 2020: COP26 in Glasgow to create a global response to the climate emergency.

This selective outline merely notes some of the more central events in the recent history of sustainable development thinking at an international level and the policy directions that are required. Nevertheless, one of the most pressing issues is finding an agreement about the meaning and application of sustainability in existing economic structures.

Defining sustainability

The question 'what is sustainability?' has led to much controversy and debate in terms of scientific concept, philosophy and practical application. The most widely accepted definition of sustainable development is: *Development that meets the needs of the present without compromising the needs of future generations* (World Commission on Environment and Development 1987: 8). While this definition sounds simple, the interpretation and application of the concept proves much more problematic. Broadly, sustainable development allows for economic development but within the parameters of resource conservation. However, the concept can be interpreted in different ways: at one extreme is economic sustainability where primarily the economy is sustained, while diametrically opposed is ecological sustainability, where the natural environment takes priority. The basic principles of sustainable development include:

1 Using resources only at a rate which allows replacement and within environmental capacity.

2 Development that does not enrich one group of people over another (between existing groups in time/space and intergenerational equity).

3 Overriding economic growth and development with sustainable growth and development (i.e. by adhering to points 1 and 2 above).

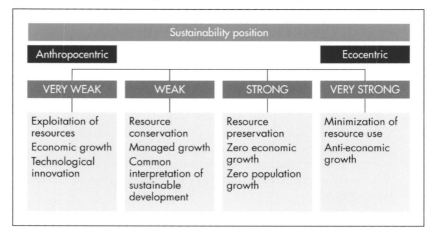

FIGURE 19.3 Degrees of sustainability

Source: Adapted from Turner *et al.* (1994)

In a world based primarily on capitalist structures, shifting to this mode of development is difficult. Therefore, achieving sustainability is unlikely under current market conditions but must be worked towards as a goal. One approach that helps to identify progress towards this goal is the concept of degrees of sustainability. Turner *et al.*'s (1994) classic spectrum of sustainable development defines positions from 'very weak' sustainability to 'very strong' sustainability, as illustrated in Figure 19.3.

Furthermore, the deep ecology movement spearheaded by Arne Naess highlights the distinction between shallow ecology and deep ecology, an idea which is reflected in tourism by Acott *et al.*'s (1998) depiction of deep and shallow forms of ecotourism. The differentiation between types of sustainability is more than a simple academic exercise: we need to be conscious of activities and practices that are labelled as sustainable and be prepared to look critically at their content and impact. More fundamentally, one of the problems of sustainable development (and sustainable tourism) is that concepts do not necessarily represent an absolute standard. So, how can we make sense of sustainable development principles in a tourism context? What, precisely, is 'sustainable tourism'?

What is sustainable tourism?

In the classic text *The Holidaymakers*, Krippendorf (1987) argued that if individuals could be persuaded to stay at home rather than go on holiday, they may be encouraged to improve their own environment rather than escape from it and damage another elsewhere. Krippendorf argues for greater 'humanism' in life, of which tourism is just one small component. The idea of humanism seeks to reverse trends of consumerism and encourage greater satisfaction in non-consumptive forms of activity. While committed environmentalists argue that truly environmentally aware individuals should spurn holidays altogether, the shift from industrial to post-industrial society has created increasingly high and diverse levels of consumer demand and expectation. Instead of finding satisfaction in one annual domestic holiday, more affluent, educated and sophisticated travellers are seeking a larger and more diverse range of tourism experiences, so fuelling the environmental crisis. Cohen *et al.* (2011), for example, discuss the phenomenon of 'binge flying'. Tourism has become an integral part of modern society, and while it may be environmentally desirable to reduce or limit tourism in the interests of climate change, attempts to do so without legislation will be futile. Commonly, sustainable tourism is conceptualized as not preventing tourism but to explore alternative ways of developing, operating and managing the destinations, facilities and services (Image 19.1) that form the fundamental part of the tourism product.

The broad response to addressing the environmental crisis as it affects tourism is the development of sustainable tourism. Since the 1980s, a growing range of international reports, actions and declarations on sustainable tourism have been published, spearheaded by the UN–WTO at an international level. This activity has generated a large volume of literature on tourism, although much of it reworks the same basic ideas (see Liu 2003; Page and Connell 2008; and Buckley 2012 for reviews). Initially, sustainable tourism was considered to be most relevant in the countryside, where the relationship between the visitor and the natural environment is most clearly observed (see chapter 21 on rural tourism). This led to a concentration on what was generally termed 'green tourism' – the 'green' emphasizing use and conservation of natural resources. In the UK, the first major event focusing on green tourism was the 1990 conference *Shades of Green – Working Towards Green Tourism in the Countryside* held in Leeds. Sponsored by the Countryside Commission, the English Tourist Board and the Rural Development Commission, the objective was to encourage good practice in rural tourism, defined as tourism that respects the environment and community. In this respect, 'green tourism' was nothing new. Walking, cycling, staying in small-scale accommodation, eating local food, using public transport, observing

IMAGE 19.1 Resort development often modifies natural coastal environments and makes them unsustainable. At Denarau Island, Fiji, concrete is required to protect the artificial sea wall

19

wildlife – these activities, encouraged by green tourism marketing initiatives, are acutely traditional. The new element is business development, research and marketing of these environmentally friendly activities. Since the 1990s, the 'green' term has been replaced by the generic term 'sustainable tourism' in recognition of the wider objectives of the concept.

Defining sustainable tourism

It is clear that sustainable tourism is a nebulous concept and to some extent has become moulded to fit the needs of conservationists, governments, communities and developers. Thus, there is no universally accepted definition, but in 2004 the UN–WTO did attempt to address this vast range of definitions by establishing that sustainability principles apply to environmental, economic and sociocultural aspects of tourism, so that a suitable balance needs to be achieved between these interconnected elements to guarantee the long-term sustainability of tourism. The UN–WTO outlined that sustainable tourism should:

- make optimal use of environmental resources (while maintaining essential ecological processes and helping to conserve natural heritage and biodiversity)
- respect the sociocultural authenticity of host communities (helping to conserve the cultural heritage and traditional values as well as seeking to engender intercultural understanding and tolerance)
- ensure viable, long-term economic operations, providing socio-economic benefits to all stakeholders
- provide for the ongoing monitoring of the impacts of tourism, allowing preventive or corrective measures to be taken when needed, as well as seeking to maintain high levels of tourist satisfaction and awareness of sustainability issues.

What this indicates is that the main remit of sustainable tourism is to find an equilibrium between the needs of the host community, tourists and the environment. This relationship is at the core of sustainable tourism principles and requires careful consideration to maximize positive benefits and minimize negative effects. As such, sustainable tourism does not imply a 'no-growth' policy, but it does recognize that limits to growth exist and that destinations must be managed with a long-term view. Clarke (1997) suggests four ways in which sustainability in tourism can be viewed:

- as polar opposites – where sustainable and mass tourism are at opposite ends of the spectrum
- as a continuum – where shades of sustainability and mass tourism are recognized
- as movement – where positive action can make mass tourism more sustainable
- as convergence – where all tourism strives to be sustainable, as epitomized in the paper by Weaver (2012) and subsequent debates in the journal *Tourism Management* over the logic of this position.

19

Swarbrooke (1999: 13) offers a further definition of sustainable tourism as 'tourism which is economically viable but does not destroy the resources on which the future of tourism will depend, notably the physical environment and the social fabric of the host community', observing the need to achieve a balance in the tourists' use of tourist resources and environments they visit and consume. The scope of these various approaches to defining sustainable tourism suggests why it has been hard to reach consensus over the meaning of the term, where two polarized views seem to encapsulate the main problem. These views consider sustainable tourism as:

1 *Development-centred*, focusing on sustaining the tourism industry and its economic value (i.e. sustaining the tourism industry).
2 *Ecologically centred*, emphasizing the natural environment and biodiversity over economic gain.

These terms are mutually exclusive and one of the challenges of sustainability has been to move towards establishing what the concept means for the diverse tourism industry and its stakeholders.

Sustainable tourism appears to be composed of two elements:

1 *Acting in an environmentally conscious way*. This relates to integration of environmental practices into everyday processes and operations, such as: using products which cause less harm to the environment, for example biodegradable washing powders and ozone-friendly cleaning sprays; conserving energy; minimizing waste

through purchasing package-free goods or composting and recycling (Image 19.2); using locally produced organic produce; and reducing the need to travel. These are practical kinds of activities in which individuals and businesses can participate.

2 *As an underpinning philosophy.* It constitutes a way of thinking about the environment where tourism takes place, respecting the landscape, wildlife, people, existing infrastructure and cultural heritage of a tourism destination. This is a more holistic, philosophical perspective. Figure 19.4 outlines a rationale for developing sustainable tourism which may be a useful framework for considering the principles used when sustainable tourism is put into practice.

IMAGE 19.2 Recycling is a vital aspect of sustainable practice

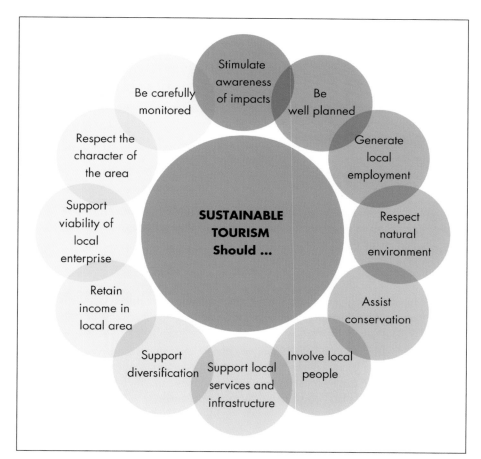

FIGURE 19.4 The role of sustainable tourism

Sustainable tourism in practice

The concept of sustainable tourism applies to a wide range of tourism ventures, operations and initiatives. The plethora of initiatives in destinations seen in a global context is a feature that Buckley (2012) attributes to reliance upon regulation rather than market measures to manage tourism. However, public sector initiatives have attempted to address market failure in relation to tourism and the environment. In practice, the delivery of sustainable tourism tends to be within two major categories:

1 Destination projects, from the setting up of small-scale social enterprises, to partnerships based on a number of interested parties working together to deliver sustainable tourism at a local, regional or even larger geographic scale.

2 Practical applications of operations and measures within tourism businesses, from micro-businesses to multinational corporations, designed to improve environmental performance. Initiatives range from simple low-cost and quick-to-implement solutions to those requiring significant capital investment, including the installation of sophisticated technology to improve environmental performance across hotel portfolios.

Sustainable tourism destination projects

Sustainable tourism projects are commonly found, and operate across a number of dimensions in time and space. Projects encompass a varied (and even disparate) range of initiatives, but what they tend to share in common are agreed objectives and/or targets usually including a set of interventions, allocation of staff to manage processes (i.e. planning, organizing, communicating changes), a clear time frame in which to achieve targets within an appropriate budget, and some mechanisms to evaluate the outcomes of the intervention. The scale of these management-related functions naturally depends on the type and scale of the initiative. Most frequently, these projects are funded and managed by local or regional government bodies in partnership with other public sector agencies, often for a limited period of time and are often in the form of:

- Regional rural projects

    These cover a large area of mainly rural districts, tend to focus on economic development with a tourism focus, and may be coupled with mechanisms for agricultural diversification, small business development and community involvement. Often, these projects are run as a partnership between public sector bodies, community organizations and private businesses with funding from larger bodies to pump-prime development.

    Example: the Alto Minho region of northern Portugal, which has a regional strategy to promote sensitive tourism development and activity that respects landscape, culture and heritage.

- District-wide projects

    Similar to regional projects in scope but usually run by a single authority (often in partnership) and covering a specific, often politically defined area or a protected area such as a National Park.

    Examples: National Park Authority projects in Kruger National Park, South Africa; Khuvsgul and Onon-Balj National Parks in Mongolia.

- Local community initiatives

    Managed by local people, sometimes in partnership with the voluntary sector and/or public sector interests, these take a 'bottom-up' rather than a 'top-down' approach and have become increasingly common in developing countries through community tourism initiatives.

    Example: the work of the Travel Foundation in Sal and Boa Vista in Capo Verde (an island off the West African coast) to bring together local interests 'to form a Destination Council, creating a culture of shared ownership and management . . . [to deliver] . . . a range of projects to support sustainable tourism practices in Sal and Boa Vista' (https://www.thetravelfoundation.org.uk/destination/cape-verde/).

- Sustainable urban tourism schemes

    Increasingly a strategy adopted by economic development and/or tourism departments in cities to reposition and rebrand tourism, enhance natural, cultural and historic features in the built environment and to stimulate a higher quality of life for city dwellers.

    Example: the Green City Initiative in Toronto, Canada; Gijion in Northern Spain.

- Destination schemes

    Building on urban tourism initiatives, declining coastal resorts, or those where environmental management has been poor, have developed regeneration strategies to engender a more sustainable approach to future tourism management. Such schemes require a holistic approach to social, political, economic and environmental change to reposition their tourism product, tackle local deprivation and address development needs alongside restoration and enhancement of physical and natural environments.

Examples: Calvià, Majorca; Malaga, Spain; Blackpool, UK. The Travel Foundation has developed the International Climate Initiative – Transforming Tourism Value Chains, led by UNEP and funded by a range of partners, which focuses on reducing tourism carbon emissions, water use and waste across the tourism supply chain in the island states of Mauritius, Saint Lucia, the Philippines and the Dominican Republic.

- Single-site visitor management

   These projects focus on a range of site-management techniques to minimize visitor impact at specific locations while allowing for visitor enjoyment and education, such as at honeypot sites, iconic attractions and World Heritage Sites.

   Examples: Niagara Falls, Canada; Uluru, Australia; Pompeii, Italy.

- Visitor attractions based on the sustainability theme, particularly those funded by grants from public sector bodies. The core attraction and built/managed elements promote sustainable principles and are designed with an educational focus in addition to fun/ entertainment aspects.

   Examples: the Eden Project, UK; the Scottish Sea Bird Centre, UK. In Paris, UGE International have installed two wind turbines at the Eiffel Tower to supply up to 10 000 kWh of electricity per year.

- Pan-country projects

   Projects that span a number of countries working in collaboration to pursue a shared vision.

   Examples: the Black Sea Sustainable Rural Tourism program set up in 2012 covering Ukraine, Turkey and Georgia, and planned to extend to Moldova, Bulgaria and Romania. A more established example is the Sustainable Model for Arctic Regional Tourism (SMART – set up in 2008) which sought to establish a number of principles for sustainable tourism (see Figure 19.5) 'to empower the tourism sector to continually innovate more sustainable tourism practices' across the Arctic region including Finland, Sweden, Canada, Alaska, Scotland, the Faroe Islands and the Arkhangelsk region of Russia.

These projects must apply the principles of sustainability to a real-world context in order to achieve credibility and the chance of long-term success in changing practice and behaviour. This process is one where the translation of ideology into policy and finally into practice is the core theme, and one that requires not just political intervention and support but innovations, applications and practical measures within the business environment to stimulate, advance and evaluate steps towards a more sustainable future.

FIGURE 19.5 Principles of Arctic tourism

Source: Developed from https://arcticwwf.org/work/people/tourism/

Tourism businesses and sustainable tourism practice

Environmental management and performance procedures are now a feature of the tourism industry but it has not always been this way. In the early 1990s, few tour operators had seriously addressed environmental issues, and most tended to follow the strategy of 'see it now before it's gone' (now debated as *last-chance tourism* in sensitive locations. See Lemelin *et al.* 2011 and Chapter 27 for more discussion on this concept). By the end of the decade, there was a greater responsiveness to environmental management and programmes for tackling problems from a business perspective which started to become more widespread. While large integrated tour operators like TUI, Thomas Cook and other conglomerates have directed resources to engage with the sustainability from several directions (e.g. environmental performance, consumer acceptance of greater commitment to the environment and corporate social responsibility measures to assist communities and resources impacted by tourism), the dominant mode of tourism production in most destinations occurs through Small to Medium Sized enterprises (SMEs), as illustrated in Chapter 12. As Kornilaki *et al.* (2019) illustrated through research on Crete, the SME is the greatest challenge from a sustainability perspective (alongside the consumer as a source of demand). Kornilaki *et al.* (2019) argue that the efficacy (i.e. the ability to produce a desired sustainability outcome) from tourism SMEs lies in two domains:

1 The importance of personal decision-making among SME owners and managers
2 The decision-making behaviour of organizations in adopting sustainability practices

although in some cases these two domains may become conflated (i.e. the term domains merge and become one as some small SMEs are owner-managed). This study shows that leadership by organizations setting the agenda as well as encouraging SME owners and managers to adopt more pro-environmental behaviours and values is necessary to shift practice further towards the objective of operating more sustainable businesses.

Thus, business responses are partially underpinned by a number of factors, including enlightened self-interest following observations of environmental decline in mass tourism destinations (such as Spanish resorts); consumer marketing opportunities to be gained from 'going green'; and, the recognition of cost savings from adopting greener practices and new technology solutions to counter escalating energy prices. Accreditation and certification schemes have been developed to assist businesses of all sizes to develop more sustainable practices and provide information to businesses as to where improvements can be introduced. In addition to the fundamental benefits of environmental improvements, such schemes add to marketing opportunities for businesses seeking a competitive edge through environmental credentials and eco-labelling.

Despite the emphasis on small scale by early exponents of sustainable tourism and the perception that SMEs might be considered more naturally as sustainable tourism advocates, larger corporations with multinational interests and access to greater financial resources have responded more quickly to pressure. Large companies representing airline, tour-operating, hotel and other travel and accommodation interests now commonly publish environmental policies and report on their performance, as well as set up initiatives (see chapters on transport and accommodation for more information). At the forefront of criticism on environmental pollution is the airline industry. While air travel can never be labelled 'sustainable', several airlines have attempted to address the sustainability agenda through a commitment to research and development, strategic investment in cleaner aircraft, new fuels, carbon offsetting schemes and funding for conservation and community projects. British Airways is a good example of an airline that has taken a lead in environmental management within the sector, as outlined by Page (2009). According to Gössling (2015), around 5 per cent of CO_2 emissions arise from tourism, and one principal strategy to address the increasing use of fossil fuels that cause the emissions is to encourage better management of carbon including promoting carbon-neutral tourism and carbon offsetting. Carbon offsetting is the process of calculating carbon emissions using tools such as the ecological footprint (see Insight 19.2) and then purchasing 'credits' from emission reduction projects. Such projects prevent the emission of or remove an equivalent amount of carbon dioxide elsewhere. In contrast, industry schemes involve carbon credits, which are a key component of emissions trading schemes, providing a way for the market to assign a monetary value to goods and services that reduce carbon emissions. So where are we at with this? A number of key studies outline the state of play with these initiatives, including:

- British Airways fund: https://www.pureleapfrog.org/british-airways-carbon-fund/
- An article in *The Conversation* (Malik and Sun 2018) which quantifies the scale of the issue
- The EU Carbon Trading Scheme: https://ec.europa.eu/clima/policies/ets_en and allocation to aviation: https://ec.europa.eu/clima/policies/eu-climate-action_en

These schemes advocate that the time has come for the Polluter Pays Principle to be enforced in travel.

In the hotel sector, adoption of environmentally friendly operations has proliferated in relation to policy and practice. One of the earliest initiatives was a proactive reference manual produced by the InterContinental Hotels

Group in 1991, giving guidelines and instructions to staff on environmental management to increase awareness of environmental concerns. The International Hotels Environment Initiative (IHE) has been operating since 1992 and is now known as the International Tourism Partnership (ITP). The ITP's Green Hotelier platform (www.greenhotelier. org) has developed from an earlier hard-copy magazine into a practical web source of advice for the hotel sector. Scandic Hotels (http://www.scandichotels.com), a large hotel chain in the Nordic region, is often cited as the industry leader in sustainability and has placed environmental policy at the core of business operations. Scandic has a strong environmental policy based on care for the environment that pervades its activities, and some of its more innovative practices include:

- close monitoring of waste, and energy and water consumption
- calculation of carbon dioxide emissions
- working only with suppliers that adhere to set environmental standards
- strict standards in relation to building and refurbishment of rooms
- operation of a sustainable social development fund.

Sustainability reporting

Performance reporting on a range of sustainability criteria has emerged as a mainstream idea for large companies and organizations. Many large tourism organizations now have environmental target and measure outputs such as greenhouse gas (GHG) emissions, water use, energy use and waste production. The World Travel and Tourism Council (WTTC) is a strong advocate for this and has produced guidance for tourism businesses about environmental, social and governance issues and the design of indicators for reporting purposes (WTTC 2017). Although this field of endeavour is still at a relatively low level of development, its scale is increasing. Various studies have begun to evaluate these activities, including Guix *et al.* (2018).

Tour operators who work at the heart of the mass tourism market are often subjected to severe criticism on the quantitative business models they adopt in relation to destinations and suppliers. While practice across the tour operator sector is variable, Budeanu (2009) argues that lack of internal resources and leadership prevent tour operators from playing a stronger role in promoting environmental actions in destination supply chains. Exceptions do exist: for example, TUI is seen as a mass market leader, promoting sustainable actions and producing annual sustainability reports (http://www.tuigroup.com). Conversely, tour operators have a bigger role to play in communication of environmental practices in host destinations where there is low awareness. One good example of this was the launch of the Tour Operator Initiative in 2000, developed with the support of UN–WTO/UNEP/UNESCO, which focused on destination co-operation and sustainability reporting, including performance indicators in sustainable tourism. Some of the largest tour operators joined the scheme (e.g. Thomas Cook and TUI), which merged with the Global Sustainable Tourism Council (GSTC) in 2014. In addition, non-governmental organizations such as the UK's Travel Foundation work with tour operators to raise awareness of environmental and social issues in destinations, and provide support, training and opportunities for tour operators seeking to engage in more sustainable activities. This is a good example of a partnership between industry, communities and non-governmental organizations working towards a common goal.

A further and relatively new area of activity is in the greening of events and festivals (see Page and Connell 2012; Jones 2018) and the increasing extension of sustainable practices in the globally expanding Meetings, Incentives, Conference and Events (MICE) industry. UNEP has produced a useful guide for meeting planners, while the Green Meeting Industry Council (GMIC) (www.gmicglobal.org), based in the USA, is an industry body dedicated to education, networking and research to assist in making the events industry more environmentally engaged.

Corporate environmental management has been seen as a source of competitive advantage and is reflected more fully in a review by Ayuso (2007) and in Insight 19.3. There are a number of tools and techniques which have been developed over the years in planning and environmental management to assess the prospective impacts of tourism projects (environmental impact assessment), measures to look at the environmental performance of businesses (environmental auditing) and the measures companies have adopted to guide their approach to sustainability (Environmental Policies and Statements). Such measures sit alongside a wider list of tools to help the sector move towards sustainable goals.

19

Business adoption of sustainable practices

A study of tourism businesses in Europe and Latin America by Tamajón and Font (2013) examined the practices adopted by businesses, which tend to be the simplest ones that are easier to take up. These are often the practices encouraged by government and NGOs, and are typically associated with activities that help businesses save money, and have an economic value to the local economy such as waste recycling, energy and water saving and encouraging customers to use local products. Types of actions were characterized as Upstream (Business to Business or B2B) and downstream (with producers), creating a sustainable supply chain management (SSCM) and promoting a new concept – the circular economy.

The circular economy

The concept of the circular economy is an emerging field of interest in many industries, notably the automotive and construction sectors but it has some salience with tourism (see Sørensen et al. 2019). The idea is one of minimizing waste by making the most of resources, as the car industry has illustrated by seeking to return many of the components at the end of their useful life to be reused in its early stages. In a more highly developed form, the notion of a car may be a series of reusable components that are replaced and returned to the manufacturer for repurposing to keep their resource use minimized. Yet these principles work on the standard linear forms of production, like making a car, and so rethinking these ideas and their application to tourism requires a different approach to resource use. Pioneering work by the Ellen MacArthur Foundation (see Ellen MacArthur Foundation n.d.) has established the scope and extent of this idea of the circular economy. The circular economy in tourism has a long way to go, as tourism has long been based on specific principles, but there is evidence that new hotel projects are beginning to embrace this idea (see Smith 2017 for more detail). One example (i.e. Airbnb) is a form of circular economy where tourists are using existing non-tourist accommodation, negating the need for new hotels and buildings, but as we will see in Chapter 20, there are examples of this causing other unintended consequences for the housing market in destinations. Most of the commentary on tourism as a circular economy industry focuses on activities promoted as sustainable tourism and so it is just new words only. This will require a fundamental rethink of the principles underpinning tourism development (e.g. circular building design and use of materials in accommodation as well as the leasing of products and services: see Jones and Wynn (2019) for a review of literature and business responses).

INSIGHT 19.2 Global environmental accreditation schemes in tourism: Greenwash or sustainable business practice?

Many Environmental Accreditation Schemes (EASs) exist in tourism, which seek to introduce a greater environmental awareness and best practice among tourism businesses. The evolution of EASs can be dated back to 1994 and the formation of Green Globe and the KEY programme in Denmark with the National Ecotourism Accreditation Programme (NEAP) in Australia in 1996 and the Green Tourism Business Scheme (GTBS) in 1997, with more recent moves to establish more specific measures such as carbon labels (see Gössling and Buckley (2016) for a review). With the proliferation of so many schemes, critics have pointed to the emergence of 'greenwashing' in tourism. Greenwash is a term coined to describe the proliferation of misleading claims which companies present about the environmental performance of their product (another term used to describe these practices is 'greensheen').

As a result of growing environmental consciousness among consumers, the EASs have sought to provide an authentic and benchmarked scheme of accreditation to avoid claims of greenwashing. This has meant that the schemes have sought to adopt scientific principles associated with environmental management to get businesses to assess their performance across their business practices in relation to issues such as waste handling, recycling, energy efficiency, water conservation and other impacts on the environment. These EASs have sought to provide a recognizable brand or logo for the members who fulfil their criteria for paid membership, to assist in advertising their products and services. This is supported to help the consumer to distinguish between greenwash green claims and those businesses that are able to legitimately verify the basis of their green credentials.

Some critics have pointed to the motivation of businesses who seek certification solely as a marketing tool (Font and Epler Wood 2007) as part of the wider sustainability business opportunity approach now being taken by tour operators to fill a demand for greener products and suppliers. Even so, as Figure 19.6 shows, there is a range of issues for tourism businesses considering joining an EAS: strategic issues (i.e. will this give my business a competitive edge?); operational issues (i.e. how much will this cost?); and what the environmental costs and benefits of an EAS would be for the business. If the business needs to understand these costs and benefits, the scope of assessment (see Figure 19.6) of these issues is very wide-ranging. Among the EASs existing in tourism, there are criticisms of the processes of accreditation where a self-audit process in which businesses rate their performance is used, and is not followed up by an annual on-site visit.

Even where on-site visits occur, low levels of business adoption have been attributed to the length of time it can take for businesses to be assessed. There is also no harmonization of the EASs globally, with some opting for a single level of certification (membership) and others creating multi-level schemes. The cost of membership is also seen as prohibitively expensive for many organizations. Of greater concern for businesses is the value of such EASs in improving their performance (over and above cost savings from improved environmental performance such as reduced energy costs). There is a great variation in how these schemes operate, and the impact at a country level (with the exception of the GTBS in Scotland and Green Key in Denmark) has been relatively modest in their penetration to tourism businesses. In many cases, the perceived barriers to joining are a reflection of how complex EASs have become. Businesses are faced with a variety of schemes and few examples exist of case studies that are able to demonstrate how membership has generated additional business and a competitive advantage that translates into an economic benefit. While the levels of businesses being targeted to join these EAS schemes has increased, the membership to date would indicate the concept is still in its infancy. Expanding the membership requires that more substantial benefits are available to members and consumers before it becomes the norm for all businesses to be members. Overall, the results from most EASs are that sustainable business practices are not yet fully developed or widely embedded in company philosophy, with some notable exceptions. There is growing evidence that many of the EASs have been perceived by tourism businesses as too complex, setting high entry levels and involving a lengthy process to gain registration. This may explain why a number of the EASs in existence have introduced pre-entry level schemes to help businesses develop an interest in this issue, to generate potential members. To try to provide clear benchmarks, specific agreed international criteria have been developed to guide international coherence on environmental measures.

Environmental guidance and criteria

There is evidence that tour operators found such guidance useful as it provided a globally binding definition of "social responsibility" formulated by the International Organisation for Standardization (ISO). In 2010, the ISO 26000 on Corporate Social Responsibility provided guidance on accountability, transparency, ethical behaviour, stakeholder interests, norms of behaviour internationally and human rights. Although there still remains limited uptake to date in the tourism sector, work is ongoing towards its adoption by larger companies. One example is Domina Coral Bay Hotel, Resort, Spa and Casino in Sharm El-Sheik, Egypt (https://www.dominacoralbay.com/en/index). *For a case study on this see ISO (2016).* The criteria used in this ISO are very similar to the Global Sustainable Tourism Council (GSTC) criteria. In 2012, the GSTC was formed to try to harmonize the wide range of EASs and to harmonize baseline standards for the various EASs, and it has consulted with 100 000 stakeholders and created criteria to set out the benchmarks against which EAS can be assessed globally (Graci and Dodds 2015).

As Webb (2015) argues, this is an interesting development and is innovative because it crosses international boundaries and is applicable to transnational corporations in an attempt to harmonize the various EAS around common criteria. However, for tourism companies and destinations, the GTSC has a wider coverage – e.g. whole destinations (https://www.gstcouncil.org/) and a list of current standards can be found at https://www.travelife.info/index_new.php?menu=standardsandcriteria&lang=en_ft.

Further reading

Font, X. and Epler Wood, M. (2007) 'Sustainable tourism certification marketing and its contribution to SME market access', in R. Black and A. Crabtree (eds.) *Quality Assurance and Certification in Ecotourism.* Wallingford: CABI.

Font, X., Walmesley, A., Cogotti, S., McCombes, L. and Hausler, N. (2012) 'Corporate social responsibility: The disclosure–performance gap', *Tourism Management*, 33 (6): 1544–1553.

Questions

1 To what extent are accreditation schemes simply a marketing tool?
2 Why might tourism businesses perceive joining an EAS as too complex?
3 Why is harmonization of EAS criteria important?
4 How has the establishment of the Global Sustainable Tourism Criteria addressed the issue of harmonization of EASs?

Tools for sustainability

While there is common agreement about the premise of sustainable development, one of the pronounced limitations has been the difficulty in finding ways to unite ideology and policy (i.e. how to take the ideas and general philosophy or approach to sustainability and then enshrine it in policy prior to implementing it in practice – see Figure 19.7). The generic approach has encompassed the development of voluntary and statutory regulations, processes and practices including a range of environmental instruments to both encourage and penalize specified environmental behaviours (known as the 'carrot and stick' approach). These tools reflect what different societies, politicians and stakeholders and the influence of stakeholders (e.g. businesses) have been willing to tolerate in shifting the status quo to a more sustainable ideology, reflected in Figure 19.3 – the degrees of sustainability a country or region is prepared to tolerate. This is where much of the current public protesting emanates from on the climate crisis: see for example the political lobby group Extinction Rebellion (https://rebellion.earth) with its radical political challenge to the status quo and its commitment to non-violent activism and protest in order to achieve three goals (based on their UK demands):

- *Tell the truth* – Government must tell the truth by declaring a climate and ecological emergency, working with other institutions to communicate the urgency for change.
- *Act now* – Government must act now to halt biodiversity loss and reduce greenhouse gas emissions to net zero by 2025.
- *Beyond politics* – Government must create and be led by the decisions of a Citizens' Assembly on climate and ecological justice (Extinction Rebellion n.d.)

The tools available to governments to engage their citizens and businesses and public sector in the shift towards a more sustainable society include a range of both restrictive and stimulating approaches, including:

- punitive laws that define unlawful environmental actions and deal with perpetrators within the criminal justice system
- requirements to engage in statutory environmental impact assessments in the course of planning for new tourism developments, such as an Environmental Impact Assessment (EIA)
- statutory designation of areas and sites to increase protection and opportunities for funding to enhance conservation and education, and prevent inappropriate development and recreation activities through land-use planning and zoning
- government taxation and levies charged on environmentally damaging activity such as flying or where activity creates an added burden on state funds to mitigate (e.g. airport taxes or tourist taxes)
- schemes offering subsidies, grants, tax reductions or exemptions, and loans to assist the uptake of new technologies in tourism operations, buildings and developments
- voluntary eco-labelling to encourage businesses to think about their environmental impacts and ways of improving environmental management performance, and to subscribe to an acknowledged system of recognition
- kitemarking, for example the British Standards Institute has developed a standard procedure for corporate environmental management known as BS 7750 (known internationally as ISO 14000/140001), entailing an annual independent assessment of company environmental practice
- voluntary codes of conduct and other information provision for tourists and tourism operators in specific destinations to promote desirable behaviour
- environmental management systems set up by companies and larger tourism operators to deal with the effects of mass tourism and travel operations on the global environment (e.g. the airlines and climate change agenda) and the activities of tour operators and hotel chains
- environmental auditing and recognition of the triple bottom line, where tourism businesses across the spectrum take stock of their purchasing decisions, management of waste, energy and water use, human resource policies, community relations, building and grounds management and a range of other resource-related impacts in an attempt to identify areas for improvement
- schemes to reward and disseminate good practice (such as VisitScotland's Green Tourism Awards)

19

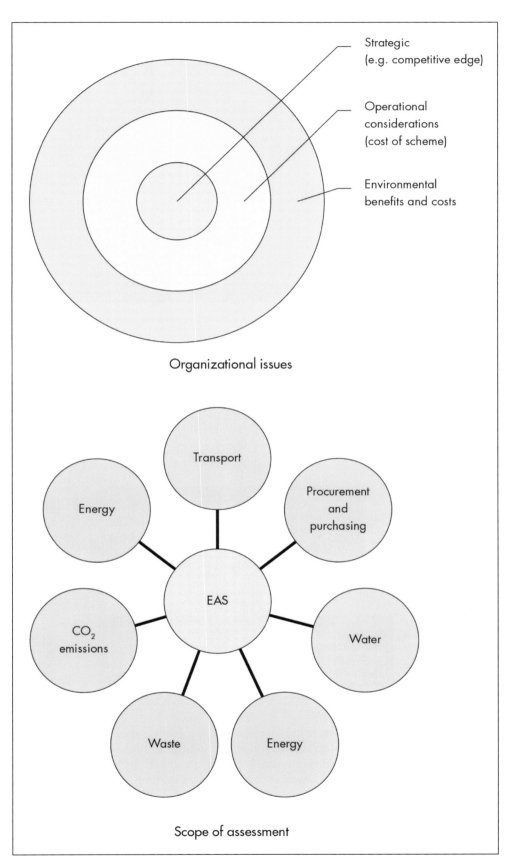

FIGURE 19.6 Key elements of Environmental Accreditation Schemes (EASs) for businesses: Organizational issues and scope of assessment

- Better education around sustainability (Image 19.3), evident in the UK with some schools now building this into their curriculum as well as embracing the tools around social marketing that have been used in the health education sector to nudge and shift behaviour (see Truong and Hall 2015).

Some of the commonly used and cited techniques and tools are detailed below.

Environmental impact assessment

One technique developed to assess the future effects of development (both tourism and non-tourism) is **environmental impact assessment (EIA)**. This is a project assessment technique which examines the adverse and beneficial impacts of a specific development used in the planning control system. The assessment covers the period from initial planning to post-development. It is an in-depth, coordinated assessment of the environmental ramifications

IMAGE 19.3 Attractions such as the Royal Botanic Gardens, Kew, London, help us to understand how protecting biodiversity is a critical issue for sustainability

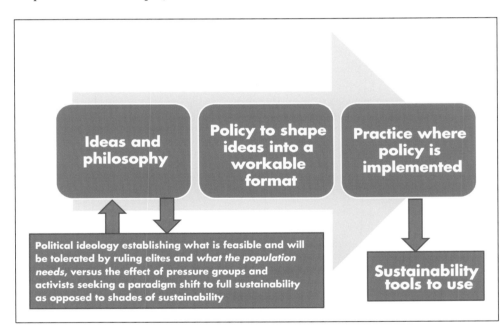

Ideas and philosophy

Policy to shape ideas into a workable format

Practice where policy is implemented

Political ideology establishing what is feasible and will be tolerated by ruling elites and *what the population needs*, versus the effect of pressure groups and activists seeking a paradigm shift to full sustainability as opposed to shades of sustainability

Sustainability tools to use

FIGURE 19.7 The Ideology-Policy-Practice conundrum in sustainability

of development, which covers not only environmental impacts but the quality of environmental management systems (Lemos *et al.* 2012). This information assists decision-makers in evaluating the consequences of a development and thus deciding whether an application should be approved or made conditional on implementing environmental management procedures. For tourism purposes, developments such as roads, airports, marinas, ski lifts and resorts, holiday villages, visitor attractions and other large-scale resort developments would require an EIA. EIA is a useful technique in principle but there are three main issues upon which one can criticize its effectiveness:

- Global implementation is patchy. While most developed nations have adopted legislation on EIAs, many less developed countries have not done so. The USA was at the forefront of EIA in the 1970s, while the European Union adopted legislation in 1985. In many countries, proposed tourism developments are subject to EIA before planning approval is given (e.g. Australia and Korea).

- While it is a mandatory requirement for large-scale development, smaller developments are not generally subject to the same process. Therefore, environmental damage is still likely to occur over the long term through the operation of smaller enterprises. For this reason, the Broads Authority in eastern England, UK, produced a sustainable development guide in 2007 which won a Royal Town Planning Institute Award on Sustainability, because it illustrated how sustainable development principles could be applied to projects (including tourism development) to reduce their environmental impact.

- EIA is only applicable to new developments, not existing operations which already cause environmental damage.

- The developer is generally assigned to collect data on the proposals, so the accuracy of the data may be questioned.

- EIA is an individual project-based approach which does not take into account wider strategic issues. Thus, EIA fails to recognize effects on an interactive and cumulative level, and does not integrate environmental, social and economic factors very effectively.

INSIGHT 19.3 The ecological footprint as an indicator of sustainable tourism and its use to manage tourism

There is a growing literature in environmental research that argues a need to develop indicators capable of accounting for the tourist's impacts on the environment. One technique developed is the ecological footprint (EF), as mentioned in Chapter 18. Ecological footprinting is a tool by which an estimate of resource consumption and waste generated by economic activity, such as tourism, can be generated in a given area. The technique examines the consumption of energy, foodstuffs, raw materials, water, transport impacts, waste generated and loss of land from development. While criticisms exist over the methods of analysis used to calculate the EF, it is now being used by public sector agencies to highlight issues of sustainability. Gössling (2002) used this technique to illustrate the EF for tourism in the Seychelles per tourist, using the common unit of measurement 'gha' (global hectares), which is the way the demand an activity places on natural resources, resulting in their consumption, is measured. In the Seychelles, values of 1.9 gha per year for the EF were 90 per cent the result of air travel. For a typical two-week holiday in the Mediterranean, the WWF study noted in Chapter 18 (WWF 2002) that a gha of 0.37 resulted in Majorca and 0.93 in Cyprus. In each case, air travel was the contributor to over 50 per cent of the EF. The value of the EF technique is that it allows you to compare the overall ecological impact of tourism products on global biological resources.

The EF has also now become central to assessing and reducing the global footprint of tourism and the debates around decarbonizing or reducing carbon emission, as mentioned earlier and to which we will return in Chapter 27. As Hall *et al.* (2015) argue, the global EF highlights the need from a sustainability perspective to not simply slow the growth of tourism – but to right-size or make it more appropriate in different contexts. Options like steady-state tourism and degrowth (i.e. putting the brakes on tourism-related economic growth) may be necessary given the:

1 The continued overconsumption of resources to meet tourism demand – which is not a basic human need, but a luxury good

2 That growth challenges to humankind such as the climate crisis mean that radical action is needed by everyone to reduce their individual carbon footprint, which tools like the EF can help us understand more fully despite the insatiable desire for taking holidays.

As Hall *et al.* (2015: 507) suggest, various components of addressing points 1 and 2 require using the EF to help assess and:

- Reduce the global ecological footprint of tourism to sustainable levels

- Address the impact of tourism of countries where the per capita EF is higher than the global average.

Further reading

Castellani, V. and Sala, S. (2012) 'Ecological footprint and life cycle assessment in the sustainability assessment of tourism activities', *Ecological Indicators*, 16 (2): 135–147.

Hunter, C. (2002) 'Sustainable tourism and the tourist ecological footprint', *Environment, Development and Sustainability*, 4 (1): 7–20.

Questions

1 What is the value of the EF?

2 What problems might exist in collecting data to calculate EF?

3 How can EF be used in a policy context?

4 What other techniques might be used to assess the impact of tourism in a destination?

19

Subsequent developments of EIA have seen the extension of this to Strategic Environmental Assessment, which requires a more strategic assessment of the plans, policies and development and consideration of alternatives based on scientific-based evidence in the new millennium, situating development in a much broader context rather than at just an individual project level.

Environmental auditing

One of the most innovative projects emanating from attempts to look at the environmental performance of existing tourism businesses is the idea of environmental auditing. Auditing is different to EIA because it evaluates existing business practice rather than potential problems. In the UK, the Green Tourism Business Scheme is the national sustainable tourism certification scheme under which businesses are assessed and graded on a rigorous set of criteria relating to a range of elements including energy, waste, transport and water. Many initiatives elsewhere follow this model, and the development of ecolabels is evident in Insight 19.2. Even some entire destinations, such as Whistler in Canada, are trying to model energy consumption to reduce tourism-related greenhouse gases (Kelly and Williams 2007) especially carbon emissions. This type of environmental evaluation is voluntary. The deficiencies in EIA procedure can be resolved to some extent by applying the two processes together; that is, EIA prior to development, then auditing following development. Auditing can provide the feedback required to assess impact prediction. One new technique gaining prominence – ecological footprinting – can be seen in Insight 19.3.

Environmental policies and statements

Many companies have developed statements about their environmental performance, policies and practices. These range in length from a sentence or two (e.g. most tour operators), or a page in a brochure, to a full booklet and even an annual report (e.g. British Airways). In many cases, very little of substance is conveyed, but some organizations provide detailed information about contributions to environmental and community work (see Mak and Chan 2006 on airlines in the Asia–Pacific region) or the assessment and monitoring of environmental impacts (see the Scandic Hotels example). The essential aspect is to ensure that policies are put into action, otherwise they are meaningless. A study by Lynes and Dredge (2006) of the Scandinavian airline sector examined how it decided upon its environmental policy. Three key motives were observed: first, a desire to achieve eco-efficiencies; second, a strategic understanding of the importance of environmental issues in Scandinavian culture; and third, the role of a senior manager as an environmental champion provided a key leadership role. However, probably the most influential catalyst for change is public policy.

Public policy for sustainable tourism

19

Public policy is about how governments achieve the goals they set themselves, the various instruments that assist in decisions on the allocation of resources and how the level of involvement or intervention on specific issues is determined, as discussed in Chapter 18. As mentioned earlier, a public policy conundrum exists in relation to sustainability as it requires significant societal changes to achieve deep sustainability rather than lighter forms. It is becoming increasingly evident from discussion around the climate crisis (see Table 19.1) that political posturing and policies that do not commit to the deeper forms of sustainability are likely to have little impact on the escalating climate crisis (although some political leaders continue to challenge the validity of the science of climate change).

In the case of sustainable tourism, it is evident from the discussion in this chapter that much of the action and activity in this area has been characterized by voluntary initiatives promoted by the tourism industry or public sector bodies. It has not been characterized by what Dredge and Jenkins (2007) describe as a *high level of state intervention* to develop policy instruments which are compulsory or regulatory in form. The low level of involvement that characterizes much of the sustainable activity is based on voluntary commitment which has shifted towards a range of mixed instruments as new measures, for example, accreditation schemes such as Green Globe (see Insight 19.2) with some degree of public support to promote the schemes. However, the reliance upon self-implementation means that participation has been limited. At a global scale, Jenkins and Mkono (2015) examine global governance and sustainable tourism, focusing on the key bodies like UNWTO and UNEP along with their contribution to developing measures to monitor sustainable tourism including what indicators to use, a number of examples we have already highlighted in this chapter. One of the key issues in moving towards more sustainable ways of planning, developing and managing tourism is how to monitor and measure both the impacts of tourism, and the outcomes of interventions to improve environmental performance. The development and use of indicators is a concept that has been promoted in tourism since the 1990s and developed on a global basis by UNWTO in 2002.

Monitoring sustainable tourism

As Jenkins and Mkono (2015: 239) argue, monitoring is a way to 'comprehend where you are, which way you are going and how far you are from where you want to be'. Since its inception in 2004 with innovative projects in China, the UNWTO International Network of Sustainable Tourism Observatories (INSTO) now comprises 26 destinations committed to monitoring and measuring the impacts of tourism. The premise of these observatories is that the data produced can be used in evidence-based local planning and decision-making processes, while best practice and lessons learnt can be shared more widely. Observatories must monitor nine core areas, as shown in Figure 19.8.

Jenkins and Mkono (2015) view indicators as an early warning system to communicate concerns and information, which was initially developed by the UNWTO in 2002 to establish the criteria upon which sustainable tourism could be monitored. The evolution of research on indicators and benchmarking (a standard by which one can measure) has been reviewed by Zeppel (2015), who critiques the various methods of environmental reporting being used. Further impetus to provide a framework in which sustainable tourism could be harnessed to develop peoples and communities beyond individual measures was provided by the UNEP with its Sustainable Development Goals (SDGs) 2015–2030, designed to be applied to all and countries structured around many of the challenges countries face (https://una-gp.org/the-sustainable-development-goals-2015-2030/). This attempt by a UN body to address global sustainable development issues was recognized by major players in the tourism industry and has now become a new agenda mentioned in many national tourism strategies.

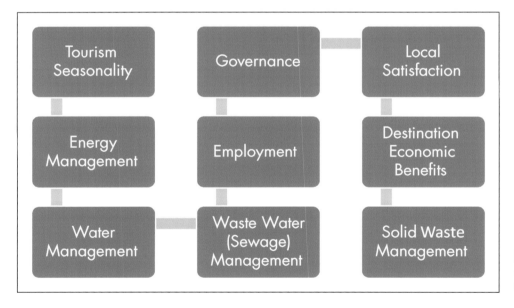

FIGURE 19.8 Core areas which Sustainable Tourism Observatories monitor

Critiquing the Sustainable Development Goals 2015–2030: What role for tourism?

Despite the widespread debating of the SDGs, much of the debate and narrative from policy pronouncements and position papers was that tourism could be harnessed as a positive tool to help with SDG1 – poverty alleviation. Yet as Table 19.2 shows, a more balanced perspective needs to take into account two other dimensions – the negative implications or impacts of using tourism in each SD goal and the complicating factor – climate change, namely global warming.

TABLE 19.2 The SDGs and their relationship with tourism

SDG	Positive relationships with tourism	Negative relationship with tourism	IPCC report: SDGs impacted by global warming
1 **No poverty**	Economic growth through tourism can help generate jobs and income, while small-scale community or pro-poor tourism schemes can help to reduce poverty	Tourism can also create poverty by land clearance to create space for tourism development, removing people's livelihoods. Tourism can also generate low-value and precarious forms of employment that create poverty	X
2 **Zero hunger**	Small-scale agricultural production may be stimulated through sustainable tourism with demand for local foods, allowing the development of supply chains that benefit small farmers	The loss of productive lands to tourism developments such as golf courses may lead to a reduction in self-sufficiency and the ability of local people to feed themselves even at subsistence level	X
3 **Good health and well-being**	Revenue from taxation could be invested in health services and well-being of local populations	Tourism taxation is rarely targeted to specific needs and is absorbed into general taxation budgets and allocated to government priorities	X
4 **Quality education**	Employment in the tourism industry requires education and training	Education and training at school level is required if employees are to benefit from more well-paid tourism jobs	
5 **Gender equality**	Jobs and opportunities for small business, such as those operated by female entrepreneurs	In many countries gender inequality exists, meaning that women are allocated less well-paid and precarious tourism employment and have fewer opportunities from microfinance institutions to be selfemployed	
6 **Clean water and sanitation**	Investment in clean water supply for tourism facilities and control of water pollution	Investment in tourism infrastructure does not necessarily filter through to local communities where exclusive resort developments may install their own desalination or groundwater pumping infrastructure only for their needs	X
7 **Affordable and clean energy**	Investment in green technology to reduce GHGs	Local people may not have the resources to make long-term household investments in green energy and will require state subsidies to transition to this form of energy	
8 **Decent work and economic growth**	Provides work and stimulates business, stimulates supply chains	Tourism may well provide new employment opportunities but the question mark exists over the quality and value of such work	
9 **Industry, innovation and infrastructure**	Tourism can assist countries seeking to move from an agrarian and subsistence standard of living for its population by providing new employment opportunities	Entrepreneurs will be the main beneficiaries of any innovation that creates new tourism employment opportunities unless a community-based model or a social innovation model of development is adopted	

No.	Goal			
10	**Reduced inequalities**	Provides local communities an opportunity to shape the nature of local development, allowing people to earn income without having to move to more prosperous economies	In many cases, tourism has been shown to perpetuate existing inequalities that are structural in nature with only limited beneficiaries of any tourism growth	X
11	**Sustainable cities and communities**	Stimulates regeneration and preservation of heritage. Investments in transportation to reduce pollution also benefit tourism	Tourism by its very nature is a fossil-fuel consumer and so it will add additional pollution and impacts by being developed versus a no-growth scenario	
12	**Responsible consumption and production**	Shifts in perceptions through greater public awareness of impacts and sustainability, alongside improved business practices and monitoring tools	In advanced societies, tourism will need to be controlled and people will have to be educated through social marketing tools to understand what their impact as tourists means for communities. This raises the question of what we mean by responsible tourism and whether we really need to take so many holidays amidst a climate change emergency, when our energy and resource needs are carbon-based	
13	**Climate action**	Tourism must reduce its carbon emissions, working towards being more carbon-neutral once alternative fuel sources are more widely available	Tourism is a very consumptive activity and not fundamental to human needs, so its contribution to climate change is a clear area for action to reduce its impact. Holidays in developed and emerging countries are seen as a right, posing issues for controlling impacts	X
14	**Life below water**	Contributes to sustainable use of marine resources – relies on healthy maritime environment	Tourism pollution directly affects coastal environments through untreated sewage and tourists' direct and indirect impacts affect the marine environment	X
15	**Life on land**	Tourism is an asset if the environment is maintained sensitively. It may help create income as an alternative to more destructive practices such as logging	Tourism has a major land take due to the scale of developments which it has traditionally been based on. Smaller-scale, ecorelated developments are one of the few areas where impacts can be minimized	
16	**Peace, justice and strong institutions**	Tourism creates encounters between people of different cultures and backgrounds and can help people come together	The sociocultural impact of tourism may generate a significant range of negative impacts	
17	**Partnerships for the goals**	Tourism may help to bring stakeholders together to establish a development path in situations where it has a bottom-up approach towards governance	In many cases, tourism does not involve the community or marginal groups and so a true partnership towards sustainable development remains elusive through the ideology-policy-practice conundrum	

Source: Adapted from UNWTO http://tourism4sdgs.org/tourism-for-sdgs/; Intergovernmental Panel on Climate Change (2018) Global Warming of 1.5c. www.ipcc.ch

Scheyvens and Hughes (2019) are highly critical of the manner in which many governments in emerging nations have embraced the United Nation's Sustainable Development Goal (SDG1) – to end poverty – and have viewed tourism as the savior of the poor, a theme we discussed in Chapter 12 and which we return to in Chapter 23. As the UN argue, 'one in ten people in developing regions are still living with their families on less than the international poverty line of US\$1.90 a day, and there are millions more who make little more than this daily amount' (https://www.un.org/sustainabledevelopment/poverty/). Yet Scheyvens and Hughes (2019) argue tourism is unlikely to make major inroads to poverty because of the multifaceted nature of that problem; there are 1 billion people living in poverty globally. This means that poverty is entrenched in many societies in the capitalist system, a system that is based on perpetuating inequality in the way resources and wealth are distributed. If tourism is to become a sustainable means of alleviating poverty, we need to consider, according to Scheyvens and Hughes (2019: 1062), whether tourism:

- Provides alternative livelihood strategies which help to reduce the vulnerability of poor communities and enhance their well-being
- Helps poor people to build their capabilities and assets
- Facilitates the empowerment of poor people and helps them to lead dignified lives in which they have greater control over their well-being
- Leads to poor people to securing their rights. (Scheyvens 2011: 25)

This remains an ongoing problem for policymakers who embed poverty alleviation as the rationale for sustainable tourism policies, since 'the available data in some cases show that tourism has impacted negatively on the lives of the poor' (Scheyvens and Hughes 2019: 1064). This reflects the structural inequalities in many societies, which are reinforced by the actions of large corporations, where investment benefits are captured by elites and the impacts are borne by the poor. Consequently, action is needed to regulate business interests so negative impacts are controlled. One key element here is in ensuring foreign ventures have a positive development impact on the country through tourism rather than exploiting the situation, expropriating profits and using highly exploitative procurement policies and supply chains. Poverty alleviation strategies linked to sustainability and tourism also need to be accompanied by labour laws that protect workers' rights and build their skill base, enabling people to help themselves out of poverty through participation in tourism.

Policy and practice gaps in sustainable tourism

In terms of international agreements on sustainability the problems in implementing real change are personified in the case of Agenda 21, one of the key outcomes of the 1992 Rio Earth Summit conference, as mentioned earlier in the chapter. Agenda 21 was designed as an international action plan or 'blueprint' for sustainable development. Signed by 182 heads of state, this plan committed national governments to consider the environment and development issues across a number of different activities and sectors, and was to be delivered and implemented at local levels by local authorities and communities working together. While tourism per se was not recognized as a specific sector at this time, it was recognized in some Local Agenda 21 action plans, for example Calvià in Majorca (see Chapter 22). The idea of Agenda 21 was adapted specifically to the tourism industry by the World Travel and Tourism Council, the UN–WTO and the Earth Council (the last is the body established to translate Agenda 21 principles into practice). As with any implementation plan, the action taken and impact upon tourism can be measured in terms of the outcomes for sustainable tourism. In relation to the impact of the adoption of Agenda 21 for the global tourism sector, a UNEP report (2003) noted that it was difficult to find many examples of local authorities implementing this agenda. The study noted only three categories of destination which had adopted Agenda 21 principles for sustainable tourism due to the pressure they were facing from tourism:

- small island states (e.g. Marie-Galante, French Caribbean)
- historic towns (e.g. Winchester, UK)
- established tourist resorts (e.g. Bournemouth, UK and Calvià, Balearic Islands).

This exercise highlights a distinct policy–practice gap, a theme we will return to later in Chapter 24, which examines tourism planning. While Local Agenda 21 plans became more integrated into sustainable development plans through time, and are now morphed into the Sustainable Development Goals, there is a continuing challenge for the development and management of tourism in the twenty-first century. As Carvalho (2001: 70) argues, we need to do more in our conceptualization of sustainable development if we are to elevate it beyond 'something that can be achieved in the current system with just a little tweaking and slight greening of the current development model'. We need a new philosophy that reconceptualizes the tourism development model, since, as Page (2019) highlights, tourism has the potential to self-destruct in localities and environments once the development process gets out of control. There are significant dangers for destinations that do not deal with the reality of tourism impacts – this is especially a challenge for countries seeking to use tourism as a tool for economic growth given the unstable nature of national economies in the current decade. One example is New Zealand, which adopted a tourism strategy (Ministry of Tourism 2007: 4) which sought to adopt a sustainability vision as an underpinning philosophy:

> *Visitors and their host communities understand and embrace the spirit of manaakitanga (hospitality)*
> *while New Zealanders' environment and culture is conserved and sustained in the spirit of kaitiakitanga*
> *(guardianship) and tourism is a vibrant and significant contributor to the economic development of tourism.*

Interestingly, the clean green image of New Zealand as a tourist destination has been challenged by the country's rapid tourism growth, alongside the climate change issue. Tighter regulatory measures for the tourism sector may be required if the planning system and voluntary measures on environmental management are not embraced fully to protect New Zealand's promotional image as an environmentally sound destination (Connell *et al.* 2009).

In Europe, much of the emphasis has shifted towards generic sustainable development strategies for the EU. It is largely up to individual governments and their local authorities to develop sustainable development plans within which tourism would fit, replacing much of the initial emphasis on Agenda 21 in tourism. To retain a tourism focus, however, the EU assembled a group of experts and stakeholders to refocus where sustainable tourism should be heading among its member states. The EU's (2007) *Action for More Sustainable European Tourism* summarizes its direction, thinking and focus for sustainable tourism at a transnational scale, where it recognizes the important role of public intervention by the European Commission, member state governments, local authorities and destination management organizations, tourism businesses, other bodies, and tourists in addressing eight key challenges for the sustainability of European tourism:

- reducing the seasonality of tourism, to remove some of the pressure points at key locations and twin- and single-peak seasonality
- addressing the impact of tourist transport, given the current debate over its contribution to climate change
- improving the quality of tourism jobs, in view of the poor perception of tourism as a career route with low wages and long hours of work
- maintaining and enhancing community prosperity and quality of life, in the face of change which reinforces the importance of community benefit tourism initiatives (as discussed in the chapter on the social and cultural impacts of tourism)
- minimizing resource use and production of waste, highlighting the green agenda and importance of recycling and waste reduction management strategies
- conserving and giving value to natural and cultural heritage in a way that recognizes the environmental ethic and is compatible with sustainable forms of tourism development
- making holidays available to all, which is a social goal of the EU but in reality may only add pressure to grow tourism in an unsustainable manner if it expands the volume as opposed to the value of tourism
- using tourism as a tool in global sustainable development, which may be a long-term ambition but is not something that the EU can easily promote without considerable culture change among consumers and the tourism industry.

The implementation of these tasks is placed on a wide range of stakeholders without a direction for the strategic implementation of these measures. In this sense, sustainable tourism policy remains a series of documents setting out broad objectives and measures that need to be embraced at a voluntary level. This highlights the individual initiatives that need to be embraced to manage tourism in a more sustainable manner, as well as raising wider issues related to the types of local plans communities and destinations need to develop to manage the future growth and development of tourism. Critics of sustainable tourism policies in some countries highlight the reasons for failure. As Rogerson (2012) noted in relation to South Africa, even with a strong policy framework, the main area of policy failure was in community initiatives where there was an absence of adequate training, capacity-building and the infrastructure support needed for local producers to penetrate the food supply chains in tourism. In other words, if businesses cannot, or will not, engage with the process of achieving sustainable tourism then it is unlikely to occur. On the positive side, however, Rogerson observed the growth in South African food quality and the greater development of increasing niche tourism markets as well as an interest in fair trade.

The issue of sustainable food sources and tourist food consumption raises several linked debates around sustainability, such as where and how food is produced, and the food miles in supply chains. This issue is relatively easy to address at a small scale but more problematic in relation to mass tourism markets. One of the least visible positive steps forward in sustainable tourism for destinations is using locally produced food to help strengthen the local economy – known as 'backward linkages'. However, there may be many obstacles to introducing more sustainable food. For example, Kasim and Ismail's (2012) study of restaurants in Penang, Malaysia found that while managers were informed, they were reluctant to invest in sustainable practices due to perceived obstacles such as inadequately enforced environmental laws and regulations, weak local supply chains and lack of consumer demand. In the UK, one good example of a major visitor attraction that promotes a sustainable food ethos is the Eden Project, Cornwall. Among its criteria for inclusion on its menus or in its shops are that food products must be local, sustainable and tell a story. The attraction uses meat, eggs and dairy produce from the local area only, home-grown salad produce and vegetables in season, and supports sustainable fisheries. Furthermore, the Eden Project works with small local businesses to produce bespoke branded products, such as ice cream. This local supply ethos is communicated to visitors by a map on the main café wall depicting the location of food suppliers. Adopting this approach has resulted in about 80 per cent of visitor expenditure in the on-site cafes remaining in the local economy. Conversely (as will be revisited in Chapter 23), in the Caribbean region, most food for tourism supply is imported and, as Eastham (2019) identifies, the disconnection between the tourism and agricultural sector creates significant economic leakage as well as environmental impact. Recognition of these negative impacts has stimulated interest in the local food economy and various initiatives have developed. A good example of a hotel that has engaged in these debates is Hotel Mockingbird Hill, Jamaica. It uses small producers from within a 90-mile radius and supports an artisan economy, reducing food miles and developing a local food economy embracing storytelling (like Eden) to portray the provenance of the food. Variability in supply means the menu changes daily and the chef looks at what they have and let it inspire the menu. Frey and George (2010) also underline the role of state intervention in relation to the implementation of measures in South Africa, such as responsible tourism as a dimension of sustainable tourism practice, along with reducing the cost of entering such schemes.

Growth management and the future for tourism and sustainability

The need to sustain tourism and recognize the challenge of sustainable development in the short-to-medium term (i.e. five to ten years) has meant that, in many destinations, the implementation of the ideas described in this chapter has been haphazard and uneven. Much of this is a result of the pressure from businesses to drive growth agendas in tourism. Gill (2004) points to legislation and planning philosophies in North America that have assisted local communities as key stakeholders to help develop their own tourism futures, assisted by a range of tools and strategies. For example, planning tools such as special districts for tourism, zoning of activity, and using planning limits on the architecture, design standards and density of development have assisted in controlling the physical manifestation of tourism development. Other destinations have used limits on the quantity of visitors to manage tourism, retain numbers within thresholds of acceptable limits and seek to achieve a sustainable balance. At an individual site level, as discussed earlier in the chapter, some resorts have encouraged the dispersal of visitors (e.g. Languedoc-Roussillon, France) while others have sought to concentrate them in specific locations within destinations (e.g. Canterbury, England). More radically, in a few locations a comprehensive growth management plan has been developed to seek to manage future tourism growth in view of the issues of sustainability (e.g. Venice, Italy; Seattle, USA). In each case the critical trade-offs are between the elements of sustainability (economic, social, cultural and environmental) to control tourism. Such a perspective recognizes the inherent conflicts between the market-driven business focus of growth and the need for balance and restraint if the destination is to prosper. For example, in England, VisitEngland has adopted a strategy for sustainable tourism entitled 'Wise Growth' to link the growth aspirations of the destination with sustainable principles. Decisions on how a destination will develop and the level of sustainability it seeks to embrace are inherently political, where public sector bodies, such as national tourism organizations and local and national governments, determine the future shape and direction of the sector. Sustainability remains a valid approach if it can be managed at a strategic level for destinations and implemented locally with specific measures and actions (UNEP 2003), particularly in relation to visitors' behaviour and their actions. For example, Buckley (2019) outlined the limited research on understanding tourist behaviour on sustainability that related to articulating a simple and understandable definition of what is meant by sustainability for individuals. Buckley (2019) suggested that we could understand tourist sustainable behaviours in two ways:

- By looking at the choice presented to tourists between various courses of action and the different environmental impacts they may have (which could also be extended to sociocultural and economic impacts)
- Evaluating the individual tourists' human behaviour through their attitudes (e.g. are they pro-environmental?) and their intention and motivations.

Several research studies have identified that pro-environment behaviour in home settings is not always replicated when people go on holiday and argue that in a tourist setting, a tourist may find it more challenging to engage in environmental behaviours simply because the facilities and services, such as recycling points, are not so easily found by non-residents. Miller *et al.* (2015), in a study of Melbourne, found that tourists may need more guidance from tour operators and local authorities to help already engaged tourists maintain their good habits on holiday. For this reason, one area of particular interest in sustainable tourism is in the use of visitor management tools to manage activity and growth in destinations.

Visitor management

At the core of sustainable tourism lies good practice in **visitor management**. Visitor management is an approach which aims to protect the environment while providing for visitor enjoyment, and is widely used to manage a range of sites including natural areas, historic houses and gardens, visitor attractions, protected sites, sacred sites, World Heritage Sites (e.g. Stonehenge, UK; Machu Picchu, Peru; and Central Eastern Rainforest Reserves, Australia). There are different methods for different types of location which work on both macro (nation, region, area) and micro (settlement, site, visitor attraction) levels. Strategic decisions about visitor management (Figure 19.9) must be made in relation to **carrying capacity**. There are four main types of carrying capacity, illustrated in Figure 19.10.

Visitor management covers a broad spectrum of strategies and tools but generally, there are three main areas – as demonstrated in Figure 19.9.

Visitor management may also be divided into two forms (Grant 1994):

1 *Hard measures* – aligned with physical and financial restrictions on access. Examples include road closures, parking fees, entrance charges, fencing, zoning and restrictions on vehicle size.

2 *Soft measures* – associated with encouraging desired behaviour rather than restricting undesirable activities. Examples include marketing and promotional material, signs, interpretation, information provision and guided walks.

A combination of hard and soft initiatives is considered appropriate in most cases. Hard measures are somewhat easier to apply and have immediate results but may not solve the problem alone.

Spatial distribution as a visitor management strategy aims to spread economic benefits of visitor activity geographically, extend recreational opportunities and experiences and reduce pressure on stressed environments. This may be achieved through a number of tools:

CONTROL VOLUME
(e.g. limit numbers, encourage alternative visit timing and locations)

MODIFY BEHAVIOUR
(e.g. codes of conduct, signposting)

ADAPT RESOURCE
(e.g. harden footpath surface, construct purpose-built facilities)

FIGURE 19.9 Summary of visitor management strategies
Source: Modified from Employment Department Group and English Tourist Board (1991)

- information packs, outlining attractions and accommodation in the wider area
- marketing areas that are less well known to the visitor
- ticketing strategies (e.g. joint ticketing, discounts, high charges)
- visitor assistants
- interpretation (e.g. trails, information, routing, tours)
- marketing of public transport links and encouraging visitors to explore new areas using more sustainable modes of transport.

In addition to protecting environmental resources, it is sometimes necessary to prevent spatial conflict – that is, between recreational users of an area. Zoning is a method of managing conflicting activities by spatial separation; it is commonly found on reservoirs and lakes where sailing, water-skiing, angling and conservation purposes might be at odds, but also form part of protected area recreation planning. The Peak District National Park in the UK, for example, is zoned into five recreational areas, indicating levels of intensity of use, from wild areas through to areas of highest-intensity recreational use. Such plans are commonly adopted by National Park services all over the world with good examples in the USA and New Zealand (Pigram and Jenkins 1996; Hall and Page 2006).

Temporal distribution aspects address how visits might be spread throughout the year rather than be concentrated on at peak times. Tools of temporal distribution are:

- timed ticketing
- promotion of out-of-season packages
- special events
- all-year facilities.

'De-marketing' is another option for areas where visitor capacity has been reached or attempts are being made to limit promotion of a vulnerable environment. De-marketing is an active policy of not marketing a location. A further method employed quite extensively to alter visitor behaviour and attitude is the publication and dissemination of codes of conduct (see Fennell and Malloy (2007) for a useful overview of codes of conduct). Friends of Conservation, for example, have produced guidelines aimed at tourists to assist in maintaining a balance between enjoyment and conservation. Entitled the *Traveller's Code*, it covers issues of accommodation, culture, dress, food and drink, out and about, shopping, transport, adventure and booking.

Much of the discussion about managing environmental and tourist resources considers the broad concept of carrying capacity (Figure 19.10), which although acceptable in theory, is criticized for its inherent difficulty in application. One of the difficulties is the decision-making process and the detailed understanding required to establish limits on resource use in specific environments at specific times, bearing in mind the seasonal nature of tourism, the seasonality of climate, vegetation change and the vulnerability of a site given seasonal and cyclical environmental change. Moreover, popular visitor sites are often fraught with political, community and commercial conflicts, which may work against the conservation needs of these fragile natural and cultural sites. The question of who has the legitimacy to decide on how many visitors are enough, or which processes should be adopted to decide on visitor quotas, may militate against site protection. Such arguments bring us to explore the difficulties in achieving sustainable tourism. These issues are evident in the prevailing concerns with the overdevelopment of destinations and the deluging of their infrastructure with visitors – a phenomenon known as overtourism. Although we explore overtourism in the next chapter in relation to the consequences for local residents in cities, a study by WTTC and McKinsey (2017) highlighted the various tactics available to destinations to address overcrowding as visitor management solutions including:

PHYSICAL

A measure of the number of tourists that may be accommodated on a site

PERCEPTUAL

A measure of the number of people that may be accommodated on a site before the visitor experience is damaged

ECONOMIC

A measure of the number of people that may be welcomed to a location before the economy of the area is adversely affected

ECOLOGICAL

A measure of the number of people that may be accommodated on a site before damage occurs to the environment

FIGURE 19.10 Types of carrying capacity

- Smoothing out the temporal (i.e. time) period over which visitors arrive in the destination, given patterns of peaking in the summer season for many destinations.
- Spreading the geographical distribution of visitors across different sites
- Making adjustments to the pricing strategies used to balance supply and demand, given that supply is a finite quantity at any point in time
- Regulating the supply of accommodation, particularly the unregulated sector such as Airbnb which can expand the seasonal availability of supply
- Limiting tourist access to key areas or regions and the range of activities (see Chapter 20 for the example of Venice).

Source: Developed from WTTC and McKinsey (2017)

Indeed, in 2019, the UK government announced an inquiry by its Environmental Audit Committee to examine the contribution of British mass tourism to climate change, given global growth of tourism which may be running counter to plans to slow global warming. The Committee set out to examine: whether the government should support sustainable tourism; whether it should assume more responsibility for the impact of UK visitors overseas; and how more sustainable travel might help reduce emissions from tourism-related activity.

Difficulties in achieving sustainable tourism: Challenges for the future

One of the main problems of achieving sustainable tourism is the lack of consensus as to what it actually means in practice. While this might seem to be an academic argument, it has practical ramifications of a critical nature because without a precise understanding of what the term means, no progress can be made towards achieving it. The challenges of sustainable tourism exist at both global and destination levels. At the destination level, Wheeller (1991: 94) states: 'Examples of positive management of the tourist influx are the exception, not the rule.' This raises the question: 'Is sustainable tourism for the elite only?' The development of new tourism has attracted new tourists. Many existing and new tourism destinations wish to attract a small number of high-spending tourists. Mass tourism is associated with low-spending, high-volume tourism, which highlights one of the essential problems in sustainable tourism: if this alternative approach to tourism is to work in protecting the environment, it cannot work in isolation. It must work for every aspect of tourism, from the Costa del Sol to the rainforests of Belize. As tourism grows apace, the answer to lessening the impacts is clearly not in attracting low-spending high-volume tourism. This is the dilemma for policymakers in destinations.

There are dangers in promoting sustainable tourism, as seen in the case of some ecotourism developments which do little to deliver benefits to local communities or protect ecological and cultural resources. Perceptions of holidays based in natural environments, such as Belize, can differ significantly from reality, in relation to tourism being harnessed as a form of sustainable development for the poor. Furthermore, green policies that focus on spreading tourist benefits, which include the temporal (widening the tourist season by encouraging off-peak visiting) and spatial (promoting a wider area for tourism) pose a potential threat to a wider range of sites. Such policies necessitate a strategic approach to the planning, management and monitoring of tourist activity and environmental change as well as capturing the benefits through robust economic analyzes. Monitoring the effects of tourism and of sustainable tourism projects needs further development in seeking to move rhetoric to measurable action. Without monitoring, it is impossible to gauge whether tourism is moving towards its sustainable goals. Criteria by which progress can be evaluated are crucial: this is becoming an accepted part of sustainable development on an international scale, and a wide range of concepts and tools exist to benchmark and assess progress at a destination level (see Schianetz *et al.* 2007).

Achieving sustainable tourism is difficult for four reasons, according to Muller (1994):

- there are too many theories and experts – too few resources and little time to act
- there is a continuing boom in tourism demand
- while there is a growing awareness of the environment, the predominance of a hedonistic philosophy means a trend towards indulgence of pleasures on holiday rather than responsibility
- a change of paradigm is needed to move towards socially and environmentally compatible lifestyles – a long and difficult process.

Sustainable tourism should be a philosophy that infiltrates the whole of the tourism industry rather than being a niche market or minority view. In addition, and from a 'real world' perspective, if sustainability has to partially rely on voluntary uptake by businesses, then it has to be profitable for businesses. Weaver (2004) points to the malleability of sustainable tourism, meaning it is a term with multiple meanings and interpretations, leading to its misuse, adaptation to inappropriate settings and as a rhetoric or veneer for some corporations in extreme cases. This is compounded by the complexity over whether tourism impacts can simply be ascribed to a cause-and-effect relationship (as discussed in Chapter 18). It may be that a sustainable project in one location can give rise to an unsustainable outcome elsewhere, even when such an impact was not intended. There is also considerable debate over what Weaver (2004) describes as the subjectivity of selecting sustainable tourism indicators. Sustainable development and sustainable tourism offer many prospective solutions for managing the growth of tourism, but this requires an enormous investment in the science of monitoring and evaluating measures of sustainability, which is unlikely to become widespread without suitable policy and planning frameworks being in place to regulate and implement these notions systematically for countries and destinations.

Further challenges in the development of sustainability in tourism focus on ethical and equity issues, for example the assessment of Western impacts in non-Western environments and the concept of intergenerational equity. New value systems are needed to cope with the thought processes required to address these issues, which lie outside of the dominant world paradigm of economic growth. The paradigm shift required to fully integrate sustainability into our existence is perhaps still some way away. Weaver (2009) describes the current situation as a 'paradigm nudge' rather than 'paradigm shift', which recognizes that despite the awareness and sympathies that are growing within tourism-generating markets, as yet there is no real demand for pro-sustainability structural change as the green economy concept has emerged (UN–WTO 2012).

There is also a growing debate on creating more sustainable lifestyles among the population who travel so that their interests and actions at home translate to their behaviour as consumers on holiday, recognizing the growing climate change agenda and implications of their impact through tourism. In this way, a greater environmental awareness and understanding of how to live greener lives becomes the dominant paradigm. However, as Stoll-Kleeman *et al.* (2001) highlighted, 'the major constraint on this notion of the sustainable lifestyle and the translation in holiday behaviour is related to a metaphor of displaced commitment'. This explains tourists' desire to travel to certain destinations, where they knowingly impact the environment, while believing that this is counterbalanced by their environmental action at home. In fact Miller *et al.* (2010) reported on very low awareness about global environmental issues among the UK travelling public, who demonstrated greater awareness of tangible issues (e.g. litter) than intangible impacts such as global warming and water equity. The UK public was generally more focused on environmental issues when they were at home than when they were on holiday. This may be justified in the minds of some travellers by presenting a 'green on balance' argument, based on the reciprocity approach: i.e. the population can 'learn' to act less responsibly towards the environment during their holidays if they have been responsible while they were at home. Consumers want to 'treat themselves' while enjoying a holiday and they do not consider environmental issues as important while they are away, reflecting short-term gratification through consumption.

Conclusion

Despite confusion over meanings of sustainable tourism, it is clear that protection of the resources on which tourism depends is central to sustainable development, but implementation involves a very complex process in different localities. It is vital to recognize this complexity and not be fooled into thinking that sustainable tourism can be achieved by devising a policy statement or undertaking one aspect of environmental management. In reality, sustainable tourism is somewhat of an oxymoron – while appropriate management is achievable at the site level, it cannot be achieved overall because of the need for travel. The best that the tourism industry as a whole can do is move towards better environmental practice. May (1991) suggests six steps that can be taken to move closer to the goal of sustainability which, while outlined at an early stage of sustainable tourism thinking, still remain relevant today:

- better understanding of the value of environments
- more complete information about environments, local values and susceptibility to outside influences
- greater attention to the regional effects of development
- use of environmental economics in relation to assessing development

- improved measurements of environmental factors for use in environmental accounting
- developments designed with long-term environmental quality in mind.

These issues have provided a continuing challenge for the development and management of tourism in the twenty-first century since Carvalho (2001: 70) argued that we need to do more in our conceptualization of sustainable development in tourism if we are to give it more meaning than 'something that can be achieved in the current system with just a little tweaking and slight greening of the current development model'. We need a new philosophy that reconceptualizes the tourism development model since, as Page (2019) argues, tourism has the potential to self-destruct in localities and environments once the development process gets out of control, according to the so-called snowball and amoeba concepts. In contrast, Mowforth *et al.* (2008: 1) argue that:

> . . . tourism can be practiced in a relatively responsible, sustainable and ethical way. But the important word here is relatively, for the notions of responsibility, sustainability

and ethics are relative to the values and perspectives of all those who participate in tourism.

Despite all the attention given to sustainable tourism since the 1980s, the evidence suggests that environmental damage has 'got worse, not better' (Gössling and Hall 2006: 305). Indeed, as Gössling and Hall (2006) emphasize, the totality of tourism activity must be considered in assessing the sustainability of tourism: for example, while an ecotourism trip that benefits a local community and has minimal impact on the natural resource base of the destination might be defined as sustainable tourism, the travel to and from the destination has to be brought into the equation, especially long-haul air travel. As such, this perspective highlights the dangers in pursuing sustainable tourism, as the travel component of tourism is not impact-free. In terms of global issues, the concepts of the green economy and low-carbon (or even carbon-neutral) tourism are rapidly becoming favoured terms for operationalizing sustainability (Image 19.4), with a renewed political onus to make sustainability work effectively in a way that it had failed to do post-1992 Rio.

One response to the difficulties presented by tourism travel is the adaptation of the 'slow' concept (Dickinson and Lumsdon 2010). Ideologically, however, we need to replace economic growth/development with a sustainable growth/development ethos (i.e. paradigm shift), a far more radical move than even the new thinking permeating the sustainable development camp under the banner of tourism in the green economy (UN–WTO 2012).

As Hall *et al.* (2015: 507) suggest, a wide range of integrated policy measures to nudge us towards more sustainable behaviour for tourism needs to include voluntary and mandatory elements, including taxation (see the discussion of Air Passenger Duty in Chapter 3 as an example), changes to consumer behaviour including ethical consumption and we need to realize overconsumption and overuse

of resources to gratify personal needs has direct and indirect consequences from a sustainability perspective. We need fundamental behaviour change and new attitudes on the part of industry leaders, as exemplified at the outset of this chapter, and a fundamental shift at government level in order to challenge elites and vested interests to reorient

IMAGE 19.4 The replacement of ageing rolling stock to reduce energy consumption from land-based transport used by tourists is now widespread in Europe

the way tourism operates globally amidst a climate crisis. Critics will immediately point to the economic context and realities of a global economic slowdown as not being conducive to developing sustainable tourism under current market conditions, but it must be worked towards as a goal. It is probably the case that a very simple idea and set of principles have been over-complicated, glamourized and pursued as one of the most overused terms in contemporary tourism.

Discussion questions

1 What role does government play in sustainable tourism development and management?

2 To what extent are multinational corporations in tourism displaying green credentials?

3 Explain the meaning of sustainability in a tourism context and suggest why this might conflict with other perceptions of sustainability.

4 Why is sustainable tourism so difficult to achieve?

References

Acott, T., La Trobe, H. and Howard, S. (1998) 'An evaluation of deep ecotourism and shallow ecotourism', *Journal of Sustainable Tourism*, 6 (3): 238–253.

Alessi. E. and Di Carlo, G. (2018) *Out of the Plastic Trap: Saving the Mediterranean from Plastic Pollution.* WWF Mediterranean Marine Initiative, Rome, Italy. http://awsassets.panda.org/downloads/a4_plastics_med_web_08june_new.pdf.

19

Ayuso, S. (2007) 'Comparing voluntary policy instruments for sustainable tourism: The experience of the Spanish hotel industry', *Journal of Sustainable Tourism*, 15 (2): 144–157.

Becken, S. (2013) 'A review of tourism and climate change as an evolving knowledge domain', *Tourism Management Perspectives*, 2 (1): 53–62.

Buckley, R. (2012) 'Sustainable tourism: Research and reality', *Annals of Tourism Research*, 39 (2): 328–346.

Buckley, R. (2019) 'Measuring sustainability of individual tourist behavior', *Journal of Travel Research*, 58 (4), 709–710.

Budeanu, A. (2009) 'Environmental supply chain management in tourism: The case of large tour operators', *Journal of Cleaner Production*, 17 (16): 1385–1392.

Busby, M. (2019) 'Capitalism is part of the solution to climate crisis says Mark Carney', *The Guardian*, 31 July 2019.

Carson, R. (1962) *Silent Spring*. New York: Houghton Mifflin.

Carvalho, G. (2001) 'Sustainable development: Is it achievable within the existing international political economy context?' *Sustainable Development*, 9: 61–73.

Clarke, J. (1997) 'A framework of approaches to sustainable tourism', *Journal of Sustainable Tourism*, 5 (3): 224–233.

Cohen, S., Higham, J. and Cavaliere, C. (2011) 'Binge flying: Behavioural addiction and climate change', *Annals of Tourism Research*, 38 (3): 1070–1089.

Connell, J., Page, S.J. and Bentley, T. (2009) 'Towards sustainable tourism planning in New Zealand: Monitoring local government under the Resource Management Act', *Tourism Management*, 30 (6): 867–77.

Dickinson, J. and Lumsdon, L. (2010) *Slow Travel*. London: Earthscan.

Dredge, D. and Jenkins, J. (2007) *Tourism Planning and Policy*. Milton, Australia: John Wiley and Sons.

Eastham, J. (2019) 'Sustainable supply chains in gastronomic tourism', in S. Dixit (ed.) *The Routledge Handbook of Gastronomic Tourism* (pp. 225–233). London: Routledge.

Ellen MacArthur Foundation (n.d.) 'What is the circular economy?' Ellen MacArthur Foundation (website). https://www.ellenmacarthurfoundation.org/circular-economy/what-is-the-circular-economy.

Employment Department Group and English Tourist Board (1991) *Tourism and the Environment. Maintaining the Balance*. London: English Tourist Board.

EU (2007) *Action for More Sustainable European Tourism*. Brussels: European Union.

Extinction Rebellion (n.d.) 'Our demands'. Extinction Rebellion (website). https://rebellion.earth

Fennell, D. and Malloy, D. (2007) *Codes of Ethics in Tourism*. Clevedon: Channel View.

Font, X. and Epler Wood, M. (2007) 'Sustainable tourism certification marketing and its contribution to SME market access', in R. Black and A. Crabtree (eds.) *Quality Assurance and Certification in Ecotourism*. Wallingford: CABI.

Frey, N. and George, R. (2010) 'Responsible tourism management: The missing link between business owners' attitudes and behaviour in the Cape Town tourism industry', *Tourism Management*, 31 (5): 621–28.

Gill, A. (2004) 'Tourism communities and growth management', in A. Lew, C.M. Hall and A. Williams (eds.) *A Companion to Tourism*. Oxford: Blackwell.

Gössling, S. (2015) 'Carbon management', in C.M. Hall, S. Gössling, and D. Scott (eds.) *The Routledge Handbook of Sustainable Tourism* (pp. 221–233). London: Routledge.

Gössling, S. and Buckley, R. (2016) 'Carbon labels in tourism: Persuasive communication?' *Journal of Cleaner Production*, 111: 358–369.

Gössling, S. and Hall, C.M. (2006) *Tourism and Global Environmental Change*. London: Routledge.

Gössling, S., Hansson, C.B., Hörstmeier, O. and Saggel, S. (2002) 'Ecological footprint analysis as a tool to assess tourism sustainability', *Ecological Economics*, 43 (2): 199–211.

Graci, S. and Dodds, R. (2015) 'Certification and labeling', in C.M. Hall, S. Gössling and D. Scott (eds.) *The Routledge Handbook of Sustainable Tourism* (pp. 200–208). London: Routledge.

Grant, M. (1994) 'Visitor management', *Insights*, A41–46. London: English Tourist Board.

Guix, M., Bonilla-Priego, M. and Font, X. (2018) 'The process of sustainability reporting in international hotel groups: An analysis of stakeholder inclusiveness, materiality and responsiveness', *Journal of Sustainable Tourism*, 26 (7): 1063–1084.

Hall, C.M. (2019) 'Constructing sustainable tourism development: The 2030 agenda and the managerial ecology of sustainable tourism', *Journal of Sustainable Tourism*, in press: https://doi.org/10.1080/09669582.2018.1560456.

Hall, C.M., Gössling, S. and Scott, D. (eds.) (2015) *The Routledge Handbook of Sustainable Tourism*. London: Routledge.

Hall, C.M. and Page, S.J. (2006) *Geography of Tourism and Recreation: Environment, Place and Space*, 3rd edition. London: Routledge.

Hardin, G. (1968) 'The tragedy of the commons', *Science*, 162: 1243–1248.

Hardy, A., Beeton, R. and Pearson, L. (2002) 'Sustainable tourism: An overview of the concept and its position in relation to conceptualizations of tourism', *Journal of Sustainable Tourism*, 10 (6): 475–496.

IPCC (2018) *Global Warming of 1.5°C*. Geneva: World Meteorological Organization. https://www.ipcc.ch/sr15/.

ISO (2016) 'Benefits in applying ISO 26000 – selected case studies as a result of the SR MENA project'. International Organization for Standardization (website). https://www.iso.org/publication/PUB100375.html.

Jenkins, J. and Mkono, M. (2015) 'Sustainable tourism legislation and regulation', in C.M. Hall, S. Gössling and D. Scott (eds.) *The Routledge Handbook of Sustainable Tourism* (pp. 234–245). London: Routledge.

Jiang, M., DeLacy, T. and Lipman, G. (2013) *Travel, Tourism and Green Growth*. London: Routledge.

Jones, M. (2018) *Sustainable Event Management: A Practical Guide*, 3rd edition. London: Routledge.

Jones, P. and Wynn, M. (2019) 'The circular economy, natural capital and resilience in tourism and hospitality', *International Journal of Contemporary Hospitality Management*, 31 (6): 2544–2563.

19

Kasim, A. and Ismail, A. (2012) 'Environmentally friendly practices among restaurants: Drivers and barriers to change', *Journal of Sustainable Tourism*, 20 (4): 551–570.

Keep Australia Beautiful (n.d.) Home. Keep Australia Beautiful (website). https://kab.org.au/

Kelly, J. and Williams, P. (2007) 'Modelling tourism destination energy consumption and greenhouse gas emissions: Whistler, British Columbia, Canada', *Journal of Sustainable Tourism*, 15 (1): 67–90.

Kornilaki, M., Thomas, R. and Font, X. (2019) 'The sustainability behaviour of small firms in tourism: The role of self-efficacy and contextual constraints', *Journal of Sustainable Tourism*, 27 (1): 97–117.

Krippendorf, J. (1987) *The Holidaymakers*. Oxford: Butterworth-Heinemann.

Lemelin, H., Dawson, J. and Stewart, E. (eds.) (2012) *Last Chance Tourism*. London: Routledge.

Lemos, C., Fischer, T. and Souza, E. (2012) 'Strategic Environmental Assessment in tourism planning – extent of application and quality of documentation', *Environmental Impact Assessment Review*, 35: 1–10.

Liu, Z. (2003) 'Sustainable tourism development: A critique', *Journal of Sustainable Tourism*, 11 (6): 459–475.

Lynes, J. and Dredge, D. (2006) 'Going green: Motivations for environmental commitment in the airline industry: A case study of Scandinavian Airlines', *Journal of Sustainable Tourism*, 14 (2): 116–138.

Mak, B. and Chan, W. (2006) 'Environmental reporting of airlines in the Asia-Pacific region', *Journal of Sustainable Tourism*, 14 (6): 618–628.

Malik, A. and Sun, Y.-Y. (2018) 'The carbon footprint of tourism revealed (it's bigger than we thought)', *The Conversation*, 7 May 2018.

May, V. (1991) 'Tourism, environment and development. Values, sustainability and stewardship', *Tourism Management*, 12 (2): 112–118.

Miller, D., Merrilees, B. and Coghlan, A. (2015) 'Sustainable urban tourism: Understanding and developing visitor pro-environmental behaviours', *Journal of Sustainable Tourism*, 23 (1): 26–46.

Miller, G., Rathouse, K., Scarles, C., Holmes, K. and Tribe, J. (2010) 'Public understanding of sustainable tourism', *Annals of Tourism Research*, 37 (3): 627–645.

Ministry of Tourism (2007) *New Zealand Tourism Strategy 2015*. Wellington: Ministry of Tourism.

Mowforth, M., Charlton, C. and Munt, I. (2008) *Tourism and Responsibility: Perspectives from Latin America and the Caribbean*. London: Routledge.

Muller, H. (1994) 'The thorny path to sustainable tourism development', *Journal of Sustainable Tourism*, 2 (3): 131–136.

Page, S.J. (2009) *Transport and Tourism*, 3rd edition. Harlow: Prentice Hall.

Page, S.J. (2019) *Tourism Management: An Introduction*, 6th edition. Abingdon: Taylor and Francis.

Page, S.J. and Connell, J. (eds.) (2008) *Sustainable Tourism: Critical Concepts in the Social Sciences, Volumes 1–4*. London: Routledge.

Page, S.J. and Connell, J. (eds.) (2012) *The Routledge Handbook of Events*. London: Routledge.

Pepper, D. (1996) *An Introduction to Modern Environmentalism*. London: Routledge.

Pigram, J.J. and Jenkins, J. (2006) *Outdoor Recreation Management*, 2nd edition. London: Routledge.

Rogerson, C. (2012) 'Tourism–agriculture linkages in rural South Africa: Evidence from the accommodation sector'. *Journal of Sustainable Tourism*, 20 (3): 477–495.

Ruhanen, L., Weiler, B., Moyle, B. and McLennan, J. (2015) 'Trends and patterns in sustainable tourism research: A 25 year bibliometric analysis', *Journal of Sustainable Tourism* 23 (4): 517–535.

Scheyvens, R. (2011) *Tourism and Poverty*. London: Routledge.

Scheyvens, R. and Hughes, E. (2019) 'Can tourism help to "end poverty in all its forms everywhere"? The challenge of tourism addressing SDG1', *Journal of Sustainable Tourism*, 27 (7): 1061–1079.

Schianetz, K., Kavanagh, L. and Lockington, D. (2007) 'Concepts and tools for comprehensive sustainability assessments for tourism destinations: A comparative review', *Journal of Sustainable Tourism*, 15 (4): 369–389.

Smith, J. (2017) *Transforming Travel*. Wallingford: CABI.

Sørensen, F., Bærenholdt, J. and Greve, K. A. (2019) 'Circular economy tourist practices'. *Current Issues in Tourism*, 1–4.

Stoll-Kleemann, T., O'Riordan, T. and Jaeger, C. (2001) 'The psychology of denial concerning climate mitigation measures: Evidence from Swiss focus groups', *Global Environmental Change*, 11 (21): 107–117.

Sustainable Model for Arctic Tourism (SMART) (2008) *Sustainable Model for Arctic Regional Tourism*. http://www.arctictourism.net.

Swarbrooke, J. (1999) *Sustainable Tourism Management*. Wallingford, Oxon: CAB International.

Tamajón, L. G. and Font, X. (2013) 'Corporate social responsibility in tourism small and medium enterprises evidence from Europe and Latin America', *Tourism Management Perspectives*, 7: 38–46.

Thunberg, G, (2019) *No One Is Too Small to Make a Difference*. London: Penguin.

Truong, D. and Hall, C.M. (2015) 'Promoting voluntary behaviour change for sustainable tourism: The potential role of social marketing', in C.M. Hall, S. Gössling and D. Scott (eds.) *Routledge Handbook of Sustainable Tourism* (pp. 246–260). London: Routledge.

Turner, R.K., Pearce, D. and Bateman, I. (1994) *Environmental Economics: An Elementary Introduction*. New York: Harvester Wheatsheaf.

UNEP (2017) 'Nudge to action: Behavioural science for sustainability', *UN Environment Programme* (website). https://www.unenvironment.org/news-and-stories/story/nudge-action-behavioural-science-sustainability.

UNEP (2019) 'Paradise lost? Travel and tourism industry takes aim at plastic pollution but more action needed', *UN Environment Programme* (website). http://web.unep.org/environmentassembly/paradise-lost-travel-and-tourism-industry-takes-aim-plastic-pollution-more-action-needed.

United Nations Environment Programme (UNEP) (2003) *Tourism and Agenda 21: The Role of Local Authorities in Sustainable Tourism*. Paris: UNEP. https://wedocs.unep.org/handle/20.500.11822/7920

19

UN–WTO (2012) *Tourism and the Green Economy*. Madrid: World Tourism Organization.

Weaver, D. (2004) 'Tourism and sustainable development', in A. Lew, C.M. Hall and A. Williams (eds.) *A Companion to Tourism*. Oxford: Blackwell.

Weaver, D. (2009) 'Reflections on sustainable tourism and paradigm change', in S. Gössling, C.M. Hall and D. Weaver (eds.), *Sustainable Tourism Futures: Perspectives on Systems, Restructuring, and Innovations*. London: Routledge.

Weaver, D. (2012) 'Organic, incremental and induced paths to sustainable mass tourism', *Tourism Management*, 33 (5): 1030–1037.

Webb, K. (2015) 'ISO 26000 social responsibility standard as "proto law" and a new form of global custom: Positioning ISO 26000 in the emerging transnational regulatory governance rule instrument architecture', *Transnational Legal Theory*, 6 (2): 466–500.

Wheeller, B. (1991) 'Tourism's troubled times: Responsible tourism is not the answer', *Tourism Management*, 12 (2): 91–96.

World Commission on Environment and Development (1987) *Our Common Future*. Oxford: Oxford University Press.

World Travel and Tourism Council (WTTC) (2017) *Reporting Guidance for Travel and Tourism Businesses*. https://www.wttc.org/priorities/sustainable-growth/sustainability-reporting/.

World Travel and Tourism Council (WTTC) and McKinsey (2017) *Coping with Success: Managing Overcrowding in Tourism Destinations*. https://www.wttc.org/-/media/files/reports/policy-research/coping-with-success—managing-overcrowding-in-tourism-destinations-2017.pdf.

WWF (2002) 'Ecological footprint'. WWF (website). https://footprint.wwf.org.uk.

Zeppel, H. (2015) 'Environmental indicators and benchmarking for sustainable tourism development', in C.M.Hall, S. Gössling and D. Scott (eds.) *Routledge Handbook of Sustainable Tourism* (pp. 187–199). London: Routledge.

Further reading

Books

Edgell, D. (2016) *Managing Sustainable Tourism: A Legacy for the Future*, 2nd edition. London: Routledge.

Gössling, S., Hall, C.M. and Weaver, D. (eds.) (2009) *Sustainable Tourism Futures: Perspectives on Systems, Restructuring and Innovations*. London: Routledge.

Hall, C.M, Gössling, S. and Scott, D. (eds.) (2015) *Routledge Handbook of Sustainable Tourism*. Abingdon: Routledge.

Hall, C.M. and Page, S.J. (2014) *The Geography of Tourism and Recreation: Environment, Place and Space*, 4th edition. London: Routledge.

Holden, A. (2016) *Environment and Tourism*, 3rd edition. London: Routledge.

Wall, G. and Mathieson, A. (2006) *Tourism: Change, Impacts and Opportunities*. Harlow: Pearson.

Journal articles

The evolution of the field is set out in the compilation of key articles:

Page, S.J. and Connell, J. (eds.) (2008) *Sustainable Tourism: Critical Concepts in the Social Sciences, Volumes 1–4*. London: Routledge.

Also see:

Gössling, S. (2017) `Tourism information technologies and sustainability: An exploratory review', *Journal of Sustainable Tourism*, 25(7): 1024–1041.

Hopkins, D. (2020) `Sustainable mobility at the interface of transport and tourism', *Journal of Sustainable Tourism*, 28(2): 129–143.

Needham, M., Szuster, B., Mora, C., Lesar, L. and Anders, E. (2017) 'Manta ray tourism: Interpersonal and social values effects, sanctions and management', *Journal of Sustainable Tourism* 25 (10): 1367–1384.

Ramjeawon, T. and Beedsay, R. (2004) 'Evaluation of the EIA system on the island of Mauritius and development of an environmental monitoring plan framework', *Environmental Impact Analysis*, 24: 537–549.

Ruhanen, L., Weiler, B., Moyle, B. and McLennan, J. (2015) 'Trends and patterns in sustainable tourism research: A 25 year bibliometric analysis', *Journal of Sustainable Tourism* 23 (4): 517–535.

19

Part 5

Trends and themes in the use of tourist resources

Having reviewed the impact of tourism in Part 4, attention now turns to a number of different forms of tourism which have impacts on the environment. This section reviews the main tourism environments which attract tourist activity and discusses the nature of tourism in each context as well as the principal issues associated with each particular form of tourism. With the development and growth of tourist destinations, a consistent theme in recent research over the last 40 years is the concept of **tourist resources**, which are consumed at specific points in time by tourists in different environments. In the following four chapters, the issue of tourist resources in specific environments is examined in a variety of different contexts ranging from the urban, through to rural, coastal and resort environments, to the less developed world. To understand the synergies and themes which unify these chapters, it is interesting to begin by highlighting a number of fundamental concepts which have evolved in both the tourism and recreational literature in the last 40 years and have influenced the way we look at, analyze and understand tourist resource environments.

Concepts and themes in the analysis of tourist resources

In some respects, the overlap between recreation and tourism is evident when one begins to try to explain how concepts have been devised to understand how tourists use certain resources (see Hall and Page 2014 for a discussion of the recreation–tourism continuum). Clawson et al. (1960) examined ways of classifying outdoor recreation and resources based on the principle of distance and zones of influence in terms of whether the resource base had a national, regional, sub-regional, intermediate or local zone of influence. This research helped explain the 'pull' of the resource, and they identified a simple model of use where three zones existed:

- A 0–16 km zone: Many resource needs for recreation can be met in terms of golf, urban parks and the urban fringe.
- A 16–32 km zone: The range of activities is greater, although particular types of resource tend to dominate activity patterns (e.g. horse riding, hiking and field sports).

- A 32 km or greater zone: Sports and physical pursuits with specific resource requirements (e.g. orienteering, canoeing, skiing and rock climbing) exist.

What Clawson *et al.* (1960) highlight is that while the majority of recreational activities are undertaken near to home, it is the more distant resources within countries and outside of countries (i.e. overseas) that are the focus of the tourist. With increased mobility, resources have become much more accessible to those tourists able to afford the cost of travel although, in terms of domestic tourism, Clawson *et al.*'s (1960) classification to a large degree is still a good analysis of the difference between recreational and tourist resource users.

For tourists, the principle inherent in this research was that visitors would use different resources depending upon their accessibility, appeal and attraction base. This has led to research which describes the features and attractions of specific resource environments. For example, inventories of the attractions and accommodation in resorts are frequently undertaken by tourist agencies, and the differences are noted in relation to the status and quality of destinations to identify the strengths, weaknesses, opportunities and threats (SWOT analysis). Much of the research on the tourist and recreationalist use of resources has been undertaken by geographers (see Hall and Page 2014 for a review) and they use specific concepts and approaches to model and classify the users of specific resources.

In Chapter 20, the significance of urban tourism is discussed as a context for many forms of tourist visit and the problems of accurately analyzing this form of tourism are explored. The impact of urban tourism on city environments and the interactions it has with the city economy are reviewed together with the nature of tourist activities in city environments. Chapter 21, in direct contrast, examines rural tourism. The problems of defining what comprises rural tourism is a major task of the chapter and the impacts and effects of this form of tourism are considered. This is followed in Chapter 22 with a review of the stereotypical tourism environment – the coastal environment and resort tourism. Chapter 22 discusses both the evolution of the coast as a context for tourism activity and its predisposition as a location for resort development, with its concentration of services and facilities to service tourist needs. Last, Chapter 23 reviews the impact of tourism activity in the less developed world, which has become a popular destination in recent years for tourist trips due to the exotic appeal and relatively low costs now offered to Western tourists through package travel. In each chapter, the nature of the form of tourism is discussed and, where possible, examples illustrating the impacts of tourism activity highlighted in the previous section of the book are outlined to show how the impacts occur in specific tourism environments.

References

Clawson, M., Held, R. and Stoddart, C. (1960) *Land for the Future*. Baltimore, NJ: Johns Hopkins Press.

Hall, C.M. and Page, S.J. (2014) *The Geography of Tourism and Recreation: Environment, Place and Space*, 4th edition. London: Routledge.

20

Urban tourism

Learning outcomes

After reading this chapter and answering the questions, you should be able to:

- appreciate the significance of cities as tourism destinations
- consider the ways in which urban areas fulfil a wide range of tourist needs
- identify why tourism has been used as a tool for urban regeneration
- develop an understanding of the complexity of towns and cities in the analysis of tourist resources.

Overview

Cities have long been the centre of tourist activity, from the early times of civilization through to their very highly developed state in the global economy of the twenty-first century, where world cities not only perform important roles as centres of business and trade but also as tourist destinations for leisure and business travellers and day trippers. Cities hold a particular fascination for tourists, from the vast, highly developed world cities through to the small historic towns where heritage, history and an intimate scale enable the visitor to feel embodied in a past landscape which has been adapted for modern-day use, as illustrated in Insight 15.3. Urban tourism is arguably one of the most highly developed forms of tourism at a global scale, since most of the major tourist gateways are urban in nature, and yet it is still a poorly understood aspect in the wider tourism system even though such gateways often control the distribution and flows of tourism to other parts of regions and countries.

Introduction

Urbanization is a major force contributing to the development of towns and cities, where people live, work and shop. Towns and cities function as places where the population concentrates in a defined area, and economic activities locate in the same area or nearby, to provide the opportunity for the production and consumption of goods and services in capitalist societies. Consequently, towns and cities provide the context for a diverse range of social, cultural and economic activities which the population engage in and where tourism, leisure and entertainment form major service activities. These environments also function as meeting places, major tourist gateways, accommodation and transportation hubs, and as central places to service the needs of visitors. Most tourist trips will contain some experience of an urban area: for example, when an urban dweller departs from a major gateway in a city, arrives at a gateway in another city-region and stays in accommodation in an urban area. Within cities, however, the line between tourism and recreation blurs to the extent that at times one is indistinguishable from the other, with tourists and recreationalists using the same facilities, resources and environments, although some notable differences exist. Therefore, many tourists and recreationalists will intermingle in many urban contexts. Most tourists will experience urban tourism in some form during their holidays, a visit to friends and relatives, a business trip or a visit for another reason.

Urban tourism: A relevant area for study?

Ashworth's (1989) landmark study of urban tourism acknowledges that 'a double neglect has occurred. Those interested in the study of tourism have tended to neglect the urban context in which much of it is set, while those interested in urban studies . . . have been equally neglectful of the importance of the tourist function in cities' (Ashworth 1989: 33). While more recent studies have examined urban tourism research in a spatial context, it still remains a comparatively unresearched area despite the growing interest in the relationship between urban regeneration (also referred to as rejuvenation by some commentators) and tourism. The problem is also reiterated in a number of subsequent studies as one explanation of the neglect of urban tourism. Despite this problem, which is more a function of perceived than real difficulties in understanding urban tourism phenomena, a range of studies now provide evidence of a growing body of literature on the topic as reviewed in Page and Hall (2002) and Ashworth and Page (2011). Yet much of the research which is published on urban tourism research remains quite descriptive, mainly case-study driven and confronted by a series of paradoxes (Table 20.1).

Interestingly, Ashworth (1992) argued that urban tourism has not emerged as a distinct research focus: research is focused on tourism in cities as opposed to being embedded in a holistic analysis of urban tourism as a distinct form of tourist activity. Consequently, research looks at the activities of tourists within cities without any recourse to why urban tourism is a unique form of tourism. This strange paradox can be explained by the failure by planners, commercial interests and residents to recognize tourism as one of the main economic rationales for cities. Tourism is often seen as an adjunct or necessary evil to generate additional revenue, while the main economic activities of the locality are not perceived as tourism-related, unless tourism is a central component of urban regeneration strategies. Such negative views of urban tourism have taken the temporary, seasonal and ephemeral nature of tourism as a reason to neglect serious research on this theme. Consequently, a vicious circle exists: the absence of public- and private-sector research makes access to research data difficult and the large-scale funding necessary to break the vicious circle, and underwrite primary data collection using social survey techniques, is rarely available. However, with the pressure posed by tourists in many European tourist cities (e.g. Canterbury, London, York, Venice and Florence), this perception is changing now that the public and private sectors are belatedly acknowledging the necessity of visitor management (see Chapters 19 and 24 for a discussion of this issue) as a mechanism to enhance, manage and improve the tourists' experience of towns and places to visit. Insight 20.1 examines the scope of many of these issues in relation to one of the world's most fascinating historic cities – Venice.

20

TABLE 20.1 Paradoxes of urban tourism research

According to Ashworth and Page (2011: 1–2) research on urban tourism is confronted by a number of paradoxes:

1 Urban tourism is an extremely important, world-wide form of tourism: It has received a disproportionately small amount of attention from scholars of either tourism or of the city, particularly in linking theoretical research to tourism studies more generally. Consequently, despite its significance, urban tourism has remained only imprecisely defined and vaguely demarcated, with little development of a systematic structure of understanding.

2 Tourists visit cities for many purposes: The cities that accommodate most tourists are large multifunctional entities into which tourists can be effortlessly absorbed and thus become to a large extent economically and physically invisible.

3 Tourists make an intensive use of many urban facilities and services, but little of the city has been created specifically for tourist use.

4 Tourism can contribute substantial economic benefits to cities, but the cities whose economies are the most dependent upon tourism are likely to benefit the least. It is the cities with a large and varied economic base that gain the most from tourism but are the least dependent upon it.

5 Thus ultimately, and from a number of directions, we arrive at the critical asymmetry in the relationship between the tourist and the city, which has many implications for policy and management. The tourism industry clearly needs the varied, flexible and accessible tourism products that cities provide: it is by no means so clear that cities need tourism.

Source: Ashworth and Page (2011: 1–2)

INSIGHT 20.1 Tourism in a small historic city: Venice

Venice is world famous as the only amphibious city. It developed towards the end of the Roman Empire and has a long history associated with a seafaring race, the Venetians, who created this small historic city, full of cultural antiquities such as the Doge's Palace (Image 20.1) and including its world-famous fifteenth-century Renaissance art. It also has a long tradition of tourism, epitomized by its popularity among the rich and leisured classes who visited in the eighteenth and nineteenth centuries. What makes Venice unusual and popular with visitors is its location on a series of islands in a lagoon (Figure 20.1), where it serves as the capital of the Veneto region of Italy. Despite economic growth in the region since the 1960s, the historic city of Venice experienced continued population loss during this period, dropping from 175 000 people in 1951 to under 61 000 in 2012 and 55 000 in 2018. At the same time, many of the city's historic buildings are under constant threat from the sea, although this is not new, and debates in the Victorian period saw poets such as Ruskin debating the modernizing influence of industrialization on the romantic aspects of the city. Among the main environmental threats facing Venice are a sinking ground level, a rising sea level, periodic flooding of the lagoon in which it is located and atmospheric pollution which impacts upon the foundations of its buildings and the very building fabric. But one of the most visible and persistent issues is the effect of tourism.

IMAGE 20.1 The Doge's Palace is a fine example of Venice's heritage

As one of the city's prominent residents, Francesco da Mosto, who fronted the popular BBC television series, Francesco's *Venice*, outlined:

Building gondolas, rowing them, blowing glass and fashioning masks were once essential livelihoods in the

economy of a great city: now they merely capitalize on the tourist industry although the very layout of the city [Figure 20.1], its canal structure and intimate urban landscape make it one of the most memorable cultural tourism experiences in Europe. (Mosto 2004: 204)

The scale of tourism is apparent from Mosto's observation that:

A reputed 15 million visitors flock to the city every year . . . and the cultural distinctiveness of Venice is threatened by the intense pressures of mass tourism. Cruise ships bring tourists right into the heart of Venice. There is much concern that this is damaging the fragile infrastructure of the city. (Mosto 2004: 206)

These visitor numbers are swelled by a large day-visitor market from other parts of Italy, especially the Adriatic beach resorts and Alpine areas, and by the concentration at key points such as St Mark's Square. Venice is saturated at key times in the year (e.g. Easter), and the police now regularly have to close the Ponte della Liberta temporarily, since the optimum flow of 21 000 tourists a day is exceeded on numerous occasions throughout the year (e.g. 60 000 at Easter and 100 000 in the summer). The diversity of people attracted to the city is evident from Montanari and Muscara's (1995) nine-fold classification of its tourists:

- first-time visitors on an organized tour
- the rich tourist
- the lover of Venice
- the backpacker camper
- the worldly wise tourist
- the return tourist
- the resident artist

- the beach tourist
- the visitor with a purpose.

While excursionists comprise over 85 per cent of all visitors to the city, additional pressures have arisen by making the destination more accessible through the advent of low-cost airlines. Since the opening up of Eastern Europe, the city has also seen an influx of eastern Europeans, with city officials reporting as many as 60 000 visitors from the Czech Republic alone, arriving in 1200 coaches in one day. In Venice, van der Borg *et al.* (1996: 314) calculated the visitor: resident (host) ratio at 89.4:1, which may explain why residents may feel besieged by the tourists. By 2018 this had reached over 550:1, reflecting the absolute saturation of visitors in a built area of 13 square miles. At key points in the year, this may be as high as 200:1 or as low as 1:1 (France 2011) but it is clear that earlier estimates have now risen sharply. The large volume of visitors who descend on Venice each year not only exceeds the desirable limits of tourism for the city but also poses a range of social and economic problems for planners. As van der Borg (1992: 52) observes:

the negative external effects connected with the overloading of the carrying capacity are rapidly increasing, frustrating the centre's economy and society . . . excursionism [day tripping] is becoming increasingly important, while residential tourism is losing relevance for the local tourism market . . . [and] . . . the local benefits are diminishing. Tourism is becoming increasingly ineffective for Venice.

A number of positive measures have been enacted to address the saturation of the historic city by day visitors, including denying access to the city by unauthorized tour coaches via the main coach terminal. Glasson *et al.* (1995: 116) summarize the problem of seeking to manage visitors and their environmental impact in Venice:

IMAGES 20.2 & 20.3 Venice has many festivals and events, some of which have a long history, including the Carnival, where masks were first worn in 1268, and which are a cultural artefact of Venice's rich and varied history
Source: Venice Tourist Board

every city must be kept as accessible as possible for some specific categories of users, such as inhabitants, visitors to offices and firms located in the city, and commuters studying or working in the city. At the same time, the art city needs to be kept as inaccessible as possible to some other user categories (the excursionist/day trippers in particular).

The city has a well-developed heritage of traditional festivals and events (see Images 20.2 & 20.3) and these attract more cultural tourists. The city's heritage includes a number of more sustainable transport solutions to cater for the tourist market, including the gondola. However, other pressures such as arrivals by cruise ship have created additional influxes of visitors, as the number of cruise ships has risen from 200 in 2000 to 500 in 2007 (France 2011) and is now around 600 a year.

This Insight is significant in that it highlights the prevailing problems affecting many historic cities around the world, which are not peculiar to Venice. While pollution is a grave problem for Venice, the greatest threat are day trippers who contribute little to the economy. Yet, as the example of Venice shows, it takes a determined political will to address the pressures posed by tourism since vested interests do not want to see the economy decline if visitors are not attracted. Probably the greatest dilemma is in reaching a sustainable solution – this desire for balance is poignantly voiced by Mosto (2004: 211): 'The future of Venice is uncertain. I hope that its remarkable history will be preserved along with its monuments, and that a balance can be found between opening up this city of wonders for modern visitors and restoring the integrity and vitality of the Venetian population'. This view is supported by the declining resident population base and prevailing concerns that the city will eventually become a people-less museum, or devoid of Venetians, as second-home owners buy apartments. In such a case it would lose much of its appeal as a living and working city (Bertocchi et al 2020).

Action for a city under siege from tourism: A battle plan

More extreme measures have been implemented in recent years, such as installing temporary gates in 2018 to separate local residents from tourists to allow the residents to enjoy their public holidays. These measures redirected tourists to other locations. Venice's mayor, elected on the mandate of dealing with the problem of tourism in the city, spearheaded a tax on tourists in 2019. From May 2019, an entrance fee of €6 a day was payable, expected to rise to €10 a day by 2022 on days when events are staged (with reductions for visitors who do not stay in the immediate region). The arguments for such a

tax were to help control the flow of tourists and to also help address:

- a reduction in the costs of tourism for businesses and residents
- the need for funding to restore the built fabric of Venice including work to address the erosion of canal banks
- to enhance security and surveillance including the cost of policing, complementing the existing steward system.

This also complements existing actions adopted in Venice to regulate and manage tourist behaviour, alongside the tourists board's Enjoy Respect Venezia campaign and measures that include:

- potentially banning sitting in public areas like St Mark's Square
- Banning swimming in the waters of Venice
- Fining people for littering
- Banning feeding of pigeons
- Banning camping.

In addition, in 2017 the city managed to get the national government to reroute cruise ships to reduce the impact on central Venice and its waterways, as residents protested about the effects of frequent visits by these vessels. This highlights the severe nature of the problems affecting the city related to tourism. The city has also put a moratorium on new hotel development and fast-food outlets, as critics point to the evolution of Venice as a living museum for visitor enjoyment, to the detriment of residents. Venice clearly represents one of the most severe examples of **overtourism** (Image 20.4), a feature we shall return to later in the chapter.

IMAGE 20.4 Overtourism is an excess of people at a destination, such as in this image of an event in Venice
Source: Venice Tourist Board

INSIGHT 20.1 continued

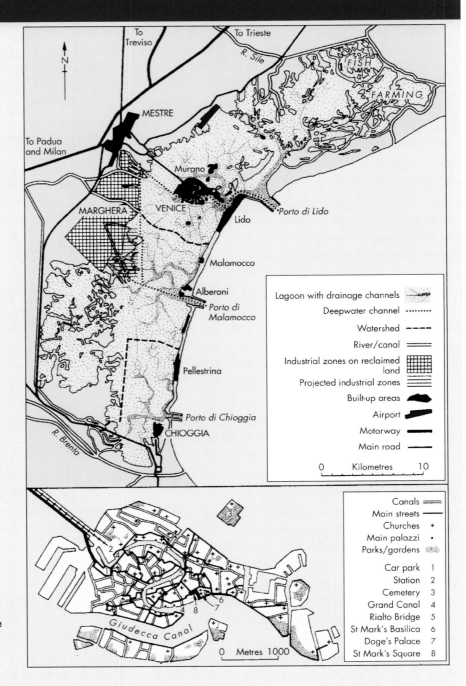

FIGURE 20.1 Location of Venice

Source: King (1987), reproduced with kind permission R. King

Further reading

France, R. (2011) *Veniceland Atlantis: The Bleak Future of the World's Favourite City*. Farringdon, Oxon: Libri Publishing.

García-Hernández, M., De la Calle-Vaquero, M. and Yubero, C. (2017) 'Cultural heritage and urban tourism: Historic city centres under pressure', *Sustainability* 9: 1346.

Seraphin, H., Sheeran, P. and Pilato, M. (2018) 'Over-tourism and the fall of Venice as a destination', *Journal of Destination Marketing and Management*, 9: 374–376.

Questions

1 Why has tourism become such a major problem for Venice?

2 What measures towards managing visitors may have a likelihood of success?

3 How can you rationalize the need to market and promote Venice for tourism and events and the needs of the city to limit numbers?

4 To what extent is Venice now a living museum available to view for a price?

Understanding the nature and concept of urban tourism: Theoretical debates

The emergence of urban tourism studies

It is apparent that there are a number of key studies which emanate from a sociological tradition (Garreau 1991; Mullins 1991, 1994; Roche 1992; Hannigan 1998), cultural studies (Zukin 1996), geography (Jansen-Verbeke 1986; Ashworth 1989, 2003; Law 1992, 2002; Dear 1994; Page 1995; Thrift 1997; Dear and Flusty 1999; Page and Hall 2002); and urban studies (Gladstone 1998). A preliminary review of any recent journal article, book or text on urban tourism will confirm these narrowly defined contributions from these disciplines remain weakly integrated, and consequently theoretical developments remain confined to the audiences they are targeted at (Ashworth and Page 2011). As Ashworth and Page (2011) argue, we need to transcend case-study analysis to focus more fully on processes, which this chapter seeks to address. Within the wider area of tourism studies, however, there has been a splintering of research activity informed by individual disciplines which frame research questions in a narrow disciplinary manner, making coherent theoretical analysis of big issues like urban tourism problematic. For example, many geographical analyzes of urban tourism have developed models and theoretical explanations predicated on the notion of space, resulting in the notion of the tourist city as a series of clustered activities with functional links that are geographically located in the urban environment. There has been a tendency for much of the published urban tourism research to be either case-study or place-specific, which has meant researchers have failed to examine these macro or theoretical issues, such as how and why urban tourism is developing as it is and where it is, and its global manifestations, particularly hierarchies of urban development.

Shaw and Williams (1994) argue that urban areas offer geographical concentration of facilities and attractions that are conveniently located to meet both visitor and resident needs alike. But the diversity and variety among urban tourist destinations has led researchers to examine the extent to which they display unique and similar features. Shaw and Williams (1994) identify three perspectives:

- the diversity of urban areas means that their size, function, location and history contributes to their uniqueness
- towns and cities are multifunctional areas, meaning that they simultaneously provide various functions for different groups of users
- the tourist functions of towns and cities are rarely produced or consumed solely by tourists, given the variety of user groups in urban areas.

Ashworth (1992) conceptualizes urban tourism by identifying three approaches towards its analysis, where researchers have focused on:

- *the supply of tourism facilities in urban areas*, involving inventories (e.g. the spatial distribution of accommodation, entertainment complexes and tourist-related services), where urban ecological models, developed by urban geographers have been used (see Page 1995). In addition, the facility approach has been used to identify the tourism product offered by destinations
- *the demand generated by urban tourists*, to examine how many people visit urban areas, why they choose to visit and their patterns of behaviour, perception and expectations in relation to their visit
- *urban tourism policy*, where the public sector (e.g. planners) and private sector agencies have undertaken or commissioned research to investigate specific issues of interest to their own interests for urban tourism.

Theoretical studies of urban tourism by Mullins (1991) and Roche (1992) are focused on the many former towns and cities with a declining industrial base that are now looking towards service-sector activities such as tourism that have the potential to generate new employment opportunities through regeneration, as discussed later. These studies examine urban tourism in post-industrial society and question the types of process now shaping the operation and development of tourism in post-industrial cities, and the implications for public sector tourism policy.

Mullins' initial research has been followed by studies which argue that a 'new urban tourism' exists in post-industrial society, based on the consumption of places. Indeed, sociologists such as Meethan (1996) suggest urban areas now see this consumption as a complex process of transforming the landscape into one of pleasure and fun. A variety of activities exist such as promenading, eating, drinking, watching events and appreciating the heritage and culture of the place. Hannigan's (1998) Fantasy City depicts many of these features in the North American city, while other studies have pointed to the globalization of such trends in the postmodern city. Critics such as Ritzer (1996) suggest that this process of globalization has led to the McDonaldization of production and consumption in such cities, meaning that in these environments one now has a similar experience regardless of location due to the process of globalization. Whatever theoretical perspective one adopts, urban places in the developed world (and former Communist eastern bloc and China) are in a process of transformation based on the consumption of tourism. Global capital has realized the benefits of investing in regeneration schemes to transform redundant areas for profit. What is also apparent is that the urban landscape of the twenty-first century is littered with symbols of globalization, such as the multinational hotel chains and hospitality brands like KFC and Starbucks, as well as a wide range of locally produced elements that retain a degree of distinctiveness for the destination. However, the competition for global investment and visitors has led to complex forms of place-marketing to promote each locality, its identity, brands and a variety of markets. For example, in Fuzhou, China, a replica of Shakespeare's birthplace has been constructed, raising issues of the cultural authenticity of the types of attraction being developed. In some cases, highly developed urban tourism resorts have evolved (e.g. Las Vegas, Australia's Gold Coast) as part of what Mullins and others have described as 'tourism urbanization'. Many of these places, solely developed through tourism, operate 24 hours a day and have a defined theme (e.g. gambling and entertainment in Las Vegas).

What the tourism urbanization studies highlight is the role of the state, especially local government in seeking to develop service industries based on tourism consumption. For example, many local authorities in Western Europe are pump-priming tourism development as a means of stimulating the urban economy, particularly where leisure and culture-based spending can be harnessed to create new employment. Consequently, one can identify the following types of urban tourist destination:

- capital cities
- metropolitan centres, walled historic cities and small fortress cities
- large historic cities
- inner-city areas
- revitalized waterfront areas
- industrial cities

- seaside resorts and winter sport resorts
- purpose-built integrated tourist resorts
- tourist-entertainment complexes
- specialized tourist service centres
- cultural/art cities
- sport cities (Page and Hall 2002).

This classification has largely been applied to the developed world, although the study by Rogerson and Visser (2007) begins to address the neglect of urban tourism in the developing world with a focus on South Africa and pointing to studies of Hong Kong, Singapore, Brazil, China, Cuba and Taiwan as well as the potential of Asian cities as convention venues. In the case of Africa, Rogerson and Visser (2007) highlight the examples in Africa of converted cities (i.e. those previously dependent upon manufacturing or other functions, and now focused on urban tourism, such as Nairobi and Johannesburg). One important category of urban place which has a major impact upon tourism is the national capital city (NCC), which often has world-city status.

20

Urbanization and city status: National capital cities and world cities as tourist destinations

There is widespread recognition among governments and transnational agencies such as the United Nations (UN) that the world's population is increasingly urbanizing. While estimates of the world's urban population vary, there is a consensus among bodies such as the UN that it will rise to 4.98 billion by 2030, dominated by growth in middle- and low-income countries, particularly in Asia. At the same time, cities make a disproportionate contribution to national economies as the focus of production of goods and services, and tourism is no exception to this as tourist gateways are predominantly large urban centres. Likewise, much of the flow of foreign direct investment (FDI) is destined to these centres, although, in advanced Western nations, lowering of trade barriers, lower transport and production costs has seen capital relocate to more profitable locations. These processes of change associated with global capital have proved to be major actors in the emerging landscapes of post-industrial and industrializing cities, as the leisure economies (tourism, leisure and the wider cultural industries) are harnessed and developed, shaping new opportunities for tourism and leisure consumption. In terms of urban tourism, these themes are not new, as shown by key NCCs, which provide a major focal point for domestic and international tourism due to the political, cultural, symbolic and administrative functions provided in such locations. The spatial clustering of many government and cultural facilities in NCCs serve a diverse group of city visitors, including business travellers and domestic and international visitors, who provide an interconnected system of tourism markets. The concept of NCCs is far from a homogeneous term: Hall (2000) identified a typology of NCCs which embraces: multifunctional cities, global capitals, political capitals, former capitals, provincial and state capitals and super-capitals. However, one useful concept here is the evolution of the term 'world city'.

World cities: A useful framework for urban tourism?

The concept of globalization is not new to tourism, but its impact on the economy, culture and politics have been widely researched in the social sciences. In urban studies, the research agenda on globalization and cities has generated a vast literature, much of it focused on the notion of world cities, a concept first advanced by Hall (1966), to describe places which dominate world business. But what exactly are world cities?

What are world cities?

The evolution of world cities has attracted a great deal of research, notably from urban geography and sociology, and with the rise of a knowledge economy, cities have become the point at which knowledge is transformed into productive activities. This is particularly the case in the advanced service sector, as global service centres like London and New York have emerged. King (1990) identified some of the principal characteristics of these world cities, including:

- Their global control function in a world economy that transcends the nation-state.
- A disproportionate number of transnational companies (TNCs) and international finance and professional services (e.g. accountancy, law, insurance and corporate services), known as producer services.
- A rise in office space to accommodate the headquarters and space requirements of these producer services.
- A concentration of global capital and investment in these places.
- Decentralization of routine administrative tasks from the world city (outsourcing).
- Deindustrialization and decline in blue-collar employment and some reindustrialization in low-wage/low-skill jobs.
- Expansion of low-level, low-paid routine work in the hospitality sector, tourism and domestic work.
- Large-scale immigration (where controls have not limited the influx), giving rise to major income and social disparities in living standards and spatial segregation of the low- and high-income classes (also by race and ethnicity).
- Gentrification of older districts and regeneration of sites for consumption.
- Economic and social polarization, increased violence and crime as well as the rise of private security and sites of private consumption (e.g. shopping malls and precincts).
- Loss of local control over the redevelopment process to attract the future of capital investment, and in particular to woo inward investment, namely footloose capital.

Many commentators merge these processes into the wider debate on the impact of globalization as a process contributing to world-city formation, and Friedmann (1986) identified 30 centres globally as world cities. Subsequent research by Thrift (1989) outlined three levels of world city:

- Truly global centres such as New York and London.
- Zonal centres, with corporate offices and links to international business flows and transactions.
- Regional centres, which are sites for corporate offices but are not connected to the international business flows.

20

Beaverstock *et al.* (2000), in contrast, devised a system of 55 world cities, with another 67 cities showing evidence of world-city formation. The important feature of the world-city hierarchy that has emerged is the linkages between each city, which connect them across geographical borders. While the contrasting explanations of the way this system functions is the subject of ongoing debate as to whether such cities coexist in a system or compete with each other, this does raise serious issues for a national tourism economy. As these world cities do function as gateways to their national tourism system in many cases, integration into an international hierarchy may disconnect them from their national urban system. Consequently, the disconnection of the world city from its local region and even its national tourism economy may raise inherent difficulties in achieving regional development goals of spreading visitor spending to more peripheral areas. Furthermore, it may also lead to a greater concentration of business travel between world cities and the predisposition of expos and conference organizers to target world cities due to their appeal and vibrant cultural industries.

Pacione (2005) argues that the cultural industries blur the distinction between production and consumption in the function of cities, in that they may sit somewhere in between. Therefore, the emergence of world cities has the potential to create a new series of geographies of urban tourism based not just on the world-city hierarchy, but on a changing internal structure of the postmodern city in terms of tourism, as Page and Hall (2002) explored. While the changing internal geographies of these cities have provided new tourism opportunities within world-city regions, this does highlight the role of globalization as a process driving such changes.

Globalization, combined with the rise of instantaneous communications, has led some geographers to claim the borderless world has emerged and the demise of geography is upon us, while other arguments have shown that globalization may 'destroy some geographies but in turn [. . .] create other new geographies. In the modern world there is always a continual movement of destruction and renewal of spaces and globalisation is its latest manifestation' (Taylor 2001: 213). One consequence of globalization and global capital, explored in Manuel Castells' work (1996, 1998), is the rise of a globally networked capitalism. One of the underlying principles in Castells' argument surrounding the networked society is the importance of connectivity for global capital to function, part of which is the transport network necessary for world cities to exist and operate. While there are many critiques and rejections of Castells' ideas and other theoretical explanations of why world cities have emerged, researchers such as Short *et al.* (2000) point to the 'explosion of interest in world cities', although tourism research has been noticeable by its absence. The main assumption has been that world cities increasingly control the global economy and concentrate financial investment and thereby affect the competitiveness of places. Various criteria have been used to identify world cities, including being a major financial centre, headquarters for multinational enterprises, being the location of international institutions, having a rapidly growing business sector, having a major centre of manufacturing, being major transportation node and population size. More recent studies seek to add quality of life, cultural attributes and attractiveness, among other measures.

Castells' work provides an initial spatial analytical framework to consider world cities, with nodes and hubs between which finance and business flow. This has profound implications for urban tourism at a number of levels. First, the dominance of world cities in the transport infrastructure and location of airline hubs raises issues of the connected and disconnected city destination in simple access terms. The world city, which is highly connected and linked to other world cities, provides a major nucleus for business travel, as already discussed, as the high-yielding sector of the tourism industry. Second, more politically derived analyzes point to the control function which this may exercise over tourism, with TNCs and other investors seeking to strengthen a market position in these world cities with their expanding markets. Third, tourism is assuming a growing political and cultural importance indirectly in relation to the ranking of world cities as places to live, work and do business. This is combined with a growing multicultural population and ethnic mix in world cities, derived from international migration, which has also impacted upon non-residential areas (e.g. restaurants and cafés) with the emergence of culturally distinct districts (e.g. Little India in Singapore and London's East End). One key element of this competition and promotion of world-city status is place-marketing.

Place-marketing and selling in world cities

Short *et al.* (2000), in line with many recent (e.g. Morgan *et al.* 2011) and some more dated syntheses (e.g. Ashworth and Voogd 1990) highlight the impact of globalization in how cities are represented and promoted. At its most simplistic level, public and private sector bodies have engaged in city marketing to attract mobile global capital, as a former public sector welfare-oriented stance has seen more entrepreneurial traits adopted to attract inward investment, most notably in tourism. As Short and Kim (1999) explain, the rise of the entrepreneurial city may begin to highlight why the public sector has embraced private sector marketing principles to create a new image for localities, districts and regions in cities as part of their repositioning, rebranding and re-imaging. This introduces a highly competitive element in place promotion, apparent in the most recent Olympic Games bidding procedure.

Here specific marketing strategies are used to attract an event and inward investment, and mirror the use of tourism and culture in the quality-of-life debates on why global capital should locate in certain world cities. Much of this highly contentious activity has been theorized by researchers such as Debord (1994) in terms of the 'spectacle', epitomized by the Olympic Games, which are seen as global events whereby a city can lay claim to global status or world-city status. Such events have a profound economic and social impact on cities, with controversial redevelopment schemes that often leave residents with a financial legacy in lieu of the urban backdrop created during the event spectacle, where landscape alteration and conflict with local communities is viewed as necessary in pursuit of global re-imaging strategies. The tourism development and activity which results during such spectacles in terms of creating new landscapes is far removed from the beneficial cultural and social exchange we expect from tourism. It is a globalized event where multinational companies and investors create an environment sanctioned by local and national planners to produce a highly commercialized and commoditized experience. This not only introduces elements of cultural globalization but may actually destroy some of the very tourism attributes that offer local distinctiveness. Hae (2018) examines how South Korea employed successful place-marketing strategies. It is possible to summarize the theoretical issues on urban tourism into the following points:

- An interconnected system of world cities assumes a transnational state, creating a global network of high-profile tourist destinations driven by business travel and the opportunities existing and proposed infrastructure offers for leisure travel.

- Many world cities and non-world cities are engaging in aggressive place-marketing and competitive strategies to retain and further their ambitions for urban status, and tourism and leisure has been integral to these strategies.

- The physical impact of inward investment and the staging of large events, often to create a global spectacle, has induced profound changes to the social and cultural fabric and landscape of many world cities. They are constantly seeking to reinvent or re-image themselves, and thereby reconfiguring tourism spaces as part of that process.

- Theoretical debates on the role of globalization in driving these changes has seen varying positions on what global and local impacts mean for specific places. Tourism is one sector that has been able to embrace the process of globalization, providing local differences and attractions that help to differentiate world cities as destinations.

- Much of the existing urban studies research on producer services point to the rise of global service centres, but in the case of tourism the networks and infrastructure which exist may shape a greater degree of core–periphery tourism patterns in nation-states where a world city exists. In some respects, this begins to have some of the inherent qualities and relationships which Britton (1982) identified in terms of the tourist enclave, where world cities and their tourism districts could continue to evolve into core-based experiences, with few functional links with their hinterland or more peripheral locations. The gateway function of many world cities in terms of globalization and in controlling the entry/exit and pattern of tourist activity may also have significant implications for national tourism organizations. In the UK, for example, over half of all overseas visitors visit London, and if the globalizing impact on the city continues, future infrastructure development may see this percentage continue to rise. Even if such visitor numbers do not rise, world cities are the flagship destinations for many countries and will certainly consume a significant proportion of a visitor's budget due to tourist living costs in these localities.

20

The market for urban tourism

Identifying the scale, volume and different markets for urban tourism remains a perennial problem for researchers. Urban tourism is a major economic activity in many of Europe's capital cities but identifying the tourism markets in each area is problematic. The principal international data sources on urban tourism are the published statistics

Primary elements		Secondary elements
Activity place	**Leisure setting**	• Hotel and catering facilities
Cultural facilities	**Physical characteristics**	• Markets
• Concert halls	• Ancient monuments and statues	• Shopping facilities
• Cinemas	• Ecclesiastical buildings	
• Exhibitions	• Harbours	
• Museums and art galleries	• Historical street pattern	
• Theatres	• Interesting buildings	
Sports facilities	• Parks and green areas	
• Indoor and outdoor	• Water, canals and river fronts	
Amusement facilities	**Sociocultural features**	
• Bingo halls	• Folklore	**Additional elements**
• Casinos	• Friendliness	
• Festivities	• Language	• Accessibility and parking facilities
• Nightclubs	• Liveliness and ambience of the place	• Tourist facilities: Information offices, signposts, guides, maps and leaflets
• Organized events	• Local customs and costumes	
	• Security	

FIGURE 20.2 The elements of tourism

Source: Reprinted from *Annals of Tourism Research*, vol. 13, Jansen-Verbeke, 'Inner-city tourism', 79–100 © 1986, with permission from Elsevier

of the UN–WTO and the OECD. Such data sources commonly use the domestic and international tourist use of accommodation as one measure of the scale of tourism activity. In the context of urban tourism, researchers must have an understanding of the geographical distribution of tourist accommodation in each country to identify the scale and distribution of tourist visits. In countries where the majority of accommodation is urban-based, such statistics may provide a preliminary source of data for research. While this may be relevant for certain categories of tourist (e.g. business travellers and holidaymakers), those visitors staying with friends and relatives within an urban environment would not be included in the statistics. Even where statistics can be used, they only provide a preliminary assessment of scale and volume and more detailed sources are needed to assess specific markets for urban tourism. Figure 20.2 describes a method of classifying urban tourists based on individual motives for visiting urban destinations, although Jansen-Verbeke (1986) points to the methodological problem of distinguishing between the different users of the tourist city. For example, Burtenshaw *et al.* (1991) discuss the concept of functional areas within the city, where different visitors seek certain attributes for their city visit (e.g. the historic city, the culture city, the night life city, the shopping city and the tourist city, to which Page and Hall (2002) have added the sport city as shown in Figure 20.3) where no one group has a monopoly over its use. Residents of the city and its hinterland, visitors and workers all use the resources within the tourist city, but some user groups identify with certain areas more than others. Thus, the tourist city is a multifunctional area which complicates attempts to identify a definitive classification of users and the areas/facilities they visit, and now the term 'tourist precinct' has been added to the existing terminology (Hayllar *et al.* 2008). Tourism precincts are broadly similar to the areas identified by Burtenshaw *et al.* (1991) but the term also describes more localized clusters of tourism-related functions in districts, precincts or quarters in cities and towns.

A study by Romero *et al.* (2002) identified the main groups of urban visitors in terms of:

- business users
- fairs and congress attendees
- visiting friends and relatives
- vacation travellers
- short-break visitors

although these markets do exhibit different degrees of seasonality.

Ashworth and Tunbridge (1990) prefer to approach the market for urban tourism from the perspective of the consumers' motives, focusing on the purchasing intent of users, and their attitudes, opinions and interests for specific urban tourism products. The most important distinction they make is between use/non-use of tourism resources, leading them to identify intentional users (who are motivated by the character of the city) and incidental users (who

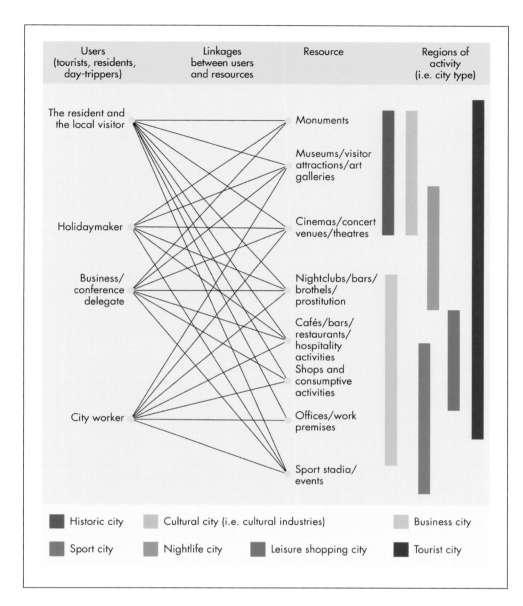

FIGURE 20.3 Functional areas in the city
Source: Page and Hall (2002), reproduced with permission from Pearson Education

view the character of the city as irrelevant to their use). This two-fold typology is then used by Ashworth and Tunbridge (1990) to identify four specific types of users:

- intentional users from outside the city-region (e.g. holidaymakers and heritage tourists)
- intentional users from inside the city-region (e.g. those using recreational and entertainment facilities – recreating residents)
- incidental users from outside the city-region (e.g. business and conference/exhibition tourists and those on family visits – non-recreating visitors)
- incidental users from inside the city-region (e.g. residents going about their daily activities – non-recreating residents).

Such an approach recognizes the significance of attitudes and the use made of the city and services rather than the geographical origin of the visitor as the starting point for analysis. This is a more sophisticated approach to understanding the tourist demand for urban areas. But it does raise a practical problem – that tourists tend to cite one main motive for visiting a city, but in any destination there are likely to be a wider range of motives beyond one principal reason to visit. It is likely that there will be a variety of user groups. This multi-use nature of urban visitors advanced by Ashworth and Tunbridge (1990, 2000) was also developed in a geographical context by Getz (1993) in terms of the tourism business district, where the attractions of the city, the central business functions and services provided in the city were consumed by three user groups: residents, workers and visitors. This makes it difficult to precisely identify the contribution of the tourist in supporting these services and resources. Yet it is evident that the economic value of such groups can be harnessed when seeking to regenerate areas to create a tourism sector.

Tourism and urban regeneration

In the postmodern city, one of the defining features of tourism is the way in which city authorities and planners have formed partnerships with investors, developers and other stakeholders to realize the development potential of tourism. One of the principal features of this approach to urban areas is the realization that, by forming partnerships, as discussed by Maitland (2002), across public–private sector interest groups, wider benefits can be achieved by turning areas into destinations in their own right such as in the European Year of Culture scheme. For example, the urban redevelopment of London Docklands since the 1980s has seen the area marketed as a destination within London's vibrant tourism economy. By adding transport infrastructure (i.e. the Dockland Light Railway and Jubilee Line) and an accommodation base along with attractions, areas formerly deemed to have been deprived have seen tourism grow, shifting the axis of tourism from the dominance of the west of London and the central tourism district.

In fact research by Conforti (1996) also highlighted the potential role of ghettos as urban attractions where they are preserved as cultural districts in cities, and in developing countries, slum tourism has evolved (Frenzel *et al.* 2012) as discussed in Chapter 15. The links between tourism and urban regeneration have gone through several transformations in thinking. In the 1980s tourism was seen as a key driver of regeneration (Figure 20.4) and various schemes were built around this premise. Although there are numerous success stories from the 1980s where tourism has helped regenerate districts of cities, especially waterfront areas, there were also many failures, In the case of the failures, this was often attributed to inadequately linking regenerated areas to the main footfall of city, to direct visitors to these new areas. To help in luring in visitors, major drawcards have been constructed in regenerated areas (e.g. an anchor project such as Bilbao's museum and Margate's Tate art gallery to generate a must-visit destination). This has led to a rethink about using a mixed economy of regeneration projects including retailing, housing and tourism to spread the risk when regenerating areas, especially waterfront districts. The argument used is that a wider range of projects may have a broader economic viability to underpin such schemes, typically with the housing conversion providing much of the investment revenue to underwrite the infrastructure investment. In many cases, this has also led to the development of a night-time economy in regenerated areas around hospitality businesses (see Images 20.5 & 20.6 of how a derelict dock area can be progressively transformed through a mixed-development model). Part of that transformation is around changing the urban tourist's perception of the locality, either by helping them to discover it or through changing negative attitudes to areas that have had a poor image previously.

20

IMAGES 20.5 & 20.6 Tourism can help to regenerate derelict areas such as this dockland area using a mixture of tourism, retail and housing to justify the regeneration benefits

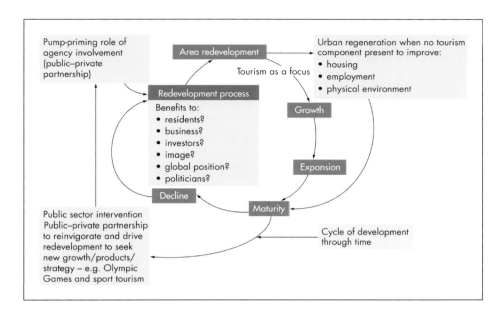

FIGURE 20.4 The links between economic, physical and social regeneration in redeveloping an urban area

The urban tourist experience: Behavioural issues

Any assessment of urban tourist activities, patterns and perceptions of urban locations will be influenced by the supply of services, attractions and facilities in each location. In an urban context, we need to try to understand how the urban visitor consumes the services and resources produced for their visit and experience. One useful framework developed in the Netherlands by Jansen-Verbeke (1986) to accommodate the analysis of what the tourist consumes and what is produced for their visit is that of the 'leisure product' (Figure 20.2). As Figure 20.2 shows, the facilities in an urban environment can be divided into the 'primary elements', 'secondary elements' and 'additional elements'. To distinguish between user groups, Jansen-Verbeke (1986) identified the primary and secondary motivations of 'tourists' and 'recreationalists' for visiting three Dutch towns (Deneter, Kampen and Zwolle). Jansen-Verbeke found that the inner city environment provided a leisure function for various visitors regardless of the prime motivation for visiting. As Jansen-Verbeke (1986: 88–89) suggests: 'On an average day, the proportion of visitors coming from beyond the city-region [tourists] is about one-third of all visitors. A distinction needs to be made between week days, market days and Sundays.' Among the different user groups, tourists tended to stay longer, with a strong correlation with 'taking a day out sightseeing and visiting a museum' as the main motivation to visit. Nevertheless, leisure shopping was also a major 'pull factor' for recreationalists and tourists, though it is of greater significance for the recreationalists. Using a scaling technique, Jansen-Verbeke (1986) asked visitors to evaluate how important different elements of the leisure product were to their visit. The results indicate that there is not a great degree of difference between tourists' and recreationalists' rating of elements and characteristics of the city's leisure product. While recreationalists attach more importance to shopping facilities than to events and museums, the historical characteristics of the environment and decorative elements combine with other elements such as markets, restaurants and the compact nature of the inner city to attract visitors. As Smith's (2015) study of events and cities illustrates, events can be an animator of the urban environment, turning the place into a must-see, as Insight 15.3 illustrated. Thus, 'the conceptual approach to the system of inner-city tourism is inspired by common features of the inner-city environment, tourists' behaviour and appreciation and promotion activities' (Jansen-Verbeke 1986: 97). Such findings illustrate the value of relating empirical results to a conceptual framework for the analysis of urban tourism and the necessity of replicating similar studies in other urban environments to test the validity of the framework and interpretation of urban tourists' visitor behaviour. Such studies also have a vital role in tourism marketing, when the elements of urban tourism are disaggregated and examined. For example, if one accepts the notion that urban destinations are competing for visitors, then these 'elements' of tourism can help to understand how consumers generate an image of the urban destination and choose to visit/not visit. The image is also influential in the intention to revisit, if the initial visit was able to meet the visitor's expectations.

20

Tourist perception and cognition of the urban environment

How individual tourists interact with and acquire information about the urban environment remains a relatively poorly researched area in tourism studies, particularly in relation to towns and cities. This area of research is traditionally seen as the forte of social psychologists with an interest in tourism, though much of the research by social psychologists has focused on motivation (e.g. Guy and Curtis 1986, on the development of perceptual maps). Reviews of the social psychology of tourism indicate that there has been a paucity of studies of tourists' behaviour and their adaptation to new environments they visit. This is somewhat surprising, since 'tourists are people who temporarily visit areas less familiar to them than their home area' (Walmesley and Jenkins 1992: 269). Therefore, one needs to consider a number of fundamental questions related to:

- How will the tourists know the areas they visit?
- How do they find their way around unfamiliar environments?
- How do they find their way in unfamiliar environments?
- What type of mental maps and images do they develop?

These issues are important in a tourism planning context, since the facilities which tourists use and the opportunities they seek will be conditioned by their environmental awareness. This may also affect the commercial operation of attractions and facilities, since a lack of awareness of the urban environment and the attractions within it may mean tourists fail to visit them. Understanding how tourists interact with the environment to create an image of the real world has been the focus of research in social psychology and behavioural geography (see Walmesley and Lewis 1993: 95–126). Geographers have developed a growing interest in the geographic space perception of all types of individuals (Downs 1970), without explicitly considering tourists in most instances. Behavioural geographers emphasize the need to examine how people store spatial information and 'their choice of different activities and locations within the environment' (Walmesley and Lewis 1993: 95). The process through which individuals perceive the urban environment is shown in Figure 20.5. While this is a simplification, Haynes (1980) notes that no two individuals will have an identical image of the urban environment because the information they receive is subject to mental processing. This is conditioned by the information signals received through one's senses (e.g. sight, hearing, smell, taste and touch) and this part of the process is known as 'perception'. As our senses may only comprehend a small proportion of the total information received, the human brain sorts the information and relates it to the knowledge, values and attitudes of the individual through the process of cognition (Page 1995: 222). The final outcome of the perception and cognition process is the formation of a mental image of a place. These images are an individual's own view of reality, but they are important to the individual and group when making decisions about their experience of a destination, whether to visit again, and their feelings in relation to the tourist experience of a place.

As Walmesley and Lewis (1993: 96) suggest:

the distinction between perception and cognition is, however, a heuristic device (i.e. something which helps one to learn) rather than a fundamental dichotomy because in many senses, the latter subsumes the former and both are mediated by experience, beliefs, values, attitudes, and personality such that, in interacting with their environment, humans only see what they want to see.

Consequently, individual tourists' knowledge of the environment is created in their mind as they interact with the unfamiliar environment (or familiar environment on a return visit) they are visiting.

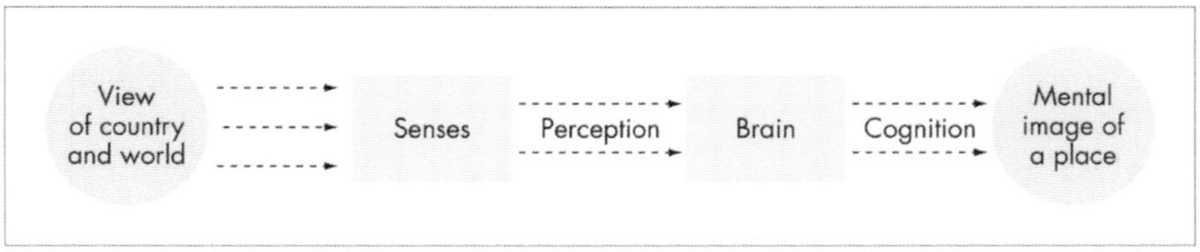

20

FIGURE 20.5 How individuals perceive the tourism environment

According to Powell (1978: 17–18), an image of the environment comprises ten key features which are:

1   A spatial component accounting for an individual's location in the world.
2   A personal component relating the individual to other people and organizations.
3   A temporal component concerned with the flow of time.
4   A relational component concerned with the individual's picture of the universe as a system of regularities.
5   Conscious, subconscious and unconscious elements.
6   A blend of certainty and uncertainty.
7   A mixture of reality and unreality.
8   A public and private component expressing the degree to which an image is shared.
9   A value component that orders parts of the image according to whether it is good or bad.
10 An affectional component whereby the image is imbued with feeling.

Among geographers, the spatial component to behavioural research has attracted most interest, and they derive much of their inspiration from the pioneering research by Lynch (1960). Lynch asked respondents in North American cities to sketch maps of their individual cities and, by simplifying their sketches, derived images of the city. Lynch developed a specific technique to measure people's urban images in which respondents drew a map of the centre of the city from memory, marking on it the streets, parks, buildings, districts and features they considered important. 'Lynch found many common elements in these mental maps that appeared to be of fundamental importance to the way people collect information about the city' (Burgess and Hollis 1977: 155) and recent studies of transport have refined this area of research in relation to cognitive maps (Golledge and Garling 2004) and mental maps (Weston and Handy 2004). Lynch (1960) found five elements in the resulting maps after simplifying the maps. These were:

1   *Paths*, which are the channels along which individuals move.
2   *Edges*, which are barriers (e.g. rivers) or lines separating one region from another.
3   *Districts*, which are medium-to-large sections of the city with an identifiable character.
4   *Nodes*, which are the strategic points in a city which the individual can enter and which serve as foci for travel.
5   *Landmarks*, which are points of reference used in navigation and wayfinding.

Pearce (1981) reviewed pioneering studies of cognitive maps of tourists, noting that visitors were quick to develop cognitive maps, often by the second day of the visit. The interesting feature of the study is that there is evidence of an environmental learning process at work. Walmesley and Jenkins' (1992: 272) critique of Pearce's findings note that:

- the number of landmarks, paths and districts increased over time
- the number of landmarks identified increased over a period of 2–6 days, while recognition of the number of districts increased from 2 to 3
- the resulting sketch maps were complex with no one element dominating them.

The significance of such research for the tourist and visitor to the urban environment is that the information they collect during a visit will shape their image of the place, influencing their feelings and impressions of it. Furthermore, this imageability of a place is closely related to the:

> *legibility by which is meant the extent to which parts of the city can be recognized and interpreted by an individual as belonging to a coherent pattern. Thus a legible city would be one where the paths, edges, districts, nodes and landmarks are both clearly identifiable and clearly positioned relative to each other.*
> (Walmesley and Lewis 1993: 98)

But among the most important issues for city managers, tourism businesses and planners, is how the visitor enjoyed their stay, particularly the level of satisfaction they derived. This is becoming a key element in the competitiveness of urban destinations, and this issue can assume an even greater complexity given the development of

20

multi-destination urban trips within and between countries. This allows the visitor to compare and contrast their experience of urban tourism. In the USA, over 31 per cent of the 6 million inbound trips by European, Asian and Latin American travellers fall into the category of urban tourism (Hwang *et al.* 2002). While such trips provide opportunities for the tourism industry to market products to such visitors, it may highlight why some cities feature prominently as self-standing destinations (e.g. Orlando), while other destinations such as San Diego are always part of a multi-city trip.

Contemporary challenges for urban tourism destinations: Protest and the anti-tourism movement

As Chapter 15 highlighted, a number of new concepts have arisen around overtourism in certain localities around the world, such as Venice. As Peeters *et al.* (2018: 22) point out:

> *Overtourism describes the situation in which the impact of tourism, at certain times and in certain locations, exceeds physical, ecological, social, economic, psychological, and/or political capacity thresholds. Psychological capacity refers to the capacity of people (residents and/or other visitors) to emotionally cope with crowding effects. Political capacity implies the incapability of local governments to grasp, manage, and govern excessive tourism growth consequences, jeopardising host community quality of life. This definition includes all forms of stress caused by high growth and volumes of visitors. It includes social (hosts, guests, citizens), physical (infrastructure, space), economic (tourism commercial zones) and ecological (noise, air quality, water use, water quality, waste . . .) aspects.*

This all-embracing definition emphasizes the basis of the residents responses to overtourism in cities where stresses from tourism create protest and an undercurrent of what Doxey's Irridex highlighted, as seen in Chapter 17 – tourist irritation. Many new terms have been developed to embody this stress, ranging from simple issues related to tourists adding to daily road congestion (Zhao and Hu 2019) to more vehement protests and attacks on tourist infrastructure such as buildings and vehicles. In the case of Japan, the rapid growth in international visitors in 2015–2018 has generated public awareness of overtourism and the government has initiated an inquiry into the problem at a regional and local level. International visitors rose by 21 per cent in 2016–2019, reaching 31 million arrivals by 2018, making it the twelfth most visited country globally. The government aims to grow international tourism to 40 million arrivals by 2020 and 60 million by 2030 and it has attracted a number of mega events like the Rugby World Cup in 2019 and Olympic Games to Tokyo in 2020 to grow visitor volumes. As the 'Invisible Tourist' (2019) outlined, a wide range of overtourism issues are now evident in Japan including: tourists being disrespectful to Japanese culture such as by taking selfies with cultural groups; the defacing of World Heritage Sites such as the Bamboo Groves in Arashiyama; too many visitors crammed into historic sites like Kyoto; tourists trespassing on private land in pursuit of Instagram photographs; the growth of Airbnb in non-tourist zones, disturbing residents. In Miyajima, the Grand Torii Gate, another World Heritage Site, has had numerous coins jammed into its cracks to bring good luck; this is further compromising the integrity of the gate structure, which now requires renovation and repainting. In essence, tourists do not respect the Japanese etiquette or understand the meaning which many historic sites have for Japanese culture, and the group-tour mentality of visitors, with the pursuit of cultural capital through photographs, has led to selfies being banned in Kyoto, and this regulation is highlighted on public information boards.

When one looks at the case of Venice, where up to 60 000 visitors day descend on the city, it is no surprise that antagonism and irritation arises at a grassroots level (i.e. among residents). The extreme form of protest against tourism (termed tourism phobia or anti-tourism) has created a political movement against tourism, as illustrated in Colomb and Novy's (2016) excellent set of case studies of different urban destinations. Figure 20.6 lists some of the cities which have experienced protests against tourism and examples of other cities where regulatory measures have been introduced to curb tourism to try to head off protests.

Apart from the inflationary effects of tourism on residents, Pinke-Sziva *et al.*'s (2019) example of Budapest and its night-time economy with its appeal to tourists, epitomizes many of the commonly cited examples of overtourism: litter, public nuisance such as urinating in public, street crime, and noise at night when residents are trying to sleep.

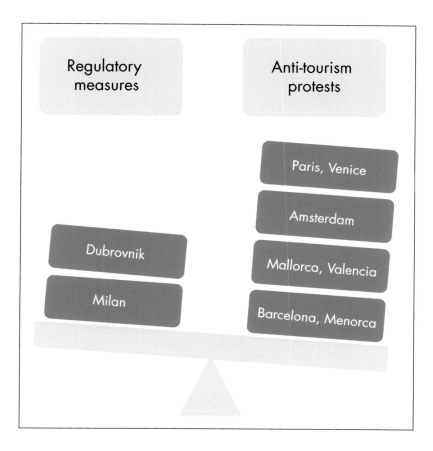

FIGURE 20.6 Sites of urban tourism regulation and anti-tourism protests

Novy and Colomb's (2016) overview of anti-tourism is an indication of the wider public discontent with urban tourism evidenced in protests to date in Barcelona. Zerva *et al.* (2019) examined the case of Barcelona pointing to the division between the *tourism-phobia* of the residents and the *tourism-philic* (meaning affinity for) approach of the Destination Management Organization promoting tourism. Evidence of the anti-tourism protest in Barcelona comprises passive protests (e.g. stickers proclaiming 'Tourism Kills the City') through to attacks on tourist infrastructure. Other examples of urban tourism protests include Amsterdam, where a resident population of 1 million is faced with 6 million visitors a year and the city has imposed a 6 per cent tourist tax and a ban on new tourist shops (e.g. cycle hire and souvenir shops) in the city, as well as a ban on Airbnb in the city centre. The effect of new peer-to-peer developments such as Airbnb has, as Adamiak (2018) suggested, created a major impact on residential areas hosting Airbnb in the 434 cities in Europe, where Paris and London dominate the stock of properties. As Peeters *et al.* (2018: 16) suggest, certain regions of Europe are at risk of overtourism including:

> the regions of Valencia, Andalucía and the Canarias in Spain, the regions of Languedoc-Roussillon and Bourgogne in France, the province of Trento in Italy, Madeira and the Algarve in Portugal, and the Ionic Isles and the Peloponnesus in Greece. The UK has five regions in the top-15 at risk of overtourism: Cumbria, Cornwall, West Wales and The Valleys, East Wales and North Yorkshire.

In these instances, the unrestricted growth of tourism is perhaps best described as a *social virus*, with no known easy cure due to the vested interests associated with maintaining a dependence upon tourism. One can draw direct parallels with one of the greatest human health risks for the next decade – the antimicrobial resistance of organisms to conventional treatment such as antibiotics. As the Health Foundation (2015) indicated, there are three principal elements to the spread of organisms (the host, environment and pathogen). In this instance we may substitute tourism as the pathogen in situations of overtourism, as 'organisms do not respect boundaries between community, primary and secondary health care, so a whole health care economy approach is vital' (Health Foundation 2015: 2). The same arguments apply to tourism, where a wider understanding of the interconnections and causes of overtourism transcend local political agendas as shown in Figure 20.7: overtourism threatens the very soul and essence of any urban place.

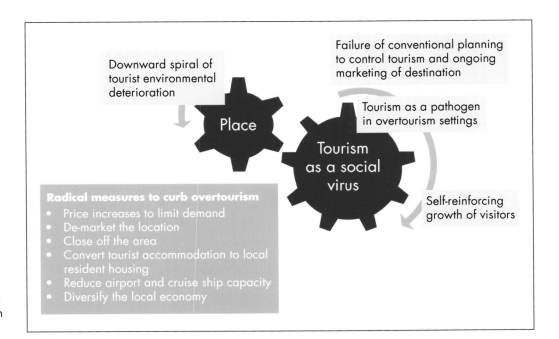

FIGURE 20.7 Tourism as a social virus in urban overtourism settings

Therefore, tourism has emerged as a social virus in overtourism locations where conventional planning and restraint have been powerless or too weak to challenge the *raison d'être* of the place – as the case of Venice shows. Here the action is still only around the margins of the problem and has effectively turned the city into a living museum, a feature that does not necessarily resonate with local people. Radical action is needed to address *tourism as a pathogen* to eradicate the effect compounded by the speed of social media communication and marketing, which accelerate the demand for visitation. One has to question why these overtourism locations still adopt a *tourism-philic philosophy* when all the evidence points to overtourism. As Figure 20.7 shows, a wide range of radical measures (some of which are listed in Figure 20.6: compare to the 100-plus policy actions listed in Peeters *et al.*'s (2018) study of overtourism) may be necessary in locations to effectively curtail the mass voluminous nature of urban tourism impacts. In such situations we see the polar opposite of sustainable tourism, where even radical measures (e.g. the antibiotic) may do little now to control the pathogenic nature of tourism, which will destroy its very lifeblood and then seek a new host (i.e. a new city) to turn into the fashionable place to visit. The sheer scale of the problem of urban tourism needs an ambitious and bold political agenda to rein in and limit or even close down tourism activity, as tourism becomes a destructive force for many of our most treasured cities.

Conclusion

Tourism's development in urban areas is not a new phenomenon. But it is only belatedly gaining the recognition it deserves within tourism studies as significant in its own right. The reasons why tourists visit urban environments to consume a bundle of tourism products continue to be overlooked by the private sector, which often neglects the fundamental issue – cities are multifunctional places. Despite the growing interest in urban tourism research, the failure of many large and small cities which promote tourism to understand the reasons why people visit, the links between their various motivations and the deeper reasons why people are attracted to cities, all remain fertile areas for theoretically informed and methodologically sound research.

The consequences for cities of not understanding urban tourism are significant, given the large-scale public sector investment in regeneration schemes and in building large facilities for events (e.g. conference centres and Olympic sporting venues), which can sometimes require major public subsidies when the markets do not materialize. Furthermore, not understanding urban tourism simply leads to missed business opportunities where common-sense issues, such as providing transport to link together the components of an attraction system to help visitors navigate and travel around the city, leads to lost spending and unviable attractions. Some cities have addressed this issue well, most notably Melbourne in Australia with its free tourist tram. Many other cities are beginning to recognize the importance of monitoring visitor perceptions and satisfaction and the activity patterns and behaviour of tourists. For the public and private sector planners and managers with an interest, involvement or stake in urban tourism, the main concern continues to be the potential for harnessing the all-year-round appeal of urban tourism activity, despite the fact that such visitors are often only short-stay. Ensuring that such stays are part of a high-quality experience, where visitor expectations are realistically met through well-researched, targeted and innovative products, continues to stimulate interest among tour operators and other stakeholders in urban tourism provision.

These concerns should force cities seeking to develop an urban tourism economy to reconsider the feasibility of pursuing a strategy to revitalize the city-region through tourism-led regeneration. All too often both the private and public sectors have moved headlong into economic regeneration strategies for urban areas, seeking a tourism component as a likely backup for property and commercial redevelopment. The implication is that tourism issues are not given the serious treatment they deserve. Where the visitors' needs and spatial behaviour are poorly understood and neglected in the decision-making process, the planning, development and eventual outcome of the urban tourism environment are affected. Therefore, tourist behaviour, the tourism system and its constituent components need to be evaluated in the context of future growth in urban tourism to understand the visitor as a central component in the visitor experience. Managing the different elements of this experience in a realistic manner requires more attention among those towns and cities competing aggressively for visitors, using the quality experience approach as a new-found marketing tool. Future research needs to focus on the behaviour, attitudes and needs of existing and prospective urban tourists to reduce the gap between their expectations and the service delivered. But ensuring that the tourism system within cities can deliver the service and experience marketed through promotional literature in a sensitive and meaningful way is now one of the major challenges for urban tourism managers.

Discussion questions

1 Why is urban tourism important as an economic activity for cities?

2 Why do tourists seek urban tourism experiences?

3 How can tourism be used to aid economic regeneration in cities?

4 To what extent do cities provide a diverse tourism product which can cater for all types of tourists' needs?

References

Adamiak, C. (2018) 'Mapping Airbnb supply in European cities', *Annals of Tourism Research*, 71: 67–71.

Ashworth, G. (1989) 'Urban tourism: An imbalance in attention', in C.P. Cooper (ed.) *Progress in Tourism, Recreation and Hospitality Management, Vol. 1*. London: Belhaven.

Ashworth, G. (1992) 'Is there an urban tourism?' *Tourism Recreation Research*, 17 (2): 3–8.

Ashworth, G. (2003) 'Urban tourism: Still an imbalance in attention?', in C. Cooper (ed.) *Classic Reviews in Tourism*. Clevedon: Channel View.

Ashworth, G. and Page, S.J. (2011) 'Progress in tourism management: Urban tourism research: Recent progress and current paradoxes', *Tourism Management*, 32 (1): 1–15.

Ashworth, G. and Tunbridge, J.E. (1990) *The Tourist – Historic City*. London: Belhaven.

Ashworth, G. and Tunbridge, J.E. (2000) *The Tourist – Historic City: Retrospect and Prospect of Managing the Heritage City*. Oxford: Pergamon.

Ashworth, G. and, Voogd, H. (1990) *Selling the City: Marketing Approaches in Public Sector Urban Planning*. London: Belhaven.

Beaverstock, J., Smith, R. and Taylor, P. (2000) 'World city network: A new metageography?', *Annals of the Association of American Geographers*, 90, March: 123–134.

Bertocchi, D.; Camatti, N.; Giove, S.; van der Borg, J. (2020) 'Venice and Overtourism: Simulating sustainable development scenarios through a tourism carrying capacity model'. *Sustainability*, 12: 512.

Britton, S. (1982) 'The political economy of tourism in the Third World', *Annals of Tourism Research*, 9 (3): 331–353.

Burgess, J. and Hollis, G. (1977) 'Personal London', *Geographical Magazine*, 50 (3): 155–159.

Burtenshaw, D., Bateman, M. and Ashworth, G. (1991) *The City in West Europe*, 2nd edition. Chichester: Wiley.

Castells, M. (1996) *The Rise of the Network Society*. Oxford: Blackwell.

Castells, M. (1998) *End of Millennium*. Oxford: Blackwell.

20

Colomb, C. and Novy, J. (eds.) (2015) *Protest and Resistance in the Tourist City*. London: Routledge.

Conforti, J. (1996) 'Ghettos as tourism attractions', *Annals of Tourism Research*, 23 (4): 830–842.

Dear, M. (1994) 'Postmodern human geography: A preliminary assessment', *Erdkunde*, 48 (1): 2–13.

Dear, M. and Flusty, S. (1999) 'Engaging postmodern urbanism', *Urban Geography*, 20 (5): 412–416.

Debord, G. (1994) *The Society of the Spectacle*. New York: Zone Books.

Downs, R. (1970) 'Geographic space perception: Past approaches and future prospects', *Progress in Geography*, 2: 65–108.

France, R. (2011) *Veniceland Atlantis: The Bleak Future of the World's Favourite City*. Farringdon, Oxon: Libri Publishing.

Frenzel, F., Koens, K. and Steinbrink, M. (2012) *Slum Tourism: Poverty, Power and Ethics*. London: Routledge.

Friedmann, J. (1986) 'The world city hypothesis', *Development and Change*, 17: 69–83.

Garreau, J. (1991) *Edge City Life on the New Frontier*. New York: Doubleday.

Getz, D. (1993) 'Planning for tourism business districts', *Annals of Tourism Research*, 20: 583–600.

Gladstone, D. (1998) 'Tourism urbanisation in the United States', *Urban Affairs Review*, 34 (1): 3–27.

Glasson, J., Godfrey, K. and Goodey, B. with Absalom, H. and Van der Borg, J. (1995) *Towards Visitor Impact Management: Visitor Impacts, Carrying Capacity and Management Responses in Europe's Historic Towns and Cities*. Aldershot: Ashgate.

Golledge, R. and Garling, T. (2004) 'Cognitive maps and urban travel', in D. Hensher, K. Button, K. Haynes and P. Stopher (eds.) *Handbook of Transport Geography and Spatial Systems 5*. Oxford: Elsevier.

Guy, B.S. and Curtis, W.W. (1986) 'Consumer learning or retail environment: A tourism and travel approach', in W. Benoy Joseph (ed.) *Tourism Services Marketing: Advances in Theory and Practice*. Cleveland, OH: American Academy of Marketing Conference, Cleveland University.

Hae, L. (2018) 'Traveling policy: Place marketing and the neoliberal turn of urban studies in South Korea', *Critical Sociology*, 44 (3): 533–546.

Hall, P. (1966) *The World Cities*. London: Weidenfeld and Nicolson.

Hall, P. (2000) 'The changing role of capital cities', *Plan Canada*, 40 (3): 8–12.

Hannigan, J. (1998) *Fantasy City*. London: Routledge.

Hayllar, B., Griffin, T. and Edwards, D. (eds.) (2008) *City Spaces Tourist Places: Urban Tourism Precincts*. Oxford: Butterworth-Heinemann.

Haynes, R. (1980) *Geographical Images and Mental Maps*. London: Macmillan.

The Health Foundation (2015) *Infection Control and Prevention. Lessons from Acute Care in England. Towards a Whole Health Economy Approach*. London: The Health Foundation.

Hwang, Y., Gretzel, U. and Fesenmaier, D. (2002) 'Multi-city pleasure trip patterns: An analysis of international travellers to the US', in K. Wöber (ed.) *City Tourism 2002*. Vienna: Springer Verlag.

The Invisible Tourist (2019) 'Overtourism: Is Japan becoming a victim of its own success?' *The Invisible Tourist*. https://www.theinvisibletourist.com/overtourism-in-japan-tourist-pollution/.

Jansen-Verbeke, M. (1986) 'Inner-city tourism: Resources, tourists and promoters', *Annals of Tourism Research*, 13 (1): 79–100.

King, A. (1990) *Global Cities: Post-imperialism and the Internationalisation of London*. London: Routledge.

King, R. (1987) *Italy*. London: Harper Row.

Law, C. (1992) 'Urban tourism and its contribution to economic regeneration', *Urban Studies*, 29 (3/4): 599–618.

Law, C. (2002) *Urban Tourism: The Visitor Economy and the Growth of Large Cities*, 2nd edition. London: Continuum.

Lynch, K. (1960) *The Image of the City*. Cambridge, MA: MIT Press.

Maitland, R. (2002) 'Partnership and collaboration in destination management: The case of Cambridge, UK', in K. Wöber (ed.) *City Tourism 2002*. Vienna: Springer Verlag.

Meethan, K. (1996) 'Consumed in the civilised city', *Annals of Tourism Research*, 32 (2): 322–340.

Montanari, A. and Muscara, C. (1995) 'Evaluating tourist flows in historic cities: The case of Venice', *Tijdschrift Voor Economische en Sociale Geografice*, 86 (1): 86–87.

Morgan, N., Pritchard, A. and Pride, R. (eds.) (2011) *Destination Brand*. Oxford: Butterworth-Heinemann.

Mosto, F., da (2004) *Venice: The Dramatic History of the World's Most Beautiful City*. London: BBC Books.

Mullins, P. (1991) 'Tourism urbanization', *International Journal of Urban and Regional Research*, 15: 326–343.

Mullins, P. (1994) 'Class relations and tourism urbanisation: The regeneration of the petite bourgeoisie and the emergence of a new urban form', *International Journal of Urban and Regional Research*, 18 (4): 591–607.

Novy, J. and Colomb, C. (2016) 'Urban tourism and its discontents: An introduction', in C. Colomb and J. Novy (eds.) *Protest and Resistance in the Tourist City* (pp. 1–30).

Pacione, M. (2005) *Urban Geography*, 2nd edition. London: Routledge.

Page, S.J. (1995) *Urban Tourism*. London: Routledge.

Page, S.J. and Hall, C.M. (2002) *Managing Urban Tourism*. Harlow: Prentice Hall.

Pearce, P.L. (1981) 'Route maps: A study of travellers' perceptions of a section of countryside', *Journal of Environmental Psychology*, 1: 141–155.

Peeters, P., Gössling, S., Klijs, J., Milano, C., Novelli, M., Dijkmans, C., Eijgelaar, E., Hartman, S., Heslinga, J., Isaac, R., Mitas, O., Moretti, S., Nawijn, J., Papp, B. and Postma, A. (2018) *Research for TRAN Committee – Overtourism: Impact and Possible Policy Responses*. Brussels: European Parliament, Policy Department for Structural and Cohesion Policies.

Pinke-Sziva, I., Smith, M., Olt, G. and Berezvai, Z. (2019) 'Overtourism and the night-time economy: A case study of Budapest', *International Journal of Tourism Cities*, 5 (1): 1–16.

Powell, J.M. (1978) *Mirrors of the New World: Images and Image-makers in the Settlement Process*. Canberra: Australian National University Press.

20

Ritzer, D. (1996) *The McDonaldisation of Society, Revised Edition*. Thousand Oaks, CA: Pine Forge.

Roche, M. (1992) 'Mega-events and micro-modernisation: On the sociology of the new urban tourism', *British Journal of Sociology*, 43 (4): 563–600.

Rogerson, C. and Visser, G. (2007) *Urban Tourism in the Developing World: The South African Experience*. New York: Transaction Publishers.

Romero, M., Ortuño, M. and Suriñach, J. (2002) 'Demand segmentation in urban tourism: Empirical evidence for the city of Barcelona', in K. Wöber (ed.) *City Tourism 2002*. Vienna: Springer Verlag.

Shaw, G. and Williams, A.M. (1994) *Critical Issues in Tourism: A Geographical Perspective*. Oxford: Blackwell.

Short, J., Breitbach, S., Buckman, S. and Essex, J. (2000) 'From world cities to gateway cities', *Cities*, 4 (3): 317–340.

Short, J. and Kim, Y. (1999) *Globalization and the City*. New York: Addison Wesley Longman.

Smith, A. (2015) *Events in the City: Using Public Spaces as Event Venues*. London: Routledge.

Taylor, P. (2001) 'Specification of the world city network', *Geographical Analysis*, 33: 181–194.

Thrift, N. (1989) 'The geography of international economic disorder', in R. Johnston and P. Taylor (eds.) *A World in Crisis? Geographical Perspectives*. Oxford: Blackwell.

Thrift, N. (1997) 'Cities without modernity, cities with magic', *Scottish Geographical Magazine*, 113: 138–149.

Van der Borg, J. (1992) 'Tourism and urban development: The case of Venice, Italy', *Tourism Recreation Research*, 17 (2): 45–56.

Van der Borg, J., Costa, P. and Gotti, G. (1996) 'Tourism in European heritage cities', *Annals of Tourism Research*, 23 (2): 306–321.

Walmesley, D.J. and Jenkins, J. (1992) 'Tourism cognitive mapping of unfamiliar environments', *Annals of Tourism Research*, 19 (3): 268–286.

Walmesley, D.J. and Lewis, G.J. (1993) *People and Environment: Behavioural Approaches in Human Geography*, 2nd edition. London: Longman.

Weston, L. and Handy, S. (2004) 'Mental maps', in D. Hensher, K. Button, K. Haynes and P. Stopher (eds.) *Handbook of Transport Geography and Spatial Systems 5*. Oxford: Elsevier.

Zerva, K., Palou, S., Blasco, D. and Donaire, J. (2019) 'Tourism-philia versus tourism-phobia: Residents and destination management organization's publicly expressed tourism perceptions in Barcelona', *Tourism Geographies*, 21 (2): 306–329.

Zhao, P. and Hu, H. (2019) 'Geographical patterns of traffic congestion in growing megacities: Big data analytics from Beijing', *Cities*, 92: 164–174.

Zukin, S. (1996) *The Culture of Cities*. Oxford: Blackwell.

Further reading

Books

Colomb, C. and Novy, J. (eds.) (2016) *Protest and Resistance in the Tourist City*. London: Routledge.

Page, S.J. and Hall, C.M. (2002) *Managing Urban Tourism*. Harlow: Prentice Hall.

Journal articles

Ashworth, G. (1989) 'Urban tourism: An imbalance in attention', in C.P. Cooper (ed.) *Progress in Tourism, Recreation and Hospitality Management, Vol. 1*. London: Belhaven.

Ashworth, G. (1992) 'Is there an urban tourism?' *Tourism Recreation Research*, 17 (2): 3–8.

Ashworth, G. (2003) 'Urban tourism: Still an imbalance in attention?', in C. Cooper (ed.) *Classic Reviews in Tourism*. Clevedon: Channel View.

Ashworth, G. and Page, S.J. (2011) 'Progress in tourism management: Urban tourism research: Recent progress and current paradoxes', *Tourism Management*, 32 (1): 1–15.

Fletcher, R., Murray Mas, I., Blanco-Romero, A. and Blázquez-Salom, M. (2019) 'Tourism and degrowth: an emerging agenda for research and praxis', *Journal of Sustainable Tourism*, 27(12): 1745–1763.

Higgins-Desbiolles, F., Carnicelli, S., Krolikowski, C., Wijesinghe, G. and Boluk, K. (2019) 'Degrowing tourism: rethinking tourism', *Journal of Sustainable Tourism*, 27(12): 1926–1944.

20

Rural tourism

Learning outcomes

After reading this chapter and answering the questions, you should be able to:

- understand the context of rural tourism and the nature of rural areas
- identify the impacts of rural tourism
- understand the need for rural tourism management and issues affecting the future development of tourism in rural areas.

Overview

For many tourists, the countryside is an attractive choice of destination. The relationship between tourism and the environment is particularly marked in rural areas. Rural areas can be sensitive to change through tourism. Changes in the environment, effects on the social fabric and economic well-being require careful monitoring. With this in mind, recognizing the impacts and planning sensitive approaches to rural tourism is a challenge for the twenty-first century. This chapter explores the concept of rural tourism and highlights some of the issues relating to different types of tourism in the countryside setting. It sets out how the subject has developed, outlining seminal thinking, and provides a synthesis of how knowledge has developed in this area. Issues associated with the management of rural tourism, including the principles for tourism in the countryside, are examined to illustrate how public agencies approach this issue.

Introduction

Rural areas have featured prominently in the development of tourism and leisure and many of the seminal works in rural studies (e.g. Clout 1972; Davidson and Wibberley 1977) recognized and developed these themes as areas for investigation. These early studies noted both the historical evolution of tourism and leisure in these environments and the continuity and changes in tourism and leisure activity which have transformed the rural landscape. In contemporary times, the countryside continues to form an important tourist destination in its own right although the links with urban areas as centres of demand continues to be a powerful force shaping these areas. The appeal of the countryside as a holiday destination is complex, linked to opportunities for a variety of sports and activities, peace and quiet, space, nature and traditional ways of life. For example, Han (2019) highlights the tranquillity associated with rural tourism and Jepson and Sharpley (2015) explore the emotional fulfilment and concept of rurality that visitors associate with the countryside. It might be argued that the countryside symbolizes a nostalgic lost 'golden age'; that it contains everything that urban areas lack. Indeed, the countryside is seen as special and deserving of protection across the world, demonstrated, for example, by the designation of National Parks. The relationship between tourism and the environment is particularly close in rural areas, which necessitates sensitive planning and management of both the resource base and tourism activity. Tourism can result in positive and negative impacts on the rural economy, environment and society.

Policy and research directions on rural tourism worldwide tend to focus on one of two emphases. First, many rural areas attract large numbers of tourists, for example National Parks in the USA which receive over 250 million visits a year. The emphasis in these areas is on visitor management. Visitor management is a management focus that aims to balance the protection of the environment with visitor experience and provision of appropriate services. The second type of rural area includes those where tourism is viewed as a mechanism for rejuvenating a declining economy or stimulating a poor economy and community. Many peripheral regions fit into this category, as Hall and Boyd (2005) show, such as Lake Plastiras, central Greece and Oberschwaben-Allgau, southern Germany. These areas may not receive many visitors, but the potential for organizing tourism services to generate more visitors and create vital income and employment is the motivating force. Keane and Quinn's (1990) landmark study recognized the significance of tourism in rural economic development and the value for local communities who engaged with development opportunities, but significant issues remain where such rural areas are remote or in 'peripheral areas' (see Figure 21.1). These arrangements are frequently used to justify state investment in rural infrastructure.

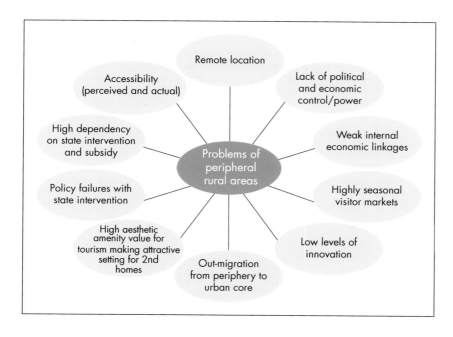

FIGURE 21.1 Problems of using tourism as a tool to develop peripheral rural areas
Source: Developed from Hall (2006)

21

Simply defined, rural tourism is 'tourism which takes place in the countryside' (Lane 1994). However, the meaning of the term remains problematic. Before we even begin to think about rural tourism as a concept, the complexity of the terms 'tourism' and 'rural' add further complications. The meaning of tourism has been dealt with already in Chapter 1, but how should we approach the definition of the term 'rural'?

The nature and scope of rurality

Defining rurality has taken much space in geographical and rural sociology texts but there is little consensus on what constitutes the phenomenon termed 'rural' (Robinson 1990; Ilbery 1997). There are three recognizable perspectives on defining rurality:

1   *Anything non-urban.* Glyptis (1991) terms this 'land beyond the urban edge'. This is known as a negative approach to defining rurality, as it implies the rural environment has few special features and transfers the onus of definition to urban commentators.

2   *Attempts to outline the elements of the countryside or the functions of rural space.* This is known as a positive perspective, as the distinguishing features are identified, such as a low-density population, visual components and forms of settlement and land use.

3   *Perception and/or user-based definitions.* The definitions are based on how individuals experience and define rurality (i.e. what people think it is). The distinction lies in the eye of the beholder. Halfacree (1995) explores the dimensions of rurality and makes the point that what one person sees in a rural area might be seen in a contrasting way by another. For example, we tend to think of the countryside as a relaxing environment, but for those who live and work there, for instance in farming, the environment is stressful and hard work.

In 1977, Cloke published the initial work on indices of rurality. Using 16 indicators, an index of rurality was constructed (see Figure 21.2). From this study, two main types of rural areas were identified. The first is the *remote rural area*, typified by remoteness from urban areas; declining, static or modestly increasing population; an ageing population; declining employment opportunities; low female activity; rates; and high per capita service provision cost. The second is the *accessible rural area*, defined by relative proximity to urban areas, rapidly increasing population, high levels of commuting, youthful population structure and high levels of car ownership. A key feature of accessible rural areas is relative economic buoyancy, with lower rates of unemployment than remoter rural areas and urban areas and growth in employment opportunities.

Moving from the more geographical approach to rurality, it is worth noting alternative perspectives on the countryside. For instance, Halfacree (1993) identifies four approaches to defining rural areas:

1   *Descriptive* – which describes the countryside using empirical data and measures, such as a census of population.

2   *Sociocultural* – which draws associations between social and spatial attributes, i.e. population density affects behaviour and attitudes.

3   *Rural as a locality* – whose defining characteristics are what makes areas 'rural' – i.e. their distinctive qualities.

4   *Rural as a social representation* – how 'rural' is perceived and relates to the social construction of the countryside by individuals and groups.

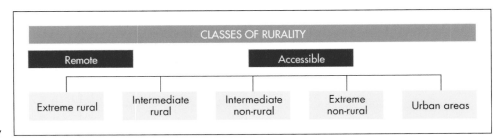

FIGURE 21.2 Index of rurality

Finally, Murdoch and Marsden (1994) present an interesting framework for thinking about the contemporary countryside and the possible outcomes as a result of change:

1 *The preserved countryside* – accessible rural areas, characterized by anti-development and preservationist attitudes.

2 *The contested countryside* – lies outside the main commuter zones. Farmers and developers have dominant interests and push proposals through.

3 *The paternalistic countryside* – large estates and tenant farms dominate. Development is controlled by local landowners with a traditional and long-term view.

4 *The clientelist countryside* – in remote rural areas where agriculture dominates but is dependent on state subsidy. Policies are geared towards local community and employment.

The concept of the countryside can be defined in many different ways. It is multifaceted, complex and dynamic. This is conveyed by Potter and Burney (2002: 35), according to whom the multifunctional countryside combines 'producing not only food but also sustaining rural landscapes, protecting biodiversity, generating employment and contributing to the vitality of rural areas'. Even so, Halfacree (1993) states that a single, all-embracing definition of 'rural' is not really feasible. Yet there is an important distinction to be made between different understandings of the term 'rural', because behaviour and decision-making are influenced by perceptions of rurality (Halfacree 1995). It appears that there are two main ways of thinking about the definition of rurality. First, as there is no unambiguous way of defining rural areas, there is no point in trying to define them. One might ask whether definitions are significant to those who live and work in rural areas. The distinction between rural and urban is deeply rooted in planning matters; therefore the definition is crucial. With the development of policy and funding for rural development, there is an increasing need to think about the parameters of rural areas.

Conceptualizing rural tourism

While rural areas are dynamic environments and change is implicit, evidenced by their use of wind farms and green energy (de Sousa and Kastenholz 2015), more radical change has been witnessed in the postwar period than at any other time before, relating to social, environmental, political, economic and technological elements of the countryside. Changes in agricultural practice and policy (intensification and modernization) through time, particularly since the end of the Second World War, have created unemployment, falling agricultural incomes and economic marginalization of smaller farms. Jenkins *et al.* (1998: 50) term the changes in agriculture as 'industrialization' and state that, in many countries and regions, farm numbers have been dramatically reduced and, of those remaining, a minority contribute the majority of farm production (in both volume and value terms). With a lack of employment opportunities, out-migration to urban areas in search of work has occurred. Lower numbers of rural residents and the subsequent reduced demand for services has partly resulted in their withdrawal. A decline in rural services has been particularly marked in rural England. Table 21.1 illustrates the level of service provision in rural parishes and villages. The situation is generally more marked in remoter areas and a major contraction in service provision occurred after 2000. For example 2000–2008, the number of rural post offices in the UK dropped from 6543 to 5158 and in 2013–2017, they were closing at the rate of one a month. This is despite the Post Office in rural areas receiving over 12 million customer visits a week.

According to the Rural Housing Federation (2017), since 2013, over 1365 English rural public houses have closed, which equates to seven a week. This is at a time of expansion in the rural population of England, which is where 20 per cent of the population reside. In addition, there were over 3000 new houses built in rural areas in 2017. Bus services also fared badly during the austerity cuts to local authority funding after 2008 by central government which saw many public subsidies on social grounds removed. By 2018, the area covered by rural bus services had fallen back to that of 1980 as risk aversion and an absence of subsidies have seen services cut. In 2013–2014 to 2016–2017 some areas of England saw a 20 per cent cut in bus services, with Wales and North West England affected the most. Some 52 rural schools closed in 2013–2016 and in the case of banks, in the UK the 17 831 bank branches in 1989 had reduced to 9500 by 2012. A further 1100 closed in 2014–2015, leaving 1500 communities with no bank and 840 with only one bank. The consequence is that many rural communities do not have easy access to banks in villages and small towns, which has reduced the opportunities for bank lending to small businesses so that they can invest and innovate. In the case of rural petrol stations, competition from supermarket discounting has created rural *fuel deserts*, as 332 closed in rural areas, many of which had been operating since the interwar and postwar years. These cuts in service provision not only affect the infrastructure, accessibility and vitality of rural communities but also make them less attractive to rural tourists when the focal points of many rural communities are closed down (e.g. the village pub). In some

21

TABLE 21.1 Rural services in 1994, 2000, 2003, 2006 and 2010

Rural service	Percentage of parishes without the service 1994 (2000 in brackets)	Percentage of households in villages*			
		2000	2003	2006	2010
Supermarket		79 (within 4 km)	78		62
Village hall/community centre	29	–	–	–	–
Permanent shop	41 (43)	–		–	–
Post office	43 (46)	85.6 (within 2 km)	–	85.2	93.3
Primary school	52 (48)	92 (within 2 km)	91	88.0	96.1
Daily bus service	71	–		–	
General practitioner	83	86 (within 4 km)	86	79.7	86
Bank/building society	94	63.9 (within 4 km)	–	63.7	51
Day care for elderly	92	–	–	–	–
Petrol station	–	89.9 (within 4 km)		88.0	94.8
Cashpoint	–	79 (within 4 km)	90		85

*The method of data collection changed in 2000
Source: Adapted from Rural Development Commission (1994); Countryside Agency (2000); Commission for Rural Communities (2010)

instances community action and volunteering have helped retain these services, but these trends are not just applicable to the UK, as other countries (e.g. USA) have observed a downward spiral in rural community service provision. Various explanations have been advanced which point to the impact of global capital restructuring to focus on larger and more profitable urban populations, alongside cuts in public support for rural services.

In some areas, there has been a repopulation of the countryside. This is as a result of a reverse migration trend of urban dwellers moving to rural areas, particularly in the accessible rural areas. In some areas, tourism and recreation have spearheaded this change, as second-home owners, retirees and countryside converts move to rural residences. The issue of second homes in the countryside has caused much debate, particularly in Finland and Canada, where a large majority of rural, lakeside and coastal homes are purchased for weekend and holiday use only. These part-time dwellers may exacerbate the problem of service provision, as the permanence of the community declines. Having explored the context of rural areas, it is evident that rural tourism and recreation have evolved partly due to an increase in supply of opportunities created by the need for a more diverse rural economy. This process is broadly summarized in Figure 21.3, which conceptualizes the problems of rural areas. Generally, this typifies the trans-European position but has wider applicability across the globe.

It is clear that it is not an easy task to accurately define 'rural tourism'. It is often described as a form of tourism that takes place in the countryside, but this is ambiguous and on further reflection points to a wide range of types of countryside and activities. A further complication is in trying to identify what is meant by rural tourism as opposed to countryside leisure. Curry (1994) clarifies this by expressing the components of countryside leisure in seven categories of which rural tourism is just one part, a point reiterated by McAreavey and McDonagh (2011). The danger of this is in thinking purely about rural tourism in terms of overnight stays. It is essential to consider the activities which tourists engage in during their stay to generate a more complete analysis. Bramwell (1994) questions whether the special characteristics of rural areas shape the pattern of tourism, creating a specific form of 'rural' tourism. In addition, the commodification of rural space which has taken place in recent years intimates rural tourism has moved into a new era, away from more simple forms of farm-based tourism to a more commercial use of the countryside (Cloke 1992). Some studies argue that we no longer need working farms to develop farm tourism, as it is the setting which is important. Commercialization and formalization of countryside experiences is evident in the range of tourist products available in rural areas. It is clear that rural tourism can vary greatly in what it purports to be. It can range from the very informal to the greatly organized product, which can be represented by constructing a spectrum of rural tourism activity and experience (see Figure 21.4). So, what are the parameters of rural tourism?

Lane (1994) outlines the special features of rural tourism. These features assist in distinguishing a more specific form of rural tourism. *First*, it is located in rural areas. *Second*, it is functionally rural; that is, based on small-scale and traditional activities and enterprises, environmental aspects and heritage. *Third*, it is rural in scale, relating to small-scale buildings and settlements. *Fourth*, it relies on the traditional qualities of the countryside and develops slowly under the control of local people. *Last*, it is non-uniform; that is, it reflects the complexity of the rural environment and has several forms.

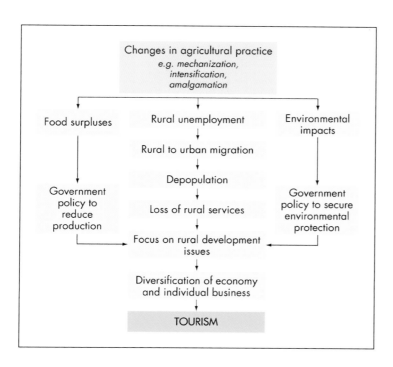

FIGURE 21.3 The context of rural tourism

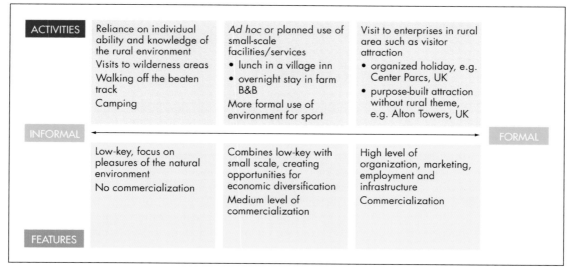

FIGURE 21.4 The rural tourism spectrum

The characteristics of the rural tourism experience that create special appeal and explain why people enjoy the countryside are:

- remoteness and solitude
- peace and quiet, relaxing environment
- adventure and challenge, opportunity to pursue sport or hobby
- health and fitness concerns, fresh air
- wildlife and landscapes, interests in the environment
- experience of rural communities, culture and lifestyles
- pleasant backcloth for being with friends and family
- a change from everyday urban life
- take part in rural activities such as conservation work
- explore historic identities, interests in heritage. (After Page and Getz 1997; Countryside Commission 1992)

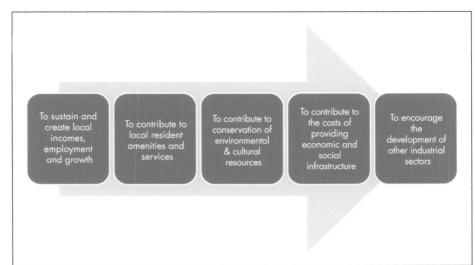

FIGURE 21.5 The goals of expanding tourism flows to rural areas.
Source: Based on Hall and Jenkins (1998)

Hall and Jenkins (1998: 28) suggest that the expansion of tourist flows in rural areas is designed to achieve one or more of the following goals outlined in Figure 21.5.

Sharpley and Sharpley (1997: 20) provide a neat overview of the meaning of rural tourism: '"rural tourism" may be defined both conceptually, as a state of mind, and technically, according to activities, destinations and other measurable, tangible characteristics'. Overall, Sharpley and Sharpley believe rural tourism to be an economic activity which both depends on and exploits the countryside.

The growth of rural tourism

According to Sharpley and Sharpley (1997), rural tourism emerged as an identifiable activity in Europe during the latter half of the eighteenth century, although it can be traced back through history. Wild, mountainous regions such as the Canadian Rockies, the Swiss Alps and the English Lake District began to attract aristocrats initially, then middle-class tourists. Thomas Cook directed the first package tour to rural Switzerland in 1863, which marked the beginning of a rapid growth in the industry in this area based on health and mountain sports. For the working classes, the countryside was viewed as a workplace until the time of industrialization and urbanization in the nineteenth century – therefore, class distinctions can be identified in the temporally uneven demand for rural tourism. Despite previous developments, it was not until the twentieth century that rural tourism became a more widely enjoyed activity, when evidence demonstrates a rapid growth in demand for and supply of rural activities. As Chapter 2 observed, new forms of technology and state promotion of tourism such as in California led to the development of rural tourism. In the 1870s companies such as Thomas Cook and the Boston-based company Raymond and Whitcomb had begun tours, and rural hinterlands such as Yosemite and other inland areas were accessed by a combination of rail and stagecoach.

Walking and cycling became increasingly popular during the interwar years in England, especially in the Pennine hills close to the major industrial centres of the north. Declining prosperity meant that there was a demand for inexpensive pursuits and membership of outdoor pursuit organizations, such as the Cyclists' Touring Club and the Youth Hostel Association. Elsewhere, increases in rural tourism participation increased along with urban migration and a desire to return to the countryside for holidays, particularly in parts of southern and northern Europe. Since the 1950s, rural leisure generally has been subject to increased participation along

IMAGE 21.1 Cycle paths through rural areas are used as a way of stimulating tourism activity along these linear routeways

with the growth in other forms of tourism (Image 21.1.). Improved mobility and increased disposable income and free time, along with an increase in supply of opportunities, have partially explained some of this increase. Other factors include a rise in environmental concern and the need to be close to nature from time to time to balance the needs of urban societies ('urban' here should be viewed in locational and psychological terms). There are also links to societal change in the form of postmodernism, which rejects modernity and reflects positively on traditional ways of life (Image 21.2). For example, Sisneros-Kidd *et al.* (2019) examined the appeal of nature-based rural tourism in the Arctic but also added a note of caution about the region developing an over-dependence on this activity.

In some European countries, especially in southern Europe, the traditional perspective on tourism in rural areas is that rural holidays are a cheap alternative to resort holidays. For example, rural tourism in Portugal has been traditionally associated with staying on farms

IMAGE 21.2 Rural businesses which embrace organic food stuffs can offer visitors a unique food experience at honeypot locations

with the farming family. In other areas, such as Germany and Austria, rural tourism has always been linked with the more affluent. There is evidence that the traditional perspective of rural holidays as a poor relation to other forms of tourism is waning. This was reinforced by a study by Perales (2002) focusing on Spain, where a new modern domestic rural tourist aged 25–44 years of age has developed an interest in consuming the rural environment. This confirmed the higher levels of education and affluence of these new groups of urban middle classes. In Portugal, for example, the Alto Minho region in the far west of the country is being promoted as a rural tourism destination based on sustainable principles, and is attractive to educated and affluent tourists. In France, a wide range of rural tourism products are available, such as the famous gîtes and *chambres d'hôte*. The rural tourism product and experience has been developed and promoted on a global scale although sometimes it has become synonymous with ecotourism or specialist interest tourism that takes place in a rural environment. Hjalager *et al.* (2018) indicated that German visitors to Scandinavia were requiring rural businesses to innovate to create products that fit the aspirations of these rural visitors. While Lane and Kastenholz (2015) review the postwar rise of rural tourism as an alternative form of tourism, they point to the new consumer markets and need for more sophisticated generational marketing as outlined in Chapter 14. However, there is an inherent danger in assuming that, because rural tourism relies on the countryside environment, it is somehow more environmentally friendly than resort-based tourism.

Rural tourists tend to be more affluent and better-educated tourists (see Countryside Commission 1992) from socio-economic groups A and B and aged 25–54, seeking high-quality experiences and products. However, the range of products that comprise rural tourism and the associated range of experiences are far too great to generalize. Looking at an overall picture of one country, the Great Britain Day Visits Survey indicates that 18 per cent of all leisure trips are taken in the countryside, which equates to around 20 million overnight trips and 335 million day visits per year. Since the 1980s, there has been a levelling off in growth in the volume of tourists but an increase in the diversity of activities and types of rural tourism. According to Defra (2009), these visits contributed £11 billion to the rural economy. Active sports participation is increasing. New activities such as snow sports, mountain biking, climbing, air and water sports are witnessing large gains in popularity, a theme returned to again in Chapter 25. Social media and Internet advertising has assisted this, by bringing cheaper yet effective materials and equipment to a larger audience. Other trends such as health promotion, the appeal of the great outdoor life, interest in the environment and increased marketing of activities all partly explain this increase. Even so, the most popular pursuit in the countryside is walking/rambling, with over 400 million walks undertaken every year by 15 million regular walkers in England.

21

Impacts of rural tourism

The aim of tourism development in rural areas is, in general terms, to provide opportunities for economic and social development. In some areas, tourism provides the main source of income and employment, as well as providing social and environmental benefits. Inevitably, negative aspects of rural tourism development are evident also. There is substantial literature on the impacts of tourism in rural areas since the 1980s (PA Cambridge Economic

Consultants 1987; Gannon 1994; Healy 1994). For example, since Estonia joined the European Union in 2004, it has seen a significant growth in tourism and in some rural areas, it has been estimated that 30–40 per cent of their income is derived from rural tourism. Much of the early tourism impact research focuses on rural areas, arguably because the relationship between tourism and the environment in the countryside is more pronounced. The positive and negative impacts of rural tourism are summarized in Table 21.2. In England, the Rural Development Commission carried out research on a sample of English rural settlements to evaluate the impact of tourism (Rural Development Commission 1996). The research found that tourism results in several benefits, the magnitude of which varies according to the settlement/community characteristics and the nature and scale of tourism activity. The benefits in general are that tourism:

- increases the range and viability of local businesses (food and non-food shops, hotels, pubs and cafés, garages, indirect spending to other non-tourist businesses)
- contributes to social and community life (encourages new businesses, provides employment, supports fundraising and community events, makes a greater choice of recreational opportunities available to local people)
- helps to maintain or improve services (health services, entertainment, banks, public transport)
- brings about environmental and/or infrastructural improvements (pride generated, revenue pays for environmental improvements, larger car parks, interpretation, enhanced visual amenity).

Several negative impacts were reported. Rising house prices, traffic congestion, parking problems, disturbance and litter were the most common aspects reported. The success of rural tourism depends on maintaining a balance between the needs of a working, living community and an intrinsically valuable environment. Lepp's (2007) study of Bigodi Village, Uganda pointed to the positive attitudes residents had towards tourism because of the opportunities it created for community development, income and improved agricultural markets (see Insight 21.1). In contrast, Liu (2006) found in a study of northern Malaysia that tourism was not adequately integrated into rural development strategies so that the quality and quantity of rural labour did not have the skills needed given the scale and pace of development. A greater emphasis on cultural understanding, cultural differences and sensitivity to religious and ethnic identity were also highlighted as essential if rural residents were to benefit from tourism development. It is with this in mind that a more sustainable and integrated approach to rural tourism has been advocated.

TABLE 21.2 A summary of the positive and negative impacts of rural tourism

Impact	Positive	Negative
Economic	Assists viability of existing tourism and non-tourism businesses	Encourages dependence on industry prone to uncontrollable change
	Creates new employment	Creates part-time, seasonal or low-grade employment
	Attracts inward investment	Incurs development costs and public service costs
	Encourages pluriactivity, helping to stabilize economic base	Leads to local land and house-price inflation
Sociocultural	Assists in viability of local services	Creates feeling of invasion by tourists; overcrowding and traffic
	Creates sense of pride	Increases crime
	Revitalizes local cultural traditions, events and crafts	Reduction in local services, e.g. food shops replaced by gift shops
	Leads to opportunities for social and cultural exchange	Import of new cultural ideas – challenges existing way of life
Environmental	Leads to environmental improvements in settlements Provides income for conservation of buildings and natural environment	Increases wear and tear on landscape features
		Creates need for new developments which may not be in keeping with local area
	Fosters awareness of conservation as worthwhile activity	Increases pollution (noise, visual, air, water, litter)
		Affects local biodiversity

21

INSIGHT 21.1 Using rural tourism as a development tool: The case of Laos

Laos, in South East Asia, experienced a major boom in international tourism in the 1990s, with its numbers of international visitors per year rising from 14 400 international visitors in 1990 to 87 000 in 1992 and 4 million in 2018. The country's market for international tourists is dominated by nearby countries (Thailand, which accounted for 2 million of Laos' visitors in 2018; 1 million visitors came from Vietnam and 500 000 from China in the same year). The country is one of the least developed countries in the world, with around a third of its population living on under US$2 a day. A study by Sunktil et al. (2009) examined the country's poverty eradication strategy and the dominant rural agricultural environment in large parts of the country, where food sufficiency remains a dominant issue. While some regions of the country have attracted a great deal of overseas aid routed through non-government agencies and charities (e.g. the Greater Mekong basin as a region identified for poverty-reduction by the Asian Development Bank), many other regions have attracted less attention. Sunktil et al. (2009) identified one rural area (Viengxay) in the Houaphanh Province, with a population of 31 000, as an interesting example of an area where rural tourism could be developed. The area reached prominence during the Vietnam War when it became a bombing target for US forces due to the Lao Communist troop concentrations in the area. To shelter from attack, residents established a hidden city in 480 limestone karst caves in the region until the cessation of hostilities. In 1990, the caves were reopened to visitors, who were predominantly from Laos. In 2005 the caves were designated a National Heritage Sire and a steady stream of domestic visitors began to visit. As Sunktil et al. (2009) highlighted,

rural tourism was at a very early stage of development and only a small proportion of villagers were deriving income from tourism. What Sunktil et al. (2009) found was a considerable interest in developing opportunities to service visitor needs, but a lack of capital and know-how to establish micro enterprises as key barriers. The area also had a lack of business support and financial aid from NGOs even though local people were predisposed towards supplementing their income from tourism. However, an important finding from Sunktil et al.'s (2009) study was that many local rural residents did not perceive themselves to be poor. The implication here is that we should not impose non-Laotian value systems upon these rural people by promoting pro-poor tourism strategies (see Chapter 24 on pro-poor tourism) without understanding and empowering them to make informed decisions that may well affect their culture, lifestyle and way of life if tourism is developed.

Further reading

Harrison, D. and Schipari, S. (2007) 'Lao tourism and poverty alleviation: Community-based tourism and the private sector', *Current Issues in Tourism* 10 (2/3): 194–230.

Roberts, N. (2015) 'The cultural and natural heritage of caves in the Lao PDR: Prospects and challenges related to their use, management and conservation', *The Journal of Lao Studies*, Special Issue March: 113–139, www.laostudies.org.

Suntikul, W., Bauer, T., and Song, H. (2009) 'Pro-poor tourism development in Viengxay, Laos: Current state and future prospects', *Asia Pacific Journal of Tourism Research*, 14 (2): 153–168.

Sustainable rural tourism

One of the inherent dangers in thinking about rural tourism is to make it synonymous with sustainable tourism. As Clarke (1998: 130) states, 'they are not, decisively *not*, one and the same'. Lane (1994) outlines why a sustainable approach to rural tourism is required. Visitors to the countryside are increasingly mobile and are able to penetrate more remote areas than just a few years ago. For example, 80 per cent of visitors to the English countryside arrive by car. Advances in modes of transport have assisted this, coupled with the increasingly sophisticated marketing of new destinations. An unknown footpath can become an overused one almost overnight as a result of an editorial in a special-interest publication or promotional literature. A threat from badly managed tourism is posed. Rural tourism may be managed by outsiders who have little understanding of the people, culture and heritage of that area. Under-management of environmental resources could lead to their ultimate degradation. Tension between conservation and rural development interests commonly exist. While one realizes there is a need to stimulate some rural economies, reliance on tourism may lead to an unbalanced economy. A sustainable approach takes a more holistic perspective towards rural development. Page and Getz (1997) state that rurality and all of its components must be preserved and nurtured because they are, in essence, the selling point of the countryside and can be used in planning and marketing strategies. Rural tourism ideally should be included as part of an integrated rural development strategy. Ezeuduji (2017) examined the critical success factors in such development strategies for rural development with a tourism component, highlighting community awareness and empowerment, leadership and community capacity building to transform local people from objects to agents of the development process. Other key success factors are building micro clusters of businesses and linkages with the agricultural sector as advocated by Sigurðardóttir and Steinthorsson (2018) in Iceland. A sustainable approach to rural tourism should be based on a multifaceted view of sustainability to achieve balanced development. Consideration of the needs of the community, the viability of the economy and the conservation of the environment should receive appropriate consideration. Similarly, improving access via public transport (Guiver *et al.* 2007) has a key role to play in reducing the ecological footprint of visitors to rural areas. A range of debates on sustainable rural transport for tourism (e.g. Smith *et al.* 2019) reveal the complexity of the issues embedded in the notion of rural travel, while Tomej and Liburd (2019) point to both the environmental and social justice arguments for maintaining a public transport network in rural areas for tourism. A good example in Devon is the weekend Dartmoor hopper bus which connects visitors arriving by rail with bus connections to visit locations in Dartmoor National Park. Similarly, the notion of rural itineraries and trails has been developed in the form of wine tours of clusters of vineyards. For example, in South Africa, where the first vineyard opened its doors to visitors in 1971, a total of 21 wine routes now exist (Ferreira and Hunter 2017). Such trails also provide opportunities for other businesses (e.g. accommodation, hospitality and tourist services) to cluster around these nodes of activity to concentrate development opportunities in the vicinity of rural tourist routeways. In the case of Europe, McAreavey and McDonagh (2011) suggest sustainability has been at the heart of policy instruments by the EU and other public sector bodies, epitomized by the EU LEADER programme. LEADER was designed to improve the competitive position of agriculture and rural economies via diversification strategies. The central strands are to build partnerships at a local level while implementing local strategies, networking and building a local skill base. Marzo-Navarro *et al.* (2017) developed this collaboration model a stage further, indicating that better integration of empowered local residents was pivotal to the success of rural tourism development. In many respects, this is not dramatically different to the underlying principles inherent in rural tourism development in China, which announced a state scheme in 2019 to select key villages to promote rural tourism. Even so, one of the prevailing concerns frequently voiced by local communities about economic development premised on rural tourism relates to issues of sustainability. For example, Ghaderi and Henderson's (2012) study of an Iranian village observed that residents viewed the negative issues of resource use and unwanted cultural impacts as outweighing any positive benefits that may arise. The study illustrated how a failure to engage local residents in sustainability debates could lead to policy failures.

The planning and management of rural tourism

On an international scale, there are a number of different strategies that can be adopted to manage rural tourism. To some extent, rural tourism is comparable to tourism in any area but there are some distinct features or other aspects exacerbated in rural locations which need to be recognized.

Issues in rural tourism management

- *The lack of statistical base.* It is difficult to establish volume and value of rural tourism as a specific market sector in a nation, and it is even harder on an international scale. Many countries have different definitions of 'rural' and will therefore collect different data. Data on rural tourism as a specific form of tourism are not easily obtainable.
- *Rural communities.* These tend to be non-uniform, for example remote versus accessible rural areas contain very different types of settlement, employment opportunities and socio-demographic characteristics. Different community structures will have diverse responses to tourism.
- *Tourism development strategies may not benefit all rural areas.* Where there is an inadequate supply of attractions and/or accommodation, tourism cannot flourish, however good the marketing strategies to attract visitors may be. Likewise, development of tourism provision by local people may not be feasible in a depressed rural economy.
- *Tourism in rural areas is highly dependent on an attractive natural and culturally interesting environment.* This highlights the need to ensure that sustainable approaches to tourism management are adhered to. Sustainability objectives may conflict with the desire to attract greater volumes of visitors to the countryside and require sensitive consideration.

Providers of rural tourism – farm tourism

One of the important issues in rural tourism is that many providers are involved in tourism part-time. For example, the main business of a farm is in managing land, stock and machinery. Running bed-and-breakfast accommodation may be an ancillary business which provides supplementary income. As the enterprise may not be the main thrust of a business, there may be a lack of skills in managing a tourism business. Many farmers are isolated, with a lack of knowledge, expertise and training in tourism, and government agencies can advise on these issues. Many UK farm tourism providers belong to the Farm Holiday Bureau, which assists in marketing, while others choose to use other channels, such as guidebooks, adverts in tourist information centres or agencies. In France, a centralized system exists, supported by the public sector, to coordinate rural accommodation bookings for over 40 000 gîtes. The Ministry of Agriculture initiated the gîtes scheme in the 1950s, giving financial assistance to farmers to restore old farm buildings as tourist accommodation. Private sector companies, such as Gîtes de France, assist in promoting accommodation and travel packages to consumers.

There appears to be much debate in the literature regarding farm tourism. A large body of literature has developed around this notion. Forbord *et al.*'s (2012) review of this literature compared studies in a variety of different countries; they indicate that farm tourism was well established in Europe by 1900 and saw a significant increase after 1945 as part of a diversification strategy. The main impetus for further growth came in the 1990s as EU agricultural policy encouraged this form of diversification; this coincided with a greater number of women on farms starting non-farm enterprises. As Forbord *et al.* (2012) observed, Austria is deemed to be the leading country in Europe for farm tourism, with a variety of trade organizations promoting this nascent activity. This has been described as a period of evolution during the 1970s–1990s where tourism on farms was gradually replaced by farm tourism as the supplementary income role transformed into a major income. As Brandth and Hangen (2011) argue, this might represent a 'repeasantization', where farming families utilize the farm resources, culture and place to help sustain the farm as an economic unit. The commoditized relationship between host and guest creates new roles for the farmer, who now contributes stories, local food and activities, with a greater emphasis on their hosting role. It demonstrates a changing relationship between tourism and agriculture (Torres and Momsen 2011). Family labour tends to be the main source of assistance in farm tourism enterprises. Successful farm tourism development requires substantive capital input, marketing, reliance on external advice and finance. Farmers face constraints from planning legislation, and farm tourism is not necessarily a panacea in terms of solving critical problems of low farm incomes or failing businesses. Jenkins *et al.* (1998) state that the returns for small farms are limited.

Criteria for success in rural tourism

According to a study undertaken by PA Cambridge Economic Consultants (1987), rural tourism can be a significant part of local economic activity. This reiterates many of the findings of the earlier studies of rural environments (e.g. Clout 1972) but, in this case, the report by consultants was used for public policy purposes. The economic rationale for rural tourism also assumes a significant role when one considers the extent of the resources which a public body such as the Countryside Agency in the UK managed and its role as a possible shaper and funder of rural tourism initiatives to promote economic development. However, total economic contribution from rural tourism depends on:

- the extent of direct and indirect benefits retained in the area
- the provision of accommodation in the area
- the existence of facilities to support tourism in the area.

We have already come across these principles in Insight 21.1, an example in which tourism is at an early stage of development. In individual businesses, success in rural tourism generally depends on a combination of a number of factors. Briefly, this includes the commitment of the proprietor; the provision of additional facilities, for which visitors are willing to pay a higher price; generating visitor satisfaction and therefore recommendations and repeat visiting; ability to promote off-peak visits, thus reducing the effects of seasonality; understanding the needs and characteristics of customers and potential customers; and the existence of an attractive natural environment and cultural/historic features of interest. Recent discussions of the suitability of branding the rural tourism product has led to various attempts to identify certain products: for example, the Farm Holiday Bureau, a cooperative, membership-owned body consisting of over 1000 farm accommodation providers in the UK, market their own products; a similar

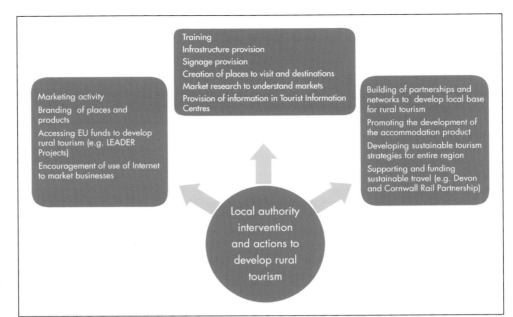

FIGURE 21.6 The local authority influence on rural tourism in the UK, 1997–2002 Source: Developed from Lane (2009)

body exists in New Zealand (the New Zealand Association of Farm Home Holidays). The aim of branding is to help identify rural tourism destinations and communicate the benefits, such as quality (Clarke 1998).

One of the foci of rural tourism strategy in general is to encourage a higher number of overnight stays and day trips. However rural areas need significant visitor spend to support employment. Attractions are particularly well suited to drawing in visitor numbers, but accommodation is needed to encourage these visitors to spend more time in that area and, subsequently, more money. PA Cambridge Economic Consultants (1987: 63) state: 'The major issue for rural areas is the creation of a critical mass of tourism facilities, both accommodation and attraction projects, which can succeed in making visitors additional to the region.' It is evident that to develop a successful rural tourism sector, particularly in more peripheral areas, there is an important role for the public sector to play. A review of the role of local authority influence on rural tourism development in the UK by Lane (2009) identified a number of positive interventions that fostered a positive range of actions and outcomes, as shown in Figure 21.6, although much of this was focused on business development.

Community involvement is an important aspect of rural tourism development. Common patterns indicate that residents need to feel tangible benefits from tourism and a degree of control over development and promotion. In the absence of perceived benefits, opposition is likely to increase (Page and Getz 1997). A 'bottom-up' approach where initiatives stem from the community is likely to lead to much less antagonism from local residents as opposed to a 'top-down' approach where an outside agency imposes a particular policy of tourism development on a community, as illustrated earlier. Many of the sustainable rural tourism projects around the world have been developed in a bottom-up way because there is a recognition that tourism is a way for local people to generate income and employment. For example, the Otago Peninsula Trust (southern New Zealand) is a voluntary organization which has taken a lead in establishing many facilities which are for the benefit of locals, the environment and visitors. So rather than its being a tool of blatant commercialism, this approach recognizes the wider developmental role which tourism can play.

Management issues

Visitor management, discussed in more detail in Chapter 19, is a key part of managing tourism in rural areas. Sharpley (2004) pointed to four key issues on the management of tourism in the countryside: access and land use issues; visitor management; land management issues; and transport issues. At regional and local levels, more precisely defined policies for visitor management can be identified. In England, the Countryside Commission

TABLE 21.3 Principles for tourism in the countryside	
Enjoyment	The promotion of the tourist's enjoyment of the countryside should be primarily aimed at those activities which draw on the special character of the countryside itself, its beauty, culture, history and wildlife.
Development	Tourism development in the countryside should assist the purposes of conservation and recreation, such as bringing new life to redundant buildings, supplementing farm incomes, aiding derelict land reclamation and opening up new access opportunities.
Design	The planning, design, siting and management of new tourism developments should be in keeping with the landscape and wherever possible should seek to enhance it.
Rural economy	Investment in tourism should support the rural economy, but should seek a wider geographical spread and more off-peak visiting both to avoid congestion and damage to the resource through erosion and overuse, and to spread the economic and other benefits.
Conservation	Those who benefit from tourism in the countryside should contribute to the conservation and enhancement of its most valuable asset – the natural environment, through political and practical support for conservation and recreation policies and programmes.
Marketing	Publicity, information and marketing initiatives of the tourism industry should endeavour to deepen people's understanding of and concern for the countryside, leading to fuller appreciation and enjoyment.

(1995) developed a wide range of different projects aimed at achieving sustainable rural tourism utilizing various visitor management practices. Many rural tourism initiatives have arisen through organizations and groups working in collaboration, mainly public and private sector partnerships. Visitor management may be aimed at encouraging certain types of desirable behaviour or limiting undesired behaviour. De-marketing, a policy of discouraging visitors, might well be part of the strategy. The Quantock Hills in Somerset, UK, are not promoted, so to help protect the area from further visits. Principles for tourism in rural areas also assist in the translation of policy to practice. The Countryside Commission, English Tourist Board and Rural Development Commission published guidelines in 1989, displayed in Table 21.3, which still hold true today and are applicable internationally. As rural tourism is in a constant state of flux, new research agendas are developing, to which attention now turns.

Contemporary issues in rural tourism

One new concept that has come into vogue for those seeking to understand the holistic nature of rural tourism is that of 'countryside capital', championed by bodies such as the Countryside Agency (now part of Natural England). The concept identifies the different components of the countryside as different forms of capital including:

- physical capital (the environmental features)
- natural capital (the built environment)
- social capital (the language, culture, people, lifestyles and food) (see Garrod *et al.* from 2006 for more detail on these components).

The concept highlights how the tourism product of rural areas can be created through the wider process of production (i.e. assembling its constituent parts) so as to show where investment in the different forms of capital will help add value to the tourism experience. This approach is gaining a great deal of credence. An example is the use of farmers' markets and festivals to develop a local differentiation of the rural experience, thereby adding value to the tourism sector but also indirectly to local food producers and the wider image of the area through the use of locally sourced products to create a tourism advantage (see Hjalager and Richards 2006 on the application to tourism and gastronomy). A key element here is understanding the tourism supply chain in rural areas and the wider interdependencies which exist, which crises such as foot-and-mouth abundantly highlight, where the countryside capital is intertwined and interrelated to such an extent that a negative impact in one area can devastate its entire supply of rural tourism. Recognizing these many interdependencies is a growing area of research on rural market towns by the Countryside Agency, highlighting the need to understand many of these fundamental links and how changes in

21

demand and consumer tastes may impact upon the countryside and service centres such as market towns. Seeking to quantify these relationships and impacts allows us to see the value of tourism and leisure to rural societies and economies. Sharpley (2004) summarized four key themes based on Roberts and Hall (2001: 220), in which the countryside is viewed as a particular destination for tourism. These themes were:

- *Change*, particularly the relationship between urban and rural places and spaces and the implications for rural destination development.
- *Transparency*, whereby all forms of tourism in the countryside can be recognized and policies and plans can then be developed to manage them.
- *Integration*, so that tourism is understood as an integral element of rural economies as well as in relation to specific types of rural tourism businesses.
- *Unsustainability*, where pursuing the notion of sustainable tourism may lead to unsustainable development in the countryside, which requires a strengthening of the environmental parameters in which tourism may be produced and consumed.

Yet a study by Hjalager *et al.* (2008) on innovation systems in Nordic tourism indicated that innovation is a key element for addressing the problems of rural tourism such as peripherality, which many rural businesses face. To create the destination products which will enable rural areas to address constraints such as peripherality and seasonality and to add value to existing products, innovation might well occur through developing value chains in rural areas. For example, the supply of local foodstuffs and products is seen as a way of retaining more value in the local economy. Networking, collaboration and public sector support were all viewed as key factors in helping rural destinations to harness innovation so as to grow the countryside capital. One other key issue is how tourism can be harnessed as part of a regeneration strategy to restore brownfield sites (i.e. sites that have been developed previously that may have lost their original purpose and so are lying unused, or may be contaminated where former industrial processes have exhausted the resources such as mining) and many local government bodies keep registers of such land. A good example of such regeneration which is the largest such redevelopment scheme of a rural brownfield site in Europe is the Cotswold Water Park (https://www.waterpark.org/) which is a 40-square-mile area with over 150 lakes located in Wiltshire, Gloucestershire and West Oxfordshire in the UK. The area was an extensive site of excavation of Jurassic limestone, created by mining leaving large craters in the landscape. Mining began to wind down from the 1970s and eventually ceased altogether, leaving a large area of water-filled lakes where the extraction had occurred. A mix of nature conservation, holiday accommodation complexes (including some innovative ecolodges) and sports activities have transformed the area since the late 1960s when the plan for transformation was first mooted, and it is now a destination that has leveraged off the branding of the nearby rural image of the Cotswold village and landscape to further expand the footprint of tourism to a much larger area, turning extensive derelict sites into reusable land.

Conclusion

It is clear that rural areas are an integral part of the modern tourism experience. Yet the principal challenge for rural areas that needs to be understood is how we ensure that appropriate forms of tourism are developed which assist in achieving the goals for national, regional and/or local rural development objectives. There is an inherent responsibility in rural tourism, whereby all those engaged in it must appreciate the long-term effects of tourism in rural areas, recognizing both the benefits and costs related to development. The relationship between tourism and the environment is particularly strong in rural areas, especially where the natural environment and resources such as National Parks create a special and highly valued location for visitors. There is also an imperative to understand to what extent tourism achieves the desired economic effects in rural areas and the criteria for a successful business strategy need careful examination. Butler and Clark (1992) recognize that tourism is not necessarily the key to rural development, highlighting concerns about income leakage, multipliers, local labour, wages and the limited number of entrepreneurs. 'The least favoured circumstance in which to promote tourism is when the rural economy is already weak, sine tourism will create highly unbalanced income and employment distributions' (Butler and Clark 1992: 175). The final point must be to emphasize the need to embed tourism within a diverse rural economy, to enable stable rural communities to exist.

Discussion questions

1 Explain why 'rural tourism' is a difficult term to define.

2 'The aim of rural tourism is to aid economic development.' Discuss.

3 Discuss the reasons why tourism may have a negative impact on a rural area.

4 Suggest reasons why tourism is more successful in some rural areas than others.

References

Bramwell, B. (1994) 'Rural tourism and sustainable tourism', *Journal of Sustainable Tourism*, 2 (1 and 2): 1–16.

Brandth, B. and Hangen, M. (2011) 'Farm diversification into tourism – implications for social identity', *Journal of Rural Studies*, 27 (1): 35–44.

Butler, R. and Clark, G. (1992) 'Tourism in rural areas: Canada and the UK', in I. Bowler, C. Bryant and M. Nellis (eds.) *Contemporary Rural Systems in Transition. Volume 2: Economy and Society*. Wallingford, Oxon: CAB International.

Clarke, J. (1998) 'Marketing rural tourism: Problems, practice and branding in the context of sustainability', in D. Hall and L. O'Hanlon (eds.) *Rural Tourism Management: Sustainable Options. Conference Proceedings 9–12 September 1998*. Ayr: SAC Auchincruive.

Cloke, P. (1977) 'An index of rurality for England and Wales', *Regional Studies*, 2 (1): 31–46.

Cloke, P. (1992) 'The countryside as commodity: New spaces for rural leisure', in S. Glyptis (ed.) *Leisure and the Environment. Essays in Honour of J.A. Patmore*. London: Belhaven.

Clout, H. (1972) *Rural Geography: An Introductory Survey*. Oxford: Pergamon.

Commission for Rural Communities (2006) *The State of the Countryside*: Cheltenham: Commission for Rural Communities.

Commission for Rural Communities (2010) *The State of the Countryside*. Cheltenham: Commission for Rural Communities.

Countryside Agency (2000) *Rural Services in 2000*. Cheltenham: Countryside Agency.

Countryside Commission (1992) *Enjoying the Countryside: Policies for People*. Cheltenham: Countryside Commission.

Countryside Commission (1995) *Sustainable Rural Tourism: A Guide to Local Opportunities*. Cheltenham: Countryside Commission.

Curry, N. (1994) *Countryside Recreation: Access and Land Use Planning*. London: E&FN Spon.

Davidson, J. and Wibberley, G. (1977) *Planning and the Rural Environment*. Oxford: Pergamon.

de Sousa, A.J.G. and Kastenholz, E. (2015) 'Wind farms and the rural tourism experience – problem or possible productive integration? The views of visitors and residents of a Portuguese village', *Journal of Sustainable Tourism*, 23(8–9): 1236–1256.

Defra (2009) *The Environment in Your Pocket*. London: Defra.

Ezeuduji, I. (2017) 'Change management for sub-Saharan Africa's rural tourism development', *Current Issues in Tourism*, 20 (9): 946–959.

Ferreira, S. and Hunter, C.A. (2017) 'Wine tourism development in South Africa: A geographical analysis', *Tourism Geographies*, 19 (5): 676–698.

Forbord, M., Schermer, M. and Grießmar, K. (2012) 'Stability and variety – products, organization and institutionalization', *Tourism Management*, 33 (4): 895–909.

Gannon, A. (1994) 'Rural tourism as a factor in rural community economic development for economies in transition', *Journal of Sustainable Tourism*, 1 (1&2): 51–60.

Garrod, B., Wornell, R. and Youell, R. (2006) 'Re-conceptualising rural resources as countryside capital: The case of rural tourism', *Journal of Rural Studies*, 22 (1): 117–128.

Ghadheri, Z. and Henderson, J. (2012) 'Sustainable rural tourism in Iran: A perspective from Hawraman Village', *Tourism Management Perspectives*, 2–3: 47–54.

Glyptis, S. (1991) *Countryside Recreation*. Harlow: Longman.

Guiver, J., Lumsdon, L., Weston, R. and Ferguson, M. (2007) 'Do buses help meet tourism objectives? The contribution and potential of scheduled buses in rural destination areas', *Transport Policy*, 14 (4): 275–282.

Halfacree, K. (1993) 'Locality and social representation: Space, discourse, and alternative definitions of the rural', *Journal of Rural Studies*, 9 (1): 23–37.

Halfacree, K. (1995) 'Talking about rurality: Social representations of the rural as expressed by residents of six English parishes', *Journal of Rural Studies*, 11 (1): 1–20.

Hall, C.M. and Boyd, S. (eds.) (2005) *Nature Based Tourism in Peripheral Areas*. Clevedon: Channel View.

21

Hall, C.M. and Jenkins, J. (1998) 'The policy dimensions of rural tourism and recreation', in R. Butler, C.M. Hall and J. Jenkins (eds.) *Tourism and Recreation in Rural Areas*. Chichester: John Wiley and Sons.

Hall, C.M. and Michael, E.J. (2006) 'Issues in regional development', in E. Michael (ed.) *Micro-Clusters and Networks: The Growth of Tourism* (pp. 7–20). Oxford: Elsevier.

Han, J. (2019) 'Vacationers in the countryside: Traveling for tranquility?' *Tourism Management*, 70: 299–310.

Healy, R. (1994) 'The common pool problem in tourism landscapes', *Annals of Tourism Research,* 21 (3): 596–611.

Hjalager, A., Huijbens, E., Björk, P., Nordin, S., Flagestad, A. and Knútson, Ö. (2008) *Innovation Systems in Nordic Tourism*. Nordic Innovation Centre.

Hjalager, A., Kwiatkowski, G., and Østervig Larsen, M. (2018) 'Innovation gaps in Scandinavian rural tourism', *Scandinavian Journal of Hospitality and Tourism*, 18(1): 1–17.

Hjalager, A. and Richards, G. (eds.) (2006) *Tourism and Gastronomy*. London: Routledge.

Ilbery, B.W. (1997) *The Geography of Rural Change*. Harlow: Longman.

Jenkins, J., Hall, C.M. and Troughton, M. (1998) 'The restructuring of rural economies: Rural tourism and recreation as a government response', in R. Butler, C.M. Hall, and J. Jenkins (eds.) *Tourism and Recreation in Rural Areas*. Chichester: John Wiley and Sons.

Jepson, D. and Sharpley, R. (2015) 'More than sense of place? Exploring the emotional dimension of rural tourism experiences', *Journal of Sustainable Tourism*, 23 (8–9): 1157–1178.

Keane, M. and Quinn, J. (1990) *Rural Development and Rural Tourism*. Galway: SSRC, University College, Galway.

Lane, B. (1994) 'What is rural tourism?' *Journal of Sustainable Tourism*, 2 (1&2): 7–21.

Lane, B. (2009) 'Rural tourism: An overview', in T. Jamal and M. Robinson (eds.) *The Sage Handbook of Tourism Studies*. London: Sage.

Lane, B. and Kastenholz, E. (2015) 'Rural tourism: The evolution of practice and research approaches – towards a new generation concept?' *Journal of Sustainable Tourism*, 23 (8–9): 1133–1156.

Lepp, A. (2007) 'Residents' attitudes towards tourism in Bigodi Village, Uganda', *Tourism Management*, 28 (3): 876–885.

Liu, A. (2006) 'Tourism in rural areas: Kedah, Malaysia', *Tourism Management*, 27 (5): 878–889.

Marzo-Navarro, M., Pedraja-Iglesias, M. and Vinzón, L. (2017) 'Key variables for developing integrated rural tourism', *Tourism Geographies*, 19 (4): 575–594.

McAreavey, R. and McDonagh, J. (2011) 'Sustainable rural tourism: Lessons for rural development', *Sociologia Ruralis*, 51 (2): 175–194.

Murdoch, J. and Marsden, T. (1994) *Reconstituting Rurality*. London: University College London Press.

Ohe, Y. (ed.) (2020) *Community-based Rural Tourism and Entrepreneurship: A Microeconomic Approach*. Singapore: Springer.

PA Cambridge Economic Consultants (1987) *A Study of Rural Tourism*. London: English Tourist Board and Rural Development Commission.

Page, S.J. and Getz, D. (eds.) (1997) *The Business of Rural Tourism: International Perspectives*. London: International Thomson Business Press.

Perales, R. (2002) 'Rural tourism in Spain', *Annals of Tourism Research*, 29 (4): 1101–1110.

Roberts, L. and Hall, D. (eds.) (2001) *Rural Tourism and Recreation: Principles to Practice*. Wallingford: CABI.

Robinson, G.M. (1990) *Conflict and Change in the Countryside*. London: Belhaven.

Rural Development Commission (1994) *Survey of Rural Services*. London: Rural Development Commission.

Rural Development Commission (1996) *The Impact of Tourism on Rural Settlements*. London: Rural Development Commission.

Rural Housing Federation (2017) *Affordable Housing. Saving Rural Life. Rural Life Monitor 2017*. Rural Housing Federation. www.housing.org.uk.

Sharpley, R. (1996) *Tourism and Leisure in the Countryside*. Huntingdon: ELM.

Sharpley, R. (2004) 'Tourism in the countryside', in A. Lew, C.M. Hall and A. Williams (eds.) *A Companion to Tourism*. Oxford: Blackwell.

Sharpley, R. and Sharpley, J. (1997) *Rural Tourism. An Introduction*. London: International Thomson Business Press.

Sigurðardóttir, I. and Steinthorsson, R. (2018) 'Development of micro-clusters in tourism: A case of equestrian tourism in northwest Iceland', *Scandinavian Journal of Hospitality and Tourism*, 18 (3): 261–277.

Sisneros-Kidd, A, Monz, C., Hausner, V., Schmidt, J, and Clark, D. (2019) 'Nature-based tourism, resource dependence, and resilience of Arctic communities: Framing complex issues in a changing environment', *Journal of Sustainable Tourism*, 27, (8) 3 August 2019: 1259–1276.

Smith, A., Robbins, D. and Dickinson, J. (2019) 'Defining sustainable transport in rural tourism: Experiences from the New Forest', *Journal of Sustainable Tourism*, 27 (2): 258–275.

Suntikul, W., Bauer, T. and Song, H. (2009) 'Pro-poor tourism development in Viengxay, Laos: Current state and future prospects', *Asia Pacific Journal of Tourism Research*, 14 (2): 153–168.

Tomej, K. and Liburd, J. (2019) 'Sustainable accessibility in rural destinations: A public transport network approach', *Journal of Sustainable Tourism*, 28 (2): 222–239.

Torres, R. and Momsen, J. (eds.) (2011) *Tourism and Agriculture*. London: Routledge.

Further reading

Books

Roberts, L., Hall, D. and Morag, M. (eds.) (2016) *New Directions in Rural Tourism*. London: Routledge.

Saxena, G. (2016) *Marketing Rural Tourism Experiences and Enterprises*. Oxford: Goodfellow.

Journal articles

Christou, P. and Sharpley, R. (2019) `*Philoxenia* offered to tourists? A rural tourism perspective', *Tourism Management*, 72: 39–51.

Ferreira, S. and Hunter, C. A. (2017) `Wine tourism development in South Africa: A geographical analysis', *Tourism Geographies*, 19 (5): 676–698.

Han, J. (2019) `Vacationers in the countryside: Traveling for tranquility?' *Tourism Management*, 70: 299–310.

Ma, X. Dai, M. and Fan, D. (2020) `Land expropriation in tourism development: Residents' attitudinal change and it's influencing mechanism', *Tourism Management*, 76: 103957.

Martinez, J., Martin, J., Fernandez, A. and Mogorron - Guerrero, H. (2019) `An analysis of the stability of rural tourism, as a desired condition for sustainable tourism', *Journal of Business Research*, 100: 165–175.

Novelli, M. and Gebhardt, K. (2007) `Community-based tourism in Namibia: "Reality show" or "Window Dressing"?' *Current Issues in Tourism*, 10 (5): 443–479.

Tomaj, K. and Liburd, J. (2020) `Sustainable accessibility in rural destinations: A public transport network approach', *Journal of Sustainable Tourism*, 28 (2): 222–239.

Yachin, J. and Ioannides, D. (2020) "Making do" in rural tourism: The resourcing behaviour of tourism micro-firms', *Journal of Sustainable Tourism*, 28 (7): 1003–1021.

21

22

Coastal and resort tourism

Learning outcomes

After reading this chapter and answering the questions, you should be able to:

- understand the importance of tourism in coastal areas
- recognize the impacts of coastal and resort tourism
- identify issues relating to the development and management of tourism in coastal areas.

Overview

Coastal areas offer some of the most desirable resources for tourism on the globe. Sun, sand and sea (the 3 S's) remains one of the most significant types of holiday in the world. However, new forms of coastal and marine recreation are emerging and increasing in popularity. This has broadened the coastal tourism product in recent years beyond resort holidays. While coastal tourism provides an important commercial sector of the tourism industry, tourism-related activities have been seen to cause negative environmental impacts. This chapter considers the importance of coastal areas for tourism, the nature of the coastal environment and the challenges for future management.

Introduction

The relationship between coastal areas and tourism is as old as tourism itself. Early tourists favoured seaside locations and made journeys to fashionable resorts to bathe in seawater to take advantage of its alleged curative powers. This was a major departure which took place in the eighteenth century; in earlier times, the sea and coast were revered as places and were even feared (Corbin 1995) (also see Chapter 2). This is illustrated by Lenček and Bosker (1999: xx) who state that 'the beach . . . historically speaking, [is] a recent phenomenon. In fact, it took hundreds of years for the seashore to be colonized as the pre-eminent site for human recreation'. The coast continues to be one of the most important environments for tourism in contemporary times, building on its established heritage. As Hall and Page (2006: 291) observe:

> The coastal environment is a magnet for tourists . . . although its role in leisure activities has changed in time and space, as coastal destinations have developed, waned, been reimaged and redeveloped in the twentieth century. The coastal environment is a complex system which is utilized by the recreationist for day trips, while juxtaposed to these visits are those made by the domestic and international tourist.

Today, for some regions, coastal tourism is the main type of tourism activity and is epitomized by the '3 S's' – sun, sand and sea. The beaches of the Mediterranean remain the most popular destination for European tourists, accounting for around 30 per cent of all tourist arrivals in Europe, although other regions of the world have highly developed forms of coastal tourism. Arguably, the coast remains the most dominant image of holiday brochures and travel programmes worldwide, epitomized by the romantic images of the South Pacific islands with their golden beaches and palm trees in the background. In the EU alone, there are 90 643 km of coastline; this is a valuable resource for tourism, with 12 991 km in Greece, 11 930 in Sweden and 17 457 in the UK. There is a growing body of research that suggests the coast is a therapeutic landscape (Bell *et al.* 2015), although there is nothing new in this idea since the early rediscovery of the coast in the seventeenth century (see Corbin 1995) as a curative location for various ills. What is different in the twenty-first century is the more holistic analysis of an individual's well-being and how visiting the coast may reinvigorate one's emotional and mental health, often associated with group interactions and activities that create a sense of pleasure.

Coastal areas are usually defined as those regions influenced by the proximity of the sea. However, other terms are in frequent use which have more specific meanings:

- the *coastline* refers to the boundary between the land and the sea
- the *coastal strip* is a narrow piece of land up to 1 km which borders the sea
- the *coastal zone*, a term which is often used in a management context, includes land and sea up to a width of 50 km – this takes in the coastal area through to the open sea.

Other definitions to consider are *coastal tourism* and *marine tourism*.

- *coastal tourism* usually refers to the type of tourism which takes place at the seaside – so resorts figure highly here
- *marine tourism* usually denotes activity that takes place in the water – such as scuba diving, sailing and jet-skiing.

Tourism at the coast

The coastal zone is of great environmental and economic significance (Bramwell 2004). The meeting of land and sea creates biologically and geologically diverse environments as well as attractive and unique landscapes which may form the basis for tourism. The surface of the earth is made up of 70 per cent ocean, and recent attention has been drawn towards the severe plastic pollution affecting the world's oceans. Estimates of the scale of the plastic problem show that:

> 8 million metric tons of plastic end up in our oceans. It's equivalent to five grocery bags filled with plastic for every foot of coastline in the world. In 2025, the annual input is estimated to be about twice greater, or 10 bags full of plastic per foot of coastline. So the cumulative input for 2025 would be nearly 20 times the 8 million metric tons estimate – 100 bags of plastic per foot of coastline in the world. (Le Guern 2019)

IMAGE 22.1 Plastic waste is now a global issue as illustrated at this marine aquarium

IMAGE 22.2 Coastal erosion may cause unstable cliffs that impact visitor access and safety

This pollution also manifests itself in the debris washed up on beaches frequented by tourists. The problem is epitomized by Nachite *et al.*'s (2019: 1) study of Moroccan beaches, where 'beach litter was mainly composed of Polymer Materials (PM), which represented 83.3 per cent of all collected items and the top three items represented 36.4 per cent of total debris, all of them belonging to plastics litter: bottle caps, crisps packets/sweets wrappers and cigarette butts' (see Image 22.1). These findings are replicated in a series of other studies of beach debris across the globe (see Rangel-Buitrago *et al.* 2019; Silva *et al.* 2018) and schemes to address the problem (see Agamuthu *et al.* 2019; Zielinski *et al.* 2019) associated with beach cleans.

Coastal tourism is growing at a faster rate than most other forms of tourism and this growth presents special management challenges, as the EU (2005) coastal zone management report highlights (https://europa.eu/), where 20 per cent of the coastline is suffering from severe impacts due to erosion (see Image 22.2). However, coastal areas across the globe face intense pressures, not just from tourism. The Organization for Economic Cooperation and Development (OECD) (1993) cite the main pressures as:

- rapid urbanization and settlement
- pollution
- tourism development
- haphazard development

which led the EU (2005) to highlight the importance of Strategic Environmental Assessment so that coastal issues are considered more fully in planning decisions, given the erosion problems (see Insight 22.1)

22

INSIGHT 22.1 Coastal erosion and the impact of coastal tourism – Holderness, Yorkshire, UK (R. Page)

Holderness is an area of coastline in East Yorkshire, stretching around 50 km from Flamborough Head to Spurn Point, with thriving tourist locations such as Bridlington, Hornsea and Withernsea. The area has an average of around 1 million visitors a year. Geologically the area is interesting because the coastline has 'soft' cliffs comprising glacial till, which is a soft boulder clay described as '72 per cent mud, 27 per cent sand and 1 per cent boulders and large pebbles' (Sistermans and Nieuwenhuis 2003).

The main form of accommodation for visitors are static caravans/caravan parks, with roughly 123 parks across the coast of East Yorkshire. This coastline is under threat due to coastal erosion (see Pye and Blott 2015), and is Europe's fastest eroding coastline with an average of 2 m of erosion annually, resulting in threats to the local community and the tourism sector. Historically, since Roman times this coastline has seen 32 settlements disappear into the sea, meaning that land loss is an ever-present problem. For example, there are 24 holiday/caravan parks in the area within 200 m of the cliff edge which are at risk of being lost to the sea. This poses major problems for the tourism sector at Holderness. As a way to cope with the effect of coastal erosion on the tourism sector, coastal retreat strategies have been implemented which include the movement of caravan parks away from the coastline. 'Roll-back' is one such strategy that has been introduced perpetuating the movement of caravan sites at least 400 m away from the cliff edge, which is estimated to allow the caravan parks to have roughly 100 years of safety from coastal erosion. Other strategies have also been implemented to protect tourist infrastructure as well as homes. One location in Holderness that is particularly reliant on tourism is Hornsea, a small town with a population of 8432 (2011 census) and which is regarded as a coastal resort with its Blue Flag beach, nature reserve and the largest freshwater lake in Yorkshire, all of which are popular with visitors. The town is steeped in local history, which has been harnessed to create visitor attractions including Hornsea Pottery, and the Hornsea Folk Museum that contains the largest collection of Hornsea Pottery in the world. These attractions have helped to maintain visitor spending of around £14.5 million, which indicates that Hornsea is dependent on tourism: 600 jobs in Hornsea are supported by tourism. The significance of tourism has reinforced the importance of hard coastal engineering strategies to protect the amenity, including a 2 km concrete sea wall, designed to provide protection for the town, resort, attractions and the 7420 caravans. The implications are that visitors should still able to visit Hornsea,

to help stabilize the tourist economy in Holderness. Yet critics point out that sea walls and coastal defences are only short-term solutions, as by 2050 it is expected that areas along the coastline will be half a metre higher due to the fact that the area is sinking by about 3 mm a year. Therefore this Insight shows that coastal environments can be very dynamic due to the physical processes of coastal erosion. Sistermans and Nieuwenhuis (2003) review the range of options for coastal management that could be adopted to protect the area in the future.

Further reading

'Hornsea' (n.d.) Yorkshire.com. https://www.yorkshire.com/places/yorkshire-coast/hornsea/essential-hornsea.

Hornsea Coastal Community Team (2017) *Coastal Community Teams Economic Plan.* http://www.coastalcommunities.co.uk/wp-content/uploads/2017/08/hornsea-economic-plan-2017.pdf.

Pye, K. and Blott, S. J. (2015) 'Spatial and temporal variations in soft-cliff erosion along the Holderness coast, East Riding of Yorkshire, UK', *Journal of Coastal Conservation,* 19(6): 785–808.

Sistermans, P. and Nieuwenhuis, O. (2003) *Holderness Coast.* Erosion case study. Amersfoort: DHV. http://copranet.projects.eucc-d.de/files/000164_EUROSION_Holderness_coast.pdf.

UKcampsite.co.uk results for East Yorkshire: https://www.ukcampsite.co.uk/sites/results.asp?county=East%20Yorkshire.

Populations are often concentrated in coastal areas: 43 per cent of the EU's population in 22 member states live in coastal regions (i.e. 196 million people). At a global scale, coastal zones account for 15 per cent of the Earth's surface but contain around 60 per cent of the world's population, and around 86 per cent of such environments in Europe are suffering from unsustainable use. In the USA, the average population density of coastal counties is five times greater than that of non-coastal counties, and beaches host 275 million visits a year. California has a large network of beaches stretching along 424 miles, shown in Figure 22.1, and serving a resident population of 35 million with an additional visitor population. The top three state beaches in 2003 were Santa Monica (7.8 million visits), Lighthouse Field (7.3 million visits) and Dockweiler (3.8 million visits) which generate US$75.4 million in travel and tourism expenditure for the Californian economy, supporting up to 1 million jobs and generating a further US$4.8 million in tax revenue. In New Zealand, Japan and the UK, no one lives more than two hours' travelling distance from the sea, and 17 million people live within Italy's coastal zone. In Denmark, 70 per cent of the population lives in coastal zones: the figure is 51 per cent in Ireland, 44 per cent in Portugal and 50 per cent in Sweden. In the UK, the 41 largest coastal towns, each with a tourism industry stretching back over 100 years, have a combined resident population of over 2.1 million and employ over 112 000 people in total. These towns employ around 11.6 per cent of the local population in tourism, although some towns employ much larger proportions of the labour force in the industry (e.g. Blackpool 19 per cent; Torbay 18.8 per cent; Scarborough 18 per cent) (House of Commons Communities and Local Government Committee 2007; Agarwal *et al.* 2018). Coastal populations in retirement resorts are growing disproportionately as the population ages in the coastal resorts of the south of England, which are popular migration destinations for retirees, a trend being mirrored in many other developed countries. For example, over 41 per cent of people aged over 65 years in the EU's 22 member states live in coastal regions. Increasing population usually results in pressure for development for both residential and business uses. Traditionally, tourism has led to development in coastal areas. People who may have spent their annual holidays in a certain resort may choose to retire to that place, creating a need for more housing. More significantly, resort tourism requires infrastructure in order to support the industry and this results in construction of new buildings, placing pressure on greenfield sites.

FIGURE 22.1 Californian beaches

Source: Copyright S.J. Page

The economic significance of marine-related industry must not be forgotten. Fishing is an important commercial element in many regions, such as Canada and Scandinavia, but raises questions of over-exploitation and indirect effects on marine ecology, although it is an integral part of the marine economy. Along the Mexican Caribbean coastline, Ruiz-Ramírez *et al.* (2019) examined the likely effects on the coastal economy of 1 and 2-m rises in sea level as a result of climate change. Their study estimated that the impact on these areas, which include resorts like Cancun, could be between US$300 million to US$1.4 billion depending on the scale of the sea-level rise which would inundate coastal areas. Tamayo *et al.*'s (2018) analysis of the Total Economic Value (TEV) of the Philippines coral reefs found that that 'annual TEV ranged from 100 to 800 million US$ with potential reef fisheries value contributing the most in the TEV, followed by reef fisheries, tourism, and WTP [Willingness to Pay] biodiversity values' (Tamayo *et al.* 2018: 63). As Spalding *et al.* (2017: 104) indicate 'coral reefs attract foreign and domestic visitors and generate revenues, including foreign exchange earnings, in over 100 countries and territories'. Therefore, these examples demonstrate the economic value of both the coastal zone and the ecological resources therein which have a powerful attraction to tourists, such as for scuba diving and visits to coral reefs.

The main issue raised by inadequate controls over coastal management is the international scale of the problems – pollution is a transnational issue and one country cannot alleviate the problem alone as the example of plastic pollution illustrates. The European Environment Agency (1998), for instance, notes that water quality, freshwater supply, fisheries, tourism, pollution and habitat deterioration transcend political boundaries and require strategic planning, and the EU has been leading initiatives on bathing water quality since 1976. Mismanagement of these issues results in what is known as 'the tragedy of the commons'.

The attraction of the coast

A variety of factors combine to form the attraction of the coast for tourism and recreation. These may be summarized as follows:

- *Natural:* the landscape of cliffs, beaches, open sea, estuaries and the sky.
- *Structural:* the townscape, architecture and tourist-related features (piers, promenades, gardens and lighthouses) (see Insight 22.1).
- *Psychological:* the meanings and values attached to the natural and built environments which gives a sense of place. For example, Sakurai *et al.* (2017) found that sense of place was a powerful influence upon attitudes towards conservation of coastal resources among residents in a Japanese coastal region.

Visitors to a coastal area or resort will be attracted by the combined elements contributing to the sense of place and the imagery associated with the area, which may focus on the beach (Figure 22.2). They will be keen to seek out desired experiences from the holiday – which might range from the need to escape urban life (the unspoilt coastline),

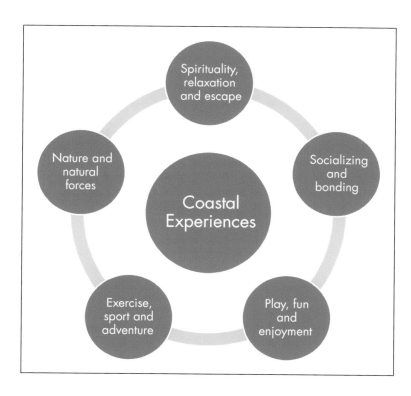

FIGURE 22.2 The elements of the coast as a tourism and leisure environment
Source: Adapted from Page and Connell (2010)

such as holidays to Bonaire, the Caribbean, to the need to integrate with others in a social setting (the resort), typified by clubbing holidays to San Antonio, Ibiza.

The evolution of coastal tourism

The coast has received much attention in the tourism literature, and three excellent surveys of the development of resorts for tourism by Towner (1996) and Walton (1983, 2000) are reviewed in Chapter 2. Researchers have studied different facets of coastal tourism including:

- the historical dimension, including sociological analyzes by Lenček and Bosker (1999) and the construction of place identities
- the evolution of resorts (e.g. Gilbert 1939; Naylon 1967) as well as disciplinary foci by geographers as an enduring theme since the 1930s (Hall and Page 2014; Meyer-Arendt 2018)
- tourist travel to the beach and tourist behaviour at the beach (e.g. Tunstall and Penning-Rowsell 1998)
- the physical and environmental aspects of coastlines as resources to be managed for tourism (e.g. Jennings 2004) including the growing concerns over climate change (e.g. Jones and Phillips 2017; Honey and Hogenson 2017; Mimura 2008; Young and Essex 2019)
- models of resort development (e.g. Pigram 1977).

Thus it is clear that this subject has been studied for many years and, as Figure 22.3 demonstrates, there is evidence to suggest that through time the beach as a tourism and leisure resource has experienced a democratization (Page and Connell 2010). As Hall and Page (2006: 292) note:

The beach developed as the activity space for . . . tourism, with distinct cultural and social forms emerging in relation to fashions, tastes and innovations in resort form. The development of piers, jetties and promenades as formal spaces for organized recreational and tourism activities led to new ways of experiencing the sea. The coastal environment, resort and the beach have been an enduring resource for tourism and recreation since the 1750s in western consciousness, with its meaning, value to society and role in leisure time remaining a significant activity space.

22

FIGURE 22.3   The democratization of the beach
Source: Adapted from Page and Connell (2010)

Yet seeking to understand how this evolution has occurred and generated resort development has led several researchers to seek to explain the essential features of coastal resort development.

Coastal resort development

Miossec's model of tourism development (1976 cited in Pearce 1995: 15) illustrates the temporal and spatial growth of a tourist region. Smith (1991, 1992) applied this model to Pattaya in Thailand and developed a tentative beach resort model, where development is observed from no development to full resort development. Figure 22.4 illustrates the model of resort development in time and space. Other studies have examined the geography of resort development

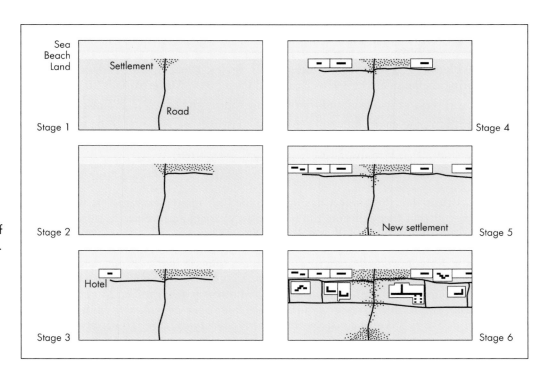

FIGURE 22.4   Model of tourist resort development.
Source: Reprinted from *Landscape and Urban Planning*, vol. 21, 'Beach resorts: A model of development evolution', 189–210, © 1991, with permission from Elsevier

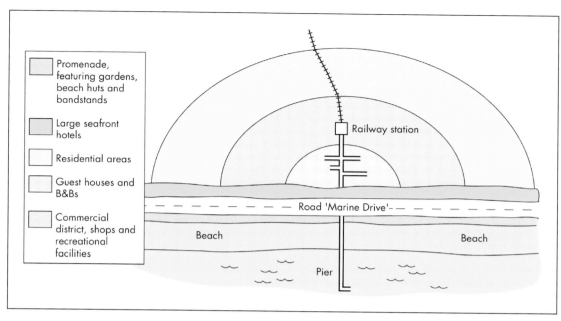

FIGURE 22.5 The basic morphology of a coastal resort
Source: Adapted from Pearce (1995)

based upon the initial ideas of Turner and Ash (1975) who viewed new resort development as a pleasure periphery. A subsequent study by Gormsen (1981) expanded upon these ideas, highlighting the importance of global capital in creating resorts with large hotel complexes or holiday villages, and King (2001) pursued the pleasure-periphery notion. Hawkins *et al.* (2002) expanded upon these ideas, illustrating the importance of globalization drivers, local and international investors, tour operators and national governments as well as local government. The role of local government has been seen as a key variable in the UK in explaining the varying fortunes of individual resorts in their ability to facilitate regeneration, given the prevailing weakness in national tourism policies to promote coastal tourism (House of Commons Communities and Local Government Committee 2007). Yet as the example of Denarau Island, Fiji suggests, not all resort development follows a set patterns. Denarau Island was developed to a masterplan (see Xie *et al.* 2013) and a distinct tourist enclave has emerged.

Aside from these evolutionary models of resort development, common structural features may be observed in coastal resorts, as indicated by Pearce (1995). The seafront, linear in form, usually consists of the beach, a promenade, a road and a line of beachfront buildings. These buildings tend to incorporate the most expensive and luxurious accommodation and restaurants, as well as some tourism retailing. Behind this first line of buildings can be found, on a graded scale of price, density and height, smaller hotels, guest houses and bed-and-breakfast establishments, which gradually merge with residential and town-centre functions. Many of the well-known coastal resorts reflect this simple pattern of development – see Figure 22.5. Additionally, in many English resorts, a classic 'T' pattern of development exists, with the 'T' being formed by the road from the railway station meeting with the promenade, which constitutes the basic structure.

In the Mediterranean, Spanish coastal resorts are often cited as extreme examples of coastal mass tourism. The reasons for this are broadly:

- inappropriate development, bearing little or no resemblance to local conditions, such as scale, style, materials
- impact on habitats and species, especially dune areas
- water pollution, most markedly sewage pollution of coastal waters
- effects on the local economy (inflation, higher land prices and in-migration of workers) and society (changes in cultural traditions, rapid changes in social composition, employment opportunities limited to lower paid work).

Torremolinos is a good example of a large-scale resort which has grown because of the rate of tourism development since the 1950s. From its origins as a small fishing village to the elite resort of the mid-part of the twentieth century to a mass-market resort with over 50 000 bed spaces, Torremolinos has witnessed extensive environmental, economic and sociocultural change. However, Torremolinos, like many other similar resorts on the Costa del Sol (Barke and Towner 2004), Costa Brava and Costa Blanca, began to lose its tourist appeal due to the deterioration in environmental quality. Less desirable tourists began to visit as prices were reduced. Some tourism development models assist in the explanation of resort growth and decline. A similar pattern of development can be discerned in Turkey where government incentives to developers led to a major expansion of resorts on the southern and eastern coastlines. Despite many of the problems of rapid tourism growth in the coastal areas, the tourism strategy for Turkey to 2023 (Ministry of Culture and Tourism 2007) views this form of development as worthy of further expansion alongside new niche markets for non-coastal tourism (e.g. thermal, cultural, ecotourism, gastronomy and other locally defined products) as marinas and fishing infrastructure are redeveloped for tourism.

According to the tourist-area destination lifecycle devised originally by Butler (1980), destinations seem to follow a pattern of development. This model is similar to the concept of the product lifecycle used ostensibly in marketing and which is illustrated in Chapter 2. The model has gained general acceptance and has proved to be reasonably effective in empirical trials. The model suggests that a newly emerging destination will gradually become known by tourists, so initially only a small number will visit. As the destination becomes more well known, tourists will visit in larger numbers and tourism providers will increase their operations – the original tourists are probably less likely to want to return by this point. Eventually, the destination becomes a mass-market resort with the inherent problems of environmental degradation, resulting in some tourists being motivated to find an alternative resort which is less spoiled for their next holiday. This leads to a decline in tourist numbers and affects the level of business in the resort. Strategies to rejuvenate the area may be required at this point to maintain or improve on the required numbers and types of visitors. Many English seaside resorts display the decline stage of the destination lifecycle, as discussed above in the case of Hastings, where public sector intervention has set about regenerating the resort. Other local authorities, in an attempt to remain competitive and entice visitors to stay, have also launched rejuvenation strategies, for example Bridlington, Rhyl and Torbay. The House of Commons Communities and Local Government Committee (2007) identified a number of European Regional Development Fund projects which have sought to rejuvenate the English coastal environment: £2.1 million at Cromer seafront to enhance access and the promenade/foreshore; £5.4 million at Southend-on-Sea to enhance the physical environment and gateway to the pier/foreshore from the town centre; £4 million at Bridlington to refurbish the former spa and to convert it to an event centre to improve the appearance of a major landmark. Other resorts have also been successful in repositioning themselves to create a USP and brand focused on a local strength, such as Newquay and its surfing appeal. St Ives has used the development of the Tate Gallery to appeal to arts- and culture-loving visitors, while Southport has developed new markets based upon golf. Many of the Mediterranean resorts, like Torremolinos, have experienced this process of regeneration, as they were built haphazardly, without planning controls or adequate infrastructure. In Majorca, a policy of demolishing outdated hotels and shabby tourist buildings has enabled the local authority to improve the physical environment of the resort through landscaping. Insight 22.2 explores this in more detail along with Figure 22.6.

Despite the example of Calvià, other commentators have argued that in many mature resorts, redevelopment is generally superficial – for example, new street furniture, landscaping, new façades – and that, while this improves the aesthetic value, it does not tackle the underlying problem of sustaining appropriate levels of growth and attracting new markets. Often, resort development is hampered by highly fragmented land ownership, existing infrastructure, utilities, development and traffic congestion. In many cases, a holistic approach to resort regeneration, while desirable, remains expensive and is often impractical. More recent attempts to understand resort developments are by Weaver (2000) and Prideaux (2000). Weaver states that after 20 years of debate, it is generally agreed that Butler's model typifies just one sequence of possible events in the evolution of a destination. Weaver proposes a broad context model which includes four types of tourism:

- circumstantial alternative tourism (CAT)
- deliberate alternative tourism (DAT)
- sustainable mass tourism (SMT)
- unsustainable mass tourism (UMT).

Seven possible scenarios are drawn up using the four tourism types (see Figure 22.7.)

22

INSIGHT 22.2 Calvià: An ageing resort with new hope for the future

The municipality of Calvià is one of the largest tourism-receiving areas on the island of Majorca, accounting for about one-third of the total flow of tourists to the Balearic Islands. In 2018 it received over 14 million visitors and a further 5.5 million domestic tourists from the Spanish mainland, with visitors typically staying 6.9 nights. It is a municipality of 143 km² with a 60 km coastline, 50 000 inhabitants, 120 000 bedspaces and 1.7 million visitors a year (Aguiló *et al.* 2005). Over 90 per cent of local revenue is derived from tourism.

Tourism development in Calvià boomed in the 1960s and has been based on short-term economic gain. As Aguiló *et al.* (2005) note, it was one of the first municipalities to experience the negative effects of mass tourism. Lack of planning regulations resulted in urban sprawl and lack of environmental regard, similar to many Mediterranean resorts. Water quality, deforestation, alien building styles and the density of development were among the main issues. Towards the end of the 1980s, the effect of this development strategy began to demonstrate negative consequences (Figure 22.6).

The long-term aim of the regeneration project was to achieve a modern coastal tourism destination offering high quality and a more appropriate bed-space capacity, and this was incorporated into the Local Development Planning Regulations. The underlying basis of future development is based on the principles of sustainability, with the environment and local community at the core. The objectives of the Local Agenda 21 plan were underpinned by a desire to improve the sustainability of the destination alongside the following strategic desire to improve the quality of tourism while assisting in the regeneration of the resort as well as making important environmental improvements and also limiting growth. Already, much work has been initiated. Seawater quality is monitored on a weekly basis, obsolete hotels have been demolished, reducing bed-space capacity and removing ugly buildings, and a proposed large-scale development has been halted. Environmental management in hotels and other buildings has been encouraged – waste recycling, reduced electricity consumption, purchase of more environmentally sound products. New planning rules have also led to de-classification of accommodation, cycle route development, the creation of green spaces and protection of heritage sites. It has also led to the reorganization of municipal management and services. A wide acceptance

of the principles of Agenda 21 has been established through broad community consultation and participation. A significant spin-off to the Calvià initiative is the transferability of the concept of environmental management and improvement to similar resorts. Indeed, Aguiló *et al.* (2005) found that prices of holidays in Calvià were now higher than for other areas of the Balearic Islands as it entered a restructuring phase using the principles of sustainability, while meeting the needs of visitors and repositioning the destination. Project Calvià 2030 is the latest strategy seeking to move the destination further along the sustainable paradigm. To achieve the shift towards a more sustainable destination, Calvià is also promoting the natural recovery of the sandy coastline by extending the revegetation of areas to retain sand and removing architectural features which interfere with sand retention. In Magaluf, a degraded area of 20 000 m² was turned into a green zone, reintroducing native plants and remodelling at a cost of €924 000 to improve the environment in key tourist areas. The municipality's 26 beaches have seen eight Blue Flags awarded, which illustrates the progress made in environmental improvements. Sharing good practice and integrating the principles of Agenda 21 in plans for sustainable development are seen as the way forward for the local authorities in Mediterranean resorts. The high level of participation of local residents in the sustainable redevelopment of the destination is combined with the provision of key publications (e.g. *Know Calvià Enjoy Calvià: Environmental Information*) to residents and

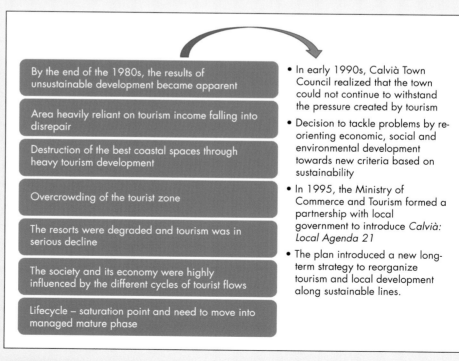

FIGURE 22.6 Consequences of unsustainable tourism growth
Source: http://www.calvia.com; Aguiló *et al.* (2005); Dodds (2007)

INSIGHT 22.2 continued

TABLE 22.1	Examples of media representations of the raucous behaviour by British tourists in Majorca and other mass destinations

Allen, F. (2017) 'ADIOS! End of an era as Brits ABANDON Majorca after hundreds of "arrogant locals" demand holidaymakers go home', *The Sun*, 27 September 2017.

Choat, I. (2018) '"Don't drink, undress or defecate in public" – how Magaluf is trying to tame its British tourists', *The Guardian*, 22 June 2018.

Couzens, G. (2019) 'British tourists top Spain's list of the worst-behaved airline passengers', *Daily Mail* (*Mail Online*), 17 June 2019.

Elliot, A. (2019) 'The science behind why British tourists behave worse abroad than at home', *The Telegraph*, 27 March 2019.

Khaleeli, H. (2017) 'From Barcelona to Malia: How Brits on holiday have made themselves unwelcome', *The Guardian*, 17 January 2017.

Penza, N. (2019) 'Idiot Brit caught weeing off Magaluf hotel balcony as yob pal encourages him to shower holidaymakers walking below', *The Sun*, 9 July 2019.

White, S. (2019) 'British holidaymakers banned from death-trap balconies in boozy tourist hotspots after Majorca death plunges', *The Sun*, 17 July 2019.

Youll, B. (2018) 'British tourists to blame for ruining Majorca rage fed up locals', *Daily Star*, 12 June 2018.

visitors, explaining the importance of this approach to tourism, making it a good example of best practice. In 2009 Calvià received a Quality Coast Award, for being the destination with the greatest number of Blue Flag clean beaches, as well as for its commitment to Integrated Coastal Plans to ensure the sustainable management of its coastal environment. By 2050, the Balearics want to be less reliant on the 70 per cent of energy consumption that arises from fossil fuels, with diesel vehicles banned from 2025 and petrol vehicles in 2035. Even so, the image of the mass resorts of Palma and Magaluf remain an ongoing problem for the island, as Table 22.1 shows, with examples of negative media coverage of British tourists' raucous behaviour. Tourist guides describe Magaluf, for example, as follows: 'This is a lively resort by anyone's standards, and has a reputation for wild nightlife, typically the British 18–30 crowd and young groups of revellers. Magaluf attracts a large number of hen and stag parties, and has a somewhat saucy reputation' (https://www.majorca-guides.info/resorts/magaluf/). So the Calvià area still has a long way to go in reimaging itself with its sustainability journey, largely because of the legacy of the pockets of 18–30-aged tourism associated with the nightlife and culture that has evolved in Palma and Magaluf. Even so, greater regulation of tourist behaviour has led to flat owners not being permitted to rent apartments via P2P mediums, to reduce house-price inflation for locals; fines of £500–£1300 have been introduced for those balconing (i.e. climbing between balconies and diving into swimming pools from balconies) and for anti-social

behaviour, and cheap drinking offers in waterfront areas have been withdrawn. Despite greater regulation, as part of its coastal analysis, Greenpeace (2013) reported that Calvià was one of the most unsustainable destinations in Spain, and emphasized the need to do more.

Further reading

Andrews, H. (2011) *The British on Holiday: Charter Tourism, Identity and Consumption*. Bristol: Channel View.

Andrews, H. (2017) 'Mass tourism in Mallorca: Examples from Calvià', in D. Harrison and R. Sharpley (eds.), *Mass Tourism in a Small World* (pp. 181–190). Wallingford, CABI.

Dodds, R. and Butler, R. (2010) 'Barriers to implementing sustainable tourism policy in mass tourism destinations', *Tourismos*, 5 (1): 35–54.

Greenpeace (2013) *DESTRUCCIÓN A TODA COSTA 2013: Análisis del litoral a escala municipal* (Destruction at all costs 2013: Analysis of the coast at municipal level). Madrid: Greenpeace.

Questions

1 What prompted Calvià to embark on its journey towards sustainability?

2 What are the main measures it has taken towards sustainability?

3 What problems does the 18–30 tourism market pose for the destination?

4 What are the long-term prospects for tourism in Calvià?

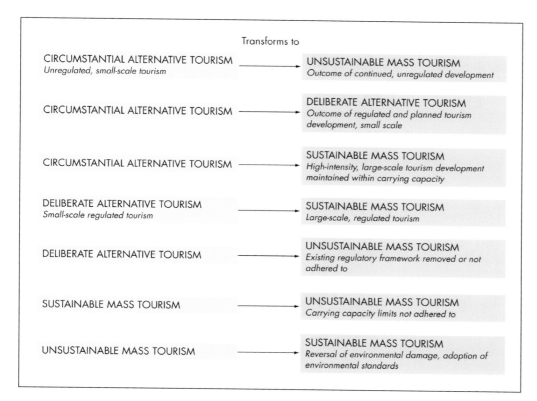

FIGURE 22.7 Scenarios of destination development
Source Adapted from Weaver (2000)

Butler's model fits the movement from CAT to UMT. The model can be used to categorize the status of tourism at a resort at the current time. Once this is done, it is then the responsibility of resort managers to consider all possible future scenarios. Desirable scenarios can then be pinpointed and worked towards. Weaver applied the model to Australia's Gold Coast, typified by high-density urban resorts, as discussed in Chapter 10. The broad context model categorizes the Gold Coast as UMT. A desired state of SMT must be worked towards with appropriate management strategies. Weaver (2012a) re-examined these ideas and suggested that Calvià represented an example of an organic path towards SMT despite ongoing issues such as water shortages, and that 25 per cent of the island's golf courses are located there and these are major consumers of water. Water remains a major constraint on development (Essex *et al.* 2004; Kent *et al.* 2002; Hof and Blázquez-Salom 2015). In addition, the groundwater is under pressure from development and a growing reliance upon costly desalinated water to meet demand. Furthermore, Hof and Blázquez-Salom (2015) point to the dogma of growth as a challenge for sustainability. Perles-Ribes *et al.* (2018) take this argument a stage further, suggesting that growth and sustainable development are a contradiction in terms with reference to the case of Majorca and residential tourism, where the focus on profit does not necessarily mean growth is inevitable or that growth is inherently good. Peeters' (2012) reply to Weaver's paper and Weaver's (2012b) response provide an interesting series of insights into the merits of the destination evolution model based around the notion of sustainability.

Prideaux (2000) proposes another new model, termed the resort development spectrum. This model identifies five phases of growth:

- Phase 1 – local tourism.
- Phase 2 – regional tourism.
- Phase 3 – national tourism.
- Phase 4 – international tourism.
- Phase 5 – decline/stagnation/rejuvenation.

Prideaux states that development is not necessarily sequential, and neither is growth automatic. Another element to the model is the inclusion of market factors. As growth occurs, new market sectors are added, which affects accommodation types, promotion, tourism infrastructure and transport modes. The move from local to international resort reflects a greater professionalization, higher investment, great diversity of attractions and availability of top-quality services.

22

The impacts of coastal tourism

Conflict between coastal tourism and the natural environment arises in a number of areas and concern has been expressed about the implications of continued growth. Effects may be observed in a social, environmental and economic context. The main environmental issue is that the marine environment is of greater ecological diversity than land environments, with the most biologically significant areas being close to shore – such as coral reefs, estuaries and wetlands. Coral reefs, for example, are said to contain a higher biodiversity than tropical rainforests (Prideaux and Pabel 2018). With increasing levels of recreational use, coastal impacts are likely to remain a significant issue, especially in view of the potential effects of global warming, as discussed in Chapter 18.

Environmental issues

Goodhead and Johnson (1996) cite some of the environmental concerns in relation to nature conservation in the marine environment. The loss of habitat is the main threat and this may arise through short- and long-term disturbance. Developments such as marinas, jetties, promenades and car parks entail loss of coastal land. There is much concern about habitat destruction and disturbance of fauna. In Norway, the building of leisure cabins and the popularity of outdoor pursuits such as boating place pressures on the coastal environment. In Finland, second-home lodge developments cause similar concerns and create opportunity costs. Intertidal and coastal land habitats may be affected by recreational activities taking place on the beach. The effects of trampling on sand dunes are, for example, well documented. On the Spanish coast, the disappearance of large stretches of dune system as a result of tourism development has resulted in an unstable coastline.

In some cases, environmental changes are necessary to sustain tourism. In Florida, demand for development has exceeded land available, so additional island waterfront has been created by infilling marshes and building finger-like extensions into the water, as at Boca Ciega Bay. Some of the barrier islands on the eastern coast of the USA are very popular tourism destinations. Barrier islands are long, thin barriers of sand separated from the shoreline by a lagoon or marsh area. Some 3200 km of coast from New York to Texas contain such islands. Before 1939, 10 per cent of the barrier islands were developed – now a large proportion is covered with resorts, houses, apartments, hotels and other services. By the early 1980s, the development rate of barrier islands took in about 24 km^2 per year. This was slowed dramatically by Congress legislation which covered small areas of undeveloped land. Erosion and coastal flooding are severe problems in this environment, often exacerbated by the groynes and sea walls that are in place to protect buildings but which have a longer-term deleterious effect on beach stability. Lithgow *et al.* (2019: 43) describe coastal squeeze as 'one form of coastal habitat loss, where intertidal habitat is lost due to the high water mark being fixed by a defence or structure (i.e. the high water mark residing against a hard structure such as a sea wall) and the low water mark migrating landwards in response to SLR [sea level rise]', meaning that habitats get squeezed into a diminishing space. Erosion necessitates beach replenishment if developments are to be protected. For example, Thuy *et al.* (2019) examined beach erosion in Vietnam and the impact of coastal squeeze on a retreating coastline, especially with the construction of a road.

The value of the tourism industry in most cases justifies spending on beach nourishment and protection measures. In Florida, the beach economy is estimated to be worth US$4 billion a year and the Florida Shore and Beach Preservation Act enables areas to development management plans to care for these environments. Miami Beach is a barrier island 16 km in length (and containing US$6 billion of real estate), naturally consisting of fine coral, shells and coarse grains of sand. Some US$60 million were spent on replenishing the beach, making a more compact surface – better for tourists and more able to withstand coastal erosion (Ackerman 1997). Yet other beach management measures may include abandonment of the site when the sand is washed away after a severe storm event, dune and vegetation restoration, and protecting the areas against inappropriate forms of development.

Hall and Page (1996) discuss the effects of tourism on the coastal environment of the Pacific islands. While similar impacts are found to exist elsewhere, impacts in the Pacific are more problematic because tourism is concentrated on or near ecologically and geomorphologically dynamic coastal environments. The main environmental impacts occur as a result of damage to mangroves and coral reefs, and this is pronounced where resort development occurs, as:

Resorts have interfered with the hydrological cycle by changing groundwater patterns, altering stream life, and engaging in excessive groundwater extraction. Coastal reefs, lagoons, anchialine ponds, wastewater marshes, mangroves, have been destroyed by resort construction and by excessive visitations and activities

22

with the consequent loss of marine life and destruction of ecosystems. Beach walking, snorkelling, recreational fishing, boat tours and anchoring have damaged coral reefs and grasses and have disturbed near shore aquatic life . . . (Minerbi 1992: 69)

In the case of Fiji, a resort complex on Denarau Island was built in drained mangrove swamps, necessitating extensive coastal protection. Effects on coral reefs are widespread. In the Maldives, for example, an airport has been constructed on a re-formed coral island, and coral is damaged by waste water from beachside hotels contaminated by chemicals found in shampoos and bathing products. As environmental impact assessments are not yet required in many less developed countries, there is less control over damaging types of development.

Wildlife issues

Effects on wildlife are notable. Shackley's (1992) study of **manatee**-related tourism in Florida (Image 22.3) is particularly noteworthy. Manatees are appealing to tourists because they are known to interact voluntarily with humans and are often attracted to marinas and harbours for food. Divers have been observed following and touching manatees and boat operators circle around the creatures in the water, both practices exacerbated by the docility of manatees. This occurs despite legal protection and published codes of conduct for visitors wishing to see a manatee. Shackley (1992) states that 'anyone who wants to ensure the survival of the species would be well advised to avoid visiting them'. The manatee, like other slow-moving marine mammals, is threatened by the use of personal watercraft. Many are hit each year by jet-skis which can operate in shallow waters, mangrove swamps and estuaries. Manatees are also subject to proportionately high levels of mortality from being struck by boats, particularly in

IMAGE 22.3 The manatees interact with humans, but are very vulnerable to careless tourist activities such as jet-skiing in shallow waters

areas where higher speeds are permitted. Birds are driven away by the noise of these machines, thus affecting feeding and behaviour patterns. Another popular pursuit which has developed recently is that of whale and dolphin watching.

Socio-economic issues

In terms of the sociocultural impacts of coastal tourism, many of the issues cited in the earlier chapters on sociocultural and economic impacts apply. A specific example of where there has been a negative effect is when local people in some areas have been prohibited from using the beaches. Some beaches in, for example, Antigua and the Gambia have become preserved for the use of exclusive beach resorts. St Thomas, an island in the Caribbean, originally contained 50 beaches but, after tourism resort development, only two were left for public use. However, the economy in coastal areas may be stimulated by tourism, creating employment and encouraging investment. The whale-watching boom at Kaikoura on South Island, New Zealand assisted in the regeneration of a declining area, reducing unemployment and raising average household incomes with the creation of new enterprises in accommodation, catering and retailing, and is a good example of how indigenous people have managed to develop a world-class tourism attraction (http://www.whalewatch.co.nz).

Protection of the coastal environment

The coast has been recognized as an environment which requires protection and sensitive management and sometimes this may involve measures to protect the integrity of the resource (Needham and Szuster 2011). As far back as 1972, countries such as the USA created legislation introducing the notion of coastal zone management, ideas which were soon adopted in Sweden, Australia (see King 2007) and later more widely. This was acknowledged as a central issue at the Earth Summit in 1992 and is reflected in the Oceans Chapter of Agenda 21. Internationally, it has been agreed that coastal nations must 'commit themselves to integrated management and sustainable development of coastal areas and the marine environment . . .' (EU 2005). The main objectives of coastal zone management are to:

- encourage sustainable use of the environment
- identify and resolve conflicts
- balance economic and environmental objectives
- adopt strategic planning function.

and these are reiterated in the EU (2005) Coastal Zone Management Strategy. The EU evaluated its progress in Integrated Coastal Zone Management in 2010 and the example of Belgium's actions illustrates the progress made. For example, in Flanders an Integrated Master Plan to protect against flooding was developed alongside measures to develop best practice in sustainable beach management. In the Netherlands, coastal tourism was reported as exceeding the volume of overnight stays in the four largest cities, reflecting the importance of interdependencies which exist between safeguarding the coastline and in accommodating this activity. In the case of the Netherlands, this has involved strengthening sea defences in eight locations so they are able to cope with the expected effects of climate change and likely sea-level rises. Many attempts have been made to assist in managing the impacts of tourism on coastal land and in coastal waters. Conservation in coastal areas is often approached through designations. Marine parks and nature reserves have been designated on an international scale covering areas as diverse as the Great Barrier Reef, Australia, to Lundy Island, off the coast of north Devon, UK.

VisitWales (2007) pursued this direction with their Coastal Tourism Strategy because £850 million of tourism spending in the country occurs in coastal areas, equivalent to a quarter of all tourist expenditure in Wales. The strategy emphasized the need to regenerate a number of coastal areas, to manage the coastal resources better and place a greater focus on quality issues to ensure they meet visitor expectations. The strategy also distinguished between the five thematic areas that need integrated management: coastal towns and resorts; the rural coast; coastal activities (including the opportunities for further development); coastal culture to identify the opportunity to promote food, cultural and heritage events; and coastal management, including the environment and conservation management. At a UK level, the Welsh example was cited as an example of best practice for coastal tourism in view of the absence of strategic direction in England (House of Commons Communities and Local Government Committee 2007).

Conclusion: The future of the coast

In *Moby Dick*, author Herman Melville wrote: 'Strange! Nothing will content them but the extremest limit of the land', which indicates that it is highly likely that pleasure seekers will continue to visit coastal areas in the future, and sustainability has emerged as the dominant paradigm in coastal planning and management, as reflected in the range of planning manuals now in vogue. This raises three issues:

- *the role of economic factors:* local communities need to earn a living wage and businesses may prioritize financial gain over the environment
- *the role of environmental factors:* the environment is the attraction in many cases, therefore it needs to be conserved
- *the role of social and cultural factors:* local people should be involved in the decision-making.

What is clear is that the market for coastal tourism is increasing, and in the USA around 85 per cent of all tourist-related revenue comes from coastal states. It is arguably the USA's leading destination product, being accessible to the large urban populations, and a historical and contemporary feature in the USA and many other societies. The coast has a special place in many of the lives of urban populations globally, as a dynamic ecosystem that accommodates a diverse range of uses. The range of products on offer is expanding and has reached far beyond the traditional sun, sea and sand experience. The emergence of marine tourism poses new threats and challenges in diverse environments: whale watching in Africa, Australasia, Iceland; diving in the Seychelles, Borneo, the Red Sea; action sports such as sea canoeing, yachting and personal watercraft use. There are even underwater hotels being built. These activities are increasing in popularity, and, if not managed carefully, will have enormously detrimental effects on the natural environment, as the example of the Pacific Islands and resort development has indicated. The rejuvenation of resorts illustrates a desire to maintain quality and to adapt to new circumstances, demonstrating a commitment to sustainable ideals. These ideals need to be embraced more fully so that sustainable management of tourism at the coast ensures that future generations can enjoy the same environments as much as the tourists of the past and today.

Discussion questions

1 Explain why coastal tourism is the most popular form of tourism today.

2 Why is a sustainable approach to coastal and resort tourism development desirable?

3 What is coastal zone management and how is it relevant to tourism?

4 Explain the evolution of coastal resorts using relevant theoretical models.

References

Ackerman, J. (1997) 'Islands at the edge', *National Geographic*, 192 (2): 2–31.

Agamuthu, P., Mehran, S., Norkhairah, A. and Norkhairiyah, A. (2019) 'Marine debris: A review of impacts and global initiatives', *Waste Management and Research*, 37 (10): 987–1002.

Agarwal, S., Jakes, S., Essex, S., Page, S. J. and Mowforth, M. (2018) 'Disadvantage in English seaside resorts: A typology of deprived neighbourhoods', *Tourism Management*, 69: 440–459.

Aguiló, E., Algere, J. and Sard, M. (2005) 'The persistence of the sun and sand tourism model', *Tourism Management*, 26 (2): 219–231.

Barke, M. and Towner, J. (2004) 'Learning from experience? Progress towards a sustainable future for tourism in the central and eastern Andalucian littoral', in B. Bramwell (ed.) *Coastal Mass Tourism: Diversification and Sustainable Development in Southern Europe*. Clevedon: Channel View.

Bell, S., Phoenix, C., Lovell, R. and Wheeler, B. (2015) 'Seeking everyday wellbeing: The coast as a therapeutic landscape', *Social Science and Medicine*, 142: 56–67.

Bramwell, B. (ed.) (2004) *Coastal Mass Tourism: Diversification and Sustainable Development in Southern Europe*. Clevedon: Channel View.

Butler, R.W. (1980) 'The concept of the tourist area cycle of evolution: Implications for management of resources', *Canadian Geographer*, 24 (1): 5–12.

Corbin, A. (1995) *The Lure of the Coast: The Discovery of the Seaside 1750–1840*. London: Penguin.

Dodds, R. (2007) 'Sustainable tourism and policy implementation: Lessons from the case of Calvià, Spain', *Current Issues in Tourism*, 10 (4): 296–322.

Essex, S., Kent, M. and Newnham, R. (2004) 'Tourism development in Mallorca: Is water supply a constraint?' *Journal of Sustainable Tourism*, 12 (1): 4–28.

EU (European Union) (2005) *Coastal Zone Management*. Brussels: European Union. https://europa.eu/

European Environment Agency (1998) *Europe's Environment: The Second Assessment*. Oxford: Office for Official Publications of the European Communities, Luxembourg, and Elsevier Science.

Gilbert, E.W. (1939) 'The growth of inland and seaside health resorts in England', *Scottish Geographical Magazine*, 55 (1): 16–35.

Goodhead, T. and Johnson, D. (eds.) (1996) *Coastal Recreation Management: The Sustainable Development of Maritime Leisure*. London: Spon.

Gormsen, E. (1981) 'The spatio temporal development of international tourism. Attempts at a centre-periphery model', in *La Consommation d'Espace pour la Tourism et sa Preservation*. Aix-en-Provence: Centre des hautes études touristiques.

Hall, C.M. and Page, S.J. (eds.) (1996) *Tourism in the Pacific: Issues and Cases*. London: Thomson.

Hall, C.M. and Page, S.J. (2006) *The Geography of Tourism and Recreation*, 3rd edition. London: Routledge.

Hall, C.M. and Page, S.J. (2014) *The Geography of Tourism and Recreation: Environment, Place and Space*, 4th edition. Abingdon: Taylor and Francis.

Hawkins, D., Lamoureux, K. and Poon, A. (2002) *The Relationship of Tourism Development to Biodiversity and the Sustainable Use of Energy and Water Resources: A Stakeholder Management Framework*. Paris: United Nations.

Hof, A. and Blázquez-Salom, M. (2015) 'Changing tourism patterns, capital accumulation, and urban water consumption in Mallorca, Spain: A sustainability fix?' *Journal of Sustainable Tourism*, 23 (5): 770–777.

Honey, M. and Hogenson, S. (2017) *Coastal Tourism, Sustainability, and Climate Change in the Caribbean: Beaches and Hotels*. New York: Business Expert Press.

22

House of Commons Communities and Local Government Committee (2007) *Coastal Towns: Second Report of Session 2006–07.* London: The Stationery Office.

Jennings, S. (2004) 'Coastal tourism and shoreline management', *Annals of Tourism Research, 31* (4): 899–922.

Jones, A. and Phillips, M. (2017) *Global Climate Change and Coastal Tourism: Recognizing Problems, Managing Solutions and Future Expectations.* Wallingford: CABI.

Kent, M., Newnham, R. and Essex, S. (2002) 'Tourism and sustainable water supply in Mallorca: A geographical analysis', *Applied Geography, 22* (4): 351–374.

King, B. (2001) 'Resort-based tourism on the pleasure periphery', in D. Harrison (ed.) *Tourism and the Less Developed World: Issues and Cases.* Wallingford: CABI.

King, B. (2007) 'The post modern resort and the pleasure periphery: The case of Australia's coastal tourism resorts', in S. Agarwal and G. Shaw (eds.) *Managing Coastal Tourism Resorts: A Global Perspective.* Clevedon: Channel View.

Le Guern, C. (2019) 'When the mermaids cry: The great plastic tide', Coastal Care (website). http://plastic-pollution.org/

Lenček, L. and Bosker, G. (1999) *The Beach: Paradise on Earth.* London: Pimlico.

Lithgow, D., Martínez, M., Gallego-Fernández, J., Silva, R. and Ramírez-Vargas, D. (2019) 'Exploring the co-occurrence between coastal squeeze and coastal tourism in a changing climate and its consequences', *Tourism Management, 74:* 43–54.

Meyer-Arendt, K. (2018) 'Tourism geographies: Geographic research on coastal tourism', *Tourism Geographies, 20* (2): 358–363.

Mimura, N. (2008) *Asia-Pacific Coasts and their Management: States of Environment.* Amsterdam: Springer.

Minerbi, L. (1992) *Impacts of Tourism Development in Pacific Islands.* San Francisco, CA: Greenpeace Pacific Campaign.

Ministry of Culture and Tourism (2007) *Tourism Strategy of Turkey – 2023.* Ankara: Ministry of Culture and Tourism. http://www.kulturturizm.gov.tr.

Nachite, D., Maziane, F., Anfuso, G. and Williams, A. T. (2019) 'Spatial and temporal variations of litter at the Mediterranean beaches of Morocco mainly due to beach users', *Ocean and Coastal Management, 179:* 104846.

Naylon, J. (1967) 'Tourism – Spain's most important industry', *Geography, 52* (1): 23–40.

Needham, M. and Szuster, B. (2011) 'Situational influences on normative evaluations of coastal tourism - recreational management strategies in Hawai'i', *Tourism Management, 32* (4): 732–740.

Organization for Economic Cooperation and Development (1993) *Coastal Zone Management. Integrated Policies.* Paris: OECD.

Page, S.J. and Connell, J. (2010) *Leisure: An Introduction.* Harlow: Pearson.

Pearce, D. (1995) *Tourism Today. A Geographical Analysis,* 2nd edition. Harlow: Longman.

Peeters, P. (2012) 'A clear path towards sustainable mass tourism? Rejoinder to the paper "Organic, incremental and induced paths to sustainable mass tourism convergence"', *Tourism Management, 33* (5): 1038–1041.

Perles-Ribes, J., Ramón-Rodríguez, A., Vera-Rebollo, J. and Ivars-Baidal, J. (2018) 'The end of growth in residential tourism destinations: Steady state or sustainable development? The case of Calpe', *Current Issues in Tourism, 21* (12): 1355–1385.

Pigram, J.J. (1977) 'Beach resort morphology', *Habitat International, 2* (5–6): 525–541.

Prideaux, B. (2000) 'The resort development spectrum – a new approach to modeling resort development', *Tourism Management, 21* (3): 225–240.

Prideaux, B. and Pabel, A. (eds.) (2018) *Coral Reefs: Tourism, Conservation and Management.* Abingdon: Routledge.

Pye, K. and Blott, S. J. (2015) 'Spatial and temporal variations in soft-cliff erosion along the Holderness coast, East Riding of Yorkshire, UK', *Journal of Coastal Conservation, 19*(6): 785–808.

Rangel-Buitrago, N., Vergara-Cortés, H., Barría-Herrera, J., Contreras-López, M. and Agredano, R. (2019) 'Marine debris occurrence along Las Salinas beach, Viña Del Mar (Chile): Magnitudes, impacts and management', *Ocean and Coastal Management, 178* (1 August 2019): Article 104842.

Ruiz-Ramírez, J., Euán-Ávila, J. and Rivera-Monroy, V. (2019) 'Vulnerability of coastal resort cities to mean sea level rise in the Mexican Caribbean', *Coastal Management, 47* (1): 23–43.

Sakurai, R., Ota, T. and Uehara, T. (2017) 'Sense of place and attitudes towards future generations for conservation of coastal areas in the Satoumi of Japan', *Biological Conservation, 209:* 332–340.

Shackley, M. (1992) 'Manatees and tourism in southern Florida: Opportunity or threat?', *Journal of Environmental Management, 34* (4): 257–265.

Silva, M., Castro, R., Sales, A. and Araújo, F. (2018) 'Marine debris on beaches of Arraial do Cabo, RJ, Brazil: An important coastal tourist destination', *Marine Pollution Bulletin,* 130: 153–158.

Sistermans, P. and Nieuwenhuis, O. (2003) *Holderness Coast.* Eurosion case study. Amersfoort: DHV. http://copranet.projects.eucc-d.de/files/000164_EUROSION_Holderness_coast.pdf.

Smith, R.A. (1991) 'Beach resorts: A model of development evolution', *Landscape and Urban Planning, 21* (3): 189–210.

Smith, R.A. (1992) 'Beach resort evolution. Implications for planning', *Annals of Tourism Research, 19* (2): 304–322.

Spalding, M., Burke, L., Wood, S., Ashpole, J., Hutchison, J. and zu Ermgassen, P. (2017) 'Mapping the global value and distribution of coral reef tourism', *Marine Policy, 82:* 104–113.

Swarbrooke, J. (1999) *Sustainable Tourism Management.* Wallingford, Oxon: CAB International.

Tamayo, N., Anticamara, J. and Acosta-Michlik, L. (2018) 'National estimates of values of Philippine reefs' ecosystem services', *Ecological Economics, 146:* 633–644.

Thuy, M. T. T., Nagasawa, T., Tanaka, H. and Viet, N. T. (2018) 'Sandy beach restoration using beach nourishment method: A case study of Nha Trang beach, Vietnam', *Journal of Coastal Research, 81* (sp1): 57–66.

22

Towner, J. (1996) *An Historical Geography of Recreation and Tourism in the Western World 1540–1940*. Chichester: John Wiley and Sons.

Tunstall, S. and Penning-Rowsell, E. (1998) 'The English beach: Experience and values', *Geographical Journal*, 164 (3): 319–332.

Turner, L. and Ash, J. (1975) *The Golden Hordes: International Tourism and the Pleasure Periphery*. London: Constable.

VisitWales (2007) *Coastal Tourism Strategy*. Cardiff: VisitWales. http://www.visitwales.com.

Walton, J. (1983) *The English Seaside Resort: A Social History, 1750–1914*. Leicester: Leicester University Press.

Walton, J. (2000) *The British Seaside*. Manchester: Manchester University Press.

Weaver, D. (2000) 'A broad context model of destination development scenarios', *Tourism Management*, 21 (3): 217–234.

Weaver, D. (2012a) 'Organic, incremental and induced paths to sustainable mass tourism convergence', *Tourism Management*, 33 (5): 1030–1037.

Weaver, D. (2012b) 'Clearing the path to sustainable mass tourism: A response to Peeters', *Tourism Management*, 33 (5): 1042–1043.

Xie, P. F., Chandra, V. and Gu, K. (2013) 'Morphological changes of coastal tourism: A case study of Denarau Island, Fiji', *Tourism Management Perspectives*, 5: 75–83.

Young, D. and Essex, S. (2019) 'Climate change adaptation in the planning of England's coastal urban areas: Priorities, barriers and future prospects', *Journal of Environmental Planning and Management*. DOI: 10.1080/09640568.2019.1617680

Zielinski, S., Botero, C. and Yanes, A. (2019) 'To clean or not to clean? A critical review of beach cleaning methods and impacts', *Marine Pollution Bulletin*, 139: 390–401.

Further reading

Books

Bull, A. (2014) *Coastal and Marine Tourism*. London: Routledge.

Meyer-Arendt, K. and Lew, A. (eds.) (2016) *Understanding Tropical Coastal and Island Tourism Development*. London: Routledge.

Journal articles

Page, S. J., Essex, S. and Causevic, S. (2014) 'Tourist attitudes towards water use in the developing world: A comparative analysis', *Tourism Management Perspectives*, 10: 57–67.

Young, D. and Essex, S. (2019) 'Climate change adaptation in the planning of England's coastal urban areas: priorities, barriers and future prospects', *Journal of Environmental Planning and Management*. DOI: 10.1080/09640568.2019.1617680

Weaver, D. (2000) 'A broad context model of destination development scenarios', *Tourism Management*, 21 (3): 217–234.

Wong, P. (1998) 'Coastal tourism development in southeast Asia: Relevance and lessons for coastal zone management', *Oceans and Coastal Management*, 38 (2): 89–109.

Zielinski, S., Botero, C. and Yanes, A. (2019) 'To clean or not to clean? A critical review of beach cleaning methods and impacts', *Marine Pollution Bulletin*, 139: 390–401.

22

23

Tourism in the less developed world

Learning outcomes

After reading this chapter and answering the questions, you should be able to:

- understand the role of tourism in less developed countries
- outline the problems which less developed countries face in tourism development
- recognize the impacts of tourism in less developed countries
- identify types of tourism which may assist communities in less developed countries.

Overview

For many developing countries, tourism is a favoured choice of economic activity. The lure of generating foreign exchange from a country's natural attractions has led many nations into tourism. Some countries are now well-established providers of tourism, such as Turkey, Malaysia and Mexico, but others such as Bhutan and Belize are more recent entrants. While most of the world's tourism activity occurs in the developed world, some less developed countries are high-volume tourist destinations with accompanying impacts and effects.

Introduction

Tourism offers an alternative economic activity to primary and secondary industries, especially if there is a lack of development choices for a less developed country. Telfer and Sharpley (2008) point to the 'tourism development dilemma' this poses: tourism may bring benefits and impacts in terms of environmental, economic, sociocultural and political issues, which means that governments and planners have to make critical decisions on the trade-offs to be made when developing tourism. These trade-offs are often politicized further when developing countries seek external capital and multinational corporations to invest in tourism. Many of the trade-offs mean that tourism will be created in one location at the expense of another as conscious decisions are made to develop tourism. In a globalized world, many multinational corporations are also seeking new locations for tourism in the developing world, but this form of tourism development may not necessarily offer the development solution which governments seek by promoting tourism. For the tourist, less developed countries (LDCs) offer a taste of the exotic, an opportunity to encounter different cultures and to experience an unspoiled environment. While most tourism movements take place between developed countries, an exploration of global tourism arrivals over time indicates that an increasing number of people are selecting holidays in LDCs. New destinations are appearing on the world market catering for a range of tourists seeking alternative holiday experiences. At a global scale, around 40 per cent of international tourist trips are to LDCs and their climate, culture and environment combine to form a tourism product for the 'new' tourist (Scheyvens 2011). Tourism to the less developed world has also seen faster rates of growth than that experienced in established and highly developed regions for tourism such as Europe. Generally speaking, LDCs are geographically located in central and South America, Africa, South and South East Asia and the South Pacific (Hall 1992). Figure 23.1 illustrates the range of destinations by volume (where data are available), although other large areas of the world, such as the South Pacific and small islands in the Caribbean, also feature prominently in tourism to LDCs (but the recent inclusion of Eastern European countries as developing countries in UN–WTO data is not reflected here, because they are at a different development stage to LDCs). Tourism in the less developed world has a long history of analysis in the social sciences, much of the work emanating initially from development studies where different disciplines examined the development posed by tourism (Britton 1980; Bryden 1973; de Kadt 1979; Dieke 2000; Dorji 2001; Harrison 1988, 1998, 2001, 2003; Mbaiwa 2005; Mitchell 2012; Oppermann and Chon 1997; Page and Dowling 2002; Pearce 1990). A number of recent studies examine tourism in LDCs including Huybens (2007) and Scheyvens (2002) seminal critique of tourism and development, In addition, a range of more geographically specific, regional studies outlined in Table 23.1. Mkono (2019), however, questions the validity of these studies in relation to African tourism where they are research studies produced by non-native African researchers. The criticisms relate to omissions such as not including the nuances and voices of local people and the complex issues associated with African culture and society. Many studies, as Mkono (2019) argues, do not

---

TABLE 23.1 Regional studies of tourism in the less developed world

Africa

Christie, I., Fernandez, E., Messereli, C. and Twinning-Ward, L. (2014) *Tourism in Africa: Harnessing Tourism for Growth and Improved Livelihoods*. New York: World Bank.

Dieke, P. (2000) *Tourism in Africa*. New York: Cognizant.

Kibicho, W. (2013) *Sex Tourism in Africa: Kenya's Booming Industry*. London: Routledge.

Mkono, M. (ed.) (2019) *Positive Tourism in Africa*. London: Routledge.

Novelli, M. (ed.) (2016) *Tourism and Development in sub-Saharan Africa*. London: Routledge.

The Caribbean

Daye, M., Chambers, D. and Roberts, S. (eds.) (2008) *New Perspectives in Caribbean Tourism*. London: Routledge.

Padilla, M. (2008) *Caribbean Pleasure Industry*. Chicago: University of Chicago Press.

Spencer, A. (2018) *Travel and Tourism in the Caribbean: Challenges and Opportunities for Small Island Developing States*. London: Palgrave Macmillan.

23

(continued)

TABLE 23.1 continued

The Middle East

Almuhrzi, H., Aliyami, H. and Scott, N. (2017) *Tourism in the Arab World: An Industry Perspective*. Bristol: Channel View.

Daher, R. (ed.) (2007) *Tourism in the Middle East*. Bristol: Channel View.

Kester, J. and Carvao, S. (2004) 'International tourism in the Middle East and outbound tourism from Saudi Arabia', *Tourism Economics* 10 (2): 220–240.

Seyfi, S. and Hall, C.M. (eds.) (2018) *Tourism in Iran: Challenges, Development and Issues*. London: Routledge.

Stephenson, M. and Ala-Hamarneh, A. (2017) *International Tourism Development and the Gulf Cooperation Council*. London: Routledge.

Timothy, D.J. (ed.) (2019) *Routledge Handbook of Tourism in the Middle East and North Africa*. London: Routledge.

Latin America

Lohmann, G. and Dredge, D. (eds.) (2012) *Tourism in Brazil: Environment, Management and Segments*. London: Routledge

Lumsdon, L. and Swift, J. (2001) *Tourism in Latin America*. London: Continuum.

Netto, A. and Trigo, L. (eds.) (2014) *Tourism in Latin America: Cases of Success*. New York: Springer.

Santanna, G. (ed.) (2011) *Tourism in South America*. London: Routledge.

The Pacific Islands

Fiyal, G. (2012) *Beachheads: War, Peace and Tourism in Postwar Okinawa*. New York: Rowman and Littlefield.

Hall, C.M. and Page, S.J. (eds.) (1996) *Tourism in the Pacific: Issues and Cases*. London: Thomson.

Harrison, D. (ed.) (2003) *Pacific Island Tourism*. New York: Cognizant.

Pratt, S. and Harrison, D. (eds.) (2015) *Tourism in Pacific Islands: Current Issues and Future Challenges*. London: Routledge.

South and South East Asia

Arit, W. (2006) *China's Outbound Tourism*. London: Routledge.

Hall, C.M. (1994) *Tourism in the Pacific Rim*. South Melbourne: Longman Cheshire.

Hall, C.M. and Page, S.J. (eds.) (2000) *Tourism in South and South East Asia: Issues and Cases*. Oxford: Butterworth-Heinemann.

Hall, C.M. and Page, S.J. (eds.) (2017) *The Routledge Handbook of Tourism in Asia*. London: Routledge.

Hitchcock, M., King, V. and Parnwell, M. (eds.) (2008) *Tourism in South East Asia: New Perspectives*. Copenhagen: Nias Press.

Lew, A. and Yu, L. (eds.) (1995) *Tourism in China: Geographical, Political and Economic Perspectives*. Boulder: Westview Press.

Li, M. and Bibu, W. (eds.) (2013) *Urban Tourism in China*. London: Routledge.

Oakes, T. (1998) *Tourism and Modernity in China*. London: Routledge.

Pablos, O., Aung, P. and Myo, Z. (eds.) (2017) *Tourism and Opportunities for Economic Development in Asia*. Pennsylvania: IGI.

Pforr, C. and Phau, I. (eds.) (2018) *Food, Wine and China: A Tourism Perspective*. London: Routledge.

Ryan, C. (ed.) (2013) *Tourism in China: Destinations, Planning and Experiences*. Bristol: Channel View.

Ryan, C. and Huimin, G. (ed.) (2009) *Tourism in China: Destination, Culture and Communities*. London: Routledge.

Singh, S. (ed.) (2009) *Domestic Tourism in Asia: Diversity and Divergence*. London: Earthscan.

Wen, J. and Tidsell, C. (eds.) (2001) *Tourism and China's Development*. Singapore: World Scientific.

Xiao, H. (ed.) (2012) *Contemporary Perspectives on China Tourism*. London: Routledge.

23

present a positive representation of Africa, tending to be extremely negative and pessimistic about the long-term prognosis for African development.

While many of the studies in Table 23.1 examine a wide range of issues associated with tourism in LDCs, much concern has been expressed regarding the impact of tourism on such nations, with the focus on the inequality between the tourist (traditionally Western, though increasingly Asian within Asia) and the host. According to Telfer (2009), over 1 billion people in the world are living in poverty, equivalent to one-sixth of the world's population, as illustrated by the United Nations *Multidimensional Poverty Index*. Telfer (2009) argues that if tourism is harnessed to assist with development objectives, it may make multiple contributions in terms of economic (i.e. improvements to GDP, employment and income generation), social/cultural (i.e. developing community self-reliance), environmental (i.e. as a basis for sustainable development) and political benefits (i.e. empowering local people, especially women). Even so, as we will demonstrate later in the chapter, there are also major gaps between these theoretical arguments

There is a great deal of debate over the term 'development': Harrison (1988: 154) argues that other criteria and motivation by governments have seen it projected as 'economic growth, structural change, autonomous industrialization, capitalism or socialism, self-actualization and individual, national, regional and cultural self-reliance'. Indeed, Spencer (2010) points to the evolution of development studies discourse (Figure 23.2), resulting in a current paradigm focused on ethical development that has contributed to new forms of alternative tourism. A further development seen in Figure 23.2 is the emergence of climate change and the declaration in 2019 in various countries that a 'climate emergency' (i.e. climate change issues) now exists, a feature we explore in Chapter 19. Telfer (2009) points to the interconnections in development theory and tourism, with the shifting focus also identified by Spencer (2010). This marked the shift from previous paradigms, labelled as modernization, dependency, economic liberalism and alternative development, but there is now a current impasse in development thinking given the lack of clarity of the purpose and long-term objectives as well as the implications of 'past development'. However, as Telfer (2009: 161) argues, development 'is also very much about power and control' as the strategies employed or growth path chosen will be ideologically determined. The outcome of development in a globalized world will also be strongly influenced by the role and level of state intervention, the role the free market plays in the development process and the power wielded by the political elite in the process. In a historical context, the evolution of such policies and influence of colonial rule is illustrated in the case of Sri Lanka in Table 23.2.

TABLE 23.2 National economic policies and tourism development strategy in Sri Lanka

Period	National economic policy regime	Tourism development strategies	Main features of strategies
Before 1948	The pre-independence open economic policy	1937 – First Tourism Bureau was established 1940 – Tourist Bureau ceased its operations due to the war	Provided services to the passengers who sailed between the West and East through port of Colombo
1948–1956	Continuation of pre-independence open economic policy	1948 – Revival of Government Tourist Bureau	Began to undertake tourism marketing and promotional strategies immediately after independence from the colonial rulers
1956–1965	Closing up the economy with the import-substitution strategy	Under the closed economy, tourism did not play an important role in the national development strategy	Under the directionless and loosely organized Tourist Bureau, there were no tourism promotional and marketing activities

(continued)

TABLE 23.2 continued

Period	National economic policy regime	Tourism development strategies	Main features of strategies
1965–1970	Partial departure from the closed economy	1966 – The government legislative body was established for the tourism sector 1966 – Introduction of the first Ten-Year Master Plan for tourism	Revival of tourism promotion and marketing strategies. Tourist Board Act No.10 of 1966, Ceylon Hotel Corporation Act No. 14 of 1966 Tourist Development Act No.14 of 1968 The plan became the blueprint for tourism development and witnessed the first tourism board in Sri Lanka The country witnessed a first wave of new hotel construction with five resort development zones
1970–1977	Closing up the economy again	No new government initiative to develop tourism	Rate of investment growth in tourism fell due to the re-establishment of import control measures. However, tourism grew rapidly as a result of previous promotional activities and the peaceful environment
1977–1996	Opening up the economy	1977 – Introduction of trade liberalization, exchange rate reforms and incentives for FDI [Foreign Direct Investment]	Sri Lanka managed to attract a large number of tourists, especially from Europe under the open economic policies. Tourism was promoted. The progress continued until 1983. Tourism became a victim of war after 1983
	The second wave of economic reforms in 1989	1992 – Introduction of the second Ten-Year Tourism Master Plan	Temporary rebound in the tourism sector and recovery of tourism arrivals with the second wave of trade reforms
1996 to date	Continuation of opening economic policies with some limitations	2002 – Signing a ceasefire agreement and creating a peaceful environment for the tourism sector 2005 – New Tourism Act 2008 – Introduction of the Third Tourism Master Plan End of war in 2009 – launching a new tourism promotion strategy 2011 – Implementation of the Tourism Development Strategy	The relatively peaceful short-term environment gave rise to an increase in tourist arrivals to Sri Lanka Closer relationship between government and private sector has built an integrated approach to tourism The tourism sector has made a remarkable recovery and it is becoming one of the fastest growing and most dynamic industries in the country due to the peaceful environment

Source: Hall and Page (2017: 354)

23

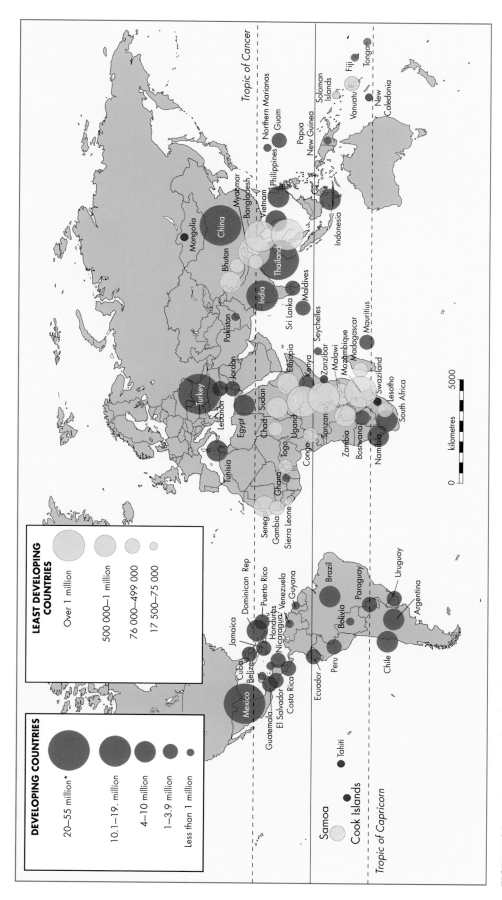

FIGURE 23.1 Tourist arrivals in less developed countries in 2018

Source: Developed from UNWTO data © S.J. Page (2019)

FIGURE 23.2 Evolution of thinking in development studies and tourism since the 1970s

FIGURE 23.3 Sub-Saharan Africa
Source: adapted from Novelli (2016: 2), reproduced with permission from Routledge

23

There is now a widely agreed consensus that any development policy should be oriented towards poverty alleviation (irrespective of the role of tourism) and in improving the human condition, as described in Chapter 19, and there has been a great deal of attention directed this theme in sub-Saharan Africa (see Figure 23.3) (e.g. Folarin and Adeniyi 2019) and Asia (Dao Truong *et al.* 2017), which we will return to later. Yet many controversies arise where external sources of capital and power (i.e. multinational corporations) become involved in tourism that may not necessarily lead to poverty alleviation. This is as much about the way tourism operates and the uneven geographical nature of economic development in LDCs (i.e. who gets what where, why and when in geographical terms) as it is about the narrow range of potential beneficiaries engaged in such a development process. This recognizes, as Steel (2012: 602) argues, that 'the relationship between tourism and development is complex and requires a holistic approach that considers the structures and functions of the tourism development process'.

The concept of development and the emergence of tourism in less developed countries

Webster (1990) defines 'development' as the replacement of traditional values with modern ones. It is a process of change and aims to achieve improvement. Theories of modernity emerged in the 1950s and early 1960s prompted by the decline of the old colonial empires. Later, in the 1970s, thoughts turned towards a theory based on the notion of dependency, which focused on the unbalanced relationship between developed and LDCs that has evolved in post-colonial times (see Hall and Page 2000; Telfer 2009).

Less developed countries – types and characteristics

Various labels exist to define LDCs. Up until recently, the First, Second and Third World categories were used widely (see Brandt 1980), but following the demise of Communism across Eastern Europe and the closing wealth gap between the First and Second Worlds, the differentiation no longer seems appropriate. The 'Fourth World' has also been used as a term to define least developed countries. Other definitions to consider are the East/West and North/South divides, and core/periphery in relation to the developed West and less developed world in geographical and economic terms. These labels are used more extensively in contemporary times to distinguish development status. Table 23.3 outlines a range of these descriptions that are commonly used.

Some of the characteristics of LDCs include:

- high birth rates and population pressures
- fast rate of urbanization
- limited economic base
- high unemployment
- low literacy rates
- low levels of industrial production
- high rates of national debt
- dependence upon overseas aid and international finance for development, with a range of donors
- low gross national product (GNP).

There are different types of LDCs and Swarbrooke (1999) outlines these as:

- *least developed countries:* average incomes less than $905 per year, literacy rates of less than 20 per cent and little industrial production. There are 41 of these countries, often termed 'the Fourth World' (Oppermann and Chon 1997) and new terminology has also been used such as 'less economically developed countries' (LEDCs) (Spenceley and Meyer 2012). These countries have endemic socio-economic problems such as poverty, low levels of education and economic vulnerability, and include many Small Island Developing States (SIDS)

23

- *developing countries:* beyond the level of least developed but still relatively poor and non-industrialized
- *newly industrialized countries (NICs):* these countries share characteristics of both less developed and developed worlds.

It should also be noted that within each category of country, there are disparities in wealth in the population, i.e. there are some very wealthy people and many poor people.

Traditionally, development has been measured in terms of economic measures such as GNP, economic growth rate and employment structure – measures of the economic wealth of a country. As understanding of the development process changed, it was realized that this measure was insufficient to show all aspects of development. The United Nations Development Programme uses the **Human Development Index (HDI)** which integrates welfare and economic aspects to produce a more holistic picture of a nation's status (http://www.undp.org). The HDI comprises three indices (that measure long and healthy life, being knowledgeable and having a decent standard of living), based on the statistical mean of each index. The Index then assigns a ranking in four groupings (Very High covering 1.4 billion people; High with 2.8 billion people; Medium with 2.7 billion people; and Low covering 926 million people). Of the 188 countries listed in the HDI, the 33 lowest-ranked countries are located in sub-Saharan Africa (see Figure 23.3 for the countries of sub-Saharan Africa).

The World Bank, however, uses economic measures only and identifies three types of country: low income, middle income and high income, and the International Monetary Fund (IMF) in 2012 listed 165 countries with a 'developing' status in its World Economic Outlook. The result is a categorization of countries according to different indicators to denote their development status. In the case of low-ranking countries such as Laos (the Lao People's Democratic Republic), the government is seeking to move from 'less developed' status by 2020 through a development strategy. A key component of that strategy is the further expansion of its tourism sector, which has seen international tourism rise from 14 000 arrivals in 1990 to over 2.5 million in 2010 largely through visitors from East Asia and the Pacific arriving by air and using land-based transport (also see Insight 21.1). This has involved almost a doubling of accommodation capacity over 2006–2010, to 30 000 hotel rooms in almost 1900 establishments.

A further approach used by the IMF uses a three-fold classification:

1 Advanced country (including Japan, USA and many of the Eurozone countries)
2 Emerging and developing economies countries (e.g. China and India)
3 Low income developing countries (subdivided into those who are heavily indebted).

TABLE 23.3 Terminology commonly used to describe development status

Label[1]	Description	North/South	Development
First World	Westernized countries, with capitalist political and economic structures	North	Developed
Second World	Less wealthy, Communist countries	North	Transitional
Third World	Poor countries	South	Less developed/developing

1 Used less extensively now, due to changes in Eastern bloc countries (Second World) and fall of Iron Curtain

23 Tourism development

Agel (1993, cited in Oppermann and Chon 1997) suggests that three stages can be identified in tourism research which typify the changing perspectives on tourism development in LDCs since the late 1950s. The first stage, from the late 1950s to 1970, was the time of great expansion and hope for future economic benefits. Tourism was considered as a tool for economic development and a generator of foreign exchange. The second stage, from 1970 to 1985, is termed by Agel as the 'disenchantment period', when the value of economic benefits was brought into question and a more critical approach to tourism development ensued. This was because many of the great hopes for tourism had not been fulfilled. The third stage covers the period from 1985 and is termed the 'differentiation period'. The

A way of obtaining hard currency to aid the balance of payments and indebtedness through admitting large numbers of Western tourists	A catalyst of social change, with closer contact between the indigenous community and the tourist	A symbol of freedom, allowing citizens to travel freely within and outside their own country
A mechanism for improving local infrastructure to cater for tourist need, thereby benefiting local people	Stimulus to commercial development, growing business tourism and small-scale entrepreneurial activity, (e.g. South Africa)	An integral part of economic restructuring through privatization, exposure to national and international market forces and transnational corporations

FIGURE 23.4 How tourism can transform an economy in the less developed world
Source: Developed from Hall (1992)

distinguishing feature of this stage is the emergence of alternative forms of tourism, such as ecotourism, with an emphasis on planning for a better future.

It is evident that the role of tourism in the development process of LDCs is subject to many debates, some of which are dealt with in this chapter. For example, one justification for tourism development is the potential benefits that may accrue to a country to assist with its development, in terms of, for instance, poverty reduction and employment growth. If tourism is viewed as a political tool, then tourism can transform an economy, as shown in Figure 23.4.

In many cases, the negative impacts are less tangible than the anticipated economic effects and often receive less attention.

The nature of tourism in less developed countries

Many studies of tourism in LDCs give the impression that the evolution of individual countries' international tourism markets is a comparatively recent phenomenon, given the relatively high rates of growth in the 1990s and new millennium. However, studies of tourism in the South Pacific and the Caribbean concur that the images of a tourist paradise are a literary creation by European and North American writers from the nineteenth and twentieth centuries, which has continued to shape the promotion of idealized images of a tourist paradise (Image 23.1). Tourism in the South Pacific has been conditioned by the process of colonization, and it is only in recent history that the independence of many island states has been achieved. A similar picture emerges in Asia and this is reflected in Figure 23.5, which depicts the former colonial past and the dominance of European powers.

Despite the strong colonial imprint on the development process in many LDCs, a number of countries have sought to develop a diversified product base for tourism. Many other niche products exist for international and domestic visitors. Tourism is least important in peripheral regions of LDCs while the core economic and political centres gain an above-average share. Enclave and all-inclusive resorts lead to the spatial concentration of tourism and its benefits, which may be minimal for the host area in the case of all-inclusive resorts. Britton's (1982) work in the South Pacific illustrates that tourism perpetuates existing inequalities in LDCs. This is explained by four factors:

IMAGE 23.1 Gangkhar Puensum mountain, at 7570 metres high, is the 40th tallest mountain in the world. For spiritual reasons, mountain climbing is prohibited, which also helps to avoid the despoliation that has occurred in other parts of the Himalayas, notably at Mount Everest.
Source: © Tourism Council of Bhutan

23

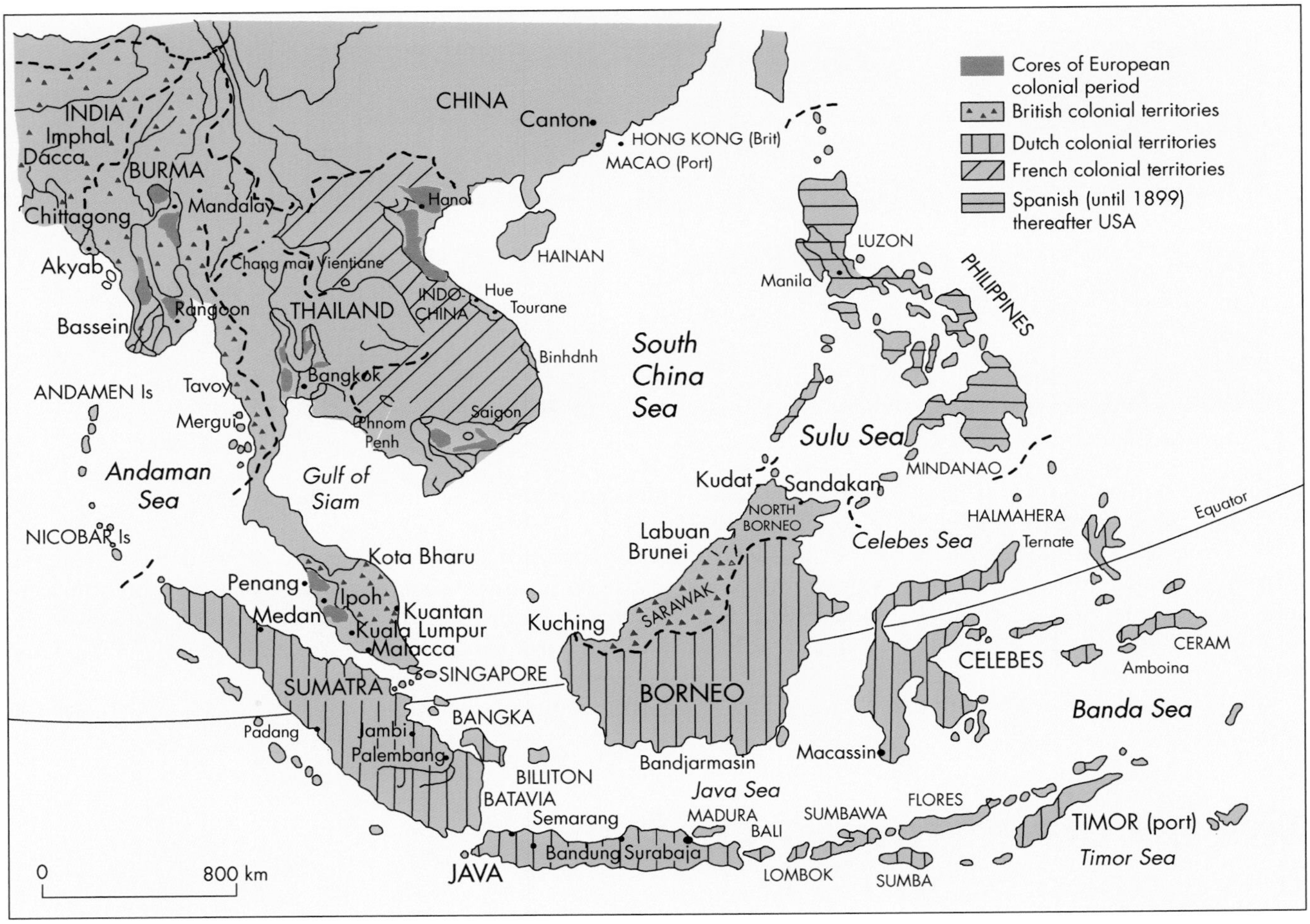

FIGURE 23.5 Asia's colonial past
Source: Hall and Page (2017: 123)

- power and influence, with tourism often controlled by foreign companies
- foreign tourist demands often not met by local service provision, exacerbating a perceived need to build luxury facilities
- general conditions of underdevelopment, such as structural disadvantages, influence the direction of tourism growth and development
- it is difficult for host communities to take control of tourism supply.

The outcome of enclave tourism is that host nations are often unable to break out of the poverty trap and the benefits of tourism do not filter through to those in need, even where luxury tourism is developed. The link between tourism and poverty is apparent from the fact that, in LDCs, tourism is a dominant feature in the poorest hundred countries and, in many countries which are recipients of aid, tourism is a dominant feature. In fact in some of the major LDC tourism destinations, many of the population subsist on less than a dollar (around 75p) a day. In many LDCs, tourism is also viewed as a long-term contributor to reducing unemployment and underemployment as an economic development option. This is one reason why current thinking and strategies to alleviate poverty through tourism (see the discussion of pro-poor tourism later) have begun to dominate the potential agendas of lobby groups and NGOs. Even so, Freire-Medeiros (2013) was highly critical of the way that poverty in LDCs has been turned into something for the tourist to gaze at, as illustrated in Chapter 15 in relation to slum tourism. Freire-Medeiros (2013: 1) succinctly summarizes the emergence of 'tourism poverty' as:

At the start of the millennium, capitalism has framed the experience of poverty as a product for consumption through tourism. In the megacities of the global South, selected and idealised aspects of poverty . . . are turned into a tourist commodity with a monetary value agreed upon by promoters and consumers in the tourism market [. . .]

with distinct itineraries developed by entrepreneurs to exploit this niche experience. As Freire-Medeiros (2013) explained, the various motivations behind this type of tourism experience are associated with middle-class romanticism of the poor, almost as a human zoo to be gazed at. There is no moral justification for this exploitation of other people's misery as a tourist attraction for profit as these people have the right to be treated with dignity and respect irrespective of their personal situation or circumstances. Such morbid voyeurism, as Freire-Medeiros (2013) explains, is yet another sign of tourism as a social virus which we introduced in Chapter 20 in an urban setting, which is where most of the slum tours occur.

Governments can directly influence the direction of tourism development but often decide not to invest in tourism infrastructure. Instead, governments often give financial incentives such as tax breaks and easing of rules on foreign labour and subsidies to foreign investors to develop facilities. Government policy tends to be centralized with little involvement of local communities. The focus tends to be on encouraging large foreign tour operators and developers to pursue tourism at the expense of indigenous operations. Traditional views on tourism can be interpreted as concentration on how much money can be generated rather than how it can be distributed to eliminate poverty in the wider population. The plight of poor countries is often ignored by tourists in search of a cheap holiday. It is one form of economic imperialism emerging in the postcolonial era as the dependency relationship with the developed world has been replicated in the tourism arena.

Conceptualizing the nature of tourism in less developed countries

Mowforth and Munt (2003) provide a framework to outline the major processes which underlie the development of new forms of tourism in LDCs. The framework consists of four elements which are outlined below:

- *Intervention and commodification:* natural and cultural resources are transformed into products for consumption by tourists. For example, visitors to Thailand can purchase T-shirts imprinted with an image of a Padaung woman wearing brass neck rings (these neck rings damage skeletal growth, but their value as a tourist attraction dictates that women continue to wear them in some areas). This example links to all the points below.

- *Subservience (domination and control):* communities and individuals in LDCs may assume subordinate roles in order to satisfy tourists and tourism development. They may have to accept low rates of pay and menial tasks in order to take enough money home to ensure survival.

- *Fetishism:* tourists remain unaware of the lives of those who serve them on holiday as commodities hide social realities.

- *Aestheticization:* objects, feelings and experiences are turned into objects of beauty and desire. Tourists may wish to experience scenes of real poverty or dangerous situations. For example, some tours take visitors to workplaces to see local craftspeople at work. What these features infer is the inherent inequality in the nature of relationships which exist and continue to develop in these contexts, as seen in the most extreme case, slum tourism.

In many LDCs, an 'uncritical faith', as Marfurt (1997) states, has led to unrestrained development and expenditure on tourism facilities. Governments often strive towards the prestige of luxury tourism developments and the associated economic statistics. Interestingly, Blake *et al.* (2008) examined Brazil's tourism economy and found that the main beneficiaries of tourism were middle-to-high-income earners. This highlighted the important role of government in using tourism revenue to address poverty among low-income households and to reduce socio-economic disparities, a theme we will return to later in the chapter. LDCs which create expansive tourism industries often create problems for their country which do not provide long-term solutions to social and economic problems. However, not all LDCs follow this path of development. Others adhere to a stricter policy of protecting culture, the environment and the local economy. Insight 23.1 outlines one of the best examples of alternative development paths – Bhutan.

23

INSIGHT 23.1 Bhutan: A sustainable route to tourism development?

As tourism has extended its global reach, many countries with heritage resources that attract domestic and international visitors are facing major challenges on how to control the insatiable appetite for iconic attractions and sites, such as Machu Picchu in Peru, where the Inca site of civilization has seen limits of 2200 visitors imposed on it to conserve its integrity from excessive vitiation. Similar debates are also facing countries that have ancient civilizations that may not necessarily survive the impact of globalized Western consumer culture. One such country which has faced these dilemmas is Bhutan, in the eastern Himalayas, with a population of 733 000, whose Buddhist culture and ancient culture has embraced tourism in a limited manner prior to the new millennium. This Insight extends that debate by focusing on the principal changes that have occurred since 2008, now that democratic parliamentary elections have moved the country towards a more constitutional monarchy. Prior to 2006, the ruler King Jigme Singye Wangchuck steered the country on a path of cautious modernization based on the preservation of Buddhist culture and a philosophy of Gross National Happiness (GNH) which is founded on four pillars that constituted a development paradigm focused on:

- Equitable socio-economic development.
- Preservation and promotion of cultural and spiritual heritage.
- Conservation of the environment.
- Good governance.

The situation relating to tourism prior to 2010 is summarized as follows:

- Tourists were first permitted entry to the country in 1974.
- Tourist numbers rose from 287 in 1974 to over 7000 a year in 1999 and have risen rapidly since, as Figure 23.6 shows.
- Under the direction of the monarch, Bhutan has been steered in the direction of sustainable growth rather than the 'boom and bust' or 'modernization at any cost' pattern.
- Tourism is recognized as a means of achieving socio-economic development, but is only acceptable within the confines of the conservation ethic which is deeply embedded in the Buddhist faith.
- Tourism has been utilized to maintain biodiversity rather than destroy it through tourism development.
- Contrary to popular belief, there is not a limit on annual tourist arrivals and not a tax on tourists – instead a tariff

exists to cover daily all-inclusive costs such as accommodation, guides and food.

- A policy of attracting low-volume/high-value tourism, using a strictly enforced set of regulations (the 'tourist tariff') covering tourism management, ensures effective translation of sustainable principles into practice.
- A brief summary of the regulations are given below:
  - visitors must travel on a pre-booked package holiday – no independent travel allowed
  - all visitors, irrespective of accommodation and choice of tour, must pay $250 per person per day in the peak season ($200 a day in the low season), which includes accommodation, food, travel itinerary, transportation, guides (the 'tourist tariff')
  - all bookings must be made through companies licensed to operate in Bhutan
  - not all areas of the country are open access to visitors, partly to ensure that religious life can continue unimpeded and partly for safety and environmental reasons, such as heavy snow
  - all accommodation must be government approved and guides must be licensed.
- Druk Air (national carrier) was established in 1981 and only one airport (Paro) exists, which helps control international arrivals.

The Tourism Council of Bhutan (TCB) rebranded the kingdom using various culturally informed straplines such as 'Happiness is a place' and 'Wake up in a place where the true essence of life exists. Come to Bhutan and be a part of our happiness' (www.bhutan.travel). Bhutan has developed tourism through:

- New destinations and products within the country (e.g. spa/wellness and adventure tourism) (though mountain climbing is forbidden as the mountains are sacred – see Image 23.1).
- Accommodation and the credit card infrastructure being upgraded.
- Setting aside over 250 acres of land for new tourism resorts.

The justification for this new direction by the TCB is that much of the hotel capacity suffers from low occupancy and is geographically concentrated, and visitation is also very seasonal. By developing new areas for tourism, the TCB aims to distribute benefits much more widely within Bhutan. All development has to fit with the GNH ideology and the tourist tariff might be raised further to fund health and education.

23

The challenges for Bhutan as a relative latecomer to tourism development are that:

- Tourist expansion is viewed positively by government bodies.
- The state wishes to keep culture and values intact but also follow a cautious modernization route.
- The government aims to control demand and tourist types through product development and cost.
- The intention is to expand the tourism sector without compromising culture and environment. This is illustrated by Suntikul and Dorji's (2016) analysis of religious festivals and attendance by visitors which is still viewed positively by residents, with such activities often concentrated in the country's iconic dzongs (elevated fortresses and sites of the monasteries (see Image 23.2). Tourism has now become the country's second largest source of foreign income after hydro-electric power generation. The country has also promoted nature conservation, with bird watching of endangered species (e.g. the black-necked crane that visits the country to nest – see Image 23.3) with a visitor centre built at Phobjikha Valley by the Royal Society for the Protection of Nature (Image 23.4).

IMAGE 23.3 Bird watching, focused on endangered species such as the black-necked crane, is promoted in this graphic representation
Source: © Tourism Council of Bhutan

IMAGE 23.2 Bhutan's sacred dzongs (monasteries) are a massive and imposing form of architecture and they form a focal point of the local community during religious festivals (Tsechu).
Source: © Tourism Council of Bhutan

IMAGE 23.4 To accommodate locals and visitors interested in observing the black-necked crane, the Royal Society for the Protection of Nature have constructed this Information Centre at Phobjikha
Source: © Tourism Council of Bhutan

Yet is it really feasible to allow tourism to keep developing under the guise of controlled sustainability, given the experiences of other countries where tourism development simply runs away and slips out of control very easily? The government is seeking to more than triple visitor numbers to 100 000, a year and it is inevitable that this may well be the first stage of a much larger association with the tourist dollar (Figure 23.6). Another example of attempts to control numbers of tourists visiting a destinations with rich natural heritage

is that of the Galapagos Islands, which have seen limits on numbers raised from 12 000 in 1971 to 30 000 in 1987 and 161 000 in 2007, and these have been exceeded to the point that over 225 000 visitors arrived in 2016, 241 800 in 2017 and 275 000 visitors in 2018, with no restrictions on visitation. Similarly, in the case of the Antarctic, visitor numbers to this pristine environment have risen from 4698 in 1990–1991 to 36 875 in 2009–2010 and 44 000 in 2016–2017, after a ban on vessels carrying more than 500 passengers in 2009. In the case of Bhutan, a brave decision needs to be taken to establish what the maximum limits to

23

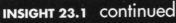

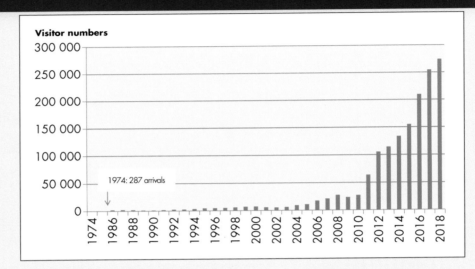

FIGURE 23.6 Tourist arrivals in Bhutan (where data exists)
Source: Tourism Council of Bhutan data

tourism are and to set these and limit the numbers. A target of 100 000 seems very high for a country with a largely rural population and limited experience of Western culture and attributes. While it is easy for a Western observer to criticize this pathway to development, it would appear that Bhutan would be well placed to fully understand the global problems associated with tourism before it sets forth on a path to development it will find impossible to reverse.

Further reading

Hummell, J., Gujadhur, T. and Ritsona, N. (2013) 'Evolution of tourism approaches for poverty reduction impact in SNV Asia: Cases from Lao PDR, Bhutan and Vietnam', *Asia Pacific Journal of Tourism Research* 18 (4): 369–384.

Nepal, S. and Karst, H. (2016) 'Tourism in Bhutan and Nepal', in C.M. Hall and S.J. Page (ed.) *The Routledge*

Handbook of Tourism in Asia (pp. 287–298). London: Routledge.

Nyaupane, G. and Timothy, D. (2010) 'Power, regionalism and tourism policy in Bhutan', *Annals of Tourism Research*, 37 (4): 969–988.

Questions

1 How has Bhutan managed the growth of international tourism?
2 What are the likely problems associated with the increasing scale of tourism development in Bhutan?
3 Is tourism an appropriate economic development strategy for Bhutan?
4 Is the Bhutan model of tourism one which other countries should implement?

Impacts of tourism in less developed countries

23

While a wide-ranging discussion of the economic, sociocultural and environmental impacts of tourism can be found in Chapters 17–19, the impacts on LDCs warrant further attention. The main debates focus around the wide gap between the host and guest as well as power relations.

Economic perspectives

A distinct philosophy was promoted in the 1960s by LDCs and the World Bank, a major source of finance for LDCs, to encourage them to invest in mass tourism. Between 1969 and 1979, the World Bank loaned about $450 million to governments in 18 LDCs. This included large-scale resorts in Thailand, Mexico and the Caribbean. But by the early 1970s (see e.g. Turner and Ash 1975) it was recognized that tourism resulted in negative as well as positive impacts and that it could not be viewed as a panacea for LDCs seeking economic expansion. The virtues of tourism development were originally extolled in many LDCs based on the idea that it is a smokeless industry, using the natural resources of a country in a non-polluting way and providing employment, increased GNP and improvements to the economy. But it soon became clear that a large proportion of tourist revenue did not remain in the host nation or benefit local communities. Employment tended to be low paid and poor quality, perpetuating the poverty experienced by many of the working population, while managerial-grade jobs were given to expatriate staff. Tourism is often an activity which can be developed relatively quickly, as in the case of the Dominican Republic (Pattullo 1996). Some countries demonstrate an overdependence on tourism to the extent that traditional industries have been abandoned in favour of a more lucrative tourism-connected trade. For example, in the Maldives over 80 per cent of the workforce depend on tourism directly or indirectly as a form of income. This makes countries vulnerable to changing markets and the vagaries of international currency. It also means that LDCs continue to depend on developed countries for their economic survival, perpetuating colonial trends of the past as tourism becomes a new form of dependency.

Leakage

Foreign exchange generated by tourism in LDCs does not remain there in sufficient volume to justify the benefits it is supposed to yield. It may go to tour companies, travel providers and accommodation providers based in industrialized nations. Many of the LDCs cannot afford the investment required to attract high-spending Western tourists and so wealthy multinational corporations grasp opportunities. The percentage of income derived from tourism returning to wealthy nations is termed 'leakage'. There are two ways in which leakage occurs in developing country economies. First, it may occur when tourists require products which the host country cannot supply. This means that the tourism expenditure leaves the country to pay for this import. This is called 'import leakage'. Second, when multinational corporations are the only source of investment capital in a destination, the profits which arise from the tourism activity are then sent back to the origin country. This is called 'export leakage'. This foreign ownership of key tourism assets may disempower local residents and remove economic opportunities. For example, over 60 per cent of hotels in Costa Rica are owned by foreign companies. More discussion of leakage can be found in Chapter 16. For example, the Worldwatch Institute estimated that half of the revenue from international tourism in LDCs leaks out to foreign-owned companies, in part through the import of goods and labour. This obscured the much wider concerns in certain destinations, such as Kenyan coastal resorts where rates of up to 70 per cent leakage occur and, similarly, in Thailand rates of 60 per cent are reported. In the Caribbean, leakage rates range from 56 per cent in St Lucia through 41 per cent in Aruba to 40 per cent in Jamaica. Import-related leakage is estimated to be between 40 and 50 per cent for many developing countries, in contrast to 10 and 20 per cent for many developed countries. Consequently, there is a strong case for the public sector and other projects, as we discuss under pro-poor tourism later, to seek to redress the loss of revenue and to retain more of it in local communities.

Social and cultural perspectives

The demonstration effect is clearly evident in LDCs. Daniel (1998) reports an example of a Thai hill village where tourism has caused community conflict and is viewed by some as cultural invasion. The younger members of the community prefer the style of clothing that tourists wear and now children wear T-shirts and baseball caps in an attempt to be like the foreigners. Young people aspire to the material standards and values of tourists but are unable to achieve them. Young males have committed suicide because they could not see a way out of their lifestyle. Cultural imperialism is evident in tourists from developed countries visiting LDCs.

Sex tourism in less developed countries

Sex tourism might be termed a form of leisure imperialism – sex tourism in Thailand and the Philippines as a form of military aggression. In the case of the Gambia in the 1990s, beach boys were performing a sexual service for female travellers: this highlights the diversity of sex tourism forms (i.e. romance, casual encounters, prostitution, sex slavery and mail-order brides). According to Kibicho (2013), sex tourism creates over US$300 million in urban remittances back to rural families in Thailand from commercial sex workers (CSWs), many of whom cater to tourists. Kibicho (2013) identified three distinct types of commercial sex worker markets, as illustrated in Figure 23.7. What Figure 23.7 shows is that sex tourism is midway between the *poverty sex trade* aimed at the local market (classified as street sex workers) and the *high-class market* at the top of the triangle, which is a small specialized segment. Sex tourism, in contrast, aimed at domestic and international tourists, based on the analysis in Kenya, targets tourist areas as well as premises frequented by tourists, where staff are aware of these activities (e.g. hotels). CSWs in these tourist settings are able to retain more income than the poverty sex workers and less than those at the high-class end of the market. The key issue here is that in some instances highly undesirable elements of sex tourism have developed, as international paedophile activities associated with child sex tourism have expanded. Organizations like End Child Prostitution in Asian Tourism (EPCAT) have been pioneers in the campaign to put a stop to this activity. 'ECPAT's mandate is to end the sexual exploitation of children through prostitution; trafficking; online and in the travel and tourism sector' (www.ecpat.org): this also includes outlining children's rights and how to get help and report cases of abuse in tourism. ECPAT's (2016) study entitled *Offenders on the Move: The Global Study on Sexual Exploitation of Children in Travel and Tourism 2016* illustrated some of the trends:

- 'Chinese men were the largest group of travellers and tourists buying sex with adults and minors in Thailand (after Thai citizens). Other hotspots for child sexual exploitation by Chinese offenders appear to be located along border areas between China's Yunnan province and Myanmar, Lao PDR and Vietnam, as well as Cambodia. They often initiate encounters with children and adult women at resorts and casinos built by Chinese corporations . . . In Cambodia, Chinese sex offenders are mostly business travellers who live in Cambodia for months or years, rather than tourists' (ECPAT 2016: 27). 'Overall tourism and SECTT [the sexual exploitation of children in travel and tourism] in the region appears to be dominated by Asian men. Along with domestic perpetrators, travellers and businessmen from China, Japan, South Korea and Taiwan are reportedly driving the development of Cambodia's sex tourism industry' (ECPAT 2016: 27).
- 'Western European countries have long been known as a "source" of travelling child sex offenders (TCSOs)' (ECPAT 2016: 29).
- In South Asia, 'The presence of female predators has long been noted in Sri Lanka, tied to relationships with "beach boys" during holidays . . . [and] . . . female child sex offenders are also travelling to Madhya Pradesh for extended stays to sexually exploit boys . . . [and] . . . Several new contexts have evolved for child sexual exploitation, in large part due to the expansion of infrastructure to accommodate larger numbers of tourists and travellers. Rather than designated red light areas, the sex trade is shifting to hotel rooms, guesthouses and rented flats in suburban areas as well as to hotels along motorways' (ECPAT 2016: 40).

These trends and patterns of activity are clearly disruptive to traditional ways of life, as ECPAT (2016) found that 1600 children were trafficked in 2007–2011 in Latin America, destined for work in sex tourism contexts. Traditional patterns of life and kinship are disrupted by tourism, but this is extreme by any measure. Local people are often driven to begging because their means of self-support have been removed through insensitive development, as EPCAT (2016) found in Puerto Rico where planned tourism zones displaced local people and their agricultural livelihoods. Such blatant lack of respect for traditional land and property rights and exogenous control of tourism businesses reflects the power which business interests have over poor people, which we discuss further below.

Katya Mira recounts the experience of backpacking in Mexico and the issue of beggars in Oaxaca city. As a tourist, she was constantly asked for money. On telling an old lady that she had no more money the rebuke came swiftly. 'You come all this way over here. You stay in hotels. You eat in restaurants. I live in a hut with no hot water and have no potatoes to feed my family. Look. Look at the holes in my skirt! You have no money? You don't know what "No money" means' (Mira 1999). To address some of these sociocultural problems, the government in Zanzibar (see Insight 25.1) recognized the need to prepare a code of conduct for tourists as guests of the country, to educate them on the local norms and cultural traditions. It is hoped that educating visitors with the support of tourism businesses will minimize offensive tourist behaviour.

Power and tourism: Colonialism and neo-colonialism

Power relationships can be identified at various levels with regard to tourism. At a macro level, the unequal nature of the relationship between developed and LDCs is illustrated by the volume, wealth and mobility of tourists from

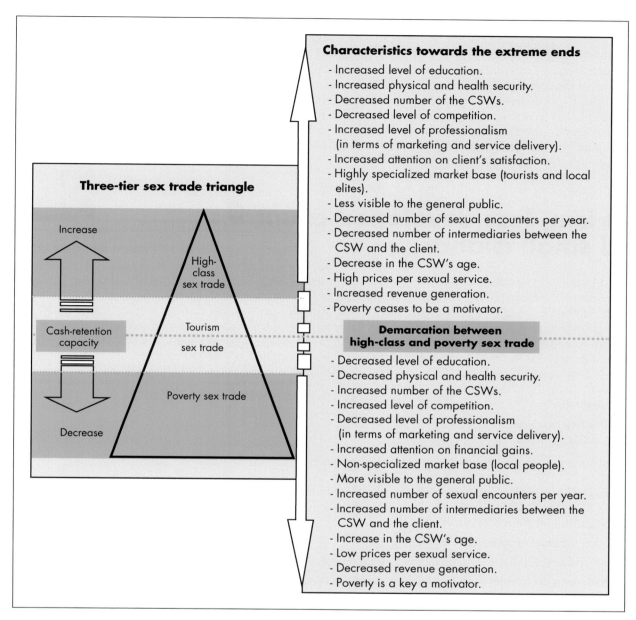

FIGURE 23.7 The sex trade spectrum
Source: Kibicho (2013: 32). Reproduced with permission from Routledge.

developed countries and also the ability of developed countries to control and gain from tourism located in LDCs (Britton 1982). At a micro level, unequal relationships clearly exist within LDCs, with a powerful minority of wealthy elite with power over poor local communities. Taking the macro issue first, this may be viewed in terms of theories of underdevelopment. As Western culture has become the dominant culture in the world, issues of power have been raised. The relationship between industrialized and non-industrialized nations is typified by a failure to recognize and respect differences (Hall 1992). The concept of development tends to assume that Western culture is applied as a standard to other nations. From the 1850s on, colonialism proved to be a valuable political instrument for controlling overseas territories with the purpose of improving the capitalist economies of the West, particularly Great Britain and France. Countries subject to colonizing powers provided cheap resources such as labour and land. From the 1960s, a new force of colonialism began to emerge. This has been termed neo-colonialism and is based on the growing power of multinational corporations. Tourism has been described as a force of neo-colonialism as it may take the form of exogenous development, controlled by overseas interests with a large proportion of income leaking overseas rather than benefiting the host nation. Scheyvens and Russell (2012) observed this process in Fiji where poverty has continued to grow, despite the growth of tourism, due to a decline in agricultural income, which is largely controlled by international markets and a neo-colonial power. It might be said that tourists have superseded the armies of the colonial powers. Britton (1982) argues that Fiji is a neo-colonial economy and illustrates this with comparisons to pre-independence and a reinforcement of associated economic patterns. As various studies of tourism planning in LDCs have shown, much of the work on plan preparation has been from aid donor countries, often on an ad hoc basis, and from the perspective of Western-based philosophies towards tourism. Concepts such as sustainable and pro-poor tourism have only recently begun to feature in the language of tourism plans for LDC, particularly in relation to tourism and small islands.

Tourism, less developed countries and small islands

Hall and Page (1996) examined the problems facing tourism in small islands, described as SIDS (see Spencer 2018 for more detail). Spencer (2018) examined the case of the Caribbean where SIDS were the most tourism-dependent countries. In the Caribbean the dominance of SIDS saw dependence measured through employment with 90 per cent of all employment in Antigua and 66 per cent in Barbados dependent upon tourism. Conversely, these SIDS in the Caribbean were also highly vulnerable to natural disasters (e.g. hurricanes) and had low levels of local production of foodstuffs for tourists, increasing the rate of leakage.

Clearly developing tourism in SIDS pose particular development challenges in LDCs including:

- accessibility
- attracting investment
- the colonial legacy and economic system
- the limited resource base to support intensive tourism.

and other studies have expanded this list of constraints to include:

- no advantages from economies of scale
- a limited range of resources
- a narrowly specialized economy, based on agricultural commodities
- small, open economies with minimal ability to influence terms of trade or to manage and control their own economies
- limited ability to adjust to changes in the international economic environment
- a narrow range of local skills and problems of matching local skills and jobs (often exacerbated by a brain and skill drain)
- high transport, infrastructure and administration costs
- cultural domination by metropolitan countries
- vulnerability to natural hazards (based on Connell 1988 and Wilkinson 1997).

Added to these problems are the loss of indigenous labour through out-migration, a dependence upon remittances and aid, and an outdated bureaucracy, derived from colonial legacies. These problems led to the use of an acronym, MIRAB (migration, remittances, aid and bureaucracy) to depict the range of issues. Not surprisingly, many of these problems were outlined in island Master Plans, such as the *Maldives Tourism Master Plan 1996–2005* (https://mymaldives.com/maldives/government/). Among the problems it highlights are:

- lack of hospitality and managerial skills
- geographical polarization of resorts from the community and concentration of ownership in a few companies
- the rapid growth of the expatriate labour force

- high economic leakages
- homegeneity within products
- dependence on a single geographical market segment
- problems related to direct foreign investments and multinational corporations
- requirement to adhere to international ethical standards in production
- deteriorating identity of Maldivian tourism products and diminishing visual quality of seascapes.

Yet the islands have around 790 000 visitor arrivals a year, and the Master Plan recognizes the social and cultural effect of this on Maldivian culture, as well as the environmental pressures and long-term problems related to climate change and the rises in sea level that could eventually engulf the islands. In 2019, a new Maldivian tourism plan was launched with a focus on more resorts being built and an attempt to diversify its portfolio of products to attract visitors seeking adventure, fun and spiritual refreshment as well as the Meetings, Incentive Travel, Conferences and Events market (MICE). The country also launched a green tax initiative in 2017, after it was first proposed in 2009. This tax charges US$6 a day for visitors in hotel and vessel-based accommodation and US$3 a day for those staying in guest houses. The country has a bold plan to become the first carbon-neutral nation by 2028 but lacks the capital (i.e. over US$1 billion) to make the shift from fossil fuels. Climate-change scientists suggest that the Maldives will disappear as a result of sea-level rises by 2100. It is also widely recognized by charitable bodies that a large proportion of the population live on around US$1, a day despite a very successful tourism sector. This raises many ethical issues for tourists who visit the islands (see Smith and Duffy 2003).

Host community issues

One of the worst **human rights** contraventions linked with tourism in recent times is that of Myanmar (Burma). This particular example highlights the stance which tour operators may take in relation to corporate social responsibility. In 1996, the pro-democracy leader, Daw Aung San Suu Kyi, who opposed the military junta, SLORC (State Law and Order Council) called on tourists not to visit the country. This was an attempt to stop foreign exchange flowing into the country and ultimately to the government. 'Visit Myanmar Year' in 1996 was SLORC's attempt to bring in hard currency through a projected 500 000 tourists (from a base of 100 000 in 1995). From 1990, SLORC tried to attract foreign investors in hotel and tourism developments, offering ten-year tax breaks and full repatriation of profits (Mahr and Sutcliffe 1996). After the grand launch was overtaken by an uprising of 50 000 student protestors and subsequent high-profile media coverage (for example, John Pilger's TV documentary *Inside Burma: Land of Fear*), tourists mainly stayed away. It was reported that local communities had been forcibly moved from their homes to make way for new tourism infrastructure, such as luxury hotels and new roads. Mahr and Sutcliffe (1996) report that people were forced to work without pay to restore the moat around Mandalay Palace. Examples of 'picturesque' ethnic peoples have been relocated to special villages where tourists can visit – an example of zooification. Despite the high-profile reporting of human rights violations and their link with tourism in Myanmar, many tour companies continue to promote the destination, highlighting the superb natural and cultural aspects but ignoring contemporary social and political issues. Ongoing opposition to such issues led to the public awareness campaign in the UK, with the Prime Minister and celebrities highlighting the use of slave and child labour in the 'I'm not going' campaign in 2005 (also see Human Rights Watch for current examples of human rights abuses in countries that are also promoting inbound and domestic tourism).

Environmental perspectives

As discussed in Chapter 19, tourism activity results in environmental damage. LDCs often contain areas of high biodiversity and environmental fragility; ecological disturbance can result in habitat damage and even species extinction. Damage, for example, to the islands and coral reefs off the west coast of Thailand (famously cited in Alex Garland's novel *The Beach*) has led to limits on day trips. On a positive note, tourism can be a force of positive change in LDCs, where tourism provides a more suitable alternative land use to intensive, commercial or environmentally damaging activities, such as agriculture, logging or hunting. For example, in the forests of Thailand, elephant keepers have turned to tourism since the logging ban left them unemployed in 1989. Tourism can also provide income for conservation purposes. The Peruvian government barred independent trekkers from the Inca Trail from 1 April 2000 in an attempt to prevent further damage to the National Park area around Machu Picchu. Access is now restricted to those on organized treks and numbers are capped at 20 000. In Mongolia, Buckley *et al.* (2008) highlight the environmental consequences of tourism in high-altitude grassland areas as well as protected areas where an absence of policy and planning measures have failed to minimize visitor impacts. In contrast, Harrison (2007) observed how the development of conservation-driven tourism at Grande Riviere, Trinidad helped to replace employment lost through the decline of the cocoa business. When leatherback turtles became protected in the 1990s, they became a major tourist attraction rather than a source of food.

One of the major growth areas of tourism that directly affects LDCs is ecotourism. This form of tourism is growing at 30 per cent compared with mainstream tourism, at about 4 per cent per annum, and thus poses a significant challenge. According to Honey (1999), nearly every non-industrialized country was promoting ecotourism as part of its development strategy by the early 1990s. Ecotourism overtook primary production as the largest foreign-exchange earner in some countries, e.g. overtaking bananas in Costa Rica, coffee in Kenya and textiles in India. There has been much debate about how ecotourism should operate; and distinctions between nature-based tourism (which may not be at all sustainable) and ecotourism which, by definition, includes benefits to local communities and protection of the environment, need to be made.

Issues of equality in tourism in less developed countries

Fair trade

One of the main questions posed is how can tourism become more equitable to those in less developed receiving countries? Tourism ought to benefit the people who live in destination areas but often does not. Fair trade is an issue that has gained momentum in recent years. A range of products are now widely available for purchase which have been 'fairly traded', such as tea, coffee, chocolate and bananas. 'Fair trade' means that the workers involved in the production of these goods have been given a fair wage and have not been subject to dangerous working conditions (for example, exposure of grape pickers to insecticides) or exploitation. Now, tourism faces a similar challenge. Organizations such as Voluntary Services Overseas (VSO) (http://www.vso.org.uk) have actively campaigned to promote awareness of fair trade in tourism.

One example of where fair trade is working effectively is in St Lucia. The Sunshine Harvest Fruit and Vegetable Farmers' Cooperative consists of 66 farmers. The cooperative coordinates production and marketing of produce to hotels on the island. An 'adopt-a-farmer' initiative is being trialled, where hotels agree to buy produce from a specific farmer at an agreed price before planting. Smallholders are being encouraged to diversify their cropping to produce a wide range of fruit and vegetables, not just bananas. Farmers have access to favourable loan rates from local banks to help them buy seed and fertilizers. This scheme has the potential to assist in greater retention of tourism revenue on the island. The integration of fair trade philosophies into tourism may be achieved in several ways via the International Network on Fair Trade in Tourism, and a very good international example is Fair Trade in Tourism in South Africa (http://www.fairtrade.travel/home/). Other ongoing research on developing local advantages in the food supply chain for the agriculture sector by Thomas-Francois *et al.* (2018) replacing the fair trade agenda. Other ongoing research on developing local advantages in the food supply chain for the agriculture sector by Thomas-Francois *et al.* (2018) is beginning to supplant the fair trade agenda by focusing on how suppliers can derive more opportunities in the supply chain. This can be achieved by hotels using more local foodstuffs.

Community-based tourism is an expanding concept in LDCs and provides a mechanism for ensuring as much economic benefit as possible remains in the host community. It also means that the community is able to control the direction and form of tourism. Many schemes are managed communally and profits are shared. Some communities work with tour operators or other organizations to promote their initiatives. Some communities operate 'village stays', where visitors stay with local families and engage in holiday activities such as bush walking, fishing, snorkelling and caving. There are many examples across the developing world, such as the Solomon Islands and Taquila on Lake Titicaca in Peru. The International Porter Protection Group (IPPG) (http://www.ippg.net) fosters the well-being of porters. Working with the trekking industry, governments and NGOs, the IPPG promotes the safety and protection of porters and collects data on deaths, accidents and injuries. Guidelines on adequate protective clothing, medical care and financial protection in relation to rescue and medical treatment have been developed to raise awareness at grassroots level. There is still much more development work and monitoring of community-based initiatives needed before any conclusions can be drawn. This is still a minority aspect of tourism provision and is seen at present as a niche market rather than a philosophy which underpins tourism management, although there are signs that a number of new perspectives are being developed in this area.

New agendas for addressing poverty and inequality through tourism

There are new ideas emerging on how to harness tourism to reduce poverty in LDCs, notably pro-poor tourism (see Scheyvens 2011) as discussed in Chapter 19 and 21, and elsewhere in this book. As the pro-poor website suggests (http://www.propoortourism.org.uk), it is an approach to tourism development designed to enhance the links between poor people and tourism so as to reduce poverty. As a concept, pro-poor tourism seeks to develop strategies which increase local employment for the poor in destination areas (including the expansion of employment opportunities for the poor), namely net benefits for the poor. According to Chok *et al.* (2007), the underlying principles of pro-poor tourism (ppt) are based upon:

- Participation, whereby local people participate in decision-making which may influence how tourism is developed and affects them.
- A holistic livelihoods approach, so that the broader impact upon people's livelihoods is recognized.
- A balanced approach to develop local people's linkages with local tourism systems and a range of products to positively enhance pro-poor initiatives.
- Wide-ranging tourism applications, so that the scope and scale of the entire range of tourism projects are incorporated into PPT.
- A detailed understanding of the costs and benefits of PPT-related development.
- Flexibility, so that tourism strategies and projects can be adapted to maximize the positive benefits.
- Commercial reality, as all PPT projects are commercially viable.
- Interdisciplinary learning of experiences and best practice from PPT and other poverty-related projects to inform and improve PPT.

To implement PPT, new methods of analysis have been developed so as to understand how interventions in the market can assist in benefiting the poor through tourism development. Organizations such as the Overseas Development Institute (ODI) in London and other similar bodies have pioneered the concept of value chains, building on the concept of tourism supply chains in Chapter 5. What the value chain idea involves is the analysis of all the activities the tourist undertakes in the destination and the spending on these activities through the supply chain to highlight how interventions can improve the flow of revenue to the poor as pro-poor income (PPI). As the ODI (2009: n.p.) argue, PPI is the 'wages and profits earned by poor households across all the inter-related strands of the value chain', so as to understand how things are now and how interventions will improve the position and impact upon PPI. A study by Mitchell *et al.* (2009: 2) of PPT in Tanzania highlighted how tourism around Mount Kilimanjaro was an excellent example of value chains working well: around 28 per cent of international package tourism spending was being captured as PPI. This is in stark contrast to the problems which Rogerson (2012) observed in high-quality tourist accommodation in South Africa, with a dependence upon imported rather than local food. What Rogerson's research highlighted was the role of a more bottom-up approach, with businesses adopting more socially responsible attitudes to reinvest in the capacity of the community through profits. Therein lies the challenge of whether you pursue a PPT or more responsible approach to tourism: the tourism sector is profit-driven and so different solutions are needed to adapt the current exploitative relationships that exist in many developing countries. One might argue that PPT is just one strand of responsible tourism, (Weeden 2013), which Frey and George (2010) describe as being focused on providing better experiences for holidaymakers and ensuring that the business opportunities that arise are beneficial to workers, businesses, the economy, society and environment. One might be forgiven for thinking that responsible tourism is just a rebranded version of sustainable tourism or that PPT is one dimension of responsible tourism. What is clear is that there are a multitude of ideas and approaches being devised on how to improve the effects of tourism in the developing world as well as the growing emphasis on corporate social responsibility (CSR) for tour operators. For example, one NGO, Tearfund (http://www.tearfund.org), is a relief and development agency which acts in partnership with Christian agencies and churches worldwide to tackle poverty. The NGO has produced

23

various reports and spearheaded different initiatives on responsible tourism, including its seminal report in 2002, *Worlds Apart: A Call to Responsible Global Tourism,* with its emphasis on the need for the tour operator sector to become more socially responsible. It has also worked in partnership with ABTA to formulate the Tour Operator Initiative, to develop a more sustainable approach to tourism via CSR with a greater focus on ethical behaviour. But other studies have pointed to the intransigence in some sectors of the tour operator industry, citing small profit margins and a limited role in destination areas compared to hotel chains. These ambitions and visionary studies such as that by Scheyvens (2002), which develop concepts like justice tourism, gender sensitive tourism and a more critical role for NGOs, the tourism industry and governments in LDCs, are certainly a refreshing, thoughtful and an alternative model for tourism development whereby communities are empowered. Even so, there is a considerable gap between the theory of PPT and its implementation and the question remains of whether it has improved the lives of poor people through tourism. Some studies claim that sub-Saharan tourism has benefited the poor (Folarin and Adeniyi 2019), especially through the development of domestic tourism in many developing countries (Llorca-Rodríguez *et al.* 2018). However, the most convincing critique remains Muchapondwa and Stage (2013: 86). Their study of Botswana, Namibia and South Africa identified the proportions of people living in poverty were 30–45 per cent in Botswana (depending upon whether the poor were in urban or rural areas); 38–49 per cent in Namibia; and 54–77 per cent in South Africa. Muchapondwa and Stage (2013: 88) concluded that 'in all three countries, the idea of using tourism as a pro-poor development strategy has yet to bear fruit', concluding that 'in the absence of meaningful benefits from tourism by the poor, taxes on tourism profits may be the simplest way through which the poor could benefit substantially from tourism'.

If one adds to this the challenge of climate change, as examined by Hoogendoorn and Fitchett (2018), these threats are heightened because many LDCs lack capital, expert knowledge and the adaptive capacity to address the problems it produces. Furthermore, they argue that the current focus on government policy is guided by the United Nation's Sustainable Development Goal 1 (to end poverty in all its forms everywhere; see Scheyvens and Hughes 2019) as we explored in Chapter 19. The poverty reduction policy imperative, as Hoogendoorn and Fitchett (2018) explain, means that climate change is further down the policy priority list because other more pressing needs, including economic growth, housing and basic services such as health provision, dominate government activity. Even so, in Africa, climate change means increasing temperatures and a growth in tourist discomfort, changes in precipitation, and an increased risk of tropical cyclones and aridification (i.e. the drying out of water supplies). For ecotourism, Hoogendoorn and Fitchett (2018) illustrate how animals, the focus of visitor interest in National Parks, are changing their migration habits to travel further for water, as well as citing increasing rates of desertification and in coastal areas, sea-level rises. For the megacities, this may also lead to a greater concentration of pollution from vehicles in these areas due to climatic conditions.

Conclusion

The last 50 years have seen a growing interest in tourism in developing countries and this has been given a considerable boost in the expansion of visitor numbers to many LDCs. The interest in poverty reduction has focused attention on equity in the relationships developed between the tourism sector and residents and workers in developing countries, including power relationships, with the most extreme example being sex tourism. A wide range of new ideas and discourses have emerged that tend to adopt one of two polarized views:

1 Tourism in the developing world is based upon inherent traits in the capitalist ideology of exploitation and the continuation of the power and control that was inherent in former colonial relationships. Consequently, new movements such as PPT and responsible tourism are simply window dressing and unlikely to make any fundamental change to the way tourism operates in the developing world.

2 Tourism can be used as a powerful tool to address issues of poverty and inequality through projects developed around notions of responsible tourism and PPT. At a national level, tourism policy leadership associated with the greater product diversification of tourism, as illustrated in Figure 23.8, may assist in creating a broader market appeal.

These two opposing views have generated a great deal of debate over which perspective is the best way forward for tourism in developing countries. It is clear that Western notions of development and modernization have been heavily criticized as inappropriate for the developing world and

23

FIGURE 23.8 Diversified product strategies for tourism in the less developed world

the most obvious notion of sustainability is a concept that many indigenous people have lived their lives around for centuries. Therefore, local interpretations of sustainability are far more appropriate than Westernized notions with little local knowledge. The principal problem is that all the lessons we have learned from the mistakes of the mass tourism that took place from the mid-1960s in coastal regions such as the Mediterranean (see Harrison and Sharpley 2017) were forgotten when tourism has evolved in the developing world. It is only belatedly that the idea of low-impact tourism has started to gain some momentum under various guises.

The future of tourism in LDCs is beset with challenges. It seems likely that the volume of tourism will continue to increase as tourists from developed countries venture further afield and those in the NICs participate more in tourism activity. Changes need to be made if tourism is to become more sustainable across the developing world. While tourism has great appeal as a mechanism for achieving economic development, appropriate policies are needed to retain sufficient tourism revenue in the host country and fair distribution within the economy. Tourism in LDCs raises complex issues and problems which have no easy solutions; it also raises many issues about the nature of the tourist experience in LDCs and future planning issues, to which we now turn in Part 6.

Discussion questions

1 Discuss the rationale for tourism as a tool for development.

2 Explain why fair trade is advocated as a way ahead for tourism in less developed countries.

3 Why is tourism described as 'neo-colonialism'?

4 How realistic is the implementation of pro-poor tourism as a development strategy for tourism destinations in LDCs?

References

Blake, A., Arbache, J., Sinclair, M.T. and Teles, V. (2008) 'Tourism and poverty relief', *Annals of Tourism Research*, 35 (1): 107–126.

Brandt, W. (1980) *North–South: A Programme for Survival*. London: Pan.

Britton, S. (1980) 'The spatial organization of tourism in a neo-colonial economy: A Pacific case study', *Pacific Viewpoint*, 21 (2): 144–165.

Britton, S. (1982) 'The political economy of tourism in the Third World', *Annals of Tourism Research*, 9 (3): 331–358.

Bryden, J. (1973) *Tourism and Development: A Case Study of the Commonwealth Caribbean*. Cambridge: Cambridge University Press.

Buckley, R., Ollenburg, C. and Zhong, L. (2008) 'Cultural landscape in Mongolian tourism', *Annals of Tourism Research*, 35 (1): 47–61.

Chok, S., Macbeth, J. and Warren, C. (2007) 'Tourism as a tool for poverty alleviation: A critical analysis of "pro-poor tourism" and implications for sustainability', *Current Issues in Tourism*, 10 (2/3): 144–165.

Connell, J. (1988) *Sovereignty and Survival: Island Microstates in the Third World*. Research Monograph No. 3. Sydney: Department of Geography, University of Sydney.

Daniel, E. (1998) 'Spirits in the village', *Orbit* (VSO) Q2: 8–9.

Dao Truong, V., Slabbert, E. and Manh Nguyen, V. (2017) 'Poverty in tourist paradise? A review of pro-poor tourism in

South and South-East Asia', in C.M. Hall and S.J. Page (eds.) *The Routledge Handbook of Tourism in Asia*, 101–118.

Daye, M., Chambers, D. and Roberts, S. (eds.) (2008) *New Perspectives in Caribbean Tourism*. London: Routledge.

de Kadt, E. (1979) *Tourism: Passport to Development*. New York: Oxford University Press.

Department for International Development (1999) *Changing the Nature of Tourism. Developing an Agenda for Action*. London: DFID.

Dieke, P. (ed.) (2000) *Tourism in Africa*. New York: Cognizant.

Dorji, T. (2001) 'Sustainability of tourism in Bhutan', *The Journal of Bhutan Studies*, 3 (1): 84–104.

ECPAT (2016) *Offenders on the Move: The Global Study on Sexual Exploitation of Children in Travel and Tourism 2016*. Bangkok: ECPAT.

Folarin, O. and Adeniyi, O. (2019) 'Does tourism reduce poverty in sub-Saharan African countries?' *Journal of Travel Research* 59 (1): 140–155.

Freire-Medeiros, B. (2013) *Tourism Poverty*. London: Routledge.

Frey, N. and George, R. (2010) 'Responsible tourism management: The missing link between business owners' attitudes and behaviour in the Cape Town tourism industry', *Tourism Management*, 31 (3): 621–628.

Hall, C.M. (1992) *Tourism and Politics: Policy, Power and Place*. Chichester: John Wiley and Sons.

Hall, C.M. and Page, S.J. (eds.) (1996) *Tourism in the Pacific: Issues and Cases*. London: Thomson.

Hall, C.M. and Page, S.J. (eds.) (2000) *Tourism in South and South East Asia: Issues and Cases*. Oxford: Butterworth-Heinemann.

Hall, C.M. and Page, S.J. (eds.) (2017) *The Routledge Handbook of Tourism in Asia*. London: Routledge.

Harrison, D. (ed.) (1992) *Tourism in the Less Developed Countries*. London: Belhaven Press.

Harrison, D. (1998) *The Sociology of Modernisation and Development*. London: Routledge.

Harrison, D. (ed.) (2001) *Tourism in Developing Countries: Issues and Cases*. Wallingford: CABI.

Harrison, D. (ed.) (2003) *Pacific Island Tourism*. New York: Cognizant.

Harrison, D. (2007) 'Cocoa, conservation and tourism: Grande Riviere, Trinidad', *Annals of Tourism Research*, 34 (4): 919–942.

Harrison, D. and Sharpley, R. (eds.) (2017) *Mass Tourism in a Small World*. Wallingford: CABI.

Honey, M. (1999) *Ecotourism and Sustainable Development. Who Owns Paradise?* Washington, DC: Island Press.

Hoogendoorn, G. and Fitchett, J.M. (2018) 'Tourism and climate change: A review of threats and adaptation strategies for Africa', *Current Issues in Tourism*, 21 (7): 742–759.

Huyber, T. (ed.) (2007) *Tourism in Developing Countries*. Cheltenham: Edward Elgar.

Kester, J. and Carvao, S. (2004) 'International tourism in the Middle East, and outbound tourism from Saudi Arabia', *Tourism Economics*, 10 (2): 220–240.

Kibicho, W. (2013) *Sex Tourism in Africa: Kenya's Booming Industry*. London: Routledge.

Llorca-Rodríguez, C., García-Fernández, R. and Casas-Jurado, A. (2018) 'Domestic versus inbound tourism in poverty reduction: Evidence from panel data', *Current Issues in Tourism*, 1–20.

Lumsdon, L. and Swift, J. (2001) *Tourism in Latin America*. London: Continuum.

Mahr, J. and Sutcliffe, S. (1996) 'Come to Burma', *New Internationalist*, 280: 28–30.

Marfurt, E. (1997) 'Tourism and the Third World: Dream or nightmare?', in L. France (1997) *The Earthscan Reader in Sustainable Tourism*. London: Earthscan.

Mbaiwa, J. (2005) 'Enclave tourism and its socio-economic impacts in the Okavango Delta, Botswana', *Tourism Management*, 26 (2): 157–172.

Mira, K. (1999) 'Postcard from Mexico', *In Focus*, 33: 20.

Mitchell, J. (2012) 'Value chain approaches to assessing the impact of tourism on low income households in developing countries', *Journal of Sustainable Tourism*, 20 (3): 457–475.

Mitchell, J., Keane, J. and Laidlaw, J. (2009) *Making Success Work for the Poor: Package Tourism in Northern Tanzania*. London: ODI/SNV.

Mowforth, M. and Munt, I. (2003) *Tourism and Sustainability. New Tourism in the Third World,* 2nd edition. London: Routledge.

Muchapondwa, E. and Stage, J. (2013) 'The economic impacts of tourism in Botswana, Namibia and South Africa: Is poverty subsiding?' *Natural Resources Forum*, 37 (2): 80–89.

Novelli, M. (ed.) (2016) *Tourism and Development in sub-Saharan Africa*. London: Routledge.

ODI (2009) *Value Chain Analysis and Poverty Reduction at Scale: Evidence from Tourism Is Shifting Mindsets*. Briefing Paper: ISSN 0140-8682. London: Overseas Development Institute.

Oppermann, M. and Chon, K. (1997) *Tourism in Developing Countries*. London: International Thomson Business Press.

Page, S.J. (2019) *Tourism Management*, 6th edition. Abingdon: Taylor and Francis.

Page, S.J. and Dowling, R. (2002) *Ecotourism*. Harlow: Prentice Hall.

Pattullo, P. (1996) *Last Resorts: The Cost of Tourism in the Caribbean*. London: Cassell.

Pearce, D.G. (1990) *Tourist Development,* 2nd edition. Harlow: Longman.

Rogerson, C.M. (2012) 'Tourism–agriculture linkages in rural South Africa: evidence from the accommodation sector', *Journal of Sustainable Tourism*, 20 (3): 477–495.

Scheyvens, R. (2002) *Tourism for Development*. Harlow: Prentice Hall.

Scheyvens, R. (2011) *Tourism and Poverty*. London: Routledge.

Scheyvens, R. and Hughes, E. (2019) 'Can tourism help to "end poverty in all its forms everywhere"? The challenge of tourism addressing SDG1', *Journal of Sustainable Tourism*, 27 (7), 1061–1079.

Scheyvens, R. and Russell, M. (2012) 'Tourism and poverty alleviation', *Journal of Sustainable Tourism*, 20 (3): 417–436.

Smith, N. and Duffy, R. (2003) *The Ethics of Tourism Development*. London: Routledge.

23

Spenceley, A. and Meyer, D. (2012) 'Tourism and poverty reduction: Theory and practice in less economically developed countries', *Journal of Sustainable Tourism*, 20 (3): 297–317.

Spencer, R. (2010) *Development through Tourism: Lessons from Cuba*. Aldershot: Ashgate.

Steel, G. (2012) 'Local encounters with globetrotters: Tourism's potential for street vendors in Cusca, Peru', *Annals of Tourism Research*, 39 (2): 601–639.

Suntikul, W. and Dorji, U. (2016) 'Local perspectives on the impact of tourism on religious festivals in Bhutan', *Asia Pacific Journal of Tourism Research*, 21 (7): 741–776.

Swarbrooke, J. (1999) *Sustainable Tourism*. Wallingford, Oxon: CABI.

Telfer, D. (2009) 'Development studies and tourism', in M. Robinson and T. Jamal (eds.) *The Sage Handbook of Tourism Studies*. London: Sage.

Telfer, D. and Sharpley, R. (2002) *Tourism and Development*. Clevedon: Channel View.

Thomas-Francois, K., Joppe, M. and von Massow, M. (2018) 'Improving linkages through a service-oriented local farmers–hotel supply chain – An explanatory case in Grenada', *Tourism Planning and Development*, 15 (4): 398–418.

Turner, L. and Ash, J. (1975) *The Golden Hordes: International Tourism and the Pleasure Periphery*. London: Constable.

Webster, A. (1990) *Introduction to the Sociology of Development*. London: Macmillan.

Weeden, C. (2013) *Responsible Tourist. Behaviour*. London: Routledge.

Wilkinson, P. (1997) *Tourism Policy and Planning: Case Studies from the Caribbean*. New York: Cognizant.

Further reading

Books

Hall, C.M. and Page, S.J. (eds.) (2017) *The Routledge Handbook of Tourism in Asia*. London: Routledge.

Mkono, M. (ed.) (2019) *Positive Tourism in Africa*. London: Routledge.

Journal articles

Muchapondwa, E. and Stage, J. (2013) 'The economic impacts of tourism in Botswana, Namibia and South Africa: Is poverty subsiding?' *Natural Resources Forum*, 37 (2): 80–89.

Scheyvens, R. and Russell, M. (2012) 'Tourism and poverty alleviation', *Journal of Sustainable Tourism*, 20 (3): 417–436.

23

Part 6

Managing tourism activities

In Part 5, the focus was on how supply and demand in specific locations culminated in different forms of tourism. At these locations, tourists would have experienced different types of products and services, and formed an overall image and perception of the locality. In Part 6 of the book, the emphasis is on that perception and evaluation of tourism, the tourism experience and how the public sector may develop plans and measures to develop, manage and where necessary intervene to control tourism. It focuses on current and future issues which may impact upon that experience, notably tourist safety and security and future trends which are emerging. Chapter 24 discusses the nature of the *tourism experience*, exploring many of the concepts and techniques used to assess how tourists rate and perceive their experience of tourism. This is a culmination of the interactions between all the chapters discussed throughout the book, where specific relationships exist that can condition and affect the way the tourist rates their holiday experience, a visit to an attraction or a destination. A starting point for Chapter 24 is how the public and private sectors seek to manage this experience through macro techniques such as planning for tourism and micro techniques by businesses at the individual visitor level. This theme is then expanded upon in Chapter 25, which examines some of the highly visible factors which impact upon the visitor experience – tourist health and safety. It is widely acknowledged that these factors are now assuming a global significance as tourism enters an age of greater turbulence. Chapter 26 provides an evaluation of a major growth area for creating tourism activity – event tourism. The chapter highlights how hosting and staging events can be used to create tourism-related activity, but it requires careful planning, management and monitoring to achieve high-quality events which add value to the tourism experience. This is followed in the last chapter of the book, Chapter 27, by a detailed analysis of the future of tourism. This highlights many of the management challenges facing the tourism industry and likely changes which will occur in tourism activity in the new millennium.

Planning and managing the tourist experience

Learning outcomes

After reading this chapter and answering the questions, you should be able to:

- identify the importance of tourism planning
- outline the tourism planning process
- indicate the key factors which interact to shape the tourist experience
- understand the importance of service quality issues in shaping the tourist experience.

Overview

The nature of the tourist as a consumer has received considerable attention in the analysis of tourism impacts and of the need for planning to control and manage it. One consequence of tourism planning and management is the need to integrate tourist needs and satisfaction to understand how tourism can achieve a sustainable future and sustainable experiences for visitors. Many of the principles of management discussed in Chapter 5 are considered in this chapter to illustrate how the tourist experience needs to be managed so as to ensure that tourists' needs and the resource base are balanced with the commercial needs of the tourism sector.

Introduction

There is a growing interest within the tourism sector on the development of concepts and mechanisms by which to understand how destinations and businesses can plan for the growth and sustainable evolution of tourism. One of the fundamental building blocks to any such strategy at a destination or business level is the need to plan for the development of tourism. This chapter examines some of the tools and approaches which the public sector uses to evaluate the best route to control and develop tourism at a destination level. Some localities have used visitor management tools to control sites and areas. What is needed is an integrated planning process which brings together different stakeholders and interest groups. These issues then have to be developed in the business plans and activities of individual tourism businesses if tourism is to pursue a direction which stakeholders wish to endorse; although reaching agreement, as Chapter 13 has shown, is far from a straightforward process. Various studies of individual countries have shown that tourism can be a transformative activity for its national economy, reflected in national economic development strategies (i.e. economic development plans). This can be illustrated by two contrasting examples from Africa. In the case of Ghana, Adu-Ampong (2018) highlighted how the country had harnessed tourism via its five-year national development plans as a key pillar of economic growth between 1964 and 2014. In contrast, Harilal *et al.* (2018) examined the central African state of Cameroon and the absence of any policy guidelines to guide development as tourism emerges as a growth sector. This is also in stark contrast to the complex evolution of tourism policy in the European Union (EU) outlined by Estol and Font (2016). It is therefore pertinent that this chapter examines the need for **tourism planning**, how it is progressed as a process and some of the features of tourism plans which set the direction for tourism planning, including the contribution of tourism policies by the public sector to guidance for tourism planning (see Table 24.1). This is followed by a discussion of the concept of the 'tourist experience', as one objective of tourism planning is to ensure that visitors are attracted, and are satisfied (if not delighted) by the experience they encounter at the destination. Indeed, many destinations are trying to promote the development of quality tourism experiences (Jennings and Nickerson 2006). This should be seen as part of the process of developing value in the experience of being a tourist, as discussed in Chapter 14, through the marketing process to meet consumer expectations.

TABLE 24.1 Key studies on tourism policy and the public sector
Andriotis, K., Stylidis, D. and Weidenfeld, A. (eds.) (2019) *Tourism Policy and Planning Implementation: Issues and Challenges*. London: Routledge.
Canadian Tourism Commission, World Tourism Organization and World Tourism Organization Business Council (2003) *Co-operation and Partnerships in Tourism: A Global Perspective*. Madrid: UNWTO.
Dredge, D. and Jenkins, J. (2007) *Tourism Planning and Policy*. Milton, Qld: John Wiley and Sons Australia Ltd.
Dredge, D. and Jenkins, J. (eds.) (2011) *Stories of Practice: Tourism Policy and Planning*. Aldershot: Ashgate.
Edgell, D. and Swanson, J. (2018) *Tourism Policy and Planning: Yesterday, Today and Tomorrow*. London: Routledge.
Elliot, J. (1997) *Tourism, Politics and Public Sector Management*. London: Routledge.
Hall, C.M. (2007) *Tourism Planning: Policies, Processes and Relationships*, 2nd edition. Harlow: Prentice Hall.
Hall, C.M. and Jenkins, J. (1995) *Tourism and Public Policy*. London: Routledge.
Jeffries, D. (2001) *Governments and Tourism*. Oxford: Butterworth-Heinemann.
OECD (2012) *Tourism Trends and Policies 2012*. Paris: OECD.
UNWTO (2010) *Handbook on Tourism and Poverty Alleviation – Practical Steps for Destinations*. Madrid: UNWTO.
UNWTO (2010) *Joining Forces: Collaboration Processes for Sustainable and Competitive Tourism*. Madrid: UNWTO.

Source: Page (2019) *Tourism Management*, 6th edition. London: Routledge.

The management and planning of the tourist experience

24

Planning is normally one task which is subsumed under the heading of management, as discussed in Chapter 5, where it was noted that the principal activities of management are:

- planning
- organizing

- leading
- controlling.

These four tasks are important for tourism destinations in coordinating the private and public sector interests (i.e. the **stakeholders**, who include the residents) in relation to the tourist experience. This is where a managing agency with a view of the 'tourist experience' can be important in ensuring that some of the potential interactions evident in Figure 24.1 are managed. This shows that planning is normally a macro-level issue which is undertaken at different geographical scales, and yet frequently fails to move beyond a broad strategy and series of objectives at the local level (although exceptions exist in resorts and highly developed destinations). It is important to emphasize that it is businesses which deal with the tourist experience, whereas, in planning terms, it is the public sector which addresses wider tourism planning issues, and rarely do the two functions get integrated so the two are optimized. Therefore, as Figures 24.1 and 24.2 suggest, there are a number of stakeholders in any given destination who can impact upon the tourism industry, ranging from the different businesses producing the supply of services and goods to the tourist (i.e. demand) and the residents. Achieving a balance between each of their needs and the viable development of the local tourism industry is a challenge and a fundamental reason for planning. Even so, local people also need to be included as a vital ingredient in the tourism planning process, as Chapters 16–19, illustrate to mitigate adverse impacts and to harness the development benefits. For example, Shakeela and Weaver (2016) pointed to the situation in the Maldives, where local people felt excluded from the tourism planning process and so were unable to participate in shaping the tourism development process.

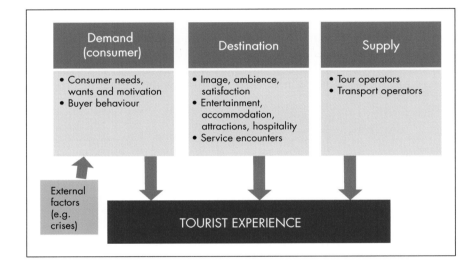

FIGURE 24.1 The influences upon the tourist experience of tourism at destinations
Source: Adapted and developed from Ryan (1997)

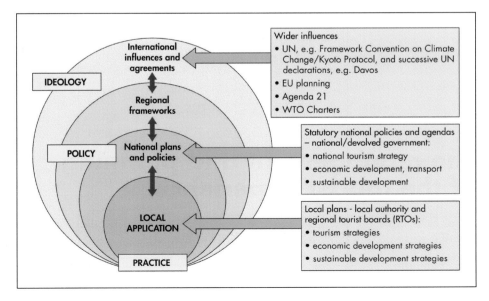

FIGURE 24.2 The scope of planning for tourism

Planning: What is it and does it exist in tourism?

According to Chadwick (1971: 24) 'planning is a process, a process of human thought and action based upon that thought – in point of fact for the future – nothing more or less than this is planning, which is a general human activity'. What this means is that change and the need to accommodate change in the future requires a process whereby a set of decisions are prepared for future action. Hall (1999: 10) argues that:

Demands for tourism planning and government intervention in the development process are typically a response to the unwanted effects of tourism development at the local level. The rapid pace of tourism growth and development, the nature of tourism itself and the corresponding absence of single agency responsibility for tourism related development has often meant that public sector responses to the impacts of tourism on destinations has often been ad hoc, rather than predetermined strategies oriented towards development objectives.

Planning is therefore a process which aims to anticipate, regulate and monitor change to contribute to the wider sustainability of the destination, and thereby enhance the tourist experience of the destination or place. What Hall (1999) and other commentators recognize is that while tourism planning has followed trends in urban and regional planning, tourism is not always seen as a core focus of the planning process at the local level.

Getz (1987) observed that there are four traditions to tourism planning: boosterism, an economic-industry approach, a physical-spatial approach and a community-oriented approach, while Hall (1999) has recognized that a fifth approach now exists – 'sustainable tourism planning' (Figure 24.3), which is 'a concern for the long-term future of resources, the effects of economic development on the environment, and its ability to meet present and future needs' (Page and Thorn 1997: 60). As Page and Thorn (1997: 61) suggest: 'In most countries, tourism planning exists as a component of public sector planning, and its evolution as a specialist activity has been well documented (Gunn 1988; Inskeep 1991)'. As a component of public sector planning, tourism planning (where it exists as a discrete activity or is subsumed within wider economic planning processes) aims to optimize the balance of private sector interests which are profit driven. In some cases this may prove problematic in getting the balance right, as Insight 24.1 suggests.

INSIGHT 24.1 Planning and small islands: Resort development in Zanzibar – local community issues

Zanzibar, off the east coast of Tanzania (see Figure 24.3) is an archipelago comprising one main island (Zanzibar Island) and a series of smaller islands, with a population of 1 million people. Tourism is a relatively new development path for the country, which became independent in 1963, and was subsumed into Tanzania. The country has a rich history of Arab, Iranian and Indian influence followed by Portuguese and British colonial rule. Tourism developed a significant presence during the 1980s as a development option, and the Tourism Commission of Zanzibar (n.d.) states that:

Zanzibar discourages any tourism that does not conserve and improve the welfare of local people. The policy emphasizes . . . responsible tourism, which has far reaching implications for the development and promotion of tourism. The objective behind the Zanzibar tourism development policy is to elaborate, taking into account

Zanzibar's own reality and vision 2020, a framework of reference which will permit the establishment of the country's future tourism development, sustainability, quality and diversification as the most important factors.

The country's development of international tourism has seen arrivals grow from 150 000 in 2006 to 376 000 in 2016, 433 000 in 2017 and to 526 000 in 2018, exceeding its own forecasts. As Quaade (2018) illustrates, this has not been without detrimental side-effects as it has placed pressure on the islands' resources:

- In terms of water consumption, a feature highlighted by Page et al. (2014), Quaade points to tourist use of water being 10 to 15 times higher than that of local residents. While 'a monthly water tax was introduced to hotels and guesthouses in Zanzibar . . . the tax was set at a flat rate regardless of the consumption meaning that it was not

24

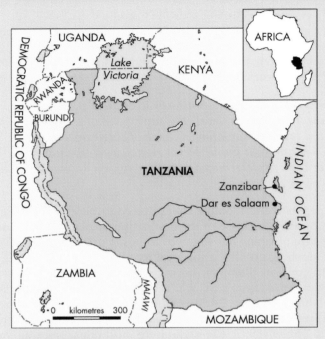

FIGURE 24.3 Location of Zanzibar in East Africa

aligned with the specific environmental problem which the tax intended to penalise to ameliorate the negative effects' (Page *et al.* 2014: 60).

- Waste disposal is a problem for Zanzibar, with the island's sewage pipes discharging 2200 cubic metres of untreated liquid waste into the Indian Ocean. While some hotels have their own sewage treatment plants, the majority of the waste is discharged out to sea. This, according to Quaade (2018) has been linked to the deterioration of the marine environment (e.g. mangrove forests, coral reefs and seagrasses). The use of single-use plastics by tourists (i.e. single-use personal items like shampoos, individual condiments and plastic lunchboxes used on tourist day trips) contributes to the problem. Quaade (2018) points to research which suggests that 80 per cent of all of Zanzibar's waste is generated through hotels and restaurants. Only 20 per cent of the island's waste is collected for proper disposal. The remainder goes to unofficial landfill and dumpsites. Although plastic bags are banned in the medieval area of Zanzibar City – Stone Town (a UNESCO World Heritage Site), and street cleaning occurs three times a day to collect rubbish, this is not the norm everywhere else.

Tourism is viewed as a key element of Zanzibar's poverty reduction plan, since 10 per cent of the island's youth are ·unemployed (Quaade 2018). Yet the country's dependence

upon tourism as a form of economic development is reflected in the fact that 27 per cent of GDP and 80 per cent of foreign revenue is derived from tourism (Quaade 2018), which employs 72 000 people.

A report by Action Aid in 2004 criticized the tourism sector in Zanzibar for 'creating enclaves of wealth' as few local people had benefited from tourism and foreign investors were the main beneficiaries. Many of the local population survive on US$1 a day on an island receiving in excess of 150 000 overseas visitors a year in a destination promoted as an island paradise. Tourism has now replaced the country's former dependence upon spices, as it accounts for 22 per cent of GDP. Much of this is beach-oriented tourism, with hotels located on or near to the island's 25 beaches. The Zanzibar Tourism Development Policy and its Indicative Master Plan for Zanzibar and Pemba sought to grow tourism by 5–6 per cent by 2005, 7–8 per cent by 2010 and by 9–10 per cent by 2020. Its vision is to 'become one of the top tourism destinations of the Indian ocean, offering an upmarket, high quality product across the board . . .' to: improve the quality of life of the population; stimulate economic growth; preserve the social and cultural fabric; contribute to the alleviation of poverty; raise service levels to internationally accepted standards; expand domestic tourism for Zanzibaris; and protect and conserve fragile ecological systems. One illustration of the impact of foreign investment is apparent from plans made in 2000 for Nungwi, on the northern peninsular of Zanzibar. It is just one example of how the interests of corporations and foreign investment have been put before the interests and feelings of local people.

The government of Zanzibar leased 57 km² (at US$1 per year for 49 years) to the British-based East African Development Company (EADC) for a US$4 billion tourist enclave. It was planning to create the biggest tourism development in East Africa: 14 luxury hotels, several hundred villas, three golf courses, a country club, an airport, swimming pools, a marina and a trade centre. The main concerns were that:

- there had been no consultation and local people had not been kept informed of plans
- 20 000 people live on the peninsula. They had not been informed whether they would have to move and, if so, whether they would receive compensation
- Nungwi is a fishing and farming community, with a few small hotels and guest houses. The opportunities for a local mixed economy which would benefit the local community were likely to be lost if this development went ahead, since Action Aid were already pointing to the problems fishermen were facing in accessing the coastline due to tourism development

- people feared the loss of fertile agricultural land and access to beaches as a result of the enclave
- water supply is an existing problem in the area, with a lack of supply and poor distribution
- no social or environmental impact studies had been carried out despite the existence of pollution of coastal habitats by untreated municipal waste.

Lobbying from the local community and NGOs halted the development but once the potential of an area has been identified, it is not likely to be long before another similar proposal, albeit of a smaller scale, will be pursued. This poses many ethical dilemmas for planners who seek to grow tourism as a development option and yet have policies which clearly state responsible tourism is to be pursued. Gössling (2001) concluded that this development dilemma really questioned the assumption that sustainable tourism can be achieved in an environmentally neutral manner.

In 2017, further plans were announced for a US$1 billion investment in Zanzibar Amber Resort; with 4.1 km² of tropical landscape and 4 km of prime Indian Ocean coastline, Blue Amber is the largest mixed-use resort development in Africa and the first of its kind on the island (https://www.blueamberzanzibar.com/). This will comprise the opportunity for non-Tanzanians to purchase residential units on a 99-year lease with the opportunity for an additional 49-year lease extension. This resort will stretch along a 4 km coastline, with leisure facilities designed to attract high spending international tourists (e.g. hotel, golf courses, a super-yacht harbour). Prices for the villas in the Blue Amber resort range from US$670 000 to US$1.7 million. The resort will be phased in over 15 years, with the initial phase opening in

2020 and is expected to generate 5000 jobs. The resort will also have a private runway, a private medical facility, an international school with 1914 villas and 3440 luxury and penthouse apartments expected to cost from US$700 000 to US$10 million. Criticisms of the project point to the poor state of supporting infrastructure for tourism (e.g. road, water, sanitation, electricity).

Further reading

Dredge, D. and Jenkins, J. (eds.) (2011) *Stories of Tourism Policy and Planning.* Aldershot: Ashgate.

Gössling, S. (2001) 'The consequences of tourism for sustainable water use on a tropical island: Zanzibar, Tanzania', *Journal of Environmental Management* 61 (2): 179–191.

Quaade, V. (2018) Zanzibar in danger of its popularity as a tourist destination, *The East African.* https://www.theeastafrican.co.ke/business/Zanzibar-in-danger-of-its-popularity-as-a-tourist-destination/2560-4614230-23ja7tz/index.html.

Questions

1 Has Zanzibar exceeded its carrying capacity as an island for tourism?

2 At what point should visitor numbers to Zanzibar be capped?

3 Is resort development the most appropriate form of tourism development for Zanzibar?

4 As Minister for Tourism in Zanzibar, what would be the top 10 actions to prioritize in the Zanzibar Tourism Development Plan 2020–2030?

According to Inskeep (1994: 6) the effective management of tourism requires certain 'organizational elements'. The most important of these in a planning context are organizational structures, which include government agencies and private sector interest groups as well as the involvement of local and regional government bodies to plan for tourism activity, and tourism-related legislation and regulations as discussed in Chapter 13. One also has to have appropriate marketing and promotional programmes together with sources of capital and finance. When a government agency engages in tourism planning, a set process is usually followed which involves a series of steps.

The tourism planning process

The tourism planning process has a number of steps comprising:

1 *Study preparation:* the planning authority within the local or regional government (it may be one national agency on small islands that do not have a complex planning structure) decides to proceed with the development of a tourism plan. Heeley (1981) observed that while a number of agencies may be actively involved in tourism, it is normally a statutory body which undertakes the plan although where a local and regional agency both develop a tourism plan, it is important that they dovetail and are integrated to ensure a unified structure to tourism. This is a problem in London, where the 33 London boroughs' unified development plans pursue different approaches to tourism (i.e. some councils promote tourism

24

development while others positively discourage it) despite the efforts of tourism agencies to coordinate their activities in tourism.

2 *Determination of objectives:* the main purpose of the plan is identified (i.e. is it pursuing a sustainable strategy to development? Is it being undertaken in response to a crisis such as saturation tourism to identify managerial measures to reduce the social, cultural and environmental impacts?). This is termed the 'goals of planning' by Gunn and Var (2002) as shown in Figure 24.4.

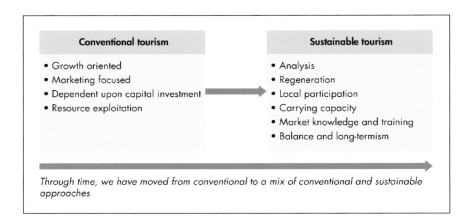

FIGURE 24.4 Conventional versus sustainable tourism strategies
Source: Developed from B. Lane (1994) 'Sustainable rural tourism strategies: A tool for development and conservation', *Journal of Sustainable Tourism*, 2 (1–2): 102–111

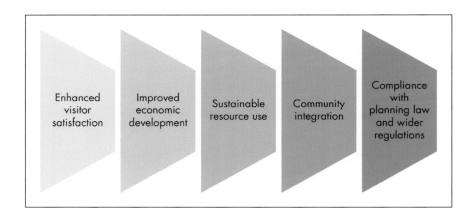

FIGURE 24.5 Goals for planning.
Source: Adapted from: Gunn and Var (2002)

3 *Survey of all elements:* an inventory of all the existing tourism resources and facilities are surveyed together with the state of development, as illustrated in Figure 24.6. This will require the collection of data on the supply and demand for tourism, the structure of the local tourism economy, investment and the finance available for future development. It will also involve identifying the range of other private and public sector interests in tourism within the destination or locality.

4 *Analysis and synthesis of findings:* the information and data collected in the previous stage are analyzed and incorporated as data when formulating the plan. As Cooper *et al.* (1998) argue, four principal techniques are frequently used here: asset evaluation, market analysis, development planning and impact analysis (especially economic impact analysis such as input–output analysis, multiplier analysis and tourism forecasting).

5 *Policy and plan formulation:* the data gathered in the previous stage are used to establish the various options or development scenarios available for tourism. This frequently involves the drafting of a development plan with tourism policy options, with certain goals identified. Acernaza (1985) argued that there are three main elements evident in most tourism policies that are germane to the tourist experience: *visitor satisfaction, environmental protection* and *ensuring adequate rewards exist for developers* and *investors*. By developing a range of policy options at this stage of the planning process, the future direction can be considered.

6 *Consideration of recommendations:* the full tourism plan is then prepared and forwarded to the planning committee of the public agency responsible for the process. A period of public consultation is normally undertaken in most Western industrialized countries. The draft plan is then available for public consultation so that both the general public and tourism interests can read and comment on it. A number of public hearings may also be provided to gauge the strength of local feeling towards the plan. Once this procedure is completed, the plan will then be approved by the planning authority and the final plan is then produced.

7 *The implementation and monitoring of the tourism plan:* the plan is put into action; this is normally seen as an ongoing process by the planning team. In some instances, legislation may be required to control certain aspects of development (e.g. the height of buildings and developments) which will need to be implemented as part of the plan. The political complexity of implementing the plan should not be underestimated. Often, the political complexion of the elected representatives on the statutory planning authority may change and cause the priorities to change also although, if an Action Plan is produced alongside the plan, it will allow for some degree of choice in what is implemented and actioned in a set period of time. At the same time as the plan is implemented, it will also need to be monitored. This is an ongoing process where the planning agency assess if the objectives of the plan are being met. The operational time frame for a tourism plan is normally five years, after which time it is reviewed. Lai *et al.* (2006) describe a gap between planning and implementation (GPI) and examined the common causes for such gaps. In extreme cases, they may lead to the failure or abandonment of the plan. For example, planners may have misunderstood the complexity of land ownership, community opposition, inadequate resources to implement the plan, and overlooked unforeseen factors. In extreme cases, a tourism plan may be little more than a paper exercise and Lai *et al.* (2006) highlighted examples of tourism plans failing in China.

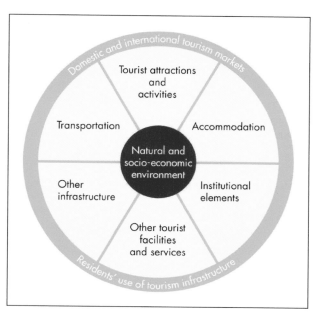

FIGURE 24.6 The elements of a tourism plan

8 *The periodic review:* the process of reporting back on the progress once the plan has run its course and been implemented. Some of the reasons for the failure of the plan to achieve its stated objectives may relate to a change of political complexion among the elected members of the planning authority (e.g. where an anti-tourism lobby dominates the local authority when the plan was commissioned by a pro-tourism council); a failure to achieve a degree of consensus between the private and public sector on how to address 'bottlenecks' in the supply of services and facilities for tourists; inadequate transport and infrastructure provision; and public opposition to tourism arising from the planning authority's misunderstanding of residents' attitudes.

FIGURE 24.7 Basic components of a tourism development strategy

Source: Adapted from Godfrey and Clarke (2000: vii)

24

This planning process is not dissimilar to that outlined by Godfrey and Clarke (2000: vii) in Figure 24.7, which shows that marketing also needs to be incorporated into the planning process, especially at the local or destination level.

Yet, as Page and Thorn (2002) show in relation to the development of sustainable tourism planning in New Zealand, while some local authorities may have plans for tourism, an absence of a regional or national plan for tourism to spread and distribute its benefits highlights the need for integration of planning between the three levels at which it commonly occurs: the national (i.e. the country level), regional (e.g. the county or state level in the USA) and the local level (i.e. the specific city, district or locality). At each level strategic vision is important (Edgell *et al.* 2008), as Chapter 13 illustrated, as planning is more than simple notions of the land-use planning that have remained a permanent feature of urban and regional planning, with the local and global processes of tourism development often overlooked.

In the real world, 'planning for tourism' is a more apt description of the way tourism is treated by the public sector, since it is frequently incorporated in wider planning considerations which influence tourism development. Whatever form of management or planning which is developed for tourism in a given locality, a strategic view will need to satisfy the long-term provision of tourist experiences that are compatible with the locality, environment and resources available to planners and managers of tourism. Therefore, with these issues in mind regarding the planning process, attention now turns to the issue of the tourist experience.

The tourist experience: Concepts and issues for planning and management

One way of starting to try to understand the tourist experience is to consider the following observations by Ryan (1997) in relation to holidays:

IMAGE 24.1 Crowding is not always detrimental to the visitor experience, as indicated by attendees disembarking from a train who are heading to the Glastonbury Festival, UK

- it has an important emotional involvement for the tourist
- there is a strong motivation for successful and satisfactory outcomes on the part of the tourist
- there is a significantly long period of interaction between the tourist on the one hand and, on the other, the place and people in the holiday destination – a period wherein the tourist can manipulate his or her surroundings to achieve the desired outcomes
- manipulative processes are part of the holiday experience and a source of satisfaction
- a number of holiday services exist, so that the tourist can select among alternatives
- holidays have a structure, whereby the tourist can play several different roles – each role may have separate determinants of satisfaction and each role may have unequal contributions to total holiday satisfaction
- it has a temporal significance not found in many service situations – it resides in the memory as a preparation for the future and is a resource for ego-sustainment during non-holiday periods.

In other words, the 'tourist experience' is a complex combination of objective, but predominantly subjective factors that shape the tourist's feelings and attitude towards his or her visit (Image 24.1). Yet it is almost impossible to predict tourist responses to individual situations, as a series of interrelated impacts may affect the tourist experience which itself is a dynamic entity, constantly subject to change. Pearce (1988)

24

suggests that the sources of satisfaction differ between more and less experienced tourists at the same location – with greater levels of satisfaction likely to be gained by the more experienced tourist. Regardless of experience, there are many factors that contribute to tourist satisfaction, some of which are beyond the tourist's control (e.g. safety, climate, traffic, noise and pollution). Many of these issues are important at the micro level (i.e. the individual tourist, place and service being consumed).

Yet the tourist experience is not just specific to holiday travel, since other types of tourists make decisions and evaluate their experiences, as business travellers for example, where certain attributes are ranked importantly in the service they consume. As Destination London (2008) suggests:

The visitor's experience begins when they are deciding where to go for their trip and continues after the trip has ended. Consequently, London needs to be exceptional in all aspects of the visitor journey; in providing the motivation to visit, in booking the trip, upon arrival, the duration of the stay, at the point of departure and in nurturing the memory. London needs to encourage its visitors to return and experience all that the capital has to offer. This has implications for marketing, information provision, skills, quality throughout all aspects of the visitor journey and the distribution of visitors.

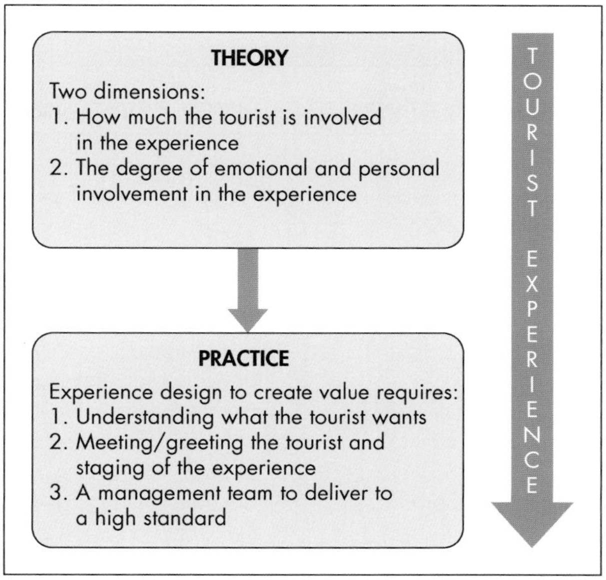

FIGURE 24.8 Designing tourist experiences

Source: Developed from Haathi and Komppula (2006)

One way to understand the tourist experience is to recognize how to design key features into the resulting experiential aspects, and Figure 24.7 highlights how to bring together both theoretical issues and more practical issues. The development of such experiential research has also led major organizations operating visitor attractions such as the National Trust in the UK to look more closely at these issues, as outlined by Calver and Page (2013).

Understanding the tourist experience is a key factor in determining the success of any tourist operation and has wider implications for the public perception of destinations, which requires appropriate tools and approaches to evaluate the tourist experience.

Evaluating the tourist experience

Despite being a key research issue in recent years (e.g. Vitterso *et al.* 2000), the study of the tourist experience remains one of the least understood fields in tourism research (Sharpley and Stone 2011). Beeho and Prentice (1997) note that the experiential aspects of tourism are often omitted from visitor survey research in favour of socio-demographic data collection and more easily identifiable issues, such as mode of transport used to access a recreation site. One of the major reasons for this neglect is that measuring the tourist experience is beset with conceptual and methodological problems, not the least of which is agreeing on the way in which the experience is framed and measured, as shown in Table 24.2 in terms of concepts and approaches used. Ryan recognized that the complexity of researching the tourist experience is due to its highly subjective nature, based on perception and cognitive views of the environment, as well as the products that tourists consume (see Figure 24.9). Otto and Ritchie (2000: 404) concur and state that in tourism, 'emotional reactions and decisions prevail'. Beeho and Prentice (1997: 75) recognize that 'visiting a tourist attraction is likely to involve a flow of experiences', which further complicates its study since there is likely to be a series of experiences rather than one focus, as tourists encounter different feelings and respond in different ways to each experiential element. This makes establishing a framework to evaluate the tourist experience a complex task which seeks to understand how tourists encounter places, people and their environment along with their responses. As Figure 24.10 shows, there are a range of perspectives to consider:

- theoretical perspectives
- operational issues related to professional practice by the tourism sector.

TABLE 24.2	Concepts used in the analysis of the tourist experience

Concept/Approach	Summary explanation
Confirmation-Disconfirmation theory	Comparing expectations and evaluations (e.g. use of ServQual).
Importance-evaluation	Use of theories such as reasoned behaviour and the multi-attribute approach.
Involvement theory	How far do people engage with the holiday experience – uses involvement theory from leisure studies.
Destination image	As shown in Chapter 14, how the visitor evaluates their experience against the concepts developed in marketing theory and how tourists construct their image of a place and the meanings inherent in these.
Theories of liminality	How the tourists transitions from the normal everyday life to a tourist experience and back again, a process, which may be characterized by different stages, roles and formalities.
Role-play approaches	As discussed in Chapter 4, this describes the roles tourists can play and adopt and involves an analysis of concepts of the extent to which familiarity/unfamiliarity and structured/unstructured experiences and stimulating/tranquil experiences are sought.
The tourist gaze	This is based on Urry's notion of the gaze and how the experience of a place is presented or framed by the tourism sector.
Authenticity	The extent to which tourists seek authentic visitor experiences.
Consumerist theories	As many tourist experiences are produced by commercially focused organizations, the experiences provided may not necessarily be authentic but are staged or manufactured.
Theories of mindlessness	Many of the activities associated with holidays are part of the ordinary way of life, so the provider needs to find ways of offering that are memorable so the tourist encounter is special.
Theories of mindfulness	Mindfulness has developed as a major concept in social psychology which relates to an individual being aware of the moment, and recognizing their feelings, thoughts and body, and has been used as a therapeutic technique, enjoying the moment. According to Tung and Ritchie (2011: 1374), mindfulness 'is a state of mind that draws distinctions, examining information from new perspectives . . .' and so the person sees many different opportunities from one situation. This means that 'mindfulness is a function of novelty, surprise, and variety and gives individuals power over their behaviours, especially in situations where they feel they have an opportunity to learn, control and exert influence' (Tung and Ritchie 2011: 1374). Mindfulness has been seen as having potential for enhancing tourist satisfaction, by presenting information to educate the visitor through different media to enhance their engagement and attention, especially where there is an emotive aspect to the information presented.
The travel career ladder	Pearce's career ladder, as discussed in Chapter 4, outlines how people develop a growing tourism career and this will shape the way they view experiences through time.
Additional perspectives:	• The experience of the holiday as a time-contingent activity in that there is a constrained period in which this activity can be undertaken. • Intimacy in the experience dependent upon whether you experience the place or event with someone else or alone/or the stage in the family lifecycle you are in. • Recreational concepts such as flow, risk and arousal all shape the way in which tourist experiences are shaped or constructed by individuals.

Source: Developed from Ryan (2011); Tung and Ritchie (2011)

24

The first step in this process is to establish the type of concepts one might wish to use to structure the notion of the tourist experience. As Table 24.2 suggests, there are diverse (and sometimes conflicting) approaches to adopt towards the analysis of the tourist experience. As Ryan (2011) demonstrates, the principal issues relate to long-standing debates about whether the tourist experience is something which is different to the everyday experience of life. Tung and Ritchie (2011) point to age-old theoretical discussions of sociologists and anthropologists such as Boorstin, Macanell and Cohen on the nature of such experiences and whether they are plural (i.e. various typologies of experience exist to fit different types of tourist). Table 24.2 incorporates these different theoretical debates and

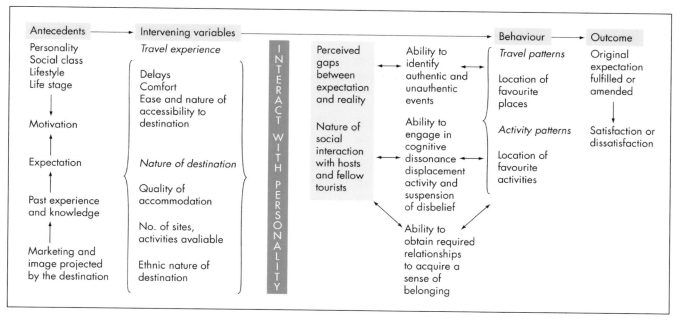

FIGURE 24.9 The link between expectation and satisfaction
Source: Ryan (2010: 42), copyright Routledge

the various methodologies used to assess each perspective. What is clear is the linkage with tourist motivation and the resulting experience in terms of satisfaction/dissatisfaction.

Research has focused on the tourist experience at heritage sites, presumably because, as Richards (1999) points out, 'heritage' alone is no longer sufficient in attracting visitors, and an understanding of visitors is a crucial aspect of ensuring future enterprise viability. Beeho and Prentice (1997) developed the use of the ASEB (activities, settings, experiences, benefits) grid analysis, a refinement of SWOT analysis (strengths, weaknesses, opportunities, threats), to gain insights into tourist experiences at the New Lanark World Heritage Village in Scotland. Experiences were found to be emotional; visitors found the village thought-provoking and overall an enjoyable educational experience. Having used the ASEB technique at the Black Country Museum, Beeho and Prentice (1997) suggest that the grid analysis method allows the experiential components of tourism to be studied. It can provide qualitative consumer insights into tourism experiences and how they might be improved at a site or destination level. The ASEB approach appears to be a feasible methodology for on-site examination of tourist experiences but would be impractical to use on a wider scale because of its open-ended nature.

Service quality and the tourist experience

Service delivery and quality is a well-established field of inquiry in the marketing and consumer behaviour literature. Tourism and recreation researchers have applied the notion of service quality in varied contexts, including outdoor recreation, hospitality, travel services and the airline industry. A number of models have been developed to evaluate quality and customer satisfaction in business operations, the most notable of which is SERVQUAL (Parasuraman *et al.* 1985). Considered as a seminal study in consumer behaviour, the basis of this evaluative framework is the difference between consumer expectation and perception of service, based on five generic service-quality dimensions necessary for customer satisfaction (see Table 24.3).

Further development of the model has led to the emergence of a range of allied quality assessment frameworks, such as HOLSAT to evaluate holiday experiences (Tribe and Smith 1998) and HISTOQUAL to evaluate the quality provided in historic houses (Frochot and Hughes

TABLE 24.3	Dimensions of service quality based on the SERVQUAL principle
Reliability	Ability to perform services dependably
Responsiveness	Willingness to assist customers and provide prompt service
Assurance	Courtesy, trustworthiness and knowledge of staff
Empathy	Display of caring attitude to customers
Tangibles	Presentation of physical facilities

24

2000). HOLSAT is designed to increase holiday satisfaction through the use of expectations/performance analysis. Key attributes of the destination are first identified and addressed, and then tourists' attitudes to these attributes are analyzed to produce a measure of satisfaction/dissatisfaction.

The HOLSAT method views satisfaction as the relationship between the performance of the holiday attributes against the expectation of the performance of these attributes as declared by tourists. Dissatisfaction is considered to have been experienced when expectations exceed the actual performance. Yet the five generic dimensions of service quality in Table 24.3 are a useful starting place for researching the tourist experience in relation to services. While Parasuraman *et al.* (1985) identified five gaps between service providers and consumers, later work suggested that another gap existed, that between the customer and the provider perception of the experience.

Gilbert and Joshi (1992) present an excellent review of the literature, including many of the concepts associated with the service quality. In tourism, it is the practical management of the 'gap' between the expected and the perceived service that requires attention by managers and the tourism industry. In reviewing Parasuraman *et al.*'s (1985) service quality model, Gilbert and Joshi (1992: 155) identify five gaps which exist between:

1 The expected service and the management's perceptions of the consumer experience (i.e. what they think the tourist wants) (**Gap 1**).

2 The management's perception of the tourist needs and the translation of those needs into service quality specifications (**Gap 2**).

3 The quality specifications and the actual delivery of the service (**Gap 3**).

4 The service delivery stage and the organization/provider's communication with the consumer (**Gap 4**).

5 The consumer's perception of the service they received and experienced, and their initial expectations of the service (**Gap 5**).

Gilbert and Joshi (1992) argue that the effective utilization of market research techniques could help to bridge some of the gaps. For:

Gap 1 – providers should be encouraged to elicit detailed information from consumers on what they require

Gap 2 – the management's ability to specify the service provided needs to be realistic and guided by clear quality standards

Gap 3 – the ability of employees to deliver the service according to the specification needs to be closely monitored and staff training and development is essential: a service is only as good as the staff it employs

Gap 4 – the promises made by service providers in their marketing and promotional messages need to reflect the actual quality offered. Therefore, if a city's promotional literature promises a warm welcome, human resource managers responsible for employees in front-line establishments need to ensure that this message is conveyed to its customers

Gap 5 – a major gap between the perceived service and delivered service should be reduced over time through progressive improvements in the appropriate image which is marketed to visitors and in the private sector's ability to deliver the expected service in an efficient and professional manner.

Such an approach to service quality emphasizes the importance of the marketing process in communicating and dealing with tourists. To obtain a better understanding of the service quality issues associated with the tourist's experience, Haywood and Muller (1988) identified a methodology for evaluating the quality of the tourist experience in an urban tourism setting.

Haywood and Muller's tourist experience framework

24

This framework involves collecting data on visitors' expectations prior to and after their city visit by examining a range of variables. It may be costly to operationalize, but it does provide a better appreciation of the visitation process than other methods and Haywood and Muller argue that cameras may also provide the day-to-day monitoring of city experiences. Haywood and Muller (1988) outline the factors to consider in evaluating the urban tourism experience (Table 24.4). These variables were selected as a result of a review of the literature on criteria for tourist attractiveness, city liveability measures and other experiential attributes. Table 24.4 indicates that there are a number

TABLE 24.4 Factors to consider in evaluating the urban tourism experience
• Unpleasantness of the city's weather during the visit
• Adequacy of standards in hotel accommodation
• Cleanliness and upkeep of the city
• The city's setting and scenic beauty
• Safety from crime
• Ease of finding and reaching places in the city
• Whether the city makes a visitor feel like a stranger
• Choice of artistic and cultural amenities
• Pleasurability of walking or strolling about the city
• Amount of crowding and congestion
• Choice of nightlife and entertainment
• Choice of good restaurants
• Pleasurability of shopping in the city
• Attractiveness of price levels
• Friendliness and helpfulness of citizens
• Adequacy of health care in case of emergency
Source: Adapted from Haywood and Muller (1988: 456) based on Connell (2002)

TABLE 24.5 Factors to consider in evaluating the garden visitor experience
• The weather conditions at the time of the visit
• The standard and quality of the garden and its features
• The tidiness and upkeep of the garden and cleanliness of facilities
• The setting and aesthetic value of the garden
• Health and safety considerations
• Accessibility of and ease of transport to the garden
• Access for disabled and less mobile visitors to the garden
• Warm and hospitable welcome extended to visitors
• Provision of information for international visitors
• The ambience of the garden as a place to walk around
• The level of crowding and congestion
• Range of events held in the garden
• Provision of a good quality tea room
• The opportunity and pleasurability of plant purchasing and other retail opportunities
• The price of entry to the garden and prices of other goods and services
• Staff helpfulness in responding to visitor enquiries
Source: Connell (2002)

of general factors which can be applied to any tourism environment which functions as a destination. It highlights the diversity of components that may contribute to the overall level of satisfaction. It is clear that some factors are less easy to control than others and also that subjective factors can affect the experience.

Although Haywood and Muller's (1988) framework relates very specifically to urban areas, it is a relatively straightforward task to rework these factors to apply to alternative tourism locations. Most of the factors listed in Table 24.3 are generic to most visitor destinations, merely requiring some rewording to make them appropriate to a particular setting. Connell (2002) adapted this framework for the visitor experience of garden visiting (Table 24.4) and modelled different elements of that experience.

What Connell (2005) acknowledges is that knowing what the customer expects is the first step in delivering quality service. Despite several attempts to delineate the features of the tourist experience, there is no specific theory or model that provides an overarching view. Yet it is evident that at a destination level, such as a country, a complex interplay of factors and organizations may be influential in shaping the tourist experience, as Insight 24.2 shows. In many evaluations of tourist experiences of products and services, the dominant element of dissatisfaction is often related to the staff–tourist encounter, and given the high human contact nature of tourism consumption, it is pertinent briefly to consider this feature.

INSIGHT 24.2 Evaluating the tourist destination experience

While the tourist experience can be modelled conceptually in relation to individual visitors, it is also possible to try to model it for a destination, as shown in Figure 24.9. Figure 24.10 seeks to try to understand the macro influences which shape tourism in a destination (e.g. demand, public sector interventions and the supply) as well as the influence of consumer behaviour and choice in selecting a country

to visit such as Scotland, where Figure 24.10 follows the customer journey (see Yachin 2018 on this concept). As Figure 24.10 suggests, a wide range of demand-led drivers influence destination choice, particularly the main motivating factors. One trend which is being viewed as important in shaping a visitor's desire to visit a destination and their expectations of the visit relates to the concept of cultural

INSIGHT 24.2 continued

capital. Cultural capital recognizes the growing affluence of visitors in mature Western economies and developing economies who possess greater levels of education, knowledge and choice of where to visit than they would in previous generations. Cultural capital suggests how visitors now communicate with their peers, in that they interact by comparing their experiences and activities. Cultural capital in this context refers to how visitors acquire value from visiting the destination and then add the experiences they gain to their social repertoire of places they have visited and can talk about; this is often communicated to peers on social media platforms such as Instagram. Cultural and social experiences in the destination are increasingly being recognized as a core element of what visitors seek, and the capital they acquire from visiting certain types of destination now affects how certain types of destinations are selected, as well as recommended through word of mouth and social networking.

The factors influencing a visit are filtered and rationalized by consumers in terms of their needs, wants, motivation and subsequent buyer behaviour to influence their choice of product, as discussed in Chapter 14. Influences upon this buying behaviour such as destination marketing and the tourism marketing process lead to product purchases and the distribution of the tourism product through various channels. As Chapter 8 has shown, transport and infrastructure development can begin to shape the visitor experience as travel to the destination commences.

The formative influences upon the type of experiences which the visitor interfaces with are influenced by subtle

and qualitative factors, through to more tangible elements such as accommodation, attractions, service encounters, entertainment and hospitality. In certain tourism settings, the ambience and environment can also be a key factor shaping the overall experience. The work of industry associations (e.g. the Scottish Tourism Forum) and sector-specific bodies such as the British Hospitality Association (BHA) can foster wider improvements and innovation in the sector, but it is at the destination level that potential exists to add value to the visitor experience. For example, a new product may be provided which attracts a new market to the destination (e.g. a new event and infrastructure to host a sport tourism event such as the World Mountain Bike Championships in Fort William). Yet at an operational level, the measurement and evaluation of the tourist experience (however it is conceptualized and developed into a measurable format), will need to be regularly undertaken. In Scotland, the Tourism Attitude Survey helps to establish many of the visitor satisfaction measures among a sample of visitors, which is fed back into the marketing process by the national tourism organization to help improve communication with the visitor.

What Figure 24.10 illustrates is the complexity of how the tourist experience is shaped and influenced as well as the multitude of businesses, organizations and bodies that can impact upon it. It also demonstrates that a lead body, which in this case is VisitScotland, needs to monitor and evaluate this experience so as to remain a competitive destination.

Human resource issues and the tourist experience

Employee performance is crucial in tourism, given the dependence upon staff to deliver many elements of the tourist experience, to add value and to delight the consumer. Since businesses are usually responsible for the tourist encounter at the micro level, these issues assume great significance for such businesses: staff can make or break the tourist experience, as already discussed. Positive interactions with staff can transform a negative experience, and there should be a constant focus on training personnel in interaction skills, as discussed in Chapter 11. Such programmes as Welcome Host, originally devised by the former English Tourist Board, and company schemes are useful to educate staff to provide quality service. The success of such programmes can be monitored through the analysis of customer comments and market research *and with the advent of social media, assessments of the tourist experience are now instantaneous*. This is part of how tourism businesses develop quality systems to ensure consistency and satisfaction with the services and products they supply. Foley *et al.* (1997) argue that systems of quality control need to be created to ensure that quality service delivery is taking place. Methods of monitoring and gaining feedback on quality include 'critical incident analysis'. This involves a detailed tracing back of service failures to discover what customers found to be unsatisfactory and how this can be avoided in the future. As Chung and Hoffman (1998: 66) state 'since the customer's perception of reality is the key factor, the analysis of service

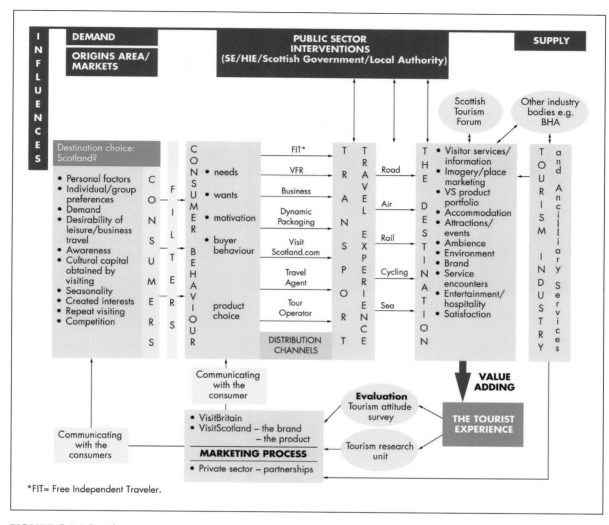

FIGURE 24.10 The tourist experience of tourism in Scotland

failures from the customer's point of view allows managers to minimize the occurrence of service failures through adjustments in operations and human resource procedures'. Another useful management tool in this context is the 'zero defect'. Everybody has a level of tolerance before deciding to make a complaint. Here the goal for the firm is to identify those tolerance levels and achieve 'zero defect', i.e. no complaints.

Quality marks also offer opportunities for guiding and forming quality expectations. National and international standards such as BS (British Standard) and ISO (International Organization for Standardization) can help businesses to design and implement quality management systems, the awarding of which can provide assurances to customers. The introduction of such standards may lead to a reduction in complaints, improved management and lessened need for third-party intervention. An important dimension in managing the tourist experience, in the context of the tourism firm, is the consideration of the aspect of service quality. To achieve this firms need the three 'S's': strategy, staff and systems. Businesses need a strategy to better understand the expectations and satisfaction of their customers and need to communicate service standards to their staff and provide them with adequate training. For employees in front-line positions this may involve dealing with stressful situations, requiring one to put on a smile and deal with an insulting customer: this has been described as emotional labour (Hochschild 1983). One consequence of emotional labour in service settings is a higher perceived level of stress for employees who may be associated with long hours of work, poor levels of remuneration and instability in employment conditions (Pienaar and Willemse 2009). This places additional demands upon the employer in the recruitment and selection of staff able to cope with these demands, as well as providing training and development so staff deliver consistent service standards. The management of difficult situations, such as cabin crew training to manage disruptive travellers (see Rhoden

24

IMAGE 24.2 A guide point on a tour adds value to the visitor experience

IMAGE 24.3 Memorable tourist experiences are crucial to encouraging repeat visits and recommendations. Palm trees and white sandy beaches in tropical locations are often the memorable elements in the stay

et al. 2008), is one example of how important investment in training and understanding of the phases in managing unruly travellers is (these are the trigger phase, escalation phase, crisis phase, recovery phase and post-crisis phase). Systems of quality may be assured through ISO standards being achieved.

Graefe and Vaske (1987) argue that the development of a management strategy is necessary to:

- deal with problem conditions which may impact on the tourist experience
- identify causes of such problems
- select appropriate management strategies to deal with problems

and that how businesses handle customers is a key element of such strategies.

Godfrey and Clarke (2000) offer a great deal of practical advice for looking after the tourist, particularly customer care in terms of adding value to the experience (Images 24.2 and 24.3), increasing the length of stay, generating positive word-of-mouth recommendation, encouraging repeat visits from satisfied visitors and differentiating the destination from competitors. They point to five interrelated themes for retaining tourists:

- a tourist-focused organization and industry
- authenticity in the experience
- provision of quality experiences and a commitment to quality by businesses
- integration in the tourism sector through cooperation to get strategic advantages over competitors
- innovation, with creative thinking and product/service development which can often be achieved by making small, incremental changes to make a difference.

In setting up a service quality standard, Godfrey and Clarke (2000) point to the importance of introducing:

- *hard standards*, where definable standards can be measured to assess progress and outcomes
- *soft standards*, where measures such as staff friendliness, courtesy and ability can be assessed.

One of the most important features here, which tourists are quick to judge, is the ability of business to handle complaints. As a result, destinations need to empower staff to address complaints in a systematic and professional manner, as discussed in Chapter 11. Godfrey and Clarke (2000) outline a number of practical tips for staff handling complaints (Figure 24.11) to ensure dissatisfied customers can have their grievance resolved.

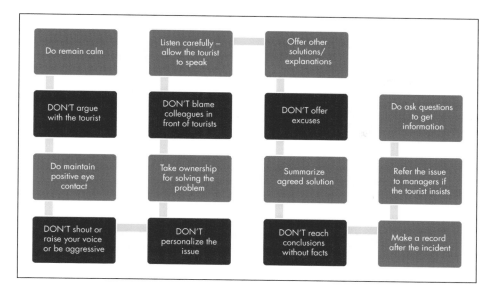

FIGURE 24.11 Selected positive and negative tips for staff handling tourist complaints
Source: Developed from Godfrey and Clarke (2000: 178)

Conclusion

The management of tourism and its different facets requires the involvement of the public sector in tourism (see Chapter 13) to ensure that private sector activities do not seek to unbalance the relationship between tourism and the resource base upon which it depends. This illustrates the need for a planning system and means by which tourism growth can be managed and controlled to achieve a more sustainable approach to tourism (see Chapter 19). Aside from these restraining motives for planning tourism, there are also important commercial and competitive reasons for developing a clear strategy for tourism in a destination, not least to ensure that the tourist experience is understood and the needs of visitors are met. Evaluating the tourist experience is a complex process which involves modelling the elements that may affect the experience and then measuring the tourists' views and attitudes, often against a scale or list of factors. This is both a time-consuming and a costly process and yet its value to the tourism industry should not be underestimated. The motivating factors (i.e. the tourist's perception of what makes them choose a particular destination); their actual activities; and the extent to which their expectations are matched by reality, all feed into how satisfying the experience of being a tourist may be. The highly personal nature of tourist expectations and satisfaction is highly subjective and changeable, making it hard for the tourism industry to create products that will guarantee satisfaction. But this is vital to the future viability and sustainability of tourism destinations, and it is not surprising that many tourism destinations are concerned with ways in which they can manage the tourist experience in order to improve it overall.

The management of the tourist experience is an absolutely vital, but complex requirement. Tourism planning is part of a wider planning process, however, where the needs of other industries as well as the local population are considered, and the tourist experience is often overlooked. Therefore, there is a need for national policies to integrate with tourism policies at the regional or local level with clear guidelines on what the tourist experience is deemed to be and how to add value to it. To be successful the wider tourism industry needs to have a strategy for understanding their customers, employ well-trained staff and have an appropriate system of quality assurance, all of which are prerequisites for achieving a prosperous tourism sector.

Discussion questions

1 Why is tourism planning needed in tourism?

2 Who is responsible for the tourism planning process and what are the stages involved in developing a tourism plan?

3 What is the tourist experience?

4 How would you develop a plan to assess the tourist experience of tourism for a specific destination?

24

References

Acernaza, M. (1985) 'Planificación estratégica del turismo: Esquesma metológico', *Estudios Turisticos*, 85: 45–70.

Adu-Ampong, E. (2018) 'Historical trajectories of tourism development policies and planning in Ghana, 1957–2017', *Tourism Planning and Development*, 16 (2): 124–141.

Beeho, A. and Prentice, R. (1997) 'Conceptualizing the experiences of heritage tourists: A case study of New Lanark World Heritage Village', *Tourism Management*, 18 (2): 75–87.

Calver, S. and Page, S.J. (2013) 'Enlightened hedonism: Exploring the relationship of service value, visitor knowledge and interest, to visitor enjoyment at heritage attractions', *Tourism Management* 39: 23–36.

Chadwick, G. (1971) *A Systems View of Planning*. Oxford: Pergamon.

Chung, B. and Hoffman, K.D. (1998) 'Critical incidents: Service failures that matter most', *Cornell Hotel and Restaurant Administration Quarterly*, June: 54–70.

Connell, J. (2002) 'A critical analysis of gardens as a resource for tourism and recreation in Great Britain', unpublished Ph.D. thesis, Department of Geographical Sciences, University of Plymouth.

Connell, J. (2005) 'Toddlers, tourism and Tobermory: Destination marketing issues and television-induced tourism', *Tourism Management*, 26 (5): 763–776.

Cooper, C.P., Fletcher, J., Gilbert, D.G. and Wanhill, S. (1998) *Tourism: Principles and Practice*. Harlow: Addison Wesley Longman.

Destination London (2008) *Improving the Visitor Experience*. https://destinationlondon2000.com/

Edgell, D., Allen, M., Swansong, J. and Smith, G. (2008) *Tourism Policy and Planning: Yesterday, Today and Tomorrow*. Oxford: Butterworth-Heinemann.

Estol, J. and Font, X. (2016) 'European tourism policy: Its evolution and structure', *Tourism Management*, 52: 230–241.

Foley, M., Lennon, J.J. and Maxwell, G.A. (1997) *Hospitality, Tourism and Leisure Management: Issues in Strategy and Culture*. London: Cassell.

Frochot, I. and Hughes, H. (2000) 'HISTOQUAL: The development of a historic houses assessment scale', *Tourism Management*, 21 (2): 157–167.

Getz, D. (1987) 'Tourism planning and research: Traditions, models and futures'. Paper presented at the Australian Travel Research Workshop, Bunbury, Western Australia, 5–6 November.

Gilbert, D. and Joshi, I. (1992) 'Quality management and the tourism and hospitality industry', in C. Cooper and A. Lockwood (eds.) *Progress in Tourism, Recreation and Hospitality Management, Vol. 4*. London: Belhaven.

Godfrey, K. and Clarke, J. (2000) *The Tourism Development Handbook: A Practical Approach to Planning and Marketing*. London: Cassell.

Gössling, S. (2001) 'The consequences of tourism for sustainable water use on a tropical island: Zanzibar, Tanzania', *Journal of Environmental Management*, 61 (2): 179–191.

Graefe, A. and Vaske, J. (1987) 'A framework for managing quality in the tourist experience', *Annals of Tourism Research*, 14 (3): 389–404.

Gunn, C. (1988) *Tourism Planning*, 2nd edition. London: Taylor and Francis.

Haahti, A. and Komppula, R. (2006) 'Experience design in tourism', in D. Buhalis and C. Costa (eds.), *Tourism Business Frontiers: Consumers, Products and Industry* (pp. 101–110). Oxford: Elsevier.

Hall, C.M. (1999) *Tourism Planning: Policies, Processes and Relationships*. Harlow: Addison Wesley Longman.

Harilal, V., Tichaawa, T. and Saarinen, J. (2018) '"Development without policy": Tourism planning and research needs in Cameroon, Central Africa', *Tourism Planning and Development*.

Haywood, K. and Muller, T. (1988) 'The urban tourist experience: Evaluating satisfaction', *Hospitality Education and Research Journal*, 12 (2): 453–459.

Heeley, J. (1981) 'Visitor attractions and the commercial sector', *Insights*, D1–D13.

Hochschild, A. (1983) *The Managed Heart*. Berkeley, CA: University of California Press.

Inskeep, E. (1991) *Tourism Planning: An Integrated and Sustainable Development Approach*. New York: Van Nostrand Reinhold.

Inskeep, E. (1994) *National and Regional Tourism Planning: Methodologies and Case Studies*. London: Routledge.

Jennings, G. and Nickerson, N. (eds.) (2006) *Quality Tourism Experiences*. Oxford: Butterworth-Heinemann.

Lai, K., Li, Y. and Feng, X. (2006) 'Gap between tourism planning and implementation: A case of China', *Tourism Management*, 27 (6): 1171–1180.

Otto, J.E. and Ritchie, J.R. (2000) 'The service experience in tourism', in C. Ryan and S.J. Page (eds.) *Tourism Management Towards the New Millennium*. Oxford: Pergamon.

Page, S.J., Essex, S. and Causevic, S. (2014) 'Tourist attitudes towards water use in the developing world: A comparative analysis', *Tourism Management Perspectives*, 10: 57–67.

Page, S.J. and Thorn, K. (1997) 'Towards sustainable tourism planning in New Zealand: Public sector planning responses', *Journal of Sustainable Tourism*, 5 (1): 59–77.

Page, S.J. and Thorn, K. (2002) 'Towards sustainable tourism planning in New Zealand: Public sector planning responses revisited', *Journal of Sustainable Tourism*, 10 (3): 222–239.

Parasuraman, A., Zeithaml, V. and Berry, L. (1985) 'A conceptual model of service quality and its implications for future research', *Journal of Marketing*, 49 (4): 41–50.

Pearce, D. (1988) *Tourist Development*, 2nd edition. Harlow: Longman.

Pienaar, J. and Willemse, S. (2009) 'Burnout, engagement, coping and general health of service employees in the hospitality industry', *Tourism Management*, 29 (6): 1053–1063.

Rhoden, S., Ralston, R. and Ineson, E. (2008) 'Cabin crew training to control disruptive airline passenger behaviour: A cause for concern?', *Tourism Management*, 29 (3): 538–547.

24

Richards, G. (1999) 'Heritage visitor attractions in Europe: A visitor profile', *Interpretation*, 4 (3): 9–13.

Ryan, C. (ed.) (1997) *The Tourist Experience: A New Introduction*. Cassell: London.

Ryan, C. (2010) 'Ways of conceptualising the tourist experience: A review of literature', *Tourism Recreation Research* 35 (1): 37–46.

Ryan, C. (2011) 'Ways of conceptualising the tourist experience: A review of literature', in R. Sharpley and P. Stone (eds.) *Tourist Experience: Contemporary Perspectives*. London: Routledge.

Schouten, F. (1995) 'Improving visitor care in heritage attractions', *Tourism Management*, 16 (4): 259–261.

Shakeela, A. and Weaver, D. (2016) 'The Maldives: Parallel paths of conventional and alternative tourism', in C.M. Hall and S.J. Page (eds.) *The Routledge Handbook of Tourism in Asia* (pp. 265–274). London, Routledge.

Sharpley, R. and Stone, P. (eds.) (2011) *Tourist Experience: Contemporary Perspectives*. London: Routledge.

Swarbrooke, J. and Horner, S. (2001) 'Researching tourist satisfaction', *Insights*, A161–A169.

Tourism Commission of Zanzibar (n.d.) *Zanzibar Tourism Policy*. Tourism Commission of Zanzibar (website). http://www.zanzibartourism.go.tz/images/joomlart/documents/Zanzibar_Tourism_Policy.pdf.

Tribe, J. and Smith, T. (1998) 'From SERQUAL to HOLSAT: Holiday satisfaction in Varadero, Cuba', *Tourism Management*, 19 (1): 25–34.

Tung, V. and Ritchie, J.B.R. (2011) 'Exploring the essence of memorable tourism experiences', *Annals of Tourism Research*, 38 (4): 1367–1386.

Vitterso, J., Vorkinn, M., Vistad, O. and Vaagland, J. (2000) 'Tourist experiences and attractions', *Annals of Tourism Research*, 27 (2): 432–450.

Yachin, J.M. (2018) 'The "customer journey": Learning from customers in tourism experience encounters', *Tourism Management Perspectives*, 28: 201–210.

Further reading

Books

Andriotis, K., Stylidis, D. and Weidenfeld, A. (eds.) (2018) *Tourism Policy and Planning Implementation: Issues and Challenges*. London: Routledge.

Edgell, D. and Swanson, J. (2018) *Tourism Policy and Planning: Yesterday, Today and Tomorrow*. London: Routledge.

Ryan, C. (1994) *Researching Tourist Satisfaction: Issues, Concepts and Problems*. London: Routledge.

Journal articles

Almeida, J., Costa, C. and Nunes da Silva, F. (2017) 'A framework for conflict analysis in spatial planning for tourism', *Tourism Management Perspectives*, 24: 94–106.

Baidal, J.A.I. (2004) 'Regional tourism planning in Spain: Evolution and perspectives', *Annals of Tourism Research*, 31 (2): 313–333.

Dredge, D. and Jamal, T. (2015) 'Progress in tourism planning and policy: A post-structural perspective on knowledge production', *Tourism Management*, 51: 285–297.

Lu, L. and Goulden, M. (2006) 'A comparative analysis of international tourists' satisfaction in Mongolia', *Tourism Management*, 27 (6): 1331–1342.

Milano, C., Novelli, M. and Cheer, J. (2019) 'Overtourism and tourismphobia: A journey through four decades of tourism development, planning and local concerns', *Tourism Planning and Development*, 16 (4): 353–357.

Mohammed, S. (2002) 'Pollution management in Zanzibar: the need for a new approach', *Ocean and Coastal Management*, 45 (3): 301–311.

Uriely, N. (2005) 'The tourist experience: Conceptual developments', *Annals of Tourism Research*, 32 (1): 199–216.

25

Tourist health and safety: Global challenges for tourism

Learning outcomes

After reading this chapter and answering the questions, you should be able to:

- understand the significance of health and safety issues in the operation and management of tourism

- identify the range of issues which may impact upon the tourist and the destination in terms of tourist well-being

- outline some of the main links between tourism and health, tourism and crime and the role which public sector agencies play in managing these issues

- explain how a tourism crisis can impact upon a destination.

Overview

Tourist health and safety is now a global theme associated with tourist travel as a wide range of threats, risks and potential hazards affect travellers. This chapter provides an overview of these threats and risks, together with a framework for conceptualizing and analyzing these issues. There is growing evidence that tourist safety, especially the role or threat of terrorism, is now one of the top ten most important world tourism issues for both travellers and the tourism sector. For this reason, tourist travel is increasingly being affected by global issues which may affect our propensity to travel, and the tourism industry in different destinations.

Introduction

Throughout the history of travel, visitors have faced the tourist-related phenomenon of leaving their home environment to visit one which they may find unfamiliar, and the associated risks and hazards inherent in their lack of knowledge associated with that environment. This highlights two interrelated themes which combine to make tourist travel unique: the pursuit of enjoyment, rest, relaxation and the use of leisure time in unfamiliar surroundings to improve one's sense of well-being (Gilbert and Abdullah 2004) combined with the associated environmental and behavioural-related risks. The underlying risks, potential hazards and safety issues which travellers face is predominantly a function of the knowledge of the individual or group travelling, and their willingness and ability to understand the information available to adapt their behaviour to reduce the potential risks. However, certain forms of tourism (e.g. adventure tourism) are based upon the notion of risk to generate an experience of being a tourist that is memorable, involving significant personal or group risk. This may take the form of seeking the enjoyment of a personal challenge posed by environmental risk (e.g. mountaineering, white-water rafting or potholing), although generalizations are best avoided when examining the different motivations and segments in niche markets such as adventure tourism. This chapter seeks to provide a wide-ranging understanding of the scope and extent of the issues associated with tourist health and safety, together with a discussion of concepts essential to understand how the notion of tourist safety and well-being are integral to tourist enjoyment and the tourist experience (see Chapter 24).

When things go wrong, a growing culture of litigation in travel and tourism can often have dire financial consequences for businesses and can tarnish the image of a destination or product. This has led to the growth of interest in practical measures to address major problems, especially crises like the Bali bombing, biosecurity risks associated with the importation of microorganisms by visitors that can harm the agricultural sector (Hall 2005), the 9/11 terrorist attack, the 2004 tsunami in Japan and the Christchurch earthquake in 2010–2011 (see Orchiston and Higham 2016). Such events can lead to major impacts on the tourism economy, environment and resident and visitor population. In 2004, the Indian Ocean tsunami led to 250 000 deaths and the WTTC (World Travel and Tourism Council) estimated that the cost to tourism would be £3 billion (but 9/11 was estimated to have cost 37.5 times that amount). The World Tourism Organization has devised practical advice for destinations to address such issues with a crisis recovery strategy, arguing that action needs to be taken:

- before the crisis, with the active preparation of a crisis management plan
- during the crisis, so as to minimize damage, as the 9/11 Insight will show later in the chapter
- after the crisis, with a recovery strategy to boost visitor confidence and active strategies to boost tourist numbers by promotion campaigns.

But these events are comparatively rare when viewed in the context of the wider issues which prevail in relation to tourist health and safety and, therefore, throughout the chapter, appropriate examples and insights illustrate the significance of tourist health and safety as a growing area of research (e.g. Clift and Page 1996) in tourism studies, as shown by the rapid expansion in articles and books in this area (see Page 2009 for a review). These issues have growing significance for both the tourist and the tourism industry as illustrated in the UN–WTO (2011) review of global tourism issues. Yet, given the complexity of tourist health and safety, it is useful to examine some of the ways this can be understood.

Conceptualizing tourist health and safety

The media are a powerful force in modern-day society and the imagery, headlines and reporting of global events have portrayed the immediacy of threats posed by terrorist groups and natural disasters (e.g. hurricanes and floods) to tourist destinations. For example, according to data from the Centre of Research on the Epidemiology of Disasters, 18 000 disasters have occurred since 1900 and the scope and extent of these is illustrated in Figure 25.1. In 2018, the greatest impact of disasters occurred in Asia where 45 per cent of them were located and where 80 per cent of deaths occurred, 35 per cent in India alone. Figures like these increasingly heighten the traveller's awareness of potential risks, but this alone will not ensure their safety and well-being, since the risk-taking behaviour of the tourist is also crucial to understanding why some individuals avoid risk while others seek risk. This was discussed in Chapter 4 in relation to tourist typologies. Tourist behaviour will directly influence the willingness of the tourist to listen to health education promotions, safety advice and the messages from the media on specific

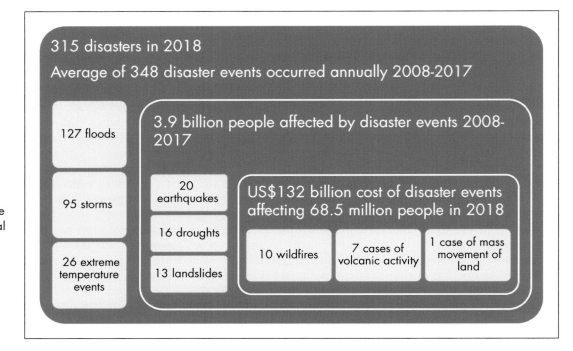

FIGURE 25.1 The scale of international disasters in 2018 Source: Developed from Centre for Research on the Epidemiology of Disasters (CRED) (2018)

destinations and activities. Therefore, the complexity of tourists' behaviour and actions needs to be understood in some organizing framework which outlines the basic assumptions and features of tourist health, safety and well-being.

Tourist well-being

Tourist well-being is beginning to be accepted by researchers and the tourism industry as an important concept in relation to tourist satisfaction, which will shape purchase behaviour and recommendations as well as the tourist experience. A dissatisfied visitor is the worst publicity for a destination or product, as word-of-mouth dissemination of the experience can damage its credibility and image. As previous chapters have shown, tourist satisfaction is a measure of the satisfaction/dissatisfaction with the product and overall experience. But this in itself does not broach the fundamental issue associated with visitor safety: who is responsible for the well-being of the tourist? Walker and Page (2003) discussed this issue, identifying a wide range of agencies and bodies who interact with tourists and who collectively have a responsibility for the tourist, as shown in Figure 25.2. This is not to suggest that tourists should not be responsible for their own actions, but the unfamiliarity with a destination means that the various agencies who interact with tourists should also have a responsibility for their well-being (Unter-Jones 2000), and thereby their resulting satisfaction/dissatisfaction with the destination and product. As the tourist experience is such a complex and multifarious phenomenon, there are a wide range of factors which can impact upon the resulting perception and satisfaction; safety and the well-being of the visitor are core elements in the experience. As Figure 25.3 confirms, tourist health and safety are essentially bound up in the wider tourist experience of the destination but few studies have explicitly discussed the roles and responsibilities of the visitor. In an age that is increasingly marked by the tendency to litigate when things go wrong (Callander and Page 2003), this debate is becoming more critical, over and above directives such as the EU's (1993) Package Holiday Directive (and subsequent revisions), which sets out who is responsible for the commercial transaction. Tourist well-being is a complex topic because it is value-laden, meaning that to some observers the tourist's experience and well-being assume a high-profile role but to others the public policy approach means that these are not issues to consider. Thus, those destinations which treat tourist well-being and seriously and coordinate many of the issues outlined in Figure 25.2 deal with incidents quickly and efficiently. Therefore, positive notions of well-being in the destination can become a potential competitive advantage. If the tourist feels safe and well looked after, and their stay is as problem-free as possible, then word of mouth on the destination disseminates positive recommendations.

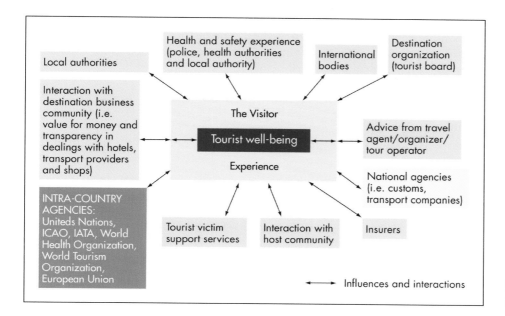

FIGURE 25.2 Influences upon tourist well-being at the destination

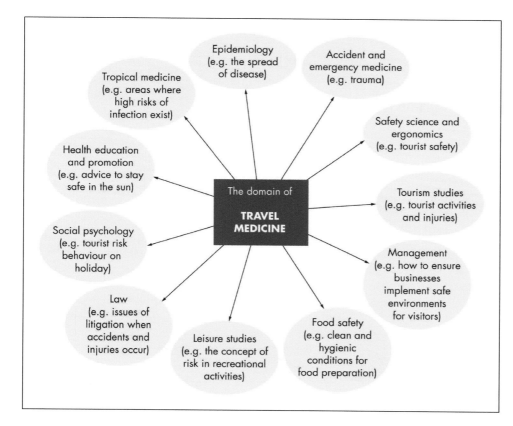

FIGURE 25.3 Subjects contributing to the development of travel medicine

The overall notion of well-being, where the reason for taking a holiday is a positive experience during leisure time, highlights the importance of understanding how important health and safety issues are. One field which has emerged as a growth area for researchers is travel medicine. However, this is not a new phenomenon, as the medical journal *The Lancet* has published articles on the subject since the 1890s. What has given the topic a boost in the period since the 1970s is the worldwide growth of tourism and travel, which has created a mobile population and various opportunities for researchers across the science and social science spectrum to study tourism from a new perspective, as Figure 25.3 indicates. The wide range of interests is also more diverse than this diagram conveys, since within medicine there are different specialisms which impact upon the study of tourism, for example accident

25

and emergency medicine, treating tourist trauma and injuries, epidemiological analysis of risks through to a growing interest in tourist travel for medical reasons. For example, the rise of medical tourism and costs of treatment in the developed world has led to the rise of medical tourists obtaining treatment in other countries such as India (Connell 2013). This has created a new dimension to travel for health and well-being.

The three key principles which underpin the role of travel medicine in tourism are:

- providing specialist medical advice to impending travellers with a view to preventing risks and morbidity associated with travel (a prevention role)
- assessment of known or likely hazards associated with a specific form of tourist travel and the prescribing of prophylactics to reduce risks (risk assessment)
- generic health advice and information to advise travellers of necessary behavioural issues associated with travel to certain areas and destinations (information role). This is epitomized, as discussed later in the chapter, by the UK Government's Foreign and Commonwealth Office's Travel Advisories of areas to which UK tourists should not travel. While such a geographical distribution of destinations to avoid will change through time, it does highlight the importance of informing potential tourists of areas of political instability and areas with a high propensity for the kidnapping of tourists (e.g. some South American destinations).

These features of travel medicine are broadly consistent with Leggatt *et al.*'s (2002: 3) attempt to define this evolving area of study:

Travel medicine seeks to prevent illnesses and injuries occurring to travellers going abroad and manages problems arising in travellers coming back or coming from abroad. Tourist health is also concerned about the impact of tourism on health and advocates for improved health and safety services for tourists.

One way of illustrating the potential scope and scale of such issues is shown in Figure 25.4. This shows that there are many high-risk/high-volume health and safety issues which impact upon tourist travel and the tourist experience which may be preventable if appropriate advice and action are offered prior to and during the visit. This highlights the importance of:

- pre-travel planning
- the trip from origin to destination
- personal safety and tourist health at the destination (Image 25.1)
- tourist health on the return to the origin area or subsequent areas they pass through, especially in the case of SARS and influenza, which was transmitted by travellers moving across borders and by air travel.

There is a considerable variability in the accuracy of information and advice offered by travel professionals in the pre-travel stage. For example, in a study of New Zealand travel agents' advice to outbound travellers to the Pacific Islands, Lawton and Page (1997) identified significant omissions and oversights. They concluded that guidebooks such as the **Lonely Planet** offered more robust and reliable information, although they were not as up to date about information on health risks and inoculations needed from GPs and practice nurses. In the UK, travel clinics and online travel advice make extensive use of global surveillance sources from the World Health Organization and the Centers for Disease Control, Atlanta, USA, and the equivalent UK body. The significance of these bodies was illustrated during the SARS outbreak (2009) and coronavirus in 2019–20 and they assumed a critical surveillance role in advising visitors on travel plans, travel behaviour and risk factors, highlighting the interconnections between tourism and health inferred in Figure 25.2 between the destination and inter-country agencies.

Figure 25.4 also shows that advice on other high-risk events such as kidnapping and crime can be obtained from government surveillance websites such as the CIA and the Foreign and Commonwealth Office in London,

25

IMAGE 25.1 Innovative new tourism experiences such as glass bottomed bridges in China may create safety concerns

as discussed later in the chapter. Low-risk events like traveller's diarrhoea, which can affect high proportions of visitors during a package holiday depending upon the destination visited, can be treated by appropriate drugs. In 2011, in the USA there were 14 outbreaks of the highly infectious and hard to kill norovirus *e-coli*, which causes acute gastroenteritis (i.e. diarrhoea and sickness), on board cruise ships calling at US ports. Outbreaks affected between 4.4 per cent and 7 per cent of passengers. In 2016, there were 13 outbreaks of norovirus and rotavirus, 11 in 2017 and 11 in 2018. Yet as the CDC (Centers for Disease Control) indicated, the scale of the issue was 74 million cruise-line passengers at US ports and 129 678 outbreaks of diarrhoea and sickness with 1:10 caused by acute gastroenteritis (norovirus and rotavirus). The severity of this

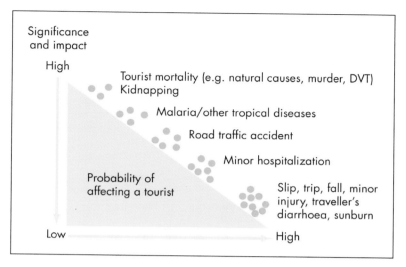

FIGURE 25.4 Tourist health and safety problems: Scale and incidence

virus has led some cruise firms to waive the cancellation penalties rather than have passengers who are vulnerable to illness travelling and contracting the virus. Norovirus is a mild and self-limiting acute gastroenteritis disease. Indeed, the extent of travel health issues is reflected in the specialist publications like the *Journal of Travel Medicine* which has highlighted that over 50 per cent of travellers returning to Australia after visiting less developed countries (LDCs) reported health problems. More worrying is the recent mutation of animal viruses which have jumped across to humans, like avian flu. Numerous studies exist in the *Journal of Travel Medicine* on the possible causes and risk factors associated with commonly reported travel health problems (e.g. motion sickness, car accidents, injuries and accidents) as well as less common events such as tourist mortality, commonly associated with cardiovascular problems.

The studies of travellers' health published in the *Journal of Travel Medicine* reveals the correlation of specific tourist groups (e.g. kidnapping of backpackers in South America) and market segments (youth travellers) in terms of car accidents as well as certain risk factors that make specific groups more likely to incur injury. The travel insurance industry is fully cognizant of these issues, and they are reflected in their premiums for specific destinations, exclusions for specific activities and the application of excesses for commonly reported health and safety issues. As any form of human activity will involve risk (Page and Meyer 1996), then injuries, accidents and safety issues will occur. For the tourism industry and the wide range of agencies who interact in this area to provide advice and information, their responsibility is to point the visitor to necessary advice. Should they choose not to take that advice or heed the warnings, the tourism sector has fulfilled its obligations. In these cases, insurance provision can often be invalidated where the 'small print' requires advice to be followed. There is a global recognition among insurers of the importance of risk assessment by destination and activities to be undertaken, and one area of growing concern among the travel sector and the travelling public is air travel and the problems this may pose. This is discussed in Insight 25.1.

Tourist health and safety problems and destinations

The seminal study by Cossar *et al.* (1990) examined the problems among over 14 000 returning Scottish holiday-makers to understand the problems they faced in the destination and the common issues they faced on their return. Thirty-six per cent of travellers reported some element of illness including diarrhoea and vomiting (18 per cent), alimentary problems (10 per cent) and respiratory problems (2 per cent) along with accidents and injuries. These figures are consistent with many of the in-house studies undertaken by tour operators on the return journey although these remain confidential to the operator. Nevertheless, subsequent studies of tourist health highlight the range and scope of problems which impact upon the tourist experience in the destination. In most extreme cases, tourist mortality may be a media issue, particularly where it is associated with crime or road accidents.

25

INSIGHT 25.1 Tourist health problems and air travel

In the pre-travel, travel and post-travel phases of tourism, air travel now plays a major role in the movement of would-be holidaymakers from origin to destination. At each stage, tourist health can actually be adversely affected (temporarily or in extreme cases permanently) rather than improved through travel. Take, for example, the journey from home to the airport and the perceived and actual stress of check-in, waiting around in crowded departure lounges, delays, and the impact upon a population with increased levels of high blood pressure. This can not only raise anxiety levels, which are high for infrequent fliers, but also may contribute towards and compound existing medical conditions.

Among the common problems associated with air travel are motion sickness, which is potentially caused (although research evidence is not conclusive) by the stress of travel (over half of travellers have a fear of flying (Abeyratne 2008)) and imbalance in the ear which causes nausea and vomiting. Yet two of the more controversial issues affecting travellers involves the onset of **deep vein thrombosis (DVT)** and the poor quality of cabin air.

DVT was in the world media (dubbed 'economy class syndrome' – Porodko *et al.* 2002) in recent years after a number of people developed the condition following a lack of mobility and cramped seating on board aircraft on long-haul flights, resulting in death or an embolism. While research is still in its infancy on the topic, high-profile court actions and media attention have led some airlines to improve the pitch of seating (the distance between the seats) to make long-haul more comfortable. Precautions for those most at risk include increased mobility of the passenger in flight, medical DVT-preventing socks, and exercises. Although the number of reported cases has been relatively low, where data exist, they have highlighted an additional problem with mass air travel. Yet this problem is much less widespread than the effect of jet lag, where long-haul travel crossing different time zones causes the body's circadian rhythms to be affected. Many remedies exist for jet lag and these are listed on popular travel websites.

The second prominent problem which has also hit the media headlines is the quality of cabin air. As the cost of providing air in flight, particularly fresh air, requires additional fuel, the quality is highly variable. As a result, the cockpit and first/business-class passengers enjoy better standards of air, leading to less dehydration, while dry eyes, throat and noses result from poorer air which is recirculated. The use of HEPA filters is recommended to improve air quality but it depends upon the budgeting for this by airline companies. Research by the UK government (UK Government Select Committee on Science and Technology on Air Travel and Health 2007) in November 2000 indicated the need for airlines to improve on-board air quality to help address the well-being issues for passengers, mirroring the lobbying by groups in the USA such as the American Cabin Crew Associations. The UK government also highlighted the need for better monitoring of these issues and to improve travel advice via the available leaflets and online advice.

Tourist road traffic accidents (RTAs) in the destination are a common non-fatal but serious health and safety issue, after more personal health issues that can be avoided by taking careful precautions on the food and water which is consumed, often following the advice: 'Don't eat or drink it if it has not been boiled, cooked or washed.' However, in the case of RTAs, these commonly result from:

- tourists being unfamiliar with local road conditions
- tourists driving too fast
- tourists being under the influence of drugs or alcohol
- tourists lacking experience of driving in other countries' terrains
- tourists failing to give way to other vehicles and to pedestrians
- driver fatigue and falling asleep at the wheel
- defects with vehicles
- poor visibility or experience of overtaking on unfamiliar roads
- following too close to other vehicles
- sudden braking or swerving
- poor weather conditions.

In many cases, a combination of factors contribute to accidents and injuries (Rosselló and Saenz-de-Miera 2011; Castillo-Manzano *et al.* 2018). Fortunately, most accidents are not serious and where hospitalization occurs it may be fewer than ten days. In Bermuda, for example, tourist RTAs had an incidence of 1.57 accidents per 1000 visitors, while among US tourist deaths abroad, 28 per cent were the result of car accidents. In contrast, these were the most common cause of death for international visitors to the USA. In Scotland, in the new Loch Lomond and Trossachs National Park, the geographical patterns of tourist accidents concentrated at specific blackspots where visibility was poor or speed combined with rapidly changing road conditions, causing serious RTAs and fatalities. Yet the most problematic issue for the national park was the volume of weekend leisure and domestic motorcyclists who rode at excessive speeds and took big risks in overtaking, leading to numerous fatalities on certain stretches of road. In fact, the UN Foreign and Commonwealth Office (FCO) observed that around 12 000 deaths occurred on Thailand's roads every year (three times the UK average), making this a major risk for British tourists. The risk increased among those riding motorbikes in Thailand as motorcycles account for 70 per cent of all road-related fatalities. While many of these safety issues are a direct result of risky tourist behaviour in the destination area, the other notable issue for destinations is tourist crime and safety.

Tourist crime and safety in destination areas

An extensive tourism and criminology literature (Jones *et al.* 2013) has been developed around the theme of tourism and crime (Walker and Page 2007; Boakyo 2012). Despite the development of many key studies in this area (e.g. Pizam and Mansfeld 2005), there is no clear evidence to support the notion that the development of tourism in destination areas leads to crime. Nevertheless, a wide range of case studies of destinations exist which highlight two important themes:

- the perceived risks of visiting a destination due to the images, perceived safety and likelihood of a safe visit
- the actual occurrence of incidents affected by crime such as robbery, assault, terrorism, murder, kidnapping and victimization.

The scope of tourist-related crime is largely undocumented in many destinations, and the less frequent occurrence of tourists victimizing local residents (e.g. including hedonistic behaviour by football hooligans travelling as sports tourists to other countries) remains even less documented, despite media attention when it occurs. One example illustrates the problem of understanding the scope and scale of the problem: in Ireland, the Irish police force, the Garda, estimate that of 6 million visits a year, 3200–3400 tourists become victims of crime. In contrast, estimates for Europe by the organization Victim Support suggest up to 8 million tourists are the victims of crime each year, which occurs almost entirely in the destination area.

A common set of behavioural issues exist for travellers: they tend to be less safety conscious when travelling, and engage in more deliberate or indirect forms of risk behaviour (i.e. visiting areas of destinations they do not perceive to be no-go or crime hot spots) and these factors make them much more liable to be victims of crime. Tourists also exhibit many visible elements which make them targets for crime including racial differences, cultural differences such as clothing type and the existence of expensive portable items such as cameras or video cameras. This combines with behavioural traits such as more hedonistic activity associated with the enjoyment of alcohol. As a result, tourists aged 15–24 years of age are most likely to be the victims of crime on holiday.

In common with other forms of criminology, predatory tourist-related crime tends to geographically cluster in areas which police identify as hot spots, notably in tourist shopping areas, resort areas and where tourists congregate (i.e. at attractions). Existing studies of tourist crime which compare rates of victimization among visitors and residents show that visitors are much more likely to be victims than local residents. This is not surprising given the behaviour of criminals, who are often opportunistic or work in organized gangs to target unsuspecting tourists. For example, Howard's (2009) study of tourists visiting Thailand found 40 per cent of visitors had experienced a hazardous event (e.g. a scam, overcharging, dual pricing, theft, robbery and drugging).

In Guatemala City, the problems of tourist-related crime were of such a magnitude that they limited tourism development when government research identified:

- robbery of visitors in the street
- attacks on tourist vehicles travelling between airports and hotels
- attacks on tourist vehicles on roads across the country

- attacks on visitors in national parks
- dishonest activities by employees in tourism-businesses towards visitors.

The government addressed the problems in the 1990s by directly protecting visitors and through preventive measures such as information and leaflets provided to tourists at the airport. A *Code of Ethics* leaflet was also provided outlining the laws and regulations relating to tourists. A tourist police force was also established to reduce crime in destination areas, a feature discussed in more detail later.

The impact on the visitor's image of the destination is severely skewed towards negative associations with a visit where criminal victimization occurs. But simple precautions which police advise visitors to take may reduce the likelihood of victimization if they take heed. However, a distinction needs to be made between the more random, unfortunate victimization and petty crime, such as handbag snatching, and the more serious criminal activity associated with binge drinking and hedonism among youth travellers (i.e. those under 20 years of age). For example, the Torbay area and its nightclub district in Devon reported numerous tourist-related criminality issues associated with alcohol. In European mass tourists resorts such as Falaraki, Greece, alcohol consumption and hedonism have been associated with predatory behaviour when a number of young females were raped, which led to a massive police crackdown on binge drinking and organized pub crawls. These severe criminal events damaged the resort's image and public attention highlighted many of the risk factors associated with youthful hedonistic behaviour. The impact of crime on destination image has led many countries and governments to establish tourist police forces. In Greece, there are 64 dedicated tourist police stations, reflecting the importance of tourism and tourists to the national economy. Among the countries now establishing dedicated police forces for tourists are: Thailand, Malaysia, Nepal, India, Fiji, Kenya, Costa Rica, Egypt, Panama, Cambodia and individual destinations such as Buenos Aires in Argentina. Many of these police forces are a comparatively recent innovation, because the value of such investment has been critical to reassure tourists. In addition, research informed by urban design is now arguing for the implementation of measures to 'design out' tourist crime victimization. This approach to tourist crime prevention through environmental design (CPTED) is now gaining momentum (see Jackson *et al.* 2011). Even so, this is unlikely to help in extreme cases of victimization such as tourist kidnapping. For example, an American tourist in Uganda was held for a US$500 000 ransom although such events are comparatively rare. Even so, the US State Department lists 35 countries in which American citizens are at risk of kidnapping, with 14 locations deemed no-travel zones, located in the Middle East, Africa and South America (https://travel.state.gov/content/travel/en/international-travel.html). But tourism and crime are probably of less significance in terms of media coverage than the impact of terrorism on tourism.

Tourism, terrorism and political instability

Tourism is a highly volatile activity which is extremely sensitive to the impact of safety and security issues. Yet, surprisingly, the study of tourism and political instability really only became a major issue for research in the 1990s, despite the seminal study by Richter (1989) and subsequent studies by C.M. Hall (1994) and the collection of papers in Pizam and Mansfeld (2005). Political instability is 'a situation in which conditions and mechanisms of governance and rule are challenged as to their political legitimacy by elements operating from outside of the normal operations of the political system' (Hall and O'Sullivan 1996: 106). Many facets of political instability exist and Hall and O'Sullivan (1996) summarized them into:

- international wars (e.g. the Croatia–Yugoslav war)
- civil wars (e.g. Sri Lanka)
- coups (e.g. Fiji)
- terrorism (e.g. the Bali bombings and Mumbai attack)
- riots/political protests/social unrest (e.g. the Palestinian uprising 2000–2002 and the Arab Spring movement, the Bangkok airport occupation in 2008 and the Hong Kong protests in 2019)
- strikes (e.g. airline strikes).

25

In each case, the impact upon tourism can be direct, in terms of the negative images the event conveys to prospective visitors via the media, word of mouth or visible government policies (i.e. civil rights abuses). One of the clearest examples of this relationship was the effect of the Chinese government crackdown on Tiananmen Square protests in 1989 which led to a temporary downturn in tourism, as negative images directly caused tourists to change their travel behaviour. Yet perhaps the most media-worthy area of attention is terrorism.

Tourism and terrorism: Critical relationships

Terrorism can take many forms, from simple hijackings, skyjackings, kidnapping, bombing of transport systems and resorts through to the new concerns over bioterrorism using undetectable germs. Among the direct effects of terrorism on tourism are:

- reduced tourism activity
- relocation of tourism to other areas
- damage to public images of tourist destinations
- economic damage to the tourism industry.

As Page (2019) suggests, terrorism is a difficult term to define given the lack of universal agreement on its precise meaning, but one useful definition can be found at *Oxford Dictionaries Online*:

> *The unlawful use of violence and intimidation, especially against civilians, in the pursuit of political aims.* (https://en.oxforddictionaries.com/definition/terrorism)

The dictionary goes on to explain that the term has its origins in the period of the French Revolution known as the 'Terror', and comes from the Latin *terror*.

Therefore, the key features in the term are: unlawful use of violence, violence/intimidation and pursuit of political aims. Terrorism can thus be situated in a continuum of political instability which at one extreme includes international wars (e.g. the Iraqi Conflict), civil wars (e.g. the Syrian conflict) through to coups (e.g. the attempted coup in Turkey in 2015), ongoing actions associated with terrorism and riots/political protests and social unrest (e.g. Tiananmen Square in 1988/89), and strikes such as those of air traffic controllers (e.g. June 2018 in France), as outlined above. Terrorism has an integrated impact in tourism destinations by affecting visitors, businesses and residents, as terrorist attacks are often indiscriminate and affect all three groups simultaneously. Terrorists may also target tourists, as in the case of the gunman attack at a Tunisian resort (Sousse) in 2015 where 38 victims, largely tourists, were killed.

Figure 25.5 provides a broad typology of some of the examples where tourism and terrorism interact. A consequence of the continued effect of terrorism in many countries is a depressed tourism industry. However, probably of greater concern for the tourism sector is the impact of a catastrophic event in countries with a low level of terrorist activity, which can devastate the tourism industry, visitor confidence and public perception, such as the case of 9/11.

As Page (2019) argued, the unpredictability of attacks in terms of time and location mean that destinations need to develop contingency plans (these are plans for various eventualities where precise measures can be put into action when a crisis occurs – a crisis management plan). This means that destinations need to understand the threat which terrorism poses for their locality or destination so they can prepare to adapt, change and operate in different ways if terrorism befalls the location. This is to ensure that the tourism sector can continue to operate and ensure care for the well-being of people affected by terrorism. It is part of a relatively new growth area of endeavour that is known as resilience planning and fits within the emergent area of emergency planning that looks at how organizations, governments and individuals can respond to emergencies such as terrorism. Resilience planning looks at how a destination can become more resilient because terrorism is characterized by focusing on a specific location (i.e. the destination, city or locale). In this setting, resilience refers to the capability of a destination to minimize losses, cope and continue to function following a shock event such as a terrorist attack. Therefore, planning for terrorist attacks requires good-quality intelligence for forward planning as well as a sound knowledge of the risks which destinations face. Such risks may also impact on visitor confidence in visiting a locality due to the fear caused by these risks or lack of confidence about personal safety, which is why there is a tendency for destinations to see a sharp drop in visitation after a terror attack. However, one key feature in tourism is the ability of visitor markets to bounce back in a one-, three-, six-month or one-year time frame (i.e. the recovery period).

Since 1970, there is growing evidence that terrorism has impacted tourism is countries which are members of the Organisation for Economic Cooperation and Development (OECD). Data from the annual Global Terrorism Index (GTI) (2017) indicates that since 1970, 10 000 deaths occurred in OECD countries, of which 26 per cent were attributed to two terrorist groups (ETA and the IRA), although OECD countries only account for 1 per cent of terrorist-related deaths. In 2016, the GTI indicated that there had been 25 673 deaths from terrorism spread across 77 countries, affecting eight of nine regions of the world. As Figure 25.6 shows, the top 20 ranked countries for terrorism are largely in the Middle East, Africa and Asia, and the GTI estimated the economic impact of global terrorism to be US$84 billion.

25

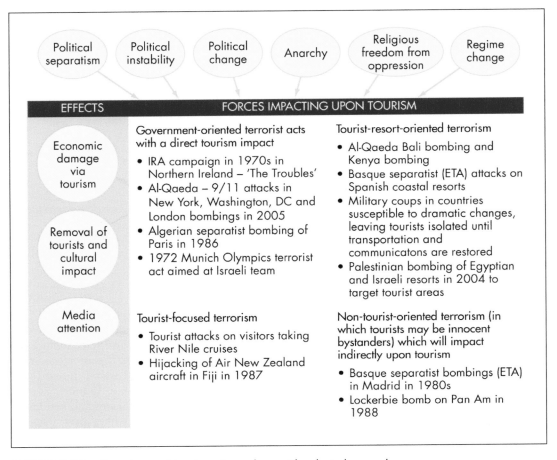

EFFECTS	FORCES IMPACTING UPON TOURISM	
Economic damage via tourism	**Government-oriented terrorist acts with a direct tourism impact** • IRA campaign in 1970s in Northern Ireland – 'The Troubles' • Al-Qaeda – 9/11 attacks in New York, Washington, DC and London bombings in 2005 • Algerian separatist bombing of Paris in 1986 • 1972 Munich Olympics terrorist act aimed at Israeli team	**Tourist-resort-oriented terrorism** • Al-Qaeda Bali bombing and Kenya bombing • Basque separatist (ETA) attacks on Spanish coastal resorts • Military coups in countries susceptible to dramatic changes, leaving tourists isolated until transportation and communicatons are restored • Palestinian bombing of Egyptian and Israeli resorts in 2004 to target tourist areas
Removal of tourists and cultural impact		
Media attention	**Tourist-focused terrorism** • Tourist attacks on visitors taking River Nile cruises • Hijacking of Air New Zealand aircraft in Fiji in 1987	**Non-tourist-oriented terrorism (in which tourists may be innocent bystanders) which will impact indirectly upon tourism** • Basque separatist bombings (ETA) in Madrid in 1980s • Lockerbie bomb on Pan Am in 1988

(Forces above: Political separatism · Political instability · Political change · Anarchy · Religious freedom from oppression · Regime change)

FIGURE 25.5 Terrorism and tourism: A typology with selected examples

IMAGE 25.2 Terror attacks in London involving vehicles ramming crowds of people walking on bridges have led to barriers being installed as an anti-terrorism measure to reduce the ability to drive into pedestrians

Yet this does not imply that countries and destinations have been inactive in seeking to stem the flow of terrorism. Many countries have paid greater attention to security measures, particularly in aviation following the 9/11 bombings of the World Trade Center in New York. The range of measures employed include seeking to reassure visitors that the location is safe despite a recognition that we are living in more turbulent times. For example, some countries such as the USA and UK issue travel advice for their citizens (e.g. the Foreign and Commonwealth Travel Advisories – see https://www.gov.uk/foreign-travel-advice, which covers 225 countries with a section on terrorism for each location). Destinations that have been affected by terrorism, such as London, have used various strategies to reduce the likelihood of terrorism; these range from improved intelligence and surveillance to reduce their vulnerability to attack; enhanced crisis management plans when attacks occur (such as the eight-minute response time for emergency services to reach the London Bridge bombing in 2017); vigilance among the travelling public (e.g. the British Transport Police

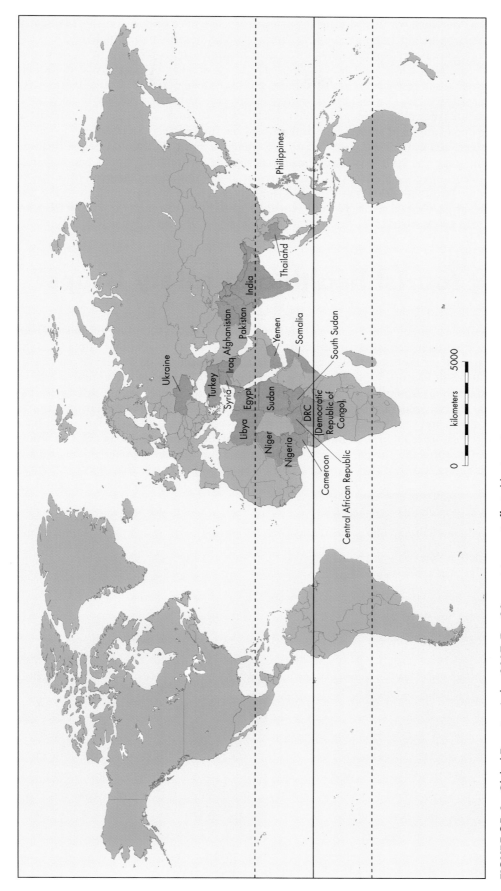

FIGURE 25.6 Global Terrorism Index 2017: Top 20 countries most affected by terrorism

Source: Page (2019) based on Global Terrorism Index (2018) data

campaign on the railway network with the slogan 'See It. Say It. Sorted.' (See British Transport Police (n.d.) for details on the publicity campaign, which includes a freephone number or text number with which members of the public can report things that do not look right, or alert train staff). Other measures include vehicle mitigation in popular tourist hotspots to reduce the ease with which vehicles can be used as terrorist weapons, as there were seven such attacks in 2017. To mitigate the risk, road restrictions are sometimes put in place (e.g. following the IRA attack on the City of London in 1993, a 'ring of steel' was introduced that involved protection barriers, CCTV cameras and checkpoints); these may also involve bollards at key venues to prevent vehicle attacks, such as the Glasgow Airport attack in 2007. Image 25.2 illustrates one example of such a measure installed on Tower Bridge in London.

Public health disasters such as the 2001 foot-and-mouth epidemic in the UK can have equally dramatic effects on the tourism industry, in much the same way natural disasters such as earthquakes, floods and volcanic eruptions do. Consequently, the sudden impact of a crisis such as a terrorist attack underlines the need for crisis planning and a contingency tourism plan (Faulkner 2001) in much the same way that hospitals have major trauma plans in the event of major disasters such as an aircraft crash. For this reason, it is useful to examine the case of 9/11 and its effect on the USA's tourism industry in Insight 25.2.

Managing tourist health and safety issues

Where destinations acknowledge that tourist safety issues are important for the wider sustainability of the tourism product, practical measures and guidelines can be offered to tourists without sounding alarmist. Where governments feel that risks need to be alerted to prospective outbound travellers, websites such as that of the FCO (http://www.fco.gov.uk) can provide targeted information. However, destination advice needs to be supplemented by good advice from many of the agencies listed in Figure 25.7 or by visiting a GP for health advice, as prevention is better than cure. But it needs to be emphasized that responsibility has to be placed with the tourist to take the advice available.

In destination areas, being prepared for a highly mobile and changing tourist population requires medical and police services to be adequately resourced. Some large tourist resorts have dedicated tourist police and natural disaster plans where the resort is in an area liable to flooding, earthquakes and disease. But at a more operational level, crime prevention in hot spots, including CCTV (Image 25.3) and a visible police presence, may be necessary. Yet tourists cannot be nursemaided so they have to be well informed of any risks they may encounter (Image 25.4).

IMAGE 25.3 Monitoring traveller safety by CCTV may reassure people about terrorist attacks

IMAGE 25.4 Local authority warning in Plymouth, UK of the hazards of tombstoning

To assist in improving the experience of visitors who are victims of crime, the initiative Tourist Victim Services in Ireland provides a model which many destinations could follow with its offering of help with:

- replacing travel and identity documents
- contacting insurers for claims and liaising with banks, embassies and airlines
- offering advice on legal support.

It is a voluntary agency set up to help redress the negative experience.

INSIGHT 25.2 The impact of 9/11 on the US tourism industry

The 9/11 crisis occurred at a time when the global tourism sector was facing an economic downturn and slow growth and although it occurred as far back as 2001, it remains one of the most globally publicized examples of a coordinated attack on travellers, many of whom were tourists. It is important to reflect on this attack, as it was a turning point in enhanced security measures for tourists travelling by air and other forms of transport. One consequence of 9/11 was that it exacerbated many of the current problems facing specific sectors of the tourism industry, such as the US airline industry, and caused them to face major financial and operational issues. However, the immediate impact of 9/11 on the global tourism industry was a 10 per cent drop in the number of tourists travelling; a 10 per cent drop in worldwide flights; a 16 per cent drop in US domestic flights; the cancelling of business travel, events and conferences, and a sharp fall in hotel-room occupancy in the USA. Theme parks were left empty. Blake and Sinclair (2003) noted the economic effects of 9/11 on income from tourist spending and loss of jobs by reducing domestic and international tourism together with the impact of no state intervention. However, the most immediate federal government response was to pass the Air Transportation Safety and System Stabilization Act which did provide federal US$10 billion credit to airlines, plus US$5 billion to airlines facing increased insurance premiums and limiting their liability arising from terrorist attack. The Act also provided US$3 billion for aviation safety. The Travel Industry Recovery Coalition advocated a six-point plan to assist tourism recovery:

- federal government should provide a US$500 tax credit for domestic travel
- expand loan facilities to small businesses
- provide a tax credit for employment in tourism
- subsidize marketing campaigns
- increase tax allowances to allow businesses to offset 9/11 induced losses against future earnings
- increase business entertaining expenses from 50 per cent to 100 per cent, which emphasizes the problems facing non-aviation businesses.

Blake and Sinclair (2003) observed the effectiveness of targeted subsidies for the airline sector rather than for more general tourism subsidies. Thus, the federal government crisis response sought to intervene to address the immediate downsizing announced by airlines post-9/11. Blake and Sinclair point to the US$30 billion loss of GDP which would have occurred through the tourism sector without the state intervention in the airline industry, which probably staved off up to 500 000 job losses. This illustrates the sudden impact of an event of the magnitude of 9/11, which not only hit business and consumer confidence but also tourism demand. Yet Goodrich (2002) also outlined the US government's travel advice warning its citizens to avoid a wide range of countries post-9/11 due to the terrorist threat posed by al-Qaeda. Many European destinations with a traditional US market were also affected. Yet the most severe effects on tourism were felt in cities such as New York, with a drop of visitors in 2001 of 5 million and a drop of US$2 billion in visitor spending, which was reflected in falling hotel occupancy rates.

What is notable about New York was the influential leadership of its mayor, Rudy Giuliani, in setting up a recovery programme which involved a media campaign to target New York visitors, day visitors and nearby leisure trippers, with an emotional and patriotic 'Stronger Than Ever' campaign which was strengthened by its winter promotion, 'Paint the Town Red, White and Blue', with special offers, discounts and incentives to build business back up again.

What the 9/11 Insight illustrates is that clear leadership is needed to redevelop tourism through a crisis management strategy, which needs to be quick, timely and highly visible, preferably with a very charismatic leader able to counter the negative fallout after a terrorist event. Above all, a coordinated approach across the tourism sector, with government funding as the US federal government provided, helps to reduce some of the short- to medium-term effects of a collapse in the tourism sector. This is in direct contrast to what happened in many of the countries which were affected by the SARS outbreak in 2002–2003, where the tourism industry's inability to formulate rapid responses, combined with media hype and misinformation, created a devastating impact on the Asian airline industry.

25

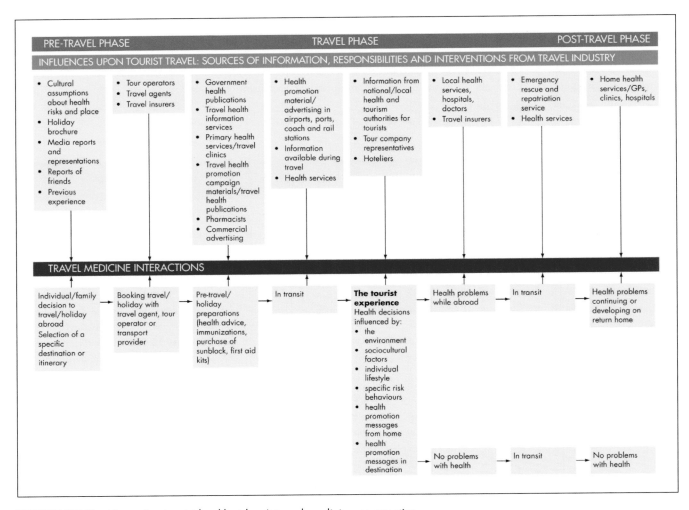

FIGURE 25.7   Managing tourist health risks: A travel medicine perspective
Source: Redrawn from Clift and Page (1996) with modifications

The tourism industry has to have a proactive approach to these issues and be committed to reducing health and safety problems, or at least in warning clients of risks (Image 25.4). After all, if tourism is an experience, and if inadequate advice is given or safety precautions are not taken, then the business may not be meeting its legal obligation of duty of care to its clients. This is becoming an increasingly contentious area of tourism, as lawyers specializing in litigation associated with such issues now feature prominently when things go wrong. Yet there is no substitute for tourists following some of the very practical advice from guidebooks and websites concerning unknown environments:

- stay in touch with friends and relatives
- consult guidebooks
- avoid dark and unlit streets
- avoid short cuts
- avoid carrying valuables around and carry a minimum of cash
- never put up a struggle against violent theft
- if hitchhiking, do so in pairs
- never tell strangers where you are staying

- always use registered taxis /official means of transport
- beware of pickpockets
- take advice from holiday reps in destinations
- do not engage in arguments and chastising of locals in public
- always defuse difficult situations by walking away

In the case of terrorism, it may be best to avoid areas targeted by known terror groups, which is where government websites may be most helpful.

Conclusion

There is little doubt that global travel has been adversely affected by terrorism, albeit in the short term; there is a tendency for the tourism market to recover quickly, implying that adverse events have a short-term impact on travel. This is evident from the effects of 9/11 and SARS on global travel. It is widely argued by travel medicine research-ers that it is the everyday concerns which tourists need to be aware of, such as the risks of AIDS, DVT and dis-eases which can be inoculated against such as hepatitis A and B. However, the global media impact of crises such as 9/11 tend to attract the bulk of attention in the media and the resources to formulate travel policy such as the new biometric scanning of travellers in the USA after the 9/11 Commission Report (2003). The creation of the US Department of Homeland Security illustrates how serious the terrorist threat is to USA travellers and for travel to the USA. But one has to put these events in perspective: it is the scale, reality and media hype that need to be disentangled to understand how relatively insignificant such events are to tourist travel, compared to the health and safety issues which tourists face every day. Even so, security is one of the most pressing issues at a global scale and is underpinned by wider problems relating to the global economy, poverty and inequality, environmental problems and other social and political pressures.

The conceptualization of tourist health and safety is com-plex, as many disciplines study it including researchers in medicine, safety science and tourism, and each approaches the subject with different perspectives and insights, as shown in Figure 25.3. The case of coronavirus illustrates how disease can easily be spread by global travel, and natural disasters are also receiving attention following the Indian Ocean tsunami in 2004. In the case of coronavirus, the World Travel and Tourism Council estimated that the pandemic could reduce international travel by 25 per cent, placing up to 50 million travel and tourism jobs at risk. But underlying all these issues is the concept of risk – what risks the traveller takes when they go on holiday, what precau-tions they take to reduce risks and how their behaviour, knowledge and understanding of tourism, health and safety interact to produce incidents and events which can spoil the tourist experience. Above all, global travel means that many of these issues affect all parts of the world, although climatic and environmental factors make some risks greater in certain parts of the world, such as the risk of AIDS and catching other diseases. Tourist health and safety are now central issues in the operation of tourism, especially given the media interest in negative events. From the tourist per-spective, their behaviour is a central element determining which places and destinations visitors travel to, and media images play a critical role in shaping this behaviour. Not surprisingly, many destinations are beginning to grasp this issue, or facets of it (e.g. tourist crime) as they wish to enhance rather than damage the image and perception of the locality, reflected in the growing number of countries and destinations establishing tourist police forces.

Discussion questions

1 Why has tourist safety and security become such a critical issue for travellers in the new millennium?

2 Outline the range of issues and problems associated with the management of tourist health.

3 What are the underlying causes of tourist accidents and injuries, and how can the tourism industry reduce them?

4 What sources of information exist to advise tourists which destinations to avoid or to take special precautions when travelling in?

25

References

Abeyratne, R. (2008) 'The fear of flying and air rage – some legal issues', *Journal of Air Transportation Security*, 1 (1): 45–66.

Blake, A. and Sinclair, M. (2003) 'Tourism crisis management: US response to September 11', *Annals of Tourism Research*, 30 (4): 813–852.

Boakyo, K. (2012) 'Tourists' views on safety and vulnerability: A study of some selected towns in Ghana', *Tourism Management*, 33 (2): 327–333.

British Transport Police (n.d.) 'See It, Say It, Sorted'. BTP (website). http://www.btp.police.uk/about_us/our_campaigns/see_it_say_it_sorted.aspx.

Callander, M. and Page, S.J. (2003) 'Managing risk in adventure tourism operations: A review of legal case history and potential for litigation', *Tourism Management*, 24 (1): 13–23.

Castillo-Manzano, J.I., Castro-Nuño, M., López-Valpuesta, L. and Vassallo, F.V. (2018) 'An assessment of road traffic accidents in Spain: The role of tourism', *Current Issues in Tourism*.

Centre for Research on the Epidemiology of Disasters (CRED) (2018) *Natural Disasters 2018*. Brussels. CRED.

Clift, S. and Page, S.J. (eds.) (1996) *Health and the International Tourist*. London: Routledge.

Connell, J. (2013) '"Current issue" in tourism: Contemporary medical tourism: Conceptualisation, culture and commodification', *Tourism Management*, 34 (1): 1–13.

Cossar, J., Reid, D., Fallon, R., Bell, E., Riding, M., Follett, F., Dow, B., Mitchell, S. and Grist, N. (1990) 'Accumulative review of studies of travellers, their experience of illness and the implications of these findings', *Journal of Infection*, 21 (1): 27–42.

Faulkner, B. (2001) 'Towards a framework for tourism disaster management', *Tourism Management*, 22 (1): 134–147.

Gilbert, D. and Abdullah, J. (2004) 'Holiday taking and the sense of well-being', *Annals of Tourism Research*, 31 (1): 103–121.

Goodrich, J. (2002), 'September 11, 2001 attack on America: A record of immediate impacts and reactions in the USA', *Tourism Management*, 23 (6): 573–580.

GTI (2017) Global Terrorism Index. http://economicsandpeace.org/wp-content/uploads/2018/12/Deaths-from-terrorism-down-44-per-cent-in-three-years-but-terrorism-remains-widespread.pdf.

Hall, C.M. (1994) *Tourism and Politics: Policy, Power and Place*. Chichester: John Wiley and Sons.

Hall, C.M. (2005) 'Biosecurity and wine tourism', *Tourism Management*, 26 (6): 931–938.

Hall, C.M. and O'Sullivan, V. (1996) 'Tourism, political stability and violence', in A. Pizam and Y. Mansfeld (eds.) *Tourism, Crime and International Security Issues*. Chichester: John Wiley and Sons.

Hall, C.M. and Page, S.J. (eds.) (1996) *Tourism in the Pacific: Issues and Cases*. London: Thomson.

Howard, R. (2009) 'Risky business? Asking tourists what hazards they actually encountered in Thailand', *Tourism Management*, 30 (3): 359–365.

Jackson, M., Inkakaran, R., Arrowsmith, C. and George, B. (2011) 'City design and its relationship with tourism crimes', *International Journal of Tourism Anthropology*, 1 (3): 195–207.

Jones, C., Barclay, E. and Manby, R. (eds.) (2013) *The Problem of Pleasure: Leisure, Tourism and Crime*. London: Routledge.

Lawton, G. and Page, S.J. (1997) 'Evaluating travel agents' provision of health advice to travellers', *Tourism Management*, 18 (2): 89–104.

Leggatt, P. Ross, M. and Goldsmid, J. (2002) 'Introduction to travel medicine' in P. Leggatt and J. Goldsmit (eds.) *Primer of Travel Medicine*, 3rd edition. Brisbane: ACTM Publications.

Orchiston, C. and Higham, J. (2016) 'Knowledge management and tourism recovery (de)marketing: The Christchurch earthquakes 2010–2011', *Current Issues in Tourism*, 19 (1), 64–84.

Page, S.J. (2009) 'Current issue in tourism: The evolution of travel medicine research: A new research agenda for tourism?', *Tourism Management*, 30 (2): 149–157.

Page, S.J. (2019) *Tourism Management*, 6th edition. Abingdon: Taylor and Francis.

Page, S.J. and Meyer, D. (1996) 'Tourist accidents: An exploratory analysis', *Annals of Tourism Research*, 23 (3): 666–690.

Pizam, A. and Mansfeld, Y. (eds.) (2005), *Tourism, Security and Safety: From Theory to Practice*. Oxford: Butterworth-Heinemann.

Porodko, M., Auer, J. and Eber, B. (2002) 'Economy class syndrome', *Internistische Praxis*, 42 (1): 169–172.

Richter, L. (1989) *The Politics of Tourism in Asia*. Honolulu: University of Hawaii Press.

Rosselló, J. and Saenz-de-Miera, O. (2011) 'Road accidents and tourism: The case of the Balearic Islands (Spain)', *Accident Analysis and Prevention*, 43 (3): 675–683.

The 9/11 Commission Report (2003) *Final Report of the National Commission on Terrorist Attacks upon the United States*. New York: Norton and Company.

UK Government Select Committee on Science and Technology on Air Travel and Health (2007) *Air Travel and Health: An Update: Report with Evidence*. London: The Stationery Office. https://publications.parliament.uk/pa/ld200708/ldselect/ldsctech/7/7.pdf.

Unter-Jones, J. (2000) 'Identifying the responsibility for risk at tourism destinations: The UK experience', *Tourism Economics*, 6 (2): 187–198.

UN–WTO (2011) *Global Tourism, Policy and Practice*. Madrid: UN–WTO.

Walker, L. and Page, S.J. (2003) 'Risks, rights, responsibilities' in 'Tourist well-being: Who should manage visitor well-being at the destination?' in J. Wilks and S.J. Page (eds.) *Managing Tourist Health and Safety*. Oxford: Elsevier.

Walker, L. and Page, S.J. (2007) 'The visitor experience of crime: The case of Central Scotland', *Current Issues in Tourism*, 10 (6): 505–543.

Wilks, J. and Page, S.J. (eds.) (2003) *Managing Tourist Health and Safety*. Oxford: Elsevier.

Wilks, J., Pendergast, D. and Leggat, P. (eds.) (2005) *Tourism in Turbulent Times*. Oxford: Elsevier.

Further reading

Books

Tarlow, P. (2014) *Tourism Security: Strategies for Effectively Managing Travel Risk and Safety*. Oxford: Elsevier.

Wilks, J. and Page, S.J. (eds.) (2003) *Managing Tourist Health and Safety in the New Millennium*. London: Routledge.

Journal articles

Castillo-Manzano, J., Castro-Nuño, M., López-Valpuesta, L. and Vassallo, F. (2018) 'An assessment of road traffic accidents in Spain: The role of tourism', *Current Issues in Tourism*.

Centre for Research on the Epidemiology of Disasters (CRED) (2018) *Natural Disasters 2018*. Brussels. CRED.

Howard, R. (2009) 'Risky business? Asking tourists what hazards they actually encountered in Thailand', *Tourism Management*, 30 (3): 359–365.

Orchiston, C. and Higham, J.E.S. (2016) 'Knowledge management and tourism recovery (de)marketing: The Christchurch earthquakes 2010–2011', *Current Issues in Tourism*, 19 (1): 64–84.

Porodko, M., Auer, J. and Eber, B. (2002) 'Economy class syndrome', *Internistische Praxis*, 42 (1): 169–172.

Rosselló, J. and Saenz-De-Miera, O. (2011) 'Road accidents and tourism: The case of the Balearic Islands (Spain)', *Accident Analysis and Prevention*, 43 (3): 675–683.

Sönmez, S. (1998) 'Tourism, terrorism and political instability', *Annals of Tourism Research*, 25 (2): 416–456.

Teye, V. (1986) 'Liberation wars and tourism development in Africa: The case of Zambia', *Annals of Tourism Research*, 13 (4): 589–608.

WTTC (2019) *Crisis Readiness: Are You Prepared and Resilient to Safeguard Your People and Destinations*. World Travel and Tourism Council. https://www.wttc.org/priorities/crisis-preparedness/.

Event tourism

Learning outcomes

After reading this chapter and answering the questions, you should be able to:

- understand the definition, nature and scope of event tourism
- identify the reasons why organizations within tourism destinations develop and host events
- outline the process of developing event strategies to encourage the tourism potential of a destination
- evaluate the impacts generated by hosting events.

Overview

In this chapter, we explore the phenomenon known as event tourism: its development, impact and use by tourism organizations and destinations to grow tourism markets. Event tourism has become a major growth industry as many destinations seek to promote and develop events to create a sense of the unique and unusual, and an ambience which seeks to portray the destination in an exciting light to potential visitors. In short, events are used to attract more visitors to destinations, although the rationale for event tourism strategies can encompass a much broader spectrum of objectives.

Introduction

According to Getz (2008: 403) the growth of the event tourism sector in recent years 'can only be described as spectacular', while event management is a fast-growing area of applied study and professional practice (Connell and Page 2010; Getz and Page 2020; Page and Connell 2020). This spectacular growth is certainly an important justification for including a special consideration of this theme as a separate chapter in relation to the management of tourist activities, even though the subject has emerged in other chapters (e.g. Chapter 9). Events can play a key role in building a more attractive and successful destination, and many destinations have embraced events as part of a wider tourism agenda. Events include a vast range of activities in the public sphere such as festivals, celebrations and themed events (entertainment,

IMAGE 26.1 Rio has developed as a key global events destination, focused on the annual carnival it hosts

sport and leisure, political, educational, arts, cultural and community events). It also includes those in the business area (such as meetings, conventions, fairs and exhibitions). Finally, events management also encompasses activities in private settings (including weddings and parties). The emphasis of this chapter is mostly on public events with a focus on the rationale for developing and hosting events in tourism destinations, the role of developing event tourism strategies, the impacts of events, and the issues which destinations face in hosting and managing events.

The promotion of event strategies to pump-prime, nurture and develop a visitor market, based upon the premise of 'attracting non-residents to the community with the expectation that their spending will contribute significantly to the local economy' (Long and Perdue 1990: 10), is now a well-established principle in event tourism. The lure of events and the benefits that they can bring has induced significant public sector expenditure to develop, underwrite and promote event-based tourism development in many locations worldwide, particularly large-scale events such as the Olympic Games. Events create a special appeal for the visitor: the limited duration and often celebratory atmosphere of events presents the opportunity to engage in the ambience of the destination beyond the everyday experiences it presents. Events also provide the opportunity for both visitors and local people to participate in celebrations, such as the Rio carnival (Image 26.1). Furthermore, events can assist in creating an event spectacle at the destination

TABLE 26.1	Examples of spectacles			
Event	Year	Number of people estimated to attend	Location	Purpose
Kumbh Mela	2001	70 million	India	Religious festival held every 12 years.
Athens Olympics	2004	• 22 000 attended opening ceremony • 2428 volunteer performers • 11 999 athletes • 4 billion watched the Games on television	Greece	Quadrennial international multi-sport event with historical roots, dating to the Ancient Greeks but hosted on a regular basis since the 1896 Games of the Olympiad.
Macy's Thanksgiving Parade	Annual	2–3 million with a further 40 million plus watching it on television	Manhattan, New York, USA	An annual event first held in 1924, characterized by large-scale street performance and designed to celebrate Thanksgiving, a blessing given to celebrate the previous year's harvest. It features large inflated balloons in special designs.

(continued)

TABLE 26.1	continued			
Event	Year	Number of people estimated to attend	Location	Purpose
Brussels Flower Carpet	Biennial event held on Assumption Day	Tens of thousands	Grand Palace, Brussels, Belgium	Event first established in 1971 in which volunteers weave a carpet out of almost 1 million begonias that are grown in Belgium.
Harbin Ice and Snow Festival	Annually in January–February	2 million	Northern China	2000 workers carve out 176 000 cubic feet of ice to create sculptures and living exhibits such as an Ice Hotel and buildings. This is based on a 300-year winter lanterns tradition from Mongolian culture and lasts for a month.
Burning Man Festival	Annual event	25 000–30 000	Nevada, USA	An alternative event where a city of people assemble in the inhospitable desert environment to celebrate the Summer Solstice and engage in communal living. The philosophy is to leave no trace.
National Association of Stock Car Auto Racing (NASCAR)	Annual event	75 million attendees over a racing season (up to 186 000 each weekend)	USA	Racing events at 32 race tracks across the USA which is the highest sporting event attendance figures globally. It is often focused on the Daytona circuit in Florida, as the home of NASCAR, which was founded in 1947, and the first race occurred at Daytona in 1948.
Speech and Protest as Spectacle	Ad hoc	250 000–500 000	USA	The National Mall in Washington has developed as the site of free speech in America. Most events are one-off: notable events were the 1963 Civil Rights March (250 000 attendees) and the Vietnam War protest event (1971) that attracted 500 000 attendees. See 'List of rallies and protest marches in Washington, D.C.' (n.d.)

Source: Events as compiled from Rockwell and Mau (2006) and other sources by the authors, reproduced from Getz and Page (2020: 244)

(Table 26.1). As Getz and Page (2020: 43) argue, 'Spectacle exists within the realm of the visual as something viewed (by "spectators", obviously); but it is larger than life, colourful, exciting and novel, otherwise we would perceive it to be ordinary and unremarkable. We are easily seduced by spectacle . . . a spectacle is a grandiloquent display of imagery evoking a diffuse sense of wonderment and awe'. In other words, the spectacle often associated with planned events has a particular appeal to tourists as animating the destination and creating a unique one-time experience of the place and occasion.

This chapter differentiates between event tourism and event management, where event tourism is concerned with the strategic context of events in realizing wider objectives (such as tourism, economic, social or cultural dimensions) and event management focuses more on the practical aspects of preparing for and staging events. Events management is a growing, specialized and commercial field (see Insight 26.1). The scope and focus of event management is wide and incorporates the 'design, production and management of planned events' (Getz 2008: 403). Event tourism is different in that although it relies on events management to develop, plan, produce and evaluate single events, it encompasses a wider strategic context of events and their impacts, and it is on this specific area of interest that this chapter focuses.

26

INSIGHT 26.1 The Routledge Handbook of Events

The recent growth in the development of event studies and its contribution to the wider growth of the event domain of study has been preceded by a vast expansion of academic and practitioner research. While this expansion of research in specialist journals (e.g. *Event Management*) and more generic journals (e.g. *Tourism Management*) combined with books and reports has culminated in a new critical mass of literature, there have been few attempts to evaluate the evolution of events-related research and its prospects for continued development. As a result, *The Routledge Handbook of Events*

TABLE 26.2 Subjects contributing to the study of events with illustrations of their application to research

Subject	Application and example of research questions that the subject might pose
Geography	• How do events as transitory phenomena transform a place in a temporary time–space context? • What use are events to re-image a locality?
Economics	• How do we use events to boost local economic growth and leverage employment expansion? • What types of economic impact and 'event effect' occur through the harnessing of event-led tourism growth?
Psychology	• What meaning do people attach to events and places and do events make their visit more memorable and enjoyable? • Does event enjoyment depend upon the emotional experience and participation of people in groups?
Political Analysis	• Who really benefits from event-led strategies in a neo-liberal state? • How are benefits from events distributed among stakeholders?
Operations Management	• How can businesses and event operators minimize risk and maximize financial return on event projects? • What managerial skills typify the most successful event organizations?
Sociology	• What types of social experience do events create for spectators? • How do events assist in community development?
Marketing	• What are the experiences which can be co-created using events to enhance the visitor experience? • How do we measure satisfaction/dissatisfaction in the event experience?
Cultural Studies	• How are events devised and constructed to appeal to popular culture versus high forms of cultural appeal? • How are events rooted in local culture?
Anthropology	• To what extent are events an authentic experience for tourists? • How does the staging of mega-events affect the guest–host encounter?
Human Resource Management	• How do event organizations ensure they have the right staff, skills and leadership to manage events? • What role do volunteers perform in event staging?
Environmental Management	• Can events be sustainable? • What measures can event organizers adopt to 'green events'?
Urban Studies	• How do the public sector use events to regenerate districts of cities? • How do events animate cities at different times of day?
Security Studies	• What types of crowd management are effective and safe in managing people at mega-events? • What security measures do the organizers of mega-events have to consider in developing a security plan?
Future Studies	• What will the event of the future look like in terms of how it engages its audience? • What role will reality and virtual reality play in the creation of event experiences?
Finance	• How will events be financed to ensure fiscal sustainability and profitability? • What role does sponsorship play in staging and hosting a financially sustainable event?
Sport/Leisure Studies	• How does the hosting of regular sporting events assist in creating a regular and loyal event audience? • How does the role of serious leisure and tourism co-exist with business-related travel?

26

was produced (Page and Connell 2020; 1st edition 2012) to act as a roadmap of the intellectual roots of the subject. It comprised commissioned essays from leading researchers in different subject areas to provide a synthesis of the events literature. Each essay reviewed many of the key concepts and debates and their engagement with the wider social science and management literature. Although this was the first major study of its kind in the rapidly expanding field of events in 2012, it is evident from the contents of the book in 2012 and 2020 that a wide range of subjects are informing the study of events research beyond the field of tourism and leisure, reflecting the theoretical agendas in social science and more operational focus of staging, operating and managing events. Table 26.2 shows this evolving domain of research is directly contributing not only to the development of an emerging event studies curriculum, but also to the formation of a distinctive area of research within its tourism and leisure studies roots. It is also apparent from Table 26.2 that many new and potentially rewarding research themes are yet to be developed within the nexus of tourism and events, including the contribution of events to the tourist experience, their long-term value in enhancing visitor well-being and the way in which event

themes may help re-image places that have lost their tourism rationale (e.g. ailing coastal resorts). Although it is often argued that much of the more applied research in events, particularly that focused on event tourism, is much nearer to the market than academia (i.e. it is aligned to industry needs) this has often been published as academic research. This, however, can lead to criticism that the research lacks intellectual rigour and depth. Whatever perspective you adopt, it is clear that events is a dominant theme within academic and practitioner environments, and it is playing a major role in leading or supporting destination development. To address criticisms of the applied nature of events research, the second edition of the handbook has remodelled its focus to also include a growing interest in critical event studies. Critical event studies adopts a more questioning approach towards the rationale, impact and effect of hosting events for tourism, reflecting the wider growth in critical social science (see Getz and Page 2020 for a more detailed explanation of this).

Further reading
Page, S.J. and Connell, J. (eds.) (2020) *The Routledge Handbook of Events*, 2nd edition. London: Routledge.

What is event tourism and why is it important?

According to Getz (2008), the term 'event tourism' was not widely used prior to 1987 (Frost 2012). Getz (1989) identified the expression 'event tourism', although prior to this researchers tended to refer to a range of terms in relation to the topic ranging from special events to hallmark events and mega-events, through to specific types of events, such as arts and cultural. As stated by Getz and Page (2014), the development of a research focus on events in tourism was weakly articulated in the 1960s and 1970s, and the initial starting point for serious academic study is attributed to Boorstin (1961) in relation to the phenomenon of 'pseudo-events'. A second influential study by Greenwood (1972) of a Basque festival highlighted the negative influence of visitors on authentic cultural celebrations. Getz attributes the first event tourism study to Ritchie and Beliveau (1974), who examined how 'hallmark events' could combat seasonality of tourism demand. In the 1980s, the field expanded rapidly and then almost exponentially in the 1990s as more journal articles and books appeared on the theme. The establishment of the academic journal *Event Management* (formerly *Festival and Event Management*) in the late 1980s also marked the evolution of event tourism as a subject area within tourism studies (Getz 2002, 2007) as a range of notable texts on the area began to be developed (see Getz 2007, 2008; Getz and Page 2020 for more detail).

Event tourism as a subject has grown for many reasons, but the range of important drivers of growth in this area of activity include the desire of tourism organizations in destinations to:

- Promote the unique and wider appeal to a visitor market that may only be attracted by a special event, particularly in the non-peak season.
- Develop a positive destination image and assist in place marketing (see Chapter 15).
- Underpin major plans for urban regeneration and grow the destination's ability to expand a visitor market around a new product base as part of a drive for local economic development.
- Try to bring the destination to life (or what Getz 2008 describes as *animating it*), linking together the attractions and tourism capacity in the area to encourage better utilization.

The variety of roles associated with event development is shown in Table 26.3.

TABLE 26.3 The role of events in tourism

Tourism development	Social and economic development and regeneration	Adding value
A way of increasing the visibility and appeal of a tourism destination, e.g.:	The event bidding process and associated spin-off benefits guaranteed by major event and partnership organizations can contribute to urban renewal and major redevelopment. Mega-events are most effective in this role, e.g.:	Used in 'animating' a destination (Getz 2008) through bringing specific features to life, which can enhance the visitor experience, e.g.:
• Events can help build destination images, for example Korea has used events extensively to shape its international image as well as promote itself as an international tourism destination since 1988 (1988 Olympic Games, 2002 World Cup)	• Regenerating post-industrial cities: for example the London 2012 Olympic Games bid included the regeneration of a significant swathe of East London, while the Atlanta Olympics created sports facilities, an urban park, low-cost housing and educational facilities	• Creating additional attractions at existing tourist attractions
• Increasing the number of visitors		• Re-enacting scenes through live interpretation of historic sites, such as battlefields, castles and other heritage sites
• Clustering of events and attractions to create a critical mass of interest for visitors	• Improving the environment, e.g. the Millennium Dome in London (now O₂ Stadium), built on an ex-industrial site, required major environmental clean-up	• Hosting living history events at historic sites, e.g. use of actors to perform scripted pieces to visitors
• Lengthening of tourist season beyond the peak season, e.g. a Spring Gardens Festival in Cornwall led to a 9 per cent increase in visitors during spring; Quebec Winter Carnival saw its off-peak season become the peak season	• Improving transport infrastructure such as airports and roads, e.g. 1984 Los Angeles Olympics	• Stimulating interest in the heritage and traditions of a destination, encouraging a better understanding of place and people
• Attracting repeat visits		• Reviving lost traditions, interests and areas, encouraging both tourist and community involvement

Event-related tourism provides a sharpened focus for destination managers and planners to help develop both the tourism markets (i.e. the demand) and the tourism capacity (i.e. the supply) with the hosting and staging of events. A good example is the European Union's annual designation of a City of Culture. This event provides a year-long celebration of the arts and culture as a stimulus to tourism, which helps to underpin the destination's plans to grow its visibility and tourism infrastructure for the longer term, so as to achieve a more sustainable tourism product base. In the case of Liverpool, the event harnessed a wide range of visitor markets from leisure travel to business travel as well as the lucrative conference and conventions market.

Bidding for events has been achieved successfully by Glasgow's City Marketing Bureau, which sought to reposition the city as an event destination, with the help of its acclaimed city branding. This example also illustrates how one destination has worked to create and foster a network of partners and stakeholders who can deliver a successful event destination image and product. The cluster of events which the city bids for and tries to attract include events related to music, the arts and culture, retail-related awards, restaurants and nightlife-related events and sports events like the UEFA Europa League, as well as environmental events such as the Glasgow River Festival. Yet events as a celebratory activity in destinations are far from a new or novel idea, as an historical appreciation of their evolution shows.

The evolution of events

Events through time have marked milestones, customs, triumphs, achievements and eras, where rituals and ceremonies can be dated back over 1000 years, while the Rio carnival has its roots in Roman times (Gold and Gold 2012). The earliest references to organized events can be traced back to ancient civilizations. In Roman times, celebrations and exhibitions of power, strength and violence – such as gladiator fights and chariot-racing events – attracted large

26

audiences, as depicted in the film *Gladiator*. The appeal of such large-scale and flamboyant events was partly related to the idea of *spectacle*, which still embodies the essence of an event.

More generally, society has long found ways to mark and celebrate times and occasions of importance to communities and individuals and expressed these in a public setting. Some of these are illustrated in the online table. Celebrations in the twenty-first century differ from culture to culture, but often mark significant dates (New Year), the changing of the seasons (winter and summer solstices), agricultural tasks (market days and harvest festivals), traditions associated with religious beliefs (Christmas and Easter), and events marked by myths and tradition (Halloween, Bonfire Night). While many events in history performed a clear celebratory role for communities and nations, in a modern-day setting Destination Management Organizations (DMOs) and tourism professionals have harnessed the powerful commercial role of events in creating a global and national impact with the creative use of media and marketing to raise the awareness and appeal of the destination to a wider potential visitor audience (Masterman and Wood 2006). In addition, more theoretical interpretations of such developments have been examined by sociologists such as Roche (2000) in relation to how mega-events are part of a global culture associated with modernization, illustrated by the pursuit of large events by developing countries. Clearly, the emergence of a modern event tourism industry has changed the way in which many events are created and staged.

Conceptual issues and classifying events

Events are a temporary phenomenon and every event is a unique combination of where and when it is held, its theme, design and style and the participants, spectators and organizers. In other words, events are of a finite length, you only experience them once and they are created by their length, setting and management (which include the staff, the design of the event and its content). Alternative definitions that have been used include the term 'special events', which Goldblatt (1990: 1) defines as something which are 'always planned, always arouse expectations, and always motivate by providing a reason for celebration'. This implies that there is something unique or special about the event experience that appeals to a different range of motivations than those generally associated with everyday leisure activities, and illustrates the importance of events in creating something which:

- appeals to the emotional elements of visitor curiosity and the search for something unusual and different
- is highly subjective
- creates a heightened sense of activity.

For this reason, a range of factors are crucial in creating this uniqueness and, as Getz (1997) suggests, successful event development may need to think about what makes an event special, including:

- *A multiplicity of goals,* where the idea of *diversity* is implicit in the creation of the event.
- *A festive spirit,* so that an ambience, joyfulness, revelry and freedom from constraint is built into the appeal, as evident in the Notting Hill Carnival in London which celebrates West Indian culture and music.
- *Satisfying basic needs,* so that it appeals to a range of leisure and tourism motivations (see Chapter 4 for more detail).
- *Uniqueness,* to create a must-see or a once-in-a lifetime opportunity to experience something.
- *Quality,* so visitor expectations are exceeded (see Chapter 25 for more detail on the tourist experience and measurement).
- *Authenticity,* so that the local community feels that it is engaged and that the event is not only embedded in their local history and traditions but also encourages them to participate alongside visitors.
- *Flexibility,* so that events which require minimal infrastructure and investment can be moved to other locations or spaces or adapted to a different market need, such as farmers' markets.
- *Hospitality,* to ensure visitors feel welcomed and special.
- *Tangibility,* where the event is the conduit and vehicle to encourage the visitor to experience the destination attributes and resources through a range of activities.
- *Theming,* to maximize the value of authenticity and increase interaction with visitors.
- *Symbolism,* where the use of rituals and symbols may give extra significance to the experience, such as indigenous music or performances.
- *Affordability,* to encourage as wide a range of visitors as possible.

26

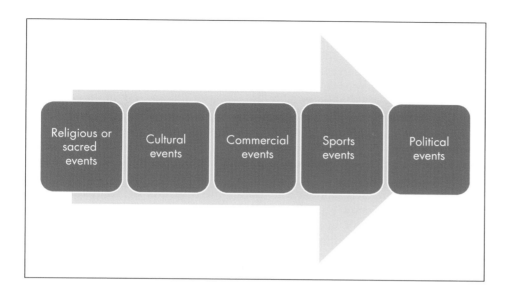

FIGURE 26.1 Hallmark event typology.
Source: After Hall (1992)

Yet alongside these elements of what makes events special is the additional use of a term within event studies – that of *hallmark events*. Hallmark events are typically a symbol of quality and are used to hallmark a destination such as the New Orleans Mardi Gras, the Rio carnival, Oktoberfest in Munich, Germany and the Edinburgh Festival. They are characterized by a high level of media exposure, positive imagery and their use to gain competitive advantage for the destination.

Hallmark events have often been interchangeably referred to, or encompass, 'special' or 'mega' events, although Hall (1992) argues that their definition is differentiated by the scale of their impact. As Hall (1992) suggests, there are five types of hallmark events as shown in Figure 26.1:

Despite the contextual difficulties of creating a typology of event tourism (see Getz 1991, 1997; Hall 1992), the most established definition of a hallmark event is that in Ritchie (1984: 2):

major one-time or recurring events of limited duration, developed primarily to enhance the awareness, appeal and profitability of a tourism destination in the short and/or long-term. Such events rely for their success on their uniqueness, status, or timely significance to create interest and attract attention.

The reasons for hosting hallmark events are varied and are well documented in the tourism literature (e.g. Ritchie 1984; Hall 1992; Getz 1997). These events are increasingly being recognized and adopted for their ability to generate significant economic and tourism benefits for the host destination. Much has been written on the impacts of these events and this is discussed later. The vast majority of these studies relate to sporting events probably because, according to Hall (1992), their higher public profile makes them the most desired events sought by tourism destinations. However, research into these events has tended to focus on measuring the positive and usually economic impacts at the expense of the overall impacts of the event (Hall 1992). There have also been attempts to define *mega-events* (Getz 1997) and it is widely acknowledged that to be defined as such, an event should have a volume of visits in excess of 1 million, capital costs should be at least US$500 million and it should be a 'must-see' event (e.g. the Olympic Games).

Festivals, by contrast, are a more traditional and contemporary form of event which Getz (1997: 8) defined as a 'public, themed celebration', and may help to maintain community values through increasing a sense of social identity, with historical continuity in the staging of the event (such as the Scottish Highland Games) as well as celebrating the survival of the local culture. One additional category to consider is that of *fairs, exhibitions, expos and shows*. These have a wide range of forms, one example is that of the rural and agricultural shows which are popular in many countries (particularly the UK, USA, Australia and New Zealand) which combine the showing of agricultural products with a trade show, parades, competitions (e.g. wood-cutting competitions) and demonstrations. World fairs and expos date back to an international agreement in 1929 with the International Bureau des Expositions, a body that sets policies for bidding and holding the world's main fairs, identified as expos. Trade shows and consumer shows are also included in this categorization of events and it is estimated that there are around 12 000 expos a year, which generate around 70 million visits annually. An associated area is the area of meetings and conferences, which is a significant area of activity and profit for many hotels and conference venues.

26

Meetings and *conferences* may range in scale and scope from conclaves (those meetings held in private/secret), through seminars and workshops which may have an educational and training function, to retreats which are away from the normal operating environment to give space for the delegates to focus and discuss issues privately, and to conferences which are interactive and associated with conferring and discussing issues. An associated type of conference is the symposium or forum, where papers are presented for discussion (e.g. academic conferences), while large events or assemblies of people are conventions, and a more international convention or summit (e.g. the World Earth Summit) may be described as a congress. The conference business is a major area of growth in the events sector and it is illustrated by the aspirations of many countries to grow this lucrative business-led form of travel (Rogers 2013). For example, South Africa's conference and meetings industry was worth between 4.2 and 4.4 billion rand for 2015. South Africa is the top business tourism and events destination in Africa, hosting 100 international meetings a year and generating around 280 000 jobs a year.

At the geographical scale of a locality or region, it is evident that there will be a mix of event forms and types and one example of this was how Scotland's main economic development agency – Scottish Enterprise (see Chapter 13) – classified events. Scottish Enterprise's *Event Good Practice Guide* identified three types of events which they have previously funded to assist with economic development objectives, and each had a varying degree of risk involved:

- *Rolling* – where an event runs from year to year. In this instance, Scottish Enterprise (SE) approaches a potential event from the perspective of both its economic potential and its business development needs and defines an exit route for its intervention prior to its involvement. This is perhaps the lowest-risk form of event.

- *One-off* – where an event is staged for a discrete period on a non-recurring basis, for example in support of the opening of a new visitor attraction. Here SE assesses the potential ability of the event to impact upon key economic criteria (e.g. net additional bed nights/expenditure) and provides support in accordance with the scale of that impact; more often than not such support is in the form of advice or funding. This is a medium-risk type of involvement.

- *Peripatetic* – where SE actively bids for 'footloose' events in a competitive environment with other locations. In this instance, SE intervention is usually twofold: it may identify the event and act as part of the bidding consortium or as a 'risk-reducer' to it; subsequently, it will often be involved in influencing the subsequent staging of the event. This is the highest-risk form of involvement.

This categorization illustrates that events do not occur in isolation but require planning, development, marketing and management at a strategic level. In the case of SE, the rationale for public sector pump-priming and partnerships is to leverage wider economic benefits through event activity. There are a wide range of motivations associated with

TABLE 26.4 Primary organizational motives for hosting events

Public sector	Not-for-profit sector	Private sector	Community groups
• To attract tourists • To attract inward investment • To demonstrate ability to mobilize resources • To engender civic pride • To achieve positive imaging • To promote economic development • To celebrate identity • To achieve a range of social, economic and environmental goals	• To attract revenue and raise funds for projects • To stimulate awareness and interest • To promote appreciation of specific features • To educate (through enjoyment) • To achieve social, environmental, economic, cultural, sport, leisure or community goals	• To enhance core business and profitability • To generate revenue off-peak and in shoulder months • To develop products and markets for commercial purposes • To stimulate consumer interest • To encourage repeat visits and increased spending • To encourage good public relations	• To raise funds for specific projects or groups • To assist in community development • To celebrate local traditions • To raise awareness of an area's attributes • To enhance an area's reputation • To keep old traditions alive • To generate civic pride • To have fun!

26

hosting events. Table 26.4 illustrates the different agendas and perspectives that various organizations bring to event development. It also underlines the importance of collaboration between public and private sector groups, including building partnership and networks which are capable of harnessing the positive benefits of such collective working towards event and destination development. Irrespective of who is planning or developing an event, to assure any degree of success it is imperative that organizations set out to plan and develop a clear strategy to articulate how and why they are pursuing events as a path towards destination development and the objectives they are seeking to achieve.

INSIGHT 26.2 Winter festivals

Many destinations around the world face a common problem of seasonality in tourist visits, where visitor numbers drop outside of major holiday periods and the main summer season. For many tourism businesses and destination managers, there is a major challenge in finding ways to extend the season, especially in the winter season either side of the Christmas/New Year holiday period (which often yields a short-term boost to visitation). This is one area where Winter Festivals in the northern hemisphere have made a major contribution to stimulate visitation and address the issue of seasonality. Even many southern hemisphere destinations have pursued this idea, such as Coolangatta's Wintersun Festival on Australia's Gold Coast. Here free ticketed events and free street parades were used to attract visitors and to boost community spirit: it is estimated that the festival now attracts 50 000–70 000 visitors a year. Other larger destinations such as Prague have used this approach post-Christmas. As Dewar et al. (2001: 523) suggest:

> Winter Festivals assume an important role in our psyche, as at low altitudes (northern and southern) winter is a time of suspension. Life slows or stops, days grow shorter, warmth is a warm fire, snow and ice lock the land in a quiet world of white. Winter has been seen as a time of death, famine and fear by many cultures. At the same time it is celebrated as a time of friendship, relaxation, good cheer and festival, a time when the fields are fallow and there is time for play. This paradox

is expressed in the ubiquitous winter festival. Christmas, solstice, or whatever the festival is, is a time to hold back the cold and dark with the light of celebration.

At a global scale, Winter Festivals are a growing trend for many destinations and have been successful in locations such as Harbin, China and Sapporo, Japan. The Quebec Carnival is reputed to be the third largest festival after Rio and New Orleans. This attracts around 65 000 out-of-state and 850 000 in-state visitors a year. In contrast, Dewar et al. (2001) point to the growth in popularity of the Harbin Festival, which grew from 250 000 visitors in 1984 to 400 000 in 1998. In the UK, a Winter Festival in north-east England in 2005 attracted an additional 25 000 visitors while Inverness in Scotland spent £250 000 on a Winter Festival in 2008. This was estimated to have generated £240 000 in additional income. The most famous winter celebration in Scotland – Hogmanay in Edinburgh, on New Year's Eve – attracts around 80 000 visitors annually and is estimated to boost the tourism economy by £30 million.

In the southern hemisphere, the major Winter Festival in New Zealand, in Queenstown is a large organized series of events over a two-week period. It combines mountain activities, night-time entertainment, free and ticketed daytime events including family and music/comedy, and food and wine events. It has a long history stretching back to 1975, and has grown from a local event to one which now has a national and international audience. It is estimated to attract 40 000–60 000 visitors a year to a small alpine community in southern New Zealand (see Image 26.2). However, with all events, issues arise over the extent to which their positive and negative impacts are felt in time and space. In particular, the immediate and long-term effect of addressing the principal problem of seasonality is often neglected by policymakers, who focus on the headline figures associated with the economic impact without considering 'who benefits/loses, where, when and why?'. While there is evidence that Winter Festivals may be a popular tool to grow a destination's off-season appeal, simply looking at the volume of visitors and deducing that this is beneficial for the tourism economy lacks sophistication and may mask the true impact on a locality and the region in which the event is staged.

IMAGE 26.2 Queenstown in New Zealand is a small community whose Winter Festival generates a large influx of visitors to the area

INSIGHT 26.2 continued

Further reading

Connell, J. and Page, S.J. (eds.) (2010) *Event Tourism: Volumes 1–4*. London: Routledge.

Dewar, K., Meyer, D. and Li, W. (2001) 'Harbin, lanterns of ice, sculptures of snow', *Tourism Management*, 22 (5): 523–532.

Page, S.J. and Connell, J. (eds.) (2012) *The Routledge Handbook of Events*. London: Routledge.

Questions

1 Why are winter events used in tourism marketing strategies for destinations?

2 What are the logistical challenges of hosting winter events?

3 How would you set about organizing a winter event in a destination? Who would you involve as key stakeholders?

4 How would you measure the success or failure of a winter tourism event programme in a destination?

Event strategies

Surprisingly few destinations have event tourism strategies or policies in place although this is rapidly changing. Australia is the most advanced country in relation to event strategies, with an event development corporation in every state. However, public sector agencies throughout the world are increasingly engaging with the idea and value of event strategies, recognizing the power of events in propelling the visibility of destinations and the tangible benefits of harnessing events to grow visitor numbers (e.g. the UK and New Zealand). One approach which is gaining interest is the use of Winter Festivals (see Insight 26.2) and the Eden Project in Cornwall (Image 26.3) has developed a summer music programme to expand its market appeal (Image 26.5). Strategic events planning for destinations enables tourism managers to identify, create and evaluate opportunities and action plans that help guide the overall direction and

IMAGE 26.3 The Eden Project, Cornwall is a project that has helped regenerate the local area. It was built in clay pits and features a strong environmental theme

assist with integrated decision-making. The process of developing an events strategy comprises a number of distinct phases, all of which require a sound understanding of a destination, its attributes, capabilities and opportunities.

The strategic planning process for events

A fundamental part of the event strategy process is the identification of objectives for event development based on an appropriate vision (Bramwell 1997). Developing a vision is a process of shaping a destination's future development using a combination of imagination and practical issues and it should raise one central question – are events a realistic focus for tourism development? Part of this process relies on consultations and stakeholder inputs, cross-referencing existing strategy documents (e.g. economic development, sport, community, cultural or tourism strategies), and an agreed understanding of what an event strategy aims to achieve.

Devising objectives: what is an event strategy for?

According to Getz (1997), event tourism objectives should assess the extent to which:

- events can be developed and promoted as tourist attractions
- support can be given to develop or assist creation of new events

- events may play a key role in extending tourism geographically and seasonally
- events may help create and enhance images of a destination

as well as wider social and cultural objectives that are related to fostering the arts, culture, sports, nature and heritage conservation and community development. Frequently, events may serve as core attractions to achieve theming, image building and marketing objectives for a destination, and to add value to attractions and resorts. In addition, an events strategy might assist in developing event tourism through a range of desired outcomes (Figure 26.2):

- encouraging repeat visits after the event
- contributing to or even creating a destination brand.

In the case of Abu Dhabi, the government's vision recognizes the role of event tourism in future development. Event tourism is viewed as a strategy for enhancing international profile and promoting international links, while encouraging private business development, stimulating economic growth and dispersing the benefits throughout the emirate. The Abu Dhabi Tourism Authority promotes the emirate as a world-class venue, and uses a specific screening process when considering event proposals submitted by promoters to ensure a fit with their strategy. For example, events should aim to raise international profile, create international media coverage and stimulate destination awareness.

Other considerations of event strategies

A strategy must identify the resource requirements including the costs of development, human resources (Hanlon and Jago 2012) and funding sources (e.g. sponsorship or grants), as well as the measures which will be taken to address negative impacts. Many organizations establish a separate sub-organization or committee, sometimes with the assistance of external expert consultants, to support event-related development, develop a strategy and implement it. Event strategies also need to undertake a careful appraisal of the resources which exist for event tourism (i.e. financial, natural, cultural, human, physical, political and technological) as well as the marketing resources needed to develop and market event tourism. Destinations typically will want to undertake a detailed review comprising a SWOT analysis (see Chapter 14) to examine:

- *Strengths:* which resources, events, related services of high quality exist?
- *Weaknesses:* is there anything that may inhibit the growth of events?
- *Opportunities:* is there anything that can be taken advantage of to increase tourism appeal?
- *Threats:* what potential obstacles exist to achieving event goals?

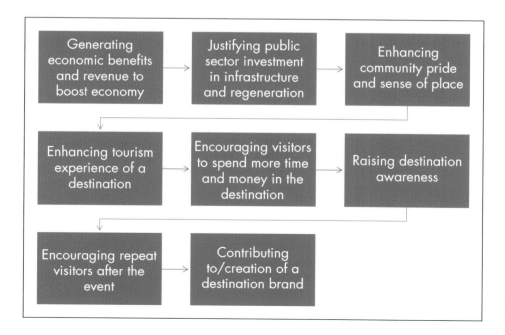

FIGURE 26.2 Desired outcomes of hosting events in a destination

Further, an assessment of available resources for event development is required, which might examine the existing demand and supply of events, including return on investment, market share and market trends. Once the preliminary steps have been undertaken, the development of the strategy can proceed and planning for specific events may begin. Strategic options for tourism destinations include:

- bidding for major events, where there is likely to be significant competition from other destinations (e.g. Commonwealth Games, and European City of Culture)
- bidding for minor and intermediate events, where there is likely to be competition from other similar destinations (e.g. conferences)
- developing new events, based on visioning and evaluation of the destination's characteristics (e.g. SWOT analysis)
- developing existing events that have potential to expand (e.g. into hallmark events)

IMAGE 26.4 Venice Beach in Los Angeles is transformed through creative arts and a rolling programme of events including live music, pop-up art galleries and a Venice Arts Crawl tour for visitors

- developing and integrating existing events to create a clustering effect and a new and interesting marketing proposition (e.g. the Edinburgh Festival incorporates a number of separate festivals, including the Edinburgh International Festival and the Fringe Festival) (also see Image 26.4 for a smaller-scale example).

These options are likely to involve undertaking a feasibility study of hosting one or more events and the implications and impacts for a destination.

Understanding the impact of the events

Seeking to assess the overall impact of any given event is a complex process which requires the event to be viewed in relation to:

- the organizing or sponsoring organizations' goals
- the effect on the local community
- the environmental impact
- the sponsors' and different partners' and stakeholder's goals
- the impact upon the local or wider economy
- the wider marketing-related benefits which are sought, including place-imaging, building tourism markets and destination positioning.

Much of the burgeoning literature on events and festivals tends to tread a familiar path, evaluating economic or other impacts to answer common research questions such as 'what was the estimated economic impact of the event?' Understanding the impacts of events is important in a public policymaking context, where it is necessary to assess the degree to which investment in individual events, or a strategy based on event development, generates the desired outcomes in a specific geographical area (i.e. nation, region, town or village – see Image 26.5). The process of and methods used in evaluating events and impacts are considered in more detail later in this chapter. Above all, it is important to understand the rationale for specific events to help evaluate the intended and unintended impacts.

A range of factors ultimately shape the impact of events, including:

- the geographic characteristics of the area
- the characteristics of the local population
- the economy and business profile of the area

- integration of events into the tourism economy
- distribution of tourist expenditure
- displacement effects

- existing tourism supply and tourist demand
- length and type of event
- marketing and profile of the event
- organizational aspects

- capital costs
- opportunity costs
- external costs.

Table 26.5 illustrates the range of economic, sociocultural and environmental impacts associated with events, which highlights that there is a balance of impacts which may occur depending upon a wide range of factors, including the event itself, where it is hosted, when it is hosted and the objectives of the event. It is apparent from Table 26.5 that the range of impacts is wide, encompassing both positive and negative effects. These impacts should also be read in conjunction with the more detailed analysis of tourism impacts in Chapters 17–20, although it is worth noting a range of event-specific effects across the sociocultural, economic, environmental and political spectrum.

Economic issues

For destinations seeking to boost the economy through event tourism, the critical issue remains the justification of event strategies in relation to the outcomes, particularly where public sector resources are employed to fund events.

TABLE 26.5 A comparison of the impact of events

Positive economic impacts	Negative economic impacts	Positive sociocultural impacts	Negative sociocultural impacts	Positive environmental impacts	Negative environmental impacts
• Increase in tourist expenditure length of stay • Employment created and sustained • New business opportunities • Sponsorship and grants attracted to fund infrastructure projects with long-term benefits • High ratio of revenue to costs • Increase in tax revenues • Media profile and increased awareness of a region • Economic legacies	• Financial input through pump-priming: opportunity costs for other projects • Displacement effect on areas outside main event core • Benefits not distributed effectively within a region's tourism economy • Cost of dealing with negative impacts	• Employment • Provision of social services • Community participation • Improved community identity and welfare • Environmental improvements funded • Housing projects, e.g. post-use of Olympic villages • Expanded trade opportunities • Increased cultural understanding	• Noise • Increased crime • Loss of community identity (Fredline and Faulkner 1998) • Loss of sense of place • Social dislocation • The effect of vandals and undesirable behaviour • Increase in retail prices • Increase in property prices and rents • Displacement and evictions, e.g. to make way for event infrastructure development	• Promote understanding of unique or special environment • Encourage participation in conservation work • Reclamation and detoxification of waste or contaminated land for infrastructure development • Enhancement of derelict areas and removal of eyesores	• Excessive consumption of resources and use of local services, e.g. water, electricity and sewage systems • Wear and tear • Litter and waste disposal • Traffic congestion and air pollution • Threat to biodiversity • Water and land pollution • Infrastructure development on greenfield sites • Damage to heritage sites

26

For example, an event tourism promoter might use the argument: 'This event will attract a lot of tourists who will spend money in the area while they are here', but the key challenge is to objectively forecast and quantify:

- how many visitors will it attract?
- how much will they spend?
- will this spending benefit local business?
- will the outcomes be positive in the short and longer term?
- what other non-economic impacts might the event generate?

Studies generally conclude that staying visitors make a significant contribution through accommodation expenditure during multiple-day events, although the magnitude of the estimated economic impacts (Dwyer and Jago 2012) depends upon the characteristics of the festival/event (i.e. the duration) and the nature of the local economy (i.e. other attractions and linkages), while expenditure on food and beverages is highest during single-day events.

To illustrate the very substantial economic effects that events can produce, the examples of Oktoberfest and the America's Cup are worthy of note. The Munich Oktoberfest in Germany is the largest annual festival in the world today, attracting around 6 million visitors from all over the world (6.2 millon in 2007). In terms of its economic impact, the 16-day festival generates approximately €955 million a year: €450 million are spent on food, drinks and entertainment within the festival grounds; €205 million on shopping, public transport and restaurants in and around Munich; while €300 million is spent on accommodation. In addition, the festival provides employment for some 12 000 people. In another example, New Zealand's Ministry of Tourism identified that the summer 2002–2003 America's Cup in Auckland generated around NZ$523 million of net additional spending, including NZ$497 million in the Auckland region. While the impact was strong at the national level, the effect of the event was negative for some regional economies in New Zealand due to reduced spending by domestic travellers, who went to Auckland rather than other domestic travel destinations. However, international visitors travelled to other parts of the country. The sectors of the economy that benefited most included sales within the marine sector, retail, and accommodation and restaurants and bars. Direct employment included just over 5000 full-time equivalent jobs (Barker *et al.* 2002a, 2002b). However, bidding for, preparing and staging events can be very costly. The massive investment required for hosting Olympic Games events is undoubtedly the best example of where the costs of the event can seemingly spiral out of control. For smaller events, balancing forecast costs against attendance and acceptable pricing is not always easy. For example, before any staging and marketing costs are considered, weather insurance to cover the cost of cancellation of the Stirling Hogmanay Celebrations (in Scotland, to celebrate the New Year) is in the region of £30 000 alone.

Sociocultural issues

Event spectators may not necessarily be tourists. Audiences at the Eden Sessions, a series of summer music concerts featuring leading musicians and bands at Cornwall's (UK) leading tourist attraction, the Eden Project (Image 26.5), comprises around 50 per cent local people. Indeed, events create a setting where tourists and local residents often come together to enjoy the celebratory ambience, although the two groups may experience events in different ways. Nowhere is this more marked than in Venice (see also Insight 20.1), where festivals form a major part of cultural life and the tourist experience. The Festa del Redentore, known as the festival of the Venetian people and in existence since 1866, has been at the centre of debates about how commercializing traditional community events can result in sociocultural effects. The festival was traditionally a local event based on religious observances, dining, boating and socializing: it was small-scale, community-oriented and meaningful. From 1978, when the city council launched a major midnight firework spectacle as the pinnacle of the festival and a greater drive towards tourism promotion

IMAGE 26.5 The Eden Project in Cornwall, UK, has developed an outdoor music programme to diversify its market appeal

began, numbers of international tourists to Venice at festival time soared. As Davis and Marvin (2004) argue, the city was unable to cope with overcrowding, numerous parties and discos and anti-social behaviour. The transformation of the festival into a tourist spectacle diminished it in the eyes of Venetian people, marking a 'truly grotesque foreign intrusion' (Davis and Marvin 2004: 246). In some cases, as Page and Connell (2020) show, residents can be displaced to make way for new infrastructure projects (e.g. new stadia) to accommodate hallmark events such as the Olympic Games, exacerbating the social and cultural impact of events on local communities.

Environmental issues

With large events, the sudden influx of large numbers of participants can cause significant impact on the physical fabric of the location, as well as capacity problems, e.g. car traffic. As the Festa del Redentore example further illustrates, the intensity of the firework display (with some 3500 kilos of pyrotechnics exploding in 50 minutes) was reported to make mosaic tiles fall off walls in important historic buildings, as well as creating air pollution. A rock concert featuring Pink Floyd (1989) resulted in a massive swelling of the tourist population (to around 200 000) which the city was unable to accommodate. Concert-goers unable to get a view scrambled onto tiled roofs to see the band, leading to a reported US$30 000 of damage and a similar amount spent on clearing thousands of tons of litter (Davis and Marvin 2004). A move towards developing and designing events in such a way that they are green and sustainable is now emerging: the staging of such events seeks to minimize negative environmental impacts. There are examples where the green message is a core part of the celebration (e.g. fair trade events, green charity events, and music and community-based festivals), or where significant attention has been given to environmental impact (e.g. UNEP's first paperless meeting in 2008, Glastonbury Music Festival (Image 24.1) and Broadway's Tony Awards) but they are the exception rather than the rule. It is clear the relative contribution of events to climate change and other environmental impacts must be managed and mitigated, implying that festival and event organizers, venues and destinations need to improve environmental performance. This is to ensure that the negative impacts of events are minimized and the benefits optimized to assist in reaching carbon reduction targets, as recognized by UNEP/ICLEI in its guidelines, published in 2009, for greening events. The future challenge is to find practical ways to reduce the associated impacts of events at both local and global scales and across the whole spectrum of events. Since the Lillehammer Winter Olympics (1994) and the emerging environmental agenda set out in Olympic bids from around the early 1990s, priorities have gradually shifted to incorporate environmental principles and technologies more widely in mega-event planning. There is a major role for the use of practical tools, such as event carbon calculators, greening guidelines, footprinting devices and offsetting schemes, and more conceptually, for examinations of how (or whether) such initiatives really compensate for environmental impacts at source. This is because the environmental footprint of events is gaining global recognition, enabling us to reduce those footprints.

Waste is one of the major problems that event organizers face. For example, around 678 tons of waste was produced from the 2004 Oktoberfest in Munich. A good example of how litter problems at events can be reduced is that of National Day Parade, Singapore's biggest celebration of the year. In 2005, the parade was launched as a litter-free event by:

- providing litterbags
- putting up banners
- posting announcements
- distributing fun packs
- distributing 250 000 wristbands bearing the messages 'Keep Singapore Litter-Free' and 'Reduce, Reuse and Recycle'.

Other problems that events create include excessive use of water, electricity and gas supplies. For example, at Oktoberfest, water consumption is around 90 000m³, which is about 27 per cent of Munich's daily need.

While events can cause environmental damage, there are some instances where the environmental agenda is a clear priority in pre-event planning. The 2000 Olympic Games in Sydney exemplified a green commitment to the event, leading to the creation of an Olympic Village as a model of environmental awareness in architectural design. Design features included north-facing buildings to provide warmth in winter and cooling in summer, and a ban on environmentally harmful gases in insulation, refrigeration and air-conditioning units. Further environmental measures included recycling, energy maximization and water conservation measures. Environmental and

26

social impact studies were undertaken and measures to protect the natural environment were put in place. To minimize traffic, all event venues were concentrated in a compact area within 30 minutes' travel from the Olympic Village.

Political issues

Events are not apolitical and can be auspicious political occasions. International contests for hosting events attract stiff competition between nations (e.g. Olympic and Commonwealth Games), underlying which is a political dimension and national prestige. Events strategies can be used as political or regime legitimization or recognition. However, some events attract protests and sanctions against host nations, where participants and sponsors identify issues of concern, most notably human rights. This was particularly high profile in the case of the 2008 Beijing Olympic Games, with worldwide protests over China's occupation of Tibet vocalized during the procession of the Olympic Torch to China. Many sporting events have been affected by similar protests, while national marketing campaigns, such as 'Visit Myanmar Year' (see Chapter 13), can affect tourist demand for destinations both positively and negatively. Whether social, economic or physical, negligible or significant, and tangible or intangible, the impacts of events are often rapidly felt. However, the legacy effect of events may not be readily understood at the time of the event and can be much more long-term in nature (Pacione 2012). Assessing the outcomes of a single event, ranging from the economic impact through to the resources required to clear up litter, is an important element of event tourism in order to improve, adjust marketing efforts for, and/or justify increased resource inputs to future events, a process known as *event evaluation.*

Evaluating events and impacts

Event evaluation can be defined as 'The process of critically observing, measuring and monitoring the implementation of an event in order to assess its outcomes accurately' (Bowdin *et al.* 2006: 413) and includes collating basic features and important statistics about the event (Getz 1994). For example, the Edinburgh International Festival in 2008 received £2.2 million public support from Edinburgh City Council and they expected to leverage £20 million of economic benefit for the destination through that operational subsidy: an evaluation of the event is the only way of assessing whether that initial investment has provided the payback required. Part of the evaluation process includes seeking feedback from stakeholders, and it is widely recognized that event evaluation can operate in three distinct stages:

- *Pre-event:* feasibility studies may be undertaken to assess the potential value and role of hosting the event and will involve the costing of creating the event, infrastructure and potential returns on the initial investment. A feasibility study is a 'comprehensive evaluation of the desirability and suitability of an event proposal' (Getz 1997: 77). It requires detailed market research, forecasting and evaluation of impacts as to whether the event is appropriate in the venue and area along with the infrastructure requirements, support required, merchandizing and licensing arrangements and creation of proposals for evaluation by other bodies to secure partnership funding.

  In terms of tourists, the feasibility study will seek to understand how the event will impact on the locality and the wider region/country. Cost–benefit analysis may also be used to determine whether initial investment in events is a worthwhile exercise based on experience elsewhere and case studies of best practice. For example, will hosting the event displace visitors from nearby destinations and attract them as potential customers at the cost of other areas? If this happens, then the initial investment may have been wasted, so the event needs to carefully assess what it is trying to do and how it will build and complement existing tourism provision and capacity to avoid too much displacement. A degree of displacement may be inevitable but event design should help to reduce this potential problem (Berridge 2012). For example, in 2003 Stirling in Scotland decided to host the World Medical and Health Games, which is a roving event (i.e. it moves to different locations each year) that typically attracts 4000 participants and their families over a one-week period. Displacement was assessed in a pre-feasibility study and a more detailed economic impact study was undertaken during the event to assess the impact, which was between £1.8 and £2.2 million for the local economy (Connell and Page 2005).

- *During the event*: monitoring the progress, mystery guests, questionnaire surveys and other assessments of consumer benefits derived from hosting the event will be used to understand the successful and immediate impact among visitors.
- *Post-event*: collation of data, feedback from stakeholders and analysis of finances, as well as impact studies. Most evaluations take place post-event and typically ask two major questions:
  1 Did the event meet its objectives?
  2 What can be improved for next time (if appropriate)?

There is also a growing international interest in the legacy effects of events (i.e. what long-term benefits does hosting an event provide for the locality it is based in), which is evident in bids to host the Olympic Games. The International Olympic Committee require all bids to prepare a plan for the legacy effects in the city-bid, although the experience of some former hosts has demonstrated limited legacy benefits for local communities, as in the case of Rio.

Brazil has pursued a tourism and events strategy associated with hosting hallmark events that are sport-focused. In 2014 it hosted the World Cup (estimated to have cost around $12 billion) and the Rio 2016 Olympic Games. The events strategy was designed to grow international tourism to over 5 million international arrivals per year, focused on a number of key markets: South American countries, the USA and Europe. Such a sport-led strategy has to be set against the well-established annual Rio carnival, which attracts over a million international visitors a year. In addition, we also have to consider the economic cost of hosting these events in relation to legacy planning. Instead of converting sport infrastructure to local people's needs, after these two major sporting events, facilities lie abandoned and decaying due to the absence of funds to convert them to local use. Add to this the environmental cost of constructing the venues for the Games such as demolishing housing in Rio's favelas (which are shanty towns or slums housing the poor) to make space for venues and infrastructure needs. Part of the explanation for the poor legacy outcome was an economic recession in Brazil in 2014–2016, leading to a drop in taxation revenue for the government and the inability of the government to service its debts. Legacy issues were a low priority at a time when public finances were severely restricted, and so poor legacy planning has meant that the benefits that were expected to accrue to residents have not materialized. Similarly, the growth in international tourism achieved through mega-events has come at major economic cost to the country.

Event research may be used to identify persistent problem areas and reduce these in order to improve the visitor experience. The most problematic area to understand is visitor satisfaction, as many factors impinge on perception and enjoyment but through evaluation and improvement, event organizers can aim to avoid critical failings. Data collection typically involves face-to-face questionnaires and surveys (see Connell and Page 2005 for an example) to assess:

- proportions of tourists and day visitors
- characteristics and motivation of participants
- catchment area of event
- visitor activities and spending
- perceptions of participants
- likelihood of making a return visit to the area after the event.

The majority of published articles in the tourism journals and *Event Management* also focus in depth on the methodological issues involved in arriving at frameworks which are appropriate for estimating economic impacts (Tyrell and Johnston 2012). Many frameworks proposed have inherent bias and problems of under and over-recording of economic data, as well as statistical concerns about the margin of error and how representative such studies are. In most cases, the data collected are based upon visitor surveys to establish expenditure (as well as motivation to visit) and so contain many of the flaws familiar to tourism researchers (Getz 1994). Yet the outcome of many studies is a level of generalization in terms of economic effect that is too imprecise to fully understand the spatial impact at a variety of scales. One interesting approach by Long and Perdue (1990) used one question on a survey instrument to assess the impact of visitor expenditure in seven areas. Where other business surveys have been employed to evaluate impacts, the level of spatial analysis in this field is notably absent since the research question familiar to geographers – *who gets what, where and when?* – is rarely posed.

In attempting to measure economic impacts, regional economic methods (i.e. input–output analysis and economic multipliers) are often used, although these models are only as useful as the data collected to validate and calibrate the findings (e.g. Breen *et al*. 2001). Multiplier analysis is one of the tools used to identify the amount of additional income generated by tourism, and can be used in an event context (see Chapter 16 for more detail) which requires

26

accurate data collection on visitor spend, and on flow of revenue through a local area (Tyrell and Johnston 2012). As many events make a direct loss, the actual financial gains for localities may only be gained over time. There is also a growing argument for evaluations of events to embrace qualitative research tools to provide more depth to the ways of evaluating issues. For example, Shipway *et al.* (2012) highlight the wider range of research methods now being harnessed such as the role of qualitative research tools (i.e. participant observation, focus groups and in-depth interviews) to complement standardized impact-related surveys.

Research from critical event studies has also highlighted the importance of understanding accessibility issues at events to ensure certain groups (e.g. people who are disabled) are not excluded by conducting accessibility audits in relation to venues and the programmes of events they offer. Other key issues such as pricing strategies at paid events also have an important bearing on event audience composition, so that events are not solely hosted for wealthy tourists to the detriment of local residents and domestic tourists. These more critical issues also need to be captured through event research to ensure that issues of inclusiveness run through event tourism strategies. This helps avoid a situation whereby events become a vehicle for resident protests focused on their impact, in much the same way as overtourism has done in certain locations.

Conclusion

This chapter has focused on the interrelationship of tourism and events. It is clear that tourism destinations throughout the world, both established and emerging, view events as a means to create, develop, animate and alter destination images and attract visitors, as well as to achieve a range of other economic, social and environmental goals. Plans for the development of events in regions (event strategies) are increasingly evident as public sector bodies recognize the power of events as a national, regional and local mechanism in tourism and economic development. What is also apparent is that events do not 'just happen': they require significant input and planning, development and execution. Event tourism incorporates a complex process of strategy creation, planning, staging, managing and evaluating outcomes.

The chapter has shown how many of the theoretical and conceptual issues dealt with in other chapters can be brought together in a practical manner, where developing successful events can assist destinations with growing their visitor economy. This will not be without impacts, which need to be understood from research and examples of events elsewhere so that examples of 'good' or 'best' practice are able to inform event strategies. Such an example is evident in Insight 15.3 in relation to how a small town in the Netherlands set about developing an event-led tourism strategy. As Getz (2008: 422) argues:

Event managers interested in developing their tourism potential should ideally become committed stakeholders in the community's or destination's tourism planning process. By working together . . . events can seek to influence the destination's positioning and brand, funding and development work, research and evaluation programs . . .

There are many examples where this has been a success from a community perspective, and it is clear that collaboration and partnerships are certainly the way forward for developing many events where multiple benefits can be gleaned by various stakeholders. However, as Getz (2008: 422) also argues, events have increasingly been harnessed for strategic reasons, mainly based on an economic development rationale. Attention has focused on destination competitiveness, how to win bids and create effective events, as well as economic considerations such as impact evaluation, return on investment and financial sustainability. However, less consideration has been levied towards environmental, social and cultural dimensions. Therefore, there is considerable scope within event tourism to build a knowledge base that links industry and academia and brings together both applied knowledge and more academic thinking to begin to address some of the weaknesses in the field which Getz and Page (2020) have identified.

Discussion questions

1 Why are events important for destinations and their tourism economies?

2 Thinking about an event you have attended, what are the features which made it 'special' and memorable?

3 What are the main social impacts of events and how might these be reduced?

4 Why is event evaluation important?

References

Barker, M., Page, S.J. and Meyer, D. (2002a) 'Evaluating the impact of the 2002 America's Cup on Auckland, New Zealand', *Event Management*, 7 (2): 79–92.

Barker, M., Page, S.J. and Meyer, D. (2002b) 'Modelling tourism crime: The 2000 Americas Cup', *Annals of Tourism Research*, 29 (3): 762–782.

Berridge, G. (2012) 'Designing event experiences', in S.J. Page and J. Connell (eds.) *The Routledge Handbook of Events*. London: Routledge.

Boorstin, D. (1961) *The Image: A Guide to Pseudo-events in America*. New York: Harper and Row.

Bowdin, G., Allen, J., O'Toole, W., Harris, R. and McDonnell, I. (2006) *Events Management*. Oxford: Butterworth-Heinemann.

Bramwell, B. (1997) 'Strategic planning before and after a mega-event', *Tourism Management*, 18 (3): 167–176.

Breen, H., Bull, A. and Walo, M. (2001) 'A comparison of survey methods to estimate visitor expenditure at a local event', *Tourism Management*, 22 (5): 473–479.

Connell, J. and Page, S.J. (2005) 'Evaluating the economic and spatial effects of an event: The case of the World Medical and Health Games', *Tourism Geographies*, 7 (1): 63–85.

Connell, J. and Page, S.J. (eds.) (2010) *Event Tourism. Volumes 1 to 4*. London: Routledge.

Davis, R.C. and Marvin, G. (2004) *Venice, the Tourist Maze: A Cultural Critique of the World's Most Touristed City*. California: University of California Press.

Dwyer, L. and Jago, L. (2012) 'The economic contribution of special events', in S.J. Page and J. Connell (eds.) *The Routledge Handbook of Events*. London: Routledge.

Frost, W. (2012) 'Events and tourism', in S.J. Page and J. Connell (eds.) *The Routledge Handbook of Events*. London: Routledge.

Getz, D. (1989) 'Special events: Defining the product', *Tourism Management*, 10 (2): 135–137.

Getz, D. (1991) *Festivals, Special Events, and Tourism*. New York: Van Nostrand Rheinhold.

Getz, D. (1994) 'Event tourism: Evaluating the impacts', in J.B. Ritchie and C. Goeldner (eds.) *Travel, Tourism and Hospitality Research*. New York: Wiley.

Getz, D. (1997) *Event Management and Event Tourism*, 1st edition. New York: Cognizant.

Getz, D. (2002) 'Event studies and event management: On becoming an academic discipline', *Journal of Hospitality and Tourism Management*, 9 (1): 12–23.

Getz, D. (2007) *Event Studies: Theory, Research and Policy for Planned Events*. Oxford: Elsevier.

Getz, D. (2008) 'Event tourism: definition, evolution, and research', *Tourism Management*, 29 (3): 403–428.

Getz, D. and Page, S.J. (2014) 'Progress and prospects for event tourism research', *Tourism Management*, 52: 593–631.

Getz, D. and Page, S.J. (2020) *Event Studies: Theory, Research and Policy for Special Events*, 4th edition. London: Routledge.

Gold, J. and Gold, M. (2012) 'The history of events: Ideology and historiography', in S.J. Page and J. Connell (eds.) *The Routledge Handbook of Events*. London: Routledge.

Goldblatt, J. (1990) *Special Events*. New York: Wiley.

Greenwood, D. (1972) 'Tourism as an agent of change: A Spanish Basque case study', *Ethnology*, 11 (2): 80–91.

Hall, C.M. (1992) *Hallmark Tourist Events: Impacts, Management and Planning*. London: Belhaven.

Hanlon, C. and Jago, L. (2012) 'Staffing for successful events', in S.J. Page and J. Connell (eds.) *The Routledge Handbook of Events*. London: Routledge.

'List of rallies and protest marches in Washington, D.C.' (n.d.) Wikipedia. https://en.wikipedia.org/wiki/List_of_rallies_and_protest_marches_in_Washington,_D.C.

Long, P. and Perdue, R. (1990) 'The economic impact of rural festivals and special events: Assessing the spatial distribution of expenditures', *Journal of Travel Research*, 28 (1): 10–14.

Masterman, G. and Wood, E. (2006) *Innovative Marketing Communications Strategies for the Events Industry*. Oxford: Butterworth-Heinemann.

O'Sullivan, D. and Jackson, M. (2002) 'Festival tourism: A contributor to local economic development?', *Journal of Sustainable Tourism*, 10 (4): 325–342.

Pacione, M. (2012) 'The role of events in urban regeneration', in S.J. Page and J. Connell (eds.) *The Routledge Handbook of Events*. London: Routledge.

Page, S.J. and Connell, J. (eds.) (2020) *The Routledge Handbook of Events*, 2nd edition. London: Routledge.

Ritchie, J.R.B. (1984) 'Assessing the impacts of hallmark events: Conceptual and research issues', *Journal of Travel Research*, 23 (1): 2–11.

Ritchie, J.R.B. and Beliveau, D. (1974) 'Hallmark events: An evaluation of a strategic response to seasonality in the travel market', *Journal of Travel Research*, 14 (1): 14–20.

Roche, M. (2000) *Mega-events and Modernity: Olympics and Expos in the Growth of Global Culture*. London: Routledge.

Rockwell, D. and Mau, B. (2006) *Spectacle*. London: Phaidon Press.

Rogers, T. (2013) *Conferences and Conventions: A Global Industry*. Oxford: Butterworth-Heinemann.

Shipway, R., Jago, L. and Deery, M. (2012) 'Quantitative and qualitative research tools in events', in S.J. Page and J. Connell (eds.) *The Routledge Handbook of Events*. London: Routledge.

Tyrell, T. and Johnson, R. (2012) 'A spatial extension to a framework for assessing direct economic impacts of tourist events', in S.J. Page and J. Connell (eds.) *The Routledge Handbook of Events*. London: Routledge.

UNEP/ICLEI (2009) *Green Meeting Guide 2009*. ICLEI. http://www.iclei-europe.org/index.php?id=greening.

Further reading

Books

Getz, D. and Page, S.J. (2020) *Event Studies: Theory, Research and Policy for Planned Events*, 4th edition. London: Routledge.

Page, S.J. and Connell, J. (eds.) (2020) *The Routledge Handbook of Events*, 2nd edition. London: Routledge.

Journal articles

Getz, D. and Page, S.J. (2014) 'Progress and prospects for event tourism research', *Tourism Management*, 52: 593–631.

Connell, J., Page, S.J. and Meyer, D. (2015) 'Visitor attractions and events: Responding to seasonality', *Tourism Management*, 46: 283–298.

Dewar, K., Meyer, D. and Li, W. (2001) 'Harbin, lanterns of ice, sculptures of snow', *Tourism Management*, 22 (5): 523–532.

The future of tourism

Learning outcomes

After reading this chapter and answering the questions, you should be able to understand:

- the role and application of tourism forecasting and its importance for tourism businesses
- the methods which can be used to understand the potential impact of factors affecting changes in tourism, including demographic and political factors
- the importance of demand and supply issues on future tourism provision.

Overview

Tourism is constantly evolving, and to understand what may affect tourism trends in the future, planners and managers need to understand techniques such as forecasting, and the range of factors likely to influence tourism in the next decade and beyond. The future evolution of tourism is uncertain, and attempting to plan for future growth scenarios poses many challenges for an industry where change is the only constant feature. A wide range of factors impact upon the future of tourism as demographic, political, economic and technological changes shape the nature, trends and participation in tourism. For governments and the tourism sector, such changes need to be recognized, understood and managed to ensure the long-term sustainability of tourism in different countries and destinations.

Introduction

Understanding how tourism can be developed, improved and be more in tune with the environmental resources it consumes is a global challenge, as shown in Chapter 19. As the futurist study by Martin (2007: 3) warns, 'At the beginning of the 21st century, humankind finds itself on a non-sustainable course – a course that, unless it is changed, will lead to catastrophes of awesome consequences', which is also a very apposite observation for global tourism. As Martin warns, describing the interconnected nature of the problems facing the planet, we are at a crossroads ('a time of transition'), at which increased tourism activity accompanies the excessive consumerism and rise in affluence in many countries, while in contrast, less developed countries face the most extreme consequences of most contemporary global problems (such as poverty, climate change, food shortages, desertification and famine). In short, we need a radical change to the way tourism operates and the impacts it induces. This means that tourism is symptomatic of many of the ills of modern society, as a consequence of its pursuit of individualism and consumption. A radical change in direction is required, and for this to happen, the stakeholders involved in tourism (tourists, destination communities and the natural, social and cultural environments affected in the destination) must look beyond the short-term 'benefits' that have characterized tourism growth and development throughout history: a new more sustainable approach to tourism is needed. But how do we begin to understand how a more sustainable approach can be developed (Gössling *et al.* 2009), if this involves considering future change in tourism? One starting point is to consider forecasting in tourism.

Forecasting change in tourism

According to Jefferson and Lickorish (1991: 101), forecasting the demand for tourism is essential for commercial operators, 'whether in the public or private sector . . . [as they] . . . will seek to maximize revenue and profits in moving towards maximum efficiency in [their] use of resources'. Archer (1987: 77) argues that:

> no manager can avoid the need for some form of forecasting: a manager must plan for the future in order to minimize the risk of failure or, more optimistically, to maximize the possibilities of success. In order to plan, he must use forecasts. Forecasts will always be made, whether by guesswork, teamwork or the use of complex models, and the accuracy of the forecasts will affect the quality of the management decision.

Reliable forecasts are essential for managers and decision-makers involved in service provision to try to ensure adequate supply is available to meet demand, while ensuring oversupply does not result, since this can erode the profitability of their operation. In essence, 'forecasts of tourism demand are essential for efficient planning by airlines, shipping companies, railways, coach operators, hoteliers, tour operators . . .' (Witt *et al.* 1991: 52). Forecasting is the process associated with an assessment of future changes in the demand for tourism. It must be stressed that 'forecasting is not an exact science' (Jefferson and Lickorish 1991: 102), as it attempts to make estimations of future traffic potential and a range of possible scenarios, which provide an indication of the likely scale of change in demand. Consequently, forecasting is a technique used to suggest the future pattern of demand.

According to Jefferson and Lickorish (1991: 102) the principal methods of forecasting are:

- 'the projection by extrapolation, of historic trends' (i.e. how the previous performance of demand may shape future patterns)
- 'extrapolation, subject to the application of . . . [statistical analysis using] . . . weights or variables'.

While additional methods may include structured group discussions among a panel of tourism experts to assess factors determining future tourism forecasts ('the Delphi Method'), more qualitative scenario-planning exercises can be used to depict future development situations (Page *et al.* 2006). The quantitative forecasting methods used in econometrics are reviewed in Song *et al.* (2009). Bull (1991: 127) notes that the most common variables used in these models are:

- number of tourist trips
- total tourist expenditure and expenditure per capita
- market shares of tourism
- the tourism sector's share of GDP.

Depending on the complexity of the methodology employed, the forecasting model may examine one dependent variable (e.g. tourist trips) and how other independent variables (e.g. the state of the national and international economy, leisure time, levels of disposable income, inflation and foreign exchange rates) affect the demand for tourist trips.

Ultimately, forecasting attempts to establish how consumer demand for tourism has shaped previous trends and how these may change in the future, often over a five- to ten-year period. At a world scale, UN–WTO forecasts predict that international tourist arrivals will grow to 1.5 billion by 2030. Domestic tourism, however, is expected to grow at a slower rate, and so be more constrained by the availability of leisure time, although some groups may have greater amounts of time (see Insight 27.1).

INSIGHT 27.1   **The senior market: A market opportunity for the global tourism industry?**

The senior market is invariably defined as those travellers in middle age and up, and has taken on increased significance in the light of what has been described as a 'greying' of the population of many Western nations. These are people who possess significant disposable income and an expectation of increased mobility reflected in greater international travel habits, as life expectancy rises. As Jang and Wu (2007) show, previous studies of the senior market have identified the various travel motivations of this group in terms of:

- rest and relaxation
- social interaction
- physical exercise
- learning
- nostalgia
- excitement
- visiting friends and relatives,

and different segments have been identified. This reflects a growing activeness of the over-50s, with around one in three taking an annual holiday in the UK, combined with increasing affluence once the family members have 'fled the nest'. Their participation in short breaks and long-haul trips as well as in adventurous holidays certainly questions many of the existing stereotypes of this market. On average the proportion of seniors makes up 25 per cent of the population in most countries, with Germany, Italy, France, the UK and Spain having the largest population in this age group in the EU.

One consequence for the tourism industry is the potential for more tailored, specialist or niche products. Even the US hotel chain, Hilton, has acknowledged the significance of this market in filling leisure capacity at preferential rates, by introducing a Senior Discounts Scheme for over-60s.

Although forecasting will never be an exact science, it is one of the bases upon which decision-makers plan to accommodate future changes in tourism and one of the best ways to understand its significance is to look at how it has been used in one country. The examination of forecasting also raises a wider discussion of the factors which are likely to influence the demand for tourism in the new millennium, and the most influential of these are now discussed. One criticism of these approaches to tourism demand forecasting is that they are not sophisticated enough to accommodate the impact of tourist behaviour change and the impact of events, as Song and Li (2008: 217) acknowledge:

Considering the enormous consequences of various crises and disasters, events' impact evaluation has attracted much interest in tourism demand forecasting research. It is crucial for researchers to develop some forecasting methods that can accommodate unexpected events in predicting the potential impacts of these one-off events through scenario analysis.

This points to the importance of scenario analysis as a valid technique to further enrich our understanding of tourism futures. Other studies such as Prideaux *et al.* (2003) reaffirmed the necessity of considering scenario analysis, given the problems of forecasting in foretelling the impact of events, and the significance of developing the domain often identified as tourism futures research. In short, scenario planning is the process of predicting multiple, plausible and uncertain futures, as briefly discussed in Chapter 3, and so is well suited to address some of the potential shortcomings of futures research, which is almost entirely based upon forecasting in tourism studies. Forecasting presupposes a degree of certainty in futures research, whereas scenario planning seeks to incorporate the principle that nothing is certain in the future: it is thus well suited to strategic planning. Examples of scenario planning in tourism include studies based on VisitScotland research by Page *et al.* (2006) and Page *et al.* (2010). For example, Yeoman *et al.* (2007) examine the question 'What will happen to Scottish tourism when oil runs out?', which also raises many wider strategic issues for the future development of tourism given its dependence upon fossil fuels. Research by Becken (2011) extends this debate to the dependence of the tourism sector on energy sources derived from oil. Recent increases in oil prices have had wide-ranging impacts on existing demand for tourism which will also extend into the future as the supply of oil decreases. There is an ongoing debate within the oil sector over whether we have reached the point of peak oil, which is the stage at which global production of oil has reached its zenith, and if we have reached it or will be nearing it soon, then long-term oil stocks will diminish while prices will rise. Although this does not take any account of alternative energy sources, the tourism sector is almost entirely dependent upon oil as a fossil fuel. To examine the long-term effects of oil price increases on tourism, Becken and Lennox (2012) focused on the potential effect on New Zealand; there the demand for long-haul travel will be affected, particularly travel to the UK, as price increases contribute to impacts on household budgets and disposable income for tourism as well as leading to more expensive holiday products.

Factors affecting the future shape of tourism trends

Within the tourism and marketing literature there is a recognition that tourism trends are influenced by a wide range of factors which are external to tourism and beyond its control (exogenous or external factors), while a range of tourism-related factors have a bearing on future trends, and examples of these are outlined in Figure 27.1. This shows that there are two broad considerations according to Cooper *et al.* (2005):

- exogenous and factors within our control
- factors outside of our control.

These two forces also impact on the tourist experience, and specific 'tourism processes of change' exist as shown in Figure 27.2. To outline some of these broad processes of change, Table 27.1 lists some of the main features which can be grouped under the following headings.

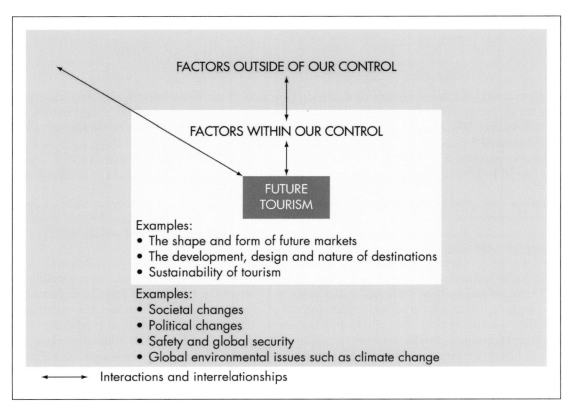

27

FIGURE 27.1 Factors within and outside of our control in tourism

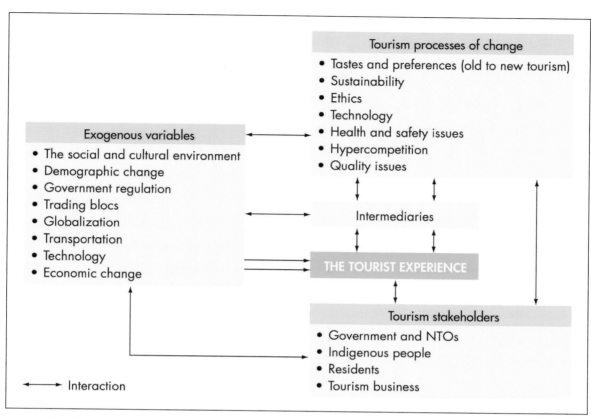

FIGURE 27.2 The future of tourism

Demographic factors

Changing tastes are affecting consumer behaviour as noted in Chapter 4, with the emergence of what Poon (1989) described as the new consumer who rejects the regimented, traditional packaged sun, sea and sand holidays in favour of more flexible holidays which are different from the mass tourism of the past. Combined with these consumer changes is a wide range of underlying demographic changes in the developed world, especially the ageing of the population, more flexible work practices, early retirement, the trend towards special interest holidays and a greater concern with the social and environmental consequences of tourism. For marketers, the shift towards generational marketing (Chapter 14) has helped to focus more closely on the attributes of specific groups for holidays.

Aside from the immediate demographic changes, there are also more profound global processes at work which are shaping future tourism trends. One such trend can best be explained as the relationship of tourism to migration: tourism can generate permanent immigration and, in turn, permanent immigration can generate a demand for tourism, particularly for the purpose of visiting friends and relatives (hereafter VFR). Many forms of migration generate tourism flows, in particular through the geographical extension of friendship and kinship networks. The migrants themselves may travel back to their country of origin for VFR or other purposes. Moreover, the migrants to a new country may be followed by their friends and relatives who choose to visit them in their new country. In the case of Vietnam, the global distribution of many family members who fled the country in the 1970s and who are now established overseas has been key to the major expansion plans of Vietnam Airlines, which seeks to grow international arrivals.

Such changes can also be related to changing lifestyles in both developed and undeveloped countries. For example, there are greater levels of prosperity among a wider range of the population and new social trends such as later marriage, couples deferring having children, the greater role of women in travel and the important role of senior travellers. All of these factors directly affect patterns of tourism, combined with the greater levels of discretionary spending among these groups on tourism. One of the main drivers of change among tourists as consumers is the pursuit of something new or unique, a different experience. This contrasts with the increasing time pressures which many in the workforce of developed countries report. The result is the pursuit of new destinations.

27

TABLE 27.1 Demographic, economic and societal changes which will impact upon the future of tourism and travel

● **Demographic changes**

- In the next 20 years, the over-50s age group is likely to become larger than the under-50s group, especially in Western nations, which are major drivers of tourism demand
- The growing segmentation of the senior market, where 60 years of age is now viewed in Western countries as the 'new 40 years old', seeking multiple travel experiences, dominating luxury travel with increased disposable income. In the UK, one in five over-60-year-olds take over three holidays a year
- Increasingly experienced over-60s travellers, with facilities and services (e.g. medical services) to support their travel needs
- Increasing trend towards single-parent families and double-income households
- Older parenting and smaller family size
- Single people comprise 32 per cent of the US market, and 29 per cent of the UK market, comprising key characteristics – ICT-savvy, time-poor, independent with individual needs but lucrative spenders
- Declining amount of annual holiday leave time taken by managerial groups (e.g. only 50 per cent take the full amount of leave in the USA)
- Rise of well-being and stress management holiday trips (e.g. revitalization of spa and treatments)
- Hedonistic behaviour, with occasional large purchases in search of quality, memorable experiences
- Increasing life expectancy which is set to rise to over 80 years of age in the next 20 years and rise of 'second homes', 'multiple careers' and importance of an ongoing workforce.

● **Economic changes**

- Growing household affluence, with rich elite (the new upper class) and growing middle class driving outbound tourism in many developing countries
- Global inequality between the consumer society – which the Worldwatch Institute estimate comprises 1.7 billion people, half of which live in the developing world – and those outside it. One illustration of consumption by these groups is that over 531 million cars exist worldwide and this is growing by 11 million a year, and US$14 billion is spent on cruising each year, a sum which could virtually eliminate world hunger and malnutrition
- A growing disparity between rich and poor in the global economy and the misallocation of resources to consumerism, including tourism.

● **Environmental challenges**

- A growing debate on sustainability, the interdependence of man and nature and the impact of excessive consumerism on resource consumption: Martin (2007) points to 7 per cent of people on earth consuming 80 per cent of the available energy.
- According to Mastyn (2001) the issues of global inequalities are replicated in patterns of tourism

consumption: 80 per cent of international tourists originate from Europe and the Americas and only 3.5 per cent of the world's population travels internationally. However, international travel will still remain an elite form of travel

- The globalization of tourism activity by large companies has seen the sustainable benefits of tourism dissipated, especially in many African countries while generating impacts which threaten the long-term resource base. This results in tourists cocooning themselves from their own impacts
- Environmental issues remain important for consumers, in spite of their limited understanding of their own impact. Global warming, climate change and pollution are key issues and will gather momentum in the next decade.

● **Patterns of travel**

- Müller (2002) outlined ten future holiday models based on a study of the future of tourism which may encompass:

  ● a growth in adventure-seeking holiday behaviour
  ● a rise in independent travellers seeking flexible holiday products
  ● the demand for more sophisticated travel products
  ● forms of relaxation, wellness and well-being enhanced tourism and recreation
  ● a growth in second-home ownership
  ● the pursuit of winter sun holiday destinations
  ● cheaper travel products, promoted by online booking
  ● more frequent and shorter trips
  ● greater spontaneity in travel decisions
  ● more mobile travel patterns, including multiple-destination trips.

● **Challenges for the tourism industry**

- Improving the quality of tourism and making it a greener product
- Widening participation to tourism via greater access, particularly for different social groups such as disabled people
- Being technologically sophisticated using ICTs to meet the needs of the online consumer and changing patterns of consumer behaviour
- Managing a more diverse industry, with a number of trends occurring simultaneously (e.g. mass tourism, elite tourism, domestic and international tourism, business and leisure travel and full service and no-frills service) and a greater disintermediation brought about by new technology
- Increased competition between destinations seeking to lure the tourist dollar while still aiming to be unique, different and customer-focused
- Changing demographic and economic trends which are challenging existing concepts of tourist motivation, leisure, lifestyle and the meaning and traditional definition of travel and tourism.

Sources: Various

Political change

Governments directly affect the pattern of travel, and can constrain and facilitate travel depending on the policies, activities and climate they promote for their citizens and visitors. In the 1990s the opening up of Eastern Europe dramatically altered the pattern of travel in Europe, leading to a demand for cultural tourism in Eastern European destinations, as improved infrastructure and opportunities for travel have created a host of new urban tourist destinations. Many of the fast-expanding destinations in the new millennium in Europe are located in these areas, as low-cost airlines, low-cost accommodation and an undeveloped tourism environment offers competition to many established west European destinations. One case in point is the rapid growth of Prague in the Czech Republic as a major urban destination. Coastal destinations like Montenegro also offer an attraction for the adventurous traveller. No one in the early 1980s could have forecast these changes and it illustrates how rapid change can be in tourism where political forces change. Conversely, destinations emerging from political turmoil, such as Vietnam after the Doi Moi reforms of 1986 and its move to market socialism (followed by today's industrial expansion), the 'new' South Africa, and Cambodia, can also provide new opportunities for tourism.

The impact of trading blocs such as the EU and NAFTA (the North American Free Trade Agreement) may contribute to a greater harmonization of travel regulations to ease the flow of travel in these new free trade areas. One also needs to recognize that the state is an agent of economic development in many countries where the secondary sector (e.g. traditional manufacturing activities) has declined and a greater emphasis been placed on the facilitation of tourism. Among some of the future issues which will impact upon the political acceptability of tourism in different destinations are:

- *community attitudes*, acceptance or non-compliance with a tourism-led strategy for economic development
- *human rights issues*, including labour rights, political oppression and the ongoing civil disturbances and war, as tourism needs a stable political environment
- *political stability of governments*, notably the ability to plan for tourism and maintain political support for its development, as political ideologies change
- *the role of international tourism companies* and their ability to generate local benefits which make tourism a viable economic proposition, rather than simply expropriating all profits from the host country (i.e. investing in the human capital of the destination)
- *the role of the nation-state versus the new trading blocs* like the EU, as more members are added and political cooperation challenges existing models of European tourism
- *the role of conflict between nation-states* (e.g. the Arab Spring movement) and the wider public perception of instability and tourism
- *newly emerging countries and regions*, such as the 48 states in Latin America, some of which have begun to develop inbound tourism, and their significance in establishing a new image for their countries via tourism development. In this instance, democracy will be a key issue in public acceptability of tourism
- *the significance of political fragmentation* and movements for alternative states within countries, and public perception of the role of tourism in adding legitimacy to their claims
- *global politics and international relations* will pose a major challenge to achieving greater political harmony and agreement between countries to ease travel and access, which will be counterbalanced by the need to address terrorist threats
- *media coverage*, where negative publicity will quickly damage visitor flows.

Technological change

Technology and virtual reality have brought major changes to tourism, by potentially enhancing the pursuit of the authentic tourism experience with entertainment-based experiences. While there are varied arguments about the impacts, despite the increasing role of technology in the everyday lives of people, it is unlikely to remove the pursuit of 'getting away' to relax in different environments and places. In terms of technology, one of the principal changes occurring globally is the continued growth of artificial environments for tourism and leisure activity. This is reflected in the global theme park industry which has grown into a US$11-billion-a-year business, with an estimated 119 major theme parks spread across the world. We now live in an information society, connected by the information superhighway; while much of the expansion in ICTs to date has been computer (PC)-based, this has now moved to mobile technologies (e.g. the smartphone). In the tourism industry, ICTs have revolutionized the organization, management and day-to-day running of businesses. ICTs have helped to reduce some of the costs of business operations. They have assisted in the globalization of tourism business activity, and the impact of the Internet is all-embracing. The use of technology in this way will certainly continue as tourism suppliers increasingly target the online booker, providing the flexibility of booking in your own home.

This new technology has been incorporated into much of the new technology since 2004 and the arrival of *smartphones* and *Web 2.0*. Thus, as these technologies have converged, portable devices have become ubiquitous and capable of enabling society to be more online and interactive. This has changed how organizations manage and market themselves, particularly how relationships are built with customers. For example, VisitScotland has over 2 million customer details on its databases for electronic and postal contact. The rise of more fluid consumers, consuming a range of products in any tourism experience, means that being able to engage with them during their tourism journey while remaining in contact will be crucial. As Chapters 6 and 11 have shown, there may also be greater future automation, with the potential use of robots in tourism (Image 27.1) although other forms of technology also remain important (see Image 27.2).

In the transport sector, technological innovations in the way aviation is organized and managed in the future will see cooperation, collaboration and mergers pursued; the introduction of driverless vehicles will be a key element in reducing costs.

Probably one of the most exciting developments in technology is the potential development of space tourism (ST). ST has been a widely debated topic since the first moon landing in the 1960s and the Space Tourism Society (http://www.spacetourismsociety.org) defines the nature of ST as:

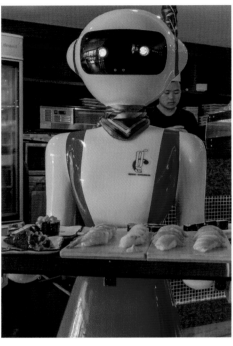

IMAGE 27.1 Humanoid robot used to serve people

- Earth orbit and suborbital experiences.
- Beyond-Earth orbit experiences (to Mars, for example).
- Earth-based simulations (i.e. Sim Experiences), tourism and entertainment-based experiences such as the NASA centres.
- Cyberspace tourism experiences.

The concept of ST received a major boost in 2001 when a US businessman, Denis Tito, joined a one-week voyage to an international space station, moving the issue from fantasy to fact. Despite the multi-million dollar cost of the experience, a number of ST companies were subsequently founded by multi-billionaires (e.g. Paul Allen, co-founder of Microsoft, and Sir Richard Branson, founder of Virgin Airlines). Their ideas range from building orbital access vehicles to lunar cruise ships and orbital superyachts, to reach a much wider market. Much of this is discussed in Spencer (2004), which depicts future scenarios for space tourism. However, space tourism is now a reality, with Virgin Galactic's proposed space tours which are imminent, *with tickets costing around US$ 250 000.*

IMAGE 27.2 The combination of theme park and film set tour at Universal Studios, Los Angeles provides a model of mixing entertainment, fun and the consumption of technology-enhanced attractions that will continue to grow in importance in the digital age

Changing business practices

What will continue to characterize the tourism industry is the pace and scale of change, with globalization and increased competition the buzzwords of the future. The growing trend towards increased efficiency in the tourism industry worldwide has led to the continued expansion of multinational chains providing services in many countries. The hotel industry is a good example of this. The many advantages of such concentration in the different tourism sectors are associated with economies of scale, the ability to resource promotional campaigns and a greater brand awareness using modern marketing techniques such as television, direct mailing and billboards. One of the most profound changes in the business environment, as Page (2009) observed, is the concept of hypercompetition, particularly in the international airline industry.

Hypercompetition and disruptive technologies

Within the global marketplace, tourism providers are constantly striving to improve their business performance. This has to be set in the context of wider changes in the operating environment of sectors such as the airline industry, which has confronted a deregulated environment, with state controls lifted to encourage competition. This has seen the role of traditional state airlines, which previously had an oligopolistic position, challenged by new entrants and competitors. D'Aveni (1998) characterized hypercompetition in this sector of the tourism industry in terms of:

- rapid product innovation
- aggressive competition
- shorter product lifecycles
- businesses experimenting with meeting customers' needs
- the rising importance of business alliances
- the destruction of norms and rules of national oligopolies.

The principal changes which hypercompetition induce are related to the way the competitors enter the marketplace and how they disrupt the existing business. They do this in a number of ways:

- by redefining the product market
- by shifting the benchmark on quality
- by offering more at a lower price
- by modifying the industry's purpose and focus by bundling and splitting industries. This can be seen in BA's response to easyJet: establishing a low-cost airline – Go – with a lower cost of operation from London Stansted Airport. However, easyJet eventually purchased the company during BA's repositioning and restructuring
- by disrupting the supply chain by redefining the knowledge and know-how needed to deliver the product to the customer, such as by exploiting new forms of technology and distribution channels
- by harnessing global resources from alliances and partners to compete with non-aligned business. This is very evident in the international airline industry now that the major global alliances have a greater degree of control over service provision,

although running parallel to such trends are global concerns about tourist safety and security, as discussed in Chapter 25.

Global security and safety

The 9/11 Commission Report, published in 2003, acknowledged that global terrorism has now made the world a much less safe place for international travel. These security concerns have had a profound effect on the volatility of international tourism demand, which fluctuated as a result of the 9/11 event and the Japanese nuclear explosion at

Fukushima in 2011, broadcast by the global media. According to the WTTC's (2002) *Travel and Tourism Security Action Plan*, to counter the threat of terrorism on global tourism there needs to be:

- *coordination of policy, actions and communications* so security and safety permeates the entire organization and leads to cooperation among employees and stakeholders. For travel advisers (e.g. travel agents), an informed decision on risks and areas to avoid is necessary rather than blanket negative images
- *measures to ensure a secure operating environment*, including the deployment of biometric measures to defeat terrorism. New technology is vital to implement security requirements
- *measures to deny terrorists freedom of action*, so communities do not make it easy for terrorists to work within them; employees' grievances in enterprises and community antagonisms should all be addressed
- *the ability to have access to and work with the best intelligence*, from staff and the public sector and communication to employees. Intelligence needs to flow in all directions, to address the terrorist threat.

These four principles highlight how a more vigilant tourism sector can help to reduce the global threat of terrorism *that remains ever present.*

Issues of concern to tourists

Ethical and moral issues

There is also a growing concern with ethical business practices in tourism, reflected in the WTO's (1999) development of a *Global Code of Ethics for Tourism*, which is wide-ranging, as Table 27.2 shows. This is a wider recognition of the complexity of tourism as an activity which has wide-ranging implications for the tourist, the tourism employee, countries and the natural environment. Linked to these issues are the legal and moral concerns with the spread of sex tourism and the impact on children, as reflected in the excellent advocacy work of the agency End Child Prostitution and Trafficking (ECPAT), discussed in Chapter 23. There is a growing body of opinion associated with the belief that future tourism development and activity needs to be founded upon a paradigm of responsibility that embodies principles of equity and is underpinned by ethical behaviour. Part of this thinking is embodied in the concept of responsible tourism, addressed in Chapter 24 and later in this chapter. It is epitomized by the work of the campaigning organization Tourism Concern, which recognized the important role tourism can play in the UN Millennium Development Goals in reducing poverty in developing countries. Tourism Concern's (2009) *Putting Tourism to Rights* report illustrates many of the problems which tourism can contribute to and exacerbate in the developing world including:

- The violation of human rights (e.g. in 2006, 7000 people were evicted from Digya National Park in Ghana to develop the area as a game reserve for tourism).
- Denying local people access to basic necessities of life such as water while supplies are diverted to hotels and to irrigate golf courses, posing access issues for local residents.
- Polluting the local environment through hotel effluent discharges and damaging the water table through excessive groundwater extraction to supply tourist needs.
- Abuse of workers' rights such as the poor treatment of porters at Machu Picchu, Peru in terms of basic living standards, and the introduction of a daily rate of US$8 a day, to reduce exploitation of this group, by the tourism organizations.

Sustainability and the environment

The topic of tourism and sustainability continues to attract a great deal of interest among tourists, governments and the tourism industry. Many new research agendas have emerged around seeking to make tourist travel and activity less carbon-dependent, as new ideas such as *slow travel* (Dickinson and Lumsdon 2010) gather momentum. Yet implementing strategies for sustainable tourism and monitoring their effectiveness remains a fundamental stumbling block which the tourism industry has to overcome. For example, consider the reality of countries in South Asia where rapid population growth, images of rural poverty and urbanization exist alongside the government's pursuit of tourism development to gain much-needed foreign currency to assist with development objectives. While existing regional surveys of the area and the respective countries of India, Pakistan and Bangladesh highlight the range of development problems facing the governments, and the policies adopted to deal with them, urbanization is a major problem associated with each country and poses major concerns for the sustainability of tourism in these environments (UN–WTO 2010). The region contains five of the world's 25 largest cities: Mumbai, Calcutta, Delhi, Karachi and Dhaka, and rapid urbanization is adding a new series of development problems for South Asia that also impact upon tourism.

TABLE 27.2 A Global Code of Ethics for Tourism

The World Tourism Organization developed a code of ethics for tourism in conjunction with its members, following their initiative to draft a code in 1997. This is a recognition of the need to enshrine many of the principles of global action on the environment and the rights of tourists and workers in writing, considering global legislation from other bodies.

The basic principles inherent in the code are:

- Tourism's contribution to mutual understanding and respect between peoples and societies.
- Tourism as a vehicle for individual and collective fulfilment.
- Tourism as a factor of sustainable development.
- Tourism as a user of the cultural heritage of mankind and contributor to its enhancement.
- Tourism as a beneficial activity for host countries and communities.
- Obligations of stakeholders in tourism development.
- Rights to tourism.
- Liberty of tourist movements.
- Rights of the workers and entrepreneurs in the tourism industry.
- Implementation of the principles of the Global Code of Ethics for Tourism.

Source: Adapted from WTO (1999)

The essential feature of sustainable tourism development identified by the WTTC *et al.* (2002: 11) was:

The challenge for stakeholders involved in all industries is to find a balance between sustenance, prosperity and people's desire to improve their financial/material well-being, with the underlying need for identity, community, religion, home and family. Travel and tourism can play a vital role in balancing these forces. It not only provides the livelihoods for both rural and urban communities, but has the capacity, when planned, developed and managed properly, to enhance community relations and build bridges of understanding and peace between nations.

Yet over eight years later, the concept of *balance* has translated into a conscious need for many destinations to grapple with the concept of growth management, epitomized in extreme cases by overtourism. For example, by 2030 China is likely to be the leading international destination in terms of volume of arrivals. This will pose problems for destinations in managing the quantity, quality and locations which visitors choose to visit. These pressures are already leading many destinations to question whether sustainability is compatible with significant volume growth in tourists. Some destinations have sought at first to limit numbers but then expanded visitor volumes (e.g. the Galapagos Islands), while others have adopted closer monitoring of arrivals to limit demand through restricting supply and capacity (i.e. growth or capacity management). Whatever strategy a destination pursues, the monitoring of growth will become a much greater issue to control tourism. The pressure of environmental awareness, climate change and political pressures to expand tourism economies will mean critical trade-offs have to be made. As the UN–WTO (2008) points out, the pressure to restrict consumption to tackle climate change will pose problems for governments and the tourism sector. Without more concerted action at government and public–private partnership level and within individual countries, tourism will continue to gain an image as a resource consumer and destroyer. In fact the debates have moved on a great way in recent years and one of the current debates around sustainability now in vogue is *decarbonizing tourism*.

27

Decarbonizing tourism – is it possible?

According to Scott *et al.* (2016), the global tourism industry is responsible for 5 per cent of global greenhouse emissions and has a reliance upon carbon-based fuels. To achieve long-term emission reductions, Scott *et al.* (2016) argue that this will require a 70 per cent reduction in carbon emissions. The distribution of emissions by sector is dominated by aviation (52 per cent), the accommodation sector (27 per cent), automobiles (19 per cent) and 2 per cent comprised of rail, buses and boats. While Scott *et al.* (2016) calculate that an additional charge of US$11 per person would help offset these emissions by 2050, critics point to the intractable nature of the problem. For example, a seminal discussion paper by Becken (2019) set out six principal challenges to decarbonizing tourism:

1   *The existing growth paradigm associated with tourism that is predicated on the notion that tourism must grow wherever it is developed.* As Figure 27.3 illustrates, at a global scale, lead organizations like the UN–WTO and World Travel and Tourism Council lobby for tourism interests. As Becken (2019) suggests, most of the member countries affiliated with the World Tourism Organization are from emerging economies and so associate tourism growth with development benefits. Becken (2019) suggests that these messages are reinforced by the UN–WTO in programmes that use tourism to reduce poverty and reduce social inequality. It is no surprise that, as Figure 27.3 shows, tourism and growth are seen as mutually exclusive. In other words, seeking to reverse the growth means we need to revisit the sustainability agendas from the 1960s and 1970s we reviewed in Chapter 19, particularly the idea that small is beautiful (Schumacher 1973), to achieve small-scale growth. This approach is at the polar opposite of the tourism-growth paradigm.

2   *There is an institutionalism of tourism interests (e.g. private sector, lobby groups, NGOs and the public sector) that promotes growth, with little commitment to long-term planning.* In other words, elites control the power base of political decision-making, making it difficult to challenge the status quo or to provide alternative futures not based on growth.

3   *The nature of policymaking seeks to retain the status quo and the growth agenda, since the institutionalism of interests often have the greatest influence on policymaking, to the detriment of citizen-engaged policymaking.* Even when alternative paradigms are considered (e.g. the green economy), the focus is still upon growth to further enhance tourism, as illustrated in Chapter 19. The green economy paradigm is underpinned by arguments that promote sustainable development as opposed to restraint/constraint or low-growth options.

4   *The improvements being made by the tourism sector to reduce emissions are inadequate, typically being piecemeal and incremental, failing to gain the momentum or level of impact needed to make significant reductions.*

5   *The tourism sector has adopted a focus on technological efficiency (i.e. leaner burn jet engines on aircraft) as the solution to reducing emissions rather than limiting growth.* This leaves the tourist as a consumer and their behaviour unchanged when in fact that is the greatest challenge. If prospective tourist behaviour can be changed, then the growth paradigm will not be fed by an insatiable demand for continued expansion of tourism supply.

6   *At a global scale, tourism is now so entrenched in the economies of most of the world's countries, that any action to stem the tide of tourism demand and supply would need a concerted global campaign.* Yet as Becken (2019) argues, tourism epitomizes inequality, with affluent consumers engaging in this activity. To make a fundamental change to the tourism-growth paradigm would require a major disruption to the tourism system, with traumatic effects on the scale that some crises have had on individual destinations and countries. As Becken (2019) rightly concludes – growth in tourism does not occur unless it is promoted.

Becken (2019) does point to a number of promising signs of change when looking at the drivers of carbon emissions of tourism (see Figure 27.4). As Figure 27.4 shows, change agents (shown in yellow on the margins of the diagram) are what Becken calls 'shifters'. While small in scale and influence, various developments (e.g. social entrepreneurship, reviewed in Chapter 12) and new ways of thinking (i.e. a shift from volume-based growth to value-based growth) may offer new directions. These ideas build upon advances in thinking in marketing. Other key initiatives suggested by Becken (2019) include:

- Taking holidays closer to home
- Using certified suppliers and more responsible organizations
- Consuming less but getting greater value from what is consumed
- Purchasing low carbon products and carbon off-setting
- Intervention of government to reinforce the ideology of more sustainable consumption patterns.

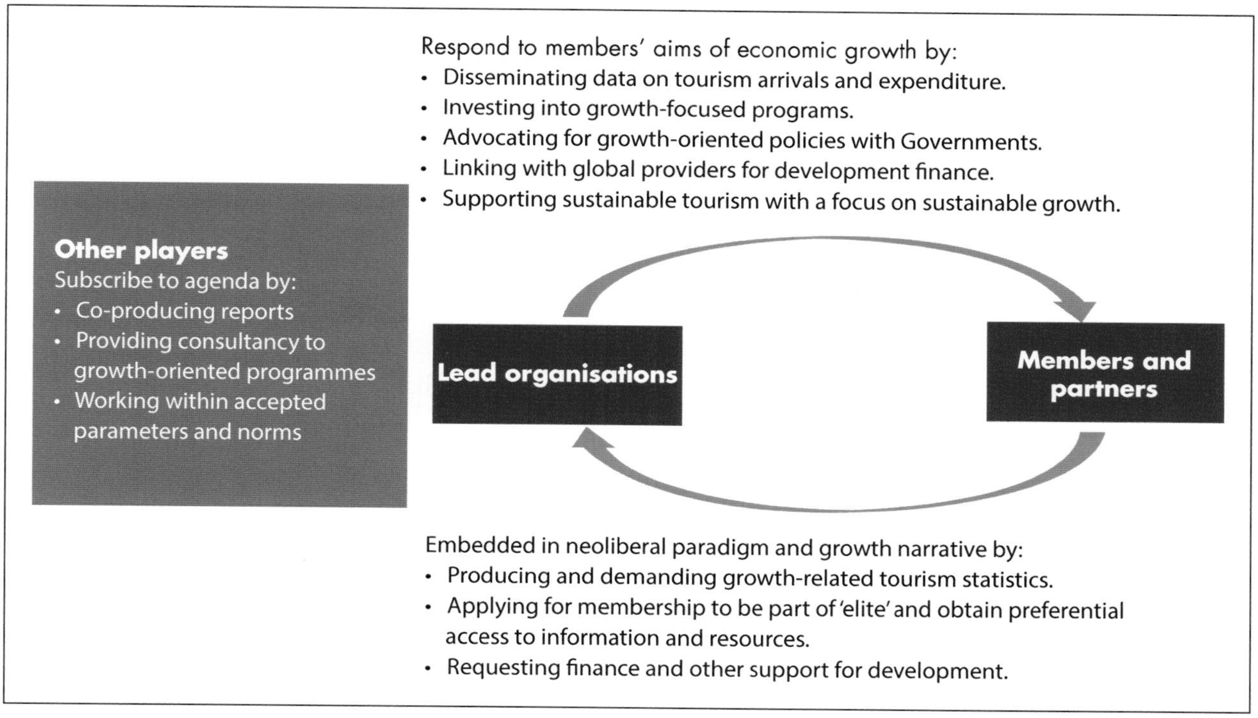

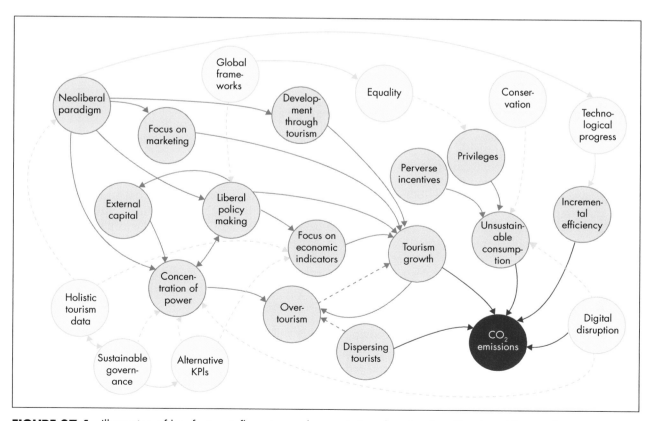

Respond to members' aims of economic growth by:
• Disseminating data on tourism arrivals and expenditure.
• Investing into growth-focused programs.
• Advocating for growth-oriented policies with Governments.
• Linking with global providers for development finance.
• Supporting sustainable tourism with a focus on sustainable growth.
Other players
Subscribe to agenda by:
• Co-producing reports
• Providing consultancy to growth-oriented programmes
• Working within accepted parameters and norms
Lead organisations
Members and partners
Embedded in neoliberal paradigm and growth narrative by:
• Producing and demanding growth-related tourism statistics.
• Applying for membership to be part of 'elite' and obtain preferential access to information and resources.
• Requesting finance and other support for development.

FIGURE 27.3 The reinforcing circle of the prevailing growth paradigm between key players
Source: Becken (2019: 4)

Global frame-works
Equality
Conser-vation
Techno-logical progress
Neoliberal paradigm
Focus on marketing
Develop-ment through tourism
Privileges
Perverse incentives
External capital
Liberal policy making
Focus on economic indicators
Tourism growth
Unsustain-able consump-tion
Incremen-tal efficiency
Concen-tration of power
Holistic tourism data
Over-tourism
Dispersing tourists
CO2 emissions
Digital disruption
Sustainable govern-ance
Alternative KPIs

FIGURE 27.4 Illustration of key factors influencing carbon emissions from tourism. The dotted lines indicate a negative feedback loop. Change factors are highlighted in yellow.
Source: Becken (2019: 11)

In 2019, Iceland announced plans to become a carbon-neutral destination by reducing its carbon footprint by 2030 to support the 2015 Paris Agreement on Climate Change (see Chapter 19). By 2040, the country aims to become carbon neutral, while the government bodies in Iceland have agreed to become carbon neutral in 2019, demonstrating leadership in the area. The carbon neutral strategy is underpinned by off-setting carbon use through planting forests in Iceland to absorb the carbon emitted through tourism. Icelandair and Air Iceland have also supported this strategy by allowing passengers to offset their carbon emissions via the Kolvidor Scheme to cultivate forests in Iceland. There are a wide range of philosophical positions on the validity of these voluntary off-setting measures from seeing them as a genuine attempt to reduce environmental impacts through to viewing them as a failure to address the real problem – changing our travel behaviour. Clark (2011) offers a very thought-provoking and challenging critique of off-setting and the philosophical and economic aspects of these growing range of measures. Whatever standpoint one adopts – the evidence is indisputable: *tourism contributes to climate change and the climate emergency and is an activity that is not a fundamental human necessity*. As the headline of Kommenda's (2019) article poignantly explains: '1% of English residents take one-fifth of overseas flights, survey shows'. This was based on the National Travel Survey of 15 000 people, carried out in 2018. Citing data from the UK's Department of Transport, the article also indicated that *10 per cent of the UK's most frequent flyers took over 50 per cent of the international flights in 2018*. And 40 per cent of the population did not take a flight at all in 2018. Kommenda (2019) also reports on the call for a progressive tax on frequent flyers. This would leave holidaymakers who are not frequent flyers less affected by measures to reduce aviation emission and pollution, since forecasts show that this will be the main source of UK greenhouse gas emissions by 2050. As illustrated in Chapter 19, a combination of nudge behaviour and government measures are necessary to address this protracted problem of excessive flying. However, as Kommenda (2019) shows, the aviation lobby is a powerful group protecting the interests of its members and to date, the aviation sector has sidestepped taking radical steps to address emissions. One has to recognize that this sector has growth as an ideology, since it supports the private and public sector interests of its members. This is evident from the continued growth of new airport construction and expansion plans globally, often using the arguments of its vital role in economic development to convince governments of the necessity of its growth agenda. This position will need to dramatically change if the impact of aviation on climate change is to be tackled. Making future growth carbon neutral is not the solution, and is little more than window dressing, as the current levels of aviation emissions also needs to be addressed. We cannot rely upon expected technological improvements in aircraft fuel consumption and more anthropocentric ideologies to address what is an ecological catastrophe. We need an ecocentric approach, where sustainability and the finite nature of environmental resources are at the heart of our thinking (see Chapter 19 for more discussion of these perspectives).

Managing change in tourism

Managing change in a fast-moving business sector such as tourism will continue to pose enormous challenges for tourism businesses in the twenty-first century. In a practical business setting, management occurs in the context of a formal environment – the organization. But the future shape and nature of global tourism organizations is changing. These organizations are becoming more fluid, moving from being place-specific to being more global as ICTs and virtual locations provide opportunities to develop less hierarchical and more interwoven series of webs. What is critical is the tourism manager's ability to be adaptable and flexible as new organizational models develop, particularly in fast-moving areas like tourism. Change is a modern-day feature of management and any manager needs to be aware of, and able to respond to, changes in the organizational environment. For example, general changes in society, such as the decision of a new ruling political party to deregulate the economy, have a bearing on the operation of organizations. More specific factors can also influence the organizational environment including:

- *sociocultural factors*, which include the behaviour, beliefs and norms of the population in a specific area
- *demographic factors*, which are related to the changing composition of the population (e.g. birth rates, mortality rates and the growing burden of dependency in consequence of the increasingly ageing population who will have to be supported by a declining number of economically active people in the workforce)
- *economic factors*, which include the type of capitalism at work in a given country and the degree of state control of business. The economic system is also important since it may have a bearing on the level of prosperity and factors which influence the system's ability to produce, distribute and consume wealth

- *political and legal factors*, which are the framework in which organizations must work (e.g. laws and practices)
- *technological factors*, where advances in technology can be used to create products more efficiently. The use of information technology and its application to business practices is a case in point
- *competitive factors*, which illustrate that businesses operate in markets and other producers may seek to offer superior services or products at a lower price. Businesses also compete for finance, sources of labour and other resources
- *international factors*, as businesses operate in a global environment and factors operating in other countries may impact on the local business environment.

Change and uncertainty are unpredictable in free market economies, and managers have to ensure that organizations can adapt while ensuring that survival and prosperity are ensured. Change may be vital for organizations to adapt and grow in new environments, and the introduction of information technology is one example where initial resistance within businesses had to be overcome. Increasingly, tourism managers are not only having to undertake the role of managing, but also the dynamic role of 'change agent'. Tourism managers have to understand how systems and organizations work and function to create desirable outcomes, often without the experience of how change will affect them. This requires leadership to embody changes and translate it into action to seize the opportunities which change offers. Two illustrations of this are how to develop new niche products and how to foster innovation.

According to Hall (2003: 18), niche tourism concerns:

- identifying and stimulating demand, segmenting consumers into identifiable groups for targeting purposes
- providing and promoting supply, by differentiating products and services from those of competitors.

One example of this has been the development of media-induced tourism, particularly film and television programme locations which can increase visitor numbers by a third in the first year after release or broadcast. This may assist with the advertising and promotion of an area using a new image. Yet even this highlights the challenge for tourism managers, where undesired effects may arise from overcrowding, congestion, excessive merchandising, local price inflation and other impacts on local communities. Conversely, the nature of tourism development is such that the ability of other areas/destinations to imitate or copy successful models of development will limit the lifecycle of new products and innovations. As a result, constant innovation is needed if niche products are to be developed and, ultimately, the niche product of today may end up being the mass product of tomorrow.

The unanswered question for many destinations with environmental limits to accommodating growth, such as Antarctica, is how do we control tourism growth? Do you control it by limiting numbers or do you have to ban it? In the case of Antarctica, scientists do not really know enough to question tourism industry claims that 28 000 visitors a year have no detrimental impact on one of the world's last wildernesses. Antarctica faces the issue of whether the shift from small-scale, scientific visits to commercial tourism is environmentally sustainable. This dilemma now faces many tourism destinations given the pace, scale and nature of tourism development. The guiding principle underpinning such critical decisions is to adopt a cautious approach and limit access where the environmental consequences are not fully understood. The problem is this runs in opposition to the prevailing commercial view of the tourism sector that this is a lucrative opportunity to cultivate a niche product. As the tourism sector has few best-practice examples of self-regulation to exercise restraint and environmental consciousness with such fragile resources, direct intervention by planning organizations is probably the only realistic option to safeguard the environment. In fact, the pressure that is developing to see disappearing wildernesses and revered locations has been described as **Last-Chance Tourism (LCT)**.

Last-Chance Tourism

Lemelin *et al.* (2012) examined destinations which were deemed to be under threat or disappearing, which included:

- Antarctica (see Image 27.3)
- The Arctic
- The Great Barrier Reef

as well as wildlife habitats that are under threat (see www.wwf.org.uk for examples). Unfortunately, media coverage of the threats posed by tourism has only exacerbated the scale of the problem as people try to visit rather

27

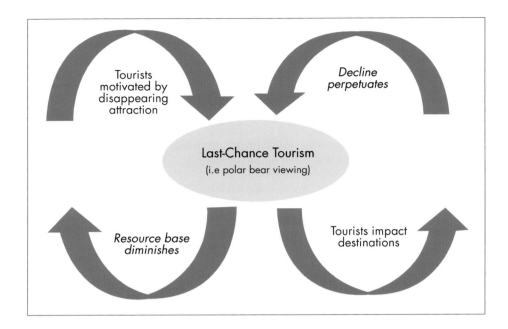

FIGURE 27.5 Model showing the paradox associated with LCT
Source: Dawson *et al.* (2011)

than exercising restraint. The compounding effects of media exposure are examined by Dawson *et al.* (2011) and Piggot-McKellar and McNamara (2017) as shown in Figure 27.5.

While Figure 27.5 shows that LCT is accentuated by populist media coverage of climate change and its effect on the landscape and attractions of natural resources, it also shows a lack of commitment by the media to sustainability. It is not surprising that critics talk of the principles of sustainability being paid only lip service by consumers and the visitor economy when the media keep emphasizing a disappearing world. In some cases, tourism is becoming less rather than more environmentally sustainable while economies become more economically dependent upon the tourist dollar. There are no easy solutions to the tourism trauma that is now being felt by many locations globally.

In 2018, the travel guide company Fodor listed key locations where overtourism was posing a range of problems, including environmental issues: the Galapagos Islands, Phang Nga National Park, Thailand, Mount Everest and the Taj Mahal. Missouri was also listed due to racial tensions; Honduras for violence to tourists; the Great Wall of China for over-visitation and Beijing for air pollution. The prevailing ideology and sustainability policies mean different things to different people. The challenge of implementing changes that will make tourism environmentally sustainable, given the prevailing hedonistic philosophy towards indulgence and pleasure at the expense of personal responsibility towards one's travel impact means planning bodies need to intervene. This raises the issue of whether alternative ways of thinking about tourism and its future direction might be important in rethinking a future pathway where the ideology of sustainability is an ideal goal to work towards BUT a more pragmatic and practical route map for tourism development exists and is based on responsible tourism. As Mowforth *et al.* (2008: 1) argue that '. . . we would not wish to promote the idea that there is a correct way to tour, to service tourists, or to develop tourism. Yes, tourism can be practiced in a relatively responsible, sustainable and ethical way. But the important word here is relatively, for the notions of responsibility, sustainability and ethics are relative to the values and perspectives of all those who participate in tourism.' As a result, we invite you to think about the future of global tourism by considering the ideology-policy-practice dilemma we present in Figure 27.6.

27 **IMAGE 27.3** Image of Antarctica to show tourist impact

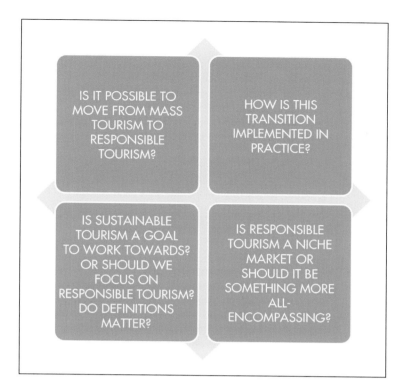

FIGURE 27.6 Ideology-policy-practice for tourism: Points for reflection

Conclusion

This chapter has highlighted a range of issues which are relevant for the tourist and the tourism sector in the new millennium since the pace of change and development in tourism is fast. In contrast, planning and developing new areas for tourist activity is a slower process, with the provision of infrastructure such as an airport expansion taking five to ten years before the project is operational. This illustrates the need for tourism managers to be realistic about the ability of resorts and destinations to accommodate visitors, with a view to assessing the appropriate carrying capacity. There are no simple solutions to developing tourism in new areas and in redeveloping tourism in areas that are flagging or have lost their sparkle. Understanding global processes of tourism combined with the individual processes affecting tourism in a given area or location is no substitute for planning. Understanding the consumer is essential and monitoring their needs and what they feel about their tourist experience remains a vital element in the tourism industry's

understanding its consumers. What is now being regarded as tourism is constantly expanding as new ideas and new trends develop, and businesses and planners need to have an open mind.

Above all else, anyone working and managing in the tourism industry will need to appreciate the need to implement new human resource policies, and ensure employees are well trained and educated as well as able to cope with change (e.g. the challenge of new technology). The tourism industry is an exciting sector to work in, even though some of the glamour and glitz associated with images of working on a tropical island may not always be met in reality. For anyone seeking a challenge and a career in a sector changing rapidly, the tourism industry offers a great deal of interesting and varied work. For the industry, promoting this image and creating a positive image of long-term career structures in both the tourism and hospitality sectors is vital to continue to attract high-calibre staff at all levels.

Discussion questions

1 What are the prospects for developing space tourism?
2 How would you set about forecasting the future market for, and changes in, tourism in a specific destination?
3 Is the future growth of tourism going to be constrained by political events and concerns over safety?
4 Will the tourist of the future be one who is environmentally responsible?

References

Archer, B.H. (1987) 'Demand forecasting and estimation', in J.R.B. Ritchie and C.R. Goeldner (eds.) *Travel, Tourism and Hospitality Research*. New York: Wiley.

Becken, S. (2011) 'A critical review of tourism and oil', *Annals of Tourism Research*, 38 (2): 359–379.

Becken, S. (2019) 'Decarbonising tourism: Mission impossible?' *Tourism Recreation Research*: 1–15.

Becken, S. and Lennox, J. (2012) 'Implications of a long-term increase in oil prices on tourism', *Tourism Management*, 33 (1): 133–142.

Bull, A. (1991) *The Economics of Travel and Tourism*. London: Pitman.

Clark, D. (2011) 'A complete guide to carbon offsetting', *The Guardian*, 11 September 2011. https://www.theguardian.com/environment/2011/sep/16/carbon-offset-projects-carbon-emissions.

Cooper, C., Fletcher, J., Fyall, A., Gilbert, D. and Wanhill, S. (2005) *Tourism, Principles and Practice*. Harlow: Prentice Hall.

D'Aveni, R. (1998) 'Hypercompetition closes in', *Financial Times*, 4 February (global business section).

Dawson, J., Johnston, M., Stewart, E., Lemieux, C. Lemelin, R., Maher, P. and Grimwood, S. (2011) 'Ethical considerations of last chance tourism', *Journal of Ecotourism*, 10 (3): 240–265.

Dickinson, J. and Lumsdon, L. (2010) *Slow Travel*. London: Earthscan.

Gössling, S., Weaver, D. and Hall, C.M. (eds.) (2009) *Sustainable Tourism Futures: Perspectives on Systems, Restructuring and Innovations*. London: Routledge.

Hall, D.R. (2003) 'Niche tourism in question: Keynote', in D. Macleod (ed.) *Niche Tourism in Question – Interdisciplinary Perspectives on Problems and Possibilities*. Dumfries: University of Glasgow Crichton Publications.

Jang, S. and Wu, C. (2007) 'Senior's travel motivation and the influential factors: An examination of Taiwanese seniors', *Tourism Management*, 28 (5): 1262–1273.

Jefferson, A. and Lickorish, L. (1991) *Marketing Tourism: A Practical Guide*. Harlow: Longman.

Kommenda, N. (2019) '1% of English residents take one-fifth of overseas flights, survey shows', *The Guardian*, 25 September 2019, https://www.theguardian.com/environment/2019/sep/25/1-of-english-residents-take-one-fifth-of-overseas-flights-survey-shows.

Lemelin, H., Dawson, J. and Stewart, E. (eds.) (2012) *Last Chance Tourism*. London: Routledge.

Martin, J. (2007) *The Meaning of the 21st Century*. New York: Penguin.

Mastyn, L. (2001) *Travelling Light: New Paths for International Tourism*. Washington, DC: Worldwatch.

Mowforth, M., Charlton, C. and Munt, I. (2008) *Tourism and Responsibility: Perspectives from Latin America and the Caribbean*. London: Routledge.

Müller, H. (2002) 'Tourism and hospitality in the twenty-first century', in A. Lockwood and R. Medlik (eds.) *Tourism and Hospitality in the Twenty First Century*. Oxford: Butterworth-Heinemann.

Page, S.J. (2009) *Transport and Tourism: Global Perspectives*, 3rd edition. Harlow: Prentice Hall.

Page, S.J., Connell, J., Greenwood, C., Yeoman, I. and Connell, J. (2010) 'Scenario planning as a tool to understand uncertainty in tourism: The example of transport and tourism in Scotland to 2025', *Current Issues in Tourism*, 13 (2): 87–137.

Page, S.J., Yeoman, I., Munro, C., Connell, J. and Walker, L. (2006) 'A case study of best practice: VisitScotland's prepared response to an influenza pandemic', *Tourism Management*, 27 (3): 369–393.

Piggott-McKellar, E. and McNamara, K. (2017) 'Last chance tourism and the Great Barrier Reef', *Journal of Sustainable Tourism* 25 (3): 397–415.

Poon, A. (1989) 'Competitive strategies for a new tourism', in C.P. Cooper (ed.) *Progress in Tourism, Recreation and Hospitality Management Volume 4*. London: Belhaven.

Prideaux, B., Laws, E. and Faulkner, B. (2003) 'Events in Indonesia: Exploring the limits to formal tourism trends', *Tourism Management* 24 (4): 473–487.

Schumacher, E. (1973) *Small Is Beautiful: Economics As If People Mattered*. London: Harper Row.

Scott, D., Gössling, S., Hall, C.M. and Peeters, P. (2016) 'Can tourism be part of the decarbonized global economy? The costs and risks of alternate carbon reduction policy pathways', *Journal of Sustainable Tourism*, 24 (1): 52–72.

Song, H. and Li, G. (2008) 'Tourism demand modelling and forecasting: A review of recent research', *Tourism Management*, 29 (2): 203–220.

Song, H., Witt, S.F. and Li, G. (2009) *The Advanced Econometrics of Tourism Demand*. Routledge: New York.

Spencer, T. (2004) *Space Tourism: Do You Want To Go?* Burlington, ON: Apogee Books.

Tourism Concern (2009) *Putting Tourism to Rights*. London: Tourism Concern.

UN–WTO (2010) *Managing Metropolitan Tourism: An Asian Perspective*. Madrid: UN–WTO.

Witt, S.F., Brooke, M.Z. and Buckley, P.J. (1991) *The International Management of Tourism*. London: Unwin Hyman.

WTO (World Tourism Organization) (1999) *Global Code of Ethics for Tourism*. Madrid: World Tourism Organization.

WTTC (World Travel and Tourism Council) (2002) *Travel and Tourism Security Action Plan*. http://www.wttc.org.

WTTC (World Travel and Tourism Council), International Federation of Tour Operators, International Hotel and Restaurant Association and International Council of Cruise Lines (2002) *Industry as a Partner for Sustainable Development*. London: United Nations Environment Programme/WTTC.

Yeoman, I., Lennon, J., Blake, A., Galt, M., Greenwood, C. and McMahon-Beattie, U. (2007) 'Oil depletion: What does this mean for Scottish tourism?', *Tourism Management*, 28 (5): 1354–1365.

Further reading

Books

Lemelin, H., Dawson, J. and Stewart, E. (eds.) (2012) *Last Chance Tourism*. London: Routledge.

Schumacher, E. (1973) *Small Is Beautiful: Economics As If People Mattered*. London: Harper Row.

UN–WTO/UNEP (2008) *Climate Change and Tourism: Responding to the Global Challenges*. Madrid: UN–WTO and UNEP.

Visa (2016) *The Future of Global Tourism*, www.visa.com.

Journal articles

Becken, S. (2019) 'Decarbonising tourism: Mission impossible?' *Tourism Recreation Research*: 1–15.

Scott, D., Hall, C.M. and Gössling, S. (2019) 'Global tourism vulnerability to climate change', *Annals of Tourism Research*, 77: 49–61.

Glossary

academic journal A periodic publication through which academic research is first reviewed by peers and then communicated to wider audiences.

ACORN Refers to 'A Classification of Residential Neighbourhoods': a database of postcodes in the UK used by market researchers.

acquisition Where one company takes over another.

adventure tourism A form of tourism based on activity, a challenge to the participant and which may have an element of risk, thrill and excitement, such as white-water rafting.

Agenda 21 An outcome of the 1992 United Nations Earth Summit in Rio de Janeiro, committing 182 countries to devise a blueprint for sustainable development at a national and predominantly local level.

angels Wealthy individuals and companies with capital to invest in new ventures.

anthropocentrism The philosophical view that humans are dominant over the natural world and natural resources exist for exploitation to secure human progress.

anthropology The study of how human societies work.

APEC Asia-Pacific Economic Cooperation Forum, an intergovernmental grouping to encourage trade, economic growth and cooperation in the Asia-Pacific region.

appraisal The formal evaluation of an employee's performance in relation to a job description and targets set to measure and monitor individual or team performance.

ASEAN Association of South East Asian Nations, a political grouping of South East Asian countries with a total population of 500 million.

Asian economic crisis An economic collapse in 1997–1998 in a number of the fast-growing economies of South East Asia, which saw those countries unable to service debts.

assets Objects that may have a cash value or be capable of being turned into cash.

ATOL The Civil Aviation Authority grants Air Tour Operator Licences, which are necessary for operating package holidays from the UK.

attraction system A concept to explain how an attraction operates in relation to the actual site, what visitors see and the information and signs relating to the attraction.

balance of payments How a country explains its financial transactions with other countries as a series of different accounts that may be in surplus or deficit.

balance sheet Statement by a limited company of the assets and liabilities it has on the last day of a given accounting period.

behavioural research The study of human preferences, perception and activities and the influences on such patterns, often conducted by psychologists.

bidding The process whereby public and private sector organizations may seek to compete for an event or conference/meeting/fair as part of a global competition to attract the lucrative market for such events. The Olympic and Commonwealth Games bids embody this process where very complex bids are prepared as part of a selection process.

biodiversity The biological variety of life on Earth, a habitat or an environment.

biosecurity The biological risks that may threaten a country, transmitted by tourists as they cross borders and enter countries.

Bluetooth A wireless technology that allows the exchange of data and information over short distances, creating what are called *Personal Area Networks*.

boosterism An approach to tourism planning adopted since the 1960s, typified by an attitude that tourism is good and of benefit to hosts, with little concern for impacts.

Bradford A former industrial city in northern England whose economy was based on manufacturing and textiles.

brand A name, sign, term or feature which a producer uses to differentiate their product from the competition.

brand image According to Kotler *et al.* (2005: 906) it is a 'set of beliefs that consumers hold about a particular brand'.

Brexit is the acronym used to describe Britain's exit from the European Union.

budget accommodation Low-cost accommodation with the minimum standards of provision of service.

built environment Places that are predominantly constructed, such as towns, cities and historic houses.

bundle of services A concept to describe how a series of services (i.e. accommodation, transport and attractions) are linked together to produce a product or offering.

business plan A detailed attempt to set out over a given time frame (i.e. one to five years) the objectives, strategy and expected profit-and-loss accounts of a business, usually prepared so a lender can assess the financial risks of financing the project or venture.

business travel Travel related to the main functions of work, including attending meetings, conferences and exhibitions, or to sell products and services.

capacity utilization How an organization chooses to use the capacity (i.e. space) it has available.

capital investment The injection of money to purchase plant, machinery or infrastructure to improve the supply/production of goods.

carbon neutral tourism An emerging idea based on evidence-based reduction and mitigation of carbon emissions from tourism activity, normally at a destination level but increasingly conceptualised at a global level. It refers to a wide range of carbon reducing activities such as promotion of low carbon or carbon free transport (such as walking and cycling), carbon offsetting schemes and more generally reducing the impacts of tourism, while providing for a high quality tourist experience.

carbon offsetting The process of calculating carbon emissions and then purchasing compensatory 'credits' that support emission reduction, often small-scale, projects, such as alternative energy schemes. The aim of carbon offsetting is to prevent, mitigate or reduce emissions, or remove an equivalent amount of carbon dioxide elsewhere.

carrying capacity The volume of use an area or resource may sustain without detriment.

cash flow The volume of cash received and amount spent.

CCTV Closed Circuit Television, used to monitor activity and as a surveillance tool to reduce criminal behaviour in public and private spaces.

census A comprehensive statistical process to enumerate the population of an area or country at one point in time, which is normally carried out at 10-year intervals.

Center Parcs A company that operates holiday villages across Europe, located in natural, often forest, settings, which provide all-weather facilities for families.

charter flight A non-scheduled aircraft flight, organized and contracted to a tour operator.

city break A holiday taken in an urban (city) location.

City of Culture An annual event in Europe where a city bids to showcase its culture and arts for an entire year. A major part of the bidding process to secure the status is how a programme of events will be provided to raise the profile of the city in question as a cultural destination. The City of Culture concept is often associated with raising the international profile of a destination which is seeking to grow its market position and to attract a wider range of visitors than it currently does.

climate change A progressive shift in the weather patterns, often linked with global warming.

Club Méditerranée (see Chapter 10) A French-based all-inclusive tour operator with its own resorts located across the world.

clustering Geographically, to congregate or group together.

coastal resort A visitor destination built in close proximity to a seaside area, usually with a beach, water environment and leisure/tourism facilities.

coastal tourism Tourism located in close proximity to a coastline, which is often linear in form and geographical distribution.

coastal zone management Integrated planning and management approach to coastal areas adopted to achieve desired environmental, social and economic objectives.

coca-colonization Reference to 'Coca-Cola', a product that has gained global sales and acts as a prominent symbol of Westernization.

co-creation The process by which a business (physical or electronically) engages the consumer in helping to create their own experience.

code of conduct A means of setting out to tourists how to behave in different environments to respect the social, cultural, economic and environmental values and resources of the host area.

cognitive A psychological term that refers to the mental processes associated with how we think and acquire knowledge, based on behavioural elements (actions) and emotions/feelings (affective components) and involving the process of perception.

cognitive map A map derived by an individual based upon the process of encoding, storing, manipulating and processing information that can be geographically referenced: a conceptual representation of place-based experiences.

collaboration To cooperate with another organization or individual on a project or business venture with agreed common objectives and outcomes.

community-oriented approach Planning tourism from a community perspective to incorporate their needs and requirements, epitomized by Murphy (1985).

competition The rivalry between different companies or organizations seeking to supply goods to a particular market.

competitive advantage A greater lead by an organization gained over its competitors by offering better value, quality, services or brands.

complementary services Those that add value or have a synergy with an existing service, such as in-flight catering on a scheduled flight.

computable general equilibrium model A tool used to model the tourism economy, which is applied in tourism satellite account models.

computer reservation system (CRS) A digital system to provide access to intermediaries to make bookings, reservations and check availability.

congestion charging A financial penalty for using a car or vehicle to enter an area that suffers with vehicle congestion.

consolidators Brokers who sell the surplus capacity of the airline sector.

constraints Barriers that prevent an individual from undertaking an activity.

consumer behaviour The actions of people (as individuals and groups) who purchase products or services for personal use.

consumption The process a consumer engages in to enjoy a product, service or other phenomenon, such as a landscape or experience.

contemporary tourism Current tourism trends and patterns rather than historical forms of tourism.

contestable market Where businesses may easily enter a market because there are few entry or exit barriers to setting up.

contract caterers Businesses providing food supplies to the hospitality sector on a pre-packed and chilled/prepared basis.

convertible bond A fixed rate bond, issued by a company, that can be converted to shares during the life of the bond or held until maturity for repayment.

core product The central feature of an attraction that visitors go to see.

corporate culture The outlook, direction and internal values of an organization which employees are expected to work towards.

corporate environmental management The process by which large corporations or companies manage their impact on the environment through environmental auditing and setting targets to improve performance. Linked with corporate social responsibility (CSR), which is a process of improving a company's impact and relationships with the people it affects.

corporate strategy How an organization positions itself to the market, and the tactics and approach it adopts.

corporate travel The travel needs of individual businesses or corporations, typically for business purposes (although it may also include incentive travel as a reward for employees).

country house A large rural residence with historical associations, often set in gardens or parkland.

creativity The use of personal or intellectual skills to develop an idea or product that is new, novel or unusual.

criminology Area of law concerned with the study of criminal behaviour, activities and its causes and effects.

cross-elasticity The percentage change in the demand for one product in relation to the percentage change in the price for the alternative product.

cultural baggage The beliefs, values and behaviour modes that tourists take with them on holiday.

cultural brokerage A bridge between the host community and visitor.

cultural history The oral and written history of a specific population group within a particular society or location.

customer service Point of interaction between an employee of a tourism operation and the purchaser/consumer.

dark tourism An interest in visiting places that have an association with death, disaster and human suffering.

data collection A process whereby information is obtained through research, which may involve primary data, such as questionnaire surveys, or the collation of secondary data sources such as published statistics.

debt The amount owed by one person or organization to another.

decision-making The process of making choices between different options.

deep ecology An ecological philosophy which values the environment more highly than human progress in industrialized nations, sometimes referred to as 'dark green'.

deep vein thrombosis (DVT) A medical condition associated with blood clotting due to immobility during long periods of inactivity, such as a long-haul flight.

defaulting loan A loan which is in arrears and not able to be repaid.

demand The number of people who choose to undertake an activity.

de-marketing A policy adopted not to promote an area, in an attempt to help reduce the number of visitors and pressure posed by its popularity.

demographic The term used to describe the population, and its study (demography).

demonstration effect Changes in the resident population of a tourism destination resulting from observing and mixing with tourists, usually used in reference to the less developed countries.

deregulation The removal of controls to stimulate free competition.

destination The combination of different tourism components (i.e. attractions, accommodation, transport, resources and the infrastructure) in a geographical location, promoted by a tourism organization.

destination benchmarking Measuring the performance of tourist destinations.

destination image The perceived and promoted elements of a destination, which determine appeal to visitors.

destination management system An electronic system that combines the tourism offering of a destination on behalf of different suppliers and stakeholders, often managed by a destination management organization.

destination marketing The process by which destinations are promoted.

destination marketing organization An organization that promotes the unique features of a destination to potential visitors, representing its stakeholders in the local tourism industry.

destination positioning A research method to evaluate the competition a destination is facing.

destination substitutability Selection of alternative destinations with similar characteristics, which may easily replace another destination.

development process The different stages through which an area or location progresses, usually associated with the social and economic improvement of a locality or country.

direct employment The jobs created as a direct result of visitor expenditure and tourism activity.

directional selling Where a travel agent tries to sell a product from their own company rather than that of a competitor.

discounted cash flow A means of capital budgeting or expenditure appraisal that looks at projected cash flows over the life of a project, and forms the basis of investment appraisal methods such as NPVM and IRR.

discretionary spending The amount of money available to an individual for spending on non-essential items, such as holidays and leisure activities.

disintermediation The process whereby existing intermediaries in the distribution channel are replaced or substituted by organizations selling tourism products directly to consumers.

displacement Movement of the host population away from their place of residence to make way for tourism development.

distribution channel A series of organizations which make a product or service available through the process of marketing.

dividend The amount of earnings distributed by a company to shareholders.

Djerba Declaration Outcome of World Tourism Organization Conference on Tourism and Climate Change in 2003, which endorsed the Kyoto Protocol on the need to reduce tourism-generated emissions.

domestic tourism Tourist travel within one's own country.

dynamic packaging An electronic tool provided by tour operators and e-mediaries to allow customers to customize a package, by picking and mixing the different components to suit their needs and budget.

e-booking An electronic booking made with an intermediary or tourism business via the Internet.

ecocentrism The view that nature must be preserved for its intrinsic values.

ecological footprint A technique to evaluate the environmental impact of human activities, which has been applied in the study of tourism.

ecology The study of relationships between living organisms and their environment.

e-commerce Undertaking business by electronic means.

econometrics The field of economics that builds complex models using statistical analysis to forecast changes in tourism and to understand how the tourism economy operates and changes under certain assumptions.

economic cycle A period of time through which an economy functions, used to identify whether conditions are conducive to growth, stagnating or in decline.

economic dependency The reliance upon a particular activity for the economy to function, such as tourism.

economic-industry approach Where tourism is viewed as a tool that government can use for economic restructuring, employment development and as an export industry.

economics The study of how the economy operates in different contexts and the importance of individuals and organizations in the function of the economy.

economies of scale To reduce the average cost of production by purchasing or producing in bulk, therefore decreasing the unit cost of the output.

ecotourism A term devised by Ceballos-Lascurain to describe tourism in relatively undisturbed or uncontaminated natural areas with the specific objective of studying, admiring and enjoying the scenery and its wild plants and animals, as well as any existing cultural manifestations (both past and present) found in these areas.

ECPAT An acronym for the non-government organization End Child Prostitution in Asian Tourism, which seeks to stop tourist paedophiles.

Edwardian An historical period associated with the reign of Edward VII from 1901–1914.

effective demand Actual or recorded levels of demand.

effectuation A concept based on the idea that the future is unpredictable but can be controlled.

e-HR The digital provision of human resource services.

elasticity of demand A ratio to measure the percentage in tourism demand and percentage change in disposable income over a set period of time.

e-mediaries Electronic intermediaries who retail travel products.

Emissions Trading Schemes (ETS) Approved systems at a country or regional level that place a cap on the amount of carbon emissions through permits and a market-based mechanism for trading unused carbon credits between members. Such schemes cover various highly polluting and energy intensive industries, such as power plants, heavy manufacturing and processing sectors, and of core significance to tourism, the aviation sector.

empowerment Providing employees with more power to deal with work issues.

enclave tourism The geographical development of exclusive forms of tourism, often involving integrated resorts, where the local population have little interaction with tourists, and economic benefits to the local area are limited.

entrepreneur Individual who undertakes to establish a business venture to make a profit, often using their own capital to take risks on whether the venture will be successful.

environment The external conditions surrounding an object, form of life or human activity.

environmental and cultural protection Measures to ensure that public resources and assets are protected from visitor damage through, for example, pollution, overuse, inappropriate use and inadequate planning controls.

environmental auditing Evaluation of business practice to examine environmental performance in relation to energy, transport, purchasing, waste, health and the local environment.

environmental bubble A term coined by Cohen to describe tourist travel within the safety of a pre-packaged, organized charter tour.

environmental impact assessment Project assessment used in the planning control system of the adverse and beneficial impacts of a specific development.

environmental policies A series of statements by companies to outline their environmental performance, policies and practices.

environmental risk Natural hazards and potential risks posed to tourists through their activities.

environmentally conscious Being aware of environmental issues and/or taking steps to reduce one's own impact on the environment.

e-tailing Electronic retailing of products and services.

ethnicity An identifiable group of people distinguished on the basis of racial, cultural, linguistic or other specific features.

e-tourism The digital purchasing, processing and delivery of tourism products and services to consumers.

e-travel The facilitation of travel by electronic means.

EU The European Union, set up by the Treaty of Rome in 1957, now comprises 15 member states and ten new member states from Eastern Europe.

eutrophication The process by which increased nutrients in the water robs the water of oxygen and leads to the death of aquatic life.

event A staged or planned occurrence, designed for public enjoyment or for the needs of a specific audience, including a fair, carnival, religious ceremony, parade, entertainment, exhibition, concert, conference, sporting occasion and special or hallmark event such as the Olympic Games.

event management The practical aspects of preparing for and staging events.

event tourism The strategic context of events in realizing wider objectives (such as tourism, economic, social or cultural dimensions).

experience economy is the economic activities associated with the value added or enjoyment derived from the 'experience' as opposed to the tangible elements of the product or service. It is a concept popularized by Pine and Gilmore.

failure rate The number or percentage of ventures likely to fail within a set time frame, typically within one year of establishment.

fair trade A movement to reform unjust trading practices, involving the payment of fair prices for goods and services to producers, and the development of equitable trading relationships.

family–life balance The relationship between the amount of work one undertakes and the ability to balance that with home and family commitments.

Fantasy City Derived from Hannigan's study to denote a city's economy in certain districts, based on entertainment, fantasy experiences, leisure consumption and cultural significance.

farm tourism A farm-based tourism enterprise resulting from diversification and often using family labour.

festival A traditional and contemporary form of event which Getz (1997: 8) defined as a 'public, themed celebration': they may help to maintain community values through increasing a sense of social identity.

financial reporting The requirement of a limited company to report its financial statements.

financial risk The likelihood of suffering a financial loss.

financier Someone who finances a project or business venture.

fiscal Financial issues.

fixed assets Also called a capital asset, an item purchased and used by a business for a projected life, such as land, buildings, plant or machinery, and is written off (depreciated) each year against profits.

flagship attractions High-profile major attractions.

flow A leisure construct suggesting that a participant can achieve a state of optimal arousal, resulting from experiences matching their skills/ability.

food and beverage The two associated sectors in the hotel sector that provide the nourishment services for guests.

foot-and-mouth Highly infectious virus spread among livestock.

Fordist The dominance of large, vertically integrated companies producing standardized products, largely based on price competition.

forecasting The process of estimating future demand and predicting future market conditions.

fossil fuels Finite energy supplies including coal, natural gas, oil and those derived from the geological processes of fossilization.

franchising The transfer of intellectual property rights, such as a trademark, brand or advice to other parties (franchisee), to allow them to conduct business with a minimum level of investment.

frontier arrival The number of people arriving at a country's borders as tourist arrivals (as opposed to migrants).

frontline staff Those who interact directly with customers, such as receptionists, cashiers, tour guides, check-in staff and tour representatives.

gamification The process of engaging people in a competition or game as a form of online marketing of a product or service.

gap year A student 'year out' of academic study or a year out of employment to travel overseas.

gateway An entry point to a country, such as a major airport (e.g. Heathrow, New York and Tokyo) or port.

geography The study of man and the environment, and how phenomena are located and organized on the Earth's surface in terms of spatial relationships.

gig economy The free market system for employment where employment is based on short-term work assignments and permanence does not exist in work, meaning it is precarious; the word 'gig' denotes the musical term to denote a short-term music event which is synonymous with this method of working.

gîte A French farm cottage used for holidays.

global distribution system (GDS) The merging of airline computer reservation systems to create global digital systems for travel bookings and reservations.

global warming The rise in average temperature of the planet over time, thought to be a result of human activity on the planet, mainly industry and agriculture, often referred to as the greenhouse effect.

globalization A process of change and development in the world economic system, affecting trading and cultural exchanges and often resulting in standardization of products and institutions.

goodwill The net assets of a business minus the total value of the business.

government Organization responsible for the management of a country's affairs.

GP A General Practitioner, a family doctor.

grading system The assignment of a category to accommodation according to its facilities and quality.

Grand Tour A circuit tour of Europe undertaken by wealthy travellers for cultural, educational and health reasons from the sixteenth century through to the nineteenth century.

green tourism Often used interchangeably with sustainable tourism, tourism based either on the environment or with environmental values in mind.

greenhouse gases Components of the atmosphere that are thought to lead to global warming, including water vapour, carbon dioxide (CO_2), ozone, methane, nitrous oxide (NO_x) and chlorofluorocarbons (CFCs).

grey literature The publication of material by commercial or non-commercial bodies such as reports, policy documents or government reports.

gross domestic product (GDP) The overall financial value of the goods and services produced by an economy over a time period.

guest Someone who stays in a location other than their own residence, who may be accommodated by the hospitality sector or by friends and relatives.

guidebook A publication by a tourist destination or travel writer to detail an area's attractions, facilities and highlights, which became popular after the eighteenth century.

hedonism The pursuit of pleasure, sometimes associated with pursuing an activity to excess, which gives immediate gratification.

heritage industry A term coined to describe the commercialization of historic attractions, events, and places for the purposes of tourism and leisure, which is associated with debates on how authentic and real these experiences are in relation to historical facts.

historic city A town or city with a large number of heritage resources.

holiday brochure A printed colour magazine (or electronic version) compiled by a tour operator to sell a holiday, featuring destinations and other products.

holiday camp A form of holiday provision with multiple accommodation units and combined social, dining and entertainment facilities, popularized by entrepreneurs such as Butlins in the 1930s. Many modern-day camps have been redeveloped into leisure parks.

holiday representative A person employed by a tour operator in a destination area to look after the well-being of visitors who have bought the tour operator's products.

hospitality Care and kindness in welcoming strangers or guests, although in industry terms it is widely used to denote the accommodation and food service sectors.

host Someone who accommodates a guest.

host–guest relationship The nature of the association between tourists and residents within a tourism destination.

hub-and-spoke operation A concept of airline operation that describes major gateways or ports of entry as 'hubs', with feeder aircraft services to outlying destinations using smaller aircraft as a 'spoke', like a bicycle wheel.

Human Development Index (HDI) The United Nations' composite measure of the state of socio-economic development in countries.

Human Resource Management (HRM) An activity focused on managing human capital (i.e. the workforce).

human rights Internationally accepted standards of how human beings should be treated by other human beings, organizations and governments.

hypercompetition Rapid pace of change in competition for products in an environment of deregulation to encourage competition.

hypothesis A proposition or assumption that can be tested through research.

IMF International Monetary Fund, an international organization of 184 countries to promote international monetary cooperation, exchange rate stability and to provide temporary financial assistance to countries with balance-of-payment problems.

indigenous people The people of a country who claim to be the original inhabitants, with an identifiable culture and society.

indirect employment The jobs created within the tourism supply sector but not as a direct result of tourism activity.

induced employment The jobs created as a result of tourism expenditure as local residents spend money earned from tourism.

induction The formal introduction to how an organization works and an explanation of the expectations, roles and responsibilities of an employee in relation to the corporate culture.

industry–education collaboration The interaction of universities, colleges and schools with the world of industry.

inflation Increase in prices in the economy and the relative fall in the purchasing value of money.

information communication technology (ICT) Hardware, software and netware used by information systems to transmit, store and manipulate digital information.

innovation An idea, product or development that consumers or other organizations view as new and novel.

input–output model A tool used to measure the impact of tourism demand on the economy.

intangible Something which cannot be seen, touched or felt.

Inter-war years The period from the end of World War One in 1918 to the outbreak of the Second World War in 1939.

intermediaries Agents in the supply chain who broker services for other producers.

internal rate of return An interest rate that equates to a net present value of zero when applied to a given projected cash flow.

international business Undertaking business at an international scale, involving investment and activities that span a number of countries.

international tourism Tourism that involves crossing an international border and a stay of 24 hours or more.

internationalization of business Business activities that occur at a global scale, and at least outside one country.

Internet Global network of computers that are independent but interconnected by digital means.

interpretation A communication-based activity to explain to visitors the meaning or significance of a place, object, culture, event or occurrence, that aims to enrich the visitor experience and achieve site management goals.

intrapreneurship Process whereby an individual or group of people within an organization envision something and make it happen, which may be radically different, exciting and novel.

investment flow The process by which capital and funds transfer from a source to a recipient.

investment risk The likelihood of an investment either succeeding or failing and the invested capital being lost.

Irridex A framework for assessing the host population response to tourism development, derived by Doxey (1975).

itineraries A planned pattern of travel by tourists, which may include stops to stay overnight en route to a destination.

Kyoto Protocol An international treaty that came into force in 2005, binding some 141 signatories in the developed world to cut greenhouse gas emissions.

Last-Chance Tourism Destinations which were deemed to be under threat or disappearing.

latent demand Demand which has yet to be realized due to real or perceived barriers.

leadership The skill of being able to use interpersonal skills to influence others to undertake what you require, particularly in a management role. It may involve liaison, being a spokesperson, negotiator and persuader.

leakage The money which flows out of the local or national tourism economy during its circulation and spending by tourists on goods and services imported from outside the economic system.

learning behaviour The process by which a person develops an understanding and image of the environment, normally studied by psychologists and other behavioural researchers.

legislation The legally binding acts and laws passed by government.

leisure product A term coined by Jansen-Verbeke to denote the nature of tourism supply in cities.

leisure society A term devised in the 1970s by sociologists to suggest that industrialized society would evolve to a point where individuals worked less and had more leisure time to enjoy.

leisure time The time left after one's normal functions (e.g. sleeping, eating, working and routines) have been completed.

lending criteria A set of conditions that an individual or business must fulfil to be eligible for funding.

licensing A managed process whereby an organization allows other companies to use its brand, logo or trademark in return for a fee.

lifelong learning The uptake of periodic training, re-training and learning opportunities during an individual's career to improve skills and career potential.

limits of acceptable change A holistic approach to carrying capacity that sets predefined limits to the amount of change which is permissible.

liquidity The ability of a company to pay its debts when they become due.

litigation Process of pursuing a lawsuit.

load factor The percentage of seats or capacity occupied by passengers on specific departures, which can be aggregated to produce a running total and average capacity figures.

Local Authorities Local government body with elected members and permanently appointed officers.

location The site or place at which a business operates.

Lonely Planet Guidebooks developed initially for more adventurous travellers, but now covering all forms of tourist activity in destinations worldwide.

long-haul Long-distance travel, typically involving a flight of over five hours.

Malthus In 1798, demographer Thomas Malthus published his essay on the Principle of Population, stating that as population grows geometrically, food production grows arithmetically, meaning that, in time, population would outstrip its food supply.

management A process of getting things done within businesses and organizations which involves four agreed tasks: planning, organizing, leading and controlling people and resources.

Management Information Systems (MIS) A system within an organization which allows managers and staff to be empowered to manage to collect information and data through computerized means, which at their simplest level may be databases that capture all the businesses customer details and their transactions.

manatee A marine mammal (also known as sea cow) found in marshy, shallow waters of America, Africa and the Caribbean, which is docile and interacts with tourists but is subject to high levels of mortality due to boat strikes.

marine park A water-based reserve with protective policies for marine life.

marine tourism Tourism activity that takes places in a water-based environment.

marketing A process, described by Kotler *et al.* (2005: 914) as a 'social and managerial process by which individuals and groups obtain what they need and want through creating an exchanging products and value with others'.

marketing campaign The mix of different marketing elements to promote a product or service to its target audience.

marketing offer The combination of products, services and experiences to satisfy needs and wants.

marketing planning A process by which an organization will analyze its resources and marketing environment to identify which direction to take.

marketing strategy The direction a particular business wishes to pursue in fulfilling its stated marketing objectives.

mass tourism High-volume tourism that appeals to a large market and can saturate a location and its inhabitants.

McDonaldization A term coined by Ritzer to denote the globalization trend associated with the fast food restaurant chain, which refers to how supply is becoming homogeneous at a global scale.

mental map A map produced by an individual based on their initial response to environmental information signals received through the senses, prior to being constructed by the brain into a cognitive image.

merger Where two companies or more agree to join another on an equal basis to create a new entity.

methodology A means by which one approaches scientific enquiry, informed by one's philosophical bent towards a subject.

ministry A department within government with responsibility for a specific issue.

MIRAB Acronym to describe the problems of the social and economic development of tourism on small islands: migration, remittances, aid and bureaucracy.

mission statement A brief statement to incorporate the purpose and objectives of an organization.

modernity A concept that describes the condition of being modern, which, in less developed countries and former colonies, developed from the 1950s and focused on the modernization of societies and economies.

modus operandi Mode of operation.

monograph A high-level academic research publication, often published as a hardback book.

monopoly Where one business or supplier is the sole provider with no effective competition.

mortgage sale Where a receiver or individual is forced to sell their house or property as an asset that may have been used to secure a loan that can no longer be repaid.

motivation The basis of human behaviour, studied by psychologists and sociologists, and concerned with the factors that makes people do certain things.

m-tourism Mobile and wireless-enabled technology that facilitates tourism information provision and bookings.

multi-day discounting A reduced price if visitors wish to revisit an attraction on subsequent days.

multidisciplinary The combination of different subject areas in academic areas to explore a common issue, such as tourism.

'must-see' places Those attractions in a destination which are high profile and iconic.

nation-state A political and geographical entity to describe the area in which a particular group of people of one or more nationalities live, often referred to as a country.

national identity (also see ethnicity) A group of people with citizenship of a particular nation, sharing basic cultural values or a common identity.

National Park A designated area where protection of natural resources is the priority and where recreation and tourism uses are accommodated through sensitive management.

National Tourism Organization (NTO) National Tourism Organization, a public or private sector body that seeks to represent the tourism interests of a destination.

nationality A legal concept used by the nation-state based on parental status, place of birth and citizenship.

natural disaster An earthquake, flood, landslip, tsunami, volcanic eruption, hurricane, typhoon or natural phenomenon related to extreme climate or weather event.

natural environment Places that are predominantly natural in form, such as countryside, mountains, national parks.

neo-colonial The replacement of former colonial exploitative social and economic relationships with a new order that simply reinforces the former patterns of exploitation between the former colony and colonizer.

net present value method A financial method used to evaluate an investment, which examines discounted cash flows (the current value of cash inflows and outflows) based on a projected rate of return for each year's cash flow.

niche market An identifiable group of consumers with particular characteristics, needs or desires, often targeted by companies seeking to supply a product or service that will appeal to that group, or that will be perceived as unique and different from the competition.

non-governmental organization (NGO) National and local groups with interests in a broad number of social, moral, environmental and economic areas, such as charitable bodies.

not-for-profit Those organizations, such as voluntary and charitable bodies, which are not in existence primarily to make profit.

OECD Organization for Economic Cooperation and Development: a grouping of 30 countries committed to democratic government and a market economy.

Office for National Statistics The UK government agency responsible for data collection on a wide range of social and economic issues.

oligopoly A limited number of suppliers who dominate the market.

opportunity costs The cost of undertaking or investing in one option at the expense of alternatives.

oral history The collection of information from individuals and families about historical events, their activities and everyday lives using audiotape, video recordings and transcribed interviews to collect their memories, recollections and accounts.

organization The formal or informal structure of an administration or system, which contains a series of functions and tasks that individuals and groups perform for the system to function.

overtourism is where the impact of tourism is so great that it overwhelms the capacity of a location to sustain the activity so that the economic, environmental and environmental capacity of the locality is adversely affected by too much tourism

package holiday The creation of a number of elements of a holiday purchased as a bundle of services, typically transport and accommodation, which are purchased from a tour operator.

paradigm A set of values, attitudes and concepts that identify a particular approach to the world or way of thinking.

park and ride A traffic management tool where visitors park in designated areas and use buses or trains to access a destination, avoiding congestion at key pressure points (e.g. city centres and National Parks).

payback The period over which a project or business expects to repay the initial investment, after which the business should enter into profit, and a more simplistic method of assessing investments than discounted cash flow principles.

perceived value Involves an individual evaluation of quality, price, reputation and emotional responses to a product by a consumer.

perception An individual's image and understanding of the environment with which they interact, based on intuition and mental constructs.

perishability Refers to a product that cannot be stored.

PEST Political, economic, sociocultural and technological analysis of the external environment in which a business operates.

physical-spatial approach Recognition of tourism's ecological basis and the need for geographical planning, epitomized by land-use planning.

place Physical location.

placeless No fixed geographical point or location.

place-making A process that seeks to generate improvements to the recognition of the place for visitors, residents and potential residents as a place to live.

planning A process to anticipate, regulate and monitor change.

policy Direction and stated objectives an organization wishes to pursue over a set period of time.

pollution A deterioration of any part of the environment due to the introduction of chemicals, substances or a process that the environment is unable to absorb without damage.

postcolonial The period following independence from a colonial power.

post-Communist countries Those states in Eastern Europe which gained independence from the former USSR after the Berlin Wall was removed in 1989.

post-Fordist The use of more specialized and flexible forms of production to respond to consumer demand.

post-industrial A phase in a region's development where its former economic rationale based on manufacturing has been replaced by an economy based on services, such as finance or tourism.

postmodern A sociological concept developed to explain changes society from the late twentieth century, which focuses on the shift from manufacturing to service economies and issues such as consumerism and popular culture and emphasizes that there is no overarching theory of how society works, as it varies from place to place.

power relationships Unequal relationships between people, organizations or countries, where one has a stronger degree of control.

practitioner Someone who practises their subject or profession rather than being engaged in academic study or research.

predatory tourist-related crime Opportunist crime perpetuated on visitors who may appear vulnerable, in unfamiliar surroundings and be different in appearance to residents.

price The charge for a product, service or commodity.

price elasticity A ratio to measure the percentage change in the quantity of tourism demanded in relation to the percentage change in the price of a tourism product.

private sector Business activities which are profit-driven and operate predominantly without public subsidies.

product lifecycle According to Kotler *et al.* (2005: 918) this is 'The course of a product's sales and profits over its lifetime. It involves five distinct stages: product development, introduction, growth, maturity and decline' and in tourism terms, an additional stage may be added in relation to destination-rejuvenation and redevelopment.

product offering The whole experience available to visitors (including the core, actual and augmented product).

production The way in which tourism services are produced (i.e. assembled together as packages), or linked through a supply chain.

production chain The integration of different supply elements into a system to provide a product or service.

productivity The output of an employee or organization in relation to the cost base of production and other inputs.

profit-and-loss account The statement by a limited company in its accounts of the profits and losses it declared in relation to expenses.

promotion The different activities that communicate the benefits of a service or product to consumers with a view to encouraging purchases.

pro-poor tourism A movement that aims to utilize tourism activity to reduce poverty in destination areas.

psychological The characteristics of an individual or group in terms of their behaviour and mental processes.

public sector The diverse range of government-related and funded bodies that work in the public interest.

public service grant A government subsidy for operating a public transport service to make it more commercially viable.

pull factor An external stimulus encouraging an individual to visit an area or place, such as destination marketing.

push factor An internal stimulus encouraging an individual to go on holiday, such as the need to have a break.

quango Acronym for a quasi-autonomous non-government department.

racking How travel agents display the products of certain company's brochures to consumers.

radiative forcing The combined effect of CO_2 and NO_x particles and water vapour, which results from airline pollution in the atmosphere and contributes to global warming.

Radio Frequency Identification (RFID) A technical term that describes new technologies associated with identifying objects as an alternative to using conventional barcodes, and does not require the object in question to be in direct contact with a barcode scanner as it uses transmitted radio signals as the means of communication.

receivership Where a lender who has a charge over a business is defaulted, a receiver or administrator is appointed to realize any assets to repay outstanding debt.

recruitment of staff A process of identifying the staff an organization needs and attracting them through advertising, word of mouth and personal recommendation, leading to a formal recruitment process according to prevailing laws and regulations (e.g. equal opportunities laws).

re-enactments Interpretation of historical events through re-creation, such as battles or domestic scenes.

re-engineering A process to redevelop an organization and to realign it to a new purpose or focus.

regional policy Government or transnational organization (e.g. EU) policy to a particular geographical region, usually with a view to aiding its economic development.

regional tourism organization A body that operates below the level of a national tourism organization to serve the needs of its members in promoting tourism in a defined region.

regulation The way in which governments manage markets and competition with controls and penalties.

rejuvenation Also used interchangeably with regeneration, it refers to the redevelopment of an ailing area or product by boosting its potential through investment and creating a new image/market.

relationship marketing According to Kotler *et al.* (2005: 920) it is 'The process of creating, maintaining and enhancing strong, value-laden relationships with customers and other stakeholders'.

repositioning How an organization or business seeks to change its market orientation from, for example, one aiming at a low-spending domestic market to a new position where it appeals to high-spending international visitors. It often involves public sector organizations who seek to change the image and appeal of the destination as part of the repositioning strategy.

research A process by which one uncovers, discovers and explores ideas, issues or a particular question to find an answer.

resilience The capability of a business or destination to minimize the losses, cope and continue to function following a shock event such as a terrorist attack or natural disaster.

resilience planning How a business or destination can become more resilient against unexpected events such as terrorism or a natural disaster at the destination, city or local level.

resort A physical location where a number of tourism-related elements occur to create a cluster of activities, often in attractive locations such as coastal areas but also in mountain, rural, city and other locations.

resort development The growth of an area through time into a tourism destination.

resort development spectrum A model developed by Prideaux (2000) to identify five phases of resort growth: local tourism, regional tourism, national tourism, international tourism and decline/stagnation/ rejuvenation.

responsible tourism Form of tourism which acknowledges that mass tourism has negative impacts for host communities and destinations, and which seeks to generate positive benefits while minimizing negative ones.

retention of staff In the long term, being able to keep employees through investment in training and valuing the role staff play in the successful operation of the business.

risk-to-reward ratio Where the capital required for a venture is assessed in relation to the expected financial gains.

rurality A condition of the non-urban environment or countryside, often based upon perceptions of what constitutes a rural area and which has been combined into 16 indicators by Cloke (1977).

SAGA A UK-based tour operator specializing in holidays for the over-50s age group.

SARS A respiratory virus which spread from China in 2002–2003 by travel.

scenario planning The process of trying to understand the uncertainty associated with the future. It focuses on three areas of research: what may happen (possible futures), what is the most likely to happen (probable futures) and what we would prefer to happen (preferable futures).

seasonality The pattern of demand for tourism, conditioned by climate, weather, daylight, price, fashion, tastes and the nature of the origin and destination area.

second home A dwelling that is owned by an individual but which is not their main residence, normally used for leisure and tourism purposes.

segmentation Matching a company's products to specific subdivisions of the market.

self-catering Non-serviced accommodation.

senior market The over 50–55 age group, also called the 'grey' market.

service debugging Removing the problems, inconsistencies and potential failure points in a service.

SERVQUAL An approach to service quality, examining how good service delivery is in relation to consumer expectations and service performance.

sex tourism Travelling with the express intent of engaging in sexual activity or gratification.

shallow ecology An ecological philosophy that pays little respect for real environmental values, sometimes referred to as 'light green'.

shareholder Someone who owns shares in a limited company or limited partnership.

small–medium enterprise (SME) A business that may typically have less than 250 employees.

SMART Specific, measurable, achievable, relevant and time-bound goals.

smokeless industry A form of economic development that does not require the construction of factories and pollution resulting from industrial production.

social class Usually taken to mean the grading of individuals on the basis of occupation of the chief income earner in a household (although social class can also refer to more intangible measures, such as education or family background).

social elite The upper and middle classes in historical terms, or, in modern society, those with the most wealth.

social entrepreneurship To use an entrepreneurial approach to make a sustained contribution to the social good as well as creating a profit through business activities to reinvest in its business mission to advance the social good agenda.

social media The generic term to describe the means by which people now share their views, interact and collaborate online including the tools used by businesses to communicate with customers and other people-to-people communications (e.g. the use of Facebook and Twitter).

social psychology The study of social influences on human behaviour, namely how people affect other people.

social tourism Providing holidays for those who would not normally have the opportunity to engage in tourism for economic or accessibility reasons.

sociocultural The combination of social and cultural elements.

sociology The study of people in society.

South Pacific The region of the world within the Pacific Ocean comprising many small islands and containing three cultural groupings: Melanesia, Micronesia and Polynesia.

spa Historically, a resort at which the visitor 'took the waters' for therapeutic purposes, either by bathing or drinking, an activity which can be dated to Greek and Roman times.

space tourism Travel to outer space, to orbit the Earth and beyond the Earth's orbit, as well as simulation and cyberspace experiences.

stakeholders Interest groups, such as businesses, residents and tourists, who are concerned with issues in an area, such as tourism.

start-up business A new venture created by an entrepreneur or other organization.

strategic alliance An agreement between companies to undertake an activity on a shared basis.

strategic planning A process to enable a company or organization to assess how it will manage to adapt to a changing business environment.

strategy A plan, ploy, tactic or approach to match an organization's or individual's capabilities with market opportunities.

stratosphere A layer of the Earth's atmosphere, from 7 km to 50 km above the Earth's surface.

supply The means by which goods and services are delivered to the consumer.

supply chain The sequence of suppliers that fit together to deliver supplies to consumers.

sustainability The goal of achieving a balance between the needs of tourism or economic development with the ability of the resource base to sustain such activities in the long term.

sustainable tourism An approach to tourism informed by the principles of sustainable development, which aims to safeguard natural resources and respect host communities, while encouraging more sensitive forms of tourism that minimize negative effects and maximize positive ones.

SUSTRANS The charitable body, short for 'Sustainable Transport', which has developed the UK Cycle Path Network.

SWOT Strengths, weaknesses, opportunities and threats analysis of the internal and external environment in which a business operates.

symbiotic relationship A relationship of mutual benefit.

system A method of examining how the different components of something fit together and interact.

target audience The consumer group that a business wishes to reach in its marketing plan.

terminal facility An airport, railway, ferry or coach/bus interchange.

terrorism The activities of extreme political groups seeking change through violent means.

TGV Train de Grand Vitesse, the French high-speed train operated by SNCF.

thanatourism A form of tourism and visitation motivated by an interest in encounters with death.

timeshare Accommodation where individuals purchase a week or more per year at a holiday property for their lifetime.

toddler tourism Travel with young children usually of preschool age.

tour operator An organization assembling and selling tourism products and services.

Tour Operators Initiative Industry-led initiative to develop a sustainable approach to tour operation.

tourism comfort indices A composite measure of mean temperature, maximum temperature, humidity, precipitation, sunshine hours and wind to assess how comfortable different environments are for tourist activity.

Tourism Concern A non-governmental organization that works to protect communities affected by tourism, particularly in the less developed world.

Tourism for Tomorrow Awards Environmental Awards sponsored by British Airways and World Travel and Tourism Council.

tourism master plan A national or subnational plan for tourism, which includes an assessment of demand, supply, forecasts, strategic issues and implementation measures.

tourism multiplier A technique to estimate the impact of tourism on an economy, using a ratio to indicate the magnitude of the effect.

tourism planning Process to determine future direction and actions for an area, region or country to achieve specified goals.

Tourism Satellite Account (TSA) An economic tool used to measure the inputs and outputs in the tourism system of one country.

tourism system A conceptual framework used to examine how tourism operates, focusing on the interaction of tourism components (i.e. attractions, accommodation, transport, destinations and tourists).

tourist expenditure The amount of money a tourist spends during a visit.

tourist experience The overall impression, understanding, rating and meaning a visitor attaches to their encounter with a specific place, event, holiday or activity.

tourist gaze A term used by the sociologist John Urry (1990) to explain the way in which a visitor observes or interacts with a tourist destination.

tourist–host encounter Instances where tourists and residents of a destination area come into contact.

tourist motivation The range of motives and factors that encourage tourist travel.

tourist night A statistical measure of how long a tourist stays in a commercial form of accommodation.

tourist receipts The amount of money received from tourist spending.

tourist resource A natural or built environment utilized for tourism purposes.

tourist role A means by which the motivation for travel can be grouped into different categories to distinguish the psychological profile of the tourist.

tourist safety The precautions necessary to minimize tourist risk behaviour.

tourist statistics Measures of tourism normally expressed as the volume, value and type of tourism, which is expressed in a tabular format.

tourist well-being The overall health and safety of a visitor, including positive and negative elements of their interaction with the destination environment.

trampling The cumulative effect of human feet on the paths and areas they visit.

trans-European network (TEN) A pan-European series of rail infrastructure projects to improve rail links and interoperability across European border areas, designed to improve the flow of people and goods.

transnational hotel chain A company that operates hotels in more than one country, with an international presence and defined brand.

travel agent An intermediary who acts as a broker between the tour operator and consumer.

travel career ladder The life history of a traveller expressed chronologically to show the development of a series of travel experiences.

travel propensity The likelihood of a group of people/individual wishing to travel.

tsunami An earthquake at sea which causes a tidal wave, as observed in Asia.

turnaround of aircraft The time involved when an aircraft lands, is cleaned, refuelled and ready for another flight, which for low-cost airlines is targeted at 26 minutes.

u-commerce Interconnected technologies to communicate with tourists that are ubiquitous, universal, unique and working in unison.

under-utilization A failure to fully use the capacity available.

undifferentiated product One which ignores market differences and aims at the entire market with one offer.

urban tourism Tourism destined for, and undertaken in towns, cities and urban resort areas.

urbanization The process of people moving to, and living in towns and cities.

User Generated Content (UGC) This describes the growth in people posting different forms of content online, typically ranging from simple question and answers to blogs, podcasts and the use of other technology to create material to share with others through mobile phones and devices, which characterizes the growth of social media and its expansion driven by UGC.

value chains The description of the *process* which firms use to bring a product, service or good from its raw state (or to describe how they assemble the ingredients or elements in an experience) to market (i.e. to the point a consumer can purchase and enjoy it). It describes how they create the final finished outcome. In tourism, this outcome is normally consumed as an experience (i.e. the overall holiday) or specific elements such as a specific service (e.g. the trip on an aircraft). In the case of tour operating, this may be divided across many connected, integrated or separate companies that are managed to provide the final outcome for the tourist. When companies are operating globally, then this will typically be a global value chain.

value of tourism The financial worth of tourism, referring to the amount of money tourism generates for a locality or country in economic terms.

venture capital Money invested in a project or business by a group of financiers who specialize in investing in high-risk ventures in return for shares in the company.

vernacular building A building constructed in a regional or local style.

victimization The feeling of becoming a victim of a crime or negative event.

Victorian The period 1837–1901, associated with the reign of Queen Victoria.

virtual reality Simulation of reality to allow a consumer to view or experience something that cannot be easily accessed (e.g. an historical event, a distant location, a protected resource or a story), using different technologies.

visa A legal document which allows the bearer permission to visit a country, issued by the destination country and valid for a certain period of time in line with the stated restrictions.

visiting friends and relatives (VFR) A form of tourism that involves the visitor staying in the home of a friend or relative.

visitor attraction A phenomenon or feature, built or natural, which is open to the public for payment or free of charge and appeals to tourists and day visitors.

visitor behaviour The way in which a visitor responds to the environment they visit, including their preferences, perception and geographical activity patterns.

visitor experience See tourist experience.

visitor management Techniques to control, direct and influence visitor behaviour and activity.

visitor payback Visitor donations or voluntary levies imposed on tourist products and services, used to fund conservation initiatives in visitor destinations.

visitor satisfaction Where a visitor's expectations have been met.

volume of tourism The actual numbers of people travelling as tourists.

Web 2.0 A term to describe the shift from the early static webpage technology of the Internet to a new stage where technologies allow people to communicate and collaborate which facilitates the creation of *User Generated Content* and development of online communities. The characteristics of the online communities are the use of new online networking tools such as blogs, technology to allow sharing of photographs and videos and other relevant information.

Welcome Host UK scheme to train frontline staff in customer service skills to meet and greet visitors.

wildlife-based tourism Visits which are associated with observing wildlife in its natural habitat.

wireless networks A technical term to describe a means of connecting electronic equipment via networks that do not need cabling, that can encompass *Bluetooth*, typically used with mobile phones, through to running computer networks and devices through local area networks without cables (i.e. *Wi-Fi*). In the case of fixed computers and devices, Wi-Fi allows communication without the conventional cabling using microwave or modularized laser light beam signals.

World Commission on Environment and Development (WCED) Convened by the United Nations and chaired by the Norwegian Prime Minister Gro Harlem Brundtland, the seminal report *Our Common Future* (1989) arose from the WCED, popularizing the concept of sustainable development.

World Tourism Organization A global organization based in Madrid, funded by the United Nations to collate tourism statistics and to provide policy advice and planning guidance to member countries and organizations.

World Tourism Organization Code of Ethics Produced by the WTO in 1999 to guide ethical behaviour in tourism.

World Travel and Tourism Council (WTTC) An organization representing around 100 of the world's leading tourism companies.

World Wide Web A virtual environment which allows different forms of text, graphics and other file formats to be accessed.

wow factor A feature or element of an attraction that leaves the visitor impressed or overawed, creating a favourable and memorable impression.

yield management Revenue management method to improve the profitability of a specific form of capacity or supply (i.e. aircraft or railway seats and hotel rooms).

Yugoslavia The country created in 1945 in Eastern Europe, which subsequently split to form Bosnia, Croatia, Slovenia, Yugoslavia and Macedonia in 1992.

Index

Note: Locators in **bold** refer to tables and those in *italics* to figures. Authors are cited where they relate to a significant idea, concept or model.